TOTAL
CHILD CARE

TOTAL CHILD CARE

From Birth to Age Five

Lorisa DeLorenzo,
M.S.

Robert John DeLorenzo,
M.D., Ph.D., M.P.H.

DOUBLEDAY & COMPANY, INC., GARDEN CITY, NEW YORK
1982

BOOK DESIGN BY *Marilyn Schulman*

Library of Congress Cataloging in Publication Data

DeLorenzo, Lorisa Mernette.
  Total child care.

  Bibliography: p. 1037
  Includes index.
  1. Children—Management.   2. Children—Care and
hygiene.   3. Socialization.   4. Child psychology.
I. DeLorenzo, Robert John, joint author.
II. Title.
HQ769.D426   649'.1
ISBN: 0-385-12593-3
Library of Congress Catalog Card Number 78-55847

This book is dedicated to our three children, Brock, Grant, and Shanelle, with love and gratitude for enriching our lives.

Authors' Note to the Reader

No one knows your child as well as you do. Books on child rearing can only be written in general terms; the information and advice does not apply specifically to your child. This is why it is important to guard against taking suggestions that books offer too literally. Your child, like every child, is a unique individual. As a parent, you know what is best, and it is hoped that the material in this book will assist you in developing your own personalized approach to child rearing.

There is no substitute for working closely with a doctor to provide good child care. By knowing your child and family, the doctor is in the best position to give you advice. This book is not intended to be used as a text for diagnosis or treatment of medical problems. It is meant to give you a general background in understanding children, their requirements and problems in the first five years of life. In some sections emergency and health care procedures are provided to assist parents in the very rare situations in which it is impossible to obtain medical advice. Although advice from a book under these unusual circumstances is better than no advice at all, assistance from a book is not as good or safe as that obtained from a physician or other trained medical professional. As suggested in the book, it is strongly recommended that parents take a first aid course in their community.

Although the examples presented in this book are based on real experiences with parents and children, their names have been changed to protect their privacy and ensure their anonymity. In writing this book we deliberated over the problem of choosing pronouns to refer to children. As a form of compromise and for the sake of readability, we have used the pronouns "she" and "he" interchangeably.

Contents

INFANCY 2

INFANCY 3

INFANCY 4

CONTENTS

INFANCY 5

INFANCY 6

INFANCY 7

CONTENTS

INFANCY 9

INFANCY 10

Contents

TODDLERHOOD 3

Contents

PRESCHOOL 1

PRESCHOOL 2

PRESCHOOL 3

Preface

In years of discussing child rearing issues with parents and professionals, we became increasingly aware that many men and women felt inadequately prepared for parenthood. Even though our society has resources for preparing people to function well in other tasks and careers, it offers little in the way of training and support to people considering or assuming new roles as parents. Being a parent is a challenging profession, yet well-organized, effective, educational materials that prepare people for parenthood are lacking, despite the large number of child care books on the market.

It was in response to this need that we became actively involved in developing new educational tools to provide child rearing information to the general public. Over eight years ago we began conducting discussion groups with parents, physicians, nurses, and educators to determine parents' needs and the ways in which we might be of assistance.

We found that the vast majority of parents are strongly committed to doing the best they can to rear their children. But at the same time they feel that they would have greatly benefited from better preparation for this important role. Parents who lived far away from their families during their child's early years were especially eager for more preparation about what to expect and how other families dealt with problems similar to theirs. Experience and information previously transmitted from grandparents to parents to children are often not available to new parents today, and this can create feelings of isolation and anxiety.

Roles have changed and are continuing to change, so that it is difficult to characterize today's family; there are wide variations in parents' ages and family structures. A high percentage of mothers work outside the home. Fathers have taken more active roles in child rearing. Single parents have unique concerns and challenges and it is often more difficult for them to seek advice from their families.

In these early discussion groups, it became obvious that parents not only wanted information on how to offer good basic care, but also had a keen interest in learning about how to deal with emotional needs, their feelings, and other common problems that face families today. They also wanted a more comprehensive and realistic view of what is involved in rearing a child. And thus, we organized small pre- and postnatal discussion groups in the early 1970s, to prepare parents for what to expect in regard to basic care, health care, accident prevention, child development, and discipline. Handouts were chronologically organized on a month-to-month basis, and parents were given the handouts approximately one month before their child reached a given phase of development. The response to these initial groups was very positive. Parents not only participated enthusiastically, but took an active part in suggesting other topics of interest.

Parents also wanted to learn about the emotional adjustments and common pitfalls involved in child rearing before they were likely to occur. They were interested in knowing whether other parents shared the same stresses and experienced similar fears and worries. When they realized that they were not the only ones having difficulties, their own feelings of guilt and isolation were reduced. Issues important to the parents we met were incorporated into our programs: family adjustments in relation to the new baby, parenthood after thirty, the single parent experience, how the arrival of a new child might affect the parents' sex life, the working parent, postpartum depression, and other similar topics.

Economic concerns were also of major importance to parents in our educational groups. Having to rear a child on a tight family budget was a common situation. A great deal of anxiety and unnecessary guilt was aroused over the fact that some parents could not afford to purchase expensive toys and fancy "educational devices." Most parents felt financial strains in varying degrees and wanted information on ways in which they could adequately provide for their children in a more economical way. In response to these concerns, part of our group discussions was devoted to ways in which parents could cut costs without compromising the quality of care that their child received. Practical tips for making baby food, reducing money spent on equipment, organizing co-operative baby-sitting services, making toys, providing a stimulating educational experience in the home, and other advice was obtained from experienced parents, physicians, and educators. Numerous suggestions over the eight years that this program was being developed were gradually added to our programs and later incorporated in this book.

As a result of the recent attention to parent-child attachment and a child's early educational experiences and environment, parents also were concerned about how best to offer their youngsters beneficial experiences early in life. They were sincerely interested in doing whatever they could to foster their children's development and provide appropriate parental and environmental stimulation, but they were also somewhat confused as to how to achieve these goals. The subjects of how to develop an early parent-child bond and help the child maximize his or her individual potential were continually brought up at the discussion groups. These concerns, too, have been incorporated into the book and highlighted in the Learning Through Play and the Total Education of Your Child sections.

The scope of the discussion groups and handouts was gradually refined and further expanded to form a comprehensive core of information about child rearing during infancy. The parents in these groups seemed excited about the new concept of being prepared for parenthood in a "total" way. They were convinced that the preparation they were receiving gave them a better understanding and appreciation of their child's unique developmental pattern; it gave them more self-confidence and brought them closer to their child. Parents felt more relaxed and capable of making the right decisions for their individual family situation. They found they were also reaping greater pleasure and fulfillment from parenthood.

Months and years passed and the children of the parents who had participated in our original discussion groups grew up into toddlerhood. These parents urged us to extend our preparatory program and materials beyond infancy to cover the toddlerhood and preschool stages of development. We received a great deal of additional encouragement in this regard from physicians and educators in the community who felt that effective preparatory materials for parents of older children were lacking.

As the volume of requests for more material grew, we were encouraged to organize our handouts into a book for commercial publication, which could reach a wider audience. So we took the material about birth to age five that had been used successfully in our parents' groups and distributed it to additional parents and an eminent group of pediatricians, obstetricians, gynecologists, psychiatrists, psychologists, and other professionals in the child care field across the country for critical review in their areas of expertise. The objective was for the book to have the widest possible application and usefulness. Over two and a half years were devoted to organizing their comments and suggestions and incorporating them into the manuscript.

After eight years of research and numerous revisions, TOTAL CHILD CARE took its final form. We hope that it will meet the need for a comprehensive, prepared child rearing program for parents in this country and abroad. Our book is designed to be used in various ways by individuals, groups of parents, or as source material for courses on prepared parenthood.

Expanding and improving parenthood education have been and still represent major challenges. We hope this book will serve as a foundation for the implementation of nation-wide educational programs on parenthood and thus improve the quality of life for children and their parents. We are actively engaged in developing programs for parenthood education, and firmly believe that courses on becoming parents and rearing children should be available to all who are interested. High school students, and even younger children, can benefit enormously from the opportunity to learn about child rearing. They will be the parents of tomorrow. It is our hope that they will be better prepared to meet the challenge of parenthood, not only for their sakes, but for the sake of future generations.

Your help is needed. By working through organizations in your community and voicing support for such preparatory programs, it may be possible for you to help establish needed facilities in your local area.

Lorisa M. DeLorenzo, M.S.

Robert J. DeLorenzo, M.D., PH.D., M.P.H.

Acknowledgments

A great many people have contributed to TOTAL CHILD CARE in a wide variety of capacities. First of all we would like to thank those professionals who themselves have made major contributions to the literature and to the concept of parenthood education. It is impossible to thank every author whose writing served as a source of ideas and inspiration, but the following deserve special mention: Jean Piaget, Erik H. Erikson, Benjamin Spock, Arnold Gesell, Louise Bates Ames, Frances L. Ilg, Lee Salk, T. Berry Brazelton, Selma H. Fraiberg, Burton L. White, and Fitzhugh Dodson.

We would also like to extend our sincere appreciation to all of the parents with whom we have worked over the past eight years. Their interest and desire to learn more about child rearing gave us a purpose. Parents were generous in offering their enthusiasm, support, time, practical tips, suggestions, and firsthand experiences. Space does not permit us to thank all of the parents individually who used the manuscript at each stage of its development and assisted in making valuable improvements in content, organization, and format. The following people deserve special mention for donating large amounts of their time and effort to reviewing major portions of the manuscript, helping us distribute it, and organizing parents' input:

Joyce Pantalone
Raffie and John Giordano
Rosann and Roger Laroche
Joetta Elia
Judy O'dell
Adrian Wisting
Susan Wood
Donna D'Amato
Eleanor and Michael Iannuzzi
Wanda Hayback
Marilyn Lombardi
Joan Reynolds
Judy Gallagher
Karen Seyfried
Ann Hinds
Cheryl Giametti
Carol Papa
Arlene Crismale

Bernadette Julia
Rosemary Higgins
Ellen DePalma
Sally Chi
Judy Donroe
Helen Lesandrine
Lori Molnar
Mary Osborne
Sharon O. Cicio
MaryAnne Gibbs
Ellen Seigel
Kathleen Rose
Heidi Millington
Regina McGowan
Leslie Tabachnick
Pam Cohen
Harriet Rosen

We are indebted to Pam Willmott, who acted as our administrative assistant. Her excellent administrative and secretarial skills and dedication above and beyond the call of duty were instrumental in making this book a reality. We also wish to extend our gratitude to Jane Badman, who served as our educational consultant and offered her expertise and numerous suggestions. The expert and highly regarded legal and

ACKNOWLEDGMENTS

Acknowledgments

management advice of Norman Resnicow and Jack Badman deserve special acknowledgment.

We gratefully acknowledge the invaluable assistance of Karen Van Westering, our editor at Doubleday. She has shown a sincere interest in promoting parenthood education and her expert guidance and direction in shaping TOTAL CHILD CARE are a testimony to her commitment. The assistance and editorial guidance of Patrick Filley during the initial development of this book is also greatly appreciated. We are indebted to them for their unfaltering faith, encouragement, and support. Without their help this book could not have been completed.

Our heartfelt thanks are extended to the following group of distinguished professionals who donated their valuable time to reviewing carefully parts or all of TOTAL CHILD CARE during various phases of its development. Their comments and suggestions based on their experience in their area of expertise were of immense value in helping this book achieve wide cross-country applicability and a high standard of excellence. Their dedication and commitment to improving methods of providing prepared parenthood education were greatly appreciated. The practicing pediatricians who offered their years of experience and understanding of parents' and children's needs in reviewing the manuscript deserve special thanks.

Louise Bates Ames, Ph.D.
Codirector, Gesell Institute of Child
  Development
New Haven, Connecticut

Carol R. Angle, M.D.
Professor of Pediatrics
The University of Nebraska Medical
  Center
Omaha, Nebraska

John W. Benton, M.D.
Professor and Chairman
Department of Pediatrics
University of Alabama in Birmingham
Birmingham, Alabama

William E. Boyle, Jr., M.D.
Practicing Pediatrician
Hitchcock Clinic
Hanover, New Hampshire

Joseph W. Brinkley, M.D.
Practicing Pediatrician
Great Falls Clinic
Great Falls, Montana

Roy Brown, M.D., M.P.H.
Associate Professor
Mount Sinai School of Medicine
  of The City University of New York
New York, New York

Barbara Bruner, M.D.
Associate Professor of Pediatrics
Emory School of Medicine
Atlanta, Georgia

Richard C. Burnstine, M.D.
Practicing Pediatrician
North Suburban Pediatrics, S.C.
Evanston, Illinois

Paul R. Crellin, M.D.
Practicing Pediatrician
The Children's Clinic, P.S.C.
Child Study Center
Billings, Montana

Thomas F. Dolan, Jr., M.D.
Professor of Clinical Pediatrics
Yale Medical School
New Haven, Connecticut

Richard A. Ehrenkranz, M.D.
Assistant Professor of Pediatrics
  and Obstetrics and Gynecology
Division of Perinatal Medicine
Yale Medical School
New Haven, Connecticut

Roselyn P. Epps, M.D., M.P.H.
Chief, Bureau of Clinical Services
Department of Human Resources
Community Health and Hospitals
  Administration
Washington, D.C.

xxviii

Geraldine Feldman, M.D.
Practicing Pediatrician
Leominster, Massachusetts

Laurence Finberg, M.D.
Professor and Chairman
Department of Pediatrics
Montefiore Hospital and Medical Center
Albert Einstein College of Medicine
   of Yeshiva University
Bronx, New York

G. J. Fruthaler, M.D.
Practicing Pediatrician
Oshsner Clinic
New Orleans, Louisiana

Kurt Glaser, M.D.
Director of Adolescent Services
Springfield Hospital Center
Sykesville, Maryland

Nelson H. Goldberg, M.D.
Assistant Medical Director
   Emergency Services
Yale-New Haven Medical Center
New Haven, Connecticut

Morris Green, M.D.
Professor and Chairman
Department of Pediatrics
Indiana University School of Medicine
Indianapolis, Indiana

Melvin M. Grumbach, M.D.
Professor and Chairman
Department of Pediatrics
University of California School of
   Medicine
San Francisco, California

James A. Hecker, M.D.
Practicing Pediatrician
Cheyenne, Wyoming

Oliver W. Hill, M.D.
Practicing Pediatrician
Pediatric Associates
Knoxville, Tennessee

Jonathan M. Himmelhoch, M.D.
Associate Professor of Psychiatry
University of Pittsburgh
Western Psychiatric Institute and Clinic
Pittsburgh, Pennsylvania

Judy Howard, M.D.
Medical Director
U.C.L.A. Intervention Program for
   Developmentally Handicapped
   Infants and Children
Los Angeles, California

Marvin O. Kolb, M.D.
Chairman, Department of Pediatrics
Fargo Clinic
Chairman, North Dakota Academy of
   Pediatrics
Fargo, North Dakota

Robert Kramer, M.D.
Practicing Pediatrician
Pediatric Associates of Dallas
Dallas, Texas

Lester L. Lansky, M.D.
Associate Professor of Pediatrics and
   Neurology
Director, Section of Pediatric Neurology
University of Kansas Medical Center
Kansas City, Kansas

Raymond E. Lesser, M.D.
Practicing Pediatrician
Kaizer Permanente Medical Center
San Diego, California

Ann C. Lichtenberg, M.D.
Practicing Pediatrician
Pediatric Associates of Cincinnati
Cincinnati, Ohio

Lewis P. Lipsitt, Ph.D.
Professor of Psychology and Medical
   Science
Director, Child Study Center
Brown University
Providence, Rhode Island

Elizabeth C. Lowry, M.D.
Practicing Pediatrician
Guilford, Connecticut

Alexander R. Lucas, M.D.
Head of Section of Child and Adolescent
   Psychiatry
Professor of Psychiatry
Mayo Clinic Medical School
Rochester, Minnesota

ACKNOWLEDGMENTS

William H. Masters, M.D.
Director
Reproductive Biology Research
    Foundation
St. Louis, Missouri

Harvey Myers III, M.D.
Practicing Child Psychiatrist
Boise, Idaho

Jack I. Novick, Ph.D.
Professor of Psychology and
    Director of Graduate Study
    in School of Psychology
Southern Connecticut State College
New Haven, Connecticut

Thomas K. Oliver, Jr., M.D.
Professor and Chairman
Department of Pediatrics
University of Pittsburgh School of
    Medicine
Pittsburgh, Pennsylvania

Howard A. Pearson, M.D.
Professor and Chairman
Department of Pediatrics
Yale Medical School
New Haven, Connecticut

Lois A. Pounds, M.D.
Associate Professor of Clinical Pediatrics
University of Pittsburgh School of
    Medicine
Pittsburgh, Pennsylvania

William O. Robertson, M.D.
Professor of Pediatrics
Director of Medical Education
University of Washington School of
    Medicine
Seattle, Washington

George B. Rosenfeld, M.D.
Practicing Pediatrician
Cheektowaga, New York

Philip M. Sarrel, M.D.
Associate Professor of Obstetrics and
    Gynecology
Sex Counselor Division of Mental
    Hygiene

University Health Services
Yale Medical School
New Haven, Connecticut

Audrey Sayers, M.D.
Director of Children and Youth Projects
State Health Department
Norfolk, Virginia

Henrietta T. Smith, Ph.D.
Professor of Psychology
Vassar College
Poughkeepsie, New York

Phineas J. Sparer, M.D.
Emeritus Professor of Psychiatry and
    Preventive Medicine
University of Tennessee College of
    Medicine
Memphis, Tennessee

Robert H. Thompson, Jr., M.D.
Practicing Pediatrician
The Children's Clinic
Jackson, Mississippi

Douglass W. Walker, M.D.
Practicing Pediatrician
Vice President for Medical Affairs
Maine Medical Center
Portland, Maine

Morris A. Wessel, M.D.
Clinical Professor of Pediatrics
Yale Medical School
New Haven, Connecticut

Governor Witt, M.D.
Associate Clinical Professor
University of Miami School of Medicine
Miami, Florida

Herbert M. Woodcock, M.D.
Associate Professor of Psychiatry and
    Pediatrics
University of Oregon Health Sciences
    Center
Portland, Oregon

How This Book Will Work for You

Child rearing should be a positive, rewarding experience for parents. Yet, for many of them this experience is not as fulfilling as it could be. They become parents with little confidence in their ability to do a good job and little in the way of practical assistance to help in their new roles. TOTAL CHILD CARE is designed to make child rearing more rewarding for parents and to help prepare them for the responsibilities they will face during their child's early years from birth to age five. There are several innovative aspects of this book that we hope will make rearing infants, toddlers, and preschool children easier and more pleasurable.

The Total Approach to Child Rearing

A major concern of prospective parents is: what do they need to know in order to be good parents? Similarly, at each new phase of their child's development parents often wonder whether or not they are well prepared or are reading the appropriate material. The burden has been on parents to determine what they should be reading at what time, or what combination of books will give them an adequate background. Unlike other books, TOTAL CHILD CARE presents a "total approach" to child rearing.

Information is organized into several broad areas, which are carried through developmental phases, appearing as they become important. These areas include: Understanding Your Child's Development, Basic Care, Family Feelings and Concerns, and the Total Education of Your Child. At the end of each phase is a Prepared Parenthood Check List designed to assist parents in following their child's unique developmental pattern and to re-emphasize some of the important areas in which they should be prepared.

Information is broken down into small segments of manageable length, which cover all of the important areas of child rearing in each phase. Thus, parents can feel confident that they are well prepared for coming events after reading a relatively short amount of material. TOTAL CHILD CARE takes some of the burden off parents, for they can learn about child rearing in the same manner in which they experience parenthood—one step at a time. By reading step by step over a period of five years, parents are able to master a vast amount of material without feeling overwhelmed. Parents can follow along at their own pace and style, using this book in the manner they find most useful.

Preparation for Parenthood Is Advantageous

Men and women who are prepared for child rearing are usually more self-confident and less troubled by guilt, insecurity, and doubt. Having a general picture of what to expect enables parents to trust themselves and be more relaxed. It is only natural for parents-to-be to have some anxieties and insecurities when faced with the responsibility of caring for a dependent young infant. But providing good basic care can be much easier, if you are prepared in advance.

The Basic Care sections provide information about meeting your child's needs, including health care, accident prevention, feeding, bathing, clothing, sleeping, and elimination at various ages. Some of the more common questions, procedures, and problems that arise are discussed, and information is presented that will acquaint you with equipment and techniques for handling your baby and assist you in making decisions.

Caring for a baby who is completely dependent upon you can be a very satisfying and rewarding experience. Ensuring that your infant's needs for nourishment, warmth, cleanliness, sleep, etc., are met will be one of your major responsibilities. As you care for her, you will not only be satisfying her basic care needs, you will also be satisfying her desire for attention and love.

The warm, close physical and emotional contact you offer during the time you spend attending to her needs is very significant. It is through this frequent, natural contact that your relationship with her will grow. Your infant's first real introduction to another human being will take place in large part through contact with you during feeding times, bathing periods, dressing times, and so forth. It is particularly important that you feel confident about your abilities, and respond to her in a natural, relaxed manner. Caring for your child need not be an area for undue anxiety and concern. After all, mothers and fathers have been doing a good job for centuries.

In order to carry out your basic care responsibilities effectively, you should have a sound understanding of how your baby's needs and abilities will change as she matures. Her behavior changes will greatly affect the nature of the care that she receives, and how the care is provided. For example, as your baby develops, her nutritional needs will change, and she will gradually require fewer feedings. She will become able to handle coarser foods, and will begin to finger-feed herself. You will have to make numerous adjustments during her first year in how her food is prepared, how it is offered, as well as alter her schedule and diet.

It should be understood that, right from the start, babies and children are individuals with different sleep and food requirements, elimination needs, etc. Your baby will have her own unique needs, which may not be similar to those of other babies whom you know, or even your other children.

One benefit of a prepared approach is that it increases parents' understanding of their children. Parents who are more aware of a child's changing needs and abilities are likely to be more sensitive and responsive to her. Learning in advance about developmental changes allows parents to be more observant of their baby's progress and to reap more enjoyment from those observations. In general, the more parents know about their child's growth, the more effective they can be at shaping her environment to her best advantage.

Parents who know how to provide a safe environment for their child during different phases of development will be able to reduce significantly the risk of injury to her. The protection of your child during the first year of life is particularly important, since she is quite vulnerable and dependent upon you for her safety. Statistics from the National Safety Council demonstrate that an alarming number of children are injured or die as a result of accidents. In fact, accidents are the leading cause of death in children. The tragedy in the statistics is that many of these accidents could have been prevented.

The purpose of discussing childhood accidents is not to alarm you, but to make you aware of the importance of taking the time to learn how to provide your child with a safe, healthy environment in which to grow. Parents in our education programs found that by being aware of the danger of potential accidents and by learning how to take simple safety measures, they felt much more at ease about caring for their children. This book will give you suggestions for how to avoid unnecessary accidents. It will provide you with the information for teaching your child the rules of safety and how to become safety conscious herself, since this is a highly significant part of any program for reducing accidents.

Becoming familiar with appropriate health care information in advance allows parents to provide a good complete preventive health care program for their child, and helps them know when and how to seek medical assistance. Parents will also be assisting their physician by being more sophisticated observers of their child's health care needs and developmental progress.

A prepared approach is extremely important in providing a good early education for a child. Many important lessons about living are learned very early in life, and these experiences play an influential role in shaping a child's development. The Total Education of Your Child sections in this book show parents how to provide a personalized education program for their child, one that will give her the best chance to maximize her potential.

As you are probably aware, many professionals agree that the first few years of a child's life are significant not only for her physical and emotional development, but also for her intellectual development. Recent research has demonstrated that children can learn from a very early point in their lives. The more sophisticated the research techniques, the earlier the age at which researchers have been able to observe and measure the child's ability to learn. These technological advances have allowed physicians to observe the fetus in the mother's womb; the fetus moves, explores its body, sucks its thumb, and carries out certain other reflex activities. It is conceivable that the infant begins to learn how to control her body, in some small way, even before she is born.

Evidence suggests that your young infant learns from birth in spite of the fact that she will be limited in her ability to interact with the world around her and restricted in her physical activities. If indeed she does learn from birth, then the type of education she receives during infancy will be largely determined by her parent(s) or the person(s) primarily responsible for her care, who determines the type of environment, personal contacts, and experiences that she will have. In most cases you will be the one primarily responsible for providing your baby with an education. This should not make you anxious; you need not have a teaching degree to be an excellent first teacher for her. Regardless of your educational or economic background, you can help to ensure that she develops to her fullest potential as an individual in a natural, spontaneous way.

Providing an educational experience for your child can be richly rewarding. Many parents in our program felt that educating their child made child rearing seem like more of a profession to them, and greatly enhanced their relationship with their child.

Promoting Early Parent-child Bonding

The importance of developing a positive parent-child bond at or soon after birth and working to maintain the closeness and strength of this attachment during early childhood is stressed throughout TOTAL CHILD CARE. This is a key concept and has been shown to promote healthy physical and emotional development. Establishing a close parent-child relationship often takes time and, once achieved, has to be nourished throughout infancy, toddlerhood, and the preschool years. The love, warmth, and physical contact that a young child needs can be well satisfied within a family setting, beginning in the earliest days of life.

A major thrust of this book is to promote a satisfying and spontaneous parent-child relationship. The information in the development, play, and education sections is especially designed to foster closeness between parent and child and to assist parents in learning to relax and truly enjoy their children. New parents often raise the question: how can they interact effectively with their young infant, whose abilities are limited? By understanding their child's developmental capabilities, they find that spending time with their baby becomes enjoyable and enriching for both parent and child. By offering her stimulating opportunities for play during infancy, you will be fostering her development in all areas, and providing her with a rich and varied learning experience.

The play suggestions are designed to supplement the developmental material by highlighting your baby's developmental abilities and allowing you to interact with her. As your baby matures, the opportunities for playing with her will increase, and the kinds of activities, exchanges, and objects that interest her will change. The play topics in Infancy 1, 2, 4, 6, and 8 will help you provide opportunities for play that correspond to your infant's changing abilities and interests. Your play with your infant should not become artificial, mechanical, or rigid. Flexibility and spontaneity are extremely important. Rather than taking the suggestions in the play sections too literally, use them as a general source of ideas. Throughout TOTAL CHILD CARE, frequent interaction between parent and child is encouraged. Emphasis is placed upon increasing parents' understanding of their child in the hope that this will enrich the ties between them.

Emphasizing Positive Family Relationships

TOTAL CHILD CARE also emphasizes individual differences in parents and takes into account the variability in family structures. The Family Feelings and Concerns section highlights the different feelings, stresses, problems, and concerns of parents in different life circumstances. Special topics are included to be of assistance to widowed, unmarried, separated, and divorced parents. Adequate preparation helps parents minimize many of the common stressful family situations that can occur during the first five years of life.

TOTAL CHILD CARE not only discusses the development of the child but also deals with the development of parents and changes in family relationships that often occur as the child grows. It is a family-centered orientation. The child's growth must be viewed within the total family picture, because the child and family are inseparable and interfamily dynamics are extremely important.

Parents' needs and feelings are every bit as important as their child's. Both need expression. This is a major concept underlying TOTAL CHILD CARE. During the different stages of parenthood, your feelings will change. You will develop in many respects as both a person and a parent. Stresses often seem less overwhelming when parents are prepared for the adjustments that have to be made and are more in touch with their own as well as their spouses' feelings.

The emphasis of the Family Feelings and Concerns section is on parents' changing reactions and feelings in relation to the various aspects of being a parent. Your awareness of possible problems and how to deal with them will offer you a fresh perspective and greater self-confidence.

There Is No One Right Approach to Rearing a Child

No one can tell parents how to rear their child. It is our hope that TOTAL CHILD CARE will help parents, as they experience child rearing firsthand, to develop the sophistication to formulate their own, individualized philosophy, which best fulfills their needs and those of their child.

There is no one theory or method of rearing a child that is "right" or appropriate for every child, or every parent. TOTAL CHILD CARE does not represent a rigid method or cookbook format. Rather, it is an educational tool for parents so that they can make their own personal choices based upon solid knowledge. Up-to-date information and alternatives are presented to assist parents in making decisions and plans.

Parents need not worry excessively about making mistakes, since there is no right or wrong. Constant guilt and worry are not productive. Effective child rearing is a learning process, not a method. Each child and parent are unique and must grow and learn together.

Children are basically resilient, and can accept imperfections in their parents, just as their parents should accept imperfections in them. Most of the errors that parents make in handling their child will not negatively affect their child's over-all development, as long as she senses their genuine love and care. Rather than dwelling on mistakes, it is important for parents to relax and trust themselves and their knowledge of their child in determining the best path to follow.

One of the goals of this book is to instill in parents a genuine respect for individual differences. No two children are completely the same, and even in the womb individual differences are noticeable, so parents are urged not to pressure their child to adhere to any set pattern of development other than her own. The variability in the development of normal children and the concept of individuality are stressed throughout TOTAL CHILD CARE. Each child has her own unique appearance, personality, and rate of development, although children usually pass through similar phases of development.

The phases discussed in this book roughly correspond to a child's development in terms of chronological age, but we have purposely avoided using "months" or "years" because the approximate ages corresponding to the phases are not meant to be used as rigid schedules for development. Some children naturally develop at a faster rate; it is also not uncommon for one child to develop more quickly in one area, such as movement skills, but to lag behind in a different area, such as language skills.

The developmental sections in TOTAL CHILD CARE were designed to take this variability into account. The material is organized to describe sequences of development in four major areas: personal-social (development of self-awareness and social skills); intellectual (development of the mind of the child and the ability to think and interact with the environment); language (ability to speak and communicate with other people); and motor (development of the ability to move and co-ordinate body activity).

In each of these areas, the child's abilities will mature and increase with time, although there can be no rigid schedule for the acquisition of new abilities. Some overlap has been incorporated into the descriptions of abilities in the phases of infancy, toddlerhood, and the preschool years to stress the variability in development.

Different Approaches to Using the Book

The material has been especially designed to enable men and women to take a prepared approach to child rearing. People with whom we have worked have found this to be a most helpful way to ready themselves for the important profession of parenting. In order for the prepared approach to be effective, read the information at the advisable times designated in the table below. Remember, there is great variation from child to child in the speed or rate at which she progresses. If your child is progressing faster than described in a given stage, or in a particular area of development, adjust your reading schedule by reading ahead. For the prepared approach to be effective, the goal is to remain one step ahead of your child's developmental progress.

The Organization of Total Child Care

	Section (Birth to 12 months)	Roughly Corresponds to the Following Ages	To Take a Prepared Approach Read During the Following Times
INFANCY			
	Preparing for Parenthood		before Birth
	Infancy 1	month 1	before Birth
	Infancy 2	month 2	month 1
	Infancy 3	month 3	month 2
	Infancy 4	month 4	month 3
	Infancy 5	month 5	month 4
	Infancy 6	month 6	month 5
	Infancy 7	month 7	month 6
	Infancy 8	month 8	month 7
	Infancy 9	month 9	month 8
	Infancy 10	month 10	month 9
	Infancy 11	month 11	month 10
	Infancy 12	months 12 to 14	month 11
TODDLERHOOD	(12 to 14 months to 2½ years)		
	Preparing for Toddlerhood		before Toddlerhood
	Toddlerhood 1	12 to 14 months to 18 months	before Toddlerhood
	Toddlerhood 2	18 months to 2 years	14 to 18 months
	Toddlerhood 3	2 to 2½ years	18 months to 2 years

PRESCHOOL (2½ to 5 years)

Preparing for the Preschool Years		before Preschool
Preschool 1	2½ to 3 years	before Preschool
Preschool 2	3 to 4 years	2½ to 3 years
Preschool 3	4 to 5 years	3 to 4 years

TOTAL CHILD CARE also enables a parent to take a problem-oriented approach. The Index and system of cross references were designed to allow parents to obtain information quickly on both major and minor topics of interest. Parents have found this approach to be useful when problems, medical emergencies, or pressing questions arose for which they needed immediate guidance.

This book has also been used successfully by parents who have organized their own informal groups to discuss child rearing issues. Parents have found that reading the material for a given developmental phase in advance and then gathering together with other parents at frequent intervals to discuss it was a very enjoyable and productive way to learn more about child rearing. Having opportunities to share feelings and personal experiences with other parents in a relaxed atmosphere helped them feel less isolated, and offered them support as well as a greater appreciation of individual differences among children and parents. The check lists at the end of each phase served as a starting point for discussion, and as a take-off point from which parents could explore other issues of importance to them.

The PREPARED PARENTHOOD check lists are an outgrowth of our work with parents. They found it very useful to focus their attention on certain highlights, and this check list format proved to be an effective method for accomplishing this. It also serves as a reminder of important actions parents should be taking, such as safety-proofing their home or arranging for their child to be properly immunized.

The check lists are designed to assist parents in being more observant of their child's behavior and following her individual developmental pattern. They encourage parents to notice not just obvious but also subtle changes that enable them to understand and appreciate their child more fully.

Another use of the check lists is to stimulate discussion of the child's development and the interplay between family and child during each phase. Mother and father can fill out the check list separately and then compare notes and talk about their answers, observations, and feelings. Open lines of communication between mother and father are stressed throughout this book, and it is hoped that the check lists will promote this by serving as a springboard for discussion and self-expression.

Preparing for Parenthood

FAMILY FEELINGS AND CONCERNS

The initial environment for the young infant and a major portion of her emotional, physical, social, and intellectual stimulation will be provided by members of the family unit. A strong, stable family provides a healthy environment in which the young child can thrive. It is sometimes easy to lose sight of the importance of the family in rearing your child. The prenatal period is one of increasing excitement, of preparation for a brand-new individual, but the baby is but part of a whole. This is the time to begin to understand that one of your primary responsibilities as a parent should be making a conscious effort to preserve a good family structure, keeping in mind that a family is only as strong as each individual member's efforts to make the family unit work.

The Family Organization

There are many types of family organizations. Probably the most familiar form today is the mother-father-child family unit. This family structure may or may not be extended to include grandparents or other relatives. Another common form is the single parent family, created through any of a variety of situations, including separation, divorce, death, motherhood apart from marriage, and adoption. Other forms of family structure also exist, such as the kibbutz model and communal organization. The type of family structure can further vary depending upon personal, cultural, and environmental circumstances.

It is important to stress that regardless of how the family is organized, the primary consideration is that an effort is made to make the family function well for parent and child. The love, human contact, care, assistance, and stimulation that the child receives from the "family" play an essential role in her total development. The value of the parent-child relationship cannot be overemphasized.

Families often go through periods of change. They experience phases of stability and relative instability and may change from one form of family organization to another. Some of these changes will reflect the child's pattern of growth and development and others will reflect the feelings of parents and the stresses of the environment.

In response to these internal and external stresses on the family, adjustments have to be made from time to time. A new balance must be achieved between each family member to adjust to new situations. The family is not static. It must be flexible enough to grow and change along with the people who comprise it.

Establishing a good family structure is one of the primary responsibilities that men and women face as they assume new roles as parents, but the stresses imposed upon the family by modern day society may make it difficult. You can help strengthen your family by becoming aware of common pitfalls and by making an effort to work out minor difficulties before they get out of hand.

The network of communication lines linking family members must remain open in order for the family to be able to survive periods of stress and crises. Only through maintaining free and easy avenues of communication can the needs of individuals continually be assessed and satisfactorily met. Co-operation, flexibility, understanding, and communication are important in relation to family life in the months and years to come.

Feelings of Insecurity Are Natural

While the transition to parenthood can be an exciting, happy time, parents usually express doubts, fears, and concerns related to assuming new roles as parents. Insecurities about a coming major life change such as the sudden switch from being a non-parent to a parent are natural and quite common. Sometimes parents find it hard to admit these feelings to either themselves or other people. Perhaps they feel that admitting their insecurity is like admitting that they might be inadequate as parents. Keeping these feelings to yourself, however, is a burden, and contributes to unnecessary anxieties that will ultimately interfere with the amount of pleasure you derive from becoming a parent.

There are many different reasons underlying the insecurities of prospective parents. Madelyn, for example, late in her pregnancy, began to express some doubts about her ability to care for the baby properly. The responsibility that men and women face in caring for a baby who will be totally dependent upon them commonly causes even the most confident prospective parents to have some doubts and worries.

Many parents-to-be worry about being able to earn enough money to support both the family and a new baby. Career conflicts also cause concern. Sheila, a hospital administrator, worried about how having a baby would affect her career, and had doubts that she would be happy staying home to care for her child on a full-time basis. She also had concerns that the baby would somehow create a distance between her and her husband and greatly alter their lifestyle.

These are common fears of prospective parents, particularly those with careers outside the home. Knowing that a baby will alter the family, most couples wonder about how their marriage will be affected, and whether or not they will be as close after their baby is born.

There can also be emotional concerns. Coreen, a single mother-to-be, feared that since her pregnancy was initially unwanted, she might not love her baby. She had had definite regrets about being pregnant early in the pregnancy, and worried that her negative feelings might have a detrimental effect upon her baby. Not all parents-to-be approach parenthood having planned for and wanting a baby. It is understandable that even though they decided to let the pregnancy run its course and keep their babies, fears and doubts about loving their babies may linger.

Unmarried, separated, divorced, and widowed mothers-to-be often worry about how they will manage to adjust their lifestyle to provide for their babies' needs and their own, both emotional and financial, and whether their babies will suffer as a result of not having a father. Prospective mothers who had not expected to rear a child by themselves usually have heightened insecurities about the unplanned-for stresses accompanying single parenthood.

Individuals about to become parents may have their own unique concerns, doubts, and feelings of insecurity that may or may not be similar to those of their spouses, or those of others they know who are also facing the transition to parenthood. Bringing your doubts and concerns out into the open can help to alleviate some of the inner tensions and worries that may be hard for one person, alone, to bear.

Whether you are awaiting the birth of your first child or your fifth, you should realize that some anticipatory worry and feelings of insecurity are natural. Try to view these feelings in a positive, rather than a negative, light. If you were not a concerned individual, and did not plan to take parenting seriously, chances are that none of these feelings would exist. By honestly admitting your feelings, and putting them into proper perspective, you will be in a better position to deal with them constructively. Once you feel more prepared for child rearing, you can look forward to assuming your role as a parent with more confidence.

Love for Your Baby May Not Be Automatic

The scene takes place in a hospital on the maternity floor. A new mother and father are overjoyed at the birth of their baby, and are overflowing with love as they handle her for the first time. Perhaps this is how you will feel. Many parents do feel love for their newborn from the moment she is born. On the other hand, with some parents, love for their baby may not be instantaneous or automatic. Sandra, for instance, was totally convinced that her love for her baby would be there the second that she saw him and held him in her arms. According to her:

I just assumed that I would feel this overwhelming motherly love for my son Darin as soon as I gave birth to him. Instead, when the doctor handed him to me to hold, I felt as if I were holding a stranger. I was really frightened by the fact that here I was, a mother, who was supposed to love my new baby, and I didn't feel any closeness or great love for him. I wouldn't tell anyone how I felt, for fear that they wouldn't understand, or that they wouldn't think highly of me. I was terrified and felt guilty over what I considered to be my own inadequacies, and it wasn't until several weeks of caring for Darin at home had passed that I began to develop positive feelings for him and love him.

In the eyes of the law, you will become a parent as soon as your baby is born. However, this biological fact of life may have little to do with becoming an emotional or psychological parent. The emotional bond between parent and newborn may or may not be automatic and immediate. In some cases this bond develops much more gradually. With you and your baby it may not be "love at first sight." Should this turn out to be the case, there is no need to feel guilty, inadequate, or panic-stricken. Other new parents have experienced similar feelings.

It may take you some time to establish warm, loving feelings for your child. After a few days or weeks, your little infant will not seem so much like a stranger. You will have had a chance to get better acquainted with her and with yourself in your new role as her parent.

Whether or not you immediately feel warm and positive toward your baby, try to make frequent contact with her as soon as she is born. Hold her, cuddle her close, and stroke her body. Skin to skin contact is important for bonding between parent and child. Talk to her and give of yourself to her, even if it feels to you as though you are continually giving and not receiving very much in return. Keep in mind that her social responsiveness in the early weeks will be limited, but be sure to look into her eyes and talk to her just the same. Through your response to her needs and through talking and touching, the two of you will be drawn together emotionally. Give your relationship time to grow. If you are patient and work at developing a close relationship with her, you will learn to love her.

Your Baby, Like Every Baby, Is an Individual

Your baby is a unique person, an individual from the very beginning. She is unlike any other person who has ever been born. She will have her own characteristic appearance, way of behaving, reactions to stimulation, and so on. If you have other children, you are likely to notice decided differences between them and your new baby.

Assuming this is your first child, you can ask any parents of two or more children about individual differences. They will probably tell you how different their children were at birth, or perhaps even before birth, and how unique they are now in their temperaments, abilities, interests, and so forth. They may even reluctantly admit that right from the start they secretly favored one child over another.

Such factors as your baby's sex, appearance, and behavior from birth may play an important role in influencing your emotional reactions to her. Daniel and Mary, for example, were hoping to give birth to a boy, and were totally convinced that their baby would be a boy. Giving birth to a baby girl came as a disappointment to them. Their disappointment actually clouded their feelings for their baby for the first few weeks, and they both honestly admitted that they were probably not as responsive to her as they would have been had she been a boy.

This couple's reaction is not uncommon. Parents' anticipation, thoughts, dreams, hopes, and wishes prior to a baby's birth are not always fulfilled at or after the actual birth. This naturally calls for adjustments from parents, and has an emotional and psychological impact upon them. Many other factors besides a baby's sex will play a role in determining a parent's feelings toward the child.

Sally gave birth to a perfectly normal, healthy baby boy. She was absolutely thrilled about this fact, and could not wait to begin caring for her son, David, at home. The first several weeks were especially hard on her. She summed up her feelings in the following way:

> I was all prepared to love my son and be a good mother, but my good feelings for him were challenged from the start. He cried constantly, and it seemed that no matter what I did to soothe him, nothing worked. He just didn't respond to me as a "loving mother." I hate to say this, but I began to resent him and didn't like him very much during the first month or so. Once he began to cry less often and respond to my attempts to soothe him, I really began to like and enjoy him.

Parents may have different reactions to their child depending upon the baby's gender, what the baby looks like, how much she cries, whether or not she is easily soothed, her activity level, and so on. One could speculate that parents whose baby cries a great deal and is hard to soothe during the first month, or has special physical problems, would react very differently if their baby were the quiet, pleasant type or required no special handling. Sometimes the labor and delivery themselves can influence parents' initial feelings for their child. A mother who experiences a long, painful, and complicated delivery may initially react very differently toward her newborn than a mother who had a very short, simple labor and delivery.

Whatever your baby is like in terms of her sex, behavior, appearance, and other characteristics, she needs love, understanding, and positive acceptance as a unique individual as well as good care. If she is not exactly what you had hoped for, or is a difficult baby to care for, try not to shut yourself off from her physically or emotionally. She cannot help being what she is, and if you can somehow manage to accept her for what she is, both of you will be off to a much healthier, happier start.

Meeting Your Baby's Needs: Meeting Your Own Needs

After a day or two of living with your child, you may be struck by the fact that caring for her is an enormous task. The stark reality of round-the-clock feedings, frequent diaper changes, coping with large piles of dirty laundry, and promptly trying to satisfy her other needs may suddenly dawn on you. Your infant will be demanding and you may initially have a difficult time not only interpreting her needs but meeting them. Her crying will be loud and impossible to ignore. You will quickly discover how annoying listening to her cry can be, particularly if your attempts to quiet her are ineffective.

Dealing with both a new baby and a different daily routine, your life may suddenly seem totally disorganized. Simply keeping up with her daytime demands may be tiring. Then add to this your loss of sleep during the night and you can pretty much count on being somewhat more exhausted and irritable than usual at the end of each day, at least until she is able to sleep through the night. You are likely to find that you have little time left over for performing necessary household chores and relaxing. If you have other children to care for besides your baby, particularly in the toddlerhood age group, meeting their daily needs for food, attention, affection, and stimulation can be an additional drain on you emotionally and physically.

Where does this leave you? Many new parents tend to become very engrossed in meeting their infant's needs to the point of losing sight of their own, and their spouse's. Angela Light put it this way:

> I put my needs and my husband Jack's needs last on my list of priorities. Between preparing Tony's formulas, feeding him, changing his diapers, bathing him, washing his clothes, and answering his cries, there was little time left for Jack and me to think about ourselves as people, or as a couple. I was a mother first, and a wife, lover, and an individual last. I suppose for the first month or so I wanted it this way, and needless to say Jack and I derived great pleasure and personal satisfaction from being with and caring for our new son. Still, I felt that if someone else had just told me to take even fifteen minutes a day to pamper myself or to consider my husband's feelings, Jack and I wouldn't have felt so much as though we'd somehow gotten a bit lost as individuals or as partners.

It is not uncommon for parents to throw themselves totally into their new roles, since they are anxious to get started, their baby's needs are pressing, and they want to do the best they can for her. Nevertheless, it is also very important to take time out each day to do something for yourself and your partner as individuals aside from being parents and as a couple. Try your best to maintain your identity and consider your needs on a daily basis. Remember that in addition to being a parent, you are a person.

Parenthood After Thirty

Parenthood for the first time after age thirty is becoming more common. For some prospective parents, the delay in having a child has been deliberate. Women who have continued their formal education beyond high school, into college, and even into graduate school and those who have worked hard to establish careers of their own outside the home are often among those who have intentionally postponed parenthood. In some cases, couples have been trying to conceive for years, but, for a variety of reasons, have been unable to. Then there are also those who had not planned on a child after thirty, or forty, but after becoming pregnant, decided to go ahead with having the child.

Individual circumstances and events that lead to parents' decisions to let the pregnancy run its course show wide variation. For some, parenthood comes as a blessed, joyful event; others do not share this enthusiasm. Even among prospective parents who are ecstatic about giving birth, insecurities and apprehensions are experienced.

CONCERNS ABOUT A BABY'S EFFECT UPON YOUR MARRIAGE AND LIFESTYLE. Couples who have been married for many years often have heightened concerns about how a baby will affect their relationship with one another. Sudden changes in daily routine and lifestyle imposed by a baby are usually more acutely felt by parents who have enjoyed years of intimacy and spontaneity, and who have achieved a certain stability and balance in their marriage.

In relationships in which both partners have well-established careers, the issue of who will assume primary responsibility for the child's care may loom large, and can be a source of tension and even friction. After many years of schooling or working, women may welcome caring for a child as a refreshing change, but this is not always the case. Fears of drifting apart from one's spouse and of losing one's personal freedom, independence, and career are not uncommon.

Communication between partners is terribly important. The best and only way to resolve possible areas of question and conflict, and deal with worries and fears, is to share your thoughts, feelings, and concerns with your spouse openly. Do this frequently, on a daily basis, at a time when neither of you is rushed or preoccupied with other issues. Take time out to talk about your relationship, and what you want from one another and your marriage. Discuss your feelings about your careers and future career goals. By keeping avenues of communication open both immediately before and after your child is born, you can be more certain of maintaining the closeness and intimacy that prevailed prior to becoming parents, and resolving minor problems before they evolve into major ones.

SETTING REASONABLE EXPECTATIONS FOR YOURSELF. Being older, and supposedly "wiser" and "more mature," parents in their thirties and forties sometimes expect to be "perfect parents," capable of handling any situation that might arise. When men and women enter parenthood with unrealistic views of their own capabilities and limitations, and set overly high expectations for themselves, this can result in enormous feelings of guilt and inadequacy after their babies are born.

Whether parents are twenty-three, thirty-three, or forty-three, they are subject to the same fears and feelings of uneasiness and of occasionally being unable to cope. These feelings are natural and should be expected. The myth of the "superparent" is, indeed, only a myth. Being human, no parent can be expected to be perfect, whatever that means. Those who try to live up to an image they have of being perfect are setting themselves up for almost certain failure. Do not expect more from yourself than you can realistically give. Be prepared to ask for help, counsel, and support whenever necessary. Your added years and maturity may be an asset in child rearing. A greater asset will lie in knowing yourself well, and having a realistic idea of your own limitations and vulnerability.

Many parents who have had children after age thirty felt that there were definite advantages to being older. They were less likely to become irritated about the minor annoying aspects of their children's behavior and were more patient with them. In most cases, having had more time to establish a firmer sense of their own identities, and to pursue careers or interests, parents could relish each phase of their children's development without feeling the need to rush their children into growing up quickly.

Parenthood after thirty has both advantages and disadvantages, according to the individuals involved. How much pleasure men and women derive from being parents in large part depends upon how much time and energy they invest in learning to enjoy their children.

Men and women over thirty for whom parenthood is not a first-time event may have the additional worry of older children in the family. An older child's or teenager's response to a new baby's entrance into the family often represents an area of concern among parents. This topic is discussed on page 182.

Your Baby May Affect Your Marital Relationship

The sudden entry of a baby into a couple's lives may be a strong test of the solidity of their marital relationship. Such a major life change is often accompanied by stress, even in cases where both partners feel positively toward one another and their baby. People react to stress in different ways. Even parents who have already had one child may respond very differently the second, third, or fourth time around.

Having to extend their attention and love beyond each other to a young infant will change a couple's marriage. It can expand their ability to give and receive love and may bring them closer together, strengthening their relationship. On the other hand, it may create added tensions and conflicts between them that, if not faced and overcome, may slowly drive them apart.

Below are a few of the more common stressful areas and experiences that parents have encountered. It is hoped that your awareness of possible strains on your marriage will enable you to recognize areas of trouble more quickly and cope with them more effectively.

Maintaining good communication with one another is of prime importance to your relationship. If feelings, both positive and negative, are shared at frequent intervals, possible minor hostilities and resentments may not have a chance to grow into major sources of conflict and turmoil. The extent to which your marital relationship is affected by your baby depends a great deal upon the two of you. During the initial adjustment period after the birth of your baby, remember that love, patience, and honesty are important.

COMPETITION AND JEALOUSY BETWEEN PARENTS. It is not uncommon for a man and a woman, who prior to the arrival of their baby had shared an exclusive relationship, to begin to compete, in a sense, with one another for the affections of their baby. Each may also become a bit jealous of the time and affection that the other shares with the baby. When one parent, say the father, spends a large portion of time working away from home, and the mother spends full time each day with the baby, the father may feel jealous of the stronger bond between mother and child. He may feel somewhat left out or resentful that he cannot establish the same kind of close relationship with his child that his wife can. Subtle competition between a man and woman over the affections of their baby is natural.

Most couples, after an initial period of adjusting to the new member of their family, find that even if one of them must be away from home during the day, each can establish a close but different relationship with the baby, adding complementary dimensions to family life. Parents should recognize that it is only natural for the baby initially to establish closer ties with the parent who consistently cares for her and spends the most time with her. Also realize that you and your spouse will each build a special relationship with your baby that cannot possibly be the same. She needs both of you in a slightly different way, and as she matures, her needs may change, altering the nature of your relationships.

Jealousy between parents can create tensions. Consider the following set of circumstances. One parent whose career has previously centered around the home elects to stay home with the baby, and the other parent who has been working outside of the home continues to do so after the birth of their baby. The parent who is absent from the home most of the day is used to having dinner prepared and awaiting him or her upon arriving home and is also used to having the exclusive attention and affection of his or her spouse during the evenings.

The entry of a new baby into their lives results in adjustments that alter their relationship and this pattern of living. The parent working away from home arrives to find that dinner is not ready as before and his or her spouse is preoccupied with caring for their baby. This parent becomes jealous, feeling that his or her partner is paying more attention to the baby, and begins to regard the baby as a rival or a possible threat to the marital relationship.

These feelings of jealousy are not uncommon, particularly for the first month or so when the parent who is caring for the infant during the daytime may become very wrapped up in meeting the baby's needs, and will not have as much time, physical energy, or emotional resources to offer a spouse. Usually this kind of problem can be ironed out over the first couple of months as the baby is gradually shifted onto a more regular schedule that is better suited to parents' patterns of living. The parent who cares for her during the day becomes more relaxed and adjusted to the routine of care. Until that time, patience and understanding on the part of both mother and father can help in easing tensions. It is important for parents to be open about discussing any feelings of jealousy that may arise, and to voice concerns if their individual needs are not being sufficiently met.

PAST EXPERIENCES MAY CLOUD YOUR FEELINGS FOR ONE ANOTHER. To your role of parent, you will bring some subconscious ideas about maternal and paternal responsibilities as well as memories of your own life as a child. Your spouse will also have ideas about parental roles as well as childhood memories. Neither of you will have any way of determining ahead of time how you will react.

As you care for your child, your spouse may be struck by the realization that you are behaving like your own parents. Similarly, you may notice for the first time that your spouse's style of parenting and behaving closely resembles that of one or the other of your in-laws.

Take the following case. Margo had never really had positive feelings for her father-in-law. She had always regarded him as being too strict, stern, and aloof. Several weeks after she had given birth to a baby girl, Mimi, Margo discovered that her husband, Rob, was acting a great deal like his father. This irritated her, and she brought it to his attention. After a long discussion, Margo and Rob realized that he was identifying with his father, and was subconsciously emulating his father's behavior. Both Margo and Rob found this to be unusual given the fact that Rob had not been close to his father and, in fact, had not seen very much of him except for major family gatherings during the past ten years.

There is a good chance that if you are a woman, you may, to some extent, act like your own mother once you assume the role of a parent. Whether or not this irritates your husband will, in large part, depend upon how he feels about your mother. Likewise, if you are a man, because you mainly identify with your father, you may respond to the paternal role in a manner much the way he did. Your wife may or may not be annoyed by this. Both you and your spouse may be somewhat surprised and even disturbed by the new personality traits and behaviors that surface in both of you after your baby is born.

You and your spouse may discover that memories of your respective childhoods can trigger in both of you all kinds of feelings, including joy, sorrow, anger, jealousy, frustration, fear, and so on. Sometimes the feelings mentioned here can be aroused while the memories remain buried. Each of you should try to discuss these feelings with the other. Support, guidance, and extra reassurance may be needed at those times.

In the event that either of you harbors feelings of resentment or hostility toward a parent of the opposite sex, these, too, may enter into your marital relationship and perhaps create tensions between you. Don, for example, had never liked his mother, and had bad memories about her. He had always regarded her as overbearing and domineering. Don's unresolved hostilities toward his mother were, without his realizing it, displaced onto his wife, Sue. When Sue assumed the role of a parent, Don's feelings and his behavior toward her suddenly changed. He began to respond toward Sue almost as if she were his mother, rather than his wife. Negative feelings for one's own parent may, in some cases, be unconsciously transferred onto one's spouse, and this can create a real source of friction or argument between marital partners.

It is important for you and your spouse to be as open and honest about your feelings as possible. Sharing them with one another and helping each other examine feelings and emotions may enable the two of you to understand each other better and also the ways in which you handle or react to your baby. Being close-mouthed about feelings and emotions may create unnecessary tensions in your lives, forming a distance between you that increases through the years.

Rearing your child will be much easier and more enjoyable if the two of you have a good marital relationship and work at maintaining it. Your relationship as a couple, and as parents, need not be constrained by memories and feelings of the past. If you can deal with them objectively, you may be able to put them into proper perspective and use them constructively in guiding you toward creating a different and more enjoyable family situation.

ADJUSTMENTS IN YOUR SEXUAL RELATIONSHIP. Some of the physical and emotional changes that occur shortly after the arrival of the new baby may affect a couple's sexual relationship. This issue is discussed in the Family Feelings and Concerns section in Infancy 1 on pages 173–77.

Possible Changes in Your Social Life

Many couples have found that certain aspects of their social life changed after they had a baby. Some of these changes may be unavoidable and others may be elective.

LOSS OF SPONTANEITY AND FEELING INITIALLY TIED DOWN. With a new baby to care for, parents often feel a loss of spontaneity in their social lives. A common complaint is that they cannot plan evenings out on the spur of the moment or respond to last-minute invitations. If you are the type of person who generally makes arrangements to go out in advance, or has a baby-sitter exclusively at your disposal, you are less likely to be disturbed by the loss of spontaneity that seems to go hand in hand with parenthood. One solution if you prefer spur-of-the-moment activities, is to try to find a baby-sitter who is usually free and willing to accept last-minute calls. This may or may not be easy, but it can help.

You may be somewhat more tied down to home for the first month or so. Your friends may not mind your bringing the baby along to their homes so that you can breast-feed her whenever this is necessary, but there is a good chance that at least for the first six to eight weeks you will find it easier to entertain friends in your own home, or else plan to get together with them between feeding times. There is also a tendency for new parents to feel more tired than usual toward the end of the day, so late-night get-togethers may also have to be pushed up a bit to early evening. Some new parents simply feel more comfortable staying home for the first month or two, and this can be helpful in strengthening the family. Eventually, however, parents will need some time to be alone as well as a break from the home atmosphere and demands of their new baby. There is no need to rush to leave your baby in someone else's care for a few hours before you are ready. It is not a good idea, however, to postpone going out alone for too many months. Short breaks from child rearing can help you put things into perspective and maintain your individuality and identity. They can also represent opportunities to re-establish closeness between you and your spouse.

SHIFTS IN YOUR CIRCLE OF FRIENDS. You may notice that your circle of friends shifts a bit after your baby arrives. This depends to a great extent upon you and your friends. You may be eager to discuss other things besides your baby when you get together with your friends, enjoying the opportunity for a refreshing change. Many parents are so excited and wrapped up in their new baby that they can speak of little else. Since childless couples and singles who have no children may be less interested in hearing details about your baby than other parents, you may feel more at ease socializing with people who have children.

Other parents may also prove to be more understanding about situations in which your baby gets in the way of your plans. There will inevitably be times when your baby comes down with an ear infection, a high fever, or a bad cough and you will decide to cancel your plans and stay home with her. There will also be occasions when baby-sitters get sick or call at the last minute to say they cannot come. Your friends who have no children may be very sympathetic and not mind your last-minute cancellations or including your child in their plans from time to time. On the other hand, your hosts may not be understanding at all.

The Single Parent Experience

This book was designed to take into account the special needs of the single parent, both mothers and fathers. Specific topics related to discipline, sexual identity, and many other issues that should be of interest to single parents are included in the infancy, toddlerhood, and preschool sections.

Having a firm commitment to the child and the family is the single most important factor that will ensure the effectiveness and success of the single parent family structure. This commitment enables single parents to achieve a healthy balance in meeting the child's changing needs as well as their own during each developmental phase.

It is very important for a single parent to be confident about handling the child, since guilt and insecurity can interfere with a parent's judgment when it comes to many issues, particularly the issue of discipline. Many single parents find that they have difficulty not only with deciding what limits are important to establish, but also with backing up those limits. This is only natural since they have no other adult to confer with regarding discipline. If this becomes a problem, a parent should discuss the subject of discipline with relatives, friends who have children, the child's pediatrician, or the family doctor.

A major concern of single parents is whether or not their child will be negatively affected by not having a second parent. There is no easy answer to this question. A great deal depends upon how the parent who rears the child handles the situation. It is generally accepted that a young child benefits from having a close relationship with a parent of the same sex as well as a parent of the opposite sex.

Assuming your baby is a boy and has no male model to identify with, it is advisable to allow him to spend some time with a male such as a grandfather, uncle, or anyone who shows an interest. Likewise, if your baby is a girl, and has no female role model, it is important to arrange for her to spend time with a woman with whom she can identify. This becomes more crucial as children grow.

Motherhood Without Marriage

The woman who becomes pregnant outside of a marital relationship is difficult, if not impossible, to characterize, since circumstances, individuals, and motives vary considerably. More women today are deliberately deciding upon this family arrangement. With the decision to allow a pregnancy to run its course and rear a child alone comes innumerable rewards and pleasures as well as opportunities for personal expression. At the same time there can be personal, familial, and social stresses along with economic pressures that have to be faced and overcome.

Motherhood without marriage can be very satisfactory for both parent and child. A woman rearing a child alone represents a family. A top priority should be given not just to preserving the family structure but making it work well for both mother and child.

There are many negative pressures on mothers who are not married, but a mother and her child can form a stable family. Love and care for the child and mutual satisfaction of needs provide the main basis for establishing a strong parent-child bond. A mother's attitude, determination, confidence, and how she handles her career as a parent and life as a total person will largely determine the effectiveness of the family. It is encouraging to see how many single mothers are doing a splendid job of rearing normal, healthy, well-adjusted children.

PARENTHOOD MAY SEEM MORE COMPLICATED AT FIRST. The questions, doubts, and insecurities almost universally experienced by all new parents are usually felt more intensely by single mothers. Expressions of disapproval and doubt from other people, particularly close relatives and friends, can heighten a new mother's concern for both her and her child's well-being.

Upon deciding to rear a child alone, a woman takes on the sole responsibility in parenthood. This can seem like an overwhelming burden, at least initially. Having emotional support and encouragement from one's family, friends, and physician can ease the burden and make child rearing easier in a host of other ways.

It is extremely important for a mother to have a realistic view of both her strengths and weaknesses, and capabilities and limitations. She should realize how crucial it is to know when to ask for help, should this become necessary. Going it alone can be rough at times, rougher than some mothers anticipate. Even the most capable of parents, married and single, sometimes need to turn to others for encouragement, support, and financial assistance.

Handling the entire job by oneself automatically means that one's personal freedom will be more limited, and more sacrifices and adjustments, both personal and financial, will have to be made. Married parents face these same issues, but usually to a somewhat lesser extent.

Single mothers often complain of financial strains. Assuming that the mother is not financially well off, and is not receiving child support, she must either decide to work and engage someone to care for her child in her absence, or she must accept state financial assistance. The issue of who is to care for the child takes on great significance for the single mother, and is often not easily resolved.

A very common worry among single mothers is that growing up without a father in the home will have an adverse effect upon the child. This does not have to happen. Boys as well as girls need to know that there are men in this world and should have opportunities to spend time with them. A mother should provide some contact with men for her child—be it a friend, grandfather, uncle, etc. It is helpful to choose a male who can establish a long-lasting relationship with the child, rather than one who will be a transient figure. Consistency in relationships is important for young children, although there should be no problem for the child in establishing relationships with several adult males.

Especially during late toddlerhood and throughout the preschool stage, a young boy needs to have regular contact with another male(s), since this will enable him to imitate and identify with a person of the same sex, serving in the capacity of a parent figure. A mother must guard against constantly showing resentment toward men, down-grading them in front of her child, treating her boy as a "substitute" spouse, or encouraging him to identify solely with her. It is also advisable to provide him with opportunities to play and form friendships with other little boys and to have them visit the house on a regular basis. A mother's attitude toward men and her treatment of them are very important, for this plays an important role in shaping her child's attitudes about men and his or her relationships with members of the opposite sex.

Once children are old enough to recognize that some children have both a mom and a dad, they can be expected to ask questions, and perhaps even express some jealousy or resentment over the fact that they only have a mother. This is only natural. A mother should not overreact to her child's comments, or become defensive and feel the need to justify the family structure or apologize for it.

The absence of a father will probably make some difference to the child who is aware of differences in family composition. This recognition of differences need not have an adverse effect upon the youngster, however. A mother should not feel threatened or try to deny that differences exist. Rather it is helpful to treat differences matter-of-factly, while showing respect for them. Treat them as you would if the child pointed out other variations in people's homes, materialistic possessions, lifestyles, skin color, and so forth. A child who feels loved and is secure in the relationship with his or her mother, and has ample opportunities to form relationships with adult males, is unlikely to feel cheated because a permanent father is absent from the home.

Separation and Divorce

Men and women who have recently been through a divorce or separation have in most cases had to make numerous emotional adjustments to the major changes in their lives. Add to this the many emotional adjustments that accompany the birth of a baby and assuming the role of a parent and it is easy to see that divorce and separation place additional stresses on new parents. Two major life changes within nine months make life that much more difficult.

There are many problems that single parents in this situation encounter. Some, of course, will be unique to their individual circumstances. Others are apt to be very similar to those of the single parent who adopts a baby or has never been married.

The insecurity, fear, and doubt that are experienced by most prospective parents are often felt more intensely by single parents who had not expected to face rearing their children by themselves. Single parents may also have feelings of loneliness and despair, particularly when familial help and emotional support are lacking. When a parent has a supportive family or close friends living nearby, this can be of enormous assistance, not only during the period immediately after the baby's birth but in the weeks and months that follow.

CREATING A HEALTHY HOME ATMOSPHERE. It is not uncommon for some bitterness or resentment to accompany a separation or divorce. Although this certainly may not be true in every case, the emotional trauma of the breakup of marital partners can leave long-lasting emotional scars. A major problem area for a divorced or newly separated parent is creating a healthy emotional atmosphere for the baby. Feelings of antagonism toward one's ex-partner may, in certain circumstances, interfere with a parent's ability to properly care for the baby or meet the baby's emotional needs.

A baby is, of course, a constant reminder of one's ex-spouse. Should a parent feel bitterness or anger toward his or her former spouse, there is a good chance that after the baby is born, she, too, will be the target of her parent's unresolved bitterness and resentment, particularly in cases where parents have repressed these feelings following the separation or divorce, or have been ashamed or reluctant to express them with other people.

Bitterness and resentment can also result in single parents being less tolerant of some of the annoying aspects of being a new parent, such as coping with vast numbers of dirty diapers and laundry, and being awakened during the night for feedings. It may also cause parents to overreact to some of the perfectly normal, but aggravating aspects of their baby's behavior such as crying and fussing, her desire for repetition, and her mealtime messes. These parents may punish their baby for the slightest reason, or in a few cases, abuse their child physically or emotionally.

It is important for a new parent who has recently been through a separation or divorce to discuss tensions, anxieties, difficulties, and feelings of bitterness or resentment openly and honestly with relatives, friends, or the family doctor. Getting feelings out and receiving support from others can help a parent put things into proper perspective. Angry and negative feelings must be channeled in constructive rather than destructive ways that might be harmful to the baby. The discussion of the single parent on pages 11–13 may also be of assistance in easing your adjustment to parenthood.

Stepparenthood

Increasing numbers of women and men in our society are assuming roles as stepparents. This can be a happy, positive step in the lives of all concerned, but may also be scary and stressful for some parents as well as their children. When a man or woman who has never been a parent marries a person who already has a child (children), many of the concerns and doubts that he or she will have are likely to be similar to those of other prospective parents. However, there is little doubt that prospective or new stepparents have some special worries and concerns, such as how to deal effectively with the child's relationship with her other or absent parent, or how the child should address them. In cases where a man or woman who has a child (children) by a previous marriage marries someone who also has a child by a previous marriage, additional concerns may arise such as how to cope with the special situation of "blended" families. Part-time stepparents will also have some concerns that are similar to those of full-time stepparents, and some that are unique to their situation.

Stepparents often wonder if there are things they can do to diminish problems or avoid pitfalls that other stepparents have faced, particularly during the adjustment period. The answer is "yes." With some advance preparation, stepparents usually feel less insecure about their new roles, more able to cope with difficulties that arise, and better able to avoid common mistakes.

The material that follows provides information and some guidelines to help answer some frequently asked questions and alleviate worries and doubts. It should assist stepparents in realizing the importance of exploring their own emotions and thoughts about their new roles, and trying to understand the feelings of other members in their new, unique family.

ASSUMING THE ROLE OF A STEPPARENT. The old stereotype of the mean and selfish stepparent that is prevalent in some books and in well-known fairy tales, such as "Hansel and Gretel" and "Cinderella," can make assuming the role of a stepparent that much more difficult. The negative images that one often associates with the word "stepparent" can put new stepmothers or stepfathers on the spot, and make them feel as though they must prove to everyone and to themselves that they do not fit the stereotype. It is understandable why a stepparent might feel anxious or insecure.

It is especially helpful for stepparents to explore and consider their feelings about their new spouse's former mate and the family's past. A stepchild is often a constant reminder of the past that their mate shared with a former wife or husband. Some jealousy and resentment are only natural. However, if this gets out of hand, it can undermine the development of a good stepparent-stepchild relationship, and contribute to numerous problems within the home.

A stepparent who marries someone who has been divorced may benefit from exploring the following kinds of issues:

How jealous and resentful are you of your spouse's former mate?

Do you feel threatened by this person?

What mechanisms have you developed for coping with negative feelings?

Can you encourage your stepchild to maintain positive feelings for and ties to the natural parent who is absent?

How do you feel about the child's visits to her natural, absent parent?

If the child makes negative comments about her absent parent, do you agree or disagree with her?

In taking on the role of a stepparent to a child whose natural parents are divorced, a man or woman should realize that it is usually in the youngster's best interest to continue loving and respecting her absent parent. The child should be able to talk openly about that parent, and should be encouraged to visit, call on the phone, or correspond by mail. If the child says negative or antagonistic things about the absent parent, it is usually best for the stepparent to try and refrain from agreeing. It is better to help the child sort out her real feelings about her absent parent. Maintaining ties to the absent parent can be important to the child.

The situation is different in cases in which a child's natural parent has died. Yet, stepparents may still feel somewhat jealous of or threatened by the deceased mate's memory. Exploring the following kinds of questions may be of some assistance:

Do you feel as though you must compete with the memory of the dead parent for the child's affection?

Are you jealous of the past or loving relationship that the child shared with her deceased parent?

How do you feel when the child talks about her deceased parent?

Do you try to help the child treasure the memory of her dead parent?

The older the child, the stronger her memory will be of her deceased parent. For the child's sake, it is important for a stepparent to encourage her to speak openly about her dead parent, and treasure his or her memory. The stepparent should try to refrain from preventing the child from looking at photographs of the deceased parent or keeping mementos or other such cherished items given to her by that parent.

Whether the child's natural parents are divorced or one parent has died, a stepparent should realize that he or she is dealing with a family that has been through a crisis. Although it is understandable that the stepparent may feel somewhat jealous of or threatened by the past, it is not advisable to attempt to compete with it. Stepparents will want to explore the past and try to come to terms with their own and the child's feelings. The events that took place and the relationships that were formed in the past will color those in the present and future, but it is the present that really counts.

STEPPARENTS CARING FOR A CHILD ON A PART-TIME BASIS. When someone marries a divorced person with a child (children), and the child lives either mainly with the other natural parent, or custody of the child is shared (joint custody), the new spouse becomes a stepparent on a part-time basis. "Part-time" stepparents have traditionally been women, but as co-parenting and other types of divided custody arrangements gain in popularity, more men are assuming this role as well. In most cases the part-time stepparent has the child mainly on weekends or vacations, or for other limited blocks of time. A stepparent's role is usually secondary to that of the child's natural mother or father.

When a stepparent is on friendly terms with his or her spouse's former mate, this can certainly make the transition from the child's primary home to her second home much more comfortable for the members of both households. However, feelings of competition, jealousy, and resentment often arise to complicate the situation and create problems of divided loyalty for the child. It is almost always in the child's best interest for her stepparent and the former mate to try at least to get along in her presence and not try to undermine her ability to remain loyal to her natural parent and still develop a good, but different, relationship with her stepparent.

A stepparent can do numerous things to make the child feel more welcome in the home. Young children often appreciate having some of their prized toys or favorite possessions or foods in their "other" home. They will also want a comfortable area(s) in which to sleep and play. Having their own special toys and areas in their second home can give them a sense of comfort and security as well as an increased sense of belonging.

It is unnecessary for a stepparent to go overboard in rearranging the home in order to please the child who does not live there full time. However, some changes will have to be made. Particularly with crawling infants and toddlers, safety becomes an important issue. It will become necessary for a part-time stepparent to safety-proof certain areas of the home or at least one room.

Discipline is a difficult issue for stepparents, since the major burden of responsibility usually lies with the spouse's former mate. A stepparent is entitled to establish his or her house rules and regulations, which may or may not be similar to those in the child's other or more permanent home. On the other hand, the young child may be quite upset by marked inconsistencies in methods of management and limit setting, and the shifts in home and rules can be confusing.

It is true that the stepparent who cares for a child on a part-time basis is placed in an awkward position. Therefore, it is generally wise not to upset the balance in the child's life by being overly strict or overly lenient. Stick to setting limits according to what is really important for the child's safety and well-being, as long as the other members of the household are not unduly inconvenienced or their rights are not infringed upon. A stepparent should try not to allow the child's bothersome behaviors to become major sources of aggravation and conflict, if they are in regard to relatively unimportant issues.

Understanding that the young child may be upset and confused when too many changes in living patterns are introduced, a stepparent should try to help the child make transitions between homes by not making major alterations in patterns in other areas besides discipline. While the child is in her second home, her daily routine, including meals, baths, naps, and so forth, should be maintained whenever possible. When there is open communication between stepparent and the spouse's former mate, it is much easier to deal with problems that might arise for the child and thus make it less stressful on the child and the family.

It is not uncommon for stepparents to feel unappreciated by their stepchildren, and somewhat resentful about having to care for "someone else's" children, especially when the visits are mainly on weekends and the youngsters arrive, eat, have to be entertained, and then leave. These feelings should be explored with a spouse and ways to reduce them, if possible, should be sought; denying their existence is not advisable.

Children whose dealings with their natural parents are limited to weekends, vacations, or other designated times may understandably want to spend some time alone with them. A stepparent should be sensitive to these needs, and perhaps even take the initiative in suggesting that the stepchild and natural parent be alone together. A jealous child may feel less threatened when the suggestions come directly from the stepparent.

Part-time parenthood does have its disadvantages, which are experienced in different ways and in varying degrees by those who assume this role. Certain allowances and compromises will have to be made, not all of which may be fully acceptable to the stepparent. It may take many visits before a child's confusion over her new stepparent and the changes in homes subsides. Given ample time, the child should start to feel more comfortable with the new arrangements, and more positively toward her new part-time mother or father.

BLENDED FAMILIES—STEPSIBLINGS. Sibling rivalry is to be expected among children who have the same parent(s). It is understandable and quite normal for every youngster to want to be the favorite, or to have the exclusive attention and affection of her parent(s). In blended families, in which children of different marriages are living together in the same home, normal sibling rivalries are often heightened.

A major problem lies in the fact that there is little time for a child to adjust to sharing her parent's attention with a stepsibling on a gradual basis. Building good relationships with another child, such as a new baby, even within the same family, takes time. However, adjustment usually occurs over about a year's time. In the case of blended families, youngsters from two separate families are often thrown together all at once, so adjustment problems can be more intense as well as prolonged. Age differences among the children can add to adjustment difficulties.

An only child suddenly brought together with several children from a different marriage (stepsiblings) may have an especially hard time adjusting. She not only has to get used to sharing her natural parent's attention with her new siblings, but also has to adjust to her new stepparent and the stepsiblings themselves. Being suddenly thrust into a larger family can leave such a child feeling overwhelmed, left out, confused, and even resentful. Parents should take special care with the child, observe her reactions, try to understand her feelings, and do their best to make the adjustment as easy as possible without pressuring her. It may take a long time before she feels comfortable in the new life situation and feels a real sense of belonging. Her stepsiblings should be encouraged to try to make her feel welcome and an active participant in household activities.

When children from different families suddenly have to live together under one roof, and probably even share the same bedrooms or at least the same living space, problems and conflicts should be expected. Quite often arguments arise over television programs, nap or bedtime hours, meals, sharing toys, and privileges. With each set of children having been used to one way of doing things, it is no wonder that problems can increase when they all have to adjust to differences in living habits.

Parents themselves will be forced to re-evaluate former styles of living, rules, and regulations. Whenever possible, compromises should be made for the benefit of each family member. In some cases parents find it best to establish an entirely new set of household rules and schedules for the "new" family structure gradually. They will have to talk often about how things are or are not working out and do their best to nip problems in the bud before they get out of hand. Keeping open lines of communication and a watchful eye out for sources of conflict can be helpful, particularly in the early weeks and months.

It is important for parents to realize that certain ways in which they treat or handle the children can intensify rivalrous feelings. Parents, for instance, may favor their own children, but may go overboard trying to deny this favoritism. In doing this, they may handle their own children more strictly and their stepchildren more leniently in an attempt to win them over. As a result, their own offspring may feel pushed out, unloved, and resentful, and the rivalry between stepchildren may increase. While it is crucial to make stepchildren feel welcomed and loved, one's own children's needs should be satisfied as well.

In those cases where parents actually feel resentment toward their stepchildren, but try to deny that these feelings exist, they may transmit this message to their own offspring, and add fuel to pre-existing rivalry among stepsiblings. Rather than acting directly on these feelings of hostility or resentment, they may, with or without realizing it, allow their natural children to express the hostility that they feel toward their stepchildren. This can occur in numerous ways. For example, by not disciplining their natural children appropriately when they pick on or abuse the stepchildren, they are allowing them to act out their own antagonism for their stepchildren. Their natural children will be quick to sense the encouragement they are getting to express resentment toward their stepsiblings. It is easy to see where this would intensify rivalry and undermine the children's ability to make a healthy adjustment to one another.

Children are very sensitive about the manner in which they are managed. They are sure to pick up on their parents' feelings of favoritism or resentment, whether or not they are actually verbalized. Parents should work toward establishing rules and a program of discipline that is applied consistently to all of the children in the home, and not try to deny preferences for their natural children. Rather than denying preferences, it is advisable to admit that they exist, and then try to minimize them.

Some stepparents have found that their natural children resent having always to share their attention with stepsiblings. It may be possible to work it out so that each parent has some special time alone with his or her natural children, and other times with the entire group. Each family situation is different, so parents may hit upon any number of possible arrangements that work the best for them and their children.

In the beginning parents often wonder if there are any ways to foster closeness among stepsiblings. Some parents have found that joint projects or special outings help to draw the family together. Perhaps everyone can become involved in planning a special day or weekend excursion to a place that all of the children decide upon themselves. Maybe all of the children can help pick out new wallpaper for a shared bedroom or playroom.

Parents should not set their expectations of themselves or their children or stepchildren too high in the early stages of living together. Sometimes new problems that arise seem overwhelming to everyone, and can place great strains on a couple's marriage. The utmost patience and consideration of feelings will be required, along with a strong spirit of determination to make the new family unit workable for all. If problems within a home or with a particular individual reach such a level that they cannot be successfully resolved despite parental efforts, it would be advisable to seek professional help.

Although blended families may face special hurdles, it is important not to lose sight of the fact that problems exist from time to time in every family. It is easy to blame every squabble or problem that arises on the fact that this is a "blended family" when, in fact, this may not be at the root of the problem at all. Overreacting to everyday conflicts and arguments that are bound to occur, particularly when parents and siblings are, in a sense, "feeling each other out" is not a good idea.

Learning to live within a blended family has its advantages, too, for both parents and children alike. Individuals often become adept at compromising, sharing, learning to get along with others, and accepting differences among people. Placing too much emphasis on always agreeing, however, may not be the right approach for a given family unit. Quite often the most stable families are made up of strong individuals who state their opinions openly.

HALF SIBLINGS. Some remarried couples, each with their own set of children, decide to have another child of their own. The new baby then becomes a half sibling or half brother or sister to the other children. In some cases a new baby seems to unite the family and offers the other youngsters a greater sense of security and stability. The children of different marriages all have a tie through the new baby. This tie can reinforce the positive feelings that stepsiblings have for one another.

At the same time the new baby may be viewed as a threat, particularly to young children under the age of five. They must share their parent further, and may be very resentful of this. Worries about being displaced in their parent's affection or being pushed out can be strong in some youngsters. Those children who are old enough to realize that they have only one natural parent in the home, while the new baby belongs to both parents, may feel more resentful of the baby.

Parents should be aware of the kinds of feelings and anxieties that can arise in young children both prior to and after the arrival of a new baby. Special care should be taken to offer young children the extra reassurance, love, and individual attention that they may need at such a time. The suggestions on pages 25–27 for preparing children for a new baby may be helpful.

WHAT TO CALL A STEPPARENT. The question of how a child should address a stepparent often arises, and there are many different ways in which families can handle the situation. This does not usually become an important issue during infancy or early toddlerhood, since the child will probably use "ma ma" or "da da," or the name that has been selected by her parents and repeated. The older toddler or preschool child, however, may be understandably confused or even upset if her natural parent is living or if she maintains a good relationship with the natural parent and is encouraged or pressured to call her stepparent "Mommy" or "Daddy" (or whatever name is used for her natural parent). The same may be true in cases in which a child's natural parent has died but her memory of him or her is still strong. Calling the stepparent by the same name that was used for the deceased natural parent may make a child feel disloyal to that parent, or as though that parent is being replaced. This can be quite upsetting for the young child, so it is often more comfortable for children to refer to their stepparent by another name.

On the other hand, when children have a poor relationship with their natural parent, or have minimal or no contact with this person, and want to address their stepparent as "Mommy" or "Daddy" (or whatever name is used for their natural parent), this might prove to be a comfortable solution for all. In some cases in which a child's natural parent has died, the child may actually express a desire to address her stepparent the same way as her deceased parent. This can be a very positive step forward in cementing the relationship with the stepparent. Some families use variations on "Mommy" and "Daddy" and find solutions in names such as "Ma," "Mommy Ellen," "Mom," "Pa," "Pop," "Dad," or "Daddy Bob." In other families children refer to their stepparents by their first names, although this may be offensive to some stepparents.

Consideration should be given to a child's feelings and also to the stepparent's feelings in deciding upon a name; everyone should feel comfortable with it. Of primary importance is the nature of the relationship between stepparent and stepchild; the label is relatively unimportant if the relationship is positive.

CHANGE OF SURNAME AND/OR ADOPTION BY THE STEPPARENT. Whether or not a stepparent should legally adopt a child is a question that often arises. This is a very complicated and emotionally charged issue for most families. There are numerous aspects to consider, such as how the child will be affected by the adoption or change of surname, how this will affect the natural father if he is still living, and whether or not the stepfather is prepared to assume financial responsibility for the child's upbringing even if the new marriage dissolves, and so forth. In considering the possibility of adoption or even just a change in surname, it is advisable for all of the adults who are directly involved to get together and discuss the situation in depth. It is sometimes wise to enlist the aid of a professional person such as a minister, priest, rabbi, psychiatrist, psychologist, family counselor, social worker, or someone else who is familiar with the family.

In cases in which a young child has been abandoned by the natural father, and feels a strong sense of rejection, adoption by the stepparent may be a good way to help the youngster begin to patch up psychological and emotional wounds, and a positive way to cement the relationship with the stepparent. Bear in mind that the nature of the relationship between stepparent and stepchild is what really counts. If the relationship is positive, then the adoption may be of benefit, but if it is not, it is doubtful that the adoption would be of value in markedly improving it. In cases in which a child has a good or ongoing relationship with the natural father, the child may wish to remain identified with him, and it is often in her best interest to do so. Adoption in this situation or a change in surname might prove to be traumatic to both parties. When a child's real father is deceased, but his memory is strong, again, it might be best for the child to keep the father's surname and to postpone adoption. A great deal depends upon the individual circumstances and the child's wishes and underlying feelings and ties to the natural parent.

Young children are incapable of making such a difficult decision on their own; they rely upon their parents to decide what is best for them. The school-aged child is more likely than the toddler or preschool child to be aware that her surname is unlike that of her stepsiblings or half siblings and, therefore, is more likely to be upset by this. Quite often parents decide to postpone legal adoption until the child is older and more capable of taking an active role in the decision-making process. If a child is upset over differences in surnames, it is usually possible for her to use her stepparent's surname at least on a temporary basis for school forms and purposes. Then she will not have to explain name differences to her contemporaries constantly or feel uneasy about having a surname different from her stepsiblings or half siblings. When she is older, she can choose to have her surname legally changed to that of her stepparent without adoption, or can retain her natural father's surname without difficulty. Again, it is crucial to give this matter the utmost consideration and thought due to the complexity of the issue.

STEPPARENTHOOD DURING INFANCY. Infants have an enormous need for verbalized love, physical demonstrations of affection, and individualized attention from a parent figure. Their dependency upon parents for emotional satisfaction and the satisfaction of physical needs is so great that they often make a fairly smooth transition from one parent to another in comparison with a toddler or preschool child. It may not take them too long to bond to a stepparent.

On the other hand, very young children are sensitive to new people and changes. Bear in mind that even in the first few months of life an infant develops bonds to the person(s) caring for her. She also becomes familiar with routines and her immediate environment, so that she may be upset when a person to whom she has become attached leaves and a "stranger" takes over. The older infant is more likely than the young infant to be disturbed by a shift in major care-givers, routines, or surroundings. A stepparent may detect signs that the child is upset such as an increase in tension outlets, crying, sleeping difficulties, appetite loss, rejection of the stepparent's offers of affection, and clinging to the natural parent.

It is not uncommon for stepparents to take an infant's initial negative response personally and feel hurt and rejected, afraid that a close bond will never develop between them. These feelings are understandable, but it is important to put things into proper perspective. A baby's initial disturbed reaction to the loss of a parent figure or a shift in care-givers should be viewed in a positive light, as an indication of her emotional development and the quality of care received thus far. A very young child's ability to perceive changes in people, routines, and her surroundings should also be taken as a positive sign. A child who formed close attachments with the natural parent who cared for her since birth should also be capable of developing a close, loving relationship with a stepparent. The length of time it will take for this to occur varies, but will depend, in large part, upon the quality of care received and the quality of time spent with her stepparent. It will also depend upon whether the child's physical and emotional needs are satisfactorily met.

It is best for a stepparent to allow the child to spend a period of time sizing him or her up. The child needs to become familiar with the stepparent's face, voice, smell, touch, and different methods of handling. Just as the stepparent wants to understand all of the child's qualities and ways that make her special, the child needs to find out what makes her new parent special, too. Guard against sudden alterations of routines, diet, and living quarters. With an older infant, proceed very slowly on matters of discipline as well. Especially in the early phases of the relationship, it is advisable to devote a great deal of time to making the young child feel loved, wanted, and secure. Even if only gradually, the child will react positively to this, and come to love her stepparent.

ASSUMING THE ROLE OF A STEPPARENT TO A TODDLER OR PRESCHOOL CHILD. Men and women assuming the role of a stepparent to a toddler or preschool child should be prepared for a certain amount of resistance as well as other possible difficulties. The older the child is, the more time she has had to build attachments to her natural parent, and become familiar with routines, living quarters, and lifestyles. Having to adjust to a new parent can be very upsetting for some children, and may be viewed as a real crisis in their lives. The reactions that youngsters in these stages of development may have and some practical hints for stepparents are provided in the toddlerhood and preschool sections of the book on pages 556–59 and 782–85 respectively.

The Extended Family Living Arrangement

Rearing a child in an extended, or communal, family living situation presents a particular challenge, especially when parents themselves have been raised in a nuclear, or traditional two-parent, family. Parents may have numerous concerns about their own feelings, the feelings of others in the group, and how their baby will be affected. They may worry that other group members will not do "right" by their child or that they will lose control over the child or have difficulty sharing their child's affections with other people. They may also worry about the possibility of the group dissolving and the effect this will have upon their child. In addition, they may have certain aims for their child and may worry that other members will interfere with them or try to shape behavior patterns and attitudes or values that are at odds with theirs.

The extended family living situation can vary considerably in size, composition, objectives, styles, requirements of members, and so forth. There are some parents who feel that this alternative living situation is well suited to their own and their child's needs. In some cases it offers more freedom, flexibility, opportunities for forming relationships, companionship, and chances for sharing child care responsibilities. However, as in any type of living arrangement there are advantages and disadvantages.

Parents who are considering this type of living situation should give the matter careful deliberation. Top priority should be given to selecting a group that is stable and can satisfy their needs and those of their children. Questions, doubts, and concerns that parents have, no matter how trivial they may seem, should be discussed with other group members, both when everyone is gathered together, and with individuals. It is important for parents to be honest with themselves about their philosophies, aims, hopes, and expectations regarding the rearing of their child, and then be open about sharing these feelings with the group to determine whether or not the arrangement is the best one for them. Parents should also be aware that other adults in the group may not know how to care for a baby, and may need to be given advance preparation as well as detailed instructions after the child is born.

Adoption

The number of couples who would like to adopt infants greatly exceeds the number of infants available for adoption. Many factors contribute to this imbalance. More than half of all single mothers are now deciding to rear their babies alone rather than put them up for adoption. The use of contraceptives and the legalization of abortion have also had a major impact in reducing the number of babies available for adoption.

Many people who have their hearts set on adopting an infant have to wait a considerable period of time, or may not even be able to adopt a baby at all. Waiting lists of couples wanting to adopt young babies are extremely long at most state and private agencies. The availability of babies can vary from state to state as well as from one agency to another within each state. Among those most often waiting to be adopted and needing permanent families are older youngsters, those with special handicaps, and groups of children coming from one family who do not want to be separated from one another. The situation often shows considerable variation from one city and state to another.

The procedure for locating approved adoption agencies can vary. Many people interested in adoption ask friends, relatives, and acquaintances who have adopted children for advice and recommendations. A more direct way to make inquiries is to contact an appropriate state government agency such as the Bureau of Children's (or Juvenile) Services or State Department of Children and Youth Services, which often operate as part of the Department of Institutions and Agencies. The exact title of government agencies will vary from one state to another. Adoption agencies, both state and private, are also listed in the Yellow Pages of telephone directories under the heading "Adoption."

ADOPTION THROUGH A REPUTABLE AGENCY. Adopting a baby through an approved state or private agency is by far the safest and most advisable approach. A reputable child placement agency normally takes great care in screening mothers who are considering giving their babies up for adoption and works with them in making sure that they have made the right decision. A good adoption agency is more likely to have pertinent medical information that can assist a case worker in placing a child, as well as adoptive parents in rearing the baby.

Approved agencies also take great care in screening applicants desiring a baby. The procedures can be different depending upon the particular agency's policy. A couple may be required to attend one or more group sessions designed to offer them information about adoption as well as help them learn more about their own feelings. A case worker is usually assigned to a couple whose interest in adoption is still strong. In the process of assessing applicants, a home study is usually required.

Even when applicants have been approved they may still have to wait for a period of time until the baby is placed in their home. The waiting period varies. During the transition or waiting period, young infants are usually placed in foster homes.

Parents adopting older babies should be aware of possible changes in their baby's behavior that can arise when she is moved from the foster home. Even during the first few months a baby can build up attachments with the person(s) who have been caring for her as well as a familiarity with routines and her surroundings. She may become upset when placed in an unfamiliar environment and cared for by "strangers." The older the infant, the more likely she is to be disturbed by changes in parent figures and her environment, although infants as young as three months may also react negatively at first.

In adopting an older child, parents should be prepared for more marked changes in behavior and personality. The older the child is, the more time she has had to build emotional attachments and become familiar with a routine, living quarters, and lifestyle. Being suddenly thrust into a new environment can sometimes be upsetting for a child. Patience, understanding, and tolerance from her adoptive parents can help her make an easier transition, and will be important in building up a good relationship. Rest assured that a child who has shown a capacity to form attachments with the person who cared for her since birth also has the capacity to form new, permanent attachments with her adoptive parents.

It is not unusual for parents whose new baby reacts negatively to them or her new surroundings to take this personally and worry that they will never be able to build up a close, loving relationship with her. These feelings are understandable. It is important, however, to put the child's behavior into proper perspective. Her reaction to the loss of people to whom she has been attached is a positive sign of her emotional development as well as of the quality of care that she has received at the foster home. The baby's ability to perceive and react to changes in persons offering her care and new surroundings can also be taken as a positive sign.

Most childless couples find that adopting a baby is rewarding and is a very satisfactory alternative to giving birth to their own child. Parents who have adopted infants have the same opportunity to derive fulfillment from child rearing and create a successful family as do parents who bear their own children.

LOVE YOUR CHILD AND TREAT HER AS AN INDIVIDUAL. How long it takes for a baby or child to adjust and come to love her adoptive parents depends upon the love and attention that she receives, as well as whether or not her other needs are satisfactorily met. A child who is made to feel secure, wanted, and loved will surely begin to react to this in a positive manner, and will come to love her new parents.

Most physicians, psychologists, and other child care experts agree that adopted children should be treated the same as biological children. They should always be respected as individuals and given every opportunity to develop to their fullest potential. All young children have similar needs for love, attention, care, stimulation, and so forth.

In cases in which a parent has adopted a child, either consciously or unconsciously, to "replace" a child who has died, particular care should be taken not to compare the two children or try to make the adopted child fit into the same pattern as the deceased child. No child wants to be brought up feeling as if she must assume the role of another child. This would be totally unfair. The tendency to compare your adopted child with the child you once had may be strong. You should make every effort not to make your adopted child aware of this, and to allow her to be herself, and accept her for what she is.

SINGLE PARENT ADOPTIONS. It is still less common for an unmarried person to adopt a child, although this situation is certainly more common than in the past. In most cases, adoption agencies prefer that a child be placed with a married couple.

However, when a child's need for a permanent parent and home is pressing, having one parent right away is thought to be more desirable than the child's remaining in an institution with a slim possibility of being adopted by a couple at some indefinite future date. There are also cases in which a child's past experiences and emotional condition make having one parent, either a male or female, more beneficial. Both single men and women are being given consideration by some adoption agencies.

INTERRACIAL ADOPTION. The number of interracial adoptions has risen in recent years. Parents who have adopted a baby of a different race or of mixed racial background often have special concerns about how this will affect their child. There is no easy answer to this question, but a great deal depends upon how parents treat the child. There may be some problems concerning the child's identity development and the process of identification with her parents. Few, if any, problems are likely to arise in this regard during infancy and toddlerhood; they often surface during the preschool stage. See also page 711.

Couples or single men and women who decide to adopt a child of a different racial background should discuss any questions or concerns openly with the people at the adoption agency with which they are working. Trained professionals who have had experience with interracial adoption can be of great assistance. Parents should also be prepared for possible discouragement, criticism, or coldness from relatives and friends. Having positive acceptance and support can make rearing a baby a great deal easier; lack of this support need not hinder parents who are confident that they have made the right decision and are prepared to accept the responsibilities of child rearing.

TELLING A CHILD THAT SHE WAS ADOPTED. Suggestions for how to inform a child that she was adopted are provided in the preschool Family Feelings and Concerns section on pages 881–82.

Your Other Children Should Be Prepared for the Newcomer

If you already have other children in your family, their emotional needs in relation to the birth of the new baby will be no less important to consider than yours or your spouse's. They will be affected by the presence of a newcomer in a much different way from you, but they will, nonetheless, be greatly affected. The entire family as a unit will be required to make certain adjustments. Each individual family member, including other children, will have to make his or her own personal and emotional adjustments.

Can you imagine how shocked a toddler or preschool child would be if her mother suddenly disappeared for several days without a word of explanation, and returned

home with a new baby—a permanent addition to the family. Some parents feel that a child anywhere from one to two would not notice if her mother became pregnant. Young children, however, tend to be highly observant as well as perceptive. They notice tiny details, such as a speck of dirt on the carpet, and they surely notice such an obvious change as their mother's enlarged belly. Youngsters have been known to sense that something in their lives or their parents' lives is changing long before they are given any explanations as to what is happening. They are not unaware of what is going on around them. Children are often very sensitive to changes in their parents' moods and feelings which can occur during the pregnancy period.

Assuming that you have another child (or children), you should treat her with the same respect that you afford your other relatives and friends. After all, she is a member of your *immediate* family. You should let her know that you are expecting a new baby and prepare her as best you can well in advance for this major life change so that she will have plenty of time to adjust emotionally and psychologically.

Even if your child is too young to understand all of your words when you tell her that there will be a new addition to your family, this does not mean that you should not try to explain through a combination of words and actions. Her feelings should not be ignored. The new baby should not come as a totally unexpected event to her. Feelings of jealousy, competition, and hostility may run high in your child when the new baby is brought into your family, but if she is properly prepared in advance, these feelings may be minimized.

PREPARING THE TODDLER. With a young child who has a limited capacity to understand verbal explanations, you will have more difficulty preparing her in advance. Still, there are some things that you can do. In the event that your child now uses the room that you want for a nursery, you can plan to shift her out of this room ahead of time. If you make the change-over at the last moment, she may feel more resentful toward the baby who invades her territory from the moment the baby enters the home. You might also bring your child to a relative's or friend's home where there is a young infant, so that she can observe the baby and the baby's care. Taking your child shopping with you when you go to purchase equipment or clothing items for the baby may also help her get adjusted. Involve her in getting the nursery ready. She may enjoy fetching things for you or holding things and handing them to you when you need them.

PREPARING THE PRESCHOOL CHILD. If your child is old enough to understand verbal explanations in regard to a new baby, you should inform her that you are expecting another child well in advance of the baby's due date. You may want to let her know before or at least at the same time you spread the news to your friends and relatives. It is better that she hears such important news from you than accidentally overhears it from someone else.

It is best not to take an apologetic attitude when breaking the news, as this may reinforce feelings of jealousy and rivalry. Let her know that you are happy about having another child and want another baby just as you wanted her. She may not react positively when she learns the news. Some children are excited and overjoyed. Others are very ambivalent and feel as though they are not wanted any more and/or that you do not love them or else you would not be having another child. Let her express her feelings without passing judgment or stressing that she should be overjoyed at the news.

You can expect her to ask questions, perhaps not immediately, but from time to time as the months pass. Her questions may be about where the baby will come from, how it got to be there, and how and where it will come out. Try to answer her questions truthfully and matter-of-factly in terms that she can understand. Do not expect her to comprehend your explanations immediately. The Sex Education section on pages 865–80 provides guidelines that may assist you in discussing sex-related issues with your preschooler.

HELPING YOUR CHILD FEEL MORE COMFORTABLE ABOUT YOUR HOSPITALIZA-TION. Another aspect of preparing your child ahead of time involves informing her that you will have to go to the hospital for a while and why that is. Any separation from you may be very difficult for her. You should make sure that someone with whom she is very familiar and whom she likes will be around in your absence. Many children feel worried, fearful, sad, and even abandoned while their mothers are in the hospital. A phone call or two from Mommy may help to reassure them that Mommy is all right, still loves them, misses them very much, has not forgotten them, and will be home soon.

Some hospitals permit young children to visit their mothers soon after the baby is born. If this is possible, take advantage of it. Have your spouse or whoever is staying with your child bring her for a visit. Seeing that you are well and having an opportunity to be introduced to the new baby in the hospital may ease the tensions for your older child after you arrive home with the baby. Remember, do not push her to love or express affection for the newcomer. Give her plenty of time to size the baby up and form her own opinions. You should not expect her to be happy or to like the baby right away. After all, how can she love or even like someone whom she has not gotten to know?

Planning in advance for the arrival of the new family member will help prevent or lessen the initial difficulties that might arise. Consideration of how your child might react to the new baby and how to deal with some of these reactions are discussed in Infancy 1 on pages 177–82.

Who Is To Take Primary Care of Your Baby?

In recent years the number of mothers who work outside the home has risen sharply. The question of who is to take primary care of the baby faces all prospective parents, particularly those who work outside the home. In some cases this question is very easily answered. Among couples to whom finances are no problem, one partner or the other may elect to remain primarily with the baby and take over the major daytime responsibility for her care. In other cases a close relative, such as the child's grandparent, may offer to care for the baby while the parents work. A growing number of parents-to-be have difficulty determining who is to take over the responsibility for their baby's care when they are not with her.

When both partners have careers outside the home they may feel that it is important for one of them to become a full-time parent, at least for a period of time. When neither partner wants to do this, it can present a problem. Sue and John Fletcher were both lawyers and neither was willing to give up a full-time career for a couple of years to assume primary care of their baby, although they both agreed that having a parent care for their baby was important. This created tensions between the two of them and also between them and their respective families.

Sue and John argued over which one should remain at home. John felt that Sue should be the person to care for their baby each day, since he felt that remaining with the baby during her "formative" years was a woman's responsibility. Sue resented what she regarded as her husband's "male chauvinist" approach, and argued that John could do an equally good job as a main parent figure and care-giver. Both of their families held the opinion that Sue should remain at home, since she was the baby's mother. They emphasized the importance of a baby's growing up with a consistent, dependable "mother figure," and intimated that if Sue did not give up her career and stay home with her baby, she would be depriving her child and making the infant suffer.

Sue began to feel very pressured and resentful of her husband, her parents, and her in-laws. She feared that once her baby was born, if she gave up her career against her wishes, she would also come to resent the baby. She was open about her feelings with her husband and insisted that some other solution to the problem be found, such as hiring a full-time baby-sitter. John felt that this was a fair compromise, and agreed to help Sue locate an acceptable "mother substitute."

For single parents the issue of who is to be their baby's primary caretaker—themselves, day care workers, or other sitters—may also present difficulties. Financial considerations may make it imperative that a parent continue to work. Those parents forced to continue working outside their homes for economic reasons, but who want to stay home with their babies, may not have many viable solutions to this problem open to them.

POSSIBLE ALTERNATIVES AND SUGGESTIONS. There are numerous ways in which to arrange for the care of a baby. Individual feelings, financial circumstances, career goals, family resources, and family structures must all be considered when determining which possible solutions or alternatives may be viable in a given situation. Below we have presented several ways in which parents involved in our educational programs have worked out their difficulties.

When both partners had careers to protect, there were different ways in which problems were resolved. In many cases women, particularly those who planned to breast-feed and who knew that they would probably need to recuperate for at least several weeks following giving birth, decided to remain at home for the first few months before returning to work.

Some couples decided that since neither partner wanted to stay home full time, they would both rearrange their schedules so that their work loads would be cut down and hours would be altered. In a few cases, each would work part time during different hours for the first couple of years so that their baby's care would be a shared responsibility. Some couples worked out daytime/evening employment.

Several couples, who were financially able, arranged for a parent figure to care for the child during the day in their absence, and then both shared child care responsibilities during the evenings and on weekends. These couples found this to be a good solution. They could not arrange flexible working schedules, and neither one could take a leave of absence and be assured of keeping his or her job. Some companies and institutions allow for leaves of absence for parents who want to stay home to take care of their baby for a period of months, or even a year. This makes life much easier on a new parent, but these companies are still the exception rather than the rule.

Single parents and couples who needed to work, in general, had fewer alternatives from which to choose. Some who had families to turn to for support took advantage of this. In a few instances new parents moved in with their parents or close relatives who offered them assistance, either financial help or help in assuming some of the responsibility of child care. In other cases, relatives such as the child's grandparent offered to care for the child during the day while the parent worked. A few single parents who were intent upon being their baby's primary caretaker decided to give up their jobs and accept state assistance.

Another alternative that some parents elected was to leave their baby in the care of a responsible individual while they worked. Depending upon individual preferences, finances, and the availability of people to serve as parent figures and the availability of child care facilities in the community, various options were chosen. Some parents decided to hire a live-in "parent figure," who in several instances became nearly fully entrenched as an additional member of the family.

Other parents decided to hire a person to come into their home solely for the hours in which they had to be absent. A few were able to find a person who offered to care for their children free of charge, or in exchange for baby-sitting on weekends or evenings. Parents choosing either of these alternatives felt that it was in the child's best interest to be reared in the familiar home environment, rather than to be removed from it for a large portion of time each day.

There were parents, for a variety of reasons, often financial, who decided to take their baby to some other person's home or to a suitable facility during the daytime while they had to work. Many left their children with women who were licensed by the state to provide day care for infants and young children in their homes. Some day care centers or day nurseries do not take young infants, but there are many that do provide care for infants. These vary greatly in availability, cost, the number of children that they take, the adult-child ratio, the quality of care provided, and so forth. Parents who lived in communities where excellent, licensed day care facilities were available, often chose to leave their child there while they worked.

In some instances where quality child care facilities were not readily available, or were too costly, or where parents preferred to have their baby cared for by people they knew personally, parents who were able to vary their working time joined together to form a day care group. Each parent in the group would take a turn caring for the other parents' children, and only had to take care of their child and the other children for a small percentage of the time during the week. If an employer would not give the parent time off to participate, still another option was for one parent to pay the other parents in the group for taking care of her or his child full time. With a little ingenuity, parents were able to solve their own problems in regard to issues related to their child's care.

SELECTING ANOTHER PERSON(S) TO CARE FOR YOUR CHILD IN YOUR ABSENCE. Throughout this book the role of the child's surroundings and early experiences in influencing her development is emphasized. The person who takes primary care of your child plays an important part in regulating the stimulation that she receives and is instrumental in helping to shape her early experiences. Assuming you are not going to be taking primary care of your child, you will undoubtedly want her to receive the best possible care from whoever will be filling in while you are gone. Your views about the ideal parent figure for your child may not be the same as another parent's, so it may be helpful to look at some of the "ideal" characteristics of a parent figure from a young baby's perspective.

Even though every baby is a unique person, babies have certain things in common and their needs when they are young are quite similar. They need an abundance of loving care. They also need physical closeness and skin contact with another human being in the form of touching, holding, stroking, and cuddling. Infants want this person to be consistent and responsive in caring for them day after day and to try to fulfill their needs promptly. All babies need this feeling of security and stability in a parent figure, for it helps them to establish a close relationship with another person and a good feeling about life.

Babies also need a great deal of individualized attention, particularly during infancy. You want the parent figure whom you select to believe in the value of giving individualized attention as well as offering early stimulation to your infant. Her parent figure should make attempts to treat her as though she is a very special, unique person.

One could speculate that babies would be more concerned with their care-giver's interest and attitude toward them, than with how much experience that person had. Still, it would be reasonable for babies to want the person caring for them to be responsible and level-headed enough to handle any emergencies that might arise and know where and how to seek appropriate help. In addition to needing love, good care, stimulation, and so forth, babies need to be safe. The individual serving as a parent figure for an infant must know how to handle the child with regard to her safety, and how to prevent unnecessary accidents from occurring.

One could go on and on about the qualities that an "ideal" parent figure for a baby should possess. Probably your best bet in selecting a suitable care-giver for your child is to get to know this person and watch him or her interact with your child. If you are selecting a person who will care for your baby in your home, you can arrange for this individual to begin work a couple of weeks before you have to leave. The person can watch how you respond to your child, get accustomed to your household routine, and most of all have opportunities to begin caring for and interacting with your child in your presence. You can judge for yourself how the person responds to your child.

In the event that you are planning to bring your baby to the person's home, you should also get to know the person in advance and observe how this individual reacts to other children for whom he or she is caring, as well as your child. If you are going to use a day care facility in your community, inquire into the possibility of observing what goes on; you can then decide for yourself what quality of care the children receive. Here also try to get to know the person(s) who will be specifically caring for your baby.

Making sure that your baby will be in the best of hands in your absence is of the utmost importance, not only for her sake, but for yours. It will be hard on you if you are constantly worrying about how she is being treated or whether or not she is happy or safe.

It is impossible for you to find a parent substitute who will respond to your baby in all instances just as you would. But you can still do your best to find someone whom you trust to have your baby's welfare and best interests at heart.

SELECTING A DAY CARE FACILITY. Most parents are aware that differences exist among child care facilities, but may be somewhat confused about judging the quality and suitability of a given care center for their child. A good way to start is to consider what your needs are as well as your reasons for sending your child. Do you plan to send your child there on a full-time or a part-time basis so that you can return to work? Are you planning to leave your child there only for a few weeks or months while you are otherwise occupied or until you are in a better position to care for her at home? Is your main reason to expose her to other children around her age? How much can you realistically afford to spend on day care? By asking yourself these and similar kinds of questions, you should have a clearer picture of what you expect from a care facility, and whether or not a given center meets these expectations as well as your budgetary allowance.

The next step is to find out as much as you can about the day care centers in your area. Some centers are privately funded, whereas others are funded by the federal government. Federally funded facilities are mainly designed to meet the needs of parents who find it economically imperative to work, and, on the whole, tend to be less costly than privately funded centers. Make sure that the center you select is licensed, and that the license is current. Do not hesitate to inquire about fees, and be open about what you can afford to pay.

In selecting a day care center that accepts children your child's age, it is important to know something about the director and the staff members. Feel free to ask what their training and experience have been, and learn as much as you can about their views and philosophy on child rearing. Talk to them and also observe them interacting with children. This will allow you to see how well they relate to children. Try to determine whether or not staff members really care about the children's needs and understand how those needs change at different stages of development.

The ratio of children to staff members should preferably be low to enable youngsters to receive individualized attention. This is an especially important issue during infancy and toddlerhood, when a child can benefit greatly by establishing a one-to-one relationship with a care-giver. Also determine the extent to which you, as a parent, can be involved. Find out if you are required to attend meetings at frequent intervals for the purpose of discussing your child's behavior and progress, and if the staff will try to assist you with problems you might be encountering with your child at home. A good facility should encourage your input and involvement, and welcome constructive criticism.

When you visit a day care facility it may help to ask yourself the following questions. Do you feel that it is clean, well maintained, and safe for your child? Is the atmosphere cheerful, friendly, and homelike? Does it have enough space, equipment, and toys for the children both indoors and outdoors? Are the children receiving adequate supervision? Do you feel that the furniture and toys are well suited to children at different stages of development? Is there a nurse who works full time at the center and can be called upon in an emergency or in case a child becomes ill? Will you be notified immediately if your child gets sick or has an accident? Are children who are ill or taking medication allowed to attend the facility? Do the children you observe there really seem to be happy and well cared for?

You will naturally be the best judge of a day care center's suitability for your child, but it is worth while trying to talk to other parents whose children have attended the facility in question. They may be willing to discuss their experiences at the center candidly. This can provide you with important information you would otherwise not receive, and might assist you in making a decision. Since your major objective is choosing a center in which your child will be well cared for, do a thorough job of investigation before making a final decision. Examine your own and your child's needs, and a center's suitability for both. Then you will not have to worry about the quality of care that she is receiving in your absence.

FINDING A SUITABLE SOLUTION FOR YOU AND YOUR CHILD. As you can see, there is enormous variability in how families deal with the issue of who is to take primary care of the child. It is important for the parent(s) to consider this question in advance. Couples should be open and honest about sharing their feelings with one another or with others in order to help minimize possible resentments after their baby is born, and find a solution that is satisfactory for all parties involved. Of primary importance is the child's welfare. If parents are not going to be their child's primary caretaker, arrangements should be made in advance to find a suitable parent figure,

31

and the utmost care must be taken in selecting a person to care for the child. A major concern should be the preservation of the integrity and stability of the family unit, whether that unit involves two parents and a child or a single parent and a child.

This discussion, of course, brings up the issue of how to select an appropriate parent figure or care-giver. Parents should also be aware of possible difficulties and emotional adjustments for themselves that may arise when they either elect to or are forced to arrange for a person other than themselves to care for their child. These feelings and possible difficulties are explored on pages 221–22.

PRACTICAL PREPARATIONS

Financial Planning: Insurance and Economic Considerations

Economic factors should be examined long before a baby is due. There is little doubt that in the vast majority of cases, parents feel financial pressures after the birth of their babies and have to make some sacrifices as a result. Realizing ahead of time that some of the luxury items and expenses to which you have been accustomed may have to be indulged in less frequently should help you get adjusted to this change in your lifestyle. You are not likely to feel as resentful toward your baby as you would if you suddenly had to make many unplanned sacrifices right after she was born.

The cost of having a baby should be considered in advance, even though you will only be able to make a rough estimate. Most parents have found that considering such costs and expenses spared them from being caught off guard at the last minute. This enabled them to make necessary financial and insurance adjustments prior to their baby's arrival so that they were less troubled by financial concerns once they became parents.

You should make appropriate inquiries to determine roughly the obstetrician's fees, and what the hospitalization period will cost, if you plan to deliver your baby in a hospital. You can also inquire about when payments will be due, and how they can be arranged. Remember that this is only an estimate, since your physical condition during and immediately after the delivery, and your baby's physical condition after birth, cannot be determined in advance.

It is advisable to arrange for maternity hospitalization insurance before you become pregnant. If you do have hospitalization insurance, check your policy over carefully to see whether additional coverage for mothers and babies with special physical problems is included. Babies, for instance, who are born prematurely or with medical problems may require placement in a newborn special care unit, the costs for which can be high.

Most major medical and group care plans cover the newborn child. Knowing the costs of medical care in advance will help you plan your options and decide on the appropriate insurance coverage for your family.

Adding a new member to your family will obviously increase the family budget. You will have to provide food and basic care needs for your infant. Using some ingenuity and a little extra effort, it is possible to reduce the cost of child rearing and still provide your child with an excellent family environment.

It is a good idea to make a list of estimated expenses and discuss the costs of having a baby with other parents. They may be able to think of expenses that you might overlook. Should the total cost seem overwhelming, try to determine possible ways in which to save. Instead of buying new baby furniture and equipment, you may decide to pick them up secondhand and refinish them. Perhaps you will be able to cut down on expenses by making your own baby food and toys, or sewing your own baby clothes.

In order to reduce baby-sitting expenses, you could decide to get together with friends in your neighborhood and form a co-operative baby-sitting pool (see pages 155–57). By discussing possible ways to cut down on the expenses of rearing a child with other parents, you may be surprised at the many practical tips and suggestions that you receive. One of the greatest advantages of advance consideration of the costs of having a baby is that you will have ample time to look for sales, hunt for secondhand items and bargains, or take the do-it-yourself approach.

Preparation for Childbirth and Parenthood Classes

Becoming a parent is a major life change that is often accompanied by stress, even among those men and women who are approaching this event with a positive attitude. Coping with this change quite often adds to people's anxieties, and makes the transition to parenthood more difficult.

In many communities there are prenatal courses available to parents given in hospital settings. Unfortunately, these classes do not usually discuss the issues surrounding emotional preparation or include follow-up sessions for parents after babies are born. Some of these prenatal courses are also restricted to members of health plans and are not open to the general public. In some instances their fees are high. In general, these classes reach far fewer people than need or want to attend them.

Courses giving instruction in natural childbirth may be available for those women and couples who are interested. Unfortunately the focus is often on physical preparation instead of a "total" approach including emotional preparation. Nonetheless, many prospective parents have benefited from attending these programs. They are often useful in familiarizing parents-to-be with labor and delivery. Many offer tours of the hospital and labor and delivery rooms.

We strongly suggest that you find out if there are any courses given in your local area and take advantage of them. Couples should try to attend the programs together. Child rearing will be a shared responsibility and both parents should be aware and informed. Having opportunities to share their feelings, concerns, and fears may bring a couple closer together and assist them in realizing the value of keeping open lines of communication not just before, but also after their baby is born.

Learning How to Pick Up and Hold Your Baby

Newborn babies thrive on being picked up, handled, held, and cuddled. You may have some questions about how to go about lifting and holding your baby properly. A young baby's back and head muscles are weak, and these areas must always be well supported whenever she is handled. Another consideration is her comfort. No baby likes to be handled roughly; you need to be gentle and make the child feel secure in your arms.

Probably the best way to gain confidence in your ability to handle a baby is to practice picking up and holding a friend's baby. Having had some opportunities to handle a baby prior to your first encounter with your own will put you at ease, and will enable you to handle her more confidently. After a trial or two, you will be an expert! In the event that you do not know anyone with a young infant, you can practice using a doll.

Even if you do not manage to get some experience in baby-holding by the time your child is born, don't worry about it. A hospital nurse will show you how. Some hospitals offer classes covering topics such as how to hold, bathe, diaper, and feed a newborn baby. These classes are available to parents who have just given birth and can be helpful in allaying their initial anxiety about the practical aspects of baby care.

Selecting a Physician for Your Baby

One of your primary responsibilities in providing the new baby with good health care will be to arrange for a physician who can assess her health and over-all development. The doctor will offer advice about how to give your baby proper care, and answer your questions concerning her medical condition and development. The doctor may be a pediatrician who specializes in providing medical care to children or a general practitioner or a doctor who focuses on family practice. In some rural communities and office practices, a nurse practitioner, physician's assistant, or other trained health professional may be available for your assistance. If you cannot afford the services of a private physician, or if one is not readily available, you may be able to have your baby examined on a regular basis at a local medical clinic or "well baby" clinic. Check with your health department for a listing of such alternative services.

If you have any questions about whom to select as your baby's doctor, and your own physician will not be acting in this capacity, he or she will probably be able to recommend a doctor for your baby. You may also want to discuss this issue with relatives and friends who may suggest one based upon their experience. Having trust and confidence in the doctor who will be caring medically for your child is crucial. It is also very helpful to choose a doctor with whom you feel comfortable. The value of obtaining the services of a doctor for your baby is more fully discussed in the Keeping Your Baby Healthy section.

Naming Your Baby

Most prospective parents have fun choosing names for their babies. Many begin narrowing down the choices just as soon as they learn that they are going to be parents. While it is not necessary to select names for your baby that early, it is a good idea to have a name for a boy and girl picked out prior to the delivery. This will make it easier for your baby's name to be entered on the original birth certificate. It can also be very awkward for you, hospital personnel, family, and friends to refer to your baby only by your last name.

With your child's future feelings in mind, try to avoid names that might cause embarrassment, and those which sound terribly babyish. A name that is cute for a youngster may not be especially well suited to an adult. If you delay in selecting a name, and one is not entered on your baby's birth certificate, do not forget to have it entered at a later date on her official record. In case you have any difficulty thinking of names for your child, there are books available with nothing but names, often giving interesting background on origins, meanings, and alternative forms of names.

Hospital Policies and What to Pack to Take with You

Prior to your hospitalization, you may want to find out about hospital visiting policies and items that you will need for you and your baby. Some hospitals provide mothers-to-be with a list. A month or more before your baby's expected arrival, gather together the few items that you will need for both of you, pack them in separate small suitcases. This can help in avoiding last-minute confusion over what to pack later on. Let your spouse know where you have put the suitcases, or else inform a friend or neighbor. Do not forget to give them a key to your home. In the event that the bags are forgotten at the last minute, they can be dropped off at the hospital for you as needed.

The type and amount of clothing you should pack for your baby to wear on the way home from the hospital will depend upon the weather. The items that you will need are minimal, and largely dependent upon your own personal tastes. The list below suggests articles to bring for you and your baby. You can use it as a general guideline in making a personalized list.*

For You:
    Sleeping garments (with front openings if you plan to breast-feed)
    Robe
    Slippers
    Underwear (nursing brassières if you plan to breast-feed)
    Toilet articles (e.g., make-up, toothbrush and toothpaste, comb and brush, hand mirror, shower cap, hair dryer, shampoo)
    Sanitary belt (many hospitals provide this)
    Something to read or to keep you occupied
    Birth announcements, pen, and stamps
    Phone/address book
    Outfit to wear home

For Baby:
    T-shirt
    Stretch suit, nightgown and booties, or other outfit
    Sweater and cap, blankets, or bunting (the weather will determine what to bring)
    Diapers—hospitals often provide disposable diapers, but if you prefer cloth diapers you'll have to bring them (2–3 diapers and diaper pins should suffice).

Arranging for Your Children to Be Cared for During the Hospitalization Period

In the event that you already have young children, they will have to be cared for while you are hospitalized. The person who cares for them may be your spouse or someone else whom they like and with whom they are very familiar. Whoever stays with them should be given a complete tour of your home, instructions for preparing meals and giving medications, and a written list of your children's daily schedules, etc., so that everything at home will run smoothly while you are away. Make sure that this person is given a key to your house several weeks in advance, and will be able to rush over at a minute's notice.

*Life will be easier for you if you bring lightweight, washable clothing.

Arranging for Someone to Assist You at Home During the First Few Weeks

After you arrive home from the hospital with your baby, you may be physically fatigued and emotionally keyed up. Because of this you may find it useful to have someone for a week or two to help care for the baby or manage the household. A parent, another relative, or friend may be of great help to you both practically and emotionally. Otherwise, you can arrange for professional help through a private employment agency or one of the community agencies such as the Homemaker Service or the Visiting Nurse Association. If you are interested in obtaining help through one of these services, be sure to make advance arrangements.

"Maternity" nurses, women who specialize in caring for new mothers and babies, can often be found through employment agencies listed in the phone book. Hiring such a person can be an expensive proposition, but some parents feel it is worth while. These nurses tend to be in great demand, and are usually booked months ahead.

You may prefer to arrange for someone to come to your home once or twice a week to help with the household chores or to baby-sit. The material on pages 155–58 provides a more thorough discussion of baby-sitters, including suggestions for how to select them.

Visitors After Your Baby Is Born

Your baby's birth is likely to be quite an occasion not only for you but also for your extended family and friends. People with whom you are close and even casual acquaintances will want to visit you and see your baby while you are still in the hospital. Depending upon hospital visiting policies, the number of visitors you are allowed to have may be restricted.

As soon as you leave the hospital, or immediately after birth, if you are delivering at home, the issue of whether or not to limit visitors to your home will arise. You may be anxious to have your relatives and friends meet the baby. On the other hand, you may feel tired or tense, and may not be thrilled about the prospect of having to entertain a constant stream of visitors.

Your baby's feelings should also be taken into account. Some new babies do not seem to mind being stared at and touched by many different people. Others seem to be irritated by the noise, fuss, and handling.

It will be up to you to determine how many visitors you want, when you want them, and how long they can stay. If either you or your baby are upset by them, or need more privacy, don't hesitate to set some limits. Initially, you may decide to keep the number of visitors to a necessary minimum, and then increase this number once you and the baby are more settled. It is advisable, in any case, to ask people who are ill to refrain from visiting until they are well. For similar reasons, you may decide to keep young children other than those in the immediate family at a distance from your infant for the first month or more.

A Place in Your Home for Your Baby

Setting aside a special area or room for your baby and getting it all arranged prior to her birth will make life a lot easier on you once she is born. Many parents-to-be take a great deal of pride and pleasure in decorating a place in their home for their baby. They want everything to be just perfect for her. What is the "perfect" room for a baby? There is no one right answer to this question.

Individual parental taste preferences and budgets play a major role in arranging a room or area for a baby, but it is more important to examine a room from a baby's point of view. A primary concern is a baby's health and safety. Your young infant will not care whether or not her "territory" has been professionally decorated. She will, however, care whether the area has been accident-proofed, is well lighted, offers her some environmental stimulation, and is not too hot or cold. Ideally, she might prefer to have a room to herself with a door that can be closed to ensure complete privacy. This is not always possible. There is no reason to think that she will suffer from having to have a roommate. In case she will be sharing with you or another child, you may want to rearrange furniture or put up a screen so that she has some privacy. More information on sleeping equipment is presented on pages 39–41. Once she begins to get about on the floor, she will naturally want freedom to move and explore. Provided her bedroom is large enough, it can double as a play area. Otherwise she can use it only for sleeping and can be given access to other larger and safe areas in your home.

Her room and everything in it will probably get a lot of wear and tear as she grows older and becomes more mobile. If you are putting up wallpaper, it is advisable to purchase the kind that can be washed. Furniture and equipment should be sturdy and simple enough to be easily wiped clean. Many parents have recommended putting indoor-outdoor carpeting on the floors while the child is young. It can be easily cleaned and provides a good non-skid surface for toddlers. Other parents on tight budgets recommended using small squares of carpeting samples taped together to make a floor covering. They can be purchased from carpeting stores at a relatively low cost. Some stores even give them away upon request. Parents who have used them claim that their multicolored rug looks great and really brightens up a room. They say that their babies loved the "feel" of the different textures.

Storage space for toys should be taken into account, since your baby will want plenty of them around. Once she begins to crawl, she will also want easy access to her toys. Many parents have suggested building low, sturdy shelves on which to store toys. Others have purchased sturdy plastic crates or wooden boxes (well sanded, please) with one end open. These "crates" can be purchased in a variety of sizes and colors, and can easily be stacked, rearranged, and added to as seems necessary.

Some parents who have the space to set an entire room aside for their babies prefer to decorate it for a young infant. Bear in mind that youngsters grow at an amazingly fast pace, and your older child may object to a "babyish"-appearing room. You may want to decorate with an "ageless" wall covering, drapery, and rug, and change the "finishing touches," such as pictures, knickknacks, and throw pillows, as your child matures. This can save you the added expense of having to redecorate as she grows older. Provided you have the inclination, an active imagination, and the time, you will be able to come up with all kinds of interesting and inexpensive ways to decorate your baby's bedroom or special area. Chances are that you will have great fun in the process. You will find further suggestions for preparing a room for her with her freedom and safety in mind in the sections on safety. Tips on providing her with a stimulating environment can be found in the Learning Through Play sections.

Equipment

Basic care equipment and a safe auto seat are important, and should be obtained before the birth of your baby. Guidelines for obtaining these items, and other non-essential but often useful equipment, are discussed below for your convenience. Safety, practicality, and economy are emphasized.

It is important for parents to be selective in the equipment they buy for their children. Placing a high value on safety and economy will put pressure on manufacturers and retailers to produce or sell only acceptable products. Being an educated consumer will be advantageous to you and your baby.

EARLY PREPARATION IS AN ADVANTAGE. There are numerous advantages to gathering the most necessary equipment prior to your baby's birth. The first few weeks at home with your infant will be very hectic. This is a time when emotions run high, routines are disrupted, and fatigue sets in. Having to rush out to buy equipment at this time can be inconvenient and more costly. Obtaining the items that you will need in advance will help you to feel more confident and relaxed during the first few days at home. You will be able to concentrate your energies on caring for your baby, enjoying her, and getting the rest and relaxation that are essential for your well-being.

Advance preparation also allows you to take as much time as necessary to survey the equipment available in your local area, and make intelligent choices. Items to be ordered can be requested in advance so that they will arrive when your infant needs them. Allowing yourself ample time to examine equipment carefully from the point of view of safety, and economy, is obviously important.

If you are buying new equipment you will have chances to get practical tips from friends and pick up items on sale. Prospective parents on tighter budgets or those who are handy will have the opportunity to make furniture, or hunt for used furniture and repair it.

Most parents begin shopping for equipment a few months before their baby's expected date of birth. Bear in mind that certain baby items may be given to you as gifts, and that your friends may offer to let you borrow some of the equipment that their children have outgrown.

SAFETY IS A MAJOR CONSIDERATION. The primary consideration when buying, making, or redoing equipment and furniture for a baby is safety. Mrs. Southwick adored antiques and put a great deal of time and effort into shopping for an antique crib that would be just perfect for her baby. She finally located a beautiful, hand-painted, turn-of-the-century crib, and proudly placed it in the nursery that she had tastefully decorated with an old-fashioned flair.

Mrs. Southwick gave birth to a healthy baby girl. Everything appeared to be going along smoothly for the first ten months. Then, gradually, she noticed several unusual symptoms in her daughter, Mary. Mary seemed to be constantly sleepy, and much more irritable than usual. Her appetite diminished, and she later began to vomit. Mrs. Southwick immediately consulted her pediatrician.

The doctor examined Mary and asked Mrs. Southwick if she had noticed Mary engaging in any new or unusual activities. After thinking about this for several minutes, she reported that she had recently caught Mary chewing on the crib slats on several occasions, but had simply pulled her away and distracted her with a toy. The doctor then asked her about the type of paint on the crib. Mrs. Southwick described the antique crib, but said that she had no idea of the type of paint, since it was so old. Her answers confirmed the doctor's suspicion that Mary had lead poisoning. She had been ingesting chips of lead-base paint on the crib over a period of several months. Blood tests revealed elevated lead levels. Mary did well after treatment, but this difficulty could have been avoided by proper selection of equipment.

It is far more important that equipment be safe than for it to be attractive in appearance. Whether equipment is new or old, it must be covered with non-toxic paint and safe in all other respects.

All items should meet the most recent federal safety standards. You can check with the National Consumer Product Safety Commission to obtain information regarding a particular product's safety by either writing them or dialing their toll-free number. The most up-to-date information from physicians and the National Consumer Product Safety Commission is included in our discussions to assist you in purchasing safe equipment or repairing used equipment. You can obtain the phone number of the National Consumer Product Safety Commission by calling the toll-free information operator: 1-800-555-1212. The current phone number for this agency is 1-800-638-8326. Guidelines for proper supervision and use of the items are also presented in order to help you ensure your child's safety in the months and years that follow her birth.

IS COST A FACTOR? Few parents are not concerned about the rising cost of living. The cost of obtaining equipment can be greatly reduced with an understanding of which items are most necessary. In the material that follows you will also find practical tips from experienced parents on how to save money.

It is important not to sacrifice an essential item such as a car seat for your infant simply because it is expensive. While there are many items of equipment that are not necessary, a car seat is not one of them.

Being budget conscious, nearly all parents will consider the price of a given piece of equipment before purchasing it. There is nothing wrong with this as long as you consider an item's safety first. A higher price tag does not necessarily mean safety and quality. Do not purchase an unsafe piece of equipment just because it is less expensive. The risk of injury to your baby is not worth the money that you save.

In the event you do not have sufficient funds to purchase a safe non-essential item, such as a baby carriage, don't make the mistake of buying an inexpensive, but unsafe one. Your baby will not miss out if you cannot afford to buy non-essential items, but she may suffer if the things you do buy are unsafe. Even if you are on a tight budget, you should have little difficulty obtaining the equipment necessary for your baby.

A BED FOR YOUR BABY. You will have to decide where your young infant will sleep. She needs a special place of her own. Her safety and comfort are the most important factors. Wherever she sleeps, there should be barriers to prevent her from rolling out, ample room for her to lie comfortably, a supportive mattress, and preferably some padding around the sides for added protection.

It is not necessary to obtain a crib for your infant right away. Until she is about three months old, she can sleep in a large, sturdy basket, a bassinet, a portable car bed, a cradle, or even in a large bureau drawer that has been removed and placed in a secure spot. After your child outgrows these temporary sleeping quarters, she should sleep in a crib. Obtaining a full-size crib is the wisest choice, since she will be able to use it until she is ready to be moved to a youth or regular-size bed. You may be able to locate a bed which converts from crib to youth bed.

Bassinet or basket. Parents often like to place their newborn baby in a bassinet or basket instead of a crib, as these can be easily carried or moved from room to room. Experts find young babies are more comfortable in a sleeping space smaller than a normal crib. The bassinet or basket must be stable and sturdy, and should have sufficiently high sides to prevent the baby from rolling out. Check to make sure that the space inside the bassinet or basket is large enough not to cramp her movements.

There should be no exposed hardware or rough, sharp edges. You may have to line the sides to prevent the baby from hurting her hands. The mattress must fit snugly.

The bassinet/basket can be used only until your infant is about three months old. As she grows older and becomes more active, there is a strong possibility that she could rock and tip it over. At the slightest suspicion that your baby has outgrown her bassinet or basket, move her to a crib.

Cribs. Crib-related accidents, some resulting in death, are more common than most people think. Until your baby is about two or three years old, she will be spending a large portion of each day sleeping and resting in a crib. It is crucial to take appropriate precautionary measures to prevent her from having a crib accident.

There are a wide assortment of cribs available on the market, in various sizes and shapes, and materials. Some are traditional in their styling, and others are modern or even ultra-modern in design and use of materials. Whether you ultimately choose a standard or non-standard size or style of crib, it should adhere to the following National Consumer Product Safety Commission regulations.

Slats on the crib should be spaced not more than 2⅜ inches apart. Those with slats spaced more widely than this pose a great danger to a baby, who could get her head caught between the bars and strangle. The best way to check for proper spacing of slats is to bring a tape measure with you when you go shopping for a crib.

All metal crib hardware should be smooth. Examine the crib carefully. Look for rough or sharp edges and exposed nails, screws, or bolts. These represent danger traps that can result in injury to the child.

Another primary consideration is to choose a crib with the largest possible distance between the mattress support and the top of the side rails. The larger the distance, the harder it will be for your youngster to climb out. Accidents involving falls from cribs are common once a child can stand. There are several ways to prevent falls. One is to make sure that the latching devices on the drop side of the crib are secure, and cannot accidentally be released.

Extensions for cribs are available. If you use extensions, make sure that the slats conform to safe spacing standards. There is no point in having the extension exceed the height of the headboard and footboard of the crib, since a child who can climb over the head or footboard can easily climb over the extension as well. As your child grows taller, stand her up next to the crib rails at periodic intervals. If the height of the side measures less than three quarters of her height, then you will know that she is ready for a shift to other sleeping quarters. Continuing to place her in the crib would be dangerous.

Any plastic wrap that is found in the crib storage or shipping carton should be immediately removed, tied into closely spaced knots, and discarded outdoors in a garbage can with a lid. Infants and small children can easily suffocate on plastic wrap that they find lying around the house if they pull it over their heads.

Mattress. The mattress that you select should be firm enough to offer your baby good support. Foam rubber mattresses are often considered to be the best, but those made of cotton and other materials will also work well. (As a temporary mattress in a basket, for example, you can use a blanket that has been cut to the appropriate size and shape, and tufted for added support and comfort.) Most mattresses that you examine in stores will be waterproof. Otherwise, you can cover a mattress with a special waterproof covering.

The mattress should be tight-fitting. A given mattress is too small if you can insert two fingers between it and the side of the crib. A baby who gets hands or feet wedged between the mattress and the crib side can get hurt.

Bed Linens. Parents often wonder about how to make up their baby's bed, and what linens they should buy. The following items are suggested for practicality and comfort.

It is advisable to cover the crib mattress with a waterproof fitted sheet to prevent moisture and urine from getting through. Even if the mattress is waterproof, some parents feel it is still a good idea to cover it as a means of extra protection. Most parents purchase two such sheets so that the bed can be made up while one sheet is being washed.

These sheets can be purchased in plain styles, or with a thin flannel backing on the top and bottom. The latter style tends to be more popular. It allows for more air circulation, and normally eliminates the need for a mattress pad to cover it, although on very hot, humid days a mattress pad may still be required.

If you don't use the flannel-backed waterproof sheets, the next step in making up a baby's bed is to place a quilted, absorbent mattress pad over the sheet. This allows more air circulation and thus helps to keep the baby drier and cooler. Two mattress pads should be sufficient, although some parents find it convenient to have a couple of extra pads on hand.

A regular sheet can be placed over the mattress pad. Fitted sheets are available, and many parents prefer them. When using non-fitted sheets, make sure that they are large enough so that they can be securely tucked in. Washable sheets that require no ironing are the most popular; the cotton knit ones afford a soft sleeping surface. Parents who have used a basket or bassinet during the early months suggest using a regular cloth diaper or pillow case as a sheet.

To help minimize the amount of wet sheets that need to be changed and washed, parents suggest placing an absorbent moisture-resistant pad between the baby's bottom and the regular sheet. This may protect the sheet from becoming wet. Several small, square pads work well, and these can easily be changed as often as is necessary.

A PLACE FOR BATHING YOUR BABY. It is not necessary to buy a special bathtub for your baby, although some parents find this to be a useful piece of equipment. Your baby will not miss anything if she is bathed in the kitchen sink, in a large oval-shaped plastic container, or in your regular bathtub with a large towel to line the bottom.

At first you will probably be giving her sponge baths. Handy, but not necessary, is a foam rubber bath mat shaped to support a baby's body. It can conveniently be placed on a counter top next to the kitchen or bathroom sink, and is skid resistant. In lieu of this you can use a folded towel, or protect your clothing and simply give the sponge bath holding the baby on your lap.

Molded, plastic baby tubs are available in most department stores. They are relatively inexpensive, and can be easily placed on a table top, making it more convenient for bathing the baby. Choose one that has a non-skid bottom surface. Some have an armrest built in. Also available is a folding bath-table combination, known as a Bathinette. This is a piece of equipment on which to bathe and dress a baby. Again, this is not really necessary.

A SURFACE ON WHICH TO CHANGE AND DRESS YOUR BABY. You will need a flat counter such as a table top or the top of a low dresser on which to dry, change, and dress your baby; a waist-high place is convenient, since you will not have to strain your back bending over. Pad the surface with a soft, folded towel or rubber pad. It is possible to purchase changing tables. Many come with barriers on all sides to prevent the baby from falling, but you can improvise and easily make your own barriers for a dresser or counter top. For safety purposes, it is very important to have such barriers. This becomes increasingly important as the child becomes more active and is able to roll over. It is possible to change your baby on a crib, with one side lowered, or on a bed or sofa, assuming you don't leave her alone. You can also change her on a blanket or pad on the floor.

INFANT CAR CARRIER. Taking proper care of your child in a car is a must. There are car carriers especially designed to protect infants traveling by car. They are constructed for infants of a certain weight, and take into account a young baby's need to recline and have adequate head support. You can have a definite impact on your child's safety simply by obtaining an infant car carrier and by being certain to use it properly. For every family planning to take their child into a car, this essential piece of equipment should be obtained before the birth of your baby. When you take your infant home from the hospital in a car, you should have her safely secured in the infant carrier.

Please take the time to get a proper crash-tested (dynamically tested) auto carrier for your infant. Your doctor should have the most current recommendations for infant car carriers that are available in your area. Some parents prefer to buy a new infant car carrier, but you can save a lot by borrowing an approved carrier from a relative or friend whose child has outgrown it.

Manufacturers' availability and the most current recommendations on infant car carriers are subject to change as new developments are made. You can obtain a pamphlet giving up-to-date information on recommended car carriers by sending $.25 and a self-addressed stamped envelope to Physicians for Automotive Safety, 50 Union Avenue, Irvington, New Jersey 07117.

Infant carriers are available in department and juvenile specialty stores and some types are also available through car dealerships. Be sure to follow the directions for installation and use carefully. Recent studies have shown that a large percentage of parents who obtain approved infant car carriers and car seats for older children do not install them properly and forfeit the protective advantage of this piece of equipment. The importance of following the directions to the letter cannot be overstressed.

Infant car carriers vary in the maximum weight of the child that they will safely accommodate. This information should be included in the instruction booklet that comes with the carrier. Most of these carriers will be outgrown in late infancy or toddlerhood, depending upon the type of carrier acquired and the weight of the child. See pages 512–13 for information on obtaining an approved car seat for the larger child.

BASIC CARE ITEMS. The following list includes items useful in bathing, dressing, and grooming your baby, as well as in caring for her health needs. They are inexpensive, and you may already have some of them in your home. It is a good idea to keep them in a convenient place such as near the dressing table or on a tray wherever you will be bathing her. Many parents place the toilet articles in a basket with a handle, making it easier to carry them from room to room.

mild soap—unperfumed to avoid skin irritation
sterilized absorbent cotton swabs and balls
blunt scissors
infant thermometer
children's-size nasal aspirator
diaper pins—if using cloth diapers
Vaseline
premoistened disposable towelettes
ointment for diaper rash
powder
washcloths (4 to 6)
towels (4 to 6)
tissues
diapers
baby comb and brush
shampoo
baby oil

EXTRA EQUIPMENT. Parents often find that certain non-essential items are useful to have. The following list is by no means inclusive, but will familiarize you with some of the more common types of equipment. These optional items are secondary in importance to those previously discussed, and you can certainly rear a healthy, happy baby without them.

Baby Scale. Some parents are interested in keeping track of their baby's weight, and thus obtain a scale especially designed for babies. This item is really unnecessary with a healthy baby who is taken to the doctor's office for regular check-ups. Baby scales are available at some department stores. Specialty shops for babies often carry them. It is sometimes possible to rent a scale from a medical supply store, assuming that your physician advises you to follow your baby's weight for a short period of time.

Diaper Bag. A diaper bag or other lightweight bag with a washable, waterproof lining in which to carry baby care items can make taking the baby visiting or shopping more convenient. Having such a bag can make traveling anywhere with a baby easier.

Portable Bassinet-Diaper Bag. A lightweight item that can be useful when your young infant is visiting other homes is a bassinet-diaper bag combination. It folds up, takes up very little storage space, and can easily be carried. Your baby can sleep in the bassinet, and you can store diapers and other basic care items in the attached bag. A portable bassinet should never be used as a type of infant auto seat. This could be very dangerous.

High Chair. A high chair is a most useful item of equipment for a baby who can sit up well, although there are lower chair and feeding tray combinations that may be used instead. (See also pages 313–14.) There are a few dangers in relation to high chairs that you should be aware of in order to protect your baby. Unless a high chair has a wide, stable base, the baby may be able to lean far over or rock and tip the chair over. The feeding tray should lock securely into place, or else the youngster may be able to unlatch it. A seat belt that is attached to the feeding tray rather than the chair itself represents another danger. Make sure that the high chair you select has a sturdy safety strap fastened to the chair. Also look for a chair that has no rough or sharp points, edges, or corners.

Buying a high chair with the safety features described above does not in and of itself provide adequate protection. Proper supervision and use of the chair are also necessary. Use this chair only after your baby is able to sit up well. Whenever you place your child in the high chair, always use the safety strap. The tray, alone, without a restraining strap, will not prevent her from slipping out of the chair. Use the strap at all times, even when you are not using the feeding tray and are pushing the high chair up to your regular dining table. Check also if the surfaces and construction will make it easy or difficult to keep clean.

Dresser or Storage Cabinet. Babies' clothing and bed linens can be stored in a closet, but most parents find it easier to store them in a dresser, wardrobe, chest of drawers, or some other storage cabinet. In making your selection, try to choose a basic style that will be appropriate for an older child as well, since it will save you the expense of having to replace it as your child grows older.

Playpen. Playpens come in a wide variety of styles and sizes. Their use, advantages, and disadvantages are discussed later in the book on pages 303–4. A major reason for using a playpen is to ensure a baby's safety during short periods when you either cannot watch her closely, or need a break from the constant responsibility of giving your full attention.

A playpen should be very sturdy, and large enough to give your child sufficient room to move about. If it is too small or the sides are not high enough, she may be able to tip it over or crawl out. Playpens with mesh netting are fine, provided the weave is very small, smaller than the size of a baby button; it is all too easy for clothing to catch onto mesh. Guard against large weave netting on which a toddler can climb or get caught. Playpens with wooden slats can also be dangerous if the slats are not secure or are more than 2⅜ inches apart. In case you already have a playpen with slats spaced more than 2⅜ inches, and cannot afford to replace it, you can take a bed sheet and weave it in and out of the slats around the entire playpen. Be sure to fasten the sheet securely.

Guard against purchasing a playpen with rough edges or protruding hardware. Make sure that the one you select has a firm floor support and a foam pad. Hinges and latches should lock securely to prevent your child's fingers from being pinched.

Making a wise selection is half of the battle. You must also be familiar with a few additional precautionary measures regarding the use of the playpen. After using it outdoors, promptly bring it back in the house to prevent rusting and sun damage.

You may want to fasten an assortment of safe, interesting objects securely onto the sides of the playpen as stimulation for your baby. If you attach these items with cords, be sure that they are less than 6 to 8 inches long to prevent them from getting wrapped around your child's neck. As your youngster grows taller, you should probably discontinue hanging toys from the sides. No strings or cords with dangling objects should be tied across the top of the playpen.

Baby Carriage. Baby carriages continue to be popular, especially in urban areas. There are many different models from which to choose. Some are multifunctional, converting to strollers or even to car beds. The majority of carriages have plain, uninteresting interiors. In order to give your baby a more stimulating environment, you can stick an assortment of colorful appliqués, photographs, picture cutouts, or even pieces of textured material or carpeting around the sides within her visual and reaching range. A few models are designed with clear panels to enable a baby to watch the changing scenery as she is wheeled along.

In selecting a carriage, look for one that is stable and well constructed. Make sure that it has good brakes and secure latches. Its canopy should lock firmly into place. Be sure that there are no rough or sharp edges and no exposed hardware. Check to be certain that there is a safety strap that is firmly attached.

The carriage should be large enough so that your infant is comfortable lying down or sitting up. It should have a snug-fitting mattress. If there are any spaces or gaps between the mattress and the frame, place bolster pillows or rolled-up towels in between the spaces. If you purchase the collapsible type, check the latch mechanisms for security. Never leave your baby unattended in the carriage.

Stroller. A useful item of equipment for taking the baby outdoors is a stroller. There are many different types of strollers available, and the stroller that you choose should be the one that best suits your needs. Lightweight strollers that fold up and are easily carried, stored, and taken in and out of cars or busses have become increasingly popular in recent years. Many have an adjustable back, which allows an infant to sit, recline, or simply stretch out. Traditional, heavier models with built-in hoods and/or side panels are also available.

The stroller that you select should have the following features to ensure your baby's safety. Buy one that is low riding or has a wide wheel base in order to prevent it from being tipped over. Stability is very important. It should not tip with your child sitting as far back as possible. The back rest should be firm and nearly vertical to offer adequate back support. The stroller should be equipped with a well-attached safety strap, which should be fastened securely every time the baby is in the chair.

Be sure that the stroller has a good brake system with adequate locks. If possible, choose one with a two-wheel brake, since this offers additional security. Do not purchase a stroller that has any exposed hardware, or sharp or rough edges. In case the stroller has a canopy, it should lock in a forward horizontal position and rotate backward and downward to the rear. When examining collapsible models, make sure that latches are secure. In the event that you want to place a shopping basket on the stroller, or in case the stroller comes equipped with one, it should be mounted in front of or centered over the rear axle. This position will be the most stable.

When your baby is in the stroller, and you are not moving it around, make sure that the brake system is engaged. Your baby should never be left on her own in the stroller, and other children should not be permitted to ride on, stand in, or pull on the shopping basket. By taking the time to purchase a stroller with adequate safety features, and supervise your baby when she is seated in it, you will be able to minimize risks to her and will feel more relaxed.

Baby Walker. A baby walker is certainly not a necessary item of equipment. There is some controversy over its use, and before purchasing one, you should read the discussion on pages 299–300 where more information is presented. Parents who purchase a walker must keep their baby's safety foremost in mind, since there are certain risks involved. A major danger is that of a baby's tipping over her walker. Another possible hazard is that her fingers might get trapped, particularly if the walker is of the older X-frame design and should suddenly partially collapse. Stairs represent a third danger to a baby who is improperly supervised.

To prevent these hazards, a baby walker should be selected with the following safety features in mind. It should be stable. Buy one with a wide wheel base that is wider and longer than the actual frame. Make sure that the walker is made of sturdy materials such as unbreakable plastic. Look for those with long-wearing fabric seats and heavy-duty stitching or large, securely fastened snaps. Coil springs and hinges should have protective coverings. The walker should not have any exposed screws, nails, or other sharp or rough points.

A final caution: Provide adequate adult supervision whenever the baby is using it. You must remain nearby your infant at all times while she is in her walker, and prevent her from going too fast, leaning too far, and maneuvering it from non-carpeted to carpeted floors or over steps without your help. Blocking stairs and temporarily removing throw rugs are additional precautionary measures that are necessary to ensure her safety.

Infant Seat. An infant seat is a plastic shell with a mattress pad designed to conform to the young infant's body. This baby chair can come in very handy during early infancy. Most parents swear by this piece of equipment, as it makes a baby easily portable, can be used indoors, and does not take up much storage space. Before a baby is able to sit up well and use a high chair, she can be placed in an infant seat. This can expand a baby's opportunities to be included in family activities when her parent cannot or does not want to hold her, and makes it easier for a parent to bring the infant from one room to another.

In selecting an infant carrier, look for one of sturdy construction, with a wide base for added stability. There are many styles from which to choose, including those that rock. The bottom surface should be made to prevent skidding. In the event that the bottom is slippery, cover it with rough-textured adhesive strips. The carrier should have a well-fastened safety strap, which should be used at all times. The device that supports the back of the seat should be sturdy and lock securely in place to prevent the seat from collapsing. Each time your baby is placed in the carrier, make sure that the supporting device is locked into place.

Never leave your baby unattended in the infant carrier. Do not place it on slippery or high surfaces. When placing on a large table such as a dining room table, set it down in the center, never near the edge. Check to be certain that all potentially dangerous objects are well out of your infant's reach.

An infant seat should not be used as a car seat. It will not offer your baby adequate protection in this capacity, unless specifically designed for car safety (see pages 42–43). Once your baby is three to four months old, depending upon her strength and activity, the infant seat may no longer be safe. If you have any reason to suspect that your baby can tip it over, immediately discontinue its use.

Front Carrier. A popular type of carrier that can be used with infants under four to five months is the front or sling-type carrier. It enables a parent to hold the baby close to his or her chest, but allows for free arm movement. This lightweight device enables parent and child to see one another, and is beneficial in terms of the baby's emotional needs as well as her need for close physical contact with her parent. Young babies are often soothed by the sound of their parent's heartbeat and the feel of their parent's body. The front-type carrier permits both of these sources of comfort.

To ensure the infant's protection, the carrier should be well suited to her size and weight, securely fastened, and sturdy. Look for strong, heavy-duty stitching and/or snaps. A primary consideration is that the carrier provides sufficient head support for the young baby. Padding will make both parent and child more comfortable.

Side carriers and unframed back carriers are also available, and considerations similar to those mentioned above should be used in their selection. Some infant carriers are convertible, allowing the child to be carried on her parent's front or back. The one you select should be safe, comfortable for you and your baby, and well designed to meet your individual needs.

Back Carrier. Parents who like to be constantly on the go, walking through the neighborhood, shopping, working around the house, or taking hiking trips, often find a back carrier to be a convenient and useful piece of equipment. A framed back carrier should not be used with babies under four to five months, or until a baby can hold up her head and her neck is strong enough to withstand bumps and jolts without resulting in injury.

The following tips should enable you to select a safe, framed back carrier for your child. Take your infant along when you go shopping, since the carrier you buy should be well suited to her size and weight.

Before you actually fasten the carrier onto your back with your baby seated in it, make sure that the leg holes are not binding, or rubbing against her legs, and are also not large enough to allow her to slip out. Your baby's back should be well supported. All areas of the metal frame near her face and head should have a soft, padded covering to prevent injury to these areas on bumpy trips.

It is imperative that the back carrier have a secure safety restraining strap or seat belt. Carriers with joints that could pinch your baby's fingers, and those with sharp or rough edges should be avoided. In examining a carrier, check to be certain that the stitching is very strong, or that there are large, heavy-duty snaps that cannot accidentally come apart.

When you are using the carrier, there will be times when you have to lean over or stoop to pick up something. On these occasions, bend down from your knees, instead of at your waist, since this will reduce the risk of your baby's falling out. Be sure that you always fasten the safety belt before taking off with her. Happy hiking!

REPAIRING USED EQUIPMENT. Those of you who plan to use older equipment will not want to compromise your child's safety, and may have questions about making the used equipment safer. The following practical tips should assist you.

There is nothing like a fresh coat of paint to brighten up an older piece of equipment. Be sure to use only non-toxic or unleaded paint. If the original paint is lead based, you should strip it off. Then you can either stain the wood or cover it with lead-free paint. Sand and smooth any rough edges. Fix ripped upholstery and tighten loose parts. Replace or repair latches, locking devices, and brakes that are not in proper working order. Vinyl tape designed for heavy-duty use can be used to cover exposed hardware and sharp edges. Check older equipment for adequate safety straps or restraining belts. Make sure that old straps are securely attached. Devise new seat belts if this is needed, and firmly anchor them.

In the event that old playpen pads or crib mattresses are mildewed, not in excellent condition, or absent, purchase new ones. If a crib mattress is in great shape, but is slightly too small, and you cannot afford to replace it, you can roll up bath towels and stuff them between the mattress and the crib sides. Used cribs often fail to meet the new safety standards for slat spacing. When slats are spaced more than 2⅜ inches from one another, do not buy the crib. If you must, then line the sides of the crib with bumper pads to cover the slat spacing. These pads should be securely fastened with no fewer than six straps or sturdy snaps. Long, dangling straps should be cut off. Remember to remove the bumper pads once your child can pull herself to a stand. This will prevent her from using the pads to boost herself over the sides of the crib. In repairing an older crib, you should also replace damaged teething bars.

Equipment Safety Features*

Crib

1. Made of safe materials—painted with non-lead paint
2. Well-fitting mattress; if 2 adult fingers can fit between mattress and crib side, mattress is too small
3. High crib sides that lock at highest position

* Based upon recommendations of the National Consumer Product Safety Commission.

4. Crib slats no more than 2⅜ inches apart

5. A latch mechanism that cannot be accidentally or easily released

6. No exposed hardware or rough spots

Playpen

1. Side slats spaced no more than 2⅜ inches apart

2. Tightly woven mesh netting through which a tiny baby's button cannot fit

3. Securely locking hinges

4. Adequate floor support and well-fitting foam pad

5. Absence of sharp or rough edges

Infant Seat

1. Bottom surface that is skid-resistant

2. Wide base for stability; sturdy construction

3. Securely locking supporting device

4. Sturdy restraining strap

High Chair

1. Safety straps that provide adequate restraint and are firmly attached to chair

2. Absence of sharp and rough edges

3. Sturdy chair with a wide base for stability

4. Feeding tray that has a secure lock

Baby Carriage and Stroller

1. Restraining strap that is securely attached

2. Secure brake system that locks, preferably two-wheel brake

3. Sturdy enough not to be tipped when child is sitting as far back as possible; check the reclining back

4. Canopy top that locks in a forward position and can be moved backward to the rear

5. If there is a shopping basket, it should be securely placed in front of stroller or centered over rear axle

6. Adequate back support; almost vertical or vertical back

7. Wide, stable base and large wheels

Infant Car Carrier

1. Must safely restrain child (pages 42–43)

Clothing

Most parents enjoy buying clothes for their baby, and many have been known to start collecting them long before this is really necessary. This can be advantageous. The earlier you start, the more time you will have to get practical tips and even hand-me-downs from your friends and relatives. Advance planning will also allow you to pick up baby clothes on sale.

The amount of clothing your baby needs will be minimal during the first few weeks. She will also outgrow her clothes very fast. Many items are likely to be given to you as gifts. For these reasons, try not to get carried away when you're shopping and purchase too many articles of clothing.

When you're ready to buy clothing for your baby, it can be a great help to make a list of the absolute necessities, and check off those articles you have already received as gifts or hand-me-downs. Take this list with you when you go shopping, so you will not duplicate something you already have. You will also avoid the inconvenience of returning those items.

The material that follows was designed to give you a basic idea of what your baby's clothing needs will be in the first couple of months, and some advice about purchasing and caring for them. When it comes right down to it, as long as your baby is comfortably dressed, it does not make a great deal of difference what or how much you buy. It is largely a matter of what clothing items you prefer.

Without doubt, the most necessary part of your infant's wardrobe is a diaper. She will need more of them than you can imagine. Most of her time will be spent dressed in diapers, with or without simple shirts or nightgowns. Outdoors, in cooler weather, a sweater and a hat are useful. In cold weather she can be wrapped in a heavy blanket or dressed in a garment such as a bunting, an all-in-one outfit which zips in the front and encloses a baby from her feet up to her neck. Many have a hood as well.

Below is a brief list of basic articles of clothing which most parents find adequate for the first few weeks. Naturally, the list can only be used as a guideline, since the wardrobe you select will depend upon your taste, your baby's individual needs, the weather, what clothing is available in nearby stores, and the size of your budget.

BASIC CLOTHING ARTICLES.

Diapers. Diapers are available in a wide variety of shapes, sizes, and materials. Disposable, fitted diapers come in several sizes and are more expensive, but are great time savers and handy for travel. Many parents swear by them. If reusable cloth diapers are used, you can select the type that appeals to you the most. You may want to purchase the large sizes, because they may be adequate as long as your baby needs diapers. Many tiny infants go through at least a dozen or more diapers a day. It is a good idea to have a couple of dozen or so extra on hand. Experienced parents frequently use non-disposable diapers as bibs, covers for their own clothing when burping a baby, and wipe cloths. More information on diapers is provided on pages 52–53.

Nightgowns. When a baby is young, and relatively immobile, nightgowns are frequently used along with diapers. It is practical to have between three and six nightgowns on hand, and be certain they have no ribbons, strings, or cords around the neck. Nightgowns come in a variety of materials, although cotton knits and jerseys are preferred because they are easily laundered and do not require ironing. They should be long enough so your baby can easily move her legs. Some have mittens on the sleeves or sleeves that can be flipped over hands to help keep a baby from scratching herself, if this is necessary. In hot weather, you can dress her in short nightgowns.

Shirts. Shirts come with or without sleeves. The length of the sleeves also varies. You will find pullover and wrap-around styles. Babies may prefer the wrap-around style, since they tend to dislike having clothes pulled over their head. Short-sleeved medium-weight T-shirts are usually sufficient, unless your home is very cold. You will need about five shirts.

Sweaters and Jackets. Have at least a few on hand. Cardigan styles are much easier to put on a baby. Some young babies are irritated by woolen fabrics, and may be allergic to them. Therefore it is best initially to avoid sweaters made of this fabric.

Caps. A knitted cap is a good choice. Do not leave your baby alone with a cap on while she is in a crib; she could possibly pull it over her face or twist it around. Wool caps may irritate your infant's soft skin and are not usually the best choice.

Clothing Items for Cold Weather. In very cold weather your baby can be dressed in a coat, snowsuit, or some other appropriate article of clothing such as a bunting. For the first couple of months, you can wrap her in a blanket or two instead.

Bibs. Bibs are available in terry cloth and other absorbent materials. Some have a plastic covering on one side with the other side of terry cloth, and you can also buy the wipe-clean types of hard plastic that need no laundering. Bibs should be large enough to protect your baby's clothing when she begins to drink from a cup or eat solid foods. Make it a habit to remove her bib immediately after each meal. Leaving her alone with it on once she gains more strength and co-ordination with her hands is not advisable, since objects around the neck can be dangerous. Diapers can conveniently be used as bibs. You can make your own if you like.

Booties and Socks. A special covering for your baby's feet will help keep them warm in colder weather. Foot coverings come in a variety of styles and weights. You will find that some styles stay on the foot longer than others. Infant tights, or "panty hose" are also useful and have the advantage of being impossible to kick off.

Dresses for Girls; Suits for Boys. If you like to dress your baby up for special occasions, you may want to have special suits or dresses on hand. They are for "show" and not at all necessary.

Stretch Suits and Overalls. Stretch suits and other similar outfits for slightly older infants are very useful and popular, since they keep a baby's feet covered. They frequently have snaps which run from the neck down on one or both sides, and can be worn day or night, indoors or outdoors. Those having snaps in the back are more difficult to put on and remove.

Diaper Liners. Diaper liners are pieces of treated paper which are worn underneath a cloth diaper, and are disposable. They are used to prevent a regular diaper from becoming soiled. Parents often find them helpful in the first month or so, and they may be money-savers. Some diaper liners are especially absorbent and designed to keep a baby's skin drier.

Waterproof Pants. Waterproof pants or diaper pants fit over a baby's regular diaper and keep her outer clothes from becoming drenched. Many parents find them useful, particularly when their baby is wearing a "dress-up" outfit. The problem with waterproof pants is that they tend to keep heat and moisture in, unless there is adequate ventilation or air circulation. This can promote diaper rash or skin irritation. Therefore, it is best to use them occasionally, for only an hour or two at a time. In case your baby has a diaper rash, it is better not to add insult to injury by dressing her in waterproof pants.

HOW MUCH CLOTHING TO PUT ON A BABY? Parents seem to feel that their babies should wear more clothing than adults, perhaps because babies are so tiny and weak. But, babies sometimes tend to be warm when adults feel that the temperature in a room is just right. Therefore, try to resist the temptation to overdress your baby, and let common sense be your guide. A good general rule is to have the infant wear as many layers, indoors or outdoors, as you yourself are wearing in comfort.

SAFETY IS IMPORTANT WHEN DRESSING A BABY. How you dress your baby is really your decision, but safety must be taken into account. All articles should be carefully selected and examined with the following principles in mind:

—clothing should not be too tight or small, since it is important that she be able to move

—clothes should not have strings, ribbons, or cords that can be pulled tightly around a baby's neck, and possibly strangle her

—clothing should not have rough or wide elastic bands or trimmings that rub against her skin and irritate it

—buttons and snaps should be sewn on securely, and these should be carefully checked periodically so as to ensure that they are not loose and cannot come off to be swallowed or aspirated

—you should not use pins or other pointed fasteners to hold together your baby's clothing if they could pop open or if she could grab or even touch them

—due to recent concerns about possible carcinogens in clothing, do not purchase flame-resistant clothing that has been treated with TRIS

—if your baby is sensitive to a particular fabric or garment, do not dress her in it

—follow the instructions on caring for clothing found on the tag, and wash all new garments as well as bed linens in a non-irritating detergent before allowing your baby to wear them

MORE ABOUT DIAPERS.

Diapering Method. There are several methods of folding diapers to put them on a baby. The method you use to fold a diaper depends upon the size of your baby and the size of the diaper. Practice diapering someone else's baby if you can, so that you will be an expert by the time your baby arrives. Here are two important practical tips to keep in mind when diapering your baby:

• Fold the diaper and put it on in such a way that the most cloth will be where your baby's urine is released and collected.

• Make sure that the diaper is not all bunched up in between your baby's legs, since this would be uncomfortable for her and puts her legs in an unnatural position.

How Often Should Diapers Be Changed? A baby's diapers should be changed at frequent intervals for obvious cleanliness purposes, and so that her skin does not become irritated. Most parents routinely change them before each feeding, since these are the times when they tend to be wet or soiled. Check your infant's diapers regularly. Some babies are more sensitive than others when their diapers are dirty or wet, so change her diapers quickly if she seems upset when they are drenched or soiled.

Diaper Care. Regular, reusable diapers need special care. Diaper services are available in most cities. If you make arrangements with one, they will give you a container in which to store soiled diapers. This service can be of great help, and can save on work, although it is obviously more expensive than doing it yourself. If you are planning to use such a service, you should make arrangements for it before hospitalization, so that a supply of clean diapers will be on hand the first time you need them.

Assuming you will not be using disposable diapers or a diaper service, you are about to embark on one of life's most tedious and seemingly never-ending chores—caring for your baby's diapers. Do not worry, because you will live through it, and more power to you if you have a lot of patience and a strong stomach!

Used diapers should be stored in a two-gallon (or larger) rust-proof pail with a lid which is partially filled with several quarts of water. It is helpful to mix some mild detergent or disinfectant into the water to help remove diaper stains. Your doctor or pharmacist can recommend a product for you to mix into the water.

Wet diapers can be put directly into the pail, but diapers soiled with bowel movements have to be cleaned a bit. The preliminary cleaning consists of emptying the stool into the toilet and, if necessary, getting it off with a knife. It may be helpful to hold the diaper in the toilet bowl while you flush, so that most of the feces will be removed.

Before you are ready to wash the diapers each day, wring them out, pour the remaining liquid in the pail down the toilet, and carefully wash the container. You can wash the diapers in a washing machine on the full cycle, or by hand, using a mild soap or detergent and very hot water. Before washing by hand, clean the diapers well and rinse them thoroughly a couple of times, or even more if your baby's skin is particularly sensitive or if diaper rash is a problem.

When the diapers have been washed, you can either put them in a machine dryer, or hang them up to dry near a window or out in the sun. After they are dry, you need not bother with ironing them, since the goal is to keep them as soft and as absorbent as possible. You may want to add a water conditioner later on if the diapers are becoming rough or are not absorbing as much urine.

LAUNDERING YOUR BABY'S CLOTHES. Initially, it is a good idea to wash your baby's clothes separately from those of other family members. Unfortunately for you, her dirty clothes will probably collect so fast that you may have enough for a full load every day, or every other day. All of your baby's clothes, including diapers, can be washed at the same time, although some people advise washing diapers and wet sheets separately. You should use a mild soap or detergent so her skin will not become irritated, and rinse at least a couple of times or more. Certain soap products tend to be less irritating to a baby's skin, even though they do not get the clothes as white as a detergent. You can either dry the clothes in an automatic dryer or hang them up to dry near a window or on an outdoor clothesline.

BREAST-FEEDING VERSUS BOTTLE-FEEDING

A pregnant woman is often asked whether she plans to breast-feed or bottle-feed her baby. For some mothers and fathers this is an easy decision, but for others, it may require careful thought and consideration. The decision about whether to breast- or bottle-feed is a personal one, taking your feelings, lifestyle, health, and opinions about shared responsibilities in child rearing into account. You may also want to consider your spouse's feelings. Breast-feeding offers several distinct advantages to both the infant and the mother. Many physicians as well as mothers strongly recommend that expectant parents seriously consider breast-feeding their babies as the method of choice.

An important factor to recognize is that you can always elect to breast-feed first, and later switch to bottle-feeding. You cannot always do the reverse. Once you have been bottle-feeding for a period of time, you cannot change your mind and go back and initiate breast-feeding. Some mothers make a hasty decision to bottle-feed and later wish that they had thought about their decision more carefully. They feel that they have missed out on the opportunity to experience breast-feeding and offer their child some of the advantages of this natural method.

You should make your own personal choice and not let others make you feel guilty if you have strong feelings about one feeding method or the other, and there are no medical reasons why the method you choose would not be appropriate. Relatives, friends, and even some professionals frequently have very inflexible feelings in regard to which feeding method is the best. Avoid letting others convince you to use a method with which you do not feel entirely comfortable.

Whether you decide to breast-feed or bottle-feed, remember that the method itself is not as important as the mother's attitude and the way in which she holds, handles, and speaks to the child. If a mother is loving and affectionate toward her baby and cuddles her closely as she feeds her, this is the most significant aspect of the feeding exchange. It is important to feel positively about the method you select and to convey to your baby warmth and love.

Breast-feeding

Breast-feeding is the natural method of providing nourishment for an infant and, on this basis alone, is the most highly recommended by both parents and professionals. Obviously, this method has been successfully used by mothers for centuries.

ADVANTAGES OF BREAST-FEEDING. Breast-feeding offers numerous advantages for both infant and mother. Some are medical and physical in nature and others are practical. Many mothers who have found breast-feeding to be a positive experience often point out that the primary advantage is a psychological or emotional one.

Human milk is ideally suited for the young infant. Nutritionally, it is the most satisfactory of all foods, being easily digestible and highly agreeable to babies in nearly all instances. Babies whose diet consists of human milk tend to have fewer allergies as well as fewer digestive and elimination problems than babies on formula.

In the vast majority of cases, a mother's supply of breast milk spontaneously adjusts perfectly to her baby's changing demands. The infant determines the milk production in that the more she suckles, the more milk will be produced to meet her growing requirements. There is little risk of forced feeding of the breast-fed infant, nor of overfeeding. This is not the case with mothers who bottle-feed. The incidence of chubby babies tends to be higher in those who are bottle-fed than breast-fed. Many physicians suspect that obesity may be more of a problem later in life among children who were fat as infants. The tendency to overfeed bottle-fed babies as well as the higher caloric content of formulas probably play a role in this.

Another major reason why breast-feeding is recommended is that this method provides an infant with added protection from illness after birth. Colostrum and breast milk contain natural immunities in the form of antibodies from the mother that help protect the young baby from infection during the first several months following birth. During this time the baby is not yet producing antibodies of her own and is more susceptible to developing an infection. Human milk offers an infant a temporary, natural resistance to certain common childhood illnesses. Antibodies are not present in formulas.

Besides being of value to an infant, breast-feeding holds many advantages for the mother. When a woman offers her breast to her baby, this is not just a physical experience, but an emotional and psychological one.

Many women who breast-feed their babies find this experience to be extremely satisfying, pleasurable, and fulfilling, not only for themselves but for their babies. The close, warm, and frequent physical contact fostered during feedings encourages physical and emotional intimacy between mother and baby, and is important in establishing a close attachment or early bond between parent and child. Many women feel that breast-feeding is an exhilarating, wonderful, and very unique experience unduplicated by other methods of offering a child nourishment. Some mothers talk about the pleasurable sensations produced during feedings, and point out their simultaneous feelings of pride, joy, and fulfillment in their own womanhood. Not all women find breast-feeding to be a positive experience, but most women consider the emotional and physical rewards to be major reasons to want to breast-feed.

Aside from emotional benefits, there are physical advantages. When a baby nurses at her mother's breasts, this encourages the production of the hormone that stimulates her uterus to contract. Breast-feeding thus hastens the contraction of the uterus and quickens its return to its former size, shape, and position in the body. This process takes longer in women who are bottle-feeding.

From a purely practical point of view, there are many advantages to breast-feeding. A major plus factor is that a mother always has a built-in supply of milk that is available on immediate demand. The time and effort required in formula-feeding are completely eliminated by breast-feeding, and this method enables a mother to respond more rapidly when her infant cries out of hunger. Middle-of-the-night feedings are easier, as well as more convenient, for breast-feeding mothers.

Breast-feeding is considered to be the simpler of the two methods in regard to taking the baby out of the home, and especially in relation to traveling. A mother need not worry about carrying special feeding equipment, or feeding in areas of the world in which sanitary conditions are poor, or milk and/or bottle-feeding equipment are not readily obtainable.

From a monetary perspective, breast-feeding is more economical than bottle-feeding. Mothers who plan to breast-feed will want to purchase special nursing brassieres, but beyond this there are no additional necessary expenses. Bottle-feeding is relatively low in cost, but depending upon a parent's financial position, it can place an added strain on the budget.

It should be most reassuring for you to remember that women throughout history have been enjoying and using the breast-feeding method successfully. This method has been proven effective. Having a knowledge of certain basic procedures and principles will make it easier for you to enjoy this natural feeding method.

ASSISTANCE WHEN YOU BEGIN. Nursing a baby is not difficult. When you are ready to begin, it may help put you at ease if a nurse, midwife, or another experienced person is on hand to provide guidance and moral support. There are some women who prefer to have privacy during initial feeding sessions, in which case do not feel bad about asking others to leave you alone with your baby.

This section is designed to help answer some of your questions, prepare you in advance for how to begin breast-feeding, and acquaint you with some of the situations you may encounter as you go along. Being relaxed, confident, and in a positive frame of mind are particularly important to this method, because tension and anxiety can have a negative effect upon your ability to produce sufficient amounts of milk.

La Leche League International was founded for the purpose of giving help and encouragement to those mothers who want to breast-feed their babies. The League believes that breast-feeding is the ideal way to initiate mother-child relationships and strengthen family ties. Their international office is located at:

9616 Minneapolis Avenue
Franklin Park, Illinois 60131
U.S.A.

The League has many community groups in the United States and abroad to offer assistance and support to breast-feeding mothers. If you are planning to nurse your baby and would like to share your experience with other mothers dedicated to breast-feeding and receive some additional instruction, you may find this organization helpful. Upon request, this organization will provide you with a list of books on breast-feeding that may be of assistance.

THE PROCESS OF MILK PRODUCTION. Having a basic understanding of the process of milk production should not only give you an appreciation of your body, but also give you more confidence in its capabilities. Each breast is composed of many milk-producing glands located in the fatty tissue of the breast. These milk glands are grouped together in clusters and are connected through ducts (pathways) to a common exit site at the hole in the nipple. These glands are at rest until a woman becomes pregnant.

During early pregnancy, large amounts of special hormones (estrogen and progesterone) are produced by the placenta. These hormones are present in the blood stream and stimulate the milk glands in the breast to grow and develop the capability to produce milk. This explains the enlargement of the breasts during pregnancy.

When your baby is born, and the placenta is delivered, your breasts are signaled to be ready to produce milk by the sudden drop in hormones previously produced by the placenta. The milk glands are primed to produce milk, but the breast needs stimulation to release the milk.

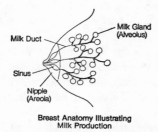

Breast Anatomy Illustrating
Milk Production

The final production and release of milk require the participation of your baby. By sucking on your areola, your infant stimulates nerve endings in the breast that send a message to the brain. The brain then stimulates the pituitary gland to secrete a hormone called prolactin. This hormone enters the blood stream and reaches the breast. It signals the milk glands in the breast to begin the production of milk and release the milk from the glands (the "let down" process). Until the milk glands are able to produce milk, the breasts release a yellowish fluid, high in protein content, called colostrum. Once the milk glands are ready (in a few days following birth) the colostrum is replaced by milk.

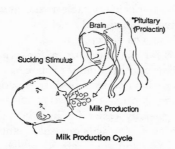

Milk Production Cycle

This interaction between mother and child to produce breast milk is a wonder of nature. Such a well-balanced process allows the child to control the amount of milk produced. The more she sucks, the more she stimulates the production of milk.

A woman who has already had a child may start to produce milk sooner than a woman who has given birth for the first time. This can vary. Generally speaking, most women begin to produce milk a few days after giving birth. Sometimes the initial milk flow is rapid and sudden, and sometimes milk is produced more slowly. In some cases new mothers do not experience the "let down" of milk until after they are discharged from the hospital and are home with their babies. The production of milk also has to do with a woman's emotional state.

It is only natural for you to wonder whether your breast-milk supply will be sufficient to satisfy your baby's needs, especially if this is your first experience with breast-feeding. Being very anxious, tense, angry, or embarrassed may actually interfere with your ability to produce milk. The ability to release prolactin and control milk production is partly controlled by the nervous system, which is sensitive to changes in your emotional condition. The importance of trying to relax, trust yourself and your body, and approach feedings in a positive frame of mind cannot be overemphasized.

For the first few days of breast-feeding, your infant may not be too hungry. Most babies need a day or two to get used to their new environment. The nourishment she will receive from the colostrum during this time should more than satisfy her. She may also receive glucose water to supplement the colostrum, especially in very hot climates where the baby may need more water. The combination of these two substances will be sufficient to satisfy her appetite for the first few days until you begin to produce real milk.

Babies normally lose a small amount of weight immediately after they are born. This can be up to 10 percent of their birth weight. This initial weight loss is natural, and not something that you should worry about. Within a week, or shortly thereafter, she will most likely gain back this weight and gain steadily during the next several weeks.

The vast majority of mothers can produce sufficient amounts of breast milk to satisfy their babies' nutritional needs completely. Your doctor will let you know whether your infant is healthy and doing well, and you will be able to see for yourself if she is gaining weight and seems satisfied. If your baby does not act hungry for a few hours between feedings, then she can be assumed to be getting enough breast milk. During the initial nursing period, the most important thing for you to do is to relax.

BEGINNING NURSING. It is becoming a more popular procedure to put a baby to her mother's breast right on the delivery table. This is beneficial, since it fosters bonding between parent and child. It is also advantageous for the mother, as was previously discussed. Nursing on the delivery table is not always possible, depending upon the circumstances of delivery, but should be encouraged.

The nursing position you select is basically a matter of personal preference. Of primary importance is for you and your infant to be comfortable and cozy. This will facilitate your milk flow and her ability to suck.

For some women, their first breast-feeding experience takes place in a lying down position. This position is often the most popular and comfortable during the first few weeks, and is generally easier for middle-of-the-night feedings. A comfortable couch or bed can be used. You will probably want to place some soft pillows under your head and back. You and your baby should be lying on the bed facing one another. It may be best to raise your arm nearest the infant over your head. Move your body in very close to hers so that your nipple is within easy reach of her mouth. Occasionally, you may have to press your breast back slightly with your fingers to enable her to breathe easily.

As the days and weeks pass, you will probably want to nurse in a sitting-up position either in bed or in a chair, although some women prefer this from the start. Cradle your infant in the bend of your arm in a semi-upright posture, with her head and back supported. Your back should also be supported. Use extra pillows if necessary. Hold her body so that her feet rest in your lap and her head is near your breast. Find a comfortable chair in which to feed your baby, and a position that suits you and her the best. Many mothers prefer to use a rocking chair rather than a regular chair. Some mothers feel that using a footstool is helpful.

Hold your baby securely and lovingly. Allow her arms to move about freely so that she can feel your body. Touching one another is an important avenue through which the two of you will be drawn together.

In order for nursing to be effective, you should initially help your baby to secure not only your nipple, but your whole areola (the dark circle around the nipple). Although she is born with a sucking mechanism, she is as inexperienced as you are at this important task. Therefore, you can gently move her mouth toward your nipple. When she feels it touching her mouth or cheek, she will automatically "root" or turn toward it and begin to suck. You will want to use her rooting reflex to your best advantage. Do not suddenly push your baby's head to your nipple. Her response will be to thrust in the opposite direction. Rather, move your nipple and breast slowly to her mouth. Tickling her a little on the cheek near her mouth may also help stimulate her to root and suck.

You should help her get the whole areola into her mouth. When she sucks on your entire areola, the milk is pushed out of the sinuses behind the areola through your nipple. By sucking on the nipple alone, she may not take in as much milk as she needs, or she may get no milk at all. This can also result in soreness and irritation of the nipple. It may be necessary to squeeze your areola between your fingers gently as you guide it into her mouth. Supporting and massaging your breast often help in getting the flow of milk started.

THE FEEDING SESSION. The best guide to follow for the length of each nursing session is your baby's desire to feed. This natural interaction is usually the best way to adjust feeding times. In the past it was felt that initial sessions on the breast should be limited to a few minutes to avoid nipple irritation, and then increased over several days. This method may not be as effective as letting your baby's desire set the nursing time.

By allowing your infant to suck when she is hungry, she will not get overly hungry and suck extra vigorously, increasing the chances for nipple irritation. Allowing the baby to nurse longer from the beginning will stimulate the "let down" reflex that helps foster your milk production. Twenty-minute feedings are usually the average time for each feeding session, and this time may be lengthened if your nipples do not become overly sore.

Many mothers prefer to offer both breasts at each feeding. Physicians usually recommend this method particularly during the time before a woman's breast-milk supply is strong. If offering both breasts, alternate the breast that is offered first at each feeding. Your physician will probably guide you as to whether to offer only one or both breasts, depending upon your condition and milk production.

Most infants need approximately twenty minutes during each feeding session, five to six times daily on the average. This means approximately ten minutes on each breast during each nursing period. It will take a little time for your nipples to adjust to the stimulation they will receive during regular feedings. Scheduling feedings and burping your baby are discussed on pages 133–37.

Bear in mind that in nursing you are not only satisfying your infant's craving for nourishment, but also her desire for extra sucking, attention, and affection. While she is nursing at your breast, you will be able to interact with her in your own special way.

Mothers who are nursing obviously cannot see how many ounces of milk their infants are consuming. This is considered by many to be one of the natural advantages of breast-feeding. A mother normally produces the right amount of milk according to her baby's needs without being aware of those needs in terms of ounces. This arrangement worked out beautifully throughout the pregnancy period when a mother was also unaware of how much nourishment her baby was taking, but always supplied the correct amount. Yet, after giving birth, many breast-feeding mothers suddenly begin to worry that their babies are not receiving adequate nourishment.

Sometimes a mother will try to determine whether her baby is getting enough to eat by looking at the size of her breasts or by examining how long the baby nurses. These things tell very little about whether or not a baby is taking in sufficient milk to satisfy her. You can learn more from observing your baby's behavior over a period of several days. Does she seem happy, content, and satisfied after feedings? Does she fall asleep shortly after and remain asleep for a few hours before awakening for her next feeding? Is she gradually sleeping for longer periods of time at night? If the answer to these questions is "yes," then you can be fairly sure that she is getting enough milk.

The best way to feel totally confident that your infant is not undernourished is to have her examined regularly by a doctor or nurse practitioner. Forget your unfounded suspicions about having an inadequate milk supply and channel your energy into a more constructive avenue such as enjoying your child.

TAKE GOOD CARE OF YOURSELF WHILE NURSING. The state of your health can influence how successful you are at nursing your infant. You should take good care of yourself during the time you are breast-feeding, not just for your baby's sake, but for your own. This means getting sufficient amounts of sleep and exercise, paying attention to the condition and cleanliness of your breasts and nipples, and keeping calm and relaxed. This also means paying attention to your diet, drinking ample amounts of fluids, and taking in the additional nutritional requirements for the lactating woman, including vitamins, minerals, iron, and calories.

The condition of your breasts and nipples is important to nursing. These areas should be thoroughly washed and dried on a daily basis, and also before and after you nurse. Refrain from touching them with unwashed hands. The idea is to keep these areas of your body clean to avoid infections of the breast and nipples, and help avoid thrush, a mild fungus infection in the baby's mouth.

Mothers who have nursed their babies report that keeping nipples very dry between feedings helps prevent them from becoming sore. They recommend leaving open the flaps of the nursing bra between feedings or allowing nipples to dry thoroughly before closing the flaps. It is advisable to avoid purchasing nursing bras with waterproof linings that retain moisture. Be sure to change soiled nipple pads frequently so that your nipples will stay dry.

A special nursing bra that is well fitted to your breasts is a must. It will provide extra support for your enlarged breasts and will help prevent them from sagging. Some physicians recommend that mothers who plan to nurse massage or exercise their nipples regularly during the latter months of pregnancy. Before you begin, it is a good idea to consult your doctor for specific instructions. Guard against massaging your nipples too often or too toughly.

Nursing your infant should not cause sagging of your breasts, assuming that you keep them well supported. After you have finished nursing, they should return to approximately their former size.

The size of your breasts has little to do with milk production. Most women, even those with small breasts prior to becoming pregnant, will produce sufficient amounts of milk. Your medical and/or psychological state has more to do with your ability to nurse. If you are planning to breast-feed, you should discuss this with your physician so you can be certain that there are no medical reasons contraindicating the use of this method.

Many mothers wonder what type of diet they will have to maintain during nursing. It is essential to realize that as the baby takes breast milk, she is depleting certain important nutrients from the mother, such as calcium, which have to be constantly replenished in order for her to remain healthy. Not only do you have to maintain a well-balanced diet, but you also should eat and drink a little extra to re-place the materials your baby is taking. On the average, lactating women need addi-tional metabolic energy (approximately 500 kcals) and 20 grams of protein daily above their usual dietary intake. In many cases the equivalent of a peanut butter sandwich on wheat bread on top of a normal daily diet can provide the additional nutrients required by the woman who is breast-feeding.

Your doctor can be of assistance in planning a proper diet, and may recommend specific vitamins designed for lactating women. Breast-feeding necessitates eating and drinking a little more, but does not require you to gain weight. For your health and that of your infant, avoid excessive eating and crash dieting. Drinking alcoholic beverages and smoking are not recommended. Before medications or drugs are taken, they should be discussed with your doctor. Drugs that you take may be trans-mitted through the milk to your infant, assuming they are of sufficiently high dos-age. Your physician can tell you whether they are advisable for you and your baby.

It is possible for you to continue eating the foods that you normally eat, although you may occasionally notice that after you eat a particular food your baby seems unusually irritable or restless, or develops a minor digestive or elimination problem such as diarrhea.

After eating a relatively large quantity of chocolate and then breast-feeding her baby, Nicholas, Mrs. Dayton noticed that he was grouchy, crying, and passing wa-tery stools. At first she was puzzled by this change in her son's behavior, but did not even think about associating his troubles with her consumption of chocolate. She continued to eat her favorite chocolate candies, and later realized that after each oc-casion on which chocolate was eaten, her nursing infant's behavior changed and he suffered from diarrhea. In an attempt to prevent further discomfort to Nicholas, and confirm her suspicions about chocolate, she eliminated it from her diet altogether. Nicholas' problems immediately cleared up and did not return.

Nursing mothers who suspect that a certain food they are eating may be causing their baby some minor difficulties should discontinue eating this food for a while. Sometimes after several weeks' waiting period, the food can then be eaten again without resulting in problems for the nursing baby. Once in a while, a mother has to leave a certain food out of her diet for months, or even during the entire time she is nursing. These minor problems, if they arise at all, will cause a nursing mother only temporary inconvenience.

BREAST-FEEDING AND MOTHERS WHO WORK OUTSIDE THE HOME. Many mothers who have interests or careers that necessitate their being away from home each day find that breast-feeding is still possible. Most women who want to nurse their babies and are fortunate to have job flexibility, plan to take time off for at least the first month or two after giving birth. It is advisable to plan for about one to one and a half months at home so that you will have time to recuperate from the delivery, get acquainted with your baby, and enable your milk production cycle to become well established.

Once your milk supply is sufficiently established to meet your infant's demands, it will be possible for you to return to work and breast-feed, too. There are many ways in which to arrange to continue breast-feeding, depending upon your work schedule and your baby's needs. Provided that your schedule permits, you might be in a posi-tion to return home once or twice during the day just to feed your baby. Some com-panies have policies which permit a nursing mother to bring her baby along with her during work hours to facilitate breast-feeding. Unfortunately, these companies are the exception rather than the rule.

Quite often mothers breast-feed their babies in the morning and express the milk (see pages 64–65) for supplement by bottle while they are at work. With a good milk-production cycle, another alternative is to supplement breast-feeding with an occasional or even daily bottle of formula during the times when mothers are not around to nurse. Then, when they return home, they can resume breast-feeding, assuming that their babies are on a regular feeding schedule.

Breast-feeding will not tie you to your home full time. Whether or not you can successfully blend breast-feeding with your working schedule will depend upon factors such as your commitment to nursing, being able to remain with your newborn long enough to establish a sufficient supply of milk to satisfy her needs, and how long you are absent from the home each day. Any questions that may arise in regard to co-ordinating your work schedule with breast-feeding should be discussed with your baby's doctor.

Some mothers who work full time find that continuing with breast-feeding represents an inconvenience. They nurse for as long as they are home with their babies after delivery, and then wean the babies to a bottle prior to returning to work. This is certainly a viable alternative.

ADJUSTMENTS IN YOUR LIFESTYLE WHILE NURSING. During approximately the first four to six weeks, it is highly important for a nursing mother to develop a good milk-production cycle. Even though both mother and father are likely to wake during the night in response to their baby's hunger cries, it will be mother's job to feed her. Accepting responsibility for the baby's feedings, and meeting her round-the-clock, frequent demands for nourishment, can be tiring and draining during the first couple of months. It can make a new nursing mother feel rather tied to the home.

Feelings of being overtired, overburdened, or tied down during the weeks following delivery are fairly common complaints among not just nursing mothers, but virtually all new mothers. Physical, emotional, and psychological changes play a role in this, and adjusting to meeting the newcomer's daily and nightly demands is enough to cause most new parents to feel tired and as though their freedom has been curtailed. Breast-feeding, by itself, should not cause extreme fatigue, signs of illness, or unintentional weight loss. Mothers who experience these physical changes should discuss them with their physician.

Most mothers who breast-feed find that this does not unduly limit their freedom with the exception of the first month or two. It is possible to continue your usual pattern of activities and either bring your baby along, or leave a supplementary bottle for her (expressed breast milk or formula) when you plan to be away from her during a feeding time.

SPECIAL CONSIDERATIONS IN BREAST-FEEDING. Occasionally a mother is unable to produce enough breast milk to satisfy her baby's needs. This is a problem that is determined by parent and physician. Often an anxious mother who has little confidence in her ability to breast-feed will give up before she has given it enough of a trial. She may listen to other people who are discouraging her from continuing to nurse, and begin to offer her baby formula on a regular basis. This can markedly interfere with her milk production. The nipples will not receive adequate stimulation and the breasts will not be emptied at regular intervals, causing a decrease in milk supply.

Sometimes anxiety alone has an adverse effect on milk production. This sets up a vicious cycle in which a mother worries that she is not producing enough milk, and this causes less milk to be produced, which, in turn, creates more anxiety. It is important to give breast-feeding an adequate trial, assuming that you have a basic commitment and really want to continue. Persistence usually brings about the desired results, since it may take several weeks before your milk production is well established.

Occasionally, there is a real problem of insufficient milk. This is the exception rather than the rule, but in such cases the doctor may offer suggestions for how to stimulate your milk supply and/or be in a position to continue nursing your baby. Suggestions might include feeding your baby more frequently to stimulate milk production, expressing milk by hand if any remains after nursing periods, or even offering an occasional bottle to supplement your breast milk. Excessive anxiety, improper diet and fluid intake, and insufficient amounts of rest may also result in a decrease in your supply of milk. Careful consideration should be given to taking good care of yourself.

Occasionally a mother who has been enthusiastic about breast-feeding and has really tried to make a go of it may be advised by her physician to change from breast to bottle because her supply of breast milk is insufficient. When a physician recommends that breast-feeding be discontinued, a mother may be left feeling that she has somehow failed in her role as a woman, and guilty that she has failed her child.

Marsha, for example, had always planned on nursing her baby. When Mark was born, she took extra special care of her body, and carefully followed her doctor's advice. After two months, she and her doctor determined that her baby was receiving insufficient amounts of milk. At first she felt down in the dumps and was worried about whether Mark would do well switching from her breasts to a bottle. However, he sucked on it vigorously and seemed to be really fulfilled and satisfied after his feedings. Suddenly he began to gain quite a bit of weight, and, for the first time, began to sleep well and appear happy during the day. Seeing him so contented and doing so well put her at ease, and made her realize that the most important issue was his well-being—not whether he got milk from her or from a bottle. Even though Marsha still wished that she could have continued nursing him, she no longer felt guilty or depressed. She had a very healthy, happy baby, and this reassured her that her and her doctor's joint decision to discontinue breast-feeding had been the right one.

A hungry baby needs and craves food, and she will easily adjust to taking milk from a bottle. Her main concern is with filling her tummy as often as she needs. This should be your main concern as well. If your doctor and you determine that your milk supply is insufficient, you can establish the kind of affectionate, intimate relationship when bottle-feeding her that you established while breast-feeding. This is what really matters anyway.

Also, you are not alone. Other mothers have experienced similar obstacles in breast-feeding. Do not, even for a moment, lose sight of the fact that the ability to breast-feed successfully does not make you a good mother. Mothering, as you know, includes far more than this! Try to discuss your feelings with your doctor, your spouse, or friends if you are feeling depressed or unhappy. They will help you to realize that your baby needs adequate nourishment as well as a mother who has a positive attitude far more than she needs to have human milk.

Still other mothers who are breast-feeding, for a variety of reasons, decide that this method is unsatisfactory for them. Perhaps they find the initial discomfort difficult to tolerate, or maybe they find it hard to relax because they are constantly worried about whether their babies are getting enough to eat.

In some cases there may be pressures on a woman from family members to stop nursing. Perhaps her spouse is feeling left out of the picture, and this plays a role in changing her mind. Sometimes older children may be jealous and put pressures on their mother to stop breast-feeding. It is not unusual for a woman to want to stop nursing because she feels tied down too much, or simply does not want to assume the entire responsibility for feeding.

At times a woman's reasons are less specific. She may simply feel generalized discontent, and believe that she would be happier and more comfortable offering a bottle. There is no reason for you to feel guilty if you decide to discontinue nursing in spite of the fact that you are producing adequate amounts of milk. You must feel satisfied and comfortable with a feeding method, since this is the most important thing for both you and your baby. If you decide to switch to bottle-feeding, it is advisable to discuss your plans with your doctor, who will give you instructions for how to wean your baby, and prescribe a formula that is well suited to her needs.

COMBINATIONS OF BREAST AND BOTTLE. Assuming that your baby is not receiving enough milk after nursing, your doctor may advise you to offer formula from a bottle immediately after you have nursed. This may work well for a while, but chances are that if you plan to continue breast-feeding, this method is not always advisable. Frequently a baby finds it easier to take milk from a bottle, and therefore comes to prefer it. When your nipples do not receive enough regular stimulation, this can decrease your production and supply of milk.

In case your supply of breast milk is insufficient at a particular time each day (with many mothers this is around dinnertime), your doctor may recommend that you offer your baby a bottle at that time in place of your breast. The doctor will tell you what kind of formula to use. You can express milk by hand, if your breasts are full (see pages 64–65). Offering an occasional bottle instead of your breasts should have no adverse effect on your ability to produce milk. Some women offer a bottle a couple of times a week. This may be a good idea, even though you have enough milk for each feeding. Should you have occasion to be away from your baby during feeding time, or in the event that you are busy or not feeling well, your baby may make a smoother transition from breast to bottle if she is familiar with using it. Fathers may appreciate this too, since it allows them opportunities to feed their babies. On the other hand, offering a few bottles a day is not advisable if you are interested in continuing to breast-feed.

EXPRESSION OF MILK. There are some occasions in which you may find it useful to empty your breasts of milk by hand or with a breast pump. In case your baby does not completely empty your breasts, your nipples hurt too much for you to nurse, your breasts are very firm and distended making it hard to nurse, or you are ill, you may want or have to get milk out. There may also be an occasion on which your baby is unwilling to nurse, or you are separated from her. You may want to empty your breasts and save your milk to give to her at a later time. A premature infant who cannot nurse can still be given your milk if you express it. In order for you to continue to produce milk, the milk in your breasts must be withdrawn at regular intervals. Proper milk drainage is very important.

Below you will find a brief discussion of how to express milk manually, and a brief description of breast pumps. These techniques for removing milk are not especially difficult to learn, but you may want to have a nurse show you the technique before you leave the hospital or have some experienced person show you at a later date.

Hand-emptying of breast milk is sometimes called manual or hand expression.

This can be accomplished by using either of two techniques. The technique most often used involves the thumb and forefinger. If you want to milk your left breast, use your left hand to hold your breast and your right hand to express milk, and vice versa. The technique in hand-emptying is to mimic your baby's sucking motions when she is nursing. You should place your left hand under and around the left breast to hold it. Put the clean thumb and forefinger of your right hand around the edge of your areola on opposite sides, and press inward and downward in quick strokes several times each minute. The object is to produce a rhythmic action that will squeeze the milk out of the sinuses through your nipple. In order to get all of the milk out of the sinuses, you will have to rotate the position of your fingers around the edge of your areola in a circle corresponding to numbers on the clock marking intervals of fifteen minutes. Do not slide them over your nipple. Even though your hands may get tired, this technique should not be painful. If you want to feed your baby right away, you can pour the milk from a clean, dry cup into a bottle that has been thoroughly washed and dried.

The second technique, which is also effective, involves using your thumb and a cup with a flared edge. Using this method, the milk is also rhythmically squeezed out of the sinuses. Your thumb should be placed on the upper rim of your areola, and the rim of the cup should be placed against the lower rim of the areola. You should mimic your baby's sucking action by pressing inward toward the sinuses and downward with your thumb half a dozen times or more each minute. Cleanliness is essential.

Assuming that your breasts are nearly but not completely emptied when you begin, hand-emptying should only take several minutes. Plan on this taking about twenty-five minutes if you begin with a full milk supply. When the milk comes out in slow drops the breasts have been emptied sufficiently and you can stop the squeezing.

Many mothers dislike using a breast pump although this can be successfully used to empty the breasts of milk. There are basically three kinds of breast pumps. One kind is operated by hand. Another uses electricity. The third is operated by water suction. The most effective of the three kinds is the electric pump, which can be purchased or rented from a surgical supply company. Some hospitals or La Leche League organizations will also rent them to parents. Your physician will assist you in selecting a breast pump if he or she recommends that you use one.

COMMON BREAST-FEEDING CONCERNS AND PROBLEMS. Sometimes women experience problems in the course of nursing. Unless women are familiar with the common problem areas, they may panic at the first unusual symptom, misinterpret symptoms, or delay seeking medical attention when it is necessary. The following material should provide background information on problems that may arise with some mothers, but whenever problems or questions arise, it is advisable to seek the advice of a physician.

Nursing When You Are Sick. A special area of concern in nursing arises when a mother is sick and is not sure whether she should continue to nurse her baby. If you have an ordinary illness that does not require hospitalization, generally you can continue to nurse your baby. Naturally, there is a possibility that your baby will catch your illness, but she might catch the same illness even if she were bottle-fed, simply from being exposed to you. In case you are very ill and are worried about your baby's exposure to you, it is advisable for you to contact your doctor in order to obtain a medical opinion. Remember to avoid self-medication without first checking with your doctor to ensure that a potentially harmful drug will not be transmitted to your baby through your breast milk.

Abrupt Weaning from Breast to Bottle.   Weaning basically refers to the process by which your breast-fed baby must gradually get used to taking milk in another way—from a bottle. The switch from offering her breast milk to formula in a bottle is normally carried out over a period of a few weeks to make the transition easier on the infant and to ensure the mother's comfort and health. There are a few unusual circumstances that can arise, making an abrupt weaning necessary. They may include a sudden hospitalization for a mother, or an out-of-town emergency that makes it necessary for a mother to leave her infant. In the event that you must abruptly discontinue breast-feeding, phone your baby's doctor for specific instructions.

Pains Can Occur When You Nurse.   It is not uncommon for women to experience some pains while they nurse, especially during the first several weeks. There is no way a mother can completely prepare herself in advance for what nursing a baby will feel like. Nipples take time to toughen and may hurt during early nursing, particularly if a baby is a vigorous sucker. This discomfort is hard for some women to bear, and is one reason why a new mother may decide to discontinue nursing. Assuming that you are intent upon breast-feeding, do not give up. The pains are temporary, and will diminish after you have had more experience.

Some women also complain of abdominal pains or cramps during the initial week or so of nursing. These cramps are usually the result of the contraction of the uterus as it returns to its prepregnant shape and position. Nursing generally speeds up this process. The contraction of the uterus is stimulated by sucking of the breast during feeding. This is a normal body response. Cramps of this nature should not cause you unnecessary concern, and are only temporary. Severe cramps or pain should be discussed with your physician.

Leaking of Milk from the Breasts.   Dribbles of milk may sometimes leak from your nipples during the nursing period. This is nothing to be concerned about as it is common, and not an indication that there is anything wrong. Small amounts of milk may come out of your breasts shortly before your baby's regular nursing time. Sometimes during the middle of the night, your baby's hunger cry may trigger some breast leaking. While she is sucking at one of your breasts, some milk may dribble out from the other. Obviously, you want to protect your clothing from being soiled. You can put nipple pads in your nursing bra, which will absorb the milk. Be sure to change the pads at frequent intervals. Some women have complained that when they were making love, small amounts of milk leaked from their breasts. This does not represent a problem for most couples, but if you or your partner are disturbed by this, you may have to wear a nursing bra to bed (see also page 60).

Whole Breast Engorgement.   Promptly contact your physician if your entire breast region suddenly becomes very swollen, hard, and sensitive. This condition, which usually occurs during the first week following delivery, can cause pain in severe cases of engorgement, and some discomfort in milder cases. Emptying of the breasts by the baby generally alleviates most cases of engorgement. When the problem is more severe, the baby may have difficulty nursing, or the breasts may become distended again immediately after nursing. Your doctor may advise you to hand-empty your breasts for several minutes before nursing, gently rub or massage the breasts, wear a tight breast support binder, use a breast pump, apply warm or cold compresses, or he may prescribe some medication to help alleviate this condition and ease your pain. Keeping your breasts well supported is particularly important if they become very swollen and distended.

Partial Breast Engorgement—Areolar Region. In some cases the areolar region, not the entire breast, can become distended or engorged. This usually occurs during the first week to ten days when the milk comes in and the milk sinuses swell. This condition is fairly common, and should not cause undue concern. The distention of the areolar area of the breast may not be too uncomfortable for you, however, the firmness of the area may give your baby some difficulty positioning her mouth around it to nurse. If this occurs, you may have to empty some breast milk by hand for a couple of minutes before you help your baby to secure your areola. This will make it less firm and more flexible so that she can begin to suck. This engorgement is temporary and will probably occur only once or twice during the entire nursing period.

Caking of the Breast. Another type of engorgement that can lead to some difficulties occurs when one area of the breast, not the entire breast region, and not specifically the areolar region, becomes distended. It often happens when the breast is not completely drained of milk and a certain area becomes overfull and swollen. This sometimes painful condition is often referred to as caking of the breast. Notify your doctor if this occurs. Your physician may recommend alternatives for treatment similar to those for whole breast engorgement. An infection may develop if milk is backed up and remains in the breast too long. Get in touch with your physician immediately in the event that you notice a warm, tender, red spot on the surface of your breast.

Mastitis. Mastitis is a different matter. It is an infection in the breast, and it is not a common problem. An infection in the breast usually produces an area of tenderness which may also be reddened and warm. Mastitis should be immediately brought to the attention of your physician.

Irritated Nipples. It is advisable to consult your doctor if your nipples become very irritated or cracked while you nurse. A mother who is unaccustomed to breast-feeding may experience some soreness of the nipples during the first few weeks. Usually this uncomfortable sensation passes. Not allowing nipples to dry thoroughly following nursing periods can result in irritated nipples, as can permitting a baby to suck for prolonged periods of time, particularly during the first week or two. Chewing on the nipples after she has finished taking all of the milk she wants can also cause them to become sore. In some cases, a nipple may be so sore that a mother finds it painful to nurse. She can offer a bottle in place of the breast and empty her breast by hand if this is necessary. Wearing a nipple guard while nursing may also be helpful until the nipple heals. A nipple guard or shield is a small, flexible, artificial nipple that fits over the breast nipple. Nipple shields can be employed to protect a sore or irritated nipple, and occasionally to assist mothers with retracted nipples. The baby sucks on the nipple guard producing suction on the underlying nipple, allowing the milk to be drawn out of the breast.

Retracted Nipples. Some nursing mothers have nipples that do not protrude or stick out beyond the surface of the breast. This type of nipple is called a retracted nipple. This is a normal variation in breast shape. The mother with retracted nipples may find that her baby has some difficulty in finding or sucking on the nipple. Sometimes simple manipulation of the nipple will cause it to stick out, making it easier for the infant to suck.

Retracted nipples are usually not a major problem in breast-feeding. There are some simple exercises that can be initiated during the last few months of pregnancy to help prevent possible problems related to inverted or retracted nipples before the baby is born. Your obstetrician should be of assistance in this.

Bottle-feeding

Bottle-feeding is a viable alternative for those women who either cannot or do not want to breast-feed. It is a well-accepted method for providing an infant with the nourishment she needs to grow. One of the advantages of this method is that a new mother does not have to bear the sole burden of responsibility for feedings.

Sharing the responsibility for child feeding is very important to some parents. Bottle-feeding facilitates co-operation in child care, particularly during the first couple of months when the baby will require middle-of-the-night feedings: mother and father can take turns, allowing the woman to get more rest. Daytime or nighttime feedings can be given by anyone. The flexibility and freedom that bottle-feeding offers are major reasons why some parents elect this method.

Another reason why some parents prefer bottle-feeding is that it allows them to keep track of how much nourishment their infant is taking in terms of ounces. Women who are anxious about how much milk their babies are consuming and overly worried about the possibility of undernourishment are sometimes more relaxed using this method as opposed to breast-feeding, even though breast-feeding is completely adequate.

There are, of course, a variety of other reasons for the selection of bottle-feeding. They often include a woman's greater familiarity with this method, lack of encouragement and support from immediate relatives or her physician for breast-feeding, embarrassment over using the breasts in this capacity, insecurities about failure to produce enough breast milk, dislike of the general idea of nursing, etc. Whether a woman's strong preference sounds valid to others, it should be respected, since it is extremely important for her to feel as comfortable and positive about feedings as possible.

Of utmost significance in bottle-feeding your baby is to provide her with warmth, security, affection, and plenty of close physical contact. Cuddling, talking, and touching are vital to the feeding exchange. The feeling and over-all impression that your baby gets from being fed should be positive, not just in regard to her hunger drive, but in regard to her emotional needs as well.

You are not alone if you have questions about bottle-feeding. Perhaps you are not sure about how to select a formula or how to prepare it. Is sterilization of the formula essential? Is it necessary to warm the baby's bottle before offering it to her? These questions are very natural, especially if this is your first baby and you have had little or no prior experience feeding a young infant. This section is designed to help answer your questions, and to prepare you to feed your baby properly. Each parent-child feeding exchange is unique, but there are certain fundamental principles and procedures that you should become familiar with before you begin to bottle-feed.

Any new task takes time to learn. It should be most reassuring to remember that women have been bottle-feeding babies successfully for years. Unlike breast-feeding, which cannot be tried in advance, you may have opportunities to get some practical experience by feeding a relative's or a friend's baby before your baby arrives, so you may feel comfortable when you actually begin.

Your baby is an individual, and her health, weight, behavior, style of feeding, and nutritional requirements will be different from other babies. Through office visits for well baby care, you will be in frequent contact with your physician, who will determine along with you whether your baby's nutritional needs are being met and whether she is healthy and gaining weight as she should. Being successful at bottle-feeding is not difficult as long as you see to it that your baby is getting all that she wants to eat and consult with your family physician along the way.

FORMULAS AND WHAT THEY ARE ALL ABOUT. Human milk is the natural food for babies. It provides the nutriments that a baby needs to grow healthy and strong. A formula is a mixture of the essential nutriments that the baby needs and is made up to be very similar in content to human milk. It normally contains milk, water, sugar, and iron, as well as other vitamins, and provides the infant with proteins, carbohydrates, minerals, fats, and vitamins essential for proper growth. Commercially prepared formulas come in powdered, concentrated, or ready-to-use liquid forms, which are extremely popular as well as convenient. The ready-made formulas are usually the most expensive.

Since your baby has her own individual nutritional requirements, your family physician should advise you as to which formula is best suited to her needs, taking into account factors such as her health, age, weight, and so forth. Assuming that you give birth in a hospital setting, your doctor will prescribe a formula before you are discharged. If you are attending a well baby or another type of child care clinic, or are seeing a public health or visiting nurse, you will also be given a recommendation for a formula. Along with the prescription, you will receive instructions for how to prepare the formula.

Follow the advice of your doctor or other trained health professional; it is unadvisable to change to another formula or alter the directions for preparing the formula unless you first consult your doctor. If for some reason you are absolutely unable to reach a doctor or nurse, and your baby appears to be normal and healthy, you can follow the instructions for formulas given on page 77. Remember that these formulas are only to be used in emergency situations.

PREPARING A BOTTLE. Babies, in the first few months, do not have their own completely developed defense system to fight disease. They often do not as yet carry in their bloodstreams enough antibodies to help most effectively fight germs and bacteria that enter their bodies unless they are breast-fed; thus they are generally more susceptible to developing infections than an older child or an adult. Maintaining clean and frequently sterile conditions when preparing foods is important to avoid infections and illness and to prevent bacteria from growing in the formula. Controversy exists over whether or not it is necessary always to sterilize formula and equipment for young babies. Your doctor will tell you if it is advisable for you to use sterilization procedures, and if so, which procedure to use.

It is not usually necessary for a formula taken out of the refrigerator to be shaken unless it is made of fresh, unhomogenized milk. Always be sure that you follow the instructions on the can or package to the letter.

The decision as to whether or not to warm the bottle before offering it is really a matter of personal preference. Breast milk is warm, and many mothers feel that bottle-feeding seems more natural and is better for their baby when the bottle is warmed. Actually, a baby can do equally as well if her bottle is warmed, taken right from the refrigerator, or offered at room temperature. However, it is less confusing for the baby if you serve the formula at one consistent temperature, since a baby who gets accustomed to having her formula served at one temperature may object when it is suddenly served at another.

If you want to warm the bottle, you can use an electric bottle warmer or simply place it in a container filled with hot, not boiling, water. You may have to rotate the bottle or gently shake it so that all of the formula will be brought to an even temperature. Always test the milk by shaking out several drops on the inside of your wrist or forearm to make sure that it is warm, but not too hot. If it feels too hot to you, let it cool down before offering it to your baby.

It is advisable to taste the baby's formula before offering it to her because if you have prepared it yourself, there is a possibility that you accidentally made a mistake. This is relatively rare, but a parent may accidentally add salt or some substance other than sugar to the formula in preparing it. In order to prevent this kind of accident from occurring, shake a few drops out on your wrist and sample it before giving the bottle. Your infant's formula may taste funny to you at first, but you will get used to it and be able to detect any variations. Using prepared or ready-to-use formulas makes this less necessary.

BEGINNING BOTTLE-FEEDING. The schedule may vary slightly from one hospital to another, but a baby usually receives her first bottle approximately ten to fourteen hours after birth. Until this time she generally is given sugar water. This satisfies her and prevents her from becoming dehydrated.

During the first few days following birth, babies tend to be sleepy and not very hungry. In the process of recovering from the shock of birth, they normally lose a little weight, which they will regain in the first week or so. Up to 10 percent of an infant's weight at birth can be lost in the first few days. This is still within acceptable limits. The weight loss is nothing for you to worry about.

There are certain pieces of equipment that you will need for bottle-feeding your baby at home. The amount and type of equipment you should obtain will naturally depend upon what is available in your area, the kind of formula your doctor recommends, and the instructions for preparation you are given. Those of you who will be using prepared, ready-to-use formulas and presterilized disposable bottles will not need to buy much in the way of equipment. On the other hand, those of you who will be mixing your own formula and following sterilization procedures will need quite a bit of equipment. It is also advisable to have some bottle-feeding equipment on hand if you are planning to breast-feed, in the event that you want to offer an occasional bottle or in case of illness or emergency. Below you will find a general guide to equipment, mainly designed as a check list for those of you who will be preparing and sterilizing formula and equipment:

Feeding Equipment Check List

nipples and caps
bottles

sterilizer (can be a deep kettle, covered pot, or electric sterilizer)
bottle rack
tongs
container (marked in ounces)
funnel
nipple and bottle brush
measuring cup and spoons
long spoon (iced tea spoons are good)
can opener (one that punches)
small pot (with a lid)
bibs

Bottles come in a wide variety of shapes and sizes. Some are made of glass, and others of plastic. Both can be sterilized. Plastic bottles are very popular for several reasons. They don't break, are lightweight, and are easier for the child who is learning to drink on her own to hold. Another reason why plastic bottles of the opaque variety are often preferred over clear glass bottles is that they prevent light from entering and destroying the riboflavin in the milk.

In selecting the size of the bottles, it is wise to purchase those holding eight ounces. While a young infant may only drink three to six ounces at a given feeding, this amount will increase later. Buying eight-ounce bottles from the start is more economical in the long run, since they can be used as long as the child still requires a bottle.

For convenience, many parents buy a plastic bottle holder designed to hold pre-sterilized disposable plastic bags or liners. At feeding time all that is necessary is to tear off one bag from the roll, fit it securely into the bottle holder without touching the inside of the bag, fill with formula, and attach a nipple. The only item that may require sterilization is the nipple, although your doctor may say that a thorough washing is sufficient. The plastic formula bags can be purchased separately. Parents often feel that the time and effort saved in using these disposable bags make them well worth their extra cost. Another advantage of these bags is that they shrink down or collapse as a baby empties formula from them, diminishing the amount of air that she swallows as she nurses.

Preparing a Formula

Your doctor will be able to advise you in choosing a formula that will meet your baby's individual needs. It is strongly recommended that you select a method for preparing a formula in close consultation with your physician since he or she will be aware of any local or environmental factors that will make one method of preparation preferable to another. Differences in disease patterns, sanitation conditions, and availability of different formulas and equipment must be carefully considered when selecting a formula. Your physician has had experience in providing proper feeding programs for babies in your community, and also knows your child's physical condition.

Discussed below are some common formula-preparation methods, covering assembly, filling, cleaning, and storing of bottled formula as well as sterilizing formula and equipment. For information on some of the more frequently used formulas, see pages 75–78. Formula preparation is not very taxing or difficult, but there is no substitute for practice. If you have friends with young children, they may be able to give you some practical suggestions and tips for purchasing and handling equipment.

HOW TO USE A NURSING BOTTLE. The basic nursing bottle consists of these major parts: bottle, nipple, nipple disc, nipple ring, and cap. When the bottle is filled with formula, the nipple disc is used to seal the bottle and keep the nipple sterile. The nipple is first inserted with the tip pointed into the bottle. The nipple disc is then placed on top of the nipple, and covered by the screw-on nipple ring. This is the storage assembly of the bottle. The contents of the bottle are completely sealed off from the air, and both the nipple inside the bottle and the formula remain sterile.

When the bottle is ready to be used for feeding, the nipple ring is unscrewed and removed from the bottle. The nipple disc is removed and set aside. Then the nipple is carefully taken out of the bottle and placed inside the nipple ring so that it sticks out through the hole of the ring. (Two ridges of rubber hold it securely in place and eliminate leakage.) It will be in position so that when the nipple ring is then screwed onto the bottle, the nipple will protrude from the top. The nipple disc is not used in the feeding assembly of the bottle. When leftover milk is going to be used at the next feeding, a cap can be put over the nipple to cover it before putting the bottle back into the refrigerator. There are special caps made for this purpose. Once a bottle has been used for feeding, be sure not to let the formula set for prolonged periods of time.

When your baby is young, most physicians recommend four- to five-ounce feedings. Your physician will assist you in determining how many ounces of formula should be put in each bottle. The amount depends upon your baby's appetite and will increase as she increases her demand for food. The amount of formula placed in each bottle should roughly correspond to the amount of milk in ounces that she takes at each feeding. As her appetite increases and the number of feedings during a twenty-four-hour period decreases, you will be putting more formula into fewer bottles. Your own common sense and your observations of her eating patterns will guide you in determining how much formula to place in each bottle.

It is important to keep all feeding equipment clean. After each feeding, bottles should be disassembled, and rinsed. Wash bottles carefully with soap and water, using a special bottle brush. Do the same with the nipple rings and nipples. It is often necessary to use a sharp pointed instrument to clean the nipple holes. Using a small cotton swab, sponge, or nipple brush to clean the inside of the nipple is often helpful. Be sure to rinse all equipment very thoroughly, and allow it to drain dry.

HANDLING AND STERILIZING FORMULA AND EQUIPMENT. The formula preparation is an ideal media for the growth of germs and bacteria. If the formula contains these organisms when it is prepared, and they are not killed during the preparation, they will grow rapidly in the formula. It is important to prevent contamination of the formula by such organisms since they may be harmful to your infant, or they may produce toxins which are also harmful. In addition, the infant is more susceptible to infections than the adult, and greater care should be taken to protect her from unnecessary exposure to bacteria and viruses.

Various techniques have been developed to eliminate contamination of the formula during preparation and storage. Some methods are better than others for different areas of the world and different family situations. Refrigeration of prepared formula significantly reduces the growth of bacteria in the formula and plays a major role in allowing the formula to be stored. Your doctor will probably recommend a method for sterilizing the formula.

Methods vary in their cost, the amount of work that they require, and how good a job they do.

A. *Terminal sterilization procedure*

Using the "terminal sterilization procedure" the formula is mixed in containers and then put into bottles. All equipment should be thoroughly cleaned in advance. The sterilization of the bottles and formula is done after the formula has been made and poured into bottles. This method is often the one preferred by some parents and pediatricians because it is simple to use and assures that the final bottled formula is sterilized. The procedure for the "terminal sterilization" method is briefly outlined below.

1. Mix the formula (you may use tap water) and pour it into the nursing bottles.
2. Place the nipples, hole facing down, in the bottles, cover them with the discs and loosely twist on the rings.
3. Put the bottles, right side up, in the wire rack in the sterilizer (or in any appropriately deep pan).
4. Put a couple of inches of water in the bottom of the pot, cover it, and put it on the stove.
5. Boil for twenty-five minutes.
6. Remove from the stove and let the bottles cool for approximately one to two hours before tightening the caps and placing the bottles in the refrigerator. Allowing the bottles to cool slowly without being disturbed often helps prevent clogging of the nipples by small pieces of crust-like material that form on the surface of the formula. Once the bottles have cooled to a lukewarm temperature, put them in the refrigerator.

B. *Aseptic sterilization procedure*

The aseptic sterilization procedure involves sterilizing the bottles and formula separately. The sterilized formula is then poured into the sterilized bottles and sealed. The sterilization of the formula is described in the section describing formula preparation on page 77. The formula can also be purchased already sterilized.

Sterilized, ready-to-use disposable bottles can be purchased. These come with or without sterilized nipples. You can also purchase sterilized, throw-away nipples. These products are ready for immediate filling with sterilized formula, but this method is rather costly.

The basic sterilization procedure of bottles and other equipment is not difficult. It essentially involves boiling all of the equipment in a large pot for five to seven minutes. You can purchase a sterilizer with a rack that can be used on the stove, or you can even buy automatic electric sterilizers that come with all of the necessary equipment. It is also possible to take a large pot with a cover and use a rack that can hold several eight-ounce bottles. Some parents prefer to use smaller bottles for water. Water bottles can be sterilized at the same time as the formula. The nipples and caps can often be fitted in the sterilizer within the rack, or can be placed in a jar with a perforated top. Be sure to place the jar and the bottles top down so that the rising steam can circulate through the bottles, and the water that condenses in the bottles can easily drain out. Other pieces of equipment that can be sterilized at the same time include spoons and tongs.

Once all of the equipment has been placed in the pot or sterilizer, and the water is added (usually two to four inches in the bottom of the pot), cover the pot and boil the water for at least five minutes or more. After boiling, allow the pot to cool. The bottles can then be carefully handled with the sterilized tongs, filled with formula, and covered with the nipple, disc, and ring. The nipple should be placed facing down into the formula so that it will remain sterile.

C. *Presterilized formula-filled disposable bottles*

There are several kinds of presterilized formula-filled throw-away nursing bottles available. These preparations are ready to use; all you need to do is attach a nipple and twist the nipple and ring to remove the protective covering and you can feed your baby. These bottles are available containing most of the ready-made formulas described below in the discussion of formulas. This method is very convenient, but also quite costly. Some parents, however, who do not use these disposable bottles regularly, recommend buying them for trips or when visiting for a weekend, since it eliminates the need for sterilization equipment and refrigeration.

D. *Presterilized disposable bottles*

There are numerous varieties of sterilized throw-away bottles. Some of the bottles come in kits containing presterilized, disposable nipples, rings, and caps. If you are not able to find presterilized nipples, you can sterilize your own nipples, discs, and rings as described in the aseptic sterilization procedure. Your prepared, sterilized formula, or ready-to-use formula, can be poured directly into these bottles. There are also sterile disposable plastic bags that fit inside the bottle, which can be filled with formula. As previously discussed, these bags are very convenient.

E. *Modified sterilization procedures*

Modern water processing procedures and the coming of the automatic dishwasher to some homes have resulted in some physicians recommending a modified sterilization procedure for bottles. In communities in which the sanitary conditions are good, it is possible to prepare the bottles for feeding in the dishwasher, providing that there is an adequate supply of hot water, good drainage of the bottles and equipment in the dishwasher, and a dishwashing detergent is used during the washing cycle. This method can be used to prepare the bottles, nipple discs, and nipple rings. It is usually not recommended that nipples be prepared in the dishwasher, but rather that they be sterilized separately, as described in the aseptic technique. However, special nipple holders are available for dishwashers, and can also be used. We recommend that this technique be used only with the approval of your physician.

The following outline summarizes the important guidelines of the dishwasher technique.

1. Thoroughly rinse off the bottles and other feeding equipment before putting them in the dishwasher, since pieces of food on them that are not cleaned off may not be removed as the equipment is cleaned in the dishwasher.

2. Load bottles with the open ends facing down, and put the discs and nipple rings in the silverware tray, or a special holder for nipples.

3. Add the specified amount of detergent and start the machine. Do not stop the dishwasher mid-cycle once you have started it.

4. Do not open the dishwasher until the dial indicates that the contents are dry.

5. Remove the feeding equipment, and with tongs in hand, assemble the bottles and nipples. You may wish to hold off adding the formula until you are ready to feed your baby.

F. Another modified procedure for bottling a formula involves the one-bottle-at-a-time approach. Some physicians and health care specialists recognize that when high standards of sanitation are maintained, and when formula is not allowed to sit for long periods of time, it is possible to avoid some of the rigid sterilization procedures described above. Good standards of cleanliness, refrigeration, pasteurized milk, and treated water are necessary for this method. The one-bottle-at-a-time technique should be used only under the direction of a physician who feels that this is an appropriate technique in your community. The basic principles and procedures to keep in mind are as follows:

1. The formula will be stored in a large, quart-size sterilized bottle with a lid, and placed in the refrigerator. If you will be sterilizing the bottle, place it top down in a large pan and place a few inches of water in the bottom. Also place the nipple, disc, and ring in the pan. Cover the pan and boil the water for at least five minutes. Let the pan cool before handling it.

2. The formula must be properly prepared in advance according to the aseptic sterilization technique described in preparation method #1 outlined on page 77, and then poured into the sterile jar. If you are using ready-to-use liquid formula, you can pour it directly into the large sterile jar. When pouring hot formula into the jar, screw the lid on loosely so that air can circulate as the formula cools in the refrigerator.

3. Immediately before you are ready to feed your baby, wash your hands well and dry them. The bottle and other necessary equipment must be thoroughly cleaned and dried as described on page 72, although this may be done several hours in advance.

4. Pour one feeding's worth of formula into the single bottle.

5. Assemble the nipple on the bottle and feed your baby right away.

COMMON FORMULAS. There are many types of formulas available. Parents find the prepared liquid formulas such as Enfamil, Similac, and SMA to be very convenient and easy to use. Most are enriched with vitamins. Enfamil and Similac come with or without iron supplement. Many physicians recommend these ready-to-use formulas to parents. Some of the other common formulas are evaporated milk formula and prepared powdered milk formula. The method of preparing each of these is described below.

Parents often find that it is useful to have a combination of different types and sizes of prepared formula on hand. The concentrates in thirteen-fluid-ounce cans, for example, are economical for everyday use. Purchasing them by the case can sometimes be cheaper than buying individual cans. Having several thirty-two-fluid-ounce cans of ready-to-use formula could be convenient if you are in a hurry. For taking the baby out or for travel, the ready-to-use formula in eight-ounce cans or the prefilled disposable bottles can come in very handy. As you care for your child, you can determine what size cans and combinations best suit your needs.

Whenever you purchase formula in cans, note and observe their expiration dates. Be sure to follow the preparation instructions written on the cans carefully. The instructions will also indicate how long the formula can safely be kept in the refrigerator. It is advisable to prepare only one day's worth of formula in advance to ensure that it does not sit for long periods of time in the refrigerator. This should also help you remember how long ago a given set of bottles was prepared. Once you remove a bottle of prepared formula from the refrigerator, it will be subject to the same contamination as would regular milk, so take care not to leave it unrefrigerated for hours, particularly on a hot day.

1. Ready-to-feed liquid formula in throw-away bottles

In any list of the most convenient formulas and methods of preparation to the least convenient, ready-to-feed liquid formula in throw-away bottles would be at the top. This type of formula and container eliminates all of the bother and extra time involved in preparing and sterilizing formula and equipment. It is truly efficient for home use, and also very handy for travel, dining out, and visiting. The bottles come in four-, six-, and eight-ounce sizes. When you have to leave your baby in someone else's care, you need not worry that her formula and/or equipment will be incorrectly prepared. With ready-to-feed prefilled bottles, there is no chance for error.

The major drawback to using formula in this form is money, and for most parents, this is an important consideration. You must pay for the extra convenience. If we were to list the ways to feed a baby starting with the most expensive, ready-to-use liquid formula in prefilled, throw-away bottles would also head up that list.

2. Ready-to-use formula

One of the most popular forms of formula is the liquid, ready-to-use formula that usually comes in quart-size cans, but also comes in smaller cans, such as the eight-ounce sizes in six packs. The formula is presterilized. Nothing needs to be added, and it requires no mixing. Formula in this form can be poured right from the container into presterilized bottles if you will be storing them for a whole day's use, presterilized disposable bottles (see page 74), or a thoroughly cleaned and dried single bottle for one feeding's worth of formula, provided you will be feeding your baby immediately (see pages 75–76).

Being able to fill a whole day's supply of bottles by pouring the formula quickly and directly from a can is convenient. Although formula in this form is less expensive than the prefilled disposable bottles, it is still more expensive than other forms of formula described below. In spite of the extra cost, many parents seem to feel that it is worth it to pay a little more for the convenience. It is important to wash and dry the top of the can and also the can opener before you open the can.

3. Liquid formula concentrate

Liquid formula in concentrated form is usually available in thirteen-ounce cans. This type of formula requires a little more time and work to prepare, since it must be diluted (watered down) with an equal amount of sterilized water.

Many, if not most, physicians recommend the concentrated formulas (proprietary formulas). They provide a happy blend of convenience and relative economy, and are routinely used by hospitals. Federally funded programs will provide proprietary formulas without charge to those who qualify. There are a few different ways in which to prepare and pour this type of formula into bottles. There are directions on the cans as to how to dilute the formula. In the health care section page 964, we discuss the fact that the baby's body is very sensitive to changes in fluid or salt balance. If you make a mistake in diluting the formula and give her concentrated formula, this may cause an imbalance in her fluid and salt levels, which can be a serious problem. Extra care in reading the instructions is crucial to your baby's well-being.

MIXING THE CONCENTRATE WITH WATER:

a) Pour the concentrate into presterilized nursing bottles. Boil water in a teakettle for five minutes. Pour the correct amount of water into the bottles.

b) Boil the correct amount of water plus two extra ounces since some will evaporate when the water boils in a pot for five minutes. Pour concentrate into the pot.

OTHER WAYS OF BOTTLING THE FORMULA:

If you use method *b* above to prepare the formula, once it is mixed in the pot, you can:

a) Pour it into a sterile quart bottle and store it in your refrigerator. When it is time for a feeding, you can pour one feeding's worth of formula into a thoroughly cleaned and dried nursing bottle, attach a clean nipple, and you are ready to feed your baby.

b) Pour the mixture into nursing bottles that you have previously sterilized by using the aseptic method described on pages 73–74.

c) Pour the mixture into disposable nursing bottles as described on page 74.

ALTERNATIVE METHOD OF PREPARATION:

You can also prepare this formula using the terminal sterilization procedure described on page 73.

4. Evaporated milk formula

Making a formula from evaporated milk is one of the more economical ways to feed a baby. Evaporated milk comes in cans. At least an equal amount of sterilized water must be added along with sugar or corn syrup as prescribed by your doctor.

Some pediatricians recommend making the formula more diluted during the first two to three weeks, mixing two parts of water to one part of evaporated milk. As the infant matures, by the second or third month, the ratio of milk to water approaches one can of milk to approximately one or one and a half cans of water, depending upon the doctor's recommendation. Most formulas also add two to three tablespoons of corn syrup or table sugar to each thirty ounces of liquid formula. The following table summarizes a typical formula:

Sample Formula
13 ounces of evaporated milk (approximately one can)
18 ounces of water
2–3 tablespoons of corn syrup or table sugar

PREPARATION METHOD #1 (ASEPTIC TECHNIQUE, WITH VARIOUS ALTERNATIVES FOR BOTTLING)

An easy way to prepare the formula is to first sterilize the water and a spoon by boiling in a pot for five minutes. Add the sugar or syrup and stir the mixture with the sterilized spoon until the sweetener is thoroughly dissolved. Wash and dry the top of the can of evaporated milk and a punch-type can opener. Punch two holes on opposite sides of the top of the can and mix the contents of the can into the pot of water. Stir with the sterile spoon. The proportion of water to evaporated milk depends on the instructions of your physician.

Once you have prepared the mixture, you are ready to choose between the alternatives previously described for bottling the formula: single bottle method (pages 74–75); pouring it into sterilized nursing bottles (pages 73–74); pouring it into presterilized disposable bottles (page 74).

PREPARATION METHOD #2 (TERMINAL STERILIZATION TECHNIQUE)

Another simple method of preparing this formula is to use the terminal sterilization technique described on page 73. This basically involves measuring the desired amount of tap water (use directions for amounts prescribed by your child's doctor) into a large, clean container. Add sugar or syrup and stir. Clean the top of the can of milk, punch holes in it with a freshly washed and dried can opener, and pour it into the sweetened water mixture. Stir the mixture, and pour it into clean, individual bottles. Complete the bottle assembly and you are ready to sterilize them.

5. Prepared powdered formula

Prepared powdered formulas are commercially available. These formulas require a mixture of a given amount of water with the powdered formula concentrate, and can be sterilized by either the aseptic or terminal techniques as described for the evaporated milk formula above. It is extremely important that the proper amount of water be added to the powdered formula. Be very careful about reading and following the directions marked on the package.

REFRIGERATING FORMULAS—PROCEDURES, LEFTOVERS, AND EMERGENCIES. Germs grow at a very fast rate in milk or formula that is left at room temperature. Formula must be refrigerated as soon as it is prepared because the cold temperature helps prevent the growth of bacteria. If not stored in individual sterilized bottles in the refrigerator, it should be stored in a large sterilized bottle such as a quart jar. Refrigerating the formula from opened cans also prevents it from rapidly becoming spoiled.

You may be wondering what to do about leftover milk if you are using prepared canned formula and do not use it all up during one day. The top of the can should be well sealed to prevent germs from entering and contaminating the formula. The can must be placed in your refrigerator. It is usually not advisable to store formula for more than a day. Be sure to follow the instructions on the can.

Under very unusual circumstances, such as in a bad storm or an electrical failure, your refrigerator may stop operating. Do not panic. Before giving your baby each bottle, you will probably be safe if you place it in a pot which has a few inches of water in it, and boil the water for about thirty minutes. Watch the water level carefully so the water does not evaporate. This will kill the bacteria. Allow the bottle to cool before offering it to your baby.

THE NEWBORN

A newborn infant is fascinating to watch. In a matter of seconds your baby emerges from her completely dependent environment in the womb to a new life of independence where her body must suddenly provide its own life-supporting functions. The details of this transition are complex and not fully understood, but it is important for every parent to appreciate the unique aspects of the newborn infant.

The newborn period is an arbitrary time from birth to approximately twenty days of life, during which your baby's body undergoes many dramatic changes. Being prepared for some of the special circumstances and minor problems that can arise should make your first few weeks as new parents a little easier and more enjoyable.

The Appearance of Your Newborn Baby

Do not be surprised if your newborn looks different from what you expected. The most important thing to remember is that it is completely natural for a baby to look rather "ugly" at birth. During the first week, your infant will make rapid strides toward developing into the cute little baby that you pictured. Her face will fill out and take on a more acceptable appearance. Shortly after birth, it is likely that everyone who sees your child will comment upon whom she looks like. Families often disagree over this issue, each feeling that the baby has a much greater resemblance to "their side." Couples themselves often pick out facial features that they believe look just like theirs, and sometimes disagree over which one of them their newborn more closely resembles. It is fun to watch how each person may see different things in the baby's appearance.

The proportion of your baby's body is also unusual. Her head is much larger for her body than an adult's and her legs and arms appear somewhat shorter in proportion to an adult's. These initial proportions are normal, and babies will gradually change into an adult-like form over the next several years.

A baby's weight is always of interest to new parents. Weights vary considerably, but most average boys weigh between 5.7 and 10 pounds and girls between 5.7 and 9.5 pounds. Some families have a history of large or small babies. Usually the first child is the smallest of your children. Older mothers also tend to have larger babies. A father or mother may boast about their big 9-pound infant, but a baby's weight at birth, if it is within normal limits, is generally not indicative of future stature or health. Babies who are too light or heavy raise some problems for your doctor, but with modern medical techniques these babies usually do just fine.

It is important to realize that most babies lose weight shortly after birth. This is due to loss of excess body fluids and adjustments to the new environment. Do not panic. This initial weight loss is expected and is not because you are taking poor care of your infant.

THE NEWBORN'S SKIN. The skin of your mature newborn infant will be covered by a substance called vernix. This is a protective covering on the surface of the skin that was present in the womb. It helps shield the baby's skin during the first one to two days of life. Vernix is not "dirt." Most doctors recommend that this whitish coating not be vigorously washed off during the first twenty-four hours of life.

At birth the color of the skin is usually bluish-gray in tone due to the poor oxygenation of the infant's blood. As the baby's respiratory and circulatory system rapidly adapt to life outside of the womb, the skin becomes a bright reddish pink. The feet and hands, however, may remain slightly blue for several days. This is quite normal—so do not be alarmed.

Some newborns' skin will be very loose and wrinkled, because of decreased fat deposits. Other infants' skin may appear very smooth because of extra fluid and fat storage. Do not be worried if your baby's skin color and texture are different or not as appealing as another baby's. In a very short time these differences balance out. There is no one "normal" type or appearance to the skin. A great deal of variation exists.

The baby's skin is sensitive to its new external environment. This can cause several minor changes in the appearance of the skin. Some of the common variations of skin coloring and changes seen in the newborn period are discussed below. Many of these changes can be disturbing to new parents if they are not aware of them.

Acrocyanosis refers to the bluish color that can persist in the hands and feet for several days. It is mainly the result of the limited development of the peripheral circulation in these areas. Some infants will develop this color change when exposed to cold surroundings. This is a harmless condition. Do not be alarmed.

Milia refers to the presence of tiny little sebaceous retention cysts which appear as little white spots around the chin, mouth, and nose. This condition is common and harmless. It disappears spontaneously with time.

Urticaria neonatorum (*erythema toxicum*) is a rash-like condition characterized by several small areas of redness with a variable diameter. Some of the red areas will have small white areas inside of them. These red blotches may be numerous and overlap each other. They may appear on the first day of life, mainly on the buttocks and trunk. They usually subside quickly, but can reappear for the first one to two weeks. This type of reaction is usually the result of the baby's delicate skin reacting to its new environment.

Mongolian Spots is an unusual name given to the large blue or purple bruise-like areas located on some newborns over the backside (buttock). They may also extend to the back and are more common among people with darker skin. Mongolian spots disappear spontaneously over the first few years of life. These marks will not disfigure your child. Rest assured that they are harmless.

THE NEWBORN'S HEAD. At first glance your newborn's head will have a shape different from what you might have expected. Molding is the term that refers to the shaping of the bones in the skull as they are squeezed through the birth canal. Right after birth some babies' heads are slightly asymmetrical because of this process. Do not be alarmed if your baby's head shows signs of molding. This is a common event and the head usually returns to its normal shape by the end of the first week.

The newborn skull is very different from an older child's. The bones are softer and are not completely joined together. The soft spot on the top of your infant's head is called the anterior fontanel. It is a region where the bones have not yet joined together. This area is somewhat more susceptible to injury. There is little to worry about in the routine handling of your infant, but some care should be exerted in handling the head of a newborn.

The head is susceptible to trauma at birth. Some babies develop a cephalhematoma (bruise of the scalp) which appears as a swelling on the surface of the scalp. Other infants may show some facial asymmetry from being pressed through the birth canal. These changes usually clear completely with time.

Head and facial changes at birth can often be distressful to the new parents. The vast majority of these problems resolve spontaneously. Your doctor will inform you if any problems exist beyond these minor changes.

THE ARMS AND LEGS OF THE NEWBORN. At birth your infant's arms and legs are proportionately short for her body size. The extremities grow and gradually catch up from six months until puberty, at which time the child takes on adult proportions. Your baby's arms and legs will be held in a partially flexed (bent at elbows and knees) position for the first several days. This position approximates the curled posture in the womb. As the arms and legs extend, she assumes the familiar posture of young infants.

Most newborns show a bowlegged posture. The heels are close together and the knees far apart when they rest on their backs. This condition is natural for many children and does not mean they will grow up with bowlegs.

You will probably take great pleasure in admiring the delicate formation of your baby's hands and feet. The tiny finger- and toenails have not fully developed at this stage. They are usually far short of the ends of the fingers or toes and are very soft and can tear off easily. Seeing such a perfectly formed tiny human being is an exciting experience, especially when you have created her.

YOUR BABY'S HAIR. As you look into the newborn nursery at your hospital, you will be amazed at the difference between babies in terms of hair growth. Some babies are completely bald, while others are born with a full head of hair. The color of the hair is also extremely variable and can change as the body develops. In general, male infants have more hair than females. It is also important to realize that if your baby is born with a thick head of hair it may not last. Much of the hair present at birth breaks off and your infant may initially lose hair. The amount of hair at birth often runs in families. If parents were "hairy" babies, they can expect the same from their child.

At birth the body is also covered with a fine, soft hair called lanugo. Most of this hair is present on the back and the face. This hair does not mean your baby will look like a gorilla. It falls out rapidly over the first few weeks of life. Some babies may keep some of this body hair for longer periods of time.

YOUR BABY'S MOUTH. Just a few comments are necessary concerning your infant's mouth. Do not be alarmed if she is born with teeth or if teeth erupt in the first few weeks of life. This does occur rarely and is most common with the lower front teeth, the incisors. The presence of teeth at birth is no cause for worry.

The mouth itself may appear somewhat unusual to you. The tongue seems large, because the chin is usually underdeveloped. If you put your clean finger or a nipple into her mouth, you will be amazed at the powerful sucking motions that your little infant can generate.

THE NEWBORN'S UMBILICUS (NAVEL). The umbilicus (belly button, navel) will have a short (one- to three-inch) dark withering stump left from the umbilical cord that was cut at birth. Most hospitals cover the stump with a purple disinfectant, which gives it a dark, almost black appearance. This stump usually falls off spontaneously between the fifth and fourteenth day of life. Very little special care is necessary for the stump, except to keep it dry. Your doctor will give you any special instructions that might be necessary in your infant's case.

THE BABY'S GENITALS AND BREASTS. The genitals and breasts of both infant boys and girls may appear slightly enlarged at birth due to the hormonal influence of the mother's blood while the baby was in the womb. The penis and testicles may appear larger than would be expected, but soon they assume a more proportionate size. It is also not uncommon for infant boys to have erections. This is completely normal and is not related to a sexual context at this stage.

Your infant girl may have a whitish vaginal discharge for the first few days. Some infants may even have a slightly bloody discharge. These conditions are not related to problems or precocious sexual development. They are usually the result of maternal hormones, which wear off in several weeks. Both boys' and girls' breasts may also be enlarged and tender at birth. Sometimes they even have a slight discharge. This is not uncommon and subsides in a short time. You should not manipulate or squeeze the breasts at this time because they may be tender.

JAUNDICE. In examining your baby, you may have noticed that your infant's skin is yellowish in color. This yellowish discoloration of the skin and the whites of the eyes is common during the first week of life and it is called jaundice. It is important to recognize that most jaundice in infants is not serious and is called physiologic jaundice. This is essentially a normal condition that usually starts during the second or third day of life. The yellowish color reaches its maximum intensity within a few days and then gradually disappears after a few more days. Once the mild jaundice disappears, medical science has no evidence that it will have any lasting effects on your child or appear again in the future.

To understand why jaundice occurs, it is necessary to discuss the infant's blood system. During life in the womb, the fetus needs more red blood cells than it does after birth. These extra red blood cells enable the unborn child to carry enough oxygen in the blood. The newborn no longer needs the excess number of red blood cells he had in the womb. Thus, the baby's body gradually destroys these excess red cells in the first few days after birth. As these cells are destroyed, the red oxygen-carrying pigment (hemoglobin) within the red blood cells is released and broken down, producing a substance called bilirubin (pronounced billy-roo-bin) as well as other pigments, which are given off into the bloodstream. These pigments are processed in the liver and removed from the newborn's body by excretion in the bile. Bilirubin has a characteristic yellowish-red color.

This process occurs in every newborn infant. If the amount of pigment released into the blood is greater than the ability of the liver to process it, the pigment will accumulate in the bloodstream and cause jaundice. The yellowish color of the skin and whites of the eyes is due mainly to the presence of this pigment in the blood. Some newborns can handle the excess pigment in the blood and not develop jaundice. Other babies cannot rapidly process the excess pigment and thus there is a short delay in eliminating the bilirubin.

Most newborns with jaundice have physiologic jaundice. Jaundice is more common in premature infants. Occasionally there are other situations that will cause the newborn's red blood cells to break down. ABO incompatibility and RH incompatibility are two of the other causes for jaundice. In these situations antibodies from the mother that have crossed the placenta and are in the baby's bloodstream can attach to the infants' red blood cells, causing excess breakdown of the cells and resulting in increased bilirubin in the blood.

If the level of bilirubin in the blood begins to rise too rapidly, your doctor will want to lower it so that it does not reach toxic levels. The doctor can follow the amount of bilirubin in the infant's blood by simple blood tests. Based on the results of these tests, and the condition of the baby, the doctor can decide whether treatment should be started to lower the level of bilirubin.

A common treatment for jaundice is to place the baby under bright lights (usually fluorescent lights). The light helps break down bilirubin that is just beneath the surface of the skin. Bilirubin decomposes in the light, and thus phototherapy (light treatment) is very useful in helping to break down excess bilirubin and allowing it to be excreted.

There have been no detrimental side effects observed in the numerous babies who have received phototherapy. The newborn's eyes, however, can be sensitive to the light used in phototherapy, so it is important to cover the eyes with blindfolds during the exposure to the light. Babies receiving phototherapy may have loose, dark greenish-brown stools and may develop a muddy-green or bronze color to their skin. These changes will pass as the pigments are excreted from the body. In rare situations, phototherapy may not be enough to lower the bilirubin levels and a procedure called an exchange transfusion may be performed. With proper observation and treatment jaundice will be controlled by your doctor.

Babies respond differently to the phototherapy treatment of jaundice. Some babies become fussy under the lights, while others sleep very soundly. It may be difficult for you to part with your newborn while she is receiving treatment, especially if she appears fussy and cries. This will decrease your parent-child contact for a few days. Try to be patient and recognize that your doctor and the staff in the hospital are aware of your desire to be with your baby and will return her to you as often and as soon as possible.

Evaluation of Your Baby at Birth

As soon as your baby leaves the womb, she must quickly begin supporting her own body functions. Some infants immediately let out a loud cry and begin to breathe spontaneously at birth. Other babies take a little longer to make this adjustment.

THE APGAR TEST. The condition of your baby will be evaluated immediately after delivery. A simple quantitative method for clinical evaluation was developed by Virginia Apgar in 1953. This test is appropriately called the APGAR test. It is based on five observations that can be quickly made in the delivery room by a health professional: heart rate, muscle tone, reflex irritability, respiration, and color. Each of the five categories is graded from 0–2. A perfect score is 10. The accompanying table explains this evaluation system.

SCORE	0	1	2
heart rate	absent	slow (less than 100)	regular rate (more than 100)
respiration	absent	slow, irregular	good, regular
muscle tone	no tone	minor movements	active
reflex irritability	no response	weak cry	strong cry
color	Blue, pale	body pink, hands and feet blue	completely pink

The APGAR test is usually performed approximately one minute after birth and then repeated four minutes later. The first score is usually lower than the second, since the infant usually takes some time to adjust to life outside the womb. Most infants receive a score of approximately 6 or more in the first minute after birth and then progress to 8 or more after five minutes of life. The five-minute evaluation is usually more valuable, since some babies take a little longer to adjust to their new environment.

The APGAR test is used to determine quickly how the baby is adjusting to her new surroundings. If your baby has a very low score at birth, this indicates the amount of assistance your infant needs to make a satisfactory adjustment to life outside the womb.

THE AMOUNT OF TIME YOUR BABY SPENDS IN THE WOMB. The amount of time your baby was carried in your uterus is called the gestational age of the infant. The gestational age can be estimated at the time of birth. The normal gestational age ranges from thirty-eight to forty-two weeks. Babies born at his age are called "term" or mature infants. Babies born younger than thirty-eight weeks are called "preterm" or premature. Those born later than forty-two weeks are called "postterm" or postmature. Obviously, it is not always possible to determine exactly the gestational age of your infant. Your doctor determines this age through a number of methods; there is often one to two weeks of flexibility in the exact gestational age as estimated by conventional methods.

Premature or postmature infants (see page 1010–13) often require special observation. If your baby is born very early or very late, your physician may want to observe her more carefully during the first few days or weeks of life and provide her with special care. Sometimes these infants have more difficulty adjusting to life outside the womb.

THE BABY'S WEIGHT AT BIRTH. Birth weight is also an important factor in evaluating your new infant. Very light or very heavy babies are usually more likely to have some difficulties adjusting to their new environments than average weight babies. Obviously, if you and your husband are over six feet tall and weighed more than ten pounds at birth, it is likely that you will have a large baby.

Reflexes and Activity of the Newborn

Your young infant will be able to thrash her arms about and kick her legs, but will be rather limited in her ability to move around. She will not be able to lift her head or roll over and will not move very far from the place where you put her. Although movements seem rather limited, she is able to perform several very impressive motor actions. She can breathe, swallow, eliminate wastes, urinate, suck, and cry. All of these actions require complex, well-co-ordinated motor functioning.

Most of these early movements are governed by reflex (involuntary) control. The young infant has not had time to develop experience in performing many complex motor actions, but is provided with a few built-in motor activities which are ready to go at birth. These reflex actions do not require voluntary (willful) control and are triggered by special events or stimuli in the baby's environment. It is fascinating to observe the remarkable ability of your infant to perform these complex tasks at birth.

Most of your baby's reflex actions are designed to serve a purpose. Some of them are for protection and others allow her to eat and drink. There are also numerous reflexes that assist in maintaining position and in co-ordinating early attempts at moving the arms and legs. The common reflexes of the newborn presented below are organized into functional groups.

FEEDING REFLEXES. The feeding reflexes are mainly concerned with co-ordinated movements of the mouth and throat. They allow the baby to obtain nutriment shortly after birth. Most of these reflexes are familiar to parents who have spent time with young infants. When you learn the simple reflexes involved in feeding, you will be able to observe them each time you feed your baby.

The *sucking reflex* is the most well-known feeding reflex. You can trigger this reflex action by putting an object into your baby's mouth. This stimulus sets off complex motor actions which allow her to suck on the object. If you put your clean finger in your infant's mouth, you will be amazed at how powerful her sucking motions can be. This reflex requires well-co-ordinated contraction and relaxation of numerous muscles surrounding the mouth. It is incredible to think that all these complex actions do not have to be learned.

Further examination of the sucking reflex is instructive for learning about reflex activity. Any simple reflex requires a stimulus that triggers the reflex. This stimulus is received through the baby's sensory system (touch, taste, and visual in the case of the sucking reflex) and automatically is channeled into a motor action. Reflexes are not controlled by the baby's own thinking process and are called involuntary or automatic actions. The sensory stimulation received by putting your finger in your child's mouth automatically triggers a motor impulse to be sent to the muscles in the mouth to begin sucking.

The involuntary nature of the sucking reflex becomes more evident as you spend more time with your infant. Obviously, the sucking reflex is designed by "mother nature" to allow the baby to draw milk from the nipple. The natural stimulus for sucking is the nipple. Since the infant does not have voluntary control over the reflex, any object (finger, carrot, etc.) can serve as the stimulus. Your infant cannot distinguish between objects which will give her food and those which will not. The reflex is automatic. Once it is stimulated, sucking begins, regardless of the stimulus.

As your baby matures, she gains more voluntary control over her actions and gradually learns to control the sucking reflex. She will learn to suck only on objects she chooses. The next time you suck on a lollipop or ice cream cone, remember that all those complex movements of your mouth which are automatic are part of your sucking reflex, which you have learned to control.

Other stimuli can also trigger the sucking reflex. Stroking you baby's lips will initiate the reflex. Your infant will suck whether she is hungry or not, because she has no control over the reflex. Most infants also derive some pleasure from the muscular contraction in the sucking movements. This is why thumb-sucking and pacifiers are so popular.

The sucking reflex is present at birth, but it still takes approximately one to two days to become well developed. At first your infant may choke or gag. It may take some practice to get the muscles working smoothly. You may also notice that there are two types of sucking patterns. The non-feeding sucking rhythm is usually about two sucks per second and this rhythm is alternated with periods of rest. Your baby may suck during sleep or in times of great excitement. The feeding rhythm is usually governed by the flow of food from the nipple. If your baby is having difficulty obtaining food, she may suck harder. Usually she settles into a continuous sucking motion with one suck per second while feeding.

The *swallowing reflex* is familiar to everyone, because it is still part of our daily functioning. Your infant is capable of swallowing, but she does it through reflex activity. The swallowing reflex is closely associated with the sucking reflex, and is triggered by the same stimuli. Once the sucking reflex is initiated, the swallowing reflex follows. Stroking the lips or putting an object in your baby's mouth will initiate sucking followed by swallowing.

The swallowing reflex is present at birth, but takes several days to develop fully. The initial co-ordination between sucking and swallowing may not be well developed. Food entering the mouth may not be smoothly swallowed. Dribbling may occur or your infant may choke. Usually by the third day the suck and swallowing reflexes are well co-ordinated and provide a steady stream of food into the baby's digestive tract.

Your own swallowing pattern is mainly reflexive in nature, but the major difference is that adults can swallow at will, and control when they will swallow. Voluntary control develops gradually over the first year. Once you begin the swallowing action, however, you also have no control over the complex contraction and relaxation of the muscles in the throat.

The *rooting reflex* is interesting to observe. It is a fascinating activity that allows your baby to find the source of food. It is essentially a searching mechanism to allow the baby to catch onto the nipple with her mouth and begin sucking.

This reflex is initiated by touching the cheek. The baby gradually turns her mouth and moves it in the direction of the object touching her cheek and "roots" or attempts to get it into her mouth and suck on it.

The baby will also turn to smells of milk or food, and can move her lips and tongue to grasp objects touching the corner of her mouth. You can have a lot of fun watching your baby follow your finger down her chin and around her cheek. She will attempt to catch your finger and suck on it.

This reflex is useful for the nursing infant. As the child is cuddled against the breast, the rooting reflex helps her locate the nipple. As you feed her with the bottle, she will be able to "zero in" on the nipple until she gets it securely in her mouth. The rooting reflex gradually disappears after the first six to eight months of life.

REFLEXES THAT PROVIDE PROTECTION. Your young infant is born with several reflexes that help protect her from the environment. In general the newborn baby is rather helpless and is highly dependent upon her parents for protection, but she has developed some simple reflex actions that assist her in interacting with the environment. You will see these reflexes being employed as you play with your baby and observe her daily activities.

Have you ever quietly sneaked behind a friend and touched his shoulder, causing him to jump "halfway across the room"? If you have, you have seen a remainder of the startle reflex. The *Moro (startle) reflex* is a sudden response to an unexpected or threatening action. It is similar to the "flight and fright" reaction of animals. This reflex allows the baby to react to her environment quickly.

The startle reflex is best observed by laying your baby on her back. Hold her by the hands and then let go suddenly. This sudden change in position will cause her to stiffen, throw her arms out away from the body, and extend her head. She may also move her legs in a jerking manner, open her eyes wide, speed up her breathing, and ultimately begin to cry. Crying, however, is not always a part of this reflex.

The startle reflex is best seen during the first two weeks of life. Some babies are much more responsive with the startle reflex than others. Gradually, the reflex diminishes, and is usually gone by nine to twelve months of life. Although this reflex is impressive to observe, it really does not do much to protect the baby, other than put on a good show for anyone standing nearby.

Your infant's eyes are protected by the *blink reflex*. Any object approaching the eye will cause a blink. Most bright lights will also cause a blink. This reaction is also seen in adults, and serves to protect the eyes from trauma. This reflex does not disappear.

Any object touching the back part of the throat will cause a gag. This *gag reflex* is also present in adults. It is responsible for preventing food from going into the airway. When the baby first begins to swallow, the gag reflex may not be well co-ordinated, and some milk or glucose water may get into her windpipe (trachea), causing her to gag and cough. This reflex is quickly developed and is present into adulthood.

REFLEXES THAT CONTROL POSITION AND MOVEMENT. During the first week of life, most of your infant's movements are controlled by reflex actions. The young baby is not really capable of supporting and co-ordinating movements of the arms, legs, neck, and trunk. These are gradually developed during the first eight to ten months of life. A series of reflex movements allow the newborn to make gross movements of her body, before her nervous system can co-ordinate them through voluntary control.

The *stepping reflex* is fun to observe. Hold your infant's body so that she is standing and leaning forward. Then move her forward and she will appear to walk, moving her feet, heel to toe, as if she were walking automatically. You will be amazed at your baby's ability to take one step after another.

This reflex is present for one to two months, and then disappears. You can also see this reflex in another way. Hold your baby in the air in an upright position, and bring her foot near the edge of a table or touch her shin to the edge of the table. She will attempt to lift her leg and step onto the table. This form of the stepping reflex is often called the "placing action."

The *tonic neck reflex* is a reflex that controls the movement of one side of the body, based on the position of the head and neck. Lay your baby on her back with her head facing you. Then twist her head gently so that her face looks to the right. At the same time, the right arm and leg will extend (stretch out) and the left arm and leg will flex (bend). Turning the neck causes changes in the position of the arms and legs.

This reflex is very interesting to observe as you dress or bathe your baby. It represents some of the early reflex connections between the arms and legs. This reflex usually disappears by the fifth or sixth month and is not seen in the older child or adult.

Place your baby on her back and push on her feet so that the legs bend at the knees. She will attempt to push you away with her legs. You can easily observe the *push reflex* while dressing your baby. This reflex usually disappears by the eighth month, although your child may always try to push you away intentionally if she thinks you are playing a game.

Here is how to observe the *traction reflex*. Hold your baby by the hands and pull her from a lying to a sitting position. She will automatically flex her elbows, brace her shoulders, and tense her neck. A newborn infant will not be able to hold her head upright as you gently pull her up to a sitting position, so you must support her head.

In performing the traction reflex you will also observe the *china doll reflex*. As you gently pull your infant up to the sitting position supporting her head in your hand, you will observe the wobbling of the head in your hand as she tries to support its weight. The infant is obviously alerted and her eyes open wide. As she reaches the sitting position, the head overshoots and falls forward. The combination of the wobbling head and wide-eyed stare resembles a china doll. This reflex is evidence of your infant's early attempts to hold her head in the upright position. By the end of the fourth to fifth month this reflex is replaced by good head control.

Stroke the palm of her hand or the sole of her foot with your finger. She will attempt to grab your finger with her hand or foot. This is a well-known reflex. Your young infant will grasp your fingers so tightly that you can pull her up to a sitting position. Be sure to support her head. The *grasp reflex* disappears by the end of the second to the fourth month.

Place your baby on her stomach and stroke her trunk along the ribs on one side with your finger or gently with an object. She will bend her back so that her bottom moves toward the side that was stroked and the trunk moves away from the stimulus. This is the *galant's reflex* and helps the baby to move her trunk. It usually disappears in two to three months.

With your baby on her back, straighten one leg and rub the sole of that foot. The opposite (free) leg will first flex (bend at the knee) and then extend (straighten out). The *crossed-extension reflex* is present for the first month and is usually gone by the end of the second month.

The *swim reflex* is fun to observe during bath time. If you carefully place your infant stomach-first into the water, she will begin moving her arms and legs as if trying to swim. Do not let her go, because although her attempts are noble, she cannot stay afloat at this stage.

MORE GENERAL REFLEXES. There are numerous other reflex actions that you can observe during the newborn period. Some of these reflexes, such as coughing, yawning, deep tendon reflexes, passing food through the digestive tract, and sneezing, will remain even until adult life. These reflexes are essential for everyday functioning. Other reflexes are present at birth and gradually disappear. Some of these reflexes don't seem to have any specific function, while others are essential for daily activity.

You can observe the *Gabellar reflex* by tapping your infant gently on the forehead, just above the nose. You will see her blink. She will continue to blink until you stop tapping. As your baby matures, she will be able to stop blinking after a few taps, but at this early stage she cannot stop the reflex blinking response.

Tap your infant on the lips. Her mouth and lips will protrude. This *snout reflex* can be fun to observe, especially since your baby will appear to be making funny faces. This reflex fades away early during the first year.

The *deep tendon reflexes* are present throughout life. Your doctor has tapped your knee many times and watched your leg jerk forward. Deep tendon reflexes are thus also present at birth. When a tendon, such as the knee tendon, is tapped, a reflex movement of the leg is set in motion. There are many of these reflexes for different muscle groups in the body.

How Sensitive and Responsive Is the Newborn?

The conception of the newborn is rapidly changing. Clinical investigators are becoming increasingly aware of the remarkable sensitivity of the young infant. Dr. Lewis Lipsitt believes that the newborn baby can discriminate different tastes. He has demonstrated that they even show taste preferences, preferring sweeter foods to sour foods.

In the past, it was believed that the newborn could hardly distinguish shapes or objects at birth. It is now thought that the newborn is visually rather sophisticated. Current research indicates that newborns see and attempt to focus on brightly colored objects held one to two feet in front of their eyes. You can see your infant follow a brightly colored object if you are patient. Her visual acuity, however, takes time to develop to its full potential.

Young infants can also smell at birth. It has been demonstrated that they can distinguish between pleasant and foul odors, although their ability to differentiate among most ordinary odors is less well developed. Babies become startled and irritable when exposed to strong, offensive odors.

Sounds are clearly perceived by the newborn. A loud, sharp sound can cause the infant to react with a startle reflex. Some scientists believe that infants can be soothed by certain types of rhythmic music. Your infant is acutely aware of the sounds in your house.

The sense of touch is also very active in the newborn. She is sensitive to hot or cold, and clearly appreciates a nice, soft diaper. The young baby is often soothed by the warmth of her mother's body as she is held close to the breast.

The world of your baby's senses provides a unique and fascinating area for you to observe and understand. You can see if your infant prefers various smells or tastes, and you can observe her reaction to resting against your warm body. These are the times when being a parent is a once-in-a-lifetime experience.

WATCHING YOUR BABY GROW AND DEVELOP

As you care for and play with your baby, you will be observing her behavior. Your child will provide you with a unique and pleasurable opportunity to watch the development of a human being. You will be able to see not only large developmental milestones (e.g., sitting, crawling, standing, walking, talking), but also the less obvious, often overlooked, changes that make your child the special individual that she is.

There are numerous advantages to being a sensitive observer of your child. One is that you will derive more pleasure from the time spent with her. Caring for an infant who cannot speak your native tongue, for example, can be more enjoyable if you are aware of developmental characteristics and subtle changes that are occurring from day to day. While feeding your baby, for instance, you can notice her feeding reflexes. When handling and talking to her, you can see her changing reactions to your voice, face, and touch. Parents who are aware of both the obvious and less obvious developmental characteristics that go along with each phase of development tend to be more sensitive to their babies' needs and interests. They are in a better position to understand and enjoy their babies to the fullest possible extent.

Recording aspects of your baby's growth and development in a special scrapbook can be a lot of fun. Some parents enjoy making daily notes, while other parents simply enjoy jotting down occasional interesting observations. By reading this book's material for each phase of development, you will have a pretty good idea of what you can expect from your child. As you interact with your baby and observe her at play, you can watch for the new developments as they emerge. Once you become a careful observer, you will be able to jot down a host of marvelous changes in your baby as she grows older.

Whether you choose to keep a detailed diary of your child's life or a less formal scrapbook on her developmental progress, you should record certain developmental and factual information. A record of her immunization schedule should be carefully kept, so that if you move or change doctors, it will be easy for you to summarize her immunization record (see page 947). You should also be sure that you have a birth certificate for your child. A brief record of developmental milestones, such as sitting, walking, and talking, can also be kept, since this information may be useful to your doctor in the future.

It is hoped that reading this book will stimulate you to spend more time interacting with and observing your child. Keeping a record of her progress can become your own documentation of the wonderful developmental process of a human being. Years from now, both you and your child may spend many enjoyable hours returning to the notes you kept about her when she was younger.

PHOTOGRAPHING YOUR CHILD

Pictures can also provide you with a record of the important events in your child's life. It is a good idea to have your camera ready before your baby is born; you will be prepared to take pictures of your newborn right after the delivery.

Several professional photographers have given us some useful tips. Picture taking is often spontaneous, but some of your best pictures will come from planned picture sessions. Parents often enjoy photographing their babies at frequent intervals during the first few months. Once your child has passed through a certain phase of development, you cannot recapture these past events. You may have regrets later on if you forget to record memorable events during the first few years.

Your young infant will be a great subject for your photographic genius. With today's simple-to-use cameras, even the beginner can obtain beautiful results. Most parents want to take several pictures in the hospital and of the trip home. Each new important development, the first bath, Grandma's first visit, or that "big" crying mouth, all provide great shots. Do not be afraid to take close-ups. Some of the best baby pictures really get in close, so you can appreciate that first laugh or that memorable cry.

The type of camera you use is up to your budget and experience. A simple and ready-to-use camera is preferable. You do not want to spend a lot of time setting dials, since you may miss a spontaneous shot. It is better to take too many pictures than too few.

Pictures are fairly inexpensive today, and can provide a great deal of satisfaction at future dates when you look back on the development of your child. She will also appreciate your keeping these photographs in an album. Be sure to record dates and comments on the pictures or in the album. You and your spouse, along with your relatives and friends, will enjoy flipping through the pages from time to time and commenting upon how far your child has come in development.

Those of you who are on tight budgets may not be able to afford to buy a camera when faced with all the other expenses associated with the arrival of a new baby. It may be possible for you occasionally to borrow a friend's or relative's camera so as not to miss capturing pictures of your child's early years.

PREPARED PARENTHOOD CHECK LIST

MOTHER	FATHER	FAMILY FEELINGS AND SPECIAL CONCERNS
—	—	What are some of the more common stresses faced by prospective parents?
—	—	Have you thought about the importance of your family to you? Your baby?
—	—	Do you have insecurities, doubts, and worries related to becoming a new parent? If so, are you making an effort to discuss them with other people?
—	—	Who is to take primary care of your baby?
—	—	Can you think of ways in which to keep open lines of communication in your family?
—	—	How do you think having a baby will affect your lifestyle? Career? Marriage? Outlook on life?
—	—	Have you prepared your other children for the new baby?

PRACTICAL PREPARATIONS

MOTHER	FATHER	
—	—	Do you know whether you have maternity hospitalization insurance and whether your policy covers mothers and babies with special physical problems?
—	—	Have you thought about whom you will select as your baby's doctor?
—	—	What area of your home will you designate as being mainly your baby's special place? How do you plan to arrange this area?
—	—	If your baby will be delivered in a hospital, have you packed two small suitcases with things for mother and the baby and placed them in a handy spot?
—	—	Do you plan to have someone assist you at home during the first few weeks?
—	—	What possible names for your baby have you selected?
—	—	Are there any preparation for childbirth and parenthood classes available in your area, and do you plan to attend them?
—	—	Have you made a list of essential equipment items and included on the list important safety features?
—	—	Do you plan to take your infant home from the hospital in a car? If so, have you obtained an infant auto seat and properly attached it to the car in anticipation of baby's homecoming?
—	—	What clothing items are most important? Do you have them on hand?

—— —— Can you remember some of the important safety features in dressing a baby?

—— —— Are you aware of your role in feedings?

—— —— Have you seriously considered breast-feeding as the method of choice before making your decision on how to feed your baby?

—— —— Do you recognize the importance of cuddling your baby close and making her feel loved during feedings?

Infancy 1

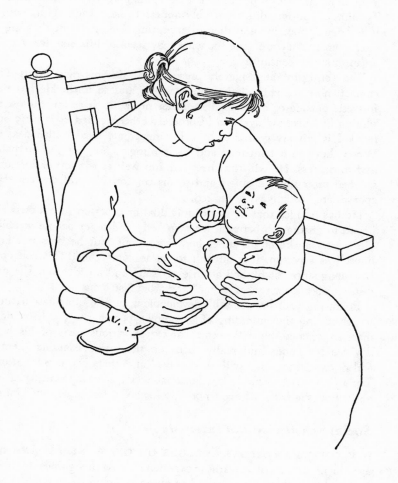

PERSONAL-SOCIAL DEVELOPMENT

Self-awareness

Your newborn baby's perceptions of himself and his social world are quite limited. To him, his surroundings probably appear to be a vague blur, with people and objects briefly appearing and then disappearing. One moment they are present and the next moment they are gone for what may seem to him like forever. There is no real organization or continuity.

The young infant is mainly preoccupied with his own needs for sleep, physical contact, nourishment, elimination, warmth, and so forth. He has not yet developed interests outside of his immediate inner needs, such as an interest in you or in exploring his surroundings, and has therefore been called egocentric or highly self-centered. His primary goal is to have his immediate needs satisfied as soon as possible. When they are not satisfied and he is hungry, hot, cold, or in pain, he is aroused and in distress. He will turn beet red and wail at the top of his lungs. When he is satisfied promptly, he quiets and seems comfortable and content. His emotional responses are, initially, very limited.

He has no idea that he is an individual or a person in his own right. He has not begun to distinguish between his own body and other people or objects around him. He is very aware of his inner body sensations, but he does not know much about himself as a person. It is difficult for us to comprehend this concept fully, since we have long since established a sense of "self" and an identity. We are clearly able to distinguish between what is "me" and what "isn't me."

Following your baby's "self" development can be quite fascinating, since you will be witnessing the unfolding of a complex person. As the baby develops and gains more experience, he will become aware of various parts of his body. He will one day see his hands and really focus on them and examine them. Then, through added experience, he will gradually learn that his hands belong to his body. Throughout the sections on Personal-Social Development, you will be learning about how the baby discovers not only his body, but discovers "himself" as a person.

Social Sensitivity and Interests

DEVELOPING A POSITIVE OUTLOOK ON THE WORLD. Professionals are in general agreement that a baby's earliest experiences have a significant impact upon his attitudes and development. In the beginning, a baby's slate is clean in that he has no preconceived ideas about himself, other people, or life in general. He has made no associations and can draw no conclusions, since he is lacking in experience. Gradually, as he gains experience, he begins to associate or link isolated experiences together, and form attitudes about them.

The first aspect of life that he probably concentrates upon is whether or not his basic physical, emotional, and psychological needs are met, and how quickly they are met. Since he has not yet developed a notion of time, initially even a delay of several minutes in your tending to his needs may seem like forever to him.

Erik Erikson, whose theories on personality development are widely respected, suggests that during infancy the baby's first outlook on the world becomes crystallized. If his needs are promptly satisfied, then he is content, and develops a positive view of the world, and a sense of basic trust and optimism. On the other hand, when his needs are not satisfied, or there are long delays in meeting his needs, the baby feels panicky, helpless, ignored, frustrated, and uncomfortable. This can result in his developing a pessimistic view of the world, or mistrust of it. The manner in which his basic needs are met is believed to be instrumental in influencing many areas of his personality development.

RESPONDING TO YOUR BABY'S NEEDS. The person or persons who care for your baby on a day-to-day basis will be providing him with his first real relationship with another person. Meeting his needs as quickly as possible is one way in which parents or parent figures can influence him positively. Some delays, such as training him to wait a while longer in the morning for breakfast after the first two months or so, will be necessary for your convenience. On the other hand, making him wait for prolonged periods of time before you meet his needs is not advisable.

The old theory about building a baby's character by letting him "cry it out" or cry for prolonged periods of time before responding to his needs is now considered by most professionals to be incorrect, and not healthy from either a physical or psychological standpoint, at least in the first few months. Some parents worry that promptly attending to their baby's needs and cries, and showering him with love, attention, and stimulation will "spoil" him. It is difficult, if not impossible, to spoil an infant during the first several months of life. In fact, you should try to respond promptly to your baby's needs for close physical contact, stimulation, nourishment, warmth, diaper changes, sleep, security, love, and affection.

THE IMPORTANCE OF PARENTAL LOVE, CARE, AND STIMULATION. Meeting your baby's needs is not enough in and of itself. More important is the manner in which you meet his needs. Tara Sapir recognized the importance of feeding her baby promptly, but did not take the time to satisfy his other needs. She thought that her young infant would not really notice the manner in which she responded to him, given his limited abilities. Whenever her son, Johnny, cried, she rushed over to him and fed him, but she was always impatient. Tara did not make an effort to see that he was comfortable, because he seemed not to care. While she fed Johnny, she was bored by his inactivity and stared off in another direction, never talking to him.

After Tara felt that Johnny had had his fill of breast milk, she took the nipple out of his mouth, burped him, and placed him in his crib. Tara was supplying Johnny with nourishment, but was not providing a warm, loving, or stimulating environment during the feeding session. As a result, Johnny became very cranky and jumpy both during and after his feedings. Mrs. Sapir seemed puzzled by his behavior, since she thought that she was satisfying his needs.

One Saturday, Tara's cousin, Martha, came over to spend the afternoon. Martha was also breast-feeding, and had a two-and-a-half-month-old son, Jeffrey. Tara could not help noticing the difference in how Martha handled her son during feedings.

Martha talked to Jeffrey as soon as she entered the room. She adjusted her manner of holding him so that he felt comfortable and secure. She gently slipped the nipple into his mouth, making sure that it was positioned properly. As he nursed, Martha cuddled him close to her body, rocked him, and talked softly to him. She watched Jeffrey to be certain that the feeding was going along smoothly. As soon as he finished, she helped him bring up the bubble. Then Martha nuzzled her face near Jeffrey's, so that he could see her, and talked to him, expressing her positive feelings for him. She rocked him until he drifted off to sleep, and then gently put him down in his bassinet.

Tara did not see why Martha spent time talking to her son and interacting with him as she did, since Tara knew that Jeffrey, like Johnny, could not understand a word. Tara thought that Martha's efforts were in vain. Yet, she also noticed that Jeffrey, unlike Johnny, was not a cranky baby. Tara finally decided to question Martha about her methods of handling Jeffrey during feedings.

Martha told Tara that it was very important to make a baby feel comfortable and stimulate him by rocking and talking to him during feedings. This helped build an early, positive bond between parent and child. She stressed the importance of working to establish a good relationship with a baby from the start, and told her cousin that feeding sessions represented opportune times to offer her baby stimulation and make him feel loved and comfortable.

Tara felt that Martha's views made good sense. Seeing how much happier Jeffrey looked than her own son, Tara decided that it would not hurt to give Martha's approach a try. The next few times Johnny cried from hunger, Tara responded to him in a manner similar to that which she had seen Martha using. Johnny gradually showed his delight by smiling and relaxing during the feedings. He immediately fell asleep afterward, happy and fulfilled. He no longer seemed cranky, and Tara was convinced that he was able to sense the difference in her method of handling him.

A young baby needs more than to have his basic physical needs satisfied. He also needs to receive attention, cuddling, and visual and auditory stimulation from his parents. Throughout the course of each day when your baby is alert, whether you are feeding him, bathing him, or changing his diapers, there are unlimited opportunities to show him that you care for him and love him. Spending time with him is important, but the quality of time that you spend with him, and the nature of your verbal and physical exchanges with him, will also facilitate his forming a close attachment to you.

A baby whose needs are fulfilled, and who receives appropriate environmental stimulation and plenty of love and affection, will gradually associate his parent with satisfaction and physical comfort. This positive association will foster a close parent-child relationship. Assuming that his first relationship with his parent or parent figure is satisfying for him, this helps him build a foundation for forming close, fulfilling relationships with other persons in the future.

If you have not had much direct contact with babies prior to the birth of your own, you may, indeed, handle him somewhat awkwardly in the first week or two. You may also feel awkward talking or singing to him and feel unsure of how much or what type of stimulation to offer him. But underlying your inexperience, you will still be conveying to him your love and affection, and this is what really counts. By trial and error you will learn more about how best to handle him and fulfill his individual needs. You will also gain experience that should enable you to understand his special method of communication.

BUILDING YOUR OWN SPECIAL RELATIONSHIP. All parents develop their own style of holding, touching, and communicating with their babies, and establish very individual and special relationships. Love, stimulation, and affection can be expressed in any number of different ways, depending upon what feels right and comfortable to you, and what your baby seems to need and enjoy. This is what makes parenting such a unique experience, and what makes effective parenting an art.

As you care for your infant during the first month, you will discover how best to comfort him when he cries. Crying babies are frequently soothed when they are rocked, talked to in a quiet tone of voice, cuddled close to their parent's body, carried around the room, given a nipple (or a pacifier), or even taken for a ride in a car. It may take a few weeks of getting to know your baby before you learn what seems to work in comforting him. Some babies are simply more easily comforted than others. His quieting down and appearing to be at peace after a crying episode can be regarded as an early form of social response on his part, assuming that you have picked him up, rocked him, or otherwise intervened in an attempt to comfort him and reduce his tensions.

Do not be frightened or upset if you cannot always soothe him or calm him down when he cries. There will inevitably be times when nothing seems to comfort him. As long as you do your best, the main thing is to remember that he is very immature, and that his behavior, in all likelihood, in no way reflects inadequate parenting. Whether or not he is easily quieted or lets his needs be known, his basic needs are similar to those of other babies. All babies need to be cared for, loved, cuddled, talked to, stimulated, smiled at, and so on. After the first few months, most "difficult" or hard to soothe babies settle down and become more responsive to their parents, so do not give up on your baby or yourself too soon. Keep working at building a good relationship with him.

Probably the first sign that you will interpret as his emerging sociability is his smiling. A closer look is likely to reveal that he smiles in response to various stimuli, perhaps a sound, a tickle on the belly, or the sight of your face, if you bend over him so that it is easier for him to see you. He may even smile when he passes gas or while sleeping. His smile is impersonal, although you may like to think that he is smiling because he feels affectionate toward you. It is doubtful that he has had time to develop positive feelings for you, although he will be steadily developing them over the next few months. His smiling and the importance of positively reinforcing the social smile will be further discussed in Infancy 2, since more babies will begin to smile after the first six weeks.

Some of you will observe your baby occasionally staring at your face, and looking briefly into your eyes. More of you will notice this in the next month or two. A baby's interest in the human face, and his smiling in response to it, is more fully explored on pages 204–5.

INTELLECTUAL DEVELOPMENT

From your baby's original environment in the dark, moist, warm womb, he is thrust into a different environment, in which he is bombarded with new stimulation from all angles. In the womb he was completely cared for and protected. As soon as he is born, his body must suddenly adjust to performing life's basic functions on its own. His body and nervous system are fairly well formed at birth, but are still quite immature. He has a brain, but he has not had a chance to use it in relation to the new world around him. He is really starting from scratch.

He is prepared and equipped to experience this new world with his five senses. He can see, hear, touch, taste, and smell. Granted, all his sensory functions are not operating at full capacity, but the fact is that he will gather information about the world through his senses from the beginning. He is a sensitive, responsive human being.

Sight

Some of the most fascinating discoveries in recent years have been related to a baby's visual abilities. His visual equipment is not sophisticated, but he can see from birth. Keep in mind that his world in the womb was dark. What an incredible experience it must be for him when he enters this new, bright environment, and sees his surroundings for the first time. It is not surprising that he is sensitive to the intensity of light. If exposed to a very bright light, he may close his eyes. When the light in a room changes, he may squint. He may even prefer a dimly lit room, since bright lights may initially bother him.

Even though your baby's visual abilities are immature, he can fixate his eyes for brief periods of time on an object held at a distance of about seven to nine inches or so in front of him. Beyond that range, images probably become blurry. He has difficulty viewing objects at various distances and focusing on nearby or faraway objects, like his hand or the object on the wall. Even though his head may be turned toward the direction of his hands while he is lying in the crib, he probably will not see them well during Infancy 1.

Nevertheless, your baby can follow a moving object for short distances, if it is moved slowly in front of him from side to side, or very slowly in an up and down direction. Mrs. Gromley was fascinated by her son Larry's interest in following objects. One morning she held a bright red ball in front of his face and moved it to the left and then to the right. Larry stared at the ball, and followed its path with his eyes. After she put the ball down, he squirmed, giving his mother the impression that he enjoyed this activity. Mrs. Gromley held up one object after another, and moved them around, just to give him a chance to practice following objects with his eyes.

After trying this "game" with an assortment of objects, Mrs. Gromley noticed that Larry followed some of them very enthusiastically, but did not respond as quickly to others. She felt that his quick responses meant that he was showing a preference for certain colors and patterns of the objects.

Your infant will enjoy having opportunities to use his eyes to track objects, and this ability will improve as he grows older. He may also be able to discriminate visually patterns from colors, and may show a preference for particular patterns. Robert L. Fantz, in a most interesting series of experiments, discovered that from birth babies show a preference for patterns over colors. When presented with a variety of different patterns, most babies show a preference for patterns similar to the human face. Perhaps this preference is significant in that it may facilitate a baby's attraction to the person caring for him, usually his parent.

Babies vary in how much looking they do and how alert they are. Most babies tend to be alert for only a minimal fraction of the daylight hours. Much of their time will probably be spent sleeping. Even when they are awake, they may often appear to be quite groggy and "out of it." If you hold a brightly colored or patterned object about seven or eight inches in front of your baby when he is awake, or put your face close to him, he is likely to become alert and excited. As you bend over to care for him, you may notice him making eye contact with you.

When he sees your face, he may smile, settle down a bit, and stop crying or fussing. Of particular interest to him is probably the upper area of your head between the bottom of your nose and the top of your head. When an interesting object appears within his restricted range of vision and captures his attention, he may even stop sucking to look at it. His ability to suck and look simultaneously is forthcoming.

Hearing

From birth, your baby will be able to hear. In fact, he will be quite sensitive to loud noises and will startle or jump in response to hearing the first presentation of a loud noise, but may not jerk or startle upon immediately hearing the same noise again. Some researchers and parents have reported that soft, humming noises, human voices, sounds of water, and sounds of the human heartbeat are soothing to young infants. It is speculated that the reason for this lies in the infant's previous familiarity with these kinds of sounds in the mother's womb. There are even some records available which purport to approximate the sounds that an infant might hear in the womb. Some people claim that these sounds can be of assistance in calming crying, irritable babies.

In terms of sound discrimination, recent research suggests that newborns tend to become quiet and listen more carefully to high-pitched rather than low-pitched voices. Perhaps this is nature's way of preparing an infant to listen closely to his mother's voice, or at least the high-pitched "baby talk" that he will probably hear from adults for the first year or so. There is some evidence that an infant is also sensitive to the location of a sound. Long before a baby is able to discriminate visually among people, he will be able to perceive differences in people by the sound of their voice.

Hearing difficulties can occur even at birth. You should be familiar with some of the simple ways to determine if your child has a hearing disability. Refer to Your Child's Hearing section on pages 982–83 for information on simple tests for evaluating your child's hearing.

Touch

Young infants tend to be particularly sensitive to touch. They generally enjoy being handled, cuddled close to their parents, picked up and carried, rocked in their parents' arms, and stroked. Their need for this kind of physical stimulation has been well documented. In fact, it has been shown that babies who are institutionalized and deprived of the frequent handling that home-reared babies usually receive are often delayed in their development, or do not develop to their fullest potential in many areas. This is not to imply that all babies in institutions do not receive sufficient handling or that all home-reared babies do.

You will probably observe that when your baby is crying or in distress, handling him quiets him down and comforts him. As a result, he may become more alert. Being picked up and gently fondled is an important form of stimulation for young babies, and it is doubtful that frequent handling and cuddling will overstimulate them, unless their sleep is interrupted. Your baby should greatly benefit from the warm, close, physical contact that you can provide. Even before he is capable of recognizing you by your voice or by sight, he may come to know you by the manner in which you handle and hold him.

Taste

The sense of taste is extremely well developed in all mammals, and the human newborn comes equipped to savor sweet tastes, which would include both mother's milk and the commercial milk preparations. Young infants definitely discriminate the sweet taste and react differently to it than to sour or bitter tastes. Moreover, they show a preference for sweet flavors in the first few days.

Drs. Kenneth R. Kobre and Lewis P. Lipsitt of Brown University have shown that even newborns suck more slowly and take fewer rest periods in relationship to the sweetness of the fluid. The heart rate even quickens to sweeter tastes. One practical consequence of some of their research in this area is that, because the newborn is capable of "negative contrast behavior," he will often turn off to a less sweet fluid after having a sweeter fluid immediately preceding it. Thus, it is not advisable to offer a newborn sucrose water from a bottle just before putting him to the breast or otherwise feeding him. As babies become older, they become increasingly tolerant of diverse taste experiences. We end up eating things like onions, pickles, vinegar, and pepper, all of which we refuse as infants.

Smell

Dr. Lipsitt and Dr. Trygg Engen have shown that infants after birth are capable of distinguishing among smells. Moreover, they can become accustomed to foul smells over a short period of time. A baby may initially react adversely to a foul odor on the first presentation, but when exposed to this smell every thirty seconds in successive trials, he will come to ignore it, even though adults may find it offensive.

Negative responses to many ordinary smells are not common in infants. While adults have strong aversions to certain odors, including some associated with bodily functions (for example, the odor of feces), there is no evidence that the newborn or the child up to two or three years of age has an active dislike of such odors. It appears that our smell dislikes are to a great extent learned.

Early Learning

The stereotype of the baby who is not capable of learning or whose mind is non-functioning during the first month or so of life has been shattered by research in recent years. Dr. Lewis Lipsitt and his associates have conducted a series of experiments which show that even in the first few days of life babies are capable of learning.

Over a series of trials babies will stop responding to stimuli (like odorants or sounds) which at first excite them. These investigators also suggest that newborns can learn to turn their heads if the stimulation is right. For example, newborns will turn their heads a certain portion of the time, about one of four times, if you touch the corner of their mouths. The head turn will be in the appropriate direction; for example, if you touch the infant's left cheek, he will turn to the left. Now if you feed the infant each time he responds in the appropriate direction to a touch on the cheek, you can increase the frequency with which the baby will do this, perhaps to as much as 80 percent. By the same token, if you now start doing the same thing on the other side of the mouth, the baby will stop responding to the first side and now turn more to the second side on which you are stimulating him.

Research by Andrew N. Meltzoff and M. Keith Moore has suggested that infants as early as a week or two after birth may be able to imitate facial expressions. Their belief is that babies can produce behaviors that they see others perform at a very early age.

These kinds of studies suggest that as a result of prior experience, babies' unlearned behaviors will be altered in response to environmental stimuli. Whether or not babies can learn at birth is difficult to determine. There is some evidence that babies are learning from the start, even when we may not see marked changes in their behavior. Perhaps the following example will help illustrate this point. Suppose you watch a television program. Afterward, your behavior does not change, and you do not talk about the program with anyone else, but you think about it. The fact that other people around you would have no way of knowing that you watched the program does not necessarily mean that you did not learn anything from it.

This same type of reasoning may, according to many professionals, apply to your baby. Initially, your baby's ability to move and vocalize is limited. However, we do know that he is sensitive to his surroundings and is gathering information about his environment through grasping, sucking, looking, hearing, smelling, tasting, and so forth. It seems quite plausible then that in spite of the fact that he cannot easily tell us what he is learning, or that we may not notice marked changes in his behavior, he is accumulating information through his sensory and motor experiences, and may be changing internally as a result of his observations of the world and his earliest experiences with it. We will look at this more closely in Motor Development (pages 110–11).

According to Dr. Jean Piaget, the baby's unlearned responses become stronger and more efficient over the first month or so as a result of environmental stimuli triggering them. Even though his behavior and ability to adapt or "accommodate" to the environment are, at best, primitive, this is nonetheless significant in terms of his future intellectual development. Piaget suggests that the baby's initial repertoire of behaviors, such as looking, sucking, and grasping, constitute the basic foundation for further sensory motor and intellectual development.

Your infant will not be doing much in the way of thinking, as you use the word (playing with ideas in the mind), but there is reason to believe that he is taking a first step forward in his intellectual development. Through sensory and motor channels he will be gathering experiences relative to his environment, and learning from them. Much of his early learning is, no doubt, taking place "behind the scenes."

LANGUAGE DEVELOPMENT

This section was designed to assist you in learning a new language—not French, Russian, or Chinese, but rather, your baby's special method of communication. From the day he is born, you will be struck by the fact that communicating with him is not easy. However, he *will* speak to you through the only means of communication available to him—crying and body language (facial expressions, gestures, postures, movements).

When he is hungry, overtired, uncomfortable, and so on, he will let you know by his crying, his body language, or a combination of the two. Likewise, when he is satisfied and comfortable, he will eat well, sleep well, gain weight, and seem generally to be in good spirits. This, too, is a subtle means of communication. His needs will be very pressing during the first couple of months of life, and since he cannot hide them, he will definitely let you know when something is the matter.

Understanding His Language Will Take Time

Do not expect to be able to understand immediately your baby's language, since interpreting it accurately will take some time. Before you have had many opportunities to observe his behavior, much of your learning will be by trial and error. When you respond to him, he will either quiet down or continue to cry. He will give you positive or negative feedback as to whether or not you correctly interpreted his needs or wants. If the first approach does not seem to work, you will try another and another until he either settles down, or you exhaust all possibilities and give up. You may be particularly confused if you have not had much experience with young infants, but even if you have, you may still not find it easy to interpret his language, since each baby will have his own unique style of communication.

All babies cry, but some tend naturally to cry louder, more often, and for longer periods of time than others. As one parent put it, "There are criers, and then there are criers!" Some babies cry every time their diapers are wet, while others act as though they could care less. Some cry and startle at the slightest sudden movement of their crib while others do not. Some cry the moment they feel the least bit hungry, while others wait to cry until they are ravenous. Some cry whenever there are several people crowding around them or handling them, while others do not seem to mind crowds or being handled. Similarly, many babies tend to make sucking movements when they are hungry, but some tend to do a lot of sucking even when they are not hungry. There are very active babies who seem to do a lot of wriggling and thrashing about even when they are not uncomfortable or frustrated, and there are others who behave in this manner only when they are in distress.

You may hear your infant making some small sounds or noises usually when he is comfortable and satisfied. The noises may sometimes sound like gurgles, grunts, or like vowels. As far as is known, the sounds do not really mean anything. Still, they are significant in that these early sounds later develop into babbling, the precursor of speech.

As the weeks go by, you will be better able to make some comments about your baby's personality and his characteristic behavior patterns. You will learn to interpret his actions. This will make it easier for you to determine what he is trying to "tell" you. By keeping track of his crying and body language, you might find that he cries and starts sucking every three hours, just before mealtimes. If three hours have passed without any crying, and suddenly he begins to cry and suck, you will have little or no difficulty interpreting his communication.

After a few weeks, you may observe a pattern emerging. You might realize that he cries every time his diapers need changing, every time he is in a crowded room, every time he gets a bath, or right before bedtime when he is obviously tired. Try to keep a mental note of the times at which he cries each day and the situation at hand, or the particular activity that he is engaged in at the time he cries, since this should assist you in interpreting his language.

The material that follows will give you a good head start in understanding your baby's mode of communication. Keep in mind that your baby will "speak" a slightly different "dialect" from every other baby. If you really intend to be an efficient interpreter, you will have to do some home laboratory work by spending time with him, listening carefully, and closely observing his behavior.

Crying

Most "first-time-around" parents are rather unprepared to cope with the frequency, duration, and intensity of a young baby's crying spells. None of their friends or relatives may have honestly discussed with them how terribly frustrating and annoying listening to a baby's crying can be. No one may have warned them about the times when their baby will cry and nothing that they do will **help to quiet him.** People may have failed to mention the feelings of worry, panic, and inadequacy that may be aroused during periods of prolonged crying. In addition, no one may have told them about the nights when they will lie in bed listening to their baby cry, and wonder if they were really cut out to be parents, or wish that the baby would go away.

Listening to your baby cry may, indeed, be one of the most irritating aspects of your job as a parent, but you must not turn a deaf ear to it. Crying is his major means of communication, and it initially serves as a signal that he needs something, or is in some physical distress. An older baby will cry more often for emotional reasons, but a young baby generally cries for physical reasons.

When he cries, you will probably notice a total body involvement. His mouth and chin may tremble, and his arms and legs may move about rather vigorously. Chances are that no tears will be produced. It will be clear that when he is crying, he is expending more energy than you do when you cry, and he is not focusing on anything else around him.

It is undoubtedly true that if a baby is regularly picked up fairly quickly after he starts crying, he begins to associate crying with comfort and being held. In most cases this should not prompt more frequent crying, except under unusual circumstances in which a baby is only held and given attention when he cries, and is pretty much otherwise ignored. (In this atypical situation a baby may cry more, simply because he needs more attention and learns that crying is the only means of getting it.) When comparisons are made among babies reared in typical home settings, babies whose cries are responded to fairly quickly cry less often after the first few months than those whose cries are not responded to as quickly.

During the first few weeks, your baby's crying may sound pretty much the same whether he is crying out of hunger, because he is fatigued, or for other reasons. You are likely to have more trouble determining the reasons for it than you will later on when his crying becomes more differentiated. Listening to him cry can be quite upsetting, but you should try to figure out why he is crying as quickly as possible, so that you can comfort him and quiet him down. Some of the most common reasons for crying are outlined below.

THE HUNGER CRY. Most young babies cry every time they feel hungry, and this means that hunger crying will occur frequently during both day and night. Sometimes a baby's crying will be interrupted by brief pauses, and it typically escalates in loudness until he is fed. Sucking movements, quivering of the area around the mouth, agitated movements, and arching of the back may accompany his loud, shrill cries for food.

Assuming that your baby is fairly regular in his feeding patterns, you may recognize after the first week or so that he cries every few hours, slightly before his feedings. However, if his feeding patterns are irregular, this makes matters somewhat more confusing. Let's say that you fed him an hour and a half to two hours ago and he did not eat very much at the time. Now he begins to cry, and you wonder whether or not to offer more food. Go ahead and try, since there is a good chance that he is hungry. Provided that he is hungry, he will take the feeding and may drift off into blissful sleep afterward.

But let's say that your baby ate very well at his last meal, and here it is less than two hours later and he is crying again. It could very well be that he is hungry again, but this is not the most likely reason. Therefore, try to determine if there is something else besides food that he needs.

Should nothing else quiet him, and his crying continues to get louder and more intense, then try offering food. If it is food that he wanted, he will take it. Even though hunger is probably the most common reason for crying during the first few months, the objective is not to pop a breast or bottle into his mouth at the slightest whimper. Rather, it is to try to determine if his crying stems from hunger or some other reason.

THE AFTER-THE-FEEDING CRY. In cases in which a baby cries regularly after his meals, and has taken in a substantial amount of food, it is unlikely that he is still hungry, since hunger crying usually takes place just before feeding times. There are several possibilities to investigate in this situation. It could be that what he has taken in does not agree with him, that he is allergic to it, or that he is having difficulty digesting it. Food allergies and intolerance to specific foods are discussed on pages 970–72.

One of the most common reasons for crying either right after a meal or half an hour or so later is that a baby has taken in a lot of air during the feeding and it is making him feel uncomfortable. Try burping him again (perhaps this even slipped your mind before), and doing a thorough job of it (see page 136). Perhaps carrying him around a bit will also help, or he might feel more comfortable being placed on his tummy, while you rub his back.

Colic may also be the reason for his crying. A discussion of colic, and suggestions for how to handle it, can be found on pages 139–40. Should your baby be troubled by colic during the first few months, you will, no doubt, be troubled as well, although in a different way. The feelings that may be aroused in parents of colicky babies are explored on pages 185–86.

Still another possible reason for crying following a meal is that a baby has not had enough food to satisfy him. Sometimes during bottle-feeding, the nipple holes are not the right size (see page 132), and this can result in crying. If you are breast-feeding, there is a possibility that your milk supply is insufficient, even though this is most unusual. Should you suspect that your breast-milk supply is not adequate to meet your baby's demands, let your doctor know.

THE THIRSTY CRY. Your baby's thirst will probably be sufficiently quenched by milk during the first couple of months, and it is doubtful that he will cry out of thirst. Nevertheless, if he is perspiring a lot on a hot day, begins to cry, and other possible reasons have been eliminated, you might try offering him some water, or juice, according to your doctor's recommendations.

Parents living in hot climates find the thirst cry much more common. When the baby sweats, he loses water and salt and may need more liquid than usual. As discussed in the health care section (page 964), the baby's water and salt balance is very delicate. You should not give your child large amounts of plain water if he is thirsty, since this will dilute his body's salt content. Liquids such as juice are preferred, since they contain salts and minerals, and thus, replace the lost body salts, as well as satisfy the baby's thirst.

THE TIRED CRY. Many babies seem to get very cranky and tense after an unusually long period of having been awake, or after a period in which they have been bounced, picked up and held by visitors, or sometimes, by even Mom and Dad. Feeling overtired and yet tense, they may find it difficult to relax and go to sleep. A combination of these kinds of feelings can prompt them to cry.

If your infant has been up for quite a while and you hear him cry, look for signs of fatigue: yawning, bringing his hands to his eyes, restlessness, or looking sleepy-eyed and fatigued. Putting him to bed may stop his crying. Also, make sure that you are not constantly interrupting his sleep to play with him or show him off, or that you are not overstimulating him when he is awake.

Some babies cry regularly toward the end of each period of wakefulness, as a signal that they are ready for some rest. In the event that your baby cries a couple of hours after he has had a good meal, there is a chance that he will stop crying when put to bed. Assuming that he is feeling well, the temperature in the room is acceptable, his diapers are dry, and he is in a comfortable position, you can leave him alone in his crib and hope that he will go to sleep with little or no delay.

Difficulty falling asleep is not uncommon, even though the child is obviously tired. In cases in which a baby continues crying after he is put to bed, you can try leaving him alone for ten minutes or more (if you can stand it), in the hopes that he will eventually settle down and sleep. After this length of time, should his crying persist, you will probably want to do something such as talk to him, sing to him, rock him, hold him close to you, carry him around, and so forth, in order to comfort him. While these stopgap measures may help as long as they are continued, you should probably avoid using them every night after the first month or two, since he may come to depend upon these external sources of comfort at bedtime long after he has the inner resources to comfort himself. This issue is more fully discussed in the Sleeping section on page 148.

THE I'M HURT OR NOT FEELING WELL CRY. Often new parents are too quick to jump to the conclusion that a baby who is crying between feedings must be sick. While this is not a common reason, the possibility does exist, especially if the crying is prolonged. Unless you recognize other signs of illness, such as those described on pages 117–18, chances are that you had best think of other possible reasons for your infant's crying.

Rare accidents such as those causing pain in which a baby is unintentionally bumped, scratched, or stuck by a diaper safety pin can happen, causing him to cry. More often than not, you will not be able to attribute his crying to these kinds of situations, but, if you do, you had better re-evaluate your treatment of your baby, and institute an intensive program of accident prevention.

THE ELIMINATION CRY. It is not uncommon for some babies to cry slightly before, during, or after they have moved their bowels or passed urine. There is not too much that you can do about the "before" or "during" cry, but the "afterward" cry may indicate that a baby is uncomfortable because his diapers are dirty or wet. Changing his diapers may help to put a quick end to his screaming. You should pay attention to your infant's stools, because a baby who is constipated, for instance, may be crying because he is experiencing discomfort or pain when moving his bowels. When a baby characteristically does not cry when he is about to defecate or during the process, and then suddenly begins to cry and strain, examine his stools (see pages 151–52). This will help you determine if his crying is from constipation or some other intestinal irritation.

THE I'M NOT COMFORTABLE CRY. When your baby is feeling too cold or too hot, there is a good chance that he will cry. The latter situation is usually the more common of the two reasons for crying. Try to avoid overdressing him or setting the temperature in his room too high, and then you will both be happier.

He may also cry because he has not been placed in a comfortable position, he is being handled too roughly for his liking, he does not like his bath, he prefers to sleep in his crib rather than his bassinet (or vice versa), his clothes are too stiff or binding, and so on. The list of reasons why he might be feeling uncomfortable could go on forever, along with the list of things that might annoy or disturb him. When he is young, his primary concern is for bodily comfort, or at least it seems that way to those caring for him.

Whenever he feels discomfort of any kind, he will probably let you know by crying. You care about his feelings and also do not like to hear him cry. Therefore, after ruling out hunger, diaper changes, fatigue, illness, and so forth, check to make sure his clothing and sleeping arrangements are adequate and suited to his comfort, and that you are handling him gently. Catering to his needs and wants at this stage is not going to "spoil" him. A satisfied baby is usually a happy baby who can focus his energy on other things besides his own bodily discomfort.

THE TENSE, JUMPY CRY. Young babies tend to cry automatically when they are startled, since this is a reflex response. It often takes much more to set one baby off than another. The "startle reflex cry" (page 86) gradually diminishes as babies grow older.

There are some young babies who startle and cry easily in response to what appears to be minimal reasons. Sudden slight shifts in position or ordinary household noises, such as that of the vacuum cleaner or of a group of people talking, cause them to jerk and cry. In general, these babies tend to be jumpy, restless, fidgety, and tense. They may never really seem to be relaxed or at peace within themselves. Such babies are frequently referred to as "hypertonic."

Should your baby be hypertonic, there are several measures that you can take that may make life more satisfactory for him, and help to stop his continual crying. What he probably needs most is peace and quiet. Therefore, you can try initially to limit the number of visitors that he has, avoid taking him into crowds, tone down your voice when you are around him, keep household noises down, and handle him slowly and tenderly. Chances are that he will outgrow this condition as he matures, but in the meantime, both of you will enjoy life more if you make an effort to offer him the kind of environment that he seems to need.

THE UNEXPLAINABLE CRYING SPELL. Many babies are subject to unexplainable crying spells during the first few months. In other words, you can search for every possible reason for your baby's crying, but may not be able to come up with one. Quite often these crying spells are sporadic in nature, and do not appear to occur at any special time of day. Occasionally, they may occur more regularly, particularly after the first several weeks. After a few weeks, you may recognize a pattern for these crying episodes. Many babies, after the first month or so, seem to have them in the evening, and in the morning, although your baby's pattern can be different.

There are many old-fashioned labels for these periods of crying that cannot be associated with hunger, fatigue, illness, wet diapers, thirst, and so on. They are generally referred to as "fretful" or "fussy" periods, and these labels still seem appropriate. Sometimes these crying spells or "fussy" periods are short-lived, and sometimes they last for an hour or more.

It has been speculated that fussy periods are a result of many things, including physical immaturity, adjustment to life outside of the womb, the need to expend energy or "blow off steam," and a baby's disposition. These reasons are all quite vague, although there is probably some truth to them. It has also been suggested that this type of crying serves a useful purpose in terms of a baby's adjustment. Perhaps this is true, too, since babies tend to have fewer of these crying spells as they grow older and mature.

The fact is that "fussy" or "fretful" periods are very common among perfectly happy, healthy, normal babies. You should not waste needless energy worrying about your baby, or searching for what you might have done wrong in handling him. It is probably safe simply to attribute fretful or fussy periods to his immaturity.

You probably will not be able to come up with any reason for his crying, and nothing may soothe him for more than a short period of time. Therefore, there is a good chance that you will begin to feel helpless, frustrated, annoyed, angry, and even resentful. Parents' success rates in quieting babies who are having a "fussy" period are not usually as high as they would like them to be. Your baby's crying will, no doubt, be hard on you, particularly if you are somewhat insecure or are not prepared for it. Try not to take it as a reflection of poor or unsuccessful parenting, or let it get the best of you.

If you are having trouble coping with his crying or are becoming too preoccupied with it, you might want to take a break by arranging for someone to take over for a few hours a day when he is most apt to be crying. This little "vacation" may help you enormously to relax and put the situation into proper perspective. Also, keep your hopes up, since in most cases there is a marked decrease in crying after the third month.

Despite the fact that little may be effective in quieting your baby for more than a short time during one of these "fretful" spells, it is important to continue to try to soothe and quiet him. Below is a list of some of the approaches that may help in quieting a fussy or crying baby. Different approaches seem to work for different babies, and it is hoped that one or more of the following will help in soothing yours.

How to Soothe a Fussy or Crying Baby

- eliminate the cause, if you recognize it (feed him, change him, put him to bed, and so forth)
- sing to him
- talk to him in a soothing way
- hold him close to your heart
- give him a gentle massage or pat him
- shift his position
- use motion (walking him, rocking him, and so forth)
- wrap him in a blanket and hold him
- put him to bed in a small space (a padded basket, a small bassinet, etc.)
- play soft music for him
- turn on the television set and place his bassinet nearby
- try a shift in his schedule

In a situation in which you have tried your best to quiet him, but nothing seems to do the trick, perhaps the only thing left to do is to put him down and let him cry. Do not administer any medications without asking your doctor. Should your baby cry for the greater part of each day, or for several hours at a time, discuss this problem with your doctor. He or she may have better luck in determining a reason as well as a solution.

Body Language

Your infant will not only communicate to you by crying, but also by his body language or actions. It is important for you to observe his movements and body positions in light of particular situations that occur. In this way, you will get some idea of how he feels, and what he is trying to tell you. His gestures may be seen in conjunction with his crying, or separately. Initially, many of his movements will be abrupt and unco-ordinated, but you will nevertheless be able to understand him better by taking note of them.

When your baby is ravenous, he may suck with his mouth, smack his lips, or stick out his tongue. He might also stretch, wriggle, and arch his back. When he has had enough to eat and is full, he has several ways of letting you know. He may make a face, spit up the last bit of milk that he took in, or simply allow it to dribble back out of his mouth. Other good indications that he has had enough to eat include turning his head away from the nipple, spitting it out, or forcing it away with his tongue.

A sleepy baby is likely to yawn, sigh, and stretch out, or later even bring his fists to his eyes as if to rub them. When he is very cold and damp or chilled, he is apt to squirm, quiver, and tremble. His body may look doubled up and stiff when he is in pain, or he may actively thrash and squirm. Wiggling, squirming, and thrashing can also indicate his dislike for a particular activity.

Your baby's whole body will move when he cries. Babies generally cry when they are hungry, in pain, uncomfortable, and so forth, so you will probably notice the gestures described above in conjunction with crying. This list is not all inclusive, but it will give you a good idea of what some of your baby's gestures may be like, and how to interpret them. As time goes by, his gestures will be easier for you to understand, and they will become more sophisticated and differentiated.

Are You Considering Introducing Your Child to Two Languages?

There are many different reasons why parents want to introduce their child to two languages very early. Parents who have learned to speak two languages fluently may want their child to learn both languages. Some parents have a strong ethnic or cultural background, and want to preserve this by teaching the child the language of their culture in addition to English. In some situations parents are not bilingual but would like their child to be in order to expand his educational background, and they feel that this would be an advantage to him. Whatever your reasons for introducing a second language, it is useful to share the experience of other parents who have done this.

There have been many studies related to bilingualism, but this area of psycholinguistics is highly complex, and at the present time, more carefully controlled research is required before clear-cut conclusions can be drawn. By learning about the more common methods of introducing a second language, it is hoped that some of your questions will be clarified, and that you will be in a better position to decide how to introduce your child to two languages. The ultimate decision as to how best to accomplish this is yours to make. A great deal depends upon individual circumstances and parental preferences.

THE PRIMARY LANGUAGE FIRST. Probably the most common approach taken by parents in our culture is to introduce English as the child's primary language from birth. Once the child becomes skillful in this language, then the second or foreign language is introduced.

Parents who were born in another country in which English was not the native language, but who now live in this country and speak English fluently, may want to introduce English as their child's primary language, particularly if they plan to remain here permanently or for a prolonged period of time. Then, after the child has mastered English as his primary language, they introduce him to their native tongue, as the child's second or "foreign language." The timing of teaching the second language is variable, but it is usually introduced during the preschool stage, when the child is very receptive to learning a second language. This approach is discussed on page 733 in the Preschool 1 Language Development section.

THE SECONDARY LANGUAGE FIRST. Parents who do not speak English very well (recently coming from another country), or feel that their children are more likely to loosen their attachment to their cultural or ethnic background by learning English as the primary language, often teach their children their own native tongue from birth as the primary language. Parents who speak English as well as their native language have the choice of introducing English as a secondary language during the preschool years, or waiting until the child attends school. Many parents who use this approach feel that their child is more likely to retain their native language and culture.

One problem with not introducing English before the child attends school is that the child may have difficulty, at first, competing with children who have been taught English from birth. This is certainly understandable. In most cases, the child picks up English rapidly, and has little difficulty performing in school once he has mastered the language. When children are given verbal performance tests in the early school years, those who are first learning English may receive lower scores than children of equal intelligence who have learned English from birth.

These differences usually disappear after the child becomes more proficient in English. However, should a child have a minor learning disability, this problem could be accentuated if English was not his primary language. Another possible problem that should be mentioned deals with peer group acceptance. In the event that a child is the only person in his class who does not speak English, it could make it more difficult for him to interact socially with his schoolmates. These possible problems are most often minor, and are naturally overcome once the child masters the English language.

INTRODUCING TWO LANGUAGES AT ONCE. Parents who speak two languages fluently (bilingualism) sometimes choose to teach both English and a foreign language simultaneously to their child during infancy. They generally believe that by introducing two languages from birth, the child will become fluent in both languages, without one or the other being dominant. Probably the most common approach to teaching an infant two languages from birth is to have one parent speak to him consistently in English, and the other parent (or another person with whom the child spends a great deal of time) speak to him in the foreign language (or native tongue as the case may be). Less preferable approaches are to speak English and a foreign language on alternate days, speak English and the foreign language consistently in separate rooms of the home, or speak both languages interchangeably.

There are certain minor drawbacks that are often associated with introducing two languages simultaneously. Children learning two languages at the same time may take a little longer to become proficient at speaking both languages than a child who learns only one. Parents using this approach may notice that their child is slightly delayed in speaking. They may also observe some interference or confusion of one language with the other. A child may occasionally use vocabulary words from one language when he is speaking in another. As the child grows older, and becomes more proficient in both languages, linguistic interference or overlap usually disappears.

MOTOR DEVELOPMENT

Reflexes Allow Him to Function at Birth

Even before a baby is born, his motor activity is already beginning to develop. The evidence has been long since recognized by mothers who can actually feel their babies moving around and kicking in their wombs. Recent research has confirmed this. The new technique of fiber optics enables scientists actually to photograph the fetus in the womb, and movies have shown that the developing fetus can kick its legs and even suck on its thumb.

At birth the infant is rather well equipped to move about. His nervous system has been programmed, so to speak, to allow environmental stimuli to trigger many reflex responses such as rooting, sucking, swallowing, crying, excretion of wastes, blinking, sneezing, startling, grasping, and so forth. Many of these reflexes have obvious value in terms of his protection and survival. Without them he would be even more helpless and vulnerable.

Reflexes allow him to function at birth without first having to learn how to move his eyes, suck, swallow, digest food, move his bowels, and so on. Reflexes are unlearned response patterns. Gradually, as his nervous system and higher brain centers develop and mature, most of his primitive reflexes, such as sucking, righting, and grasping, begin to fade. He slowly gains more voluntary control over his body, and learns to suppress primitive reflex activity. Still, a few reflexes are never lost. Even as adults we continue to sneeze, yawn, and blink by reflex action. A more complete description of many of the infant's reflexes was presented in the Newborn section on pages 84–88.

Even though your infant's reflexes are working at birth, they may not be operating at full efficiency. As stimuli from his surroundings trigger his reflex responses, they gradually become stronger and more co-ordinated. After he is several weeks old, you will probably notice that his body is functioning more smoothly. He will breathe more regularly, suck more strongly, and spit up, startle, gag, and sneeze less frequently. In essence, his reflexes become more organized as he becomes accustomed to life outside the womb.

He may also become more efficient at rooting and aiming his mouth directly toward the nipple. This suggests that he is learning to distinguish it from the bottle or skin area around the areola, despite the fact that it is thought that he only remembers objects that reappear within a brief period of time. He is, if only in a small way, showing an ability to adapt to the environment.

When Alice Turner first began breast-feeding, she noticed that her son, Ben, had some initial difficulty finding her nipple. He often groped at the breast tissue around her areola, and she had to guide the nipple into his mouth. After the first three weeks, Ben no longer seemed confused at feeding times. As soon as Alice placed her breast near his face, Ben immediately opened his mouth and aimed it toward her nipple. Alice was convinced that Ben knew the difference between her nipple and the areas around it, and she correctly took this as a sign that Ben was learning from experience.

You will notice that when he is crying, your baby's entire body actively responds. The same whole-body reaction occurs when he sucks, or feels abrupt temperature fluctuations. Much later in the first year, you will notice that his whole body is no longer involved when he cries, takes in food, or is subjected to abrupt changes in light, temperature, or sound. His responses become more specific and localized and he will no longer use up a great deal of energy when crying or sucking.

Your infant's response patterns are generalized, and many different stimuli can trigger his reflex activities. He may suck in response to a light, a loud noise, a tickle on the cheek, or feeling a nipple. As his nervous system matures, and with added experience, he gradually becomes more discriminating.

His Other Abilities Are Quite Limited

Your baby's motor behavior is mainly controlled by reflex responses, and his abilities otherwise are extremely limited. Reflexes control most of his arm, leg, and hand movements, although he may wiggle, squirm, kick, and wave his arms and legs around, usually in a rather jerky, awkward, and purposeless fashion. His control over his body is so limited that when you place him down in a certain position, it is doubtful that he will be able to shift from that position easily. Still, if he is the active sort, he may manage to move a bit by squirming, pushing with his legs, or abruptly flinging himself from a side to a back position. Much of the time when he is lying on his tummy, he may assume a frog-like or a fetal position, with his rear end held up in the air a little and his legs either spread out and flexed or tucked under his body. As the weeks pass he will gradually begin to lie flatter on the mattress.

On his back, after the first several weeks, you will observe that he assumes the "fencer's" position. Both of his hands will be held in a closed or fisted position. His head will be turned to the side, most often to the right. On the side to which his head is turned, both his arm and leg will be stretched out or extended. On the opposite side, his arm and leg will be held in a flexed position. The position of his head generally determines the position of his arms. This posture is due to his tonic neck reflex.

Infancy 1 babies are weak. They have very little head control. It is possible that you will see your baby moving his head slightly from one side to the other, but the ability to turn it with ease or look over his shoulder is lacking. His head is overly large as compared to the rest of his body, and this, coupled with the fact that his head and neck muscles are very weak, makes it hard for him to turn and lift his head. On his stomach, he may be able to lift his nose off the mattress for a second or so, but maintaining this position other than momentarily is incredibly difficult for him.

When lying on his back, your baby may not be able to raise his head at all, due to the fact that his front neck muscles lack sufficient strength. If you make use of his grasp reflex to pull him to a sitting position, or prop him in this position, you will observe his head and trunk slumping. It is important to refrain from lifting him in this manner on a regular basis, and to make sure that his head is well supported whenever you are lifting and carrying him.

When you open his hand, which is usually held in a fist position, and insert your finger, he may automatically clench his fist tightly around it. This is his grasp reflex in action.

Mrs. Cantini was holding her newborn baby in the hospital when her three-year-old daughter, Liz, entered the room. This was the first time Liz had seen her tiny brother, Bruce, and Mrs. Cantini wanted to give her preschooler an early opportunity to get acquainted with him. She encouraged Liz to try to shake hands with Bruce, and told her to pry open his fist gently and insert her finger. Liz approached her brother hesitantly, and carefully opened his tightly closed fist. As soon as she placed her finger in Bruce's hand, he grasped onto it very tightly, and did not let go of it as she moved her arm up and down. Liz was thrilled by Bruce's response, and took it to mean that he was happy to meet her. She did not realize that Bruce's grasping was simply an automatic, uncontrolled response.

It is doubtful that your baby gives his hand more than a brief glance at this stage, even though it is held in front of his eyes. As his eyesight matures and as he gains more control over his arm, he will not only begin to look at his arm, but later will co-ordinate looking at it with moving it. Eye-hand co-ordination will develop in the months to come.

Occasionally he may bring his hands to his mouth and even suck on his fist. He may also thrash about actively and aimlessly with his arms when lying on his back or when held in your arms. As his nervous system matures, and as he gains weight and exercises his muscles over the first month, he will grow stronger and seem less limp.

LEARNING THROUGH PLAY

Since your baby is likely to be really alert for only a small portion of the time each day, his capacities for movement and active interaction with people and objects are extremely limited, and he will not be in a position to do much playing on his own. Nonetheless, it is important for him to receive appropriate stimulation, particularly that which you can provide. He is a sensitive human being, capable of seeing, hearing, feeling, tasting, smelling, responding to stimulation, and communicating with you in his own primitive way. These abilities provide links between himself, you, and his surroundings.

One of the most important ways in which you can strengthen these links, promote his development, and enrich your relationship with him is through playing with him. You will be helping him "come out of his shell." You can offer him the kinds of sensory stimulation that should increase his awareness of and interest in you and the world around him.

Play Will Be Fun

Anything that your baby enjoys when he is awake and alert can be considered to be play. It may take several weeks of spending time with him and getting to know him before you will be able to determine which kinds of stimulation and how much stimulation he prefers. His "tastes" in relation to stimulation may be very different from another baby's. One baby may seem delighted whenever he is handled and picked up by a variety of people, while another may enjoy this form of stimulation only in very limited doses. Some babies show a preference for visual stimulation, while others may appear to derive the most pleasure from physical or auditory stimulation. Since a major purpose of play is that your baby derives pleasure from it, you should try to take his individual needs, capabilities, and "tastes" into account when playing with him. This general rule of thumb will apply throughout early childhood.

Your baby will not be taking ordinary objects, noises, and sights for granted as you do. Each thing that he sees, each noise that he hears, and each object that he feels will be new and fascinating. With so many novel experiences to absorb via his five senses, it is doubtful that he will be bored. You will not be hard pressed to come up with something new to interest him as you might be with an older preschool child. Just the sound of your voice may captivate his interest and bring him pleasure.

Playing with your baby and offering him a variety of sensory experiences will probably come very naturally to you, whether or not you have had much prior experience in being with babies. You might sing to him, talk to him, cuddle him close, nuzzle your head to his tummy, run your fingers from his head to his toes, stroke his soft skin, or rock him in your arms while whispering in his ear. There is no one method of playing with a baby that is "right" or "best." Each of you will develop your own, special ways of playing with your baby depending upon what feels natural and enjoyable for the two of you.

There is, furthermore, no one time of day that needs to be set aside specifically for the purpose of play. Spontaneity is extremely important. Play with him whenever he seems to be receptive to it. Obviously, if he is terribly hungry, uncomfortable, or sleepy, being played with and stimulated will be the furthest thing from his mind. On the other hand, you need not feel as though you must button up your lips and not play with him at mealtimes or bath times. In fact, since much of his waking time will center around being fed, bathed, and changed, these activities will present you with marvelous opportunities for playing with him.

You can take advantage of numerous chances throughout each day to stimulate him. You need not worry that you might spoil or overstimulate him, unless, of course, you keep interrupting his sleep to play with him, or he indicates that he would rather have some peace and quiet.

Keep in mind that the suggestions below for various sensory experiences should be used mainly as guidelines or take-off points from which you can go on to devise your own methods of enjoying your baby, depending upon his individual needs and yours.

Suggestions for Stimulating and Playing with Your Baby

TOUCHING

Pick him up often and hold him close to you, since physical contact is an essential form of stimulation for babies.

Infancy 1

• Take hold of his hands and help him to feel various objects, textured materials, your facial features, his own features and body parts, and warm and cold substances.

• Say nursery rhymes such as "this little pig went to market" or "pat-a-cake" that involve touching parts of his body.

SEEING

• Hang a mobile to the right and left side of his crib about eight to twelve inches from his face. You can easily make your own mobile by cutting out various shapes from cardboard, and stringing them from the crib. You can paint, glue, or draw brightly colored patterns of high contrast (e.g., facial patterns) on the cardboard shapes. This will give him something interesting to look at while he is lying in the crib. Make sure that he will be able to see the patterns from his lying down perspective.

• When you go into his room to check on him, bend way over him, with your face near his so that he can see you. Look into his eyes when you talk to him and smile!

• When you carry him in your arms, take a tour around your home. Hold various objects and toys near enough to his face so that he can see them.

• Occasionally you may want to change the position of his crib in his room, or change his position in the crib so that he will have a change of scenery.

• Hold his hands near enough to his face so that he can see them.

• Take a brightly colored, patterned toy, hold it at a distance of about eight or so inches from his face, and slowly move it from side to side and up and down to give him practice in visual following.

HEARING

• Talk, sing, and hum to him often. Vary the pitch, tone, and volume of your voice. It is highly important that he hear human speech from the beginning.

• Expose him to everyday household noises such as the sound of the television, vacuum cleaner, radio, stereo, etc.

• He may enjoy listening to music.

SMELLING

• You may want to introduce him to different scents to stimulate his sense of smell.

MOVING

• His movements are mainly reflex actions, and one activity that you may enjoy might involve eliciting some of his reflexes so that you can observe them. For example, you can take advantage of his grasp reflex and place a rattle in his hands, or stroke the balls of his feet and observe his toes curling in.

• You may want to circle his arms around or move his legs up and down a bit to give him some exercise.

KEEPING YOUR BABY HEALTHY

Providing for your baby's health care needs is not a difficult task. The advances in medicine over the past forty years have made it possible to prevent or minimize many serious childhood illnesses. These advances have played a significant role in ensuring the health of young children.

After birth, your baby will be carefully examined by both your obstetrician and baby's doctor. This is a routine procedure in hospital deliveries. If your baby is delivered at home, you should arrange to have your child examined by your doctor shortly after birth. As you recover from the delivery, most hospitals observe the baby through the nursing staff and by follow-up visits by your pediatrician.

You can play a major part in keeping your baby healthy by taking advantage of preventive medicine. Providing your infant with good nutrition, maintaining a safe environment, and keeping him clean are but the first steps in ensuring his health. Have him examined regularly by a physician or other competent health care professional; by working together with your physician, you will be assuring that your child receives the benefits of modern medicine. This type of health care, designed to prevent illness, is called well baby care. Before reading further, study the special index on page 944, which indicates what topics are covered in the Health Care Guide.

Well Baby Care

The home environment that you offer should promote both physical and emotional health. The basic care sections in this book and the advice of your doctor will assist you in meeting your baby's physical needs. Seeing that your baby's emotional needs are satisfied is also an important part of well baby care. Establishing an early positive bond with your baby will help ensure his healthy development. Infants need a great deal of love, attention, and physical contact. You should offer your baby an abundance of emotional support.

REGULAR WELL BABY CHECK-UPS. Be sure to have your baby regularly examined by a doctor. Some doctors work with other highly trained health care professionals such as physicians' assistants, nurses, and nurse practitioners. Most communities also have well baby clinics, which you can use if you do not have a private doctor. These clinics usually will see the young infant for the first year of life, and often have facilities for follow-up visits during toddlerhood and the preschool years.

Schedules for visits vary slightly from one physician to another. During the first six months of life, doctors usually want to examine the baby more frequently. Following your infant's initial physical examination shortly after birth, the doctor will examine the baby before you take him home from the hospital, if you gave birth in the hospital. A follow-up check-up in two weeks and at approximately one month of age is often suggested. Following these examinations, monthly check-ups are usually arranged for the next several months. Each visit will include a complete physical examination. Your baby's height, weight, and head size will be measured and immunizations against childhood diseases will be given at appropriate times. The doctor will ask you about your baby's behavior at home. Then your doctor will be able to evaluate his progress and make recommendations to assist you in keeping him healthy.

By observing your baby from day to day, you will have a thorough picture of how he is developing. You will also be aware of changes in his personality and bodily functions. It is helpful to keep a mental or written note on these observations and bring them along when you visit the doctor. Also jot down questions that you have. This will allow you to present your doctor with useful information about your baby and be able to discuss his progress and your concerns.

TESTS TO PREVENT ILLNESS. PKU (Phenylketonuria) is a rare genetic disease resulting in the absence of an enzyme to break down a certain chemical in the body. The enzyme defect causes increased levels of the substance phenylketone in the blood, which then appears in the urine. A simple test for this disease can make the diagnosis. It is important to detect this condition early in life, since left untreated it can cause mental retardation. PKU can be treated by a special diet. If this diet is started early, the child can develop normally. Many hospitals test the blood of each newborn child for PKU. This test picks up most cases, and is usually repeated at two weeks of age. A third PKU follow-up test on the baby's urine is then done at approximately one month of age. Some hospitals and doctors also test the baby's blood for thyroid function and a condition called galactosemia. Your doctor will advise you about these tests or other appropriate tests that are part of well baby care.

Babies with Special Problems

Sometimes babies are born with certain problems requiring special attention, care, or treatment. Parents often want to become familiar with these special situations if they arise so that they will be better prepared to cope with them. Most of these problems are medical in nature, and will be thoroughly discussed with you by your physician. A few of the more common situations that may arise include premature, low birth weight, postmature, and handicapped babies.

As a result of many new advances in modern medical science, there is a great deal that can be done to assist babies with special problems in leading normal, happy lives. There are also many organizations and support groups to assist parents in caring for babies with special medical problems or minor physical difficulties. Individual topics related to the "special" baby are discussed on pages 1010–13.

Sick Baby Care

It is almost impossible to prevent illness completely during the first year of life. All normal babies occasionally get minor illnesses. Sick baby care is directed at recognizing early signs of illness and knowing how and when to seek medical assistance.

First-time-around parents often express uncertainty about knowing when to contact their doctor. With added experience, parents usually become good judges of what symptoms require a prompt call to the doctor. They also learn that some situations are not as pressing, and can be discussed at the next well baby check-up.

When you leave the hospital with your healthy baby, you have already overcome many of the medical problems that occur in the first few days of life. You can feel confident that your child is in good health. The type of illnesses that he will encounter over the next few months are usually minor, and the majority of babies do very well.

It is useful to be familiar with some of the common illnesses and problems of infancy so that you will be prepared if they arise.

Consult the Health Care Guide (pages 944–1060) for additional information on the following topics:

Fever and taking a temperature
Colds, ear infections, and common respiratory illnesses
Diet during illness
Problems with digestion
Common elimination problems
Allergies
Rashes and common skin problems
Contagious and infectious diseases
Eyes and visual problems
Babies with special problems
The handicapped child

HOW TO RECOGNIZE WHEN YOUR BABY IS SICK. Babies, like adults, have changes in their personalities and activity when they are ill. You would have little difficulty in recognizing that an adult was sick by the way he or she acted. The secret to recognizing when a baby is ill is to understand how a baby behaves when he is sick. Babies differ in their responses to illness depending on their own personalities and the nature of the illness. But there are some common changes in babies' behavior that indicate they are sick.

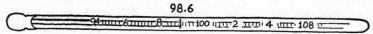

Sudden or unusual changes in behavior, appearance, breathing, temperature, and body waste products can be indicators of illness. You should easily be able to detect these changes as you interact with your baby. The accompanying chart summarizes some of the more common signs of illness. Your physician or his or her associates may want to expand this list based on their knowledge of your own particular circumstances. Upon detecting significant changes in your baby's behavior, you should seek medical advice. Knowing when and how to contact a doctor is a major part of sick baby care.

The list below indicates some obvious as well as more subtle signs that your baby is sick. You would not want to overreact every time your baby has a crying spell or decides he is not hungry. In interpreting your baby's behavior, make use of good common sense and look for changes in normal patterns of daily activities.

Signs of Illness

CHANGES IN BEHAVIOR
- Baby is not alert or does not respond
- Excessive crying or irritability as if in pain
- Sleep difficulties

CHANGES IN APPEARANCE
- Excessive flushing of the face
- Very hot dry skin
- Unusual paleness
- Marked sweating
- Very watery or dull eyes
- Appearance of rashes

CHANGES IN BREATHING
- Difficulty breathing
- Coughing
- Sneezing

Infancy 1

- Hoarse crying or breathing
- Runny nose

CHANGES IN BODY TEMPERATURE
- Fever
- Shaking chills

CHANGES IN BOWEL OR BLADDER FUNCTION
- Vomiting (not spitting up)
- Diarrhea
- Bloody urine or bowel movements
- Prolonged changes in elimination patterns

CHANGES IN FEEDING BEHAVIOR
- Prolonged loss of appetite
- Refuses or spits up all feedings

Some symptoms, like rashes and vomiting, are easily recognized and clearly indicate that something is going on and that your baby might be ill. Other less obvious changes will also attract your attention. Fussiness, minor sleep difficulties, or slightly diminished activity may be signs of illness, but require further consideration. If these less obvious changes occur, you should see whether your infant is functioning normally in other ways.

Mrs. Hughes noticed that her young infant, Peter, was very irritable. This was a clear change in his usual behavior. She watched him carefully to see if anything else had changed. His temperature was normal and he was eating well. She did not observe any other signs of illness.

Over the next few hours Mrs. Hughes noticed that Peter's irritability always followed his feedings. Since he seemed fine otherwise, she suspected he was not sick. Burping him a little more often after each feeding put an end to his fussiness. Mrs. Hughes was relieved that Peter's altered behavior was the result of a little extra gas that needed to be brought up.

When you suspect your baby is not acting normally, but does not clearly seem sick, this is the time to observe him carefully. By being alert, you can observe your baby's behavior, breathing, bowel and urine function, appearance, and temperature. If these other aspects seem fine, he is probably doing well. Minor illnesses will usually become obvious, and you should see signs that your baby is sick.

CONTACTING YOUR DOCTOR. New parents often want a list of reasons for calling the doctor. This is understandable, especially if they have not had firsthand experience with a young infant. Having a general list of signs of illness that should be brought to their physician's attention seems to put them at ease. Using your own good judgment, you will be able to recognize when your baby needs medical assistance. Your doctor may give you his or her own guidelines for calling for medical attention. Some physicians have a list of important signs that they feel require an immediate call, while others feel that it is better to discuss these signs with you and let you use your own common sense. No one list can possibly take into account every situation in which it would be wise to call a doctor. The main point is to recognize unusual changes in your baby's appearance and behavior.

The following list was developed with the assistance of several practicing pediatricians; it is by no means inclusive and should be used only as a very general guide. Your physician may wish to modify the list, taking into account your personal situation. Space is provided at the end of the list for you to record any additions that your doctor wants to make.

GUIDELINES FOR CALLING THE DOCTOR

Sudden or marked changes in behavior

A baby who does not respond or seem alert should receive immediate medical attention. When you see less obvious changes in behavior, such as fussiness or irritability, these may or may not be signs of illness. If symptoms like these are persistent or excessive, you should discuss them with your doctor.

Signs of pain

In a young infant the major sign of pain is prolonged persistent crying (page 105). Colic is one of the most common causes. Your physician will advise you about this condition and will probably suggest that it is not necessary to call for every colic episode once the diagnosis is made (see pages 139–40). An older infant may indicate pain from an ear infection (see pages 957–58) by holding his ear.

Fever

A temperature of greater than 100° F in a baby less than two months old should be brought to the attention of your doctor. Fever and how to take a temperature are discussed on pages 951–54. Not all babies have a fever when they are sick, so you must use good judgment. If the infant has other signs of illness, but does not have a fever, you will still want to seek medical attention. Your physician may want to give you specific guidelines for how to interpret your baby's temperature.

Diarrhea

Marked or prolonged passage of watery stools should be brought to your doctor's attention. More mild forms may be less urgent, but your doctor should be consulted. Diarrhea is discussed on page 964 and should be reported early.

Vomiting

Unusual or persistent vomiting should be reported to your doctor. Occasional spitting up of formula is not considered vomiting. See pages 962–63.

Cold

Many doctors prefer to be notified of a baby's initial cold in the first few months. More generally you should report the cold if it is rather severe or the child develops any unusual symptoms. See pages 954–55.

Marked loss of appetite

Sudden and prolonged loss of appetite should be reported. It is not necessary to be concerned if your child refuses an occasional feeding and otherwise appears fine. Persistent spitting out of food or refusal to eat for several feedings on a given day should be brought to your doctor's attention (see pages 954–55).

Difficulties with breathing

Difficulties with breathing, bark-like cough, or other marked changes in breathing should be brought to your doctor's attention (see pages 954–55).

Signs of bleeding

Bloody urine and blood in vomitus or stools should be reported to your doctor.

Head trauma

Any severe head injury, especially if it results in changes in behavior, loss of consciousness, or fever should be evaluated by your doctor.

Appearance of rashes

Diaper rash is the most common rash in infancy and is not an emergency (pages 974–76). Rashes from contagious disease such as measles and rubella can be prevented with proper immunizations. Any other sudden or unusual rashes should be reported to your doctor.

Head enlargement

Rapid enlargement of the head or soft spot in the skull (fontanel) should be reported immediately.

Prolonged lack of urination or bowel movements

Lack of urination for more than twenty-four hours when feedings are continuing as usual should be reported rapidly. Prolonged absence of bowel movements for more than three days should be brought to your doctor's attention to rule out blockage (see pages 964–65). Some babies normally pass bowel movements every three to four days. Once it is clear to you and your doctor that this is your baby's pattern, there should be no cause for concern.

Eye problems

Eye injuries or infections (crust or pus-like material in the eye) should be brought to medical attention.

Emergency situations

Emergency situations such as extensive bleeding, poisoning, persistent nose bleeds, convulsions, and other injuries, should be immediately reported. (See Health Care Guide, pages 985–1003).

Additions suggested by your doctor

BE PREPARED WHEN YOU CALL YOUR DOCTOR. When new parents call their doctor to ask for advice or report an illness, they often feel disorganized in presenting pertinent information about their child. There are several aspects of a baby's behavior that parents should observe and be prepared to relate to their doctor. If an infant is vomiting, for example, parents should note the amount, frequency, and color of the vomitus. If a baby has a fever—how high was his highest temperature and how long has it been elevated? This type of approach will allow parents to convey important information that assists the physician.

Many new parents find it useful to have a check list to help them evaluate their child's condition. Physicians also find it helpful for parents to be able to give them a clear explanation of the child's illness.

SICK CHILD CHECK LIST

Temperature is _____.

Temperature has been elevated for _____ hours.

Baby is _____ lethargic _____ restless _____ irritable.

Breathing is _____ normal _____noisy _____difficult _____ rapid _____ slow.

Baby is _____ hoarse _____ coughing _____ sneezing.

Baby's appetite is _____ good _____ bad. (He has skipped _____ feedings.)

Bowel movements are _____ normal _____ abnormal. (color_____ consistency _____ odor _____ frequency_____)

Urination is _____ normal _____ abnormal. (color _____ frequency _____ painful _____)

Baby has vomited: force _____ amount _____ color _____ frequency _____.

Body movements are _____ normal _____ abnormal. (twitching _____ stiffness _____ immobility _____ convulsions _____)

Appearance is _____ normal _____ flushed _____ pale _____ perspiring _____ rash. (color _____ itchy _____ patchy _____ even _____)

There are signs of pain _____ crying _____ screaming _____ ear pain.

Eyes are _____ normal _____ watery _____ red.

Additions:

TAKING CARE OF A SICK BABY. Most childhood illnesses are self-limiting in nature and usually take a few days to run their course. Working with your physician will allow you to take advantage of modern medicine and minimize or eliminate much of the discomfort that accompanies some of these minor illnesses. Your Child's Medicine Chest (pages 945–46) presents guidelines for getting simple basic equipment and materials that will be useful in caring for your child.

Medications that are given improperly can be harmful or ineffective. Although parents often gain experience in managing colds or other minor illnesses, it is best to allow the doctor to make a diagnosis and prescribe treatment. Knowing what is causing an illness can be very complex and requires a great deal of professional training.

Mrs. Croft's two-month-old son Jonathan developed a mild cough. His doctor examined him and took a throat culture. Jonathan had a mild viral cold and his doctor prescribed some cough liquid to help relieve his congestion until the cold went away. He recovered quickly and did not need much of his cough medication.

Several months later Jonathan developed a similar cough. Mrs. Croft assumed he was just having another mild cold, since it was the cold season and he was having symptoms similar to his previous cold. She gave her son his old cough medicine to help relieve his symptoms. The medicine helped for a few days, but his cough got worse and he seemed much sicker. Mrs. Croft became concerned and called her doctor. When the doctor examined him and obtained a throat culture, it was clear that Jonathan had a bacterial throat infection. He needed an antibiotic and not simply a cough liquid. Given the proper medication, Jonathan did well, but he could have recovered sooner if he had been placed on the right medication from the start.

The same signs of illness can be produced by very different causes. You should always obtain your physician's advice before giving any medication to your young infant, and never use medications prescribed to treat a previous illness.

Medications can occasionally cause side effects such as fever, rash, kidney difficulties, a low blood count, and allergic reactions. Fortunately, these complications are rare, but medicines should only be used when necessary.

ALLERGIES DURING INFANCY. Some babies are prone to develop allergies, especially if their parents have a history of allergic problems. The Allergies section on pages 970–72 discusses the common allergies of infancy and suggests possible ways of trying to avoid them. Babies rarely, if ever, develop allergies to breast milk. Some babies, however, do develop allergies to cow's milk or certain prepared formulas. If you have a strong history of allergies, it would be worth while to discuss this with your baby's doctor when you are selecting a feeding method for your baby.

It is important to keep in mind that your baby still has not completely developed his natural defenses against common infectious diseases. You should attempt to protect him from unnecessary exposure to sick adults or children.

what is

Emergency Baby Care

Emergency care is the third component of good child health care. Emergencies are rare, but they can occur. With a small amount of effort, you can easily be prepared for them. Learning how to handle emergency situations can minimize the risk to the baby, and should not create, but rather diminish anxiety or fear in parents.

No one wants to face an emergency situation. By taking the appropriate measures to prevent accidents and offer good well baby care, nearly all avoidable emergencies during infancy should be prevented. In the rare event that an emergency does arise, you should find the following information useful.

Specific information on common emergencies during infancy and childhood is presented in the Health Care Guide (pages 985–1003) for quick reference.

No parent can be expected to remain completely calm in an emergency situation involving his or her child. While some anxiety is natural, it is important not to panic, and to try to think clearly about the appropriate steps to take. When an emergency occurs, you should evaluate the situation and determine the proper course of action. Knowing how and where to seek medical help as well as how to administer first aid until assistance arrives are the most important aspects of preparing to deal with emergencies in a level-headed fashion.

HOW AND WHERE TO GET IMMEDIATE HELP. Getting immediate help in an emergency is made much easier by having all the phone numbers and appropriate information on a prepared card. After completing the list given below (see also page 948) attach it to an obvious place near your phone. You should also carry such a card with you in your wallet at all times and leave a copy with your baby-sitter.

The Emergency List has two purposes. The first is to make sure that you know where and how to get in touch with your doctor, the hospital, police, fire department, poison control center, and other important sources of help. By writing down this information, you not only have it for easy access, but you are also sure to look into such facilities as the poison control center in your area in advance.

The other major purpose of the list is to serve as information for others who might find your child first, following an accident. In case you are away from home and an accident occurs, the baby-sitter or guardian will have all the necessary information available. Your child's allergies, medications, and illnesses should be clearly listed. If your child does not have any of these conditions, write down "none" in the space provided.

Always leave the Emergency List with your baby-sitter and give the phone number and address where you can be reached. This point cannot be overemphasized. Too many parents do not take the time to inform baby-sitters how to get assistance in case of emergency.

Until assistance can be obtained, it is important to know how to provide supportive care and administer simple first aid if necessary. The First Aid and Acute Medical Problems section on pages 985–1003 presents basic guidelines. Being skilled at providing regular and emergency care is a very useful asset. It is recommended that you take a local first aid or CPR (Cardiopulmonary Resuscitation) course to help you become well trained in these techniques.

EMERGENCY LIST

Child's name _____

Address _____

Phone _____

Parent's Name(s): Mother _____

Father _____

Parent's Work Phone: Mother _____

Father _____

Doctor: Name _____

Address _____

Phone _____

Poison Control Center Phone: Day _____

Night _____

Hospital: Name _____

Address _____

Phone _____

Nearest Emergency Room: _____

Phone _____

Local Emergency Phone Number (if available, e.g., 911): _____

Police: Phone _____

Fire Department: Phone _____

Pharmacy: Name _____

Phone _____

Person to be contacted if parents not available: Name _____

Phone _____

Current Medications: _____

Allergies: Medicine _____

Foods _____

Other _____

Illnesses: _____

_____

Other: _____

_____

HOW TO ENSURE YOUR BABY'S SAFETY

Many parents look upon accidents as always striking other people's children—not their own. Unfortunately, until their child has had a "close call," or an injury from an accident has occurred, some parents never take the time to read about accident prevention or to take necessary safety precautions.

Accident prevention is an important topic because parents can directly affect the safety of their child. Being safety-conscious, however, does not mean being anxious about your baby's every move. Ensuring your baby's safety is not a difficult task. Using good common sense and making an effort to prepare in advance, you will be able to keep your baby safe. Protecting your infant from avoidable accidents should become second nature to you, enabling you to spend less time worrying about his safety and more time enjoying his company.

Prevent Car Accidents

The major cause of accidental death in children is car accidents. The infant is especially susceptible to injuries in the car if he is not properly protected in an acceptable seat or carrier. Even short stops or accidents that may not injure adults can be very dangerous to a baby who is held in a passenger's arms or laid on the seat in an improper carrier.

Mr. and Mrs. Abate were taking a Sunday drive with their infant son. Mrs. Abate was holding him on her lap in the front seat. Suddenly, a driver, who obviously did not see them approaching, pulled out of a side street. Mr. Abate had to slam on the brakes to avoid a collision. Mr. and Mrs. Abate sustained no injuries, since they were just thrust forward in their seats. Their son was much closer to the dashboard, because he was on Mrs. Abate's lap. He hit his head against the dashboard as she was thrown forward, sustaining a large bruise.

Although Mr. and Mrs. Abate were conscientious parents in most other respects, they completely ignored safety precautions in the car. The injury to their son was unnecessary. Knowing how to travel safely in a car with a child can prevent this type of accident.

Guidelines for using and obtaining a proper infant car carrier are presented in the equipment section on pages 42–43. This seat will protect your child and make it much easier to drive without interference. Strapping a baby in an improper infant seat or placing him in a small bed on the seat is not acceptable. Sudden stops or turns can cause these holders to fall or slide. Adult seat belts or harnesses are not suitable for infants and can be dangerous. It is also not safe for an infant to be held in someone's arms while riding in a car.

Always be sure that the infant carrier is properly attached to the car seat, because a child could sustain injury if a sudden stop or minor impact caused the carrier to fall off the seat. Take the few minutes extra time to be sure you know how to attach your infant carrier to the seat (usually with the seat belts). Be ready in advance so that when you take your baby home from the hospital you have an approved infant car carrier. (See also Traveling with Your Baby, page 155.)

Prevention of Burns

Burns are the second most common cause of accidental deaths or injury to young children. The majority of these accidents can be avoided or greatly reduced in severity by taking some very simple precautions to prevent fires and burns.

—Flush out-of-date medications down your toilet. Rinse out bottles before throwing them in the trash.

—If not already properly labeled, mark medicine containers with his name and the date of purchase.

—Keep track of the time when you give medicines by jotting them down on notes on the bathroom mirror, refrigerator, or other places that you frequently see.

FALLS

—Keep side rails up when you are not there.

—Take necessary precautions so that he cannot squirm, wriggle, or roll to the side of a crib, changing table, bed, couch, or other place and fall.

—Hold him securely when carrying or handling him.

POISONS

—Do not allow him to suck or chew on any items covered with lead-base paint (especially old toys).

—Do not store poisonous or inedible substances in food or beverage bottles or containers (e.g., gasoline in Coke bottles).

FIRE AND BURNS

—Hot beverages (coffee, tea, soup, etc.) should never be placed near your baby.

—Keep a fire extinguisher in a handy spot (preferably in or near the kitchen) and keep it up to date.

—Plug electrical outlets with blank covers or tape.

—Frayed electrical wire and cords should promptly be replaced.

—Do not smoke around him.

—Be sure to protect him, especially his eyes, from overexposure to the sun.

PETS

—Keep pets away from your baby unless you are there to protect him.

—Have your pets periodically treated for worms and fleas, and vaccinated for rabies and other diseases.

WHEN YOU LEAVE HIM IN SOMEONE ELSE'S CARE

—Make sure that the person is old enough and is responsible; this means doing screening in advance.

—Do not forget to post an emergency check list (see page 123) near the telephone, and a number where you or a relative or neighbor can definitely be reached.

—Be certain to give the person explicit instructions for your baby's care and the giving of any medications.

—Call once or twice while you are gone to make sure everything is okay.

WHEN YOU TAKE HIM AWAY FROM HOME

—Do not leave your infant alone or with a stranger when traveling.

—Be sure to bring along necessary equipment so that you won't have to put him in an unsafe place.

—Placing your baby in a securely fastened, well-designed auto seat is essential when riding in a car. The least safe place for an infant in a car is riding in the front seat in his mother's arms.

—Avoid

FEEDING

—Every family member should take an active part in protecting your baby and eliminating potential dangers. You cannot do the entire job on your own without their

—Carefully

full co-operation. Young children in particular, who are ignorant about a baby's capacities and limitations, may unknowingly jeopardize your efforts to protect your baby.

Mrs. Preston had difficulties when her two-year-old, Corinne, tried to pat and hug her new baby brother. Corinne did not know her own strength, and handled the new baby too roughly. She had to be taught to touch the baby very gently, and also kept away from him unless her mother was around to supervise.

Toddlers and preschoolers should be shown as well as told how to gently touch and handle a new baby. After the first demonstration and explanation, parents should stay with them to make sure that these important lessons have been understood, and are being followed. Young children should not be expected to know how to treat an infant, nor should they be expected to know anything else about a baby's capabilities. Do not expect your toddler or preschool child to follow your instructions, because their ability to take instruction is also limited. It is important to be present when your child is playing with the baby to supervise their interactions.

Mr. Swenson reported that his three-year-old son, Pete, tried to feed his new baby sister bits of food from his own dinner plate. This was Pete's way of expressing affection and making social contact with his sister. He obviously did not mean her any harm, but was totally ignorant about what kinds of food a baby can and cannot eat safely.

In some cases an older child who is jealous of a new baby may intentionally try to harm the infant. The baby must be protected from older children, particularly toddlers and preschoolers. Your other children should be given at least some information about how to conduct themselves in the presence of the baby and what kinds of things to avoid doing.

Family members can work together to make a home environment safe. Not just for the baby's sake, but also for the sake of each and every person living under the same roof.

FEEDING

Getting Roles and Responsibilities Straight

YOUR BABY'S PART IN FEEDING. Before you actually start feeding your infant, it is important to get roles and responsibilities straight. Although your tiny infant will be totally dependent upon you to see that he is adequately nourished, he will take a rather active part in the feeding exchange. He is born with sucking and swallowing reflexes, and a natural ability to let you know when he wants to be fed through vocalizations and "body" language. When you provide him with adequate amounts of food given in the proper form, he will suck until he is satisfied. Then he will relax, and most likely fall asleep feeling fulfilled. On the other hand, when he is not provided with enough food, he is likely to finish what he is offered and cry out for more food. His internal bodily sensations indicate to him when he is hungry so that he can signal this to you. He "knows" and lets you know when he has had enough to eat. Like all infants, he is an individual and will have his own "timetable" for feedings that best suits his needs.

YOUR PART IN FEEDING. Your role will be to satisfy your baby's needs by offering him enough food in the proper form and responding appropriately to his communications that he is either hungry or full. Another important aspect of your role is to keep the atmosphere friendly and non-pressured. When your baby feels relaxed, it will be much easier for him to digest his meal. No one enjoys eating when rushed, tense, or in unpleasant surroundings, especially not a tiny infant whose internal drives are so strong that he has to expend great amounts of energy when he eats. This accounts for perspiration during feedings. Your young infant has no real ability to wait, adapt, or postpone his meal until a comfortable mealtime atmosphere is available.

WORKING TOGETHER IS THE KEY. You will essentially be working along *with* your infant to ensure that he gets proper nourishment and all the food that he wants to eat. Together you will develop a comfortable, satisfactory arrangement that will enable him to grow and develop. Neither one of you is in complete charge of the feeding exchange, since you both have different roles and responsibilities. Mutual respect and co-operation are required.

Keeping your responsibilities in feeding in mind throughout infancy, and also during the toddler and preschool stage, will prevent you from trying to take over your baby's responsibilities. Thus you will realize that coaxing, pressuring, or forcing him to eat is not part of your job. If you used these tactics, you would be infringing upon his individual rights and responsibilities to decide how much he wants to eat.

Many feeding problems stem from the fact that well-meaning parents often try to take over their child's part in feedings. They coax and pressure him to eat more than he wants. He tenses up and rebels by losing his appetite and eating less. What could have been a low-keyed, pleasant feeding atmosphere turns into an occasion for arguments and bad feelings. The parent-child relationship suffers. This can easily be prevented if you stick to your responsibilities and allow your child to carry out his responsibilities without your interference. Both of you will be much happier. Your relationship with him will remain a positive one which is not clouded by bad feelings on either side.

Feeding Techniques

A full discussion of both breast- and bottle-feeding is found in Preparing for Parenthood, pages 54–78. What follows is specific information on feeding patterns, scheduling, and possible problems.

FEED YOUR BABY WHERE YOU ARE THE MOST COMFORTABLE. It is advisable to start feeding your baby wherever you can make yourself most comfortable. Choosing a quiet place is often helpful so that distractions can be kept to a minimum. It is a good practice to gather all of the equipment you will need ahead of time, and have it close at hand before you begin. Spend an extra few minutes getting yourself in a positive frame of mind before interacting with your baby. If you are anxious or upset, he may be able to sense that you are tense. This may interfere with your ability to nurse, or his ability to eat or digest the breast milk or formula.

HOLDING YOUR BABY DURING FEEDINGS IS IMPORTANT. In order to maintain a warm, affectionate interaction with your baby, and provide him with the close physical contact that will make him feel loved and secure, it is important to hold him lovingly during his feedings. Most mothers prefer to sit in a comfortable armchair or rocking chair and hold their babies in a similar position to that which would be used in a sitting-up breast-feeding position (see page 58). This is the most popular position, but you may want to try others, depending upon what feels the most comfortable for you and your baby. Whichever position you select, make sure that you hold your baby close to you.

Propping the bottle is not recommended. Never leave your baby to eat on his own. He is too weak and helpless to manipulate the nipple or bottle by himself, or shift his position if this becomes necessary. There is a chance that he could choke or experience other difficulties if left on his own. Cuddling and affection are important aspects of the feeding exchange, and for this reason, as well, propping the bottle is not acceptable.

HOW TO HOLD THE BOTTLE. The manner in which you hold the bottle depends upon the type of bottle that you are using. Using a classic bottle, you would hold the bottle so that the nipple is lower than the rest of the bottle. Make sure that the nipple is constantly full of formula, otherwise he will take in air, not formula.

New bottle equipment is now available enabling the bottle to be held in an upright position. Special, inexpensive devices that work like a straw can be purchased to fit most standard, wide-neck bottles. They fit onto the nipple and are designed to reduce the air swallowed as the infant nurses. The infant sucks on the upright bottle and the milk goes up into the nipple.

At first you may have to help your baby to get the nipple properly positioned in his mouth. Ease it into his mouth rather than poking or shoving it. It is not necessary for you to keep pulling the nipple out of your infant's mouth. Let him take control of the flow of formula, and stop sucking whenever he wants. He will have his own individual sucking pattern. You do not have to worry about this aspect. If he pauses for a bit, or stops sucking for a moment, he may resume again after this brief pause. You might try gently turning the bottle in his mouth or slightly pulling it away, since this slight movement may stimulate him to resume sucking.

BURPING YOUR BABY. How to burp your baby is discussed on page 136.

HOW MUCH FORMULA TO GIVE YOUR BABY. Many mothers wonder how much formula their babies need. Remember that all babies are individuals and have different needs as well as different appetites. Some babies take approximately the same number of ounces of formula at each feeding. Other babies have appetites which are much less predictable. The number of ounces of formula your baby takes can vary on a daily basis, or from one meal to another, depending upon many factors.

It is best to give your baby as much formula as he wants to take at each feeding. Always put a little more formula into his bottle than he usually takes just in case he is slightly hungrier at a particular feeding. The aim is to provide him with plenty of formula so that he can take what he wants. It is not advisable for you to encourage him to take a lot of milk in a short time or to pressure him to take more than he wants. Allow him to consume what he wants and needs, since this is *his* responsibility.

HOW LONG SHOULD FEEDING SESSIONS LAST? There is no one answer to how long feeding sessions should last. A lot depends upon how hungry a baby is, and his style of eating. There is variability in the duration of feedings. Fast eaters may gobble up their formulas and be satisfied with feedings of ten minutes or less. Slow eaters and dawdlers may take as long as half an hour to forty-five minutes. In general, there is no reason to prolong a feeding beyond forty-five minutes. In the majority of cases, your baby's look of satisfaction and relaxation will be the best sign that he has taken in enough formula to meet his needs. After a few weeks, you will be able to more easily judge by his behavior pattern when his appetite is satisfied.

DIFFERENT STYLES OF NURSING. All babies have their own personalities and their own style of nursing. One baby will suck very vigorously until he has emptied both breasts or his bottle. Another will take his sweet time and take brief catnaps during the nursing period. Some have the annoying habit of drifting off to sleep immediately after they are positioned at the breast or bottle and begin to suck. A few, who experience initial difficulty in securing the breast or bottle or take in very little milk, become fussy, angry, or give up and cry or go back to sleep.

The restless, fussy, and sleepy baby may make feeding times more difficult on a mother or father. Situations in which a baby just does not seem interested in nursing, or does not nurse well, can naturally cause a mother who is breast-feeding to become concerned and uneasy. This, in turn, can affect her ability to nurse.

It is reassuring to know that there is a better than even chance that the young infant will gradually outgrow these trying behaviors as he matures over the first month or two. There are a few suggestions that you might find helpful.

Try to remain calm and in a positive frame of mind. Your infant simply is very immature, so there is no reason for you to think that you are doing anything wrong and feel bad. Keep in mind that excessive worry and tension may interfere with your flow of milk, if you are breast-feeding.

If you are breast-feeding and he has difficulty securing your areola, do your best to help him get the entire areola at the beginning of each nursing period. In case you are bottle-feeding, check to be sure that the nipple holes are not plugged, and that they are large enough to allow milk to flow through them easily. See page 132.

Whether you are feeding by breast or bottle, check your position too, to make sure both you and your baby are comfortable, and that his head is held higher than his body. Be certain that you are holding the bottle properly. Examine the entire situation and see whether you can come up with any reasons why he is not nursing well. Sometimes you may be able to locate a problem and, with a minor adjustment, correct it very easily.

Should your baby start to drift off to sleep or squirm around restlessly after nursing only briefly at one breast, try offering him the other breast. This change may make it easier for him to take in milk. If you are bottle-feeding, sometimes rotating the bottle in his mouth, tickling his cheek or chin, or giving it a gentle tug away from his mouth may encourage him to resume sucking. Some babies just cannot seem to stay awake for the entire nursing period.

Falling asleep after he has sucked for a few minutes, your baby may stay asleep for a short time and then awaken and start sucking vigorously again. There is no real need to stop the feeding, although this behavior can prolong it. Guard against letting feedings drag out beyond forty-five minutes whether you are breast- or bottle-feeding, but especially if breast-feeding, since this can result in sore nipples. When he is really hungry, you will be the first to know.

After five to ten minutes of nursing some babies drift off to sleep and then wake up and begin to cry the moment they are placed in their cribs. In this situation, a baby has probably taken in sufficient nourishment to tide him over for about two hours. Try burping him if he starts to cry. It could be that he has taken in a lot of air and simply needs to bring it up. He might also be crying just because he is irritated or just having a bad day. You can try to wait and not put him back to your breasts or offer him a bottle, but you would not want to ignore his crying if it is really out of hunger.

Individual differences among babies' nursing styles make each mother-infant feeding exchange unique. Some of you will initially have it easier than others. After a few weeks when both you and your infant have gained in experience and had time to adjust to one another, feeding will not seem as confusing.

SPECIAL CONSIDERATIONS IN BOTTLE-FEEDING. The size and number of the nipple holes will determine the flow of milk. The nipple holes should be large enough to allow your baby to take in milk easily when he sucks, but not so large that milk just pours out of them in a continuous stream even when he is not sucking. There is a greater chance that the nipple holes will be too small than too large. If they are too small, your baby will have to exert more effort to get any formula. He may get annoyed and fatigued before finishing his feeding and drift off to sleep, unfulfilled and still hungry, but physically exhausted.

Hold the nipple up to a light to examine the holes. In the event that you hardly see any light coming through the nipple, this is a sign that the holes are too small or too few in number. Another way to check is to tilt a full bottle as you would during a feeding. If all that comes out are slow drops of formula, this also indicates that the holes should be enlarged. In such a situation, first check the cap of the bottle. Loosen it slightly and see whether the milk flows out more easily. You can make adjustments in the size of the nipple holes, if this does not happen.

Nipple holes that are too small can be enlarged, or new holes can be made. An easy method of enlarging nipple holes is as follows. Obtain a fine sewing needle. Take hold of the dull end with a small pliers or stick the dull .end into a potato. Sterilize the needle by holding the fine point in a candle flame or in the flame of a gas stove. Wait until the needle tip turns red, let it cool a minute or two, and then poke a hole in the nipple with it. Go slowly and test your results. Avoid enlarging the holes too much or poking too many new holes, since the milk may begin to pour out in a fast, continuous spray or stream. When this occurs, you have gone too far. A steady flow of drops is what you are aiming for.

As your baby gets older, the nipple holes can be further enlarged. Nipple holes that are too large may be compensated for by tightening the cap on the bottle. This sometimes helps to make the milk flow out more slowly. If this does not help, save the nipples for later use.

It is advisable to check the condition of the nipples from time to time, especially as your baby grows older. Some children chew on the nipples, and after a while the nipples can begin to fall apart, making it possible for a baby to swallow a piece. Nipples that are not in good condition should promptly be replaced.

There are a variety of nipples available in most stores. When you go to purchase them, you will notice that some are designed for the young infant, and others for the older baby. Also note that nipples can be purchased according to their intended use for water, juice, and even thin cereal.

Nipple holes with an X-shaped cut on the top are less likely to become clogged than other types with just holes. You can buy this kind of nipple, or make the special cuts in the nipples that you already have. Press the tip of the nipple together and with a fine, sharp scissors or single-edge razor blade, make two right angle slits on the top. Holes that have become clogged can be unclogged with a fine needle before they are sterilized.

BABIES OUTGROW THEIR FORMULAS. As your baby grows older, his nutritional requirements will change. His diet will have to be adjusted so that it continues to satisfy his individual needs. How will you know if he has outgrown his formula? This is a difficult question which can only be answered properly by consulting your physician and discussing your baby's behavior.

From observing your baby's behavior, you may notice that he is crying more often because he is hungry, is demanding feedings at more frequent intervals than in the past, and/or is gobbling up his regular amount of formula in no time and still hunting for more to eat. Whenever it is appropriate, your doctor will prescribe a formula change. Do not make adjustments in formula on your own since this may result in digestive difficulties or other problems.

Common Considerations in Breast-feeding and Bottle-feeding

FEEDING PATTERNS. Given two babies born on the same day, it is doubtful that they will get hungry at exactly the same times each day and need or want exactly the same amount of food. There is no one schedule that is well suited to every single baby or for that matter every single parent. One baby may initially need to be fed every two hours. Another may want to eat every three or four hours. Still another may want food at completely unpredictable times.

The second important aspect related to feeding schedules is the young infant's immature body and strong hunger drives. New infants have a shortened stomach-emptying time and as soon as the stomach is emptied, the child feels hungry again. The younger and smaller the infant, the shorter is the emptying time, and the more frequent is the desire for food. Premature infants and low birth weight infants are fed as frequently as every two or three hours, whereas full-term infants usually average about every three to four hours.

Your baby is not capable of eating three meals a day as you do. He gets hungry at very frequent intervals during both day and night, and usually cries from hunger at those times. He has extreme difficulty adapting or waiting awhile, because he is very immature and mainly governed by his strong inner needs, a major one being a need for food. When the young baby gets hungry, he does not just want food, he craves it.

Because of an infant's immaturity, you cannot expect more patience from him than he is initially capable of giving. Since, as we have seen, his earliest experiences in regard to such an important area of his life as feeding may influence his attitudes and feelings about his environment, you will undoubtedly not want him to associate long periods of crying and feelings of being ignored or anger with you with meals. In order to avoid this negative association and for his own well-being, you should be responsive to his hunger cries. Do not make him wait for long periods of time for food when he is really famished.

As the infant grows older and his body matures, he consumes more at each feeding and requires fewer feedings. In the majority of cases, a baby's mealtimes also become more regular. It is easier after the first month or two to predict his feedings, and, therefore, scheduling meals at regular intervals should be possible.

So far we have been concentrating upon babies' needs, but parents have needs, too, such as the need for rest, relaxation, and peace and quiet. During the first few months, parents' needs are usually at odds with their baby's needs. They cannot be responsive to the baby's needs without sacrificing a bit. They must do the adjusting, compromising, and adapting in the short term. This seems like the most logical solution until their infant becomes capable of adapting.

Just as soon as a baby begins to be capable of waiting for a while for his feedings, and being shifted to a more regular schedule, parents can take advantage of this. They can gently guide him into a feeding pattern that suits their needs, and, at the same time does not ignore his individual eating patterns.

Parents who do not mind feeding their babies whenever they are hungry can continue to follow their lead. The aim is eventually to have everyone satisfied, without one person compromising a great deal more than the other.

COMMON SENSE APPROACH TO FEEDING SCHEDULES. The initial feeding schedule in the hospital will depend partly upon whether or not your infant will be placed in a nursery or in your room. He will probably be brought to you every few hours if kept in a nursery. If you are at home or using a rooming-in situation in the hospital, you can usually feed him whenever he appears to be hungry. In some hospitals mothers are not awakened for middle-of-the-night feedings so that they have more of an opportunity to rest.

Your doctor will discuss scheduling feedings with you before you are discharged from the hospital. Based upon your baby's physical condition, and also your lifestyle, the doctor may suggest a feeding schedule that best suits both you and your baby. In case you are delivering at home, you can call your physician and arrange for an appointment so that your baby can be examined and you can discuss an appropriate feeding schedule.

There are numerous approaches to feeding schedules. As long as a schedule is somewhat flexible and a baby is not left crying out of hunger for long periods of time, it should work well for both of you.

Given that an infant is not really capable of adapting to any real extent to parents' needs, pediatricians frequently advise that he be fed as often as he is *really hungry* during the first several weeks, not necessarily each time he cries, since he may sometimes cry for reasons other than hunger. This is sometimes referred to as a "self-demand" schedule.

Should a baby sleep for more than three and a half to four hours during the daytime without awakening and wanting to be fed, parents can wake him and feed him in an attempt to guide him toward a more regular schedule. At night, on the other hand, if a baby goes for four hours without demanding a feeding, it is usually recommended that parents refrain from waking him. The aim is to have him drop night feedings just as soon as he is able to do so.

After a period of about a month or two, a baby matures and his hunger patterns begin to change. He can go for longer stretches of time between meals, and can sleep through the night without awakening and wanting to be fed. Some babies, of course, will quickly develop more regular feeding schedules, while others continue to have rather unpredictable patterns beyond the first six to eight weeks.

After the first month or month and a half, if your infant still demands very frequent feedings during both day and night, you and your physician may decide that it is time to guide him toward a more regular pattern. You would do this by trying to hold off offering him food until three and a half to four hours have passed since his last feeding. Sometimes offering some water or small amounts of fruit juice will be sufficient to tide a baby over until his next feeding. Gradually, you will also try to get him to sleep through the night without needing to be fed, by not giving him nourishment as soon as he starts to cry out of hunger. Let him cry for about ten minutes or so, and see whether he will fall back to sleep. If not, offer him some water, since this may satisfy his appetite.

Young infants will experience growth spurts at periodic intervals, and at those times may require larger amounts of milk to satisfy their increased appetites. Parents who are bottle-feeding can simply place a couple of extra ounces of formula in the bottle if they notice that their baby suddenly wants to be fed at more frequent intervals. Nursing mothers, on the other hand, may have more difficulty adapting to their baby's new milk demands. When a growth spurt occurs, for several days they may have to nurse their child more frequently in order to build up their milk supply.

A nursing mother whose baby has been feeding at intervals of every four hours, for instance, may, after about a month and a half (this will vary), suddenly notice the child wants to be fed every two and one half to three hours. Rather than jumping to the conclusion that her milk supply is insufficient, she can discuss this situation with her baby's doctor. In all likelihood, the infant is experiencing a growth spurt, and if the mother feeds him at more frequent intervals for a period of time until her milk supply increases, he will once again stretch out to longer intervals between feedings. This situation can be especially disturbing to a nursing mother who is anxious for her baby to shift to a more regular schedule with fewer feedings. But realizing why a slight regression is occurring should help to put her mind at ease.

It is not uncommon for mothers who nurse to complain more than bottle-feeding parents about having difficulty getting their babies onto a regular schedule. However, it is important also to understand that a woman's milk supply can vary from feeding to feeding, and may be diminished at certain times of the day. This will naturally affect her baby's eating pattern and schedule. Bottle-fed babies, on the other hand, have a steady amount of formula offered at each feeding, and may thus have an easier time adjusting to a more regular schedule.

Babies differ as to the age at which they are ready to omit the middle-of-the-night feeding. Most are willing to forego it within the first three months. Parents of babies who are able to give up the middle-of-the-night feeding after three or four weeks are very lucky, indeed. Keep in mind that before you allow your baby to sleep through his last late evening feeding, it is usually advisable to encourage him to give up his middle-of-the-night meal. If he has not as yet given it up, but is capable of foregoing his late evening feeding, you should wake him up for it. Otherwise, he is almost sure to be famished during the night.

Some babies will cry and become irritable when a more regular schedule is initiated by their parents. Listening to a baby cry is unnerving for most parents, particularly in the middle of the night. You may have to grin and bear it or else wait for a week or two and then try again.

The kind of feeding schedule that you select is not as important as seeing that your baby's needs are met, and that as he matures, your needs are also considered. You should not be overburdened with very frequent daily feedings or unnecessary feedings during the night. After all, if this continued, you would be exhausted as well as resentful. No matter how irregular your infant's hunger patterns are during the first several weeks or the first few months, he will probably establish more regular patterns shortly thereafter, so do not give up hope.

Below are listed some of the more common feeding schedules. You will develop your own, personalized feeding schedule depending upon your baby's needs, his readiness to adapt, and your lifestyle.

Four-hour schedule: feedings at 6 A.M., 10 A.M., 2 P.M., 6 P.M., 10 P.M., 2 A.M.

Substitute four-hour schedule: feedings at 7 A.M., 11 A.M., 3 P.M., 7 P.M., 11 P.M., 3 A.M.

Three-hour schedule (four hours at night): feedings at 6 A.M., 9 A.M., 12 noon, 3 P.M., 6 P.M., 10 P.M., 2 A.M.

BURPING YOUR BABY IS NECESSARY. All babies take in some air when they suck on a breast or bottle. Air that gathers in a baby's belly causes him some discomfort, and may interfere with his ability to finish his meal. Your baby is not capable of completely bringing up the air on his own, so he will be relying upon you to help alleviate his discomfort.

Babies differ in how much air they swallow, and how often they need to be burped. Frequently, those who eat very fast and vigorously take in a lot of air during the first part of a feeding. They may pause during the feeding and look mighty uncomfortable, or even pull away from the nipple. It is not necessary to interrupt their meal by burping them if they make no indication that this is a problem, but some babies require this, even as many as two to three times. It may take a couple of weeks for you to determine how often your baby needs to be burped. The only thing to do until you are more experienced is to stay "tuned in" to his behavior. The majority of babies need to be burped after their feedings, and nursing mothers can try burping their baby before they shift to the second breast, as well as after the feeding.

There are several ways to help your baby bring up swallowed air. The most common way is to hold him up to your shoulder with the front of his body against yours, and gently rub or pat his back. You can also slowly lower him face downward on your lap and massage his back or sit him up in your lap and pat his back or rub his belly. You can experiment with these methods in order to find the most effective way of burping him.

In case your infant does not bring up the air right away when you try one or more of these methods, do not panic. You can try lying him on his back for only a minute or two and then holding him to your shoulder. Many experienced mothers have found this variation to work well. Place him face downward on his crib, if nothing else seems to work, and he may eventually burp on his own. If you have been unsuccessful in burping him, avoid placing him on his back. This position makes it difficult for him to bring up air, and there is a chance that he may bring up milk that could make him choke.

When you burp your infant, he may dribble and bring up some food along with the air. Do not worry about this, since it is common, particularly in bottle-fed babies. Place a diaper or some other material over your shoulder when you burp him to protect your clothes from being soiled.

SPITTING UP MILK AFTER FEEDINGS. Spitting up small amounts of milk is quite common during the early months. Just be sure that you are not overfeeding him by pushing him to take more milk than he wants, since he may be spitting up the excess, along with burping. Make sure that you are burping him frequently enough.

As long as your doctor tells you that he is gaining weight satisfactorily and is healthy, relax. Chances are that in spite of the fact that it seems that he is spitting up a lot of milk, he is only spitting up a very small portion of his total milk intake. Sometimes when the feeding atmosphere is tense, rushed, or unpleasant, a baby will have difficulty digesting his meal, and will bring up more milk than usual when he burps. Quite often a baby's digestive system is simply not working efficiently or smoothly during the first several weeks, and it has nothing to do with the feeding atmosphere or parental handling. As he matures, he will probably spit up less frequently. In some cases, a change in formula may be needed so that it is more easily digested by your baby, although you should refrain from making formula adjustments without the advice of your doctor.

Spitting up large quantities of milk after each feeding and/or forcefully projecting food from his mouth after feedings should be brought promptly to the attention of your physician. This is clearly not the routine type of spitting up.

ADDING SUBSTANCES TO THE DIET. *Vitamins* are essential food substances and are usually found in the full natural diet. Infants who are only receiving milk do not receive a full diet. Even though breast milk contains certain vitamins, it does not contain all of those that are currently recommended. Most prepared infant formulas are fortified with iron and enriched with vitamins. It is unlikely that prepared formulas need to be supplemented with additional vitamins.

Whether a baby is being fed by breast or bottle, physicians may still recommend that additional vitamins be given, usually vitamins C, D, and A and iron. Adults can get these vitamins by eating a variety of foods, and maintaining a well-balanced diet without supplementation. Babies, however, are limited in their ability to digest different food. They may not get the vitamins needed, depending upon the type of formula given, because they are receiving a limited milk diet. Special attention must be given to ensure that they are receiving sufficient amounts of those vitamins lacking in the milk.

Before you leave the hospital, your doctor may prescribe a vitamin preparation for your baby, and give you instructions for how to give it. The vitamins, unless provided in the packaged formula, generally come in a small bottle with a dropper and are squeezed into the side of the baby's mouth before a feeding on a daily basis. They are not squirted toward the back of his throat, since this could cause choking or gagging. Giving your baby his daily vitamins is an important part of your regular basic care regimen. Be sure to stick to the exact dosage that your doctor prescribes.

Fluoride is another substance that pediatricians occasionally recommend as a supplement to a baby's diet. This substance is beneficial for the teeth, since it makes them stronger and helps in preventing tooth decay. In many cities, fluoride is regularly added to the public water supply and some doctors feel that it is unnecessary to give additional fluoride. Many physicians advise parents to offer fluoride during the early months even if city water contains it. If your doctor feels that it would be valuable for your baby to receive fluoride, he or she will probably give you a prescription and specific instructions before you are discharged from the hospital. In many cases a doctor will prescribe a vitamin preparation that also contains fluoride.

Provided that a baby is eating regularly, he will be taking in enough fluids to satisfy him. Offering *additional fluids* may not be necessary except when he has a fever or is in a very warm climate or room, causing excessive water loss because of excessive perspiration. Some thirsty babies like to take a few ounces of *water* between feedings, while others refuse it. Sometimes offering some plain or slightly sweetened water will help to keep a baby who is hungry between meals satisfied, but if he wants something more substantial, giving him water will not do the trick. Avoid offering water just before a meal, since this may decrease a baby's appetite.

Knowing that your supply of water is acceptable (check with your local health department), your doctor may tell you that it is all right to offer your baby tap water from a bottle. In some cases physicians feel that it is safer to boil the water for several minutes (approximately 5 minutes) and then let it cool until it is slightly warm or reaches room temperature before offering it. This kills any bacteria or other organisms.

A sufficient quantity of water can be boiled each morning and then poured into very clean or sterilized bottles, depending upon what your doctor recommends. If you are adding small amounts of sugar or corn syrup to the boiled water (approximately ½ teaspoon to 16 ounces—check with your doctor on the amount), be sure to taste the water before giving it just to ensure that you have not added the wrong substance by mistake.

INTRODUCTION OF SOLID FOODS. Around the turn of the century, the common practice was not to begin a baby on solid foods until the first year of life had passed. Over the last fifty years, doctors and parents have introduced solid foods at earlier and earlier times in the infant's life. They found that some babies, even as early as two to six weeks, could take solid foods and do well on them.

Several reasons were given for starting solid foods during the first half year of life. Some physicians felt that the baby who started solid foods during this time found it easier to get used to them than later in infancy, when he became fussier. They also felt that solid foods could add substances to the diet that were not found in milk in high quantity, especially iron. Parents enthusiastically took to giving solid foods earlier and earlier because this reflected that their babies were more "mature." In fact, how soon a baby began taking solid foods became a competitive issue among some parents.

The experience doctors and parents have gained over the last twenty years in starting babies on solid foods in the first few months of life has indicated that this is not the time to introduce solid foods into the child's diet. It has been realized that there were few, if any, benefits for the baby in starting solids early, and, in fact, many babies developed difficulties in tolerating solids before they were ready.

Although some babies can accept starting solid foods at an early stage, the immature digestive system of most young infants before six months of age cannot handle many of the more complex food sources, such as starch, that are present in solid foods. Some of these complex substances will pass right through the digestive system and out with the bowel movement, providing little or no additional nutritional benefit over milk to the child. Doctors have also demonstrated that human milk and formula supplemented with the appropriate vitamins and minerals provide more than enough food source for the first six months of life, making it unnecessary from a nutritional point of view to introduce solids before the age of six months.

Many babies have difficulty digesting solid foods at an early age. They become colicky and irritable when forced to take a solid diet. Babies may also more easily develop problems with bowel movements when taking solid foods in the first several months.

In children who are susceptible to developing allergies, introducing solid foods early is more likely to cause an allergic reaction. In general, the older the child is when receiving a new type of food, the less likely he will be to develop an allergy to it.

Infants who are fed solid food early seem to have a high incidence of being overweight. Overfeeding an infant may increase the number of fat cells in the body that develop during this stage of life. Doctors now believe that if an infant develops a large number of fat cells due to overfeeding early in life, this can sometimes lead to problems of obesity later in adulthood.

The American Academy of Pediatrics recommends that solid foods be introduced after the first six months of life. For this reason, our discussion of how to introduce solid foods is presented in Infancy 6 on pages 304–13.

ABOUT WEIGHT GAIN. Many parents are naturally curious about how much weight their baby is gaining, particularly parents of premature babies who tend to feel very relieved and proud each time their baby gains even a tiny amount of weight. The infant is growing at a very rapid rate, particularly during the first six months. This is the fastest growth rate once the baby is born. The growth rate for premature infants is even more rapid during the first month or two after birth. It is important to recognize that the premature birth weight is less than a term infant's and this difference in weight often takes as much as a year or two to be made up.

Remember that a baby's weight, like an adult's, can vary from day to day. It is the over-all weekly and monthly trends in your baby's weight which should be followed, not his daily fluctuations. Following your baby's weight gain can be enjoyable, but it should not become an obsession. Weigh him once, or at the most, twice a week. Most doctors say that it is unnecessary for parents to chart daily weights. When you take your baby for his regular check-ups, he will be weighed and your doctor will let you know if he is gaining satisfactory amounts of weight.

COLIC. The term "colicky" baby is often used to describe a baby who cries a lot, and seems cranky and irritable. Such a "colicky" baby, however, may not necessarily have the condition known as colic. Generally speaking, a baby with colic cries a great deal during the first few months. His cries are loud, piercing, and shrill-sounding. He often thrashes about as he cries, and takes in a lot of air, resulting in abdominal distension. His body may become rigid at times, and he may raise his knees toward his chest and pass a lot of gas, looking as though he is experiencing pain.

Sometimes his screaming and crying lasts for several hours at a stretch, and often it seems that nothing his parents do to try to comfort him or calm him down is effective for any length of time. Often he cries harder after, rather than prior to his regular feedings, and in many cases he is a good and vigorous eater. In fact, he may gobble up his meal very quickly, and in doing so may take in a lot of air. He may constantly look tense, irritated, and uncomfortable. He may also seem overly jumpy or sensitive to changes in his surroundings.

Unfortunately, the cause of colic is still somewhat of a mystery in medicine. Doctors often speculate that colic occurs when a lot of air is swallowed and gets lodged in a baby's intestinal tract. This causes him discomfort and cramps. Some professionals attribute colic to the fact that a baby's digestive system is not yet working smoothly, or to an overly sensitive intestinal tract. Still others claim that improper handling at feeding time or an overly tense and unpleasant feeding atmosphere contributes to the condition of colic. Babies with colic are not usually sick. Quite to the contrary, in the vast majority of cases these babies seem to be quite healthy. They are gaining weight at acceptable rates and are developing well.

It is not uncommon for a baby who generally seems happy, healthy, and contented to have one or more brief digestive upsets or spells of colic during the first few months of life. Some babies appear to be more or less regularly in distress from colic throughout the first three months. Most instances of colic seem to disappear almost "magically" after the third month of life, regardless of the various therapeutic regimens tried, although a rare baby with severe colic may be troubled by it for a few additional months.

Contact your pediatrician or family doctor if your baby develops symptoms of colic. Sometimes a doctor, based upon his or her years of experience in dealing with colic, will prescribe a medication, an adjustment in formula, or other measures in order to help this condition. In addition, your doctor can reassure you that there is nothing physically wrong with your baby.

Since air in a baby's intestinal tract is believed by many to be a main cause of colic, it is useful to be certain that you are doing an effective job of burping your infant at feeding times. You might try burping him after five or ten minutes of sucking, for example, particularly if he eats quickly. Stick to the ten minutes maximum on each breast during each feeding, since in sucking on an empty breast he will take in a lot of air. In bottle-feeding, make sure that the nipple holes are the right size. If they are too small, your baby will take in air as he works hard at drawing out milk. Nipple holes that are too large result in the milk coming out too fast, causing difficulty in swallowing, gagging, and cutting down on sucking time.

Another positive step to take is to be certain that the atmosphere at feeding times fosters good digestion. It may be best to feed your baby in a private place, away from noises and distractions, where both of you can have some peace and quiet.

Caring for and living with a "colicky" baby is not easy, and may greatly trouble and disturb you. Feelings of anger, resentment, helplessness, insecurity, and so forth, are commonly expressed by parents of babies who develop colic. These feelings and emotions are important to recognize and put into perspective. See pages 185–86 of the Family Feelings and Concerns section.

THUMB-SUCKING IN EARLY INFANCY

Thumb-sucking is a common occurrence among babies, but not every baby will engage in this activity. Some babies begin sucking their thumbs in the first few weeks, although most start more commonly during the first few months. In lieu of or in addition to thumb-sucking, fingers or wrists may also be sucked.

Many Possible Reasons for Thumb-sucking

Controversy exists over why thumb-sucking is initiated and what it signifies. There can be many reasons for its occurrence. One can speculate that babies suck their thumbs because they are hungry, because they have to satisfy their need to suck, because it helps to make them more relaxed, or because they derive pleasure from it.

It is often thought that babies who are fed every three, as opposed to four, hours, and who are breast-fed will be less prone to sucking their thumbs. They tend to receive more sucking satisfaction in early infancy. Yet, these babies may also suck their thumbs in the early months for no obvious reason. Thumb-sucking has been visualized in utero and in the newborn nursery so there may be a certain reflexive aspect or several explanations for it.

Handling Thumb-sucking

In the early weeks, you should check to see whether your baby is thumb-sucking out of hunger. Make sure he is getting enough to eat. Also make sure that you do not cut short his feedings. Allow him to determine when he has had enough sucking.

This is easy for nursing mothers, whose babies do tend to have more opportunities to satisfy their sucking need during feedings. With bottle-fed babies, this is more difficult. Once the bottle is emptied, it is taken away, even though they may desire further sucking. If they continue to suck on an empty bottle, all they will take in is air, and this will make them feel very uncomfortable.

When a bottle-fed baby grows older and is strong and efficient enough to empty the bottle in about ten, as opposed to twenty, minutes, parents may find him doing extracurricular sucking on his thumb. This is a fairly common time for thumb-sucking to begin. A positive step to take in trying to increase the time it takes for him to empty the bottle, and thus increase total sucking time, is to purchase new nipples so that the holes are smaller. The baby will therefore have to suck longer and harder to get his milk.

As the baby grows older and requires fewer feedings, parents sometimes notice the emergence of thumb-sucking. In the event that a baby begins to suck his thumb just after one feeding has been eliminated, this could indicate that he is not receiving sufficient sucking to satisfy his need or desire. If it is not too inconvenient to keep the feeding going awhile longer, allowing him to have this extra opportunity to suck may result in a decrease in thumb-sucking. Going slowly on dropping feedings with a baby who does a lot of thumb-sucking is a good idea.

Whatever the reason may be behind thumb-sucking, many babies do it in spite of the fact that they are happy and receiving plenty to eat as well as ample attention and stimulation. Thumb-sucking represents a normal aspect of a baby's development. Initially, babies use their sucking and rooting reflexes when they suck their thumbs. As babies develop after the first few weeks, they may happen to suck their thumbs as they explore with their mouths.

Thumb-sucking is nothing for you to worry about at this stage, so relax. There is really nothing that you have to do about it. It is very common for young infants to suck their thumbs, and this is certainly no indication that you are doing anything wrong, or that your baby is unhappy. Many happy, healthy babies do some extra-curricular sucking, so try to ignore this activity. More information on thumb-sucking later in infancy is presented on pages 332–33.

Do Not Confuse Thumb-sucking with Teething

During the period of time when babies begin teething, often after the first three to four months, they may begin to nibble and gnaw on their thumbs and/or fingers. Chewing on the fingers serves as a natural outlet for them at this time, and does not necessarily mean that they have developed thumb-sucking as a habit. Babies who have been thumb-sucking prior to the teething period are often seen frequently to alternate between gnawing and sucking on their fingers, unlike the other babies who do no sucking and simply chew. There is a good chance that the real thumb-suckers will continue sucking beyond the age at which their teeth erupt while the other babies may discontinue finger chewing once the teeth come in.

PACIFIERS

A pacifier is a flexible, rubber nipple attached to a flat, round disc. Whether or not parents should allow their babies to suck on pacifiers is a touchy issue around which there exists quite a bit of controversy. Some professionals claim that a pacifier can be quite useful during the early months: It may provide extra opportunities for sucking that many or even most babies require; it may satisfy a baby when he starts to cry or gets irritable before his regular feeding times; and may keep a baby from sucking on his fingers or thumb.

Professionals who advise against offering a pacifier claim that it does not keep a baby from sucking on his thumb. They also claim that it is frequently used improperly by parents when they offer it in place of food when a baby is really hungry, or they stick it in his mouth every time he begins to get cranky.

Discuss the pros and cons of pacifier use with your baby's doctor, if you are wondering about whether or not to offer a pacifier to your baby. Provided that it is used appropriately, it is doubtful that offering a pacifier will in any way be harmful for your child, and it may offer him extra opportunities for sucking. There are several pacifiers in recent years, however, that have been proven to be dangerous. If the disc is not large enough, there is a possibility that a baby could swallow it and choke on it. Or, when there is liquid in the pacifier, it may leak out, and this could be dangerous. Check with the Consumer Product Safety Commission in your state to be certain that the pacifier you select meets proper safety standards.

There is an added consideration regarding the misuse of pacifiers. If the pacifier is dropped and becomes contaminated, it represents a means of introducing dirt or germs into your baby's mouth. It is important to keep his pacifier clean. Do not place a pacifier that has dropped to the floor back into his mouth. Take a minute and wash it first. More information on the use of pacifiers is presented on pages 333–34. Be sure not to attach a string or cord to the pacifier, since it may get tangled around the neck.

There are several styles of pacifiers available in most larger drugstores or children's stores. Some pacifiers are traditionally shaped, others claim to be shaped more like a mother's nipple, and still others are called orthodontic exercisers. If you have any questions regarding which to buy, you can check with your baby's doctor. A baby may also have his own preferences. Nursing mothers who want to offer a pacifier may find that when an occasional relief bottle of formula is given, it is a good idea to have the bottle nipple shaped like the pacifier nipple. This is because a baby who becomes accustomed to sucking on a pacifier of a certain shape may more readily take a bottle whose nipple is similar to the pacifier.

THE BABY'S TEETH

A few babies are born with teeth. This is not very common. Eruption of teeth in babies is more likely to begin when they are about six months old. There is wide variation in the age at which babies cut their first teeth. Familiarize yourself with the information on teeth in Infancy 6, pages 314–17, if your baby cuts his first tooth at any point during the first five months.

BATHING

In keeping your baby clean it is best to rely upon good common sense. Many parents prefer to bathe their babies every day, although you may find it more convenient to do so every other day. Certain areas of his body which get dirty very quickly (mainly the area around his mouth and organs of elimination) should be cleaned as often as necessary. This generally means more than once a day. Many parents find themselves using disposable, moist towelettes to handle some of the frequent small clean-up jobs.

Keeping the diaper area clean is one of the more unpleasant but necessary responsibilities that goes along with being a parent. Although you do not have to race to wash and change him the moment you feel or smell wet or soiled diapers, it is advisable to change him without a long delay. Prolonged contact with bodily waste products can result in irritation to sensitive skin, secondary infections, and rashes. Washing the diaper area with soap and water on a regular basis, and drying it thoroughly before putting on a fresh diaper can help prevent rashes from developing.

Giving a baby a bath is really quite a simple procedure. After a few practice sessions giving a friend's baby or even a doll a bath, you will be as much of an expert as anyone. Many of you will also have an opportunity to bathe your baby with the guidance of a nurse before being discharged from the hospital.

Keep in mind that since bathing your baby will be part of your daily routine when he is awake, you should try to make this experience as pleasant as possible. The close physical contact and the interaction between you at bath time will be an important avenue through which your relationship will build. Many parents find that talking and singing to their baby during bathing and changing procedures help to relax him, making these necessary activities more enjoyable and more of a social experience.

Bathing Equipment

A modest amount of basic equipment will be necessary for bathing your infant. See page 43 for a list of basic care items, including items necessary for bathing.

There are various types of soaps and shampoos from which to choose. Select mild products that will not irritate your baby's delicate skin or eyes. Many parents enjoy applying lotions and powders to their baby's skin after a bath, although this is usually not necessary. If you use baby lotion, be careful to hold your child securely, since he will be slippery. You can ask your pediatrician or pharmacist to recommend a soap, shampoo, lotion, and powder, if you are in doubt about which to buy.

Safety at Bath Time

Accidents can occur at bath time, if a parent fails to take the proper safety precautions. The guidelines in the How to Ensure Your Baby's Safety section should allow you to prepare in advance to prevent avoidable accidents. Never leave your baby alone in the tub while you go to get other equipment or answer the phone. A baby can drown in a few inches of water. You will also need to support him securely. Being aware of bath time safety will make it much easier to be relaxed when bathing your infant.

Giving Your Baby a Bath

Before you actually start giving him a bath, check to be sure all of the items you will need are within easy reach, including towels and clean clothes. Use warm water. If the water feels too hot to you (use your wrist or elbow to test it), it will be too hot for your baby. After you are through rinsing, use a soft towel to pat him dry immediately.

Many parents make it a habit to take the phone off the hook during bath time so that they are not tempted to answer it and are not disturbed. If you feel that you must answer the phone, doorbell, or whatever, wrap your baby in a towel and carry him with you. Never leave him by himself in the tub. You can bathe him in the kitchen, bathroom, his bedroom, or any other place that is convenient and warm. Avoid bathing him in cold, drafty areas, or uncomfortably hot rooms.

Whichever type of bath you will be giving, sponge or tub baths, there are certain things to keep in mind. Bathing a baby after his feedings is generally not recommended, because too much stimulation at this time can cause him to spit up his meal. He may also want to sleep after his dinner. Sometimes giving a bath during his fussy period helps to relax him. Be sure to keep a firm but gentle grip on his body since this will prevent him from slipping, and will make him feel more secure.

After you have had some experience in bathing your baby, you will develop your own preferences about tub versus sponge baths, how best to hold him, when to give the bath, and what bath products to use. There is a great deal of flexibility. Whether or not you will start giving him tub baths right away, or sponge baths until his navel has healed is an issue that your physician will discuss with you. Many doctors claim that either type of bath is really all right, although some prefer that sponge baths be given initially.

SPONGE OR TUB BATHS. There is nothing like plain old soap and water to keep him clean and fresh-smelling. Avoid getting soap or especially shampoo in his eyes. Try to buy a shampoo that does not burn the eyes. His scalp does not really need to be washed with soap on a daily basis, although you may still want to rinse it with water each time you bathe him.

The basic procedure in giving a bath is to hold him securely with one arm and wash and rinse him with the other. Many professionals and experienced parents advise beginning with his scalp and moving downward, but the order in which body parts are washed is not really very important. Be sure to rinse him thoroughly. Pay particular attention to rinsing his scalp well to prevent a sticky film from developing.

You can give a sponge bath on your lap or anywhere else. Obviously, holding him directly on your lap will mean that he is not the only one who will be getting a bath! Protect your clothes (floors, too, if necessary) with a plastic tablecloth or covering, and place a folded towel on your lap so that he will be comfortable and cannot slip off accidentally. There are foam mats specifically designed for use in giving sponge baths. They are contoured to fit the infant's bottom and do not slip out of place once they are put down on a counter top. Many mothers swear by them. A sponge bath is a fun time to interact with your baby.

Prior to giving a tub bath, line the bottom of the tub, sink, or other container with a towel, bath mat, or special bathtub decals so that it will not be slippery. Make sure that the water is comfortably warm before placing your infant in it. Use only a few inches of water. Should the water temperature change after a couple of minutes and feel too cool, do not add hot water to the tub while he is in it. Lift him out, add the hot water, test it, and then lower him back into the water.

CARE OF SPECIAL AREAS. Most parents are slightly nervous when giving their child his first bath. They are afraid they might hurt their "fragile" infants. They are especially concerned about washing certain areas of the body.

In washing your baby's body, be sure to get into the creases. You need not worry about hurting him by gently washing the fontanel (soft spot) on top of his head where the several bones that form the skull have not as yet joined. This area is protected by a membrane made to withstand normal handling. It is not advisable to stick a cotton swab or anything else deep into his ear canal or nostrils. Gently cleaning the entrance to these areas and all around the outside is sufficient.

If your baby is a boy and has been circumcised, it will probably take several days for his penis to heal. Some doctors recommend treating this unhealed area with a special ointment or Vaseline, and covering it with gauze for added protection. Check with your doctor, who should give you specific instructions for care following circumcision. If your baby boy has not been circumcised, your doctor may recommend that you gently pull back the skin over the tip of the penis (foreskin) so that you can wash the head of his penis, and so that adhesions do not develop. It is best to follow his or her advice.

Your baby's navel will probably take about a week to heal. Follow your doctor's instructions about whether or not to wash this area. Keeping it clean and dry should hasten the healing process. Do not cover it with medications or dressings unless your pediatrician recommends this. Exposure to the air should help keep the navel dry and allow it to heal naturally.

In the event that the scab over the navel is accidentally pulled off as it rubs against clothing, the unhealed area may bleed a little. Do not worry about this. Should you notice any secretions coming from the unhealed navel, try to keep it drier by exposing it to the air as much as possible. Dab it clean on a daily basis using a sterile ball of cotton and some alcohol. Redness or swelling of or around the navel may indicate a slight infection. You should contact your doctor.

Try to keep your baby's nails trimmed so that he will not be able to scratch himself. You can use a nail clipper or, preferably, a small, blunt-tipped scissors to clip them whenever necessary. If you have trouble clipping them while he is awake because he protests or moves around too much, you can probably trim his nails while he is asleep. It is important to keep his nails clean, since one of his favorite activities during infancy may be to suck on his fingers. Later in infancy he may even suck on his toes.

SLEEPING

Supporting Your Baby's Need to Sleep

Each baby has his own individual requirements: one may sleep for twelve hours a day and another for sixteen hours or more. Generally speaking, your baby will determine how much sleep he needs. All you have to do initially is support his natural tendencies to sleep by putting him in his crib or other safe sleeping area, not disturbing him once he is asleep, making sure that he is in a comfortable position, and seeing to it that he is not too hot or cold while sleeping.

Young infants' sleeping patterns are often related to their feedings. Many infants who are satisfied and relaxed after eating fall asleep directly, although some will remain alert for quite a while before drifting off to sleep. If your baby is one who does not fall asleep right after a meal or who remains awake for larger portions of the day, you need not worry that you are doing something wrong. As long as indigestion or illness does not seem to be a problem, and he is gaining sufficient amounts of weight, chances are that he simply does not require more sleep. As babies grow older and require less sleep, sleeping patterns will become more independent of other activities such as eating. In the first few weeks or so, you can probably expect your baby to sleep for a large portion of each day and for several hours between feedings.

AN ATMOSPHERE CONDUCIVE TO SLEEPING. Try to put your baby in a room that is neither too hot nor too cold while he sleeps, since this will help to ensure his comfort. Even though he will be able to fall asleep with lights on, you may want to dim or turn off the light in his room. It is not necessary for everyone in the household to tiptoe around and whisper so that he will not be disturbed. In fact he can and should get used to sleeping through normal, everyday noises. The television, radio, and stereo can be turned on at a reasonable volume as long as he does not appear to be bothered by the noise.

Getting him used to a silent household during the first month or two is not really the best thing for him in the long run anyway. When family members finally return to making their usual noises, he may have a great deal of difficulty sleeping through them. Feel free to do what you normally do while he sleeps, keeping in mind that an unreasonable noise level would disturb anyone's sleep, not just his.

BABIES MAKE STRANGE BEDFELLOWS. It is not advisable to allow your baby to sleep with you or you and your spouse. This could be dangerous for him if you accidentally roll over on him or if a pillow or blanket somehow covers his face and obstructs his breathing. Besides, many babies make quite a bit of noise when they are sleeping, and, of course, wet their beds. It should also be mentioned that a baby who gets used to sleeping in his parents' bed during the first six months or so may strongly object when this arrangement is discontinued. The problem of dependency that often arises can be avoided by arranging for your baby to sleep by himself from the very beginning. All in all, babies make strange bedfellows, and for your baby's safety do not take him to bed with you.

Some parents like to keep their baby's basket, crib, or bassinet in their room, assuming that his presence does not interfere with their intimacy, sex life, or need for privacy. There is nothing wrong with this approach, and it can be very convenient at feeding times. Most professionals advise that a baby be moved to his own sleeping quarters by the time he is five to six months old, if not earlier. A baby beyond that age who has become accustomed to sleeping in his parents' bedroom may loudly complain about sleeping anywhere else. This can create unnecessary problems for both him and his parents.

It is best for everyone concerned to get him used to sleeping alone from the start, or after the first few months, preferably in his own bedroom. When space is a problem and he must have a roommate, try to hang up a curtain or other room divider so that they will have some privacy and cannot easily see one another. Once a baby becomes more of a social person, he may refuse to fall asleep as long as there is another person in the room whom he can see. His desire for company may outweigh his desire and need for sleep. It is helpful to separate his sleeping quarters somehow to ensure some privacy.

SLEEPING POSITIONS VARY. There are differences of opinion about the best sleeping position for a young infant who may not be able to change his position once he is placed a certain way. The alternatives include placing him on his stomach, back, right side or left side (with firm pillows or rolled towels supporting him on either side). Even though your newborn is not likely to be able to voice a preference for a certain position, his comfort seems to be the most important factor. A few babies do show a preference for one of the above positions from the start. Most will not develop a preference for several weeks, after which time they may be reluctant to sleep in any other position but their favorite.

Until such time as your infant becomes opinionated, we suggest that you and your doctor decide how best to position him for sleep. In case your doctor has no strong recommendations, and your baby has no obvious preference, you should use your own judgment. Actually, it does not really seem to make a great deal of difference which position you use.

It is doubtful that the initial consistent use of one or another position will have any long-lasting negative effects. As an important safety reminder, be sure to burp your baby properly before placing him in his crib, particularly if using the back position. This will minimize his getting into rare but possible problems related to gagging or choking on his vomit, or breathing it in. Burping him well after his meals will also reduce the discomfort he might feel upon going to bed with a lot of air in his stomach. This again becomes more important in conjunction with a position on his back, in which he will have more difficulty bringing up the air.

HOW AND WITH WHAT TO COVER YOUR BABY. Many parents prefer to dress their babies in sleeping bags which are made of many different materials from lightweight to heavyweight. These "bags," selected in the appropriate fabric according to the temperature in a baby's room, eliminate the need for other blankets or covers. In a sleeping bag, a baby will have plenty of room to move around. He will be fully covered, so that you will not have to worry about the possibility of his kicking off blankets during the night.

Any other types of coverings that you put on his bed should be pulled smooth, tucked underneath the mattress, and pinned or clipped in areas that are not accessible to your baby's hands. The object is to prevent the blanket from bunching up on his bed in the middle of the night as he kicks and wriggles, possibly covering his face and obstructing his breathing.

SAFETY AT BEDTIME. The common hazards that exist when a baby is put to bed can be eliminated if a parent knows what preventive measures to take. Guidelines for purchasing safe cribs and mattresses are presented on pages 40–41. It is highly important that you read this material and follow the suggestions. Additional safety rules to keep in mind were presented on page 126.

What to Do If Your Baby Has Trouble Falling Asleep

If your baby has difficulty falling asleep, there are several tricks you can try:

> sing to him or hum a lullaby
> turn some soft music on the radio or stereo
> give him a gentle rubdown or a brief massage
> tuck him in snugly, or hold him close to your body
> rock him, pat him, or gently move his crib back and forth

The only problems with these approaches are that once these patterns are used on a routine basis over a period of a few months, they are hard to break. It is up to you whether or not to make use of them. Feel free to use any of the above techniques suggested by experienced parents, or some of your own.

What to Do If Your Baby Awakens in the Middle of the Night

Throughout the first few weeks, you can count on your baby awakening around 2 or 3 A.M., or some other time during the night, crying out of hunger. With a very young infant you will want to respond promptly to his cries for food. When it is not food that he wants, try to determine if he needs a diaper change, fewer or additional coverings, a shift in position, or some other concrete adjustment. Do not feel bad if you cannot determine a reason for his crying. Simply try to soothe him and chances are that he will soon return to sleep.

Establishing a Bedtime Routine

During the first few weeks, you will mainly be following your baby's individual sleeping pattern and trying to support it. After about a month or two you will probably want to begin to steer him gently in the direction of a sleeping schedule that is more convenient for you and allows you to get the rest at night that you need. Since his sleeping patterns are likely to be related to his hunger patterns, how to work toward establishing a sleeping schedule that is well suited to both your needs and his was discussed in the Feeding section on pages 133–35.

As his requirements for sleep diminish and he becomes more capable of adapting to your schedule, it is advisable not only to devise a suitable schedule, but to stick to it. Experienced parents who have been fairly strict about putting their babies to bed at regular hours report time and again that this is the best approach. Their babies quickly became accustomed to their routine. The parents were assured of having predictable "free" times during the day and night around which they could plan their work or recreation.

Even on the occasions when their babies did not actually fall asleep when put into their cribs, these parents still stuck by the routine. This gave them opportunities to do other things and gave their babies opportunities to rest. Most of you will probably find that establishing a fairly firm sleeping routine works well for you, too, and will help to avoid many unnecessary hassles and conflicts with your baby as he grows older.

PATTERNS OF ELIMINATION

Your baby has no control over his organs of elimination, and thus urinates and moves his bowels by reflex action, not by a conscious, voluntary action as you do. This is one major difference that you will notice once you begin caring for him and cleaning up his messy diapers during both day and night. Cleanups will occur at frequent intervals, no doubt, too frequent for your liking.

Assuming you have not had much experience with young babies, you may be quite surprised or even concerned about the appearance of your baby's stools, since their consistency and color will be markedly different from yours. This difference is partly due to the fact that his intestinal tract is still immature, and partly due to the fact that his diet is limited to milk.

The material in the Patterns of Elimination sections will give you an idea of what you can expect in terms of a baby's bowel and bladder function. Having this basic knowledge should put you more at ease, and assist you in recognizing any major changes in his stools or elimination patterns that might indicate an illness or intestinal problem.

Bowel Movements Are Different at First

Within one full day after he is born, a baby should have his first bowel movement. His stools during the first day or so will not look like those that he will pass thereafter, since they will mainly consist of meconium; a rather thick, green-black colored substance that has collected within his body while in the womb. All babies should defecate within twenty-four hours after they are born. The nurses or physicians in the hospital will be sure to check on your infant's first bowel movement. If you deliver your child at home and he does not pass a bowel movement within the first twenty-four hours, you should contact your physician. After the first few days, when the meconium has passed out of his body and he takes in more milk, his stools will gradually become lighter in color and less sticky.

Color of Bowel Movements

The color of bowel movements varies, depending upon whether a baby is breast-fed or bottle-fed. Breast-fed babies' bowel movements tend to be light green to light yellow in color. On some occasions they may appear slightly darker or lighter in color. Bottle-fed infants usually have light brown to yellow stools. You will easily see that your infant's stools are different in color from your own. There can be slight variations in the color of stools depending upon the kind of formula offered to the baby. Iron-supplemented formulas can turn the stools dark brown to almost black in some children.

Consistency and Odor of Bowel Movements

The consistency or texture of babies' bowel movements will differ. Breast-fed babies usually pass soft, loose stools that may look like thick or watery paste. They are very rarely hard. The stools of bottle-fed babies are usually rather lumpier (like scrambled eggs), slightly bulkier, and stickier in texture than breast-fed babies' stools.

Breast milk often has a mild laxative effect, and, as a result, babies on the breast rarely have a problem with constipation. Constipation is more commonly seen among babies taking formula. Assuming you are bottle-feeding, you may notice that your baby's stools have an unpleasant odor, something on the order of milk that has turned sour. This is nothing to worry about. If you are breast-feeding, your baby's stools will probably not have as strong an odor.

The Number of Bowel Movements a Day Varies

Babies on the breast usually pass more bowel movements a day than those on the bottle. It is not unusual for a breast-fed baby to move his bowels after each feeding. The need to move the bowels after taking in food mainly stems from the "gastrocolic" reflex. This reflex stimulates the intestines to push out bowel movement that is in the rectum when food is put in the mouth. Some parents are under the impression that the food coming out in the stool after a feeding is the same as that which their baby just took in. This is not the case. Eating simply stimulates the reflex that activates the bowels to eliminate any feces already in the rectum. If no feces are in the rectum, then eating will not stimulate bowel movement at that time.

Some newborn breast-fed babies do not defecate after each meal, perhaps moving their bowels from four to six times a day. Bottle-fed babies usually defecate between two and four times per day, although some may only defecate once or as many as five times a day and still be perfectly healthy.

Generally by the time babies on the breast or bottle are about three months old, they defecate less frequently than during the first few weeks. One baby may defecate twice a day, another once a day, and still others once every two days or more. There are babies who will pass a bowel movement only once in several days. This is less common, but can be perfectly normal. As long as a baby seems satisfied, and there are no indications that he is sick or in pain, you need not worry that something *must* be wrong with him. Your baby may establish a pattern of elimination that is quite different from your own, or from your other children. Each infant establishes his own pattern. If you are concerned about the frequency of your baby's stools, consult your baby's doctor.

Babies Have Different Styles of Defecation

Babies may behave quite differently when they defecate. There is the "pusher," who seems to bear down in an attempt to force out a bowel movement. Next there is the "strainer" who appears to be having a mighty tough time of it. The baby "beet" turns red in the face just as he passes a bowel movement. Then we have

"Mr. Fussy," who acts grouchy and whimpers or cries each time he defecates. "Mr. Gas," naturally passes a lot of gas, and finally there is the "squirter," whose bowel movements always seem to come out with quite a bit of force. Your baby will fit into one or more of the above descriptions, or he may have his own unique "style" of defecating.

Most parents of "strainers" become a little concerned, since they fear that their child is constipated or in great pain. Some babies have a natural tendency to strain or act grouchy with the passing of each movement. In most cases, this is simply the baby's style, and is nothing to worry about. On the other hand, if your baby does not usually strain when he passes a movement, and then suddenly begins to do so after several days of not passing one, pay attention to the appearance of the stool when it is finally passed. Straining after several days without the passage of a stool, followed by a movement that is unusually hard or loose and watery, suggests that the infant may be having a mild digestive difficulty or a touch of constipation. Constipation is a much more common problem among bottle-fed babies, and fairly rare among breast-fed babies. Your doctor may prescribe a change in your baby's diet or a mild medication to help alleviate these conditions.

Be on the Lookout for Marked Changes in Baby's Stools

Marked changes in a baby's stools can be a sign of illness. That is why it is important for you to observe your baby's stools, and be on the lookout for marked changes. It is very helpful to keep track of the frequency, color, and texture or consistency of his stools over the first couple of weeks so that you will know what kind of stools are typical or characteristic for him. Jot this down in a record-keeping book or make a mental note.

Although an occasional mild case of diarrhea is not uncommon, and does not represent a serious problem, persistent or excessive diarrhea may result in a baby's losing large amounts of body water and salt, causing him to become dehydrated (lose body water). This type of diarrhea may also be a sign of illness. Frequent passage of watery stools should be brought to the attention of your physician. Your baby is very sensitive to changes in the amount of his body water and salt, and thus persistent or rapid loss of water and salts through diarrhea can pose a serious health threat if left untreated (see page 964).

Baby's stools may look black. This is not uncommon in infants receiving iron supplements. Black, red, or frankly bloody stools can indicate a disturbance in the digestive tract and should be brought to the attention of your physician. Stools that are excessively foul-smelling and very mucousy should also be mentioned to your doctor.

Breast-fed babies tend to have loose stools, so you need not jump to the immediate conclusion that your baby has diarrhea. Wait and observe them, comparing their consistency, and appearance with his typical stools. Should you notice marked changes or still be concerned, then ask your doctor. If a baby is started on solid foods, his stools change temporarily, often becoming looser and more greenish in color until his body, specifically his intestinal tract, has had time to adjust to the new diet. This is nothing to be concerned about. Solids are not usually introduced until after six months of age since the baby's digestive tract is more prepared to handle them at this time. See page 305 for a further discussion of possible changes in stools when solid foods are added to an infant's all-milk diet.

Occasionally, when a baby's stools are hard, small spots or streaks of red blood may be interwound amid the mass. This may indicate that he has a crack or irritation around his rectum. This could be a small cut or a special type of minor irritation called an anal fissure. See page 966 for further information about anal fissures.

Should you notice major changes in your baby's stools at any point in time, the safest and most advisable course of action is to discuss these changes with your doctor. Bloody or very unusual stools should probably be saved in a clean container, in case your doctor wants to examine them more carefully. Do not plunge ahead and try to treat diarrhea, constipation, or any other major change in your baby's patterns of elimination without your doctor's prior consent, since changing a baby's diet, or giving him suppositories, enemas, laxatives, or other medications can be harmful.

Urination

Within twenty-four hours or one day after a baby is born, he will urinate for the first time. His initial output of urine often has a pinkish or reddish tinge to it, and this should not be a cause for undue concern. If two days have passed and your baby has not urinated, let your doctor know.

Initially, when your infant urinates, he will probably produce much smaller quantities of urine than he will after a week or two. This is because his fluid intake is minimal. Once he is consuming larger amounts of fluid, his urine output should increase proportionally. You may find that his urine production varies from one day to the next. This variation is normal. On a hot day, for example, when he perspires more than usual, his urine output may be less substantial than on a cold day.

You will be constantly changing your infant's wet diapers, since he will be urinating at frequent intervals. This can be tedious at first, but after a few weeks, you will get used to the routine. There is no need for you to worry if he squirms, makes a face, or fusses when he urinates, since some babies behave this way, even when they urinate while sleeping. An occasional baby will cry after urinating. Changing his diaper may quiet him.

Undressing or changing your infant or giving him a bath at a time when his bladder needs emptying may lead to your being sprayed with urine, particularly if your baby is a boy. Many parents who have been through this experience know that the spray of urine may be so powerful that it can even hit the wall next to the crib or changing table. As a practical tip, covering yourself with a washable apron, keeping clear of his aim, and putting washable wallpaper on the wall most likely to be sprayed may help save extra cleaning chores.

EXPOSING YOUR BABY TO THE ELEMENTS

Sunbaths

Most parents are naturally curious about when they can take their babies outside for a sunbath. Exposing babies to the sun for limited periods of time can be healthy, but you should be aware that prolonged direct exposure to sunlight may be harmful to the skin and eyes. You must be especially careful with your young infant, because his skin can easily be burned. Sunburns may be very dangerous and in order to guard against them, you should expose your baby to the sun a small step at a time.

While there are no hard and fast rules, it is thought to be safe to begin exposing your baby to the sun or giving him sunbaths when he weighs approximately ten or eleven pounds. The temperature and weather should naturally be suitable for sunbaths. Some babies are annoyed by sunlight hitting their faces, and others do not seem to mind it. If your baby does not like having the sunlight hit his face, you can expose the rest of his body.

Most physicians advise limiting an infant's first sunbath to no more than a couple minutes (one minute on his back, and one minute on his stomach) with his eyes shielded. Each day thereafter, you can increase the time of his sunbath by a couple of minutes, if he does not get overheated. Once his sunbaths last anywhere from half an hour to three quarters of an hour, most physicians suggest not increasing them any further.

In case you are beach lovers and plan to bring your baby along, it is best to keep him entirely in the shade for most of the time. Even when he is ready for some fun in the sun, be sure to shield his eyes and limit his exposure. You can gradually lengthen his sunbaths, but watch him carefully for signs that he is overheated. Outdoors in hot weather, it is not wise to keep your baby in a carriage or bassinet if the sunlight is intense. In these carriers, the cooler air will probably not reach him as well as it would if he were held on your lap or placed on a blanket on the ground. There is, therefore, a greater likelihood of his getting overheated.

If you are interested in giving your baby a sunbath during the wintertime, this is also possible. He can, for example, have a sunbath in a sunny room near a window, providing the temperature of the room is suitable. It is advisable to limit his sunbaths in the wintertime, just as was suggested for the summertime. Always make sure your baby is not chilled. It is important to keep in mind that sunburns do not usually show up until several hours after a person has been exposed to the sun, so be very careful when giving your baby sunbaths.

Bringing Your Baby Outside for Some Fresh Air

It is a good idea for everyone to go outdoors and get some fresh air now and then. There are no hard and fast rules as to what age, when, and for how long to take a baby outdoors, although the following general guidelines may be useful. Doctors usually suggest waiting until a healthy baby weighs approximately eight or nine pounds before taking him outdoors. They caution parents against taking the baby outside in freezing temperatures or very cold, damp, or windy weather. A baby's first outing should be limited to about an hour or so depending upon the weather. Naturally he should be appropriately dressed.

As the baby gains weight, the time he spends outdoors can be gradually increased. When a baby weighs about twelve or thirteen pounds, he can be taken out in freezing weather for limited periods of time, providing he is properly dressed and it is not too damp or windy outside. Again, the time he spends outdoors can be slowly increased as his tolerance builds. Noontime is a good time for him to get some fresh air in the winter months, since the sun is likely to be the strongest then.

In case you want your baby to get some fresh air, but prefer to stay indoors, you may simply want to open the windows in his room. In the wintertime you should make sure that he is dressed warmly enough. You should also initially limit the time during which the windows are open to less than an hour.

Whenever you take your baby outdoors, watch him carefully. If he looks chilled, bring him back inside. Since there are no strict guidelines to follow, it is best to use good common sense.

TRAVELING WITH YOUR BABY

Many parents shy away from traveling with their babies for several reasons. One is that carrying the extra equipment necessary to pack can be cumbersome. Depending upon the mode of travel you select and the nature of the area in which you are traveling, bringing a baby under a year old along may be inconvenient. Another common reason for not traveling with a baby is that you will not have as much privacy, since it is usually far more economical to share a room with your baby.

In spite of these drawbacks, young babies tend to make good travelers. The ease with which you can travel with a baby largely depends upon where you are going, how long you will be gone, the type of transportation you will be using, and the accessibility to refrigeration, grocery stores that carry baby foods, and laundry services. Most babies are lightweight enough to be easily carried. In fact, they are quite portable. They are usually not disturbed by sleeping in unfamiliar surroundings as long as their needs are satisfied. Quite often parents who have traveled with their young babies say that the rocking motion and background noises of boats, trains, planes, and cars actually soothed their babies. Many of these parents claim that their babies had little or no difficulty sleeping wherever they were taken. Most major hotels will supply cribs upon request.

Equipment

There are many products and multifunction equipment available that make traveling with a baby easier and more convenient. Ready-to-use infant formulas in presterilized disposable bottles that do not require refrigeration, despite their cost, are a blessing for parents who want to avoid the time, effort, and special equipment necessary for preparing formulas from scratch. Disposable diapers and liners are very convenient. Jars of baby food, cans of fruit juice, and snacks such as teething biscuits or crackers do not take up very much room in a suitcase. It is advisable to pack some of these items in the event that it takes you longer than you anticipated to find a grocery store that carries these food products.

Other products such as throw-away wipe cloths, bibs, and towelettes make keeping a baby clean relatively easy and convenient. If you are traveling in the United States, you need not overload your suitcases with these products, since most food stores, drugstores, and department stores carry them. Parents who have taken many trips with their babies suggest purchasing an insulated diaper bag, and buying a carrier (front, side, or back) for toting your baby around during your daily sight-seeing adventures (see pages 47–48).

In case you are planning to travel by bus, train, or plane, you may want to inform them that you will be taking your baby. Inquire in advance if there are any special services or facilities for infants available at the major terminals. Most airlines, for example, provide bassinets for babies. Many allow parents with children to board the plane early, and will assign them seats so that they will have more room. At the major airports there are usually special nursery areas with a few cribs and changing tables. Whichever mode of travel you select, it is advisable to request a direct or "express" trip that does not require stopovers and changes in transportation along the way.

Clothing does not usually represent too much of a problem with young babies. Washable clothing that requires no ironing is the wisest choice. Sweaters with hoods often come in handy. Be sure to take climate changes into account when deciding what to pack. Also bring along several small washable toys for your baby. Include his favorite toys as well as a few new ones.

Many large restaurants and cafeterias are equipped to accommodate the needs of babies. Quite often they keep a supply of high chairs on hand, for older babies. If you ask to have your baby's bottle or solid food warmed, you may be surprised at the staff's willingness to please.

Finding baby-sitters when traveling can be a problem. In many major hotel chains in the United States, baby-sitters are available upon request through the hotel. The same criteria presented on pages 29–30 and 155–58 in selecting someone to care for your baby, whether you are home or traveling, should be used, if at all possible. It is usually safer to take your baby with you wherever you go, but the ultimate decision is yours to make.

It is generally more difficult to travel with older babies. They tend to be more easily upset by changes in their routines, strangers, as well as unfamiliar places. They also have very strong desires to be moving about and practicing their new skills. Most parents find that it is much easier to travel with babies under the age of about five or six months, but, again, this depends largely upon the individual baby and the nature and duration of the trip.

Safety When Traveling

Your baby's safety is of utmost importance when you travel. When traveling by car, you should be using an appropriate infant auto seat as discussed on pages 42–43. Your little one should never be left alone in the car. All items should be cleared off the back seat ledge and the front ledge to avoid their flying in all directions should the car stop suddenly. Ashtrays should be cleaned and doors should stay locked to prevent the older child from opening them. Safety rules on planes, trains, boats, and other forms of transportation should be observed.

You may want to discuss your travel plans with the doctor if you are planning an extended vacation or a trip to another country. The doctor will be able to advise you of any special immunizations that might be required and may recommend a mini-medicine chest to take along, depending upon where you are going. It is also important to know about the water supply in the area you are visiting and ask if any adjustments should be made in preparing your baby's formula. A little planning in advance can often make the trip much safer and more enjoyable.

BABY-SITTERS

Sooner or later you will need the services of a baby-sitter. It is good for you to have a break from your baby now and then, if for no other reason than to give you some privacy, some time out from care responsibilities, and a chance to relax. Your child may also benefit, because it will give him an opportunity to get accustomed to people other than you.

There are several important aspects of engaging the services of another person to care for your child in your absence that warrant your consideration. These aspects are broken down into brief topics for your convenience.

Infancy 1

Finding and Selecting Baby-sitters

The easiest way to find a baby-sitter is to ask your friends and neighbors who have children if they can recommend one to you. They may even have teen-agers of their own who have done a lot of baby-sitting or they themselves may volunteer to baby-sit with your child occasionally if you return the favor. If you have parents or relatives living nearby, they might be willing to care for your child occasionally. If you have a teen-ager, he or she may also be willing to baby-sit. Other sources you might turn to are as follows:

local high schools
church groups
employment or social service agencies
the YWCA
the Red Cross
a local school of nursing or college

A viable alternative to hiring a baby-sitter is to form a co-operative baby-sitting pool with friends who live in your apartment complex or neighborhood and who also have youngsters around your child's age. There are many different arrangements that can be worked out so that baby-sitting services can be shared or exchanged. This can be a good way to cut down on the cost of sitters. Make sure, however, that their child rearing practices are at least similar to your own so that you do not have to worry about how your child is being treated in your absence. While some limited exposure to varied methods of handling may be beneficial, if the other parents' methods of discipline and handling are very different from yours, this can set up conflicts.

Selecting a suitable baby-sitter is not always an easy task. It is best to choose someone with whom you are familiar, or someone who is highly recommended by a person whose opinion you value. It is not advisable to hire someone whom you know nothing about, except, perhaps in emergency situations.

For your baby's sake and for your own peace of mind, always try to meet potential baby-sitters in advance. Talk with them and ask any questions that you feel are necessary. It is also a good idea to introduce them to your child, and observe their reaction. After all, how they respond to your child and how he reacts to them is what really matters. Check their references to see whether or not the other people they have worked for have been satisfied.

Some of the factors to consider are as follows:

Is the person old enough and mature enough for the job?
Does the person really like children?
Is the person responsible and dependable?
Does the person have an understanding of children?
Can the person be trusted to follow your instructions and act appropriately in case of an emergency?
Does the person have good common sense?
Is the person in good enough physical shape to keep up with an active child?
Does your child like the person?

SHOULD A BABY-SITTER BE A WOMAN? This is a very difficult question to answer. Most of the time, women are the ones who offer their services as baby-sitters. However, there are a number of men (teen-agers on up in age) who are now available for such jobs. Since women are assumed to know more about caring for children, and have more experience, parents generally feel more comfortable selecting them as baby-sitters. The "traditional" male and female roles in our society are beginning to change, and selection should be made on an individual basis, regardless of a person's sex. In fact, in the case of a fatherless child, the child may benefit from having a male figure, particularly a consistent male baby-sitter, spend time with him.

In hiring baby-sitters you should always discuss the cost of their services, payment arrangements, and the issue of transportation. It will be easier on your child if you regularly use one or two baby-sitters. A constant stream of strangers into your home may be upsetting. Using only one or two consistent sitters will enable him to get to know them and feel more comfortable while you are away.

Letting the Baby-sitter Know What You Expect

Once you have selected one or more suitable people to care for your child, there are several additional important things for you to do, including letting the baby-sitter know what you expect in your absence. Here are some brief suggestions:

Familiarize the sitter with your home. A brief tour of where items such as the telephone, refrigerator, your child's room (also toys, clothing, etc.), first aid kits, fire extinguishers, flashlight, etc., are located should be part of the "initiation." If the locks on your doors are tricky, show how to operate them. The same holds true if you have a burglar alarm system. Should you live in an apartment building, point out the location of the fire escape.

Always post an emergency list of phone numbers by each phone in your home. An example of such a list is given on page 948. It is important to discuss this list with your baby-sitter so that he or she can act appropriately in an emergency situation. Knowing where to call for help will avoid confusion in the rare situation where this is necessary.

Familiarize your baby-sitter with child care routines. You may want to pay the sitter to visit your home in advance so that he or she can watch you handle your child, and can care for him under your supervision. Specific instructions for formulas, other foods, diets, medications, etc., should not only be discussed, but should be written down.

Make a notebook containing a list of "Everything your child would like his baby-sitter to know." Be sure to include items such as:

where you will be—when you will return
a phone number where you can be reached
your child's daily schedule
any special dietary considerations or instructions for preparing foods
medications that have to be given and instructions for proper use

Ask your baby-sitter to read the appropriate safety check lists in this book, but remember that it is your responsibility to accident-proof your home and give explicit instructions in this regard. Familiarizing your baby-sitter with accidents that are common with children your child's age may help him or her in taking safety precautions in your absence.

Be sure to discuss the issues of telephone use, having friends over at your home, eating, and watching television on the job. Be clear about what you do and do not want.

Let your baby-sitter know that it is not safe to open the door when the doorbell rings. If you are expecting a visitor, tell the sitter the person's name.

It is a good idea for you to call home at some point while you are out, just to check to see that everything is all right. As a matter of courtesy, you should inform your baby-sitter that you will do this.

If you have made plans to be home at a certain time, and discover that you will be detained, always call to let your baby-sitter know. Do not forget to pay overtime expenses.

Always make sure that your baby-sitter arrives home safely. If no transportation is available, you should drive your sitter home.

Find another baby-sitter if your child seems particularly upset or frightened by a certain baby-sitter. After all, his feelings about the matter should definitely be taken into account.

PETS

Parents often wonder what to do about pets. You must take certain precautionary measures for your infant's sake, if you have a cat or dog. A tiny, helpless infant is defenseless against such an animal. The possibility that your pet may scratch, bite, or jump up on your baby and harm him is a real one. Therefore, you will have to closely watch your pet whenever your baby is around, and prevent it from entering your baby's bedroom when he is sleeping or otherwise alone.

An older infant or toddler is not mature enough to be expected to care for a pet. Young children up to the age of about three, in fact, must be closely supervised when they are around family pets for their own sake and the animal's sake. Young children quite often have little awareness of how to interact with animals. They may not realize that a playful pinch, squeeze, or a tug on an animal's tail may result in an animal scratching or biting in retaliation. Toddlers can be taught to handle a pet "gently" and "make nice" to them, but precautionary measures must be taken to ensure the child's and the pet's safety. Caged pets such as birds and fish generally make appropriate pets when there are youngsters in the home, although parents must assume the entire responsibility for the care of these pets.

Preschool children are often quite fond of pets, and are more capable of being taught how to handle and conduct themselves around animals. Hamsters, fish, caged birds, guinea pigs, and turtles generally make fine pets for children, and youngsters can learn about many things in relation to pets, including how they reproduce. Still, a preschool child should not be expected to assume charge of caring for a pet.

Those of you who have a pet such as a cat or dog should make sure that it is healthy, and that all of its inoculations are kept up to date. You should be prepared to assume the complete responsibility for its care. When your child is young, it is wise to supervise his association with your pets. Many parents love animals and want their children to get accustomed to them and feel positively toward them at an early age. This can be a rewarding experience for children, and if handled properly, can be a safe one. When visiting friends or neighbors who have pets, care must also be taken so that there will be no risk to either your child's wellbeing or that of the animal.

DISCIPLINE

Parents as well as professionals may have completely different philosophies on discipline. Some believe in the old saying, "Spare the rod and spoil the child," while others feel that children must be permitted full freedom during early childhood. Given the wide spectrum of opinions and variations in philosophies and convictions, it is apparent that discipline is a highly controversial issue.

What Are Some of the Common Approaches to Discipline?

There are many different approaches to discipline, although the common approaches fall into three basic categories:

The very strict approach
The very lenient approach
The middle-of-the-road approach

Theories about disciplinary tactics have changed through the ages. Around the turn of the century, the very strict approach was quite popular. Then, after the Second World War, there was a swing to the opposite extreme and the very lenient, or "permissive" approach gained in popularity. At present, the middle-of-the-road approach appears to be the most popular among many parents. In order to give you an idea of these three philosophies, they are briefly outlined below.

THE VERY STRICT APPROACH. Parents using this approach set very strict limits and controls on their child's behavior, and enforce them with a "heavy" hand or by force. They do not tolerate rebellion or "back talk," and are always in full control. Their authority is unquestioned. Their child's compliance with their commands must be complete and immediate. The basic philosophy behind this approach is to set firm and inflexible rules on behavior patterns that will be adopted by the child.

THE VERY LENIENT APPROACH. Parents using this approach give their child total freedom of action and expression. Basically he is permitted to do as he pleases, since there are either no limits or very few limits placed on behavior. Even if his behavior infringes upon others' rights, his parents do not try to limit it. Their child is free to act upon his impulses no matter what the outcome. Parental authority is not strong, and it is rarely exercised.

THE MIDDLE-OF-THE-ROAD APPROACH. Parents using this approach lie midway between the very strict and the very lenient. They respect their child's individuality and need for some freedom, but they do not allow him to infringe upon other people's rights. They can say either "yes you can" or "no you can't" to him depending upon the particular situation at hand.

Parents do not expect more from him in terms of obedience than he can realistically give at any given stage of development. The limits that they impose and enforce are justifiable and reasonable in their number and nature. Their expectations and demands are in line with his capabilities and his temperament, both of which may change as he passes from one developmental phase to another. They do not hesitate to exercise their authority as his parents when they feel that this is necessary, although they also do not blindly impose their wishes on him because they are his "parents."

Selecting a Method of Discipline

Discipline is very much a personal matter. Parents and children are individuals, and there is no one philosophy or approach that could possibly be "right" or well suited to every parent and child. You must ultimately decide upon an approach that takes into account your personal ideas and convictions. You must feel satisfied and comfortable with whichever approach you select, and not merely select an approach based upon what someone else has told you is the "best" approach.

After reading the three philosophies of discipline mentioned above, you may decide that you favor one in particular, a combination of them, or none of them. However, this issue deserves further attention. You should carefully examine your own feelings, your spouse's feelings, and, naturally, your baby's temperament and capabilities.

WHAT DOES DISCIPLINE MEAN TO YOU: WHAT ARE YOUR AIMS? One of the most helpful things for you to do is to determine what discipline means to you, and what the aim of a program of discipline should, in your opinion, be. Many parents feel that a program of discipline should educate or teach their child socially acceptable ways of behaving so that he is generally well behaved, can get along with other people, and can function in a society in which there are hundreds of rules and laws, both written and unwritten. This implies that he must be educated in self-control.

Disciplining a child, in short, involves training or guiding him in what you feel is the "right" or "proper" direction. What is "right" in the eyes and mind of one parent may not be so to another, and this is why you should make up your own mind. Assuming that you want your child to obey your every command to the letter, and to do so immediately after you give an order, your program of training will differ greatly from that of another parent whose main objective is to rear a self-regulating individual.

Most parents are concerned about their baby's future adjustment as an adult, and therefore view discipline in a positive light. Discipline imposes some structure, direction, and organization to a child's life. Most people, both parents and professionals, believe that disciplining a child is a major responsibility for parents during early childhood, and a major avenue through which concerned parents can show their child that they care about him. A child's adjustment from living mainly within the boundaries of his home to functioning outside the home sphere will be much easier for him if he gets his first training in discipline from his parents.

Infancy 1

YOUR PAST EXPERIENCES MAY INFLUENCE YOUR PHILOSOPHY. Try to remember back to when you were a child. Think about how your parents disciplined you. Were they strict, permissive, or middle-of-the-road in their handling of situations? Did they share the responsibility for discipline, or did one parent do most of the disciplining? Did they agree or disagree on controversial issues in regard to methods of discipline? Did they believe in punishment, and, if so, what kind? What attitude was conveyed to you by their approach to discipline? What aspects of their approach did you like, and what aspects did you dislike? In the event that you would like to do things a little differently with your child, what things would you change, and why?

Asking yourself these and similar types of questions about your upbringing can be very helpful and enlightening. Most experienced parents reluctantly admit that they often find themselves handling situations very much like their parents, particularly when snap decisions and spur-of-the-moment judgments have to be made. When you begin to discipline your child, all sorts of memories about your own childhood and the way in which your parents disciplined you may be aroused. Some of these memories may be pleasant, while others may be unpleasant, or even painful.

Your past experiences may influence the way in which you handle your own child, so try to recall them and examine them both objectively, and subjectively. Remembering your parents' disciplinary approach as well as your reactions to it may make you more aware of your own feelings and convictions in regard to discipline. They may also influence the philosophy about discipline that you want to adopt.

Let's say that you basically agree with your parents' philosophy. Then you will probably want to follow suit and take a similar approach. You may actually find that disciplining your child comes rather naturally to you. You may not really have to stop and think too much about what you are doing each step along the way.

On the other hand, if you view certain aspects of your parents' discipline program in an unfavorable light, then you will want to alter your philosophy so that it is more in line with your own beliefs. As a result, you may not initially feel as at ease or as secure in your approach, since your experience with it has been limited. You will probably have to guard against overreacting or swinging to the opposite extreme in an attempt to avoid making whatever mistakes that you feel your parents might have made.

It is important to re-evaluate your program of discipline at frequent intervals to determine its effectiveness. Should you determine that it is not working out as well as you expected, be flexible about making necessary alterations. A good program of discipline is not static, since it must take the baby's changing needs and capabilities into account during each phase of development.

DISCUSS THIS SUBJECT HONESTLY WITH YOUR SPOUSE. If you are married, you should definitely discuss your feelings about discipline with your spouse. Be as honest with each other as you can from the start. Very often parents do not agree on disciplinary methods, upon the goal of discipline, or upon the methods used to enforce discipline. One parent may lean toward a more lenient approach, while another may favor a stricter approach.

Mr. and Mrs. Benson had different philosophies of discipline. Mrs. Benson was the major disciplinarian, since she spent more time with Arthur, their son. She was the stricter of the two parents, and saw the value of early training. During the first two and a half months after Arthur was born, he had frequent unexplainable crying spells throughout the daytime and evening hours. Mrs. Benson would always try to determine a cause for the episodes, but she could never seem to find a reason for his crying. She showered him with attention at such times and picked him up and rocked him.

After Arthur was three months old, his crying really got on Mrs. Benson's nerves, and she decided to discourage him from these crying spells by ignoring them. All day long she would give him her attention whenever he was not crying, but would ignore him when he cried unnecessarily. This seemed to work fairly well during the daytime. However, when Mr. Benson came home at night, he would rush over to pick Arthur up as soon as he started to cry. All of Mrs. Benson's efforts to discipline Arthur during the day were undermined by her husband. This led to friction between them. By talking over the problem, Mr. Benson realized that he could bend a little and try not to reinforce his son's crying episodes. The Bensons were able to talk over their differences and develop an approach they could agree on.

Both parents should give the issue of discipline some serious thought. It is not to be taken lightly, since your approach will underlie your general handling of your child. If you and your partner do not agree in your philosophies, try to come to some sort of compromise. Many future problems and arguments may be eliminated by discussing your differences and working them out early.

It would be naïve to think that the two of you will never disagree over issues of discipline in the future, but it will be helpful to recognize each other's feelings, and come to a general agreement as to your approach. Do your arguing in private. Try to back each other up in front of your baby. Mutual co-operation is important. Support one another, and life will be much easier for the two of you, as well as for your baby. When your older infant senses that one of you is more lenient, and will "give in" under pressure, rest assured that he will cleverly take advantage of the "lenient" parent, and will play one of you off against the other. Avoid letting him have the opportunity to "divide and conquer" by sticking together on issues of discipline and by backing one another up, at least in his presence.

TAKING YOUR BABY'S PERSONALITY INTO ACCOUNT. In formulating your approach to discipline, take your child's personality into account. Each baby is an individual from birth, and the kind of approach that is effective with one child may not be as effective with another. One child can adapt easily to changes in his routine, while another is more conservative about changes. One child is very regular in his patterns of behavior, while another has irregular or unpredictable patterns. Getting a baby with unpredictable patterns to adapt to a regular feeding schedule in the first month, for example, would be going against his nature. Similarly, getting an extremely active baby to lie still while you are changing his diapers would be difficult.

You must learn something about the person you are attempting to educate or train, if your program of discipline is to be successful. The goal is not to remake the child completely or go against his nature. Rather, it is to work within the basic framework of his temperament and his make-up in order to guide him.

There are some babies who, by nature, are easier to guide and train, and others who will be more difficult. Even if you already have other children, you are likely to find that the training methods that worked well for one may not work well for the next.

TAKING HIS CAPABILITIES INTO ACCOUNT. Your baby will change enormously over the next year, and some of the methods of discipline that you initially adopt will no longer be appropriate as he grows older. It would not be reasonable, for example, to expect a young infant to have any idea what the word "no" or "don't touch" means, but it might be appropriate to expect a young toddler to respond to these words.

For your program of discipline to be effective, it must be suited not only to your baby's needs and temperament, but also to his capabilities. Your expectations should also be adjusted to go along with his level of performance. At certain stages of development you are likely to discover that he has become either easier or more difficult to manage. Both in the developmental and the discipline sections throughout this book we will inform you of possible changes in his behavior patterns. Knowing about these changes in advance should assist you in adapting your methods of discipline so that their effectiveness will be maximized.

Discipline During Early Infancy: Birth to Six Months

Professionals hold varying opinions on whether or not disciplinary actions should be applied during early infancy, since the child's awareness of his parents' approval or disapproval of his actions is limited. They also feel that disciplinary actions that delay or block the satisfaction of the baby's needs may undermine the development of trust in his parents. Other professionals feel that discipline in early infancy can be effective if initiated in proper forms. They suggest that babies are capable of learning and responding to training almost immediately after birth.

The decision of whether or not to begin active discipline shortly after birth is up to you. Some parents feel that it is important to establish a program of discipline right after birth, by instituting rigid feeding schedules. They believe that disciplinary measures during early infancy are necessary for good habit and character formation. Other parents prefer not to initiate disciplinary actions until the baby is older, between three and six months of age. They feel that during early infancy the baby is not really aware of his social environment, nor is he capable of adapting his needs or desires to a rigid schedule at this early stage.

Despite controversy over the exact time to introduce disciplinary measures in infancy, there are certain principles of discipline that should be considered right after birth. Developing a strong parent-child relationship is an important foundation for establishing an effective discipline program later in life. It is also important for parents to realize that their baby cannot be expected to understand right from wrong or simple commands during early infancy. These two major principles are discussed below.

How you discipline should be a personal decision taking into account your own feelings and the individual characteristics and needs of your baby. The material in this and other discipline sections during infancy should assist you in developing your own personalized approach to discipline.

BUILDING UP A POSITIVE RELATIONSHIP WITH YOUR BABY. One of the most valuable steps that you can take during early infancy is to focus on building up a positive relationship with your baby. The all-important basic foundations of love, respect, and trust are established very early in a child's life. These foundations can be of great assistance to you in disciplining your baby later in infancy, toddlerhood, and the preschool years.

By offering your infant love and attention, and by being consistent and prompt in responding to his needs, he will learn to trust you and become emotionally attached to you. He will also come to realize that you have his best interests at heart. The rules and limits that you impose on his behavior as he grows older are thus likely to be accepted without his feeling resentful, and without his questioning your underlying motives. Caring about you will make him strive harder to please you. Part of this will entail following your rules and staying within the boundaries you set. As a result of establishing a close, positive relationship with you, he will learn the value of respecting and showing concern for other people's rights and feelings.

Now is the time to begin working on developing a good relationship with him. It is not too early to be thinking about the future. The rewards that you will reap from this, both now and in the months and years to come, will be tremendous.

YOUR BABY DOES NOT UNDERSTAND RIGHT FROM WRONG. Your baby cannot be expected to comprehend what you say to him. He will not understand the difference between "good" and "bad," "right" and "wrong," or "yes" and "no." It will be a long time before he has any idea of what these words mean, and clearly becomes aware of your approval and disapproval of his actions, although he can get some sense of your disapproval by the tone of your voice.

When he is doing something that bothers you, you cannot expect him to understand when you tell him to stop doing it. His lack of responsiveness will occasionally be very irritating to you. Mrs. Bannister's son, Andy, had been crying for an hour during the night, and all of her attempts to quiet him did not work. With each passing minute she got more and more frustrated and annoyed, but did not know what to do.

Unfortunately, this mother's alternatives for further action were limited. If she yelled at him, he probably would not respond, because he would have no idea of what she was saying. If she spanked him, he would not know why she hit him. Furthermore, her screaming and spanking would only add to his discomfort or pain, and give him further cause for crying. Her hands were tied.

This inability on your baby's part to comprehend what aspects of his behavior annoy you, and to exercise self-control, is likely to be one of your biggest "gripes" during early infancy, and rightly so. It is important, however, to keep in mind that your child is not doing this intentionally.

A baby who cannot even understand rules should not be punished for breaking them. Most professionals agree that punishment should not be meted out to a young infant. If your baby did something that was irritating, and you retaliated by screaming at him, spanking him, withholding his next meal, or depriving him of your attention and affection, these actions would be inappropriate. They might also undermine his sense of trust in you and put a damper on the relationship that you share.

A certain amount of patience and restraint on your part will be necessary, particularly during early infancy. This will be easier on some of you than others, especially if you have trouble controlling your temper or tend toward physical expressions of anger. You must remember that you are dealing with an infant, not an older child who understands the difference between right and wrong and who is capable of exercising self-control.

PUNISHMENT. Punishment rarely becomes a major issue during early infancy. According to most professionals, punishment should only be employed when a child clearly understands the rule or limit that his parent has established, and deliberately disobeys or violates the rule. It is unfair to punish a child who does not realize that he is doing anything wrong.

Babies, even those from nine months to a year of age, have limited self-control and comprehension of language. As the child matures and becomes more aware of the difference between acceptable and unacceptable behavior according to his parents' standards, punishment may be employed by some parents as a means of enforcing their program of discipline. The difference between punishment and discipline and some basic principles of punishment are discussed on pages 327–31.

INTRODUCING DISCIPLINE DURING EARLY INFANCY. The choice of whether or not to introduce disciplinary measures in early infancy is a matter of personal preference. During approximately the first five to six months of life, the child has limited locomotor skills. The common areas in which parents often feel the need for discipline are mainly related to constant demands for their attention, unexplainable crying episodes, fussing during necessary activities, and feeding and sleeping difficulties. Regardless of the age at which you decide to take some initial disciplinary action, the topics below should be of assistance to you in training your child.

Helping Him To Establish Good Habits. During the first month or two, your baby's ability to adapt to a regular routine that fits into your lifestyle is, at best, limited. As he matures, however, his body will begin functioning more smoothly. Steering him gradually into living patterns that nicely coincide with yours will subtly teach him that there are certain aspects of his life that must be structured in order to live in harmony with others in the family.

You can also establish a more regular routine for feeding, bathing, sleeping, and so forth, and try to stick to it. Predictability and consistency in his daily schedule should promote good living habits at an early age. This should also help to prevent unnecessary arguments in the future over going to bed, taking a nap, and so on.

Even during the first few months, babies may voice their dislikes for certain activities. Some babies fuss, cry, and squirm whenever their hair is washed, or whenever they are given a bath. To discontinue bathing them because they are protesting would lead to very dirty, smelly babies. They can learn very early that there are some things that have to be done, even though they may not like them.

Should your infant fuss when you try to carry out certain necessary activities, you may have to ignore some of his objections, and show him that you mean business. Keep a firm hold on him if he is kicking and squirming, and carry on in a calm and confident manner. Let him know that you understand his dislikes, but "tell him" that it is necessary to proceed for his own good. This is not to imply that you should not take his preferences into account, but when it comes to necessary activities such as brushing his hair or keeping his body clean, you probably will have to be firm.

Not Responding To His Every Whimper. During the first few months, as is discussed in several other sections, it would be a mistake to ignore his crying and fussing because this is his major way of communicating to you that he needs something, or is in some sort of distress. You need not be particularly concerned about the possibility of spoiling him simply because you respond promptly to his real needs.

But what if he continues to cry or fuss for no apparent reason after the first few months? Some babies who are capable of sleeping through the night, continue to cry each night for no apparent reason. Others cry each evening just before bedtime for no reason that you can determine. Still others fuss on and off during the day, again, for no obvious reason. In this situation you can take some disciplinary action to try to discourage unexplainable crying or fussing.

The first step is not to rush to your older infant the second he begins to fuss or cry. Wait for ten minutes or so to pass. If he does not settle down, or his crying escalates in volume and intensity, go to him and try to figure out why he is crying. Be sure he is not sick or in pain. Provided that you cannot find a legitimate reason, and have done a thorough check, you can reassure him, leave him alone, and then ignore him if he continues to cry or fuss.

Consistency In Your Handling Is Important. For your baby to understand that you will not tolerate fussing or crying for no good reason, you will have to be consistent in your handling of him each time he cries or fusses unnecessarily. If you ignore his evening fussing for three days, and then shower him with attention on the fourth, your behavior will teach him that by being persistent he can get what he wants. Consistency in your response to specific situations is important when trying to get some message across to him, and is an essential aspect of an effective approach to dicipline.

The repetition and predictability that a consistent approach offers helps babies and young children to learn more easily the lessons of discipline. It also adds a certain stability to their lives and makes them feel more secure. Inconsistency or vacillation over discipline can result in anxiety, insecurity, and more provocative, testing behavior on the part of children. Most children seek guidelines, direction, and limits.

Children who can rely upon reasonable and consistent external limits, rules, and routines learn to live within those boundaries. They can relax, knowing that they can trust their parents to respond in a certain predictable way in particular situations. This gradually enables them to formulate their own internal controls and personal boundaries over the first five years. Consistency in discipline will become even more important once your baby begins to crawl or move about across the floor, and you must teach him that there are certain objects that he can or cannot touch.

You Cannot Devote 100 Percent Of Your Attention To Your Baby. All babies need an abundance of love, cuddling, affection, and individualized attention. They thrive on these "gifts." During infancy it is hoped that your baby will receive these "gifts" in large doses. However, sooner or later as he grows older and stays awake for longer periods of time each day, he will necessarily have to learn that you cannot possibly devote 100 percent of your time and attention to him whenever he is awake.

There will be times when you have other important things to do besides attending to him. During these times he will have to learn to be resourceful. One aspect of your program of discipline will probably involve training him to be on his own for short periods of time during the day when he is awake and you either cannot, or do not want, to give him your full attention.

Once he is about three to four months old, you can do this very easily by placing him in a playpen, or another safe place. This does not mean that you should ignore him completely. You can talk or sing to him, put his playpen in the room in which you are working, check on him from time to time, and let him know that you still care about him and are thinking of him even when you are otherwise occupied.

Another aspect of his training will involve getting him used to being around other people when you are not around. If you work outside of the home, he will be forced to learn that you cannot always give him your attention. Even when you are at home, however, you can see that he spends some time with other people, particularly your spouse and your other children, but also, occasionally, a neighbor, a friend, or a baby-sitter when you have to go out. Getting accustomed to being around other people from an early age will be beneficial for him in many ways.

POSTNATAL ADJUSTMENTS

Women who have just given birth will have to make several adjustments, both physical and emotional in nature. It is important that a mother be aware of some of these adjustments and understand how essential it is that she take good care of herself for her own sake and the sake of her family.

Maternal Care

YOUR FEELINGS. Whether or not this is your first child, you may feel on top of the world after delivery and ecstatic about your new baby and new role as a mother. On the other hand, you may feel somewhat depressed and anxious for a while. Not all mothers experience the "blues" (commonly referred to as postpartum blues) after giving birth, but some do. You should certainly be aware of the possibility. Postpartum blues and other emotional considerations are more extensively discussed on pages 170–72. Whatever your feelings are, you should try to share them with your spouse, close friends, physician, or other people. Do not hesitate to ask for a little extra assistance and emotional support, if you think it might help.

FATIGUE. It is common for women to feel tired following delivery. As a new mother, you should be sure to get adequate amounts of relaxation and sleep in order to regain your strength. This may not be easy in the beginning, with frequent feedings, diaper changes, and so forth. Try to include time for a short nap or two in your daily schedule. It is often wise to take a nap while your baby is sleeping.

It is not advisable to overwork or overexert yourself. Even though you may wish to get back to your normal routine and pattern of work immediately, try to make a gradual return, doing a little more each day as long as you feel up to it.

DIET. Some of you will have put on unnecessary pounds while you were pregnant, thinking that they would automatically disappear after delivery. Your doctor can recommend a diet, if you are heavier than you would like to be following delivery. If you are breast-feeding, you will have to maintain a well-balanced diet that concentrates on adding back the elements your baby depletes when he nurses. You will find a more extensive discussion of a nursing mother's diet on pages 60–61.

BODY CONDITION. Whether or not you are breast-feeding, your doctor may recommend that you perform certain postpartum exercises daily, once you feel up to it, in order to get your body back into shape. Walking, sit-ups, bicycling exercises, and exercises that are focused on the abdomen are among those often suggested.

After giving birth, your body will begin returning to its non-pregnant condition. Your uterus will start contracting and decreasing in size shortly after delivery, so that by about two weeks or so following delivery, it will have almost returned to its pear-shaped normal size. This process occurs more rapidly in women who are breast-feeding, because a baby's suckling releases the hormone that stimulates the uterus to contract. You may experience some pain or discomfort as your uterus contracts. If so, consult your doctor, who may prescribe a medication to ease the pain. Mothers who are breast-feeding should definitely not take any medication to alleviate the pain without first consulting a doctor, due to the possibility of harmful oral medications reaching their babies through the breast milk.

As your uterus shrinks in size, you will have a discharge called "lochia" from your vagina, composed of clots of blood, mucus, and tissue. This bloody discharge, which generally lasts through the first couple of weeks, will probably change in color from blood red to light pink to light yellow, until it disappears. In the event that this lochia smells very bad or remains bloody, inform your doctor. An obvious increase in bleeding from the vagina after the first week should be reported. Sanitary napkins will be required for at least the first couple of weeks. Be sure to change napkins frequently. It is not advisable to use tampons during this time.

Should you not plan to breast-feed your baby after your delivery, your doctor will probably recommend specific ways to suppress your supply of breast milk. Your breasts will gradually begin to return to their normal shape and size. If you plan to breast-feed, your breasts will remain somewhat enlarged until you wean your baby.

BOWEL MOVEMENTS. Many women after delivery wonder whether they will be able to pass a stool without tearing or overstretching their stitches, if they have any. You need not worry about this, as long as you do not strain in moving your bowels. The best thing to do is to relax, eat well, get some exercise, and drink adequate liquids to help stimulate your movements. Constipation is not unusual. Your doctor may recommend a change in diet, a milk laxative, an enema, or a suppository to alleviate the situation. Take no medications or laxatives without consulting your doctor if you are nursing. A stool softener may be recommended. Hemorrhoids, dilation in the veins around the anus and rectum, can produce added discomfort. This problem should be discussed with your physician.

URINATION. Most women experience no difficulty urinating after delivery. If you have had a hard time passing urine while in the hospital, a doctor or nurse may catheterize you in order to release the urine. This process is not usually painful. It involves putting a small rubber tube through the urethra into the bladder and releasing the urine. Should you feel any pain when you urinate at later times, be sure to inform your physician.

PERSONAL HYGIENE. A doctor or nurse will give you instructions regarding your personal hygiene after delivery. Instructions may include things you should do to prevent infection around your vagina, since the period immediately following delivery is a time when infection might occur. Your doctor will probably recommend that you wait a week, or sometimes longer, before taking a normal tub bath, but will suggest other alternatives for bathing. Breast-feeding mothers should review the information on page 60 regarding breast care.

CARE OF EPISIOTOMIES. Episiotomies (an incision made at the time of delivery to enlarge the opening through which the baby passes and prevent undue stretching and tearing of the tissues) are often performed during delivery. Many women, after delivery, experience tenderness, soreness, discomfort, or pain as the result of their episiotomy. Sitz baths are often recommended. A hospital staff member or your doctor may also give you instructions for after you leave the hospital about what you should and should not do in the region where there are stitches. Sitting on an inflatable, doughnut-shaped ring is often more comfortable than sitting on a chair. Cold treatments until the swelling subsides and heat treatments thereafter to reduce soreness may be recommended. Follow the instructions that you are given.

FAMILY PLANNING. Those mothers who are interested in family planning are often curious about the resumption of ovulation, menstruation, and methods of birth control after delivery. The time at which menstruation will be resumed can vary from woman to woman. Bottle-feeding mothers may have a period within the first couple of months postpartum, whereas in breast-feeding mothers, menstruation is often delayed, and sometimes returns only after weaning is initiated. Whenever menstruation returns, your period may be somewhat irregular for a while. Discuss any questions that may arise in relation to menstruation with your gynecologist.

According to Dr. Philip Sarrel of Yale University, ovulation can occur as early as twenty-eight days postpartum in non-breast-feeding mothers. A delay in ovulation normally accompanies breast-feeding, although it can occur as early as forty-two days postpartum. Once ovulation has begun, it is possible for a mother to become pregnant. Conception can occur even in the absence of menstruation.

Some parents are misinformed about breast-feeding as a form of birth control. They mistakenly believe that because a woman is breast-feeding, she cannot become pregnant. Breast-feeding does not preclude conception, as those women who have become pregnant while nursing discovered. You cannot count on breast-feeding as a trusted method of birth control.

Always consult a gynecologist if you are considering a form of birth control, and be sure to inform your physician that you are breast-feeding. If you have been accustomed to taking the "pill" as your method of contraception and are going to breast-feed your baby, you should be aware that birth control pills are not recommended. This type of oral agent can be transmitted to the baby through the breast milk, and may affect a mother's breast-milk supply. There are other reliable methods of contraception that can be employed in lieu of birth control pills that your physician can discuss with you.

POSTPARTUM EXAM AND RESUMING SEXUAL RELATIONS. Resuming sexual relations after delivery is discussed on pages 173–76.

Your physician will arrange for you to come in for a postpartum check-up within a month or month and a half following delivery. Be sure to keep this appointment. Any unusual symptoms or pains that worry you before the scheduled exam should be brought to your doctor's attention via telephone. Before resuming sexual intercourse, your doctor should examine you. If you feel up to having intercourse before the examination date, call your doctor, who may arrange to see you earlier.

CAESAREAN DELIVERIES (C-SECTIONS). Mothers who delivered by C-sections will experience abdominal pain for the first few days or longer after delivery. Sometimes pain will be felt in the shoulder region, as a result of minor irritation of the diaphragm by gas or blood that may accumulate under the diaphragm. As with any operation, your doctor will be able to give you medications for pain if necessary, and advise you on what to eat in the hospital. During the first day, you will be fed intravenously. Gradually, over the next few days you will be put on a regular diet.

The stitches in the abdomen will be removed at an appropriate time, usually after a week or more. If the stitches are the type that dissolve by themselves, they will not have to be removed. Delivery by C-section is very common and should not cause you undue concern. It will take you a little longer to regain your full strength and your hospital stay will also be a little longer than following a normal delivery.

The decision to deliver the baby by C-section is often made just prior to delivery. This makes it difficult for a woman to prepare herself emotionally and fully understand what is involved in this operation. Questions related to the effect of this operation on the ability to have future children, resume sexual relations, or other concerns may arise. In most C-section deliveries the mother's functioning after recovery will not be different from a normal delivery. Discuss any concerns with your physician, who is aware of your individual case and is best able to answer your questions.

Postpartum Blues: Temporary Feelings of Depression After Giving Birth

It is not unusual for women to experience "the blues" or a mild, temporary depression following the birth of their baby. These feelings of depression may follow the delivery of a first baby or subsequent ones. This fairly common type of mood change is often referred to as the "baby blues," because of the usual close association between giving birth and the onset of this mild emotional "low."

Many of you will never experience a downward mood swing in the weeks following your delivery, but since some of you will, this topic warrants your attention. By learning something about the "baby blues" and by realizing that you are not the only one to experience them, it is hoped you will be better prepared to cope with them should this become necessary. According to Marsha Dolan, a new mother:

In retrospect, the worst part about feeling depressed after my baby was born was the fact that I was totally unprepared for it. I thought I was the only woman in the world who had those feelings. I was frightened and felt very isolated. If I had only been made aware of the possibility of having the "baby blues" ahead of time, I think that I would have felt less shocked, panicky, bewildered, and alone. Had I been aware that other women have also experienced feelings of depression and have gotten over them, this would have been most comforting and reassuring at the time.

This feeling of depression frequently emerges around the third day postpartum, although the onset can vary. Some women are hit with the "blues" a few weeks or months after their baby's birth. In some instances women feel very "high" immediately following their delivery; their spirits are elevated, only to find that a couple of days later their mood has swung to the opposite extreme. Approximately one to two months after delivery, some mothers also experience a first or second brief mild depression, possibly as a response to the realization that motherhood is a more difficult, time-consuming, and even less glamorous profession than they had anticipated.

THE "BABY BLUES" CAN VARY IN INTENSITY. Women experience the "baby blues" in varying degrees. In most women the depression is mild and short-lived. For several days they may feel gloomy, tense, restless, desperate, grouchy, and insecure. Some women feel inadequate, apprehensive, unloved, and ugly. Many mothers find themselves sobbing or constantly on the verge of crying for no apparent reason. A few have bad dreams, nightmares, and frightening thoughts of suicide or about harming or leaving their babies. These thoughts quite often cause mothers to feel terribly guilty, and as a result, they may try to make it up to their babies by being overly affectionate and attentive to them. Sometimes women's anger and hostility in response to their baby or themselves are projected onto their spouses, other family members, or even their doctors.

With most women these feelings are not incapacitating and usually pass after several days, although in exceptional cases, the depression may persist, be more severe, and may interfere with normal functioning. If you still have this feeling of depression after several days, or if it seems to be escalating or interfering with your ability to function normally, you should definitely seek help in dealing with it. Your physician should be able to assist you, or may recommend a psychiatrist or other mental health professional in your local area. It is essential not only for your sake but for your baby's sake that you receive prompt medical attention in an attempt to overcome this problem as quickly as possible.

FACTORS THAT MAY CONTRIBUTE TO FEELINGS OF MILD DEPRESSION. Unfortunately, the cause of the "baby blues" is still unclear to the majority of physicians. In addition to the major life stress of having a baby, there are physiological and hormone changes that may contribute to or trigger the mild depression. Differing individual circumstances that exist prior to, during, or after delivery must also be taken into account.

It is not uncommon for women who are happy about becoming mothers, and who are well adjusted, "normal," and healthy, to experience the blues. Some of them simply feel let down after their babies are born, since the long-term build-up of anticipation prior to delivering a baby passes very quickly after the actual event. The delivery itself may even seem anticlimactic. The realization of the responsibility and hard work that go along with having a baby may first strike a mother after her baby is born. This can contribute to feelings of panic, doubts about her ability to assume the role of a mother, and depression.

Emotional and physical fatigue may also play a role. When a woman has little support from friends or family, or has little in the way of help after she arrives home, she may feel overwhelmed by the demands of a new baby. This may deepen her feelings of apprehension and despair. In some cases mothers 'are worried sick about their babies' health, especially if they are born prematurely or with a physical problem or handicap. In other instances mothers are simply disappointed over their baby's appearance or gender, and this, too, may set the stage for or contribute to the "blues."

SUGGESTIONS FOR EASING STRESSES. We cannot offer specific suggestions for how to prevent the "baby blues," but you can make some arrangements prior to your delivery to make life less stressful after you give birth. These include getting someone to help you at home afterward, keeping your daily routine flexible so that you will have ample time to accommodate your baby's pressing needs and unpredictable schedule, getting sufficient amounts of rest and relaxation, eating a proper diet, and initially limiting extracurricular commitments.

There is no reason to feel guilty, embarrassed, or ashamed about feeling blue; not all new mothers are happy and cheerful. Be honest and open about expressing your feelings. Sharing them with your spouse, physician, or some other understanding person may enable you to receive the extra support and reassurance that you may need until your depression lifts.

New Fathers May Also Feel on Edge

New fathers may also go through a temporary period in which they feel anxious or mildly depressed, although to a lesser degree than mothers. There will, of course, be no accompanying physiological or hormonal changes. In many cases mild or fleeting feelings of apprehension, loneliness, and depression and/or feelings of being left out or neglected have been gradually building up during the pregnancy period when their wives have been the main focus of everyone's attention. They seem to feel rather unimportant. These feelings may escalate at the time of their wives' hospitalization and delivery, even if they are happy at the prospect of becoming parents.

Most hospitals permit men to observe and participate at the time of the delivery, and this helps to prevent men's feelings of being lonely, left out, helpless, and unimportant. Both parents should be encouraged to handle and care for their newborn actively from the start. After the delivery, though, new fathers may not be encouraged to become actively involved in their newborn's care immediately, and may in fact not be able to visit except at certain designated times. Mothers on the other hand are encouraged to participate in their newborn's care from the beginning, and thus have a head start in gaining practical experience as well as in building a relationship with their babies.

THE RESPONSIBILITY OF BEING A PARENT CAN CAUSE ANXIETY. After their babies are born, some men are first struck by the additional responsibilities that accompany fatherhood. Many new fathers, like new mothers, feel frightened, inadequate, and rather overwhelmed by the sudden entry of a new baby into their lives. The disruption of their normal home routine may increase their anxieties. Some men are resentful that their privacy at home has been invaded, particularly if a relative, family friend, or nurse is present in the home for the first couple of weeks acting in the capacity of a "mother's helper." Worries about their baby's health, especially when some real medical problem exists, can contribute to fathers' blues, as may disappointment over the baby's physical appearance or sex.

New fathers often find themselves being leaned upon by their wives as sources of emotional support and practical help with household tasks. They may receive little in the way of support or affection themselves, particularly if their wives are preoccupied emotionally as well as physically with their child. In cases in which their wives are having downward mood swings or ambivalent or negative feelings about their baby after giving birth, fathers may bear the brunt of their wives' hostility or anger.

FEELING HELPLESS AND LEFT OUT. For a variety of reasons, fathers are sometimes reluctant to offer assistance in their baby's care, even though they may desperately want to be included and involved. Sometimes their hesitation is simply a matter of inexperience in dealing with babies or insecurity about their abilities in this regard. Lack of sufficient reassurance and encouragement from their spouse may be a factor. When a new father is, in subtle ways, forced to take second place to a mother-in-law, friend, or nurse, or stay in the background for the first several weeks following delivery, feelings of depression or of being unimportant may be heightened. It is also not uncommon for men to feel some resentment and jealousy if their wives are devoting more attention, time, and energy to their baby than to them.

The adjustments that new fathers have to make are no less important than those of new mothers. Men who are actively involved with their wives during labor and delivery, and those who immediately take an active role in their baby's care, may not experience the "blues" as intensely as those who do not. Nevertheless, the hospitalization and postdelivery periods are stressful, and new fathers feel the pressures in varying degrees.

Do speak up, if you feel you would like to be more involved in your child's care, but for whatever reasons are not. Your early involvement is crucially important for your own sake, and your baby's. Through early participation in his care, touching, and eye contact, the two of you can establish a close bond that may be much more difficult to achieve later on in infancy. Similarly, if you feel as though you are not receiving the support, attention, or reassurance that you need, do not be embarrassed, ashamed, or hesitant to ask for it. Not all new fathers experience the "blues" and those who do may experience them immediately, or in the weeks or months following their baby's birth. Usually these feelings are only temporary, and subside after an initial period of adjustment.

Your Sex Life

Parents have concerns about the resumption of their sex life following the birth of their baby. The addition of a new member to the family disrupts the family's normal routine and the atmosphere in the home. This is a time of transition, when the whole family system is altered. Couples' relationships are often affected by these changes. Events and feelings are often easily exaggerated during this time. Sharing feelings and making an effort to keep things in perspective will make it easier for you to resume a satisfactory sexual relationship.

RESUMING SEXUAL RELATIONS. Many physicians recommend to their patients that sexual relations, specifically intercourse, not be resumed until after the mother's first medical check-up following delivery. The time for this check-up mainly depends upon your doctor's preference. Most doctors see new mothers around three weeks to a month and a half after delivery.

During the delivery and postpartum period, a woman's body undergoes physical and hormonal changes. In the weeks after their babies are born, women commonly experience a certain amount of fatigue and discomfort, particularly women who have had a difficult delivery. The difficulty of the delivery and the size of the episiotomy will have an effect on how a woman feels, and how quickly she will be able to resume normal functioning after giving birth. There can be great variability in the time it takes for a mother's vaginal area to heal, and for her to regain her strength. Some women are able to resume sexual intercourse within three weeks after giving birth. There are other women who are not fully healed and not ready to have intercourse even at six weeks.

As you recover after giving birth, your body will be undergoing numerous changes in the healing process. It is advisable to let your doctor examine you before having intercourse. In the event that your vaginal area feels fine, you are not having a vaginal discharge (lochia), and you feel ready to resume sexual relations before your scheduled doctor's appointment, call your physician and discuss your situation. An earlier appointment may be made, or your doctor may tell you to go ahead and have intercourse. Knowing your medical history, your doctor will give you appropriate advice. If your delivery was very simple and you required no episiotomy, or a small one, your doctor may recommend that you rest for a couple of weeks and then gradually resume sexual activity when you feel ready.

The main things to consider are your health, comfort, and feelings. There are some women who feel physically ready for intercourse before they feel emotionally ready. Feelings should be considered and respected.

MINOR DIFFICULTIES RELATED TO INTERCOURSE. Most couples have no difficulty resuming satisfying sexual relations following delivery, but some experience minor problems. Difficulties that arise are often due to the physical and hormonal changes taking place in a woman's body, but others may be due to alterations in lifestyle and the stresses that usually accompany having a new baby.

Some women experience discomfort during intercourse lasting for several weeks up to several months following delivery. Women who experience minor pain often find that varying their position for intercourse eases their discomfort. In a few cases, tearing of the ligaments supporting the uterus during the delivery results in minor pain in the pelvic region. These problems normally diminish with added time, but if pain persists, it should be brought to the attention of your physician.

Vaginal dryness is another minor problem that may arise. This is more common in women who are breast-feeding, and may persist for six to eight months. Vaginal lubrication normally accompanies sexual arousal, and a couple comes to expect this. When intercourse is attempted following delivery, insufficient lubrication of a woman's vagina can come as an unwelcome surprise.

A man may take this as a sign that his wife is not sexually aroused, even though the opposite is the case. A lack of lubrication can make intercourse quite uncomfortable for both partners. It can also be a sexual "turn off."

A simple solution to this problem is to use a lubricant, either saliva or a jelly for this purpose. Using a lubricant should alleviate the vaginal dryness, and make sexual intercourse more comfortable. Your doctor may have other recommendations, so you are wise to discuss this problem with him or her.

SEXUAL SATISFACTION WITHOUT INTERCOURSE. During the early weeks after a baby is born, a woman will be healing and trying to recuperate from birth, and both she and her spouse will be finding life very different from before. It will be several weeks or more before intercourse will be possible, but this does not mean that parents cannot feel sexually satisfied during the interim period.

Sexual satisfaction does not equal intercourse; the two do not necessarily go hand in hand. Even though you cannot have intercourse, you can continue to enjoy warmth and intimacy in bed. This will not take the place of intercourse, but it will help to ease tensions. Sometimes it is much better, since neither of you will feel any pressure to perform. Warmth, sensuality, support, love, and affection can be expressed in countless numbers of ways, and at any time, depending upon your individual needs and preferences.

Masters and Johnson and Dr. and Mrs. Sarrel, well-known authorities on human sexuality, emphasize the many ways in which a man and woman can feel closeness and sensuality without necessarily feeling the need to have intercourse. Caressing, cuddling, kissing, stroking each other's bodies, and massaging one another with oil or lotion are some of the countless ways of achieving sexual and emotional satisfaction. You and your spouse can discover your own special ways of satisfying one another's needs and deriving pleasure during those times in which you either cannot or do not want to have intercourse.

Communication, both physical and verbal, is crucial in maintaining intimacy after your baby is born. Sharing your feelings, ideas, fears, doubts, and sexual problems will help to strengthen your relationship. It is important to talk frequently about yourselves as individuals, as parents, and as sexual partners. Free and comfortable communication will help prevent the major changes in your lives from creating a distance between you. Also make an effort to do things together, particularly things that you both enjoy.

Having fun together and spending some time alone is vital to your relationship. When parents feel good about themselves, their relationship, and their sex life, they will also feel more positively toward their child. Finding pleasure in each other will help to set a positive tone for family life, and will make life more enjoyable for every member of your family.

SEX AND THE NURSING MOTHER. Breast-feeding a baby does not necessarily affect your sexual relationship with your spouse. Some couples, however, have noticed that breast-feeding does affect their relationship, and it might be helpful to be aware of common experiences.

It is not uncommon for the breasts to secrete milk during sexual stimulation or at the time of orgasm. This is a very natural response. Many couples are not bothered by this flow of milk, while others find it somewhat undesirable. Wearing a bra or nursing pads that provide some pressure may decrease the milk flow or absorb it. These articles of clothing may make love-making seem less natural for some. Having sex shortly after you nurse your baby may help prevent leakage of large quantities of milk.

Some women note that their breasts seem less sensitive to their husband's stimulation now that the breasts are engorged and producing milk. This is not a cause for concern, and should not greatly interfere with the over-all satisfaction that you derive from your total relationship with your spouse.

ROMANCE AND SPONTANEITY. Romance and spontaneity are often considered to go hand in hand. With a new baby in the family, many couples experience a loss of spontaneity in their sex lives. Parents often speak of how they are suddenly forced to contend with elaborate baby care routines and feeding schedules, anticipate every move, and forget about sudden changes in plans or spur-of-the-moment decisions about when to make love. They often find that being practical and calculating when it comes to deciding when and where love-making will occur takes away from some of the excitement and romance.

In the event that you feel your sex life is suffering because of lack of spontaneity, one solution is to plan for it. At first, this suggestion may seem to be contrary to the obvious meaning of the word "spontaneity." However, if you arrange ahead of time to enlist the services of a baby-sitter occasionally, or leave your baby at Grandma's house for an evening, this will enable you to be as spontaneous as you like about making love.

It often takes a little more planning ahead for spontaneity, but most couples feel that it is well worth the effort. Once your baby's schedule becomes more regular and predictable, it will be easier to be spontaneous during those times when he is sleeping or napping. Remember that romance need not always involve or lead to sexual intercourse. An unscheduled candlelit dinner can sometimes add more excitement and spice to your relationship than making love at four o'clock in the afternoon in the middle of the living room floor.

FEELING TOO TIRED FOR SEX? Fatigue is a factor that can definitely interfere with a parent's sex life. Meeting the constant demands of a baby during the day and night can leave you feeling pressured and drained of all energy to do anything but the bare minimum. There will be times when your baby is sleeping, but chances are that you will spend that time trying to catch up on your own sleep, cooking, cleaning, laundry, and other necessities of life.

Getting up for feedings at frequent intervals during the night can make a parent too tired to respond to sexual advances. The tension, responsibility, and demands of being a new parent can lead to the regular complaint that "I'm too tired for sex!"

Laurie Cole, a new mother, had this to say about the first two months after her baby daughter was born.

Responsibilities piled up tremendously. I could never get myself ahead of schedule so that I had time to relax and unwind. There was always something left that I had to do. When it came time for sex at the end of the day, I was so exhausted that I couldn't seem to get myself in the mood. Sex, although I felt the need for it, became simply one more daily activity that, quite frankly, drained me a lot. When Jim came home from work, he was nearly always in the mood for sex. Me? I could have cared less. All I wanted was to be left alone so that I could relax and catch up on much needed sleep.

When intercourse becomes "just one more responsibility," then the pleasure and satisfaction derived from this form of sexual expression will be greatly diminished. Husband and wife should be considerate of each other's feelings, needs, and physical limitations. This is particularly important during the first few months after the baby's birth. Feelings of fatigue usually pass as the baby's needs become more predictable, and as parents feel comfortable about having someone else occasionally stay with the baby while they get some relief. In the event that one partner's complaint of being too tired for sex persists, and seems to be used as an excuse, then it would be advisable for a couple to examine the situation and try to determine the underlying reasons. Seek the help of a trained physician or counselor if this becomes necessary.

PREOCCUPATION WITH A NEW BABY. Amid all of the excitement, decisions, feedings, and so forth, that go along with dealing with a baby for the first time, you must not ignore your own needs or those of your spouse. You should make time to talk about yourselves as individuals, your lives together, and your sex life. Even if your desire for sex has diminished, you should realize that your spouse's desires may not have. You should attempt to gratify them out of consideration for him or her.

It is not uncommon for parents, mothers in particular, to become overly preoccupied with their new baby, especially if it is their first child. In some cases a new baby becomes the major focus of a parent's energies and attention, as well as the major topic of conversation. When both parents feel this way for a while, this may not present any problem, but when only one parent becomes rather obsessed with the new baby, this can create tension and perhaps arouse the other parent's resentment and jealousy.

Sarah Goodhue became totally wrapped up with her new son, Sean, for the first several months following his birth. This led to some friction between her and her husband, Gary. According to Gary:

All Sarah talked about was our baby, Sean. Every phone conversation, dinner conversation, and bedroom conversation centered around Sean—how well he sucked on her breasts, how many times he wet his diapers, how long he cried during the afternoon, what his bowel movements looked like, and on and on and on. I didn't mind all this talk about Sean for the first few weeks, because I was excited and wanted to know everything that happened or that he did while I was at work. After a while, though, I resented the fact that Sarah was paying more attention to Sean than to me. She lost her interest in sex, and nothing else seemed to matter to her except Sean. She even made me feel like I was being selfish for wanting to make love. I hated the fact that I had to compete with Sean for her attention. Things were really tense between us for four months. We rarely spent any time alone together, and had sex only a handful of times. After Sean was four months old, Sarah calmed down, and no longer seemed as preoccupied with our son. Things between us gradually got better.

It is easy to become wrapped up in a new baby, to the exclusion of everything and everyone else in your life, but you should guard against allowing this to happen. It is extremely important to strike a balance among meeting your baby's needs, your own needs, and your spouse's needs, if stability in your home and marriage is to be maintained. During the first few weeks after your baby is born, it is only natural that he will be the center of attention and the main topic of conversation. At the same time, it is important to consider your spouse's feelings and sexual needs, and re-establish the closeness and intimacy that are vital to your relationship and happiness.

YOUR FIRST CHILD'S REACTION TO THE ARRIVAL OF THE NEW BABY

Bringing a new baby into your family structure will necessarily have an effect upon your first child. Many parents worry about how their child will react toward the new baby. There is no one answer to this question. Reactions among children vary considerably.

One child may be elated and another may be depressed. One may act friendly toward the newcomer, while another may express open antagonism and even lash out at the baby physically. One child may regress, while another may act more grown-up. An occasional child may become silent and withdrawn. Still another may seem indifferent or in good spirits for a month or more and then, suddenly, a rush of negative feelings may come pouring out.

How a child is affected and how he expresses his feelings will depend upon factors such as his age, how dependent he is upon you, the closeness of your relationship, the amount of time you normally spend with him, his emotional maturity, whether or not he was properly prepared in advance, and how you handle the situation. Feelings of unworthiness, jealousy, insecurity, and mild depression are fairly common among children in regard to the arrival of a sibling. Less common are feelings of happiness, joy, and positive acceptance. In some instances a child's feelings vacillate from positive to negative.

You should not be surprised if your child has some ambivalent or negative feelings in regard to the new baby or has difficulty adjusting to having a sibling, particularly if he is less than three years old. This is not to say that all children will be upset when you arrive home with a baby. Likewise, this is not to imply that all children will have nothing but positive feelings for their new sibling. Rather it is to bring to light the possibility that a child under age three may be more threatened by the new baby and less able to cope with this life change as effectively as an older child.

It may, indeed, be difficult at first for your other child to adjust to the reality of sharing your affection and attention with a newcomer, just as you may have some initial difficulty giving of yourself to your new infant while still meeting the needs of other family members. Rest assured that difficulties experienced initially will be resolved if you give your older child some extra love and reassurance, as well as ample time to make an adjustment and begin building up a relationship with his sibling. In time, your child will come to accept the new baby, although he may or may not be completely happy about this.

Reactions of Children Under the Age of Three

A child under the age of about three, who is still very dependent upon his parents, may feel the loss of their time, affection, and attention more intensely than would an older child. Generally speaking, a child past the age of three is more independent, and has friends and perhaps even a life of his own, so to speak, outside of the home environment at nursery or elementary school. He has already worked through some of the problems of independence from his parents, and, although he may be closely tied to them, he is not as dependent as a toddler would be for companionship, going to the toilet, and so forth.

THE TODDLER MAY HAVE TROUBLE SHARING YOUR ATTENTION AND AFFECTION. A new baby is more of a threat to a toddler, whose day revolves a great deal around his parents. The abrupt transition from being a major focus of his parents' energies, attention, and love, to having to share all of this with a baby or even, perhaps, take second place to the baby for a few months, may be highly disturbing to him. In many cases younger children show an instant dislike for their new sibling, and resent the baby's presence. A child younger than three does not have the same intellectual equipment as an older child to deal with the situation. He may have great trouble trying to understand exactly what is happening, and in doing so, may misinterpret events and other people's actions and responses.

NEGATIVE FEELINGS WILL BE EXPRESSED IN BEHAVIOR. Toddlers and even many young preschool children are lacking in their ability to express their feelings in words. Any negative feelings that they have are likely to be expressed through their actions. The normal amount of negativism and rebellion that nearly every toddler and young preschooler express may become centered around and directed at the new sibling. The possibility that the child who is disturbed by the baby's presence may strike the baby or try to harm his sibling physically is very real. Parents should understand that this is due to his limited capacity to express anger and aggression through language as opposed to direct actions. Nevertheless, such behavior cannot be tolerated. Adequate provisions and precautionary measures must be taken to prevent harm from coming to the new baby (see page 511). Teasing, poking, and grabbing away the baby's toys are also fairly common ways in which the toddler or preschool child may express dislike of his sibling.

REGRESSION. Several important developmental milestones are generally achieved during toddlerhood, including walking, developing toilet habits, "first" independence, and speech. A major stressful event in a toddler's life such as the arrival of a new baby can, in some instances, result in a temporary regression in behavior. A toddler who has just learned to walk, for example, may briefly return to crawling. A child who has mastered the use of the toilet may slide backward for a time and soil or wet his pants. Children who are perfectly able to speak may begin to talk "baby talk." Some children who feel that they are being neglected or are not "wanted" as much as the new baby decide that if they become more like a baby their parents will love them again or pay more attention to them; this prompts requests for the breast or bottle, their return to crawling, talking like a baby, or wetting their pants, and their increased dependency.

DESTRUCTIVE BEHAVIOR. Some toddlers become destructive. A toddler who is feeling unloved, rejected, and angry that his parents are not devoting as much time to him as they used to may begin to break toys and other objects in the home as a way of venting frustration, and as a way of attracting their attention. He knows that they will not ignore his behavior. He may act up whenever he feels left out or as though he is being ignored. There are also many other ways in which a child may attempt to get more attention, such as showing off or throwing temper tantrums.

GIVE YOUR TODDLER TIME TO ADJUST. Young children's feelings of jealousy, rivalry, and resentment in relation to the arrival of a new baby are fairly common. Your child may not have these feelings, and may have little or no difficulty adjusting but most youngsters under age three will have to make numerous emotional adjustments in the days, weeks, and even months after the baby is born.

Try to understand the reasons why your toddler reacts the way he does to the baby. Make sure that your own behavior is not giving any real substance to his feelings of jealousy, being neglected, or unloved. Giving him a little extra love, affection, individualized attention, and reassurance that you are still there for *him* may help in making the difficult adjustment to sharing you with a sibling a little easier.

Reactions of Preschool Children

An older preschool child around three or four years of age is an entirely different person from a year-and-a-half-old child or a two-year-old in many respects. In addition to the differences previously mentioned, one of the major distinctions lies in his greater understanding of the events that are taking place and his ability to talk about them, verbally express his feelings, and ask questions. His reaction to the new baby will, to a greater extent than with a child under three, depend upon whether and how well he has been prepared in advance for the baby's arrival, and how his parents handle the situation afterward. He is still immature. Even though he has been prepared in advance and has had ample time to get used to the idea of having a new baby in the home, there is no real way of predicting ahead of time how he will react to the reality of the new baby.

FEELING UNLOVED AND REJECTED. It is not uncommon for a child to feel unloved or unwanted. He may think that he must have done something terribly wrong for his parents to want another baby to "replace" him. He may be very jealous and resentful of the newcomer. His anger over the fact that his parents "betrayed him" may be directed at the new baby. Several parents have heard statements that their preschoolers have made to the effect that they wanted their parents to "take the baby back," "get rid of him," or "throw him away."

EXPRESSING ANGER TOWARD THE BABY. These kinds of negative feelings may prompt the child to lash out at the baby by making him cry, poking, teasing, and even hitting him. Parents, in response, may have to put a stop to this firmly, but at the same time can assure the child that they understand the feelings underlying such unacceptable behavior. The preschool child clearly knows what he is doing, and is more capable of exercising self-control than is a toddler.

DISAPPOINTMENT. Preschool children, in some cases, have been told by their parents that the new baby will be a perfect playmate for them. These children may be very disappointed when they see the baby for the first time and fully realize that the baby is tiny, helpless, and not at all capable of playing with them. These youngsters are likely to feel let down and even angry at their parents for misleading them.

Sometimes a preschool child has definite feelings about whether he wants the baby to be a girl or a boy, and may, through his immature and magical kind of thought process, believe that because he wishes it were so it will be so! This child may be terribly let down when the baby does not turn out as he had expected. The baby's sex may contribute to a child's feeling mildly depressed about the baby's entry into the family.

THE PRESCHOOL CHILD SHOULD BE PERMITTED TO TALK ABOUT HIS FEELINGS. There are many different reactions that a child may have and feelings may be expressed in different ways. The point is that he will be affected by the baby and he should be given opportunities to voice his feelings. He cannot control his feelings, although he can control aggressive actions toward the baby, you, or other children. Parents should try to encourage rather than discourage their child to talk about his feelings, even though the comments are very negative.

Some parents tend to deny their child's feelings simply because they do not like what they hear. When a child says, "I hate that baby, so send him back to the hospital," a parent may reply, "How can you say such bad things about your baby brother whom you *know* you love." Such a parent is trying to make the child deny his real feelings, and is making it difficult for him ever to express how he truly feels.

HELPING HIM ADJUST TO THE NEW BABY. When you finally bring the baby home, recognize your older child's need for a big hug and kiss. He will want to know that he is still loved and is still important. Tell him how much you missed him while the two of you were apart. Give him the time and individualized attention that he needs from you, not from Daddy, Grandma, or Grandpa.

If your child has a negative reaction to the baby's arrival, you should try to understand his reactions and the feelings behind them. His feelings are very real to him. Examine your own behavior, too. Perhaps you are not giving him enough time and affection. It could be that you are inadvertently overlooking or not satisfying his needs. Maybe you are not giving him enough opportunities to express his feelings openly, or are not allowing him to be as involved in the baby's care as he would like.

He may need your extra reassurance and affection during the transition period. Be sure to give him opportunities to hold the baby with supervision, and let him help you tend to the baby, but refrain from pressuring if he expresses a desire to keep his distance. Even having chances to perform simple tasks, such as bring you the baby's bottle or diapers, may make him feel less left out and excluded. Give his feelings and needs due consideration by allowing him to express them without your passing moral judgment on them or denying them.

Do whatever you can to make him feel less lonely, unimportant, left out, and neglected. In case you cannot devote equal time to him and the baby, let him know why. Explain to him that when he was a baby, he had very pressing needs for food, cuddling, attention, and so forth, and that you devoted a great deal of time and attention to him. This may be a perfect time to take out a photograph album and show him pictures of what he was like when he was a baby. The fact that you took so many pictures of him may boost his ego and self-esteem, and convince him that he is wanted and important.

Playing with dolls, and perhaps a doll house or other related equipment, may serve as a marvelous outlet for him while you tend to the baby. He can mimic your actions or express feelings and possible frustrations and aggressions when playing with dolls that he may be unable to express toward the baby or toward you. You may want to purchase these special playthings prior to the baby's delivery date and then present them to him upon your homecoming as a gift. Remember that the newcomer will be receiving all kinds of gifts and attention from visitors. Receiving a special present from you can help to downplay the older child's feelings of jealousy and being left out, and may keep him happily occupied while visitors are doting over the new baby.

Some children become upset when they observe their mothers breast-feeding. Seeing the intimacy between their mother and the baby may heighten their own feelings of the loss of this intimacy or of being left out. If such is the case with your child, try to respect his feelings. Some mothers find it helpful to read to their child and allow him to cuddle up to them during the nursing session. This gives the child the attention and closeness that he feels he is missing, and helps to minimize jealousy and resentment.

REMEMBER THAT EACH CHILD HAS DIFFERENT NEEDS. It will be impossible for you to divide your time, attention, and affection equally between your older child and your new baby. They are different people with different needs, and should be treated as such. Promises that you may make to your preschool child about being loved equally as much as your youngest or treated equally are almost sure to be broken. Rather than making such promises, show by your actions that you recognize your older child's individual needs and are responsive to him.

Rivalry and jealousy among siblings are common and to some degree should be anticipated. It may take quite a while for your preschool child to get accustomed to having the new baby around, or he may adjust to this very quickly. By staying in close touch with his individual needs, rivalry between siblings and possible problems and difficulties will be minimized.

The Reaction of Older Children or Teen-agers to the Baby

Teen-agers' reactions to a new baby's arrival can range from positive acceptance to strong jealousy, resentment, and even embarrassment in front of their friends and acquaintances. When an older child or teen-ager reacts negatively to the infant, a great deal of patience, understanding, and reassurance on the part of parents will surely be required. A happy attitude about the arrival of the new baby can make it easier for the older child to accept the baby, too. When parents convey their own concerns about how the baby may disrupt family life, or are apologetic to the older child, this can create added difficulties. Parents' attitudes and the manner in which they handle the situation with the older child, both prior to and after the baby is born, will greatly influence the older child's feelings and responses. As in the case of younger children, adequate preparation can help minimize difficulties.

POSSIBLE FEELINGS OF REJECTION. Older children and teen-agers sometimes feel rejected and neglected after a new baby arrives. In some cases their feelings are based upon fact. There is often a tendency among parents to ignore the older child and devote more attention to the new baby. This, to some extent, is to be expected, particularly in the first few months, but when carried to an extreme, can encourage sibling rivalry and even give substance to an older child's feelings of being unloved, unwanted, and neglected.

LET YOUR TEEN-AGER HELP BUT DON'T PRESSURE. An older child can be of great assistance to parents in caring for the new baby. It is important to take advantage of an older child's desire to be involved and willingness to help out. On the other hand, when no interest is expressed, it is best not to make demands upon the older child.

Parents sometimes take it for granted that their teen-ager will baby-sit for the new baby. A great deal of resentment can build between parent and teen-ager when parents force or pressure a teen-ager into baby-sitting against his will, make too frequent requests for this service, and offer no remuneration for the services rendered. A responsible teen-ager who is interested in baby-sitting on occasion should be offered first option of this job, but should always be treated with the same respect as would an outsider assuming the job.

ALLOW YOUR CHILD AMPLE TIME TO ADJUST TO THE BABY. Given ample time, the older child or teen-ager will more than likely come to accept the baby, but on his own special terms. Given the wide age difference between children, it may be difficult for the older child to feel really close to the baby. They will develop their own relationship, which will be most comfortable for them. Pressuring an older child to like the baby and play with him is usually not the most advisable approach. Let your child determine how to begin building a relationship with the baby in his own style, and at his own pace.

THE EMOTIONS OF PARENTHOOD

New Parents Have to Be Good Diplomats

One thing that you can pretty much count on as a new parent is the fact that, whether or not you ask for it, other people will offer you advice regarding the handling of your baby. People who have had experience in rearing children, including your parents, in-laws, other relatives, friends, neighbors, and new people to whom you are introduced, may flood you with suggestions, criticisms, and stories about their own experiences as parents. Most of the advice that you will receive will be offered by those who mean well.

LISTENING TO OTHER PARENTS CAN BE HELPFUL. You may benefit greatly from talking about child-rearing issues with experienced parents. Practical tips on burping, soothing a crying baby, clothing and equipment, choosing toys, setting up a nursery, and so forth, can make life a bit easier and less confusing in the beginning. Comments and suggestions that they give you may prove to be very helpful. Just hearing others describe difficulties or problems that they encountered as new parents and how they found suitable ways of coping with them can put you at ease when questions and minor difficulties surface, especially during the first few weeks.

INSECURITY ABOUT TAKING ADVICE. Many new parents are very touchy about advice, even advice that is tactfully offered with the best of intentions. Try not to be threatened when people give you advice. This may or may not be easy for you. Perhaps you lack self-confidence and are insecure about your ability to do a good job as a parent. Maybe it is important for you to prove that you are independent and can "go it alone." You are certainly not alone, if you fit this description.

IT IS USEFUL TO KEEP AN OPEN MIND. When approaching any new task or profession, especially the profession of being a parent, it is advisable to keep an open mind about advice that you receive from others, and to permit them to express their opinions. There is usually much to be gained from listening to the "voice of experience." In many instances you may find that you can benefit from their experience and put what you have learned from them to good use in avoiding common pitfalls and problems.

There will be times when you feel that a person's advice does not apply to your situation or is inappropriate, given your baby and individual circumstances. You may occasionally be offended by someone's critical remarks, especially if that person offered them in what you feel was a tactless manner. Learn to be a good diplomat. When you feel that the advice you have gotten is clearly wrong, let the person know that you are grateful for his or her suggestions. Then do whatever you feel is right.

YOU RESERVE THE RIGHT TO REAR YOUR CHILD AS YOU THINK BEST. In dealing with close relatives who are continually nagging you about ignoring their advice on methods, philosophies, techniques, religious practices, or whatever, it may be best in the long run to sit down with them and have a frank discussion about your feelings on the issue. Hear them out and consider what they are telling you. If you do not plan to follow their advice because it goes against what you feel is best for you or your child, let them know that you appreciate their concern, but that you must do what you feel is right.

Try to explain your point of view. Perhaps you will be able to make them understand why you feel the way you do. Open rap sessions like this may help to clear the air. They know, just as you should, that the ultimate decisions concerning the rearing of your child are yours to make. As his parent you hold this privilege. In the event that tensions and arguments between you and close relatives over the manner in which you are rearing your child escalate to the point where life is becoming miserable, it may help to discuss family problems with a professional such as your physician, a minister, rabbi, or family counselor.

You should not feel compelled to follow other people's advice if you have given it due consideration and determined that it is wrong or detrimental for you and your baby. You and your infant are individuals as well as a family, and what works well for someone else may not work well or may not apply to your family. Rather, you reserve the right to determine what is "right" for you, depending upon your needs and those of your child.

Life with a Difficult Baby

Some babies are simply more difficult to live with and handle than others. Babies who cry a great deal, are hard to quiet, do not appear to be very responsive to parents' attempts to calm them, or are not in perfect health usually make life stressful and hard on parents, particularly during the first few weeks and months. Try as they might, parents may have trouble getting off to a good start with their baby. They may bend over backward in an attempt to soothe, comfort, and quiet him, but he may continue to squirm, fuss, cry, as though he is annoyed at them for even handling him.

A DIFFICULT BABY CAN AROUSE ALL KINDS OF FEELINGS AND EMOTIONS. How does this make a new parent feel? There is no easy answer to this question. Those who had doubts or insecurities about their abilities to be good parents or those who were not overjoyed at the prospect of becoming parents often feel frustrated. Feelings of resentment toward their baby are not uncommon. Many also feel emotionally drained and exhausted, especially if crying persists for long stretches of time during the night and the baby requires special handling. Some parents, feeling "trapped" and angry at their baby, wish that they could send or give him away. Fleeting thoughts of dropping or harming the baby may plague them and make them feel guilty.

Quite often a baby's constant crying is interpreted by parents to mean that they are doing something wrong or that the baby does not need or love them. A baby's continual fussing and crying may result in his parents not wanting to have very much contact with him. Babies who are easily comforted and who are responsive to their parents' efforts to show them attention and affection give parents the kind of feedback that encourages them to continue in this regard. A baby's persistent crying and lack of responsiveness may actually drive his parents away. It is only natural for parents to make less of an effort when their efforts seem in vain or go unrewarded. Ignoring the baby is no solution and may initiate a vicious cycle whereby parents avoid responding to him, he becomes less responsive to them, and they, in turn, back away even further.

Parents who feel anger or resentment toward their baby usually feel very guilty and ashamed about such feelings. They may try to suppress or deny these emotions or keep them all bottled up inside so that other people will not discover their true feelings. The fear is that others will think that they are not doing well in their role as parents or will not understand the circumstances. Keeping feelings to oneself, denying that they exist, or suppressing them may only serve to increase one's sense of anxiety and frustration. Feelings of guilt may be heightened if parents start to wonder whether this baby represents some kind of punishment for wrongdoings in their pasts. It is not uncommon for parents to ask the question "Why me?"

Hearing from other parents how easy their babies are to manage and how enjoyable their babies are to have around can also make parents feel miserable. A difficult baby can put all kinds of extra pressure on parents and can cause many strains on family relationships. Sometimes parents place the blame for their baby's behavior and their own misery on one another. Blame becomes a major issue and fingers get pointed. Fatigue and irritability interfere with lines of communication. If one parent felt even the least bit pressured into having a child by the other, the former may feel very resentful and direct much hostility toward the latter. Preoccupation over their baby's condition may result in parents letting their own needs go unsatisfied, heightening feelings of frustration.

PUTTING THINGS INTO PERSPECTIVE. Feelings of exhaustion, exasperation, and anger need to be expressed. There is no need for you to feel guilty about your feelings, if you are the parent of a difficult baby. You must realize that your baby is not consciously or purposely attempting to make your life unhappy and complicated. He cannot help being the way he is, and is unaware of the impact he is having upon you. You should not take your anger and frustration out upon him. Neither should you place blame upon yourself or your partner. No one is really to blame, anyway.

Maintaining a sense of perspective in your life is the key. Try to avoid becoming overly preoccupied with your difficult baby. Share your feelings with people who will not put you down and who can offer you support and reassurance. Your doctor may be of some assistance. Work at channeling your anger in constructive ways and making your life more pleasurable. Take time out to relax and rest. Spending some time away from your baby alone or with your spouse or friends may help. Putting the situation into proper perspective may also put you more at ease and may prove to help other family members as well. Keep responding to your baby, giving him affection, attention, and stimulation. He needs all of these and especially your love, even though it may not seem apparent to you. You should also not lose hope because your "difficult" baby is likely to become more enjoyable as he grows older.

YOUR FEELINGS IN RELATION TO YOUR BABY WHO HAS COLIC. Should your baby be plagued by colic (see pages 139–40) during the first three months or so, this will undoubtedly affect and probably disturb you a great deal. Depending upon the intensity or severity of the condition, all kinds of troubling emotions or feelings may be aroused. You may begin to believe you are doing something wrong or doubt your ability to handle your infant properly. Mrs. Connolly, who was breast-feeding her baby, Tommy, had this to say:

> I couldn't bear to see him having such obvious trouble. He didn't seem to be getting any pleasure out of life and I began to blame myself for his difficulties. I worried a lot about whether or not my breast-milk supply was adequate. This made me very tense and anxious whenever I fed him. This only made the situation worse, since my high anxiety, according to my doctor, hindered my milk flow.

Feelings of self-blame along with anxiety are quite common. They can be especially bothersome to mothers who are nursing, as in Mrs. Connolly's case, possibly interfering with normal milk flow. Blaming yourself is very unconstructive. More than likely, you are doing a fine job as a new parent, and your guilt feelings are totally unfounded.

Mrs. Murphy made the following remarks:

> I hated to hear my daughter, Karen, screaming for hours. She constantly cried, squirmed, and behaved as if she were in pain. I was going crazy with guilt for the first two weeks alone in the house with Karen, so I asked my hus-

band, Larry, to take his vacation from work early, just to help me. As soon as he began to care for Karen, he began to understand my feelings much more so than before. Nothing we did to try to comfort or quiet Karen seemed to work. Larry began to feel as guilty as I did. We began to wonder if we were inadequate as parents. We felt helpless and very boxed in.

In many cases parents secretly ask themselves the question "Why?" Their feelings of helplessness and frustration sometimes turn to anger and resentment. As Daria, a teen-aged mother put it:

I had figured that being a parent was going to be a bowl of cherries. Oh, how naïve and terribly wrong I was. My son screamed frantically for hours during the day and night for the first couple of months, and this really began to get to me. I felt constantly drained, physically and emotionally. It was as if maybe I was being punished for having him without being married. I hate to admit it, but for a period of several weeks, I wished he would go away and never come back. That's how miserable I felt caring for him.

Resentment toward the baby is often felt, although rarely do parents share these feelings with others for fear of being labeled as "unfit" or overemotional and immature. It is far healthier to verbalize resentment than to try to bury it, lest it build to the point where you take it out on your baby.

Coping with a colicky baby often causes parents to wonder whether they were cut out to assume this role. Comments about this from relatives or friends, even when made in jest, can heighten parents' own doubts and insecurities.

According to Cynthia Mellon-Browne:

I had always thought that I would make a wonderful mother, although my own mother and mother-in-law often kidded me that I was more suited to be a career woman than a mother. After I brought Mimi home from the hospital, she developed colic. I couldn't help taking her discomfort and misery personally. To make matters worse, my relatives kept making sarcastic remarks like, "I told you you weren't cut out to be a mother," and kept giving me advice about what I was doing wrong. The more I tried to soothe Mimi whenever my relatives were visiting, the more she cried and thrashed. This made me feel so embarrassed and also insecure, because at times I couldn't help wonder if maybe they were right about the fact that I wasn't cut out to be a mother. There were many days in which I felt like screaming along with Mimi; that's how upset I was. Whenever she pushed me away from her or screamed when I tried to soothe her, I felt personally rejected.

Feelings of guilt, inadequacy, and anger are common among parents of babies who have colic. It is difficult for parents not to take their baby's behavior personally, and not to resent him. It may seem as if he is deliberately behaving this way in order to get back at them for some unknown reason. Embarrassment about their baby's behavior often enters in, too, particularly in new parents. It is hard to swell with pride and joy over a new baby who is screaming and acts as though he is in pain. Coping with those people who feel obliged to offer their advice and who are quick to point out what they feel you are doing wrong is also not easy. The situation can become worse when parents become tense, irritable, and start to blame one another. Sometimes a baby senses this family tension and hostility, and becomes even more irritable and fussy.

MAINTAINING A SENSE OF BALANCE. Try to view the situation objectively and to put it in the proper perspective before things get out of hand and minor incidents are blown way out of proportion. Your baby is not intentionally acting this way. His behavior is the result of colic, not a willful attempt on his part to embarrass or get back at you for something you have done wrong. Blaming yourself, your spouse, your baby, or even your doctor for this situation will bring no improvements, and can cause more trouble.

It may be difficult for you to feel "close" to your baby during the first three months. You may feel as though your entire relationship with him is dependent upon your giving, rather than receiving, but do not stop giving even though he seems to reject your attempts to soothe him, swaddle him, offer him affection, or play with him. Stick with it. Most cases of colic, as we have said, disappear after the first three months. Rest assured that the quality of your life and your baby's life, as well as the quality of your relationship with him will improve.

Try your best to grin and bear it, and get plenty of rest and relaxation. Many parents who have been in this situation recommend getting out of the house for a few hours a day if possible. Even brief "breathers" away from your baby may be especially relaxing, and should help prevent you from becoming too preoccupied with his behavior, and too depressed about life circumstances.

Are You a Potential Child Abuser?

Men and women approach parenthood having had varied backgrounds and experiences in life. Some have had happy childhoods and marriages, and others have not. Many have positive feelings about becoming a parent and others have mixed feelings or negative feelings. Past and present situations are bound to have an influence upon the way a parent handles a new baby.

There are, of course, times when every parent feels a bit overwhelmed and frustrated. In response to this parents may become irritable, angry, resentful, and even depressed. This is only natural. There are numerous ways in which human beings react to stress. Unfortunately, there are situations in which parents abuse their babies, either consciously or unconsciously, as a reaction to stress.

CHILD ABUSE TAKES MANY FORMS. Just as there is no one explanation for why parents abuse their children, there is not just one form of abuse. Some parents physically abuse their children. Others abuse their children in less obvious ways; for example, through verbal abuse and emotional or nutritional neglect. All too often parents lose self-control and use their innocent children as outlets for their own anger, frustrations, tensions, and aggressions. In some cases they are actually unaware of what they are doing until afterward when they see bruises, welts, or other negative effects of their actions on their child. Sometimes parents deny the fact that they are child abusers. When abuse takes place in subtle ways, parents may not realize that their actions or harsh comments are having a profoundly harmful effect on their child.

AWARENESS OF THE PROBLEM IS IMPORTANT. As a parent or a parent-to-be, you may be wondering why such an unpleasant topic was even mentioned. It was not brought up in order to frighten you and leave you with the impression that you must never show irritation toward your child or express anger toward your baby. After all, parents are only human. They are bound to get frustrated, angry, and irritable at times, and it is healthy for these feelings to be expressed. This topic was discussed in order to make you aware of the fact that in unusual cases parents have

Infancy 1

expressed these feelings in ways which are harmful to their babies. Perhaps as you are handling your baby, you will be more inclined to think twice before acting in ways which could affect him negatively.

It would be unrealistic to anticipate that you will never err in rearing your baby and that you will never get angry with him unjustifiably or take your frustrations out on him, as this is sometimes inevitable. Feeling guilty or burying your feelings can be just as harmful to your baby. Occasionally, justified verbal expressions of annoyance or anger can relieve your frustration and help clear the air, but expressing anger by means of overly rough handling, prolonged ignoring of the child, extreme punishment, constant verbal abuse, or emotional neglect are considered to be forms of child abuse that are potentially very harmful.

GETTING HELP IF YOU NEED IT. The vast majority of you will have nothing to worry about. If, however, you are feeling as though your emotions or thoughts about hurting your baby are getting out of hand and that there is a possibility that you might abuse or physically harm your baby, immediately call someone over to stay with the baby and then leave the house until you have better control of yourself. In case you continue to have a problem controlling your feelings, it is advisable to seek professional help, both for your own sake and the sake of your family.

You will probably do well to discuss your problem with your doctor first, who may be able to recommend a psychiatrist or other mental health professional. In some communities there are child abuse "hot lines." Parents who are having difficulties in this regard may dial a specific number on the telephone and speak to a counselor who is specially trained to deal with problems related to child abuse. Also, some communities have clinics or organizations such as Parents Anonymous set up purposely for parents who abuse their children and want help with this problem. Parents meet frequently in small groups led by a trained professional and have opportunities to discuss feelings and problems.

MULTIPLE BIRTHS

Multiple births refers to having two or more babies at the same time. While this is the exception rather than the rule, it is a common enough occurrence to warrant special attention. In spite of the fact that being blessed with more than one baby at once is not a problem in and of itself, the situation can complicate parenthood in many ways, other than just financially.

Prospective parents are usually informed well in advance of the delivery date that they are giving birth to more than one baby, due to the fact that doctors have several ways of detecting multiple births during the pregnancy period. A physician, upon examining a pregnant woman, may hear two or more separate fetal heartbeats or may actually feel two or more babies in her abdomen. Ultrasound examinations can also confirm multiple births. However, it is not always possible to make this determination before delivery.

Twins are the most common of all multiple births, and there are two types, "fraternal" and "identical." Boy and girl twins are always fraternal, although fraternal twins can also be alike in their sex. These babies are as different as any two babies born in the same family, since they develop from two separate eggs. Identical twins, on the other hand, come from one egg and are always of the same sex. Many twins are so alike in appearance that even their parents may initially have a difficult time telling them apart.

Extra Worries Prior to the Babies' Births

Knowing ahead of time that multiple births will occur can increase parents' worry and anxiety about being able to love and care for more than one child. Naturally, many parents also worry more about the increased demands on their time and energy, and alterations in lifestyle that necessarily come with having more than one baby at a time. It should be reassuring to know that although parents who have had more than one baby at once agree that it requires more work and personal sacrifices and adjustments, especially at the beginning, they generally feel that the rewards are terrific.

During the pregnancy period, when concerns, doubts, and insecurities can be very strong, it should help to share them openly with your partner, relatives, friends, and your physician. You may need to receive additional support and understanding from these people, and should not hesitate to ask for it. Advanced planning and preparation should greatly cut down on anxieties prior to the babies' births, and also make things easier for you during the postpartum phase. If you know of other parents who have given birth to twins, triplets, and so forth, it may be a good idea to contact them. They will probably be more than happy to offer practical tips and share experiences that may prove useful to you in the weeks, months, and years that follow as you rear your own babies.

There may also be special organizations for parents of twins, etc., in your community that may be of assistance in a variety of capacities. Your doctor or department of social services may be able to put you in touch with such an organization.

Numerous Adjustments After Your Babies Are Born

The postpartum period can be especially stressful for new parents of more than one baby. This is often a time when emotions are strong. Countless physical, emotional, and psychological factors will play a role in how a parent feels, making each situation unique. It is not uncommon for babies of multiple births to be born prematurely and small. It is often necessary for them to be separated from their parents for a period of time and placed in a newborn special care unit. This, of course, can increase parents' worries and anxieties, particularly when the babies' health and/or survival is at risk. Feelings of fear, depression, helplessness, and emptiness, coupled with worry, are commonly experienced, and should be talked about frequently with those people who you feel can provide comfort and emotional support. Remaining in close touch with your doctor is strongly recommended.

Help for You at Home

Parents who give birth to two or more babies will need all of the help they can get immediately after bringing the babies home. Coping with one new baby is often hard enough. Coping with more than one, especially in the early weeks, can make life even more hectic and stressful. Parents should definitely try to arrange for a relative, friend, or other preferably experienced individual to stay for as long as is necessary in order to help out with the care of the babies and/or the housework.

Dirty bottles and laundry can pile up incredibly fast. It usually seems as though the work load is never-ending as well as overwhelming, especially if there are other young children in the home. You will greatly appreciate having even part-time help to ease your burden. Sharing child care responsibilities with a helper(s) is often a necessity, and is highly recommended.

One major way in which to cut down on extra work is to find short cuts. Streamline each task so that it requires only a minimum amount of time and effort. Provided that you can afford it, make use of all possible conveniences. Disposable diapers, diaper services, and automatic washers and dryers in the home can be of great help. Even making use of frozen dinners, take-out food services, and paper cups and plates can decrease your work load during the first several months, until some semblance of order in the routine and home can be established.

Do no more than you have to in terms of housework. It is far more important for you to devote a large portion of time to caring for and enjoying your babies, and getting sufficient amounts of relaxation and rest, than devoting your time to keeping a spotless house. No one will expect you to have the tidiest home on the block with more than one new baby on your hands. People will understand.

You should try to figure out ways to streamline baby care routines as well. The number of full baths that you give your babies can be cut down considerably, as long as faces and diaper areas are cleaned daily or as often as necessary in between baths, and your babies' skin seems healthy. Depending upon how many babies you have, and what kind of household you run, each of you will find the most expedient ways to approach giving baths, changing diapers and clothes, offering nourishment, and tending to each child's other individual needs.

Parents will naturally wonder about methods of feeding and feeding schedules. A mother who wishes to breast-feed may be able to work things out, depending upon her breast-milk supply, how many babies she has, and their individual needs. Doctors will discuss alternatives for breast-feeding, and advise a mother as to how she can best proceed with this feeding method.

Feeding schedules are sure to be rather hectic in the early weeks. Since babies of multiple births are often small, they may require more frequent feedings, perhaps every two to three hours. Different feeding schedules for different babies may be required for a while, further complicating the situation. Many parents try to get their babies onto fairly predictable, reasonable schedules as early as they can in order to avoid having feedings go on at all hours of the day and night. Your physician should be of assistance in scheduling feedings and making adjustments. He or she will also recommend formulas for you to use, if you plan to bottle-feed or use a combination of breast and bottle, depending upon your convenience and your babies' needs. Many parents find that sterile disposable plastic bottles, or bottles with presterilized "bags" to hold formula, ready prepared formulas, and electric sterilizers save them an enormous amount of time and energy, and are worth the extra expense. An automatic dishwasher will come in very handy.

Whichever feeding method is used, trying to feed more than one hungry baby at a time is difficult, especially if they are crying. It is quite a feat to train babies to wake half an hour or so apart, but an occasional parent of twins or triplets may have success with this. Mothers who breast-feed have been known to feed two babies at the same time, but some find this awkward or uncomfortable. As you can see, parents who have help initially are much better off than those who do not.

Equipment

Purchasing new equipment for two or more babies can be very costly. To avoid this expensive proposition, parents often hunt for secondhand furniture that they can refinish, try to borrow necessary equipment, or at least look for items on sale. There are shops for children carrying specialized strollers, carriages, and feeding chairs and tables for twins and even triplets. These are expensive, and some styles do not fit through normal door openings. You will be the best judge of whether or not a particular item would be useful, but it is a good idea to talk this topic over with other experienced parents who have had multiple births.

For the first couple of months, it is unnecessary to have one crib per child. Two young infants can share a crib, and a partition across the middle is easy to make at home. As the babies grow larger and more active, each will need his own crib. One dressing or changing table should be sufficient. An infant seat will come in handy for each baby. A playpen can be shared by two, but having two playpens is ideal. Having one or more bassinets on hand is a good idea. When the time comes, two high chairs or feeding chairs with trays will be necessary.

It is best to purchase a bare minimum of equipment in the beginning. You can always obtain more later on if the need arises.

Clothing and Toys

In cases of multiple births, parents often wonder whether or not it is advisable to dress the children alike. There is no easy answer to this question, since there are happy, emotionally well-developed children who have been dressed alike, and those who have been dressed differently. A major factor to consider is the children's individuality.

Sometimes in dressing children alike there is a tendency for parents and other people to treat them alike. Children may find it more difficult to develop a firm sense of their individual identities apart from one another. Parents' attitudes toward their children and children's attitudes and perceptions of themselves are probably the most important consideration.

Many parents find that it works well to dress the children in similar outfits but of different colors. This eliminates some of the problems in selecting clothes. It also helps to give the youngsters as well as other people the impression of not being identical. Again, each situation is different, and you will want to take individual factors into account in selecting clothes.

Toys can be another source of concern among parents. Purchasing identical toys for children from the start and maintaining this policy as they grow older is usually not the best approach, since it often leads them to expect that they will always receive equal treatment in regard to materialistic possessions. This can heighten rivalry among youngsters and can also be a very expensive proposition.

For the most part, it is a better idea to buy them different, but similar toys, perhaps with the exception of certain playthings such as tricycles that are most difficult to share. Even then, these special possessions may be purchased in different colors to help avoid confusion. Name tags or labels can also be useful in keeping the ownership of toys straight, and preserving each child's sense of personal property and identity. Being matter of fact about giving children different toys and expecting them to do some sharing of playthings helps them to accept this more willingly, and reinforces the value of co-operation.

Additional Considerations

Parents who have more than one baby at once are bound to have rough going at times. Contending with normal routines of baby care can leave them exhausted and with little time for rest and sleep, not to mention having to cope with more than one baby fussing, crying, or catching a cold at once. Parents will necessarily have to be more practical in devising short cuts in managing their day-to-day affairs. They will also have to make an extra effort to keep in touch with their own feelings and those of their spouse, and to set aside times when they can be alone together.

In spite of the fact that babies may be alike in appearance, all babies, as you know, are individuals with different personalities and needs. It is easy for parents sometimes to get into the habit of treating their children exactly the same, simply because they look alike or were born at the same time. Some parents become so wrapped up in trying to be fair and not show favoritism, that their attention and affection become too predictable, rigid, and forced. It is wise to keep in close touch with each baby, and be responsive to his own individual cues, needs, interests, and capabilities rather than to plan out a system for treating them impartially. Every child deserves to be loved and needed for what he is, to spend time alone with his parents occasionally, to develop friendships and interests apart from his brothers or sisters, and to develop in early childhood a firm sense of his individuality and uniqueness.

YOU WILL PLAY AN IMPORTANT ROLE
IN YOUR BABY'S EDUCATION

Before your child is ever exposed to a formal school setting, he will be learning about himself, his environment, people, life in general, and a host of other things too long to mention. In many subtle ways, you will be instrumental in educating him, shaping his attitudes and behavior patterns, setting an example for him to follow, and regulating the kinds of stimulation to which he is exposed. Your home will be an informal type of school, with you acting as the primary teacher. Through your daily interactions with him and by the way you arrange your home, you can encourage or discourage many of his actions, habits, feelings, attitudes, and skills.

You will still play an important role in your baby's education, if you work outside the home and/or leave your baby in the care of another adult(s) in your absence. During the time that you spend with him, even if this is primarily in the evenings or on weekends, you will be teaching him many things in subtle, as well as not-so-subtle ways. Knowing that his earliest experiences will influence his development, you should try to make sure that he will be receiving a good education in your absence. This can be accomplished by selecting a "parent figure" or day care facility that will offer him the kind of early stimulation and educational experiences that you yourself would provide if you were taking care of him on a full-time basis.

It is important to consider your feelings and objectives in regard to his education, and then discuss this subject with the person(s) who will be caring for him while you are away from home. Let them know what types of interactions and experiences you would like them to offer your baby, and why. Be explicit, since their ideas about "good" child rearing practices may not coincide with yours. As your child's parent, you have the right to decide what type of care and education he will receive. Even though you cannot expect another person to treat him the same as you would in every situation, you can expect that person to respect your wishes, and do his or her best to carry them out. The main thing to remember is that your baby's educational process begins at a very early age, and that either directly or indirectly, you will be instrumental in providing for his education.

Learning about the important role that parents play in their baby's education makes some parents feel insecure about their ability to function well in the role of an educator, particularly those parents who never liked school or never did well in a formal classroom setting. You are not alone if you are uncertain or uneasy about your ability to do a good job as your child's teacher. However, you do not need a degree in order to provide a beneficial educational experience for your baby.

Most parents have the natural ability to provide a good education for their babies because they love them, care about them, and spend a great deal of time with them. Parents have the opportunity to get to know their babies better than anyone else, and to understand their feelings and needs. Parents also have the opportunities to offer their children plenty of personalized attention.

It is highly doubtful that the love, special lines of communication, individualized attention, and spontaneous guidance that parents can offer their babies in the relaxed, home environment could ever be matched by a trained teacher in a formal school setting. By caring for your baby in a manner that tells him you are responsive to his special needs, and by giving him plenty of love and attention, you will automatically be offering him a great deal of early stimulation that will foster his development.

There are also some specific ways in which you may be able to encourage or discourage your baby's acquisition of particular skills, and facilitate his learning. Much that is involved will come naturally to you, and you will find numerous suggestions in the Total Education of Your Baby sections as well as other sections in this book. It is hoped that this material will help make your job as an educator easier and more enjoyable for you, and more beneficial and pleasurable for your baby.

THE IMPORTANCE OF THE PARENT-CHILD RELATIONSHIP

It may seem trite, but perhaps the most important way in which to provide a young infant with a beneficial early education is to concentrate upon building a good relationship with him. Parents who are sensitive to their babies' needs and interests as they grow and develop will be in a much better position to shift the ways in which they respond to their babies and alter their home environments so that the abilities their children have acquired can be utilized and practiced, and so that their youngsters will have enough challenge and stimulation to encourage the development of new abilities. Their babies are likely to be more receptive and responsive when they try to teach them new things.

HOW TO STIMULATE YOUR BABY'S MIND

Through your baby's five senses, he will be taking in information from birth. Thus, it seems reasonable to conclude that the manner in which he is cared for, and the type of environment in which he is reared, will influence what, and possibly how much, he learns. It is well accepted that babies need stimulation. However, how much and what kind of stimulation are appropriate depend upon a baby's individual needs and preferences.

Bear in mind that your baby is quite helpless, and will not be in a position to seek out stimulation or control the stimulation that he receives from his surroundings. He will be relying upon you to offer him parental stimulation, and to arrange your home and his routine so that when he is awake and ready for stimulation, he will have plenty of physical contact with you, and something interesting to look at, listen to, and so forth.

When your baby is feeling cold, tired, hungry, or otherwise uncomfortable, his awareness of sights, sounds, and people in the environment is likely to be severely restricted. It will be difficult for him to focus on external stimulation when he is crying or in distress and concentrating on his inner needs. Being uncomfortable and crying, he will not be as alert as when he is comfortable and content.

One could reasonably speculate that the more time a baby is alert, the more time he will have to take in new sights, sounds, and experiences, and learn from them. By doing your best to meet your baby's needs and answer his cries fairly quickly, you will be helping to ensure that he will be alert as much as possible. This should help him maximize his opportunities to learn.

As your baby grows older, he will become increasingly alert, aware, and responsive to people and his surroundings. Through seeing, hearing, swiping, grabbing, feeling, tasting, and smelling he will grow more familiar with his environment. His growing curiosity will emerge more clearly, and it is advisable for you to try to foster it and support it. It is hoped that you will not only play with him, but will design his familiar surroundings so that he receives ample sensory and motor stimulation. His early sensory and motor experiences, as discussed in the Intellectual Development section, will serve as the foundation for later intelligence. Through playing and moving around he will be continually making new discoveries and learning. This is a major reason why it is important to help him make the most of his early play experiences.

HOW TO STIMULATE YOUR BABY'S LANGUAGE DEVELOPMENT

Anything you say to your infant is fine, as long as you say something. Hearing the sound of the human voice is of prime importance to a baby's development of language. Your talking will capture your young infant's attention, and your speech will play an important role in the development of his attention. You will notice that even as early as two months of age he will turn his eyes and head to the source of a sound when he hears a voice. His visual attention is "grabbed" by the voice and he quickly stares at the sound's source or location in space.

Talking to him is also important for other reasons. Before he is able to recognize you by your appearance, he will probably recognize you by the sound of your voice. Talking to him from the very beginning should make it possible for him to discriminate between you and other family members or strangers before he is able to do so by sight.

It makes absolutely no difference what you say to your infant, since he will not understand a word of it. You can ramble on to your heart's content without fear that he will find you a boring conversationalist. Talk to him often whenever he is alert. Your one-sided conversations with him as you feed, wash, change his clothes, and play with him are crucially important. Sing and hum to him, too, if you like. He will be an appreciative audience, even though he cannot tell you so in words.

Besides giving your baby opportunities to hear your speech, it is a good idea to expose him to a wide variety of sounds, including music, ordinary household noises (the sound of the radio, television, vacuum cleaner), and toys that produce noise when moved. This will stimulate his sense of hearing, and heighten his interest in sounds.

Once your baby of two or three months begins to babble, it is very important to reinforce him positively for producing these sounds, since these primitive sounds will later develop into words. Once he begins producing non-crying sounds to attract your attention and initiate social contact, you should realize the value of consistently responding to his sounds. It is important for him to learn the value of using his voice and "speaking up" when he wants or needs something. Responsiveness on your part will help to reinforce this lesson.

HOW TO STIMULATE YOUR BABY'S PERSONAL-SOCIAL DEVELOPMENT

Your role in stimulating your baby's personal-social development is highly significant. As was previously mentioned, all babies need to have consistent contact with another human being(s) who cares for them. In most cases this is his parent, although it may be any person who is willing to assume this role. This person should recognize the value of offering consistent care and being responsive to the baby's cries and needs. The most basic need is for an abundance of love, attention, and physical contact. A baby's first relationship with another human being should be positive and satisfying.

In the event that you will not be caring for your baby the greater part of each day, it is crucial that you select a parent figure who will satisfy his needs in your absence, and give him a feeling of being loved and special. This feeling of being loved by a consistent parent figure will provide him with a marvelous security base, and will serve as a foundation for the development of further social relationships with other people in the future. Providing your baby with a warm social environment is probably the most valuable gift that you can offer him.

The importance of parent-child contact cannot be overemphasized. A valuable way to maintain frequent contact with your baby and make his life more pleasurable and satisfying is to play with him affectionately. Playing with him, especially as he becomes more responsive to you, should be great fun for you as well. The suggestions for games and activities in the Learning Through Play sections should stimulate your ideas.

More importantly, be spontaneous in your interactions with him. Do what comes naturally and comfortably. Learn to really enjoy him and appreciate the time you spend together. This will enhance your relationship and promote not only his social development but his development in all areas.

Usually in the second month, a baby's social smile emerges. One way to promote his social development is to reinforce him positively whenever he smiles, since this should result in his smiling more often. More about social smiling is presented in the Personal-Social Development section.

Through your baby's contact with other people and toys and objects, he begins to develop an awareness of himself. Some of the highlights of this long, slow process are brought to your attention in the Personal-Social Development section. Initially, you can assist in giving your baby a feeling of being important by promptly and consistently answering his cries and meeting his needs.

As he grows older, you can help him learn that by his actions he can positively influence his environment. Suggestions for games and activities designed to foster such a feeling in him are offered in the Play sections. By offering him a variety of objects to play with and explore, he will have opportunities to compare his own body with other objects, and thus begin the process of differentiating himself from his surroundings. You will find discussions of how introducing a mirror into your baby's play will heighten his consciousness of his own facial expressions, gestures, and body movement. You need not worry that allowing your baby to play in front of a mirror will result in his turning into a supreme egotist; at this stage simply having opportunities to see his reflection in a mirror will increase his self-awareness.

HOW TO STIMULATE YOUR BABY'S MOTOR DEVELOPMENT

You will play a less influential role in your baby's development of motor skills as compared to his development of language, intellectual, or social skills. The early environment that you provide for him will markedly influence his development of speech and personal-social skills. Motor development, on the other hand, follows more of a programmed course, and is highly dependent upon the rate at which he gains control over his muscles and nerves.

Still, there are several things that you can do to promote the development of motor skills. What you will essentially be doing is supporting his tendency to develop specific abilities when he is physically ready, by giving him plenty of opportunities to practice those abilities. For example, in Infancy 2 to 4, by placing your young infant on his abdomen for a period of time each day, he will have chances to practice lifting his head. You can also give your baby positive feedback by praising him each time he masters a new skill, and offer him assistance in learning new tasks, if this seems necessary.

Of crucial importance is to make sure that your baby has freedom of movement. He will need ample space in which to move and try out his new abilities. The clothing that he wears should not limit his movements.

There are numerous activities and suggestions for encouraging both gross motor and fine motor skills presented in the Learning Through Play sections. As your baby matures, he will show an increasing interest in exercising. By giving him suitable outlets for exercising, and engaging him in activities that go along with his emerging abilities, you will be providing a positive setting for the further development of motor skills.

EXPANDING YOUR EDUCATIONAL PROGRAM TO MEET YOUR BABY'S CHANGING NEEDS

As your baby develops, his ability to learn rapidly expands. It is important that you recognize your young infant's growing need to learn. To satisfy his natural curiosity and desire to learn, you will need to provide him with stimulation that is appropriate for his developmental progress. Your program of education will be constantly growing and expanding as your child matures.

If you read the developmental sections at each phase of your baby's growth, you should be well aware of how he is changing in the many different aspects of development. The material provided in this section should assist you in creating your own, personalized educational program for your child. Particularly in Infancy 4, 8, and 12 there are additional guidelines for educating your growing baby.

PREPARED PARENTHOOD CHECK LIST

MOTHER	FATHER	UNDERSTANDING YOUR BABY'S DEVELOPMENT
――	――	Do you try to respond promptly to your baby's needs and inter-act with him verbally and physically in a manner that makes him feel loved and secure?
――	――	Are you aware of the importance of the continuity of parental love, care, and stimulation in establishing a close parent-child bond?
――	――	Have you noticed your baby occasionally staring at your face and looking briefly into your eyes?
――	――	Does your infant usually calm down and stop crying in re-sponse to your attempts to soothe him?
――	――	Are you aware that your infant's five senses are operating from birth?
――	――	What types of stimulation are you offering your infant?
――	――	Are you able to observe any patterns emerging in your baby's crying or body language?
――	――	Do you respond fairly quickly to your baby's cries?
――	――	Have you considered the possibility of introducing your infant to two languages?
――	――	Do you talk to your baby as you care for him?
――	――	Are you aware of the importance of your baby's reflexes in al-lowing him to function at birth?
――	――	Do you know how to trigger and observe some of your infant's reflexes?
――	――	Are you spontaneous in playing with your baby?
――	――	Have you been taking advantage of the many opportunities to play with your infant as you tend to his needs?
――	――	Do you realize the value of playing with your infant in terms of fostering closeness between you and strengthening your relationship?

		BASIC CARE
――	――	Are you aware of the importance of good nutrition, proper basic care, and a warm parent-child relationship in preventing illness?
――	――	In what ways does well baby care begin in the home and how is it continued by regular visits to the doctor?
――	――	Do you know how to recognize when your baby is ill and how to seek medical advice?

Infancy 1

—— —— Have you become familiar with some of the common medical problems that occasionally arise during infancy and made an attempt to learn simple first-aid techniques?

—— —— Did you fill out the Emergency List, copy it, and place one near the phone and another in your wallet?

—— —— Have you obtained an approved infant car carrier and correctly attached it to your car so that your baby's first car ride home from the hospital will be safe?

—— —— Do you know how to prevent burns?

—— —— Are you familiar with the items on the Safety Training Check List?

—— —— Why should every family member take an active role in keeping your baby safe?

—— —— What will your role be in feeding your baby?

—— —— Have you familiarized yourself with some common feeding techniques?

—— —— Are you aware of the basic procedure in giving a sponge or tub bath?

—— —— Do you know how to care for certain areas of your baby's body (eyes, ears, nose, navel, genitals, nails) which are quite sensitive and/or require special attention?

—— —— How can you support your child's individual needs for sleep?

—— —— Do you know what to do if your baby has trouble falling asleep or if he awakens during the night?

—— —— Are you aware of how different a young infant's elimination patterns are from an adult's?

—— —— Have you considered the importance of watching for changes in the frequency and appearance of your baby's bowel movements?

FAMILY FEELINGS AND CONCERNS

—— —— What is your philosophy on discipline?

—— —— Have you been focusing on building a positive relationship with your baby, knowing that this will assist you in disciplining him later?

—— —— Are you fully aware that your young infant cannot be expected to understand right from wrong or obey even simple commands?

—— —— What are some common areas in which parents often feel the need for discipline during the first six months or so?

—— —— How do you feel about being a new parent? Have you discussed less than positive feelings with your spouse or close friends?

—— —— Are you familiar with the "baby blues" that are experienced by some new mothers, as well as the feelings of tension and mild depression sometimes felt by other family members?

—   ——   What effect, if any, has your new baby had upon your sex life?

—   ——   In what special ways do you and your spouse achieve sexual and emotional satisfaction without intercourse?

—   ——   Have you been making an effort to consider your own and your spouse's feelings and needs, and re-establish closeness and intimacy?

—   ——   If you have an older child, how has he or she reacted to the new baby?

THE TOTAL EDUCATION OF YOUR BABY

—   ——   Are you aware that your baby's educational process begins at a very early age, and that you will be instrumental in offering him a beneficial, pleasurable educational experience?

—   ——   Have you been taking your child's individual preferences and abilities into account in your educational program?

—   ——   How often do you talk to your baby and hold him?

Infancy 2

PERSONAL-SOCIAL DEVELOPMENT

Self-awareness

Throughout the first month and a half to two months of life, a baby may lie with her head and eyes turned toward her outstretched arm, but she may not appear to be looking at her hand. Prior to the age of about two months, her visual equipment makes it difficult for her to see clearly anything outside a very limited range. As her eyesight matures, she will find it easier to focus on nearby objects. Limited visual range, in large part, accounts for her delay in seeing her hand, even when it is positioned near her face.

Your baby's discovery of her hand is an event that you will not miss. Once she zeros in on it, she will gradually spend more and more time looking at it, with obvious interest and concentration. This discovery will add a new dimension to her self-awareness. As she realizes that her hand belongs to her body, she will gradually recognize that it is different from other objects that she touches and brings to her mouth to taste and explore. Most babies will be finding their hands in the third month, and a further discussion of this topic appears in Infancy 3.

Social Sensitivity and Interests

A baby in the second month does not know that she is a human being. Your infant's ability to interact with you and express her emotions is still very limited. Nevertheless, you will notice that she is growing slightly less preoccupied with her bodily functions, and is becoming more aware of and interested in the people and objects in her surroundings.

BABY'S SOCIAL SMILE. One of the most dramatic new developments, guaranteed to prompt some reaction from you, is the emergence of your baby's social smiling. At some point during Infancy 2, and definitely by Infancy 3, she will begin to look and smile directly at you and other people. Many parents say that their baby's first smiles made them feel kind of warm all over, and was the highlight of the second month. There is surely something special about a baby's smile that captivates everyone who sees it, and makes them smile back.

When you appear at the side of your baby's crib and she sees you and gives you a big smile, you may understandably conclude that she is smiling because she knows you and is happy to see you, or is grinning because she feels good. She may, indeed, be smiling for those reasons. Researchers have observed that a baby will smile in response to a sculpture or a mask of a person's face, or to a picture of a human face, even when facial features are distorted and grotesque-looking, or the face is frowning. One afternoon, Carrie's Uncle Hank, with his mustache and scowling face, bent over her crib and stuck out his tongue in an attempt to frighten her. Carrie's parents expected her to start crying, but to their surprise, she smiled back at Uncle Hank.

Carrie's reaction is not unusual. Impersonal or indiscriminate smiling to a human face or representation thereof will probably continue for several more months. Your baby will gradually become a more observant smiler, putting a grin on her face mainly when she sees you or other familiar and important people in her life. Frequent social smiling is likely to become more noticeable in Infancy 3.

Even though your baby's smile may not be directly associated with you, it is advisable for you to smile back at her, pick her up, or show your delight in other ways. These rewarding responses on your part can actually foster more frequent smiling. If babies are not positively reinforced when they smile, their smiling is apt to diminish, and eventually disappear. Even at this early stage, the feedback you offer her in response to specific actions can promote or discourage certain social behaviors.

SHE'S GETTING TO KNOW YOU. Your baby is able to remember experiences and images of people and objects for only very brief periods of time, but she is slowly getting to know you, and is beginning to connect you with particular activities such as feedings, diaper changes, baths, and so forth. Assuming that you have been consistent in fulfilling her needs, she will associate you with tension reduction, pleasurable stimulation, satisfaction, warmth, and comfort. This positive association forms the basis for her trust in you and her attachment to you.

Consistent contact with you since birth is enabling her not only to make positive associations but also establish certain special response patterns specific or peculiar to you. She learns that when she produces a particular sound or cries in a particular tone, you come into her room to see what she wants. She also uses particular body movements and facial expressions when you are holding her, as opposed to when your partner or other people are holding her. In fact, she may now recognize your voice, your smell, your touch, and your method of handling her. She may be soothed by your talking, humming, manner of holding her, or even by the sight of your face alone.

Mrs. Chase left her two-month-old son, Alan, for a few hours with a person unfamiliar to him. According to the baby-sitter, Alan cried and acted irritated from the time his mother left the house until the moment she returned. When Mrs. Chase went over to Alan and picked him up, he immediately became quiet and began to smile. His mother was very pleased that he recognized her and missed her when she was gone.

Not all very young babies have this reaction, but it is not uncommon, especially among infants whose major social contact has been with one parent. They clearly discriminate between people and the way they are handled.

THE LITTLE SHOW-OFF. Your infant is becoming more sensitive to you and other family members as the weeks and months pass. When people play with her and give her their focused attention, she may actually work to keep this attention by smiling, making some sounds, and waving her arms. She may even keep this routine going for fifteen minutes or more, if she receives applause and encouragement from her audience. You will see more of this type of behavior over the next few months as she becomes more social.

INTELLECTUAL DEVELOPMENT

Longer Periods of Wakefulness and Alertness

Your baby will now stay awake and appear alert for longer periods of time. Previously she may have had only very brief periods of wakefulness during the daytime. Now she will remain awake for about twenty minutes each hour, although the length of babies' alert periods can vary considerably. When her needs have been met and she seems satisfied, she will naturally pay more attention to the outside world than if she is hungry or in some sort of discomfort. The fact that she can remain awake longer than before and is more alert affords her more opportunity to interact with her surroundings.

Gathering More Information About the Environment

CURIOSITY. It may appear to you as if your baby is actively seeking out stimulation. This is her way of showing her curiosity. When you and other people hover over her crib and talk to her, she may stare wide-eyed at you, smile, and become all excited. Her whole body will be activated, and she may even wriggle or strain as if to respond to you. Her periods of responsiveness are growing in length, particularly when other people are nearby and paying attention to her.

She seems much more interested in environmental stimulation than during the past few weeks. She will stare intently at objects within her still-limited range of vision, and try to follow them. When you and other people have left her room, she may listen carefully to sounds, and suck on her fingers. Even though her experiences with her new environment have been limited, the getting-acquainted process has begun.

SIGHT. Your infant's interest in looking at her surroundings has increased. She may spend relatively long periods of time gazing about, and if an object comes into her visual range, she will examine it with obvious interest and sober concentration. She is now able to focus on objects at slightly greater distances. Some professionals have observed babies following attractive, large, moving targets that are up to several feet away from them. This suggests that babies are capable of seeing objects clearly at a more distant range, but it is not certain that they can focus well on objects at distances beyond one to two feet. Beyond that range, their focusing ability is questionable and objects may become fuzzy or blurry.

Their ability to track or visually follow a moving object is increasing. Head and neck movements are gradually becoming co-ordinated with eye movements. As a baby follows a moving target with her eyes, her head may turn in the same direction. She may now be able to track an object in a much larger arc, perhaps of 100 degrees or even more, if she is able to turn her head to look over her shoulder. You will probably notice her blink response. Quickly move a toy in front of and close to her face, and she will blink her eyes.

As your infant's ability to focus her eyes or "converge" on nearby objects improves, she will find her hand and stare at it. Her discovery of her hand, which should take place in this phase or the next, is discussed further in the Personal-Social Development section on page 226. Once she has "found" her hand, she will spend a great deal of time looking at it. Her interest in staring at her own hand, much like staring at other objects, is evidence of her growing curiosity.

If you have hung a mobile on her crib, you may also observe your infant staring intently at the objects, especially when they are moved. She may even begin to bat or swipe at them with her hands, although this may not occur until Infancy 3 or 4. Simultaneous staring and swiping provide additional opportunities to gather information about her environment.

Your Infancy 2 baby's favorite sight may be your face, other people's faces, and cutout pictures of faces. If she is presented with both toys and people's faces to look at, she will probably prefer to watch the faces.

HEARING. When your baby hears a sound, you are apt to see her looking in the direction of the sound. If you call to her from the door to her bedroom, where she cannot see you, but you can see her, you may notice that she turns her head and looks toward you.

She is probably able to recognize the sound of your voice, since it is the voice with which she is the most familiar. Stand away from her crib with another person and carry on a conversation. She may pick your voice out from among the others. When she hears you talking she may smile and look toward you. When an unfamiliar person speaks to her, she may not react or her smiles may turn to frowns and she may turn her head away from them.

TOUCH. As a result of having had frequent contact with you over the past month, your baby has gradually learned more about the special manner in which you hold, handle, and fondle her. She can probably pick you out from a group of people on the basis of how she is handled. Once she begins to manipulate objects, exploration with her hands will be one of her favorite pastimes.

A Higher Level of Intellectual Development

During Infancy 2 and 3, the baby begins to function at a slightly more sophisticated level of intellectual development. At this new "level" several of her previously isolated or fragmented actions become co-ordinated. Seeing and hearing are put together as the baby looks toward the source of the sounds that she hears.

A baby's mouthing and sucking on objects represent an important channel for investigation and perception during early infancy. By now, her fist or fingers may be put into her mouth regularly. It is doubtful that there was any intention to do so on her part the first time this happened. Nevertheless, she may suck vigorously on her hand, find this activity quite pleasurable and soothing, and repeat this behavior pattern over and over again. This is significant.

Her regular sucking on her fingers, co-ordinating her hand with her mouth, is not an inborn behavior pattern or instinctive response. This pattern of action was acquired as a result of experience. It provides evidence of learning. The repetition and strengthening of this activity, according to Piaget, constitute a higher level of intellectual function than was characteristic of the one-month-old. In this new phase of intellectual development, which roughly corresponds to the time from Infancy 2 to 4, the repetitive nature of your baby's activities can be observed.

You will probably be able to see other evidence of learning, particularly learning that has taken place in relation to feedings. Patsy Driscoll had been breast-feeding her daughter, Trudy. One evening, Patsy was extremely tired, and was trying to take a nap when Trudy began to cry out of hunger. Patsy was simply not up to breast-feeding, and, besides, her nipples were rather sore. She therefore decided to give Trudy a bottle in lieu of the breast. When Patsy tried to offer Trudy the bottle, Trudy squirmed and made no attempt to suck. Patsy tried to insert the nipple into Trudy's mouth, hoping that Trudy would take it, but she cried and turned her head.

By this time Patsy was aggravated and exhausted, and so she called her husband, Roger, for assistance. She thought that he might have better luck than she in getting Trudy to take the bottle. Roger was thrilled at having a chance to feed his daughter, and gladly offered to take over. Patsy stood nearby as Roger attempted to feed Trudy. No matter what Roger tried, Trudy still refused the bottle. Patsy was so annoyed that she finally left the room, leaving Roger to cope with Trudy alone.

To Roger's surprise, soon after his wife left him and his daughter alone, Trudy began to suck. At first she sucked slowly and seemed to be puzzled by the bottle. After a few minutes, her sucking became more vigorous, and she enthusiastically emptied the bottle.

Trudy's response was not unusual, particularly since she was breast-fed. A baby builds up strong associations during feedings. When the only person who has been feeding her from birth has been her mother, she associates Mommy with being fed, and may refuse to suck if another person tries to offer her food.

Babies who are breast-feeding will not only associate Mommy with being fed, they will also associate Mommy with a particular method of feeding. As a result, when Mommy tries to give them a bottle instead of the breast, there is a strong possibility that the bottle will be refused. Interestingly, though, they may be willing to accept a bottle from Daddy, as long as Mommy is not around.

There is little doubt that your infant is learning from experience, and making associations. When she is crying out of hunger and you pick her up and hold her in the nursing position, she may suddenly stop crying, as if she expects to be fed. Or she may stop crying the moment she hears you enter her room or sees you. You may also notice that she immediately begins to suck as soon as she sees her bottle or the breast. These noticeable changes in her behavior, and others that are explored in the developmental sections, clearly indicate her increasing awareness of her surroundings and her learning from previous experiences.

LANGUAGE DEVELOPMENT

Crying

Your baby's communications are similar to those in Infancy 1. Still, you may notice a few changes. Her crying should now be easier for you to interpret. You have probably begun to recognize some patterns emerging. Parents often notice that their baby's crying sounds differ depending upon whether she is hungry, tired, annoyed, or simply in a cranky mood. You are likely to note variations in the tone, pitch, and intensity of your infant's crying. By this time her crying will probably be accompanied by a flow of tears, unlike the tearless crying during Infancy 1.

Unexplainable crying spells continue. These episodes can still take place at any time, but with many babies, "fussy" periods occur quite regularly each evening, often around the dinner hour. As was previously discussed, you can try any number of the tactics outlined on pages 106–7 in order to try to quiet your baby down, but you may inevitably discover that nothing works. Sometimes babies' crying spells are so intense that they actually turn beet red to purple in the face and look like they are going to explode. Some babies even appear to have stopped breathing, but they will not actually pass out. Their breathing will resume after a very brief pause.

These episodes are enough to scare even the most confident parent to death, but they look more serious than they really are. All parents can really do is to try to bear up under the strain, and not lose hope. These aggravating and anxiety-producing crying jags will eventually be outgrown.

You may notice a slight decrease in the amount of time your baby devotes to crying. Perhaps she sucks on her fist or fingers, looks around at her surroundings, smiles, or listens to sounds instead. As she comes further "out of her shell" in Infancy 3, crying should markedly diminish.

Non-crying Sounds

You are likely to hear your infant producing more gurgling and cooing, or babbling, sounds. Her sounds, at first, are quite simple in nature. They may sound like "ah," "eh" or other vowels, but it is much too early for her to be producing any word sounds. Once she really begins to produce sounds, she is apt to become quite interested in listening to her own sounds, even the sounds that she makes with her own saliva. Try to imitate her sounds and smile, since this should encourage her to produce them more frequently. These early sounds will gradually develop into more sophisticated vocalizations that more closely resemble real speech, and it is important to reinforce them positively.

MOTOR DEVELOPMENT

Reflex Activity

Your baby still moves mainly by reflex responses. Most of her reflexes can be elicited, and some such as her rooting, sucking, and swallowing reflexes have become stronger and more co-ordinated. Her tonic neck reflex is still present, as you will observe it when you place her on her back.

Some of her reflexes are gradually beginning to diminish. Her grasping reflex is one of them. Her startle or Moro reflex response may also begin to fade, and thus she may not jump or startle as frequently as in the past. Minor, sudden changes in the environment may not bother her as much or cause her to jerk her body and cry. Reflex walking may also become harder to observe as she approaches Infancy 3.

Gross Motor Activity

BEGINNING TO CONTROL THE HEAD. The Infancy 2 baby is beginning to gain some control over her head. When she is lying on her abdomen, she may start to hold her head in more of a center, or midline position, as opposed to a right or left side position. Her hands and forearms may occasionally be held so that she can rest some of her weight on them.

Your child may make regular attempts to lift her face off the mattress when lying on her stomach. Despite poor muscle strength, she may manage to lift it momentarily. Success with this task varies from child to child, but your baby will most likely be able to raise her head a few inches off the mattress for a brief period of time. When you hold her up or prop her in a sitting position, you may also see less head bobbing and slumping than before, but head drooping is still quite prominent.

When lying on her back, your infant may suddenly turn her head from one side to another, but she does not yet hold it in a center position, and turns it only in a limited range. While on her back, she may strain to lift her head off of the mattress, but this task is extremely difficult for her to manage, since she still lacks strength in her front neck muscles.

BODY MOVEMENT. It continues to be hard for your baby to move about. She has not gained control over her trunk and leg muscles. She cannot roll over or sit up. Yet she may squirm, arch, and wiggle around a lot, dig her heels into the mattress, and push. In the midst of these activities she may actually move her body for very short distances. Now is the time to begin taking safety precautions to prevent avoidable falls, lest she catch you off guard and inch her way to the edge of a bed or changing table and fall.

The thrashing, waving, and circling movements of her arms may be somewhat less jerky than before. As she exercises her arms and gains muscle strength, her movements will become smoother. Similarly, her leg movements may become slightly less abrupt. The position in which she holds her arms while on her back is still rather restricted by the tonic neck reflex. Her arms will appear to move more smoothly than her legs.

Fine Motor Activity

Your baby is beginning to gain some control over her hand movements. Previously, her hands were mainly held tightly clenched, but gradually they are opening and being held in a more loose-fisted position. When you touch her hand with a spoon, she may open her hand and grab hold of it. The spoon may remain in her hand slightly longer than before.

Her arm movements, in large part, seem rather purposeless, but she may start to bat at an object held close to her. You may also notice her bringing her hand to her mouth more often than before, or perhaps for the first time. She may still suck on her fists, but now that she is outgrowing her fisted position, she may suck on her thumb or other fingers. Her initial attempts to get her thumb into her mouth may be awkward and comical to observe. Her aim may not be very good, causing her to miss her target on the first few tries.

Her eyesight is improving. Either in this phase or the next she may actually take more notice of her hands. She is also better able to track objects visually and focus on nearby objects. This is more fully explained in the Intellectual Development section on page 230.

LEARNING THROUGH PLAY

Through play, your baby will be constantly making new discoveries. Her play will involve moving, looking, hearing, feeling, tasting, and smelling. Note that these are exactly the same avenues through which she learns. Over the next two months, she will be awake and alert for longer spans of time than in Infancy 1, and there will be many other new developments taking place that should make playing with her more pleasurable for you.

You will see progress in every area of development. Her eyesight is improving. She is gaining more strength and more control over her head and body. Sounds that she produces are becoming more obvious. Her reflex patterns are becoming more co-ordinated. Her interest in and curiosity about the world around her is growing. In addition, she is becoming more sociable and receptive to your attention day by day.

By playing with her, you will be able to heighten her consciousness of people and her surroundings, and give her outlets for her lively curiosity and opportunities to practice her new motor skills. As her interest in exploration increases, it will be important for her to have opportunities to satisfy her desire to learn. Spending time with her and arranging her immediate surroundings so that she receives adequate amounts of sensory and motor stimulation can answer her individual needs.

You can continue to follow the suggestions for stimulating and playing with her that were outlined in Infancy 1. Since there will be new developments occurring over the next couple of months, however, we have made an addendum to the list of suggestions. As she grows older and gains more control over her arms and hands, she will become more interested in exploring toys and objects. Thus, what toys to buy her will become a major consideration.

Toys

If someone asked you to free associate words with the word "play," chances are that you might say "toys" or "fun." Many people immediately think of toys when they hear the word "play" mentioned. A toy should be something that is enjoyable to play with. However, your idea of what a toy is and your baby's idea of what constitutes a toy may be completely different. It is doubtful that you would classify objects such as tissues, swatches of textured material, keys, or small cardboard boxes as toys. Yet, your baby may be fascinated with these ordinary household objects once she begins to reach out and grasp things.

From the start, you should realize that in the months to come your baby will enjoy playing with the most ordinary household items as much, if not more, than store-bought toys. As she plays, she will be getting more acquainted with her environment. Exploring objects that she sees in your home will bring her pleasure and will satisfy her curiosity. Therefore, you need not rush out and buy her a toy chest full of expensive or "educational" toys. Every object in your home that she can manage to touch and grab, from a cup to a box, will be something new to her, and will be "educational," because she will be learning about them and her environment through having opportunities to handle and explore them.

In spite of the fact that there are hundreds of "toys" in your home, you will, no doubt, want to buy her some store-bought toys. Many parents really enjoy choosing toys for their children. There is such a vast selection from which to choose that parents are often in doubt about which kinds of toys to buy. Below you will find some general tips for selecting toys.

SELECTING APPROPRIATE TOYS. Toys are for fun, discovery, and growth. One of the most important factors in choosing toys for a baby is to select those that are appropriate for her, taking into account her interests, abilities, and safety. Store-bought toys are generally labeled as to whether they are appropriate for infants, toddlers, preschoolers, adolescents, or adults. It is important to pay attention to these labels, but do not rely too heavily upon them. Children of any given age differ widely in their needs, interests, and capabilities. A toy that is designed to appeal to a baby from six to twelve months of age may appeal to a younger infant or a toddler. The best way to ensure a toy's appropriateness for your child is to remain in close touch with her at each stage of development. Spend time with her. Watch her closely as she acquires new skills. Pay attention to her interests and which types of toys and objects she enjoys most.

Obviously, you will occasionally err in your selection of toys. If you purchase a toy, hand it to her, and several moments later she loses interest in it, do not force her to play with it because "this toy cost me ten dollars and there are plenty of children who don't have any toys who would be thankful to have this one!" She should be the one who decides whether she is interested in a particular toy, not you. As is often the case, the toy she may cast aside on one day may become her favorite plaything the next day, or the following month. Perhaps as she grows older and her interests shift, she will come back to these toys with renewed enthusiasm. The main objective is to follow her lead in choosing toys, rather than insisting that she play with a particular toy that *you* feel is "good" or "right" for her.

At various points throughout the remainder of the Learning Through Play sections in this book, we will offer suggestions for objects and toys that may be appropriate during particular phases of development, taking into account the child's interests and abilities. However, you should use these lists only as guidelines, since your child's unique needs, capabilities, and preferences for toys and activities should be considered.

Safety Is of Utmost Importance in Choosing Playthings.   It is essential to consider your child's safety first whenever toys are concerned. Unnecessary accidents and injuries resulting from inappropriate selection of toys, unsafe toys, and inadequate parental supervision occur daily. Your baby will not be capable of making judgments in relation to her own safety and well-being, and thus you must make them for her. The Safety Training Check List in the How to Ensure Your Baby's Safety sections provide you with many guidelines and suggestions regarding the use of toys.

Knowledge of your own child and good common sense must enter into the picture. Common sense should tell you that a year-old child, even one who is highly advanced in her intellectual capabilities, is far too young to be playing with number games or difficult puzzles. Similarly, since infants tend to put everything that they get their hands on into their mouths, common sense should tell you not to purchase toys that could be swallowed.

Even though you may have good common sense and may make your child's safety your number one consideration in choosing playthings, you should not expect the same from relatives and friends. They will, no doubt, be buying some toys for her over the next few years. We urge you to examine them carefully, just as you would toys that you yourself select. Ask yourself the following kinds of questions: Are they well made? Are they appropriate for my child? Are they totally safe? If after close inspection you determine that a particular toy is too complex and might be frustrating for your child, is potentially dangerous, or simply does not meet your high standards, do not proceed to give it to her for fear of hurting someone else's feelings.

Assuming that a given toy is safe, there are additional factors that you should consider. Adult supervision will frequently be necessary when your child is playing with toys. If your infant happens to grab hold of a toy that belongs to your older children, she may be injured. Playthings that are strewn on steps or scattered around the house may be tripped over by both youngsters and adults. Housekeeping will be your responsibility, since you cannot expect your infant to put her toys in their proper places after she is finished playing with them. Remember that a smashed or broken toy can be very dangerous. A toy that has been left outside to rust and rot can be equally hazardous. Proper parental supervision and good housekeeping in regard to the use of toys are both necessary for your child's safety. Should you have any questions pertaining to the quality or safety of a toy, you may want to contact the Consumer Product Safety Commission in your state. In addition to answering these types of queries upon request, they may send you pamphlets providing guidelines for selecting safe, appropriate toys for children.

Suggested Playthings
   rattle
   wooden blocks
   plastic measuring cups and spoons
   ball (soft)
   sponge toys
   small stuffed animals
   teething toys
   squeeze toys
   small pieces of carpeting
   an assortment of small cardboard boxes
   cradle gym

An Infant Seat

Carrying your baby around with you from room to room as you go about your work would be impractical, as well as tiring. The alternative is to leave her in a safe place such as in her crib. This is fine, but from her point of view, a crib is a rather boring and unstimulating place in which to spend a good portion of her waking time. An infant seat (see page 47 for a description) is a very useful item that will enable you to tote her around from one room to the next. She will benefit from having changes of scenery, and more opportunities to be close to you or included in family activities.

Suggestions for Activities

PRIMITIVE CONVERSATIONS. Usually between the ages of two and three months, babies begin to babble. As you care for your baby, talk to her whenever she is alert. If she produces a sound such as "ah," smile at her and imitate her. The value of this activity is fully described in the Language Development section.

FOLLOWING OBJECTS WITH HER EYES. Hold a brightly colored, attractive object over her head as she lies in her crib. Move it slowly in a circular or figure-eight motion. If you have hung a mobile over her crib, jiggle the objects to make them "dance." She can follow the movements of the objects with her eyes.

FUN WITH MIRRORS. Hold a mirror about seven inches to a foot away from her face so that she can see herself. Talk to her about who she sees.

LOOKING AND TURNING TOWARD THE LOCATION OF A SOUND. Hold a rattle or some other noisemaker several feet away from her and shake it. See whether she turns her head and looks toward the direction of the sound. Slowly bring the rattle close to her so that she can see it. Circle it around her head, from side to side, and in various other directions. This should give her practice in co-ordinating hearing, seeing, and head turning.

LOOKING AND HEAD RAISING. As she gains more head control and strength in her arms, she will enjoy repeatedly raising her head from the mattress to get a better view of her room. To give her some practice in looking and lifting her head, place her on her abdomen. Hold an attractive object in front of her face and gradually lift it upward so that she will have to raise her head a few inches to keep the object in sight.

LOOKING AND SWIPING. A valuable device that you can purchase for your baby of two and a half to three months is called a cradle gym. Once she begins to use her arms to swipe, it will be important for her to practice swiping at objects hanging over her while she is lying on her back in her crib. If you are handy, you may want to make a cradle gym, but make sure that it is sturdy, be sure that there are no strings or ropes that your baby can pull down on her or get tangled in, and suspend only safe objects from the "gym."

Be certain that you remove any flimsy mobiles that you may have suspended from either side of her crib because they may be dangerous once she begins to grab them.

Dangle a variety of small, interesting objects over your baby, or in front of her. If she makes an attempt to reach for them, give them to her.

FEELING. Take advantage of your baby's interest in touching by giving her a variety of different textured fabrics, pieces of carpeting, and objects to handle. You might run her hand over each object and tell her something about the object at the same time. You might also run her hands over her own face and body and touch her hands together as a means of increasing her self-awareness.

KEEPING YOUR BABY HEALTHY

In the past, many children suffered from the effects and complications of polio, diphtheria, whooping cough (pertussis), and tetanus. These diseases brought fear into the hearts of parents.

Today it is no longer necessary for children to suffer from these diseases. Modern medical science has developed vaccines that can prevent these illnesses from striking a child. There is no reason for your child to be at risk. It is your responsibility to arrange with your doctor or appropriate health professionals for your child to be properly immunized during infancy.

What Is Meant by Immunization?

The most effective way to prevent infectious disease is through immunization. Immunizing substances, called vaccines, are available for several infectious diseases. Preparing vaccines is complex and varies from one disease to another. In general, vaccines are developed from the agents that cause or trigger the disease. These altered agents still stimulate the body's defenses against the disease, but do not produce the disease itself. At the time of this writing the American Academy of Pediatrics recommends that seven vaccines be routinely used to immunize children against the following infectious diseases: diphtheria, tetanus, pertussis (whooping cough), polio, measles, rubella, and mumps.

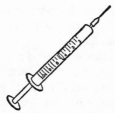

Vaccines are given to the child by mouth or by injection. The method of administration depends upon the type of vaccine. The vaccine arouses the body's defense system (the immune system) to produce antibodies or other types of resistance against the substances in the vaccine. The same defenses triggered by the vaccine are ready to fight off the particular disease for which the vaccine was prepared.

Some vaccines produce permanent or very long-lasting immunity against specific diseases while others produce resistance that does not last as long. Repeated immunizations ("boosters") at appropriate times can maintain the body's readiness to fight off illness and develop strong resistance to certain diseases.

Providing a Proper Immunization Schedule

The best way to ensure your child's immunity against certain diseases is to provide her with a proper immunization schedule or program. The accompanying table on page 217 presents the schedule for routine immunizations of normal infants in the Americas, as currently recommended by the American Academy of Pediatrics. The recommended schedule for immunizations during the first five years of life is presented on pages 947–48 and space is provided there for recording when your child receives these immunizations. It is important to keep good records of your child's immunizations, since this will be important health information to have later in life.

The immunization schedules presented here may be modified or supplemented depending upon the needs of individuals and groups, or the disease patterns in different areas of the world. As new vaccines or methods of administration are developed, your doctor will recommend appropriate alterations in this schedule.

The routine immunization of normal babies is initiated at approximately two months of age. The DTP (Diphtheria, Tetanus, and Pertussis) and TOPV (Trivalent Oral Polio Vaccine) vaccines are given at this time. DTP is a combination of three vaccines and is given by injection. The DTP vaccine is also abbreviated DPT. TOPV is a vaccine against the three types of polio virus and is given by mouth.

The DTP and TOPV vaccines are given again at approximately four and six months of age. The third oral polio immunization may be optional depending upon the risk of polio in your area. You should make arrangements with your doctor to receive these immunizations at the appropriate times during well baby care visits. Be sure to keep your appointments.

Do Not Take Immunizations Lightly

Unfortunately, there are some parents who mistakenly believe that immunizations are not that important. They feel that diseases like polio, diphtheria, pertussis, and tetanus no longer exist or exist only in other areas of the world. As a result, they often fail to have their child properly immunized.

Even though the incidence of these diseases has been greatly reduced by large scale immunization programs, they still exist at the present time and children need to be protected against them. It is tragic to see a young child needlessly suffering or being permanently harmed by polio or other diseases that could have been prevented by proper immunizations.

The importance of providing your child with proper immunizations during infancy and childhood cannot be overemphasized. This is one area where you can have a direct effect on your child's health and welfare. Do not put your child at risk. Take advantage of the immunizations that are readily available from your doctor or local public or private health facilities.

Possible Reactions to Immunizations

Some children have mild reactions to immunizations. Most reactions are minor and rarely require medical assistance. The following list describes some of the more common reactions.

RESTLESSNESS AND LOSS OF APPETITE. Your child may become fussy and restless for one to two days after an immunization and refuse to eat. These symptoms are more common at night. Do not force the child to eat. Beverages such as water or strained fruit juices (if okayed by your baby's doctor) can be encouraged. These reactions are usually very brief and pass quickly.

FEVER. Some children run a slight fever, especially with the DTP immunization. This is rather common and reflects the baby's reaction to the vaccine. Your doctor may recommend treating the fever with baby aspirin or a liquid antifever preparation. Never give medications unless specified by your doctor. A fever that persists or is very high should be brought to the attention of your doctor.

LUMP. A mild swelling or lump may develop at the injection site. The swelling usually only lasts for a few days and is not a cause for alarm.

Use Common Sense. The above list of minor reactions to immunizations gives you some feeling for how the baby may respond. If these symptoms persist, or other symptoms arise, consult your doctor. Do not forget that your child could also be sick from some other cause.

Recommended Immunization Schedule for Normal Infants[1]

AGE	IMMUNIZATION
2 months	DTP and TOPV
4 months	DTP and TOPV
6 months	DTP and TOPV[2]

HOW TO ENSURE YOUR BABY'S SAFETY

Even though your baby's abilities are still highly limited, she can often do more in the way of squirming, flipping over, and moving around than you may anticipate. Therefore, prevent your baby from squirming off the dressing table or other high places, and take other necessary precautions to ensure her health and safety as outlined in the Safety Training Check List presented on pages 125–27.

FEEDING

You are probably feeling more relaxed and confident about your ability to feed your baby. Some of you will take a bit longer before you feel 100 per cent at ease, but this is not unusual. Time and added experience will help. By now you have learned many things about your baby's feeding style, and how to make yourself comfortable and more efficient at breast-feeding or bottle-feeding. As you feed your infant by breast or bottle, you will be more accustomed to her behavior. You will be in a better position to stop feeding her when she indicates that she has had enough to eat. Many babies at this stage will be satisfied after a nursing period of about half an hour.

You will be enjoying the feeding exchange to a greater extent than before, now that you have the feeding method well underway. Probably the most important aspect, other than seeing to it that you are offering your baby plenty of food when she

[1] This schedule is based on the recommendations of the American Academy of Pediatrics, Report of the Committee on Infectious Diseases. Your doctor will advise you of any modifications or supplementations to this schedule for your child's individual needs.
[2] The third TOPV immunization may be optional depending upon the incidence of polio in your area.

is hungry, is the quality of your interaction with her during feedings. You will, of course, do this in your own special way, taking care to ensure that she receives plenty of love, affection, cuddling, and auditory stimulation such as talking or singing.

As you take your baby for her regular visits to the doctor or well baby clinic, she will be weighed and examined. If you have any questions about how she is doing on her feedings, be sure to ask them. Your physician will also discuss with you any changes that should be made in the bottle-feeding formula. You can assume that you are producing sufficient amounts of breast milk unless you learn otherwise from your doctor.

Again we wish to remind you that your baby is different from other babies, and nutritional requirements and diets among babies may vary considerably. Your doctor will advise you as to how best to satisfy your infant's food needs. The material in the feeding sections throughout this book should not be used as a substitute for the care and advice of your physician.

Fewer Feedings—More Milk at Each Feeding

As your baby gets older, she will not have to have food as frequently as before. She will take greater amounts of food at each feeding period. She will become more regular about when she wants to eat, and it will be easier for you to predict her feeding times.

Some babies during this phase will still have rather irregular hunger patterns and continue to require food at very frequent intervals. This is nothing to worry about. Naturally, unpredictability of feedings will inconvenience you and make it harder for you to plan your days, but by next month you can pretty much count on greater regularity. Try to be patient and tolerant.

Keep track of your infant's schedule by jotting down feeding times if she still requires very closely spaced feedings. Bring your notes with you when you visit your doctor. This may help the doctor determine whether she is getting enough to eat, and if certain adjustments are advisable.

GIVING UP THE MIDDLE-OF-THE-NIGHT FEEDING. Some babies have already dropped their middle-of-the-night feeding, while others will not be ready to do so until Infancy 3. Often when a baby weighs between ten and twelve pounds, she suddenly no longer needs to be fed during the night, although there is some variation in this. Parents wait impatiently for their baby to drop this feeding, and are no doubt overjoyed when they can finally get a decent night's sleep.

As the time approaches for the baby to begin sleeping through the night, you can try to hurry the procedure along using the following suggestion. Give the dinnertime or 6 P.M. feeding earlier, around 5 P.M., and the evening or 10 P.M. feeding later, around 11 P.M. Many parents find that a gradual shift to these approximate times facilitates the process of establishing a schedule without a feeding during the night, as well as the eventual shift to three meals a day.

Some babies still require a middle-of-the-night feeding, despite outside encouragement to give it up. In this situation, it is best to be patient and continue to satisfy the baby's real need for more frequent nourishment.

GIVING UP THE LAST EVENING FEEDING. A few babies will also begin sleeping through the last evening feeding at 10 or 11 P.M., in addition to being able to sleep through the night, but most will not be dropping this feeding until Infancy 3 or 4.

ADJUSTING TO YOUR BABY'S CHANGING NEEDS. When a baby's appetite increases, and her feedings decrease in number, certain adjustments have to be made.

If you are breast-feeding, your breast-milk supply will naturally increase to meet your child's changing need for more milk, although you may have to feed her more frequently for a few days. In some cases, a woman may not produce sufficient amounts of milk to meet her baby's greater demands. If you suspect that your milk supply is not completely adequate, discuss your concerns with your doctor. Together you can decide whether or not your baby's nutritional needs are being met.

If you are bottle-feeding, you will offer fewer bottles, and divide up the amount of milk that your child usually takes during a twenty-four-hour period according to how many ounces she generally consumes at each feeding.

Appetite Fluctuations

Babies have different appetites and it is impossible to predict exactly how many ounces a baby will take at each feeding. Some fluctuation in appetite is normal and nothing to be alarmed about. Parents who are bottle-feeding and can observe the number of ounces their babies are taking are apt to worry when the amount they take varies from one feeding to the next or from day to day. Breast-feeding mothers, on the other hand, may be less aware of appetite changes.

Try not to be too concerned about how much your baby is eating. As long as you offer enough food, she will eat as much as she needs. Do not coax or push her to eat larger quantities than she desires, since she may get annoyed and eat less or have trouble digesting the food she has eaten. Stick to your responsibilities and let her be the judge of how much she eats. Call the doctor if she is refusing meal after meal.

Weaning from the Breast

The decision as to when to stop breast-feeding is usually a matter of a mother's personal preference, and does not usually occur for many months. In some cases, however, it is necessary to wean a baby from the breast at this early time. Some mothers consider weaning their babies from the breast during the first few months for a variety of different reasons or for medical reasons. If you are considering weaning or must wean early, discuss your plans with your physician. We strongly recommend that your decision to wean be made in conjunction with your physician, who can offer advice as to how best to accomplish this. The main discussion of weaning appears on pages 280–83.

BATHING

By this time bathing should have become part of your regular routine and should be going along quite smoothly. As your baby gets older, you may want to give a full bath in a tub or other suitable container assuming you have not already done so, although some parents prefer to give a sponge bath for the first few months. If you find that bathing her every day is drying out her skin, try an every-other-day schedule.

Even though most babies probably enjoy their baths, some babies cry a lot at bath time. If your baby cries each time you give her a bath, try to examine the situation carefully to try to pinpoint a reason for this. Are you holding her securely? Is the temperature of the room too cold? Are you washing her so vigorously that her delicate skin is becoming irritated? When you soap up her scalp, is any shampoo getting into her eyes? Try to find a cause, but if you cannot, do not worry. Some babies simply do not like taking a bath, and may continue to cry. The only thing to do is to try to ignore her crying, and do the best you can to soothe and comfort her. Also try to get her bath over with as quickly as possible.

SLEEPING

Now that your baby is growing older, you will probably notice that her sleeping habits are changing. Assuming that she has not already begun to sleep through the night, she may do so at some point during Infancy 2, if not of her own accord then with a little gentle prodding from you. Refer back to pages 134–35 for suggestions for how to accomplish this. Not all babies are ready to sleep through the night in the second month. With some this is more easily accomplished in Infancy 3.

If you have been keeping your baby in your bedroom at night, you may want to shift her to sleeping in her own room, particularly if you find that your presence is interfering with her desire or ability to sleep, or vice versa. Once she has begun to sleep through the night, she will probably take two or more daytime naps, depending upon her individual need for sleep.

RETURNING TO WORK OUTSIDE THE HOME

Some parents have decided prior to their baby's arrival to return to work outside the home, either out of necessity or for reasons of personal preference. Others consider returning to a job or pursuing a career outside the home only after a month or several months of staying home to care for their baby. Regardless of individual family structures, parents who leave their babies in the care of another person for a large portion of time each day may find that certain emotional adjustments have to be made as a result.

Feeling Guilty and Unhappy

Many parents, particularly those who have little or no choice but to work, are unhappy about the fact that they have to be separated from their babies. It is not uncommon for parents who decide to work outside the home and leave their child in someone else's care to feel bad or guilty. Sometimes family members, pediatricians, and even child psychologists discourage them from other careers, contributing to a heightened sense of guilt. Some parents who had not anticipated feeling bad about being separated from their baby discover only after caring for her that leaving her with someone else is very difficult on them emotionally. They miss being with her while they are apart, and find themselves feeling depressed over the separation and longing to be abe to spend all their time with her. Psychologically, they remain full-time parents, despite the physical separation.

Guilt feelings can trouble parents who are not their baby's primary caretaker. They may feel that by not assuming full-time care of their child they are neglecting her, even though these feelings are not grounded in fact. Parents, who for reasons other than economic necessity, decide to work outside the home and have some lingering suspicions about not having made the right decision, are likely to be particularly troubled by remarks or subtle hints from others that they are uncaring, irresponsible, or unfit to be parents. On the other hand, parents who are confident about their decision and are certain that their babies are in the best of hands in their absence are not as likely to be upset over other people's reactions.

Adjustments Have to Be Made

Regardless of whether or not the decision to return to work was willful or could not have been avoided, parents may have some difficulties adjusting emotionally to the situation. It is not uncommon for parents to become jealous and even resentful of the person whom they have enlisted to care for their child. The feeling that they are easily "replaceable" is hard for most parents to take. In many situations in which parents work full time away from home, their baby naturally comes to build up a closer attachment with the parent figure caring for her, rather than her parents. Young babies have very short memories and may initially react to their natural parents as though they are strangers.

Parents may begin to wonder, "Am *I* really her parent?" or "Is she really *my* child?" They may also have doubts as to their own importance in child rearing. Jealousy between parent and caretaker can arise, causing some friction and resentment. Parents may even try to compete with the caretaker for their own child's affection by being overindulgent or overly lenient with her whenever they do spend time together. If parents leave their child with in-laws or their own parents, and their relationship with their relatives is not what they themselves would call "the best," they may feel even more threatened, dependent, and insecure about their youngster's relationship with them.

Most of these difficulties and minor problems can be easily worked out. After an initial period of adjustment, some problems are naturally resolved. Sometimes parents who feel bad or guilty that they are not spending enough time with their child are able to rearrange schedules to enable more parent-child contact. If your baby is asleep when you return from work, you, along with the adult caring for her in your absence, might work to ease her onto a schedule that will shift her bedtime back an hour or more so that you can spend time with her in the evening. You can also arrange to keep her last feeding in the evening (10 or 11 P.M. feeding) beyond the age at which it could have been discontinued so that you can feed her yourself and have a chance to be more involved in her care. You will find a way to spend more time with her, provided that this is really important to you. Perhaps you can even arrange to take your lunch hour at home, or can arrange to get out of work early a couple of days a week, if you make up the time at night when your baby is sleeping. Let your superiors at work know how important it is to you to be able to spend a little extra time with your baby. You may find that they are willing to assist you in this regard.

You will find that it helps to talk about your feelings and problems with other parents whose jobs and careers take them outside their homes. They may not only be very sympathetic of your position and feelings, but may be able to offer you suggestions for how to iron out minor difficulties based upon their own experience. If problems related to your having to leave your child in someone else's care escalate to the point where you cannot deal with them, it may be helpful for you to seek some guidance from your doctor or another professional.

PREPARED PARENTHOOD CHECK LIST

MOTHER	FATHER	UNDERSTANDING YOUR BABY'S DEVELOPMENT
—	—	Has your baby's social smile emerged?
—	—	In what way is your baby getting to know you?
—	—	Does your infant respond positively to your attention and affection?
—	—	Has your baby's interest in looking at her surroundings increased?
—	—	Do you see any signs that your infant is learning from experience in relation to feedings?
—	—	Is your baby's crying easier for you to interpret?
—	—	Has your infant had any unexplainable crying spells or fussy periods? When do they usually occur?
—	—	Have you heard your baby producing any non-crying sounds?
—	—	Is your baby making repeated attempts to lift her head off the mattress?
—	—	Are your infant's hands held in a more loose-fisted position than in Infancy 1?
—	—	Are you aware of the major considerations in selecting safe, appropriate toys for your baby?
—	—	Have you been spending time with your baby and arranging her immediate surroundings so that she receives ample sensory and motor stimulation?
—	—	What types of activities and interactions does your infant seem to enjoy the most?

BASIC CARE

MOTHER	FATHER	
—	—	Why is it so important to have your child properly immunized and what are the dangerous diseases that can be prevented by starting to immunize your baby at this time?
—	—	Have you made arrangements for your child to receive the appropriate immunizations at this age? If you have not, be sure to contact your doctor and make an appointment.
—	—	Is your baby moving to fewer feedings and taking more milk at each feeding?
—	—	Have you been offering your baby ample stimulation at bath time?
—	—	How do you plan to steer your baby gently toward a sleeping schedule that is more convenient for you?

FAMILY FEELINGS AND CONCERNS

MOTHER	FATHER	
—	—	Are you aware of some of the emotional adjustments that may be required if you return to work outside the home?

223

Infancy 3

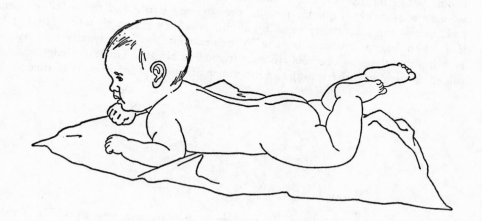

PERSONAL-SOCIAL DEVELOPMENT

Self-awareness

I'VE REALLY FOUND MY HANDS. By Infancy 3, your baby will have already found his hands. When he first really sees them he may look rather surprised. In fact, if he happens to wave them quickly past his eyes he may startle and try to follow their path, wondering where they came from, and how they got to be there. His familiarity with human anatomy is virtually non-existent: he initially has no way of knowing that the hands he sees are an extension of himself. This knowledge will be gained through extensive testing and experimentation over a long period of time.

Once he has found his hands, he is likely to stare at them very often. The serious expression on his face should be amusing to observe. He will watch his hands as he moves them, straightens them out, and swipes at objects with them. He carefully tests out his new equipment, and learns about what he can do with his hands—with a part of his body. He will look closely at his fingers. Touching his hands together and wiggling his fingers at the same time produces a unique sensation that he frequently tries to maintain and repeat.

Sucking on his fingers may reduce his tension and soothe him. Mr. Harrow noticed that his son often sucked on his fingers immediately prior to falling asleep, when he was frustrated, or wound up. His son seemed to relax as he sucked on his hand. At first he became concerned that this habit would lead to vigorous thumb-sucking, but he noticed that his son did not abuse this activity and used it to relax himself.

Thumb-, fist-, or finger-sucking is a common means by which babies calm themselves. Some psychologists speculate that a baby's sucking on his fingers represents an attempt on his part to recall the satisfaction and pleasure he derives from sucking on the nipple during feedings. They suggest that parents view this behavior as a healthy, constructive outlet, and an indication of their baby's resourcefulness. A further discussion of tension outlets and thumb-sucking is presented on pages 331–35.

An infant's interest in playing with his own hands and fingers can keep him occupied for relatively long periods of time. When you hold your baby, he may grab your hand and fingers, and carefully look them over. He may even look back and forth between his own hand and yours, in what appears to be an attempt to compare them. This is part of how he begins to learn that he is similar, but also different from you and other people. At this early stage he is not at all clear about the fact that he is a separate person. By gradually studying his own body and comparing it to yours, he will learn this lesson in time.

FINDING HIS FEET. After your baby focuses on his hands, finding his feet will probably be the next step. Prior to the third month, he may have stared right past his feet and not seen them. Now that his eyesight has improved, it is easier for him to see objects at various distances and focus more clearly on nearby objects. One day soon he will discover his feet.

At first his foot may appear to be just another object that someone has left in his crib. He will gradually learn that he can move his feet, and elevate them a little. The first time that he kicks the side of the crib with his feet while watching them, he may seem quite surprised to learn that he feels pain. Previously he may have been unaware that he had feelings or sensations in his feet. After an experience or two like this, there will be no doubt about his growing awareness of this "new" part of his body.

Your baby will stare at his feet in a similar manner in which he stared at his hands and fingers. Older babies often play with their feet and toes. An infant's awareness of his feet as part of his body will increase as he moves them around, stretches them out, and later realizes that he can kick objects dangling from his mobile, causing them to swing. Learning what he can do with his legs, feet, and toes adds to his self-awareness.

Social Sensitivity and Interests

An Infancy 3 baby is more capable of expressing his feelings than in the past. His range of emotions is still quite limited, but there should be little doubt in your mind that he has feelings. When he is happy and feels good inside, he will smile frequently and spontaneously. In fact, most babies at this age who have had tender, loving care from birth tend to smile a great deal.

In the event that your baby was a "crier" from birth, you are likely to notice that his crying is diminishing. He still lets out loud wails when he is angry, hungry, fatigued, or frustrated, but he does not cry as often as before. He is beginning to cry as a means of expressing feelings, as opposed to crying mainly out of tension from pressing physical needs or discomfort.

Marcy Weiner noticed her son, Orin, crying more often in an attempt to get her attention. She also noticed that his cries varied to a greater extent than before, according to different situations or what he was trying to communicate to her. When he was really raging mad or in physical distress, he screamed or cried at the top of his lungs. When he was lonely, upset by something she did or failed to do, and simply wanted attention, he fussed, whimpered, or cried in a different way. He learned that this special cry brought her back to his room.

You are likely to notice similar changes in your baby's cries. They are becoming more differentiated, according to what he needs or wants. As his ability to communicate his feelings and needs increases, you will feel less confused about what he wants when he cries.

A baby's social crying or crying for attention may be willfully started or stopped. When he is placed in his crib, but does not want to be alone there, he might cry in an attempt to get you to return, just so he can have your company. While crying, he will probably listen carefully to household sounds, and the sounds that you produce when you talk or walk. At the sound of your footsteps, he may suddenly stop crying, because he anticipates your entry into his room. You will notice that his social crying is purposeful, and cleverly aimed at drawing you to him.

GETTING TO KNOW HIM. Over the past couple of months, you have become a much better judge of what your infant wants or needs. Part of this stems from the fact that the two of you have gotten to know one another better, and part stems from the fact that he is more capable of communicating his needs. The expressions on his face, his body positions, hand gestures, and sounds, all serve to clue you in on not only his needs, but also his feelings.

When he is excited to see you, or all wound up about some activity, he breathes heavily, moves his whole body, grins from cheek to cheek, and opens his eyes. He may even strain his head forward and reach out with his arms when he is happy to see you and wants to be held. Strangers will not get this same treatment. At the sight of unfamiliar faces, he may seem frightened and upset. He may glare at them cautiously, size them up, and then turn his face away.

By his responses, you may be able to tell when he is happy, uncomfortable, pensive, uncertain, lonely, excited, and angry. It should be interesting for you to observe how quickly he can shift from one emotional state to another. One moment he may be highly distraught and screaming at the top of his lungs, and the next moment he may smile and appear to be satisfied and content. This sudden shifting from distress to satisfaction is characteristic of young babies.

HE'S BECOMING MORE OF A SOCIAL PERSON. Your baby is more sensitive to you and other family members. He may now be able to pick out your voice when he is in a room in which other people are also talking.

Carolyn Bunk brought her three-month-old son, Martin, to an informal cocktail party. She placed Martin's bassinet in the middle of the room, and began to socialize, always keeping an eye on him as she moved about the room. After several minutes, she saw Martin straining, as if he was trying to locate the sound of her voice. A couple of minutes later, she noticed him struggling to lift his head and turn it in her direction. He then began to make special sounds in what appeared to her to be an effort to attract her attention. She was so delighted and touched by his behavior that she quickly returned to him, picked him up, and gave him a big hug and kiss.

Repeated opportunities to hear your voice, frequent contact with you, and improving perceptual abilities enable your baby to discriminate between your voice and others. Should you notice him trying to locate the sound of your voice and turning in your direction, you will undoubtedly be delighted as was Martin's mother. This can be taken as a sign of the progress your baby is making, as well as the headway you are making in building a close relationship with him.

There should be little doubt that he is becoming more attached to you, assuming that you have been a consistent figure in his life from birth. He is likely to behave very differently around you than when around other people, even other family members. His smiling at you, making special sounds and gestures when you are near him, and his attempts to get you to play with and pay attention to him should convey that you are someone special, and that he derives pleasure from being in your company.

He may also be able to recognize other familiar figures in his life, such as your spouse and his brothers or sisters. When they play with him and try to amuse him, he may become active, produce sounds, and smile. Socializing and being around people has become more important to him. So important that he may sometimes get upset when it is time for bed and being alone.

A PARENT CAN BE A STRANGER. A baby's memory is short. Thus, he may sometimes regard family members, other than the parent who cares for him consistently, as strangers. This can be disconcerting to them, and may be taken as an insult. Once his memory improves, he will have no trouble remembering them and will be more responsive.

Mr. and Mrs. Harper both had active careers and hired Anna to care for their son, Robert, for most of the day. The Harpers loved their son, and looked forward to playing with him each evening. At around three months of age, Robert began to cry each night when his parents played with him, but was quickly quieted when Anna picked him up.

The Harpers were very hurt at first by their son's behavior. They felt he really did not love them, and that they were being replaced as parents by Anna. In discussing the situation at length, they realized that Robert was showing a normal behavior pattern. His memory was not long enough to remember his parents' affection from day to day at this early stage. Robert saw Anna all day and thus clearly recognized her as the person meeting his needs. As Robert's memory improved in Infancy 6 to 7, he became much more responsive to his parents and really looked forward to playing with them every evening.

Given that his ability to remember people and experiences is not well developed at this time, it is easy to see why continuity of care is important to the infant. Through repeated contact with at least one individual performing routine basic care activities and providing love and affection, he can count on several things. One is the fact that someone loves him and is affectionate toward him. He can also be certain that his needs will be met. When his cries are answered, he realizes that his crying has an impact upon someone, and that he can trust that person to come when needed. He feels secure knowing that there is a certain routine or predictability in his life. This makes for a happy and contented baby.

The parent or parents not providing for his daily needs should not feel hurt at his attachment for his main provider. This is a healthy, natural sign that his needs are being met, and that he is satisfied. He will gradually learn that other people also love and care for him.

INTELLECTUAL DEVELOPMENT

Your baby is no longer as preoccupied with his own inner bodily states and needs. He shows more interest in what is happening around him. His sleep requirements have diminished considerably, and thus he is awake and alert for longer periods of time during the day, perhaps as long as three quarters of an hour. Much of the time when he is awake he will probably appear to be bright-eyed, attentive, and responsive. He has surely become more "in tune" with the outside world.

Greater Interest in the Environment

An Infancy 3 baby readily accepts the challenge of finding out more about the outside world, with greater determination and enthusiasm than in previous months. He is also more well equipped to absorb new experiences, interact with the environment, and learn.

This fellow has a lively curiosity. He is interested in looking at objects and people. The mobile dangling from his crib attracts his attention. So does your voice, and particularly your face. Once he sees his hands, he becomes curious about them too. His growing curiosity needs an outlet. He not only wants to look and listen, he now wants to bat at and feel objects within his reach, and, perhaps, bring them to his mouth for further exploration.

IMPROVING VISUAL ABILITIES. The infant's visual capacities show rapid expansion, and this enables him to get a much better look at things. His eye and head movements are gradually becoming more co-ordinated, as is his blink response as objects quickly approach his face. He is much better able to focus both eyes upon nearby objects, as well as see objects at further distances than in previous months. In fact, as he approaches four months of age, he may be able to get a clear view of objects all over his bedroom. This should give him a fresh, new perspective on his surroundings.

Following objects is much easier now. He shows an improved ability to follow slowly moving targets both from side to side, and up and down without losing track of them. It is likely that the objects and people he follows are seen more clearly.

His ability to focus more distinctly on nearby objects and keep both of his eyes zeroed in on a target is significant. Now he will do more than give nearby objects, such as his hands, a quick glance. He will stare at them intently, and perhaps really pay attention to them for the first time. Small, detailed, nearby targets will attract his attention, and he will quickly and carefully examine them. There is little doubt that he is becoming a more sophisticated observer. Around this age, as he opens his fist a little, he will have something new to look at—his fingers. Your infant will be quite fascinated with staring at his moving fingers.

LISTENING. Your baby will listen attentively to all kinds of sounds, and is apt to turn his eyes toward their sources. He may particularly become quiet and attentive when you talk to him or he hears the sounds of your footsteps heading in his direction. He pays attention to close-by noises as well as those that are further away. His interest in his own sounds is also growing.

MOUTHING OBJECTS. The mouth is one of your baby's main organs for exploring his surroundings. One of your infant's favorite activities may be sucking on or gumming his own fist or fingers. He may start to bring other small objects that he holds to his mouth as well. As he samples objects in this manner, he learns more about them. He discovers whether objects are smooth or rough, whether they taste good or bad, and whether they are small or large.

This hand-to-mouth behavior enables him to learn many things about himself and objects. After sampling first his fingers and then objects, he can make comparisons. His hand-to-mouth response pattern will increase as he becomes more capable of reaching out to grab objects.

REACHING OUT FOR OBJECTS. In the months to come he will increasingly use his hands to explore objects. Initially, his abilities in this area are limited. His hands are there, but they are not of much use to him, since he has little or no voluntary control over them. As he gains control over his hands, he will wave them around, move his fingers, and play with them. He will reach out toward nearby objects and try to grab hold.

He Is Learning More Each Day

You will see more evidence that your baby is combining or co-ordinating simple behaviors. He not only looks at objects, but he simultaneously hears the sounds they produce. He regularly turns his head and eyes toward the direction of a sound.

Visual-motor co-ordination has already begun. He moves his hands, and simultaneously watches them. Thus, looking and moving, together, give more information about himself and his surroundings. Objects are not only looked at and moved, they are also increasingly brought to the mouth for sucking. Looking, moving, and sucking become co-ordinated.

At some point as your baby moves his hands, he may accidentally discover that when his waving hand hits an object hanging over his crib, something very interesting happens; it moves. He will want to repeat this behavior just to be able to observe this interesting change in his environment.

This type of behavior, which becomes even more prominent in Infancy 4, is very different from his behavior in the past. Previously, he seemed to repeat simple actions such as sucking and making a fist for their own sake. In other words, there appeared to be little intention or purpose to this behavior, and he seemed not to be very interested in seeing what effect, if any, his movements could make on his surroundings. By the end of the third month, or early in the fourth month, his behavior is becoming somewhat more purposeful. After he discovers that the movement of his arms or the wriggling of his body produces some interesting change, he seems to repeat the action intentionally in order to maintain that change until he either gets fatigued or bored. This behavior, even if only in a small way, shows he is becoming more goal-directed and his interest in making frequent contact with nearby objects will increase in Infancy 4.

Throughout the time you spend with your infant, you will notice more evidence that his actions are less focused about himself and more directed toward his immediate surroundings. In the Personal-Social Development section you read about how he will try to attract your attention and how his interest in interacting with you is increasing. It is clear that his attention is gradually progressing outward from himself to objects and other people.

You will see evidence of his ability to make associations, and differentiate between people and things. He recognizes people, mainly you and other close family members, and when he sees you, he smiles, becomes excited, and babbles. He may even recognize one or two familiar objects such as his bottle or a rattle.

LANGUAGE DEVELOPMENT

Language development basically involves active language learning (learning to speak) and passive language learning (learning to understand what is said). As progress in language development is followed through each successive phase, both of these aspects of language learning will be explored.

Active Language Development

CRYING MARKEDLY DECREASES. Assuming that your baby has been a real "crier" over the past couple of months, you should be overjoyed to discover that the total time of his crying has noticeably decreased. This seems to occur with the majority of babies, even with those who have been troubled by colic. A few babies will continue to cry a great deal for another month or two.

This transition from a great deal of crying to a relatively small amount may have begun during Infancy 2 but generally becomes more obvious at this time. Your baby has begun to find other outlets for his energy besides crying. Along with being more alert during the daytime, he is more interested in the outside world. He listens to sounds, gazes at people and objects, and reaches out to make contact. He is more capable of amusing as well as calming himself by looking, listening, batting objects, sucking on his fingers, and producing new sounds. His body seems to be adjusting well to this new life outside of his mother's womb, and he is growing up. All of these factors may account for the amazing decrease in crying that occurs around the third month.

CRYING FOR ATTENTION. Crying for attention may now surface as one of your baby's reasons for crying. Some professionals refer to this type of crying as "spoiled" crying, but this label leaves a rather sour taste (no pun intended). A need for attention can be just as good a reason for crying as bodily discomfort or hunger, especially during the first few months. When parents have not given their babies enough satisfying human contact and attention, it is only natural that their babies will cry out for it. Crying for attention would seem a "real" reason under these circumstances. It is also a justifiable reason for crying when parents only offer attention to their baby when he is crying. Their baby learns to connect crying with being picked up, and cries regularly just so that someone will pay attention to him.

On the other hand, some babies who have received a more than sufficient share of love and parental stimulation cry out of sheer habit. Perhaps they were troubled by colic or some other condition during the first few months and were used to being picked up, carried about, or rocked whenever they cried.

Should your baby continue to cry because he misses the extra attention you offered during the first couple of months, there is no reason for you to be upset with him. Once you understand his point of view, you can see that it would be hard for him if you abruptly stopped rocking or carrying him around when he cries. He is still immature and his reasoning ability is extremely limited. It is likely that your sudden change in treatment of him might baffle him. Therefore, it is a good idea to withdraw your extra attention gradually. Little by little you can begin to set firmer limits on his crying.

When he cries at bedtime, for example, you can spend a few minutes calming him down. Let him know that you understand what he wants, but that it is important for you to leave so that he can get his sleep. Then leave the room, even if he is still crying. He will eventually learn to quiet himself, even though it may take him a week or two. In the meanwhile, to reinforce the lesson that you want him to learn, do not go back into his room. If you do, your inconsistency in handling the situation may confuse him.

Babies who cry because they want attention, usually stop crying the moment they hear the sound of their parent's footsteps coming toward their room, or when they see their parent's face. Those who are crying for other reasons will have trouble turning their crying on and off at will. It is not uncommon for all babies, at some point or another, to cry for attention, or because they want company, particularly at bedtime. Generally, the more aware they become of people and activities, the less they want to be cut off from either or both at bedtime. It will be up to you to determine whether or not your baby's crying for attention is legitimate, and to react accordingly.

OTHER SOUNDS. Sounds other than crying are heard more often at this time. You may hear your baby chuckling, gurgling, making loud shrill sounds and cooing sounds. Usually by the third month, babies begin to put their sounds together in the form of babbling. Vowels are combined to make sounds like "aa" and "oo."

These sounds are repeated over and over again, often in a rhythmic, song-like fashion. As your baby practices producing sounds like "oo oo oo" he may vary the volume, tone, and pitch. In other words, he will probably "play" with the sounds that he produces.

RESPONSIVE BABBLING. Your baby may now begin to babble in a responsive way when you talk to him and smile, as though trying to answer you or participate in the conversation. This type of vocalization in response to your speech or social gestures represents an important step forward in terms of his language development. Gradually, this type of verbal exchange will become more sophisticated, and will evolve into what is called "conversational babbling." His babbling will begin to resemble actual sentences more closely, and even though he will not actually be saying "real" words, it will sound as though the two of you are carrying on a conversation. The use of his voice in response to your talking and smiling represents a point along the long path from the production of the most primitive, meaningless sounds, to the mastery of speech and the ability to carry on a real conversation.

Passive Language Development

A stronger interest in sounds and people's voices is apt to emerge during Infancy 3. When you speak to him, he will become alert, listen carefully to what you say, and look at your face. It is still too early for him to be able to understand what he hears. Nevertheless, there is some evidence that he will begin to pick up on certain word sounds, and even recognize some of the different syllables that he hears. He may also begin to sense your feelings or moods by the tone of your voice. When you sound terribly upset, he may begin to cry, as if he can sense your mood.

As your young infant practices using his voice, he is likely to seem a bit surprised by his own sounds. After producing each new sound, he may stop for a moment with a wide-eyed look on his face, and then continue practicing. Hearing the sound of his own voice is a new experience, and adds another dimension to his self-awareness.

MOTOR DEVELOPMENT

Reflex Activity

Your three-month-old is taking steps toward gaining more voluntary control over his own actions. Many of his primitive reflex responses are fading and disappearing as his higher brain centers work to suppress these automatic patterned behaviors. He no longer startles as easily, since his Moro (startle) reflex is slowly disappearing. It will probably be much harder for you to elicit his walking reflex.

When he is lying on his back, he is no longer obliged to assume a "fencer's" posture, since his tonic neck reflex is fading. By Infancy 4 it may be gone forever. Once free of this reflex, he will be able to hold his head in a center or middle position, and his posture will be more symmetrical. His hand position will no longer be bound or influenced by his head position, and he will therefore be freer to move his hands as he pleases, independent of his head movements.

Previously, if you stimulated the corner of his mouth with your finger, his rooting response was clearly observable. Now when you try this, you may notice that he does not immediately or automatically turn his head toward your finger and try to grasp it with his mouth. Rather, he hesitates a bit as he sizes up the situation, and may seem disinterested, if what he sees is not a nipple.

In regard to reflex grasping, you are likely to observe an important change. The tight, closed position of the hand is giving way to a more open position. It is more difficult to trigger his grasp reflex, since it is fading.

Gross Motor Activity

HEAD CONTROL. Your infant is still limited in what he can do with his body, but he is slowly gaining more control. One of the areas in which rapid progress can be seen is in head control. As was previously mentioned, he can finally hold his head in a center position when lying on his back, and can move it freely from side to side in a much broader arc. He has better control over the movements of his head, and it is easier for him to lift it, although he may only sustain this position very briefly.

When he is lying on his stomach, he can raise his head more than a couple of inches off of the mattress, and can keep it up more than for only a moment or two.

Beverly Allen walked into her son Patrick's room expecting to find him sleeping. Instead, she saw him repeatedly lifting his head off the crib mattress and looking around his bedroom. Patrick's determined efforts to raise his head, without any outside encouragement, convinced Beverly that having opportunities to examine his surroundings was very important to her child. By watching her son's activity, she also noticed that he had not gained as much control over his arms and legs as he had over his head and neck. Beverly had read that babies gain voluntary control over their heads very early, and that later they develop control over their arms and, eventually, their legs. Seeing this developmental progression in Patrick interested her, and she made a note of her observation in the special record-keeping book that she had set aside for this purpose.

You may observe your baby lifting his head fairly high off the mattress and holding it up for some time so that he can get a good look at his surroundings. This activity is important to him. In order to make it possible for him to have ample chances to practice lifting his head, you can place him on his stomach frequently when you lay him in his crib.

Support him in a sitting position, and you will still see his head slump forward or fall backward, but in general, it will be less wobbly. He may strain to keep it erect, but it sways in spite of his valiant efforts to the contrary.

MORE STRENGTH IN HIS ARMS. Another sign of increasing strength can be seen in relation to your baby's arms. Formerly, his arm muscles were extremely weak, making it hard for him to push his chest up and rest part of his body weight on them when on his stomach.

During Infancy 3, he may frequently do "mini-push-ups," resting his weight on his forearms and/or hands. In this position, in which his chest is held off the mattress, he may also be capable of holding his head vertical to the mattress, but only for brief periods of time. Another activity that he enjoys is scratching his mattress or other flat surfaces. He may shift his weight so that much of it is resting on one side of his body, leaving the other hand free to scratch. He probably likes this activity because of the noises that are produced.

MORE STRENGTH IN HIS LEGS. His leg muscles are also stronger than they were. Direct evidence for this lies in the fact that he can now lift them a little off the mattress or a changing table, something that he probably found hard to do before. One of his treasured activities on his tummy may involve elevating his legs, spreading his arms out to his sides, arching his back, and lifting his head. In this position he may rock and move a bit, and actively wave his arms and legs.

Place him on his tummy so that his feet can press up against the back of the crib. He will thrust his feet against the crib, using all of the power in his legs that he can muster. If you support him under his arms in an upright position, he may love to bounce up and down and step, and may even briefly support much of his own weight.

HE LIKES TO EXERCISE. Your baby's body is no longer as unco-ordinated, weak, and floppy as it was. He seems to like to exercise, and he does so by engaging in activities like kicking, swiping, batting, and raising his head. He also squirms, arches, wriggles, and thrashes about with his arms and legs, sometimes with such great strength that he moves about, turns his body over to one side, or even flips himself over. It may be another month or more before he is able to roll over, although there is a possibility of his performing this feat during this month.

He is gradually gaining trunk control during the latter half of this phase. When you hold him in a sitting position, he will try to help maintain his balance, but his trunk muscles are not sufficiently developed to enable him to sit up straight or hold his head erect. Therefore, it is unadvisable to keep him in this position more than briefly.

By now he may have a strong opinion as to whether he likes to be placed on his tummy or his back. In fact, if you fail to place him in his preferred position, he may squirm, whimper, or cry.

Fine Motor Activity

In Infancy 3, your baby will gain more voluntary control over his hands. Grasping, once done automatically, is now difficult for him, since he must actually learn how to perform this task. He makes many attempts to grab toys that are held near his hand. Many of his tries may be unsuccessful, but he will not seem to mind.

Batting and swiping at objects within his arm's reach are becoming two of his favorite activities. His aim is not very accurate, since good eye and hand co-ordination are lacking. Hold an interesting toy over the front of his body. He will get all excited and thrash about with his arms at his sides. Gradually, he may bring them together in front of his body as he attempts to reach for the toy. His reaching, however, is far from being controlled and efficient.

His eyesight once again shows improvement, and he is beginning to co-ordinate looking with reaching, as is more extensively covered in the Intellectual Development section. It will probably be another month before visually directed reaching is more fully established.

Your infant is bringing his hand to his mouth more easily and frequently than in previous phases. At this point, he is probably sucking on his thumb or fingers as opposed to his fist. Now that hands are no longer held in a fist, his thumb and fingers are becoming separate entities that can be played with, stared at, and sucked, but his fingers are not particularly useful to him.

FEEDING

As your baby becomes increasingly alert and responsive to you, feeding him should become more enjoyable. By now, both breast-feeding and bottle-feeding should be progressing very smoothly. Even though your baby may still need a little assistance in taking the nipple, he will not need as much help as in the past. As always, allow your doctor to determine along with you whether your breast-milk supply is adequate, or whether any formula or other dietary changes are in order.

A Decrease in Appetite May Be Noticed

Some babies' appetites begin to diminish during Infancy 3, although this usually occurs between Infancy 4 and 6. With some babies there is an obvious lag in appetite, and with others there may be no lag at all. Babies usually want or need to eat less as their weight gain slows down. Do not be alarmed if you notice that your infant seems slightly less enthusiastic at mealtime. The main problem that may arise when parents become overly concerned is that they often begin to pressure him to eat more than he wants. Continual nagging or pressure on a baby at mealtime can lead to problems in the area of eating. In Infancy 4, on page 257, you will find suggestions for how to avoid unnecessary feeding problems.

Fewer Feedings

Many babies will now need to be fed less often. Most will be sleeping through the middle-of-the-night feeding, much to their parents' relief. Some babies, having dropped the feeding during the night, will indicate that they are also ready to drop the late evening feeding at 10 or 11 P.M. Those who are not yet ready should be ready during the next two months.

Some parents like to awaken their baby for this last night feeding, particularly if they work outside the home during the daytime. This feeding offers them a good opportunity for close contact that would otherwise be missed. They may also want to keep it going if the baby seems to need more sucking satisfaction and is regularly looking for something to suck or is regularly sucking on his fingers or blanket.

As your baby takes fewer feedings, you will also notice that his pattern of feedings is becoming more regular and stable. This is what many parents have been waiting for, since greater predictability in terms of mealtimes makes it much easier for them to plan their daily schedules. Many babies will now be on a four-meal-a-day cycle.

BATHING

By now you should be confident and an expert bath-giver, which will put you and your baby at ease. There are essentially no changes in the bath procedure, but as your baby's activity increases, you should pay even closer attention to the safety precautions mentioned in Infancy 1. His moving body and circling arms may make it harder for you to hold him, especially when he is soapy. Be certain you have a good grip on him at bath time.

Some babies continue to dislike having a bath, but they can learn even at this early stage that certain things in life, like taking a bath, are necessary. If your baby objects violently to having his bath in a regular bathtub, you can try bathing him somewhere else, such as in a Bathinette, or giving him sponge baths instead. The objective is to keep him clean, and the means by which this is accomplished are not as important as the end result.

CLOTHING

If your baby spends time in a playpen and your home is cold, you may want some covering for his feet in the way of socks, or want to buy outfits that come in one piece, like jumpsuits with attached feet. These garments can be purchased in cotton, jersey, or terry cloth, and many parents swear by them. Make sure that these outfits do not restrict his movements, since freedom to move is important. As he spends less time sleeping in his crib, the shift will gradually be made away from nightgowns to jumpsuits and other similar garments. As always, it is up to you to expand his wardrobe as you see fit.

SLEEPING

Your baby should now be capable of sleeping through the night and may sleep much more soundly than in previous months. In case he is not capable of spontaneously sleeping at least six to eight hours each night, you should probably take appropriate steps to encourage him to do so (see pages 238–39). Most babies awaken very early in the morning, much too early for many parents' liking. Should your early riser inconvenience you, try gradually to wait longer before going into his room after he starts to whimper or cry, with the hope that he will quiet down and perhaps even go back to sleep. Should his crying be loud and persistent, you will not be able to sleep through it anyway. Chances are that his needs are real and should be met.

Middle-of-the-night Waking

In the event that your baby awakens each night and cries, try to hold off going to him for a few minutes and see whether he will settle down and return to sleep. If he does not stop crying, and you cannot discover any apparent reason for his crying, at this point you may want to reassure him, briefly comfort him, and then leave his room.

Letting him cry without going to him will not be easy for you, but if you can try to grin and bear it for several days, he may eventually learn that his crying will not prompt an immediate reaction from you. He will learn to quiet himself when he awakens during the night, or may stop awakening altogether.

Again, there are no hard and fast rules on dealing with this problem. If you cannot stand to hear him cry or he seems in real distress, you need not feel guilty about going to him. Every parent will handle this problem a bit differently, depending upon the individual case at hand. The main thing to keep in mind is that as your baby grows older and becomes more socially inclined, your presence becomes more positively rewarding to him. He may make a habit of waking during the night and crying just to have your company or see your face. Refrain from responding to his crying, night after night, or you will be positively reinforcing this behavior and may never get a decent night's sleep.

Once you are fairly certain that all he wants is company, you should be firm in your approach to his antics. Bear in mind that middle-of-the-night waking may persist longer than is necessary if your baby is still sleeping in your room. Switching him to his own room where he will not automatically see you the moment he awakens may be a necessary step toward trying to solve this problem.

Time for a New Crib

If your baby has not yet outgrown his bassinet or basket, at some point during Infancy 3 or 4 he will probably grow too large and active to be placed in it safely. Vigorous activity, such as rocking, may cause his bassinet to tip over.

Now is the time to be planning ahead and making arrangements to shift him to a crib in the near future. Another reason for making a shift to a crib is to give him more room to move about at night. Freedom of movement is very important during both day and night.

PARENTING IS ONLY ONE DIMENSION
OF YOUR LIFE

An issue that often arises in the course of small group discussions among parents is that of maintaining your individuality and a life of your own as a person apart from being a parent. Many parents have talked about how their own parents became overly involved with them to the point where their lives revolved solely around them. Then when they left "the nest" so to speak, their parents felt a terrific loss of identity and purpose. Many men and women have also talked about how after they became parents they also became so wrapped up in their children that they began to lose sight of the fact that parenting was only one aspect of their lives as people.

There is a tendency for some parents to lose sight of their own needs as individuals apart from being parents. Being a good parent does not necessitate your being a self-sacrificing martyr. Your needs and feelings count. You are entitled to have a life of your own apart from your life as a parent, if you so desire. Being a parent is only one of several dimensions of your life as a person. If you are feeling "incomplete" as a total person, motivate yourself to take the necessary steps to fill the empty area in your life. For some parents this means hiring a baby-sitter twice a week just to be free of child rearing responsibilities. For others it involves finding an interesting hobby, enrolling in an adult education class, taking a part-time job, taking work into your home, joining a club, or returning to your former job or career.

It is most often the parent who stays home with the child who may, at some point, express feelings of being "locked in," "unhappy," "bored," "unstimulated," or "unfulfilled." In some cases parents with these complaints may be centering their entire lives around their child and not giving their own needs any priority. Parents who are unhappy staying home with their babies may miss their former jobs or careers and the stimulation that accompanied working or establishing interests and activities outside the home. A rather common complaint among parents who assume primary care of their baby is that they miss having contact with other adults. It is interesting, though, that many of these parents have done little or nothing to initiate such contact.

Another common gripe among parents is a loss of privacy in the home. Most often this gripe surfaces during the latter part of infancy, once the baby begins to crawl. This complaint is also commonly heard during toddlerhood. As one mother put it:

> My whole house was my territory, and yet I was the only person in the household who had no particular area that I could truly call my own. My baby had her bedroom, my older child had his bedroom, and my husband had a workshop in the garage all to himself. I had no special place, and yet, in one sense, I had every room in the house. It's hard to describe how I felt, other than to say that I felt a loss of privacy and individuality. In the midst of being a mother and a wife, I somehow lost track of "me."

Find a room or even a corner of a room to call your own, if you feel a loss of privacy. Rearrange the furniture or partition the area off to afford yourself maximal privacy. This room or area can be decorated to suit *your* tastes. It can be your special hideaway.

In some instances parents begin to feel unneeded, unimportant, and unfulfilled as their baby becomes more independent. For the first six months or so, when their baby is highly dependent upon them, they may be very satisfied with their lives. Then, as their baby begins to acquire the ability to hold and drink from a cup, move across the floor, finger-feed himself, and so forth, parents may feel as though he does not need them as much as before. These kinds of feelings often arise around the time at which weaning occurs.

Parents who for whatever reason feel bored, or feel a loss of privacy or individuality, sometimes become jealous and resentful of their spouses or their friends who work outside the home. In fact, they may think that other people consider them to be dull and uninteresting simply because they themselves feel this way inside. Being unhappy with their lives may result in feelings of resentment toward their children, even though it would be unfair to place the blame for this upon them. These feelings may also result in their giving less attention or poorer quality of care to their children, and creating a home atmosphere in which their resentment and dissatisfaction affect every family member.

Parents who assume the major role of caring for their baby sometimes lose sight of the significance of their role. Parenting is really an important profession. Being a parent is one of the most challenging and rewarding careers that a person can choose. Learning about child development and growth, observing the child change from day to day, and participating in his upbringing can be highly stimulating, fulfilling, and enlightening. Rearing a child and assisting him to reach his fullest potential as an individual can really be as stimulating and interesting as a parent wants it to be. Parenting is one of the few professions that enables a person to be his or her own boss, and allows for creativity, flexibility, and self-expression. Like every profession, there are some aspects that are boring and require hard work and personal sacrifices. Some drudgery exists no matter what job a person undertakes.

Surely other family members will be affected by your unhappiness. Chances are that everyone else will be happier once you find a way to increase your own satisfaction. In addition, you will probably approach the "parent" aspect of your life with renewed enthusiasm, and will derive more enjoyment from the time you spend with your baby, if you have a positive self-image and are happy with yourself.

PREPARED PARENTHOOD CHECK LIST

MOTHER	FATHER	UNDERSTANDING YOUR BABY'S DEVELOPMENT
——	——	Has your infant discovered his hands and fingers? Does he spend time staring at and playing with them?
——	——	How does your baby communicate his feelings?
——	——	Does your infant seem to recognize your voice and/or your method of handling him, and behave differently around you than other people?
——	——	During your infant's periods of alertness, what seems to be his favorite activity?
——	——	Is your baby beginning to co-ordinate simple behaviors such as looking and hearing, or looking and moving?
——	——	Has your baby's crying decreased?
——	——	Have you heard your infant producing babbling sounds?
——	——	Does your baby ever cry for attention?
——	——	Have you observed any of your baby's newborn reflexes beginning to fade?
——	——	Is your baby making rapid progress in gaining head control?
——	——	Have you observed your infant doing any "mini-push-ups"?
——	——	Does your baby like to exercise?

		BASIC CARE
——	——	Does your baby sleep through the night without needing to be fed?
——	——	Is your infant's pattern of feeding becoming more regular?
——	——	Now that your baby is becoming more active, are you paying closer attention to safety precautions at bath time?
——	——	Can your infant sleep through the night? If not, are you aware of how to encourage this?
——	——	Has your baby outgrown his bassinet or basket? Are you planning to move him to a crib in the near future?

		FAMILY FEELINGS AND CONCERNS
——	——	In what ways do you try to maintain your individuality and a life of your own as a person apart from being a parent?

Infancy 4

PERSONAL-SOCIAL DEVELOPMENT

Self-awareness

EXPLORING HER BODY: LEARNING WHAT IT CAN DO. As your baby gains more voluntary control over her body, particularly her arms and hands, she will begin to explore her face, and learn more about the features of her body. She may either purposefully or by accident lift her arm and bring it to her head, and explore her hair and facial features. Running her fingers around her ears, eyes, nose, and mouth, and even yanking on her wispy hair will produce feelings that may surprise her. With some babies, greater hand control leads to more time spent on finger- or thumb-sucking.

Once your infant begins to bat at objects dangling from her crib mobile, causing them to swing or move, or push toys in her crib away from her, she will learn something about how her hands can produce changes in her surroundings. You are likely to notice her reaching for toys first with one hand, and then the other. This leads to the realization that she has two separate arms and hands that can do essentially the same things.

Experimentation with her hands and objects leads to more knowledge about them and increased awareness of her body. The information that your baby is now gathering will eventually enable her to realize that she is distinct from objects in her surroundings, a separate entity.

MIRROR IMAGES MAY SURPRISE AND CONFUSE YOUR BABY. Parents often enjoy holding their babies up to a mirror and observing their reaction. A young baby who is just beginning to discover her limbs and facial features knows little about her overall appearance. She probably will not recognize her reflection in the mirror. In fact, when you hold your baby up close to a mirror, she is likely to be quite surprised. She may smile, or startle, when she moves her arm and sees an arm move in the mirror, or when she smiles and sees the face in the mirror smiling too. It will be many months before she recognizes her mirror image as being herself.

Seeing your reflection in the mirror, she may recognize you and smile or babble. When she turns away from the mirror and looks back at you, she is apt to be confused at having seen two of you. In an attempt to figure out what is going on, she may look back and forth between you and your mirror image. Then, if you say something to her or move while holding her, she may suddenly turn and look at the "real" you, thus suggesting her recognition of the difference between the "fake" and the "real thing." A clearer recognition will more likely be made in Infancy 5.

Social Sensitivity and Interests

Spending time with your infant is likely to be more pleasurable and fun now that she clearly knows you and enjoys your company and attention. She will appear to be more interested in being around you and other familiar people. She seems like more of a real member of the family. When family members pay attention to her, or play with her, she is likely to become very active, talkative, smiley, and excited. Her obvious delight and interest in socializing, and her positive reaction to social stimulation, give everyone around her good reason to play with her, pick her up, and smile back at her.

GETTING YOUR ATTENTION. Your baby may have made some attempts in previous months to capture and maintain your attention, but you can expect more of this now and in months to come. Having learned what kinds of behavior and sounds cause you and others to go to her and give her attention, she may produce them intentionally when she wants company. Each baby learns which sounds and behaviors are most effective in accomplishing her goal. One baby may cough, another may giggle, and another may cry or squeal. Your infant's efforts to draw your attention away from someone or something else represent a significant step forward in terms of her social development.

There will be times when you are busy and cannot immediately respond to her pleas for attention, but it is important to reinforce this behavior positively. Mrs. Rogers, the mother of four-month-old Doyle, was busy baking in the kitchen when she heard Doyle making the special sounds that he always produced when he wanted her attention. As much as she wanted to drop what she was doing and go to him right away, this was not convenient. Rather than ignoring him, she told him that she would be with him as soon as she could.

This mother's approach to handling the situation was good. She communicated to her son that she acknowledged his signal, and she was responsive to him, even though she was busy. There is no need or reason for you to have to drop whatever you are doing and run to your baby the moment she "calls" for you. On the other hand, by saying something back to her in reply, this will help put her at ease and show her that you care about her feelings.

SOCIAL GAMES. Along with your infant's greater interest in socializing may come an interest in social games, particularly those involving imitation. If she makes some babbling sounds, and you smile and imitate her, she may delight in producing the same sounds over and over again, providing that you keep up your end of the game. Babies and parents will develop their own special social games, according to what they enjoy. Once you have devised a game involving a particular sound, she is likely to produce it whenever she is in a playful mood, or wants to be the focus of your attention.

A REAL, HEARTY LAUGH. During Infancy 1 to 3 your baby smiled and produced gurgling sounds when she was happy or excited, but did not really laugh aloud. Either in this phase or the next, you will hear her laugh out loud. Frequent giggling and laughing is fairly common among babies, assuming that they have been receiving plenty of social stimulation.

Keep in mind that babies have very different personalities, and some simply smile and laugh more than others. If your infant is not doing a lot of laughing, you need not jump to the conclusion that you are doing something wrong. A fairly certain way to get your baby to laugh is to tickle her. At this stage she may immediately smile and giggle in response to being tickled, whereas in previous phases this form of stimulation probably did not produce this reaction, even though she felt it. Her new response to being tickled probably goes hand in hand with her growing interest in socializing.

INTELLECTUAL DEVELOPMENT

Improved Sensory-motor Abilities: Yield New Views of the Not-so-new World

Your baby's visual abilities are reaching maturity, and she will be able to view her surroundings more extensively than in previous phases. Everything is likely to be seen in color, and she may even develop preferences for certain colors. Many different visual abilities have matured over the past few months, including ability of the eye to adjust to various distances, to see one image rather than two, to follow moving targets, to perceive depth, and to see color. Her eye and head movements are more well co-ordinated, enabling her to follow a moving object more easily and turn quickly to look at an object that catches her attention.

More is known about visual development than the development of other senses, although babies' sense of taste, smell, and hearing are also becoming more fully developed. Usually at two or three months, a baby will turn her head and eyes in the direction of a familiar voice. She will now listen carefully to other sounds she hears, even those coming from a distance, and will orient her head and eyes toward the location of the sounds.

An infant's increasing body control along with her more fully developed eyesight will facilitate more opportunities for interaction with her environment, and gathering more information about it. Her improved ability to lift her head while lying in her crib will enable her to examine her own body. From a propped sitting position, she can also do more people and object watching. Her new ability to reach for and take hold of objects allows for greater appreciation of and more active involvement with the outside world. Along similar lines, her emerging ability to roll enables her to benefit from shifts in scenery as she wishes.

Growing Curiosity and Interest in the Environment

Your baby is more interested in her surroundings. Her crib mobile, the colored pictures hanging on the walls or ceiling in her room, her own hands, fingers, and feet, and objects or toys that she happens to be holding will attract her interest. She will stare at your face as you approach, and pay close attention to your facial expressions and movements. Examining toys and objects will help her learn about their color, size, distance, design, detail, and so forth. When lying on her stomach, she will repeatedly struggle to lift her head to see about her.

Listening to sounds and voices is another way of exploring. When given a toy that produces noise, such as a rattle, she will shake it to continue hearing the sounds. Her previous indifference to playing with this toy has probably given way to new enthusiasm and utter delight with it. The sounds that she herself makes are also apt to interest her. Upon hearing other people speak or sing, she will pay close attention.

Reaching, swiping, and grasping become methods for making contact with the outside world of objects. Along with growing voluntary control over hand and fingers comes a stronger attraction to toys and objects. As she holds, turns, and fingers the surfaces and crevices of objects, she learns more about such things as their shape, texture, weight, and size. This is a time when you should place only safe objects within her reaching range, since all reachable objects are apt to be of interest to her.

Objects handled will be brought to her mouth where they will be further explored. In her mouth, they will be tasted, gummed, and sucked. As is more fully described in the Personal-Social Development section, her switching between sucking on fingers and/or toes, and objects, helps her to distinguish between herself and her surroundings. Co-ordinated behaviors of sucking and looking, moving and looking, and listening and looking are quite prominent.

Interest in Her Actions and Their Effects

The effects of your baby's activity on people and objects are becoming a prime area of interest to her. When she does something and a new or interesting reaction follows her action, she will frequently repeat the action in an attempt to produce the same event.

One afternoon, George Brewer was hovering over his four-month-old daughter's crib, and making funny faces at her in an attempt to get her to laugh. In response to her daddy's funny faces, Christine giggled and actively moved her legs around. As she kicked and squirmed about, the hanging mobile over her crib began to swing and jingle, catching her attention. The movement and sound of the mobile overhead delighted her, and she kept squirming and kicking just to keep seeing this interesting result of her activities. Having associated her kicking with the movement and jingling sound of the mobile, she repeatedly kicked whenever she was placed on her back in her crib and wanted some fun.

Your baby will be taking more interest in her activities and their results, and her behavior will seem more deliberate and intentional. You will see evidence of this each day in a variety of circumstances and situations. An important aspect of her self-awareness and ability to interact with the environment involves her learning that she can make things happen by connecting her actions with the changes that they produce.

LANGUAGE DEVELOPMENT

Active Language Development

Your baby is beginning to realize that her non-crying sounds capture people's attention as well, if not better, than crying. She is learning to use her voice to draw people to her when she wants company or attention. The fact that you come quickly when you hear her sounds is likely to make her giggle with delight at her own cleverness.

In Infancy 3, your baby probably began to respond to your voice by producing sounds. Her babbling, a type of social response, will be more obvious during this phase. When you talk to her as you hover over her crib or seat her on your lap facing you, she may "answer" you back with sounds of her own. She is likely to continue this primitive "conversation" as long as your interest in this activity holds out.

Her enthusiasm for using her voice will be heightened if you imitate the sounds that she can produce. Games in which you imitate her babbling sounds and then she, in turn, mimics your sounds, should be pleasurable for both of you. Already she may be able to echo several sounds that she hears you make in imitation of her sounds. In the months to come, she will imitate sounds that she has never before produced. Imitation should be positively reinforced and encouraged at an early age, since it is an essential aspect of learning to speak.

Your baby may not do much in the way of responsive babbling or mimicking your imitation of her sounds until she approaches Infancy 5. She may babble away and experiment with her voice in private, but keep quiet when you or others are around. This is nothing to worry about, since she will gradually learn to "talk" in your presence.

When your infant is excited and happy about something, she may giggle, laugh out loud, make high-pitched sounds, and babble. When she is annoyed or mad, she may grunt, growl, or cry. Her facial expressions and gestures will show greater variation as she gains more control over parts of her body. These gestures will frequently accompany her sounds, making it easier for you to understand what she needs and wants.

Babies most often produce vowel-like sounds, but a few consonant sounds may now be heard. Your baby will produce a greater variety of sounds as she experiments with her voice in the weeks to come.

Passive Language Development

Your infant may now derive a great deal of pleasure from waving her rattle and playing with other noisemaking toys, indicating her heightened awareness and interest in sounds. When she hits objects against her crib or feeding table, or lets them drop to the floor, she will listen intently to the noises they produce. She will also be more aware of voices and household noises such as the noise of the cuckoo clock, the doorbell, the vacuum cleaner, the television, and so forth. One of her favorite pastimes is likely to involve listening to the sounds that she herself produces.

MOTOR DEVELOPMENT

Reflex Activity

Neonatal reflexes are continuing to fade. Your baby's grasping reflex, for instance, is vanishing. Her tonic neck reflex has disappeared, so that while on her back she can easily keep her head facing upward, although she may prefer the asymmetrical side position while lying on her back. More willful control over many parts of her body is becoming evident during this phase.

Gross Motor Activity

HEAD AND ARM CONTROL. The Infancy 4 baby is a much stronger and more active person than she has been, even though her ability to move is still rather limited. One of the areas in which you will observe marked improvement is in her head control. Your baby will now reap the visual and personal pleasures that accompany her increasing ability to hold her head upright. Place her on her stomach and you will see her lift her head high off the mattress more easily, at approximately a ninety-degree angle. She may stay in this position for relatively long periods of time. This allows her to get a much better look at her surroundings.

You will also observe your baby push her chest up, supporting herself on her forearms and/or hands. Her head is held high, and is less wobbly. She may frequently turn it from one side to the other, giving her a broader view of the room. Large arm muscles are much stronger, but both forearms and hands are necessary to support her in a push-up posture. Occasionally, you may observe her leaning her weight on only one arm, leaving the other, usually the right, free to scratch or reach. Mini-push-ups will be practiced repeatedly, and you will notice her growing interest in using her arms.

Now that the tonic neck reflex has vanished, her body is positioned more symmetrically when she is lying on her back. Her head can easily be turned from side to side, allowing her to follow an object or person that interests her. It can also be raised upward and forward a little, enabling her to look briefly at hands and feet.

MORE LEG STRENGTH. A marked increase in leg strength will be observed. While lying on her back she can elevate her feet, at least a little. A few youngsters will already be grabbing their feet with their hands and examining their toes, but the ability to bring the feet all the way over to the mouth does not usually come in this early. It more commonly emerges around Infancy 7.

Some of your child's feats will surprise you. Frequently she will kick and thrust out with her legs and feet, and perhaps even inch forward a bit. If you hold her in a standing position, she will probably support some of her own weight, but still only very briefly. During the next half year or so, as preparation for standing, her leg muscles will become more powerful and well developed.

ROLLING TO HER SIDE, THEN ALL THE WAY OVER. Another new development to watch for is rolling over to her side. This accomplishment becomes possible as her trunk muscles grow stronger. Your infant may begin to turn from her back to one side or the other during Infancy 4. Then, one day, either in this phase or in Infancy 5 or 6, she will roll all of the way from her back to her stomach.

Rolling over is a fairly complicated task which involves the co-ordination of the muscle actions in her neck, shoulders, trunk, arms, and legs into one movement. Previously, your baby moved one muscle system at a time, such as when she lifted her head, or waved her arms about. Isolated actions are now beginning to be put together into a more complex movement pattern so that she can roll over. When your infant turns her head, the rest of her body is influenced. In rolling over, you will see her turn her head and shoulder to one side toward the mattress, arch her back, twist her torso and hips in the same direction, and curve her arms and legs toward her belly.

Initially, rolling over is somewhat like a reflex action in that she probably will not think about what she is doing. The turning of her head automatically causes the rest of her body to activate and turn in the same direction. This is sometimes referred to as a "righting" response.

OTHER ABILITIES. When your baby is lying on her back and you offer her your hands, she will grasp them and help to pull herself into a sitting position, unlike earlier times when she may have made little or no effort to help. Her back is held much firmer, although you may still see some hunching or slouching. She has much better control over her head, and freely turns it every which way, even though her trunk muscles are not very strong. With sufficient support from you she may maintain a sitting position for as long as ten to fifteen minutes before getting fatigued.

Pull her from a sitting to a standing position and notice the effort she makes to help. You are likely to observe her pushing with her legs and trying to lift her rear end. In a standing position, she will hold her head steadier and more upright.

One of your infant's activities on her abdomen may include arching her back, lifting her head, extending and raising her arms and legs, and rocking back and forth. This activity will delight her. She may keep this up until she collapses from exhaustion.

On her abdomen, she can scoot, wriggle, and push with her arms and legs, and may flip her body over to one side. You must take care not to underestimate her ability to move. In order to prevent falls, never leave her alone on any chair, table, or bed unless there are adequate barriers to prevent her from rolling or falling off the edge.

Fine Motor Activity

You will notice a definite increase in eye-hand co-ordination. Your baby is likely to spend a lot of time watching and playing with her fingers. She now has the ability to grasp an object even if it only lightly rubs against her hands. She will keep her hands more open, ready to reach out and grab things.

Janis Knoll was bending over her daughter's crib, getting ready to change Colette's wet diaper, when Colette suddenly reached up with her right arm and took a swipe at the animal figure dangling from the crib mobile overhead. On Colette's first try, she missed hitting the animal by several inches. After persistent efforts to hit it, she finally succeeded. Janis observed her daughter's awkward attempts to make contact with a target, and was surprised at how inaccurate Colette's reaching really was.

As you watch your infant swipe at or reach for objects, you, like Janis, are likely to be struck by the imperfection in your baby's aim. Frequent missing of her target stems from her poor co-ordination and control. Given another couple of months and added practice, her aim will show marked improvement.

Observe how your infant's palm works against her fingers. If you place a bit of dry cereal in front of her on a tray, you will notice how inefficient her grasping really is. She may lower her hand over it and try to swipe at it in an attempt to bring it closer to her, but she cannot control her thumb and fingers in order to pick it up.

Once an object is in your baby's hands, it will be carefully watched and probably moved to her mouth. Near the end of Infancy 4, she may even be capable of alternating hands to grasp a toy. More information on eye-hand co-ordination, eye-head turning co-ordination, and other aspects of fine motor activity is provided in the Intellectual Development section.

LEARNING THROUGH PLAY

As your baby gains more control over her body and becomes more aware, alert, and sociable, her play becomes more active. Over the next two months, you will notice that she is devoting more time to play, and that she responds more enthusiastically when other people play with her. Her ability to reach and grasp is improving, and this enables her to make more frequent hand contact with people, objects, and toys. One of her main interests will be to explore objects. Toys begin to take on more importance as her ability to grab and handle them grows. Toys and objects left within her arm's reach will no longer simply be visually explored. They will be grasped, looked at, waved around, listened to, turned, and brought to her mouth. As you know, through her dealings with a variety of objects, her intellectual abilities will expand. Manipulation and investigation of toys and objects are major avenues through which she learns, and this is why she will profit from having ample opportunities to handle all different kinds of objects and playthings.

Having sufficient amounts of both environmental stimulation and parental stimulation are crucial for her development in all areas. She will greatly enjoy having you take an interest in her and her activities. Social exchanges between you and her are important, and the exchanges that she may enjoy the most are likely to involve imitation of simple sounds and actions. She is fast becoming a more receptive, responsive, and participating "audience," making playing with her even more enjoyable than in previous phases.

Use of a Playpen

Even though play with you is extremely important, she should have opportunities to play and explore on her own. Now that she will be awake for longer periods of time during the day, you may find that a playpen is a very useful piece of equipment. It certainly will afford her more freedom of movement and opportunities for exercise than would a crib.

The playpen can fairly easily be moved from one room to another, so that even when she is playing by herself, she can see you, and feel more a part of family activities. You can place several playthings and interesting objects in her playpen to keep her happily occupied and mentally stimulated. When you place her in the playpen, you will not have to worry about her safety, and by setting up the playpen in the area of your home in which you are working, you will still be able to maintain contact with her.

There is some controversy about the advisability of using playpens. Most of the objections to its use center around keeping a young baby in it for prolonged periods of time each day. It is not advisable to put your baby in a playpen, with no interesting playthings, ignore her, or leave her there long enough for her to become bored. Rather, use it sparingly during those times in which she is awake and you do not have the time to give her a great deal of attention, or have more important things to do.

Place a few playthings in the playpen, within her reach, as opposed to ten or fifteen. Placing too many toys at once in the playpen may be overstimulating. Return to her at frequent intervals. Talk to her, play with her for a minute or two, and make a shift of playthings if this seems necessary.

Most importantly, do not use the playpen as an excuse not to pay attention to your baby. It is true that a playpen can give you extra freedom. When you place her in it, you will be assured of her safety, and will have opportunities to do other things. However, for your baby's sake, do not abuse this piece of equipment.

It is useful for your baby to learn that you cannot devote 100 percent of your time during the day to playing with her. By placing her in a playpen for short periods each day, she will learn to be resourceful and occupy herself with solitary play. On the other hand, by leaving her in it too long, she will not only become bored and frustrated but will also come to regard the playpen as a restrictive device or as a form of punishment. These problems can be eliminated by using the playpen properly. See also page 383 on the advisability of playpens once a baby begins to locomote across the floor.

Use of a Bounce Seat or Jumper

There are several bounce seats or jumpers available for infants. A canvas seat is suspended from a metal frame or support such as a doorway. A spring device is built into the suspension so that a baby sitting in the chair who pushes down on the ground with her feet will bounce up and down in the seat. Many babies enjoy bouncing and stepping down with alternating feet, and this apparatus capitalizes on babies' desires for this type of exercise.

In recent years, some pediatric bone specialists (orthopedists) have questioned the use of this type of apparatus and advised against a bounce seat or jumper because of possible injury to the baby's bones that may result from excessive, vigorous, and continuous bouncing. We therefore recommend that you ask your physician about the advisability of a jumper for your child before purchasing one.

Suggested List of Playthings

The suggestions for playthings provided thus far continue to be appropriate for a baby at four and five months of age. Again, it is worth re-emphasizing the value of placing appropriate objects and toys within your baby's arm's reach so that she will be able to practice reaching and grasping and simultaneously satisfy her curiosity.

Suggestions for Activities

Over the next several months, your baby's awareness of the results of her actions and "cause" and "effect" relationships will be expanding. Thus it is important for her to realize that when she produces certain sounds or performs certain actions, there is an interesting outcome. She will be learning that she can make things happen. One of the objectives of several of the activities suggested below is to impress upon her that she is important, and that her actions produce results.

OBJECT PERMANENCE GAMES. The Infancy 4 to 5 baby is lacking in the concept of the permanency of objects. The following activity will allow you to observe her reaction to objects that are out of her view. Hold her on your lap. Take a plastic, non-breakable cup or toy and allow her to play with it. Then take it away from her. While she is looking at the cup, let it drop from your hand to the floor. See if she looks at the place from which it dropped or bends forward and turns her head downward to look for it on the floor. Chances are that she will make no attempt to "search" for the lost object, even after several repetitions of this game. In another couple of months, play this game with her again. Notice how differently she responds. She will begin to look for an object that has been dropped. This will provide you with direct evidence of the fact that she is starting to realize that objects she cannot see still exist.

SIMPLE PEEK-A-BOO. While your baby is lying on her back, bend down over her, smile, and talk to her. With a handkerchief in hand, cover your face for a moment or two. Then remove the cover and say, "Peek-a-boo, I see you!" Repeat this several times. Next, put a handkerchief over her face and see whether she reaches up and pulls it off. If she does, smile and say a few words of praise, or "Peek-a-boo, I see you!" Provided that she does not remove the hanky after a moment or two, take her hand in yours and help her uncover her face. This activity should give her practice in reaching and grabbing, and should help her realize that her actions bring positive results.

MIRROR PLAY. The value of mirror play in heightening your baby's self-awareness, knowledge of the space behind her, and ability to make discriminations is discussed in the Personal-Social and Intellectual Development sections. You can devise many games involving mirrors. When allowing her to play in front of a mirror, or when introducing a hand mirror into her play, we urge you to take proper safety precautions and to supervise her whenever she is around mirrors. Hand mirrors should be unbreakable.

IMITATION GAMES. There are any number of imitation games that you can play with your baby, depending upon her preferences and responsiveness. You might play games involving the imitation of laughs, coughs, arm movements, facial expressions, or thrusting of the tongue. Many babies enjoy having their parents imitate their babbling sounds.

These games are valuable in terms of a baby's language and personal-social development. Your baby quickly learns that when she wants your attention, she will probably get it by babbling a certain sound, coughing, or doing whatever it is that the two of you do when you play. If you are consistent in responding to her attempts to attract your attention, she will realize that her actions can positively influence your behavior.

REACHING GAMES. While your baby is lying down, or held on your lap in a sitting position, dangle a toy or some other object in front of her slightly beyond her arm's reach. If she makes an effort to reach for the object, give it to her and allow her to play with it. This will give her practice in reaching.

A SIMPLIFIED TUG OF WAR OR PULLING GAME. A modification of the game of tug of war may be fun for you and your baby. Hold a toy or object in front of her within her reaching range. When she gets her hands on it and tries to pull it toward her, pull it slightly away from her so that she will have to pull harder in order to bring it toward her. If she makes an effort to pull, let her have the toy, otherwise take it away for the moment. This exercise will give her practice in reaching and pulling, and will enable her to realize the positive results of her efforts.

LOCATING THE SOURCE OF A SOUND. This is a fun game to play that will enable you to observe and reinforce your baby's ability to turn her head toward the location of a sound. Take a bell or some other noisemaker and stand behind the doorway to her bedroom so that you can see her, but she cannot see you. Jingle the bell and see whether she turns her head in your direction (toward the location of the noise). If she does, come out from behind the door and let her know that you are pleased about her ability. Hand her the bell or noisemaker and let her play with it.

KEEPING YOUR BABY HEALTHY

Sometime during the fourth month, your child should receive a second set of immunizations. The second DTP and TOPV immunizations will be given. Refer to the earlier chart on page 217. Check with your doctor or health clinic to arrange for an appointment.

HOW TO ENSURE YOUR BABY'S SAFETY

Now that your baby is older and beginning to reach for objects and squirm, scoot, and even roll over, these new abilities must be taken into account in preventing accidents. She will do a lot of sampling of objects with her mouth. Most things that wind up in her hands are almost certain to be placed in her mouth. It is crucial that objects and playthings within her reach be completely safe and too large to be swallowed. It is also important to take precautions to prevent her from falling off a high place.

In the course of your safety efforts during this new phase in your baby's development, you must be careful that you are not limiting her chances to handle and sample objects with her mouth, since this activity is of prime importance in fostering curiosity and learning. You will also not want to curtail her freedom of movement, since this activity allows her to practice new skills and learn about her surroundings. Your main goal should be to offer her freedom to move within safe boundaries, and to give her a variety of safe objects to handle. This can be accomplished by anticipating your baby's new abilities before they develop and preparing in advance to allow her to learn these new skills in a safe environment.

Below is an addendum to the Safety Training Check List presented in Infancy 1 (pages 125–27). It is hoped that the items on the check list will help you expand your safety program. The items previously included continue to be appropriate for your baby at this phase of development, so review the former list before reading the new one. Some of the items that deserve special attention at this time are repeated.

Even if your baby is not reaching out with her hands, wriggling her body, or rolling over, she will soon acquire these new abilities. The idea behind this program of accident prevention is to be prepared in advance.

Additions to the Safety Training Check List

GENERAL RULES

—Pay particularly close attention to crib rails and other bars to prevent unnecessary falls.

—Be sure to fasten the safety strap on her infant seat and high chair.

—Keep any objects small enough to be stuffed into her mouth and swallowed far away from her.

—Never leave the following types of ordinary household objects near her:

scissors

knives

paper clips

letter openers

tablecloths that hang over the edge of a table

ropes

hanging plants

string

tape

smoking equipment

cosmetics

medications (pills, chewable laxatives)

nuts

popcorn

bathroom products (soap, cleaning powders, shampoo)

sewing equipment (pins, needles, thread, buttons)

objects covered with lead-base paint

furniture polish

cleansers or detergents

shoe polish

drain openers

insecticides

electrical equipment and wires

marbles

jacks

FEEDING

Your Little People-watcher

You may now begin to notice that your baby is more distracted at mealtimes, mainly because her interests in people-watching, playing, moving, and "talking" are growing. Your infant may seem as interested in playing at mealtimes as she is in the food you offer. This can result in her nursing for briefer periods of time at the breast or bottle.

She will probably take all the milk that she needs in the first five minutes or so of nursing, but if you are breast-feeding, you may find that decreased stimulation of your nipples results in diminished milk production. Nursing in a private place, away from all distractions, or nursing her more frequently, may help to promote your milk production and increase the supply. In bottle-feeding, you may also find that keeping distractions to a minimum results in your child's taking more milk.

Teething May Affect Nursing

When a baby is teething, she may experience some discomfort or even pain when she nurses. She may stop after a brief nursing period and wail as if she is in pain, pause several times in between nursing, or decide to stop nursing altogether. In breast-feeding, you may find that it helps her to pause for a short while after nursing for a few minutes, start in again, and then pause again. Bottle-feeding often proceeds more smoothly and may be less uncomfortable for a baby when the nipple holes are temporarily enlarged so that she does not have to work as hard to take in milk.

Most often, teething difficulties will diminish after a period of about three months. If your bottle-fed baby finds it just too uncomfortable to nurse, you can try offering milk to her from a cup. For some babies this works effectively until their discomfort while nursing subsides.

Decrease in Appetite

Slight decreases in appetite are fairly common among infants between four and six months of age, although decreases can occur after six months in some babies. Do not become alarmed if your baby does not seem to be as hungry as in the past. Babies may be satisfied to nurse for shorter periods of time on the breast or bottle, or they may reject a meal or two now and then. As long as your baby seems to be healthy and happy, and your physician tells you that your infant is gaining weight as expected, there is no reason for concern. Sometimes a lag in appetite indicates that a baby is ready for fewer feedings, in which case she will probably take more milk at each meal than she would if she were offered more frequent feedings. When your baby's appetite begins to slacken, you may be tempted to urge or coax her to eat more than she wants. This can lead to difficulties in the area of eating.

How to Avoid Unnecessary Feeding Problems

Occasionally unnecessary feeding problems arise because parents have failed to keep their responsibilities and their baby's straight. Refer to Infancy 1, pages 128–29, if you have forgotten who is responsible for what in the area of feeding. There is nothing wrong with some mild encouragement in getting a baby to eat, but quite often parents go overboard, and begin to nag, coax, insist, push, and even force their baby to eat more than she wants. Parents sometimes lose sight of their responsibilities, or become too emotional about the feeding situation, even to the point of begging, scolding, and showing great frustration when their infant refuses to eat as much as her parents would like.

Doctors often remind parents that the child knows how much she needs. Bottle-fed infants and those who are inappropriately given solids early, with strong parental pressure to eat more, may become overweight as well as rebellious at mealtime. This can be avoided with careful feeding early in infancy, leaving the child to determine how much food she wants to eat.

It is a rare parent who can honestly report that he or she has never used exaggerated, emotional, and sneaky tactics to get a baby to eat a little more. The real difficulties are more apt to arise when a parent uses these tactics frequently. The baby can become annoyed, angry, and resentful. Who would not under these circumstances? After a while, a baby may react negatively to being fed, and in the long run may become a very choosy eater, eat smaller amounts, or develop poor eating habits. Continual pressure on a baby at feeding times should be avoided. If you remember that how much food your baby wants to eat is *her* responsibility, you will be able to avoid many unnecessary feeding problems during the next year and during early childhood.

BATHING

Your baby is much more energetic, so bath time will probably be messier than before. She will wave her arms about and splash when held in a sitting-up position, and splash and kick when placed on her back or belly in an inch or two of water.

You are bound to get wet, so be sure to protect your clothes or wear old ones. To make sure that your squirming infant does not slip, hold her carefully. She may like to have some appropriate plastic or sponge toys to play with in the tub. Being occupied with her toys, she may be easier to wash.

You are not alone if your baby is one who cries during the whole bath period. Chances are that your efforts to talk and sing to her have been in vain, and you feel frustrated and annoyed each time bath time rolls around. Mrs. Richmond, the mother of four-month-old Lenny, discussed with some friends the fact that Lenny always screamed whenever she put him in the tub. Her friends, having had similar experiences with their infants, suggested that she take a bath with Lenny as a possible solution.

At first Mrs. Richmond thought that her friends' suggestion was rather silly, but after several more days of listening to Lenny's crying at bath time, she decided to give it a try. One afternoon, she climbed into the tub and held him securely on her lap. Much to her surprise, Lenny did not cry, and, for the first time, seemed actually to like his bath. For the next month this mother continued to bathe with her son. She found that bathing together was enjoyable for both of them, and represented a time when they could share a special closeness. Assuming that all of your attempts to soothe and quiet your infant during baths have failed to bring the desired result, you may want to try this, too. Note that there is some danger of slipping with the baby when getting out of the tub, so be sure to place skid-resistant bath mats both inside and alongside of the tub.

SLEEPING

You are likely to notice some changes in your baby's sleeping habits during Infancy 4. She will probably sleep longer at night, anywhere from about ten to twelve hours, and may take only a morning and afternoon nap, each lasting about an hour and a half to two hours. Some babies will still take an extra nap, provided they need it. Gradually, your baby is becoming more capable of sleeping later in the mornings, assuming that you have been encouraging her in this direction. Rather than cry as soon as she awakens, she will probably move around in her crib, make sounds, or amuse herself in other ways for a while. At this stage her sleeping periods are becoming more and more independent of other activities such as eating.

She may still cry before she goes to sleep, but chances are that you will observe less crying and more playing both prior to sleep, and after she awakens in the morning or after her naps. It is hoped that you have established a fairly regular routine for bedtime and naptime, or are working toward this goal. Firmness and consistency at bedtime and naptime will certainly be helpful in making the transition from waking to sleeping as smooth and problem-free as possible. Since babies are larger and more active, they need room to move about when they sleep. If you have not already done so, you should probably move your baby into a large-sized crib that will be adequate until she makes the shift to a regular or youth bed.

PATTERNS OF ELIMINATION

Some babies have now settled down to a more regular pattern of elimination. The most common pattern is for a baby to defecate once or twice per day, often following a meal. It is important to note that there can still be wide variations in this pattern. You have become familiar with your baby's pattern of elimination over the past three months. Do not be surprised if her frequency of bowel movements is different from your neighbor's child of the same age. Babies, like adults, have their own individual patterns of elimination. Some perfectly normal infants only pass a bowel movement every other day or sometimes they may not go for two or three days. If this is your baby's regular pattern of elimination, do not be concerned or try to force her into a more frequent pattern. Babies tend to take care of their bowel movements rather well when they are on a proper diet.

COMPARING NOTES ON CHILDREN'S PERFORMANCES

Parents who get together inevitably begin comparing notes on their children's abilities, despite the fact that they know that their child is an individual, different from any other child. As a result of such comparisons, one parent usually goes home feeling mildly depressed and insecure. Obviously this parent is the one whose child is not yet doing what the other parents claim their children of the same age are doing.

According to Mrs. Travers:

> I used to get very nervous and upset after getting together with my friends who had babies my daughter's age. They constantly compared notes on what each child was doing, and would brag about how smart or advanced their children were. My child was developing well according to my doctor, and yet my friends' children were always ahead of her in what they could do. They smiled first, babbled first, and rolled over before Marie did. I couldn't help wondering if maybe my friends were doing something that I hadn't done or should have done for Marie.

Doubts about whether or not you are doing right by your infant and are handling her as well as you could be are common. Hearing of other babies' advanced abilities can cause insecurities and self-doubt to surface, despite your doctor's reassurance that your child is fine and doing very well.

In some cases parents' insecurities about themselves cause them to feel embarrassed about their infant. They look upon her lack of performance as a poor reflection upon them. To boost their own egos, they begin to pressure their child into doing more than she is capable of doing, in the hopes of making themselves look better.

Mr. Lattimer made the following comments:

> My brother and I had always been in competition with one another as we grew up. Once we got married and had children, the rivalry seemed to get worse. It just happened that our kids were born two days apart. Whenever we got together we couldn't help comparing notes. His kid was constantly showing mine up, and this infuriated and embarrassed me. After our talks, I used to go home and try to push my son Mark to perform, and then get mad at him and frustrated if he wouldn't. Finally my wife made me realize how immaturely I was behaving. She showed me an article in the paper about how each child is an individual who shouldn't be pushed to do things that he isn't ready to do. I guess I finally saw the light.

It is important to avoid getting caught in the unfortunate trap of continually comparing your baby with other babies her age or even with your other children, and then drawing what will probably be inaccurate conclusions about her intellectual or other capabilities. A baby who can roll over at three and a half months is not necessarily going to be brighter or a better athlete than one who rolls over at five months. A baby who smiles a lot and babbles constantly is not necessarily going to turn out to be more socially adept than one who does not do much smiling or babbling. Chances are that you will always find a child who performs faster than yours if you search hard enough. Likewise, you are bound to find some children who are developing more slowly than yours.

It is only natural for you to be concerned about how your baby is doing in relation to other babies of her age, but avoid trying to push her to do things before she shows any signs of being ready. This is not to imply that it is unadvisable to encourage your child to acquire new skills. Rather it is to point out that there is a difference between encouraging and nagging or pushing. There is little to be gained from forcing and much to be lost. Whether your baby is very quick to acquire new abilities, or is slower to acquire them, you should respect her as an individual. The fact that she is not developing at as fast a rate as your friends' or relatives' babies does not mean that you are not as good a parent, or that she is not as good a child.

Your main concern should be to love and accept your baby for what she is, to make her feel as though she is special, and to help her to achieve her full potential as an individual. When you get together with other parents and the topic of conversation turns to children, do not sit there feeling sorry for yourself or resentful of your baby if the other children seem to be a step or two ahead in their development. Find something nice to say about your baby. After all, she is a superstar in your opinion, even though so and so's baby is ahead of her in reaching, rolling over, cutting a tooth, or whatever.

TELEVISION

Do not be surprised if one day, while you are working in a room with the television on, your baby intently begins to watch television. Your infant may be especially captivated during the commercials when the volume is increased and the music and sounds tend to be very lively. You will quickly realize that television will intrigue most infants at an early age.

Television can greatly enhance a baby's world of perception beyond the boundaries of her home, since it represents additional sources of visual and auditory stimulation. Most children are not greatly affected by the content of the programs before one year of age, although most authorities suggest that you avoid programs in which scenes of brutality, violence, and horror abound.

The time when television becomes more a concern for parents is after the child is able to comprehend the nature of the program. Obviously, this is a variable age depending upon the development and the maturity of your child. After the first year and a half to two years of life, some parents begin to consider what shows their children are watching, and monitor television viewing more closely, although most youngsters, even at that age, normally spend relatively little total waking time watching television. During the preschool stage, children become more interested in television viewing, and this is a time when parental monitoring of programs becomes more important.

To the infant, television represents an added avenue of receiving language stimulation. This is considered by some parents to be valuable, particularly during those times of the day when parents are unable to give their children their full attention. According to many parents, watching television is entertaining for the child, and is like having a built in "baby-sitter" in the home.

Regular use of television as a "baby-sitting service" is not recommended. Parents who rely heavily upon television as a source of entertainment and stimulation for their infants without providing parental stimulation are doing their children a disservice. Television, despite its possible virtues, will not help your baby to master her own skills. It should not take the place of verbal interaction and involvement with her. It should also not take the place of indoor or outdoor play and more educational and creative-type activities. It is up to you to determine what place television should take in your baby's life, if any, and to monitor the time your infant spends in front of the television set. The topic of violence on the screen in relation to the young child is discussed on pages 776–77.

BROADENING YOUR EDUCATIONAL PROGRAM

Your baby's continued developmental progress over the next several months will necessitate the expansion of her educational experience. The need for providing adequate stimulation for her is becoming more apparent. Your awareness of some of the ways you can broaden your child's educational program to meet her changing needs should assist you in helping her develop to her fullest potential and derive more pleasure from everyday experiences.

HOW TO STIMULATE YOUR BABY'S MIND

One of the ways in which you can stimulate your baby's mind is to try to support her interests, and help her satisfy her curiosity. Up until the age of about eight months, most babies lack the ability to crawl or move across the floor. They are in the prelocomotor stage, and are more reliant upon their parents to provide them with stimulation than they will be once they can crawl around their homes and constantly seek out stimulation for themselves. Your role in stimulating your baby's mind will be very active, since you will be providing her with experiences that she would otherwise probably not have.

This is not to imply that she is a passive little person. Quite to the contrary, she will be looking around actively, listening to sounds, reaching out to bat, swipe, and grasp objects within easy reach, gumming objects that she holds, and trying to interest you and other people in socializing with her. One of her main interests over the next several months will be in playing with objects and toys and finding out not only what she can do with them, but what their properties are.

Stimulating her mind will involve exposing her to a wide variety of household objects and toys of different sizes, textures, shapes, and weights that are near enough to her so that she can reach them. It will also involve providing her with frequent changes of view, rather than keeping her confined to her crib in her bedroom for most of the day. Another way to foster her intellectual development is to play with her often, and talk to her as you engage her in different activities.

There are several specific suggestions for playthings and play activities presented in the Learning Through Play sections to assist you as well as heighten your enthusiasm about providing her with sensory and motor stimulation. You should try to make sure that the objects, toys, play activities, and stimulation that you offer are in line with her level of performance and individual preferences. This necessitates your watching her closely to learn what interests her and what bores her.

Structure your infant's daily routine so that she has plenty of chances to practice her new skills, experiment with objects, look, hear, taste, smell, feel, and interact with you and other people. The varied kinds of stimulation to which she will be exposed will support her increasing curiosity about her world and tendencies to want to make new discoveries. Most of you will be stimulating your babies' minds in very natural ways in the course of spending time with them, without ever having to think about the results of your actions. When your baby cries after her nap, for example, you will probably go over to her, pick her up, carry her to another area of your home, and play with her or talk to her as you hand her a toy. This type of comfortable, informal exchange between you and your baby is invaluable in terms of her intellectual development.

You need not rush out to buy your baby the latest "educational" toys that you have seen advertised on television. It is far more important to spend time with her, enable her to watch you and other people as you do things around the house, provide her with many different objects to explore (ordinary household objects will interest her), and make sure that she is not bored, than it is to give her expensive, "educational" toys and do no more than feed, bathe, and change her diapers. No toy can equal the stimulation and encouragement that you can provide while she is young. Giving her objects and toys to play with is important, but your sincere involvement with your baby is a better means of stimulating her mind as well as her language and personal-social development.

HOW TO STIMULATE YOUR BABY'S LANGUAGE DEVELOPMENT

Stimulating language growth should be easy and enjoyable. Most parents do this naturally in the course of spending time with their babies. Below are a few specific suggestions that can serve as guidelines.

Speaking to Your Baby

In the course of tending to your baby's everyday needs and playing with her, you should speak to her about what is happening or what you are doing. As you are feeding her, you might tell her about the spoon, or talk about the foods she is eating. While you are giving her a bath, you can talk about water, the washcloth, soap, which parts of her body you are washing, and so forth. When you dress her, you might name the articles of clothing for her. Talking to her about objects that she can see, touch, smell, taste, and hear—objects that are physically present to her senses—is a very valuable practice, and one which we hope you will adopt if you have not already done so. In general, it is more beneficial to talk about the present, rather than past or future events. Your baby lives in the immediate present, and will have an easier time learning language if your speech is related to what you are doing with her at the time.

Speaking with Your Baby

Verbal exchanges of babbling sounds between you and your baby are very important, as has been pointed out. When you hear her babbling, you can get into the habit of mimicking her sounds. Games that center around the imitation of sounds are valuable, and numerous suggestions for activities involving "primitive conversations" and those that foster language development are presented in the Learning Through Play sections.

As she grows more aware of your voice, she will also become sensitive to changes in its tone. When you are angry or annoyed by her behavior, you will raise your voice. Your baby will gradually be able to judge from listening to the tone of your voice whether or not you approve or disapprove of her actions, or whether you are happy or unhappy. The tone of your voice becomes an effective instructional tool that will take on even greater importance between Infancy 8 and 12.

Speaking with Others in the Presence of Your Baby

It is advisable to get into the habit of including your baby in family conversations, and allowing her to be present when you speak to other people. This is an indirect way to foster her language development, but one that is nonetheless important. Even though the vast majority, if not all, of what you say will go over her head, she will have many opportunities to observe facial expressions, hand gestures, and postures, and can learn indirectly that language is an effective means of communication.

HOW TO STIMULATE YOUR BABY'S PERSONAL-SOCIAL DEVELOPMENT

Show Your Baby that You Love Her

Once again we feel that it is worth while emphasizing the importance of conveying to your baby that she is loved, that her needs will be met, and that she is special to you. There is no one way in which to get this message across to a baby, and you will do this in whatever way seems natural and comfortable to you. Parents who tend not to be very physically affectionate will want to make a conscious effort to fondle and cuddle their babies, since young babies need physical shows of affection, particularly during the time when verbal expressions of affection are often lost on them. Being responsive to your baby's needs and cries is, of course, a major avenue through which you can show her that you care about her.

It is hoped that you are playing with her often, since this, too, is a valuable means through which you can express your love, offer attention, and maintain closeness. Through frequent verbal and physical contact with your infant, you can continue to establish very special lines of communication with her.

Encouraging Your Baby to Get to Know Other People

One way to expand your baby's repertoire of social skills is to give her opportunities to be around and get acquainted with people other than yourself, your spouse, and your other children. You can introduce her to relatives, friends, and even casual acquaintances. There is no reason not to include your baby in your social activities occasionally, as long as your friends are receptive to the idea, and the circumstances are appropriate. Taking your baby along when you go out will not only expose her to many other people, but can be much less of a strain on your budget than having to pay a baby-sitter every time you want to leave the house.

On the other hand, leaving her in someone else's care from time to time while you go out during the day or in the evening may be beneficial, since she will have opportunities to get accustomed to different faces and voices. Some parents are reluctant to go out and leave their baby with an unfamiliar person. For the first six months or even longer, they never hire a baby-sitter or spend any time away from their child. Spending short periods of time away from a baby, however, can be important, not only for your baby but also for you. Short separations not only enable an infant to learn about other people, they enable her to learn the important lesson that when you leave you always return. Separations also strengthen her resourcefulness by exposing her to new situations in which she must learn to adapt.

Now is an opportune time to begin getting your infant accustomed to spending time with people other than immediate family members. By the time she is around eight months old, she may react with fear at the sight of strangers (this occurs earlier in some babies). Having had ample chances to spend time with unfamiliar people previously should enable her to cope more effectively with these encounters as she grows older. Most babies at four and five months are very sociable and responsive. They usually do not mind and may enjoy being played with and held by different people. You can support your baby's natural sociability by expanding her social interactions to include dealings with many different people.

Promoting Your Baby's Self-awareness

You may want to begin naming parts of your baby's body as you dress, bathe, change, feed, and play with her. As you are putting on her socks, you can encourage her to look at her feet while you say, "This is your foot." While you are bathing her you might say, "Now I'm washing your hands, legs, hair," etc. It is advisable to get into the habit of teaching her the names for parts of her body.

You can also point out the similarities between your body and hers. Say the word "mouth" as you feed her, and then take her hand in yours and let her feel her own mouth and then yours. These types of body naming and body comparison games should help to promote her self-awareness and make her more conscious of both her separateness from you and the similarities between you.

HOW TO STIMULATE YOUR BABY'S MOTOR DEVELOPMENT

Of prime importance is enabling your baby to have freedom of movement, and opportunities to practice each new ability that she acquires. You can also offer her encouragement when she shows signs of readiness to move on to new abilities. Be sure not to push her to acquire new abilities before she is capable or shows any interest in developing them. Numerous suggestions for playthings and activities that go along with and foster each new ability that emerges are provided in the Learning Through Play sections. Use your own best judgment as to when to introduce the various activities and games, according to your baby's level of performance and preferences.

It is important to avoid holding your baby back or stifling her development of new abilities. Her movements should not be restricted either by her clothing or by lack of space. A baby who is confined in a small area such as a crib for the greater part of the day, or is restrained for long periods of time in an infant seat or other chair, will not have ample opportunities to exercise and move. By offering your baby room in which to move, and engaging her in activities that enable her to practice her new abilities, you will be fostering her motor development. Her drive to try out her emerging motor skills will be enormous, and you can develop many new ways to interact with her while stimulating her desire to learn.

PREPARED PARENTHOOD CHECK LIST

MOTHER	FATHER	UNDERSTANDING YOUR BABY'S DEVELOPMENT
——	——	Has your baby begun to explore her face with her hands and fingers?
——	——	How does your infant react when you hold her up to a mirror?
——	——	Does your baby make more attempts than before to capture and maintain your attention?
——	——	Have you heard your baby laughing aloud?
——	——	In what ways does your baby express an interest in you and in objects?
——	——	Does your baby's behavior seem more purposeful in small ways?
——	——	Is your infant taking more interest in the consequences of her activities?
——	——	What evidence do you see that your baby is using her voice to draw people to her when she wants attention?
——	——	Does your baby babble in a responsive way when you talk to her, as if to answer you back?
——	——	Is your infant showing a greater interest in objects that make noise such as a rattle, doorbell, or the television?
——	——	In what ways is your baby a stronger and more active little person than she has been?
——	——	Is your infant making repeated attempts to reach out for objects and grasp them?
——	——	Are you on the lookout for your child's ability to roll over to her side?
——	——	Is your baby devoting more time to play and responding more enthusiastically when people play with her?
——	——	Are you supporting your baby's new abilities to reach and grab and her interest in exploring objects?
——	——	Have you engaged your infant in play activities designed to help her realize that she is important, and that her actions bring results?

BASIC CARE

MOTHER	FATHER	
——	——	Have you arranged for your baby to receive her second set of immunizations?
——	——	Have you familiarized yourself with the additions to the Safety Training Check List?
——	——	Is your baby more distractible at mealtimes? Why?

— — Has your baby shown a decrease in appetite?

— — Does your baby like to have one or two appropriate toys to play with in the tub?

— — Is your infant more capable of amusing herself both prior to going to sleep and after she awakens?

— — Are you trying to set a fairly regular routine for bedtime and naptime?

— — Has your baby's pattern of elimination become more regular?

FAMILY FEELINGS AND CONCERNS

— — How often do you compare your baby with other babies her age? Why are constant comparisons not a good idea?

— — Do you make a sincere effort to respect your baby's individuality?

THE TOTAL EDUCATION OF YOUR BABY

— — How do you plan to expand your child's educational program to keep up with her changing abilities?

— — Are you seeing to it that your infant has plenty of chances to practice her new skills, experiment with objects, look, hear, feel, and interact with you and other people?

— — Do you realize the importance of spending time with your child and offering her different kinds of stimulation in a natural way, both parental and environmental?

Infancy 5

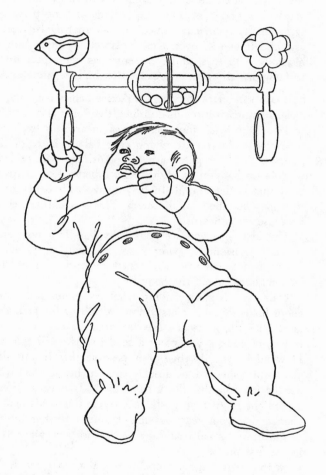

PERSONAL-SOCIAL DEVELOPMENT

Self-awareness

EXPLORING HIS BODY. Your baby is probably becoming more interested in his own body, and when he is interested in something, he naturally wants to explore it. He may still spend relatively long periods of time playing with his hands and fingers. Occasionally, you may notice him alternating between playing with and mouthing toys and fingers or even toes. This activity gives him a chance to compare parts of his body with toys, and represents another aspect of the kinds of experiences that will one day allow him to realize that he is separate and different from objects.

DISCOVERING HIS GENITALS. Active babies may not only touch and play with their facial features and hands and feet, they may also discover their genitals. Some babies will not zero in on their genitals as an area for exploration for several more months. One day while you are giving your baby a bath, or changing his diapers, you may see him touch or play with his penis. He will probably strain to lift his head or wriggle his body in an effort to get a better look at his hands on the new part of his body that he has found. In playing with his penis, or as you wash it while bathing it, it may become firm and erect. This is a natural, common response that represents no cause for concern.

The first time you see your baby handling his genitals, you may be rather surprised. Occasionally, parents are not only surprised, but shocked and disgusted. Every parent will react differently depending upon his or her own inhibitions (or lack of them) about the body.

Your baby is simply doing what comes naturally to him, exploring and learning about his body. He wants to find out about his genitals, just as he learned about his hands, mouth, and ears. His sex organ is a focus of self-exploration as is his nose, unless, of course, you plant a seed in his mind that this part of his body is taboo. How might you do this? It is possible that if you slapped his hand, scolded him, acted quite shocked, or quickly covered his genitals with a towel or diaper he might get the message that this area of his body is very different from other areas. The result might be that he would not try to touch his genitals again, but there is a good chance that your reactions might arouse further interest in this area. Interest that would have normally subsided if he had been allowed to satisfy his natural curiosity in the first place.

At this early stage it probably will not make much difference how you react to his attempts to explore his genitals, but it is advisable to recognize that many attitudes about life and "self" are shaped very early in one's life, and that you will be influential in shaping your child's attitudes, quite often in very subtle ways. Try to refrain from instilling in your baby the notion that a part of his body is dirty, bad, or not to be explored. He needs to have opportunities to find out about every part of his body that he can touch and see. This is an important aspect of self-awareness and forming positive, healthy attitudes about the body.

MIRROR PLAY. Seeing his reflection in the mirror is apt to be more enjoyable for your baby than in previous phases, and he may smile, laugh, and babble when he sees his own image. This type of obvious pleasure and interest at seeing his reflection appears to be characteristic of a majority of babies this age. He may also show you by his responses that he recognizes the difference between his own image and yours.

Social Sensitivity and Interests

EXPRESSION OF FEELINGS. Your infant will find it easier to express his feelings as a result of his greater awareness of people, improved ability to produce a variety of sounds, greater variety of facial expressions, and improved control over his body movements. The occasions on which he feels the need to cry are diminishing. When he does cry, he will probably do so as a means to an end that he has in mind. His crying usually has more of a purpose, a main one being as a way of communicating his feelings. You will be better able to know when he is frightened, angry about something you have done or refused to do, disgusted, excited, or sad.

MORE ATTEMPTS TO SOCIALIZE. Being with people and at the center of their attention becomes more important to your Infancy 5 baby. He will make further attempts to get and hold your attention and socialize with you. If you take him visiting and park his playpen in a room in which there are many people in addition to family members, he may try hard to capture your attention. His ability to distinguish between familiar and unfamiliar people has improved. When he finally locates you or other family members in the room, he may hold out his arms, babble loudly, and grin. It will be obvious that he recognizes you and wants your company.

When you are talking on the phone, and he feels left out, he may begin to produce particular sounds in an attempt to make you focus your attention on him. When you are entertaining in your home and he is jealous that he is not the center of attention, he may babble to try to capture your or your company's attention. Getting no response, he may keep producing sounds in a louder and more demanding way until you finally have to stop your conversation and pay attention to him. His use of sounds in order to make social contact and command attention is significant, and you will notice more of this in months to come.

IMITATION. Imitation is a major avenue through which a child learns. Your baby may now be mimicking some of your facial expressions and sounds. If you notice this, you should try to reinforce it positively. Social games involving imitation, previously described in Infancy 4, are a good way to foster more imitation, and are apt to be more appealing to him at this time.

ANOTHER INDEX OF SOCIAL DEVELOPMENT. Your baby is highly self-centered, but it will be clear to you that he is growing more interested in other people, toys, and objects. Over the next few months, he may decide that he likes one toy or object in particular, and become quite attached to it. It may be a specific blanket or a truck. Each baby selects his own favorite. He often likes to take his favorite toy to bed with him, and cries loudly or puts up a real struggle when someone tries to take it away from him.

A baby's attachment to a toy or object, according to most professionals, should be viewed in a positive light, since it provides evidence of his resourcefulness and his ability to offer affection to a "thing," in addition to his parents. A baby's "security" toy seems to offer him just that—security. The fact that he becomes attached to a toy as he grows up and becomes more independent from his parent is interesting. His favorite toy, it seems, helps to alleviate his frustration, comfort him, and assist him in feeling less tense when he is separated from his parent at bedtime or nap-time.

It is usually a baby who has become attached to his parent and who feels satisfied with the relationship who will be able more easily to direct his affection further than the parent-child relationship. Your baby's attachment to a special toy or object should be viewed as another sign of his progress in personal-social development.

UNEASINESS AROUND STRANGERS. An Infancy 5 baby knows the difference between familiar faces and voices and unfamiliar ones. He may behave differently depending upon whether he is with you and other family members, or with strangers. Some babies become withdrawn or shy around unfamiliar people, and even show dislike for them. This is nothing to worry about and is evidence that their ability to discriminate among people is improving.

Uneasiness around strangers is more common during the second half of the first year, and is more fully discussed on pages 289 and 335–36. If you have not been introducing your baby to people other than immediate family members, now is a good time to do so, since it is advisable for him to become accustomed to being around different people. Also try to give him opportunities to get used to being in unfamiliar territory. As he grows older and becomes even more aware of the distinction between "familiar" versus "unfamiliar," he may react quite strongly to meeting strangers, being left with a baby-sitter, or having to sleep at Grandma's house overnight. By giving him chances to be with unfamiliar people, and to get used to different places, his emotional discomfort in novel situations may not be as marked as it would otherwise be. This may make it easier for him to cope and adapt.

INTELLECTUAL DEVELOPMENT

Your baby's periods of being awake and attentive have lengthened, so that he may now be up and alert for as long as two hours or more at a time during the day. He is no longer satisfied to be lying in his crib and simply looking about and listening. He wants to be exploring nearly every object within reach or even within sight. He also shows a greater interest in touching parts of his own body. This is quite a change in behavior from that which was observed during Infancy 1 and 2. You now have the makings of a little pioneer on your hands, although his curiosity about his surroundings still exceeds his ability to translate curiosity into action.

More Co-ordinated Behaviors Allow for Further Explorations

When you observe your little one in action, notice that his eye-hand co-ordination is rapidly improving. Real mastery of visually directed reaching, in which the eye directs the hand to move quickly and skillfully to grasp an object, may be yet to come, but he is making swift progress in that direction. By watching closely, you will see him stare at a nearby toy, lift his hands in the general direction of the toy, and look back and forth between his hand and the toy. He will gradually move his hands close enough to be able to clasp it.

This two-handed reach is surely not very efficient. His lack of accuracy can be clearly seen in his occasional missing of the target for which he is aiming. Sometimes his hands are clasped too far beneath, above, behind, or in front of the target. Nevertheless, he will make frequent contact, and with additional practice, his aim will improve markedly.

This new use of his hands to reach a goal plays an important role in the further development of intelligence. Man's well-developed eye-hand co-ordination and manual dexterity, in addition to his use of language, set him apart from other animals. Your baby's visually directed reaching is still new, but it nonetheless represents a signficant step forward toward the goal of more mature intelligence and problem-solving behavior.

Greater Interest in Toys and Objects

As visual, manual, and body control increase, so does your baby's interest in toys and objects. He wants to grab them, finger them, turn them every which way, shake, and mouth them. He is no longer satisfied simply to watch his crib mobile and bat at the dangling objects. He has a driving need to grab those objects and bring them to his mouth. When he cannot accomplish this, or when a toy is left slightly beyond his reach, he will become very frustrated.

Through playing with objects, he gathers more information about them. He learns a great deal about their qualities and properties, how they are different from him, and what he can do with them.

An infant learns that his actions—like lifting an arm and hitting a mobile—can affect objects in his surroundings. He does something, and something happens or changes as a result. Gradually he learns to separate the action from the result. He also learns about simple time sequences such as "before" and "after."

As your baby looks at and feels a variety of objects, he becomes more familiar with them. He learns to recognize more of them. Previously, if you hid part of a familiar object such as his favorite toy behind a box, he might not have recognized it. Now he may immediately recognize the object after only seeing a part of it.

The Infancy 5 baby is beginning to discover that objects have certain stable characteristics. For example, as he handles an object and moves it toward his body and then away from it, he learns that its shape does not change, even though its appearance changes at various distances.

One of the most interesting concepts in relation to objects that he does not completely understand is the concept that objects continue to exist even when he cannot see, touch, or hear them.

The Most Sensational Disappearing Act in Town

The world to us is a fairly organized place. One of the reasons for this is that we have a concept of the permanency of objects. We know, for example, that the glass we just put on the kitchen table will continue to exist even when we are not looking at it or handling it. Should we lose our car keys, we still know that they exist—somewhere—and we try to search for them. When a friend walks out of our house and we do not see him for a day or two, we do not conclude that he has somehow magically vanished into thin air.

Your baby, during the first half of infancy, does not have such a well-developed concept of the permanency of objects. When an object is out of sight, hands, or mouth, he generally perceives it as being permanently gone. This is why he does not really bother to search for an object that drops from his hands, or why he looks down only briefly and then seems to forget about it. To him, an object that he cannot see, hear, or feel has somehow magically vanished. Over the first six to eight months, as he gains more experience in dealing with objects, and as his intellectual abilities improve, he will gradually learn that objects have a stable, permanent existence. He may develop a notion of the permanency of very familiar objects with which he comes into repeated contact each day, the bottle, breast, or his parent, long before he perceives other objects and people as having a permanent existence.

Imitation

It is during the last half of the baby's first year that imitation really begins to blossom, but even now, you may notice him mimicking your prominent hand motions, facial expressions, and sounds more frequently. This activity will be of vital importance to him in relation to his further intellectual, personal-social, and language development.

LANGUAGE DEVELOPMENT

Active Language Development

EXPERIMENTATION WITH SOUNDS. Your baby will continue to produce the sounds that you heard earlier, and may experiment further with altering these sounds as well as making new ones. Experimentation with sounds is carried out differently from one child to the next. Each baby seems to adopt his own style of sound "play."

One baby will experiment wherever he is, while another who does not practice too much around other people will babble away when he is by himself. One baby will enjoy producing loud sounds, while another devotes his practice time to soft sounds and variations in tone, pitch, and range.

Even at this early stage, given a group of babies of the same age, you may be able to distinguish the "talkers" from the more quiet ones. Babies become interested in producing and experimenting with sounds at different ages. Some babies—those who are not doing much in the way of playing with sounds—are simply more interested in looking, listening, reaching, or other activities. Their time for sound production will come.

HE MAY OCCASIONALLY PRODUCE SOUNDS WHICH RESEMBLE WORDS. As your baby experiments with various combinations of vowel and consonant sounds, he may utter a sound such as "da da" or "ba ba" (which often sounds to parents like baby talk for bottle). You will be thrilled if you happen to hear him say something that sounds like a real word. When Mr. Blyden heard his five-month-old son utter "da da," he rushed to his baby's side, grinning and looking proud and absolutely delighted. Mr. Blyden repeated the word "da da" several times, hoping to hear his son say it again. His son, however, did not repeat it. He obviously did not associate the meaning of the sound, "da da," with his father. Mr. Blyden was still happy with his son's new sound. In time the child will eventually learn that this sound refers to his father, but in the meantime Mr. Blyden was having fun anyway.

Your baby's first "words" are usually produced accidentally, in the course of his sound play, although they may be produced as he mimics other people's sounds. Chances are that he has no idea that he said a real word, and no idea of the meaning of the word. The ability to say a word appropriately, with an understanding of its meaning, takes time to develop.

POSITIVE REINFORCEMENT OF HIS SOUNDS IS IMPORTANT. When your baby eventually utters sounds that resemble real words, the fact that he does not know their meanings should not matter much to you. A celebration is in order, but try to include him in it by going to him, picking him up, giving him a big hug and a squeeze, repeating his sounds, or doing something else that conveys to him how happy you are. By giving him positive feedback for the sounds he produces, you will be encouraging him to repeat this combination of sounds. He will keep producing specific word sounds, because he learns that following this behavior, you will reward him by smiling or some other positive response.

Initially, the objective of this positive reinforcement is simply to encourage him to produce more sounds, and to imitate your sounds. As he practices uttering sounds, he will master them, and thus feel competent and successful. He will also devote more time to listening to your voice, imitating your inflections, and parroting simple words. Offering him positive feedback also has further educational value.

When he initially utters sounds, they are not specific to any language. Some of them may resemble sounds used in speaking English, French, German, or other languages. When he produces sounds that more closely resemble those in your native tongue, you will probably react more enthusiastically. Your positive response to the sounds in your native language encourages those sounds to be repeated. The other sounds that are not positively reinforced gradually begin to disappear, until he has acquired the basic sound patterns for learning to speak your language.

GAMES INVOLVING IMITATION OF SOUNDS. Your baby is apt to derive a great deal of pleasure from games in which you imitate his sounds, and then he repeats them. Try occasionally to introduce different sounds into this verbal exchange. He may listen carefully and try to copy them. Some babies, on the other hand, enjoy this sound imitation game only if their parents continue to imitate sounds that they themselves have already uttered. When parents introduce new sounds, these babies get very quiet or look unhappy. Some infants prefer to learn new sounds on their own, since in private they may devote a great deal of time to experimenting with different combinations of sounds.

VOCALIZATIONS HELP HIM EXPRESS HIMSELF. Expressing himself through a variety of sounds is easier. By his grunts, laughs, shouts, whimpers, and growls, in combination with his body language, you will have a pretty good idea of whether he is happy, pleased, annoyed, or unhappy. As he produces different sounds, you react differently, and he learns to associate your reaction with various vocalizations.

At this time he may begin using his voice more often, other than to cry, as an attention getter. This can be irritating, particularly when you are speaking on the phone or talking to someone else in your home and he begins producing sounds to divert your attention to him. When he feels that you are ignoring him, his sounds may get more demanding or change to cries.

Passive Language Development

Even when your baby is not producing sounds, he will still be doing some behind the scenes language learning. As you and other people speak, he will be observant of your voice inflections, the movements of your mouths, your facial expressions, and gestures. He registers all of this now, and will try to duplicate what he has seen and heard in the weeks and months to come.

All kinds of sounds may interest him, even sounds of animals and inanimate objects such as clocks. He may particularly enjoy manipulating toys and objects in such a way as to produce different sounds. Playing with sound-producing objects such as bells, noisemakers, or rattles, or banging spoons or cups on his feeding table, may bring him a great deal of pleasure. He may also enjoy listening to "talking" records and all kinds of music.

MOTOR DEVELOPMENT

Reflex Activity

If you stroke the sole of your baby's foot, his toes will probably continue to curl as if he is trying to grasp your fingers, and this type of response may continue for about the next six months. Touch the palm of his hand, and he is less likely to curl his fingers in a grasping motion, since reflex grasping is giving way to voluntary grasping. His rooting reflex may still be seen, but usually only when he is sleeping. Most of his primitive reflex responses are now being suppressed by the development of higher brain centers.

Gross Motor Activity

Even though your baby is not yet what you would call mobile, you will see definite improvement in his body control. As you have probably observed, his development has been generally progressing from his head to his feet. He first began gaining good control over his eyes, head, and arms. Then he started to develop increasing ability to control the muscles in his torso and lower back. Now he is also beginning to do more with his legs, since his leg muscles are stronger. His actions, in general, seem more directed because he is slowly learning to control his body.

HE ENJOYS A POSITION ON HIS ABDOMEN. When you place your infant on his stomach, you are likely to see him resting the weight of the upper part of his body on his hands with his chest and torso elevated, and his knees tucked under him. He will be able to raise his head and chest high off of the mattress more easily, now that his arm muscles are stronger. His head and shoulders are now steadier and held in a more upright position.

Now that his leg muscles are becoming stronger, he will use his legs in daily activities more frequently. You may see him pushing hard with them in order to move a bit, and pivoting with the help of his arms and hands. On his stomach, he will enjoy stretching his arms and legs. Rocking back and forth in a "seesaw" fashion is fun for him.

ROLLING OVER. Your baby will probably be able to roll over from his stomach to his back and vice versa, and he may do this constantly, despite his limited comprehension of the actions involved in this movement. This ability may not emerge until Infancy 6 in some babies. Lying on his stomach, your infant may attempt to move across his crib or playpen mattress by rolling over and over, turning and twisting his body, and rocking forward and backward. Still, he cannot get very far.

ON HIS BACK. On his back, he is better able to lift his head and shoulders to see his feet, but cannot yet sit up. He may try to move about by squirming and pushing his legs against the mattress or the back of the crib. Most babies dislike being placed on their backs, and chances are yours will, too. Because he likes to look around the room, he finds this back position prohibitive. However, he may keep himself occupied by reaching out to grab toys hanging above him, or raising his feet so that he can watch them.

SUPPORTED SITTING. He will probably be able to sit with pillow support for longer periods of time. When he is seated, his head may no longer fall forward or wobble as much as before. With better control over the muscles in his torso and lower back, he sits much straighter than before. While supported in a sitting position, he may be able to reach out for a toy. He tries to sit up as straight as he can. Without support, chances are that he will slump forward.

As you pull him from his back into a sitting position, he will help pull up his body by moving his head forward, bending at the waist, and bringing his legs in toward his stomach.

SUPPORTED STANDING. You can more easily pull your baby from a sitting to a standing position. When you try this, notice that he holds his head in line with his body, extends his legs, and pushes down against the mattress in an attempt to help. When you support him in this upright position, he will bear some weight on his legs, bounce, and stamp.

Fine Motor Activity

One of the most obvious, exciting, and significant developments is your baby's improving ability to reach and grasp objects. Reaching and grasping becomes a smoother motion as well as more accurate. He now has better arm and hand control, and also better eye-hand co-ordination. Visually directed reaching has been discussed in detail in the Intellectual Development section. He still finds it difficult to pick up small objects, but he will acquire this ability over the next several months. You will notice him bringing many objects that he grabs to his mouth, and that he is gaining co-ordination.

HOW TO ENSURE YOUR BABY'S SAFETY

The Safety Training Check Lists compiled thus far continue to be appropriate for an Infancy 5 child. Some of you have been using an infant seat occasionally to support your baby over the past several months. By the fifth month a baby is gaining more control over his body and more strength as well as weight. He is more active, and thus this type of seat is probably no longer safe, since he may easily tip it over. Besides, he needs freedom of movement and may wriggle and squirm to get out of the restraining device. The infant seat is also not adequate car protection, and you are advised against placing him in an infant seat when you take him for a ride in the car.

Any other chairs that you may purchase or have already obtained should be well anchored and weighted down at the bottom to prevent them from being tipped over by your active baby. If your baby, when placed on the floor, is already able to crawl or use some other ingenious method of getting around, we suggest that you read ahead to the next discussion on How to Ensure Your Baby's Safety on pages 301–4 for further comments.

FEEDING

More Activity at Mealtimes

As your baby's ability to swipe at and grab objects improves, and his interests in play and exploration increase, he will become more active during mealtimes and less interested in sucking and eating. When feeding, he may bite or play with the bottle nipple or your breast nipple after only a relatively short nursing period. He may also want to place his hands on breast or bottle, and stroke them. Playing with or biting your nipple instead of sucking on it can be quite uncomfortable and even painful. These actions probably indicate that he has had his fill of milk, anyway, so do not feel guilty about setting limits on this kind of behavior by sharply saying "no" or "don't," or by ending the nursing period.

Weaning

Weaning, as was previously mentioned, refers to the transition from taking milk by sucking on a breast or bottle, to taking milk in a different way, from an unbreakable glass or cup. Weaning is usually a very personal issue, based upon what feels "right" and is most convenient for you, and upon when your baby shows a natural readiness to give up sucking on the breast or bottle. This discussion of weaning in Infancy 5 is purely for educational purposes to prepare you in advance for this event. It is not meant to encourage early weaning.

THERE IS NO ONE "RIGHT" TIME TO WEAN EVERY BABY. Doctors' advice varies about the timing of weaning. Most physicians recommend that weaning take place during the latter part of infancy. In their opinion, weaning a baby early may be particularly frustrating for him, since his need to suck will not be sufficiently satisfied. Many psychologists claim that too early weaning may prolong a baby's sucking desire, and lead to fixation on oral gratification or other emotional problems later on. This has yet to be scientifically proven. As long as you do what feels right for you and follow your baby's lead, there is no need to worry about negative effects of weaning.

Until a baby is between approximately nine and eleven months old, his sucking instinct is usually still present, and that instinct may need to be satisfied until that age. Gradually, as the sucking instinct diminishes and his digestive system, mouth, teeth, and jaws develop more fully, he becomes able to chew, swallow, and digest coarser foods and drink milk from a cup easily. At that point, usually two or three months before a baby's first birthday, or shortly after he is a year old, weaning is quite appropriate.

Both a parent's feelings and a child's needs and feelings should be taken into account in deciding when would be an appropriate time for weaning to occur. It is important to recognize that because of individual differences, some babies accept taking their milk in a cup well before they are a year old, and some require a bottle or want to continue nursing at the breast until they are well into toddlerhood.

Breast-feeding mothers who are very much enjoying this experience may not want to give it up until their babies are about a year old. Some even continue to nurse into the child's second year, feeling that breast-feeding offers them and their child a special time for shared closeness. Occasionally, mothers offering the bottle may have similar feelings in wanting to continue giving it into the child's second year. Other mothers are anxious to encourage their child's shift from breast or bottle to cup, viewing this transition as a kind of milestone for their baby, and as a way of satisfying their own need for more convenience.

Perhaps you are planning to return to work outside the home or are going back to school and feel that you want to wean before this. Or you may have a variety of other reasons for wanting to discontinue breast- or bottle-feeding at a certain time. If you have a definite plan as to when you want or have to wean, it would be advisable to inform your doctor about a month in advance. The doctor can help guide both you and your baby in making an easier transition.

HOW WILL YOU KNOW WHEN YOUR BABY IS READY? At some point your baby will probably begin to nurse for shorter periods of time on the breast or bottle. Giving him opportunities to drink from a cup may cause him to have a greater interest in using it, or show no objection to taking milk from it. One day, very suddenly, he may simply seem to lose his enthusiasm for breast or bottle, and turn his head away from it when it is offered or push it away after a very brief nursing period. With some babies a loss of enthusiasm or interest is more gradual. A few young children never seem to indicate that they have had enough sucking. In these cases parents will eventually have to make this decision for them.

FROM BREAST TO BOTTLE OR BREAST TO CUP? Advice sometimes varies in regard to how a baby should be weaned. Some doctors advise breast-feeding mothers to wean straight from breast to cup—not from breast to bottle. More physicians recommend that a baby before the age of nine months or so be weaned to a bottle first and then to a cup. It all depends upon whether or not a baby is able to drink from a cup and is willing to do so. Bottle-fed babies will be weaned to a cup. It is early to wean a baby to a cup during this phase, so do not be too disappointed if your baby refuses to take milk from it, and continues to demand the breast or bottle.

HOW LONG DOES WEANING TAKE? Most physicians advise allowing anywhere from a week and a half to three weeks and strongly suggest that the transition be a gradual one. Weaning may require some psychological adjustments for you. If breast-feeding, your body will also have to undergo a physical adjustment. For your health and comfort, the shift should be made slowly. Guard against rushing weaning into one week, or you may have difficulties with your breasts, and may experience some discomfort. Allow at least two weeks.

Keep in mind that although weaning from bottle to cup can be accomplished very suddenly, for your baby's sake try to make a gradual shift. Some babies want to have one bottle, particularly an evening bottle until they are two years old or older, even though they readily drink milk from a cup during their regular meals. There is no harm in this.

Some babies, during the process of being weaned or shortly after they have been weaned, suddenly want to return to breast or bottle, particularly when they are emotionally upset or sick. Assuming this presents no real problem, you may decide to accommodate your baby. On the other hand, you can surely find many other ways of offering him comfort until he feels more secure and independent. It is best to make a decision to wean and then stick by it, especially in the case of mothers who are breast-feeding. Switching back and forth in feeding methods may be confusing to a child, and in the case of mothers who are breast-feeding, this may not be feasible. Depending upon when and how you wean, it may become obvious that your baby simply is not ready for more independence. You may have to postpone weaning for a month or two and then start again.

There are several emotional factors which are important for you to consider, since weaning is a time of transition for you. These emotional considerations will be discussed on page 285.

WHEN IS A GOOD TIME TO INTRODUCE A CUP? It is advisable to introduce a cup while the baby is still taking the breast or bottle. This will give him a chance gradually to get used to taking his milk in a way that is different from a nipple, and will make the transition easier on him when the time comes. The exact age at which you begin to offer milk from a cup is not really important. Some physicians recommend starting when a baby is between five and six months old, although this is rather early. Most babies have an easier time managing if the cup is introduced when they are between seven and nine months old. Begin by offering small amounts of liquid, and do not be too discouraged if your baby refuses to drink his milk this way. There is no reason not to wait for another month or so and then try again. He will eventually learn. As long as you let him get used to it well before you plan to wean him, there is no reason to pressure him to use a cup right away.

WEANING FROM THE BREAST. The main idea is to go slowly and eliminate one breast-feeding session at a time. Stick to this schedule a few days or more before dropping another breast-feeding session, so that your body will have time to adjust. When you begin, it is advisable to drop the feeding at which your baby is likely to be the least hungry. You may hand-empty your breasts for a brief period of time, or allow your baby to nurse for half a minute or less if they feel very full and are causing you any discomfort. Hand expression should alleviate the discomfort.

Provided you cannot consult your doctor, you can follow the brief guidelines below, recommended by experienced mothers, for the order in which breast-feedings may be eliminated. You should vary this method according to your own comfort and supply of milk. In dropping breast-feedings, take your infant's appetite and your comfort into consideration. Just as your milk supply naturally increases as your baby's demand for food increases, nature will see to it that your breast-milk supply is turned off with diminishing feeding times, if this is done slowly.

You may find it easiest to start by eliminating the lunch time breast-feeding, if your baby is on a three-meal-a-day schedule. Assuming you feel comfortable, then gradually continue to eliminate the other two breast-feedings. In case your baby is on four meals a day, you might find it helpful to begin by dropping either the second or third breast-feeding before dropping the first or last. If you are still breast-feeding five times a day, you might begin with skipping the suppertime breast-feeding. Wait a few days, and then drop the second morning feeding. After this point, use your own judgment about which breast-feeding to eliminate next.

WEANING FROM THE BOTTLE. The main idea is to go slowly and eliminate one bottle at a time. Allow a few days to pass after dropping one bottle-feeding before you eliminate another. Watch your baby's reaction to see whether he accepts this. If he does not protest too loudly, continue to drop other bottles until he is taking all milk from an unbreakable cup or plastic glass.

BATHING

Even though the bathing procedure has remained unchanged, you may notice how differently your baby behaves during his baths. He is no longer content to sit quietly as you go about the business of washing him. He will want to kick his feet, grab at the washcloth and soap, and reach out for other bath products around the tub. You should be certain that only safe, non-breakable items are left along the rim of the tub.

As playing becomes more important to him, he will enjoy playing in the tub with bath toys. Try not to rush him out of the tub if he really enjoys babbling, splashing away, and trying to sink his float toys. He will like having a few extra minutes to play after you have finished washing him.

SLEEPING

Most babies are able to sleep through the night, but some babies wake during the night full of energy and ready for activity. Assuming your baby is one of them, he may comfort himself with activities such as rocking, rolling, or squirming. If he cries loudly enough to awaken you, and refuses to quiet down after about ten minutes (or as long as you can wait), you may have to spend a few minutes comforting him and helping him settle back to sleep. Again, guard against making a habit of this unless you are willing to have your sleep interrupted on a nightly basis. Occasionally a baby may find it easier to sleep at night if he has a late evening play or exercise period, but discontinue this if it gets him too wound up and overstimulated. A late evening feeding for a couple of weeks may help, although this, too, should not be continued long enough to become a nightly ritual.

A few doctors advocate restraining an active baby by utilizing a sleeping harness at night, but most feel that it is important for a baby to have freedom to move around, as long as he is in safe territory. An active baby will shed his covers at some point during the night. This need not present a problem since he can be dressed in an appropriate sleeping bag or other garment so that extra coverings for his bed are not necessary.

Babies are usually quite anxious to be up and on the go very early in the morning. This may present problems if other family members are not accustomed to waking at the crack of dawn. Try to ignore your infant's crying if he wakes earlier than you like, since this will convey the message to him that he must learn to be more resourceful and find ways of amusing himself until you are ready to get up and go into his room in the morning.

EMOTIONAL CONSIDERATIONS IN RELATION TO WEANING

Weaning (see pages 280–83) often necessitates more of an emotional adjustment in mothers than they anticipate, particularly in mothers who are breast-feeding. There comes a time when nearly every baby expresses his indifference to the breast or bottle or pushes it aside when it is offered. When this first happens, it is difficult for mothers who have been breast-feeding not to take their baby's sudden change in attitude toward the breast personally. A personal interpretation is certainly understandable, but there is no need for you to feel guilty or annoyed when your baby refuses your breast. While the physical tie (in the true sense of the word) with you is coming to an end, the emotional bond still keeps you together. Whether or not your baby is sucking on your breast, he will continue to need to feel close to you during his feedings, as well as at other times. He needs, in essence, to be "mothered."

There are mothers who experience a brief, mild depression when breast-feeding comes to an end. It is similar to the "baby blues," but usually milder and of shorter duration. As in the case of mild postpartum depression, a physiological adjustment based on hormonal changes frequently is part of the depression that accompanies weaning. When weaning is rushed, it is much harder for a woman to make both a physical and an emotional adjustment. Weaning your baby gradually will help make the shift less traumatic.

When weaning takes place, bottle-feeding mothers may also experience feelings of no longer being as important in their baby's life. These feelings, again, are natural and understandable. Many mothers, whether they are feeding by breast or bottle find the feeding exchange fulfilling and emotionally satisfying. They often speak of how close to their infants and how needed they feel during feedings. During the time of weaning, it is easy to see why many mothers find it difficult to adjust immediately.

During weaning some mothers also become jealous of their baby's relationship with his father, especially when the father-child bond is strong. This can place an emotional strain on a mother. If these mothers only recognized how their babies still need them, and need to be "mothered," perhaps these jealous feelings could be put into proper perspective and more easily resolved.

Occasionally a mother who takes pleasure in her baby's dependency upon her will continue to breast-feed or offer the bottle far beyond the age at which her child expressed a willingness to drink milk from a cup and at which the vast majority of children in our culture have been weaned. Such a mother should examine her feelings and life circumstances in an attempt to determine why she feels the need to hold her child back from becoming more grown up. Delaying weaning in spite of a child's readiness to move to greater independence is not in his best interest, and may contribute to adjustment difficulties at a later age.

PREPARED PARENTHOOD CHECK LIST

MOTHER	FATHER	UNDERSTANDING YOUR BABY'S DEVELOPMENT
——	——	Is your infant taking a greater interest in exploring his body and socializing?
—	——	Why does your baby find it easier to express his feelings?
—	—	Has your baby become attached to a "security" object or toy?
——	——	Does your infant frequently bring objects that he grasps to his mouth for further exploration?
—	—	Have you observed evidence that your baby lacks a good concept of the permanency of objects?
—	—	Is your baby producing and experimenting with a variety of sounds?
—	—	Have you been positively reinforcing your baby when he babbles?
—	—	Do you try to play games involving imitation of sounds or mouth movements with your infant?
—	—	Does your baby prefer a position on his tummy rather than on his back?
—	——	Many babies like to be supported in a standing position. How does your baby react to being held upright?
—	—	Is your baby's reaching and grasping becoming smoother and more accurate?

BASIC CARE

—	—	Why is your baby's infant seat probably no longer safe?
—	—	Is your infant more active at mealtimes?
—	—	Are you aware of some of the important considerations in weaning?
—	—	Have you noticed how much more active your baby is at bath time?
—	—	Does your baby ever wake up during the night? How do you handle this?

FAMILY FEELINGS AND CONCERNS

—	—	Are you aware that weaning a baby is often an emotional event for mothers?

Infancy 6

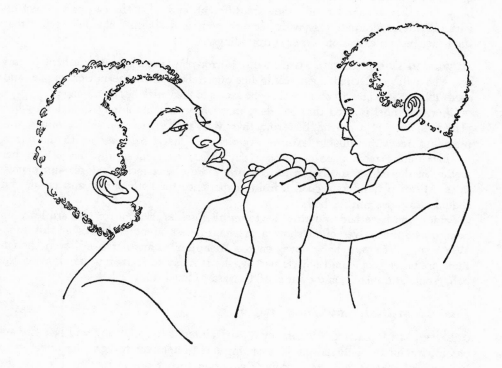

PERSONAL-SOCIAL DEVELOPMENT

Self-awareness

Your baby's awareness of herself continues to expand as she explores, plays, experiments, and learns. She is becoming more conscious of the different parts of her body, how they are similar, how they are different, and what she can and cannot do with them. Her alternate play with her own body and objects helps her realize that she is not just an extension of her surroundings.

MIRROR PLAY CONTINUES TO BE FUN. Mirror play often fascinates a baby of this age. She will get excited upon seeing her own reflection in the mirror, giggle, and even "talk" to it. You will observe that she seems to recognize her own image.

Cheryl Mandel noticed that her daughter, Mary, was absolutely fascinated when placed in front of a mirror. Believing that Mary's play in front of the mirror was providing her with valuable learning experiences, Cheryl held her up to the mirror in their dining room once or twice a day. Mary enjoyed seeing herself and her mother in the mirror and began to recognize more of her facial features and expressions. Mirror play offers a good learning experience for both parent and child, and should also prove fun for both.

Babies who have had opportunities to see themselves in a mirror and are learning more about themselves often show a greater interest in other babies at this time. When you place your baby down on the floor next to another baby, even though there are other people and objects nearby, she is likely to focus her attention on the baby, smile at the baby, and even bend forward to touch him or her.

Social Sensitivity and Interests

GREATER SOCIABILITY. An Infancy 6 baby's interest in socializing will be more apparent. Interacting with people is becoming more important to her. Her attempts to make social contact and draw people's attention to her are increasing. One of the main ways in which your baby will accomplish this is through babbling. By now she has probably learned which particular vocalizations capture your attention and bring you to her, so naturally she repeats them loudly whenever she feels like seeing you. In addition to expressing her feelings of delight and anger through sounds, she will use hand gestures, body positions, and facial expressions.

IMITATION AND SOCIAL GAMES BECOME MORE PROMINENT. Your baby's attempts to mimic other people's behaviors, especially their vocalizations, facial expressions, and gestures, will be more purposeful and obvious. Many babies are thrilled by the Peek-a-boo game. You may notice her copying your movements by placing her hands to her face or covering it with a blanket or napkin. Her deliberate imitation of others and your positive reinforcement of her behavior is significant in terms of continued progress in personal-social development.

If you have older children, you may notice how much more attached your baby seems to them—even more responsive to them than to you. Mrs. Tolkin reported that her baby son, Jeremy, occasionally put up a struggle when she tried to change his diaper or feed him, but would readily respond when his eight-year-old brother stepped in to take over. Babies may thoroughly enjoy being around, playing with, and even trying to imitate their siblings.

Interacting with older brothers and sisters is a valuable experience, and should not be curtailed unless the baby's physical safety is at risk. By playing with siblings, a baby will grow both as a person, and as a social being. She will learn more about the similarities and differences between herself and other people, how to get along with others, how to capture others' attention, and how to build relationships with them.

STRANGER ANXIETY. There is a strong possibility that you will notice a rather dramatic change in your baby's reaction toward unfamiliar people. You may no longer see her smiling at strangers and accepting their presence without much reservation as she might have in the past. Instead, she may suddenly glare at them and if not reassured by your presence, act fearful and begin to cry. This type of reaction toward unfamiliar people is commonly referred to as "stranger anxiety."

Not all babies show stranger anxiety, although it is commonly seen between the ages of about six and eight months. It may be noticed earlier or later with some babies. A baby's fear response toward unfamiliar people often becomes more intense around the eighth month. It is interesting that stranger anxiety frequently arises around the time when babies become better able to recognize the faces of their parents and immediate family members, and can discriminate between these familiar faces and those of strangers. Although the reasons for this response are not clearly established, it could very well be that this new ability to discriminate is what causes their alarm by making them aware of strange faces.

In cases in which babies have been accustomed to being around or being cared for by many different people from a very early age, this fear of strangers may be much less marked, or even non-existent. Individual differences in upbringing, personalities, and perhaps even biological differences can play a role in influencing babies' sensitivity to unfamiliar people.

Stranger anxiety is a common phenomenon, so you need not be unduly concerned if your baby's reaction to strangers is less than friendly. Even a family member who she sees for only a limited period of time each week may receive similar treatment. She is very immature, and her negative or fearful response should not be taken as a personal insult. Given enough time, her opinions and responses will change and become more mature.

The most advisable approach to take if you notice that she is sensitive to new faces is to refrain from overreacting, remain nearby, and try to reassure and comfort her. Give her as much time as she seems to need to look them over and calm down. Forcing unfamiliar people on her, or getting angry at her for embarrassing you, can make the situation worse. Offer explanations to Grandma, Uncle Dick, or whoever triggers her response. Chances are that once she has stopped crying and has received your reassurance, people can approach without her becoming upset.

INTELLECTUAL DEVELOPMENT

Eye-hand Co-ordination Improves

Your baby's eye-hand co-ordination is improving. When an object catches her attention, she will probably reach for it faster and more smoothly than before. Most of the time she will keep her eyes peeled on the target of interest as she reaches out to grab it, but occasionally you will see her shut her eyes as she reaches. Place a toy within her reach, and she will probably be able to pick it up with greater ease than before. Her improved reaching and grasping enable more frequent, sophisticated contact and play with objects.

Exploration of Objects Continues

When your baby is alert, she will exhibit a strong desire to handle and grab all nearby objects. Holding an object, she will turn it around, run her fingers over it, bang it on her feeding table, and wave it around. She will also look at it from various perspectives, listen carefully to the sounds it produces, and, naturally, put it into her mouth for additional testing.

Putting objects into her mouth is an essential aspect of her investigatory activities. Curiosity motivates her to explore anything and everything from a teething biscuit, to a piece of wrapping paper. As she reaches for and explores objects, you will observe that she is more determined than before, and better able to concentrate or stick with a task.

An emerging interest in relation to objects is dropping them. Your baby may start to drop small toys, feeding utensils, and food items over the edge of the table while she is seated in your lap or high chair. When she has dropped everything there is to drop, then she may cry or screech until someone picks the objects up and gives them back to her. Dropping things becomes a game to her, and she will probably keep this up until the person who is stuck in the position of retrieving all of the dropped objects is either too exhausted or annoyed to continue. This interest is more likely to show up in Infancy 7 to 12.

Repetition Is Important

Your infant's activities are gradually becoming more intentional or purposeful. After she has performed some action and has seen the results of it, with those results in mind, she works to achieve them again. Her goal is to keep making something happen, after she has discovered the means to accomplish it.

You will notice how interested she has become in repeating certain actions, such as dropping objects, pushing them, or moving her body around to cause her crib mobile to sway or other objects to move. She keeps these activities going so as to observe the effects or results of her behavior. Repeated trials of an activity seem to help her learn what has happened, and remember it. As a result of experiences in dealing with objects, the next time she comes in contact with the same objects she is better able to remember what actions were performed on them, and what results were produced. Her memory definitely shows improvement, particularly in relation to people and objects with whom she has had consistent contact over the past six months.

As she deals with objects she not only learns about their properties, such as what sounds they produce when they are dropped, she also learns about cause and effect relationships. Performing simple actions on objects and watching the consequences will become more prominent over the next several months.

You will notice that your baby becomes alert, strains to lift her head to bend forward, and waves her arms when she sees her bottle or your breast, but does not respond this way when you hold up a stuffed animal or another object. These kinds of changes in her behavior provide evidence that she is learning more about the world around her.

LANGUAGE DEVELOPMENT

Active Language Development

You are likely to hear your baby babbling continuously, whether she is lying still, attempting to move around and sit, or playing. She seems to need to practice expressing herself orally, both when she is happy and satisfied and when she is irritated and angry. As her voice equipment matures, and she devotes more time and effort to repeating certain sounds in her repertoire, her articulation of them will improve. Experimentation with babbling also enables her to broaden her range of sounds.

In the past, most of your baby's babbling may have sounded like vowels, although some consonant sounds are likely to have been heard. As she plays with sounds, more consonants will be accidentally hit upon and repeated. You may hear her coming up with combinations of vowels and consonants such as "ga ga," "da da," "fuh fuh," or "goo goo." It is interesting that babies, in general, tend to utter "da da" before "ma ma." Since mothers, on the whole, tend to be more actively involved in their baby's care, it is frequently taken as an insult to them when their baby says "da da" first. However, producing sounds that require movement of the lips as in "m" seems to be more difficult for babies than producing sounds that call for back of the throat action such as "ga," or tip of the tongue against palate action as in "da."

HER FIRST WORD. Your infant may now utter a sound or combination of sounds that resemble a real word. Perhaps she will come up with sounds that resemble "da da" or "bye-bye" or "bay bee." Hearing your first baby finally say something that sounds like a real word is a once-in-a-lifetime experience. Do not be disappointed or concerned if your baby does not produce sounds that resemble words. Babies don't usually produce such sounds or say any words meaningfully until they are well into toddlerhood.

The topic of a baby's first word has generated a great deal of discussion and speculation. Some theorists believe that the first words babies utter are related to bodily needs or things that gratify them. Substantial evidence for this, however, seems lacking. Many babies have been known to utter "da da" or "ma ma" as their first words, but there are many other words that are uttered as first words, including "pretty," "ball," "no no," and so forth.

THE REASONS FOR CRYING MAY CHANGE. The reasons why your baby cries may show some changes during the last half of the first year. Previously, she mainly cried when she was hungry, tired, or in some sort of physical discomfort. She will still cry for these reasons, but she is better able to wait for her meals. Her tolerance for minimal physical discomfort seems to be greater. She has long since adjusted to life outside the womb, and the frequent unexplainable crying spells that were common during the first few months of life are now much less common.

Around this time she may tend to cry more often for emotional expression. When she is very angry, sad, or jealous, she may cry. Being more sensitive to other people's moods, she may also cry when she sees that other people are extremely upset or are crying, particularly other babies.

A common reason for crying during this phase is frustration. Babies seem to have one-track minds when it comes to something they want. When faced with obstacles, or when an activity that they are enjoying is curtailed, they will become quite frustrated and probably start to cry. Restricting their movements or placing toys slightly beyond their reach can also cause them to cry out of frustration.

There is still another aspect of frustration crying with which you should become familiar. Babies, on the whole, tend to cry more often prior to accomplishing developmental milestones such as sitting, crawling, and walking. With each new skill that is acquired, emotional as well as physical adjustments must be made. Unfortunately, there is not too much you can do for this type of crying except be understanding and supportive. Once each milestone is mastered, this crying will probably diminish.

Babies also cry more often because they are lonely or bored. It is common for them to start crying when their pleas for attention or company are not acknowledged, when bedtime rolls around, or when they are put in surroundings that lack stimulation.

As babies grow older and become more mobile, the chances of their getting into mischief or having an accident increase considerably. Babies who can crawl are subject to scrapes, bruises, scratches, and splinters, and as a result, crying from pain or hurt emerges more strongly during the next six months.

Crying that is prompted by the approach of strangers, or being in a strange environment, will become more noticeable over the next several months. This type of crying was more fully explored on pages 289 and 335–36.

By this point you are probably much better able to determine why your infant is crying. She may have a special cry when she is lonely, bored, frustrated, angry, frightened, and so forth. Her facial expressions and gestures, which now are more purposeful and varied, will help you pinpoint the reasons for her crying.

Passive Language Development

UNDERSTANDING WORDS. Babies are not born with an understanding of what words mean, but they gradually begin to associate words with the people, places, and objects that the words represent. Simple words that your baby hears regularly are likely to be learned first. Infancy 6 babies may show by their behavior that they understand the meanings of words such as "mommy," "baby," "daddy," "bye-bye," "ball," or "bottle."

When a baby first says a word, this does not necessarily indicate her awareness of its correct meaning. Mr. and Mrs. Caplan were delighted and surprised when their six-month-old daughter, Kiki, said the word "da da" for the first time. They immediately jumped to the conclusion that she knew what this word meant, but later realized that this was not the case when Kiki said "da da" to her mother, her toy, and her two-year-old brother. Mr. and Mrs. Caplan decided to try to help Kiki learn the meaning of the word "da da." Whenever she said this word and her father was around, either he would go over to her, smile, and say something to indicate his delight, or Mrs. Caplan would point to him and repeat the word. On the occasions when Mrs. Caplan was alone with Kiki, she kept a loose snapshot of her husband within easy reach so that she could show it to Kiki whenever her daughter said "da da."

These parents did a fine job of assisting their baby in making the association between a word and the person it signifies. With extra encouragement and help, a baby will find learning the meanings of words easier and more enjoyable.

At every stage of development you will notice that your infant's comprehension of words is far greater than her ability to say them. In fact, she may say little or nothing in terms of actual words throughout the next year or so, but will grow to understand many words, commands, and simple conversations. Shortly after your baby begins to connect a few words with their meanings, her understanding of simple orders and directions will improve.

INTEREST IN SOUNDS. Your baby's interest in different sounds is likely to become stronger as she becomes more aware of her own sounds and experiments with them. She seems to derive much pleasure from hearing her own voice, other people's voices, and all kinds of household noises as well as music. The sounds that she can produce when interacting with toys and objects take on greater significance as her enjoyment of sounds grows.

Her attention is often grabbed by sounds she hears. When she hears music, for instance, she may briefly stop making sounds to listen. Voices, however, particularly high-pitched voices (generally women's voices), may be even more effective in catching her attention and stimulating more babbling after her initial pause to listen.

MOTOR DEVELOPMENT

Reflex Activity

It is much harder for you to elicit and observe your baby's primitive reflexes, since most of them are being suppressed and replaced by voluntary movements. Now that she has greater control over her body, her movements will seem less automatic, and more intentional.

Individual Differences Become More Noticeable from Infancy 6 to 12

Variability in babies' acquisition of new motor skills becomes even more apparent from midway to the end of the infancy stage as compared to the first five phases of infancy. Noticeable differences can be seen in the rate, order, and manner in which motor skills are acquired.

Each baby displays her uniqueness by setting her own pace and establishing her own style and order. Assuming that your baby is making rapid progress in motor development, you will no doubt be thrilled. On the other hand, if she is a late "bloomer" in this particular area, you may feel somewhat impatient, disappointed, or even embarrassed, particularly when other people insist on discussing their baby's feats, and you have no exciting news to relate along the same lines.

There is no need for you to try to push your baby to accomplish certain physical tasks before she seems able or willing to do so. Chances are that this will only make both of you more frustrated, and will not serve to speed up her acquisition of skills.

All that you really need do is to make sure that she receives plenty of encouragement and opportunities to practice her motor skills and move about. Follow her lead. Try not to become preoccupied with her progress or her lack of it. Rather, be as supportive as you can. This variation in the acquisition of new motor skills is a normal part of human development.

Gross Motor Activity

You will notice how much stronger and more co-ordinated your baby is becoming. A great deal of her time may be devoted to exercising parts of her body. While on her stomach, she may repeatedly push her chest and head up by straightening and stiffening her arms, and resting her weight on her hands. This position can be sustained for longer periods of time, since her arm muscles are more well developed than before. She may even shift her weight over to one arm and hand and reach out to grasp a toy with her free hand. When supported by two arms, notice how her head turns in all directions. She does not want to miss things that are going on around her.

On her back, your baby may lift up her head and shoulders to get a better look at her feet. Quite a lot of time is apt to be spent playing with her hands and feet. Elevating her legs and bringing them up and over her body is easier for her now, but many babies do not acquire this ability until Infancy 7. You may also see her arching her back and throwing her head backward to get an upside-down look at her surroundings. Kicking and pushing down and out with her legs may be one of her favorite activities when she is on her back.

ROLLING. Rolling over from her back to her stomach and then reversing the roll to make it complete are apt to be among her recent accomplishments, but remember that some babies lag behind at this activity. Once rolling is mastered, practicing may become one of her treasured pastimes. As she practices, her movements will become smoother.

SITTING. Previously your infant needed full support when in a sitting position. Now that her trunk and lower back muscles are stronger, she may sit well with only partial support. She may be able to lean forward or to the side and then straighten up again, and also reach out for toys in front of her without losing her balance. If you remove the support momentarily, she may even be able to sustain this position without slouching forward.

Some babies can already sit without support once they are helped to this position, while others still have difficulty sitting even with some support. Should your baby seem uncomfortable or straining while in the sitting position, it would be advisable to place her on her abdomen or back. She may not be fully ready to stay in the sitting position. Rest assured that she will learn to sit. Give her plenty of time to work up to this task slowly, at her own pace.

Some Infancy 6 babies make many attempts to sit up by themselves. Chances are that your baby, like most babies, will not really master this for another month or more. On the other hand, if she is advanced in her motor development, she may cleverly begin to maneuver herself into a sitting position by rolling over, bending at the waist, pushing on the floor with her hands, and hoisting her body upward. She might also raise her head, shoulders, and torso by resting her weight on her forearms and knees in a crawling position and then awkwardly try to get into a sitting position.

SUPPORTED STANDING. Many babies, anxious to exercise their leg muscles, love to be supported in a standing position. When Liz Pake tried to pull her son, Claude, to a sitting position, he pushed down on the mattress with his legs and stiffened at the waist in an obvious attempt to stand, rather than sit. This desire to get up to a standing position is common during this stage, and you are likely to notice it emerging when you offer your hands to help your child sit. With substantial support under her arms, your baby may bounce and stamp, and even momentarily bear some of her own weight.

Standing may become very important to your baby. You can anticipate her making numerous requests to be held up or making several determined attempts to pull herself to a standing position in her playpen or crib either in this phase or shortly thereafter. If you lift her to a stand at the side of her crib, and place her hands on the rails, she may stand by herself for a short period of time.

LOCOMOTION. A few exceptionally active babies may begin to crawl short distances on the floor, but this ability to move does not usually emerge until approximately the eighth month. The baby's increasing mobility will be discussed in future Motor Development sections.

Fine Motor Activity

Your baby has more control over her arms and hands, and she will have a great need to exercise them and try them out on objects. As her ability to sit without using arms and hands increases over the next month or so, she will use them while sitting to grab, explore, and manipulate objects. You will begin to see her reaching for an object with one hand, although most of the time she probably uses both hands. Being more accurate in grasping, she may no longer have to circle an object with both hands in order to grab hold of it. Her grasp is still unskilled, but you may notice that she is slowly beginning to grasp objects between her thumb and first few fingers. Even though she has better luck in grasping small-sized objects, she continues to have great difficulty picking up a tiny-sized object or particle. If you place a very small piece of cheese, the size of a raisin, on her high chair tray, she will probably smash down on it with her whole palm and try to bring it toward her with an inward sweeping motion involving her whole arm.

She will examine objects by turning and twisting her wrists, shaking the objects, banging them, and bringing them to her mouth. She may also transfer objects from hand to hand, and hold an object in each of her hands at the same time. If you offer her another object, however, she will probably let go of one of those she has in order to grasp it.

You will see much evidence of her improving eye-hand co-ordination and developing manual dexterity. She reaches for objects that catch her attention quickly and smoothly.

LEARNING THROUGH PLAY

Over the next two months you will notice that your baby is spending a greater portion of her waking time playing. In fact, she will probably love to play both on her own, and also with you and other people. When she plays on her own, she may be happier if she is positioned so that she can see you.

Exploration of toys and objects is becoming increasingly important to her. As she becomes more skillful with her hands and fingers, she will be able to hold and manipulate objects more comfortably, and transfer them back and forth between her hands. A favorite activity among babies of this age is dropping objects. While seated on your lap or in a high chair, your baby will probably derive a great deal of pleasure from picking up small objects and dropping or throwing them to the floor. Naturally, once all of the objects within reach have been thrown overboard, it will be your job to retrieve them. Chances are that you will tire of this activity long before she does.

Many babies of this age show an interest in small objects. Having a good supply of such objects in the home may keep them happily occupied for relatively long periods of time. It is hoped that you will provide your baby with a variety of small-sized objects of different shapes, textures, colors, etc. Again, you need not purchase such items at a toy store, since ordinary objects that you have at home will be equally, if not more, fascinating to her than those you might buy. She will enjoy banging the objects on a table, waving them about, repeatedly picking them up, bringing them to her mouth, turning them in all directions, and listening to their sounds as she shakes, bangs, and drops them. These activities enable her to make new discoveries about the properties of objects, and compare objects with one another.

In her play with objects, you are likely to observe her emerging interest in fitting one object inside of another. "Nesting" objects such as plastic cups or bowls that are graduated in size will make wonderful toys for her between Infancy 6 and 12. Stacking toys are also appropriate for babies of this age. Another activity that many older babies enjoy involves dropping small objects such as wooden cubes into a wide-mouthed plastic jar or pot, and then pouring them back out and starting all over again. The objects and activities mentioned above not only give her opportunities for exploration and learning, they also provide opportunities for her to practice the simple manual skills that she has acquired.

Once your infant is able to sit without having to rely on her hands for balance, it will be much easier for her to sit on the floor and play with objects scattered around her. As her trunk muscles become stronger and better developed, she will be able to twist her body around while seated, lean forward or sideways to reach objects and toys, and then sit back up without toppling over. Added control over her body means that her play will become more active in nature. Using her body, she will perform various actions on toys and objects, and will be focusing to a greater extent upon the results of those actions.

A portion of her playtime will probably involve playing by herself, but she will also love to engage in play activities with you and other family members. Nursery games, like peek-a-boo or simplified hide-and-seek, and games that involve imitation of sounds and simple movements are especially enjoyed by babies. Your involvement in some of her play activities is important, not only in terms of its value in relation to her over-all development, but also in terms of bringing the two of you together and strengthening your relationship.

Suggested List of Playthings

The playthings suggested on page 213 will still probably be enjoyed by babies at this stage. Below are a few additional suggestions for playthings:

> nesting toys (small, graduated plastic cups or measuring equipment)
> stacking toys (empty cardboard boxes with lids, lightweight large blocks)
> a variety of small objects (small pie tins)
> toys that make noise (rattles, squeeze toys)
> bath toys (sponges, plastic animals, and toys too large to be swallowed, cups)
> simple jack-in-the-box
> wide-top plastic jar
> pots and pans with lids
> wooden spoon
> old magazines
> unbreakable hand mirror

Suggestions for Activities

TRUNK TURNING. The following activity can be introduced once your baby can sit without using her hands for support. Hold her favorite toy, or a toy that produces sounds when moved, slightly behind her to her left or right and shake it. She will have to twist her trunk around in order to reach and grab it. If she makes an effort to get the toy or object, give it to her. Alternate between presenting it to her left side and her right side. This will give her practice in turning both her head and torso toward the location of a sound, and in reaching and grasping.

SOLVING A SIMPLE PROBLEM. There are many games that you can devise that will give your baby practice in finding solutions to simple problems. For example, place an attractive small-sized toy or object that cannot roll in the center of a piece of paper about the size of a diaper. Place the paper within her reach, but far enough away so that the toy itself is beyond her reach. Encourage her to get the toy. Obviously, in order for her to get her hands on the toy, she will have to pull the paper toward her. If she seems puzzled by this simple problem, do not be discouraged. What to you seems simple, to her may seem like a complicated problem. Show her how to solve the problem, and then encourage her to practice what she has seen. Through this activity she will get practice in reaching and grabbing, and will learn how to get an object that she cannot reach by using an object that is within reach.

SIMPLIFIED HIDE-AND-SEEK. Many babies enjoy simplified games of hide-and-seek. You might take her favorite toy and hide it underneath a bath towel while she is watching. Ask her to find or get the toy. Should she seem puzzled, uncover the toy and let her play with it. Next, hide it again. If she still seems confused, or makes no attempt to find it, uncover the toy again and allow her to play with it. Then hide it once more, but only partially, so that half of the toy is hidden under the cloth. Again, encourage her to get the toy. After a few trials of hiding it partially, then hide it completely and see if she can find it. Do not be too disappointed if she does not catch on easily. This type of game may be of assistance in helping her to realize that objects still exist, even though they cannot be seen.

SOUND PRODUCTION AND IMITATION. Earlier games mainly involved her producing a sound, and your imitating that sound. As she gets older, you can shift the emphasis in language-imitation games so that you say a sound that you have heard her practicing on her own, and then she imitates you. If you make sounds that you have never heard her produce, she may start to imitate them as well.

SEPARATION GAMES. Games in which you and your baby are separated for brief periods of time may help her realize that when you leave her, you will come back. Repetitions of and variations on the type of game suggested below may help her learn to cope more effectively with short separations from you. Pick a time to play the following game when she is alone in her room. Knock so that she will see you. A moment after she spots you, hide behind the door so that she will not be able to see you. Then, in a moment or two, stand in the doorway again so that she will see you once again. You can also vary this game by hiding behind a couch, chair, or other piece of furniture.

PEEK-A-BOO. Peek-a-boo involves hiding your face with both hands, and then removing your hands, smiling, and saying, "Peek-a-boo!" or "I see you!" You can also take your baby's hands in yours, cover her face with them, remove them, and say, "Boo!" Soon she will take an active part in this game by hiding her face with her hands. This game helps her to learn that people are permanent—that you can disappear and then reappear.

NURSERY GAMES. Below are a few examples of nursery rhymes and songs that your baby may enjoy. Be sure to use appropriate gestures that correspond to the rhymes. You can also play records of nursery rhymes, but she will undoubtedly like your involvement in her play more than simply listening to records.

This Little Pig
This little pig went to market;
This little pig stayed home;
This little pig had roast beef;
This little pig had none;
This little pig said, "Wee, wee, wee!"
All the way home.

Pat-a-cake
Pat-a-cake, pat-a-cake,
Baker's man!
Bake me a cake,
As fast as you can.
Pat it, and turn it
And mark it with T,
Put it in the oven
For Tommy and me!

One, Two, Buckle My Shoe
> One, two,
> Buckle my shoe;
> Three, four
> Shut the door;
> Five, six,
> Pick up sticks;
> Seven, eight,
> Lay them straight;
> Nine, ten,
> A big, fat hen.

Row, Row, Row Your Boat
> Row, Row, Row your Boat,
> Gently down the stream.
> Merrily, Merrily, Merrily, Merrily,
> Life is but a dream!

Use of a Walker

A popular piece of equipment that you may consider purchasing when your baby is around six to eight months old is a "walker." A walker is basically a sturdy frame with a seat in the center. The frame rests on wheels. When seated in a walker, a baby's legs should touch the ground. When she moves her feet, the walker will move, too. A walker takes advantage of a baby's natural desire to exercise her legs and investigate her home. While seated in the walker, she may be able to move all over your home and reach out to grab all kinds of objects, particularly as she approaches the age of six or seven months. Many babies really enjoy being placed in a walker, and some love this device so much that they protest being taken out of it.

A major disadvantage of a walker centers around the fact that if you allow your baby to use one, you will have to pay close attention to where she is and what she is doing as long as she is in it. The walker will give her access to areas and objects in your home that would otherwise not be available. Thus, her safety may be at risk unless you offer proper supervision. In addition, if you will be purchasing a walker, be sure to select one that is tip-proof, sturdy, and safe in all respects (see page 46).

Another possible disadvantage of a walker is that a baby may become overly dependent upon it. When a baby is permitted to use one for hours each day, she may come to rely upon it as a type of crutch. Without her walker, she may feel helpless and very frustrated. There is a possibility that rather than putting her efforts into learning to sit and move around on her own, she will come to rely upon this device to do the work for her.

You should weigh the advantages and disadvantages of allowing your infant to use a walker, based upon her unique needs and capabilities, before purchasing or borrowing one for her. Permitting her to use such a device will not necessarily foster early walking, although there are some parents who claim that their babies walked early as a result of using a walker.

299

The main thing to keep in mind if you decide to let your infant use a walker is to place her in it for short periods of time during the day, and to offer her close supervision during those times. Once she begins to acquire locomotion on her own, it is far better to encourage her to practice her locomotor skills than to permit her to rely upon her walker as a means of moving through your home.

KEEPING YOUR BABY HEALTHY

Immunization Reminder

Sometime around the sixth month, your child should receive a third DTP immunization. The TOPV immunization may also be given at this time, but this is optional, depending upon the incidence of polio in your area. Your doctor will determine if the third TOPV is needed.

Allergies to New Foods

As new foods are introduced into the baby's diet, there is a possibility she will develop an allergy to the new food. Infants with a strong family history of allergies are especially susceptible. The discussion of food allergies in infancy on pages 971–72 and how to introduce new foods carefully on pages 304–5 should be of value in helping to avoid the development of allergies in a sensitive infant.

HOW TO ENSURE YOUR BABY'S SAFETY

Greater Mobility Must Be Anticipated

Over the next six months your baby will become increasingly mobile. Her curiosity will also be rapidly growing, prompting a passion for exploring. She will want to maneuver her body into all the small spaces and areas of your home, and handle, throw, and investigate practically every object that she can possibly grab.

SHE HAS A DIFFERENT VIEW OF OBJECTS. The home area viewed from your baby's eyes is completely different from your perspective. You have no interest in or desire to empty wastebaskets, tug on the long cords that open and close the drapes, or drink the liquids from the bottles under your bathroom vanity. She does. You would not dream of pulling out and emptying all of the objects from the space under the kitchen sink or throwing a glass vase sitting on your living room end table. To her these objects and activities are especially inviting.

You are aware of what is "safe," but your infant is not. She has no awareness of the dangers of playing with knives, smelling glue, drinking cleaning fluids, eating pills or moth balls, or tugging on certain objects such as tablecloths, which could send china, silverware, hot liquids, and lighted candles down on her. Your baby has no idea that these objects are not safe for her to play with.

SHE CANNOT UNDERSTAND SAFETY RULES. Your baby's capacity for judgment is extremely limited. She does not perceive danger, or understand why particular objects must not be eaten or touched. One of the major ways in which she continues to learn is to manipulate objects and put them into her mouth. Anything that she manages to grab hold of or pick up, including tiny specks of dirt, razor blades that she finds in bathroom waste cans, garbage, pills accidentally left on a nightstand, nuts in the candy dish, soap flakes, and jacks or marbles from her brother's games (the list is endless) will be brought to her mouth for tasting and probably swallowing. She cannot discriminate between edible and inedible substances. The cigarette butts that are left lying around in ashtrays may look like candies to her, although when eaten they may cause a gastric upset.

Your attempts to instruct your baby not to touch or handle certain objects will not prevent her from playing with them. It is useful to begin telling her about objects in her surroundings, but throughout infancy you cannot expect her to understand your warnings fully or heed them. Thus, you must arrange her environment so that she can explore and develop safely.

Time for a New Car Seat?

Your baby may soon be outgrowing her infant car carrier. When she is more able to sit up and no longer easily fits into her infant auto seat, you should obtain a proper child car seat. This piece of equipment will allow you to continue to ensure her safety in the car.

Guidelines for obtaining a safe car seat are provided in the equipment section on pages 512–13. It is important to be sure that you fasten this seat to your car properly and use it whenever you take your child for a ride.

Providing a Safe Place to Develop and Learn

Your infant cannot understand danger and will not be able to take care of herself. You must provide her with a safe environment so that she can play and practice her new skills without being exposed to unnecessary dangers. Parents find that taking the time initially to plan for their baby's safety during this phase is well worth the effort.

The experiences and confidence that a child who has ample chances to explore and move in a safe home will build are invaluable in terms of her development in all areas. This is why professionals and educators in this field urge parents to create a safe home for their babies and toddlers. Having the ability to investigate her surroundings and to practice her new motor skills freely, she gains familiarity with ordinary objects around her and confidence in herself. She also finds outlets for her unbelievably strong curiosity.

It is really your living space inside your house, and outside in your yard, that you will have to safety-proof. Safety-proofing basically involves removing possible dangers and potential sources of accidents for a baby. For some of you this will be more difficult than for others. It all depends upon the arrangement of your home. The Safety Training Check Lists provided in previous sections and in Infancy 7 should serve as a guideline for some of the major safety considerations during this phase.

Safety-proofing your home for the mobile infant involves removing breakable and valuable objects and locking them up, taking down books and trinkets from low tables and bookshelves, covering low electrical outlets, padding sharp edges on low pieces of furniture, and other similar measures. It is helpful to view your home from your child's point of view (on the floor) and remove any potentially dangerous objects.

In many respects, this is asking a great deal from parents. You will have to change some of your living habits if you are the type of person who frequently leaves potentially dangerous objects such as medications or smoking or sewing equipment lying around during the daytime on tables, couches, or other easily accessible places. It will mean that each and every day you will have to make a concerted effort to clean up after each and every activity, and put potentially harmful objects and substances away in high up or locked cabinets.

In homes which are not designed to meet a baby's needs and are not safety-proofed, a parent must constantly hover and prevent the child from touching all of the breakable, sharp, and otherwise potentially dangerous items. The parent must also limit the baby's movements, lest she dirty the unprotected couch or bump her head on a sharp piece of furniture. This can be draining on the parent, and incredibly frustrating on a child who hears "no" and "don't" every time she moves or reaches for an interesting object. The child feels inhibited in satisfying her strong needs to handle and investigate. A parent cannot take his or her eyes off the child for even a couple of seconds, since the baby may have an accident or may break a treasured object.

The minimal sacrifices you have to make initially to safety-proof your home will be offset by the fact that you will not have to spend as much time worrying about your baby's safety and well-being. The time and energy that will be required in disciplining, warning, and punishing her will be kept to a minimum. The amount of effort you will save in terms of unnecessary anxiety, and the increased freedom that you and your baby will enjoy in your safe home, should outweigh the temporary inconvenience of safety-proofing your home.

Should You Safety-proof Your Entire Home?

There is no easy answer to this question. Some of you will want to safety-proof every room in your home. Having freedom and safety to move all over a house as she matures would seem best from a child's point of view. Nothing is likely to please your baby more and foster her over-all development than having ample opportunities to explore your home, and put her physical abilities to good use. Your infant, however, does not need to explore every room in your house, and will have more than enough to satisfy her curiosity in one or two safety-proofed rooms.

Some parents find safety-proofing their whole home too great a sacrifice. This is certainly understandable. For many, this is simply impractical, if not impossible, particularly if space is limited, or if you want to keep one or two rooms intact for entertaining purposes.

There is no need to feel guilty if you either cannot or do not want to safety-proof your entire home for your baby, as long as you safety-proof one or more rooms, such as her bedroom or playroom, or one area within your home so that in it she will be free to roam around. The kitchen and bathroom should also be safety-proofed, since she will necessarily be going into and out of these rooms. Other areas can then be made off-limits unless you are prepared to watch her. Lock doors to these rooms or place gates or barriers at their entrances so that there is no possibility of her crawling or, later, walking into them. Such a compromise should be satisfactory to both you and her.

Short Breaks from Constant Supervision

Parents find that it is not possible to watch their child all day long; they need some time off to relax or talk to a friend on the phone. To get a break from supervising their infants, many parents put them in a playpen. This is often a good tactic if used properly, and can be beneficial for both parent and child.

Try to maintain a stimulating environment for your child while she is awake. By providing appropriate toys and colorful decorations in the playpen, you can be sure that your baby will have plenty to keep her busy for short periods of time. It may even be useful for her to take a break from long range exploring to concentrating on more quiet play with toys.

Do not confine your baby in a playpen for long periods of time, since she will surely get bored and frustrated. Being confined there on a regular basis can put a damper on her curiosity and drive to learn. Using the playpen for short periods of time can be helpful for you, but do not abuse these kinds of restraining devices.

FEEDING

Breast- and Bottle-feeding

As you nurse, you may notice that your baby is placing her hands on the breast or bottle. She is making some effort to be more involved, even if only in a small way. You will want to encourage your bottle-fed infant to hold the bottle when she is ready. At this early stage you had better keep a firm grip on the bottle.

As babies begin to cut their first few teeth, they will want to practice using them. This can present some problems for mothers who are breast-feeding. It is usually painful for a mother when her baby bites on her nipple, and a natural response is to yell "no" or "stop that." This quick response is usually sufficient to get the message across to the baby that biting will not be tolerated, provided it is used consistently. An alternative approach is to discontinue the feeding session promptly as soon as any biting occurs. In some cases in which the baby persists in biting, weaning may be indicated.

Introducing Solid Foods

TIMING FOR ADDING SOLIDS. As we have seen, solid foods are not necessary before six months of age, from the point of view of the normal infant's growth and developmental requirements. Breast milk or formula supplemented with vitamins and iron is sufficient to satisfy the baby's nutritional requirements. According to the American Academy of Pediatrics, solid foods are not recommended until after the age of six months.

There is a certain built-in flexibility to take into account. Each baby has her own particular appetite and physical condition. The "right" time for solid foods to be introduced into a baby's diet is when the child is no longer satisfied with milk alone. This can vary from infant to infant. Any time after the sixth month that your baby shows signs of readiness is a good time to begin.

The decision to start adding solid food should always be made in conjunction with your doctor. Taking both your observations of your baby and a knowledge of her health into consideration, the doctor will advise you of dietary additions and alterations that are best suited to your infant.

ADDING SOLID FOODS ONE AT A TIME. Solids should be introduced one at a time with a period of time in between each addition. This is the most important point to keep in mind. Some babies have an allergic reaction to particular foods which may not show up until a few days or a week has passed. Allowing a week or so before the introduction of another new food enables easy identification of sensitivities which may occur. In cases in which a mixture of new foods is given and an allergic reaction occurs, it is much more difficult to determine which food is causing the difficulty. In addition to the problem of sensitivities toward certain foods, the introduction of a single (not mixed) food at a time will permit the mother to identify the infant's likes and dislikes.

A family history of not only egg allergy, but of any sort of allergic phenomena, including asthma, hives, hay fever, etc., should alert parents to starting various foods cautiously and slowly. There is no rush.

Some babies regularly vomit up a food to which they are sensitive. Others pass a lot of gas or develop a rash; the color and consistency of their stools may be noticeably altered. If a baby shows a sensitivity to a food, it should be stopped for a while and perhaps reintroduced later on. Sensitivities to foods generally diminish as a baby gets older.

Professional opinion varies as to the order in which solid foods should be introduced. There are those doctors who advise starting with cereal, those who advise starting with fruit, and those who advise starting with meat, etc. Your doctor will instruct you as to what the first food given should be, and what foods should follow.

SPOON-FEEDING SOLID FOODS. Parents who are first beginning to introduce solid foods sometimes wonder whether initially to put cereals and other solids into the bottles (with or without formula). This is both unnecessary and unadvisable. The nipple holes would need to be enlarged, and giving a baby food this way can lead to her gagging and choking. As soon as your baby is started on solids, introduce her to taking it by spoon.

When you begin, you can hold your baby on your lap so that she is in a nearly upright position, or feed her in an infant seat. Both of you should be comfortable. You can also put her in a high chair. Since this experience will be new to her, she may feel more secure being held close to you.

Experienced parents have recommended starting with a baby-sized spoon, or a demitasse (small coffee) spoon. Initially, your infant may push the food out as soon as you place it in her mouth because of the novelty of either the spoon, the food, or both, but within a short time she will get used to taking food from a spoon.

For both of you, spoon-feeding will be a new experience, so do not expect everything to work smoothly at first. You can expect spoon-feeding to be a bit awkward until you have had time to practice and master the technique. In the beginning, messes are inevitable. Have a washcloth handy, protect your baby's clothing with a bib, and protect your own as well.

The main objective is to make this new experience a positive one for your baby. This means allotting enough time so that you do not have to rush. It is helpful to talk and smile at her so that she will feel happier and more relaxed. Maintaining the social aspects in spoon-feeding is important. Also see that distractions are kept to a minimum.

HOW MUCH SOLID FOOD TO OFFER. There is no "right" amount to offer, since one infant's appetite and desire for solids may vary considerably from another's. It is usually best to start with solids in very small amounts, observing a baby's reactions, and then slowly increasing the quantity if the infant seems to enjoy it and wants more.

Mrs. Jefferson was anxious to have her son, Vernon, move to solid foods. The first occasion on which she introduced Vernon to cereal, she offered him a heaping teaspoonful at breakfast. He made a face in protest, and immediately spit it out, dirtying her clothes. This frustrated her. She shoveled in another heaping teaspoonful of cereal. Again Vernon spit it out. After several more unsuccessful attempts, Mrs. Jefferson ended the feeding session, angry and even more frustrated.

Around noontime she tried once more to have him take the cereal, using the same technique as before. Vernon not only repeatedly spit out whatever she offered, but screamed and thrashed about, pushing the spoon away with his hands to prevent it from being put into his mouth. The more Vernon protested, the harder Mrs. Jefferson tried to push him to eat. This set up an unfortunate pattern at mealtimes, marked by resentment from her as well as her baby.

When solids are introduced rapidly, and are given in large amounts from the start, babies are almost sure to reject them.

One or two baby-sized tastes, given at a time when your baby is hungry, might be enough for starters. Consider yourself lucky if your infant accepts this without putting up a fuss, spitting it out, or giving you the "evil eye." Try not to be too disappointed, annoyed, or discouraged if she spits back the food or protests. It may take a while before she gets used to the new feeding utensils and the new taste and consistency of the food.

Some babies take readily to solids and others act as though they would rather starve than eat them. Proceed at a slow pace and refrain from pressuring your baby to eat. After a few days of giving her only a spoonful or two, provided that she is a willing candidate, you can gradually increase the amount you offer according to how much she wants to eat.

In cases in which an infant rejects the solid food offered, you might postpone giving it for a couple of weeks and then reintroduce it very slowly, only once a day. Keep control of your emotions, and realize that there is no reason to try to push solid foods before your infant is willing to accept them.

Many babies take anywhere from one third to one half of a jar of baby food, although others will want more. It is your baby's responsibility to eat as much as she wants, and to let you know when she has had her fill.

AT WHAT FEEDING SHOULD YOU BEGIN? It probably makes little difference at what feeding you begin, as long as the timing is appropriate. Obviously, you would not want to offer solids if your baby is in a particularly bad mood, or is not the least bit hungry. Trying to find a time when she is most apt to be receptive to this new experience should not be too difficult. Some parents have found the first morning feeding to be appropriate, but babies may be most receptive to solids at completely different feedings.

Many parents find it best to introduce solids at midday to encourage the move to the "big" meal at lunch time. When cereal is the solid begun first, it can be moved to be associated with the morning bottle. Meat or fruit can be given around noontime, and cereal can be offered again with the late afternoon bottle, setting the pattern for three meals a day. For the next addition to the diet, parents often give a vegetable along with meat at lunch time.

Experienced parents suggest that when cereal is offered in the morning, it is a good idea to offer fruit juice as a mid-morning snack. If a 10 A.M. bottle is still required, the juice can tide a baby over until her bottle is ready. Again, you and your physician, together, can decide upon an appropriate time for the addition of solids into your baby's schedule depending upon her needs and preferences and your convenience.

MILK BEFORE SOLIDS OR SOLIDS BEFORE MILK? Physicians often hold varying opinions as to whether solids should be offered after the breast or bottle, or before them. Your doctor will probably state a preference. In some cases a baby becomes very indignant and refuses to eat even a bit of solids unless she has had her familiar breast or bottle first. Should this occur, it is best to respect your baby's preference.

Some breast-feeding mothers have found that offering solids first took away their baby's appetite for breast milk. Decreased sucking time also resulted in decreased milk production. If you are breast-feeding, keep this in mind. Many doctors and parents find that it is best to allow the infant to suck on the breast or bottle for a while until she pauses for air or seems to have taken all she wants, and then offer her the solid foods. This enables the baby to satisfy her sucking reflex. In the case of breast-feeding mothers, this approach usually enables them to maintain a good milk production cycle.

MAKING YOUR OWN BABY FOOD. The vast majority of supermarket chains carry a wide variety of baby foods in jars. These foods are carefully and specifically prepared so that they are appropriate for babies. Many parents swear by them since they come in ready-to-eat forms, do not require refrigeration, and are terrific time-savers. In most food stores you can also find precooked cereals with directions for how to mix them to an appropriate consistency for an infant.

Some parents, however, prefer to make their own baby food. Making your own food is certainly more economical and not all that difficult, although it does take a bit more time and thought. Other advantages are that parents can provide their babies with fresh and highly nutritious foods and a greater variety of foods. Parents who prepare their own baby food often derive great satisfaction from knowing that they are helping to ensure their children's proper nutrition and growth. Today's parents are more concerned about the possible effects of food additives and colorings on their children (see the discussion of possible effects of food additives on the child). By preparing their own baby foods, parents have more control over the types of foods and food additives that their children will be eating.

There are several principles regarding food preparation that you should be familiar with whether or not you plan to make all or part of your baby's foods. The following information can serve as a general guideline.

Equipment for Feeding Your Baby. It is not necessary for you to purchase expensive equipment in order to feed your baby solid foods. You probably already have on hand many of the essential items, with the exception of a high chair or a low chair with a feeding tray. You will need the following items:

a small-sized spoon
bibs
unbreakable cup
unbreakable dish/bowl
a feeding chair

More specific information on spoons, cups, and feeding chairs is provided throughout this section. Some parents wonder whether or not they will need a specific feeding dish for their baby. This is not really necessary, since any small unbreakable dish can be used. There are special baby feeding dishes available in a variety of styles. Some have a compartment on the bottom that can be filled with hot or cold water to help keep the food at the desired temperature. There are also triple compartment electric warming dishes. Some parents receive these as gifts, and find them useful. However, they are rather expensive.

It is important to understand that if you plan to use a warming dish, you should warm the food immediately before feeding your child. Bacteria can multiply rapidly in warm temperatures, so make sure that food is not left in the dish for long periods of time, and only warm as much food as you feel your child will eat at a given meal. Foods that you eat cold can be served to your baby.

The Consistency and Taste of the Solids. Obviously, since your baby has few (or no) teeth with which to chew, careful attention must be given to the texture of the foods she is offered so that she does not choke and can easily digest them. This is the reasoning behind offering a baby at this phase only strained or puréed solids.

Some parents have found initially that mixing a little formula, milk, evaporated milk, fruit juice, vegetable juice, or even water with a food makes it more acceptable to babies, and easier to swallow. If you are using precooked cereal, for example, you could add a little more milk than the instructions on the box suggest. Adding formula or milk to the solids may make the "strange" substances seem more acceptable.

When preparing your own baby food you may find that a purée is too thin and watery. In this case you will want to add something to thicken it. A few of the nutritious thickeners include powdered non-fat dry milk, ground wheat germ, hard-boiled egg yolk, and cooked whole grain rice cereal. Before adding any thickener, be sure that your baby's doctor has already had you introduce this food into her diet with no resulting allergy.

Keep in mind when preparing food that babies tend naturally to dislike very strong-flavored, bitter, highly salted, and sour foods. Recently, the food companies have taken out all additives, including salt and sugar, from their jarred baby foods. These additions had originally been introduced to please the parents' palate, not the baby's. It has been found that such additives are not healthy. When preparing your own baby food, remember that your baby will do best on very bland foods, so do not expect always to like the taste of the dishes that you prepare for her.

Preparation Equipment. The kind of kitchen equipment that you use in preparing your baby's meals will largely depend upon how much time and effort you want to put forth, and whether or not you can afford to purchase special equipment to make food preparation more convenient. In considering whether an item that you do not have on hand is worth buying, think about its usefulness for preparing food for other members of your family, not just your baby.

For a limited period of time, you will be offering your infant finely puréed foods. Gradually, when your baby shows her readiness, you will begin offering coarser purées, finely diced foods, finger foods, and then table foods. Before many of the modern cooking appliances and conveniences were available, parents managed very well with only knives, forks, spoons, and strainers in preparing baby foods. These can still be used, although using these tools alone is time-consuming and taxing.

Food mills or baby food grinders are fairly inexpensive, and make puréeing many cooked foods or soft raw fruits less of a chore. An electric blender is an invaluable aid to parents. If you can afford to buy one or borrow one for several months, you will find that baby food processing can be quick and easy. Foods can be prepared in either small or large quantities, and you can vary their consistency by pressing a button.

Food processors are more expensive than blenders, but they have virtually revolutionized the processing and preparation of both raw and cooked foods. They are incredibly fast and convenient to use. In addition to other advantages, larger quantities and varieties of food can be processed at one time, and they allow for greater control over the consistency.

Many parents feel that having either a blender or food processor in the home is extremely convenient for preparing baby foods as well as foods for the whole family. They also feel that the money they saved in preparing their own baby food outweighs the initial expense of the specialized equipment.

There are several other relatively inexpensive items that should also come in handy. Most of them you probably already own. A paring knife or vegetable peeler (with a slot in the center of the blade) is useful for removing the skins or the outer layer of fruits and vegetables. For cleaning vegetables and fruits, a stiff brush works very well. A juicer will help in obtaining fresh citrus fruit juices. Manual juicers are inexpensive, and should suffice. Electric juicers and juice extractors are quite costly and not necessary items. Those of you who do not have an electric blender may want to buy an egg beater for making a variety of egg or fruit drinks. A good, sharp chopping knife is a must.

Cooking Equipment and Methods. To cook your baby's food, you can, with some alterations, use the same methods you use to cook for yourself. Bear in mind, however, that some cooking methods preserve important minerals and vitamins more than others. When vegetables, for instance, are boiled in water, many of the vitamins and minerals will wash out into the cooking water. Cooking with high heat, chopping foods into small cubes before cooking, and cooking foods for prolonged periods of time should be avoided whenever possible, since these methods also destroy many of the nutrients in foods. Nutritionists usually recommend steaming as the method of choice for preserving the nutrients and helping foods maintain their natural color and taste.

Parents who do a lot of steaming often recommend purchasing a steamer/blancher for this. Instead of buying a special steamer, you can purchase an inexpensive item called a steam basket. It is adaptable to most pots, and allows an ordinary pot with a tight-fitting lid to be used as a steamer. Some parents have found that a small colander put inside a pot also works well. A pressure cooker will steam foods much faster than an ordinary steamer pot, but this piece of equipment is not necessary. An electric crock pot can also be useful, but again, this is a luxury item for those who can afford it.

Aluminum foil, see-through roasting bags, and baking dishes with lids make it easy to cook foods in the oven. Baking foods slowly at a 325° F oven temperature in covered ovenproof containers will help to preserve nutrients and soften foods so that puréeing them is easier. It is best not to add water, so that the foods can cook in their own juices.

Handling Foods and Storing Them. Whenever you handle foods, make sure that your hands and fingernails are clean. Although it is unnecessary to sterilize utensils and cooking equipment, they should always be thoroughly cleaned prior to their use. Food grinders, blender and cutting blades, strainers, and cutting boards tend to collect bits of food, so pay special attention to these items. Wash all tops of cans before opening them.

If foods are not properly stored, potentially harmful bacteria can rapidly grow to levels that can jeopardize your baby's health. In many instances it is possible to detect foods that have spoiled. They frequently have foul or unusual odors, areas of mold growing on them, rancid flavors or unusual tastes, or slimy coverings on poultry or meats. If you observe any of these signs of spoilage, throw out the food immediately.

Foods that can be stored in your kitchen cabinets, pantry, or basement should be tightly covered and kept dry. This will keep them as fresh as possible. Vegetables should be stored uncovered. Although you may want to stock up on cereals, for instance, that you find on sale, it is not a good idea to go overboard. The longer the item sits on your shelf, the more likely you are to forget about it, and the more likely it is to lose its freshness. Pay close attention to dates on packages, boxes, and cans, and perishable items. If an item is marked that it is best if used before a given date, be sure to heed the markings.

All of the foods that you have cooked as well as perishable items and many fresh foods need to be stored in your refrigerator. With the exception of tomatoes and fruit, the foods should be properly wrapped, covered, or placed in airtight containers. Guard against saving small amounts of leftover food in non-see-through containers or wrappers and then forgetting that they are there. Cooked foods that have been puréed for your baby and then refrigerated can spoil very easily. Plan to use them within a twenty-four- to forty-eight-hour period from when you prepared them or else discard them. If you have any doubts about the length of time that a certain food has been in the refrigerator, do not take a chance on offering it to your baby. It is a wise general rule to make a habit of checking for possible spoilage of a food item before giving it to your baby.

Many of you will probably be offering your baby some foods that you have prepared yourself, and some baby foods that you purchased in jars. Most infants will not be eating an entire baby food jar of vegetables, fruits, or meats. In order to prevent foods from spoiling, and for general health reasons, it is advisable to transfer a small portion to a bowl, and put the tightly covered jar into the refrigerator. The food in the jar should not spoil under refrigeration for a couple of days. Do not put the leftovers from the bowl back into the jar. The spoon which has been in your baby's mouth has, of course, touched the food remaining in the feeding dish. Later, when your baby is capable of polishing off a whole jar of baby food, you can feed her directly from the jar.

A freezer is a good place to store cooked or raw foods that you have prepared for your baby. By preparing large amounts of baby food from foods that were sale or seasonal fruits and vegetables, you can save money as well as valuable time and effort. Leftovers from the family lunch or dinner can be processed for your baby and then conveniently placed in the freezer. Even though it is possible to store some foods for several months to a year, it is advisable to plan on frozen baby food being used within one month's time. You may want to obtain a special chart that lists various foods and the recommended freezing storage times.

It is extremely important not to refreeze baby food made from foods that have previously been cooked, frozen, and then thawed. In order to maintain a food's moisture and quality, be sure that it is wrapped in airtight containers, heavy-duty aluminum wrappers, plastic sealed storage bags, or other appropriate freezer wraps.

According to many experienced parents, an excellent way to store puréed baby food in the freezer is to pour it into plastic ice cube trays, wrap the trays, and freeze them. Large quantities of vegetables, meats, etc., can be prepared, frozen in the trays, and then transferred to large clear plastic storage bags. Labeling and dating the bags is a good idea. At feeding time you can remove as many "food" cubes as you feel your baby will want, and heat them or let them thaw at room temperature. This is a convenient method of storage that takes up relatively little freezer space.

OFFERING WELL-BALANCED MEALS. A very important aspect of feeding your baby is to offer her a selection of nutritious foods from the four basic food groups:

> meats and other protein foods
> fruits/vegetables
> cereal/grains
> milk/dairy products

If you offer her a variety of foods from these groups in serving portions sufficient to satisfy her food requirements, her diet will eventually become balanced. The essential nutrients in foods that are necessary for growth include vitamins, minerals, fats, carbohydrates, and protein.

Once your baby is eating foods from each food group, then you can plan a well-balanced daily menu using the following as a guide. Breakfast would include cereal, fruit, and an egg. For lunch you would offer a food high in protein, vegetable, and fruit. A typical dinner would include cereal/protein, vegetable, and fruit. Foods from these categories can actually be served at any time each day, but are presented in this manner for your convenience. This daily menu guide assumes that a baby will also be drinking about three to four cups of milk/formula/breast milk or taking other dairy products as milk substitutes. In addition, your doctor may prescribe vitamin supplements to be given each day.

FRUIT JUICE. Some babies occasionally want something more substantial than water between meals, and fruit juice makes a good between-meal snack. Often it is initially diluted with extra water, at least for the first several days. After this, assuming a baby likes it, the concentration can be gradually brought up to full strength. Strained fruit juices for babies can be purchased in cans and transferred to sterilized or thoroughly cleaned bottles. Some juices are available in presterilized throw-away bottles. After a couple of months, juices can be poured into a clean cup and offered to a baby a small sip at a time, in order to accustom her to drinking from a cup.

Many babies take a liking to apple juice for starters, although there are many fruit juices from which to choose. Unless your doctor advises you otherwise, steer away from giving orange juice in the beginning, since it is not uncommon for young infants to have an allergic reaction to it as well as all other citrus juices.

CEREALS. In your supermarket you will probably find a variety of precooked cereals for babies from which to choose. All that is required in their preparation is to mix them with milk or formula. Provided your doctor leaves the selection up to you, it is advisable to start with a single grain cereal, such as rice or corn, which many babies readily accept. Steer away from wheat, since babies tend to develop sensitivities to this cereal more than others. Mixtures of cereals should gradually be introduced after your baby does well with the individual grain cereals used in a particular mixture. Many precooked cereals are enriched with thiamine and iron, both valuable nutrients and important additions to a baby's diet.

VEGETABLES. Vegetables that are either fresh or frozen can be well cooked, and then puréed. Fresh vegetables are the best choice from a nutritional point of view. Canned vegetables that have been puréed or strained are also fine to offer.

A wide selection of vegetables is available in baby food jars in ready-to-eat forms, for those who are not preparing them at home. Some of the more strongly flavored vegetables, such as onions or spinach, may not be readily accepted. More mild-flavored vegetables are usually enjoyed by babies. Corn tends to be difficult for babies to digest, so you might want to hold off on corn until your baby is older, and her digestive system is more mature.

Many parents have become unduly alarmed after seeing their baby's stools or urine after she has eaten beets. It is not uncommon for a young baby's urine to be reddish-colored after eating beets. Some small pieces of beets that have not been fully digested can also get mixed in with her stools, giving them the appearance of being spotted with red blood. This is obviously not indicative of any problem. If you notice red pieces of beets or any small pieces of vegetables in your baby's stools, you will know that there is no reason for undue concern. Watch closely for other changes, however, including marked changes in bowel movements, rashes, or chapping, and discontinue offering a particular vegetable for a while if these symptoms develop.

MEATS. Finely ground plain meats provide important minerals and vitamins, and are an excellent source of protein for a baby. You can prepare your own meats, or purchase specially prepared meats that are available in ready-to-serve forms in grocery stores.

Plain meats are more bothersome to prepare. Raw beef can be scraped with a knife or processed and then placed in a small metal container which is put inside of a saucepan of boiling water, and cooked until the redness is gone. You can also broil, boil, or bake meat and put it into a baby food grinder or food processor. Again, some babies have an easier time swallowing meat when it is slightly watered down with a small amount of milk. Be sure to trim off the fat, and avoid giving your baby fatty meats. Although meats used to be among the last foods introduced into a baby's diet, some doctors now add them in the beginning, or as a second food.

EGGS. Many babies are sensitive to eggs until they are around five to eight months old, so you may want to hold off on eggs. Then start off with only the yolk, since the egg white often gives a baby the most difficulty. Mash the yolk well, and add a little milk if it seems too sticky or thick. Egg yolks are another excellent source of protein and iron. Prepared egg yolks in ready-to-serve forms are also available in jars. When there is a family history of allergy to eggs, they may be avoided altogether until a baby is about a year old.

FRUITS. Most babies like the taste of fruits, and may accept fruits more easily than cereals or other foods in the beginning. That is why many doctors recommend offering fruits as a first solid food. There are numerous varieties of plain, ready-to-eat fruits that are available, so you should not have any difficulty finding one or more that your baby enjoys. Begin with the plain fruits, one at a time, before progressing to mixed fruits. If your baby really likes fruits, feel free to offer them more than once each day. Some fruits can be either mildly constipating or can act as a laxative, so if your baby has elimination difficulties, try to discontinue giving the fruit in question or cut back on the amount that you offer. Usually, but not always, constipating fruits include pears, bananas, and apples. Fruits that usually have a laxative effect include plums, prunes, apricots, dates, peaches, and figs. Hold off offering strawberries until she is older, since many young babies are allergic to them.

If the doctor gives you the "green light" to start fruits, then you can take the fresh or frozen fruits you have in the house, steam or stew them, and strain, grind, or purée them finely. Fresh, very ripe bananas can be offered without having to cook them if they are mashed to achieve a smooth consistency. Mixing in a little formula should help a baby to swallow it. When offering canned pineapple, peaches, pears, or some other fruit, it is advisable to purchase the unsweetened varieties, drain off the liquid, and then process the food to the desired consistency.

WHAT IF YOUR BABY REFUSES SOLID FOODS? It is not uncommon for parents to find that their infant has initial difficulty taking solid foods. This is a new experience for the baby, and may take some getting used to. Some babies relish solid foods after several days of getting used to them, and others may protest or resist eating them even after a week or two of their parents' persistent offers and encouragement. The process of adding solid foods is gradual, and there is a great deal of variation among children in regard to their tolerance of solids when first introduced.

Some infants put up a great deal of resistance to taking solid foods for several weeks to a month or more. This often causes concern for their parents. They worry whether their child will get enough nourishment from the formula or breast milk alone to supply her growing nutritional needs.

It is important to recognize that your infant can continue to receive sufficient nourishment from formula or breast milk well beyond six months of age, but the child's requirements for iron and a few other minerals and vitamins may not be supplied by this form of feeding. This does not pose any significant problem. Your doctor will enrich this liquid diet with the necessary iron and vitamin supplements.

For those parents whose babies take longer to accept solid foods, there is no need to be concerned. The child will do very well on the supplemented liquid diet until she is ready to expand her diet to include solid foods. It is best to refrain from becoming annoyed or angry and pressuring her to eat solid foods against her will. By taking a casual, gradual approach, your baby is more likely to accept the transition to solids when she is ready.

RESPECTING YOUR BABY'S PREFERENCES FOR CERTAIN FOODS. Some babies, even during this month, take a liking to certain foods and show a dislike for others. One baby loves apples but refuses to take pears. Another may enjoy eating peas and carrots, but protests against green beans and broccoli. Often when a baby does not like a particular food she will spit it right out of her mouth, turn her head, or keep squirming so that it is impossible to feed her.

Provided your baby's likes and dislikes become clear to you, it is advisable to go along with her wishes. There is no one particular food that is crucial for her to eat in order for her to remain healthy. There is such a wide selection of foods within the meat, cereal, fruit, and vegetable categories, that you can certainly find at least some foods that appeal to her individual tastes. It is not worth getting into arguments over foods that she does not like at this stage.

Introducing the High Chair

Holding an active little child on your lap while you try to spoon in solid foods successfully can be quite a challenge. Some parents are able to continue with this position, but many of you will find it much easier to spoon-feed when your baby is sitting in a chair of her own, either a high chair or a low table and attached chair combination.

There are three important rules of safety to remember when using a high chair. First, it should only be used when your infant can support her back well enough to sit up in it. Second, you should use a sturdy high chair with a broad leg span so that it cannot be easily tipped by your baby. A third safety precaution is always to harness your infant in the high chair to prevent her from standing and from slipping under the tray and falling.

Some of you will prefer the lower table and chair. This is safer in some respects, because there is less chance of a baby's falling or tipping it over than with a high chair. As long as adequate safety precautions can be taken with a high chair, many parents prefer using one, since it can be conveniently pushed near the regular kitchen or dining room table so that baby can join in at mealtimes.

Introducing the Cup

Infancy 6 or 7 is a good time to introduce your baby to drinking from a cup. Any small, unbreakable drinking glass or cup will do. Some babies find it easier to use cups with handles. Experienced parents often suggest purchasing a cup specially designed for babies who are learning to use a cup and are likely to have many accidental spills. These cups come with a lid to prevent liquid from spilling, and have a spout that fits into the infant's mouth. Once the baby becomes more proficient at drinking from the cup, the lid and spout are removed.

Parents often begin offering very small amounts of juice or even milk in the cup. Do not be surprised if your baby objects to the cup and refuses to let you help her drink from it. It takes infants time to get accustomed to using a cup, so introduce it slowly, and do not rush. It is not uncommon for a baby to take fruit juice or water from a cup willingly, but not milk. Again, avoid pressuring her to drink milk from it against her will.

Sometimes babies do better with a cup when they have had numerous opportunities to play with it before any liquid is poured inside. While you are spoon-feeding your infant, it may be a good idea to allow her to hold a cup. This will not only be enjoyable for her, but should keep her hands occupied, making your job easier.

In a casual way, you can start to show her how to hold the cup and position her mouth on it. Let her practice without liquid first. Then, try pouring in less than an ounce of liquid, and offer her a single sip at a time. She may prefer to hold the cup herself. Unless you are using a spill- or tip-proof cup, you should control it, although you can let her keep both hands on it. More liquid can be added according to how much your baby is willing to take.

Whether or not you use a spill-proof cup, she will eventually have to or demand to manage it by herself. Placing an old shower curtain under her feeding chair will protect your floors and make cleaning up her inevitable messes much simpler and easier. Give her as much independence as she wants and can handle. Cup-feeding during this phase can be very messy, but with added time and practice your baby's ability to drink from it will improve. In the event that she strongly protests against drinking out of a cup, forget about using it for a few weeks and then gradually reintroduce it again, perhaps only once a day.

THE BABY'S TEETH AND TEETHING

The Age at Which Babies Cut Their First Teeth Varies

Eruption of teeth in babies usually begins around this age. This can vary widely from child to child, and some babies will not have any teeth until they are a year old or older. It is difficult to predict at what age a baby's first tooth will appear. In some cases the timing or appearance of teeth seems to follow a hereditary pattern.

Early, average, or late appearance of teeth in a healthy baby is generally believed to have nothing to do with whether a baby is developing well. Some parents mistakenly believe that the earlier the eruption of teeth, the brighter the child will be. You cannot assume that your baby is of superior intellect simply because she teethes early, at three months of age. Likewise, you cannot assume that your baby is slow or behind intellectually if her first tooth appears when she is fourteen months old. There is wide variation in the age at which teeth break through the gums. You need not become overly concerned if your baby does not cut her first tooth during the first year, or even later.

After cutting their first tooth, some babies cut on the average of one tooth during each successive month, until they have a full set of twenty teeth, generally established by the time they are between two and three years old. This is not the case with all children. Again, the rate of cutting teeth and the age at which a full set is acquired varies from child to child.

When a baby has ten teeth in each of her jaws, her first set will be complete. This first set of teeth is often referred to by different names such as the "baby," "primary," "deciduous," or "milk" teeth. This primary set will remain until approximately the age of six, around which time they will fall out and be replaced by a new set of sixteen teeth in each of her jaws. The second set of thirty-two teeth is often called the "secondary" or "permanent" teeth, which will hopefully remain intact for the rest of her life.

The Order of Tooth Eruption Can Also Vary

There appears to be somewhat less variation in the order of tooth eruption, but this too can vary from one individual to the next. With many babies, their two lower incisors appear first, followed by four upper incisors. These six teeth are often cut by the age of a year. After some lapse in time, perhaps a few months, six additional teeth may erupt. First two more lower incisors, and the four first molars may appear. The molars are not situated directly adjacent to the incisors. There is usually a space between them for the sharp, pointed teeth, commonly referred to as the canines or "dog" teeth. These teeth generally erupt after a lapse of a few more months. Following the four canines, a baby generally cuts four more molars. These teeth are called the second molars, the last of which appears around two and a half years of age.

Babies React Differently to Teething

Babies' reactions to teething also can vary. Some babies tend to salivate more while teething, causing them to drool or cough more to clear the excess saliva from their throats. Occasional loose bowel movements may be observed. Some parents claim that their infants always had a run of watery, frequent stools when they were teething. They may experience some discomfort if their gums are sore, tender, or swollen. Frequently when a tooth begins to pierce a baby's gums, a moderate amount of swelling and redness on the area of gum around the tooth can be noticed. This may cause a baby a certain amount of discomfort. With some babies there are no noticeable signs of redness or swelling. Sometimes a baby appears grouchy, has difficulty sleeping through the night, or shows a slight loss of appetite. She may also find it uncomfortable to suck on the breast or bottle as was discussed on page 256.

A baby may experience all of the above, a few of these difficulties, or none at all. If these behavioral changes do appear, they may be observed anywhere from a few months prior to the actual eruption of a tooth, to a couple of days before it erupts. In general, babies tend to be slightly more affected around the time that their first few teeth erupt, than when later teeth break through their gums.

Some of the behavioral changes that can accompany teething also look like signs of illness. Teething is not related to a disease process. Fevers, severe loss of appetite, vomiting, and other signs of illness should not simply be attributed to teething. The child with a fever of 101° or more should be checked for something other than teething. Fever is not associated with normal teething, and should be considered a sign of illness, although minimal elevations are often found. The main point to remember is not to neglect an illness because you attribute your baby's change in behavior to teething. If your baby has any problems or develops any symptoms that you suspect are signs of illness, discuss this with your doctor.

Helping the Baby Who Experiences Discomfort from Teething

For most babies, teething causes discomfort. When they are uncomfortable or in pain, babies become cranky, fussy, or irritable. You will have to be patient and understanding if such is the case with your baby. Should you notice that she is having difficulty with excess saliva, having trouble sleeping, or that her gums are irritated, there are several things you can do to try to make her life more satisfactory. These measures are described in the material that follows, and may help temporarily to decrease her irritability.

IF YOUR BABY LOSES HER APPETITE. Some babies show a slight loss of appetite while teething. There is nothing to worry about if your baby loses her appetite for a few days. Continue to offer her regular amounts of food. When she is hungry, she will eat. There is no need to coax her to eat if she is not hungry. Be patient, and reread the material on pages 256–57 in the Feeding section.

IF YOUR BABY DROOLS A LOT OR IS TROUBLED BY INCREASED SALIVA. When a baby sleeps on her stomach and drools a lot, her sheets may become soaking wet. In situations in which her face is in prolonged, frequent contact with a wet sheet, a face rash may develop. Change her sheet as often as is necessary, or to save work, place a diaper on the sheet. Make sure it is tucked securely under the mattress and change it at regular intervals. If your baby sleeps on her back, increased saliva may collect in her throat and cause her to cough during the night. Raising the head half of the mattress may help. Drooling during the daytime is fairly common. You can help her cope with this by keeping a box of tissues handy and wiping her face at frequent intervals.

Excess saliva that collects in your baby's stomach during the night may need to be brought up before she takes any food for breakfast. When you offer her breakfast before she has had an opportunity to spit up the saliva, she may refuse to eat or eat and then bring up her breakfast along with the saliva. Give her a little water or juice upon waking, rather than solids. Let her bring up the saliva with these fluids. Later, once the saliva has been cleared out of her system, she will probably be able to hold down her breakfast.

IF YOUR BABY'S GUMS ARE UNCOMFORTABLE OR SORE. Should your infant's gums become sore while she is teething, gentle pressure on them may help alleviate the discomfort. Pressure on a baby's gums seems to make them less painful. This is why babies who are teething frequently like to bite down, chew, or gnaw at their fingers, or any other objects that they can get their mouths on, including furniture, window sills, and brittle plastic toys. For her safety, you should offer her only appropriate objects such as teething biscuits, plastic unbreakable toys, or rubber teething rings. Chilled raw vegetable sticks can be given before any teeth erupt. Feel free to massage her gums gently with your clean fingers, if this helps her.

It is not advisable to give any medications by mouth, or to apply any medications to her gums without the doctor's prior advice. Your doctor may recommend medications that can alleviate some of the pain, if this is indicated. Never pierce or cut into the swollen gums. This does not help the tooth erupt and can lead to infection and other complications. If you become frustrated in handling your teething child, talk to your doctor about your concerns.

IF YOUR BABY AWAKENS DURING THE NIGHT. Should your baby feel uncomfortable during the night, she may awaken and cry. This may stem from the fact that she is teething. You can hold off going into her room in the hopes that she will settle down after a short period of time and go back to sleep. When crying persists, you can go to her and try to comfort and reassure her. After her teeth have appeared, you should discontinue whatever middle-of-the-night routine was established while she was teething. Otherwise, she may continue waking during the night just to have your companionship and attention. Neither of you will get the rest that you need if this pattern is allowed to develop.

Tooth-grinding

Occasional tooth-grinding may occur as a baby acquires teeth. This is normal. When a baby is tense or anxious about something, she may also grind her teeth as a way of reducing tensions or frustrations. Most babies outgrow this behavior after a while, and it is not something that should cause you undue worry.

Care of Your Baby's Teeth

Once your baby's teeth erupt, you should try to help her keep them clean and as free from decay as possible. It is advisable to discuss the care of your infant's teeth with your dentist. The dentist can recommend simple measures for early tooth care. Usually all that is necessary is occasionally to offer a little water after meals to rinse the teeth and avoid foods that promote tooth decay. Be sure that your child is receiving fluoride as a dietary supplement or in drinking water since this will help protect her teeth from decay (see page 137).

Many dentists like to see children twice a year after their primary set of teeth has come in. It is advisable for you to ask your dentist when your child should have her first visit. Dentists often suggest a first visit when a child is between two and three years of age. Further discussion of care of the teeth is provided on pages 503–4.

BATHING

Your baby will continue to be quite energetic and active during her baths. She will probably delight in playing with her toys or kicking and splashing water everywhere. If you have followed a set procedure in bathing her, she may anticipate some of your actions as you prepare her for a bath and when you actually bathe her.

Mr. Hawley reported that as soon as his son, Zachary, was lowered into the tub, he leaned forward to grab the washcloth and soap. One day when the washcloth and soap were not in their usual spots on the rim of the bathtub, he looked disturbed and searched all over the bathroom with his eyes in an effort to locate them. Several weeks later, Mr. Hawley noticed that as soon as he mentioned the word "bath" to his son, and carried Zachary into the bathroom, he would begin to smile, giggle, and yank at his diapers in an obvious attempt to remove them.

There is a strong possibility that you will see evidence that your baby anticipates her clothes being removed when you say the word "bath." She may also indicate an awareness of each step in the bath routine through her actions and reactions.

This is a phase during which to be sure to keep your baby's fingernails trimmed and clean. Along with toys and objects, her fingers will regularly be put into her mouth. The same goes for her toenails.

CLOTHING

You will notice some changes in your baby's behavior while you are dressing her. She may play around with some articles of clothing, especially her socks or booties, and even manage to yank them off. At certain times, it may seem as if she anticipates some of your actions in dressing or diapering her, an indication of her improving memory. Over the next several months, she will become more actively involved in the dressing routine.

Provided your baby moves about quite a bit in her crib, you may find it helpful to put her in a garment with legs and attached feet at night, rather than worry that she will crawl out from under the covers or kick them off. Sleeping "bags" or outfits shaped like a sack are also suitable, although a crawling baby will find them too confining.

Now that your infant is older and much more active, and will be playing for longer periods of time each day on the floor in a playpen or outside, you may want to dress her in outfits other than stretchsuits or pajamas. Many mothers purchase durable, washable playsuits or overalls that have snaps around the crotch and legs to allow easier diaper changing. Corduroy and denim are fabrics that are sturdy and require minimal care. Sunsuits and sleeveless T-shirts plus her diaper will be appropriate for play outside in warm weather, although when it is hot, a diaper alone should be appropriate. In cooler weather, T-shirts, overalls, socks and perhaps sweaters will keep her a little warmer.

As she becomes more active, it is important to check her clothing size and the way her outfits fit frequently. They should not fit too snugly, since she needs to be able to move around freely, especially her arms and legs.

Some parents, particularly those who are impatient or overly concerned about their baby's progress in motor development, have already purchased a pair of shoes for their baby in the hopes that she will "need" them soon. It is too early at this time to concern yourself with shoes. Should you be intent on buying shoes at this early age, before your child is walking, keep in mind that the only reason for buying them is to protect her feet. Any lightweight shoes with soft, flexible soles that are not too small or too large will serve this purpose. Actually, if floors are suitable and safe, many parents let their children go barefoot indoors until late in toddlerhood. More information about shoes is provided on pages 443–45.

SLEEPING

Around this time you may have some trouble getting your baby to sleep at night. She may prefer to move around in her crib actively, perhaps sitting up, rolling over, or squirming about on her abdomen. Your difficulty in getting her to lie down and go to sleep may be due partly to the fact that she is dying to practice her new motor skills and be on the move. It may also be due to the fact that she enjoys being around you and other family members and dislikes not having any company at bedtime.

Rather than setting the precedent for future problems at night by allowing her to stay up past her regular bedtime or permitting her to sleep in your bedroom, it is advisable to be understanding, but nevertheless firm. You can tell her that you know that she would rather not go to bed, but that you must insist upon it. Leave her room after your good-nights and kisses, even if she is not lying down, ready for sleep. Chances are that after she has tired herself out from all of her activities, or from crying, she will lie down and fall asleep. Dress her in an appropriately warm sleeping garment, so you will not have to worry about covers. The other alternative is to tiptoe into her room once you are certain that she is asleep and cover her.

Waking during the middle of the night is a rather common problem between Infancy 5 and 8. Some babies who get up during the night are resourceful enough to play, move, or "talk" for a while, and then quiet themselves so that they can get back to sleep. Others get themselves so wound up that they cannot seem to settle back down to sleep and, thus, cry for their parents. Still others simply wake because they feel lonely and want their parents' company and attention. Handling middle-of-the-night waking was previously discussed on pages 238–39. Bear in mind that by being oversolicitous in regard to night waking, you may encourage your baby to continue with this pattern.

Infancy 6 babies usually take two naps a day. Parents often try to keep both naps going, even if their babies do not actually fall asleep but play quietly in their cribs. This gives them a much needed and appreciated "breather" during the day. In order to have your baby continue taking two naps, be firm about putting her in her crib at her regular naptime, and then go about your own activities. She may fuss and never actually sleep, but most babies learn to play on their own provided their parents don't give in and take them out of their crib before naptime is over. In the event that your baby is quite active, and seems to need less sleep during the daytime, you may decide to let her give up one nap, assuming that she does not look too tired during the day, and you don't find this too inconvenient.

PATTERNS OF ELIMINATION

Your infant's pattern of elimination has become well established over the past several months, and you will be very familiar with her own particular habits. Many parents will begin to introduce solid foods during Infancy 6 and this may cause some minor changes in the infant's regular pattern of elimination.

Solid Foods May Cause Changes

Possible changes in a baby's stools resulting from the addition of new vegetables and other solid foods to her diet are described on pages 304 and 312. Once a bottle-fed baby is no longer taking formula, or the sugar in her formula is removed, she may initially become constipated, since sugar has a mild laxative effect. Your child's physician will advise you about what measures to take to alleviate this condition if it should develop. Changes in your baby's bowel movements clearly reflect changes in her diet. It may take a little time for her digestive system to become used to these minor dietary changes, but with some patience you should not have any problems in expanding her diet.

Early Attempts to Condition a Baby to Use the Toilet

Developing toilet habits is a task that is usually accomplished when a child is around the age of two, although the age at which a child learns to use a toilet can vary. Some of you have probably heard stories about babies who have been fully trained between the ages of about six months and a year, and may be wondering about the advisability of initiating training efforts during the second half of the first year.

WHAT DOES EARLY TRAINING INVOLVE? There are some babies who will begin to defecate and possibly urinate at very regular and fairly predictable times each day over the next six months. Some parents try to take advantage of this predictability in attempting to "toilet train" their infant. Early training efforts involve placing the baby who is capable of sitting up on a toilet or potty chair a minute or two before she normally "makes," allowing her stools or urine to be deposited in the toilet bowl. Some parents can also tell that their baby is about to defecate by her facial expression, fussing, facial coloring, or special sounds. When they see such signs, they quickly place her on the potty.

Training efforts at this early stage do not involve teaching a baby to learn the procedure or steps involved in this task. She does not have control over her organs of elimination and is not intellectually capable of remembering the steps involved in learning toilet habits. Although a baby may become "conditioned" to defecate soon after she is placed on the potty, just as she can become "conditioned" to wait for a period of time before breakfast is served, she does not consciously co-operate in her parents' efforts, nor understand what is happening or what they are attempting to do.

ADVANTAGES OF EARLY TRAINING. The major advantage of placing a baby on the potty at an early age is that parents who succeed at conditioning her to use it have far less work cleaning up soiled diapers and a messy baby, and can save a few pennies on laundering. In some cases babies who are regularly placed on a potty or toilet may come to feel comfortable with this piece of equipment. This familiarity with the potty may facilitate future training efforts when they are older and able to understand what is happening.

DISADVANTAGES OF EARLY TRAINING. Many professionals feel that there are more disadvantages than advantages in attempting to toilet train a baby who is under a year of age. The baby who is placed on the toilet and becomes conditioned to defecate shortly thereafter is not really "trained" in the true sense of the word, since she is not conscious of the procedure, or physically ready to control her bowels or bladder. Parents cannot help a child develop good toilet habits until she is ready and wants to learn how to use a toilet of her own accord. In the case of a young infant, it is the parents who are doing all of the "learning," not the baby. They are learning to place their baby on the toilet in time for her urine or stools to land in the bowl.

There are some parents who place their baby on the toilet and make her sit there for more than five to ten minutes, hoping that she will "produce." The child may become bored or angry at being forced to remain on the seat•for prolonged periods of time (who wouldn't in her place?), particularly if she has a driving need to keep moving or even to stand. Her failure to "produce" as expected may result in parents' nagging, scolding, or punishing her. This can lead to negative associations with the toilet. Toilet training can become an area for conflict and much resentment, and cause greater resistance on a child's part to acquire good toilet habits later on in toddlerhood, when she is able to understand what toilet training means. Punishment should not play a role in toilet training, and a baby should not be forced to sit on a potty or toilet for more than a few minutes, since she may come to regard the toilet as a place in which she is restrained against her will.

Problems may also result if parents who succeed in conditioning a baby to defecate on the toilet expect her progress to continue. Early success in toilet training usually does not proceed forward along a straight and narrow path. Quite often a baby who has been quite regular in her patterns of elimination between eight to ten months may suddenly become more irregular. She may begin to resist defecating when she is seated on the toilet as she approaches her first birthday and finds it difficult to sit still.

Parents who have been "successful" may have misinterpreted this success as meaning that their baby had really gained control over her bowels and was willingly participating in their training efforts. When their child later becomes irregular or resists defecating on the toilet, because she needs to be active and standing, these parents may claim that she is deliberately behaving poorly in an attempt to spite them. They may become upset with her over her poor performance, or may punish or scold her for what seems to them like deliberate "failures."

Parents' frustration or disappointment and disapproval may upset their baby, who does not even understand why they are mad at her. These angry parental reactions are clearly out of place and reflect a lack of understanding of their child's abilities. Later on in toddlerhood, when parents try once more to toilet train her, she may deliberately refuse to co-operate because of these initial bad experiences.

THE ULTIMATE DECISION IS YOURS TO MAKE. The real mastery of learning to use the toilet necessitates that a child have control over her organs of elimination, and have a desire to learn to use the toilet or go along with her parents' educational program. With most children, this occurs between the second year and the first half of the third year, with bowel control generally preceding bladder control.

Throughout the first year of life, elimination usually occurs as a reflex response, rather than a voluntary one. This is why most professionals advise against training during the first year, and suggest that parents wait until toddlerhood before starting to encourage their child to acquire good toilet habits. At that time the child is more anxious to imitate the things that grownups do, and is more likely to be gaining some awareness of bodily functions as well as bowel control.

Ultimately, the decision as to whether or not to place your baby on the potty during the first year is yours to make. Should you want to begin conditioning your baby early, avoid becoming emotionally involved with her failure to perform as you expect, or her "good" performances. Do not keep her on the toilet for more than several minutes, and try to treat the whole process as casually as possible, rather than making a big issue of it. With any signs of resistance or rebellion on your baby's part, it is advisable to stop placing her on the potty and wait until she is older.

It is best to relax. When your baby's nervous system is sophisticated enough and she is more mature, she will convey her readiness to you (see pages 522–26). Until this time, try to be patient. Young children essentially teach themselves to use the toilet when they are ready and want to be more grown-up in their elimination behavior. It is important not to force your child to do something that she is not ready to achieve, just to satisfy your own needs or to keep up with your neighbors' efforts.

DISCIPLINE

As your baby matures and becomes more independent and active, the need for expanded methods of controlling her behavior may become necessary. The material in this discipline section introduces certain concepts and techniques of both discipline and punishment that may be of use to you at any point in time between Infancy 6 and the end of infancy. Further comments on discipline will be discussed in later sections where they are more appropriate.

Disciplining the Mobile Baby Is More Difficult

Discipline is much less of an issue during early infancy than it is during later infancy. Once your baby begins to move across the floor, disciplining her will become more difficult. A more mobile baby causes many new stresses that never emerged during early infancy. All of a sudden your baby will become more independent of your control. She will have strong desires to move, explore, and touch nearly every object that she can grab. Two major new problems surface at this point.

One is the problem of the baby's safety. There are many potentially dangerous objects and areas in every normal home situation. In cases where a baby is allowed complete freedom to explore her home environment, and proper safety precautions are not taken to accident-proof the home, parents will find themselves having to watch and limit her actions constantly. This is not only time-consuming, but also very frustrating for both parent and child. On the other hand, even when parents do a thorough job of accident-proofing their home, they cannot possibly remove every risk of danger to their baby. She can still head for the controls on the stove or oven, get her fingers caught in a swinging door, or fall off of a chair, and so forth. Keeping your infant safe will be a primary objective of your program of discipline during the latter half of the first year.

Another problem that may surface is that objects in the home may be damaged. Depending upon parents' individual home situations, they may have many treasures or valuable objects, or very few. Even in homes in which there are not many expensive items with personal value, there will still be a risk of possible damage to furniture. Floor and table lamps can be knocked over, upholstered furniture will receive a lot of wear and tear, and toys may be thrown, causing other objects to be broken or damaged.

Anxiety and worry about your baby's safety and the safety of objects and furniture in your home may come to a head at some point over the next few months as she acquires new motor skills. You will have to place some restrictions and limits upon her behavior, especially when her safety is in danger. A discussion of her abilities and some of the techniques of discipline that may assist you in educating and managing her are presented in the material that follows.

Keep in mind that a few physically active babies will begin to locomote as early as six or seven months of age. Many more will begin during Infancy 8 and 9. This early discussion of discipline as related to the mobile baby is included at this stage so that you will be prepared to manage your baby appropriately.

What Can You Realistically Expect from Her?

It would be unrealistic to turn your baby loose in your home (assuming that she is mobile and that you have not accident-proofed it), warn her not to touch all of the valuable or potentially dangerous objects and to stay away from certain rooms and danger areas, and then expect her to follow your verbal commands. Your concept of how she *should* behave would be completely out of line with her nature and abilities.

It is part of your infant's nature to want to touch, grab, drop objects, and investigate. Her curiosity is strong. Her primary motivation is probably to satisfy her own needs and desires, and her approach to this is a determined and single-minded one. Your baby's ability to block her own impulses and actions and exercise self-control is extremely limited. It will be a long time before she is capable of regulating her own behavior.

Your baby's comprehension of your words is, at best, minimal, as are her abilities to perceive danger and distinguish between valuable and non-valuable objects. Her intellectual capacities are a far cry from an older child's, and her memory is very short term. When she is warned not to touch specific objects or to stay away from specific areas, she may not understand these verbal warnings. Even if she did, she might not remember them from one moment to the next.

You should not, as was previously mentioned, expect more from her than she is able to do. She cannot possibly live up to your standards or expectations of how she should act if they are far above her abilities. Setting realistic expectations is a first step toward an effective program of discipline.

Useful Techniques in Discipline

Given your baby's limitations, you are probably wondering what disciplinary actions you can take in order to avoid having to restrict her movements severely, and spend a great deal of your time and energy acting as a "police person." The following techniques have been used successfully by many parents.

MAKING ADJUSTMENTS IN YOUR HOME: ENVIRONMENTAL DISCIPLINE. One of the most effective steps that you can take to foster your baby's over-all development and simultaneously make your job as a disciplinarian easier is to arrange your home so that it is more suitable to her needs and abilities. Realizing that she cannot understand your verbal warnings, you simply have to remove important or unsafe objects from her reach and do a complete job of accident-proofing your home. The issue is explored in depth in the How to Ensure Your Baby's Safety sections of this book. By temporarily making adjustments in the arrangement of your home to suit her needs and abilities, you will not have to watch her every move, and will save on hundreds of no's, don'ts, and stops.

You will come up with numerous ways in which you can arrange your home to make disciplining less taxing and time-consuming. The inconvenience should be well worth the effort. You need not worry that you are "giving in" to your baby, or are skirting the main issue, which is that of seeing to it that she behaves properly. Actually, what you are doing is making certain adjustments in your home life so that everyone concerned will benefit, rather than trying to force your baby to conform to the standards of behavior that you would expect from an older child.

TAKING ADVANTAGE OF HER DISTRACTIBILITY. Even though your baby will be growing less distractible over the next six months, she will still be rather easily lured from one activity to another. A useful technique in getting her to stop doing something that might be dangerous or that is bothersome to you is to divert her attention away from that activity by engaging her in another that is more acceptable or less dangerous.

Lillian Vogel turned her eight-month-old daughter, Francine, loose on the living room floor. Francine headed right for the lamp cord and started to pull on the wire. Rather than scolding, warning, or punishing her, Lillian dangled Francine's favorite toy in front of her, picked her up, and engaged her in another activity that she always enjoyed.

By substituting acceptable for unacceptable activities, Mrs. Vogel saved scores of no's and don'ts each day and no longer was constantly angry with her infant. You, too, can adapt your techniques of discipline to take into account your baby's nature and abilities, and thus make life easier on you, and more pleasant for her.

A STERN VOICE AND SHARP COMMAND MEAN BUSINESS! Long before your baby is capable of understanding your words, she will begin to get some idea of whether you are pleased or displeased about her actions by the tone of your voice and the feeling with which you speak. When she is doing something that you disapprove of or that is irritating, you can begin to convey this message to her by raising your voice.

Once she becomes more mobile, you should definitely begin helping her learn the meanings of the words "no," "don't," and perhaps one or two additional simple commands such as "stop," "hot," and "hurt." The task of teaching her to understand and obey these commands is likely to be a slow one. The way in which you introduce the words can influence not only how quickly they are learned, but also whether or not they will be heeded.

At six months of age it is not likely that your baby will respond well to verbal commands, but in time she will respond more regularly to your spoken direction. In the early stages, your words alone will not be enough to stop her from persisting in some dangerous or unacceptable activity. You will have to take advantage of environmental discipline, her distractibility, or removing her from one area of your home to another. At this time direct intervention on your part will probably be much more effective than verbal commands, but teaching her to associate words such as "no" and "don't" with certain off-limits objects and areas is an important aspect of her education in discipline. The following suggestion may be useful in your early attempts to teach your child the meaning of simple verbal commands.

Let's say that your baby is crawling toward the fireplace screen that you have decided is a "forbidden" object to touch, and is just about to touch it. In a very stern tone of voice, and while restraining her from moving any closer to the screen, you can look her in the eye and say, "No, no" or, "Don't touch." Let her know that you are not kidding. When you order her not to touch something, or use the word "no," it will help to get the meaning across if you accompany the words with appropriate facial expressions and hand motions such as shaking your head from side to side or pointing to her hand.

In training your infant to learn what these brief, sharp commands mean, you should initially limit your use of them to a few specific objects and situations, perhaps only when her safety is at stake. Do not use "no, no" constantly throughout the day, or use it for trivial reasons. Save it for important matters, or, after a while, the word will lose its meaning and effectiveness. Be *consistent* in letting her know when her actions are unacceptable or are potentially dangerous by raising your tone of voice. After many repetitions in different circumstances, she will be able to sense when you are displeased and when you really mean business. In time she will also learn the meaning of the words "no" and "don't."

TAKING COMMAND. In case environmental discipline and distracting your infant have failed in getting her to discontinue her unacceptable behavior, an obvious solution is to pick her up and take her away from a dangerous or undesirable activity. This approach often leads to crying and kicking. These responses may be avoided by attempting to distract her with another activity after you have removed her from the bothersome one. In the early stages, this is probably the most effective form of controlling your baby's behavior. As she develops and her vocabulary and intellectual function expand, this form of discipline will give way to discipline that is more verbal in nature.

Punishment

By using the disciplinary techniques suggested above, you should have little need for physical punishment during infancy. However, as babies become increasingly active, independent, and assertive, and begin to develop some awareness of their parents' approval or disapproval of their actions, parents sometimes feel the need to punish whenever their other means of discipline have failed to control their child's unacceptable behavior. Due to the wide variability among babies and tolerance levels of parents, some parents feel like punishing during early infancy, and others may not feel like punishing until well into toddlerhood.

It is difficult to predict whether or not you will, at some point over the next six months, feel the need to punish your baby. Most parents, at one time or another, find it necessary to punish their babies. A few may never punish their babies, and others may regularly use punishment whenever their babies break their rules or go beyond their limits.

As you try to control your child's unacceptable actions, you will be frustrated by having to repeat your disciplinary measures constantly for the same problem. Mrs. Michaelson was the mother of an extremely active six-month-old son named Roger. According to Mrs. Michaelson, Roger was difficult to tolerate during the day. He often screamed at the top of his lungs when he wanted attention. His mother usually tried to distract him by giving him toys or other playthings that he enjoyed. When this approach failed, as it generally did, she sternly told him to "stop crying" in a loud tone of voice, in an effort to display her displeasure at his behavior.

Despite all of her attempts, he persisted in crying unless she stopped whatever she was doing and paid attention to him. This became highly frustrating, and also embarrassing when she had company. Mrs. Michaelson was so upset and drained by her son's behavior that she wanted to use physical punishment to deter him from crying.

Many parents, like Mrs. Michaelson, occasionally feel extreme frustration and anger because of their inability to control their child's bothersome behavior. In some cases this frustration may prompt parents to use physical punishment.

There is enormous variability in opinions about whether or not punishment is justifiable during infancy, and if it is justifiable, how and when to employ it as a means of enforcing your disciplinary measures. Most parents and professionals would agree that punishment, or at least physical punishment, is not advisable during early infancy (pages 165–66). The use of punishment often comes into question between the age of six to twelve months. As your baby develops, your own feelings, and your child's nature, will determine how you approach the question of whether or not to punish your baby during later infancy, and if so, how to go about it.

The following information on punishment has been organized to assist you in formulating or clarifying your own ideas on this subject. This material will be useful to you in developing a personalized approach to the use of punishment to enforce your methods of discipline. As you handle your baby, particularly in the presence of other parents or relatives, you are likely to receive plenty of advice about the pros and cons of punishment, as well as suggestions for specific methods and techniques. Being more aware of the subject of punishment should enable you to be more confident in handling possible criticism from other adults as well as handling your baby.

THERE IS A DIFFERENCE BETWEEN DISCIPLINE AND PUNISHMENT. Some parents make the mistake of equating discipline with punishment, but the two terms don't mean the same thing. Discipline is a means of teaching your baby about your rules, limits on her unacceptable behavior, and expectations of how she should and should not behave. If she should deliberately violate these rules, limits, or expectations, this is where punishment comes into the picture, since it represents a penalty for intentional breaking of the rules established by your program of discipline. Punishing her may be one method that you can employ to enforce the rules that you set down.

LOVE AND PUNISHMENT. Your child should always sense your love underlying your punishment. After all, you are attempting to teach her certain acceptable patterns of behavior because you care about her. Punishment is employed because you care enough about her to want to help her alter undesirable behavior patterns. It should not be allowed to damage the parent-child relationship. Provided that your child feels your love and affection, punishment should not interfere with this feeling. Constant use and abuse of punishment can be damaging to your relationship with your child. The positive aspect of this relationship is sure to be one of the most effective aids in discipline, so it would be self-defeating to undermine this bond by excessive or inappropriate punishment.

WHAT ARE YOUR OBJECTIVES IN PUNISHING YOUR CHILD? Think about what punishing your child is supposed to accomplish. Most parents use punishment when their child has done something wrong and they want to teach her that if she does the same thing again she will be punished. They expect that she will avoid the improper behavior in the future, and avoid the punishment that she knows she will receive if she steps out of line. In this context, punishment is used to enforce your framework of discipline by serving as a deterrent to unacceptable behavior. It should be instructive in helping the child learn not to engage in specific unacceptable activities.

By thinking about punishment and when it is justifiable, you will probably conclude that it is wrong or cruel to punish a child who had no idea that she did anything wrong or was not capable of conforming to her parents' rules and expectations due to lack of developmental maturity. For this reason, it is important to avoid setting your expectations too far above your infant's abilities, because it is unlikely that she will be able to live up to them. She will continually, according to your standards, be violating your limits or misbehaving, and you will find yourself constantly having to punish her. Punishment in this context would be difficult to justify. No matter how hard your infant tries to please, she would not be in a position to alter her behavior since she does not have the necessary abilities to do what you expect.

The importance of establishing realistic rules and expectations based upon your baby's capabilities cannot be overemphasized. By reading the development sections in this book and by observing her behavior, you should be better prepared to set appropriate and reasonable standards of behavior.

It is not uncommon for parents to vent their frustrations on their children, and it is important to be aware of this possibility before punishing your child. Andrea Samuels was going through a very rough period with her husband, Mark. She rarely expressed her resentments and hostility toward him for fear of possibly losing him. After he left for work each morning, she would be terribly tense, angry, and frustrated. Normally, she regarded her daughter Terry's crying for her attention in a positive light, but because Andrea was so anxious, upset, and preoccupied with her marital problems, she began to use physical punishment by spanking her daughter regularly for her behavior. Although hitting her child alleviated some of the anger and frustration that she felt, this form of punishment was inappropriate considering her daughter's behavior.

It would be a rare parent who could truthfully claim that he or she never took personal frustrations out on his or her baby, even though the baby's behavior did not warrant this kind of treatment. In most cases this occurs very infrequently. The parent recognizes the mistake that was made and makes immediate amends. No harm is done to the child.

There are some cases, as in the example above, in which a baby is regularly punished inappropriately, or used as a substitute target for her parent's frustration. This should be avoided at all costs, since it can have detrimental effects upon the child.

Another situation that may arise involves a parent punishing as a way of seeking revenge. Mr. Keaton was feeding his eight-month-old baby and was highly aggravated by his daughter's behavior. She was enjoying playing with her food and throwing it on the floor during feedings. He became so frustrated by her lack of response to his initial pleas for her to stop playing and eat her meal, that he took the food away and decided to "show her who's the boss" by slapping her hands and refusing to feed her for twenty-four hours to teach her a "good" lesson. He was obviously frustrated by his daughter's refusal to respect him as a figure of authority, and was punishing her to "get even" or seek revenge.

Not realizing that his daughter was not intentionally playing with her food to disobey his commands, he took her behavior as willful defiance. His daughter, however, was doing what many babies of her age do. Exploring and playing with food are activities that are very common at this stage. In addition to taking her behavior at mealtime personally, his expectations of how she should behave were unreasonable, and his punishment was thus overly severe.

Before punishing your baby, carefully evaluate your motives and objectives. Punishment is not effective when used as a means of venting frustration that should be directed elsewhere, or when employed to seek revenge. It can be effective when used properly as an educational tool, but when it is used inappropriately, it borders on subtle forms of child abuse.

METHODS OF PUNISHMENT. There are many different methods of punishment, and you will develop your own according to your child's behavior and your personal philosophy. Among the most common methods are isolating a child from social contacts, not giving a child something that is important to her, and using physical punishment. To give you a brief idea of how these methods can be employed, each one is discussed below.

Isolating a Child from Social Contacts. Sometimes a child persists in some unacceptable or undesirable behavior because she receives reinforcement for it by people who are present. When a child is in a family group or company is present, she may behave in an improper manner to receive attention or a reaction from the crowd. Assuming that normal disciplinary measures are not effective in getting her to alter her behavior or act properly, a parent might isolate her for a short period of time in her room or some other place where she will be alone.

Ten-month-old Lindsay Butler often behaved poorly on purpose when she was eating with the rest of the family. She threw her food, purposely spilled her milk, and giggled afterward at her own antics. Her father warned her to stop misbehaving by using short, sharp commands, but getting attention, even of this nature, seemed more important to her than altering her behavior. As a form of punishment, Mr. Butler made her eat by herself in the kitchen until she was ready to conduct herself in a more reasonable fashion when eating with other family members.

The motive underlying this father's punishment was quite appropriate, as was the form of punishment that he employed. The punishment was linked to his baby's misbehavior, was not overly severe, and was truly designed to teach her the difference between acceptable and unacceptable behavior. He believed that the primary reason for her misbehavior was getting attention, and that by removing the source of attention at mealtimes, she would correct her behavior so as to be permitted to eat with her family again. Soon after Mr. Butler instituted this form of punishment, Lindsay's behavior improved.

The objective of isolating a baby from other people is that she will miss being in the company of others and will behave more reasonably the next time so that she will not have to be isolated again. Some parents carry this to an extreme and keep the child isolated from other people not just temporarily, but for prolonged periods of time, or on a regular basis. This is not advisable, nor is it healthy in terms of a child's emotional and social development.

Not Giving a Child Something That Is Important to Her. When a child repeatedly disobeys, a parent might warn her that if she persists in her unacceptable behavior, the parent will either take away or deny her something that is important to her. This type of punishment will not be effective, however, unless your child really feels that you are depriving her of something that she considers important.

Assume that your eleven-month-old baby loves to listen to records. One afternoon she deliberately plays with your record player, even though she understood that she was not supposed to touch it. You warn her that if she touches it again, you will not let her listen to any more records that day. Again she touches it, and thus you deprive her of the opportunity to hear any records for twenty-four hours.

This punishment, after many repetitions, might motivate her to respect your rule not to touch the record player in the future. When she does not respect it, she knows her wish to listen to records will be denied. Again, it is important to point out that if the child is too young to understand your verbal rules, or is incapable of exercising self-control, it is unfair to expect her not to touch certain expensive pieces of equipment, and you should avoid the need for punishing her by keeping this equipment from her reach.

This specific type of punishment is more successfully employed with toddlers and preschool children, but it may be effective with babies as well. Most infants consider receiving parental attention to be very important. Many parents, utilizing this form of punishment, deprive their infants of their attention for short periods of time following their babies' misbehavior by ignoring them.

Using this technique, you give your baby an incentive for altering her responses to maintain parental attention and approval. This can certainly be an effective method for shaping a baby's behavior patterns. Given the significance of parental attention to a baby, however, it is extremely important not to withhold attention or affection for prolonged periods of time. Doing this would not only be damaging to the parent-child relationship, but might also have negative consequences for the child's over-all development.

Using Physical Punishment. Some parents spank a child's buttocks, or slap her hands when she deliberately breaks a rule. Spanking is generally the most common form of physical punishment, although its advisability with children under a year of age is questioned by some parents and professionals. When a child clearly understands that she is not supposed to touch the controls on the television set, and deliberately touches them, a parent might warn her that if she touches them again she will be spanked. Thus she has a choice. She can behave properly, or suffer the consequences. Assuming that she proceeds to touch the controls again, a parent might then spank her lightly on her hands or behind, in the hope that she will associate being spanked with her unacceptable behavior, and avoid it in the future. Gentle spanking or slapping makes it clear to the child that her parent means business.

The need for physical punishment throughout late infancy should be minimal, especially since the child cannot usually understand the reason for punishment. In the event that you feel the need to use physical punishment regularly, or find that you have on more than one occasion bruised or inflicted severe pain upon your infant, you should make a careful evaluation of your reasons for using physical punishment. You should seek advice from your physician or local center for child abuse if your behavior in meting out physical punishment is excessive and difficult, or impossible, for you to control.

GENERAL GUIDELINES FOR USING PUNISHMENT. The different methods for punishment described above may be employed occasionally to enforce your program of discipline. For punishment to be effective, there are several important factors that must be taken into consideration as to when and how the punishment is administered.

Punishing the child immediately after she misbehaves will allow her to associate the punishment with that particular behavior. When she acts in a certain way, she immediately sees the results of her actions. She can connect "cause" and "effect." If you delay punishing her for several minutes or hours, she may forget what it was that she did wrong, and when she receives the punishment, she may feel that you are being unjust.

A severe punishment should not be employed for a minor misdeed. If your child, who is normally well behaved, begins to act up when company comes, it would be inappropriate to isolate her for the rest of the day in her room. By carrying a punishment on too long, or with severity disproportionate to the child's behavior, your child may resent you and may not learn the intended lesson. Bear in mind that her memory is extremely short term. A punishment that is prolonged probably would not serve any significant purpose, and might be destructive rather than constructive. Good judgment and common sense are the best guides.

A child during infancy cannot usually understand verbal warnings completely, but it is important to *try warning her by other means of discipline* (as described previously on pages 325–26) *before instituting punishment.* By distracting her or using strong verbal commands, you may be able to avoid having to resort to punishment. Before you punish her you should attempt to warn her by raising your hand or using a loud, firm tone of voice. Warning before punishing will become increasingly important as her comprehension of language improves. Once she is able to understand your warnings, she can choose either to obey you, or suffer the consequences. By warning her in advance, you are at least giving her some control over the situation.

Most importantly, remember that *well-designed, reasonable punishment teaches the intended lesson.* Should you decide to employ punishment in your program of discipline, evaluate your baby's behavior after every occasion on which she has been punished. Try to determine whether or not the punishment employed was successful. Should you find that your punishment is not helping to achieve the desired objective, you will want to discontinue it in favor of other disciplinary techniques. By regularly evaluating your methods of discipline, you will be better able to get across the intended message to your child in an effective way.

WAYS THAT INFANTS RELEASE AND REDUCE TENSION

Some infants during the last half of the first year engage in different activities to help them cope with tensions. One baby, for example, may suck her thumb as a method of soothing or comforting herself. Another child may roll her head, or get up on her hands and knees and rock back and forth in her crib, making a lot of noise. Others may stroke a piece of soft fabric repeatedly, bang their heads against the side of their cribs, tug on their ear lobes, or finger their hair. Sometimes the same baby will engage in more than one of these tension-reducing activities.

Such behaviors, which allow infants to release tension and excess energy, tend to cause parents concern. Parents sometimes consider these actions to be indications that a child is abnormal, unhappy, or very insecure. Some parents even feel guilty if their child exhibits such behaviors, because they feel that somewhere along the line they have failed to provide their child with enough love or security, a proper home environment, or good handling.

Most psychologists view these behaviors as normal, natural, and useful resources for helping a child live with everyday tensions that all babies experience in growing up. They suggest that parents think of their child's behaviors in this light, rather than thinking of them as bad habits, and that they treat these behaviors casually, and not become upset by them.

Normal children will outgrow these activities as they mature. Parents should be patient, and not make their children discontinue such behaviors. In fact, most authorities feel that the less a parent does and says about a child's tension-reducing behaviors, the greater the likelihood that she will outgrow her need for them as soon as possible. Quite often a baby will use these tension-reducing behaviors during particular stages of her development when she has a lot of excess energy, is nervous, bored, unhappy, or having sleeping difficulties.

The second half of the first year is a time when many children utilize tension-relieving behaviors. Your child may never exhibit such tension "outlets," or she may develop them during toddlerhood or during the preschool years. It is not uncommon for some tension-reducing behaviors to emerge, then diminish, and then emerge again later in a child's life. Keep in mind that the frequency, intensity, and type of comforting behavior may vary from child to child. The more common tension outlets seen in infancy are discussed below.

Thumb-sucking

Some of the possible reasons for thumb-sucking during the early months were presented on pages 140–41. The same reasons may underlie the older baby's thumb-sucking, with perhaps a few differences. As a baby grows older, it is less likely that she sucks her thumb or finger out of hunger. It is also less likely that she sucks because she has not received enough sucking on the breast or bottle during early infancy, once thought to be a major reason for the occurrence of this behavior in the first five to six months.

Thumb-sucking is commonly seen when a baby is fatigued, tense, unstimulated, or having a hard time getting to sleep. This activity is often used by a baby as a means of soothing, calming, or comforting herself. Thumb-sucking may also represent the infant's desire to re-create the satisfying feeling and security that she felt when she was cuddled in her parent's arms and fed by breast or bottle. Thumb-sucking that is associated with sleep seems to help the child during the changeover from being active and alert to sleeping. It may also help her deal more effectively with anxiety and loneliness aroused during separations from her parent.

A rather common time for thumb-sucking to emerge is just prior to the baby's accomplishment of major milestones in development. A couple of months before an infant learns to sit up, crawl, or stand, she may experience more than the usual amount of inner tension and frustration. Thumb-sucking may help her reduce the tension and frustration. In many cases the baby's use of thumb-sucking diminishes as she becomes more occupied with motor activity and masters new abilities.

THUMB-SUCKING MAY BE ASSOCIATED WITH GROWING UP. Thumb-sucking in many cases is thought to be associated with a baby's becoming more independent. Between the ages of about six months and a year, babies begin to sense their separateness from their parents. While they are motivated to grow up and become more independent, this desire is sometimes countered by periods of insecurity and a need to cling to parents or return to previously used tension-reducing behavior patterns.

At times it seems as though a baby wants both independence and dependence. This is where thumb-sucking may come into the picture. Sucking may serve as a way of gaining security and reducing tension. A baby who wants to grow up still needs the security and comfort that her parents provide. Yet, to cling to them constantly would be like giving up the progress toward independence made thus far. The child may therefore use thumb-sucking as a means of recalling her parents' image and thus reducing the loneliness and anxiety that she feels. Once she feels more comfortable with separations and her own independence, this type of thumb-sucking will be outgrown naturally.

OTHER RHYTHMIC PATTERNS SOMETIMES SEEN WITH THUMB-SUCKING. Thumb-sucking is sometimes accompanied by other rhythmic activities, such as twirling the hair, rubbing the nose, or fingering a fuzzy toy or soft fabric or blanket. These combined activities are seen commonly as the baby prepares for sleep, but may also occur when she is tired or tense during the daytime. In most cases these accompanying activities decline as the child outgrows thumb-sucking. They are common and should not arouse undue parental concern.

HANDLING THE THUMB-SUCKER. Parents sometimes overreact to the baby's natural use of thumb-sucking as a tension outlet. They may forget that they are dealing with a baby, and envision their child as a three-, four-, or five-year-old still sucking her thumb in public. This worries them, along with the possibility that this activity could cause permanent harm to their child's teeth. Some parents therefore try to intervene in an attempt to put a stop to this "bad habit" before the baby grows older.

When thumb-sucking is strong parental intervention is rarely helpful in getting the baby or young child to stop sucking, and in some cases may aggravate the situation. Thumb-sucking seems to have to run its own course with each child. Punishing, scolding, applying foul-tasting substances to the thumb, and using finger restraints are not advisable. These tactics can be very frustrating for an infant, and may cause increased tension that results in a heightened need to suck. Such methods are rarely effective.

Thumb-sucking in the infant is common, and should not be a cause for undue concern. Probably the best course of action is to overlook it, treat it casually, and avoid calling the baby's attention to it. When thumb-sucking seems to be associated with a particular state in a baby, such as boredom or fatigue, parents can try to correct the underlying cause, rather than the symptom. Offering her a more stimulating environment or putting her to bed a little earlier may help. Trying to find ways to make the infant happier, less tense, and more satisfied is a constructive approach. Even in babies who are happy and satisfied, thumb-sucking can still be seen. Therefore, there is no need to worry if an underlying cause cannot be pinpointed. Be patient. Thumb-sucking will eventually be outgrown when the child herself is ready to give it up. As long as thumb-sucking is outgrown before the permanent teeth come in, around age six, there is no need to be concerned about its effect on the bite or alignment of the teeth. More information on thumb-sucking in toddlerhood can be found on pages 537–38.

Pacifiers

The reasons why an older baby continues to want to use a pacifier are similar to those for thumb-sucking. However, parents should check to be sure that they are offering their infant enough attention and other kinds of stimulation, since a lack of these may underlie a baby's continued reliance upon a pacifier.

Provided that this is not the case, parents can be on the lookout for indications that the baby is ready to give up the pacifier. Older infants sometimes spit the pacifier out after a few minutes, or even as soon as it is placed in their mouths. This can be taken as a sign of readiness to give it up. In this situation, parents can try gradually not to offer the pacifier. If the child clings strongly to it, however, taking it away will be very frustrating for her and she may cry until it is placed back in her mouth.

In this situation it is probably best to let her use it until she outgrows it on her own. Many babies give up the pacifier as they approach their first birthdays, but there are some who still demand it in toddlerhood.

Tongue-sucking

Tongue-sucking is another type of rhythmic pattern that may emerge during the last half of the first year. It is not as common as thumb-sucking and other tension outlets, but also tends to arouse parental concern. In many cases this activity is not very obvious, and parents may not even be aware that tongue-sucking is going on, unless it is accompanied by loud sucking noises or noticeable rolling of the tongue.

Parental intervention is not usually effective, and there is little that can be done to prevent this activity. Calling the infant's attention to her tongue-sucking is not the most advisable approach. It is probably best to ignore the activity and try to find ways to make the child feel happier and more fulfilled.

Body-rocking

Body-rocking is a fairly common tension outlet during late infancy. In many cases it emerges around the time that a baby learns to get into a rocking position on hands and knees. This is usually around nine to ten months. While remaining in one spot, the infant rocks forward and backward, sometimes so vigorously that the crib squeaks or moves.

This activity is often seen at bedtime, and may be used as a natural means of releasing excess energy, tension, or frustration. It may also be used as a means for inducing sleep. Rocking can also occur during the night or in the daytime.

Gentle rhythmic back and forth movements do not arouse as much parental concern as more vigorous, noisy movements that may even awaken parents during the night. This tension outlet can vary in intensity, and does not usually indicate that anything is wrong with an infant who is doing well in all other areas of her life.

When the rocking is strong enough to shake the crib, parents should check to make sure that it is sturdy enough to withstand the wear and tear. If a child is actually able to move the crib around the room, it can be bolted to the wall or floor. Placing a thick rug that is fastened to the floor underneath the crib is an alternative that can sometimes work well.

Rocking movements are usually outgrown by the child in due time. They should not arouse excessive parental concern, since they represent a common form of tension release during infancy. Parents may want to look for possible reasons for this activity. Is some cases a child who rocks may be doing so because she feels undue pressure or tension, but there are many cases in which perfectly normal, happy children employ this outlet during a particular phase of development for no apparent reason. Body-rocking during toddlerhood is discussed on page 541.

Head-banging

Head-banging worries and tends to disturb parents more than the other tension outlets seen in infancy. They are often frightened by the noise as their infant hits her head against a hard surface such as the headboard or sides of her crib. Their baby's appearance after a vigorous period of head-banging can also frighten them, since she may be left with bruises, bumps, or even welts. It is rare that further harm than this comes to a child after a head-banging episode.

In order to protect the child from hurting herself, and to reduce the noise banging generates, heavy pads can be placed around the inside of the crib. If necessary, a thick rug can also be placed under the legs of the crib and fastened to the floor to prevent the crib from moving. Upon seeing the baby banging her head, a parent can pick her up and try to comfort her, but it is not a good idea to call undue attention to this activity by acting overly sympathetic or upset. Distracting the child with a game or toy may work well.

In a child who otherwise seems happy and is developing well, occasional head-banging should not be a cause for alarm. It may simply emerge as a natural form of release during times when she feels tense or angry. Parents whose child continually engages in vigorous banging should talk the situation over with their doctor. More information on head-banging is presented on page 541.

Head-rolling

Head-rolling is another rhythmic activity in which a child simply rolls her head from side to side or back and forth while lying on her back as she gets ready for sleep, or when she is fatigued during the daytime. Occasionally noises or sounds accompany head-rolling. This behavior is normal and should represent no real cause for concern if the child seems well adjusted. With some children this behavior persists into the preschool years.

Physically punishing a child for head-rolling generally does not help. This can lower a child's self-esteem and make her angry and frustrated. Rather than trying to eliminate the behavior itself, a better approach would be to find some other outlet that the child enjoys. At night, perhaps you could cuddle her close and read or sing to her. During the daytime, you could engage her in a fun activity or encourage her to play with a favorite toy. If head-rolling occurs when she is tired, putting her to bed earlier may help.

Other Tension Outlets

There are other ways that infants may release and reduce tension. Some of these include the use of a security object, throwing temper tantrums, having breath-holding episodes, frequent handling of the genitals, and biting. These tension outlets are more common during toddlerhood, and are discussed on pages 534–42. In the event that your infant makes use of any of the above outlets, the information and suggestions provided in the toddlerhood section should be helpful.

PARENTS' REACTIONS TO BABIES' STRANGER ANXIETY

Around the age of six months, many babies begin to react with fear when strangers approach. This can have different effects upon parents. Some parents who are taking primary care of their babies are actually delighted, in a sense, when their baby acts shy around strangers. This indicates to them that their baby clearly knows who her parent is, making them feel loved and important.

Other parents who are very outgoing themselves may not look as kindly upon this change in their babies' behavior. They try to force babies to adjust to strangers and spend time with them, hoping that this approach will help their children get over the fears as quickly as possible. These parents may be unsympathetic and hand their infants over to a stranger despite their children's protests and fearfulness.

To a number of parents their children's stranger shyness is an embarrassment. Coreen, the mother of six-month-old Shirley, made a special trip cross-country to show Shirley off to her grandparents and relatives whom she had never seen before. Unfortunately, the trip did not turn out as well as Coreen had expected. Shirley's grandparents and relatives, naturally thrilled to see the newest addition to the family, all wanted to pick Shirley up, hold her, and shower her with affection. Shirley was very frightened by them, and screamed and clung to her mother from fear each time her relatives approached. Coreen found herself apologizing for Shirley's behavior, and was quite embarrassed by the whole situation, even though she understood the reasons behind her daughter's reaction.

There are some parents who are quite upset by their child's stranger anxiety for entirely different reasons. Parents who are not home full time caring for their babies may discover that the babies react to them as strangers. This happened to Eleanor and Martin. Their daughter, Carrie, had not really seen too much of them during her first six months, since the two of them worked full time outside of their home. Carrie had become very attached to Mrs. Snow, the woman caring for her every day. Although in past months Eleanor and Martin had been aware that Carrie felt closer to Mrs. Snow than to them, she had always accepted them and had never cried when they took over late in the evening. Suddenly, Carrie's reaction to her parents changed. She cried and looked frightened whenever they approached. This was difficult for them to deal with emotionally.

Eleanor and Martin took their child's reaction personally and were very hurt. Their hurt feelings coupled with the guilt they felt prompted them to reassess their lives in relation to their daughter. Eleanor volunteered to take a leave of absence from work for a year so that she could spend more time with Carrie.

Carrie's reaction to her parents is not all that unusual. Parents who are away from the home or from their child for most of the day may find that she responds to them negatively, or looks upon them as though they are strangers during this phase. Bear in mind that babies' memories are still very short term. Perhaps the only way to alleviate this situation is for parents to try to be with their infant more often or to be more patient. Stranger anxiety, as discussed more extensively on page 289, appears to be a developmental phase that some babies pass through. A baby's negative response toward her parents is hard for them not to take personally, but she is in no way reacting this way to make them feel guilty or to express her dislike of them. As a baby's memory improves during infancy, she will begin to remember her parents and will not react to them as strangers.

PREPARED PARENTHOOD CHECK LIST

MOTHER	FATHER	UNDERSTANDING YOUR BABY'S DEVELOPMENT
——	——	Is your infant showing stranger anxiety?
——	——	What social games do you and your baby enjoy playing?
——	——	Does your baby enjoy mirror play?
——	——	Is your baby showing a strong desire to handle and examine nearly all objects within reach?
——	——	Have you noticed your infant becoming more interested in repeating certain actions such as dropping objects, reaching, or kicking?
——	——	Has your infant accidentally hit upon a sound that resembled a real word? Did you offer her positive feedback?
——	——	Is your baby crying more often now for emotional reasons?
——	——	Are you aware that babies tend to cry more often out of frustration and tension prior to reaching large developmental milestones?
——	——	Have you seen evidence that your baby understands the meaning of one or more very familiar words?
——	——	Does your baby enjoy listening to your voice, music, noise-makers, or her own sounds?
——	——	Are you aware that individual differences in motor development become more noticeable during the latter half of infancy?
——	——	Have you seen your baby rolling over?
——	——	Is your baby able to sit well with support?
——	——	Can you identify your child's favorite toy or activity?
——	——	Is exploration of toys and objects becoming increasingly important to your infant?
——	——	Are you providing your baby with a wide assortment of safe toys and objects with which to play?
——	——	Does your baby try to attract your attention when she wants you to play with her?

BASIC CARE

MOTHER	FATHER	
——	——	Have you arranged for your infant to receive her third set of immunizations?
——	——	Are you aware of how to minimize the development of food allergies when introducing solid foods?

—— —— Are you anticipating your baby's increasing mobility and curiosity in planning to update your program of accident prevention?

—— —— Your baby may soon outgrow her infant car carrier. Have you obtained an approved auto carrier for the larger baby?

—— —— Do you realize the benefits of providing your infant with a safety-proofed home environment?

—— —— When you need or want to take a break from supervising your baby, how can you ensure her safety?

—— —— Are you aware of how to introduce solid foods?

—— —— Have you thought about making your own baby food?

—— —— When do you plan to introduce your baby to a cup?

—— —— Are you paying special attention to the cleanliness of your baby's fingernails and hands, since they will be into everything, especially her mouth?

—— —— Do you frequently check the fit of your baby's clothes to make sure that she is able to move around freely?

—— —— Does your baby resist going to sleep at night? Are you firm about her bedtime?

—— —— What types of changes in your child's stools may arise as a result of the introduction of solid foods into her diet?

—— —— Why is it usually best to hold off helping your child develop good toilet habits until the second year?

FAMILY FEELINGS AND CONCERNS

—— —— Why does discipline become a more important issue once your baby becomes more mobile?

—— —— What are some of the useful techniques in disciplining the infant?

—— —— Why is it beneficial to establish reasonable, realistic expectations, and be consistent in discipline?

—— —— Are you familiar with common forms of punishment and the general guidelines for using punishment?

—— —— What specific behaviors serve as tension outlets for your baby?

—— —— Are you bothered by your infant's methods of reducing or discharging tension? How do you respond when you see these behaviors?

—— —— If your baby is showing stranger anxiety, what is your reaction to her behavior?

Infancy 7

PERSONAL-SOCIAL DEVELOPMENT

Self-awareness

FURTHER BODY EXPLORATION. Some babies do a great deal of investigating by poking at things and their bodies with their fingers. All areas within reach will be investigated, his ears, nose, and even genitals. Even babies who prior to this time may not have done too much in the way of exploring their own bodies may now show an increased interest in this activity.

Your baby will be actively experimenting with his body in other ways. He may spend time looking at and playing with his hands and feet while sitting. As he begins to move a little on the floor, and plays with toys and objects, he learns about the potentials of his body, and what things he is not yet capable of doing.

HE MAY KNOW HIS FIRST NAME. At some point during this phase, or shortly thereafter, you may become aware that your infant knows his first name even though he cannot say it. Mr. Flager was talking on the phone while his son, Brad, was playing with a toy. In the course of the conversation, he mentioned his son's name. Brad stopped what he was doing, became alert, and looked in his father's direction. Mr. Flager was surprised, but recognized his son's ability to respond to his own name. After he hung up the phone, he tried calling out Brad's name from different corners of the room to see if his son would respond and clearly Brad was able to distinguish his name. This recognition was a sign of his increasing awareness of "self." In this phase or during Infancy 8 to 12, you will be able to observe your child's growing response to his own name.

RECOGNIZING HIS FACE. Seeing a moving mirror image or movie of himself can heighten your baby's awareness of his body, and reinforce the inner sensations that accompany movement. Now he may babble with great enthusiasm when he sees his image, and may even stretch his hand out toward his image to pat it. Some babies clearly recognize their own mirror images. You may realize this if you see your baby grinning at his mirror image, but not at other people's images.

Show him a snapshot of himself. He may smile, babble, and reach for it. When shown a picture of another young baby on a food label or in a magazine, he may have a similar reaction, perhaps because he recognizes the similarity between other babies and himself, or he may show a preference for his own image.

BODY SIMILARITIES AND DIFFERENCES. When you hold your infant, bend over to play with him, or tell him something, he may show a more definite interest in exploring your body. With his hand or fingers he may investigate your ears, eyes, nose, and mouth. Following this, he may return his hand to his face and do the same thing to himself. Exploring first your body and then his own enables him to draw comparisons and helps him to learn that he is similar to you, although different.

Imitation games should also increase his awareness that he can do things with his face, voice, hands, and other body parts similar to those that you and other people do. If you repeatedly rub your hands together, stick out your tongue, or scratch your head, you may notice him attempting to do the same. He finds mimicking your behavior great fun. He may also make more attempts to imitate the actions of his siblings and other babies with whom he comes in contact.

Social Sensitivity and Interests

AN EMOTIONAL ADJUSTMENT. A baby's greater mobility has a profound impact upon both him and his parent. When he begins to move around on the floor in his own special style, this can be both a thrilling and frightening experience for him. On the one hand he has been building toward this major developmental step for some time, and having acquired the necessary control and determination to take this step will give him an enormous sense of personal accomplishment and achievement. On the other hand, he will be exposed to all kinds of new environmental stimuli, some of which may prompt feelings of uneasiness or anxiety. Ordinary household noises that he paid little attention to before, such as the sound of the garbage disposal or the vacuum cleaner, may now scare him. The awareness of his emerging ability to separate a little from his parent and the increased independence that comes with new mobility may also frighten him.

The inner tensions that he feels as he approaches each new developmental task make him irritable. His personality may be happy and outward-going on one day and cranky and withdrawn on the next. Try to understand his feelings and recognize that he is going through some difficult adjustments.

Mr. Beeson took great pride in bragging about his son Paul's good nature. He was quite surprised one day when Paul suddenly became a "different person." Paul was irritable and did not seem to respond to his father's attention or play. Mr. Beeson was puzzled. Paul was doing fine, was not sick, and seemed to have everything he needed. Finally it occurred to him. Paul was just beginning to crawl, and clearly became more moody and irritable following his exploration on the floor. Apparently this new experience was creating some inner tensions. Mr. Beeson gave his son extra comfort and support during this phase, and as Paul mastered this new challenge, his old jovial personality seemed to return quickly.

During these periods of increased tension, your child will be strongly attached to you and may be very insistent about having your attention, even when other family members are quite anxious to hold and play with him. When both of you are in the same room, and he seems engrossed in some play activity, he may still keep one eye on you at all times, or frequently glance in your direction. He may want you to stay close by him throughout the day. His clinginess and constant demands for your attention may more than occasionally annoy you.

He seems to need to keep track of you within the home. When he is left alone in his room, he may frequently call you and anxiously wait for a reply so as not to "lose" you. Leaving him in someone else's care for relatively brief periods of time, or

341

leaving him alone in his bedroom at night, he may become quite upset and fearful. Any separation from you may disturb him. A baby's new ability to move away from his parent seems to heighten his awareness of his parent's whereabouts and the possibility that he or she will leave and not return.

Your baby's dependency and demands on your time may be bothersome, frustrating, and draining, but this behavior is a compliment to your parenting and his attachment to you. What he is really communicating to you is that he needs you, cares for you, and feels secure when you are near. Your support during these difficult times of adjustment will make it easier for him to cope with each new developmental challenge.

HE'S MORE ASSERTIVE. As your infant grows older and more independent, you can expect him to become more assertive, and to "tell" you in no uncertain terms what he wants, when he wants it, what he likes, and what he does not enjoy. During this phase he is more aware of his influence over you and other members of the family. Producing certain sounds enables him to command people's attention. When he is in trouble and cries out to you, you will come to his aid, and when he makes a sound and reaches out in the direction of his favorite toy or bib, you will get it and hand it to him.

Assuming that you cater to his reasonable demands, he will probably be satisfied for a while and leave you in peace while he plays by himself, until he makes a new request. Through his past and present experiences in dealing with you and other people, he is learning to use you as a resource for getting what he needs and wants. This is important in terms of his social development. Knowing that his behavior influences your reactions is very important to the further development of his self-concept.

A BEGINNING SENSE OF HUMOR. Have you noticed that your baby is developing a sense of humor? Some things that he does may be both irritating to you and highly amusing to him. His attempts to call you back into his room for no special reason when you are obviously busy with something else may be annoying, but to him, this is a funny game. When you repeatedly return to his room expecting to find him in trouble, only to find him laughing and grinning over his success in "tricking" you, at least a part of you may appreciate that his teasing is a sign of his emerging sense of humor. His "fresh" behavior may have a rather delightful and naïve quality to it; at least some parents speak of it in this light.

INTELLECTUAL DEVELOPMENT

Further Ability to Interact with the World Around Him

Over the past several months your baby has been acquiring the necessary abilities that will enable him to interact more easily with his environment. His eyesight has markedly matured, and he can quickly and accurately locate the source of sounds.

In previous months, although his curiosity was strong, it was very difficult for him to express it directly through action, due to the fact that his motor abilities were so limited. He is now gaining more voluntary control over parts of his body, and this enables further movement and exploration. Once he can sit up without having to use his hands to support himself, it will be possible for him to reach out and explore his immediate surroundings more easily.

He will now be able to handle a single object with both hands. He will transfer objects back and forth between his hands, and, in doing so, compare them as well as his hands. As his thumb begins to work opposite his fingers in the months to come, his ability to pick up smaller objects, as well as manipulate them, will improve. His more fully developed sensory and motor abilities allow for further exploration. This is one of his primary interests.

Interest in Small Objects

Your baby's interest in small objects is probably becoming noticeable. He is likely to be especially attracted to toys or objects that are less than six inches in size. Sitting or lying on the floor or in his playpen or crib, he will enjoy having several such toys around him. As he manipulates them, he will pay attention to their properties.

Even small crumbs and pieces of dirt may fascinate him. At mealtime, when crumbs and mini bits of food accumulate on his bib or feeding tray, you are likely to see him staring at them and even, perhaps, unsuccessfully attempting to pick them up. At bedtime, you may see him fingering or looking intently at pieces of fuzz that have come from his blanket. Naturally, since tiny objects and particles may be easily swallowed, care must be taken to provide him with safe objects to explore. In the event that he is spending time on the floor, the area around him should be vacuumed and kept clean lest he discover wads of lint, tiny pebbles, or bits of peanut shells to eat.

Greater Interest in Dropping Objects

While seated in his chair or in an upright position on the floor, one of your baby's favorite activities will now be dropping or flinging objects. You will see much more dropping of objects now than in previous phases.

Roz Baker, trying to capitalize on her son Roland's interest in using his hands, gave him a piece of toast to hold at mealtime. Roland gladly took the piece of toast, examined it for a minute or two, and then dropped it from his high chair onto the floor. Not wanting him to eat food that had landed on the floor, Roz immediately handed Roland another piece of toast. Again he looked at it and then tossed it overboard. After three more instances of this, Roz became frustrated and angry. She was just about to scold her son when her husband, Fred, came home. Roz told Fred how annoyed she was at Roland's behavior, and said that he needed a scolding to teach him a lesson.

Fred was sympathetic, but urged her to realize that dropping things in a repetitive manner was Roland's way of learning. He also helped her understand that Roland was doing something that babies his age normally do, and was not deliberately trying to aggravate her. So as not to waste food and have to clean up the mess on the floor, Fred suggested that Roz spread out an old large sheet underneath Roland's high chair. Roz was defensive about taking Fred's advice at first, but after she had relaxed for a moment and calmed down, she realized that he was right. From the start, she found the sheet quite useful. After each meal, she shook it outside, and whenever it got really dirty, she washed it. Roz still found Roland's constant dropping of objects somewhat bothersome, but tried to take it in stride, knowing that through this activity he was practicing his new abilities and learning more about himself and the objects he dropped.

Nearly all babies go through a phase during which they enjoy dropping objects; after they drop something, they usually look down to see where it has gone. In the event that a child does not spot the object right away, he will make no further attempts to hunt for it, and will probably think that it simply vanished. Until he learns that objects out of view still exist, it is doubtful that he will try hard to search for bits of food or objects that he has dropped.

Interest in Containers

Another activity that emerges during the last half of the first year is putting objects into containers and boxes and then pouring them out. Give him several small objects and some kind of container such as a cardboard box or large plastic bowl. He may enjoy dropping items into the container, and then dumping them out and starting again. This activity is likely to delight him, particularly in the months to come. This "game" gives him opportunities to practice picking objects up and releasing them, and helps him learn more about spatial relationships such as the difference between "inside" and "outside."

Interest in Sounds

Over the past couple of months you have observed how much more interested your infant has become in sounds. He may be particularly attracted to toys that produce noise when they are moved. Rattles are especially enjoyed at this time.

His repetitive banging behaviors will allow him to hear the noises an object handled in this manner will produce. As he bangs first one object, such as a spoon, and then another, such as a squeaky toy, on a hard surface, he will be able to compare their sounds. He also learns about what noises objects produce when they are dropped.

Your infant is also growing more interested in his own sounds, and may do quite a bit of experimenting with sound production. His interest in imitating sounds is increasing as well. This fascination with sound is more fully discussed in the Language Development section.

Learning About the Effects of His Actions

An Infancy 7 baby's primary interest continues to be seeing what effects his actions have upon people and objects. This interest has been steadily building over the past few months. When he was around three months old, he seemed fairly content just to bat at or try to reach for objects. The act of repeated batting, for example, in and of itself, seemed to be his major focus. A few months later, his interests shifted to discovering what changes his actions produced, and then repeating those actions. It seems as if each time he acquired a new motor ability, he devoted time to practicing it for its own sake. Once the new motor skill was mastered, his interests shifted to learning what new changes he could bring about using the new skill.

At this stage your baby is constantly trying out many different new abilities on objects. He reaches, grasps, pushes, strikes, bangs, kicks, mouths, drops, and throws them, and then carefully observes the consequences of his actions. Through repetitions of these simple means-ends response patterns, such as pushing and reaching, his actions and abilities are strengthened and grow more familiar to him. Toward the end of this phase, or during Infancy 8, your infant may first begin to combine or co-ordinate these familiar response patterns in order to solve simple problems.

LANGUAGE DEVELOPMENT

Active Language Development

Your baby's vocalizations are increasingly used in a deliberate fashion. You will hear him make sounds as demands for your attention, or babble in anticipation of an activity such as being changed, fed, taken outside to play, put in the tub, or placed in his crib. If he is in a sociable mood, he will babble continuously, giggle, and even squeal. He may use particular sounds when he wants to call you, your spouse, or his brother or sister.

You may hear your infant mutter some sounds that resemble "ma ma," "da da," his brother's, or his sister's name. He might also consistently say a certain sound for a specific person, toy, object, or activity, but the sound itself is not likely to resemble that person's or object's name in the least. His sounds cannot be found in a dictionary, but he is beginning to use them meaningfully, as primitive names or labels, and this represents progress.

More consonant sounds are used and may even be heard as frequently as vowel sounds. He is likely to be able to produce several syllables such as "da," "lu," "ma," "ti," and "boo," which he repeats in his babbling. He may say several different sounds in one breath, or say the same sound over and over again.

Previously, many of the sounds he produced involved back- or middle-of-the-throat activity. At this stage he is likely to devote more practice time to using the tip of his tongue against his palate. He may utter more sounds such as "ta ta ta," "na na na," and "da da da." The front of his mouth is slowly being put to use for sound production. Out of further play with his voice will come new sounds, more well-defined syllables, and steadier control.

Your baby's play with sounds will sometimes occur when you or other people are around, but he is likely to practice more when he is alone in his crib. If you peek into his bedroom after you have tucked him in for the night, or early in the morning, you may observe him gurgling, squealing, and babbling not only to himself, but also to his favorite toys. However, you need not be overly concerned if most of your child's efforts are being aimed at practicing his motor skills rather than practicing with his voice.

The importance of repetition to your baby will be particularly obvious in relation to his progress in language development. Each new sound that he produces may be repeated for several days or weeks. After a few hours, his repetition of sounds may irritate you, particularly if he is repeating the special sound that he has come to associate with you.

The fact that you consistently answer or respond to "ma ma," "da da," or whatever sound he has connected with you is important. Word sounds bring him a sense of being in command, as he realizes that he can influence people with his voice. Through this type of practice and repetition of sounds, he learns more about his voice, and how to put new abilities to better use.

There is a good chance that your baby will begin to cry whenever he is around strange people or is in strange territory. This type of crying frequently accompanies "stranger anxiety," which is discussed in the Personal-Social Development section. This kind of crying does not occur with all babies, but it is common. As a baby becomes more accustomed to being with people other than immediate family members, and being taken out of the home setting, stranger anxiety, and the crying that accompanies it, will diminish.

Passive Language Development

Infancy 7 babies' interests in sounds, particularly their own, continue to emerge more strongly with each successive month. Your baby listens to his own sounds and people's voices, and will be entranced by the sounds coming from the radio, television, or record/tape player. His awareness of sounds has increased, and his various reactions to them show that he is clearly differentiating among sounds. Certain sounds, such as the sound of a lawn mower or ambulance, may frighten him, while other sounds, such as the sound of music or talking, may delight him.

As your infant listens to sounds, he tries to locate their source. He observes your face, closely watches your every move, listens to the tone of your voice, and probably senses the feeling with which you speak. When he hears you say something, he may also try to pick out a few familiar words. It is possible that he understands some simple words, and you will be able to judge whether or not this is true by his reactions. At earlier ages he might have been frightened by low-pitched voices, but he has probably gotten over this by now, and may enjoy hearing them. Fathers will be pleased by their babies' new attraction to their voices.

MOTOR DEVELOPMENT

Gross Motor Activity

Your baby is not only stronger, but also more able to change posture and positions. You are likely to observe an increase in his movement. He seems to need to be in constant motion of one sort or another.

He will have good control of his head, neck, shoulder, and arm muscles. Since there has been a "head to foot" or cephalo-caudal progression of body control, he will also begin to have better control of the muscles in his trunk, lower back, and legs. Along with greater control will come better co-ordination of various parts of the body.

When he is lying on his stomach, he can change positions with relatively little difficulty. He will be better able to lift his head and chest, and support his weight on only one hand so that he can grab toys and explore with the other. He may repeatedly push up on his hands and knees, and set himself in motion by rocking forward and backward.

Lying on his back, your infant can more easily raise and crane his head forward in an attempt to sit; or he might try to grab his feet with his hands. He can elevate his legs high off the mattress and sustain this posture for longer periods of time. An interest in toe-sucking may emerge in some babies, while others will play with objects instead. They will kick their legs and squirm in an effort to get going. Your baby will probably strain to get up to a sitting position, since he wants to be able to see everything, but this task is still apt to be very difficult for him to master.

SITTING. Your baby has better control over his trunk muscles. Once you sit him up, he may now sit all by himself, holding his head erect and his back firm for several minutes or more. When you pull him to a sitting position, you are likely to see little or no head wobbling or slumping. When he is sitting, since he may no longer always need to use his hands for support and balance, they can be used for playing with toys. He may also be able to lean over and then sit back up again without falling.

You may see him maneuvering himself into a sitting position on his own. From a half resting position on his side, he may push on the floor with both arms and gradually achieve a more upright position. Or he may get up on his hands and knees in a crawling position, flop backward on his rear end, and then swing his legs around in front of him.

Parents whose babies are not able to sit up well without support at this phase sometimes worry that something might be wrong. Jannine Young, the mother of seven-month-old Tim, invited her new neighbor, Sondra, over for lunch. Sondra, the mother of a three-year-old daughter and a seven-month-old named Andy, brought her son along to Jannine's home while her older child attended nursery school. Sondra placed Andy down on the floor beside Tim, and the two mothers chatted while they watched their infants. After several minutes, Jannine saw Andy getting into a sitting position. She could not help comparing his performance with her son's, who was not able to sit up by himself without her assistance. She began to worry about Tim, and wondered why he was not sitting as well as Andy.

Sondra noticed the concerned expression on Jannine's face, and questioned her about it. Jannine reluctantly admitted that she was concerned about Tim's inability to sit. In a sympathetic tone of voice Sondra explained that she had had similar concerns about her first child, who was not able to sit up until she was nine months old. Sondra went on to say that her daughter, now three, was among the most physically active and athletic children in her nursery school class. She urged Jannine not to be concerned about Tim's inability to sit alone at this age, and not to compare her son with Andy, who had always been early at acquiring motor skills.

After listening to what Sondra had to say, Jannine felt reassured. She realized that although Tim was not yet sitting up by himself, his development was certainly within normal limits. Tim mastered this task over the next few months.

There can be wide differences in babies' sitting abilities, so you should not become upset or unduly worried if your baby is not able to sit without support. He may not be ready to do this until he is well along into Infancy 8 or even 9. If he has difficulty sitting up, it is advisable not to keep him in this position for long periods of time, since this may cause some straining of the muscles in his torso and lower back.

STANDING. Your baby may now make some effort to help you when you pull him into a standing position. He might straighten out his body, try to lock his knees, and push down, lifting his rear end off of the mattress. He may enjoy being pulled to a stand so much that he constantly demands this particular type of exercise. He is likely to bear more weight on his legs than in the past, although his major interests may lie in bouncing and stamping his feet. Chances are that your baby will be able to stand fairly well when clutching on to your hands or something else such as a piece of furniture. A very active, determined baby will even begin to pull himself up, using the bars of his crib or playpen in order to reach a standing position on his own, but most babies will not acquire this ability for some time. Once your baby pulls to a stand in the crib, for safety reasons it is advisable to lower the crib mattress.

PREWALKING LOCOMOTION. Some babies begin focusing their efforts on locomotion. At first, they will probably be awkward, inefficient, and slow in attempting to move across the ground. Your baby's initial efforts to get going are bound to amuse you as he struggles to keep himself moseying along, inch by inch. Babies' preferred methods of locomotion can show wide variation, but many begin by moving about on their bellies, turning, wriggling, and pulling with their arms. A few will actually bring their legs under them, get up on their knees, and begin to go forward or backward on forearms and knees, with their stomachs held close to the floor.

Locomotion on the floor is a complex task. Since a baby's shoulder and arm muscles are stronger and under better control than his leg muscles, his first attempts to move may involve pulling and tugging with his arms. His legs will drag behind, not being much of a help to him. As he practices, he will gradually begin to use his legs more efficiently, although you will notice that he has difficulty co-ordinating the movements of his arms and legs. He will move very unsteadily, and you will probably notice him taking a few nose dives as his wobbling arms and legs collapse.

Many names have been used to describe the baby's prewalking locomotion. Most parents recognize the baby's movement across the floor as crawling. More important than worrying about specific terms is observing your baby's individual style of loco-motion.

Babies who are not quite as active may also show a definite interest in locomotion, although they may take their sweet old time about it. They may start in a lying down position on their backs. Every now and then they may lift their rear ends and push against the surface with their feet. In this manner they may move a few inches at a time, like a little worm.

Keep in mind that although movement of this type may begin to emerge during this phase, many babies do not start to move across the floor until Infancy 9 or 10. A few babies never really locomote on the floor, and simply sit, and later stand and walk. You need not become alarmed if your infant's activities do not include mov-ing across the floor. Perhaps he is concentrating more of his efforts on becoming proficient with his hands. In the event that he has started to make attempts to get around on his belly, you should not expect him to move very far or fast.

Fine Motor Activity

Once your infant can sit all by himself, he will have many more opportunities to explore and play with objects. His eye-hand co-ordination shows definite improve-ment, and he gets plenty of practice, since his desire to look at objects and grab them is very strong. His eyes help to guide his hands in quick, smooth, and accurate reaching and grasping. Since his two-handed grasping is no longer necessary, he is much better at grabbing small objects with either hand. When holding only one ob-ject, he may enjoy transferring it from one hand to the other and then back again.

He can pick up small objects such as wooden cubes more easily, but the more skillful type of grasp in which the thumb and forefinger work like a "pincer" to pick up crumbs or other tiny particles may not emerge for another couple of months.

HOW TO ENSURE YOUR BABY'S SAFETY

Now is the time to expand your efforts to eliminate possible sources of danger in and around your home. To do an effective job, you must imagine yourself in your baby's place and go from room to room thinking of the places that he would wander into, the drawers and cabinets that he would open, and the objects that he would touch, drink, pull, smell, eat, etc. Remember that even the tiniest of objects (pins, onion peelings accidentally dropped on the kitchen floor, paper clips, etc.), and the most ordinary objects (keys, money, ashtrays, and so forth) will arouse his curiosity and fascinate him, and will be put into his mouth.

Eliminate the sources of danger that you find as you go along. Be compulsive in your search, and double check after a day or so to be certain that danger areas have not been unintentionally overlooked. Other family members can help you in your search and assist you in removing potential sources of danger. Small children must be told not to leave tiny objects such as jacks, marbles, or dice lying scattered on the floors, since a baby may attempt to eat them. Even if they are told, it will be your responsibility to make sure the floors are safe. Every member of the family should make an effort to be safety-conscious. It is helpful to make a concerted effort each month to consider these principles to be sure that they become second nature to you.

Keeping One Step Ahead of Your Baby

Your baby is now beginning to become more mobile. In the next few months his ability to move around your house and get into new areas will greatly expand. Safety-proofing your house, as described in Infancy 6, was the first step in preparing for his newly emerging abilities. It is also important to expand your Safety Training Check List to keep up with his new skills. The additions to this list, presented below, should assist you in anticipating these changes and prepare you to better protect your baby for the remainder of infancy.

Safety Training Check List

GENERAL RULES
—Put your baby in a safe place unless you can give him your full attention.
—Keep all small-enough-to-be-swallowed, poisonous, breakable, and treasured objects far away from him, preferably in very high, locked cabinets.
—Lock doors, and put up gates or other barriers at stairways and at the entrances to rooms that are not completely safety-proofed.
—Clean up after each activity so that potentially dangerous items are not left lying around where he can get to them (sewing kits, handbags, smoking equipment, silverware, books, records, stockings, nail polish, tweezers, etc.).

KITCHEN
—Do not allow your baby access to the kitchen when you are not around to supervise.
—Keep him far away from you when you are cooking.

—Make the stove and other appliances, both large and small, off limits to him at all times.

—Keep pot handles turned inward toward the back of the stove so that he cannot grab them. Try to use the back burners.

—Remove or cover control knobs on the stove when not in use.

—Avoid using tablecloths that hang over the edge of the table. From a baby's point of view, tablecloths are made to be pulled.

—Place containers with hot liquids in the middle, rather than near the edge, of your table.

—Clear all cleansers, other poisonous or dangerous substances, and sharp, breakable, or dangerous cooking equipment and utensils out of low drawers and cabinets, and store them in very high cabinets.

—Install special child-proof latches inside cabinets and drawers to allow you but not your child access to such places.

BATHROOM

—Do not allow your baby to play in the bathroom, or wander into it alone.

—Keep all medicines and other everyday products (cosmetics, deodorants, shoe polish, soap and soap powders, bathroom cleaners, etc.) in locked cabinets or those with safety latches, preferably those that are high off the ground.

—The American Academy of Pediatrics has warned that some commonly sold mouthwashes in the large-size containers hold enough alcohol (25 percent) to kill a two-year-old child. They suggested that these products be sold in child-proof containers. However, some of these mouthwashes may not yet be bottled in child-proof containers. Thus, you should carefully read the labels of mouthwash products. If the mouthwash contains alcohol, it should be treated as a medicine or poison and kept away from children. This example emphasizes the need to read labels on products in the home during the phase when your child is highly subject to accidental poisoning.

—Do not allow your baby to manipulate the water faucet in the tub or sink.

—Make sure you have not left any potentially dangerous objects on the floor, the counter tops, around the tub, or anywhere else when you are ready to leave the bathroom.

—Discard razor blades in a safe container—often supplied with the blades. Never put razor blades in the waste basket.

FURNITURE

—If pieces of furniture have sharp, protruding edges or corners (such as glass table tops), tape padding on the edges or pointy spots to protect your baby from getting hurt. For a toddler, the coffee table is usually the most dangerous item of furniture in the house.

—Swings, bounce chairs, high chairs, and other types of equipment, should be weighted at the base so that he cannot tip them over.

—Be sure to close all drawers immediately after you have taken items from them.

—Clear coffee tables and other low pieces of furniture of dangerous items such as loose change, pills, candy, nuts, pens and pencils, breakable dishes, and smoking equipment including ashtrays, etc.

DOORS

—Closed doors may not prevent a baby from entering an off-limits area once he learns to twist doorknobs, so purchase special child-proof safety latches and/or knob covers, or place locks high up, out of his reach.

—Pay particular attention to doors leading to stairways, the basement, the garage, workshop, sewing room, and attic.

STAIRS
—If there is no door to close leading to stairs, put up a strong, sufficiently tall gate or barrier that cannot be tipped over by him, and in which he cannot get a part of his body trapped (head, fingers, etc.).

WINDOWS
—Make sure that there are locks, window guards, or child-proof safety latches on windows, especially if you live on the upper floors.

CLOSETS
—Arrange closets so that objects do not fall down when the door is opened.
—Moth balls (often mistaken for candy) and other poisonous materials (rat poisons, etc.), as well as mousetraps, should be cleared off the floors and stored in locked cabinets.
—Do not leave plastic bags covering clothes; a child can suffocate in them.
—When not in use, close doors to closets, and be sure to install special child-proof latches to keep your baby out.

TOY CHESTS AND OTHER STORAGE CHESTS
—Put child-proof locks on chests that do not have adequate ventilation. Get rid of chests that do not have a cover that can be easily opened from the inside, since children love to hide inside chests. They can be dangerous or fatal if chests do not have adequate safety features.

TOYS
—Safety should be the number one consideration when choosing toys.
—Kiddie cars and other ride-on toys should be stable so that he cannot tip them over.
—Do not put several large toys in his crib or playpen, since a baby who can climb may pile them up and get out.

MEDICINES
—Medicine caps should be "baby-proof."
—A baby should not be told that medicines are candies as a way of getting him to take them.

POISONS
—Make sure that all poisonous substances are kept far from your baby's reach, or in locked cabinets.
—Never put poisonous or non-edible substances in empty food containers (i.e., soda bottles).

GARAGE, WORKSHOP, BASEMENT, ATTIC
—These places should all be off limits to your child because they generally contain numerous poisonous substances (gasoline, fertilizer, insecticides, paint), dangerous equipment (lawn mowers, hedge cutters), and sharp tools. They may also contain old garbage cans, trunks, and refrigerators in which children love to hide.
—Try to put all poisonous substances and sharp tools in locked boxes, and cover large equipment. Keep all potentially dangerous objects out of reach. When you take your child with you to these areas, keep your eyes on him at all times.

YARD

—Keep all drains, wells, and pools covered; pools should be fenced in, and gates to them should be locked at all times (use child-proof locks).

—Always supervise him when you are barbecuing. Keep him far away from the grill, fire, barbecue utensils, coals, and lighter fluid.

—Do not allow him to eat dirt, flowers, grass, wild mushrooms, or other plants, or berries. See also pages 377–78 on dangerous house plants.

—Keep him far away when the lawn is being mowed or when bushes are trimmed (a rock may fly out from under the mower and injure him).

—If you have to leave your child alone outside momentarily in a playpen or fenced-in "safety-proofed" area, always watch him from inside your home.

BURNS AND FIRE

—Make sure all electrical outlets not in use are plugged or covered.

—Do not leave him alone in a room with an open fire in the fireplace (all fireplaces should be covered with secure screens which cannot be opened or tipped over by him).

—Watch your baby carefully when he is in any room with a fireplace or wood-burning stove, even when it appears that the fire is dead.

WEAPONS

—Weapons and ammunition should always be kept in a locked drawer or cabinet far from your baby's reach.

—Firearms should not be loaded when stored in the home.

FEEDING

Appetite Fluctuations

Your baby's appetite will occasionally fluctuate according to several factors. When he is very hot, tired, in a bad mood, sick, or having trouble sitting still, you are likely to see decreases in his desire for food. Weather changes often cause fluctuations in appetite, as do growth spurts. Growth often occurs in spurts rather than steady and progressive increases, and when there is a growth increment occurring, there may be an increase in a child's desire for food. Your child may demand more food or an extra meal now and then, or reject a meal. There is usually no reason for undue concern on your part over normal variations in his appetite from meal to meal or day to day.

Keep in mind that severe and prolonged refusal to eat and rejection of food may indicate the start of an illness, and should be mentioned to the doctor. As a parent, you are in the best position to determine when an appetite change is related to an illness, particularly if it is associated with a fever. You can associate the fall-off in eating with the beginning of an infection.

Upon noticing that their baby's desire for food has declined, parents are usually tempted to coax, nag, and pressure him to eat "just one more spoonful." It is advisable to avoid the temptation to exert pressure on your child to eat more than he wants during episodes of diminished appetite, since this can result in more adamant refusals to take what is offered.

Playing at Mealtimes

Eating is a time for fun for many Infancy 7 babies, and this activity will be a mess, as far as you are concerned. Active babies are not happy taking an entirely passive role at the table. They want to be more involved at mealtimes, and are dying to use their hands. Your baby may try to grab on to or swipe at his food, his spoon, or his cup, and this can result in food landing on his lap, your clothes, and all around the chair. Experienced parents who have learned their lesson the hard way usually use an apron or some other plastic covering to protect their clothes and have also devised some protection for their floors, too.

Babies of this age are sloppy, and understandably so. They are learning to reach and grab, and want to experiment with and learn about whatever is within their arm's reach—this includes food and feeding utensils. You can probably expect your baby to stick his hands into his juice, and throw and smear some of his food. This is his way of trying out his abilities, and finding out what he can do with food besides eating it.

Standing by and watching him make a mess will require patience on your part. You will have to lay down the law when things get out of hand, but try not to get too angry with him because during this phase of life he needs to have an opportunity to explore—it is all in the nature of the game. By making an effort to understand the value of his play at mealtimes, it will be easier for you to tolerate some of his antics.

Placing a large-size bib on your baby at feeding time is a necessity. Parents often find that certain types of bibs are more helpful than others at this stage. There are stiff plastic bibs, for instance, that are turned up at the bottom, making a "shelf" to catch messes and dropped food. These are especially handy for travel. Cloth-backed plastic bibs are also useful since they can be wiped clean after each meal and laundered whenever a thorough cleaning is required.

Involvement in Spoon- and Cup-feeding

You will notice your infant's growing desire to be involved in the feeding exchange. He may make several determined attempts to take the spoon away from you. After you load it, you will have to beware! Even though it will be a long time before he is able to spoon-feed himself, you can allow him at least to feel as though he is taking a more active part in eating by letting him hold on to and play with an extra spoon while you feed him. He will enjoy playing with it, and banging on his feeding tray. This should satisfy his desire for greater participation.

Some babies who prior to this time showed little or no interest in drinking from a cup will suddenly want to use or play with it. You may notice that your infant has an easier time positioning his lips to it in order to take a few sips, if he has been practicing drinking from a cup for some time. He may also make some attempts to hold it and drink from it on his own. Since he is still lacking in control, you will have to keep your hands on it. Even if you have given him a "spillproof" plastic cup, there are apt to be some resulting messes.

Foods That Can Be Eaten with the Fingers

Finger-feeding is a skill that emerges long before spoon-feeding in children. Your baby may soon be willing to eat teething biscuits, crackers, toast, and perhaps some small bits of foods that he can grasp and put to his mouth. Once he acquires the ability to pick up small toys and objects between his thumb and fingers, you can begin to encourage him to feed himself bits of food during part of the meal.

All babies are clumsy and messy when they first begin self-feeding. Food will accidentally drop out of your baby's hands on the way to his mouth, landing on the floor. It will also end up being smeared on the feeding table as well as on his face and hair. His lack of sufficient finger control makes self-feeding a difficult task for him during this early phase.

Some babies will not be ready for finger-feeding for several months, but many will be anxious to begin actively using their hands in Infancy 7 and 8. Babies who show a beginning interest should be encouraged to practice, and praised for their efforts, despite their poor performances.

In order to prevent your infant from choking on the food and from making huge messes, place only one or two tiny pieces of very soft food on his tray at a time. Let him take these first before offering any more. Giving very small quantities of food at any given time also helps to prevent a baby from becoming overly frustrated when he is learning to finger-feed, and reinforces his successful attempts, since he can easily see that he has cleaned off his feeding tray. More food can be added depending upon how well he is able to manage.

Parents often offer large pieces of toast and crackers as the first finger foods. After the baby learns to handle these foods well, a variety of others can be offered, depending upon what foods the doctor advises. Some of the common finger foods are cubed parboiled celery or carrots, small pieces of soft cheese, tiny pieces of peeled, soft fresh fruit, such as banana, plain cookies, and dry cereal. Be sure to consult your doctor before giving any chopped or diced foods or new foods, since your baby may not yet be ready for them, and may gag or choke.

Your child's interest in manipulating bits of food will increase throughout the remainder of the infancy stage. Once this interest becomes obvious, you should respect it. Worries that in feeding himself an infant does not consume as much food as he does when fed by an adult often lead parents to interfere with the child's attempts to self-feed. With a baby whose desire to participate actively during meals is strong, parental interference will probably be met with protest, resentment, dawdling, and refusals to eat. It is advisable to follow your baby's lead in regard to self-feeding, letting him participate in accordance with his desire and capabilities. Often after several minutes of self-feeding, a baby will then allow his parent to spoon-feed him the remainder of the meal.

The Vegetarian Infant

Vegetarianism is becoming more popular, and parents often wonder about using this diet with their babies. It is important to discuss your feelings about offering your infant a vegetarian diet with your doctor. In most cases there is no problem with an infant eating a vegetarian diet, as long as it is varied among the vegetables, and some allowance is made for milk and/or eggs, fish, and so forth.

Your physician is in the best position to guide you, since he or she is familiar with infants' growth patterns and the requirements for minerals and vitamins. The vegetarian diet is often lacking in iron and vitamin B complex, but you can make up for this by giving supplements.

SLEEPING

Your baby's pattern of sleep will probably remain much the same as in Infancy 6. Since the amount of sleep required varies from child to child, there can be no strict rules as to how much sleep a baby should have. Assuming that you are flexible about schedules and give him opportunities to sleep during the day and night, he will use them as he sees fit. If he dislikes going to sleep, an attitude common in babies, and is stubborn about turning in when he is fatigued, you will have to pay attention to cues that he is tired. Should your infant begin to yawn and put his hands over his eyes, or become very grouchy, you had better get him to bed, even though he objects. Signs of fatigue should not be ignored.

All of this need not become a problem. Simply train him to adhere to a consistent nap and bedtime schedule. You have the upper hand when it comes to his sleeping schedule. Giving in to his pleas to forego his nap and stay up way past his bedtime is okay once in a while, but if done too often, you will be giving him the upper hand. This will lead to continued problems at naptime and bedtime. In most family situations, the best approach is to stick rather closely to a regular sleeping schedule.

Your baby may insist upon having a favorite toy or special object with him at bedtime. There is nothing wrong with responding to this request. For safety reasons, you should not allow him to have a large toy, or even a pile of smaller toys in his crib. Babies can easily push a large toy to the corner of their cribs, or pile several smaller toys at the corner, climb up on them, and pull themselves over the top of the crib bars. Keeping this in mind when you put him to bed should help to prevent unnecessary falls from his crib.

DISCIPLINE

Try Not to Become Too Nervous About Discipline

Parents who are either afraid of spoiling their baby or are afraid of being so strict as to repress or make him hostile toward them may be so preoccupied with not making any errors that they become extremely anxious. Worried about the possibility of making mistakes, or failing to do the "right" thing, they may let their guilt or anxiety interfere with their good judgment. This can be a serious problem.

Try to be confident in disciplining your child, and do not lose sight of the fact that there is no one right approach. Realize the importance of your direction and guidance to your baby and that he cannot judge for himself what he should or should not do, and what is dangerous or not dangerous. The objective of your discipline is not for you to be the master and he the slave, or vice versa, but to work with him in helping him learn to regulate his own actions.

Underlying whatever approach to discipline you adopt should be your message that you love him and are doing what is best for him. You need not be too worried about the outcome of your program of discipline as long as you are doing what you are doing because you love him and are genuinely concerned about his well-being. Even though you will inevitably find that you have occasionally mishandled a situation in disciplining him, just as he will make some errors as he learns to distinguish "yes" from "no," and "do," from "don't," do not let your own errors upset you. One mistake, or even several minor mistakes, in handling him will not make him turn into a spoiled brat or a repressed, resentful child.

Excessive worry and doubt about doing what is right can cloud your thinking and better judgment. Having confidence in your ability to discipline him will make him more confident that "If my parent said this is for my own good, it must be true." Keep the ultimate goal of your training program in mind, since this will minimize the possibility of heading in an undesirable direction as a result of fear, excessive worry, or guilt over isolated incidents.

It Is Easy to Become Impatient

Disciplining your baby is not something that you can devote your time to only on certain days of the week, and only for several months. Discipline is an area of education that requires a full-time effort on your part over a long period of time—many, many years, in fact.

Once your baby becomes more mobile, and you begin to initiate more active and serious training efforts, you may get rather impatient after a month or so of seeing little, if any, progress. The main thing is to try to be patient with your baby. An effective teacher is not one who gives up easily when the student is not responding immediately to the curriculum. Rather, the teacher offers guidance and training, repeats the lessons over and over again, and allows the student to digest the information at his own pace without pressuring or forcing him to learn the material faster than he is able.

Given a relaxed atmosphere, proper guidance, ample encouragement, and sufficient time, the student will eventually learn the lessons, even though perhaps not as quickly as the teacher had hoped. Your efforts to guide your baby in what you feel is the "right" direction are worth while and crucially important, and if you are patient enough to continue and not give up, you will eventually see positive results.

POSSIBLE EFFECTS OF NUDITY IN THE HOME ON A BABY

Some parents who are in the habit of walking around their homes in the nude, or only partially clothed, are concerned about possible negative effects that this might have upon their baby. No well-controlled scientific studies have been done to determine clearly the effects that nudity in the home environment have upon young children. In general, it is best to use your own good judgment, since this is a personal matter.

Some parents are very modest about their bodies and prefer to keep fully clothed except when they have complete privacy. Others are less modest and feel very comfortable and relaxed about sometimes being nude in their home and taking baths or using the toilet in front of their babies.

Most psychologists agree that it is very doubtful that seeing his parents in the nude will have any damaging effects upon a baby. In fact, many feel that this practice may give the baby a natural, healthy attitude toward the naked human body, and opportunities to learn about human anatomy in a natural way. In general, while your child is very young, you need not be concerned about harm coming to him if you regularly undress in front of him, take a bath with him, or allow him to see you naked in your home. Further information on nudity in the home with older children appears on pages 629–30.

PREPARED PARENTHOOD CHECK LIST

MOTHER	FATHER	UNDERSTANDING YOUR BABY'S DEVELOPMENT
—	—	Do you notice evidence that your infant recognizes the sound of his name?
—	—	Does your baby frequently reach out to explore your body?
—	—	Are you aware that babies often become more tense, irritable, and clingy just before trying to master large tasks such as sitting and crawling?
—	—	Is your baby especially attracted to small toys and objects?
—	—	Does your infant make a game of dropping objects and waiting for you to retrieve them? What do you think he is learning from this?
—	—	Are you aware that one of your baby's primary interests is seeing what effects his actions have upon people and objects?
—	—	Has your infant associated any particular sounds with you, other family members, or familiar objects and begun to use these sounds as "primitive names"?
—	—	Are you aware of the importance of repeating sounds to your baby?
—	—	Does your baby cry whenever he is around strange people or in a strange place?
—	—	Is your infant better able to change postures and positions?
—	—	When lying on his back, can your baby grab his toes?
—	—	What evidence do you see that your child is gaining further control over his trunk and back muscles?
—	—	Is moving about on the floor one of your baby's newly emerging interests?

BASIC CARE

—	—	In safety-proofing your home, do you imagine yourself in your baby's shoes?
—	—	Have you familiarized yourself with the expanded Safety Training Check List in preparation for your infant's emerging mobility and changing abilities?
—	—	In what ways is your infant becoming more involved in the feeding exchange?
—	—	If you are thinking of offering your baby a vegetarian diet, do you know how to go about this?
—	—	Are you aware of the danger in allowing your baby to have a large toy or even a pile of smaller toys in his crib?

PREPARED PARENTHOOD CHECK LIST

Infancy 7

FAMILY FEELINGS AND CONCERNS

— — Do you feel confident in your ability to discipline your baby?

— — Are you patient with your infant and willing to repeat rules and warnings constantly?

— — What are your feelings on nudity in the home and how this might affect your baby?

Infancy 8

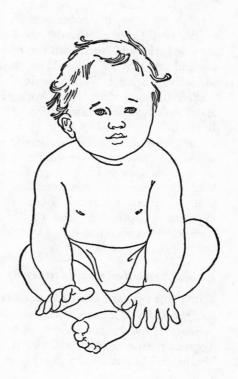

PERSONAL-SOCIAL DEVELOPMENT

Growing Self-awareness

Throughout Infancy 8 your baby will continue to learn more about her body through direct experimentation and exploration. She will discover that she can do similar or different things with the two sides of her body. Using one hand to hold an object, she will reach with the other to get another toy. As she plays with toys, she will find that she can hold two toys at once, one in each hand, or can hold one toy with both hands. While moving her head and body into different positions, she realizes that her view of the world changes. Comparisons between her own body and inanimate things continue, as will her comparisons of other people's bodies and her own.

Your baby is becoming more conscious of the ways in which your sounds, expressions, and movements are similar to her own. Along with this consciousness may come an increase in her attempts to imitate you and other people. Some babies particularly concentrate upon mimicking the behaviors of other babies whom they see. One can speculate that this is because babies have become more aware of their own appearance, movements, and vocalizations, and are thus better able to recognize similarities between themselves and other babies.

Social Sensitivity and Interests

SHE'S BETTER ABLE TO EXPRESS OPINIONS. As your baby's awareness of herself and her ability to influence other people increases, she becomes more "vocal" about her wants. Her ideas about which toys, activities, and foods she likes or does not like are becoming more definite, and she is becoming more opinionated. She may protest vocally and physically if you try to get her to do something that she does not want to do.

Put her in a playpen against her wishes, or try to take an object that she wants to play with out of her hands, and she will put up a fuss and get angry. As she learns more about which of her behaviors are most likely to influence your actions in a desired direction, she will use them in a purposeful and manipulative way.

HER INTEREST IN YOU STEADILY INCREASES. Older babies and toddlers are very interested in the person who spends the most time with them each day. In most cases, this person is their parent or parent figure. In a situation in which a baby's care and stimulation have been divided between two or more parents or parent figures, she may be interested in each of those people, although there may be one person, in particular, to whom she is most attracted. Assuming that you are the person primarily responsible for her care during the day, you will notice that she has become quite attached to you over the past several phases. Through your interactions with her, the two of you have, and will continue to build up, a strong, close relationship.

Upon waking, she may spend a good deal of time engaged in activities that center around your own. Even when happily occupied in solitary play, she may glance up frequently to look at you. If you leave her room, she may attempt to crawl after you. Her desire to be with you and follow you in the home stems from the fact that you are important to her and make her feel happy and secure.

She is becoming more sensitive to your moods, your approval and disapproval, the tone of your voice, and your gestures and postures. Quite often she may extend her affection to you in a very friendly, loving manner that is guaranteed to warm your heart. When you least expect it, she may nuzzle up close to you, put her arms around you, look you in the eye and smile.

Knowing that you will come when needed, she has learned to count on you for help. When she is in trouble, or needs an adult's assistance, she will naturally call out to you. Throughout the course of each day she will also "ask" you for many things that she wants, perhaps a favorite toy, her bottle, food, a cookie, the pleasure of your company, or your attention. She will become alert when you call her name and talk to her, and will listen carefully to what you say as she plays in one area or crawls around exploring your home. She is learning how to annoy, tease, trick, and make you laugh.

ESTABLISHING SOCIAL SKILLS. Over the next year your baby will be developing a rather broad and complex repertoire of social skills. In many respects you will influence what types of social skills she acquires, not only through direct teaching, but also more informally through setting an example and subtle daily contact with her. Your role as an educator in relation to the area of social development is more fully explored in the Total Education of Your Baby section on page 389.

ANXIETIES. This is a time when stranger anxiety may possibly increase in a baby who has previously shown this reaction. A baby's anxiety about strangers can persist throughout her first year, and even into her second. Usually stranger anxiety diminishes as a child grows older, becomes more accustomed to new faces, and becomes more sociable. Stranger anxiety was previously discussed on pages 289 and 335–36.

A new fear often surfaces around this time, but can occur earlier or later. This is the fear of being separated from parents or the person whom the baby has come to know the best. A baby who has recently learned to move around the home becomes more aware of the fact that she can separate herself from you. She also has become more aware of when you move away from her. The ability to discriminate between you and other family members and her greater understanding of separations make her afraid to be apart from you.

Your infant may become panicky and cry upon being separated from you, even for brief periods of time such as when you leave the room in which she is playing or leave her bedroom at night. Even though you know that you will return, she is not sure of this. The thought of losing you frightens and panics her.

It is commonly believed that the stronger the emotional bond or attachment between parent and child, the more intense her separation anxiety will be. Babies who have not established a close emotional bond with a parent, or who have had several inconsistent parent figures, may react much more mildly, if at all, to being separated from them. If your baby becomes mildly or intensely upset when you leave her, this is a sign that she has become attached to you.

Sensing that you are about to leave her with a baby-sitter, she may protest loudly and cry in an effort to try to get you to stay. Then she may continue after you are gone. Finally, she will probably calm down and socialize with the sitter, until she hears your car pull up the driveway, your footsteps on the porch, or your key in the door. All of a sudden, she may begin to cry again. This may be a manipulative tactic on your baby's part to make you feel guilty about leaving her, or perhaps seeing you again reminds her of how upset she was when you left.

Some babies are much more sensitive to separations than others. Try to be understanding if your child has a very difficult time dealing with short separations from you. This type of vulnerability to short separations may make you want to think twice about taking a long vacation without her in the next several months, or going back to work full time, if these kinds of separations are not necessary. A separation from familiar surroundings, such as a move to a new home, might also upset her at this time. Unless necessary, you might want to postpone a move until she is older and better equipped to cope with it.

Handling Separations. Separations may be difficult for your baby, but there are a few ways in which you can help her learn to adjust to them. In selecting baby-sitters, try to choose someone with whom she is familiar. Allow her to spend some time getting to know the person before you leave her alone with the sitter. See pages 155–58 on baby-sitters. As you get ready to leave, try to prepare her for your departure. Tell her that you have to leave, give her a big hug and kiss, and do your best to reassure her that you will be back. Then leave promptly with a smile and a confident look on your face.

Your child may also become afraid that you will leave her in a strange environment. In situations in which you take her out of the home to new places, try to offer her some advanced preparation to ease the shock. Hold her and reassure her as best you can, if she seems frightened. Give her as much time as she needs to get used to unfamiliar people or places. Then she will probably allow strangers to approach, and may want to do a little exploring on her own of her new surroundings, as long as she can see you.

Helping your child deal with short separations at home may make it easier on you when you actually have to leave the house. You can initiate games along the order of peek-a-boo or hide-and-seek. Through these games, she will learn that after you leave, you always return. Such games can be very valuable to a baby in helping her adjust to short separations. By being sensitive to your child's individual reactions to separations and by trying to prepare her in advance, these traumatic experiences will be less painful for both you and your infant.

INTELLECTUAL DEVELOPMENT

Curiosity

Your baby will be extremely curious about nearly anything and everything from the piece of dirt that she finds on the carpet to the control panel on your television. All of the objects that she has seen, but has until now been unable to reach due to limited locomotor abilities, will soon become targets for further exploration. Her strong curiosity has been evident for some time, but she has had little outlet for it other than in visual and auditory exploration, unless objects were placed within her reach.

Between now and your baby's first birthday, as she becomes able to move along the floor from one room of your house to the next, new opportunities for exploring will be available to her. Previously unreachable objects will be reached, and previously unexplored areas will be investigated. You are likely to be surprised at the ordinary objects that she finds fascinating, such as an old magazine, an ashtray, a telephone wire, a door, and the electrical outlet on the wall.

Moving and exploring objects and spaces in her home are the primary avenues through which your baby learns. These sensory and motor experiences are crucial to the further development of her intelligence. While it is extremely important for your infant to have ample opportunities to crawl and investigate her surroundings, she must be able to do so safely (see pages 386–87).

An infant's exploratory behavior is really interesting to observe. Once she begins to move about across the floor, she will first scan a room with her eyes, and then try to decide where to head and what to touch first. To her, every room represents a new, exciting, unexplored territory, and every object is attractive.

When you look around your living room, you probably take many features and objects for granted. She wants to run her fingers over the carpet, pull the books and objects down from the shelves, and crawl on the couch. She also wants to play with the wires on the floor, yank on the curtains, pull objects out of drawers, and swing the cabinet doors back and forth. These kinds of activities help her become more familiar with her home.

It is clear that no one is telling her to be interested in this or that, or is rewarding her for such behavior. She needs no external positive reward for learning. Your baby explores and learns because she derives incredible pleasure from this. She thrives on exploring.

Exploration of Your Home

LEARNING ABOUT SPACE. Once your infant is able to move in one manner or another across the floor, there are hundreds of new things that she will learn including, naturally, how to travel from one space to another. She will also learn many things about spatial relationships, such as distance, how to crawl under a table, what a corner is, how to crawl around a piece of furniture to get to the other side, how to get somewhere in a room and then retrace her movements in the opposite direction, and so forth. New locomotor abilities will greatly increase her awareness of space and movement.

Exploring your home will also heighten your baby's awareness of specific locations or positions of objects. She will learn where the telephone, couch, coffee table, chair, door, cabinet, and so forth, belong or are positioned in the room. She will gradually form a mental "picture" of the over-all room and objects in it so that if she later enters it and an object such as a candy dish has been moved, or a new object has been placed in the room, she may immediately perceive the alteration and head directly toward it. This mental "picture" of the entire scene, or perception of the "whole" is commonly referred to as a memory of "gestalt."

As she gains more experience in dealing with objects, she will also learn about spatial relationships among objects. She learns to place one object inside another, or several wooden cubes "inside" a plastic bowl. Then she learns to pour them back "out." Your baby discovers that when she places several toys in a box it becomes "filled." When she removes the toys from the box it is "empty." She also finds out how to line up blocks "next to" one another to compare their size.

It is clear that through her movements and manipulations of objects she is gathering the kind of information that will enable her to interact more effectively with her environment. These experiences serve as the foundation for future intellectual development and the formation of concepts.

FURTHER DISCOVERIES ABOUT OBJECTS. Your baby is likely to devote much time to experimenting with her hands, and finding how to use them in dealing with objects. At mealtimes she may attempt to pick up pieces of bread, fruit, and crackers. While holding them in her hand she will stare at them, turn her hand so that they can be examined from all angles, drop them, pick them up again, and bring them to her mouth. Exploration of food tends to prolong mealtimes and make them messier, but these experiences help her learn.

Objects that you deem ordinary arouse your infant's curiosity. She wants to find out about their characteristics—which ones are rough-textured, which ones shatter when dropped, what kinds of noises are produced when she bangs them or shakes them, and which ones roll when pushed. Holding one object in each hand, she can compare them. She finds that a tissue is lighter to hold than a block or that one object can be torn but another cannot. She gathers information about size, shape, texture, weight, color, quantity, and so forth.

Your baby also learns that certain properties of objects do not vary under changing viewing conditions. Even when she squints her eyes, looks at objects from different angles, or the lighting in the room grows brighter or dimmer, she slowly learns that the shape, size, and color of objects are not altered. This type of lesson is not learned overnight. It takes much experience in dealing with objects for these "lessons" really to sink in. She is still interested in her own actions and their effects upon objects, but she appears to be concentrating upon the actual qualities of various objects more than in the past.

Over the next couple of months, as your infant becomes able to grasp or pick up very small-sized objects between her thumb and forefinger, she will be in a better position to examine and explore tiny objects more fully and to sort them more easily. A "pincer-like" grasp will facilitate further experimentation with small objects. Once acquired, her interest in small objects and tiny specks of things is likely to increase.

LEARNING ABOUT THE PERMANENCY OF OBJECTS. Generally, between six and twelve months, a baby begins to sense that objects go on existing even when she is not looking at them, but it is not until the toddlerhood years that the concept of the the permanency of objects is fully developed. The process of separating herself from objects and other people is lengthy as well as time-consuming. An Infancy 8 or 9 baby who can put an object down, turn her back on it, and later turn around and immediately pick it up again is showing some small signs of recognizing that it keeps existing even when she is not handling or looking at it.

Take a favorite toy away from your infant and quickly hide it behind your back. She may become angry and try to look for it. This, too, indicates progress toward developing a notion that objects are permanent.

While your baby is looking, take an object from her and hide it under a box. In this situation, some Infancy 8 babies will try to find the object, but others will simply seem puzzled by its disappearance. At this early stage, an infant may begin to sense that objects have their own, separate existence, but she still relies heavily upon immediate sensory perceptions of them. You may be able to play some simple hide-and-seek games with her, but you should not be too surprised if she finds these games very difficult. Over the next several months as she learns more about the permanency of objects, her ability to play hide-and-seek should improve.

LEARNING ABOUT TIMING. Your baby has no real concept of time, as you think of this term, but she is slowly developing an idea of sequence. She learns that in order for an object dangling from her mobile to swing, she must push it. In order to achieve the desired result or goal, some action must be performed "first." When she observes the after-effects of an action, this helps her to remember what prompted it, and she may remember her own behavior in the immediate past.

You may see further evidence that she is developing a primitive sense of time. While seated in your lap, she may drop an object. A second or so after she drops it, she may make a face or blink her eyes as if she anticipates the noise that will follow as the object crashes to the floor. She may also anticipate certain other events.

When she hears the sound of a car pulling up the driveway, she may look or move toward the door in anticipation of someone's entrance. When you open the closet door to grab a coat or sweater, she may cry in anticipation of your leaving her. The sound of the refrigerator door opening and closing may prompt her anticipation of lunch or dinner. You are likely to see other signs of her anticipation of future events as you watch her during the day.

Simple Problem-solving

Either during this phase or soon thereafter, your baby will begin to solve her first problems, even though they are extremely simple ones when viewed from an adult's perspective. The infant is not yet ready to think through a problem by manipulating ideas in her mind. Rather, she learns to combine one behavior pattern with another to come up with a new action that can "solve" a problem.

Leonard Glasgow was watching his daughter, Meg, moving about on the living room floor. He noticed her glancing ahead at a saucepan lying about three feet away from her. A foot or two in front of Meg was a large stuffed animal, blocking her pathway to the saucepan. Meg approached the stuffed animal with a look of determination on her face, lifted her hand, and pushed it aside. Once she had clear access to the pan, she moved forward, reached for it, and pulled it toward her, smiling with delight.

Mr. Glasgow took this series of actions as a sign of Meg's intelligence. He had never noticed her behaving like this before, and was proud at the realization that she had solved the problem of how to reach the pan. What Meg did to solve this problem was to combine familiar, simple response patterns and use them to obtain her goal. Previously she mastered the act of pushing an object, reaching for an object, and pulling an object. Now she used these responses in a new way, in a purposeful way, to obtain a specific object—her goal.

The baby did not simply push an object to watch it move as in the past—the effect of her action upon the stuffed animal was not her primary interest. Rather, she pushed it because it was obstructing her path to the pan. Once it was pushed aside, she paid no more attention to it, and moved forward to reach for her goal and pull it toward her.

As you watch your infant playing you will see more purposeful behaviors. Her actions will indicate her determination to reach some goal. You can try the following experiment with your baby. Hold her favorite toy in one of your hands, and put your other hand between your baby and the toy, making it serve as an obstacle to the toy. Chances are that she will try to push away your empty hand in an attempt to reach the toy. At earlier ages she may have done nothing, or she may have tried to move around the obstacle (your free hand), but she would probably not have tried to displace your hand.

The intentional pushing aside of an obstacle to reach a desired object appears to be one of the earliest signs of "intelligent" behavior. The baby who is able to use previous response patterns to solve simple problems, and whose behavior is becoming more goal-oriented has progressed to a more sophisticated stage in intellectual development. This stage of sensory and motor or "behavioral" intelligence generally lasts for several months, or until a baby is approximately a year old.

Your baby's concentration on reaching a goal may be evident in numerous daily activities. At lunch time she may try hard to feed herself bits of food and hold her bottle or cup. The following little game should enable you to readily observe her emerging ability to solve problems of a simple nature.

While she is watching you, cover your face with a cloth. To solve this problem, she must remove the cloth in order to see your face again. Simple hide-and-seek or peek-a-boo games may be helpful in giving her practice in early problem solving.

LANGUAGE DEVELOPMENT

Active Language Development

Your baby will probably babble often. By listening closely, you will hear a variety of sounds, since her range has rapidly increased. She will spontaneously practice vowel and consonant combinations, often repeating them for her own pleasure. As she practices, she alters their pitch, loudness, and inflection. As she gains further lip control, "m" sounds as in "more" or "ma ma" will be heard more frequently.

Some babies' two-syllable sounds will resemble words, but most Infancy 8 babies will not realize that they have said a "real" word. A few babies will say words such as "mama," "dada," and "bye-bye" specifically or meaningfully, but you should not expect this, since most babies will not say real words, or use them meaningfully, for many months.

An occasional parent may be surprised to hear his or her infant imitating the sounds that an animal or object makes, and using these sounds as a name for it. The Dannon family had a pet mynah bird named Lispy, who regularly made screeching sounds. Eight-month-old Gina Dannon was very interested in watching Lispy and listening to his sounds.

Mr. and Mrs. Dannon were in bed one Sunday morning and were awakened by screeching noises coming from Gina's room. Frightened that Lispy had escaped from the cage and was in their daughter's bedroom, they scrambled out of bed and rushed to her aid. To their surprise, instead of finding Lispy flying around her room, they found Gina screeching away with delight. In the weeks that followed, she produced screeching sounds whenever she wanted to refer to their pet bird, as though she had given it this name.

Some babies seem to be quicker than others to associate sounds with the animals or objects that they represent. The ability to "name" animals or objects by their sounds comes in at different ages, but often emerges toward late infancy or during toddlerhood. It provides evidence that a baby has taken an important step forward in her language as well as intellectual development.

IMITATION PLAYS AN IMPORTANT ROLE. Many babies are now enthusiastic about imitation games involving the exchange of nonsensical sounds such as giggles, coughs, tongue clicks, simple babbling sounds, or even made-up words. Your baby may not mind it when you introduce a new sound or word in the context of playing sound imitation games. In fact, she might imitate it right away.

Some young babies are more inclined to mimic sounds than others. They delight in parroting many simple sounds and even words that they hear, although they have no idea what the words mean. Others do not do as much imitating of new sounds and words, preferring to learn them on their own. Individual styles in learning to speak often show marked variation.

You may notice your infant trying to imitate your facial expressions, lip movements, hand motions, and sounds, if she is taking an interest in imitation. One day she may concentrate on sounds. The following day she may focus on hand motions, and so forth, until she has each aspect down pat. Then, when she feels confident enough, she will put isolated pieces of behavior together. This is a long, slow process that will be carried out and refined over the next several years, but many of the basics involved in speech are being gradually acquired during infancy.

Passive Language Development

Parents of babies who are doing little in the way of vocalizing or imitating sounds sometimes jump to the incorrect conclusion that these babies are not making much progress in language development. Even babies who are not very vocal are still making steady strides forward in their passive language development. By knowing what to look for, you will be in a better position to appreciate the progress that your infant is making. She is likely to turn around to locate the sound of a voice, and also turn toward you or other people when she hears her name mentioned. A similar response will be observed when the television is turned on, or when the doorbell or the telephone rings.

When your infant hears you or others speaking, she is likely to pay close attention, and her face and eyes may light up when she hears familiar words. Several words that you use often are apt to be understood, particularly words like "no no" or "don't," since these commands tend to be given with accompanying gestures that help to reinforce their meanings. She is likely to get some sense of the meaning of your words when you express disapproval by listening to your tone of voice and inflection, and watching your motions and expressions.

HELPING HER UNDERSTAND WHAT WORDS MEAN. For a word to be meaningful to your baby, she must associate it with the appropriate person, activity, or object that it signifies or labels. There are several ways in which you can help her with this difficult, time-consuming task. The most obvious, as well as important, way to offer assistance is by talking to her often. Try to use simple language, and speak slowly and distinctly. Hand gestures will add further meaning, and allow her to put what she hears into a broader framework. Repeat words and phrases often. Repetition is a very effective teaching technique when it comes to conveying the meanings of words. The word "dish" will eventually come to mean something to your baby if you say it often and point to a dish or pick one up at the same time. Wherever you are, in your home, in a park, in a store, and so forth, use this technique to help her understand the meaning of words and how to label people, toys, objects, places, and animals that she sees.

Even though she will not imitate these word labels after you say them, she will be forming associations and taking in information that will later be put to good use in toddlerhood, once she really begins to talk. This activity should be carried out in a relaxed, natural way that makes it enjoyable for both of you.

Infancy 8

MOTOR DEVELOPMENT

Gross Motor Activity

SITTING. Your baby's torso and lower back muscles are now much stronger. As a result, she will do pretty well at unsupported sitting, and will be able to sustain this posture for relatively long periods of time. Her ability to maintain her balance is rapidly improving to the point where she may lean forward or sideways to pick up objects while sitting and then regain her balance with little difficulty.

She may also find it easier to maneuver herself into a sitting position, although probably not from a position on her back. The ability to shift from a sitting to a crawling position and vice versa is emerging, and this provides direct evidence that her co-ordination of body parts is improving.

PREWALKING LOCOMOTION. Locomotion can be seen with many Infancy 8 babies. The days when you observed your baby lying inactively on her stomach or back for long stretches of time are probably over. She will need and want to be continually moving around, exercising her muscles, and practicing her physical skills. In order for her to have ample opportunities to practice, she needs plenty of space in which to move.

Most babies are now starting to get around on the floor. There are unlimited ways in which a baby may locomote, although a crawl-like movement is the most common.

When an infant first starts to locomote in this fashion, she will do so rather awkwardly and inefficiently. It may take a few days to several weeks for her arm and leg movements to become better co-ordinated. Additional time will be needed for her to gain speed, for her to learn that going forward is faster than moving backward, and for her to learn to pivot to change directions. Once she really polishes her performance, there will be no stopping her. The baby will turn in all directions, and begin to follow her parent. She will also start to crawl while holding on to a toy in her hand or even her mouth.

There are also a variety of other methods of locomotion that one might see. Some babies will move across a room by rolling over and over and twisting as they roll so as to change direction. Others get up on their hands and knees, rock forward and backward. Later, they flop forward. Several of these "flops," one after another, can move them along, slowly but surely. Some babies bounce or scoot along while they are sitting. They may push with one leg while the other is flexed, and pull hard with one outstretched arm (the opposite). While this method is certainly not as effective as crawling, it does have its advantages. Once a baby gets where she wants to be, she is in a perfect position for immediate playing and exploring.

Again, do not become overly disappointed or discouraged if your infant is not yet moving across the floor. There can be wide variation in both the age at which locomotion emerges, and in the styles in which babies move. Not all babies will be mobile during Infancy 8.

STANDING. Your baby may now show a greater interest in standing. When you pull her up into a standing position, she will probably make a more concentrated effort to help you out by holding her body straight and lifting her rear end. In a smooth and quick motion, she will be up on two feet, and bearing some of her own weight.

You are apt to notice her continual efforts to pull herself up to a standing position while holding on to your legs, her playpen, her crib, or another piece of furniture.

On her way up, she is likely to stick out her backside, and her legs will wobble a great deal. Struggling to pull herself all the way up, hand over hand, she may accidentally let go and come tumbling down. This will not discourage her for too long, since she will make repeated attempts until she has mastered this task. Once she manages to pull herself all the way up, she may not have the foggiest idea of how to get back down, and may cry for help. You will probably have to teach her how to get down from an upright position into a sitting position, and demonstrate this several times, until she gets the idea.

Fine Motor Activity

A more refined type of grasp in which your baby can pick up tiny objects between her thumb and index finger may now be emerging. She may frequently stare at her hands as she touches these two fingers together and then brings them apart, as if she recognizes the value of these wondrous tools. She will move her hand accurately toward a tiny object such as a bit of toast and attempt to pick it up. Once she has done so she may then drop the piece of toast, simply so that she can pick it up again. Practicing this new, more sophisticated grasp seems to be very important to her, and you are likely to see her repeatedly dropping objects and then trying to grasp them.

After Joseph Haire had nearly finished feeding his eight-month-old daughter, Marianne, he placed a small piece of cheese on her feeding tray, just to see whether or not she would be able to pick it up. Marianne stared at the food for a minute, and then tried to reach for it. She held her thumb and forefinger out stiffly in what seemed like a perfect grasping position. As she neared her target, she opened her hand, swiped at the cheese with her palm, and brought the cheese toward her in a sweeping motion, causing it to fly off of the tray onto the floor. Joseph was amused by Marianne's awkwardness, and continued to place several more pieces of cheese on her tray. No matter how hard she tried, Marianne could not control her fingers well enough to pick up the small pieces of cheese.

Thumb and index finger grasping is not fully developed in babies during this phase. They gradually become more skillful at using a pincer grasp later on in infancy. Lacking sufficient finger control, most Infancy 8 babies have great difficulty attempting to pick up tiny chunks of food or pea-sized objects, although their lack of success does not stop them from trying.

You, too, may enjoy watching your child's early attempts at picking up very small items. It is helpful to give her some opportunities to practice, and after she has eaten her dinner might be a good time to begin. Over the next several months, her grasping of objects will show a great deal of improvement. You will be able to observe her continued progress at mealtimes. While she is learning, try to be tolerant of the messes that she creates.

Your infant may continue to have difficulty holding on to an object such as a spoon for more than several minutes at a time before it drops from her hand, and is also likely to have trouble handling more than one object at a time. If she is holding a wooden cube and you offer her a second, she will probably drop the one she is holding to grab the second. It is possible that she will begin to handle two objects simultaneously, one in each hand, but being able to hold more than one object at a time is a difficult task that does not usually emerge during this phase.

LEARNING THROUGH PLAY

Your baby will be changing a great deal over the next several months. You will see improvements in her memory and in her ability to solve simple problems and make associations and discriminations, as well as in her gross motor skills and manual dexterity. Her understanding of simple words and directions, ability to mimic sounds and perhaps repeat a few words, and so forth, will also be expanding. These new skills will have a direct bearing on her play activities; as she gains more control over her body and becomes more mobile, her play will become more active, her curiosity will be very strong, and she will seek out both stimulation and learning.

With each new skill that she acquires, the range of games and activities that you can introduce will expand enormously. Her greater responsiveness to you when you interact with her and teach her how to play different games should make the time spent with her very rewarding. Although she will spend a lot of time playing by herself with toys and objects, she will also enjoy activities which involve you and appreciate your showing an active interest in whatever she is doing.

Try your best to adjust playthings and activities to suit her moods, interests, and individual needs. Follow her lead, and be flexible. Should you suggest an activity that does not appeal to her, avoid pressuring her. When you are engaged in some activity and she shows signs of being bored, quickly shift to another.

Watch closely for signs of fatigue. Babies are often so driven to keep moving and playing that they go overboard, and do not know when to stop and rest. When you notice your baby getting tired, shift from vigorous play activities to quieter ones, such as looking at picture books or listening to records.

In order to afford her maximal play opportunities, you should arrange for her to have plenty of space in which to play and explore both indoors and outdoors, and should provide her with a wide variety of playthings for pleasure and learning. As we have seen, safety-proofing your home or at least a large room and an area outside (if you have a yard) is a must.

As far as playing with other children goes, you should not expect too much from her during the remainder of her first year. It may be a good idea to take her to a playground, park, beach, or a friend's house occasionally so that she will have a chance to see and meet other babies and young children, but chances are that she will prefer solitary play or play with you rather than play with others. You should not push her if, like most babies her age, she shows little or no interest in making social contact with other babies.

You will notice that even routine activities such as eating, taking a bath, and getting dressed or undressed set the stage for play. In her play activities during meals and at bath time, she may create some messes, but if you realize how play helps her learn, perhaps you will be slightly more tolerant of her behavior.

It should really be fascinating for you to watch your infant play, and to think about how her behavior has changed since the time she was only a few weeks old. You have watched the unfolding of a remarkable series of events and are no doubt proud of her progress in development. It is hoped that the list of activities and games suggested below will not only bring you and her a lot of pleasure and foster her development, but will also make it easier for you to observe the tremendous strides she has made and will continue to make as she nears her first birthday.

Suggestions for Playthings

plastic pail or waste can to house a variety of safe toys and small objects
paper—old newspaper, wrapping paper, greeting cards, magazines, department store catalogues
dolls and cuddly stuffed animals
pull toys (those that make noise are terrific)
take-apart toys (simple ones with only a couple of parts)
old hats (babies love to admire themselves in a mirror wearing their parents' old hats)
wooden cars and trucks (small- to medium-sized)
large basket or cardboard box for filling and dumping
large non-toxic crayons and paper for scribbling (don't leave her alone with crayons or she may try to eat them!)
books (preferably those made of cloth or heavy cardboard since they will have to withstand a lot of wear and tear)
hammering and pounding toys
small soft ball

Look ahead to the toddlerhood Learning Through Play sections where you will find many more suggestions for playthings that you may want to introduce as your baby approaches the end of the first year, but remember that her safety should be the primary consideration in choosing toys for her.

Suggestions for Activities

Below are listed some new activities that you may want to introduce over the next several months. Be sure to take your baby's interests, capabilities, and needs into account. Some of the activities below will be better suited to a baby between ten and twelve months, so judge for yourself their appropriateness for your baby, and the age at which you wish to introduce them. You may want to look ahead to the toddlerhood Learning Through Play sections where further suggestions are provided.

HIDE-AND-SEEK FOR THE CRAWLING BABY. Once your baby is able to crawl or move across the floor, more sophisticated games of hide-and-seek can be played. You can hide under a table, behind a counter, or behind a door, and encourage her to find you, or she can hide and you can find her. Even though you will have no difficulty finding her since she probably will not do a good job of hiding and will make a lot of noise, do your best to take your time in seeking her out. Try to act surprised when you "find" her. She will enjoy feeling as though she has fooled you!

RETRIEVING OBJECTS. Here is a game that should give your baby practice in crawling. Roll a ball or a toy on wheels a few feet in front of her and encourage her to retrieve it. An older baby who is able to understand simple commands can be told to "go and get it" (a familiar object). This will not only give her practice in crawling, but also in following verbal directions. Be sure to praise her when she returns with the object you asked for, since this will make her feel proud of her achievements.

CHASING YOUR BABY. A simple game of chase can be played with a baby who can crawl. She gets a head start, and you scramble after her on your knees. Take your time in catching up to her. It will make her feel good to think that she can get away from you.

OBJECT PERMANENCE GAMES. There are variations on hide-and-seek games with objects that can be played with the older baby. Instead of hiding her favorite toy under a towel, enabling her to see the form of the object underneath, you can make the game more difficult by putting the toy, while she is watching, in a dresser drawer, a cabinet, cardboard box with a lid, or a large pot with a cover. Then encourage her to try to find it.

A variation on this game that will also give her practice in hand and finger control is to wrap her favorite toy in some tissue paper and then hand it to her and encourage her to unwrap the present and find the object. This will also give her opportunities to imitate you.

THE OBSTACLE COURSE GAME. This is a game that will give your baby practice in crawling and will help her to realize that her actions are worth while. Obtain two or three large cardboard boxes. Cut off both ends (top and bottom), line them up in a row, and tape them together with masking tape. Place your baby at one end, and an attractive object at the other. See whether you can interest her in crawling through the "tunnel" to reach the object at the opposite end.

CLIMBING GAMES. A baby who can crawl may enjoy practicing crawling up and down several steps. You can also make a simple "bridge" by placing a smooth, flat board across two sturdy building blocks or old department store catalogues. Arrange the "bridge" so that it is about four inches off the floor. Seat her on one side of the "bridge" and place a toy on the other. Encourage her to climb over to get the toy.

SIMPLE PIGGY BANK GAMES. A baby around ten months to a year may delight in practicing picking up objects between her thumb and forefinger, and then releasing them. You may want to play the following game to give her practice in using her new pincer-type of grasp, and also to reinforce her growing understanding that objects that she can no longer see do not cease to exist.

Obtain a cardboard container with a lid such as a Quaker oatmeal container. Cut out a *large* slot in the lid so that a flat cardboard circle (about the size of a large poker chip) will fit through the slot. Cut out about twenty "poker chips" from heavy cardboard, and place them next to the "piggy bank." You can also use large buttons or real poker chips. Encourage your baby to pick up the "poker chips" and place them in the "bank." If necessary, show her how to do this.

Once all of the "chips" have been placed in the bank, encourage her to retrieve them by removing the lid of the "bank" and pouring them out. Should she have difficulty manipulating the "chips," you can use small wooden cubes or a variety of other small-sized objects, and simply enlarge the hole in the lid so that you are certain the objects will fit through. This activity will also help her learn something about spatial relationships. When she holds the "chips" in the incorrect orientation to the slot, they will not fit through the hole, but when she lines them up they will go in easily.

FILLING AND EMPTYING A CONTAINER. Many babies of this age enjoy emptying out boxes and waste cans, and then examining each "treasure" that they find. In order to capitalize on this interest, you can collect a wide variety of small-sized objects, junk mail, old wrapping paper, and so forth, and fill up a plastic pail or waste can. Chances are that your baby will love to empty the contents, and you will not worry about the "garbage" she finds and plays with, because you will know that each object in the can is safe. This activity may also enable her to realize the difference between "full" and "empty," and "inside" and "outside."

BUILDING A SKYSCRAPER. The following activity should give your baby opportunities to practice picking objects up and releasing them, and should also increase her awareness of spatial relationships. Show her how to build a "skyscraper" out of two wooden blocks. Then encourage her to imitate you. You should not expect her to accomplish this task, although she may put forth a valiant effort which may eventually lead to success. You may also play this game using cardboard boxes of various sizes.

STACKING GAMES. Nail a wooden pole about a foot tall perpendicular to a square, flat board. Show her how to stack stale bagels, or other objects with holes in the middle, on the pole. Graduated stacking toys can also be made or purchased.

WATER PLAY. Most babies enjoy playing with water in the bathtub or with a tub and water outside in the yard. To enhance water play you can provide your baby with washcloths, sponges, and different-size plastic cups and containers. Rubber or plastic animal-shaped toys are also appropriate for bath time play.

SAND PLAY. Older babies may love to play with sand and combinations of sand and water. Some suggestions for sand play are provided on pages 497–98 in the Toddlerhood sections.

NAMING GAMES. To help foster your baby's language development, get into the habit of pointing to people and objects, or holding up objects and saying their names. When you take her to a department store or grocery store, there will be hundreds of objects to name for her. She should be learning that every person and object has a name. Once she shows signs of associating specific names with the correct people and objects, you can say a name and have *her* point to the person or object. A similar game can be introduced as she grows older to help her to learn to characterize objects as being "big," "soft," "hard," "cold," "hot," "sharp," "dirty," or a specific color.

READING TO YOUR BABY. Your older infant may enjoy having you read to her from simple storybooks containing large, attractive pictures of familiar people and objects. You can hold her in your lap as you read. Point to each picture, and say its name. You can also "read" to her from magazines and catalogues with pictures, and show her how to turn the pages as you go along. The value of this type of activity in fostering her language development is discussed on page 388.

SCRIBBLING. Spread out some old newspaper or other paper on the floor, and gather together one or two large non-toxic crayons. Scribble something on the page and then encourage your older baby to scribble, too. Do not expect her to scribble, though. She may have difficulty holding the crayon, and it may be some time before she learns to scribble or imitate a simple mark that you make first on a piece of paper. However, this activity will increase her familiarity with various writing and drawing instruments. You may want to draw a picture of various people or objects with whom she is familiar, and then name them as you go along.

PAT-A-CAKE. *Pat-a-cake* is a nursery game that many older infants enjoy. Your baby may like the motion, rhythm, sounds, and the fact that you are involved. Other co-operative nursery games such as *This Little Pig Went to Market* are also appropriate and enjoyed by parents and babies.

MUSIC ACTIVITIES. You can allow your baby to listen to all different kinds of music. She may love to bounce, rock back and forth, clap her hands, or bang some spoons on a table or pot as she listens to the beat. When she sees you do the same, this will increase her enthusiasm for listening to music.

HOW TO ENSURE YOUR BABY'S SAFETY

As your child becomes more mobile over the next several months, she will gain access to new areas of your house and want to put almost everything in her mouth. Minor accidents and the ingestion of non-food substances become more prominent toward the end of infancy, but do not really reach a peak until toddlerhood.

It is useful to be prepared in advance to try to prevent these accidents from occurring. Reviewing previous How to Ensure Your Baby's Safety sections and reading the material on lead poisoning on pages 1004–5 should be of assistance to you at this time. You may also want to read the section on poisoning on pages 1000–3 to familiarize yourself with how to handle this situation if it arises.

Safety-proofing your home must be repeated at regular intervals, and you should be "thinking safety" during the course of each day. Review the Safety Training Check List on pages 350–53 and be sure that you are taking appropriate safety precautions. Keep in mind that at this stage preventing accidents requires more effort and foresight. Make sure that your baby is in a completely safety-proofed area and that it is impossible for her to get out of this area if you have to leave her alone for a short time. It is also advisable to check on her at regular intervals during the day, especially if she is quiet, since silence often serves as a clue that a baby has gotten herself into mischief or trouble.

Now is a good time to begin educating your baby about safety. At this early stage, her ability to comprehend what you are saying or trying to teach her will be extremely limited. Nevertheless, by setting limits on her behavior, you will be helping her learn that there are certain things she can do, and certain things she cannot. When she behaves in unacceptable ways, or heads in the direction of a dangerous place or object, say "No," or, "Don't touch" in a tone of voice that tells her you *mean* it. You cannot expect a baby of this age to heed your verbal warnings, so continue to reinforce what you say with physical techniques of discipline and accident prevention. These techniques include picking her up and carrying her away from a dangerous object, distracting her, substituting a safe object for the unsafe one, or placing her in her playpen for a period of time. Building the initial foundation for her education in safety now will help make it easier to teach her in the future.

Questions About Plants

Growing house plants is a common hobby in many families. Parents often ask about what safety precautions they should take to prevent their child from being harmed by eating some of their house plants. This is a reasonable question, since plants are often kept on the floor in reach of the crawling infant, and since many cases of infant and toddler plant ingestions are reported by physicians each year. In fact, plants, potting soil, and fertilizers are among the most common toxic substances ingested by infants and toddlers.

Of the thousands of reported plant ingestions each year, the majority of infants suffer either no ill effects or very minor ones from the small amount of material that they usually ingest. It requires large amounts of the majority of these plant toxins to produce serious effects. Fortunately, most cases of plant ingestion result mainly in stomach upsets.

To be on the safe side, some parents completely avoid growing toxic plants while their children are too young to know enough to leave them alone. Other plant enthusiasts limit their plant collections to areas of their home that are strictly off limits to their child. Another solution is to use hanging plants that are well out of the child's reach; however, once she can climb, even these plants may have to be moved. Most common fertilizers and potting soils are not seriously harmful in the amounts that can usually be ingested by an infant. These substances, however, should clearly be treated as poisons and kept out of the reach of your child.

Some of the more common house and garden plants that are toxic include (this list does not include all poisonous plants):

Asparagus	Jimson Weed
Azalea	Juniper
Bleeding Heart	Larkspur
Castor Bean	Laurel
Christmas Pepper	Lily of the Valley
Crocus	Mistletoe
Daffodil	Monkshood
Daphne	Mushrooms (some)
Deadly Nightshade	Nightshade
Dumbcane (Dieffenbachia)	Oleander
Elderberry	Philodendron
Elephant Ear	Poinsettia
English Ivy	Privet
Fox Glove	Red Sage
Geranium	Rhododendron
Golden Chain	Rhubarb
Ground Ivy	Rosary Pea
Holly	Star of Bethlehem
Hyacinth	Tulip (blue)
Iris	Wisteria
Jessamine	Yews

If your child has eaten all or parts of a plant, immediately call your doctor or the Poison Control Center for your local area.

FEEDING

Appetite Fluctuations

Some babies' appetites will continue to be somewhat irregular. They may demand an extra feeding now and then, want to skip a meal or split it into two or more parts. In case your baby seems hungry at the beginning of each meal, but loses enthusiasm toward the end, you may want to try offering her solid food first, when she is most likely to eat.

It is best not to urge or force a baby to eat when she occasionally wants to forego a meal. Simply take the food away, with as little display of disappointment or annoyance as possible. Whatever you do, guard against giving her food two hours later because you are worried that she will starve to death. This will only show her that she can alter her mealtimes as she pleases and, ultimately, can make you do what *she* wants. Eating substantial amounts of foods between meals could take away her appetite for the next meal. Wait until the next usual meal before offering any more food. By that time, she may be hungry enough to eat.

The Transition to Three Meals a Day

The time you decide to make the shift to offering your infant only three meals a day depends upon her readiness to give up the fourth meal, and upon whether or not this alteration in her feeding schedule is convenient for you. Babies vary in the age at which they are ready to make the transition from four to three meals. Once a baby is on a fairly diversified diet of solid foods in addition to milk, she is probably ready for three meals a day, and can be encouraged by her parent to make a gradual adjustment. They usually indicate their readiness by eating less at mealtimes (perhaps two out of the four) or by refusing to take one of their four meals.

Occasionally a baby gives no indication of readiness, being perfectly content to stick to the four-meal-a-day schedule. There is no reason to alter your baby's schedule if she is comfortable with four meals and this arrangement is not inconvenient for you. A baby who is famished and yelling because she is hungry at the end of each four-hour interval is not yet ready for a shift in schedule.

In spite of indications that a baby is ready, the adjustment to three regular meals may not always be quick and easy. In some cases babies who no longer seem to require a fourth meal nonetheless awaken an hour or more earlier than the rest of the family, crying from hunger. An appropriate way to handle this situation is to offer babies milk or juice to take the edge off their hunger, and hold off giving the solid foods, such as cereal and fruit, until the rest of the family eats breakfast.

Another situation that can arise in the course of shifting a baby to three meals is that she might get hungry right before bedtime and not be able to go to sleep. Experienced parents suggest offering the baby a little extra milk. This often satisfies a child's hunger, enabling her to settle down to sleep. Offering a baby a bottle in bed at naptime or bedtime to help her sleep is definitely inadvisable. Most dentists advise against allowing milk or other sweetened liquids to coat the teeth during sleep. This is more fully covered on pages 503–4.

The three-meal daily schedule that you select should be designed to meet your baby's needs as well as your own and your family's. What works well for one family may not be the best schedule for another. A baby who is eating at approximately five-hour intervals often wants a snack between breakfast and lunch, and between lunch and dinner. You may need to include a morning and afternoon juice break in the schedule that you design.

Eliminating Sugar from the Formula

A baby who is consuming a substantial amount of solid foods in addition to formula may be ready to have the sugar eliminated from the formula, particularly during a period of sudden loss in appetite, or when a baby is overweight. The sweet taste of sugar can decrease an infant's desire for solids, as well as add extra calories that she probably does not need. Your doctor will let you know when and if it is appropriate to remove the sugar, and how to go about eliminating it gradually so that your baby will hardly detect its absence.

When Can Sterilization Be Discontinued?

Those of you who have been sterilizing formula and equipment should let your doctor decide when you can stop sterilizing everything. Generally speaking, if you have a safe water supply, adequate refrigeration, and are no longer preparing formula to keep in bottles, you can probably discontinue sterilization procedures. Immediately before a feeding you can wash the equipment, remove the milk from the refrigerator, and pour it into the bottle or cup. If you are using canned evaporated milk, and your doctor says you no longer have to boil the water, you can simply mix the milk and tap water in the clean bottle or cup.

Experimentation with Food and Eating Utensils Continues

As you feed your baby, you will probably observe how fascinated she is becoming with the food itself, as well as the spoon and cup. Some babies will even be trying to drink from a cup on their own, and a few may succeed in this. Your infant may act as though she prefers to play, explore, and experiment at mealtime, rather than eat. The look of obvious concentration on her face as she moves a few pieces of her food around her tray, smears it on her face, gets some in her mouth, spits it out and stares at it, is enough to make you either laugh with amusement or become annoyed with her antics. There are those babies who are content to sit quietly and manipulate pieces of food, or tinker with their spoon and cup. Some babies take to throwing food and utensils, and forcefully blowing or tossing liquid from their cups around the room, making the entire area around their high chair look like a pigpen.

For babies who have not had prior opportunities to explore and experiment with their food, these activities may be beneficial learning experiences, though not every parent is cut out to stand by and watch a grand mess being made. If these are your baby's first exploratory experiences in eating, you may want to protect her clothes and your floor and let her experiment as she sees fit.

You can expect her to be moving on to more grown-up eating behaviors, if she has already had ample opportunities to mess and play in previous months. She will not automatically know how to behave in acceptable ways at mealtimes unless you teach her. Teaching a baby is a slow process, but even at this early stage there are a few things that can be done in order to get your message across.

A baby who intentionally tries to tease, test, show off, or provoke you and other family members by flinging or dropping food and eating utensils around the room needs to have some limits set. You can sharply and loudly say "No," or "Don't," or "Stop, now." In the event that she does not respond appropriately, you can feed her by herself rather than with the family. Social isolation may be an effective motivator for her to clean up her act.

The Social Aspects of Eating with the Family

Feeding your infant at the family dining table can benefit her in many ways. She will be exposed to much conversation, some of which will naturally be aimed her way. Mealtimes present good opportunities for family members to speak with her, not in baby talk, but in normal, ordinary conversational tones. This provides her with good language stimulation, and as time goes on, the child will understand more and more of what is said.

In most families, mealtimes together offer natural opportunities for socializing. Babies enjoy receiving attention from family members, and usually get plenty of this during meals. Being included at the regular family gathering can provide your infant with an important source of social stimulation.

Some babies do not eat as well with the family as they do alone with one parent. They often get too distracted and spend more time playing and trying to get attention than eating. A baby's presence at family mealtimes can make things more inconvenient for the parent feeding her, and more hectic for everyone else as well. In this case, it may be best for everyone to feed the baby beforehand, and then simply allow her to sit at the dinner table while other family members eat.

BATHING

In case you have not been bathing your baby in the family tub, now is a good time to make the shift. She has gained much more control over her body, and her rocking and vigorous activity in the Bathinette may knock it over. You may also have to switch to undressing and dressing her on a sturdy, well-anchored dresser top, bathroom or kitchen counter, or bed, rather than on a small changing table.

Use good common sense and keep your baby's safety foremost in mind at bath time. Should she make attempts to play with the water faucets, give her plenty of interesting bath toys to play with instead. Do not allow her to work the controls, since many children have been burned as a result of turning on the hot water. Keep one hand and one eye on her at all times; if you leave her alone for even a second or two, faster than a flash she could get her hands on the faucets or slip and fall. Bath time should be a safe time as well as a fun time.

CLOTHING

The Infancy 8 baby's increased mobility may necessitate some minor alterations in her wardrobe. The clothing she wears indoors should be loose-fitting enough to permit easy movement as she crawls around the house. A crawling baby, whose elbows, knees, and feet are continually rubbing against a floor or carpet, may need some protection for these areas of her body. Overalls made of denim or corduroy tend to be very durable. Long-sleeved T-shirts will help to protect her elbows, and socks, booties, or elasticized slippers can be used to cover her feet.

An active infant can be hard on her clothing. If you find that the feet, knees, and elbows of her outfits are wearing out, there is no need to spend money on new clothes. You can simply cover the worn areas with iron-on patches that are available in a variety of materials. Corduroy or vinyl make good replacements for the elbows or soles of an outfit. Making your own patches out of leftover pieces of material is easy and even cheaper.

Your infant will probably enjoy taking off her socks and fooling around with other articles of clothing. Now that she is more skilled at grasping, and is more active, she may challenge your ability to get her into and out of her clothes. If she puts up a struggle, you will have to be firm. Try to get her dressed or undressed as quickly as possible, or distract her with a favorite toy while doing so. Her desire to keep active may make her resent having to lie still on her back during necessary diaper changes.

SLEEPING

Your baby's sleeping pattern will be very similar to Infancy 7. With the exception of naps, there are not many changes in schedule between months 8 and 12. Getting her to settle down to sleep may present more problems. She may be much more interested in playing, socializing, and moving about than in going to bed. You should try to handle bedtime in a matter-of-fact manner without waiting to see signs of fatigue, or waiting for her to indicate a desire to turn in. It is best to remain consistent and firm about keeping regular naptime and bedtime schedules, since very few babies ever ask to go to bed when they are given the freedom to make this decision.

If your baby wakes during the night, grabs on to the crib bars, pulls herself to a stand, and does not know how to get down, she may cry out for help. The first few times this happens, you can show her how to get down by bending at the waist and plopping to a sitting position. After you are convinced that she has mastered the new technique of getting herself down from a standing to a sitting position, then you can stop going to her at night, despite continued crying. She will eventually learn how to occupy herself in the middle of the night, assuming that you encourage her to by not responding to her crying. Teaching a baby to be more independent during the night is not always easy on parents, but it is important for her to develop her own ways of calming herself, and for you to get a good night's sleep.

DISCIPLINE

Probably during Infancy 8 or shortly thereafter, your baby will be able to get around on the floor. This would be an appropriate time to initiate a more active training program to help her learn that there are some things that she cannot do and should not touch. Refer back to Infancy 6 for a more detailed discussion on this topic.

There will undoubtedly be occasions when you are not or do not want to be in a position to offer her close attention and supervision. At these times it will be necessary for you to put her where she will be safe. A playpen may be a handy, safe place in which to put her, but it is not advisable to keep her hemmed in a play-pen or other cramped space for long periods of time. As a viable alternative, you may decide to accident-proof at least one room of your home, perhaps her bedroom or a playroom, and place a gate with a child-proof latch at the entrance to the room so she cannot possibly wander away.

Generally, the more freedom she is permitted to have, the more restrictions on her behavior you will have to impose. You should not expect her to act as though she likes these restrictions. Being only human, and having very strong desires, she will undoubtedly balk and do some protesting, at least on the surface. Do not be intimidated by her protests or her expressions of annoyance and frustration. Chances are that you would react in a similar manner if you were in her shoes. Do what is necessary as far as setting limits. Let her know that you hear and understand her complaints, but that you must impose certain necessary restrictions for her own good.

If you have already begun using the words "no" and "don't," and have been making a concerted effort to teach her the meaning of these words, you may occasionally notice her responding appropriately to your commands. You should not expect her to obey them all of the time, however, or expect too much from her in terms of staying within the limits you established. Remember that her understanding and ability to block her own impulses are extremely limited. Be patient.

The Stresses Accompanying Discipline

It is doubtful that babies who have learned to crawl will be happy to remain in one area for very long. Many parents are awed at how fast their baby is transformed from a passive little creature who did not object to lying in her crib, to a little "house-wrecker" who is crawling about and intent upon getting her hands on everything.

The stresses that accompany the baby's new ability to crawl are greater than they have been in the past. The simple fact that she is able to crawl away from you when you call can be stressful. Each new major step that the child takes toward more independence means added risks of danger for her, and probably more worry for you. Many parents find themselves worrying a great deal over their baby's safety. A crawling baby may also place numerous demands on you in terms of your time and the sheer physical stamina required to keep up with her travels and perpetual motion.

Discipline also becomes a more important issue. Assuming more of a role as a disciplinarian may be hard upon you, particularly if you are a single parent. Those of you who receive little in the way of help and support from someone else, such as a spouse, may feel the strains of your crawling baby more than you would otherwise.

Once your child is able to get around on all fours, your home will no longer be your "castle." You can kiss good-bye the days when it always looked neat and clean, for its appearance will undoubtedly change. Your baby will be exploring every area, depositing her toys and objects at random and leaving them scattered all over the place. She may even destroy your prized possessions, if you do not remove them, or manage to get hold of them before she does.

You may be disturbed by your child's increasing mobility and curiosity, if you pride yourself upon the appearance of your home. Once you remove most "finishing touches" from your living room, where you entertain guests, and this area becomes scattered with your baby's toys, it may look more like a hurricane hit it than a picture in a decorator's magazine.

Your greatest consolation will probably be in the fact that allowing your child ample chances to explore her home environment freely and safely is valuable to her. The sacrifice you make will only be a temporary one, until she grows older. Further discussions of the stresses that often go along with a more mobile child appear on page 473.

As the baby becomes more and more active and independent over the next several months, a need for further parental limits and controls will emerge. You may find that you and your spouse do not always agree on how best to manage your infant or upon the limits that you want to establish. This can create tension and friction. Many experienced couples speak of the arguments that they had over disciplinary techniques and methods of handling their baby. Quite often one parent claims that the other undermined his or her program of discipline. In most cases this problem was created because one parent was more lenient. Sometimes this results in their baby learning which of the two of them is the more lenient, and playing up to the lenient parent whenever there is any disagreement over rules, in the hopes that this parent will relax the rules or "give in."

Single parents may also experience some tensions and stresses in relation to discipline. Sometimes the single parent who works may feel a bit guilty about not spending enough time with his or her child. During the time spent with the baby, the parent may become overindulgent in an attempt to "make it up" to her. These feelings of guilt can interfere with a parent's willingness or ability to establish necessary controls.

Many single parents have expressed uneasiness about setting limits: they often say that the single parent has a tougher time disciplining, because there is no one to consult or turn to for support in making decisions and establishing rules and limits. This can lead to feelings of confusion and insecurity.

Another problem among single parents or couples who have to leave their baby in someone else's care during the day is that they worry about what disciplinary measures the person caring for the baby is taking in their absence. In some cases parents discover that they disagree with the methods of handling used by this person, and this leads to conflicts that are sometimes not easily resolved, particularly if the person happens to be a close relative.

Parents in every family structure may feel added pressure and strain when the issue of discipline begins to take on more importance toward the latter part of infancy and particularly during toddlerhood. Some controversy over methods of handling is likely to arise between parents themselves or between parents and the person taking primary care of the child. There is no one right approach to discipline and each person will have his or her opinions on the subject. The only way to begin to resolve differences of opinion is to be honest and open about how you feel.

When you are in disagreement with your spouse, try to work out some kind of compromise. Bear in mind that discipline should be a shared responsibility. Mutual participation in decision-making as well as enforcing the rules is important.

Should you disagree with how the person caring for your baby is handling her, it is advisable to make your feelings known. Be explicit about how you believe your baby should be managed and give reasons why you think your approach would be best for her. Keep in mind that since you are the parent, you reserve the right to determine how she should be handled. Discuss this issue with the person caring for your baby. If you find that the person persists in handling your baby in a way that you feel is unacceptable, you may have to consider finding someone else to do the job. You cannot expect someone else to handle your baby exactly the same way you would, although you can expect that person to do his or her best to respect your wishes as your baby's parent.

BROADENING YOUR EDUCATIONAL PROGRAM

Once your baby begins to move across the floor in her own special style, you should broaden your educational program to meet her changing needs. From the age of about eight months to the end of the first year, she will undoubtedly display a lively curiosity about herself, your activities, objects, and her surroundings. Her desires to practice new abilities, keep in fairly constant motion, keep tabs on your location in the home, and discover as much as she can about objects will emerge quite strongly. One of the major objectives of your educational program will be to support these natural interests and give her ample opportunities to learn. She will need both your encouragement and your help.

HOW TO STIMULATE YOUR BABY'S MIND

It is important at this time in her development to offer her plenty of freedom to move about in your home and interact with objects. In order to maximize her opportunities to move and learn, while also minimizing the possibility of accidents, you should accident-proof your home. Avoid keeping her contained in a playpen or other confined area for many hours each day.

One of your baby's main interests will be in examining and manipulating objects, so toys can be an important way for her to improve her skills and make all kinds of discoveries about the properties of objects. In the Learning Through Play sections there are lists of appropriate objects and playthings for babies. By observing your own baby and noting her preferences for objects you can select numerous additional safe and stimulating playthings.

Many suggestions for games and activities designed to promote your baby's intellectual development are also presented in the Learning Through Play sections. Some of the games are meant to help your baby realize that objects have a permanent existence. Others will give her practice in finding solutions to simple problems. Some center around helping her understand the relationship between her actions and their results. Still others involve encouraging her to imitate you. Through imitation you will be teaching her many different things. It is hoped that these activities will not only be enjoyable for you and your baby but will also be mentally stimulating for her.

TEACHING THROUGH IMITATION AND SETTING AN EXAMPLE

The second year of life is the time when imitation emerges very strongly and becomes a highly effective avenue through which to teach your child such things as how to brush her teeth, use a toilet, and get dressed. Imitation begins to emerge very early in infancy and steadily builds throughout the second half of the first year. It is important for you to be aware of your role as a model for your baby. In many ways she will be emulating your behaviors; this is discussed more fully in the Intellectual and Personal-Social Development sections.

As she nears her first birthday, you will notice her mimicking your facial expressions, hand movements, perhaps your words, and possibly even the manner in which you express frustration and anger. There are many subtle ways in which you will be shaping her mannerisms and attitudes by serving as an example for her to follow. Assuming you are a fanatic about keeping neat and clean, you may notice that she has adopted some of your attitudes. Gladys March, who fit this description, observed that her baby disliked getting her hands dirty at mealtime and refused to play with sand and water, since this was a messy activity.

There are also many not-so-subtle ways in which you will be teaching your infant through imitation. When you want to help her learn how to feed herself with her fingers, how to get down from a standing position, how to use a new toy, or how to stroke another baby or family pet, you can show her how these things are done, and then encourage her to do the same. Your baby, whose understanding of language is very limited, can be taught many new tasks and skills by observing your actions and then attempting to mimic them.

There is no need for you to feel overly self-conscious in front of your baby simply because you realize that you are setting an example for her to follow. Still, you might think from time to time about the kind of example you are setting. Should you notice her picking up some of your "bad" habits, you might decide to alter your behavior in the hope that she may change hers. Remember, too, that other children in the household serve as important models. They will play a large role in her education, since she will be learning many things from them during the time they spend together.

TEACHING YOUR BABY ABOUT BEHAVING IN RESPONSIBLE WAYS

Most parents are interested in helping their babies learn to conduct themselves in reasonable and responsible ways. This is something that cannot be accomplished in a short period of time; it is a long, slow process of continued education. This type of education should begin very early in a child's life and revolve around the programs of discipline and accident prevention that parents establish. These areas are discussed in their respective sections in the text, with suggestions for how to convey messages to your baby about acceptable versus unacceptable behavior and safe versus unsafe ways of acting. It is hoped that your awareness of the importance of these two areas of your baby's education will heighten your enthusiasm for being an effective and patient teacher.

HOW TO STIMULATE YOUR BABY'S LANGUAGE DEVELOPMENT

Naming Games

A fun activity that can be engaged in any time and any place involves naming objects and people for your baby while she is looking at, touching, or holding them. This activity can be very valuable in fostering her understanding of the meaning of words, and later, generally in her second year, in broadening her speaking vocabulary.

Reading to Your Baby

Reading aloud to your baby is likely to be a pleasurable experience for you and an activity that she enjoys. You can read to her at any time, although you may find that it is especially appropriate to do so just before she goes to bed. The aim of reading to your baby is partly to provide language stimulation, and partly to instill in her an early, positive attitude toward books. It is especially helpful to hold her on your lap or snuggle up close to her when you read. The closeness that you and she share will make this activity more enjoyable.

Short, simple stories about familiar people and objects are appropriate for babies. It is advisable to select books with large, colorful pictures of *real* people and objects —things to which she can relate. As you read to her, you can show her how to turn the pages, and even let her help you hold the book. Books made of heavy cardboard or cloth make good choices, since they can generally withstand a lot of wear and tear. Her main interest is apt to be in the pictures, so be sure to identify them for her.

Encouraging Your Baby's Ability to Follow Directions

Once your baby has learned to associate several names with the familiar objects that they represent, you might wish to play simple games in which you ask her to "get" these objects, which should be close at hand. You should keep these games at a very simple level. Asking her to bring you an object that she can see at the other side of her crib, or an object that she is holding, will soon be within the range of her abilities.

HOW TO STIMULATE YOUR BABY'S PERSONAL-SOCIAL DEVELOPMENT

Your baby is growing more sensitive and becoming increasingly responsive to you. Over the next year or so she will be developing social skills that she may carry with her throughout early childhood. In very subtle ways, you will be teaching her many things about herself, social relations, and other people. It is important for you to try to be somewhat objective about what behaviors and attitudes you are helping to shape in her.

Are you allowing her to monopolize your time and attention? Do you respond to her every whim? Are you right there to offer her your help, even though she has not even made a genuine effort to try to do something first? Do you yield to her requests and demands each time she protests against doing something that you want her to do or that is important? Are you allowing her to take advantage of you?

Asking yourself these and other similar questions will help you think about the way you treat her. If you feel that you are being overindulgent or oversolicitous in handling her, then you can try to alter your responses to her in an attempt to nip a possible future behavior problem in the bud. Think about what type of person you would like her to be, or what type of child you would not like her to be. Then try to do what you can to shape in her the attitudes and behaviors that will help her to develop into a child who is pleasant to be with, who likes to be with people, who can respect you as a person and as a figure of authority, who can be affectionate, who can do things for herself yet come to you when she really needs help, and so forth. There is no magic formula for making a baby turn out the way you would like, and even if there were, it might not be advisable to use it, since it may overlook the baby and her individual personality and needs.

You must develop a relationship with her that feels free and easy, and "right" for both of you. There is no need for you to be nervous every time you respond to her, interact with her, or make a mistake in handling her. It is highly doubtful that any one encounter could have that much impact upon her future social development. On the other hand, recent research has suggested that during the earliest years, patterns of social interaction that a baby develops with her parents may be generalized to other people with whom she comes into contact, and with whom she builds relationships in the future. Your awareness of this is important, since much of your baby's time will be spent with you, and since you may, indeed, be the major focus of her social world.

HOW TO STIMULATE YOUR BABY'S MOTOR DEVELOPMENT

Over the next several months, one of your baby's major areas of interest will be to practice her emerging gross and fine motor skills until such time as they are mastered. Giving her maximal opportunities to move around your home and engage in activities that will promote both large and small muscle development is important.

The Learning Through Play sections offer suggestions for playthings, equipment, and activities designed to promote her motor development and afford her chances to exercise. Keep your baby's need to move and practice her new motor skills in mind when you discipline her and safety-proof your home. Giving her ample freedom to move within certain necessary limits is central to her growing knowledge of her own body, awareness of spatial relationships, familiarity and ability to adapt to her surroundings, and development of self-confidence.

Occasionally one comes across a baby who, according to her parents, seems content to sit rather than locomote across the floor. Assuming that a baby is capable of crawling, it could be that she is content in a stationary position because her parents have not encouraged her enough to move. If parents cater to their baby's every whim, and are right there to bring her toys or whatever she seems to want or need at any given moment, she may not be sufficiently motivated to move in order to get what she wants. Sometimes when parents deliberately refrain from bringing everything their baby wants to her, and simply leave her on the floor where she will be in a position to get her own toys or objects, it serves to motivate her to crawl. Parents might also put their baby on the floor, dangle her favorite plaything several feet away, and encourage her to attempt to get it.

The purpose of this tactic should not be to tease a baby. Rather, it should be to encourage her to want to get going. The slight frustration of the situation may give her an incentive to crawl. On the other hand, if it appears that a baby is clearly not, yet, ready to crawl, the suggestions above are not advisable. The baby would undoubtedly find the situation very frustrating, since she would not be in a position to do anything about it.

Using your own imagination and ingenuity will be important in developing an educational program for your baby. As she begins to get more active, you will have quite a challenge to keep up with each of her new abilities. The time you spend interacting with her and encouraging her to develop to her fullest potential during this first year will probably be a most cherished and rewarding experience.

PREPARED PARENTHOOD CHECK LIST

MOTHER	FATHER	UNDERSTANDING YOUR BABY'S DEVELOPMENT
—	—	Is your baby more opinionated and assertive?
—	—	Has your infant's interest in you steadily increased?
—	—	Does your baby have difficulty dealing with separations from you? How do you handle this?
—	—	Are you offering your infant ample opportunities to learn through exploring your home?
—	—	When you take a favorite toy away from your infant and quickly hide it behind your back, does she make any attempt to look for it?
—	—	Have you observed your baby's emerging ability to solve problems of a simple nature?
—	—	Do you play games with your baby to give her practice in early problem solving?
—	—	Does your baby enjoy playing imitation games involving the exchange of nonsensical sounds?
—	—	Do you see your child trying to mimic your facial expressions, lip movements, and gestures?
—	—	Have you been helping your baby understand what words mean by using the "naming" technique?
—	—	Can your baby sit without support, or does she still need some assistance?
—	—	Is your infant starting to get around on the floor or making attempts to move across the floor?
—	—	Does your baby, like most, have trouble grasping tiny objects?
—	—	Have you noticed how much more active your baby's play is becoming?
—	—	Do you try to adjust playthings and activities to suit your baby's moods, interests, and individual needs?
—	—	Are you arranging for your infant to have plenty of space in which to play and explore, and providing her with a wide assortment of playthings for pleasure and learning?
—	—	Is your baby responsive to you when you play with her and teach her how to play games?
—	—	Can you readily observe the progress your baby is making in development as you play together?

BASIC CARE

—	—	In what ways are you trying to educate your baby about safety?

—— —— Are you taking any safety precautions to prevent your child from being harmed by eating some of your house plants or gardening supplies?

—— —— Does your baby's appetite fluctuate often? Do you ever try to coax or pressure her to eat more than she wants?

—— —— Has your infant shown signs of readiness to shift to a three-meal-a-day schedule?

—— —— Have you observed your baby experimenting with food and eating utensils?

—— —— Do you give your baby opportunities to eat with the family?

—— —— Have you had to switch to bathing your baby in the regular tub for safety purposes?

—— —— Does your infant put up a struggle when you change her diaper or try to get her dressed?

—— —— Is your child's wardrobe suitable for an active, crawling baby?

FAMILY FEELINGS AND CONCERNS

—— —— Are you helping your infant learn that there are some things that she cannot do or should not touch?

—— —— Do you feel added pressure and strain between you and your baby's other parent over the issue of discipline?

—— —— When areas of disagreement arise between the two of you about how to handle your baby, do you express honest opinions and try to come to some kind of compromise?

THE TOTAL EDUCATION OF YOUR BABY

—— —— Is your older infant displaying a strong curiosity about herself, your activities, objects, and her home? How are you helping her satisfy her curiosity?

—— —— Does your baby have several of the following interests: practicing her new abilities; keeping active; keeping tabs on you; discovering as much as she can about objects?

—— —— Have you been supporting your child's natural interests?

—— —— Do you make learning new things enjoyable for your baby?

Infancy 9

PERSONAL-SOCIAL DEVELOPMENT

Self-awareness

Your baby is now more capable of recognizing his own image. Mr. Ebersole handed his son, Jimmy, a photograph taken a week earlier at Jimmy's Aunt Suzy's home. In the snapshot, Jimmy was playing on the floor with his eleven-month-old cousin, Candy. Upon examining the picture, Jimmy's face lit up with delight. He smiled broadly, uttered some sounds, and pointed to his image.

Appropriately, Mr. Ebersole took this as an indication of Jimmy's recognition of himself in the picture. Once your baby can recognize his reflection in a mirror or his image in a photograph, this will add still another dimension to his perception of "self."

Social Sensitivity and Interests

NEW FEARS AND INSECURITIES. As your baby becomes increasingly mobile, more independent, and more attached to you, he is susceptible to developing new fears and insecurities. Now that he will be moving around on the floor to a greater extent, he will be exposed to new objects, places, sights, and sounds. Babies cope with additional stimulation in different ways. Some are understandably frightened, while others are not. Quite often babies who are first beginning to crawl around their homes and crawl up a few steps experience feelings of insecurity. Fears related to heights are not uncommon among babies, and fears of loud noises such as the sound of lightning, thunder, sirens, and the noises produced by the vacuum cleaner are also fairly common. Fears related to taking a bath in the tub may also surface.

Helping Your Fearful Baby. You will have to be especially patient and understanding about your baby's insecurities and fears. Rather than trying to force him to overcome them quickly or overprotecting and pitying him, it may help to offer him reassurance and encouragement during this vulnerable period. In the event that he crawls up on a low couch and is afraid to get down, you could give him a gentle hug, offer some understanding, and help him learn to overcome his fear by showing him how to crawl down from the couch. Let him climb down several times while you are there to give him added security, self-confidence, and assistance, if needed.

Should he be afraid of the vacuum cleaner, you can hold him in your arms while you vacuum, talk to him about it, and reassure him that there is nothing to fear. You can also try turning off the motor and letting him examine the vacuum while you hold him. Perhaps you can also show him how you operate the switch, and thus control the noise.

The sound of thunder or other loud noises may frighten him. In this case, hold him and spend a few minutes cheerfully reassuring him that he will not be hurt by them. The warmth of your body plus the sound of your voice should soothe him. Try not to overreact to his fears, or offer too much pity or sympathy. He will overcome his fears more quickly if you offer appropriate reassurance, but also act cheerful and confident in a way that communicates to him that there is no reason to be afraid.

Each baby has his own way of overcoming a fear. One baby will like to confront his fear directly in an attempt to overcome it, but you should not force yours to do so, if he makes no move in this direction. Another infant will be helped by having an opportunity to explore a feared object while his parent holds him. Still another will try to reduce his fears by acting them out in play situations. A baby who has recently fallen from a high step may try to cope with this frightening experience by repeatedly pushing his toys over the edge of the step.

You will be the best judge as to how to help your baby overcome fears or insecurities, taking into account his own personality and style of overcoming fears. A fearful baby is, in most cases, less fearful when his parent is nearby. If your baby develops a fear, he may want to cling to you for security and protection, and may seem to be more dependent upon you. Satisfying his needs in this respect, without going overboard, will give him that extra bit of security that will enable him to regain his confidence.

GREATER SENSITIVITY TO PEOPLE AROUND HIM. Your baby will not only be more sensitive to heights, strange places, and loud noises, he will also be more responsive to people's movements, moods, and feelings. He will sense whether you are in a good mood or a bad mood. When the home atmosphere is tense, he may reflect it by also becoming more tense and irritable or by retreating to a corner to play by himself. Sensing that family members are happy and relaxed, he may try to capture their mood and want to play with them.

He is becoming more receptive to what people say to him and to their attempts to show him new ways of doing things. He is also doing more in the way of mimicking other people's behaviors. Awareness of what is happening around him is increasing with the passing of each month.

He May Misinterpret Your "Signals."   As a result of your baby's immaturity, and his self-centered outlook on life, he may sometimes misconstrue your anger or hostility for your partner or some other member of the family as being directed at him. You will notice him listening carefully when you speak, and watching your facial expressions and movements. Even though you are not mad at him, he may think that you are and begin to act frightened, retreat to a corner of the room, hide behind a chair, or pout. In the event that you are not one to hide your emotions after an argument, you should guard against letting him think that he is to blame or that he has done something wrong. A short hug or kiss may be all that he needs to reassure him that you are not mad at him.

INTELLECTUAL DEVELOPMENT

Better Concentration and Greater Determination

As your baby plays and uses all of the skills he has acquired to explore his surroundings further, you will see greater determination in his behavior. When he is engaged in a particular activity, he may concentrate intently upon it, being less distractible than before. He may work constantly at some task, giving it his full attention until he has become skillful at it. He will not readily give up or lose interest when an obstacle impedes his path toward a goal. Instead, he tries to overcome obstacles, because he knows what he wants and is determined to get it. Nine-month-old Ronny was playing close to his two-year-old sister, who stood blocking his path toward a toy that he wanted to reach. Rather than forgetting about obtaining the toy, he tried to push his sister aside so he could continue crawling toward his goal. In order to test your baby's ability to deal with an obstacle, hold a piece of cardboard in front of a toy that he wants to reach, and see if he tries to knock it down.

Being able to concentrate more fully, ignore distractions, and remove obstacles help your baby accomplish tasks at which he would have previously failed. You will notice his greater desire to achieve certain goals in different situations throughout the day. At mealtime you might see him trying very hard to feed himself, despite the fact that he is not very good at this. He is still distractible, and his powers of concentration do not match yours, but he is making progress in this area, and is becoming more goal-oriented. His ability to take the necessary simple step toward some goal that he wants to achieve, without getting distracted or giving up, provides evidence of this.

More Complete Exploration of Objects

During Infancy 9, you will probably see your child trying to grasp small objects between his thumb and forefinger. This thumb and forefinger grasp will become more refined in the months to come, allowing him to pick up, hold, sort, and examine tiny particles, objects, and bits of food more carefully than before. You may even see him picking up one object such as a wooden cube, and trying to place it directly on top of another cube.

Jonathan Daniels was playing with his son, Jason, when he first noticed Jason trying unsuccessfully to pile one block on top of another. Thinking that Jason would benefit from having a correct model to follow, Jonathan attracted Jason's attention, and slowly built a small tower of blocks. Then he encouraged Jason to imitate him. Jason's pincer grasp was developing, but he was awkward in grasping the block. He was also lacking in control, spatial perception, and the co-ordination necessary to place one block on top of another. He tried very hard to copy his father's actions, but never succeeded.

After watching his son struggle at this task and continually fail, Jonathan realized that what Jason needed was not a correct model to follow, but more time and added manual skill. Seeing that Jason was becoming frustrated at his own lack of success in piling blocks, Jonathan drew his interest away from that activity toward another that he knew his son would enjoy.

Building a small "tower" requires a child's utmost concentration, as well as a fair degree of fine motor skill. A few babies will be able to construct a tower of two cubes during this phase, but most will not experience success with this for several more months. A baby must first be able to pick up a small cube, hold it directly over another cube so that it is correctly aligned, and then carefully release it so that, in the process, he does not accidentally knock over the structure. This seems like a simple task to you, but to your infant, it will be very difficult. Given added maturity and ample opportunities to practice, your baby will eventually build his first tower.

Your baby's use of his thumb and forefinger as a "pincer" in picking up objects indicates an important differentiation in the use of his fingers. Further differentiation will be seen as he starts to use his forefinger in explorations to poke at objects, cracks in the wall, holes in a piece of cheese, and his belly button. This poking and index finger pointing will become more noticeable in Infancy 10 and 11.

As he practices using his hands, and watches them as he examines and plays with objects, he begins to get a better sense of spatial relationships. As he plays, he will alter the position of his hands according to the size and shape of the objects that he reaches out to pick up. Attempting to grasp a small object, he is likely to reach for it with his thumb and index finger. Getting ready to grab a big object, he will approach it with both his hands, because he recognizes from past experiences in dealing with large objects that two hands are necessary. Your baby will grab on to a pencil, pen, or a crayon, but will not hold it as you do, since he is still lacking in manual control as well as knowledge about how to handle drawing instruments appropriately. When you make some marks on a piece of paper with a large crayon, he will probably watch you with interest, and may even make some awkward attempts to mimic your actions.

As your infant handles objects, he will enjoy moving them up and down, and away from his body, and then close to his face. You will also notice him turning them, and looking at them upside down, or while he is squinting. By examining objects under these different circumstances, he becomes more aware of the fact that objects have permanent shapes, sizes, and colors no matter how he looks at them or how far away they are.

He Learns More About Space as He Travels

As your infant moves from one area of a room to another and then back again, or travels from one room to another, the space in your home becomes more familiar to him. He learns something about the distance between the kitchen and the living room, and between the sofa and the television set. He also figures out how to crawl around obstacles, such as chairs, in order to get where he wants to go.

In trying to get from one area of the kitchen to another, your baby may well discover that the fastest route involves crawling underneath the kitchen table. This provides evidence of his greater understanding of the space in your home. He has an idea in mind of a specific place to go, and remembers past travels in deciding what is the best way to get there.

A baby who is just beginning to climb, stand against the side of his crib, and step out while holding on to his parent's hand, learns more about up and down directions. Actually being able to crawl up and down from a low piece of furniture, or crawl up a flight of steps, gives an infant a new awareness of height. This awareness can initially frighten a baby or make him feel somewhat insecure.

Having freedom of movement is crucial to your infant's awareness of space and other important concepts. As he acquires new skills and added mobility, new opportunities for exploration, learning, and accomplishment will be open to him. He will accept them with pleasure.

Further Signs of Intellectual Development

Slowly but surely you have been growing more aware of the progress your baby has made in his ability to remember things, make connections between people and events, imitate a few of your behaviors, and adapt to his environment. Each day you may be struck by the fact that he is learning something new—perhaps a new game that you have been trying to teach him.

You may be surprised by the fact that he remembers his doctor's office even though he has not been there for two months. As soon as he gets onto the examining table, he may begin to cry and cling to you. You may also be amazed at the fact that he remembers how to wave "bye-bye" and play "pat-a-cake" even though you taught him these tricks the day before.

His ability to understand, remember, and correctly carry out your simple commands that he go and retrieve some specific object not too far away and within sight is also a sign of progress. As a result of past experiences, he has learned that when he gets and brings you the object you asked him for, you will praise him or show your delight. Thus, when he successfully brings you a toy, he will expect your smiles of approval.

Now that his memory is improving, and he has had more experience in dealing with objects, he may have an easier time finding an object that he has seen you hide under a cloth, or a lost object that he wants. It seems that images of objects are being retained for longer spans of time. He is slowly becoming more aware that objects that are out of his sight still exist, even though it will be a long time before he becomes fully aware of this.

Imitation is now more evident. You will notice him deliberately mimicking some of your behaviors. This is more fully described in the Personal-Social Development section. Imitation is becoming an avenue through which you can teach him various things.

LANGUAGE DEVELOPMENT

Active Language Development

STAGES IN LEARNING TO SPEAK. Babies must master three general tasks before they can speak: learning how to pronounce words correctly, building a repertoire of meaningfully used vocabulary words, and putting those words together into sentences. All of these tasks are difficult and time-consuming. Each task, once mastered, usually leads to the next. Occasionally children do not imitate words or say much of anything, and then suddenly begin to put words together to form sentences. Most babies, however, tackle each task in order. There is always some overlap, of course, because throughout a person's life he is constantly broadening his repertoire of words, discovering what those words mean, and learning how they are correctly used in sentences.

At this stage in your baby's life he is probably working on the first task, learning to pronounce words. He does this by actively listening to others speak, trying out new sounds, experimenting with them, and attempting to mimic people's lip movements. He may also be imitating your words, if he is an early talker. Simultaneously, he is working on learning to understand the meaning of some words.

A few babies may already be speaking in brief, single word sentences. They may say "out" and point to the window, thus meaning that they want to go outside. These babies are in the minority, for one word sentences generally emerge during toddlerhood.

A baby tackles each basic task in learning to speak at his own rate, and in his own style. Given a group of babies of the same age, you may notice that some are able to say several simple words, mostly in imitation of words that they have heard their parents or brothers and sisters use often. Others simply make gurgling, grunting, or unintelligible babbling sounds. Individual differences in language development become much more apparent during the last half of the first year.

In order to help your baby learn to pronounce words correctly, there are several things that you can do. One is to speak slowly and clearly. Another is to encourage him to practice making sounds, and to give him positive feedback when he does. When he says something that resembles a word, say the word again for him so that the correct pronunciation will be fresh in his mind when he copies it again. By saying the same word several times, you will be giving him constructive help. Keep in mind that he is still lacking in tongue and lip control. Therefore, his pronunciation of words is likely to be less than accurate for a long time.

HE'S BETTER ABLE TO EXPRESS HIMSELF. You will notice your infant attempting to express his needs and feelings through vocalizations. He develops special sounds that communicate his desire for food, a favorite toy, attention, sleep, or company, and so forth. His more varied babblings, grunts, shouts, and cries convey certain meanings that only someone who spends a great deal of time with him will be able to understand. You will know when he is pleased, displeased, lonely, irritable, bored, angry, frightened, or excited by the different sounds he produces along with his facial expressions and gestures, which are now more sophisticated, appropriate, and varied.

In his babbling, you are likely to hear more double syllable sounds such as "da da" and "ma ma." He may repeat each double syllable sound with a brief pause in between as if he is saying words. He may also utter a wide variety of single syllable sounds over and over again in a series such as "ga gu ma ley" or "ga ga ga ga."

"PSEUDO" CONVERSATIONS. Your infant babbles and plays with sounds when he is alone, but will probably babble in the presence of other people to a greater extent than in previous phases. After you speak to him, he may reply by babbling. His sounds may be uttered in segments that sound like short sentences, and his voice inflections may be quite appropriate. When you say something, and he replies, it may appear that the two of you are actually carrying on a conversation, or a "pseudo" conversation, even though he is not using real words. Real conversations will one day emerge from these "pseudo" verbal exchanges, and they represent a step in the right direction.

Passive Language Development

Despite your baby's inability to talk, he can probably understand some things that are said to him, and respond accordingly. He may scramble away from you when you say, "Time for your *nap*," or "It's time for *bed*." He may also be able to respond appropriately to a few simple commands or requests such as "Bring me your shoes," or "Don't touch my purse." Some familiar words that refer to activities such as eating, going outside, bathing, and playing special games may also be understood. These words might include "more," "cookie," "juice," "bottle," "bye-bye," "hot," "water," "peek-a-boo," "out," or "door."

MOTOR DEVELOPMENT

Gross Motor Activity

SITTING. Your baby will probably be able to sit well in a chair, and may be able to sit without any assistance for a much longer period of time than in Infancy 8. He is likely to try to perfect this skill by testing several different ways of getting into a sitting position. He may attempt a sitting position from a rolling or side position, or he may assume crawling position first, and then maneuver into a sitting position. Some babies will experiment with a few different methods before they figure out which they like the best. It is much easier for your infant to get into a sitting position, pivot around while sitting, lean over to reach for a toy, and then recover his balance, and scoot along in this position.

PREWALKING LOCOMOTION. You will not fail to recognize your baby's desire to be perpetually moving around, and how much more skillful he has become at locomotion. It is doubtful that you will see him spending much time, if any, on his back, or flat on his stomach. On his abdomen, he will probably be extremely active. He is likely to move from one place to another at a very fast pace, even while grasping a toy in one hand.

There are many variations in styles of prewalking locomotion that are used by babies. One may hold his abdomen close to the ground, push out with his legs, and reach out to grab things, pull, or change directions with his arms. Another might support his weight on his forearms and knees, and get around in this manner. Some babies support their weight on their hands and knees, holding their arms straight and their shoulders and tummy high off the ground as they move. In still another type of movement a baby gets up onto his hands and feet with his rear end protruding in the air. Your baby's individual style of prewalking locomotion is the one which best suits his special needs and motor abilities, so there is no need for concern if his method of moving is unlike that of the baby next door.

STANDING. By the end of Infancy 9, your child will probably be able to pull himself up to a standing position by grabbing on to the bars of his crib or the sides of a piece of furniture, although he may not accomplish this task for another month or so. Remember that his first few attempts will involve great concentration and effort on his part, with both hands clutching on to a piece of furniture in order to help hold up his weight. Standing may be so important to him that he relentlessly practices this new activity. He is apt to be able to stand fairly well with you holding his hands or supported by a piece of furniture. He may stand all by himself for brief periods of time.

An extremely active baby is likely to begin making attempts to get into a standing position without using furniture for support. This is unusual in Infancy 9, so do not expect your baby to try this feat. From a stomach position a baby may push up on his hands, hesitantly place one foot and then the other on the ground, gradually extend one arm after the other to his sides for balance, straighten his legs, lift and straighten his trunk, and stand alone. His first few trials at standing all by himself may prove to be unsuccessful, but he will not be too discouraged, since his desire to master this task is likely to be very strong.

CRAWLING OVER VERY LOW OBJECTS. Occasionally, an Infancy 9 baby will attempt to climb up and down from very low objects, less than a foot in height. Most babies do not try to climb, even over low objects, until they gain more skill and confidence over the next several months.

In the event that your infant is capable of crawling up a flight of steps, chances are that he will panic at the top, since he will not know how to get down. You should closely supervise him if he has begun to crawl up a flight of stairs, lest he get into trouble. You should also teach him how to back down stairs, or place sturdy gates at the bottom and top of stairways so that there will not be any chance of his falling when you are not around.

Fine Motor Activity

In Infancy 8, your baby probably tried picking up small objects and bits of food, but was unsuccessful at this type of sophisticated grasping. His eye-hand co-ordination now shows considerable improvement. He may successfully pick up a raisin or string, and in another month or two he will be able to pick up a tiny crumb.

Your infant's wrist and hand action are much more sophisticated than before, and you will see him turn, twist, and rotate his wrists. He varies the position of his hands when he goes to grasp objects depending upon their size and shape. Holding one object in each hand and then banging them together in front of him is a relatively new activity that he enjoys.

At this time you may notice him using his forefinger more often. This is more fully described in the Intellectual Development section. His use of his index finger in this manner is indicative of greater differentiation in finger use in the months ahead. Gradually he is using one finger for one purpose, and a different finger for another reason.

HOW TO ENSURE YOUR BABY'S SAFETY

As preparation for your baby's ability to crawl up on objects such as chairs and stand up, now is the time to make sure that potentially harmful objects are locked and/or stored in places beyond his reach. Do not underestimate a very clever and physically advanced baby's ability to drag a lightweight chair over to a shelf, crawl up on the chair, and grab an object that was supposed to be off limits.

Once your baby is capable of crawling up steps, part of your educational program should include showing him how to back down. You can also show him how to climb down from low beds, couches, or other pieces of furniture that he has climbed. Demonstrate how to accomplish these tasks several times, and then supervise him while he practices. Having these simple skills may help to prevent falls.

In educating your baby about safety, be sure that you are not overusing verbal warnings such as "no" or "don't touch," and are using them mainly for educational purposes when he is reaching for an off-limits object, or heading toward a dangerous area. By limiting the use of these words, and using them only when you really mean business, they will be more instructive and meaningful to him.

Another aspect of your educational program should include training him to put toys away where they belong after he is through playing with them. Do not expect to see miraculous results. He is simply too young. Show him where his toys are kept, and encourage him to help you pick them up and put them in boxes or other containers by making a game of this. For a long time to come, you can expect to be picking up after him, but there is no reason not to start gently steering him in the right direction at an early age.

FEEDING

Breast- and Bottle-feeding

You will notice how quickly and efficiently your baby is emptying milk from the breast or bottle. Some babies will now be attempting to hold their bottles by themselves as they suck, and actually do quite a good job of this. Occasionally a baby who can surely hold his own bottle will make no effort to do so, insisting that his parents continue to feed him. Taking a passive role and having his parents feed him his bottle gives a little extra security that he needs at this phase of development.

There is great variation in the timing of the weaning process from one child to the next. During the remaining months prior to their first birthday, many babies will indicate to their parents that they are less interested in nursing at the breast or bottle, and more enthusiastic about drinking milk from a cup, but some babies will still be very content to nurse. There is no reason not to continue with the breast or bottle if your baby enjoys this, as long as you pay attention to indications that he is ready to make a shift.

When a baby is not ready for weaning he may flatly reject taking milk from a cup, even though he knows how to drink from it, and accepts taking liquids other than milk from it. The baby may also cry hard and long and constantly reach for the breast or repeat "ba ba" for bottle for hours at a stretch. Mrs. Steinbach said that her little boy was so angry with her for weaning him from the breast that he intentionally tried to scratch and bite her nipple. There is little doubt that a baby who is not willing or ready to be weaned will make his wishes known.

You need not feel awkward about this, or pressured to wean simply because your relatives or friends have all weaned their babies prior to this age. You must do whatever seems "right" and most comfortable for you and your child. If you try to wean him and discover that he needs more time at the breast or bottle, try to be flexible enough to respond to his needs.

Expanding Your Baby's Diet

Most babies have now become accustomed to consuming a good variety of solid foods including plain vegetables, fruits, cereals, and meats. Egg yolk and food products such as cottage cheese and yogurt may also be among the foods that a baby eats in addition to milk. Most babies are ready for some new taste experiences, and possibly slightly coarser textures. As always, your doctor should advise you of alterations in your baby's diet and the coarseness of the foods offered.

MIXTURES OF FOODS. Once a baby has readily accepted a variety of single foods within each of the four major food groups, you might want to mix foods together to add further variety to the diet. Many of you will want to make your own mixtures of foods at home, using family and table foods slightly modified for spices and texture. You can prepare nutritious, suitable mixtures such as beef stew for your baby to eat without much bother. This is also more economical than buying commercially prepared, jarred baby foods.

Meats, vegetables, and fruits, in different combinations, are also available in baby food jars. Some, with ample portions, such as in "high meat dinners," are intended for use as an entrée. Other combinations, or soups, can be used as a side dish, not in place of meat or another main dish high in protein.

NEW SOURCES OF STARCH. Your doctor may now suggest the introduction of various macaroni dishes or pastas, and potatoes that have been baked or boiled and mashed. Obviously, if your baby is overweight or does not need these extra starches, your doctor may advise holding off on them. Macaroni or potatoes are often mixed in with the various combination dinners or soups that you can buy. If you are serving them to your family, you can give your baby small quantities, too. Often when eating potatoes for the first time, some babies dislike or have trouble swallowing them. In order to make mashed potatoes easier to swallow, mix them with a little more milk than is ordinarily used, obtaining a loose, runny texture.

"FINGER" FOODS FOR MORE INDEPENDENCE. Most Infancy 9 babies enjoy picking up foods with their hands and chewing, biting, and sucking on foods, particularly if they are teething. You may offer your baby finger foods, as they are sometimes

called, such as stale crusts of bread, pieces of toast, graham crackers, plain cookies, or teething biscuits, and so forth. He will enjoy "working" on these foods as a part of his regular meal or in between meals. Many experienced parents have found that offering their child a finger food to hold on to during regular meals makes feeding him easier.

WHAT ABOUT DESSERT? In selecting a wholesome dessert for a baby, or anyone else, most dieticians would probably recommend fruit, either steamed, baked, or soft fresh fruits with the skins removed. In order to broaden your baby's taste experiences, you may want occasionally to serve plain gelatin desserts, custards, milk puddings, or milk and starch puddings such as rice pudding. Puddings made for babies come in ready-to-serve forms in jars or cans, which make convenient snacks when on an outing, or you can make your own. You can add some powdered milk when you prepare the puddings, or pour milk on them when served. Provided your doctor says that it is all right to introduce sherbet, ice cream, and other desserts, feel free to offer them now and then for variety.

COARSENING THE TEXTURE OF BABY'S FOODS. By the time your baby celebrates his first birthday, he will most likely be eating bite-size pieces of foods that adults eat, rather than puréed or strained food. Over the course of the next several months, your doctor may recommend that you gradually offer him some coarser foods that are lumpy or chopped. Introducing them early will give him plenty of time to get used to new consistencies, and will make the transition easier for him.

There are a wide variety of chopped foods, sometimes referred to as "junior" foods, available in ready-to-use jars. These are the right consistency for older babies, but feel free to use family or table foods. When you first introduce chopped (junior) foods, do not serve every food in this consistency. Introduce a chopped food every now and then when your infant is hungry and in a good mood. By making a slow transition, he will probably be more willing to accept it. At first, mash up the chopped food so that it is fairly smooth. After he takes this form, slowly mash less and leave more lumps.

Even though he does not have many or, in some cases, any teeth, he will still be able to manage chopped or lumpy foods with his gums. By making a slow shift from puréed to chopped, he will also be less likely to gag or reject them. Should the child have great difficulty handling or accepting coarser foods, return to puréed and strained foods and reintroduce chopped foods after a month or two. There is no real rush.

The Choosy Eater

Most babies have developed obvious likes and dislikes for particular solid foods. Sometimes offering your baby a disliked food in combination with one he likes may make it more appealing. If the taste is not well disguised, he may turn against the food you combined it with, too. There is no need for you to insist on any one food that is disliked. With so many different kinds of foods to choose from, you can certainly find one that he will willingly accept.

Learning to Eat by Himself Is a Slow Process

There can be considerable variability in babies' skills with their hands and with their demands to participate during meals. Many will want to take a more active, independent role at mealtimes, but do not become concerned if this is not the case with your infant. Some young ones are simply happier in a more passive role, and are more secure being fed for the time being. Sometimes babies feel independent and brave enough to try to carry out one aspect of feeding on their own, such as managing a cup, or feeding themselves with their fingers, but are not ready to tackle everything by themselves.

It is generally a good idea to offer your baby as much independence as he shows you he wants and can handle. There is no urgent reason why he has to do things for himself in this area. Let him progress at his own rate, in his own style, without pressuring him.

It can occasionally be difficult as well as trying on your nerves to be patient while your baby is learning to eat. Try not to become overly impatient about his lack of co-ordination and manual skills. As he grows older and has more opportunities to practice, his abilities will show marked improvement. In the meantime, neatness and accuracy in self-feeding should not be expected.

BATHING

Now that your baby's memory and ability to make associations are improving, he will anticipate many of your moves as you get him ready for his bath, and wash and dry him. As soon as you put him in the tub and reach for the washcloth, he may turn his face away in an attempt to escape having it washed. Assuming that he does not mind having his face washed, he may lean forward toward the washcloth in an attempt to make things easier for you. When it is time to have his arms and legs washed, he may lift them and hold them out straight. This can work both ways, however. In the event that he dislikes his bath, he may deliberately put up a struggle and refuse to extend his arms and legs, making your job more difficult.

Give your baby the opportunity to handle the washcloth and soap on his own. You may see some amusing results. He may toss the soap out of the tub, or it may slip out of his hands and plop into the water. The splash may get you wet and no doubt delight him. He may also make some clumsy attempts to wash himself, although headway in this area will be slow. If you have given him cups or other containers to play with in the tub, do not be surprised if he fills them with soapy water and tries to drink from them.

Occasionally, a child who has enjoyed his bath until this time may suddenly show a fear of it. He may cry as soon as he sees the bathtub, and tightly grasp the side of the tub or his parent for security after he is placed in it. Even his bath toys may no longer interest him since he is too frightened and insecure to let go of his parent or the sides of the tub to play.

Keep the water shallow and see whether this helps to put him at ease. Sometimes lining not only the bottom but the sides of the tub with bath mats or towels makes it less slippery, and helps to allay a baby's fears. You might also try taking a bath with him and holding him in your lap or giving him a sponge bath for a while until he seems less afraid. There is no sense forcing a fearful, struggling baby into the tub. Chances are that his fear will be short-lived. In the meanwhile you can be considerate of his feelings.

CLOTHING

During Infancy 9 you may have even more trouble than before trying to get your baby to be still long enough to change his diapers and clothes. He will want to be moving about constantly and may complain loudly about being placed on his back. You will have to work quickly and keep a firm hold on him. Give him an interesting object to play with while you go about dressing him, since this should help at least to keep his hands occupied. Actually, getting him to lie still in order to be changed will become more and more difficult as he nears his first birthday.

Your infant may be well aware of your set routine in dressing him. He may be a helpful participant, sticking out his arms and legs when you hold up his shirt and pants, or he may tease you by becoming limp or rigid, refusing to help. If you have already put your child in shoes, he may enjoy playing with them and carrying or dragging them around by the laces. Many children become fascinated with their shoes, and even resent those times when they must part with them. Mr. Grober reported that his little boy, Mark, regularly took his shoe to bed with him, and insisted upon playing with it each night before drifting off to sleep. This attachment to shoes is not uncommon among older infants, and should be respected.

DISCIPLINE

Setting a Good Example Is an Important Aspect of Discipline

Over the next few months, and increasingly over the next few years, an important point to remember is that what a child sees is what he will do; what he hears is what he will repeat. While this oversimplification of the situation does not give him much credit for being independent and unique in his thoughts or actions, it is true, nevertheless, that he learns a great deal from emulating you. This has a direct bearing upon the subject of discipline.

As the old saying goes, "What is good for the goose, is good for the gander." You are an adult; you are older, wiser, and more experienced, and are therefore entitled to say things and behave in ways that your baby should not. You are also entitled to certain privileges that he cannot or should not have. This really goes without saying. On the other hand, there are some things that you should not expect him to do if you yourself do not do them. If you are not polite to other people, how can you expect him to be courteous as he grows older? In the event that you destroy household objects whenever you lose your temper, you should not be surprised if he does the same, long after he is old enough to have learned the value of respecting property. He will have no idea that he is supposed to imitate certain of your behaviors and not others. Therefore, he is bound to mimic your bad habits as well as your good ones.

Eleven-month-old Larry was a very early talker. Copying his mother's speech, he began to use "bad" words. One evening, quite to his mother's surprise and dismay, Larry said the word "Damn." How did his mother react? She shook Larry and angrily shouted, "G-d dammit, you son of a b———. I never want to hear you use the word 'damn' again." Larry had obviously learned this word from his mother, who set one standard for her conduct and another for her child's. It is important to establish fair and realistic limits that will make it easier for you to discipline your child.

ARGUMENTS BETWEEN PARENTS

As babies grow older and more aware of what goes on around them, parents often wonder whether their child will be negatively affected by seeing them arguing with one another. There is no easy answer to this question. Factors such as how often arguments occur and the nature and severity of the exchanges will have a bearing upon how the child is affected.

It is a rare couple who can honestly say that they never argue. If your baby or even young child occasionally sees you and your partner having a routine, "civilized" argument or verbal disagreement and later sees you make up and resume normal relations toward one another, it is doubtful that he will be negatively affected.

Arguments and disagreements are a normal part of life. In some respects they are probably beneficial. Watching people who love each other get angry and express their emotions, and make up afterward, helps your child realize that anger is not something a person must never express. He will also realize that people can still love and respect one another despite occasional arguments. In the long run this may help your child to cope with his occasional feelings of anger and resentment without feeling overly guilty, ashamed, or frightened about these feelings.

Severe, Prolonged Arguments Are Not Beneficial for the Child

"Uncivilized" arguments in which parents lose control, become destructive, or physically and verbally abuse one another can have a traumatic effect upon a child. He may be very upset after hearing or seeing such arguments, and feelings of fear, confusion, and insecurity may result. After all, his parents, whom he loves, represent a very important security base for him. A toddler or preschool child may somehow feel that he is the cause of his parents' arguments, even though these feelings are not substantiated by fact. He may feel very guilty and unworthy as a result. Some children develop fears and have bad dreams and nightmares after witnessing "uncivilized" arguments.

This kind of argument should, with due respect to the child, be carried on in private. If "uncivilized" arguments are a frequent occurrence in your home, perhaps the two of you should seek professional help before your innocent child suffers.

Just because a child is not present at the scene does not mean that he is totally unaware of the tensions between his parents. Children are very sensitive to the moods and feelings of their parents and may sense that they are not getting along despite parents' efforts to conceal their arguments and feelings.

Some parents whose marriages are not working out well and who feel that a separation or divorce would be best for the two of them, wonder whether they should maintain the marriage solely for their child's sake. This issue is complex. If you and your spouse are faced with this question and cannot deal effectively with it alone or you are having any doubts, you should discuss problems with a professional person such as a marriage counselor.

PREPARED PARENTHOOD CHECK LIST

MOTHER	FATHER	UNDERSTANDING YOUR BABY'S DEVELOPMENT
——	——	Has your baby developed any new fears or insecurities? How can you help him overcome them?
——	——	Does your infant sometimes feel that your anger at another person is directed at him? Why?
——	——	In what ways is your baby more sensitive to people whom he sees on a regular basis?
——	——	Can you see greater determination and more direction in your baby's activities?
——	——	What evidence do you see that your infant is better able to remember things, make associations, and adapt to his surroundings?
——	——	Are you familiar with the three general stages in learning to speak?
——	——	Does your infant attempt to express his needs and feelings through vocalizations?
——	——	When you say something and your baby replies, does it appear that you are carrying on a conversation, even though he is not using real words?
——	——	Can your baby understand any words referring to familiar activities?
——	——	Does your infant make attempts to get himself into a sitting position?
——	——	Is your baby becoming more skillful at prewalking locomotion?
——	——	Have you seen your child trying to pull himself to a standing position?

		BASIC CARE
——	——	Have you made sure that potentially harmful objects are locked and/or stored in places beyond your baby's reach?
——	——	What steps are you taking to expand your program of educating your infant about safety?
——	——	Has your infant shown any signs of readiness for weaning?
——	——	Are you aware of some of the main considerations in expanding a baby's diet?
——	——	Does your infant have a fear of the bathtub? How do you handle this?
——	——	Is your baby well aware of your set routine in dressing him? Does your child try to participate in dressing?

Infancy 9

FAMILY FEELINGS AND CONCERNS

—— —— Do you ever stop to consider what type of example you are setting for your child?

—— —— Do you and your spouse argue mainly in front of your baby or in private?

—— —— What effect, if any, do your arguments appear to be having upon your child?

Infancy 10

PERSONAL-SOCIAL DEVELOPMENT

Self-awareness

MINE VERSUS THINE. As a baby grows more aware of herself, she also grows more aware of her own possessions and belongings. Having a sense of what toys or objects are "hers" may begin to arise at this time. Mrs. Purpura became amazed at her daughter Helen's sudden aggressive behavior.

Helen was playing with her box of toys when her older brother walked by and picked up her toy car. Suddenly, Helen became red with anger and protested loudly until her brother put back the toy. Previously she did not seem to mind people taking some of her toys, but at this time she became very possessive. Mrs. Purpura recognized that her daughter was beginning to learn what objects belonged to her.

A notion of possession may be emerging during this phase or the next, but the concept of property rights will not be well established for several years. Having a better idea of what materialistic objects belong to her reflects your child's emerging sense of identity.

BODY POINTING AND LABELING GAMES. If you have not already started playing games naming body parts with your baby, now is a good time to begin. Point to various parts of your own body, or to parts of a doll's body, and say the appropriate names (nose, ear, eyes, etcetera). Then point to parts of your baby's body, doing the same thing. This helps to make the child more aware of her body and the labels for body parts. She also becomes more conscious of the similarities between her own body and other people's bodies.

Your baby may begin to point as you name parts of the body. She may even be able to point correctly to her own major facial features or hands and toes as you ask her, "Where are your ——?" or "Point to your ——." A baby may correctly point to her parents' or a doll's body parts, if parents encourage her to do so by asking her the above types of questions. Some infants will not be able to point to the correct parts of the body when questioned, but as they approach one year of age, many more are able to participate in this game, having some understanding of the word labels for parts of the body.

LEARNING ABOUT THE IMPLICATIONS OF HER ACTIONS. Through months of acting and then observing the results of her actions, your baby is gradually becoming more aware of some of the consequences or results of her own behavior. In essence, she is becoming more "self"-conscious. She may appear to be more sensitive to your praise or disapproval of her actions. Her looking to you after she has done something "right" or "wrong" in order to see your reaction implies that she is growing more aware that you are separate from her, and that you have certain expectations for her.

Much of the time she will attempt to live up to your expectations in order to gain your approval and stay in your favor, but sometimes, when she wants to do something contrary to what you want her to do, she will persist in trying to get you to change your mind. Her sensitivity to your expectations and reactions helps her to define her own personal limits, and realize more clearly that you are separate from her.

SHE'S MORE ASSERTIVE. Again, you will notice that your infant is more capable than before of asserting herself. She can express her likes and dislikes. She is likely to show her refusal by shaking her head from side to side, or even saying "No," or making a specific sound that indicates refusal. A baby's awareness of the real meaning of "no" is probably limited.

Your baby is slowly learning that her opinions and plans are occasionally at odds with yours. Her voicing those opinions, balking at your commands, or stubbornly refusing to comply with your requests can be taken as a further indication of her growing self-awareness.

EMERGING SEXUAL IDENTITY. There is a good chance that a large part of how you have been reacting to your baby from birth has been based upon her sex. Some parents tend to use more terms like "sweetheart," "honey," "gorgeous," "dear," and so forth, when addressing baby girls than boys. From the time that their babies show an interest in toys, they often buy girl babies dolls, and boy babies cars and trucks.

Parents usually tolerate more aggression from baby boys than girls, and do not become as upset when baby boys break or are rough with toys as they would if baby girls did the same thing. Similarly, parents often try hard to shield baby girls from getting dirty, but allow boys to have more opportunities to "mess." When boy babies imitate their fathers, older brothers, or male relatives they receive all kinds of positive encouragement and feedback, but when they imitate females, they receive very little positive feedback.

Many parents are quite selective about which behaviors they will reward or not reward, depending upon the baby's sex. By positively rewarding and encouraging only certain behaviors, those behaviors tend to be repeated. Parents can, and quite often do, encourage or discourage their baby's actions and imitations depending upon whether the child is male or female. Their reinforcement of particular behaviors is believed to have an influence upon their baby's continued imitation of and identification with males or females, and hence, a baby's "sexual identity." If you have been selective about reinforcing your baby's imitations and spontaneous behaviors, you may now begin to see her doing more imitating of Mommy, or behaving in what you feel is a "feminine" manner (if your baby is a boy, you may notice the opposite). A baby who spends a great deal of time with one parent will probably be more inclined to imitate that person's behavior.

It is clear that the way parents treat their children has an effect on how they regard male and female roles. The way you handle your child is a personal matter, but you should be aware of your influence.

It will be some time before a baby's sexual identity becomes more clearly established. This normally occurs during the preschool years. At first, a baby begins to imitate her parents' behaviors. If she is positively reinforced for imitating one parent, she may continue to imitate mainly that parent, and gradually come to identify with the parent. Later, her identification is likely to be incorporated into her personality and self-concept.

Social Sensitivity and Interests

GIVING AND RECEIVING AFFECTION. Your baby will probably be quite receptive to your affectionate smiles, embraces, and kisses, and will offer her affection to you by throwing her arms around you, hugging you, and giving you a kiss. This behavior, long awaited by you, should naturally help to cement your relationship, and make you more responsive to her. Some babies are not as receptive to their parents' displays of affection for them, or as readily able to give affection to their parents. This is partly due to individual personality differences and environmental differences. In a home in which family members are free and easy about showing affection for one another, and for the baby, a baby may also be more inclined in this direction, but this is not necessarily so. Several children within one family often respond very differently.

Attachment to certain toys and objects will now be more noticeable. Your baby may have definite "feelings" for one or more of her toys, and behave quite warmly and affectionately toward them. You are likely to see her "talking" to them softly, carrying them with her wherever she goes, hugging and kissing them, and even rocking them in her arms. Her ability to extend her affection to toys is evidence of her social development, and is a testimony to the quality of the relationship you have established with her. Her close, affectionate relationship with you has given her social skills and feelings that she can now extend to others, at this stage, mainly to her toys.

IMITATION. Imitation, as was previously pointed out, begins to flourish in the latter part of a baby's first year, and plays a significant role in her personal-social development. You are likely to notice more attempts on your baby's part to imitate your behavior, even when you are not intentionally encouraging her to do so.

At the family dinner table, she may pick up a napkin and wipe her face with it in imitation of you. After her bath she may grab a hairbrush and try to brush her hair the way you do. As you go about your daily chores, she may enjoy having an old rag so that she can "dust" along with you. If you are finicky about getting dirt on your hands or clothes, you may notice that she is developing a similar aversion to getting dirty.

A baby may also devote some time to mimicking her brother's or sister's behaviors. This can get her into some trouble if she sees them painting a picture and attempts to do the same. She will learn quickly that there are many things they can do that she cannot. Many babies are quite persistent about trying to perform tasks that are beyond the range of their abilities. They struggle for long periods of time, getting more frustrated by the minute. Others have a better notion of their own limitations, and shy away from tasks that they have determined are too difficult.

Your infant may also focus her attention on other babies. She will watch their every move, and then try to mimic their actions. Mrs. Lisk brought her ten-month-old daughter, Regina, to her sister's house for the afternoon. While she was there, Regina seemed to observe her aunt's fourteen-month-old son, James, intensely.

When Mrs. Lisk was home later that evening, she noticed that Regina was making funny faces at her. She had never done this before and her mother was puzzled. Then Mrs. Lisk remembered that James had been making faces at Regina for a short time that afternoon. Regina had obviously observed his behavior and was trying to imitate it. Her ability to copy people she has seen but who are no longer present helps her expand her skills, and is evidence of her mental development, specifically the improvement of her memory.

GREATER RESPONSIVENESS AND INTEREST IN SOCIALIZING. An Infancy 10 baby's interest in socializing continues to increase. She particularly enjoys playing social games like chase the crawling baby, peek-a-boo, hide-and-seek, and pat-a-cake games. Her improving ability and interest in imitation make her a better candidate for all kinds of games and activities. With several demonstrations and your encouragement, your infant may learn to wave "bye-bye" and throw kisses.

She will also express her wish for your attention or company when she is playing. Now that she is better able to express what she wants, she will frequently point to things, vocalize in a loud tone of voice, and then wait for you to bring the desired objects to her. She will pay close attention to all of your actions and expressions, and may be quite sensitive to your moods as well as your smiles of approval or frowns of disapproval.

LEARNING TO COPE WITH BROTHERS AND SISTERS. After months of being rather helpless against brothers or sisters, your infant gradually develops the social skills that enable her to "fight back" when mistreated, or at least to try to defend herself and protect her possessions. Prior to the time she became more mobile, her brothers or sisters had free roam of the house, and could easily trick her and pull her toys away, knowing that she could not do much of anything about it except cry.

Once she becomes more mobile and begins to crawl around the house, she can invade "their" territory, and becomes a threat to them. Over the past few months, she has been watching them carefully, imitating them, and picking up their tricks. She will be better able to stand up to them, and will protest loudly and struggle if they try to swipe her toys. When she senses that they are irritable, angry, or in an aggressive mood, she may stay clear of them, or stick close to you, so as not to bear the brunt of their hostility.

Fights and tensions between brothers and sisters, particularly when close to one another in age, are quite common. This is not to give the impression that all closely spaced children do is argue and fight, or that they do not get along. There are family situations in which children a year or two apart in age act as real companions and are genuinely delighted to be in each other's company. This, however, is often the exception rather than the rule. If you feel that your children's interactions are having negative effects, you may have to make some shifts in schedule or in the arrangement of your home so that the two of them will have their own private territories.

You are likely to notice occasions on which your older child behaves affectionately toward the baby, and occasions on which they play happily together. The older child may also be an excellent teacher for the baby, taking time out to show her things and helping her learn new words. In spite of their frequent squabbles, they have probably grown somewhat attached to one another. Sometimes you may even be struck by the fact that in the midst of their fighting they actually seem to be having a good time.

Unless your baby is obviously being bossed and dominated by your older child, or unless her physical safety is at risk, you may discover that it is best to let them try to work out their own differences. You should not leave the infant alone with a young child, since he or she may unwillingly or willingly hurt the baby. Be present to watch. Their games may be interesting and enjoyable to see as well as educational for them. Your infant obviously cannot hold her own with your older child, but you will notice how much more assertive she is in her **contact with her** brother or sister.

INTELLECTUAL DEVELOPMENT

More Vigorous Explorations

Your baby is likely to be more determined to master every new challenge. She will concentrate hard as she engages in various tasks, and is apt to become angry or frustrated if you cut her investigatory enterprises short or get in her way. She is taking slow, but nevertheless steady, steps toward maintaining her interest and concentration in specific activities.

Her ever-improving eye-hand co-ordination and finger control may now make it possible for her to pick up small objects for more close examination, if she has not already accomplished this. It is interesting that around this age many babies start to use their index fingers to a greater extent than before to further explore their surroundings. With her index finger rigidly extended, your baby may begin poking and probing at everything in sight. She will run her finger over the surfaces, edges, and corners of objects, and probe into cracks, holes, and crevices. If you happen to have access to a typewriter and hold her on your lap in front of it, she may delight in trying to press down on the keys. As she uses her forefinger to explore a variety of objects, she will learn into which ones she can insert her finger and which ones have no holes. This index finger probing heightens her awareness that some objects are hollow, and some are solid.

Your infant's ability to use both hands simultaneously to engage in different tasks should become more noticeable. She may begin to use her right hand more often for reaching and examining objects, and her left hand for sucking or holding objects. She may now be able to hold on to two small objects in one hand as she moves around a room.

PLAYING WITH OBJECTS. One of her favorite activities is likely to be putting objects into a receptacle, and then trying to fish them out again. If you supply her with a variety of wooden cubes or other small objects and a plastic food container or wide-mouthed, non-breakable jar, she may sit for relatively long periods of time repeatedly filling and emptying the container. This activity gives her practice in picking up and releasing objects and in pouring objects from the container. She is likely to stop at various points along the way as she is filling the container, lift it with both hands, and rattle it. This gives her a chance to find out if louder or different noises are produced when more objects are in the container.

As she experiments with putting things into other things, she may seem puzzled by the fact that given two objects such as measuring cups, the larger measuring cup

will not fit into the smaller one. Similarly, as she experiments with piling one or more objects on top of one another, she is likely to be somewhat surprised to learn that when a large cube is piled on top of two smaller cubes, her structure tips over.

At this early stage, your baby seems most sensitive to very large differences in the size of objects. Her perception of small differences in size does not seem to be as well developed. She may be able to place a group of graduated rings on a peg, but may stack them in incorrect order. As she plays with objects, she continues to learn more about spatial relationships. She enjoys taking objects apart, and then attempting to put them back together. Babies often zero in on old pans with lids and old percolators as prime targets to disassemble, and seem fascinated with these objects.

EXPERIMENTING IS FUN. When your infant moves around a room with a toy car in her hand, she learns to roll it forward and backward. Then she takes this information and applies it to new objects. Let's say you place a Lazy Susan in front of her. At first she may try to push it forward and move it backward. After some trial and error experimentation with it, she will eventually learn to push sideways, and to take her hand away from it at the appropriate time so that it will spin, rather than stop. Each new object represents a challenge in learning.

Infancy 10 babies often seem to be somewhat more conscious of numbers. Your baby may like to hold two objects apart, arms extended to her sides, and then bang the objects together in front of her. When she searches for the mate to your slipper or her own sock, this may indicate an early awareness of the difference between "one" and "two."

If you watch her as she tinkers with objects, you will see her intentionally performing a variety of actions on an object to see how her actions affect the object, to learn more about the characteristics of an object, and to practice her manual skills. She explores the inside bottoms of jars with her fingers, waves objects around, knocks them down, bangs them against the table top and floor, and shoves them and watches to see if they roll. When she happens to be playing in the kitchen, you may see her repeatedly opening and closing or swinging your low cabinet doors back and forth.

Knobs, caps, and jar lids will also be explored. This is the age when she will be fascinated by the control knobs on your stove, radio, and television set. She knows that when she turns the knob, something happens, and she may frequently approach these objects, in spite of your warnings to the contrary. If you accidentally leave a tube of shampoo or cream lying near the edge of your bathtub, she may have a terrific time exploring this object. If she can unscrew the cap, she will not be able to resist the temptation of squeezing it, much to your dismay. Whenever her ability to unscrew the lids of jars and bottles emerges, this may get her into a great deal of trouble, unless you have adequately safety-proofed your home. Her curiosity, mobility, and lack of knowledge and experience make for a delightful, but potentially dangerous combination.

Around this time your baby may become more sensitive to the up versus down spatial positions of certain objects. She may recognize when an object is correctly or incorrectly positioned. When she sees a glass or some other object turned upside down, she may immediately rush to turn it over. After she empties a cardboard box filled with pots, pans, and other playthings and notices that some of the objects are overturned, she may rather compulsively turn each one right-side up. She may also turn magazines and books right-side up before "reading" them and may learn to start at the front cover and proceed to the back cover.

Memory Improvement

Some Infancy 10 babies begin to develop a longer lasting memory for objects, activities, and people that were once seen, but are no longer within view. Believing that his daughter's memory was improving, Mr. Thatch decided to play a game with her that would allow him to test her memory. While Mimi was watching, he hid her favorite red ball in a low dresser drawer in her bedroom. Then he distracted her with other activities. Ten minutes later he asked her to get the red ball. She crawled over to her dresser and reached for the drawer handle. She had, indeed, remembered where her father had hidden her ball.

Some Infancy 10 babies, like Mimi, have a fairly good memory for hidden objects or people whom she can no longer see, but this is the exception rather than the rule. Most babies will not develop this kind of concept or memory until toddlerhood, so do not be discouraged if your infant is not showing the same kind of memory improvement as did Mimi Thatch. If you carefully watch your baby's behavior, you will undoubtedly notice signs that she is able to retain information for longer periods of time than in the past, although dramatic improvements may not be seen this early.

LANGUAGE DEVELOPMENT

Active Language Development

You can expect to hear your infant doing more vocalizing than in previous phases. As she becomes more assertive, she often uses her voice to make her demands known and emphasize how she feels about something. Your baby may now begin to hum to music, and you are likely to hear her trying to imitate many sounds. Do not be too disappointed if she is not imitating your words or saying any words on her own. A few babies talk before the age of one, but many more do not.

Some babies will be continually repeating sounds and words. Ruth Clark recently learned how to say "hi." When her parents first heard this word, they were most enthusiastic and encouraging. Ruth was so delighted with her new word, and so anxious to practice it, that she constantly repeated it for several days. She answered "hi" to every question asked of her.

Mr. and Mrs. Clark eventually grew tired of hearing the "hi," and stopped responding to Ruth as enthusiastically as before when she repeated it. Suddenly, she learned another new word, "out," which once again got her parents excited and rekindled their enthusiasm for encouraging her further.

Babies are sensitive to how their sounds affect people around them, particularly their parents. They carefully observe their audience's reactions, looking for signs of approval, enthusiasm, and encouragement. When these signs are obvious, they have good reason to continue repeating a new word. When they notice signs of disinterest or lack of enthusiasm after a week or two of seeing positive responses, this may prompt them to move on to another word that brings more desirable results.

Your baby will take note of your reactions when she produces sounds. It is important to be aware of the influence that your praise of certain sounds and words has upon her speech, specifically the frequency with which particular word sounds are repeated.

GESTURES WITH WORDS. Part of the excitement of learning to say words such as "no" and "bye-bye" for a baby stems from being able simultaneously to use the appropriate gestures used in conjunction with these words. As a baby learns to repeat the word "no," she is likely to learn to shake her head, and as she says "bye," she will open and close her fist. The enjoyment she derives from mastering the gestures accompanying these words will equal, if not surpass, the pleasure derived from the words themselves.

DON'T FORCE HER TO PERFORM. In the familiar setting of her home, your baby may vocalize continually, but take her to someone else's home for a visit, and she may refuse to say anything. This is a rather common response, and should not cause needless worry or concern. It is best not to pressure her to "talk" or show off her talents if she seems uncomfortable around unfamiliar people or uneasy in new settings. In response to too much pressure, babies sometimes become more stubborn and unco-operative about vocalizing.

Around this age you may notice your baby becoming frightened and crying whenever she is separated from you. This crying is similar to the crying that accompanies stranger anxiety in that it appears to emerge with a certain developmental "phase" of life and then diminish when this "phase" is outgrown.

Passive Language Development

Your baby will now be focusing more deliberately on comprehending the conversations and commands that she hears. She will listen to words in an attempt to pick out familiar ones, and may know the names of immediate family members, pets, and several frequently used objects. Many babies will now understand and obey simple directions such as "give the soap to me," "don't touch," and "no." When they hear the words "bye-bye," "kiss," "hug," "peek-a-boo," or "pat-a-cake," they may respond with the correct hand motions and actions.

A few babies may also understand the names for certain parts of their bodies. If you ask your baby, "Where is your mouth?" she may point to her mouth if she has learned this word. How well your infant responds to questions in which she is asked to point to parts of her body will largely depend upon whether or not you have made a concerted effort to teach her the names for her facial features and major body parts.

MOTOR DEVELOPMENT

Gross Motor Activity

SITTING. Your baby has probably perfected her sitting ability to the point where she can sit alone well controlled for as long as she wants or has to maintain it. From nearly any position, crawling or standing, she may now maneuver herself into a sitting position more easily. Sitting is fast becoming a position from which she can move on to other activities such as crawling or standing. Even if she has not already begun to sit unaided prior to this time, she will now begin to do so.

PREWALKING LOCOMOTION. The infant's former method of moving across the floor was probably one in which her belly was held rather close to the ground. Having gained in muscle strength, tone, and co-ordination, she is now likely to hold her torso and bottom higher off the floor. Her weight will mainly be supported by her hands and knees or hands and feet. This is a more efficient position for getting around. Notice how much faster she can move, and how much easier it is for her to follow you around.

STANDING. Many Infancy 10 babies will be making determined efforts to stand. Stella Jackson carried her ten-month-old daughter, Marcia, into the nursery, while Marcia cried and struggled to get free because she did not want to go to bed. Despite Marcia's resistance, Stella was matter-of-fact about putting her child to bed at her regular hour. She put Marcia down in her crib and began to tuck her in.

As Stella was arranging the covers, Marcia rolled to the side of the crib mattress, grabbed hold of the crib bars, and began struggling to pull herself up to a stand. Placing hand over hand, Marcia managed to stand all the way up. Then she turned to her mother with a triumphant grin. In the process of turning, she accidentally lost her grip on the crib rail, and came tumbling down on her fanny.

This minor spill did not put a damper on Marcia's enthusiasm, for a moment later she pulled herself up again. Marcia had made repeated attempts to stand during the past month, but had never been successful before. Knowing how important standing was to her daughter, Stella clapped and cheered Marcia on, taking obvious pride in her latest accomplishment.

Once a baby takes a strong interest in standing, she is likely to want to practice this frequently during the day, and even at night, until she has mastered this ability. You may notice that your baby has less difficulty pulling herself to a stand, holding on to the sides of her crib. Her arm, trunk, and leg muscles are stronger than before. She is likely to practice getting herself to a stand repeatedly, holding on to anything for support.

Once she is standing, she will probably be able to maintain this position while holding on to something for support for longer periods of time before tiring, although some difficulty will be experienced in getting down from a standing position. Your infant can probably stand on her own very briefly, and may even be able to stand alone well.

STEPPING SIDEWARD. In a standing position, you may see your baby step sideways (cruise) or stamp her feet while using the sides of her playpen or another piece of furniture for support. She will place one foot, and then the other, timidly at first, until she gains more confidence. Over the next couple of months, she will gradually gain speed, and may hardly need to hold on to pieces of furniture except to maintain just enough contact with her fingers to give some security.

You will notice your infant making a valiant effort to place her feet just where she wants them to be, although her first efforts may be so awkward that they make you laugh. She may also take some steps while holding on to your hands. If she is very active, she may even begin to step out unsteadily on her own, although most babies are not yet ready to walk.

Fine Motor Activity

Your baby may be much more adept with her hands, and will continue to work on developing her manual skills. She no longer has to use a whole-arm and shoulder movement in order to grasp an object. She now uses only a wrist and hand movement when grasping. She has made progress in her thumb and forefinger grasp, enabling her gradually to perform more precise tasks, such as picking up crumbs, sorting small objects, pulling strings, or plucking a guitar.

Your infant will begin to do different things with each hand at the same time. The left may be used to hold the objects that the right picks up or explores or vice versa. With some babies performance of different tasks with both hands simultaneously is marked, and with others this may not be commonly seen. If a baby's right hand, for instance, is constantly used mainly for "active" tasks such as exploration or picking up objects, and the left is mainly used to carry objects, it would not be surprising for her gradually to develop greater dexterity with her right hand.

It is getting easier for your baby to hold more than one object at a time. She may be able to hold two small objects, such as wooden cubes, at the same time in one hand. Letting go of small objects that she is holding may be somewhat more difficult for her. The ability to release objects easily will improve as her nervous system matures. Her immature ability to release objects may make it hard for her to roll a ball back and forth with another person, or to construct towers with her blocks.

HOW TO ENSURE YOUR BABY'S SAFETY

Babies will be moving in any number of different styles at this time, but two things are certain: they manage to get around at an amazingly fast pace, and they are curious about everything. Put their mobility, their curiosity, and their naïvety about danger together and you get *accidents*. You must supervise your baby closely in order to ensure her safety. Be sure to review the Safety Training Check List on pages 350–53, and continue to do what is necessary to give her opportunities to roam, investigate, and learn without risk to her safety.

As soon as she begins to stand alone, you should train her not to stand on couches, beds, or other places from which she could fall. Teach her that furniture should be used only in appropriate ways. If she is beginning to walk, read ahead to the next phase where additional precautionary measures to take for babies who can walk are presented (page 441).

FEEDING

Solid Foods

Your baby is now eating a much wider variety of solid foods, both plain foods and combinations of foods. You should be staying in rather close contact with your doctor to ensure that your baby's nutritional requirements are adequately fulfilled, and that new foods are continuing to be introduced at appropriate times. Keep in mind that now, more than ever before, babies may be on totally different diets. Remember the importance of offering your infant wholesome foods to eat, and making the atmosphere at mealtime cheerful and low-keyed so that it is conducive to eating and good digestion.

A WELL-BALANCED DIET. You will be offering your baby (and yourself) a variety of foods from within the basic groups or categories of foods (see pages 311–13). There is some question about the need for a diet to be balanced over each twenty-four-hour period, particularly with young children who get on "kicks" of certain food preferences. Rather than worrying when your infant does not want to take a well-balanced meal at each feeding session, simply offer her foods from among the four categories, and chances are that over a week's time, her over-all intake of food will be well balanced. The fundamental point is that the diet should be balanced over several days or a week, not necessarily on a meal-to-meal or day-to-day basis.

TEXTURE OF THE SOLIDS. You have probably been gradually serving your child coarser foods. At this time feeding her should be less work for you since you can offer many of the same foods that you eat after chopping, dicing, or cutting them up into very small pieces for easier handling and digestion. Most babies are well able to handle "junior" foods, although some foods may still have to be mashed well and diluted with a little milk or water. Each baby will proceed at her own individual pace.

Not on Three Meals a Day?

Some babies who have not been firmly encouraged to give up their late evening feeding may still be waking up for it each night, even though their parents find this bothersome. The vast majority of babies who are eating fairly substantial amounts of solid foods, and who are gaining weight at a satisfactory rate, have no real need for this additional feeding and will probably profit from giving it up.

Providing you wish to discontinue your infant's late night meal, you will have to be firm about this. When she wakes and cries, do not offer any food. Simply try to ignore her crying and tell her quite frankly that she is old enough to be eating three meals a day. Stick to your guns, and do not offer her this meal. Eventually she will not awaken for it. This approach usually works with most babies, but occasionally infants continue to demand this feeding, in which case parents may have to postpone a three-meal schedule until Infancy 11 or 12.

"I Want to Do It Myself!"

Most babies will insist upon taking over at least some of the responsibility for feeding themselves, although as mentioned in Infancy 9, babies will move toward more independence in eating at different rates, using different approaches. Many who have previously shown an interest and have had opportunities for practice will be drinking with little assistance from a cup and eating on their own with their fingers. Others will be attempting to do the same, but will need more time to become skillful.

Be prepared with washcloth and mop in hand to clean up the incredible messes your baby, learning to eat, will create. In cutting down on unnecessary work, take a tip from experienced mothers and be sure to save newspapers or a plastic dropcloth to spread out in at least a five- to ten-foot radius around your baby's high chair. Sampling, testing, smearing, and manipulating her meals may seem to give her much greater enjoyment than eating them.

It is important to give your baby some freedom to exercise her new abilities and to be more independent. On the other hand, when she is clearly playing and dawdling rather than eating, feel free to let her know promptly that this is not what mealtime is all about by ending the meal. When her need to practice feeding herself results in too grand a mess, or too much playing instead of eating, you can offer her an empty dish, a spoon, and a cup to play with and to use for "pretend" eating.

Not all babies are ready or have the desire to "do it myself." They seem perfectly content with the arrangement in which their parents do all of the work, and they sit back and enjoy eating their meals with no headaches. There is no reason not to continue spoon- or cup-feeding such a child, but be sure that you are not overlooking her signs of wanting to be a more active participant at mealtimes and that you are giving her chances to be more actively involved.

When Is It Time to Give Up the Formula?

Your doctor will advise you as to when you should discontinue giving your baby formula. Once bottle-fed babies have progressed to the point where they are getting necessary nutriments from many other solid foods, they often do not need formula anymore. After the formula is discontinued, your doctor will recommend shifting to whole milk, a lowfat milk, or a commercially prepared beverage designed for older babies who are eating solids and no longer need formula. This lowfat drink is enriched with vitamins and minerals, and is available in concentrated liquid form or ready-to-use quart cans.

BATHING

Your baby will most certainly be actively participating in her bath, even if her goal is *not* to co-operate with you. It could be that she feels as if she is ready to wash and dry herself. In spite of her attempts and good intentions, her abilities are rather limited in this department.

Her insistence upon crawling around or even standing in the tub can make washing her quite a struggle. You will have to watch her very closely so that she does not slip, fall, or bang her head. You may have to resort to giving sponge baths for a while if she simply refuses to stay still.

In the event that you have recently begun to wear a raincoat with a hood at bath time, you are not alone. Seriously, you may find that every exposed object in the bathroom is drenched with water after her bath. She will probably slide back and forth in the tub with such force that she sends water flying in all directions. She still will love to splash. She may repeatedly slap her palm down into the water, each time harder than before, as she concentrates upon making the water travel as far as possible. Once she has perfected her splashing technique, beware! Part of the fun of the bath, at least from her point of view, entails playing with her bath toys, and flinging them over the side of the bathtub. Some limits may have to be set so that bath time messes do not get out of hand. A friendly word of advice: it is a good precaution to place several large towels on the bathroom floor, particularly around the tub, where the most water is apt to collect. More than one parent has discovered that water on the bathroom floor seeped through to the ceiling below.

CLOTHING

Now that your baby is more aware of the dressing routine, and her ability to make associations is improving, she is likely to behave in a more appropriate manner when you dress her. When she sees you take out a T-shirt, she may immediately respond by lifting her arms, since she associates this action with your putting on her T-shirt. She is also likely to make correct associations with pants, socks, and shoes, responding by stiffening and lifting her legs and feet. This co-operation on her part will make dressing her a little less taxing. She may also associate pajamas or a blanket with going to bed, or a jacket or cap with going "bye-bye" or "out," and actually crawl to get these clothing articles as a signal to you that she is ready for bed or wants to play outside.

You may see your infant tugging at her clothing in an attempt to get them off. She is probably skillful at yanking off her hat, socks, and shoes, and may be successful with other items as well, including her diapers, so beware! Offer her a hat, scarf, empty handbag, or some other article of clothing that belongs to you, your partner, or an older brother or sister. She will enjoy wearing it as she plays.

SLEEPING

Your baby's continued resistance to going to sleep and her middle-of-the-night waking may represent problems during Infancy 10. She may have so much nervous energy and such a burning need for activity that she seems completely disinterested in taking a nap, lying still at night, and sleeping through the night. Rocking, headbanging, and other tension-releasing behaviors may be seen before a baby falls asleep or when she wakes during the night. These behaviors are discussed on pages 331-35.

The best way to handle a baby who resists taking a nap or going to bed in the evening is to be firm with her. Put her in her crib at her regular nap or bedtime with a favorite small toy or two, and leave her alone. If she cries for a long time, use your own judgment about checking on her, bearing in mind that firmness is very important. You need not be concerned about whether or not she actually falls asleep, as long as you give her appropriate chances. Some babies, as has been mentioned before, are simply able to get by with less sleep than others. If your baby is ready to forego one of her naps, you can encourage her to engage in quiet, more subdued activities during the regular nap hour.

DISCIPLINE

Encouraging Good Behavior

Sometimes parents place too much emphasis upon the negative aspects of discipline (e.g., saying, "No," "Don't," or punishing their baby when she breaks the rules), and not enough emphasis on the positive aspects (e.g., rewarding her for "good" behavior with such things as a nod of approval, an affectionate squeeze, or a few words of praise). A baby who only receives attention and recognition when she disobeys commands or violates acceptable standards of behavior may keep this up because the attention, albeit negative, that her parents offer is more than she would receive if she behaved properly. On the other hand, a baby who receives attention, approval, and acceptance when she is well behaved, or is making some headway in that direction, will be more inclined to keep this up and not misbehave.

The use of the word "reward" needs some clarification. We are not referring to bribery for good behavior by promising a baby that if she stays "in line" you will love her or give her a special treat or buy her a present. The reward we are speaking of is not indicated to her ahead of time to motivate her to behave properly. Nor is it a material object. Rather, it is your spontaneous show of approval after she has behaved properly. This does not necessarily mean that you should never give her a treat or a gift as a reward for good behavior. This will certainly do no harm if it is done occasionally, and without bribing her with it. However, for the most part, her reward for good behavior should involve not only the pleasure and satisfaction she will derive from carrying out your command successfully, but also your positive acceptance and approval at its completion.

Just as your show of disapproval after she has done something wrong can discourage her from repeating her action, your show of approval after she has done something you wanted her to do can encourage her to continue along the same lines. Your disapproval and approval will probably have little or no effect upon her behavior if your relationship with her is not close or regarded by her as satisfying and rewarding. Generally speaking, a child who loves her parents will strive to live up to their expectations of her in order to receive their approval.

Even though this example has been oversimplified in order to make a point, the value in maintaining a close, loving relationship with your baby cannot be overstressed. This is not to imply that every time she fails to heed your "don'ts" or breaks the rules of the house, she does not love you, respect you, or care what you think of her. As was previously mentioned, her comprehension of language is limited, her memory is short, and her desire to satisfy her wants is incredibly strong. Breaking rules and going beyond the limits you set are part of how she learns about the rules themselves, the difference between being "good" and being "naughty," whether or not you are consistent, and whether or not her persistence may result in your relaxation of the rules.

The major point is not to forget the positive side of discipline. When someone that you care about compliments you on a job well done, this may motivate you to try to continue doing your best. You will be proud of your own achievement as well as flattered that someone took notice of your efforts. The same general principles can be applied to your baby as a way of encouraging her good behavior. When she shows signs of occasionally being able to respond appropriately to your simple commands, or obey your "no's," you should let her know how proud you are of her, even if only through your smiles.

DEALING WITH YOUR BABY'S SEPARATION ANXIETY

One of the most difficult aspects of your baby's behavior now may be her reactions to being separated from you. You should anticipate that her fear and anxiety about separations will have an emotional impact upon you, assuming that you have built up a close relationship thus far, and have taken an active role in rearing her. A parent may feel very sorry for his or her baby, even when leaving is necessary, such as at bedtime. A baby's crying, clinging, and frightened expression can prompt all kinds of guilt responses in her parents, particularly if parents have any doubts as to whether they are devoting enough time to being with their child.

Belinda, for example, felt guilty about the fact that her work took her away from her child during the day. Still, she had established a very close relationship with her son. When her son, Gershwin, reached the age of ten months, he became terribly upset every time she left to go to work or left him to go out on the weekends. He also cried for prolonged periods of time after Belinda left his bedroom at night.

Gershwin's reaction heightened Belinda's guilt feelings about not being able to care for him full time. As a result, she began to take him to bed with her at night and began to cut down on the time she spent with her friends on the weekends. After a month or two it became clear to her that her son was becoming more and more dependent upon her. Gershwin's separation anxiety was not diminishing. She slowly became angry at him for keeping her so "trapped," and began to feel resentful. Feeling this way about him made her feel even more guilty than before, and finally she decided to discuss her feelings and problems with her doctor, Dr. Snow.

Dr. Snow was very understanding about Belinda's feelings and helped her to view the recent events more objectively. He told her that many of her guilt feelings were unnecessary and suggested that she was overreacting to her son's anxiety over necessary separations from her. This was not beneficial for either of them. He said that her actions were not really helping her son learn to cope with necessary separations from her, but rather were fostering his increased dependency. Dr. Snow advised her to come and go as she normally did and to discontinue taking her son into her bed at night. He also suggested that she spend a little extra time reassuring her son whenever she had to leave him, but not be apologetic about having to leave or wanting to leave. Belinda felt very reassured after speaking to her physician, and afterward was able to cope with Gershwin's separation anxiety more effectively.

Many parents, like Belinda, feel guilty about leaving their children and overreact as she did. Other parents feel that their baby should be acting more grown-up, and are not sympathetic to their baby's feelings. Going overboard in either direction may not be particularly helpful to the baby. Rather, it is important to understand that your baby's anxieties about separations from you, even when brief or unavoidable, are very real to her. It is also important to recognize that while she needs your understanding, she must learn to adapt and cope effectively whenever you have to leave for work or for several hours here and there.

PREPARED PARENTHOOD CHECK LIST

MOTHER	FATHER	UNDERSTANDING YOUR BABY'S DEVELOPMENT
——	——	Is your baby growing more aware of her own possessions and belongings?
——	——	Have you begun playing any body-pointing and labeling games with your infant as a way to foster her self-awareness?
——	——	Does your baby seem more conscious of your approval and disapproval?
——	——	Would you say that your infant is affectionate?
——	——	Do you see evidence of your baby's growing interest in learning by observation and imitation?
——	——	Have you noticed your baby using her index finger to poke at and explore objects?
——	——	Is your infant showing an interest in containers?
——	——	What evidence do you see that your baby is becoming more aware of the space in your home?
——	——	Is your baby doing more vocalizing than in the past?
——	——	When your baby utters sounds, does she pay attention to her audience's reactions?
——	——	Can your infant respond appropriately to a few simple directions?
——	——	Is your baby faster and more efficient at moving across the floor? In what ways has your baby's method of prewalking locomotion been perfected?
——	——	Does your infant make determined efforts to stand?
——	——	In a standing position, does your baby experiment with stamping her feet or moving a step or two?
——	——	Have you observed your baby's thumb and forefinger grasp, or "pincer" grasp, emerging or becoming more efficient?
——	——	Is it getting easier for your baby to hold on to two or more small objects at once?

BASIC CARE

MOTHER	FATHER	
——	——	Are you offering your infant adequate supervision without stifling her drive to explore and learn?
——	——	Do you offer your baby a well-balanced diet?
——	——	Have you been gradually coarsening the texture of your infant's foods?

—   —   Are you giving your baby some freedom to exercise her new abilities and be more independent at mealtimes?

—   —   Does your baby actively participate at bath time?

—   —   Can your baby take off a few articles of clothing by herself?

—   —   Does your child associate certain clothing items with particular activities?

—   —   How do you handle your baby's bedtime or naptime resistance?

FAMILY FEELINGS AND CONCERNS

—   —   Have you been rewarding your baby for her good behavior by showing your approval?

—   —   If your baby is showing separation anxiety, what emotions does her behavior arouse in you?

—   —   How do you handle situations in which you either have to or want to leave your baby for short periods of time?

Infancy 11

PERSONAL-SOCIAL DEVELOPMENT

Self-awareness

LEARNING MORE ABOUT HIS BODY. As your baby moves around in your home and tests his new abilities on toys and objects, he will learn more about his body and what he can and cannot accomplish. When he stands up holding on to furniture, and takes a sideways step or two, he is apt to observe his feet carefully. When he practices pushing objects around, throwing them with each hand, and transferring them back and forth, he discovers more about both sides of his body, and what actions are possible with each side.

He becomes more conscious of the fact that he can do something with one hand, and, at the same time, engage in another task with the opposite hand. Learning about the two sides of his body is another aspect of his growing self-awareness. You may even see him showing a preference for using the right hand or foot for one type of activity, and the left hand and foot for another. Perhaps he uses his right hand for reaching, grabbing, and poking objects, and the left hand for clutching at a chair (if standing) or holding a toy (if in a crawling position). Some babies show a hand or foot preference at an early age, although in most cases a clear preference develops later in toddlerhood or during the preschool years.

BECOMING MORE OPINIONATED AND INDEPENDENT. Part of your infant's emerging sense of identity involves becoming more conscious of his own feelings and opinions. He is slowly learning that he is a person in his own right, with a mind of his own. He is discovering how best to voice his opinions and influence people to give him what he wants. Although there is a great deal of variability in the development of obstinate behavior, your baby may begin to develop a negative attitude over the next several months.

If he is verbalizing at this age, he may play and experiment with the newly found expression "No," and repeat this word over and over throughout the day. At first it has little appropriate meaning for him, but after a while he becomes able to use it meaningfully. When you offer your baby the kind of juice or cookies that he does not like, he may clearly and loudly say, "No," or vigorously shake his head from side to side. He likes the feeling of independence and the influence that this new gesture or word affords him. This negativism, which may surface during this phase, is a normal aspect of his personal-social development.

The word "No" has special meaning to your baby. When he begins using it or a similar gesture or sound to express his contrary opinion, you may feel angry at him for his "back talk" and obstinacy. What he is doing, however, is announcing his newly found independence, and separateness from you. This is significant. He is slowly discovering himself, his own ideas, and his separateness as a person. Each time he shakes his head and says "No" to you, or refuses to go along with your wishes and limits, he is testing his will against yours. This is an important aspect of learning about himself and you. Babies begin showing some negative behavior as they approach their first birthdays, although in many instances the first real displays of negativism do not occur until toddlerhood.

432

LEARNING MORE ABOUT THE IMPLICATIONS OF HIS ACTIONS. Once the meaning of the word "No" dawns on your baby, and he begins to use it for himself, he will be more conscious of this word when you use it. He is learning more about the consequences of his own behavior, and whether or not he is living up to your expectations. Having been "good," or having done something that you have asked him to do, he will seek your praise and approval. When he wipes his dinner plate clean or drinks all of his milk, he is likely to turn to you waiting for a smile and hold out the empty plate or cup in anticipation of your nod of approval.

Likewise, it is becoming clearer to him what it means to be a "naughty" boy. He will expect your disapproval or punishment after he has done something wrong. When crawling toward the wire that you warned him not to touch, he may glance around the room with a rather guilty and sneaky facial expression. Should he catch your eye, he may back away looking frightened, as if waiting for you to scold him. He might turn on the stereo, and then, immediately afterward, scramble away to a corner of the room as though he knows he is the guilty party, and is trying to escape your reprimands by hiding. When you walk in and go over to him, he may look up at you with embarrassment, or with a fearful expression on his face.

Social Sensitivity and Interests

MORE INDEPENDENT, AND YET MORE DEPENDENT. One aspect of his behavior that may puzzle you is his simultaneous need to be independent from you and dependent upon you. On the one hand he may act as if he resents your attempts to help him do things. When you offer him assistance, he may look angry, say "No," and push you away. He obviously wants to do more things by and for himself, with minimal or no help from you.

On the other hand, in the midst of his pushing for more independence, he may suddenly want to cling tightly to you, and refuse to help himself, even though both of you know that he is capable of doing so. He may crawl into your lap and want to be babied and rocked, especially if a stranger approaches. He may also burst into tears when you leave him alone, even at bedtime.

It would appear that you represent a security base for him. When you are around, he feels confident, secure, and courageous enough to leave you briefly and welcome more independence. However, he can only be independent for short periods of time before he has to scramble back to you. Offer him support, understanding, and a few words of encouragement. This will give him the simple reassurance and security that he needs to go on to face new challenges.

YOU ARE MOST IMPORTANT, BUT HE'S INTERESTED IN OTHER FAMILY MEMBERS, TOO. Your baby's attachment to you and interest in you is obvious. He will imitate your behavior, try to engage you in his play activities, crawl after you around the house, and make many bids for your time, attention, and affection. Still, he is interested in other family members, too. When one parent works during the day, an infant may wait impatiently until he or she returns, and offer quite an affectionate greeting. His attention, at that time, may quickly shift from you to your spouse, especially if he mainly associates you with daily routines, and your spouse with play activities.

Many Infancy 11 babies display a marked interest in their fathers or the working parent. Children especially enjoy rough play, piggy-back rides, and being bounced or tossed into the air. In homes where a father works during the day, a baby may regard Daddy as a refreshing change each evening and may shift his bids for attention and affection from his mother to his father as soon as Daddy comes home each evening. The reverse would be true if the mother worked outside the home during the day.

With brothers or sisters, too, your baby will be more sociable. He will copy their behavior, and be quite attentive when they try to teach him things. On the other hand, now that he is becoming increasingly assertive, more arguments and fights are likely to ensue, particularly if your other children are only a year or two older.

HE LEARNS MORE ABOUT HIS INFLUENCE OVER YOU. Your baby is learning how to tease you, get your goat, and manipulate you so that he can have his way. He may deliberately try to get your attention or prompt a reaction from you by tugging on your newspaper when you are obviously trying to read, calling you at the top of his lungs, or reaching for an "off-limits" object when you are busy talking on the phone. If you have a sense of humor, you will surely have to rely upon it to see you through those days when his antics might otherwise make you angry.

His teasing, testing behavior, and attempts to manipulate you may not always have a playful quality to them. In an effort to get his way, he may deliberately throw a temper tantrum

TEMPER TANTRUMS AND HOW TO HANDLE THEM. Temper tantrums often emerge as the baby nears one year of age, although they are more commonly seen in toddlerhood. When a baby does not get his way, or is very frustrated or angry, he may lose all control, cry, turn red, hold his breath, pound his fists, and kick. Your reaction to his violent outbursts of anger and frustration may influence how frequently they occur. Sometimes an infant can get so excited that he holds his breath, turns blue, and even passes out for a few seconds. This can be very frightening when you see it for the first time. This behavior is not harmful and requires no special care (see page 1024 for a discussion of breath-holding spells). Knowing what is involved in a breath-holding episode can make it much easier to handle in the event that it occurs during infancy.

Mrs. Wolfe took her son, Lloyd, with her to a department store. As she was carrying him through the aisles, a toy on the shelf caught his attention. He pointed to it, vocalized in a demanding tone of voice, and strained toward it. She told Lloyd that he could not have the toy, and kept walking. He screamed at the top of his lungs, and squirmed so hard in protest that she had to put him down on the floor. Once on the floor, Lloyd kicked his feet and banged his fists. Mrs. Wolfe was not only embarrassed but also taken aback by her son's behavior, since she had never seen him act this way before. She quickly went to Lloyd to try to soothe him, offered him sympathy, and then gave in to his demands to have the toy.

From his mother's reaction, Lloyd learned that this behavior worked successfully and enabled him to satisfy his wish. Being rather bright, he began to throw temper tantrums every time he did not get his way, as a method of trying to manipulate his mother and force her to give in to his demands.

Behavior that brings positive results is likely to be repeated. However, punishing a baby is not a wise alternative, since this can increase his anger and frustration. The most effective approach is to try your best to keep calm, and ignore him. When your baby discovers that you are not offering him sympathy or are not about to "give in," this behavior will lose its effectiveness. There is no harm done if, in response to the first few temper tantrums, either now, or in the future, you overreact to them or get upset and fulfill his demands. However, unless you do not mind dealing with frequent tantrums, you will probably want to ignore successive temper outbursts.

Ignoring a tantrum, particularly if it is thrown in a public place, when you have company in your home, or when you are talking on the phone, is not the easiest thing in the world. In the long run, you will have a much harder time dealing with your baby if you overreact or give in to his temper tantrums. Ignoring them is definitely the lesser of the two evils.

Just about every child occasionally throws a temper tantrum, particularly in toddlerhood. Keep in mind that your baby is still emotionally immature and unable to talk about his anger or frustration. Instead, he must discharge anger and tensions through physical avenues. It will be fruitless for you to try to reach him in the midst of his tantrum. He will be too out of control, emotionally, to respond. It is best to wait until it is over before you approach and comfort him.

Try to determine if there is any reason, besides his not getting his way, for his tantrums. Perhaps he is frustrated because he wants to move and explore, and you are keeping him penned up in a playpen. There could be any number of reasons for a tantrum, or none that you will be able to determine. Examining possible reasons for his outbursts may enable you to pinpoint a cause, and, if possible, try to eliminate it. It could be that he is simply more tense, since tensions often surface just prior to the age at which a baby learns to walk. While there may be little that you can do to prevent temper tantrums from ever arising, you can certainly try your best to refrain from encouraging them. Remember, babies and young children do not throw temper tantrums unless there is an audience!

INTELLECTUAL DEVELOPMENT

Experimenting with the Properties of Objects

Now that your baby's hand and finger skills are becoming more refined, he will derive more pleasure from play and investigation activities. As he experiments, he will also be focusing to a greater extent upon each new object, and trying to find out about its individual characteristics. He seems to be trying to discover what makes each object "tick," and whether it is similar to or different from other objects.

Eleven-month-old David Levin dropped a variety of objects, one at a time, into a cardboard box, and appeared to be highly interested in the different noises each object produced when it hit the bottom. Then he removed the objects and started all over again using different containers such as a saucepan, a basket, a waste can, and a jar. In this way he became more aware of small differences in noises.

You will notice your infant actively dropping objects to the floor just to see what will happen to each one. This helps him to learn that the same action produces different results depending upon the individual qualities of the object. He will discover that some objects such as balls will bounce, water will splash, metal objects will produce a loud noise, and tissues will not make any noise.

This type of comparing will involve many actions such as banging, shaking, pushing, and so forth. As he experiments, he slowly builds up the kinds of experiences that enable him to recognize differences in size, shape, weight, consistency, depth, texture, and so on. He also learns more about the quantities of objects, whether objects are hollow or solid, whether objects are empty or full, whether they are inside or outside, and whether they are right-side up or upside down.

At this time you will see evidence of improvement in his ability to associate certain sounds or other characteristics with appropriate objects. He may try to "bark" when you point to a dog, make "engine" sounds when he sees a picture of a large truck, or point toward the sky when you say "airplane." He may also raise both hands, loosely clenched, toward his mouth and tilt his head back when you show him a picture of a cup.

Learning About What Makes Things Happen

As a result of repeated experiences with objects, your baby's ability to associate cause with effect shows improvement. If he happens to lean against a large cardboard box and it moves forward, he will immediately recognize that he caused it to slide. Sometimes he performs certain actions over and over again just because he wants to practice simple motor skills, but much of his repetition is for the sake of producing interesting results. He may enjoy turning the television set on and off, turning on an electric light by tugging a string, and flicking a light switch. He may also enjoy rolling a ball back and forth, and opening and closing doors. Repetition of these activities helps him to associate cause and effect.

In his dealings with you and other people, he is growing more aware of the outcome and some of the meanings of his behavior. He is beginning to sense when he has been a "good" boy or a "bad" boy, and anticipates either your approval or your disapproval, depending upon his actions.

During infancy, a baby's concept of what makes things happen is highly self-centered. He thinks that all events are caused by his own movements or actions. Mr. Stone arrived home one evening after a trying day at the office, and found his neighbor's car blocking his driveway. He had politely asked his neighbor, Mark, to move the car on three previous occasions, but this time he was really angry and therefore had it out with Mark. Mr. Stone was still fuming when he finally entered his house.

Upon hearing the car pull up the driveway, eleven-month-old Terry had crawled over to the door in anticipation of his daddy's entrance. As soon as Terry saw the angry look on his father's face, he scampered away with a frightened look on his face and hid behind a chair, as though he expected his father to spank him. Mr. Stone was rather puzzled by his son's behavior, but after a moment or two it dawned on him that Terry thought that he was angry at him.

The notion of an event taking place independently of his own world was foreign to Terry, as to other babies at this age. The child's self-centered notion of what makes things happen will persist throughout Infancy 12, and even into toddlerhood. It will gradually be outgrown as he develops the ability to look at things that happen around him from a more objective perspective.

Learning More About Spatial Relationships

Your baby may now take a greater interest in observing movements of objects. He may roll his ball from one area of a room to another, scramble to get it, and then try to roll it back to the original place. Or he may empty out the contents of a box, a cabinet, or a drawer, and then perhaps try to fit the objects back inside. Taking objects apart and emptying cabinets and drawers are favorite activities among older infants, although it will be at least several more months before they have the desire and ability to put things back together correctly.

Babies also enjoy hiding things and then finding them. They may be able to find an object through one move or displacement in a room, but it will be a long time before they are able to find an object whose location has been changed several times.

LANGUAGE DEVELOPMENT

Active Language Development

Your baby's babbling is sounding more and more like real speech, despite the fact that his vocalizations make little or no sense. His babbling mimics real speech. After you talk to him or ask him a question, he will babble in reply. His tone of voice, inflections, facial expressions, postures, and hand motions will make it seem as though he is really trying to tell you something. This kind of babbling is often referred to as "expressive jargon," the precursor of real speech.

Your baby is still more likely to imitate you when you make sounds that he uses, but he is probably starting to imitate more new sounds, and even, perhaps, words. As he vocalizes, you may periodically hear him say an actual word sound or two. He may or may not know that he has said a real word. Many babies can now use at least one word, having an understanding of its meaning, but do not be discouraged if your baby is not saying any words. There is a great deal of variability in this developmental area.

Infancy 11 babies who can say a few words in addition to "ma ma" and "da da" are early talkers. These babies may already be using one word, often with a gesture, to convey a complete thought. A baby who says "cook" and points to the box of cookies on the kitchen table is using a one-word sentence to express "I want to eat a cookie." One-word sentences normally do not appear this early. In most cases they emerge during toddlerhood.

Passive Language Development

As you speak, your infant will continue to concentrate on understanding your words. He will gaze at your face and perk up when you say specific words such as "ball," "spoon," or "shoe," that are associated with activities or objects which are routine or familiar. He will also look at whomever says his name in the course of a conversation.

When you say the names of certain objects, he may show you that he understands what the names represent by his responses. If you say "airplane," he may point upward. When asked to "go and get Big Bird," he may successfully bring you his favorite stuffed animal, and beam with pride at his own accomplishment. Most babies will now be able to understand several simple requests or directions and respond appropriately. Sometimes they will understand commands such as "no, don't touch," but will pay little or no attention to them.

MOTOR DEVELOPMENT

Gross Motor Activity

SITTING AND LYING DOWN. Your baby should be able to get himself into a sitting position with very little effort, although he will most likely get into this position only when he is tired and wants a breather. You may hardly ever find him lying on his back or stomach except when he is sleeping and napping, and he will quickly shift from these positions once he is fully awake.

PREWALKING LOCOMOTION. You will see your infant moving about quickly and in a well-co-ordinated manner on all fours. He will get around so fast that you may have difficulty keeping up with him. As he moves, he will probably hold his body higher off the ground than before, supporting his weight on his hands and knees or perhaps feet.

From a position on all fours, he may begin to climb everywhere, including up the stairs, unless safety gates are used. Going upstairs while you are with him may not present much of a problem, but going downstairs probably will. At times you may find him at the top of the steps, confused as to how to get down. He can learn, and probably should be shown, how to back carefully down a flight of steps.

You could make the stairs off limits by putting up a gate, but eventually your child will be old enough to want to go up and down by himself. At this time you can teach your baby how to crawl backward, bearing in mind that he will need parental supervision on stairs. Even though he may initially refuse to go backward, he will eventually practice when he feels more confident, and is determined to get down the stairs once he has climbed to the top.

STANDING, CRUISING, AND WALKING. Your baby may constantly want to be up on two feet, and this may be dangerous if he stands in his high chair, stroller, or the bathtub. He may also want to stand while you are trying to get him dressed, or trying to get him to lie down and fall asleep. It makes no difference to him where he stands, as long as he is standing.

Probably for the first time, he will stand alone sometime during the next several weeks. Mastering this task may be so all important to him that he practices and struggles at it day and night. As he practices standing and stepping sideways (cruising) over the next couple of months, he gains the added muscle strength and upright balance that will enable him to walk.

Individual differences in babies' performances will be quite pronounced during Infancy 11. Many babies will still be unable to stand alone, while a few will be walking without support. Both are normal. When a baby is physically ready and his desire to take a few steps on his own is very strong, he will devote an enormous amount of energy and time to learning to walk. Until then, any efforts to push him to walk can be fruitless and frustrating for all concerned. Even if your baby is not the physically active type, he will still be gaining the muscle strength, co-ordination, balance, over-all body control, and energy that will be necessary for walking in the months to come.

He is probably capable of pulling himself to a stand while hanging on to something, and will most likely stand alone, although perhaps only momentarily. Your baby can now stand very well while holding on to something, and his new self-confidence and stability may enable him to drop down into a squatting or stooping position and then come back up again without wobbling and falling over. While standing, he may be able to turn his body around a bit.

You are likely to see him stepping sideways around his playpen or crib, holding on to the side edges for security. Mr. Press saw his son, Nate, taking sideward steps while placing his hands on the seat of the couch as a basis of support. Taking pleasure in his son's activities, and wanting to be more involved, Mr. Press offered Nate his fingers, to lure him away from relying on the couch as a type of crutch. Nate hesitantly grasped his daddy's fingers, and slowly took step after step, gaining confidence with each move forward.

Feeling that Nate was ready to try walking on his own, Mr. Press gradually withdrew his fingers until he and his son were only maintaining finger-tip contact. Finally, this father moved his fingers completely away from Nate, expecting him to keep walking. The moment Nate was on his own, however, he lost his balance entirely and fell.

Keeping physical contact with his father gave this baby the added bit of security that he needed to continue walking. Walking alone is a major motor development and a big step toward independence for every child. Until a baby or toddler feels confident and secure, he is not likely to step out on his own without touching either a railing, a piece of furniture, or a parent's hands for added security.

As a baby begins to stand alone and experiments with walking, he will frequently fall down. Falls and bumps are a necessary part of learning to stand alone and walk, so it is best to anticipate them and try to take them in stride when they occur. Your baby will not be especially bothered by these spills, so neither should you.

It is quite possible that your baby will be taking a few steps all by himself. Wobbly, at first, with his feet positioned wide apart and his hands raised for balance, he will place one foot in front of the other, and hopefully you will be there to root for him and praise him for his great achievement. Most babies will not begin walking alone until Toddlerhood 1.

Even though your baby may be walking on his own, a frightening or emotionally upsetting experience may temporarily result in his switching back over to walking hanging on to furniture or prewalking forms of locomotion; should this be the case, there is no need to punish him or push him to perform. When his desire to walk alone is strong enough, he will quickly get going again.

Fine Motor Activity

Your baby's eye-hand co-ordination enters into nearly all of his activities. He is becoming much more skillful with his hands and fingers. His grasping of both large objects and crumb-sized particles is more direct and efficient, and this enables him to derive more pleasure from his play activities.

His hands are becoming more useful to him in bathing, dressing, feeding, and exploration, too. You will notice that his manipulations of objects and food are more deliberate and sophisticated. Further examples of his fine motor activity can be found in the Intellectual Development, Feeding, and Clothing sections.

HOW TO ENSURE YOUR BABY'S SAFETY

Between the ages of about twelve and fifteen months most babies will begin to step out and walk on their own. As your baby's horizons for movement expand, you must also expand your program of accident prevention. Below is another addendum to the Safety Training Check List for the older baby or toddler who can walk. Parents sometimes make the mistake of giving a baby who can walk too much responsibility and freedom. An Infancy 11 or 12 child still has a very short memory and can easily forget warnings. He still is extremely limited in his ability to recognize danger and must be carefully supervised. Remember that the responsibility to ensure his safety rests upon your shoulders, not upon his.

FLOORS AND RUGS
—If your floors are slippery, scuff up the bottoms of your infant's shoes so he will have better traction.
—Remove, hide, or securely anchor electrical cords over which he might trip.
—Make sure old floor tiles are not curling up so that your baby cannot trip on them.
—Be certain rugs are securely tacked down to your floors and steps.
—Carpet stairways (small carpet squares are inexpensive) or place no-slip step guards on each step to prevent him from slipping and falling. Padded carpeting on stairs and stair landings, especially the basement stairs, reduces injury and is a good safety investment.

CARS, DRIVEWAYS, AND STREETS
—Do not ask for trouble by allowing him to play in your driveway, the street, or in any area where automobiles are parked, unless you are standing next to him and are watching him carefully.
—Look all around and underneath your car before starting it, to eliminate the possibility of a young child's presence.
—Be especially careful when pulling into your garage and when backing up, since a small child may not be seen at first glance.
—Do not allow him to play with the lighter, ignition, emergency brake, or power window buttons in the car.
—Lock your car when not in use to avoid the possibility of his climbing into it.
—Hold him, or at least hold his hand, whenever you are crossing the street or walking through a parking lot.
—Be sure to fasten your child's safety belt or harness before you drive.

FEEDING

Your baby's diet will probably not change very much just now, although your doctor may suggest that you offer him new foods in different mixtures from within the four basic food groups. His schedule will also show no change. The vast majority of you will have made the gradual shift from strained and puréed food to chopped or diced foods. Many babies will be finger-feeding themselves quite well and drinking on their own from a cup. Some will even be trying to use a spoon. These babies are still in the minority at this point.

Over the past several phases we have emphasized your baby's increased participation at mealtimes. This continues to be a time when babies need to experiment with food and eating utensils. They have a burning desire to investigate and do things by and for themselves. You still cannot expect them to be very precise or neat. In the midst of this shift in feeding responsibility, you will have to be especially tolerant and supportive.

As your baby goes about learning how to feed himself, there may be many days on which he gets annoyed if you interfere. On other days he may become irritated when you refrain from helping him. You will have to be flexible. Judge by his behavior just what your position in feedings will be. His changing between wanting to be independent and wanting to be dependent will make patience on your part all the more important.

Appetite and Between-meal Snacks

Most Infancy 11 babies continue to have good appetites, although some tend regularly to eat less at one meal, for example at breakfast, than at other meals. This is no reason to worry. When your infant is not hungry, he can afford to forego a meal occasionally, as long as your doctor says that he is healthy and is gaining weight at a satisfactory rate. Keep in mind that as your baby learns to eat by himself, his need to test things out during mealtimes may be as necessary to him as eating. He may not consume as much food as he did when you were feeding him his complete meal. Rest assured that when he is hungry he will not dawdle or even object to your offers of help.

Babies who get hungry in between their regularly scheduled meals may want to have a midmorning to midafternoon snack. There is no harm in giving a hungry baby who is a good eater a snack, as long as it is not offered too soon before his next meal. On the other hand, when a baby is misbehaving at mealtimes or is eating very little, it is a good idea not to offer him snacks between regularly scheduled meals.

Independence in Eating

Your baby's need for more independence in eating should become more obvious to you. Many babies will want to feed themselves with their fingers, at least in the beginning of their meal. Some will persevere until their entire plate is empty, although some will get tired or discouraged midstream and accept a little help from a parent at that point. Polished performances in self-feeding are usually yet to come, and inaccuracy should be expected until more skill is acquired.

A baby's personality and individual style may, to some extent, influence how much responsibility he wants to assume for eating. If he is the type who forges ahead despite all obstacles, he will want to do everything by and for himself, even though he is not very skilled. On the other hand, a baby may be overwhelmed by the task at hand and give up after a while, or continue to let his parent feed him until he is surer of his abilities.

Sometimes a very neat baby who appreciates cleanliness will not attempt to feed himself because he is hesitant about getting his fingers dirty. There is the other type of baby who plunges in and enjoys getting food on his hands, face, hair, and lap. Try to be patient and supportive of your baby's own special way of behaving during meals, and responsive to his individual needs for testing his abilities, exploration, independence, and dependence.

Many babies will be anxious to try their hand at manipulating a spoon and cup. Some will manage to do a fairly decent job of drinking on their own from a cup, although few will be capable of doing the same with a spoon. Skill with a spoon takes much longer to be acquired. Those who attempt to use a spoon often get very frustrated by their own lack of control. It seems that soon after they load it, the food slips off on the way to their open mouths. An unusually advanced baby will be able to handle a spoon more adeptly, but the majority will not be able to spoon-feed with any degree of accuracy until they are well into toddlerhood.

Babies who want to try their hand at using a spoon can be given some time to play with it, perhaps after they are nearly finished with their meal. A baby who shows a strong interest in imitation and spoon-feeding himself can be taught how to use the spoon, one step at a time. Do not expect him to be successful in mimicking your use of the spoon. Manipulating a spoon properly is a complex task for a baby to undertake.

Need to Stand During Meals

Babies can continue to be placed in high chairs for their meals. Some babies who are fidgety will have difficulty sitting still. They may set their high chair into motion and try to stand up in it. Even if the high chair is well anchored, and is equipped with a safety strap, your baby may still be able to knock it over. To ensure his safety, place him in a low chair with attached feeding table or tray for his meals.

CLOTHING

As your baby's activity level increases, check to make sure you are not overdressing him, since too much clothing may cramp his movements or cause him to become overheated.

Footwear

Now that your baby will be spending more time standing and even attempting to walk, it is important to discuss the subject of wearing shoes. When he is learning to walk, he will benefit from going barefoot or wearing shoes with flexible, leather soles. Being able to "grasp" the floor with his feet will give him more stability and help him exercise the muscles in his feet. Assuming that your floors are safe (are not rough, do not have splinters, pieces of glass, sharp pebbles, etcetera), and not unusually damp or cold, you can allow your baby to go barefoot indoors for another year or two. He can also go barefoot outside, providing that these surfaces are safety-proofed, if this is possible. If you take him to the beach, he may enjoy going barefoot.

Naturally, when your child is toddling and is outdoors in cold weather, or otherwise walking on streets or sidewalks, he will need shoes. It is important that the shoes he wears be well made and fitted to his foot size. Many doctors advise starting out with shoes which have medium-soft soles, and soft leather uppers, because flexible shoes will allow feet more freedom of movement. Later on, once a child has begun to walk well, he can be outfitted with harder sole shoes. There is some controversy over whether a youngster is better off in flexible shoes, or firmer, higher shoes.

There are shoes in which the heel or rear portion is formed by the sole coming up and over. These do not have any ankle support, and should be avoided. Those infant shoes where there is a single seam in the back portion of the shoes, independent of the sole, are better. This becomes important as soon as shoes represent more than a covering, particularly when the infant needs some ankle support in order to walk with stability. It is best to ask the advice of your pediatrician or family doctor, who can recommend a shoe that is suited to your child's needs.

If the soles of your baby's shoes are smooth, it may make it more difficult for him to walk on slick or highly waxed floors. In order to prevent him from slipping and sliding, you can put small pieces of double-stick tape on the soles, or use a piece of sandpaper to rough them up a little, since this will give them more traction.

There are numerous guides to buying shoes, but your best bet is to go to a children's shoe store that has been around for a long time, and consult a salesperson who has had plenty of experience in fitting children's shoes. Always bring your child with you so that the salesperson can measure his foot and select the correct size shoe. Keep in mind that well-fitting shoes are important, and are not necessarily the ones that cost more.

An occasional child will have problems with "toeing in." Parents may or may not be able to observe this, depending upon the extent or nature of the problem. The child's doctor usually detects such foot problems during well baby or child examinations, and may even detect them in early infancy. The doctor then makes recommendations for ways to correct the problem.

Sometimes straight-last shoes are recommended as a corrective measure in children who "toe in." These shoes are symmetrical and can go on either the left or right foot. They are also identical in shape, having no in-flare or out-flare. Depending upon the nature of the problem, other types of corrective shoes, arch supports, or other corrective measures may be recommended.

If the child's doctor feels that some correction is required, he or she will write a note or prescription for the shoes. A parent will then bring the prescription detailing the correction to a shoe store. Not all children's shoe stores carry corrective shoes, so it is a good idea to phone a shoe store before making a trip out there. The length of time a given child will be required to wear corrective shoes is variable, and is determined by the child's doctor.

Young children outgrow their shoes at an unbelievably fast rate. A child younger than a year and a half may outgrow his shoes every month or two. After that age, he may outgrow them a little less frequently, but still every few months. You need not buy shoes that cost more because they are "long-lasting." What you should get into the habit of doing is checking your baby's shoes every three weeks or so, to make sure that they still fit his foot. Check his shoes when he is standing. There should be about a half-inch space between the end of his toes and the tip of the shoe. The shoe should be wide enough so that his foot is not cramped. Should you notice any hard skin, blisters, or pink or reddened spots on his feet which are due to rubbing or pressure, chances are that his shoes no longer fit.

Young children go through their socks just as quickly as their shoes. It is advisable for you also to check your baby's socks from time to time, to make sure they still fit. When he is standing up, they should protrude a fraction of an inch beyond the tips of his toes. If they are too tight and short, they may cramp his feet.

SLEEPING

Sleeping difficulties, while not apparent with all babies, persist with some babies or surface for the first time. Separation anxiety, discussed on pages 363–64, may heighten a baby's resistance to go to bed or trouble sleeping during the night. His increased locomotive abilities coupled with his desire for constant activity may also add to his resistance to go to sleep, as can discomfort from teething.

Should your baby seem anxious or upset about being separated from you at bedtime, he may need a little extra understanding and reassurance by whatever methods you elect to offer. On the other hand, avoid going overboard in the sympathy department or being too lax in handling bedtime or night waking, since this can encourage future problems in this area.

Many babies will now be ready for only one nap during the day, and some will occasionally refuse even one nap. Maintaining at least one nap or even a quiet play or rest period is very important to many parents.

DISCIPLINE

Sensitivity to Your Approval and Disapproval

Your baby's growing awareness of how his behavior affects other people's reactions plays an important role in his response to your program of discipline. His increased consciousness of simple cause and effect sequences, of the results of his actions, and of your reactions to his behavior, are crucial to his learning whether he has behaved in an acceptable or an unacceptable manner. He is probably starting to understand what you mean when you emphatically say "No" or "don't touch," even though he may not always obey these commands. He is slowly beginning to sense which actions you approve of, and which you don't.

When he has been successful in following your orders to go and bring you his shoe, he may scramble to your feet, drop the shoe in front of you, pull himself up on your legs, and look as though he is waiting for you to comment on what a good job he did, or to show him that you approve. Similarly, when he reaches for an "off-limits" object, he may peer over his shoulder to see whether you are around. Provided that you are not in sight, he may grab the object, seemingly aware that you would not approve. In the event that you happen to "catch" him with the "forbidden fruit," he may even have a rather frightened look on his face, as if he is anticipating your anger, or else have a devilish gleam in his eye indicating that he is testing you.

His possible attempts to seek your approval after he has been "good," as well as his look of fear or defiance after he has been "naughty," indicate that he is learning and responding to your discipline, even if only in a small way. Clearly he still has a long way to go, but these signs that you may notice either now or sometime soon, should be viewed in a positive light.

Your Baby May Start to Test Your Rules and Limits

At some point during Infancy 11, and increasingly as your baby grows older, he will begin to tease you or test your "No's" or "Don'ts." You should expect this testing behavior, since it is a necessary aspect of his learning about the limits you have established in regard to his behavior, and how consistently and adamantly you intend to enforce them.

The following example involves an eleven-month-old baby, although it might, in principle, apply to a toddler or even a preschool child. One day while Mrs. Marsh was in the kitchen, her son, Bradley, crawled over to the stove, pulled himself up, reached with his hand, and turned the control knob. Mrs. Marsh responded appropriately by restraining his arm and saying, "No, don't touch that," in a tone that meant business. However, Bradley had not fully learned or understood the lesson about not touching the controls. He reached for the knobs on the stove with his other hand, just to see if his mother would react the same way as before. Again, Mrs. Marsh sternly said, "No, don't touch."

All Bradley learned up to this point was that he should not touch the knobs on the stove *when* his mother was in the room. But he needed to do further testing to more clearly discover exactly what it was that he did that caused his mother to say, "No, don't touch." When he was at a relative's home he wandered into the kitchen and tried touching the knobs there. Eventually, after much experimentation and testing, he finally realized that the knobs of stoves were definitely off limits, since his mother had been watching him and her reaction to his behavior was consistent.

You are likely to observe your baby testing your limits, and experimenting to determine exactly which of his actions prompt your "No's," and whether you will be consistent and firm in your reaction. If you allow him sufficient opportunities to test out your "No," this will help him to differentiate between acceptable and unacceptable behavior. Once he clearly understands what he can and cannot do, he will probably feel proud and secure, since he will have a better sense of where he stands.

Sticking by him while he tests each limit that you set, and having to repeat each lesson many times a day, is not an easy or an enjoyable way to spend your time. There will be situations when you feel as though he is deliberately testing you to make you suffer. You should understand that his repetitious behavior is a necessary part of his learning about limits, rules, regulations, and boundaries. Unless he experiments with you and your rules, important lessons may be learned incorrectly or never learned. Keep in mind that some of his testing behavior may be in fun. He has learned which of his actions prompt a reaction from you and may repeat them just for the sheer fun of influencing your behavior and seeing how you respond. If you understand some of the reasons behind his testing behavior and the value of this behavior in terms of his development, it may not irritate you as much as it would otherwise.

YOUR FEELINGS IN RELATION TO TEMPER TANTRUMS

Dealing with temper tantrums can be very trying. According to Mrs. Lange:

The day that my son threw his first temper tantrum, I had had a very rough day and wasn't in a particularly good mood. In fact, I was irritable and tense. Suddenly, as I was trying to get him dressed, he flopped to the floor and began to scream and kick. I was really annoyed at his behavior. My annoyance, plus the fact that I was already anxious and in a bad mood, prompted me to take my frustration and anger out on him. I spanked him. Instead of quieting down, he lost more control and screamed and kicked louder and more actively than before. I felt like wringing his neck, but instead, I slowly regained my composure and walked out of the room. Thank God, this seemed to do the trick. Ten minutes later he crawled over to me and gave me a hug. Both of us had lost control, and I guess we each felt sorry afterward. I couldn't help losing my temper, and I guess he couldn't help losing his either.

Children's temper tantrums often arouse feelings of anger in parents. It is difficult to remain pleasant and calm when you are watching your infant explode, particularly when you are rushing to get somewhere, are not in a good mood, or have had a rough day. In helping your youngster learn to control his emotions, you must set a good example. Refraining from losing your emotional control and overreacting to his behavior is very important, although usually not easy.

Feelings of Fear

The child's first temper tantrum can sometimes frighten parents, especially those who are unprepared for the possibility of one occurring. Mrs. Urbano talked about her feelings about her daughter's first temper tantrum.

> The first time I saw my daughter, Terry, throw a temper tantrum, I have to admit that I was frightened. In fact, in the back of my mind I worried that she might have been having a seizure. I got very upset and immediately rushed over to her to help calm her down. I felt sorry for her and gave in to allowing her to stay up past her bedtime. Unfortunately, she began to throw temper tantrums every night just when it was time for her to go to bed. After the first two tantrums I wised up and ignored her, but I'll never forget how scared I felt the first time I saw her lose control.

It is not unusual for parents to mistake a first temper tantrum for a seizure, especially since they are likely to be caught off guard, and perhaps emotionally drawn into the event. Seeing a child lose all emotional control sometimes reminds parents of their own susceptibility to losing control when under great amounts of stress. This may be scary, particularly to those parents who tend to have difficulty controlling their own angry and aggressive impulses.

Feeling Embarrassed

Parents usually find that the temper tantrum thrown in a public place is the most nerve-wracking and difficult to handle. Mr. Ash had the following comments about the first time his son threw a temper tantrum:

> I remember very well the time that Don threw his first temper tantrum. I had taken him with me to the grocery store. He wanted a special kind of cereal, but I didn't want him to have it since it was loaded with sugar and I felt that he would be better off with another brand. This is what set him off. There he was throwing a temper tantrum in the middle of the aisle. I had read about how to handle temper tantrums and thus decided to ignore him. All of a sudden there were swarms of people gathered around watching. I was really embarrassed by the whole thing. I felt that maybe people thought I was a cold-hearted guy because I ignored Don. It was hard, but I didn't give in. Several minutes later Don quieted down and the people finally went about their own business. Boy was I relieved.

It is hard not to feel embarrassed when your child has a temper tantrum when you are entertaining guests in your home, or are out in public. People will stare, and sometimes even express their disapproval of the manner in which you are handling your child. As long as you feel that you are dealing with the temper tantrum properly, do not take other people's criticisms to heart.

Feelings of anger, sympathy, and embarrassment are common. Rest assured that you are not alone if you have a hard time accepting or dealing with this aspect of your baby's behavior. If you feel as though you did not deal especially well with the first tantrum, there is no reason to feel bad or guilty. Certainly there is no need to panic. In the future there are sure to be other occasions on which your child will become angry or frustrated and throw temper tantrums. Suggestions for how to handle temper tantrums are presented on pages 434–35 and these should be of assistance to you. Breath-holding episodes can prompt similar reactions in parents as do temper tantrums. Suggestions for handling these episodes are given on pages 434–35.

IF YOUR CHILD IS A "SLOW" DEVELOPER

Parents' positive and negative feelings are often closely related to their babies' progress. When a baby is developing at a fast pace, parents are naturally proud and happy. Many take this as a sign of having "good parents." Parents of a baby who is slow in achieving developmental milestones such as sitting, crawling, and so forth, or who is lagging behind his peers in his general development, are likely to be rather unhappy and inclined to take this personally.

There are many other feelings besides unhappiness that may be aroused in parents of "slow" developers. Two common feelings are guilt and anger. This prompts some parents to try to urge their baby to surge ahead in his performance, even though there are clear indications that he is not ready to master a new skill. A few parents may even yell at their child and punish him for being slow to achieve certain skills.

It is not unusual for parents to be ashamed of their child, particularly when other parents comment on how quickly their youngsters are developing. Such comparisons of children's achievements are bound to leave a parent of a "slow" developer feeling jealous, resentful, and mildly depressed. In some cases parents also feel guilty. They may start to blame themselves for their child's lack of rapid progress. A few parents may even begin to wonder if they are somehow being punished for past mistakes in rearing the child, or have, as one parent put it "passed rotten genes on to him."

It is easy to lose sight of the fact that there are as many slow developers as there are fast developers. As long as parents are doing their best to rear their child and meet his needs, there should be no reason for them to doubt their adequacy as parents or question the quality of care that he has received. In cases in which parents are worried about their child's pace of development, their best bet is to discuss their concerns with their family doctor, who will determine whether or not the infant is progressing at a normal rate. If the doctor feels that the child is developing at a rate that is within normal limits, parents should do their best to relax and simply respect their baby's individuality. Every baby will progress through each phase of development at his own pace and in his own fashion.

Of major concern is parents' attitude and treatment of their child. Frustration and resentment should not be directed at him. He should not be made to feel inferior since this could result in his developing a poor self-image and feelings of inferiority. He needs to feel that his parents love him for what he is and one way to accomplish that is not to pressure him to excel beyond his capabilities.

PREPARED PARENTHOOD CHECK LIST

MOTHER	FATHER	UNDERSTANDING YOUR BABY'S DEVELOPMENT
—	—	In what ways is your infant both independent and dependent?
—	—	Is your baby more aware of the consequences of his own behavior and whether or not he is living up to your expectations?
—	—	Has your infant's interests in other family members increased?
—	—	Does your baby try to manipulate you to get what he wants?
—	—	Are you aware of how to handle a temper tantrum?
—	—	Does your infant experiment with the properties of objects? How?
—	—	Is your baby's ability to associate cause with effect improving?
—	—	Does your baby's babbling sound like real speech, even though his vocalizations make little or no sense?
—	—	Is your infant mimicking new sounds that you introduce?
—	—	From a position on all fours, is your infant beginning to crawl or climb everywhere, including up the stairs? Have you shown him how to crawl back downstairs?
—	—	Is your child able to stand well on his own, holding on to something for support? Is he beginning to stand alone without support?
—	—	Have you seen your baby stepping sideways around his playpen or crib while holding on to the rail for support?
—	—	What evidence do you see that your baby is more skillful with his hands in bathing, feeding, playing, and undressing?

BASIC CARE

MOTHER	FATHER	
—	—	Do you know how to expand your program of accident prevention as your baby begins to step out and walk on his own?
—	—	In what ways is your baby demanding more independence at mealtimes?
—	—	Can you see obvious signs of improvement in your baby's ability to feed himself with his fingers?
—	—	Are you aware of the important factors in buying shoes for your child?
—	—	How often do you plan to check your baby's shoes and socks for proper fit?
—	—	Does your baby seem anxious or upset about being separated from you at bedtime?

450

FAMILY FEELINGS AND CONCERNS

—— —— Is your infant becoming more sensitive to your approval and disapproval of certain of his behaviors?

—— —— Has your baby begun to test your rules and limits? Why is this a normal, very important aspect of his education in self-control?

—— —— What are some of the common feelings and reactions that parents have to their babies' temper tantrums?

—— —— Parents often have trouble dealing with temper tantrums. Do you find it hard to cope with this aspect of your child's behavior?

—— —— Are you inclined to take your baby's developmental progress personally?

—— —— If your baby is a "slow" developer, have you discussed your concerns with his doctor?

Infancy 12

PERSONAL-SOCIAL DEVELOPMENT

Self-awareness

Your baby has made great strides in self-awareness. She is conscious of several parts of her body, such as her major facial features, her arms, hands, fingers, legs, feet, toes, and genitals, and is probably able to point to them when asked. She has gained voluntary control over much of her body, recognizes how her actions can alter her surroundings, and learned to make her body work for her. Through movement and manipulation of objects in her environment, she has realized that it is possible to perform different activities simultaneously with her right and left hands, but it will be a long time before she learns "right" from "left."

As further evidence of self-awareness, your baby can respond when someone calls her name, and can probably recognize her own reflection in a mirror. Through observing other people and imitating their behavior, she has discovered both similarities and differences between herself and them. Her ability to regulate her own behavior is still doubtful, but she is showing ever-improving patience while her meals are being prepared, and is adapting to certain parental expectations of her.

By now she has become even more aware of what she wants than before, and is more capable of expressing her opinions. She is intent upon "telling" you as well as the other children in your family when she likes something and when she does not.

Her awareness of her own feelings has increased, and you will see her express many different emotions and moods. Along these lines, she seems to be more able to recognize your emotions and moods. Among her repertoire of social skills are pretending that she is hurt, has a "boo boo," or is in need of help, just to get your attention and have you shower her with sympathy. Other skills include pleasing you as well as getting you angry, and manipulating you to get you to satisfy her wants and whims. As she tests your limits and your tolerance of her behavior, she learns more about her own limitations and your "image" of or expectations for her, both of which help to define her "self" further.

Your baby is slowly separating herself from her environment, and from you, even though this distinction is probably still somewhat unclear to her. Through displays of negativism and rebellion, she learns more about the differentiation between "her" and "you," and her own individuality and autonomy. During toddlerhood, her position as an independent person, separate from all other people and objects in her world, will be more fully recognized. Even though your infant has made much progress in the area of self-awareness, there is still much for her to learn about her body, and her "self."

Social Sensitivity and Interests

It was not too long ago when your baby had no idea of who her family was and was mainly concerned with her own needs and body sensations. Being highly aware of family members versus strangers, she now relates to each family member differently. She likes to socialize and be at the center of attention. Your baby is more sensitive to others' feelings, more emotionally tied to her family, and enjoys being included in family activities. She imitates family members and learns from them.

454

Your infant has a well-developed sense of who you are, what you look like, and what you mean to her. Whenever she needs assistance or something else, she calls you because she knows you care. Her ability to extend her love and affection to you by hugging and kissing are quite obvious. To her, you probably represent everything: love, care, familiarity, security, and trust all rolled into one.

Your moods, touch, voice, facial expression, praise, and disapproval are better understood by your baby than in the past. She knows how to communicate with you through a varied combination of sounds, perhaps words, and "body" language. It is easier for her to tell when your mind can be changed, and when you are not about to budge or be persuaded to give in to her. She senses when you are at the end of your rope and about to explode.

Your baby is growing more independent of you day by day, although she continues to depend heavily on you in a variety of respects. You can expect her still to want to climb into your lap and cling when she is in unfamiliar territory or when strangers approach. This never really stops, even in adults, at least on an emotional level. Separations from you may be terribly difficult for her to handle at this point. In the midst of her charging ahead at full speed, there will be demands for you to baby, hold, cuddle, carry, and rock her. As you move around in your home, she may be like your little shadow, trailing close behind and imitating your behavior.

This is a time when you must follow your baby's lead. When she wants more independence, you must let her go. On the days when she wants some extra support and reassurance, do not hesitate to satisfy her needs for fear of making her overly dependent upon you. You will be giving her the understanding and security that will allow her to move on once again toward greater independence. By taking your lead from her, you will be able to make appropriate adjustments in your relationship according to her changing needs.

INTELLECTUAL DEVELOPMENT

Your baby at one year is an active explorer who is interested in everything, and determined to maneuver herself into every accessible area of your home. Once she begins to stand, take a few steps on her own, and walk, there will be no stopping her. Opportunities for further travel will be nearly unlimited. She will somehow manage to walk, worm, and squeeze herself into places in which you never imagined you would find her, just to hide from you or have a good look around. No area will remain unexplored. Over the past year, her curiosity about her surroundings has rapidly increased. She searches actively for new experiences, stimulation, and challenges.

She's More Sophisticated in Her Dealings with Objects and People

An Infancy 12 baby has learned many things about objects during this past year, and her interest in them has steadily increased. She knows how to play with objects, put them to use for her own benefit, separate and combine them, and handle as well as carry more than one at a time. Her more skillful and appropriate use of objects shows up throughout the course of her daily activities.

You will notice your infant making scribbles with a large crayon, trying to use a spoon to feed herself, and drinking on her own from a cup. Other fairly new accomplishments with objects may include piling objects on top of one another, stacking pierced wooden cubes or rings on a peg, and even, perhaps, matching simple pictures of familiar objects. As a result of her past experiences with objects she has learned to associate cause with effect better, to discriminate among objects, and to use them more appropriately.

With all of the knowledge your baby has gained, there is much that she still wants and has to learn about objects. During this phase, you will notice her investigating their characteristics and functions further, exploring their differences and similarities, and observing how they can be displaced in space. She will continue to perform various actions on them to see the outcome, and practice simple hand and finger skills on them.

HER MEMORY HAS IMPROVED. Images of objects appear to be more permanently stored in your baby's mind. Her memory for absent objects shows improvement. You might see her reaching accurately for objects even with eyes averted or shut, showing not only her better memory for the position of objects, but also a notion that they exist even when she is not looking at them.

Objects are no longer perceived as part of her body; they are regarded as separate from her. After watching you place one of her toys under a box or a blanket, she may immediately uncover it. Your infant may try hard to locate an object that you have hidden when she wasn't looking, although her search may only involve hunting for it in the place where she last saw it. You may also see her hiding objects and then recovering them a day or two later. Her concept of the permanence of objects, however, is still not as fully developed as it will be later in toddlerhood.

SHE HAS LEARNED A GREAT DEAL FROM YOU. There is little doubt that your infant's sophistication in everyday social situations has dramatically increased. You will notice more deliberate and precise imitations of your behavior and sounds. Andrea Mussen had been trying for the past month to teach her daughter, Louise, how to wave "bye-bye," but it was not until Infancy 12 that Louise was consistent in responding appropriately to her mother's requests to wave good-bye to people.

One afternoon Andrea invited some friends over. When they were about to leave, Andrea encouraged Louise to "wave bye-bye" to them. At her mother's prompting, Louise raised her arm stiffly and repeatedly opened and closed her fist. Andrea was delighted at Louise's response, and took pride in knowing that she had helped her daughter learn her first "social grace."

Your baby, like Louise, is probably showing evidence of having learned many things from you, such as how to wave good-bye or give hugs and kisses. Through observation and imitation, she is also learning how to eat by herself, wash and dry herself, and remove some articles of clothing at bedtime. She may even be repeating words that she hears you use, and playing many social games. Your patient efforts to teach her things are surely bringing positive results, making parenthood very enjoyable.

Her understanding of language and ability to communicate needs and wants have also blossomed in the past few months, largely due to your continued efforts to talk to her and foster her language development in many different ways. Your simple directions and requests are now likely to be understood, if not followed. To a much greater extent than before, words are being correctly associated with people, animals, and objects. She can point correctly to many objects when you ask her to or when she spots pictures of them in magazines, on food boxes, or in books. Your baby's progress in this area provides further evidence of your caring and well-invested time and energy, as well as her desire to learn from you.

YOUR BABY IS MORE ADAPTIVE. In essence, your baby has learned to deal more adaptively with her surroundings. During the past year, she has acquired many of the necessary simple mental and physical skills that will facilitate more complex and sophisticated learning in the future. Through her daily interaction with and exploration of people, toys, and objects, she is continuing to learn how to learn.

The many skills acquired thus far will serve as a preparation for more complex living experiences and challenges that your child will encounter during toddlerhood. At each stage of her life, new abilities will become part of her old repertoire of skills, thus broadening her horizons for personal growth and accomplishment. Intellectual development is really a building process, and her sensory and motor experiences over the past year have paved the way for her to reach a higher level or new stage of intellectual development, which you will read about in Toddlerhood 1.

LANGUAGE DEVELOPMENT

Active Language Development

Your baby's expressive jargon resembles actual speech so closely that a stranger who hears you and your baby carrying on a "conversation" from a nearby room might actually think that your infant can talk. Nearly everyone will have a difficult, if not impossible, time trying to make sense out of her jargon, but you are likely to have at least occasional success understanding her, knowing her as well as you do.

Babies' vocabularies can vary widely during this phase. Some infants will not be doing much "speaking" but will understand some of what they hear, and respond appropriately to simple requests. There are Infancy 12 babies who will have relatively broad vocabularies, but they are definitely in the minority. There is no need for you to be too disappointed if your child is not yet saying words, as long as you are positive that she can hear and can imitate a few sounds. For many children, talking really begins to develop in toddlerhood.

Passive Language Development

You will be aware that your baby can understand many more words and phrases than she can say, particularly if she is not saying much of anything. This is true of all babies, even those who are early talkers. A fun way to appreciate the progress she is making in comprehension is to initiate activities in which you ask her to point to objects in a room or bring them to you. Correct responses on her part will provide substantial evidence of her understanding of language.

When you speak to your baby, she is likely to recognize many words that she hears, and comprehend their meanings. Her ability to connect words in her mind with the people and things they represent shows a great deal of improvement. From the quality and expression of your voice, she will clearly sense whether you are pleased or disappointed with her actions, whether you are in a good or a bad mood, or whether you are relaxed or tense. Even when what you say is beyond her simple level of understanding, she may still get some sense of it by your tone of voice, actions, and the particular situation at hand.

MOTOR DEVELOPMENT

Gross Motor Activity

As you think back over the past eleven months, it will be apparent how far your baby has come in her motor development. Once a relatively immobile, dependent infant whose actions were almost entirely determined by primitive reflexes, she now has voluntary control over her body, and is perpetually moving around.

PREWALKING LOCOMOTION. Locomotion on all four limbs is speedy and easy for her. Moving is likely to involve hands and feet being used for body support. At any time now she may be shifting to walking, although even after she has begun to walk she may still use prewalking forms of locomotion when she has a particular goal or location in mind and wants to reach it as soon as possible.

CLIMBING. High off the ground on all fours, your baby is in a favorable position for climbing, and you are likely to observe her climbing up steps, on chairs, beds, couches, and so on. Heights are not likely to frighten her very much, since she is not only brave but also very curious about what is in your cabinets and drawers. Assuming that she is pretty good at climbing, you should read pages 348 and 356 on how to prevent possible falls from the crib. A great deal more climbing will be seen during toddlerhood.

STANDING. Your infant may finally be able to stand unaided. Her next move will then be to practice getting into a standing position without hanging on to anything for support. Once this is mastered, she might practice stooping or squatting and then standing up again. Soon she will polish every aspect of standing and will move on to bigger and better things.

CRUISING AND WALKING. Infancy 12 babies are often seen walking sideways while holding on to furniture. Upright locomotion has definitely become your baby's goal. Naturally, whenever she steps out, her first attempts at walking are bound to be quite awkward. Attempting to walk without your assistance, she will have a very tough time maintaining her balance without plopping to the ground.

Walking will require her total concentration. If she is striving to reach a specific goal several feet away from her, this may help to motivate her to take an extra few steps. Falling probably will not bother her in the least, for she will be up on two feet again quickly, practicing with endless determination until she can get wherever she wants to go. The expression on her face will testify to her concentration, determination, and delight.

Once your baby begins to step out on her own, she will tirelessly practice this new skill whenever she can. Her incredible drive to take step after step will demonstrate how all important this task is to her. She needs no outside reward for walking. The pride and sense of accomplishment that she feels upon taking each step are enough of a reward for her.

Not all Infancy 12 babies are ready to walk. Parents of babies who are not making attempts to walk sometimes lose sight of this when they see or hear about other one-year-olds toddling along on their own. Concerns about a child's inability to walk by age one are common. The fact is that walking alone, for the majority of youngsters, is a milestone that is reached during Toddlerhood 1. There is no reason to worry or feel concern if your child does not begin to step out by herself at twelve or thirteen months. She will learn to walk according to her own individual rate of development. Until that time, try to be patient with her and relax. Focus on her strengths, rather than weaknesses that may not even exist. Also concentrate on really enjoying the few remaining days, weeks, or months before your child enters a new, walking phase that will bring about many changes in both of your lives.

Fine Motor Activity

Think back to the time she was born, and you will remember how she kept her fists clenched, how her arm position was tied in with her head position, and how her eyesight was limited. Gradually her hands opened up and were used for swiping, batting, and later visually directed reaching. Looking at her manipulatory behavior today, you will be struck by the rapid progress that she has made during the past year. She is becoming more agile day by day.

She no longer uses whole arm movements and a crude grasp. Her reaching and grasping movements have been greatly refined. Now that her thumb-forefinger grasp is more well controlled and efficient, she will be able to handle small objects and tiny particles more easily and neatly. Without much effort she can pick up a raisin or a small wooden cube, put it inside a small box, and then quickly remove it.

Having refined her ability to grasp and hold on to objects, your baby will now be developing the ability to release them more efficiently. You are apt to see her picking up small objects, one by one, dropping them deliberately, and then picking them up again. Her growing ability to let go of objects smoothly and easily will allow her to roll a ball to you more easily. She was previously unable to participate in this activity. She may also be able to place one block directly over another in order to build a two-block structure.

By now your infant may be able to hold on to more than two objects at a time. When she is holding an object in each hand and you offer her still another, she may place one of the two objects in the bend of her left elbow in order to grab for the third with her right hand. Using this clever approach she can hold on to even more than three objects at once.

You will also notice further signs of improvement in her fine motor co-ordination. She will probably be able to scribble with a crayon, although her artistic abilities are, at best, quite limited during Infancy 12. She may also be able to remove an article of clothing or two. Her ability to use her hands for finer or more delicate tasks and work with tools is still limited, but the progress that she has made thus far is nonetheless significant.

KEEPING YOUR BABY HEALTHY

Toward the end of infancy, your doctor will want to give your child a test for tuberculosis. Tuberculosis is a treatable contagious disease and is discussed on pages 968–69. This test, called the tuberculin test, will indicate if your child has been exposed to tuberculosis. It is a useful screening test to help the doctor be sure that your child stays in the best of health. Record the results and date of this test on the chart on page 947. Your doctor may also want to check your child's blood for anemia or other changes as part of a routine preventive medical screening.

HOW TO ENSURE YOUR BABY'S SAFETY

Overprotection

As your baby develops new physical skills, your ability to limit her actions in order to keep her safe, on the one hand, and permit her freedom to practice her new skills, on the other, will constantly be challenged. This is not always easy on parents. Some parents worry about the possibility that they are overprotecting their babies.

Parents who are overprotective persist in shielding their baby from harm long beyond the age at which she is perfectly capable of ensuring her own safety in certain areas. The child often becomes overly dependent and fearful of ordinary situations in which other children her age would not feel uncomfortable. During a child's first year, overprotection usually does not represent a major problem, because she is incapable of protecting herself, or even recognizing dangers. Parents must do this for her. Still, you should not go overboard trying to control your child's behavior, and must establish a happy medium between letting her go to do what she pleases and limiting her freedom for her own well-being. This is where the value of safety-proofing your living space enters into the picture.

By providing her with safe home surroundings, she has more freedom and you do, too. You do not have to stand over her like a hawk ready to pounce when she makes the slightest move toward a dangerous object. Since protecting her every move is not necessary, it is doubtful that you have to worry about being overprotective.

Teaching Your Baby to Be Safety-conscious

It is hoped that you are continuing to help your child learn to obey certain safety rules and to follow your warnings. A child who is well disciplined is usually safer, so be certain to pay attention to your methods of discipline, particularly now that she is becoming more aware of what it means to be "good" versus "naughty," and since her ability to remember things is increasing. In time, although not for another year or two, your early efforts to teach your child to behave in ways that will keep her safe will begin to bring desirable results. Until that time, you should keep training her, repeating the rules of safe and responsible conduct, and reminding yourself that this is not all in vain!

TEACHING YOUR CHILD TO SWIM

Around the time that your youngster begins to walk, when placed on her stomach in an inch or two of water in the bathtub, or held under her chest in the air, she may circle her arms, wriggle her trunk, and kick with her legs in a manner which resembles swimming motions. Her movements will probably be similar in nature to the reflex movements you observed after she was born. See pages 87–88.

Chances are that at this age, the infant can be taught some fundamentals of swimming rather quickly and smoothly if you are interested in having her learn to swim. You may find some swimming classes for infants and young toddlers advertised in your local newspaper, intended to take advantage of the child's natural ability to swim.

Whether or not it is advisable to teach a youngster to swim at this early age is an issue over which there is much debate. The youngster around a year of age frequently has no fear of water, and does not usually perceive the possible dangers. People who advocate teaching babies to swim often claim that a baby who is not afraid can be taught to swim much more easily than a child closer to two or three years old who has developed a fear of water. The baby's "swimming" behavior, which greatly facilitates her learning to swim, will disappear if it is not reinforced and encouraged, so many people feel that this is an opportune time to teach her to swim.

On the other hand, some people feel that because the baby or young toddler has no fear of water, teaching her to swim is a potentially dangerous proposition. Having no awareness of the potential for drowning but knowing how to paddle about in a limited way, a youngster may confidently jump into deep water or travel from shallow to deep water in a pool to practice swimming. She is likely to be unaware of the dangers of water that is too deep, and unaware of her own limitations.

Perhaps more important than whether or not you should teach your youngster to swim at a very early age, which is basically a matter of personal preference and the availability of classes and pool facilities, is the issue of her safety. A young child should be given an adult's *undivided* attention and supervision whenever she is in or near water.

A child who can swim must be *carefully* watched at all times while in or around a swimming pool by a parent or trained lifeguard, and should be prevented from traveling into the "deep" half of a pool. Drownings are more common than some parents would like to think. The best way to prevent them, at any age, is to take proper safety precautions. This is crucially important with young children who do not have a clear notion of their own limitations, who are unaware of the possibility of drowning, and who can easily "get in over their heads" both literally and figuratively.

A condition that occasionally develops in children who spend a great deal of time in the water is called swimmer's ear (see page 1035). It is advisable to discuss with your doctor your plans to take your young child swimming. The doctor should be aware of any unusual water-related illnesses that might occur in your community, especially if you plan to swim in lakes or other non-chlorinated bodies of water. With modern filtration and purification of swimming pool water, pool-originated infections have been essentially eliminated, but it is still best to check with a health professional who is familiar with possible water-related infections in your area.

Flotation Devices

Each summer you will see many children wearing or using various flotation devices in swimming pools. If you decide to purchase a flotation device for your child, it is important that you recognize their potential dangers. Do not assume that once your child is strapped into a flotation device that she is safe. In fact many of these floats can actually be dangerous. Thus it is imperative that you *never* leave a young child unsupervised in the water, even if you feel she is protected by a flotation device. The false sense of security that these products often produce can pose a threat, especially for the young child.

Since there are so many brands and new designs for flotation devices, it is best to have a general understanding of how to select a good device rather than having a recommendation for a specific product. An important feature to look for is that the flotation part of the apparatus can be securely strapped on the body. Poorly designed products do not provide well-made straps or fasteners and thus they often slip off the child, especially when wet. Some devices that attach the float to the back of the child can become very dangerous if the child bobs from an upright position in the water to a face-down position. The float may make it very difficult for the child to right herself and lift her face from the water. Some safety experts prefer flotation devices that attach to the arms.

By selecting a well-made product that does not slip off your child when wet, the possible dangers from flotation devices will be minimized. Even if your child is using a properly fitted device, however, you should always stay with her in the water. Being there to offer adult supervision is the best way to ensure her safety in the water.

FEEDING

A Decline in Appetite

The second year often brings with it an expected decline in appetite. As the child's growth rate slows down, her nutritional requirements change. Your infant's weight has approximately tripled in the past year, and will normally only increase by four to five pounds from age twelve to twenty-four months. This means that she will be eating smaller quantities of food in comparison to what she has been taking in during previous months. You should not become unduly concerned when your child takes smaller portions of food or seems disinterested in eating three or even two substantial meals a day. All you can do is continue to offer her plenty of food, three times a day, and not worry about how much she wants to eat.

There are other factors that may also play a role in the reduction in the amount of food that your child eats. Some of the disinterest in eating that surfaces in Infancy 12 can be associated with the child's increased mobility and interest in her surroundings. Sometimes teething discomfort puts a damper on her appetite. Your infant's desire to be standing and constantly on the go may make it difficult for her to sit still at mealtimes. Her lack of skill in feeding herself and refusal to let you help can also result in decreased food consumption. Strong food preferences may result in her only "picking" at her meals, particularly those that are not specially designed to cater to her specific preferences. The amount of food that is eaten should be determined by your child—not you.

The Choosy Eater

In describing their baby's eating behavior during this stage, parents often use the words "fussy," "choosy," "picky," and "finicky." Many babies, indeed, become more particular and assertive about what they will and will not eat. They are no longer as hungry as before, and now take their time, look over the food on their dish, and figure out what looks good to them and what is not as appealing.

Once they hit upon a food that they like, they may be quite insistent upon having it for breakfast, lunch, and dinner for several days. When their requests are denied, they may refuse to eat altogether. Food preferences usually grow stronger as a child becomes more independent and realizes that she has a mind of her own. Stating her likes and dislikes is one way of convincing both herself and her parents that she is her own individual, not merely an extension of them.

Your child may dislike some food for a week or two and then change her mind. She may want nothing but one particular food every day for lunch and dinner for five days, and then abruptly refuse to eat it on the sixth. The most sensible approach in dealing with the young, choosy eater is to refrain from making a huge fuss over food choices. When a certain food is refused, you can find a substitute that is agreeable to her, as long as this isn't too inconvenient. Experienced parents caution against pressuring a baby to eat a disliked food. This may result in her developing a more long-lasting dislike of that food when she might have changed her mind about it in a week or two.

The Time for Feeding Herself Has Arrived

Beginning around the twelfth month, babies want to take over more responsibility for feeding themselves. Many are doing quite a good job with their fingers, and are able to drink on their own from a cup, even though perfection is still yet to come. Some are even doing a fairly good job with a spoon, although most need much more practice and time with this utensil.

Allow your child to do as much as she can by herself. Remain nearby to help out in case she needs it and is willing to accept it. Do not feel rejected when she has difficulty managing the entire meal on her own, but will not let you feed her. Simply permit her to set the pace and then follow her lead. Most of you will be taking a behind-the-scenes role in feeding your youngsters. Some babies are a bit slower to become independent in eating and may still require help. Even those who can do things by themselves may occasionally want to be fed. This temporary step backward should be accepted without making them feel babyish or immature. The push for more responsibility does not always continue along a straight, forward road. Sometimes for each few steps forward, a child will take a "baby" step backward.

Eating Problems and How to Avoid Them

Starting about now and continuing throughout the second year, eating problems often arise. Many of them can be avoided or at least kept to a minimum. Listed below are some of the common eating problems, the possible reasons for their occurrence, and suggestions for preventing them from becoming major problems.

COMPLAINT: A child is not eating enough.

A baby at one year does not have to eat as much as before in order to grow and stay healthy. She wants and takes less food, and is often satisfied with only one or two meals a day. If her parents are unaware that she needs less food, they may become upset when she wants to skip an occasional meal, or eat smaller quantities of food at a meal.

Parents often want to decide how much their youngster should eat, rather than the other way around. When she does not eat the quantity of food that they have decided is the "proper" amount, they become annoyed and worry that she is undernourished. Their clean-your-plate-or-else attitude makes their child angry, and she gets back at them by eating less, or by strenuously resisting their efforts. We have the early makings of a poor eater.

Be aware that decreases in appetite at this stage are common, as are daily or weekly fluctuations. Avoid getting emotionally involved in the amount of food your child eats or does not eat. This is her business. Also avoid establishing a "clean plate" policy, since this can contribute to unnecessary tensions and hassles at mealtimes. Offer enough food so that it is possible for her to satisfy her appetite, and let her determine when she is satisfied.

It is advisable to keep an accurate record or food diary of *everything* your child eats and drinks to document if, in fact, she is *not* eating. Most of the time parents' claims that their child is not eating are really unfounded. It may only seem that she is not taking any food, when she is really eating satisfactory amounts over the long run. In the event that based on the record of her food intake you still have concerns about her food consumption, discuss them with your doctor.

COMPLAINT: She is not eating a certain food that you want her to eat or is "good" for her.

There are many reasons why a child may refuse to eat a particular food. Perhaps she simply does not like its taste or finds it hard to chew. Maybe her parents are putting too much pressure on her to eat it, and so she rebels by refusing it. It could be that she finds the appearance of this food unappealing and cannot bring herself to eat it. Her parents become angry. They feel that this food is crucially important to her health and well-being, and thus they try to force her to eat it or bribe her to eat it. They may try to disguise its flavor by mixing it with a food that she likes. She is not easily fooled by their sneaky tactics, and courageously refuses to eat the "combination." From this point on, she may forevermore refuse to eat that food, even though her former dislike may have only been short-lived. She may also come to dislike the food used to disguise the disliked food's taste.

Offer your child a wide variety of nutritional foods, and expect that she will like some and dislike others, just as you do. Rather than force the foods on her that she dislikes, offer her those that she likes within each food category. Remember, youngsters often go on temporary food "binges," and change their minds about the foods. Take these in your stride, and avoid getting into arguments over such minor problems.

Strongly voicing her food preferences, and being stubborn about giving in or changing her mind, is her way of saying, "Hey, folks, I'm a separate person with my own ideas about what I want to eat, so pay attention to me and give me some control over what I want to eat now that I'm more independent!" As long as there are so many foods to choose from within the four basic food categories, you should not have any trouble giving her foods she likes and at the same time satisfying her needs for wholesome foods and a well-balanced diet (even though from one meal to the next it may not seem that her diet is well balanced).

One word of caution. Some firm limits may have to be set on how much catering to her likes you want to do. When it is highly inconvenient for you to prepare meals for her that are different from the rest of the family's, then you will have to let her know. Give her the food that you have prepared, and also give her a reasonable period of time in which to eat. Casually take it away if she will not touch it. Sooner or later she will realize that your needs are important, too. Do not worry that she will starve to death. After skipping a meal or two she will probably be so famished that she will gobble anything, even her not-so-favorite foods. As long as you offer plenty of food at regular mealtimes, there is no reason for you to feel guilty.

As a final word of caution, you should avoid catering to her preferences if this entails eating dessert instead of her main meals, or eating unwholesome, undesirable foods rather than nutritional foods. Catering to her likes is all right as long as they are reasonable. Since you are the one in command, you can have the final say as to what is *reasonable*.

COMPLAINT: She is stalling, dawdling, and taking too much time to eat.

A child who is not yet efficient at feeding herself cannot possibly eat as fast as an older child or an adult. She needs more time in which to practice feeding herself with her fingers, drinking from a cup, and using a spoon. You should not expect her to finish with the rest of the family. Give her ample time so that she does not feel rushed and can learn to eat at her own pace.

On the other hand, some children may deliberately stall, dawdle, and take their sweet time because they know that this annoys their parents. When this is the case, you can calmly take away her meal after you have given her a reasonable length of time in which to finish. Chances are that after a few such incidents, she will learn to finish her meal in an appropriate length of time so as not to have to leave the table hungry. Bear in mind that if time deadlines are set there is a problem, since most infants have no reference point with time except the here and now. A concept of time is slow to be developed, so a deadline is not very useful when employed inflexibly.

COMPLAINT: She plays during mealtime instead of eating.

A child who plays instead of eating during her meals may be having difficulty concentrating. Children of this age tend to be highly distractible. When there are toys readily available, or there is a lot of noise, conversation, movement, or people around, your baby may naturally begin to pay more attention to whatever is going on around her, rather than eat her dinner. Feeding herself is still a rather new activity, to which she must devote her full concentration and effort. She has great difficulty concentrating on more than a single task at once. She may be better off eating by herself in a place where distractions can be eliminated.

Some children, even those who are isolated while they are learning to eat by themselves, will still persist in playing at mealtimes. They deliberately smear, throw, or spit out their food, and toss eating utensils overboard onto the floor. Some experimentation with food and eating utensils can be expected, but there is a limit to how much playing at meals should be tolerated. Quite often the playing begins after the child has eaten enough to satisfy her appetite, at least for the moment. Rarely will a ravenous child play with her meal, since she will be concentrating upon shoveling it into her mouth. If and when your child starts to play deliberately during meals, you can warn her that unless she stops playing, you will have to remove her food. This may motivate her to settle down, but if not, then calmly take away her meal. She will get the point after a while.

In some cases a child who is eating with the rest of the family deliberately acts up and plays or shows off in order to get attention. When she irritates and annoys everyone into commenting on her behavior, or reacting negatively to it, then she has accomplished her goal of getting attention. It is advisable initially to try to ignore her antics. You can also get good results from feeding her alone at mealtimes until she is willing to behave more politely.

COMPLAINT: She is too messy when she eats.

Some parents who complain about this are overly concerned with cleanliness, and expect a polished performance from their children when it is not possible. They fail to recognize that children who are first learning to feed themselves are bound to be sloppy and messy because they are lacking in skill and control. On the other hand, some children who are quite capable of handling utensils without a lot of spilling, or who have perfected their ability to feed themselves with their fingers, like to throw food deliberately, and mash and spread it around. To minimize this problem, when you are sure that your child is being willfully sloppy, calmly take away her food. She is too young and unskilled for you to expect neatness from her, but you can expect her to refrain from being intentionally messy at mealtimes. Soon she will learn that if she does not clean up her act, she will have to leave the table hungry.

AN ADDITIONAL WORD ABOUT EATING PROBLEMS. Many unnecessary arguments occur when parents overreact to normal shifts in a child's eating patterns, and treat normal behavior as problem behavior. Problems may also arise when parents set definite expectations as to how much and what kind of food they feel their child should be eating. Then, if she does not or cannot meet these rigid standards, parents get upset, and begin to lose sight of where their responsibilities end and hers begin. Whether these expectations are right or wrong, realistic or unrealistic, arguments and tensions can build to the point where mealtimes become a tug of war, with resentments on both sides building.

The brief suggestions for how to avoid eating problems emphasize the importance of setting realistic expectations, and not letting emotions interfere with objectivity. If you are disturbed by your child's eating habits, it is advisable to try to keep a cool head, and examine the situation carefully. Rather than possibly antagonizing her to the point where she will become more rebellious or resistant to change, casually take the necessary steps that should help alter her behavior, or prevent it from occurring in the future.

Expanding Your Baby's Diet

By this time your baby is probably eating many of the same foods that you prepare for yourself, with a few exceptions, naturally, and eating foods in chopped or diced consistencies. Prior to this age, most babies' diets were relatively limited. There were several reasons for this. One major factor was the baby's limited ability to digest foods easily. Another consideration was her greater susceptibility to developing sensitivities to particular foods. Still another factor that influenced her diet was that it generally takes babies more time than older children and adults to get accustomed to new tastes and consistencies. These factors still apply, although to a lesser degree, to the child from one to two years of age. As the child grows older, she can be given a much wider variety of foods from within the major food categories. Let your physician advise you about changes in the structure of your child's diet, or any matters pertaining to what new foods to introduce. We will only very briefly discuss some of the main considerations in constructing a diet for a youngster between approximately one and two years of age.

Most children can begin to have some fresh, uncooked vegetables (celery, carrots, green beans, etc.) and more raw fruits (grapes, oranges, pears, tangerines, etc.) that have been pitted, peeled, and chopped into very small pieces or diced. She can also be given more kinds of dairy products (cream, buttermilk, etc.), starchy vegetables such as cooked cauliflower, stronger-flavored vegetables that she may have rejected at earlier ages, and a broader variety of meats.

Since eating habits are formed early in life, it is best to accustom a child to lean meat as well as chicken and fish early on. Hamburger and skinless hot dogs can be given, but these are not the best quality meat. Fatty foods can be offered on occasion, but should be discouraged on a regular basis, as part of a program of establishing good eating patterns. Even the types of baked goods that she can now be offered may be considerably expanded.

As you continue to add to your child's diet gradually, avoid foods that are known to cause allergic reactions. Offer those that are more easily digested. Some of the foods that tend to be more difficult for youngsters to handle include heavily fried foods, dried beef, corn, very fatty or greasy foods, such as bacon or sausage, spareribs, rich foods such as lobster meat or éclairs, oily or salty fish, and so forth.

A baby's ability to chew her foods well and handle food chunks is still limited, so there is a possibility that she may choke on foodstuffs such as nuts or popcorn. These are not recommended for a young child. It is also not advisable to offer dried fruits such as figs, dates, apricots, and so on, to a youngster of this age. They are generally introduced when a child is around the age of two.

Raw berries are sometimes hard for a child to digest, and strawberries, for instance, can still cause more allergic reactions than other fruits. Fresh, uncooked berries, and also raw melons, are usually not given until a child nears the age of two, and at that time are pitted and introduced only in very small quantities. Many youngsters also develop sensitivities to chocolate. It is advisable to hold off on chocolate in any form until a child is two.

Stimulants such as tea or coffee are not recommended. Most youngsters are quite active and energetic enough without these beverages. In addition, coffee and tea can also discolor a child's teeth. There are other foods and "sweets" that doctors commonly advise parents to include only in very limited quantities, if at all. Nearly all of you know what these foods are, but here is a very brief list to serve as a reminder: candy bars, soda, ice cream, highly sweetened foods and syrups, filled pastries, jams, sugar, cakes, and cookies—need we go on? These foods do not add important nutrients to a child's (or an adult's) diet, are high in calories, and in addition, may promote tooth decay. It is definitely better to avoid offering these foods, except, perhaps, on special occasions or celebrations, and to avoid giving them in between regularly scheduled meals since they can diminish a child's appetite. Be sure to set a good example for your child, because if she sees you constantly nibbling on these foods after or in between meals, she is apt to want to follow suit.

Small amounts of fats and oils have probably been included in your child's diet as a source of energy. Fats and oils include such items as margarine, butter, and salad oil. Many doctors recommend the continuing use of a vitamin preparation. It is vital and should be a regular supplement to a child's diet.

Continued Demands for an Evening Bottle

It is not uncommon for a child who drinks milk from a cup during her daytime meals to express a desire for an occasional bottle or even one bottle a day, particularly after dinner, or before she goes to bed. This is not indicative of "immaturity" or any psychological problem. There are many children who will ask for an occasional bottle throughout the toddlerhood stage. Unless you or your doctor have strong reasons for not going along with her wishes, there is no pressing need to insist that she give up this single daily bottle, if she persists in asking or pleading for it. Remember that allowing a child to have a bottle in bed is not recommended. Refer to page 379.

BATHING

As your baby becomes more interested in washing herself, she will probably settle down a bit and become a little less preoccupied with constant, vigorous movement, and creating "water messes." Using a washcloth effectively will require her full concentration. Although she may manage to rub her belly or dab at her face with it, she is not yet ready to be trusted to do a thorough cleaning job. A dab here and a rub there does not a clean baby make!

In spite of her lack of skill, if your baby insists upon grabbing the washcloth away from you when you wash her, try giving her one of her own. She may not be satisfied with anything but the "real" thing. This is a time when you can try to capitalize upon her desire to mimic some of your actions.

Using yourself as a model, you can show her how to wash each easily accessible part of her body, and then encourage her to do the same. Do not expect perfection. What to you is an incredibly easy task is a difficult one for her. Your baby will appreciate the time and interest that you are devoting to her bath time "education." Being able to hold and use her own washcloth will give her a feeling of independence and accomplishment, as well as being more grown-up like you.

For several days she may insist upon "washing" herself, and suddenly, she may toss her washcloth aside and passively wait for you to wash her. A baby's conflicting wishes to be both independent and dependent often become obvious in the basic care areas. Your best bet in handling her sudden changes of heart is simply to follow her lead and try to satisfy her needs at any given time. Encourage her to manage small tasks by herself when she shows you that she is ready, but do not push her to do this if you see no signs of a desire on her part to become more independent.

CLOTHING

Your child will probably be more helpful and involved in putting on and taking off her clothes. As she experiments with her new abilities, she will enjoy removing clothes rather than putting them on, since undressing is a much easier task for her. Some youngsters will be able to remove every stitch of clothing. This can be annoying to parents.

Some children pull off their diapers immediately after a bowel movement and play with their feces. Perhaps the best way to solve this type of problem is to take the necessary steps to prevent it from occurring. You can dress your baby in outfits and pajamas that zip up the back, since the zipper will probably be impossible for her to reach. Outfits that snap in the back are also helpful, although you may have to pin them shut to ensure that she cannot yank open the snaps. Another possible solution, although generally less foolproof, is to keep a closer eye on her and get to her before she removes her diaper. See also page 684.

The Right Clothes Encourage Independence

Most babies at this stage will not be able to dress themselves, but they often make attempts to do so. Over the next two years, as your child becomes more co-ordinated and skillful with her hands, she will want to become more independent in dressing, and will gradually learn to dress herself. There are cloth "books" and other toys designed to encourage hand co-ordination and dressing skills. They enable a child to practice using snaps, buttons, zippers, shoelaces, etc., and learn necessary practical skills that will help her learn to dress herself. It is useful to buy clothes designed to make it easier for her to learn how to dress and undress herself. Below is a brief list of the kinds of features to look for in selecting clothes that foster self-help.

SNAPS:
Snaps that are securely fastened and large-sized are easier for a child to manage. Outfits that snap in front are the wisest choice.

ELASTIC WAISTBANDS:
Trousers and skirts with elastic waistbands are easy for a child to step into and out of, but make sure that the elastic isn't too binding.

ZIPPERS:
Front zippers are the simplest to work (this goes for adults, too!).
A small piece of rust-proof metal or large ring attached to the zipper makes it easier for a child to pull.

Zippers that are designed to release material immediately when it is caught will make for a happy child, a happy parent, and longer-lasting clothes.

BUTTONS:

Buttons that are large, relatively flat, not slick surfaced, and few in number are easiest to manage.

BUTTONHOLES:

Make sure buttonholes are large enough so that a child will have no trouble buttoning.

NO FASTENERS:

Actually, it may give your child a real feeling of success in the beginning if you encourage her to wear T-shirts that she can easily slip over her head, since there are no fasteners to worry about.

SLEEPING

A baby's determined efforts to get up on two feet and walk during the day may contribute to greater reluctance to take a nap or go to bed. No baby appreciates being forced to discontinue an enjoyable activity in favor of lying still in her crib and going to sleep. This is particularly true when staying in constant motion and being with her family are very important to her. By putting yourself imaginatively in your infant's shoes, it should be easier for you to understand her nightly objections at bedtime.

The tension, energy, and enthusiasm generated within a baby who is concentrating her efforts upon learning to walk are difficult for her to turn off abruptly at naptime or at night. This may be a major factor underlying her sleeping difficulties and vigorous activities in the middle of the night. It is not uncommon for tension outlets such as rocking to emerge during Infancy 12. Should your infant's tension outlets prove to be bothersome, review pages 331–35 where suggestions for handling these behaviors are provided.

Most children do not make concerted attempts to climb out of a crib until toddlerhood. A baby who is extremely active and physically advanced may attempt to climb over the crib bars during Infancy 12. Without elaborating upon the possible dangers to a baby imposed by a fall from her crib, suffice it to say that it is necessary to prevent falls of this nature. Should you even suspect that your baby is capable of climbing out of her crib, read ahead to page 513 for suggestions on how to prevent crib falls.

PATTERNS OF ELIMINATION

Most babies defecate once or twice each day, although each baby still has her own characteristic pattern of elimination. Some children's bladders will be maturing and retaining urine for longer spans of time, enabling them to remain dry for a couple of hours, usually during their naptime. You may not notice this until your baby approaches the age of a year and a half to two years of age. An occasional child at this age may be able to sleep through the night without urinating, but most will need to be changed upon waking.

Considering Toilet Training

Due to the fact that your baby has shown great progress in other areas, you may feel that she is capable of learning to use the toilet. Ordinarily, children of this age are not ready to develop good toilet habits. Some children show small signs of readiness for training during Infancy 12. They may be regular in their pattern of elimination and somewhat more aware of the internal feelings that signal the need to defecate, or that go along with the process. They may develop positive feelings about their stools, which they may regard as part of their bodies, make some special sound just prior to defecating, or indicate a desire for soiled diapers to be changed immediately. A few babies at this age will be interested in using the toilet, and both boys and girls may want to play with their feces or urine. Babies who become interested in putting small objects into and out of bowls, cups, boxes, or other containers, may also be interested in learning to deposit their stools or urine in the "big" container, namely the toilet bowl, assuming that they are encouraged to do so.

Should you see some small signs of interest and readiness on your baby's part, and wish to begin encouraging her to learn to use the toilet, do so very gradually. It may be a good idea to begin teaching her to associate words with the process of defecation or urination. See page 525 for how this can be initiated, but do not expect her to catch on right away. Over a period of several months she will gradually learn words such as "pooh pooh" or "pee pee," and begin to link them with the process of elimination.

In the event that you began sitting your baby on the potty several months ago, you may now find that she protests against this, or fights your attempts to get her to sit still. Even though she sits down on the potty without making a fuss, she may not defecate until after she gets off the potty and is standing.

Keep in mind that your baby is still lacking in control, and may have such a great need to stand and move around that it is simply easier for her to stand up to defecate. Try to understand that she is not willfully trying to annoy you. She will find it easier to sit still as she gets older. Do not be concerned about her "accidents" or poor performances. Signs of unco-operativeness at this age should indicate to you that she is not ready. It is best to wait until she is well into toddlerhood, has more control over her bowel and bladder functions, and is more interested in acting "grown-up" before making earnest attempts to teach her to use the toilet.

In spite of the fact that you were encouraged by the progress she made in the past, remember that you were the one who was responsible for the success, not her. Most psychologists and experienced parents advise parents to postpone the whole issue of training until the child indicates both physical readiness and a desire to become trained. This combination of factors usually surfaces during toddlerhood. For a more extensive discussion on how to help your child develop good toilet habits, see pages 522–26.

DISCIPLINE

As your child progresses from infancy to toddlerhood, your job as a disciplinarian is likely to become more difficult. Once she begins to walk, you will be rather suddenly struck by her greater independence from your immediate control. A child who can walk can also open doors that are off limits, get away from you when you call, climb up on chairs to reach high up "forbidden" cabinets, and so on.

Your infant's greater mobility is not the only factor that may make disciplining her more stressful. She is also becoming more assertive, and perhaps even negative as described in the Personal-Social Development section. Her awareness of herself as a person separate from you, with ideas and opinions of her own, is just beginning to surface and will become more clearly established during toddlerhood. The ramifications of this awareness are widespread. She will begin to express her opinions more actively, insist upon getting her way, and test herself out against you and your expectations. These are a few of the major ways in which she goes about the long process of establishing her separateness and her autonomy.

This is an age when she may refuse to eat her lunch, deliberately test your rules, try your patience, refuse to take a nap, and throw a temper tantrum when you insist that she do something that she does not want to do. The next few months may be frustrating for both you and her. Keep in mind that she is still quite immature, and limited in her capacity to understand your commands and regulate her actions. She is only beginning to comprehend what you mean by the words "No," "Don't," "dirty," "hot," "hurt," and so on, and it will be a long time before she fully comprehends their meaning in relation to her actions. She has only recently become more conscious of your approval and disapproval, and you should not expect a great deal from her in terms of obedience.

On the other hand, it is important to set down clear rules and regulations (make sure that they are reasonable) and enforce them firmly and consistently. You will be helping her enormously by giving her behavioral guidelines to follow since she cannot yet set personal direction and controls for herself. Later in childhood she will begin to incorporate many of your external controls and rules into her own internal system for self-guidance—her conscience—but during the interim period, you should continue to provide parental limits and controls.

Due to your infant's lack of speech and limited ability to comprehend verbal rules, you will find that physical means of discipline (e.g., distraction, carrying her away from one spot to another) will be far more successful than verbal means. Some children are obviously more difficult to handle than others, and a few of you may find yourselves wanting or having to punish your child physically. If you are feeling the need to enforce what you say with physical or other kinds of punishment, review some of the basic principles about punishment on pages 330–31. You should also benefit from reviewing the information on handling temper tantrums presented on pages 434–35, and on handling feeding problems presented on pages 464–66, since Infancy 12 is a phase in which both temper tantrums and eating problems are likely to surface.

YOUR JOB BECOMES MORE STRESSFUL AS YOUR BABY MAKES THE TRANSITION FROM INFANCY TO TODDLERHOOD

Your child may be a considerable drain on you physically and emotionally and upon other members of the family as well. You may constantly have to struggle in an attempt to get her to stay within the limits you have set, while not being too overcontrolling or restrictive. Managing her is apt to be very trying. Coping with sibling rivalry and demands from more than one child may make life doubly hard on you for a while.

The issue of disciplining her is likely to come to a head, and like many parents, you will realize that it is not easy to straddle the line between being too permissive and too controlling. While it is important to give her some freedom and "breathing room," it is necessary also to be firm with her and establish clear limits and rules. This is the time when you may find yourself arguing with your spouse over methods of discipline, and the added stress of dealing with your child's behavior may create tensions between you.

As a result of the pressures and strains that accompany your job as a parent, you will occasionally feel frustrated and a bit overwhelmed. This is a time when a few parents may be pushed to the point of lashing out at their babies, and losing control of their tempers. These parents may cross over the line that separates strong discipline from child abuse, sometimes without even being aware of it.

Parents should realize that the temptation to abuse children generally increases as they enter the toddlerhood stage of development. Feelings of anger and frustration, however, are no excuse for abusing a child. Parents should make every possible attempt to find acceptable outlets for these feelings. If you are fearful that you will act upon your feelings or abuse your child, you should discuss this problem with your doctor, who should be able to assist you in seeking appropriate professional help.

PREPARED PARENTHOOD CHECK LIST

MOTHER	FATHER	UNDERSTANDING YOUR BABY'S DEVELOPMENT
——	——	Is your baby able to recognize her reflection in a mirror or a photograph of herself?
——	——	In what ways has your infant's emotional range expanded? Can you easily identify her feelings?
——	——	Have you noticed that your baby is becoming more and more assertive?
——	——	Does your baby respond differently to each member of her family?
——	——	Are you granting your infant more independence in accordance with her wishes and capabilities?
——	——	Would you describe your infant as an active explorer who is interested in just about everything?
——	——	What examples can you give showing your baby's memory improvement?
——	——	Do you notice your baby deliberately trying to imitate your actions and sounds?
——	——	Is your baby receptive to your efforts to teach her many things?
——	——	Are you able to understand what your infant is trying to tell you, even though her vocalizations make no sense to other people?
——	——	Is your baby able to say one word meaningfully?
——	——	When you ask your baby to point to familiar objects or a few parts of her body, is she able to respond appropriately?
——	——	In what ways is your infant trying to polish her standing ability?
——	——	Can your baby take a step or two while holding on to your hands or pieces of furniture?
——	——	Is your baby beginning to focus her energies on learning to walk?
——	——	What evidence do you have that your baby's thumb and forefinger grasp is more well controlled and efficient?

BASIC CARE

——	——	What is the best way to guard against overprotecting your baby?
——	——	Are you continuing to teach your infant to be safety-conscious and to obey your warnings and limits?

—— —— Could you describe your baby as a "choosy" eater?

—— —— Is your infant doing a good job eating with her fingers and drinking from a cup?

—— —— Are you giving your baby chances to spoon-feed herself?

—— —— What are some common eating problems? Do you feel that your baby has one? How do you handle this?

—— —— Have you noticed your baby's growing desire to wash herself in the tub?

—— —— In what ways does your baby participate and help at dressing and undressing?

—— —— Do you try to select clothing that fosters your child's independence or self-help?

—— —— Is your baby showing greater reluctance to go to bed? What factors do you feel underlie this reluctance?

FAMILY FEELINGS AND CONCERNS

—— —— Is your job as a disciplinarian becoming more difficult? Why?

—— —— Are you setting clear, reasonable rules and being firm and consistent in enforcing them?

—— —— Have you seen any positive results of your program of discipline?

—— —— Do you, like most parents, occasionally feel frustrated and angry that you are unable to control your baby as easily as in the past?

—— —— Are you aware that the temptation to abuse a child generally increases as youngsters enter toddlerhood?

Toddlerhood 1

PREPARING FOR TODDLERHOOD

The toddlerhood stage is turbulent and stressful but brings with it many unique pleasures and rewards. Toddlers are very interesting, likable little individuals. Once you get to know and understand them, it is easier to accept their imperfections and more fully appreciate their energy, curiosity, offers of affection, and zest for life.

Toddlerhood is divided into three phases that roughly correspond to the ages of twelve to eighteen months (Toddlerhood 1), eighteen to twenty-four months (Toddlerhood 2), and twenty-four to thirty months (Toddlerhood 3). This is a difficult time to fit the child into rigid developmental phases. The three phases of toddlerhood represent a general developmental trend that each child goes through at his own pace. Since the child may be slightly behind or ahead of the descriptions in a given time period, parents should read ahead if necessary in individual areas that may apply to the special characteristics of their child.

The most dramatic change that occurs during toddlerhood is the child's ability to "toddle" or walk by himself. This new achievement gives him an entirely new view of himself and his world. Added mobility affords him expanded opportunities for investigating his home and a considerably greater degree of independence from his parents. Along with the toddler's remarkable ability to walk, come pressing urges to keep moving, to practice his new skills, and find out more about his surroundings by manipulating toys and objects.

Play and exploration become very prominent activities during this stage and serve as outlets for the toddler's strong inner drive to make new discoveries. Sensory experiences and movement provide stimulation for the child's developing mind and are to be encouraged. On the other hand, giving the toddler full freedom to express his curiosity would be placing his safety at major risk.

Toddlerhood is a prime time for accidents, given the child's strong curiosity, lack of self-control, and inability to avoid danger. Keeping him safe without stifling his desire to learn and impeding his over-all development looms as a major challenge and concern among parents. Within each family setting, parents will have to try to establish a successful balance between offering their toddler freedom and limiting his actions.

Rapid expansion in the toddler's intellectual abilities are reflected in nearly every aspect of his behavior. The emergence of early forms of thinking during toddlerhood represents a significant step forward in development. Evidence of the child's broadening intellectual capacities will be abundant. Parents will see noticeable improvements in his memory, ability to imitate them, ability to engage in simple pretend activities, and his abilities to understand language and to speak.

The toddler makes the remarkable transition from producing sounds that are difficult, if not impossible, to decipher to producing real words and short sentences. His new ability to talk is one of the most exciting developments. It prompts immeasurable joy and pride in his parents. The toddler not only learns to use words meaningfully, but his understanding of conversations, questions, and directions shows rapid improvement, and makes him a truly different, more responsive human being.

The toddler develops a new awareness of himself and his abilities. He learns about the influence that he holds over his parents and brothers and sisters and realizes that he is like them in some ways, but also different and separate from them in others. He also becomes more aware of his own independence and feelings of happiness, anger, frustration, aggression, accomplishment, and sexuality.

One of the major hurdles that the toddler faces is to establish himself as a separate and independent person. Each toddler goes about accomplishing this task in his own individual way, at his own pace, and in his own style. Toddlers commonly demand to do more things by themselves, become more assertive, and almost seem to enjoy giving their parents a hard time. This struggle for independence that more clearly emerges toward the end of toddlerhood is often described as the "Terrible Twos." As the toddler strives to achieve greater independence and personal control, a conflict is usually set up between him and his parents. The intensity, nature, and timing of the clash between parent and child vary from one family to the next, but the family tensions and stresses that emerge during toddlerhood are universal.

The child wants to do as he pleases, but he also wants to please his parents. Along with his emerging sense of independence, there are feelings of insecurity and longings for continued dependence. His recognition of his ability to separate from his parents prompts in him courage, on the one hand, and fear of separations on the other. These opposing feelings and desires that arise within the toddler frequently result in unpredictable actions, rapid mood swings, and heavy reliance upon channels for alleviating tension, excess energy, and frustration. Toddlerhood represents a stage in which temper tantrums often reach a peak, and tension outlets such as thumb-sucking, rocking, head-banging, and blanket-rubbing are commonly seen.

It is during toddlerhood that parents make major attempts to discipline their child and teach him to behave in an acceptable manner. They make more concerted efforts to help him learn right from wrong and "do" from "don't." Parents also try to help him control his aggressive actions, develop good toilet habits, and obey rules and requests.

A toddler who wants to do things by and for himself and demonstrate his autonomy does not easily accept his parents' attempts to control his behavior and make him conform to their expectations of how he should act. In order to convince both them and himself that he is his own person, and define his own boundaries as an individual, he finds it necessary to defy some of their orders, test their limits, and rebel.

Toddlerhood is not an easy time for parents or their child. Internal and external pressures that the child experiences make life more difficult and complex than in infancy. The toddler's increased demands, rebellious nature, and poor ability to regulate his emotions and actions make handling him more challenging. This is a stage in which parents find it useful to give additional attention to matters pertaining to

Toddlerhood 1

family feelings and the needs of each family member. Realizing that the child's testing, negative behavior is a natural aspect of his development often helps parents exercise extra patience until their youngster passes through this stage.

Just as a toddler should be given the right to make mistakes, assert himself, express his feelings, needs, and emotions, and occasionally explode in anger or frustration, his parents are entitled to these same rights. Parents must not only set reasonable and realistic expectations for their child's behavior, but also for their own. Given the storminess and stress of this stage of development, and the temperamental nature of the toddler, it is quite common for parents occasionally to feel extremely frustrated, angry, and overwhelmed. Even the most loving, caring parents are likely to experience difficulties in handling their toddler.

In trying to meet the challenges and do right by their toddler, parents will sometimes wonder if they mishandled certain situations. This is quite normal and natural. It would not be healthy to waste needless time worrying or feeling guilty about those errors. A toddler who senses his parents' love and care will not only overlook their occasional mistakes, but will thrive in spite of them. Learning to relax, understand the toddler's special qualities, and truly enjoy spending time with him will be important goals for which to strive during the exciting stage of toddlerhood.

PERSONAL-SOCIAL DEVELOPMENT

Getting to Know Your Toddler

Toddlerhood is a time for many changes in your child's abilities and these will have a profound impact upon her personal and social development. She will gradually acquire many new skills, and will want to practice them without having anyone or anything get in her way. You can count on the fact that your toddler will want to investigate her surroundings and move toward greater independence. This desire is normal and necessary if she is to leave infancy behind and enter the world of toddlerhood. It is not surprising that some stormy weather and friction often arise during toddlerhood. Many new skills are blossoming forth at once, and this makes life more complicated.

YOUR TODDLER IS A SENSITIVE PERSON. A toddler is in some ways quite fragile. She will try to fulfill her desire to do what she pleases, but what she wants to do is not always acceptable to you. You will try to change her behavior and shape her values, attitudes, and personality characteristics so that they are acceptable and appropriate. This involves helping her learn about acceptable forms of behavior by initially working to get her to alter her unacceptable actions. For instance, you will keep her from exploring areas of your home that are dangerous or off limits, and you will also try to get her to stop throwing food at mealtimes. This relatively new form of "training," which will become much more important later in toddlerhood, creates many conflicts for your toddler, who takes pleasure in exploring "forbidden" areas and doing as she pleases. To learn acceptable behavior she must frequently be told what she should and should not do. Your insistence that she discontinue behaving in a way that she finds gratifying seems to pressure her much more during toddlerhood.

This pressure is not easy for her to deal with, and at times it may confuse her and make her feel insecure. Your young toddler will be limited in her ability to control her behavior, and you must be patient and not expect too much from her. If she is punished constantly, always told "No" as she explores, and seldom praised for her good behavior, the result may be feelings of resentment and a lack of self-confidence. She may also be robbed of her natural desire and enthusiasm for learning about her surroundings. Her needs to explore, become more independent, and gain self-confidence must be kept in mind as you spend time with her and guide her.

BEGINNING TO BECOME MORE INDEPENDENT. Perhaps the major task for a toddler is realizing that she is an independent person. According to Erik Erikson, a well-known psychoanalyst, toddlerhood is a crucial stage for the child to acquire a sense of independence, self-esteem, and competence. Your young toddler is beginning to develop a sense of her own uniqueness and independence. You will notice that she makes many more demands to do things for herself, even though she is often not capable. For example, she may insist upon dabbing her body with the washcloth at bath time, and may be determined to hold her own cup or spoon at dinner. She may also try taking off her clothes. Despite your offers to help her, she may often refuse your assistance. Her assertiveness may surprise you. In her own way she will show you that she wants to be more independent.

She will no longer be as compliant and willing to go along with what you suggest. In fact, she may occasionally seem obstinate and pushy. For instance, if you are trying to dress her, but she wants to keep moving around, she may put up a real physical struggle in an attempt to get her way. Her resistance to your wishes can be very annoying.

Most children pass through a rebellious phase, although they do so according to their own inner timetables. Some toddlers begin to say "No" and defy their parents just as soon as they learn to walk. Others behave this way toward the middle of toddlerhood. More commonly, children enter a phase of contrary and obstinate behavior when they are closer to two and a half.

To acquire a real sense of herself as a separate and unique individual, she must resolve the struggle between doing what *she* wants and what you and society want her to do. In toddlerhood, when her desire to explore and test things out soars to new heights, she may clash with you. You should allow her to take some part in decision-making and grant her a reasonable amount of freedom to explore and investigate her environment so that she can make many new discoveries, practice her new abilities, and gain self-confidence. Feeling confident and competent, she will be able to approach new, challenging situations with enthusiasm and without being too fearful. Children of parents who are overprotective or too restrictive may become overly frightened or dependent and unable to surge forward and feel comfortable in new situations.

All children need to feel loved, wanted, and special. They also need to experience a sense of accomplishment and to have their accomplishments recognized and complimented. At this time in your child's development, when she is beginning to develop a sense of being an independent person, it is important to avoid making her feel inferior or inept. You should praise her accomplishments, and organize your home so that she can explore, master new skills, and become confident of her abilities without constant reprimands and restraints.

THE ROAD TO INDEPENDENCE IS OFTEN BUMPY. The push for independence may not always be steady or continuous. This is what makes this time all the more difficult for a toddler and her parents. The child who realizes that she can leave her "nest" and "test her wings" may also be afraid of being separated from her parents.

At times she will be brave, and will be determined to do things by herself. Her courage, however, may be short-lived. Like any person developing a new skill, your child will have moments of fearfulness and insecurity. Some examples may help to illustrate this point. A young toddler was taken by her father over to their neighbor's home. They entered the front door and she immediately began exploring the room in a very self-assured manner. Moments later, she burst into a flood of tears when she realized she had lost track of her father. She suddenly lost her confidence and demonstrated her dependency upon her father for security and emotional support.

In another case, a seventeen-month-old boy became very obstinate with his mother after his bath, insisting that only he could have the towel. He protested and cried when his mother attempted to finish the job and dry him thoroughly. The next day, however, he made no attempt to dry himself, and refused to leave the bathroom until his mother dried him. His desire to do things by himself the day before demonstrated his developing self-assurance. However, his assertiveness was as new to him as it was to his mother. His refusal to dry himself the next day was an indication that it would take time before he felt comfortable and secure taking care of things for himself.

Although your child will be gradually becoming more assertive and demanding, she may turn to you periodically, wanting to be cuddled, fed, held, and soothed, needing extra support and reassurance. You can offer her the love and security that will help her tackle each new challenging task. A strong family base provides the solid emotional foundation that allows your child to move steadily out on her own.

PERSONALITY VARIABILITY. Over the next few months your child's personality and social style will become even more well established and individualistic. At this stage, you will undoubtedly notice personality differences between her and other children of the same age. In her second year she will be capable of displaying many more emotions and showing more complex social skills than she was in her first year.

Although children become more aware of themselves as separate individuals and begin to want to do more things for themselves during toddlerhood, each child will handle this in her own style. Mr. Foster, a forty-five-year-old salesman, made the following comments about the marked differences between his two children:

"My first child, Eric, was subtle about his need for more independence. He gradually made us aware that he was an individual who had his own ideas, but he never was all that difficult to manage. Jonathan, our second child, was unbelievably different. From the moment he began to walk at fourteen months, he was a real 'hell-raiser.' He constantly said 'no' to everything, and did the opposite of what we wanted him to do. Life was a constant struggle for a while. When I look back on it, it's hard to believe my two boys were raised under the same roof!"

This variability in children's personal styles and personality characteristics becomes more pronounced during toddlerhood. Being aware of your toddler's individual personality is the key to getting to know and really understand her.

Parents are usually concerned when their children go through this negative phase, since it often causes problems with discipline and is a source of tension in the home. Although most do not enter this phase until Toddlerhood 2 or 3, some, as described by Mr. Foster, can develop this rebellious behavior at an earlier age. If your child is becoming obstinate and defiant at this time, we suggest that you read ahead to Toddlerhood 2 where the subject of negativism is discussed in more detail.

TEMPER TANTRUMS AND BREATH-HOLDING. Temper tantrums and breath-holding episodes can accompany a child's expressions of negativism, and also reflect the inner tensions that occur during toddlerhood and the preschool stages. These behaviors are more commonly seen as a child approaches the age of two, and are thus discussed in Toddlerhood 2.

Self-awareness

Your child was not born with a sense of identity. During infancy, the first major chapter in her life, she began to find out about herself. In her explorations, she discovered her hair, fingers, feet, genitals, navel, and facial features. She gradually became conscious of her body, although not on a sophisticated level, and also began to distinguish between herself, objects, and her parents. Her ability to answer when someone called out her name was an important step in her continued identity development. Through a process of trial and error she learned that she could affect her surroundings. Your loving care and responsiveness to her needs enabled her to trust you and feel good about herself and her surroundings.

Your toddler will go on to find out more about herself that will affect her self-image. Two processes will be working together as she does so. First, a child's self-image grows out of her awareness of her body, her actions, and the feelings that go along with whatever she does. The second factor shaping her self-image is the feedback she gets from her environment, her parents, and her siblings along with all other people with whom she has contact. How people react to what she does influences the way she feels about herself.

New abilities emerge during toddlerhood, including initial language, locomotion on two feet, some degree of independence, and bowel control. How these abilities develop for the child, and the extent to which she experiences success will greatly affect how she feels about herself. Whenever she masters a new skill, she feels competent and proud. If she is unable to become adept at these abilities or experiences great difficulties in regard to these areas, she is apt to feel a loss of self-esteem and may begin to question her ability to do well.

Although there are clearly certain things a toddler can and can't master, she herself is only vaguely aware of her limitations. She often thinks she can accomplish more than she really can, tries to do what she can't, and begins to insist upon doing things for herself. For example, she may want to feed herself, or dress herself. Her abilities, however, may not be up to her desire. Trying to feed herself may result in a huge mess. Putting on her clothes will also prove difficult, since she has not yet developed the necessary motor skills to perform this task. Her sense of what she can do may drop a notch or two, when she realizes that the task she has undertaken is too difficult for her. Persistent failure can result in feelings of self-doubt and frustration.

Your reactions to her failures and frustrations will influence her development of a positive self-concept. In attempting to become more independent, she will obviously have to experience failure in learning to perform new tasks. By providing encouragement and understanding you will be able to assist her in not letting her small defeats keep her from striving ahead. If she becomes frustrated or upset, a few words of encouragement and an affectionate hug may go a long way in helping her learn that she is loved in spite of her limitations. It is important that you make your child feel strong and independent as a separate person who is good and deserving of your attention and affection.

Social Sensitivity and Interests

Although your child is now a toddler, she is rather immature in her social abilities; she still deals with people more through physical, rather than verbal, interactions. Children of this age are assertive, and often make many non-verbal demands for what they want. They may, for example, pull their parent's hand toward the door when they want to go outside or point to a toy on the shelf that they can't reach. Some may cry and lose their tempers, when they don't get what they want. Children who develop speech early will use verbal signals to tell their parents what they want. After being put to bed, a child may repeatedly call out "Mama" or "Dada" to get her parents' attention. At times your toddler may not be particularly pleasant to have around, because she may be displaying this type of demanding behavior. It should be of some consolation to know that her repeated requests are indications that she is developing a mind of her own.

Interacting with you or the primary person caring for her will be one of your child's major interests. Attempts will be made to capture your attention. She may cry if you ignore her or follow you wherever you go. Occasionally she will come to you wanting help, when she can't accomplish a task on her own. She may look helpless or frustrated, while seeking your support and affection. It is advisable to use common sense in regard to these pleas for assistance. Even though you may become annoyed at times by her clinging behavior, try to realize that she needs your affection and contact to handle the new stresses that she faces. A brief caress or a soothing word will often be all that she needs in reassurance before she goes on to her next activity.

Your child will also come to you when she wants to express affection or displeasure. Parents are eager to accept affectionate kisses and hugs from their children. Physical expressions of anger or displeasure, however, are not generally well tolerated. Toddlers will cry incessantly, throw a temper tantrum, give a mean look, or even strike out at their parents when they are very angry. Your child comes to you to express her emotions, because you are the center of her social contacts. It is important for her to share her feelings, positive and negative, with another person. Through these interactions she will be developing her ability to communicate and socialize with others. Gradually, over the next few years, she will learn socially acceptable methods of expressing her feelings from you.

You will notice how eager your child is to imitate your behavior or her older siblings' actions. Imitation will be an important avenue for her in learning how to behave. She may especially enjoy mimicking your laugh, cough, hand gestures, or other mannerisms.

Your child's interactions with her peers is emerging, but is still limited. At this early phase there tends to be some interest in other children. Toddlers may carefully observe each other and examine each other's playthings, but they usually don't play with one another for long periods of time. The major social interactions of the young toddler are still almost exclusively with her parents or the primary person caring for her.

Her ability to interact with other adults is gradually improving. She will probably not be as uneasy around strangers as in the past. Unfamiliar people may even receive a warm response, providing you are right there for support. Your presence will afford her a great deal of security in new social situations.

SEPARATION ANXIETY. By now you are probably familiar with separation anxiety, since most children, during the second half of infancy, become fearful or upset when they are separated from their parents, particularly their mothers, even for brief periods of time. Separation anxiety is also common in children during toddlerhood, especially at bedtime. If you see signs of separation anxiety in your child, look ahead to the discussion of this subject in Toddlerhood 2.

A WORD ABOUT SIBLING RIVALRY. It is commonly believed that children within one family are always jealous, negative, and competitive toward one another. Whether or not this is true is subject to debate. However, it is important to understand that the arrival of a new baby in a family may be upsetting to a toddler. Sibling rivalry is discussed in the Family Feelings and Concerns section on pages 177–82.

INTELLECTUAL DEVELOPMENT

The Developing Mind

The child's previous intellectual functioning produced circular or repetitive behavior in which she repeated an action over and over again to observe a given result. This simple, repetitive behavior satisfied her curiosity. She did not seem to have the desire or ability to experiment further with her actions and appeared content to deal with her environment just by repeating a variety of behavior patterns.

Toddlerhood 1 marks the beginning of a stage of more vigorous experimentation. Piaget's observation of his own children and others led him to the conclusion that this developmental phase is characterized by a newly acquired intellectual ability to deal with the environment on a more active and sophisticated level.

At this higher level of intellectual development, the child's interests expand and are not limited to the same action producing the same effect. She now approaches a new object with her previous experience and develops new patterns for dealing with the object in an attempt to see what results are produced. Through active play and experimentation with behaviors and objects, the child will discover new ways of solving problems and learning about her surroundings.

You will see marked progress in your child's ability to remember things and deal with objects. Her desire to play with toys and familiar objects will become more evident during toddlerhood.

GREATER PURPOSE IN YOUR CHILD'S ACTIONS. Watching your child at play should provide you with opportunities to see evidence of the gradual change and improvement of her intellectual skills. She is likely to be much more interested in playing with her toys than in the past. She will manipulate, pick up, drop, push, spin, and handle objects in countless ways. It is as if your child is actually searching for new experiences, and you may marvel at the often humorous, sometimes puzzling reaction she has to her own actions.

Her activities seem to be less random than in previous stages and appear to be directed by some underlying goal. Your child may want to move objects from one side of the room to another. This directed action indicates that her mind is taking on a new "goal-oriented" dimension.

In attempting to accomplish her goal of moving a block, for example, she may experiment with numerous ways of moving it. At first she may push it across the room on her hands and knees. She may then find that by pushing the block with her foot she can also move it, but may have difficulty with this task at this age. By co-ordinating some of her previous experiences in dealing with blocks, she may try to drop and toss the block, and experiment with throwing the block in front of her, developing the initial stages of throwing objects.

These activities are different from the child's earlier experiences with her blocks in which her play was not directed toward a specific goal or purpose. Through experimentation the child eventually learns the best way to move an object across the room, and gains more knowledge of her environment.

It is important to realize that you are seeing the further development of her memory, which allows her to approach each new object with some recollection of her previous interactions with either this or similar objects. Being able to draw on past experience, your child will begin to vary her prior response patterns so that they become more appropriate for dealing with each new object that she now encounters.

LEARNING THROUGH MOVEMENT AND SENSORY INPUT. Your child will still do a great portion of her learning via sensory and motor activities, so try to continue to provide her with opportunities to familiarize herself with her home and the objects in it. You should also be sure that she receives sufficient language and sound stimulation by reading to her, talking to her, allowing her to listen to music, and encouraging her to say words. Language will not only help your child to communicate her thoughts to other people, it will also help her to organize and develop them. By spending time and showing interest in her, and letting her know that you are proud of her, you will be encouraging her to learn more.

Concept of Objects

During toddlerhood the notion of an object having existence beyond one's ability to perceive it is more definitely established. The following example should help illustrate the concept of object permanence and how to observe it in your young child.

You and your child are straightening up her playroom and she sees you take her Teddy bear and place it in the toy chest. Fifteen minutes later, if you say, "Debbie, go get your Teddy bear," she will most likely remember that you placed it in the toy chest. She will be able to find it there even though she does not see it.

Debbie's ability to find her toy demonstrates that she has taken the next major step in memory development. Previously she would have searched in the toy chest only if she had been playing with or reaching for the bear at the time it was hidden. If she was only looking at the bear, and not physically interacting with it, she would not have later searched for it in the toy chest, but would probably have looked for it where she had most recently played with it. In later infancy the object's existence was still linked to the child's touching or acting upon the object. In Toddlerhood 1 Debbie has developed a more lasting memory of the object that is no longer tied to her physical dealings with it.

Try to observe the development of your child's memory by playing the following game with her toward the end of Toddlerhood 1. While she is watching, take her ball and place it inside a cookie jar. If you ask her to find the ball a short time later, she will probably open the lid and grab the ball. Now try a more difficult task. Put the ball back inside the cookie jar and take the jar behind the couch. While behind the couch, hidden from your child's view, take the ball out of the jar and put it behind the couch. Then bring the empty jar back to her and ask for the ball. She will most likely open the jar expecting to find the ball inside. When she discovers that the cookie jar is empty, she will be quite bewildered and surprised.

The Toddlerhood 1 child may not search behind the couch for the ball, since she may not, as yet, be capable of following an object such as the ball through multiple movements around the room. She is not able to handle all of the information about the ball's complex shifts in position in her head. The ability to follow more detailed object movements doesn't usually emerge until later in toddlerhood.

What Makes Things Happen

The Toddlerhood 1 child looks at what goes on around her from a very narrow perspective. She still relies heavily upon her parents to satisfy her needs, and like a supreme ruler, whenever she wants something, she expects them to fulfill her requests. The world, from her immature, limited viewpoint, revolves around her actions, needs, and desires.

When she sees things happen, she quite naturally links them to herself. Her mother appears before her because she wants her mother's companionship, not the other way around. A napkin blows off the dining room table, not because a draft in the room carries it off the table onto the floor, but because she happens to be looking at it at the time. Although it is difficult to know exactly what a Toddlerhood 1 child is thinking, the self-centered view of her environment that developed in infancy still greatly influences her view of the world. For the most part she thinks that things happen because she wants them or causes them to happen. Her new view of objects as things that continue to exist even when she isn't looking at them marks the beginning of her increasing objectivity in understanding her surroundings. She may have some idea during this phase that objects can move without her influence, but it will not be until Toddlerhood 2 and 3 that this idea emerges more clearly. At this point, her views of what makes things happen are still closely related to herself.

Concept of Space

Your child spends a great portion of her day moving about from place to place in your home, handling objects, looking at things, and comparing them. Through her movement, observation, and manipulation of objects, she is learning more about interrelationships between objects, and is gradually becoming more familiar with space in your home. As she moves around the room, you will see evidence of her growing knowledge of space.

She may show you that she knows where certain familiar objects are kept. From her toddling around tables and chairs to get to a toy, it can be suggested that she is aware of some simple spatial relationships. Your child puts visual, tactile, and auditory sensory input about her environment into an organized framework, so that she can learn more about the space around her and the floor plan of your home.

Although your child is learning more about spatial relationships, the following example may help to demonstrate that her abilities are still very limited.

A fourteen-month-old child was playing with a ball in the living room. She pushed the ball vigorously and it rolled underneath a day bed and out the other side. She bent down to look for it at the base of the bed and became frustrated when she was unable to find it. This child did not realize that if the ball was not under the bed, it must have rolled out the other side. She had not developed a clear understanding of the spatial relationship of the bed and the room. It is not until later in toddlerhood that the child can follow an object through different movements or displacements in space.

Concept of Time

In spite of the fact that your toddler usually cannot talk about time, she is becoming more aware of time relationships. During the course of each day, you will notice that she seems to sense that one event follows another in her daily routine. If her bath time always follows dinner, she may directly head for her sponge toys after she finishes eating, in preparation for her bath. She senses or anticipates the event that is to follow, demonstrating a primitive understanding of the concept of time. At this age, however, she is mainly concerned with the present, and does not have a good notion of either past or future events.

Learning Through Imitation

Your toddler's ability to remember events and associate actions and mannerisms with people helps her to imitate others more accurately. There seems to be greater purpose in her imitative behavior, and she is apt to mimic your actions and words more than she did in infancy.

Mary, a little toddler who loved to follow her mother around as she cleaned house, was given a child-sized mop and broom set for her birthday. One afternoon while her mother was sweeping the kitchen floor, Mary watched carefully and then grabbed her own small broom and began to sweep. At first she held both hands tightly around the base of the broomstick and pushed it along. She immediately put the broom down, glanced intently at her mother, and then picked up the broom again, this time taking care to see that she held it in the same way as her mother.

Your child may now make further attempts to eat, bathe, dry, and undress herself. She is also apt to enjoy mimicking you as you work around your home and yard. Imitating your behaviors, such as sneezing and smiling, and repeating words that she hears you say, will become one of her favorite pastimes. Imitation will play an increasingly important role in your child's development over the next several years.

LANGUAGE DEVELOPMENT

One of the exciting developments to watch for in toddlerhood is the emergence of elementary speech. Speech is beginning to develop, although most young toddlers can say only a few words. Occasionally words arise from the child's nonsense talk. By listening carefully to your child "speak," you will probably hear them.

Your toddler's vocabulary will be expanding over the next several months. Individual differences in children's language abilities will become more prominent during this phase. If your child is an early talker, she may already be saying simple sentences, but if she is like most children in Toddlerhood 1, she may not be doing much talking except for a few words. Even if she isn't saying words, the sound sequences that she is producing probably resemble the rhythm of speech, particularly when you are not standing in the same room with her.

Some toddlers who are early talkers may be repeating many words that they hear other people using. They may know, for example, how to ask for objects, toys, or foods that they want. As your child's interest in mimicking your speech increases, you can take advantage of this and teach her new words. Through imitation, her vocabulary will gradually increase.

Active Language Development

When your child plays or toddles around your home, you may hear her "speaking" to you, yourself, and her playthings. Most of what she says will still be undecipherable. "Conversations" with her stuffed animals, dolls, and other playthings may increase as her play becomes more socially oriented and imaginative. At times it may seem as if she is giving herself and her toys directions to do this or that. It may appear at other times as if she is asking herself or her toys questions.

You will observe that recognizable words are being produced more often than in the past. Praise your child when you hear these first words, or positively reinforce her in other ways. This will motivate her to keep saying the words, and will help her learn that they are an effective means of getting and holding your attention as well as getting things that she wants or needs. When a child learns a new word, she often repeats it throughout the day to practice using it or perhaps just to hear her own voice. She is generally her own most appreciative audience, since, after a while, her parents may find her constant repetition grating on their nerves.

Your toddler is now likely to be imitating words that she hears you using. She may also mimic simple words that she hears on records, television, radio, or tape recorders. You may even hear her imitating the sounds of animals, trucks, airplanes, or sirens. One toddler, according to her mother, began to imitate "bird" sounds, since they had several birds as pets. The vast majority of children will now be saying "Mama" and "Dada," as specific names. More than half of the children of this age will have vocabularies larger than this.

Some children will now begin to produce brief sentences consisting of one word, for example: "Up!" or "Out!" A few may start to use simple two word sentences, having both a noun and a verb. Parents may hear simple questions or statements such as "Mommy go," "Daddy up?" and "Truck go." A few toddlers may be using longer, more complex sentences if they are early talkers. Although their grammar is likely to be incorrect, they won't know it.

Most young toddlers are able to understand a large portion of what their parents say. Their ability to speak, however, is at an elementary stage. When toddlers try to explain or say something, and cannot make their parents understand, they are apt to get angry and upset. If you sense that your child is upset because her ideas are there but she cannot put them into sentences, you may be able to help by offering her the words she doesn't have at her command. By using this technique appropriately, you will be helping her learn new vocabulary words and promoting her intellectual development.

Passive Language Development

Your child's understanding of language continues to increase during Toddlerhood 1. In addition to her ability to follow your simple commands and directions, she may understand the meaning of questions such as, "Are you thirsty?" or "Are you hot?" She may show you that she knows what you're saying by her actions or, even perhaps, by her verbal responses.

As your child learns a new word, she may use it in a broad sense to describe or classify more than a single object. If, for example, she learns the word "truck," she may say the word "truck" whenever she sees not only a large truck, but also a fire engine, a jeep, or a bus. She has appropriately named these large vehicles that move, but she has not developed the ability to differentiate between each object. This type of generalization and grouping is likely to be seen frequently until your child is able to separate and describe objects with greater sophistication.

You will see numerous examples of physical forms of communication in your child. Children continue to indicate their needs and wants through their facial expressions, hand movements, and body positions. When they want something, they often point to the toy or object. Squirming away, for example, usually indicates their dislike of a person or an activity. Non-verbal communication becomes more highly developed as children grow older and become more aware of people around them.

MOTOR DEVELOPMENT

Your child will be making the transition from crawling to walking. Walking is now becoming your child's usual method of getting around, although she may sometimes return to a position on hands and feet when she's rushing to get somewhere. Once she is able to walk, she will probably refuse to be kept in a playpen, crib, or other confining space. She will want to be roaming around, inside and outside, upstairs and downstairs. Her desire to move is apt to be very strong, and she will be on the "go" perpetually. As she becomes more confident about her new skills, she will want to climb up and down furniture, your lap, and the stairs, and will love to carry, move, and drag objects and toys.

When your child can walk fairly well, she will be much less under your direct control. If you turn your back on her for even a moment, you might find that she has disappeared from the room and wandered upstairs or outside. You will have to keep her in one safe area, or offer constant supervision if you allow her freedom to move about the entire house.

Now that your toddler has developed the ability to move and control most of her body, you will begin to see more and more co-ordinated motor activity. When she was first able to turn over, she was beginning to co-ordinate the muscles in various parts of her body into a smooth movement. During this phase you will see further evidence of co-ordinated movement patterns. She will begin to develop more complex motor activities such as throwing, walking backward, and sitting in chairs, by co-ordinating both fine and gross motor activities. It will be educational to observe your toddler's early attempts at these complicated movements.

Gross Motor Activity

WALKING. Your child will be walking fairly well, although she is probably not very sure-footed. Gradually, as she has more opportunities to practice, she will become better at maintaining her balance; she can then lower her hands and use them to carry toys and objects as she travels.

She still toddles with feet spread far apart to maintain her balance, but moves ahead with greater assurance. Depending upon their personalities, some toddlers go forward with great gusto and courage, while others are much more timid. In spite of your child's improved ability to walk, you may notice that she has difficulty in starting, stopping, or turning corners.

If your child falls down or trips fairly frequently, this is nothing to worry about. Many toddlers stumble, lose their balance, and trip, although they rarely get seriously hurt as an older child or an adult would if they fell down. Toddlers tend to be flexible and relaxed as they fall, whereas older children and adults are generally rigid and stiff.

CLIMBING. Using your hand, a wall, or a railing for support, your toddler may be able to walk up a flight of stairs awkwardly. At first, she will lift one foot up and place it on the step above. Then she will bring the other foot up on the same step before continuing on up the flight of stairs. It will not be until approximately age three that a child is able to walk up a flight of stairs in an adult-like fashion. Some toddlers in this phase still prefer to go upstairs on hands and knees or hands and feet, in a modified crawling position.

Walking down a flight of steps is a much more difficult task, which she probably won't accomplish until she has learned and feels confident about going up. Until that time, she may hesitantly go down backward on hands and knees or hands and feet, turning her head and looking over her shoulder to see where she's going as she descends, step by step. She may go down in a highly comical seated position, bumping from one step to another on her rear end.

SITTING ON A CHAIR. It will be interesting for you to watch the various clumsy ways in which your child approaches and seats herself on a chair, because she is not as certain of the space behind her as the space in front of her. She is apt to climb up frontward on her knees, holding on to the back of the chair for support. Then she will twist her body around to face in the right direction, and finally bring her feet down. When she attempts to seat herself on a low chair with no back, she may move backward toward it inch by inch, looking over her shoulder or under her torso at the seat until she is directly up to it. When she feels sure that she will not be lowering herself onto the floor in front of the chair, she will then sit down. Later, when she is better able to co-ordinate her body movements and to judge distances and spatial relationships, she will have more confidence in her movements.

ATTEMPTING TO KICK A BALL. Your toddler may now attempt to kick a ball. In order to do this, she must stop walking directly before reaching the ball, balance herself on one leg, and move her other leg backward and then forward. Although her intentions may be good when she first tries to kick a ball, she will not be able to co-ordinate her body movements to match her intentions. Unable to stop as she approaches, she will probably run right into the ball with her feet, or miss it entirely. Even once she becomes able to stop and balance her weight briefly on one foot, she may accidentally kick the ball forward as she brings her other leg backward. The ability to kick a ball is an indication of a toddler's improved balance, co-ordination, and sense of timing. Most children will not successfully kick a ball forward until they are closer to two years old.

ATTEMPTING TO THROW AND CATCH A BALL. The ability to throw a ball is dependent upon a child's ability to co-ordinate her arm and hand movements, and to release an object. In infancy your child was able to move her arm up and down in a casting type of movement. She then became more skilled at picking up a small ball, but was only able to hold on to it very briefly before it dropped out of her hands. Gradually she became able to hold on to it for longer periods of time, but was unable to release it whenever she wanted. Now she is beginning to co-ordinate her arm and hand movements, and is further developing the ability to let go of an object whenever she wants. You will see her intentionally throwing an object such as a cup in order to practice her new arm motion.

Her first attempts will be rather crude, although most amusing for you to observe. She may let go of the ball too early as she brings her hand backward toward her body, causing the ball to be flung to the ground. Depending upon where she releases the ball in the process of moving her arm, it will fly in all directions, making it impossible for you to play a game of catch with her. Over the next several phases, she will gradually develop the ability to control her release, and to time it properly so that she can throw a ball overhand in the direction in which she intends it to be thrown.

Most parents find it enjoyable to start playing ball with their children at an early age. You might find yourself intrigued by her lack of co-ordination and timing in grasping an object that is thrown to her; when you toss a ball to her, she may bring her hands together either too early or too late. Even if she manages to bring them together at the proper time, she may not be able to arrange her hands in such a way as to clasp the ball. As her co-ordination, understanding of space, and sense of timing improve, she will begin to grasp it in the air. Thus, don't expect too much from her during this phase.

WALKING BACKWARD. Your child may begin to add a few new maneuvers to her repertoire of activities, now that her stability and co-ordination have improved. She will probably be able to walk backward. This is a more complex action than going forward. When she begins to walk backward, she will do so awkwardly and hesitantly, and may often lose her balance and plop to the ground. It is understandable that she would prefer to go forward, since in this direction she can go faster. She relies heavily upon visual cues to maintain her balance while walking, and when she walks forward she can see where she's going; when she walks backward there is much uncertainty.

RUNNING IS YET TO COME. Before very long, you are apt to see your child not only walking, but walking very rapidly. At this time a toddler isn't usually capable of running. In true running, a child's body is suspended in air for a brief period of time. A young toddler doesn't possess the leg strength and balance that are required to lift both feet off of the ground simultaneously. Although your child's rapid walking may begin to look more and more like running movements toward the end of Toddlerhood 1, you will notice that at least one of her feet always remains on the ground. It is not until later in toddlerhood that children really begin to run.

Fine Motor Activity

BLOCK-BUILDING. Signs of your child's increasing ability to release objects can be seen when you watch her at play. At this time she is likely to be able to pile one or more blocks on top of one another successfully. Her first attempts to align a block correctly and set it down were probably very awkward. She was apt to have misjudged where to place it and plopped one block over the other, causing them to fall over. Even if she placed the block properly, she might have knocked it over in the process of releasing it. Building a tower of two blocks is a complicated task involving fine motor control and co-ordination of several actions. In order to accomplish the task, your child must be able to pick up a small block between her thumb and forefinger efficiently. Then she must be able to place it directly on top of another block. Finally, she must be able to release the block smoothly and easily so that it stays in place.

You will also see other examples of your child's increased finger dexterity and better ability to release an object. She may now be able to fit a square block into a square hole successfully. She may also be able to drop a pea into a cup easily.

MANUAL DEXTERITY. In addition to your child's improved ability to release objects, you will see other signs of improvement in the way she co-ordinates and uses her hands. With a felt-tipped pen grasped awkwardly, she will probably begin to scribble. Make a simple mark with a pen on paper (e.g., a straight line) while she's watching. See if she tries to copy the mark that you made. Her abilities to draw are extremely limited, so don't expect too much.

She is becoming more adept at feeding herself with her fingers and can often put finger foods such as cut-up pieces of cheese or fruit into her mouth skillfully. You will also notice less clumsiness in her handling of simple utensils. She may do a much better job of drinking from a cup on her own, but until she gains further manual control, some spilling should be expected. You should enjoy watching her attempts to use a spoon. If she manages to get food on the spoon, it will often be spilled or smeared on her face. Observing your child's progress in feeding herself throughout the remainder of toddlerhood will allow you to appreciate the dramatic improvements in her manual dexterity.

LEARNING THROUGH PLAY

Play Is an Essential Ingredient in Your Toddler's Life

One of your important responsibilities during toddlerhood will be to provide your child with opportunities to play by herself, with you, with playthings, and later with other children. Through play, she will find out many things about herself and the world around her. Your toddler needs to be able to interact with her environment through sensory and motor activities. If she is denied such experiences, her opportunities for acquiring learning skills will be cut short severely, and her intellectual as well as other abilities will probably begin to lag behind her peers. Before toddlers can move to a higher level of intelligence in which they manipulate symbols and ideas in their minds, they must have had sufficient prior sensory and motor experiences. Play is a major avenue through which your toddler will learn and acquire the building blocks for future development in all areas.

Toddlers Make a Game Out of Everything

For your young toddler, play has truly become a pleasurable activity in its own right. As she varies her old reactions to her toys and actively discovers new ones, she turns almost every new behavior into a pattern of play. Take, for example, a little girl with a ball. She first approaches the ball and interacts with it as she has in the past. She pushes it on the ground, carries it from place to place, and drops it. While playing with her ball, and trying to get across to the other side of the playroom, she varies her arm actions when dropping it and, in doing this, learns to throw the ball in an awkward fashion. This new arm action of throwing fascinates her. She practices throwing with great interest and amusement. She repeatedly picks up the ball and every other small object that she can grab and throws them around the room, laughing with delight. This little toddler made a "game" out of throwing, and this new activity kept her happily occupied for nearly half an hour. Like other toddlers during this phase, as soon as this child discovered a new behavior or way of interacting with her toy, she turned it into a play activity and created a new "game" around it.

Selecting Toys for a Toddler

The number one consideration in selecting toys for your toddler is her safety. It is important to emphasize the fact that toddlers may still put everything into their mouths, and therefore you must choose toys that are not small enough to be swallowed. Toys with small parts that can easily break off and be swallowed should be saved until your child is older. Toddlers are not ready to play with jacks or marbles. Equipment and toys must be safe, and even when your child is using safe toys and equipment, you should be around to oversee her activities.

Toys and equipment should be suited to your child's abilities and interest. If your child dislikes picture books, it would be a mistake to push them on her because you feel that they would be "good" for her. Use the age levels marked on toys as a general guideline, but rely on your own common sense and knowledge of your child in judging whether or not a toy is suitable for her.

Toys which are unstructured in nature are usually better at this age than toys that do one specific thing. A set of wooden blocks, for example, is a marvelous toy for a young child, since blocks offer opportunities for an endless number of play activities. The child can throw them, bang them together, pile them one on top of one another, and so forth. After closely examining her blocks, she will develop games to play with them. Toys that allow the child to practice her newly found skills and to be creative are extremely valuable. Although a doll that talks may hold a child's interest for a short while, a doll that doesn't talk will probably be just as much fun and may be more beneficial for your child in the long run. She will be able to be creative and imaginative in making the doll say what she wants it to say when she begins to talk. Through the child's own initiative, she will play with her doll, rather than the doll doing all of the work for the child.

You should look for play equipment that your child can manipulate without your help. Your toddler will want to do many things on her own, without your assistance or interference. It is therefore important for her to have playthings that foster independence. If you have to direct all of her play activities, this can promote dependence and rob her of opportunities to learn on her own.

Another characteristic of a good toy is that it can be used both indoors and outdoors. Since your toddler will love to move, shove, drag, and carry her toys around the house, it is a good idea to select playthings that are light enough for her to be able to move without your help. When you walk into a toy store and are examining the toys, you will notice that some playthings promote various areas of your child's development: physical, intellectual, personal-social, language, and combinations thereof. It is a good idea to select playthings that your child will enjoy and, at the same time, will help her develop new skills.

One Man's Junk Is Another Man's Treasure

Parents often make the mistake of rushing out to buy their toddler expensive toys, thinking that this is what will interest and benefit her the most. In doing so, parents overlook the fact that toddlers are absolutely fascinated with common household objects. They love to play with materials and equipment found in their homes, and this includes what to you may seem dull and uninteresting. The objects that you usually throw away, such as old picture catalogues, egg cartons, empty milk cartons, cans, cardboard boxes, crumpled-up pieces of wrapping paper, and so forth, will be interesting playthings for your toddler. Those of you who hate to throw anything away and who save everything, including junk, are now in luck. The old saying that one man's "junk" is another man's "treasure" is especially true during toddlerhood and the preschool years.

One of your toddler's favorite pastimes may be emptying out your waste cans, and exploring the discarded objects. If you get into the habit of saving boxes, paper, coffee cans, old clothes, and other items that you would normally give away or throw away, you will find that they will come in very handy as playthings and art materials for your young child. Buying expensive toys may be enjoyable and fun, but those of us on tighter budgets need not feel left out, since there are numerous varieties of wonderful homemade toys that are just as good.

Old cardboard boxes, for example, make terrific toys. Your toddler can stack medium-sized boxes to make towers. She can pile numerous objects in a box, and then have a grand time removing them. By cutting windows out of a large box and a slit for a door to open and close, your child will have a playhouse. A few different-sized boxes make perfect nesting toys. Several boxes when strung together with a piece of rope will make a fine first "train." By keeping the open end facing up, your child will be able to put objects such as her ball and wooden blocks in each "train car."

Take a small cardboard box or container and partially fill it with large empty spools of thread. Tape down the lid (make sure that it is well fastened). Your child will now have a noisemaker to shake when she hears music. Attach a piece of rope to the filled container and it can easily be transformed into a pull toy. By cutting a square hole in the top of an empty box, your toddler can practice dropping objects such as blocks into the slot. The variety of toys that can be made from ordinary cardboard boxes, and the activities that can arise from using these containers, is virtually endless.

Making toys for your child not only saves money, but can give you an opportunity to exercise your creative talents. Besides cardboard boxes there are other safe and inexpensive household items that will make excellent playthings. A little imagination goes a long way. In making toys for your child, be sure to remember the importance of her safety when she is using them. Especially avoid using small objects that can be swallowed and toxic substances, since she is likely to chew on most of her toys.

Expanded Play Area

You may be very tempted to keep your toddler in a playpen during her play periods. After all, if she's confined to a playpen, your job will be much easier. You won't have to worry about safety-proofing your home, or keeping your eye on her. Thus, you will have more time to do the things that you want to do during the daytime. But, at what cost to your child?

Most toddlers will now complain and cry when they are put in a playpen. Your child has a driving need to be out and about, pushing things, carrying large objects, shoving, climbing, and exploring her environment. This is the way she learns. She will no longer be happy when she's confined to a limited area such as a playpen. She'll need a larger area in which to play. Your toddler's new gross and fine motor abilities need an outlet in exercise and play activities. If you provide a stimulating home environment, you will be fostering both her motor and her intellectual development.

Whether she is inside or outside your home, she'll need more room. Thus, you should offer her play space both inside your home, and outside in the yard or park. Giving her freedom to move around will have a positive effect upon her over-all development. The playpen can be used on occasion to allow your child to play with less supervision, but if you can minimize her confinement, you will be helping her to grow.

Exploration Activities with Objects

Toddlers spend much of their time interacting with objects—more time than they spend interacting with people. Many of your child's dealings with objects will involve exploration. She will stare at them intently and examine them from all angles. She will grab objects, carry them from place to place, throw them, listen to the sounds they produce, combine them, pull them, push them, and even stuff them into her mouth. For her safety, small toys and objects that could be swallowed must be kept out of her reach.

In this way, she will be practicing new skills. When she looks at pictures in a magazine, for example, she will be developing the skill of turning pages. Exploring her bowl of cereal will give her experience in picking up tiny objects. Playing with her ball, she will get practice in throwing and dropping, and even in interacting with people if she attempts to play catch. The more chances she has to practice her newly found skills, the more proficient she will become. The feelings of competence that she experiences when she has opportunities to interact with objects and manipulate them are invaluable. As she gets older, she will devote increasing amounts of time to mastering simple skills such as those discussed above.

Play with Water, Sand, Dirt, and Combinations Thereof

Most toddlers delight in playing with water, sand, and dirt. Digging, pouring, and splashing will give young children a great deal of pleasure. These experiences, although messy from your point of view, will be very enjoyable and educational for your toddler.

Nature's play materials are not only easy for you to provide, they are inexpensive and don't take up storage space inside your home. These natural substances do not just include water, sand, and dirt; they also include grass, leaves, rocks, sea shells, and an endless variety of other substances. Although adults often take these natural resources for granted, children are fascinated by them and are often highly motivated to play with, handle, and discover the properties of these materials.

WATER PLAY. Children of all ages usually love to play with water, and there are endless possibilities as to what your child can do with water. Be sure to dress her in old clothes. Water play can take place outdoors if the weather permits. Fill up a wading pool with a couple of inches of water and let your toddler splash about to her heart's content. You might also simply offer her a bucket or some other container of water and let her take it from there. Indoors you can utilize the bathtub or kitchen sink. If bubble bath is not irritating to her skin, this can make water play even more fun.

Your child will naturally want some equipment for her water play. Now is your chance to utilize all of those old pots, pans, plastic cups, sponges, and plastic squirt bottles that you have been saving.

Water play can be very satisfying to your child, but it can also be very dangerous. You will have to supervise her when she's in the bathtub, and take all other appropriate safety precautions whenever she's playing with water or near water.

SAND AND DIRT PLAY. One of the most useful items for outdoor play that you can provide for your child is a sandbox. You can easily make a sandbox yourself or buy one secondhand. If you have a large shallow container with drainage, you may want to dig a hole in your yard for the container and fill it with sand. Cups, toy shovels, plastic containers, old baking tins, and other similar objects will make your toddler's play with sand more enjoyable. Water added to sand will enable her to fashion it into cakes, mountains, and castles when she is ready. If you live near any public beaches or playgrounds with sandboxes, you can easily take your toddler there to play. Old clothes are recommended for sand play.

Youngsters tend to be intrigued by dirt. With dirt and a little water, children can enjoy hours of messing and oozing. A few spoons, sticks, and a toy shovel for digging will add interest to their play with dirt, and will keep them happily occupied for relatively long periods of time. But, let's face it, many parents are opposed to letting their children play with dirt. Why? Because dirt play makes for a messy child, dirty clothes, and a dirty house. Dressing your child in old clothes and keeping her dirt play limited to a specific area outside the house should eliminate your major objections.

Vigorous Play Activities

Children will want to practice their physical skills, and will especially enjoy activities such as pulling, toddling, and climbing, which allow them to exercise their large muscles. They will also love to crawl over things. A wooden plank, supported by a building block at either end, raised several inches off the floor is an excellent item for a child. At this stage she can crawl over it, or push her cars along this "highway." Later she can use it as a homemade balance beam. Small-sized furniture is another much-used item. Your toddler can push it around, drag it, and sit on it. Four-wheeled kiddie cars in which she can sit and move about are also excellent choices for toys. She will probably prefer these large-muscle activities to fine motor activities.

PULL TOYS. Toddlers love to pull or drag anything attached to a string or rope, since this allows them to practice their new motor skills. Pull toys are inexpensive to make, but rather expensive to buy. They can be made from simple objects in your home, securely attached to a string or rope. Wheels are not really necessary. Pull toys that produce sounds will be thoroughly enjoyed. You can use measuring cups, wooden spoons, empty food or milk cartons, and so on, when making pull toys.

BALLS. Play with balls of various shapes and sizes will give your toddler a great deal of pleasure. She can roll them, throw them, watch them bounce, and retrieve them. Balls that you buy should be large enough so that they cannot be swallowed. They should also be unbreakable. Lightweight, plastic beach balls, round rubber balls, and toy footballs are among the most popular with young children.

TODDLERS ARE FASCINATED BY STAIRS. If you live in a ranch-style home or apartment, you'll discover that when your child visits other homes with stairs, the stairs become the focus of her attention. Stairs provide toddlers with opportunities to practice climbing. It is unusual to find a toddler who doesn't like to climb. Naturally, you will have to watch your child carefully to prevent accidents from occurring on steps, but there is no need to keep her off stairs altogether unless you are not there to supervise her. If there is no stairway in your home, and your toddler loves to climb stairs, you can easily purchase a small, sturdy step stool, or three-step wooden stairs, at a hardware store or toy store.

More Subdued Activities

Even though your child will want to be in constant motion most of the time, there will also be moments in which she'll engage in a quieter variety of activities. She will enjoy playing on the floor with graduated cups, stacking cones with colored wooden rings, and wooden blocks. These kinds of toys will help her develop concepts such as "in" and "out," "larger" and "smaller," size, shape, and number. Hammering and pounding toys are also enjoyed by toddlers, along with a whole host of other toys including dolls and stuffed animals.

LOOKING AT BOOKS AND PICTURES. Most toddlers enjoy looking at books, especially ones which have bold, colorful pictures of familiar things. Books should either have hard, stiff pages, or they should be made of cloth, since they will have to withstand a lot of wear and tear from your youngster. She will also enjoy "reading" old magazines, toy or clothing catalogues, discarded letters, and so forth.

Many parents fill their child's bedroom walls with pictures, since they realize that toddlers enjoy looking at interesting things. In addition to hanging cartoons or children's pictures, some parents hang reproductions of Picasso, Rembrandt, Monet, and other famous artists. Why not introduce your child to famous paintings at an early age? Posters or large photographs can also make excellent wall hangings. A photograph of your toddler that has been blown up to poster size and hung in her bedroom is an excellent way to personalize her room, or one area of a room, if she is sharing it with another child.

One good way to help your child learn about objects in her environment, and to stimulate her vocabulary growth at the same time, is to make picture cards. Cut out realistic colored pictures of objects and animals from magazines or other sources and paste each on a small piece of cardboard. As you show them to your child, name them for her and talk about them with her.

LISTENING TO STORIES AND MUSIC. Your child may love to listen as you read simple stories to her. She may also enjoy nursery rhymes and poems. Reading to her can be an invaluable activity as long as she is interested. Many young toddlers, however, won't sit still long enough for you to read to them. A toddler may also like rhymes such as "pat-a-cake," since she can associate words with arm, hand, and other body movements.

Most toddlers derive pleasure from listening to music. At this stage your child may not show a preference for a particular type of music or record, but as she gets older she may develop these preferences. While she is young, it's a good idea to expose her to a wide variety of music.

Children often enjoy rhythmic songs, especially those that have a clear, singing voice, but anything goes. Music from different cultures, rock and roll, soul music, or classical music may all be pleasurable listening for your child. There are many excellent relatively inexpensive records available for young children. You can also make use of the radio. While she listens to music, you can encourage her to "dance," or bounce to the beat.

Play in the Kitchen

Toddlers love to play in the kitchen. This room fascinates them because there are plenty of drawers to pull open (filled with interesting objects), knobs to turn, and cabinet doors to open and close. The kitchen, as you know, can be a dangerous place for a toddler. Therefore, you will have to safety-proof this room as well as keep a constant eye on your toddler when she is there. She may insist upon playing in the kitchen while you work or cook. Rather than keeping her out of the kitchen, you may want to clear out a low cabinet in a corner of the room far away from the stove, and stock it with a variety of safe plastic containers and cooking utensils. She can play safely with her own utensils. If you have no extra storage space, you can fill a cardboard box with cooking equipment, and this may keep her happy and out of your way. As you prepare dinner, she will be delighted to pretend she is cooking along with you, or she may enjoy banging on and experimenting with her pots, pans, and wooden utensils.

A Well-rounded Diet of Play Activities

Ideally, children should be offered a balanced diet of play activities. The image used is apt: your child needs playtime for healthy growth as surely as she does edible nourishment. You should guide her and suggest changes in activities from vigorous play to quiet, more subdued play. Try to see to it that she has at least a couple of rest periods a day so that she doesn't get overly fatigued. You may find that it works well to have one quiet period before lunch, and one in the afternoon. Rest periods are important, particularly in cases where a child refuses to take a nap. Most toddlers will accept a quiet play period even though they protest against going to sleep. If your child is expending great amounts of energy climbing, trotting, and dragging small pieces of furniture around, and appears to be getting tired, you might suggest that she listen to a story, look at a picture book, or watch you prepare lunch. A well-rounded daily play program should foster all areas of development, and allow you to observe the remarkable abilities of your toddler.

Suggested List of Playthings

Below you will find a suggested list of playthings for Toddlerhood 1 and 2 children. The list is presented mainly to give you a general idea of the types of playthings that children enjoy. There are innumerable toys and objects that can be bought or made, and it is impossible to list all of them. We hope that this list will trigger your imagination, and that you will respect your own toddler's needs, interests, abilities, and preferences for certain types of playthings and activities.

hammering and pounding toys
pull toys
push toys
dolls
doll carriage
cardboard boxes in all shapes and sizes
books—made of cloth or cardboard
old magazines or picture catalogues
balls
stuffed animals
wooden trucks and cars
stacking toys
child-size jungle gym
water toys—containers, plastic boats, sponge toys, rubber animals
sandbox and appropriate equipment for sand play
dirt play equipment—toy wheelbarrow, shovel, containers
kiddie cars
small wagon
hollow wooden blocks
toy telephone
nesting toys
pots, pans, wooden spoons
large paint brushes
plastic containers and unbreakable jars with lids
toy sweeping set
three-step stairs
assorted colored paper and material
child-size shopping basket
play vacuum cleaner

KEEPING YOUR TODDLER HEALTHY

Well Toddler Care

The very rapid growth rate of infancy is beginning to slow down, but the toddler continues to grow at a steady pace. You may notice that her body proportions are beginning to change. In infancy the head made up a much larger proportion of the total body size than in the adult. During toddlerhood the body grows more rapidly than the head and your child's body proportions begin to approach those of an adult.

PROVIDING THE BUILDING BLOCKS FOR GOOD HEALTH. Offering your active toddler good nutrition is an important aspect of providing health care. Being well nourished gives your child the needed energy to resist infections and disease, as well as the strength for maintaining her active play schedule. Guidelines for providing good nutrition and the common problems that can arise in eating during toddlerhood are discussed in the Feeding sections.

Proper body cleanliness is important to your child's health and teaches her about keeping her body healthy. Proper care of the nails, hair, skin, and teeth are obvious and important aspects of providing good health care. Your toddler will learn a great deal by imitation, and her observation of your hygiene habits will be influencing her attitude toward her body. Baths, teeth brushing, nail cutting and cleaning, and shampoos will be much more easily tolerated if your toddler knows that these functions are also part of your daily routine.

PREVENTING ILLNESS BY IMMUNIZATION. The importance of the proper immunization of your child was stressed in Infancy 2 on pages 215–17. During toddlerhood your child's immunization program must be continued to protect her from specific diseases.

The immunization schedule recommended by the American Academy of Pediatrics, Report of the Committee on Infectious Disease for the first five years of life is presented on page 947; space is provided for recording where and when your child receives these immunizations during toddlerhood. Keeping good records of your child's immunizations is an important part of well child care.

It is recommended that normal toddlers be routinely immunized against measles, rubella (German measles), and mumps. These contagious diseases (discussed on page 969) can be prevented by proper immunization. To be most effective, the measles vaccine should not be administered earlier than fifteen months of age. When there is a high risk of exposure to measles before fifteen months, it may be given earlier. Your doctor will advise you of the proper time for your toddler to be immunized against measles in your area. If it is necessary to receive this immunization before fifteen months of age, the child should be revaccinated sometime after fifteen months of age to ensure long-lasting immunity.

Mumps and rubella vaccines are routinely administered with the measles vaccine after fifteen months of age. These vaccines are usually given in combined measles-rubella plus mumps or measles-mumps-rubella vaccines.

It is also recommended that toddlers receive DTP and TOPV immunizations at

502

approximately eighteen months of age. These immunizations will strengthen the child's protection against diphtheria, tetanus, pertussis, and polio.

What if immunizations were not started in infancy? It is not too late to start now, if you have not provided your child with this protection. The DTP, polio, measles, rubella, and mumps immunizations can be started at older ages. Do not hesitate to contact a doctor and begin, if your child was not properly immunized during infancy.

If some of your friends or relatives have children who have not been immunized against these serious childhood illnesses, you might discuss the importance of immunizing their children with them. It is shocking, but there are parents who neglect to immunize their children against these diseases. The young child cannot make this decision for herself. Unprotected children are at risk for developing serious illnesses. One of the great tragedies of this age is to see a young child crippled by polio, when we have such a simple, complete immunization against this disease.

Taking Care of the Toddler's Teeth

You can begin to teach your child why her teeth are important and help her learn to take proper care of her teeth when she is very young. Many dental problems can be avoided with good early care. There are three major considerations in protecting and ensuring the proper development of your toddler's teeth: good diet, brushing, and the first dental exam. This is a prime time to pay attention to her diet. It is also a time to begin brushing her teeth and arranging for a check-up exam with your dentist.

A PROPER DIET CAN HELP KEEP TEETH HEALTHY. Most dentists feel strongly that the longer certain foods, especially starches and sugars, are left on a person's teeth, the greater the risk of tooth decay. It is best to keep between-meal snacking to a minimum. Refined sugars and sweet foods, when eaten regularly, or held in the mouth for prolonged periods of time, can undermine the sound development of teeth.

Along with a reduction in glucose in the form of simple sugars in the child's diet, water fluoridation is a key to dental health. Fluoride in the water supply is a major deterrent against dental caries. Topical fluoride or mouthwash and vitamins with iron and fluoride may be recommended by your dentist or doctor, especially if your drinking water does not contain fluoride. Vitamins also help promote the healthy development of the teeth. Although a small amount of fluoride in the diet is good for the teeth, too much fluoride can cause discoloration of the teeth. Thus, do not use additional fluoride without the advice of your dentist.

BRUSHING THE TEETH MINIMIZES TOOTH DECAY AND OTHER PROBLEMS. After a baby begins to acquire teeth, parents often wonder about when to start brushing their child's teeth. Some dentists recommend that a parent start brushing a baby's teeth just as soon as a tooth erupts, and suggest brushing after every meal with a specially designed toothbrush for babies. On the other hand, most dentists claim that regular brushing can be put off until a child has most of her teeth. They suggest that the appropriate time to encourage brushing is when the child is about one and a half to two years old; at that age a child enjoys imitating what grownups or older siblings do, and will probably think that brushing her teeth is fun. Prior to the time when a child shows an interest in brushing her teeth, parents can offer her water after meals to help rinse off major particles of food that stick to her teeth.

At first your toddler will be awkward with her toothbrush, and her clumsy attempt to brush may be messy and inefficient. Demonstrate how to brush properly, and show her how to rinse out her mouth. Given ample time to practice, she will become more skillful. Encouraging her to brush after every meal will be met with less resistance if you do the same or brush with her.

YOUR CHILD'S FIRST DENTAL EXAM. Most dentists recommend that a child's first check-up be arranged after all of her primary teeth have come in. This is usually between ages two and three. Your own dentist may want to see your child a little earlier or later.

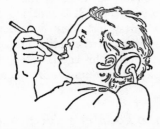

The objective of the first visit may just be for the dentist and your child to get to know one another. During this time the dentist will be able to examine the condition of your youngster's teeth. He or she will confer with you about the findings of the exam and may advise you about how to care for your child's teeth at home. The dentist will also discuss a schedule for regular examinations for your child and provide instructions for proper brushing techniques.

Many adults have grown up with a fear of the dentist, and it is important to try not to convey your own worries to your youngster. Dentists are developing more effective techniques for reducing anxiety and encouraging children to feel positively about regular dental check-ups. Before taking your child for her first dental exam, it is advisable to prepare her in a positive way for what to expect.

SETTING A GOOD EXAMPLE IS IMPORTANT. Along with being great imitators of their parents' behavior, toddlers and preschoolers are also very impressionable. When they see their parents brushing regularly after meals, eating wholesome foods, and having a positive attitude about going to the dentist, chances are that they will want to follow their good example. As a result they will be learning good dental habits at an early age.

Common Illnesses and Problems During Toddlerhood

Most of the common illnesses and problems that arise during toddlerhood are minor and self-limiting. Having had experience in recognizing illness and phoning your doctor during infancy, you know what this involves. The signs of illness in toddlerhood are very similar to those seen in infants. There are some differences in the types of health problems that occur, and those that warrant special consideration are discussed below.

Toddlers and preschool children commonly develop many more colds or minor upper respiratory tract infections than infants. It is not unusual for a toddler to have anywhere from four to eight colds per year. Being prepared to handle these minor illnesses can make caring for a sick child easier and less worrisome (see pages 954–59). Ear infections, sore throats, and fever often go along with colds and respiratory infections. It is important to be able to recognize when an ear infection is developing so that you can obtain medical assistance as described on pages 957–58. Prompt medical care can help avoid chronic ear infections and prevent impairment of hearing.

Sore throats are seen more often during toddlerhood and preschool and should be evaluated by your doctor. It is important that your doctor examine and culture your child's throat to determine if a beta hemolytic streptococcal infection is the cause (pages 958–59). This type of sore throat occurs fairly commonly, and if left untreated can lead to rheumatic fever and other complications. Having your doctor evaluate your child's sore throats can help prevent these problems from developing.

Some toddlers develop very high fevers from even minor illnesses as discussed on pages 953–54. Learning about how to handle a high fever can make the management of this problem easier if it arises.

During toddlerhood, accidents are common, and bumps, cuts, and bruises may occur frequently; occasionally, an accident may require prompt medical attention. Parents find it useful to be prepared to handle minor accidents and administer supportive first aid care. The information in the Health Care Guide on pages 985–1000 in the First Aid and Acute Medical Problems section will be helpful.

The toddler is prone to putting almost anything into her mouth. This makes her more vulnerable to ingesting potentially harmful substances. Now is an appropriate time to learn about poisonings (pages 1000–5) and the special problem of lead poisoning (pages 1004–5).

Other health-related problems that can arise are also discussed in the Health Care Guide. This information should be used only as a supplement to the regular care and advice of your doctor. One of the best ways of ensuring your child's continued good health is to have her examined regularly by your doctor and develop a good relationship with him or her.

GIVING MEDICATIONS TO THE CHILD. It is often difficult to get the toddler to take medicine prescribed by a doctor. There are a few simple suggestions that may come in handy.

It is usually easier to give the child a liquid medicine, since it is not as difficult to swallow. Although some toddlers will accept a teaspoon of liquid medicine, others may resist either because they refuse to take medicines in general, or because the medicine tastes terrible. This problem can often be overcome by mixing the medication with a drink that the child likes. It is usually advisable not to mix the medicine with a standard beverage that the toddler has every day, since she will probably detect the slight difference in taste. Try to use a different juice or soda that she likes, but doesn't have too often.

Most of the more common medications for children come in pleasantly flavored liquid. Occasionally it may be necessary to use another form of medication. Pills or capsules present a more difficult task.

Toddlers are commonly not able to swallow pills. It is usually necessary to crush the pill with a spoon. A capsule can be opened or broken. Mixing the crushed pill or the capsule contents with applesauce, pudding, or cake may make it much more appealing. Some parents prefer to mix the crushed pill with a strong-tasting drink such as orange juice or grape juice. Most toddlers will eventually take their medicine given a little extra time and ingenuity on the part of parents.

HOW TO ENSURE YOUR TODDLER'S SAFETY

The number of accidents often reaches new heights during toddlerhood. Toddlers are determined to try new things out for themselves, to get their hands on just about everything, and to explore every possible area into which they can wander. At the same time their ability to recognize and avoid danger is still very limited. A toddler does not realize that the pencil that she grabbed from the desk could pierce her eye if mishandled. She is not aware that she could be poisoned if she eats or drinks the substances in the bottles underneath the bathroom sink. The pills left on her mother's nightstand may look like candies to her. When she looks at a small wading pool she thinks about having fun, not the possibility of drowning. While concentrating on watching her brother back his new little red sports car out of the garage, she may fail to realize that she is standing in the middle of the driveway, or that the car could run over her and possibly kill her.

Your toddler has new locomotor abilities, a high level of curiosity, and a love for adventure, but she is limited in experience, impulse control, and the ability to recognize potential danger. She is a prime candidate for accidents. One of your continued responsibilities during her toddlerhood will be to ensure her safety. You can accomplish this by safety-proofing your home, by disciplining your child and teaching her about being safety-conscious, and by setting a good example for her to follow.

The Toddler Needs Freedom Within Limits

Knowing that a toddler wants to satisfy her curiosity by touching and exploring, but doesn't know the difference between safe and unsafe places, objects, and activities, you must make a major decision. You can choose to arrange your home environment so that it is suited to your needs, or so that it is temporarily safety-proofed and suited to your child's needs. Since you have been through the pros and cons involved in this decision during infancy, you should recognize the importance of this temporary inconvenience to you and decide to provide a safe environment for your child. This approach to accident prevention is well worth the effort because it allows you to spend less time worrying about your child, and more time enjoying her. It also allows for a happier, more relaxed atmosphere in the home. Furthermore, it doesn't undermine your child's self-confidence and curiosity about her environment. Restrictions to help ensure her safety should be limited in number and offered within an over-all atmosphere of freedom. In this way they are more likely to be accepted and respected by your child.

A Toddler Should Be Careful, Not Fearful

It is essential to a child's progress and future development that she learns to be careful and to become aware of what is safe versus unsafe. You should, however, avoid making your child too fearful and afraid to learn or try new things by overprotecting her. Once you have safety-proofed your home and surrounding grounds as carefully as you can, relax and don't watch over her like a hawk. She needs to be allowed to make some mistakes and learn from them. Although you can prevent her from having major falls from windows, beds, stairs, and changing tables, you cannot save her from all minor falls, spills, and scratches. Both you and your child will have to realize that these minor types of accidents are a necessary part of growing up and becoming more independent.

Safety-proofing Your Home

Making your home as safe as possible for your toddler will involve considerably more effort and ingenuity on your part than were required during infancy. Now that she can walk, her exploration will obviously be more vigorous, and she'll be able to get into places in which you never imagined you'd find her. If you have been following the guidelines set forth in previous sections, and have been safety-proofing your home and yard at frequent intervals, then you have a good head start. Most of the items on the "safety check lists" provided on page 441 will be appropriate during toddlerhood, and it is recommended that you carefully reread them and follow them. It cannot be overemphasized that home situations, parents' habits, and children differ, and therefore you must individualize your approach to accident prevention.

SAFETY-PROOFING FROM YOUR TODDLER'S POINT OF VIEW. It will probably be helpful at this point for you to explore your home and yard the way your toddler would. This will enable you to recognize and eliminate all hazards unique to your own house. Try to think like a curious toddler. Every room in your home will present new challenges, and ordinary household objects can be terribly fascinating.

Start with one room of your home and look for interesting material—either solid or liquid—that she might put into her mouth. Be sure to explore all of the cabinets, especially the low ones. Don't forget that your toddler will still be doing a great deal of exploring with her mouth. Small interesting objects, such as pills, marbles, nuts, and bits of garbage in waste cans, will probably be chewed on and swallowed. She is unaware that she could choke on them or that they could make her sick. If your toddler found liquids in attractive bottles or containers, she would undoubtedly attempt to drink them to find out what they taste like. It is not unusual for an occasional toddler with free access to the bathroom to play in or even try to drink the water in the toilet. Warnings marked on the labels of poisonous or potentially poisonous substances will be of no value. Don't forget to check for poisonous plants (see page 378).

If you were thinking like a toddler, you would love to touch and play with every interesting object you saw. Carefully look around the room and take note of all objects of possible attraction. Dangling cords and ropes, for instance, might be fun to play with. Your toddler wouldn't realize that if she got herself tangled in them she could be strangled. Electrical outlets might also attract her attention. Perhaps she would take her wet fingers and try to stuff them into the plug outlet, unaware that she could be electrocuted.

Her attention would be caught by a low bookshelf within easy reach filled with glass figurines. She might think that it would be fun to handle each object and then throw them in all directions to see what noise they made when they hit the floor. A toddler's experience with glass has been limited. She wouldn't know ahead of time that the figurines could break, and that handling the glimmering pieces of glass on the floor might cut her.

Your toddler might see an interesting variety of breakable objects, sharp and pointed objects, light pieces of furniture that she could easily trip over, or a fireplace with a movable screen that deserves investigating. Maybe she will spot a tablecloth hanging over the edge of a table or pot handles on the stove within reach just "begging" to be pulled. She will need to practice using her hands and won't be afraid of challenges. Thus, she will probably want to twist the knobs on the stove, and try to open doors, jars, medicine bottles, and windows.

A toddler tends always to be in a hurry to get from place to place. Sharp corners on furniture are a common hazard and can lead to bruises, cuts, and even more serious injuries. There are special devices available that you can attach to sharp table corners to buffer them. Some parents have found that pieces of gauze attached with adhesive tape serve a similar purpose.

As you slowly and carefully tour your home, and your surrounding home territory, eliminate possible hazards that your toddler might encounter by removing them, locking them up, or storing them in high cabinets well beyond your child's reach. Certain areas, such as the kitchen and bathroom, warrant special attention. Other areas like the garage, basement, workshop, and darkroom, which cannot be completely safety-proofed, should be off limits to your toddler, unless you are with her and are prepared to give her your *undivided* attention and constant supervision.

Being warned that she isn't supposed to open the doors to certain rooms and wander into areas such as the attic, the basement, or the workshop may further arouse her curiosity about these places. She isn't sure if you really mean what you say, doesn't understand the reasons for these restrictions, and can quickly forget verbal warnings. She will probably want to try to get into these places to explore and will make attempts to open the doors that lead to them. If she finds any of them unlocked, she'll discover many objects of interest to her—objects that you definitely do not want her investigating. You should use locks and child-proof barriers to block off these areas.

It is important that at least one room of your home, such as her bedroom, offers your child complete freedom and safety. When you temporarily need some relief and/or cannot supervise her, you can allow her to play there, knowing that she'll be safe and in comfortable surroundings.

The small amount of time that it will take to tour your home from your toddler's perspective will be worth while. If you have grade school children or teen-agers at home, encourage them to make the grand tour with you. Once you have met your responsibility in safety-proofing your house, you will not have to worry as much about your child, and she will have more fun and freedom.

BE SAFETY-CONSCIOUS EVERY DAY. It is essential that you continue to be safety-conscious all of the time. After completing each daily activity, make sure that you haven't left potentially dangerous objects and substances in unlocked cabinets and/or places within your toddler's reach. A cleaning solution accidentally left near the tub in the bathroom, for instance, can poison a child who drinks it. Several peanuts left on the floor after an evening of entertaining can be extremely dangerous to a toddler who puts them into her mouth and chokes on them. If parents accidentally leave cigarettes and matches lying around, the child may attempt to imitate smoking, and cause a fire.

A minute or two is all it takes to clean up after each activity. Glance around the room to be certain nothing dangerous has been left. Once you become accustomed to thinking "safety," you will do this automatically.

Know How to Select Safe Toys

Selecting safe toys for your toddler will make it much easier for you to ensure her safety. It is crucial for you to consider her safety in relation to playthings, since so much of her time will be involved in playing with toys. When you purchase toys, make sure that they are:

well designed
appropriate for your child's age, capabilities, and preferences
not covered with toxic paint
well constructed
flame retardant/flame resistant
washable/hygienic

According to the U. S. National Consumer Product Safety Commission, there are seven major danger areas to avoid in relation to toys. Become familiar with these danger signs so that you can recognize them and select toys that are safe for your child.

1. *Projectiles.* A projectile is any object that can be propelled through the air, such as an arrow, dart, or rocket. These toys can cause severe injuries, especially to the eyes. Even arrows with rubber suction cups are dangerous, since it does not take the child very long to remove the protective tips. Never allow your child to play with adult projectile objects with sharp points.

2. *Toys That Produce Loud Noises.* Toys, such as cap pistols and guns, that make loud noises can produce sufficient noise levels to impair hearing if held close to the ear. The law requires that these types of toys carry a protective warning on the box, but don't just go by the warnings. Check every toy yourself for potential noise dangers.

3. *Sharp-edged Toys.* Toys with sharp or rough edges should be avoided, since these edges can cause cuts. Easily broken toys made of brittle materials can also be very dangerous, since they will have sharp edges when broken.

4. *Toys or Parts That Can Be Swallowed.* Small toys, such as dice, marbles, or jacks, can be dangerous if they are swallowed and block the child's airway or lodge in her ears or nose. Small parts on larger toys are potentially harmful if they can be broken off. Stuffed toys that can be ripped apart may contain stuffing that can be swallowed. Small noisemakers in squeeze toys are a favorite to be removed and swallowed. Inspect each toy to be sure that it is well made, and that your child can't open the toy or pull off parts. Remember that a toddler will put anything and everything into her mouth.

5. *Pointed Objects.* Pointed objects such as knives, scissors, pins, knitting needles, letter openers, and even pens and pencils are potentially dangerous. Examine each toy carefully for sharp points, even those that do not seem to have sharp points at a quick glance. An easily removed tire from a toy car may reveal a sharp, pointed axle. The arm of a toy doll may come off revealing a pointed fastener that connects the arm to the body.

6. *Electrical Toys.* Electrical plug-in toys can be very dangerous during toddlerhood, and are not recommended. Toddlers are not ready to assume the responsibility of properly handling plug-in toys. Battery-operated toys should be inspected for safe construction, and all warnings on the box or toy must be carefully read.

7. *Inappropriate Toys*. Toys that are designed for older children can be dangerous in the hands of a toddler. Some of these items include chemistry sets, sharp tools, or yard equipment.

Before buying a toy for your child, inspect it carefully. Be sure it does not have one of these seven danger signs. It should be sturdy and able to take the stress of her play activities.

Toys received as gifts can also be dangerous. Apply the same standards of safety when inspecting these gifts as you would in buying a toy. Don't be too embarrassed to prevent your child from playing with the new toy from Grandma or other close friends or relatives if it does not meet your safety standards.

Take Advantage of Locks and Other Preventive Barriers

Now that your child can quickly wander away from you, it is worth re-emphasizing that child-proof locks, gates, and other physical barriers will be effective in prohibiting her from entering areas in which she should be supervised. Bathroom doors that can be locked from the inside can be hazardous. It is advisable to remove the lock temporarily, or place tape over it. Another approach is to put a lock high up on both the outside and the inside of the door. The outside lock will prevent your toddler from entering when you are not with her to supervise. Most importantly, adjusting the locks in this manner will prevent your child from locking herself in, which could be frightening for her, as well as dangerous. You might want to readjust the locks on other doors as well, particularly doors to dangerous areas that cannot be completely safety-proofed.

On the subject of locks, it is advisable to leave a house or apartment key with a neighbor or place it outside (if you live in a private home) or in a garage, if there is access to it when the house is locked. More than one parent has placed a child in a playpen and left the house momentarily to take garbage out, only to discover that he or she has accidentally been locked out.

Stable safety gates can also be very useful at the top and bottom of stairways, especially if you live in a several-story home. These gates can also be placed at the entrance to basement and attic stairs. Caution should be taken to select gates in which a small child's hands or fingers cannot get caught.

Windows are a potential source of danger for a toddler, especially if you live in a multiple-story house or apartment. Your child is not safe just because the windows are above her reach. A child can certainly push a stool or a table over to a window, climb up, and then reach it. It is advisable to purchase window guards, child-proof locks, or locked screens (never the adjustable ones you insert into an opened window).

Teaching Your Toddler to Be Safety-Conscious

You cannot protect your child from danger forever. Eventually she will have to begin to assume responsibility for her own safety. Making an effort to help her become safety-conscious when she is young will enable her to be better prepared to recognize and deal with potentially dangerous objects and situations later on when she begins spending time playing outdoors with other neighborhood children.

Below are some suggestions for ways to teach your toddler to be safety-conscious. Keep in mind that a well-disciplined child is usually a safer child. It is up to you to establish your own "teaching" method, and alter it as your child becomes older, more mature, and better able to comprehend what you are trying to do. Remember that a child of this age is not capable of perceiving dangers or protecting herself. Continue to keep her in safe places, or be willing to give her your total attention, but try to initiate safety training, especially in Toddlerhood 2 and 3.

SIMPLE WARNINGS CAN BE HELPFUL. Be consistent in your use of certain words and phrases to warn her of dangerous areas, actions, or situations. Warnings like "stay away," "cut," "hot," "sharp," "ouch," "no," "dirty," and "don't touch" are easy for a toddler to learn and comprehend. Take care not to overuse these warnings throughout the course of each day, or else they will come to mean little to her.

HANDLING MINOR MISHAPS. It is important to refrain from rewarding your toddler after very minor accidents that could have been avoided. Offering her a lot of sympathy, hugs and kisses, or small presents when she is upset after an accident is not advisable. By doing this, you will not be helping her learn a lesson or providing her with an incentive for preventing the same kind of mishap the next time.

A toddler who has had a minor accident that could have been prevented should be told why the accident occurred and how to prevent it in the future. Use simple words that she can comprehend. You can even act out the situation and demonstrate how she can avoid another accident, if your verbal message seems to puzzle her.

CONCENTRATE ON OBVIOUS DANGER AREAS. Toddlers love to climb up and stand on furniture. This can be dangerous, and a prime source of unnecessary falls. It is possible to encourage her to sit rather than stand on furniture such as chairs. This can be done simply by saying, "Chairs are for sitting," and then firmly sitting her down.

Children who are climbing up and down stairs or through rooms filled with furniture are likely to have accidents. Tell your child to take her time walking up and down stairs, and make sure that she learns to hold on to railings. Also try to teach her to slow down and when she is navigating her way through areas of your home that are filled with obstacles.

Warning young children not to handle specific tools or utensils such as scissors or knives occasionally stimulates their curiosity about these objects, and heightens their desire to play with them when their parents are not watching. An effective way to get around this is to demonstrate how to use these objects properly, and then let your toddler practice to her heart's content using toy models. Allowing your youngster to play with a toy model can often work well in keeping her away from the "real," dangerous objects until she is mature and intelligent enough to handle them properly.

THE TODDLER AND A YOUNG INFANT. Leaving a toddler alone with an infant can be potentially dangerous. Toddlers, especially in Toddlerhood 1 and 2, do not understand how to conduct themselves around a new baby. Feelings of jealousy over the attention paid to the infant may even arouse feelings of anger in the toddler. Many parents have seen their older child play very roughly or occasionally even hit their younger brother or sister.

It is advisable to supervise your toddler when she is playing with an infant. You can help her understand that she must be careful with the baby by telling her things that she can understand. Telling her that the baby is "soft" and must be handled gently is commonly expressed by parents. Showing the child how to approach the baby slowly and stroke her lightly will also help teach her how to handle the young infant. Many toddlers learn to take great pride in "caring" for their younger brother or sister.

TEACHING RESPECT FOR ANIMALS. Pets can provide great pleasure for your toddler, but they can also be dangerous. Toddlers often treat a pet like a new toy. They may try to push it around the floor or pat it very hard. They do not mean to hurt the animal, but occasionally the pet will become angered by this rough treatment and fight back with a scratch or bite.

Not allowing the toddler who plays roughly with her pet to be alone with the animal is one way of avoiding minor accidents. Attempting to show her how to stroke the animal gently without abusing it may also be effective. With some precautions and supervision, a toddler can play safely with her pet.

SAFETY BY EXAMPLE. Your toddler, who spends much of her time around you, will be mimicking many of your actions, particularly as she enters Toddlerhood 2 and 3. An effective way to help her learn to be safety-conscious is to set an example for her to follow in this regard. Therefore, when she emulates your actions, she will be copying the kinds of patterns that will enable her to avoid unnecessary accidents.

Safety in the Car

All toddlers who ride in cars should be placed in an approved, crash-tested (dynamically tested) auto seat or protected by an approved auto shield. Automobile collisions are a leading cause of injury and death in children. Young children are more vulnerable than adults to injury in accidents for several reasons. Their bone structure differs. Their body proportions are not the same; their heads are disproportionately large. Children's vital body organs are not as well protected, and their center of gravity is also higher than an adult's. Special safety restraints help to protect them in case of collision by distributing crash forces over a larger body area.

Obtaining a special auto safety restraint for your toddler is a must if she has outgrown her infant auto carrier. Seeing to it that your toddler is protected whenever she is taken for a ride in the car is one of your primary responsibilities.

A protective shield attached to the auto seat around the front of a child's body can be successfully used to protect the toddler and is the restraint currently preferred by many safety experts once the child can sit up without support. Parents find the safety shield is also easy to use. With an older child who is very active or difficult to manage, however, there is a possibility that she might slide through the shield or climb out of it while the car is in motion. In such cases parents should reconsider the effectiveness of this type of restraint and switch to the "traditional" car seat.

The protective value of any car restraint or seat is dependent upon its being properly fastened to the car, and upon the safety straps being fastened. You should buckle up your toddler each time you place her in the car. When purchasing or borrowing an approved car restraint, be sure to read the instruction booklet for guidance on installation and proper usage.

In determining what type of auto safety restraint to purchase, it is advisable to consult your doctor. He or she should have access to the most up-to-date recommendations for restraints available in your area. The manufacturing, types, and availability of car restraints and the most current recommendations are always subject to alteration as new research and developments occur. A way to obtain the most current list of approved restraints is to send $.25 and a self-addressed stamped envelope to the Physicians for Automotive Safety, 50 Union Avenue, Irvington, New Jersey 07.117.

Climbing Out of the Crib

A few children may now be capable of climbing out of their cribs. Parents should be aware of the possibility that their child may attempt to climb out, risking the chance of falling and sustaining an injury. Therefore, depending upon the kind of crib they have, parents can lower the mattress, raise the sides of the crib, or add extensions to the sides of the crib. Do not underestimate your child's ability to get out of her crib, and keep a close watch on her motor development so that you can take the necessary precautions.

TRAVELING WITH A TODDLER

Traveling with a toddler can be fun, despite inevitable inconveniences. The pleasure that many parents derive from taking trips with their toddler often outweighs the disadvantages. There are several important factors to consider when taking short trips or vacations with your child. Toddlers are more aware of changes in their surroundings than infants, and tend to be more sensitive to changes in living quarters or their routine. Older toddlers, in particular, may be more easily upset by these changes.

It can be difficult for parents to travel with a toddler, because of her reactions to change and her demanding nature. With an understanding of your child's needs, and some advanced preparation, you may avoid unnecessary problems and have a more enjoyable trip.

Preparing Your Toddler for a Trip

A week or two before your departure date, tell your child about the trip. Make it seem like fun and excitement. Tell her when and where you will be going, and do not forget to reassure her that you will be with her throughout the vacation. An older toddler, who is better able to understand verbal explanations, can be told about some of the specific destinations and types of activities that you have planned.

Involving your older toddler in discussions about the trip, and in shopping and planning for it, may be fun for both of you. She will enjoy looking at colorful brochures of the places that you plan to visit. Try to involve her in packing as well. She can assist you in small ways such as holding items to be packed for you, or getting items for you from her room. She may even like to place a few of her favorite toys in a bag or small, lightweight suitcase.

In planning your vacation, it is a good idea to select a few side trips to places that your toddler will enjoy, such as a zoo, park, children's museum, or amusement grounds. Knowing in advance that there is an activity planned especially for her enjoyment may give her something to anticipate.

Youngsters are sometimes fearful of various forms of transportation such as busses, trains, and airplanes. One mother, knowing that her son was afraid of airplanes, bought him several toy planes and encouraged him to play with them. She also read him a couple of stories about planes, and promised to sit next to him on the flight. By the day of departure, many of her son's fears had been allayed, and he actually seemed to enjoy the plane ride.

This mother displayed advance planning and careful consideration of her youngster's feelings. It is not always possible to predict a child's fears of a specific form of transportation ahead of time, but this kind of approach may be helpful in preparing a child for a trip and making traveling more enjoyable.

Making the Child Feel at Home in New Surroundings

There are several ways to help make unfamiliar surroundings seem less threatening to your child. By staying close by her throughout your adventures, she will feel much more secure. You can also pack a few of her favorite toys or "security" objects.

One father, whose little toddler was rather upset at having to sleep in strange beds, packed her favorite pillow, blanket, and stuffed animal. Whenever they changed motel rooms, the first thing he did was to unpack his daughter's security items and arrange them on the bed. This lessened her anxiety and helped comfort her at bedtime.

It is important to bring along at least a few small, familiar toys with which your toddler can play. This will help to keep her happily occupied and stimulated during the inevitable dull moments of your trip.

A Secret Bag Especially for Your Toddler

Besides packing her familiar toys, also plan to take a "secret" bag filled with new objects and playthings. All children love surprises and especially like to receive a new toy when they are feeling bored or unhappy. Parents who have successfully employed the secret toy bag approach suggest that for maximum effectiveness it is advisable to refrain from offering a toddler more than one new toy at a time.

Take her age, special interests, and capabilities into account when deciding what to put in the bag. You may want to include colored paper and large crayons for scribbling, storybooks, an old magazine, small wooden cars, large empty spools of thread and a shoelace for stringing, sponge toys, junk jewelry, picture cards, and so forth.

Nutritious snacks can also be placed in the secret bag. Individual packets of crackers, cookies, and raisins are ideal, as are small cans of juice. Small boxes of dry cereal also make a fine snack. Avoid bringing foods that are messy, sticky, or those that will spoil.

Secret bags can save the day on lengthy plane, bus, train, and car rides when your active little toddler will not have opportunities to move around. New items can be added to the bag whenever necessary as you travel from place to place.

What to Pack

It should not be very difficult to pack for your toddler. Most toddlers do not really care what they are wearing, as long as they are not too warm or cold, and are able to move around freely. What to pack will naturally depend upon anticipated changes in climate, baggage limitations, and length of your trip.

In most cases it is advisable to plan for at least three changes in clothing and underwear. While one outfit is being washed, the other can be worn. The third can serve as a spare. Items that can be easily washed and cared for, and which require no ironing, are the best for travel.

Packing several laundry bags is a good idea when traveling. There may not be enough time to allow hand wash to dry before you are on the road again, and wet things can be put into a laundry bag. Some parents deliberately travel with some clothes, especially underwear, that are on their last legs and can be thrown away after use, if laundering is a problem.

It may be necessary to include special items such as a raincoat, sweaters with hoods for cool evenings, and so forth. Try to anticipate these items in advance. Chances are that you can buy them along the way should this become necessary, but this can be inconvenient as well as costly.

Disposable diapers are very convenient for travel. Parents who are toilet training their toddlers will probably want to pack a supply of diapers and training pants. Young children who are used to one special potty chair or bathroom may be upset by changes imposed by travel. Try to get your toddler used to different toilets ahead of time to minimize problems in this regard while vacationing. When traveling by car, it may be possible to bring along her potty chair or a flat child's toilet seat that adapts to a standard toilet seat, enabling the child to sit on it.

Wipe-clean bibs and disposable moist towelettes come in very handy. These items, along with toilet articles, including your toddler's special no-sting shampoo, bubble bath, hairbrush, toothbrush, lotion, and powder, can be packed in a special flight bag or small washable carrier. Also pack her child-size eating utensils and small plastic cup. A rubber mat or pad is another convenient item to have. It can be placed under your child when her diapers are changed, or laid inside the bathtub to prevent her from slipping.

Providing for Freedom of Movement

Toddlers almost always resent being forced to sit still and remain in one place for extended periods of time, since this goes against their nature. They consider having to sit still boring, making them restless, and unhappy. Taking your toddler's need for space into account when traveling can make the trip much more enjoyable for all concerned.

On long plane flights, for instance, you can plan trips to the bathroom at frequent intervals, even if neither of you needs to use the facilities. This will give your restless toddler chances to stretch out, walk, and explore. Car trips can be broken up into short intervals of a couple of hours, with ample rest stops in between.

During stopovers, whether you are traveling by train, plane, bus, or car, give her ample opportunity to release pent-up energy and roam around while you keep a close eye on her. Pick any wide-open space and let her zoom around to her heart's content, even if the stopover is only a few minutes.

Ensuring Your Toddler's Safety While Traveling

A few special safety precautions are worth considering when traveling. Toddlers who are left alone in unfamiliar places can quickly get into mischief or wander off. Old buildings, hotel rooms, and waiting areas can be dangerous to an unsupervised toddler.

An initial effort at safety-proofing your hotel room will allow you to be more relaxed. Books of matches are usually provided by hotels and left on the nightstand or desk within easy reach of most toddlers. Removing them and other potential hazards such as a letter opener is a place to start. It is a good idea to bring along a roll of adhesive tape. A strip of tape can be placed over the lock on a bathroom door to prevent your toddler from locking herself inside. It can also be used to cover low electrical outlets.

Most major hotel and motel chains will provide cribs on request. Be sure to take precautionary measures to prevent falls. If you cannot obtain a crib, placing a mattress on the floor is a useful tip.

When traveling by car, appropriate safety restraints are strongly recommended for your child. It is also useful to install child-proof door locks on your own car.

If you are renting a car, try to make sure that the car has appropriate safety belts and restraints. In case you are in a strange city and don't have access to a special toddler auto seat, your child can ride in the back seat with an adult who can offer supervision. Make certain that a safety belt is properly fastened around her. By taking appropriate safety precautions, your toddler will be safe, and you will be more relaxed and able to enjoy your trip.

Camping

Camping has become an increasingly popular and relatively inexpensive way to vacation with young children. Through camping, it is possible to enjoy family togetherness and introduce children to the wonders of the outdoors. Family camping trips can be a refreshing change from city life for parents and toddlers.

The best way to camp with a young child is to make all necessary preparations in advance and select camping grounds carefully, since facilities vary. There are campgrounds with running water, gas, toilets, hot showers, laundry facilities, telephones,

and emergency stations. Other camping grounds are lacking in these types of facilities. By investigating camping grounds ahead of time, it will be possible to locate one with facilities to suit your family's needs.

It is important to plan for your toddler to have an appropriate place to sleep. A portable crib will work well, but in the event that it is too cumbersome to pack, she can use a sleeping bag. Be sure to purchase one that is washable and waterproof. Many toddlers enjoy using a sleeping bag, particularly when their bags are positioned next to their parents'. You should make sure that your child cannot get out of the camper (or tent) while you are sleeping.

In deciding what clothing items to pack, it is most important to include items that will ensure your child's warmth and comfort. One-piece, zippered, flannel sleeping outfits, long-sleeved shirts, jeans, sweaters with hoods, jackets, warm socks, scarves, rainwear, hats, gloves, and boots are among the clothing articles that parents often include when cool weather is anticipated. It is better to pack too many warm clothing articles than too few.

Assuming that you are toilet training your toddler, and she is used to one potty chair, you might want to bring it along. An alternative is to train her to use a regular toilet well in advance of your trip, and select a camp site with toilet facilities. Parents who really plan to "rough it" will have to accustom their toddler to urinating and defecating outdoors.

Be sure to take appropriate safety precautions when camping. Bring along a paperback guide to medical care, a good first aid kit, and one of those kits to treat insect stings as well as insect repellent you can spray on a child's clothing. Always keep a close eye on your child so that she does not wander away and get lost, and keep her away from open fires, barbecues, and other potentially dangerous areas and substances. Make sure that she is outfitted with a good life jacket, and that she uses it if you plan to do any boating.

Young children's adventurous natures often blend nicely with camping. The simplicity of many camping sites and the freedom of the outdoors is well suited to their needs. Hiking, exploring, and playing with dirt are activities that most youngsters enjoy. While camping with your toddler, try to take advantage of opportunities to help her develop an early appreciation for nature and a respect for the environment.

Health-related Considerations

When traveling in a foreign country or any area in which the water supply may be unsafe, you can purchase sterilized water in bottles. Mix this with powdered milk, or canned evaporated milk, if your toddler is still taking an occasional bottle. Your physician will advise you of necessary inoculations and recommend other ways to ensure your child's good health on the journey. Assuming that you plan to be in one area for an extended period of time, he or she may also be able to recommend a physician to call in case any questions regarding your toddler's health should arise. If you will be traveling in a foreign country, you can probably obtain a list of doctors from the American embassy in that country.

Baby-sitters

Toddlers often have difficulty dealing with separations from their parents. Being left in unfamiliar territory with a stranger can be quite upsetting to a young child. It is usually advisable to take your toddler with you wherever you can. If you must leave your child for a period of time with an unfamiliar baby-sitter, it is important to check on this person's reliability. Most major hotels have reliable baby-sitting services for guests. Parents in a strange city often find such services helpful in a pinch.

EATING

Many Toddlerhood 1 children will be more finicky in regard to the foods they eat. The basic framework of your child's diet is unchanged, although you will be gradually offering her additional types of foods to keep expanding her experiences with new foods.

In regard to self-feeding, children may be at different stages. Some children will be feeding themselves very well with their hands, whereas others will still be awkward and clumsy in their self-feeding techniques. Very few will be able to feed themselves well with a spoon.

Most large department stores carry feeding "trainer" sets, including a spoon, fork, and knife for young children. It is much easier for a toddler to handle these small-sized utensils, and the forks and knives usually have blunt edges which offer some protection. There are also spoon and fork sets specially made of curved plastic for beginning eaters; the structure of these supposedly aids in getting food into the mouth.

The Toddlerhood 1 child should be shown how to use a spoon. Toward the end of this phase, or early in Toddlerhood 2, you can introduce a fork. It should be fun for you to observe your child's efforts in this regard. With a camera in hand, you may be able to capture the expression on her face when the food on her spoon slips off as she quickly tries to bring it toward her open mouth, or when she accidentally drops the spoon or tips it over. Have a napkin or wet washcloth nearby as well, since by the end of each meal, her face and hands are apt to be smeared with bits of food.

Appetite Fluctuations

Chances are that your toddler's appetite will be similar to her eating habits in Infancy 12. Since one- to two-year-olds require less food than they did during infancy, do not be alarmed if you notice a general decrease in your child's appetite. A parent can choose what a child can eat, but only a child can determine how much.

Feeding problems and suggestions for handling them were previously discussed on pages 464–66. If you feel that your child has a problem in this area, you might wish to review this material. Any worries that you have about your child's eating behavior are best talked over with your doctor.

Weaning

Many toddlers who still are drinking from a bottle can now be weaned to a cup. Some toddlers who are able to drink from cups will continue to want their bottles, particularly their nighttime bottle. For convenience sake, parents often let the children continue taking bottles. If you definitely would like your child to discontinue her bottle, you could take a straightforward approach and simply refuse to give it to her, telling her that she's "grown-up" now, and that bottles are for "babies" only. Refusing to give her the bottle may result in whining or crying for several days until she adjusts to a new lifestyle without it. However, she will adjust eventually, so try to be patient.

Some parents would like to see their children give up their bottles, but are not unduly upset by the fact that they still seem to want them. There is no real problem here. It should be noted, however, that many dentists do not recommend sucking on bottles for lengthy periods of time between regular meals, especially after children are about a year old. They also do not recommend tucking them in bed with a bottle to help them fall asleep. This is because the presence of sweetened substances in the mouth, such as milk (with sugar added), for prolonged stretches of time is believed to result in additional tooth decay. Allowing a child to suck on a bottle at nap and/or bedtime also tends to delay complete weaning.

Additions to Your Child's Diet

When your child was around a year old, your doctor may have recommended that you introduce certain new foods into her diet. Many of you will be gradually continuing to add new foods at this point. You may find it helpful to review the discussion of new additions to your baby's diet (pages 466–68). You will find more information about a child's diet in Toddlerhood 3.

The Vegetarian Toddler

Parents who are vegetarians often want their toddlers to follow a vegetarian diet. Well-balanced meals can be offered with combinations of vegetables, fruits, grains, and milk products.

It is important for growing children, as well as adults, to have an adequate amount of protein and B vitamins in their diets. In planning a vegetarian diet for your child, it is usually advisable to offer her vitamin B supplements, since this vitamin is not often found in high levels in a vegetarian diet. Some families add fish to their child's diet as an additional source of protein. You should discuss dietary plans with your child's physician.

CLOTHING

You may find that although your child is more capable of helping to dress and un-dress herself, she may be less co-operative. This is probably because her mind is on playing, and because she doesn't like to sit or stand still for very long. The toddler's testing behavior may make getting her dressed a real hassle. A firm, matter-of-fact approach may be helpful.

She is still more interested in and more skillful at taking off her clothes than get-ting dressed. She will most likely be able to take off some of her clothes, but will have great difficulty in undoing fasteners. Putting on clothes is a harder task for her to master. She will usually learn to take clothing off before she learns to put it on. Attempts may be made at dressing. She may try to put on her socks. Even though she probably cannot get them on straight, this will not bother her at all. Just having managed to put them on will give her a sense of personal achievement.

Some Practical Tips for Buying Clothes

Since children outgrow their clothes so quickly, it is a good idea to purchase clothes that leave room for growth. Below is a brief list of some of the clothing features which indicate possibilities for growth.

1. hems
2. waistbands that stretch
3. self-lengthening cuffs
4. seams and tucks that can be let out
5. overalls with adjustable suspenders
6. knitted materials that have some "give" to them

If you examine the tags on articles of clothing, you will notice that some manufac-turers point out these features. Any article of clothing that has at least some of these features may allow for months of extra wear.

For safety reasons, it is desirable to purchase fire-retardant clothing. A chemical called TRIS, previously used to make clothing flame-retardant, is no longer on the market, since this substance poses a health danger. Be sure to read clothing labels carefully. Many other safe methods of making clothing flame-resistant are now becoming available.

SLEEPING

A Regular Schedule

Parents are usually in agreement that it is best to keep the toddler to a consistent bedtime and naptime. Children who have been used to definite daily and nightly routines are likely to sense when it's time for a nap or time for bed. They are apt to accept these facts of life more willingly than a child who hasn't been put to bed at regular hours. If, by playing up to her parents and stalling, a child can persuade them to let her stay up fifteen minutes longer each evening, she will surely continue this pattern, and bedtime may become very unpleasant.

Keeping a child to a schedule does not mean that you have to be inflexible. There may be evenings when you allow your child to convince you to let her skip her nap or stay up past her bedtime because of special circumstances such as holidays. This occasional relaxation of the rules may be good for the child. However, unless you are prepared to cope with frequent conflicts and hassles over her naptime and bedtime, it is advisable to maintain a consistent schedule.

The schedule that you establish should be well suited to both you and your child, not necessarily what you have read in a book. Many parents who work away from home during the day often wish to spend as much time as possible with their children during the evening hours. If they arrange the child's schedule so that her bedtime is at 7 P.M., for example, this would mean that they wouldn't see much of her at night. Thus, they may decide to ease the child into a schedule with a longer nap around 3 or 4 P.M. This may enable her to stay up later at night, without jeopardizing her sleep requirements.

Bedtime Resistance

Many children are not difficult to handle at bedtime, but rarely do children ever elect to go to bed of their own accord. A child may cry or get upset, but if parents are confident and firm, the child should settle down more readily.

It is not uncommon for children to want to sleep with their favorite toys or objects, such as blankets, dolls, Teddy bears, or even articles of clothing, including hats or shoes. They may strongly resist going to bed unless they can take their sleeping toy with them. These objects help children feel less lonely and uncomfortable after their parents have left their bedrooms.

If your toddler cries or fusses at bedtime, try to be patient with her. At this age her fussing at bedtime reflects her insecurity about being separated from you or possibly her dislike of having her play activities come to an end. You can show her that you understand her reluctance to go to bed, but at the same time you can be firm about her bedtime hours.

Delays in Going to Sleep

Some children will not automatically fall asleep after being put in bed. They play for a while before falling asleep, especially the energetic type. Assuming that your child does not fall asleep quickly, it is best not to go back into her room to check up on her. Seeing you again may cause her to have even more trouble settling down to sleep. If you must return to make sure all is well, try to wait until you're fairly sure she's asleep.

Sleeping Difficulties

Active children often have trouble sleeping through the night, although occasional episodes of sleeping difficulties are common among all children. Children differ in what helps them get back to sleep. Some children may "talk" or play with toys for a while until they calm themselves and are able to fall back to sleep. Others may cry and refuse to go to sleep again until their parent comes to the rescue and attempts to comfort them. If a child has trouble sleeping at night and her parents proceed to rush to her bedside, they may make the situation worse. She may learn that when she has trouble sleeping, they will come to her aid. Under normal circumstances (unless she's ill or in real need of assistance) it's a good idea to hold off going into her bedroom. She may be able to settle down and fall back to sleep on her own. She must learn to calm herself at night, rather than rely upon her parents to do the soothing.

Taking a Nap

Most children of this age are not rebellious at naptime. Some, in fact, may get their bedtime toy and their favorite blanket as an indication that they are ready for a nap. There are children who will fall asleep right away, whereas others will play, hum, and "talk" to themselves before drifting off to sleep. Parents may have to insist or argue with their child to take her nap, particularly if she kicks or rebels, or cries during her entire nap period. If this is the case, there is no use trying to force a child to fall asleep. It may be better to allow her to get up and play quietly. You may also want to read her a story if both of you enjoy this activity. Allowing a child to listen to the radio or a record is often a good idea. Some children even seem to become conditioned to certain records which induce relaxation and eventual sleep.

DEVELOPING GOOD TOILET HABITS

How to teach your child good toilet habits is one of the most controversial and most discussed issues in child rearing. There are numerous books and pamphlets devoted entirely to how to toilet train a child, and some of them even offer quick-training techniques which are "guaranteed" to work in a week's time or less.

You will find that opinions vary greatly as to how toilet training is best accomplished. There are some pediatricians, for instance, who recommend fairly rigid and elaborate procedures in training. Others offer more flexible, general guidelines that attempt to coincide with the child's capabilities and interests. A few doctors advise parents not to toilet train at all, based on the assumption that children will essentially train themselves when they are ready and interested in imitating their parents or older siblings.

Teaching good toilet habits to your child should be relatively easy and problem-free, despite your initial insecurity, or warnings to the contrary from other people. It is most important to have the utmost confidence in your ability to do a good job. Well-meaning advice from relatives, friends, and even total strangers should be politely accepted and considered, but the fact is that every family situation and child is unique. Knowing yourself and your toddler as well as you do make you the expert.

The material that follows in the Toddlerhood 1 to 3 sections on toilet habits will assist you in establishing a personalized approach that seems comfortable and right for you and your child. There is no one correct way to teach good toilet habits, nor is there an exact age at which teaching should be initiated. By relying upon your own good judgment and the feedback that you receive from your child, you will be in the best position to do an excellent job in teaching good toilet habits.

Learning to Use a Toilet Is a Big Step for Your Child

When a child learns to use the toilet, she will have taken a major step forward. Toilet training is a developmental milestone. Initially, babies have no control over their organs of elimination, so they pass a bowel movement (defecate) and urinate by reflex action, automatically. As they grow and mature, they gain more control of their bowels and bladders. In other words, your child will develop the ability to respond independently and willfully to bodily feelings or urges that she has to "make" or use the toilet.

You can assist your child in learning to control her urges to defecate and urinate, and teach her that her bodily waste products belong in the toilet. Even though toilet training represents a major step in terms of her development, helping a child achieve bowel and bladder control is very similar to helping her learn to master many other important tasks; each child will establish her own pace for learning to use the toilet, although children usually pass through similar stages along the way.

Keep a Relaxed Attitude About Helping Your Child Develop Good Toilet Habits

The manner in which training is accomplished will be influenced by your attitude. If you approach toilet training in a patient, casual, and matter-of-fact manner, both you and your toddler will be much better off. There is no need to rush or to start teaching your child before she is ready. By doing this you may make training a pressure situation. When your child fails to live up to your unreasonable expectations, she can be left feeling inept, upset, and frustrated. By pressuring her to do what she cannot or by reprimanding her for lack of control, you may trigger in her feelings of hostility, rebellion, obstinacy, or perhaps even fear. Keep your expectations in line with her abilities and the learning atmosphere low-keyed and friendly.

On the other hand, by being overly worried about arousing your child's resentment, you may ignore her signs of readiness and wait too long to train her. If you do not assist her in learning to use a toilet when she is ready, you will be cleaning her soiled clothes long past the age when she could have been trained easily.

You should try to avoid passing on to your child any negative feelings that you might have in regard to elimination. A few parents have rather unhealthy attitudes about elimination, and experience feelings of disgust or embarrassment when tending to their child's soiled diapers. You should make a special effort not to use phrases such as "icky pooh pooh," or "dirty Mary" constantly. The organs of elimination and the genitals are located near one another. According to many psychologists, negative attitudes acquired by a child about organs of elimination may spread to the sex organs. If a child comes to feel that organs of elimination are bad or shameful, she may have difficulty developing a healthy attitude toward sexual functioning. Defecation is a necessary and natural function, and, therefore, parents should try not to teach a child otherwise in toilet training.

Part of adopting a healthy attitude is understanding how toilet training usually progresses. Realizing that setbacks along the way are normal, for example, you won't overreact when your child performs well or has lapses in control. You will be more patient and relaxed, and so will she.

Try to abide by your child's own inner feelings in regard to her urges to defecate and urinate and her own personal "pace" for mastering this task. Using her training progress as a basis of comparing your child's abilities to those of other children or taking toilet training personally will do more harm than good.

BOWEL TRAINING IS DIFFERENT FROM BLADDER TRAINING. Toilet training involves learning to control the release of both urine and stool. The child's ability to control each of these functions does not always develop at the same time. Bowel training usually can be mastered before bladder training. Most children have an easier time achieving bowel control. These two aspects of toilet training warrant special attention and will be discussed separately.

Since it is unusual for children to control the release of their bladder before age two, bladder control is discussed in Toddlerhood 2.

It is often recommended that bowel training be initiated when a child is able to walk to a toilet by herself. This usually occurs in her second year. She should show signs that she is physically capable of controlling her bowel movements as well as a willingness to accept your direction. This readiness generally emerges during toddlerhood. Thus, many parents initiate toilet training between the ages of around a year and a half to two and a half, with the majority beginning at about two years of age. Be flexible. Don't try to push your child to toilet train early. Some very normal children are not ready until two and a half to three years of age. The best advice is to follow your child's lead.

Your child will be ready when she develops voluntary motor control over certain muscles called sphincters, which regulate the release of stools from her rectum (anus). Control is gained when the body develops the muscle and nerve co-ordination required to allow the child to move her bowels through her own effort. Most children gain control of the release of their bowel movements during their second year.

Another important component in your child's readiness is her willingness to accept guidance in toilet training. No child can be easily or successfully trained unless she is willing to co-operate. How will you know if your child is willing? There are several ways. You will probably notice how anxious she is to imitate you, to please you, and to do what is expected of her. You will also notice her growing awareness of bowel movements and the use of toilets. She may be able to say the words for bowel movements such as "BM," "pooh pooh," "do do," or "dudy" that you are using. She may also indicate a dislike for soiled diapers, and may begin to signal you after she has had a movement or when she is about to have one. These are all indications that your child is getting ready to respond to your toilet training efforts. Most children begin to demonstrate these signs of willingness to co-operate toward the end of the second year.

Children not only differ in the age at which they are ready for training, they also differ in the time it takes them to achieve this big developmental step once parents begin training. One child may take several months or more to accomplish this task and another may accomplish it in a matter of a couple of days or weeks. A few children, through imitation, simply train themselves when they are ready, having had little or no specific parental guidance. Once you are aware of signs that your child is ready to learn to use the toilet, then you can initiate a personalized program of training.

SUGGESTIONS FOR HOW TO PROCEED WITH BOWEL TRAINING. If you have already had experience with toilet training a child, or have your own sound plan in mind, feel free to use it. Your pediatrician may also give you specific instructions for toilet training based on experiences with other children and a knowledge of your child. The method you use is not as important as selecting the right timing for your child, and adopting a good attitude toward toilet training. There are several important principles to keep in mind:

• Take your lead from your child's natural "urges" in determining when to place her on the potty. Don't put her there when *You* want to.

• Try hard not to create unnecessary friction over bowel training or make a big issue of it.

• Give her positive feedback whenever she is successful, but don't go overboard in offering affection.

• Do not use harsh words or punitive measures in your toilet training program. Avoid punishing her for lapses in bowel control.

For those of you who have no plan in mind, we have set forth a general guide to bowel training. You should tailor any toilet training program to meet your child's individual needs and abilities.

The first step is to teach your child to associate a word with her bowel function. Among the words that parents often select are "pooh pooh," "do do," and "BM." Assuming that you choose the former, you could start using it repeatedly whenever you change your toddler's soiled diapers, or if she normally grunts or strains right before she passes a bowel movement, you could tell her that she is making or just about to make a "pooh pooh." After a while, depending upon the child, she may say the word "pooh" after she has moved her bowels. Later, she may say the word when she is passing a movement, and, still later, just before she passes a movement. Each step in the right direction should be taken as an accomplishment.

A potty chair should probably be obtained when your child begins to train. It is easier for a small child to sit on her own potty rather than on a large toilet. Having her feet touch the ground may give her the added bit of leverage and security that she may need. Before you actually begin training her, it is often a good idea simply to place the potty in the bathroom or in her room. Let her examine this new piece of equipment or strange-looking "toy." Casually, you can tell her its name and use. While playing, she may sit on it. This would be a good time to tell her that her "pooh poohs" belong there. If she doesn't try getting on and off the potty, show her how. This initial getting-acquainted period with the potty may make her less confused and frightened when she actually uses it for the first time.

Not all children will take to the potty chair. One mother purchased a potty for her two-year-old son, Andy. Andy refused to sit on the potty, because he said "baby chair, me no baby." Andy had been allowed to watch his parents using the regular toilet, and he wanted to imitate them in every respect. Andy's mother was able to train Andy without the use of a potty chair.

When initiating training, many parents prefer using a flat "insert" that fits on the regular toilet. It is specially designed for small children, easier to travel with than a potty chair, and takes into account some children's desire to sit on the "big" toilet like the grownups they know. A step stool placed in front of the toilet will allow easier access, and acts as a footrest for the child's comfort.

To help her really understand what she is supposed to be doing on the potty, you can let her watch you or another family member going to the bathroom, or at least watch you "pretend" to be defecating. Imitation can be a very useful teaching device in toilet training. When you do start to notice signs that she is ready and interested in learning to use a potty, you can put her in training pants. Training pants are similar to regular underwear. They usually have an elastic top so that they can be pulled down easily. To help prevent unnecessary messes if the child has an "accident," training pants are made of heavier, more absorbent materials, such as terry cloth. Wearing training pants may make her feel more grown-up. They can serve as positive reinforcement for her initial successes, and motivate her to want to use the potty. On the other hand, it is advisable not to put her in training pants if she shows no indication of being ready to be trained. This might indirectly pressure her to master a task before she is capable, and result in her feeling as if she's failed you when she soils the training pants.

Try to ignore her "accidents" or at least remain casual and calm about them. Toilet training should be carried out in as relaxed an atmosphere as possible.

Some youngsters are frightened by the flushing toilet, as described on page 631, and seem to look upon their "pooh poohs" as part of themselves or as special "possessions" that they are hesitant to part with in the toilet. Other children are not frightened by the toilet flushing, and are rather intrigued by this piece of equipment. In fact, they may play with it out of curiosity, and repeatedly flush it themselves as they explore its moving water and loud noise. If your child is afraid of the toilet, you can wait until she has left the bathroom before depositing her product in the toilet and flushing it.

Once she has become accustomed to using her potty, it is a good idea occasionally to introduce her to the regular toilet. Having some familiarity with it will make it easier when you take her out of the house and do not bring her potty along.

Bowel training is generally achieved over the course of several months during the second year and part of the third year. It does not always follow a continuous, forward course. While a child is gaining voluntary control over her sphincter muscles, and learning to use a toilet, 100 percent control cannot be expected. Most likely, she will have occasional lapses. These lapses or "accidents" will most often occur when a child is very excited, overly tired, wrapped up in play, tense, under stress, ill, or away from home.

In some cases a child who has been trained for quite some time may begin to soil her pants again when a new baby is brought home. Perhaps she is so worried and upset that she has difficulty controlling herself. She may also feel as if she's being ignored, so she makes a BM because she knows this will attract attention to herself. Some "accidents" are common, and should be tolerated. Belittling or reprimanding a child because "she should have been good" or because she is "purposely being mean" can make a situation worse. Any new skill takes time to master, so be patient and rest assured that these lapses will gradually diminish as she matures.

Occasional difficulties may arise in the course of bowel training, including constipation, stool smearing, and refusal to train. These problems are not usually encountered during this phase, and are therefore discussed in Toddlerhood 2. If your child is training early, you can read ahead to this material.

DISCIPLINE

Teaching Acceptable Behavior

Most parents place a greater emphasis upon teaching acceptable behavior in toddlerhood, as discussed more fully in the Personal-Social Development section. They earnestly begin to teach the child values and behaviors that are acceptable and appropriate to her society. The child, during toddlerhood, is developing in many areas which allow her to become more independent, and to assume a more active role in relation to people and objects in her environment. Her desire to explore is great, and she wants to test her new abilities. This often gets her into trouble. As she attempts to satisfy her own needs, she occasionally finds that her parents are not pleased with her behavior. In fact, they make numerous attempts to redirect and change it. This often creates conflicts.

Discipline is an essential aspect of teaching good standards for conduct. The child who is continually allowed to "do as she pleases" will not be motivated to regulate her own behavior in terms of the rules and regulations that her parents have established and will not learn to respect the feelings and rights of others. Discipline, essentially education in self-control, is necessary for your young toddler.

Don't waste needless time and energy worrying about what your parents, your neighbors, or your child is thinking when you discipline your child or enforce your limits. You must set limits, make decisions, and discipline her based upon what you feel is right for her. No one but you is in the best position to determine this. If you feel confident handling your child, she will sense this and more readily follow your guidelines. She will be looking to you for guidance and answers. So relax and trust your own ability to exercise authority.

Parent-child Relationships and Discipline

Of great help in disciplining your toddler and preschooler will be maintaining a positive relationship with her and showing her that you respect her individuality. Your toddler is becoming more aware of your approval and disapproval, and the difference between being good and being naughty. The love you share with your child will motivate her to want to co-operate with you. Caring about what you think of her, she will want to gain your approval to stay in your favor.

Your child is also showing more signs of wanting to imitate your behavior. Wise parents will take advantage of these natural tendencies in their child. Lacking in experience, language, and self-control, and wanting and needing to assert herself, your child will frequently annoy you and break rules. Because you love her, you will tolerate her immaturity and firmly steer her in the proper direction. At times you may need to be stricter than you'd like, simply to teach her a lesson. Occasionally you will explode and may even punish her without good cause. Nevertheless, as long as she knows that you love her, and that you respect her as an individual, she will try to obey your rules without feeling threatened or resentful toward you.

The Need for Clear and Consistent Rules

One of your major responsibilities will involve educating your child to behave appropriately. Your child's newly found freedom and strong curiosity may even endanger her life, if some of her activities are not restricted. She will be relying upon you to make your home safe. For your part, if you do not assume the responsibility of disciplining her, you should count on her having needless accidents, having valuable objects in your home broken, and living with a toddler who has little respect or consideration for you and other family members.

Most toddlers find security in knowing clearly what they can and cannot do. Ambiguous or inconsistent rules can confuse them. They want to know how far they can go. If they are not told, they must constantly test and provoke parents, perhaps in an attempt to find out just what they can get away with. Children who are labeled as spoiled often show more of this irritating, testing behavior. It is almost as if they are behaving that way deliberately, in an effort to force their parents to say "No" to them, and punish them for poor behavior. A child who is provoking her parents is usually asking them to set limits for her, something she cannot, as yet, do for herself.

The toddler is learning about her separateness from other people, and part of this includes learning about her own limits and boundaries. If parents do not discipline their child and make their expectations clear, she may have difficulty developing her own personal limits, distinct from those of her parents.

Parents who set clear-cut guidelines for their child's behavior will, in effect, be saying to her that they are offering outside regulation until she eventually becomes able to control her own behavior. Most children are somewhat relieved when their parents establish definite rules and regulations and, as a result, they are motivated to incorporate them and utilize them in developing their own control system. Learning to govern one's own behavior takes a great deal of time. The experience of listening to your repeated warnings and being punished or scolded for unacceptable behavior will gradually enable your child to learn how, and in what situations, to control her own actions.

Individualize Your Program of Discipline

As your child becomes more curious about her surroundings and more independent, each day may bring new tests of your ability to manage her. In trying to establish an organized approach to discipline, you may first turn to other experienced parents, perhaps relatives or friends, for guidance. No doubt, you will receive plenty of advice as to how they handled their children during toddlerhood.

Even though you know that your child is unique, and different from your friends' and relatives' children, you may still try to employ their methods of discipline with your child. Chances are that many of their techniques will not work well with your child. Although you may find other people's advice to be very helpful, it is advisable to take the time to examine what your own goals are. There is no one method of discipline that is right for every child. Be aware of your child's individual personality and needs, so that you can devise a personalized method of discipline.

If you have already reared a child, don't expect your second toddler to respond to the same methods of discipline as your older child. Even though each of your children is raised in the same family, each one is probably very different. It is important to establish a positive, individualized approach to discipline that does not undermine your child's emerging self-concept and sense of self-esteem.

One common mistake that parents make is expecting too much from a child in relation to good behavior. Whether or not your child can live up to your expectations partly depends on her abilities and upon how much you expect from her. There is a better chance that your child will be able to follow your directions and adhere to the limits you've established, if you keep your rules to a minimum and your expectations at a modest level.

It certainly helps to learn about how your child's ability to understand your directions and control her behavior changes and grows from phase to phase. The material in the developmental sections, as well as the material in these discipline sections, will give you a general idea of what you can reasonably expect from your toddler as she develops. However, you must carefully observe your own child as she grows older to ensure that your expectations are not too far above or beyond her abilities. This approach will increase the probability that your methods of discipline will be effective.

You should also take into account various environmental circumstances which may affect the child's ability and/or willingness to conform to acceptable behavior patterns. A new addition to your family, a terrifying experience, a move to a new home or room, or a separation or divorce are just a few of the numerous adjustments in her environment which may affect a child and cause changes in her behavior.

Although clarity, firmness, and consistency in discipline are necessary, flexibility is also an important component of a good educational program in acceptable behavior. Flexibility will enable you to alter your discipline techniques if need be as your child changes from within, and in response to her surroundings.

Techniques in Disciplining the Young Child

The fact that every family situation is unique cannot be overemphasized. There is enormous variation in what parents expect from their children and how effective they are in getting their children to adhere to their expectations. There is also variation in children's abilities and willingness to live up to their parents' standards. Although we will offer you some suggestions which may serve as guidelines, it will inevitably be your responsibility to define limits for your toddler, and enforce those limits when necessary.

LIMIT "NO" AND "DON'T TOUCH" TO WHAT'S REALLY IMPORTANT. A child who is confronted with a constant barrage of "No No's" every time she moves may soon begin to ignore them. Parents must establish rules but how many, and which ones? There is not one answer to this question. You will have to come up with your own list of limits you expect your child to observe.

The best tip that can be offered is to limit your verbal warnings to things which are absolutely necessary and important. You may even write out a list of rules that you want your child to observe (e.g., don't play with the controls on the stove, don't throw food, don't hit baby sister, and so forth). Then examine it closely. Is every item really important? Only you can decide. From your child's point of view, life is difficult enough without having to learn and observe a million and one rules. It is easier for a child to stay within the bounds you've set and co-operate willingly, if you keep your "No No's" and "Don'ts" to a minimum.

At this stage in your child's life, she will probably be difficult to handle. Although she will be better able to understand what you say to her, a mere "No No" from you may not be sufficient to keep her in line. Therefore, you will probably find that verbal methods alone will not be adequate in managing her.

TAKING ADVANTAGE OF YOUR CHILD'S DISTRACTABILITY. If your toddler is involved in some activity that is either potentially dangerous, irritating, or "off limits," you will find it helpful to divert her attention and substitute a more acceptable activity that she enjoys. This approach will be more effective than giving lengthy instructions and explanations that she won't understand. Since she likes to interact with you and is apt to be attracted by a favorite toy or object, diversion or distraction will probably work well in managing her. By redirecting her activities so that they are more in line with what you feel is acceptable, you will not be compromising your ultimate educational aims in discipline. Quite to the contrary, one of the major lessons a young child must learn is how to accept new or different outlets for her unacceptable impulses, and find new ways of enjoying herself.

It may be difficult, at times, to get your toddler to accept a substitute activity for the "forbidden" one. Patience and firmness on your part will surely be required. A curious toddler, for example, begins to take books down from the shelf in the den. She then proceeds to tear one page at a time. To distract her from this unacceptable behavior, she must be offered an equally attractive activity which satisfies her normal curiosity and need to explore. Such a child, for example, may be content if she is provided with a pile of construction paper, cardboard sheets, or used colorful wrapping paper to do with as she pleases. The distracting activity must be exciting to the child.

Bear in mind that substitute activities should not be so similar to the unacceptable activity as to be confusing to the child. Giving her magazines to rip rather than books, for example, would not get the desired message across, since magazines are often perceived as books in a child's mind. The child could have difficulty telling which objects are okay to rip, and which are off limits.

USING SHORT COMMANDS. Ideally, you should only set limits which you can justify to your child and to yourself. As your child gets older and becomes more capable of understanding what you say to her and the reasons why a particular behavior is dangerous or unacceptable, it will be important to offer her explanations. On the other hand, "reasoning" with a toddler and offering her drawn-out explanations about why she shouldn't touch an electrical outlet or stove will get you nowhere, since they are beyond her comprehension. Giving a short, sharp order and picking her up and carrying her away from an object will be a much more effective technique.

Parents who feel that they owe their toddler an explanation about every limit they set are probably feeling guilty about imposing limits and are having some difficulty assuming the role of an authority figure to their child. A matter-of-fact approach and some firmness now will be most effective. Later on, when verbal methods of discipline begin to replace substitution and distraction, explanations and "reasoning with" your child will be more appropriate. Trying to reason with a child who can't understand is futile and frustrating.

When you want your child to follow verbal directions, say her name, be very emphatic, and use a minimum number of wisely chosen words. Saying something like "Mary get your hat!" will undoubtedly motivate a young toddler to a greater extent than a long, complicated explanation about why it is important for her health to put on a hat in cold weather.

When you give commands, back your words up with actions, since it will help get your message across to your child. For example, your child begins to climb upstairs to her bedroom. You emphatically say, "Don't go." To back up your command you immediately pick your toddler up and carry her away from the steps and into the play room. The physical action of lifting her away from the unacceptable activity will reinforce your verbal order. If she goes back to the steps immediately afterward, repeat your response. Consistency in handling your child will help teach her that the steps are off limits.

THE IMPORTANCE OF ENVIRONMENTAL DISCIPLINE. Arranging your home and schedule to make restricting the child easier is an effective method for keeping your child's behavior in line. This form of management, which we have already considered, becomes increasingly important during toddlerhood for two main reasons:

1) The toddler has a very strong desire to touch and play with everything she sees.

2) The toddler is more capable of getting away from you and wandering into dangerous and "forbidden" areas of your home.

The toddler does not have sufficient self-control to quench every impulse to handle or touch dangerous or precious objects in your home. She also does not have a sufficient command of language to enable her to understand your explanations as to why she shouldn't touch various objects or wander into certain areas. To avoid a lot of unnecessary arguments, to ensure the safety of your child, and to protect valuable objects in your home, it is advisable to arrange areas of your home so that your child can play freely without danger to herself or to your possessions (see pages 324–25). By the time she is three or four years old she will be better able to regulate her own behavior and more capable of using and understanding language. At that time you may want to give her more freedom of access in your house. Objects can be returned to their proper places, and doors can be unlocked. In the meantime, environmental discipline can be extremely effective.

HANDLING AGGRESSION. Kicking, screaming, biting, hitting, and other physical as well as emotional outbursts are among the more frequent ways a toddler expresses anger and aggression. Up until the age of about two and a half to three, the young child is generally not able to inhibit her aggressive impulses and find substitute outlets for aggressive behavior.

Nellie, for instance, at seventeen months, demonstrated jealousy and anger when her mother left for a week's stay at the hospital and returned with a baby sister for her. At first Nellie began to regress and act like a baby again. She wanted to be the prime focus for her parents' attention and affection instead of her new sister. Her parents did not want to reinforce this infantile behavior, and therefore they ignored her pleas for the bottle and so forth. Nellie became increasingly jealous of the baby, and her anger and frustration built to the point where she swung at the baby and scratched the infant's cheek.

Although Nellie's mother understood the reasons for Nellie's aggressive behavior, she could not allow it to continue for fear that the baby would be harmed. Nellie's ability to speak was not well developed enough to enable her to express her anger verbally. Therefore, she had to express it physically. When her parents prevented her from striking the baby again, she needed another physical outlet for her aggression. She began to hit other family members. Nellie's parents did not know how to handle Nellie's aggression, which didn't seem to subside.

How can you handle aggression in youngsters too young to talk? Parents cannot allow a toddler to continue to hit, bite, kick, or scratch a young infant or anyone else. Therefore, they must actively control these actions and not condone this kind of behavior. On the other hand, by restricting the child's direct expression of aggression in one form, in this instance hitting, the child must find another action for letting out her aggression.

Parents can encourage a child to express her angry and hostile feelings toward others through indirect action. Providing her with a baby doll that she can strike may be one way in which the child can release her aggression without harming anyone. Many psychologists, in fact, suggest that parents provide their toddler with a substitute target for her aggression, such as an inflatable dummy, a punching bag, or a pillow with a crude face drawn on it to resemble a person. The child can then scratch, punch, and kick this substitute target whenever she is angry and has to discharge her aggression. As soon as the child acquires a greater ability to speak, parents are urged to teach her more sophisticated ways of handling aggression, chiefly through encouraging her to talk about her anger and hostility (pages 687–88).

Males appear to have a somewhat more difficult time learning to control their aggression than females. Perhaps this is partly innate, and partly the result of environmental learning. Aggression in males is often condoned to a greater extent than aggression in females. In general, fathers may have a harder time dealing with toddlers' aggressive actions than mothers, and may find themselves wanting and sometimes having to react to their children's outbursts by hitting, spanking, or slapping them. One of a parent's responsibilities during late toddlerhood and the preschool stage is to teach the child how to handle aggressive feelings. Simply by setting yourself up as an appropriate model for your child to imitate, you will be fostering the notion that violent and aggressive actions are not acceptable and must be controlled.

TEMPER TANTRUMS. Temper tantrums, an obvious indication of the child's frustrations, appear now and then throughout toddlerhood. They may become more frequent around the age of two and a half, and then gradually subside around three. When a child's activities are stopped or redirected, she may feel anger and frustration, which she releases through a temper tantrum. Sometimes the most mild suggestion from parents is enough to trigger one of these outbursts. Temper tantrums and how to handle them have been discussed previously on pages 434–35 and are discussed again in Toddlerhood 2 (pages 536–37, 590).

HOW TO HANDLE NEGATIVISM. Obstinate, rebellious behavior is more characteristic of the older toddler, although it may emerge, to a limited extent during Toddlerhood 1. A toddler's negativism creates special problems in disciplining her. Specific suggestions for managing the child who is entering this "negative" phase of development are provided in Toddlerhood 2 on pages 621–22. If your child enters this phase early, you should find it helpful to read ahead.

PUNISHMENT DURING TODDLERHOOD. Nearly all parents will probably find it necessary occasionally to punish their children when their youngsters deliberately break rules. Some will feel like punishing their children, although they may refrain from doing so for various reasons. A few fortunate parents may never have to resort to punishing their children, if they are able to handle them successfully using other methods.

Sometimes parents who never felt the need to punish during infancy may find that they are now spanking their child once in a while, or depriving her of a privilege in order to alleviate their frustration and show that they mean business. Between the ages of two and three, when the child may become extremely difficult to manage, the frequency with which parents spank their children may reach a peak. Increased punishment may also be seen in Toddlerhood 1. Those of you who believe in punishment, and those of you who didn't believe in it before, but have recently changed your minds (you are not alone), should refamiliarize yourselves with the discussion of punishment in Infancy 6 on pages 328–31.

After you have punished your child, it is important to determine if a particular punishment has been effective. We suggest that you ask yourself the following questions:

1) Did your child's behavior warrant it?
2) Did it accomplish your educational objective without causing any serious side effects?

If your answer is "yes" on both accounts, chances are that you exercised good judgment. If your answer is "no" to both questions, perhaps you should re-examine your motives for punishing your child, as well as your approach to discipline in general. Lastly, if you answered "yes" to the first part and "no" to the second, we suggest that you reread the material on punishment on pages 330–31.

In regard to spanking, probably the most common form of physical punishment, it is important to be aware that many parents spank toddlers simply because they think that the toddlers are deliberately behaving poorly. The parents of eighteen-month-old Julia, for instance, were very angry when they found her in the kitchen taking garbage out of the waste can and dropping it all over the floor. Thinking that she was willfully doing this to spite them, her mother rushed over to Julia and spanked her. A three- or four-year-old child, engaged in the same activity, would more likely have been deliberately behaving badly, and would have known it. An eighteen-month-old toddler, such as Julia, however, was simply exploring, without any intention of spiting her parents. She was not deliberately behaving badly, and her behavior was quite normal for a toddler her age.

Parents sometimes make the mistake of treating normal behavior as if it were problem behavior. By spanking a child when she is merely acting normally, parents may arouse her anger, confuse her, and create a problem where none really exists.

It is worth mentioning, again, that if your fundamental relationship with your child is good, then it is doubtful that an occasional well-deserved spanking will do anything to harm this relationship. However, if the spanking is severe, simply given because you are angry at someone else and are taking it out on your child, or given because you are feeling helpless or bossy, there is a greater chance that it may do more harm than good. Most parents who supervise their toddlers and arrange their home environments so that they are well suited to their toddlers' needs, find that disciplining them is much less taxing, and the need for punishment is kept to a minimum.

PUNISHMENT AND CHILD ABUSE. It is important to emphasize that as the need for punishing the child increases, the potential for child abuse also becomes greater. Child abuse is a major social problem, and deserves every parent's attention. This subject is explored in the Family Feelings and Concerns section on pages 562–64.

Parents' Guilt Feelings and Discipline

Parents' guilt feelings can interfere with their ability to make decisions about disciplining their child. For example, sometimes parents feel guilty about neglecting the child because they have to work outside the home and/or must leave the child in another person's care during the day. When they come home at night, they may be overindulgent in an attempt to "make it up" to the child. Parents may or may not be consciously aware of their feelings of guilt. They may fail to establish firm limits because they feel guilty or may set their expectations as to how their child is capable of behaving far below her abilities. Their toddler begins to get out of hand, and they try to be calm and understanding, while they are really feeling upset and frustrated on the inside. They may also "pretend" that they simply do not notice what is happening, and do not warn or discipline her for fear that they will lose her love or make her resentful.

The child usually seems to be aware of her parents' hesitation to say "no" to her. She also appears to know when her behavior is getting out of control, and this may make her uncomfortable. In an attempt to find definite limits, she may begin to tease, test, and provoke her parents to an even greater extent, as if to force them to lose patience with her and impose limits with a scolding or spanking.

Even when parents finally respond to her pleas for limits by threatening or punishing her, they may still feel guilty about losing their temper, and may not follow through on their threats. They may also ignore her the next time she starts to act up, take back a punishment before it has been fully carried out, or allow her to "talk back" to them while they are in the midst of reprimanding or punishing her.

It is important for parents having this kind of trouble to try and determine the underlying cause of their guilt feelings, and objectively pinpoint the situations in which they are too lax. Then they can work toward establishing firmer limits, and will be more prepared to enforce them with punishment, whenever necessary. Once parents can manage to offer firmer controls and properly and consistently enforce rules, chances are that their child's provocative behavior will subside, and she will once again respect them as authority figures.

WAYS THAT TODDLERS RELEASE AND REDUCE TENSION

Tension-releasing behavior patterns, such as thumb-sucking, rocking, and temper tantrums are common during toddlerhood. Throughout this stage your child will be striving to achieve some independence. The tasks that she faces are not easy. Increased awareness of her surroundings and herself, demands from you that she act in acceptable ways, and new responsibilities will create conflicts and additional stresses.

The increasing negativism and rebelliousness that emerges even more strongly between Toddlerhood 3 and Preschool 1 produces further sources of frustration and anxiety. You can expect to see an increase in tension-releasing activities at that time, although they may be seen intermittently throughout toddlerhood. The normal process of growing up is accompanied by some degree of frustration and tension, which is reflected in the child's behavior. Understanding these patterns and knowing how to deal with them effectively can alleviate your own tension in handling your child during this difficult time. The discussion and suggestions that follow apply to Toddlerhood 1 to 3.

TENSIONS NEED TO BE RELEASED. The toddler somehow has to release pent-up tension in order to relax. Her ability to talk about tension and cope with frustration is extremely limited, and she relies mainly upon discharging these feelings through physical actions.

Her constant motion and play during the day will be an important avenue for releasing these tensions. She can also release her emotions through such behaviors as throwing temper tantrums, sucking her thumb, banging her head, or rocking in bed. These behaviors often arouse parental concern and worry that something is wrong with the child.

Mr. Archie was quite disturbed by his son Seth's behavior. After the family had moved to a new home, twenty-month-old Seth began to suck his thumb, both at home and in public. Mr. Archie thought that Seth had outgrown his thumb-sucking in early infancy. He looked upon his son's activity as an indication that Seth was babyish and insecure, and became intent upon ridding Seth of his bad habit. Many parents express similar concerns about their toddler's "bad" habits, but they are useful to the toddler when she is under stress or is bothered by something.

The toddler's use of tension outlets may be easier to understand if you examine how adults commonly rely upon them. Mounting pressures at work or in the home frequently prompt adults to release tension verbally through statements such as, "I can't take it anymore," "I give up," or "I'm a nervous wreck." These verbal outcries help discharge anxiety and frustration, and are usually considered more acceptable than physical outlets.

Physical forms of release are also very common. Violent actions such as kicking doors, pounding fists against the wall, and throwing something across the room are common. Foot-shaking, finger-tapping, and hair-pulling are other more subtle forms of physical release. The widespread use of alcohol, tranquilizers, and cigarettes to relieve nervous tension indicates the dependence on these agents to help reduce anxiety.

SUGGESTIONS FOR HANDLING TENSION-RELEASING ACTIVITIES. Occasional thumb-sucking, temper tantrums, body-rocking, or other tension outlets discussed on pages 331–35 should not produce concern. These kinds of activities are very common during the toddlerhood years, and do not indicate that your child has a serious emotional or psychological problem.

Knowing that these behaviors can be useful to a child, it is advisable to ignore them rather than draw attention to them by punishing or trying to eliminate them. They usually pass within a few weeks or months as the toddler feels less pressured and more relaxed.

Children who rely heavily upon tension outlets may cause considerable concern to their parents. When these activities are seen several times a day, or frequently used in public, they are more difficult to ignore. In these cases most parents want to take some form of action in an attempt to control their child's behavior.

Persistent scolding, restraining, or punishing the toddler for her behavior is often futile. Some parents find that punishing even increases the frequency of tension-releasing activities. This is not surprising, since punishment only heightens the tension that the toddler experiences.

The child's frequent or persistent reliance upon physical outlets for tension generally indicates that she is experiencing more pressure and frustration than usual. In planning what measures to take to improve the situation, you should first determine if there are any excessive pressures on her that could be causing her to make greater use of outlets for tension. You may be able to pinpoint an obvious source of stress or an upsetting event that is making her feel more anxious.

There are many possible causes for stress during toddlerhood such as the arrival of a new brother or sister, moving to a new house, separation from a parent, or pressures from older siblings. Very restrictive disciplinary techniques, fear of physical punishment, or overly pressured toilet training methods represent a few areas in which parents can contribute to their toddler's tensions. Even activities that do not directly involve the child, such as marital disputes or arguments with relatives or friends in her presence, may create additional stresses upon her.

Taking your toddler's sensitivities and needs into account, and examining your family environment, you may be able to find some reason for her increased frustration and tension. Discussing these issues with your spouse or your child's physician may also help you to determine possible sources of added stress. By making attempts to eliminate stressful areas in her life, you will be taking a major step in helping her overcome the need to use tension-releasing activities.

It is not always possible to locate an obvious source of stress. In these situations it is usually best to be supportive of your child. Extra reassurance and affection can be helpful in allaying her anxieties. A relaxed attitude and patience on your part are important.

Temper Tantrums

A common form of discharging tension and frustration is the temper tantrum. In late infancy a baby may have had frequent crying spells and breath-holding episodes as an early form of temper tantrum. With the merging of independent and negative behaviors seen during toddlerhood, temper tantrums become more frequent and exaggerated.

Normal, healthy toddlers occasionally throw temper tantrums. Children commonly flop to the floor, kick, pound their fists, hold their breath, and scream. There are variations in the manner in which tantrums are carried out, depending upon the child and the intensity of her outburst. See also the discussion of temper tantrums in Infancy 11, pages 447–49.

Outbursts of temper usually arise when a toddler is overly fatigued, angry, frustrated, anxious, or confused. She may also throw tantrums as a way of expressing negativism. Despite the numerous factors that may account for or trigger temper tantrums, it is not always easy to pinpoint a reason for their occurrence. For no apparent reason, the child may occasionally blow her stack and lose control. Even minor reprimands by a parent may result in a temper tantrum. Some children are "set off" more easily than others.

Temper tantrums during toddlerhood do not indicate psychological abnormalities. Parents need not waste time worrying that somewhere along the line they have gone wrong in handling their child if she throws a tantrum every now and then.

However, temper tantrums are a definite source of irritation to parents, and they can also be a source of embarrassment, as any parent whose child has had a temper tantrum in front of other people knows. Coping with these outbursts is not the easiest thing in the world. Many times, out of anger and frustration, parents themselves will feel like throwing a temper tantrum, too.

DEALING WITH TEMPER TANTRUMS. The following suggestions may be useful in handling temper tantrums. Trying to reason with your child or encouraging her to regain self-control when she's in the midst of a tantrum will usually get you nowhere. She'll be in such an emotional state that she won't respond to logic or reason.

Most parents find that the tantrums usually end more quickly and occur less often when they consistently ignore the outburst. Letting your toddler have what she wants or offering her attention during the tantrum may encourage her to use this behavior continually as a means of getting your attention.

Punishing or severely scolding a child does not work with most toddlers as a means of controlling or preventing future tantrums. She may be further antagonized or frustrated by reprimands to the point where she retaliates by creating more of a scene. Punishments may also increase tensions and cause more frequent outbursts.

By remaining in control of your emotions and not encouraging your child's temper tantrums, you will be helping her learn to control her behavior. You will have to be patient with her since this is an outlet for her frustration and anger during toddlerhood. By bearing with your toddler and handling her tantrums properly, she will outgrow them.

BREATH-HOLDING EPISODES. Occasionally, in a fit of rage, frustration, or defiance, a child may hold her breath. These breath-holding episodes can occur alone or as part of a temper tantrum. Sometimes a child may lose consciousness momentarily, and this can be very frightening.

While holding her breath, the child does not get any oxygen from the air. She becomes faint, and may pass out. If your child loses consciousness during a breath-holding episode, she will immediately begin to breathe by reflex action. There is little or no danger to her from a breath-holding spell.

Thumb-sucking

Thumb-sucking is a common tension-releasing activity during infancy and toddlerhood. It frequently reaches a high point early in Toddlerhood 2. A child may suck her thumb during the day for several hours and continue at bedtime or nighttime. As the child enters Toddlerhood 3, a decrease in thumb-sucking during the day is often noticed, although nighttime thumb-sucking may still be strong.

This outlet for the toddler's tension may be used on and off by her depending upon how tense she feels. She may suck her thumb more frequently when she is anxious, lonely, bored, or fatigued. Thumb-sucking often appears nightly, just before bedtime. It seems to be a natural way for youngsters to comfort and calm themselves as they prepare for sleep.

Thumb-sucking should rarely cause concern in parents, since it is so commonly seen in toddlerhood. Sucking the thumb is not a sign of a disturbed child. Many normal, happy children suck their thumbs when they feel tense or need to soothe themselves.

Parents often wonder if there is anything they can do to stop this habit. The most successful approach is first to determine if your child is under any increased stress. The common pressures discussed on pages 481–83 should be considered. Attempting to alleviate her tension and providing a relaxed, affectionate environment will often result in a decrease in thumb-sucking. However, some children seem to suck their thumbs for no apparent reason. Not making a big issue over the habit and letting it work itself out often brings the best results. Even the worst thumb-suckers eventually outgrow this habit.

Parents of children who regularly suck their thumbs for hours each day may become impatient and want to do something to stop this activity. It is important to recognize that most measures initiated at the height of a child's sucking are usually not effective. Even in these situations, the best results are obtained by waiting and being patient.

If you must take action, you are apt to be more successful if you wait for a natural decrease in thumb-sucking rather than trying to hasten its decline when your child's need for it is strong. This decrease may become apparent in Toddlerhood 3. At this time there are a few things that you can do that may help her overcome her reliance upon this tension outlet.

You can try to take note of when and under what circumstances your child engages in this activity. This may offer you some good information about what prompts her to suck her thumb and may enable you to eliminate that source. A child who sucks her thumb whenever she is bored may not suck as often if she is given additional stimulation at those times. If thumb-sucking is associated with fatigue each evening, shifting the child's bedtime to an earlier hour may help.

Other measures such as putting gloves on the child's hands, applying foul-tasting substances to her thumb, and tying her hands are not very successful in reducing thumb-sucking and are not recommended. Parents who use these techniques often find that the child's need to employ this tension outlet increases, since these measures are frustrating and put her under added tension and pressure.

Attempting to control and prevent thumb-sucking by embarrassing, verbally belittling, and severely punishing a child rarely have any positive results, especially during toddlerhood. They should be avoided since they can shatter a young child's sense of personal pride and self-esteem and heighten the pressures and tensions that she feels. Further stress in her life can also contribute to an increase in thumb-sucking.

Thumb-sucking is one of several tension-releasing behaviors and may simply need to run its natural course. It often persists throughout the preschool years with some children, despite parents' attempts to encourage them to give it up. Given enough time, children outgrow their need to suck their thumbs of their own accord. In the meantime, parents should be patient.

Security Objects

Security objects (favorite things, accessory objects) are things that the child cannot part with or uses as a source of comfort. The most well known is the security blanket. Other favorite objects include Teddy bears, dolls, toys, and pillows. Many infants and toddlers develop an attachment for a special object and find security in carrying it or taking it to bed with them. Stroking, pulling, or fingering the object is often seen, and represents an additional rhythmic tension-releasing activity. Children may also derive comfort and enjoyment from the feeling of having something all to themselves.

The pressures and tensions that go along with growing up and becoming more independent may cause toddlers to want to return occasionally to the security and dependence that they experienced in infancy. Snuggling up to a soft comforter such as a fuzzy blanket or stuffed animal appears to fulfill their need. Physical closeness to a special object may remind them of the closeness that they had with their parents when they were held as infants.

Parents are fairly tolerant about their child's requests for a certain object. Friction develops when the child refuses to give up the possession or demands to take it out in public. This can be a problem when you want to wash the object. It also embarrasses some parents to let their child be seen with such a dirty, shabby object in public.

Wanting a security object is not problem behavior and should not be treated as such. In most cases the child eventually gives up the object on her own, making parental interference unnecessary. It is unreasonable to take these possessions away from your child completely, or to punish and ridicule her for clinging to them.

Some parents find it useful to put reasonable limits on when and where their child can use her security object, without altogether depriving her of it. From the start, it can be made clear to the child that the object cannot leave the home. This works in many cases, but some children will put up quite a fuss. If a child is so strongly attached to an object that she does not respond to this kind of limit, it is better not to force the issue.

The texture, smell, color, and appearance of the special object are easily recognized by the child. Attempting to substitute a new comforter or washing her old, shabby one may not solve the problem. She may immediately detect the difference, create a scene out of anger and frustration, and have trouble sleeping.

Some clever parents use foresight to solve this problem. It is often possible to sneak the object away from the child at night while she is asleep, or during the day when she is not using it. By doing this from the beginning, and washing the object at frequent intervals, she is used to a clean, fresh object and will not detect a change when it is washed. Using your imagination and knowing your own child, you may be able to come up with other possible solutions.

Security objects can play an important role in soothing your toddler. Trying to respect her attachment to an object is often the best approach. Tolerating her needs may be easier on both of you than expecting her to give up her dependency.

Requests Before Bed

The Toddlerhood 3 child frequently makes numerous requests for crackers, the toilet, drinks of water, and comfort from her parents after she has been tucked in bed and left alone. These demands can also be seen to a lesser extent in Toddlerhood 1 and 2. Bedtime requests can be considered a type of tension outlet, although they are not similar to other tension-releasing behaviors in form. The toddler's requests may reflect her insecurity and anxiety about being apart from her family.

The tension she experiences over separations prompts her to make many excuses to call her parents back to her bedroom, and keeps her from falling asleep easily.

Demands usually diminish early in the preschool stage, and do not represent a major problem. Suggestions for dealing with presleep requests are offered in the Sleeping section on page 616.

Genital Play

It is not unusual for toddlers to handle their genitals occasionally when they are nervous, excited, or upset. This normal, natural activity for reducing tension should not cause undue concern in parents. Very frequent or prolonged genital handling is often a reflection that a child is experiencing more than a usual amount of stress and tension. In such cases parents should make attempts to alleviate the stress and pressure that may underlie their toddlers' excessive genital play. This topic is more fully discussed in the Toddlerhood 2 Sex Education section on pages 626–30.

Aggressive or Destructive Activities

The acquisition of improved motor abilities allows the toddler to express or release her anger and frustration with more aggressive and sometimes destructive activities. This behavior usually becomes evident in Toddlerhood 2 or 3, but its expression is variable. Aggressive activities tend to be more prominent in active children.

Aggressive or destructive activities take two major forms. One type is directed at people, and the other is directed at objects, such as toys, furniture, or clothing. To some extent all toddlers display these activities in various degrees, since this is a common way to discharge tensions and frustrations.

Expressions of aggression toward others may include biting, hitting, or pushing. One mother was very concerned when her daughter, Farah, bit her on the arm while refusing to go to bed. At first the mother was hurt that Farah would want to cause her pain. Then she realized that this outburst was not directed against her as a parent, but was an expression of frustration and anger at not getting her way.

Aggressive outbursts are often directed at other siblings or playmates. This can lead to fights. The toddler is very limited in her ability to control these outbursts. Try to be tolerant of her behavior, and not overreact to it.

Destructive or aggressive activities toward objects can take many forms. Breaking a toy in a fit of rage is probably the most common. Messing up their room by emptying drawers or scattering their playthings is sometimes seen. Some children even try to pull off their clothes or the slats on their bed. Others may push around or tip over light pieces of furniture. The possibilities are endless.

Parents find these outbursts difficult to tolerate and are usually anxious to bring them to an end. Like the other tension outlets, these activities usually run their course and should generally be handled like other outbursts (pages 536–37). Specific suggestions for handling undesirable aggressive or destructive behavior are given in the Discipline section (pages 531–32). Providing the child with other more acceptable outlets for her tensions can often help minimize these activities. The child can be gradually taught that certain behaviors are unacceptable.

Rocking Movements

The rhythmic rocking movements that may have been initiated in the second half of infancy (pages 334–35) may continue into toddlerhood. Crib- or bed-rocking is often seen during Toddlerhood 1 and 2 and usually begins to decline in Toddlerhood 3. Some children employ this form of release more than others, and may continue bed-rocking into the preschool years.

Bed-rocking can be a gentle rhythmic back and forth movement or it can be more vigorous as the child grabs the sides of the crib and causes the whole crib to shake. In some cases the child can actually move the crib with his rocking. Bed-rocking can be noisy and some parents can hear their child rocking herself to sleep.

Rocking movements can also be seen during the day. Some toddlers will sit or stand and rock back and forth. This activity, like bed-rocking, can vary in intensity. Although these behaviors often arouse more parental concern in toddlerhood than they did in infancy, they are part of the child's natural tension-reducing activities. Some children make more use of rocking than other forms of tension outlets.

Body-rocking runs a natural course and will usually decline and stop without your interference. It should be handled like any other tension outlet (pages 535–36). By following earlier suggestions for stabilizing the crib, you will not have to worry that the child can tip it if her rocking is severe. These movements do not indicate that something is wrong with your child, if she seems happy and well adjusted otherwise. However, persistent and excessive rocking movements may indicate that your child is under emotional stress. It is advisable to discuss your concerns about excessive rocking with your child's doctor, rather than punishing or restraining her.

Head-banging

Head-banging causes great concern to most parents. This activity may begin in the later part of infancy (pages 334–35) and may continue or begin in toddlerhood. It usually diminishes or stops by Preschool 2 or 3. Most children do not cause themselves serious harm from head-banging, but occasional bumps and bruises can occur.

Occasional head-banging in a child who at other times seems relaxed and happy is not a reason for concern. Try not to draw attention to this activity. Padding the sides of the crib may help prevent bruises. Vigorous banging against a hard surface should not be allowed to continue. It is usually best to pick up the child and take her away. Try not to become excited or overly upset, but, instead, distract the child with a favorite activity. You should discuss this issue with your doctor if the head-banging is severe or doesn't stop. The general guidelines for handling tension outlets (pages 535–36) will be useful.

There are some children who bang their heads because they feel very frustrated or angry. Attempt to determine what triggers this activity. If a cause can be found, eliminate it. Head-banging can also occur for no apparent reason. Distracting your child, engaging her in other activities, and soothing her usually helps. See also the information on hyperactivity (pages 551–52).

Head-rolling

Head-rolling can begin in infancy or toddlerhood. It is a well-known form of tension release and should represent no real cause for concern. This activity is discussed in Infancy 6 (page 335).

Nail-biting

Nail-biting is not usually seen in toddlerhood, but it may occur in Toddlerhood 3. This activity is more commonly used as a tension release during the preschool phase. Nail-biting is discussed in the Preschool 1 section on pages 766–67.

Tongue-sucking

Tongue-sucking is much less common than thumb-sucking, but can occur with some children. This activity was discussed in Infancy 6, page 334. It should be handled in the same manner as thumb-sucking, and is a normal tension outlet during toddlerhood.

FEARS

Everyone at some point in his or her life has experienced the feeling of fear. Fears are a common reaction to certain events or circumstances in our environment. Psychologists often describe fear as being a type of feeling or emotion that is generally associated with the anticipation of pain, physical or psychological distress, or uncertainty about what lies ahead in the future. It is usually accompanied by certain behavior and physiological reactions such as pounding of the heart, a queasy feeling in the stomach, increased perspiration, or trembling.

Fears are quite common during early childhood. One child may differ somewhat from the next in what she fears, although studies by Gesell and others of thousands of normal children have revealed that at different ages there are similarities among children's fears. Some fears often arise at certain ages and follow a developmental pattern. Keep in mind that there is a great deal of variability in the emergence of fears.

Many professionals believe that because of their immature thought processes young children, especially from about one and a half to five, are more susceptible to fears than older children or adults. Sunny, a seventeen-month-old toddler, had a negative reaction to the entry of a new baby brother into her family. One morning, while her mother was tending to the baby, Sunny walked over to her brother's crib, pointed to the baby, and said, "Away, away," in an angry tone of voice. That afternoon the baby developed a severe cold and, as a result, had to be admitted to the hospital for tests and close observation. In response to the sudden disappearance of her brother, Sunny became very withdrawn. She wandered around the house with a terrified expression on her face, as though she believed that her wish for her baby brother's departure had actually caused him to get sick and disappear.

Developing thought mechanisms of the young child can lead her to believe that her own wishes or thoughts can cause actual events to take place. The child creates a magical world in which there is no clear distinction between reality and make-believe. Imaginary threats of danger and make-believe figures come "alive" in the child's mind, and can seem real.

Children's lack of a strong sense of reality enables them to enter the world of make-believe without realizing that they have gone beyond the boundaries of what is real. Adults can also enter an imaginary world, but they are normally aware of the difference between fact and fantasy. Given the fact that reality and fantasy are not clear divisions in a child's mind, she can easily come to some frightening conclusions about her surroundings. A child may think that people cause thunder and lightning, or that the old, twisted tree in the back yard is a monster. She does not understand the absurdity of these thoughts. As the child's imagination develops more fully, she has to deal with both fears of real substance and fears of imagined dangers.

Understanding Your Child's Fears

Children's fears are often reactions to actual events. In most cases parents feel that this type of fear makes sense. Sixteen-month-old Amy, who was scratched by a cat, afterward developed a fear of cats. Raymond, after slipping and falling in the bathtub, refused to take a tub bath for several weeks.

Fears which seem to parents to have no obvious association with actual events are common during early childhood. Karen, for instance, began to cry and run away each time her mother turned on the vacuum cleaner. Her mother could not understand why. Karen had previously enjoyed watching her mother vacuum, and had even liked to hold the handle while her mother pushed it along. As Karen's imagination developed, something new began to trouble her. She feared that she could be sucked up like dirt into the vacuum. She was not able to recognize that she was too big to be picked up by the vacuum. It was not until Karen's mother tried to think like a toddler, who does not have a clear understanding of spatial relationships, that she began to understand why her daughter suddenly became fearful.

From time to time during toddlerhood, your child may become temporarily afraid of things which, to you, seem non-threatening or absurd. Your first reaction to her fears may be to laugh, or to let her know that she is being babyish and immature. However, you should acknowledge the fact that her fears are real to her, and try to understand them.

The number of possible fear reactions that your child may develop are great. The material that follows discusses the more common fears that toddlers develop. Some of these are more prominent in early toddlerhood, although many apply to the entire phase.

FEAR OF ANIMALS. A child's fear of an animal may develop after she has been scratched or bitten, or in some way threatened. Sometimes when parents are particularly afraid of dogs or cats, their toddlers develop the same fear. In some cases in which a child has a bad dream about an animal, she may wake up believing that her dream was real. As a result, the next time she comes in contact with that animal, she may appear frightened by it.

Fears related to the appearance, size, sounds, or movements of animals are very common in toddlerhood. The loud bark of a dog, the roar of a lion, the appearance of a bear at the zoo, or the sudden movement of a squirrel across the lawn may terrify a toddler.

Large animals are often more frightening to toddlers than small ones. A child may calmly hold or approach a puppy or a kitten, but become fearful at the sight of a large dog or full-sized cat. A dog or cat may not frighten her as long as it is kept at a distance or contained by a fence, but the child may tremble with fear when the animal is nearby or if she is forced to approach and pet it.

Being held by a parent when in the presence of the feared cat or dog often helps to allay the child's fears. Buying her a puppy or kitten or a toy animal may be helpful. Reading her short, simple stories about animals with accompanying pictures may also alleviate her fears. In cases where these approaches fail, a parent may have to keep the child at a distance from the feared animal for a short while until her fear subsides. In most children, fear of a particular animal is short-lived.

FEAR OF THE DARK. One of the most common early childhood fears is a fear of the dark. It frequently emerges between the ages of about two and three, but it may emerge earlier. This fear tends to outlast most other fears that arise around the same time, and may persist far beyond the preschool years. A child's fear of the dark often creates sleeping difficulties. Methods of dealing with this are provided in the Sleeping section on page 679.

FEAR OF STRANGERS. Fear of strangers, usually referred to as stranger anxiety, is frequently seen among young children during toddlerhood and even during the preschool phase. This fear may center around unfamiliar people, objects, or new situations. Stranger anxiety, also exhibited during infancy, seems to reach new heights between the ages of one and two, since the child is more aware of both herself and her environment, and is better able to contrast familiar from unfamiliar faces and surroundings. Unfamiliarity tends to breed anxiety and insecurity, whereas familiarity brings with it reassurance and security.

Confronted with a strange person or new situation, the child may feel threatened and shaken. She may cry, regress to more immature ways of behaving, try to hide behind her parents, and become withdrawn. Suggestions for dealing with stranger anxiety are presented in the Personal-Social Development section on pages 289, 335–36.

FEAR OF SEPARATION FROM A PARENT. Fear of separations from mother and father is quite common in toddlerhood, and seems to become more prominent during Toddlerhood 2. This fear is often exhibited at bedtime, although it may be seen anytime the child is separated, even if only briefly, from her parent. Usually the child becomes anxious when she anticipates being separated, and begins to cry, cling, or panic. Separation anxiety is discussed more fully on pages 594–96, where suggestions for handling the toddler are presented.

FEAR OF FALLING. The number of times a toddler falls in the span of several hours may be astounding. Most youngsters take minor falls lightly, and are immediately up and about again. Some children become fearful of falling and hurting themselves, especially after they have recently had a hard fall, and their parents have been overprotective.

A parent who overreacts to his or her toddler's minor falls often tries to curtail the child's normal explorations out of fear that she will be injured. This reaction may encourage a child to become afraid of her surroundings or of falling and hurting herself. There is no reason not to console and reassure the child who has fallen, but parents should take care not to overprotect her or make too much fuss over inevitable everyday spills.

FEAR OF THE BATH. Fear of the bath is common during toddlerhood and even during the early preschool years. A child who has enjoyed taking a bath previously may suddenly become frightened of the tub and resist getting into it. Her fears may center around falling or slipping in the tub, getting soap that stings into her eyes, or hearing and seeing the water swoosh down the drain. The fears related to taking a bath are discussed in the Bathing section on pages 614–15.

FEAR OF SUDDEN MOVEMENTS AND CERTAIN NOISES. Fear of sudden movements, such as the quick opening of a door, the unexpected charge of a dog after a cat, or the popping up of a clown from a windup toy box, is often seen in young children. As the child's awareness and knowledge of her environment broadens during the second year, this fear gradually diminishes.

Certain noises also appear to frighten young children. The sounds produced by sirens, thunder, flushing the toilet, and the vacuum cleaner are among those most commonly feared. Fear of the toilet flushing often emerges around the time toilet training is initiated. This specific fear is discussed in Toddlerhood 2 on page 631.

In cases where a child appears to be frightened by the sound of the washing machine, vacuum, or lawnmower, it is generally helpful either to use them when she is not around or to allow her to keep her distance from them until her fears subside. Sometimes buying a child a toy model of these objects helps to allay her fears. She can play with them and make her own "sound effects."

FEAR OF THE DOCTOR. Many children have a fear of the doctor, and in most cases this is not hard to understand. During the first year and a half, the child receives several injections and sometimes has unpleasant experiences at the doctor's office; it is only natural for her to resist visits to the doctor, because of this. It is difficult to overcome completely most children's negative or fearful reaction to visits to the doctor during toddlerhood. Your reassurance during check-ups may help lessen your child's anxieties. It is also advisable to prepare her in advance for routine medical check-ups.

FEAR OF GOING TO THE HOSPITAL. Occasionally a young child must be admitted to the hospital for tests, treatments, or an operation. Fears about being hospitalized, being in an unfamiliar environment and examined by unfamiliar people, and perhaps experiencing pain, are well founded and certainly understandable. There are many things a parent can do to help alleviate a child's fears and make hospitalization less of a traumatic experience for her. Suggestions are presented on pages 1020–23.

Helping the Fearful Child

There is no way that parents can completely protect or prevent their child from developing fears. Although you will probably try to shield your child from overly frightening or unpleasant experiences, you will not be able to protect her from all anxiety-producing situations.

Most children develop fears at various times during toddlerhood and the preschool years. The fact that these fears develop is probably not as significant as how they are overcome. Even the young child between one and two has developed some skills that can be employed in dealing with fears. A child who is afraid of falling, for instance, may repeatedly act out this situation. She may practice falling on her soft bed or on the couch. By re-enacting a fearful situation under circumstances that she can control, her fear may gradually decrease.

Your role in dealing with your fearful child should be to encourage and help her to utilize her own inner resources for coping with a particular fear. Make a sincere attempt to determine what is frightening her, since understanding her fear is the first step in helping her eventually overcome it.

HOW LONG SHOULD A FEAR LAST? Children naturally tend to avoid feared objects or situations. They may also cry and show signs of panic. How long they continue to avoid feared objects or situations, or exhibit overt symptoms of fear, may depend partly upon a child's personality and partly upon how frightened she is. Some children's fears are very short-lived, while other children have fears that may last for several weeks or months. Even if you did nothing to help your child overcome her fears, chances are that she would get over them on her own, but it might take longer. Much unnecessary tension and many arguments may be eliminated by trying to locate the source of her fear, and helping her find ways to resolve it.

Sometimes it is not important that a particular fear be resolved immediately. It is not imperative for a toddler who is afraid of the water to learn to swim. On the other hand, from a practical point of view, it is important that a child who is afraid of the toilet get over this fear. Should your toddler develop a specific fear that continues for what you feel is too long a period of time, or is interfering with her normal routine or living habits, there are things you can do to help her get over it.

BE SENSITIVE TO YOUR CHILD'S FEELINGS. Be patient with your toddler. Do not make fun of her fears, scold her, or punish her for them. Some parents feel that the most effective method of getting a child over a fear is to force her to face it immediately and directly. In a case where a child is afraid of dogs, they might suggest bringing her to a dog kennel and forcing her to be around dogs. While this approach may work for a few children, it certainly does not take the child's feelings into account.

Try to be sensitive to your child's feelings, and do not become impatient with her if the process of resolving a fear takes longer or is more complex than you had anticipated. Go slowly, and do not force her. Results are not always seen right away. With a young child, trying to explain why a fear should not really exist probably will not work, since she is too young to understand. However, reassuring words from you may help calm her down and may allay her fears.

TAKING ONE STEP AT A TIME. You can help your toddler gradually get used to a fearful situation or object by taking one step at a time. Let's say that she fears large cats in the neighborhood. First you might let her get accustomed to being around a kitten, and then gradually let her get comfortable around larger cats. Sometimes keeping a feared object at a distance while the child is busy playing with toys or doing something she likes may make the feared object less frightening. There are some children who do better by facing their fear more directly (with a parent's help), and getting it over with. Each child and situation are different, and may require individual techniques and solutions. Whatever your feelings, try to be patient and reassuring.

FEARS ARE USUALLY SHORT-LIVED. Most fears are temporary. In many cases they are followed by a brief period in which a child may even be overly attracted to the situation or object she recently feared. A child who was recently petrified of dogs may suddenly turn around and be overly attracted to every dog she sees, wanting to approach them and pet them.

The temporary attraction to formerly feared objects represents a natural part of a child's method of overcoming her fears. By exposing herself to the feared object, she is, in a sense, desensitizing herself. Under these circumstances, try to give her your close supervision and support. Once her fear is really resolved, she will be neither overly afraid of the formerly feared object, nor will she have to prove to herself that she can approach or touch it.

Differences in Susceptibility to Fears

Some children are simply more fearful than others. There appear to be individual differences in susceptibility to fear, although the factors that account for these differences are not clear. Innate as well as environmental factors are often believed to be involved.

Mrs. Jamison threw an elaborate birthday party for her two-year-old son, Nick. He had always enjoyed watching a popular children's television program in which there were several animal characters. To surprise Nick, she rented a costume of his favorite animal character for the party. At the party were several children between the ages of one and five.

When Mrs. Jamison put on the costume and entered the room, she was surprised to find her son screaming with fear at her arrival. As she looked around the room, she noticed other children's reactions to her costume. Some of them were obviously terrified, while others seemed not to be surprised or afraid. Even some of the older children appeared to be fearful, while some younger children laughed and readily approached her.

This mother was puzzled by the fact that this costume turned out to be a potential source of fear for some youngsters, but did not cause the same reaction in all of the children. After talking with other parents at the party, she realized that along with many other individual differences in children's development, there is variability in children's susceptibility to fear and in what causes fear reactions.

You will undoubtedly have opportunities to observe this variability for yourself. Suppose you discover that your toddler seems to have more fears than other children her age. This is most likely due to her own, inborn threshold for fear, and probably has little to do with the way in which you are handling her. However, there is a possibility that her environment or relationship with you and other family members is contributing to her increased susceptibility to developing fears. When parents are overprotective of their toddler, are unusually demanding, or have many fears themselves, the result may be that their child develops more fears than might normally be expected.

Fears and Anxieties Are Not All Bad

Some people feel that fears and anxieties are undesirable and should, therefore, be eliminated. These unhealthy emotions, they say, are common indications or symptoms of an emotional problem. Although intense and very frequent fears and anxieties that interfere with a person's ability to function can often be a sign of an emotional problem, in most cases, feelings of anxiety and fear are natural and healthy. They can even be constructive. Some fears, for example, can actually play an important role in accident prevention. Fear of being hit by a moving car, for instance, can make a child want to avoid riding her tricycle onto a street where there is traffic, and to learn to observe traffic signals when crossing a street. A fear of being burned can motivate a child not to play with the knobs on the stove.

Fears can motivate people to take safety precautions. Mild anxiety and fear may be useful in helping a child learn to behave in an acceptable manner. Fear of parental disapproval, for example, can motivate a child to obey certain household rules.

Obviously, there are fears and anxieties which are less useful and which may exceed what most people would recognize as being "normal" limits. A child, for example, who is bitten by a dog, may be very frightened the next time she comes in close contact with a dog. In fact, she may try to avoid dogs for a while. This is perfectly natural and very understandable. If this child refuses to go outside the house for months, or becomes so paralyzed with fear that she has difficulty functioning on a daily basis, her reaction represents a major problem.

This type of intense anxiety and fear is easily recognized, and is not very common. If your child's fear or anxiety is extremely intense, appears to be severely interfering with her normal life, or cannot be overcome even with your help, it would be advisable to seek professional guidance.

HANDLING A TODDLER IS A DEMANDING PROFESSION

As compared with when she was an infant, your toddler will create extra work, worry, and demands on your time. Her new ability to walk will make it harder for you to control her. Increased responsibility for accident prevention and discipline will add to your load. At this time parents often feel as if they have advanced to a higher level job in which there are more pressures and causes for anxiety. Parenting during toddlerhood is a most demanding profession, and its responsibilities, requirements, and hours exceed most other jobs.

It is not unusual for parents to misinterpret their feelings of fatigue and being overworked. Some parents assume that these feelings reflect their inability to handle the job of being a parent effectively. Quite often they do not realize that the majority of parents of toddlers have similar feelings and are experiencing the same types of difficulties.

The extra work that your toddler creates may be difficult for you to tolerate, particularly if she is an energetic child. Over the course of a couple of hours, you will probably pick up numerous toys and put them back where they belong, only to watch your toddler immediately pick them up again and leave them scattered around the house. You will find that keeping up with your child's messes and demands will create a great deal of frustration. One mother expressed her feelings about handling her son in the following way:

> I always knew where Barry was, since he constantly left a trail of toys behind him. This infuriated me. No sooner did I finish putting away his toys and straightening up my house, then he was making another mess. Sometimes lying in bed at night I would think about the events of the day and what had been accomplished. In the back of my mind I knew Barry and I had done many enjoyable things together and that he was learning from his play and travels. The thing that stood out the most in my mind was that I had spent most of the day straightening up the house, picking up Barry's toys, and rearranging the clutter so that no one would trip if they walked into the living room.

It is easy for parents to lose sight of their child's need to interact with a wide variety of objects and to engage in repetitive and often messy activities. This behavior is invaluable in terms of her educational experience. The routine day-to-day chores that are necessary to allow your child to learn through play can occasionally wear down even the most dedicated parents. Knowing that your efforts are not in vain and are important for your child's development should help to alleviate some of the inevitable frustration that accompanies being a parent of a toddler.

In addition to being frustrating and annoying, caring for your young toddler can also be exhausting. At the end of each day you may find yourself feeling overly tired. Even parents who pride themselves on being in top physical condition often find that several days at home with their toddler can be a fatiguing experience. A father of a fifteen-month-old toddler, who was home with his daughter during his summer vacation, put it this way:

> I had always been interested in athletics during high school and college, and considered myself to be in good shape. Boy, was I ever mistaken. Trying to keep up with Suzy's pace is impossible. At the end of an afternoon with her I'm absolutely exhausted. I don't know how other parents manage, but I feel like I'm ready for a rest home.

It is not uncommon for the parent working outside the home to underestimate the amount of work and energy required to take care of a toddler. Being home with your child is certainly a demanding and often exhausting career, but one which offers many rewards.

The responsibilities of parenting during toddlerhood are also significant. Many challenging decisions concerning the management of your child must be made. During this phase, parents typically feel more concerned about their ability to ensure their child's safety. The mother of a sixteen-month-old toddler expressed her concerns as follows:

> My daughter, Andrea, is extremely active. I worry about protecting her and what could happen if I leave her alone for even five minutes. Even though I take safety precautions, I can't help but worry. I have to constantly keep an eye on her, and this is especially hard when the phone rings and I want to talk to someone. If I pick up the phone in the kitchen, faster than a flash she wanders away into the living room, so I drop the phone and run there to grab the extension so I can keep an eye on her. No sooner do I start talking again, when I find that she's disappeared into another room. Lord, she tires me out. Most days I count the minutes until her naptime when I can flop myself down into a chair, finally close my eyes, and stop worrying.

It is true that toddlerhood is a prime time for accidents. Thus, it is only natural to be concerned about protecting your child. Although there are no easy solutions to counteract the added responsibilities of ensuring her safety, it certainly helps to do as thorough a job as you can to safety-proof your home, and make use of locks on doors and gates if you wish to keep your toddler on a certain floor or out of particular areas. This should cut down on the amount of time you spend worrying about her safety.

Like any demanding profession, rearing your toddler can occasionally wear you down. Feelings of being pressured, taken for granted, or overworked are experienced by virtually every parent. It is important not to deny and repress these feelings. Talking about them with your spouse, friends, or relatives may help to relieve the tension. Occasionally, you might want to leave your toddler with a relative, baby-sitter, or baby-sitting pool and get away for a while. An evening or afternoon all to yourself once a week or more may be "just what the doctor ordered." Having an opportunity to transfer the responsibility for her care to someone else for brief periods can be relaxing and rejuvenating for both mind and body. If nothing else, it will give you a chance to catch up with household chores, hobbies, friends, or whatever else has been sliding while you attempted to keep up with your toddler.

WALKING LATE–TALKING LATE

Few parents can honestly say that they have never gotten together with other parents and compared notes on how their respective children were progressing. It is also safe to say that most mothers and fathers want their child to stand out in terms of being the brightest, the most talkative, or the most physically able in such comparisons. During toddlerhood, individual differences among children become more obvious. Personalities of toddlers and learning styles become more sharply defined. However, comparisons between youngsters tend to focus on walking and talking as the major developmental milestones.

There are parents who are able to keep such comparisons in their proper perspective. They realize that these wide differences in rates of development are normal, and they are not especially bothered by them. On the other hand, when some mothers and fathers learn that their child is developing more slowly in a given area, such as walking or talking, they are highly disturbed by this information. Mr. Joyce, for example, whose fourteen-month-old son, Terry, was not yet walking, made the following remarks:

> I can't help wondering if Terry is normal, or if there is something I'm doing wrong as a parent. Every time I get together with my friends, all I hear about is how their children are walking well. It's embarrassing for me whenever our conversations shift to talking about our children. Terry is obviously the slowest in the group, and this disturbs me.

Mr. Joyce's concern is natural, but his son's slower progress should not cause unnecessary anxiety. Learning about your child's development will help you put things into perspective, but even parents who are aware of normal variability often need reassurance.

Mrs. Dorman was a psychology major in college and had studied child development. Despite her knowledge, she still became emotionally involved when her daughter was slow to talk. She expressed her concern by saying:

> I worry a lot about my daughter, Daria. She seems pretty normal and happy, but she just doesn't talk. When I'm at home with her it doesn't bother me at all, but whenever I have coffee with neighbors who have children Daria's age, and hear about how many words their kids can say, I really get uptight. It's gotten to the point where I just keep my mouth shut whenever other parents get on the subject of kids. Pretty soon, I may stop getting together with them, because I don't think it's good for me or Daria. Lately I've been trying to push her to talk. I know that I shouldn't be doing this, but I felt that this approach might work. It hasn't. She doesn't say any more than she did three months ago, and I think both of us are getting more frustrated. I suppose I'd better let well enough alone and let nature take its course. I pray that she isn't retarded.

When it's your child, it is often difficult to be objective. Mrs. Dorman discussed her feelings with her husband and other parents, and was gradually reassured. She was able to put things into perspective. Daria turned out to be an active talker by two and a half years of age.

It is not uncommon for parents to feel somewhat insecure or guilty about the fact that their child is not progressing at as fast a pace as some other toddlers or preschool children of the same age in a particular developmental area. Even when they are aware of the variation in children, they may wonder if they are doing right or wrong by their child. Very often parents worry that something is drastically wrong and that children who are slower to master walking or talking will be physically or intellectually slower later in life, although, in the vast majority of cases, that is a false premise.

Do not allow other parents' comments about the fast rate at which their children are developing to play on your insecurities about your own abilities as a parent, or your child's development. Think in terms of your child's over-all developmental progress; placing undue emphasis on one ability or another makes it easy to lose sight of the total picture of your growing child, which will be the best indication of how well your child is developing. Any specific concerns that you have about her development should be taken up with her physician.

IS YOUR CHILD HYPERACTIVE?

The term "hyperactive child" has been used to describe a particular group of children who have essentially normal verbal abilities, but who have difficulties with concentration and fine motor function. This name can be very misleading, since it is not specific. Many children are very active, but do not have the hyperactive child syndrome.

Parents who have a very active young toddler and have read about the hyperactive child syndrome may become very concerned and anxious over the possibility that their child might have this condition. Be reassured that the vast majority of toddlers are preoccupied with keeping themselves in constant motion. As described in the Development sections, your young toddler will have a strong need to explore, manipulate, run, climb, talk, and even "annoy" you. She will certainly appear hyperactive in comparison with her previous behavior.

There are very few parents who do not feel exhausted after spending several days, full time, with their toddlers. A sudden surge of increased activity and negativism are a natural part of your child's development during toddlerhood. Some parents mistake their child's normal behavior as a symptom of this hyperactive condition. The following example may help to illustrate this point. Mrs. Arthur, parent of a very active little toddler named Stewart, had recently read several magazine articles on hyperactive children. In these articles, the authors emphasized the fact that hyperactive children have very short attention spans, constantly shift from one activity to the next, rarely sit down, and have difficulty performing tasks that require fine motor co-ordination. The authors also stressed the fact that medications and shifts in diet can help to calm hyperactive children and make them more manageable.

After reading these articles, Mrs. Arthur became very anxious and concerned over Stewart's behavior, which seemed to her to fit the description of the hyperactive child. Activities that she had previously regarded as being normal now seemed to her signs that something was wrong with her son. This, coupled with the fact that she was having trouble managing Stewart and keeping up with his active pace, heightened her fears. Her worries and frustrations increased to the point where she began to punish him for the slightest offense, and would try anything she could think of to restrict his activities. The harder she tried to alter his normal activities and keep him still, the more defiant and rebellious he became.

These problems precipitated a visit to her pediatrician. Mrs. Arthur told her doctor that she was convinced that Stewart was hyperactive, and wanted to know if there was some medication that he could prescribe in order to alleviate her son's terrible condition. After giving him a complete physical exam, the pediatrician recognized that Stewart was a normal, healthy toddler. He reassured Mrs. Arthur that there was no reason to treat her son with medication.

The doctor also explained to Mrs. Arthur that even children who have the hyperactive child syndrome can do well with only a minimum of assistance. He emphasized that the time this condition becomes a problem is when the child cannot concentrate in school and thus has difficulties learning. Medications and closely supervised teaching methods can then be used to correct this difficulty in concentration, allowing the child to get a good education. The doctor reassured her that Stewart was doing fine and that she should not worry about her active toddler, especially at this early stage.

Mrs. Arthur was glad she had discussed this concern with her pediatrician because she felt relieved and was much more relaxed in dealing with Stewart. Stewart was more active than most children his age, but he gradually became easier to manage as he entered the preschool years.

The wide variability in children's behavior during toddlerhood can often cause a parent with an active child to think that the child may be having physical difficulties. If you are concerned, discuss it with your pediatrician. Your doctor will give you a broader perspective.

Hyperactivity rarely becomes a problem during toddlerhood. This condition should be considered more fully when the child is older and enters school, since it is important to be sure that she is able to concentrate on her lessons and will not fall behind her class. The hyperactive child syndrome is discussed in more detail in the Health Care Guide (pages 1006–10).

PROBLEMS IN SHARING DISCIPLINE

As the need for discipline increases during toddlerhood, it is not unusual for couples to have difficulties sharing responsibilities for disciplining their child. This can create tensions within the family. Several of the more common problems that may arise are examined below. Your awareness of these pitfalls may assist you in avoiding them in your family.

Resentment for Having to Bear the Major Burden

The parent who stays home during the day with the child often has to carry the major responsibility of discipline; when the child misbehaves, this parent is there and must immediately decide what to do. The person doing most of the disciplining in the family may be regarded by the child as the "mean" one. This parent may resent being the person who has to punish the child while the other parent is not involved.

One couple had a great deal of difficulty resolving this problem. The mother happened to be at home with their child during the day, while her husband commuted to work. She had to put up with her son's constant demands. Each evening, by the time dinner was ready, she was exhausted and wanted to share her frustrations with her husband. When he came home each night, he was too tired to want to listen to a detailed accounting of what went on all day with his son. He especially did not want to be involved in the household problems, since he felt he had his share of problems at work. This heightened his wife's feelings of resentment.

She became increasingly irritable and annoyed about carrying the full burden of discipline and care of her son. This hostile setting led to many arguments and bitter feelings. Variations of this type of problem are fairly common. Parents who do not openly discuss or respect each other's feelings about sharing the responsibilities for their child can develop hostilities and feelings of resentment toward one another. This creates a distance between them and an unpleasant home atmosphere for each member of the family.

Inability to Discipline

Another problem can arise when one parent tries to shirk the responsibilities of discipline and place them onto his or her spouse. A parent who is home full time caring for a child may feel that the parent working outside the home should assume the role of an authority figure for the child. The at-home parent may postpone punishment of the child, leaving it for the other parent to handle when he or she gets home. The latter frequently comes home to face a lengthy discussion of limits and rules which have been violated by the child during the course of the day and either punishes the child that night without understanding the full scope of the situation, or becomes aggravated at being placed in this awkward position.

Meanwhile, the child who has been warned that she will be punished when the parent comes home has been fearing his or her return all afternoon. By the time she is punished, she has long forgotten why, and all she feels is anger and resentment toward the parent. Understandably, the working parent quite often resents being put in this position.

Mr. and Mrs. Johnson were having difficulties sharing the responsibility for discipline. Mr. Johnson regularly spent most of the day with their son, Ben. His spouse would leave at 7:30 A.M. each day, and not return home until 6:30 P.M. Mr. Johnson had many unpleasant memories of his childhood, and resented his own father's strictness and harshness in handling him. Being placed in the position of disciplinarian for Ben for most of the day was intolerable. He refused to punish Ben for breaking rules. He feared that if he set firm limits and reprimanded him for stepping out of line, Ben would grow to dislike and resent him.

Mr. Johnson felt strongly that his wife should assume the major responsibility for disciplining Ben and left this job for her. Mrs. Johnson declined and never seemed to understand all of the circumstances surrounding Ben's violations. She could not justify punishing him for infractions that took place hours earlier.

Unless parents can come to some understanding of the child's need for immediate feedback about her behavior, this type of problem may result in further tensions between parents, and difficulties in handling the child. The person caring for the child during the day should recognize the importance of assuming the role as an authority figure for her. There is no need for parents to equate an authority figure with strictness or harshness. At this stage the child actually needs and expects her parents to provide guidance in the form of setting consistent boundaries for her conduct.

The "Dr. Jekyll-Mr. Hyde" Syndrome

The child quickly learns how much naughty behavior she can get away with in the presence of each parent. She senses the limits of their patience and tolerance. If she knows that one parent is much more lenient than the other, this may result in the "Dr. Jekyll-Mr. Hyde" syndrome. She will behave like an "angel" with the strict parent, and like a "beast" with the lenient one.

The Kleins, parents of a sixteen-month-old son, were having trouble dealing with him. Mrs. Klein was upset because her son always misbehaved in her presence. It was hard for her to be with him all day. He did not behave badly when cared for by his father. Mrs. Klein felt that her son was deliberately acting up in front of her. This made her angry, and she began to think of reasons for his behavior. At first she thought that he was doing this to spite her, but realized that this was unlikely at his age. She decided that she must have done something wrong in the past to prompt her son's misbehavior. Feelings of inadequacy as a mother preoccupied her thoughts.

Each day when Mr. Klein came home from work, Mrs. Klein, feeling frustrated and overwhelmed, would complain about their son's unacceptable, provocative behavior, expecting her husband to sympathize and support her. Instead, he offered little in the way of sympathy. He treated her as if she were a "hysterical female" who was overreacting to the situation. He often told her that he found it hard to believe his son's behavior could change so drastically within the course of each day, since the boy was always well behaved in front of him.

This lack of understanding from her husband, coupled with her growing sense of helplessness and frustration, heightened her feelings of inadequacy in handling her son. It also contributed to constant tensions between her and her husband. Communication lines between them broke down, and she felt increasingly alienated from both her husband and her son.

When one parent does not set and enforce limits and the other parent does, the child can sense this, and may behave very differently with the two parents. The lenient parent, like Mrs. Klein, may find that her child misbehaves much more in his or her presence. It is important to recognize that the child's behavior reflects the current lack of adequate discipline, and not an inherent inability to be a good parent.

Playing One Parent Against the Other

Another difficulty can arise as a result of parents taking different approaches to discipline and disagreeing with one another in their child's presence. The child quickly learns to play up to the sympathy of the more lenient parent, so that she may be able to escape being reprimanded by the parent who enforces the rules. The problem is that this is frequently a source of conflict among couples, and can result in numerous arguments. Instead of working in co-operation with one another to achieve a common goal, parents end up working against one another, and feeling as if they are enemies.

Mr. and Mrs. Taylor had very different approaches to discipline. Mrs. Taylor believed in a strict approach, while her husband regularly took a lenient stance. These differences were sensed by eighteen-month-old Andrea.

One evening while Mr. and Mrs. Taylor were playing cards in the living room, Andrea wandered over to the stereo set in the far corner of the room and began fiddling with the records, despite her parents' warnings that she would be spanked if she did. By the time her parents recognized what was happening, she had scratched one of their favorite records. Mrs. Taylor was furious, and walked over to Andrea with an angry expression. Andrea, sensing what was about to happen, quickly walked over to her father, gazed up at him with a pathetic, frightened look on her face, and clung to him for protection from her mother.

Mrs. Taylor told Andrea that she deserved a spanking, and was going to get one. Mr. Taylor immediately jumped to his daughter's defense, urging his wife to forget about the incident. The two of them got into a heated argument over the issue of discipline. This was not unlike the other arguments they had been having at increasingly frequent intervals over the past few months.

When couples disagree over approaches to discipline, and do not present a "united front" to the child, they may find themselves facing problems much like those that the Taylors experienced. Disagreements over approaches to discipline should be discussed in private, and attempts should be made to come to some compromise that is satisfactory to both parties.

If an on-the-spot decision involving how to manage the child must be made by one parent, the other parent should back this ruling up in the child's presence, saving disagreements until later, when the child is not around to overhear them. Taking a unified approach in front of your child not only eliminates opportunities for her to play one of you off against the other, but also makes it easier for her to learn the lessons underlying your program of discipline.

Mother and Father Should Share in Discipline

It would be unrealistic to think that all conflicts about discipline during toddlerhood and the preschool years could be avoided if mother and father shared equally in the responsibility for discipline. It would also be naïve to assume that disciplining a child could be a completely fifty-fifty proposition. One parent or the other necessarily spends more time with the child, and automatically assumes the greater responsibility for setting and enforcing limits. But parents should be aware of each other's position, and try to share responsibility for their child's education in self-control. Discuss possible conflicts about discipline, and do not try to shirk or shift this responsibility onto one another. This approach should help minimize unnecessary conflicts and arguments.

THE IMPORTANCE OF THE FAMILY IN TODDLERHOOD

To a young child, the family is vitally important. It provides her with a sense of security and belonging. Her family satisfies not only her basic needs, but also her emotional needs for love, warmth, attention, and physical closeness with people who care about her.

In toddlerhood the child's relationship with her family changes from what it has been in the past. She becomes more emotionally attached to her parents and solidly entrenched as a family member. She is also better able to operate more independently within the sphere of her family, learn from other members, and give of herself.

Toddlers derive a sense of identity from their families. Through interactions with parents and brothers or sisters they begin to realize that they are separate individuals who are like other family members, but also different from them. A toddler's perception of herself and her body is in large part influenced by the feedback and treatment she receives. The child's roots lie within the family, and during toddlerhood she begins to identify closely with its members, particularly her parents.

The manner in which family members treat one another and conduct themselves both inside and outside the home offers the toddler insight into how to get along with other people. Rules and regulations set forth for her, and the approach to discipline that her parents take, play an important role in teaching her the difference between acceptable and unacceptable behavior. In Toddlerhood 2 and 3 she begins to learn their standards for conduct and starts to internalize these behaviors gradually in the form of a conscience.

Within the family setting, the child receives an informal education that she will carry with her throughout her life. Through direct teaching efforts as well as everyday experiences with family members, she will learn countless lessons about other people, herself, and animate as well as inanimate objects. The kind and amount of encouragement, opportunities for discovery, and stimulation that family members offer her will greatly influence her development.

A toddler's social world primarily centers around her immediate family. Separations from her parents are difficult for her to deal with, and contribute to feelings of insecurity and anxiety over the possibility of being left alone. The anxiety that many toddlers experience when apart from their parents is a testimony to their need for the security and love that their families offer.

The child's ability to leave the home and venture out on her own for short periods of time is not well developed in toddlerhood. Older toddlers will be acquiring the skills and abilities that will enable them to begin to separate from their parent(s). The family not only prepares the toddler to function well within it, but also provides her with the security base and basic preparation that will eventually enable her to leave and function well outside of it.

Given the importance of the family to a toddler, parents should take pride in working to preserve the family and be certain that it is responsive to the individual needs, rights, and feelings of each member. Families vary considerably in their composition, size, and way of operating. Regardless of the type of family you have, offering your toddler a stable, loving family base should be very rewarding.

STEPPARENTHOOD DURING TODDLERHOOD

When someone marries a single person with a toddler, this person will become a stepparent to the child. The general discussions about assuming the role of a stepparent previously provided in the Preparing for Parenthood section on pages 14–22 should be of assistance to prospective or new stepparents of toddlers. The toddler's reactions to a stepparent can be similar to an infant's in some respects, but age and added experience can make a difference in how readily the child accepts and adjusts to a new parent. Some of the special concerns that stepparents often have about the toddlerhood stage are explored in the material that follows. It may also be helpful to read the section on stepparenthood during the preschool years (pages 782–85), particularly when older toddlers or toddlers who are talking are involved.

Toddlers, like infants, are still very dependent upon their parents for the satisfaction of emotional and bodily needs. This dependency can work to a stepparent's benefit. When a stepparent is able to fulfill a child's needs, she is likely to be receptive to her new parent's efforts on her behalf, and may, after making an initial adjustment, respond very positively to this parent. It may not take too long for her to become attached to a new parent who offers genuine love and attention, and good basic care.

The older the toddler, however, the greater is the likelihood that the stepparent may run into resistance. Many toddlers have mixed feelings or even negative feelings about their parent's remarriage, at least initially. A toddler will naturally have a stronger attachment to her natural parent(s) than would an infant, and will also be more sensitive to and disturbed by shifts in major care-givers, routines, and surroundings.

How any young child responds to a new parent will depend upon numerous factors beside her age, such as how she has adjusted to the natural parents' divorce or the death of one parent, how old she was when the crisis occurred, how painful this was for her, what type of relationship she has with her natural parent(s), and how the introduction to the stepparent is handled. Other factors, including the child's personality, temperament, and ability to understand her parent's need to remarry, will also play a major role in her response. Still another highly significant factor is how the stepparent feels about and relates to the child.

Children who are strongly attached to one parent may initially have tremendous difficulty sharing that parent with a third person, particularly when he or she is presented as a new parent. Feelings of jealousy are common and natural, even in a child who seems to need love and security from another parent figure. Be aware that the child may strongly resent the fact that her natural parent's attention is no longer directed toward her alone, and feel threatened by her stepparent's involvement in the family. This resentment can result in efforts to cling to her parent and create friction between her parent and stepparent. It is not unusual for a jealous young child to cry, whine, throw temper tantrums, and act up in other ways in an attempt to get more attention from her natural parent or drive the prospective or new stepparent away.

It is common for a toddler who has "lost" one parent either through divorce or death to worry a great deal about the possibility of losing her other parent. Seeing this parent become seriously involved with a new adult may lead her to believe that her parent no longer wants her, and may arouse in her a sense of rejection as well as a fear of being left alone. The toddler who cannot express her feelings through words will express them through her behavior; she may become overly clingy and emotionally upset over even brief separations from her natural parent, or she may become overly obedient, thinking that if she is very good, her parent will not want to abandon her.

A youngster may also be resentful because she regards the stepparent as someone attempting to be a substitute for her natural parent, who in her mind can never be replaced. In the event that the loss of her parent was very painful, and she is not fully able to accept the fact that this person is not coming back, it is understandable why she might reject her new stepparent. Accepting this person may be very difficult for her, since, in her mind, this would be very unfair to the natural parent and might make that parent angry at her.

Toddlerhood is a time when children will be working through the issues of establishing their independence and voicing their separateness as individuals. It is also a time when parents try more actively to train the child to use the toilet and stay within the boundaries they have established for her behavior, and so forth. The entry of a new stepparent into the child's life, if not viewed positively by her, can be a very upsetting experience that may interfere with the ease with which certain of the toddler's personal goals are achieved.

For example, a child who is just beginning to voice her independence from her only parent is told that she will have a new parent. Out of a fear of losing her natural parent, her behavior may markedly change. She may regress to infantile behavior and refuse to help feed and dress herself or cry for prolonged periods of time whenever her parent leaves. Other children who are upset by their parent's remarriage will show this in other ways. They may become withdrawn, refuse to become toilet trained, make requests for the breast or bottle after having given it up, cry more often, rely heavily upon tension outlets, have nightmares, throw frequent temper tantrums, and so on.

Both the child's natural parent and stepparent should carefully observe her behavior and be on the lookout for signs that she is unhappy or experiencing difficulties adjusting. Should signs of trouble such as those mentioned above persist despite parental attempts to alleviate her anxiety, it may become necessary to discuss this with her doctor.

Gradual introduction of a prospective stepparent during the courtship period is usually the best way to prepare the toddler and enable her and her stepparent to get to know one another. Once the decision about the marriage is finalized, some simple explanation should be offered to the child. A toddler's ability to comprehend the events that are occurring or the explanation itself is apt to be limited, but her parent should try to help her understand that "so and so" is going to be her new mommy or daddy and will be living in the same home. Rather than taking an apologetic attitude, which can heighten or give substance to a child's wariness, the parent should talk about the marriage as a happy event. It might be said that in time, it is hoped that the child will learn to love her new stepparent, and will be much happier having another parent in the home. It might also be appropriate to offer some reassurance that her natural parent will continue to love her, and will be there whenever she needs him or her. The child should also be told how to address her new stepparent. Suggestions for dealing with this are provided on page 20.

The transition period in which the toddler has to adjust to having two parents in the home is apt to go more smoothly if the stepparent refrains from going overboard on physical demonstrations of affection or gift-giving as a way of "winning the child over." The child may be confused or threatened by these efforts from a person whom she does not know very well, and may turn away from them. Slow, genuine advances should be made by a stepparent and small tokens of affection can be given according to signs from the child that she is ready to accept them.

Toddlers are often upset by alterations in their living patterns. They usually like to cling to familiar ways of doing things. Therefore, it would be advisable for a stepparent to become very familiar with the toddler's daily routine and preferences before making changes. If and when alterations are made, go very slowly.

A stepparent often has his or her own opinions about managing the child, and they may differ from those of the natural parent. In this case some compromising by the parents may be necessary. Particularly when toddlers are involved, it is important for parents to be consistent in their program of discipline, and to back each other up, at least in the child's presence. Children who sense that their parent and stepparent are at odds on matters of discipline or punishment, and who are unhappy with the new parental arrangement may try to play one parent off against another in an attempt to "divide and conquer." This is why presenting a "united front" is advisable.

Stepparents who are afraid to discipline and are overly lenient in their eagerness to be friends and not antagonize their child or spouse should also be prepared for trouble. Young children, especially toddlers, need adult guidance and often push parents to the limits of their patience and tolerance until they have to set down rules and regulations. Stepparents who go to great lengths not to discipline are not doing a favor to their spouses or their children.

Not all children have feelings of resentment or anxieties in regard to having a new stepparent. It is possible that a child will like her stepparent and accept him or her from the start. She may be thrilled at the prospect of having an intact family once again, and having an opportunity to fulfill her strong need for developing another bond with an adult who will be a permanent person in the home. She may also remember how unhappy her remaining parent was after the divorce or death, and be pleased at the happiness the stepparent has brought to this parent.

BEGINNING OR RETURNING TO WORK OUTSIDE THE HOME

The reasons parents decide to seek employment outside the home differ. Some parents who are caring for their children on a full-time basis decide to supplement this career by working outside the home because they want additional stimulation.

Economic pressures may arise while your child is in the toddlerhood stage, making it necessary for both parents to bring in an income. A discussion of economic pressures was presented in Preparing for Parenthood (pages 32–33), but certain of these pressures may take on new dimensions in toddlerhood.

Wanting to Supplement Child Rearing with Another Job

Some parents decide to supplement their career of child rearing by returning to work during the toddlerhood stage. The reasons for this vary greatly: dissatisfaction, resentment, unhappiness, social isolation, boredom, pressures of rearing a toddler, wishes to obtain more money, or a desire to return to one's former career.

Parents are often torn between not wanting to leave their toddlers, and wanting to fulfill their own needs. They should closely examine their motivation for wanting to work outside the home, and weigh their own needs against those of their child.

Toddlers benefit greatly from individualized attention. A toddler is more than just emotionally tied to her parent; she has also developed special lines of communication and complex patterns of daily social responses with this person. In many ways she is still quite dependent upon her parent. The important developmental tasks that she faces of establishing her separateness and self-confidence are often accomplished more easily when a parent is physically present.

Making Your Own Decision

You should carefully consider your decision to work outside the home, and what effect it might have upon your toddler. There is no one else who is better equipped to make this decision than you. If your needs to leave full-time child rearing are quite strong, and are in some ways interfering with the quality of care that you offer your child, you and your child may be better off if you work outside the home.

Being away from your toddler for a period of time each day may enable you to gain a new perspective on child rearing. You may even discover that your enthusiasm and enjoyment of her actually increase.

A toddler needs a loving, responsive parent figure who enjoys caring for her. Parents who resent or are unhappy caring for their toddlers on a full-time basis are not likely to be able to fulfill their children's needs unless they totally repress their own. A substantial number of women pursue a career in addition to motherhood and are able to do a credible job of handling work and a family.

There is little doubt that for some parents, separations from children are traumatic experiences. Insecurity over the possibility of losing the closeness to their child, and of finding that a "replacement" can do a better job, can make leaving the home even harder upon parents. These feelings, worries, and concerns are natural, and very common. In many cases a mother who has to leave full-time child care for an outside job is more disturbed by this than her child.

As long as a child is looked after by someone who cares about her and is responsive to her needs, there is no reason for a parent to be unduly concerned about her welfare, or feel guilty about not being physically present all of the time. A child who is happy and well cared for during her mother's temporary absences from the home will sense her love and genuine concern even when she is not around. A mother's love in her child's heart will not be replaced, even by the most efficient, responsive parent figure. Provided that your toddler is secure in your love, well cared for while you are away, and knows that you will soon be back, you need not worry about her reaction to your absences or the possibility of losing her love.

If there is no pressing financial need to work, it is not uncommon for a parent, especially a mother, to receive strong pressure from a spouse, parents, or other relatives to remain at home. In trying to motivate a mother to change her mind they may use words and phrases such as "remember your obligations," "your child needs a mother," and "don't shirk responsibility." Unless a mother is very confident about her need for outside work, pressure of this sort can make her feel guilty, worried, and selfish, and ultimately cause her to change her mind about working. If you feel your decision to work is the right one, do not let pressure from other people interfere with your plans or induce guilt. Some parents have found that denying their own needs and remaining at home to care for their child fostered resentment that probably had more of a detrimental effect upon the child than a separation imposed by an outside career would have.

Part-time Versus Full-time Employment

Given the toddler's reactions to separations, in cases where a parent has the option of working part time, this would be preferable to full-time employment. Lengthy separations will be much harder upon her than shorter ones.

Parents who plan to work part time and have some flexibility in how they can arrange their work schedules often wonder if it is better to work three full days, or five half days. The latter schedule would probably make it easier to maintain continuity in the parent-child relationship. Many parents find this to be a satisfactory working schedule, although each situation warrants individual consideration.

Preparing Your Toddler for the Separation from You Is Important

Having made a decision to work outside the home, it is important to prepare your child in advance for the fact that you will be apart from her. A child who can understand simple verbal explanations should be told of your plans in advance, perhaps a week or two before you leave the house.

Gear what you say to her level of understanding. An older toddler may want to know concrete facts such as where you will be, and when you will come home. Adequate explanation and emotional support can alleviate unnecessary tensions and problems.

Dianne, the mother of twenty-month-old Drew, found that the following approach to preparing her son worked well. She sat down with him one morning and explained that she would be leaving him for part of each day, beginning the next week. She compared her job and work schedule to his daddy's, since this made the concept of her coming and going easier for him to grasp. She told him that his grandmother would be coming to their home to care for him. Dianne also said that although they could no longer have lunch together, she would still eat breakfast with him each morning, and would be home in the late afternoon in time to have dinner with him. Finally, she emphasized that she loved him very much and would miss him while at work.

Conveying this message to your toddler is extremely important. Exactly what you say to her is not as important as the attitude and feeling that come across in your words.

Finding Someone to Care for Your Toddler

A discussion of some of the options available to you for ensuring that your toddler will be well cared for in your absence can be found on pages 636–39. Ideally it would be best to leave her in the care of a very familiar, capable person whom she likes. Being with a person whom she knows will help to reduce the anxiety she feels when you are away.

The utmost consideration for your toddler's feelings and needs should be shown in determining who will care for her. Having trust and confidence in this person should also be a top priority. If you know that she is happy and that her needs are being fulfilled in your absence, this will eliminate much of the guilt and worry that you may feel about leaving her.

Preserving a Sense of Stability and Continuity While You Are Gone

Maintaining a sense of continuity and familiarity in your toddler's life is another important consideration. A toddler who has difficulty dealing with separations may be markedly disturbed by constant shifts in the person caring for her. Try to consider this in making your arrangements.

It is not unusual for a child who is upset over separations from her parent to feel even more anxious upon being placed in unfamiliar surroundings. Remaining in her home offers her a certain sense of security, familiarity, and comfort. Although it might be ideal for a toddler to be cared for by a familiar person who comes to your home or cares for her in another home in which she feels comfortable and secure, this arrangement is not always possible or economically feasible. Should there be a choice between arranging for her to be with a familiar person away from your home, or an unfamiliar person in your home, the former would more than likely be the better choice.

THE BATTERED TODDLER

Horrifying as it may be, there are parents who regularly abuse their toddlers. They may do this without realizing it or having any intention of doing so. Bruises, broken bones, and psychological trauma resulting from severe beatings, social isolation, emotional deprivation, or even more bizarre forms of punishment are not as uncommon as you may think. Negligence can also be a form of child abuse. Leaving a young child unattended in a potentially dangerous area can frequently result in accidents, some of which may cause permanent physical damage and even death.

The potential for child abuse seems to be strong during toddlerhood. A toddler's assertiveness, testing behavior, and need for constant supervision may be extremely hard on her parent's nerves. This may result in the parent's feeling the need to rely, to a greater extent than before, upon punishment as a means of control. Feelings of anger and frustration over a child's behavior, although common, are kept under control by most parents. Some, however, cannot control their emotions and abuse their children.

Mr. Walters, the owner of a successful printing business, had been abusing his child for many months before it was brought to his attention. This forty-year-old father had always been dissatisfied with himself. He had dreamed of owning an influential local newspaper, but, for a variety of reasons, had never "made it." Feeling that he was a failure in life, because he never achieved his life's dream, drove him to have overly high expectations for his son, David.

This discontented father vowed to train his son early to be a winner. When David began to become demanding and assertive during his fifteenth month, Mr. Walters found it impossible to tolerate what he felt indicated his son's disrespect and disobedience, and was committed to molding his son into line. He attempted to accomplish this by using the methods he was most familiar with, beating David with a strap whenever he misbehaved or mildly refused to comply with his commands. Mr. Walters had frequently been whipped by his own father as a child, and believed that physical punishment and discipline were one and the same.

Blinded by his unrealistic expectations of his young toddler, he whipped David several times each week and applied so much pressure that his son was regularly left with welts, cuts, and bruises. Although Mr. Walters saw the strap marks on David's body, his emotions and thought processes were so out of control that he could neither stop himself nor recognize that he was abusing his son.

David's mother realized what was happening, but was so afraid of her spouse's temper that she said nothing to relatives or friends. She also feared reporting her husband's problem to the child protection agency, since she believed that their son would be taken away from them. Day after day David was kept at home so that no one would see the obvious marks on his body. Mrs. Walters prayed that her husband would come to his senses, and meanwhile devoted her energies to nursing her son.

Their neighbors, the Bells, heard David's screams day after day and suspected that he was being severely beaten. Yet, initially, they felt that they had no right to interfere or make accusations for which they had no real proof. For two months they said and did nothing, but they continued to suspect the worst. One afternoon, while they were having an outdoor barbecue, David wandered into their yard. Mrs. Bell was appalled at his condition. His arms and legs were covered with welts and cuts. She immediately reported it to the child protection agency in their local area. Her only regret was that she had not reported her suspicions earlier, since this would have saved David from a great deal of unnecessary suffering.

The Walters' situation was not unlike numerous other instances of child abuse that occur in many communities. With professional help, it is often possible to rehabilitate the family. At first Mr. Walters was angry and shocked that he was being accused of abusing his child, whom he claimed he loved dearly. After discussions with professionals at the child protection agency, he realized that he was indeed abusing his son. With proper treatment, he was gradually able to control his emotions and set more realistic expectations for his son's behavior. Parents who abuse their children are frequently unable to help themselves, and need professional assistance. Reporting child abuse is important. If you suspect child abuse either in your own family or among friends or neighbors, do not hesitate to contact your local child protection agency or police department.

Parents who occasionally feel that it is necessary to spank, and who do so without applying power or pressure enough to harm or bruise the child physically, and don't keep this up too long, needn't be concerned about child abuse. On the other hand, parents who use too much force or use potentially dangerous objects when employing physical forms of punishment, and afterward (either that day or the next) notice bruises, welts, cuts, or scratches on their child's body as a result, should immediately realize—or be shown—that they have punished their child too severely.

Depriving a child of emotional or physical stimulation is also a form of child abuse. Parents who temporarily withhold their love and affection by showing disapproval in order to teach their child a lesson in obeying rules, do not have to worry that they are harming their child. On the other hand, parents who regularly withhold their love and affection for extended periods of time, isolate a child in a locked closet, or prevent a child from having any social contact in order to punish her, are also abusing their child. As a result of such deprivation, a child may be psychologically, socially, and intellectually scarred.

Mrs. Nuland, a twenty-eight-year-old homemaker and mother of an active toddler named Lester, was having marital problems that resulted in her abusing her son. Mr. Nuland was rarely home at night because of his business schedule, and this upset her greatly. She suspected that he was not really spending time at the office, but was having an affair. Her anxiety was further heightened because her sexual relationship with her husband had been very inadequate over the past two months.

As a result of her preoccupation with personal tensions, she was much less tolerant of Lester's normal exploratory nature, constant motion, and persistent demands for her time and attention. She reacted by punishing him excessively for what would be considered acceptable behavior during this stage. Whenever Lester got on her nerves, she would lock him in a hall closet and force him to remain there by himself, for several hours at a time. Situations like this in which she isolated and ignored him were occurring almost every day.

Her concern about her difficulties in controlling Lester luckily outweighed her embarrassment in talking to others about her problem. She had the good sense to discuss her discipline problems with other parents. They appeared shocked when she told them that she had been locking her son in a closet and indicated that this was an inappropriate form of punishment. Putting a child in a dark, isolated room for hours at a time is a very severe form of punishment. Mrs. Nuland finally realized this, but said that she thought this punishment was less severe than spanking her child.

As a result of these discussions, Mrs. Nuland also realized that Lester's activities were far from abnormal. With her friends' help, she became aware that she had been overreacting to her child's behavior, and treating it as if it were a problem. She also recognized that her anxieties and preoccupation with her marital problems were interfering with her judgment and ability to manage her son appropriately.

By discussing their marital problems together, this couple was able to improve their relationship. Mrs. Nuland learned from her spouse that her fear that he was having an affair was unfounded. Once Mr. Nuland recognized her strong desire to have him home during the evenings, he arranged his work schedule to spend more time at home. As her marital problems lessened, Mrs. Nuland felt less tense during the day, and was better able to discipline her son. She learned to use other more acceptable forms of management. Thus, the Nulands were very fortunate.

Every parent should be familiar with the topic of child abuse, even though it is an unpleasant subject. It is tragic when a young child, who has no control over her environment or choice of parents, is battered and possibly "scarred" for life. If you find that you are using excessive physical punishment, or have strong urges to inflict pain upon your child, stop and re-examine both your reasons for punishment, and what is happening in your life that might prompt these feelings. Talk to your physician if you think that you have or feel you are at risk of abusing your child. Your knowledge of the subject of child abuse should also alert you to the crucial, and possibly life-saving importance of reporting suspected instances of abuse. It is hoped that public awareness of this serious problem will help diminish the incidence of child abuse.

ENJOYING PRIVACY WITH YOUR SPOUSE

A couple will want to be alone together at times; this is necessary to keep their relationship alive and satisfying. Working toward maintaining closeness, intimacy, and open communication is often hard to manage with an active toddler in the house. Once your child is walking, talking, and getting into everything, it may become harder to sneak away to a place where you and your partner can have some privacy and some intimate moments together. Your child will probably follow you around the house, making constant demands for your attention and affection. A toddler can sometimes be an intruder, not through any fault of her own. She generally wants to be the center of attention and is not aware of the difference between the type of relationship that her parents share and the relationship that they have with her. The toddler's strong, constant bids for attention and affection are normal.

As Mr. Banet put it:

Every time Meg and I would try to hug and kiss one another on the living room couch, my son Dougy would climb all over us. He was jealous of the attention Meg and I paid to each other, and the only time she and I could be really alone was after dark behind closed doors. Even at mealtimes, it was impossible for either of us to talk without Dougy interrupting us. I really began to resent the fact that Dougy was interfering with my relationship with Meg.

There are times when nearly every couple wishes they could be alone again—just the two of them, the way it was before they had a child. These occasional feelings are very natural, and not something about which you need to be ashamed.

A loss of privacy occurs from the day you bring your child into your home, although it usually becomes an issue of greater significance once your child is able to walk. When parents feel a loss of privacy in matters related to interpersonal communication or to sex, this can become a problem. Once communication between partners breaks down, chances are that their sexual relationship will suffer.

Spending Time Alone Is Important

There are several things you can do to ensure that you and your partner have more privacy, without severely restricting your child's freedom. One approach is to arrange your child's schedule so that she is occupied when the two of you want to be left alone. For example, if you really feel the need for a quiet mealtime two nights a week, you could arrange to feed your child ahead of time, and put her to bed before you eat.

Still another approach is to institute or join a baby-sitting co-operative with neighbors, or arrange to leave your child in someone else's care occasionally. You can even drop her off at the baby-sitter's house and return home to enjoy privacy. Taking a short vacation without your child, even for a day or a weekend getaway is also a way to spend time alone.

Making love with a third person in the home can affect people in different ways. Some parents find it inhibiting. They worry that the sounds may be overheard by their child, and they therefore strain to control themselves. These parents may not feel free to let loose because they fear that the child will come barging into the room at any time. Other parents find that the presence of a third person in the house adds an element of secretiveness and excitement to their sex life.

Concerns About the Child Walking In

Once their child can walk, parents often worry about the possibility of their toddler or young child walking in on them. This is not an everyday occurrence, but is definitely a possibility when parents do not lock the door to their bedroom.

Carol Blake, the mother of two-year-old Peter, talked about a recent incident during which Peter walked into her bedroom while she and her husband, Ralph, were making love. According to this mother:

One evening Ralph and I were both really in the mood to make love. After putting Peter to bed, we made our way to our bedroom, closed the door behind us, and began to make love. Just then the door opened and in walked Peter. My first reaction was one of shock and guilt. I felt like a child who was caught doing something I shouldn't have been doing. I apologized to Peter, jumped up from the bed, and asked him to please go back to bed.

Later, I felt very angry at myself for reacting the way I did. Was there any reason for me to feel guilty about having sex with my husband, or wanting some privacy? Obviously, the answer was no. There was no need for me to feel like I had to apologize to Peter for my behavior. He should learn to respect my need for privacy. Even after I resolved the question of privacy in my mind, however, I wondered if Peter would in some way be very confused by what he saw.

A young child cannot be blamed and should not be reprimanded for walking into her parents' unlocked bedroom while they are making love. Many parents allow their children to move freely in and out of their rooms, but a child cannot be expected to *know* when her parents need privacy; she must be taught. Toddlers and preschool children tend to get into every room in their homes, even when doors are closed. The only way to assure your privacy is to lock the doors to rooms you do not want her to enter. It is worth while establishing certain firm rules about when your child may or may not enter your room.

When a child enters her parents' room while they are having intercourse, there is a good chance that they will be embarrassed and unsure of what to say. This is understandable. There is no need, however, to make apologies for your behavior, or take a defensive stance. If you feel like being more direct and telling your child to "please leave right now," that would probably be better than apologizing, but it is advisable to guard against making her feel rejected or very uncomfortable.

To avoid leaving your child feeling confused or upset, you could give her some explanation of your actions, either immediately or later on that night or the next day. Since you know your child best, you will be a good judge of how to tell her and how much information to offer. A preschool child will require a more sophisticated explanation than a toddler, since she is not ready for details and facts about sex that might confuse or upset her.

You might center your explanation around the fact that when a married couple love each other very much, they like to be close physically, and this involves kissing, hugging, and touching one another's bodies. A simple explanation such as this will probably be sufficient to satisfy the child's curiosity. In case she wants to know more, you can offer further information, keeping in mind the difficulty a young child has in comprehending feelings and facts related to sex.

From the Young Child's Perspective

Those parents who are inclined to make noise while having sex should recognize that the vocalizations and/or movements might be interpreted by a young child as indications that you are fighting or physically hurting one another. Therefore, it is advisable to be somewhat discreet in your sexual practices, for your child's benefit, and for your own. You could move your child to a room as far away from yours as possible, or soundproof your walls, but these suggestions are difficult to implement for most people. Parents usually decide that it makes more sense to wait to make love until after they are certain that their child is asleep.

A young child can become confused and upset if she associates making love or being intimate with aggressive noises or movements. To avoid problems, it is best to get into the habit of locking the door to your room at night, or whenever you generally make love.

HOW TO STIMULATE YOUR CHILD'S MIND

Your child's capabilities will expand enormously during toddlerhood, enabling you to broaden the scope of her over-all education. She has a driving curiosity, and wants to learn, test things out by herself, and become a competent person. One of your major responsibilities during this stage will be to help satisfy her curiosity and see to it that she has sufficient opportunities to learn.

This section applies for Toddlerhood 1, 2, and 3. There are obvious differences in abilities when comparing a child in Toddlerhood 1 with a child in Toddlerhood 3. In reading the topics and suggestions that follow, you will notice that some are more appropriate for the young toddler, and others more well suited to the older toddler. Judge for yourself when to introduce certain activities and ideas depending upon your child's capabilities, needs, and preferences. This section highlights the major areas that you should consider in developing your own educational program.

The guidelines offered will foster closeness between you and your child, and support her natural desire to learn. Helping your child receive a positive, informal educational experience in the home will not only be rewarding for you, but will provide her with the foundation for future development and learning.

Stimulating Curiosity

Your toddler's boundless curiosity will propel her to touch, taste, smell, listen, and look at her surroundings. It is this curiosity that underlies her strong drive to explore and experiment. Help your child by conveying to her that it is good to be curious and that you are enthusiastic about her adventures in learning. You can also provide her with an interesting area in which to play. It should contain a wide variety of sounds, sights, and objects that can be manipulated, piled, and moved.

Teaching About the Properties of Objects

During the child's second year, as described in the Intellectual Development sections, objects begin to have more permanent qualities for her. She becomes able to find toys and objects even when she did not see them being hidden. She will also begin to follow them through a sequence of displacements in space. One way in which you can help reinforce your child's realization that objects are permanent is by playing games in which you hide objects and then ask her to find them. Your toddler will be manipulating a variety of objects in your house. Provide her with opportunities that will enable her to learn about the properties and permanent qualities of objects.

Early in toddlerhood, before the concept of object permanence has fully emerged, your toddler is likely to have more difficulty finding objects that you hide. She will also be slow in getting objects for you. Several months later, if you observe her interactions with objects and play hide-and-seek games with her, you will be aware that the concept of object permanence is being more firmly established. Hide-and-seek games and discussions about the qualities of objects, such as color, shape, and size, will usually be of great interest to her in Toddlerhood 3.

Encouraging Exploration and Experimentation

Through her explorations your child will be building up sensori-motor experiences that are necessary to lay the foundation for the emergence of higher modes of thinking. Many psychologists feel that the more sensori-motor experience a child has during the first year and a half of life, the greater will be her opportunity to develop intellectually. Whether or not this is completely true is a controversial point. However, it is advisable for you to encourage your child's exploration by providing her with a safe play area in which to master new skills and make new discoveries. This is the first step in the development of her thinking process.

HOW TO PROMOTE EARLY THINKING

It is usually during the latter part of toddlerhood that early forms of thinking emerge. Your child will start to manipulate symbols and ideas in her mind. She will gradually begin to solve simple problems, and think about possible actions and their results before making any moves. This significant change in her ability to think will enable you to take a more active role in fostering her intellectual development.

Providing your child with opportunities to accumulate a wide variety of sensori-motor experiences is the first step. Now you can go one step further and help her more fully to understand these experiences, make associations and generalizations, and learn the words (symbols) for objects that she sees. This can be accomplished by offering her explanations about things, and answering her questions.

When she comes to you wanting to know something, be enthusiastic. This will encourage her to ask more questions. Bear in mind that in Toddlerhood 1 and 2 her questions may not necessarily be verbal in nature. She will make inquiries through facial expressions and body language. Become aware of her interests and talk to her about them. This will expand her knowledge and demonstrate your enthusiasm. As she becomes more verbal, give her simple, but complete answers that will help her learn, not just "yes" or "no," or one-sentence answers. Don't give her the impression that you'd rather not be bothered.

Another way to help her learn from her experiences and become aware of concepts is to talk to her about the activities that you engage in together. When she's watching you work, shop, or even relax, tell her something about what you're doing, and the purposes behind your actions. Early in toddlerhood she may have trouble understanding even your simple explanations, but this is no reason not to offer them to her. Hearing you speak to her is helpful in stimulating her language abilities and desire to communicate. It is also a way of making her feel important. Later in toddlerhood you will notice that she will be more responsive to your verbal stimulation, and may begin to interact with you, using a few words of her own.

When you talk to her each day, you can help her develop an understanding of time, space, and cause and effect relationships. Try to help her learn about time relationships by saying things like, "Daddy will take you for a ride in the car after dinner," or, "Let's finish up our household chores this morning so that this afternoon we can go to the playground." Pointing out sequences of events in your daily activities will gradually increase her awareness of time. Repeating these kinds of explanations during the course of the day, or from one day to the next, will assist her in learning about this concept. Slowly she will realize that certain activities follow others during the day. She may be able to anticipate dinnertime by going to the table when she sees you putting out place mats, if you regularly do that just before dinner.

You can help her recognize spatial relationships by talking about them. As you attempt to park your car, you could say, "Our big car will never fit into this small parking space, so we'll have to find a larger parking space somewhere else." When playing together on the floor with measuring cups, you can call attention to the fact that "The small cup will fit inside of the large cup, but the large cup cannot fit inside of the smaller cup, because it's too big and there isn't enough space." These kinds of casual comments will enrich her daily activities.

Cause and effect relationships can also be pointed out. When you go to turn out the light, point out to her that when you move the switch the light goes off. Taking her for a drive, you can explain to her that when you turn the key the car will start. Keep your explanations at the simplest level.

Grouping objects according to their similar properties is a fun way to stimulate your child. Wherever you are, you can point out how objects are similar. For instance, you can tell her that an apple and an orange are fruits, a pancake and a pizza are both round and flat, and string beans and lettuce are both vegetables. This activity is much more effective when directed at the objects that she sees and interacts with every day.

It is important to emphasize that her ability to deal with the concepts of time, space, cause and effect, size, shape, color, and so on, is very limited. You should not expect her to grasp these concepts fully during toddlerhood. The development sections discuss the gradual progress that she is making in this area. Your explanations at this stage will mainly provide an enjoyable way to interact with her and help build a foundation for her future understanding of these concepts.

HELPING YOUR CHILD DEVELOP HER INTERESTS

Every individual has his or her own special interests. As you spend time with your toddler, you will notice the things which seem to attract her attention. Many younger toddlers focus on investigating their surroundings, practicing new physical abilities, and interacting with and watching their parents. Older toddlers appear to have similar interests, although new ones may arise. They often show interest in speaking, developing their manual skills, playing with toys, being around other children, using blocks and other materials to make "creations," watching television, and using their new elementary powers of imagination in make-believe play activities.

You will not only observe your child's general interest patterns, but will also discover that she has one or more favorite pastimes. It is important for you to respect your child's interests and encourage them. There are many ways in which you can let her know that you are enthusiastic about her preferences. Try to engage her in activities which will enable her to build upon them and expand them. If she likes to play with letters, you can provide her with printed material so that she can point to various letters, serve her alphabet soup, or buy her lettered blocks. A child's interest in small, movable objects, such as trucks, can be supported by buying her several trucks, pointing them out while riding in the car, talking to her about them, and reading her a simple story about them at bedtime.

It would be a mistake to concentrate solely or too heavily on one particular preference to the neglect of other important interests. Maintain a healthy balance in your child's total educational program, and encourage her general and specific interests.

HOW TO FOSTER VERBAL ABILITIES

Teaching Through Talking

The significance of talking to your child as often as possible was emphasized in infancy. Talking often both to and with her continues to be of prime importance. A child who has been exposed to conversation is more likely to be encouraged to develop her language skills to their fullest potential. Your child learns to speak by listening to others, imitating them, and practicing her new abilities.

Encouraging Imitation of Words and Sounds

Your toddler will be very interested in imitating your words, as well as sounds that she hears in her environment. Perhaps the best way to encourage her to imitate your words and sentences is to reinforce positively her efforts in that direction. Smiling, giving her a joyful hug, or a few words of praise may be all the encouragement that she needs. You can also promote imitation by saying a word, telling her to repeat it, and then saying the same word again.

Word imitation games will not only be fun for your toddler, they will also help her develop language skills. Through these games she will be exposed to many new words. Language games encourage children to learn new words, and offer them immediate feedback as to whether or not they are pronouncing words properly.

Teaching That People and Objects Have Names

One of the most effective ways to foster the development of language is to teach your toddler the names of objects that she sees in her surroundings, and the names of people with whom she interacts. This can be done anywhere and at any time. In addition to telling her the names of objects and people, you can also label their properties. For example, when you hand her a new stuffed animal, you might say to her, "Here is a big, cuddly brown Teddy bear for you to play with"; or if you are handing her an apple, you might say, "Here is a red, shiny apple." You can point out colors or concentrate on shapes and sizes. Once your child starts speaking, you can point to various objects and encourage her to tell you their names. You can also ask her to tell you the colors of different objects.

Knowing the names for objects and their properties will give your toddler word power. It will enable her to express her feelings and ideas to others more easily, and will also foster her ability to think. During the latter part of toddlerhood, and the early preschool years, your child will be trying to learn the names of many objects and will be increasingly able to manipulate these symbols in her mind. By teaching her that people and objects have names, you will not only be increasing her word power, but you will also be increasing her thinking power.

Reading to Your Child Can Be Enjoyable

Reading to your child is a good way to stimulate language development. If she is enthusiastic about your reading to her, by all means carry on. Begin with simple stories about people and experiences she can relate to, and also make up stories in which her name is used.

As your older toddler or preschool child listens to stories, she may enjoy looking at pictures, naming them, and asking questions about the characters or events. She is likely to want you to repeat the same story until you are bored to tears with it. Her continued fascination with the same stories indicates that repetition is important for her. Through such repetition, her familiarity with specific ideas, the over-all meaning, and sound patterns will increase. There are many good books written especially for this age child. Always try to pick stories to suit her interests and her level of understanding.

Young children sometimes have a hard time sitting still while their parents read. They may also seem bored or disinterested. A child who either cannot or does not want to sit still and listen to stories should not be forced to do so. Such a youngster may prefer hearing short poems, rhymes, or jingles.

Books are not the only source of reading material. You can read to her from magazines, picture catalogues, and food packages. Whenever you venture outside your home, you can tell her what the signs and billboards say. All of these activities should stimulate her interest in words and language. They should also be fun for you and her.

The Magic of Learning Through Sound

There are additional ways to provide your toddler with auditory stimulation. You can turn on the radio, allow her to listen to children's records, give her or make simple musical instruments, and attempt to teach her simple children's songs and nursery rhymes. Encourage her to listen to ordinary sounds such as the rustling of leaves, footsteps, ticking of a clock, opening and closing of doors, sounds of traffic, and ringing of church bells. Her awareness of sounds and her interest in listening to them is an important aspect of language development.

HOW TO TEACH YOUR CHILD TO LISTEN AND FOLLOW DIRECTIONS

It is important for your child to develop listening skills and the ability to follow directions. Providing her with auditory stimulation, such as described above, will draw her attention to sounds. A good way to encourage her to listen to what you have to say is to speak slowly and distinctly. Use language that is appropriate for or slightly above her level of understanding. Emphasize important words and use hand gestures and actions to get your message across. If you want her to close the back door, you can say, "Milly, please *shut* the *door now*," while you point to it and take a step or two in the direction of the door.

Playing games in which you ask her to do various tasks will also assist her in learning to follow directions. Ask her to shut the door, open the door, bring you your shoes, put her toy away where it belongs, dance, say a word, bend at the waist, put her truck under the chair, and so on. When she is able to follow simple, one-task directions, try increasing the number of tasks to two toward the end of toddlerhood. You might tell her to put a napkin on top of the table and then put it on her lap. Once she has mastered many two-task directions, gradually increase the number of tasks even further. These types of games will help give her practice in listening and following directions. They will enable you to observe the development of her understanding of language, and her ability to hold more than one idea in her head at one time.

HOW TO ENCOURAGE PHYSICAL DEVELOPMENT

One of the most important things you can do to encourage your child's physical development is to offer her freedom to move around in safe territory. A toddler needs space in which to walk, run, and explore. She will desperately want to exercise and practice her new locomotor abilities until she has become adept at them. It is not advisable to restrain her or restrict her movements except for certain occasions in which it is absolutely necessary. Make sure that her clothing does not restrict her possibilities for movement. Arrange your home and your yard so that she has opportunities to move around freely. This will also help her build self-confidence.

Equipment to Promote Large-muscle Development

Another way in which to promote physical development is to give your toddler access to play equipment designed to foster the development of large muscles. This category of equipment includes items such as a low jungle gym, large blocks, and balls. More information about appropriate equipment for toddlers is given in the play section(s) on pages 498–99. You can also play simple games, such as tag, that encourage movement. These pleasurable activities will also give opportunities to put her new gross motor abilities to good use.

Equipment to Foster Small-muscle Development

You should see that your toddler has ample opportunities to practice using her small muscles. Children frequently love to work with their hands. Materials such as wooden blocks, very simple puzzles, and raisins will serve as fun toys to play with and manipulate, using her hands and fingers. You can also show her how to turn pages of a magazine or book. She will want to practice picking up and releasing objects. Observe her at play, and you will see that she often repetitively picks up and drops objects. Through these activities she will be learning how to co-ordinate her eyes and the fine movements of her hands. Further suggestions for equipment and activities can be found on pages 499–500.

HOW TO PROMOTE SELF-AWARENESS, SOCIAL SENSITIVITY, AND SELF-WORTH

Reinforcing Feelings of Individuality and Self-esteem

Your child will be clarifying for herself and you that she is a unique and independent person. She will be making a sharper distinction between what is "her" and "not her." Knowing that she will be working hard to achieve greater independence, you should be supportive of her efforts and respect her emerging individuality, even if the way she goes about it is not always to your liking.

There are many ways in which you can help her to realize more fully that she is an individual. One way to increase her self-awareness is to teach her the names for parts of her body. Show her how her body is similar to yours, but also separate and different from yours. Another way is to support her efforts to do things by and for herself. Allow her to assume more independence in dressing, eating, and bathing, without undue interference. Doing this will foster her feeling of self-reliance and self-sufficiency. Also grant her freedom to learn that her actions can affect the environment.

To increase her awareness that she is a separate person who counts, allow her to make simple choices and decisions. The younger toddler has not had much practice in making decisions. She is likely to have difficulty making them. The older toddler will be more capable of choosing between two alternatives. You might ask your child whether she wants to wear blue pants or yellow pants, whether she wants a hot dog or a hamburger for lunch, or whether she wants to play indoors or outdoors. It is possible to give many choices in the course of a day's time. These choices may not really matter to you but will make her feel as if her opinions are important.

Promoting Self-expression

An older toddler's rebellion and testing behavior need to be expressed. You should allow your child freedom, within reasonable limits, to express negativism. Negativism in toddlerhood is a normal, positive sign. By giving your child some leeway to rebel against your wishes and oppose your commands, you will be helping her realize that she is an independent individual. This is not to suggest that you give up your control and authority as parents. Occasionally allowing her to "win" when the two of you are "battling it out" over a trivial matter will fortify her feelings of self-esteem and independence.

Teaching About Property Ownership and the Rights of Others

Part of your toddler's task of separating herself from the environment involves becoming aware of what belongs to her and what doesn't. She has a lot to learn about property ownership and rights. You can help her acquire a better ability to distinguish her own belongings from items that belong to others. One way to assist in this is to name various objects such as articles of clothing and other personal possessions. Point to them or pick them up, as you tell your toddler to whom they belong. Pick up her shoes, for instance, and say, "These are Carla's shoes." Then pick up her father's shoes and say, "These are Daddy's shoes." Also teach her the words "his," "hers," "yours," "my," and "mine."

Labeling objects with her name can help you teach her property ownership. You can write her name on certain toys, boxes, cabinets, or bookshelves which you have filled with "her" objects and playthings. Name tags can help her to keep better track of what is hers. Although her sense of ownership will be emerging more clearly during toddlerhood, it will not be well developed for quite some time. During the preschool years she may occasionally take something that doesn't belong to her, and may appear to "forget" the lessons you have taught. You should be willing to repeat lessons in what *does* and *doesn't* belong to her and tolerate her forgetfulness. It will take a long time before she develops a definite sense of property rights.

Helping Build Self-confidence

Toddlerhood is a prime time for you to help your child feel self-confident and important. It is crucial for a young child to develop self-esteem. By setting reasonable expectations for her behavior, she will be able to meet and master many tasks more successfully. If you set expectations far beyond her capabilities, her inability to meet them can contribute to feelings of self-doubt, frustration, and inferiority.

Your praise and recognition of both small and large accomplishments will also foster a sense of personal pride in achievement as well as a sense of being a competent person. She will be pleased when you compliment her on a job well done. You can smile or nod your head in approval when she puts forth a good effort to finish a task. When she has difficulty with a task or fails, a few sympathetic words from you and a hug will convey the message that you still love and support her, even when the "chips are down."

It is also important for you to give her as much independence in certain areas as she shows that she is capable of handling. Eating is an area in which youngsters often wish to assert themselves. A young toddler who displays a strong desire to feed herself with her fingers should be given some opportunities to do so. Later in toddlerhood you can arrange her room to foster self-sufficiency. This will assist her in successfully learning to master new skills. Low bookshelves and hooks in the closet will make it much easier for her to put away her toys and hang up her clothes. By helping her learn to assume some responsibility for her own care and belongings, she will develop a sense of pride in mastering new tasks. Teaching simple activities that she can see to completion will build her self-confidence. Be patient and supportive when helping her learn new skills. Given enough time, she will be successful.

Teaching Social Skills

The ability to communicate effectively with people, get along with others, and develop rewarding friendships are not just inherited. They must be learned. Many of these social skills are acquired during early childhood, although they will be further refined throughout your child's lifetime. You will be instrumental in helping her acquire these important social skills, since she will spend a great deal of time with you.

The kind of relationship that you establish with her, and the patterns of interaction that you encourage and discourage will greatly influence her development of social skills. There is no one best way to teach her social skills. Your spontaneous and natural interaction with her and her contact with other people will comprise a large part of her social education. Allowing her to socialize with your relatives and friends on casual visits, weekends, or holiday get-togethers will broaden her exposure to other people. Her social education will not only stem from her firsthand experiences. It will also be enhanced by her observations of how people interact with each other. To help stimulate your imagination in the various ways in which you will be fostering her social development, the following ideas are provided.

- Enable her to express her feelings and emotions spontaneously.
- Be affectionate toward her and encourage her to be affectionate to you.
- Respond to her genuine needs for assistance.
- Provide opportunities for her to meet and spend time with other people.
- Teach her basic social graces, such as saying "hello," "good-bye," "please," "thank you," and other simple phrases.
- Gradually educate her to be able to adapt to other people's wishes, wait, take turns, and share.

Learning to express feelings, and get along with other people is a slow, continuous process. You should not expect too much from your toddler, since she is just in the beginning stage of developing her social abilities. Despite her limitations, it is important to recognize that during this stage she will be acquiring fundamental social skills and attitudes about people.

Being natural and relaxed with your child, and truly enjoying the time you spend together, will enable you to continue to develop special lines of communication with her. These rewarding social interchanges between you and her will be invaluable in helping her learn to derive pleasure from interacting with you. This positive feeling that she has toward you will then be generalized to others with whom she comes into contact.

Providing Peer-contact

Although the younger toddler is not likely to be very interested in other children her age, the older toddler will be more social and interested in her peers. During

Toddlerhood 2 and 3, it is advisable to allow her to play with children in your neighborhood, or take her regularly to a park, a playground, the beach, or anywhere else where there are opportunities for her to play with contemporaries. You may even wish to get together with other parents and form a play group of your own. See page 656 for a discussion of play groups. Do not forget that when children of this age are playing together they need close and effective adult supervision.

Teaching by Setting an Example

Your toddler's interest in and willingness to imitate your behavior will be of great assistance in teaching her about herself, other people, and how to function in life. Imitation is a tool for teaching, so take advantage of it by helping her learn how to dress, feed, wash, and groom herself. Through imitation, especially in Toddlerhood 3, you can help her slowly learn to perform many simple household chores such as putting away toys and setting the table. Imitation can also be valuable in promoting language learning, learning how to interact with and get along with other people, and learning self-control. Your child in Toddlerhood 1 probably won't imitate you at every turn, but by Toddlerhood 3, imitation will be very prominent and much more accurate.

The importance of setting a good example to follow cannot be overemphasized. Your child will be quick to copy both your virtues and your vices. If you are rude to other people, generous in your use of four-letter words, and have trouble controlling your aggressive or violent impulses, you will see this behavior reflected in hers. Your behavior will influence hers whether it is good or bad. You cannot expect her to ignore your "bad" side and imitate only your "good" side. This is not to imply that you should be paranoid about what aspects of your behavior your child will be mimicking or that you should change your personality or behavior patterns. However, you should be aware of the fact that you are the primary model for your child. The example you set will influence her behavior, both now and in the future.

HOW TO TEACH SELF-CONTROL

Setting Firm, Clear, and Consistent Limits

Your toddler needs freedom to express her feelings and explore your home, but she also needs firm, definite limits and clear guidelines for how to behave in an acceptable manner. For her own good, you must establish such boundaries, and be prepared to enforce them with punishment when she ventures beyond the boundaries and breaks rules. You should be very firm and not back down, but, at the same time, you should guard against making her feel inferior, and causing her to lose face. The Discipline sections offer numerous suggestions for managing your toddler and helping her learn the difference between acceptable and unacceptable behavior.

Promoting Love-oriented Discipline

It is important to remember that the kind of relationship that you establish with your toddler will influence how difficult or easy it will be for you to discipline her.

Try to maintain a positive, satisfying relationship with your child. Her love and respect for you will motivate her to care about what you think of her. By showing her in countless ways that you love her and respect her autonomy, chances are that she'll strive to live up to your expectations, which should be realistic, and try to follow your directions and rules without feeling resentful or antagonistic toward you.

Limiting No's and Don'ts

A child who is constantly bombarded by her parent's "No's" and "Don'ts" is likely to ignore them. She may stop exploring and lose interest in many activities. It is advisable to limit your "No's" and "Don'ts," and use these words only for important things, and when you really mean them.

Utilizing Environmental Discipline

In handling your toddler, you may find that she responds much better to environmental discipline than she does to verbal discipline. Environmental discipline involves arranging your home to make managing her easier. Put locks, gates, and other kinds of barrier devices to work for you. How to use this effective technique is discussed in detail on page 531.

Initiating Manners Training

Although you cannot expect too much from the child in Toddlerhood 1 and 2 in regard to having good manners, toddlerhood is a time to begin teaching manners slowly. As part of your early training program, she can be taught to wipe her mouth and hands after eating. Once she is able to talk, teach her to say "please" and "thank you," but realize that some prompting from you will be necessary. Manners are acquired over a long period of time. Once they are learned, they become an important, natural part of a child's dealing with other people.

Giving Responsibilities in the Home

Your toddler can be given certain minimal responsibilities in your home. You can, for instance, encourage her to help you put away the groceries and also her toys when she's through playing with them. As an older toddler, she can also run simple errands for you inside the home and assist you in straightening the house. Early involvement in these household chores can help give your child a sense of responsibility and pride in accomplishing simple tasks.

HOW TO TEACH RESPECT FOR OTHER PEOPLE

Even though the toddler is a bit too young for explanations about respecting other people and their differences, it is important for you to set a good example for her. Toddlers can easily pick up on derogatory slang words for religious, racial, and ethnic groups, and then repeat them. They can also sense how their parents interact with people who are in some way different. You should realize the value of not passing your prejudices on to your child by teaching her a positive respect for others and their differences at an early age. See pages 935–37 for further suggestions.

HOW TO DEVELOP PRACTICAL SKILLS

Teaching Household Tasks

There are several simple household tasks that you can begin to teach your older toddler. Gradually show her how to open and close cabinet doors and drawers properly, help you set the table, help dry plastic dishes and bowls, assist in dusting large pieces of furniture and helping around the yard. Roger, a twenty-seven-month-old toddler, derived great pleasure from sweeping up leaves with his toy broom, right next to his father who was cleaning up the yard. Although Roger was not a skilled worker, he was having fun and learning a new job.

Such opportunities to develop their manual skills also give children a chance to learn practical things. It also helps them learn important lessons in orderliness and cleanliness and understand that there is a proper way to approach and complete a task. Once your child has mastered these simple skills, she will feel very proud of herself, and her successes will boost her self-esteem.

Teaching Basic Care

Toddlers begin to want to assume more independence in the basic care areas. They may be quite adamant about doing many things by and for themselves. To help your child gradually take over some responsibility for her own care and needs, you should show her the correct way to perform simple basic care tasks such as buttoning large buttons, zipping zippers, buckling buckles, washing and drying her hands, fastening snaps, feeding herself with a spoon and later a fork, and brushing her teeth and hair. The younger toddler will have much greater difficulty with these tasks than the older toddler of two and a half, but she can still be shown how to do them and given opportunities to practice. She may think that learning these jobs is great fun, since she'll be better able to emulate you.

Many of these activities will help your child develop eye-hand co-ordination and manual control. Since a toddler's hand and finger skills are not well developed, you should not expect her to be proficient at these tasks. It is advisable to go very slowly, and break each job down into small successive steps. Let her have unlimited opportunities to practice. When she has completely mastered the first step, this will give her a sense of accomplishment. Then you can show her the next step. Teaching in this manner, one step at a time, ensures that she will be successful. Her own pride over each small success will motivate her to continue. The feelings of happiness and pride that will be experienced when she learns how to take over some of the responsibility for eating, dressing, grooming, and so forth, will make the time and effort that you expend well worth it.

HOW TO EDUCATE YOUR TODDLER
ABOUT HEALTH CARE AND SAFETY

Teaching Your Toddler to Be Safety-conscious

Toddlerhood is an excellent time to begin teaching your child how to avoid danger, and handle herself in a responsible manner to prevent unnecessary accidents from occurring. A well-disciplined child who is able to follow instructions is usually a safer child. The objective of early training in accident prevention is not to make your toddler fearful of her surroundings. It is to prepare her to recognize and handle potentially dangerous objects and situations both now, and later when she goes out of your home and is away from you. Numerous suggestions for how to help her become safety-conscious are provided in the accident prevention section on pages 510–12.

Although you may not see her making rapid progress as a result of your educational program, don't stop trying. It takes a long time, and added maturity, before these kinds of lessons can be fully learned. Remember that your toddler is not capable of recognizing dangers or protecting herself. This is your responsibility.

Teaching Cleanliness

Few parents would argue that it is important to teach a child cleanliness. Cleanliness not only refers to one's body, it also refers to one's home environment. Toddlers learn the value of being neat and clean in large part by observing their parents and imitating their behavior. A little boy who sees his father regularly wash his hands before eating and brush his teeth after each meal will probably mimic this behavior.

You can encourage your child to wipe her face and hands with a napkin when they are dirty. Try to teach her to avoid some unclean things at inappropriate times. Gradually instill in her the lesson that she wipe her messy shoes before entering your home. Let her assist you in cleaning house, and so on. Another way in which to teach about the value of cleanliness is to buy her a toy dustpan, mop, and broom set. She will enjoy imitating you as you sweep the floors, and indirectly learn the importance of keeping a clean house. Toddlers love messy activities such as playing with dirt and clay, but they should be taught that there are appropriate times and places for "messy" activities, and that in general cleanliness is important.

TEACHING RESPECT FOR THE ENVIRONMENT

Now is a good time to begin teaching your toddler to respect the environment. She can be taught not to litter. By placing empty soda cans or apple cores in a waste can when you're out on drives or on a picnic, you will be setting a good example for her to follow. If you see litter in the park, you might comment on the value of putting litter in appropriate receptacles so that the park will stay clean. Learning to respect our natural resources even at this early age can help instill in her an awareness of her environment.

You can also begin to help her develop an appreciation of nature by taking her on short hikes, walks around the neighborhood, or weekend camping trips. Encourage her to observe the colorful flowers, examine rocks, and admire the beautiful scenery. The wonders of nature provide free toys and experiences that will offer her pleasure as well as varied stimulation. If you appreciate nature and respect the environment, chances are that she will, too. See also pages 775–76.

HOW TO UTILIZE PLAY AS AN AVENUE FOR LEARNING

Through your toddler's play activities she will practice her abilities, exercise her body and her mind, and accumulate experiences. It is very important to offer her opportunities to engage in many different kinds of play activities, and keep them well balanced. By offering a well-rounded program of play, you will be fostering her over-all development. Numerous suggestions for play equipment and activities are provided in the Learning Through Play sections.

HOW TO TEACH USE OF THE TOILET

Toilet training represents one aspect of your total educational program. Suggestions for how to help your child gain control over her bowel and bladder functions, and learn to use the toilet are presented on pages 522–26.

HOW TO PROVIDE SEX EDUCATION

Conveying Attitudes About the Body

Your reactions to your child will influence the attitudes that she develops about her body and herself as a person. It is particularly important to convey positive messages to her at an early age, since this is part of sex education in a broad sense.

You do this in several different ways. One way is to give her positive feedback in order to help build self-confidence and self-pride. Another way is to teach the names for all external parts of the body in a natural way. Try to avoid making her feel guilty, bad, anxious, or dirty for expressing an interest in genitals or handling them. Instill in her a good feeling about herself, and a healthy, positive feeling about her body.

Shaping Attitudes About Relationships

Sex education also involves conveying to your toddler attitudes about non-sexual relationships between people of the same sex as well as those of the opposite sex. She will receive this subtle form of sex education through daily interactions with you and also with other family members. These early experiences are very important, since they will help shape her attitudes about relationships with other human beings. An extensive discussion of sex education during toddlerhood is presented in Toddlerhood 2 (pages 624–30).

HOW TO HELP YOUR TODDLER ADAPT TO NEW SITUATIONS

Coping with New Situations

It is not uncommon for young children to have at least some difficulty adjusting to strange people and places, particularly if their exposure to non-family members has been minimal during infancy. One way in which you can help your toddler get accustomed to being with strangers is to let her adjust to them at her own pace. In order to ease the transition from home to a strange environment, such as a waiting area in an office, it often helps if you bring along one or two of her favorite toys. Strange places may seem more inviting and less threatening when she has some familiar objects from home to bridge the gap. If you are not with her when she meets new people or is exposed to new situations, she may feel anxious and insecure. You can help her become more adaptive by remaining close to her when she meets strangers and is exposed to new experiences. With you nearby, she'll feel more secure and at ease, and will gradually begin to interact with strangers and investigate unfamiliar surroundings.

Helping Your Toddler Cope with Separation Anxiety

Separation anxiety often reaches a peak in some children during toddlerhood. With some toddlers it may simply have to run its natural course, although there are a few suggestions for helping your child cope with separations from you. Hide-and-seek games are sometimes helpful in showing that even when you leave her or she leaves you, you do not leave forever. Another way to help her cope with necessary brief separations is to prepare her in advance for your departure, reassure her that you'll be back, and then leave without hesitation. You cannot, nor should you, feel guilty about not being with her 100 percent of the time. She must learn that important fact of life. On the other hand, try to be understanding about her feelings, which are very real, for this too will help her deal with necessary separations from you and become more adaptive.

Helping Your Toddler Adjust to a New Member of the Family

Many adjustments will have to be made by your toddler upon the entry of a new baby into the family structure. She will eventually adapt to having a sibling, but whether she adjusts well or poorly, depends, in large part, upon how you handle the whole situation. Therefore, if you are expecting another child, we suggest that you reread pages 25–27 in Preparing for Parenthood, and also pages 177–79 in Infancy 1, where guidelines for helping your child adjust to a new sibling are presented.

FIELD TRIPS CAN BE FUN AND EDUCATIONAL

Short trips to various places in your community can be fun for both you and your toddler, and educational for her at the same time. Especially during the latter part of toddlerhood (Toddlerhood 3), you can plan all kinds of new adventures for her. The list of places that your toddler will enjoy visiting is virtually endless. Visits to the local butcher shop, zoo, farmer's market, police station, library, pet shop, shoe repair, fire station, airport, truck stop, and so on, will broaden her range of firsthand experiences, and will give you interesting source material for conversation.

Although a shoe repair shop or butcher store may not be exactly your idea of a delightful afternoon outing, remember that these places will be interesting to her. There she will see new things, hear different sounds, and meet new people. When you take her to various places, direct her attention to small details. Talk to her about what she sees and hears, and encourage her to ask questions or point to whatever captures her interest. These outings can greatly enrich her education.

THE NURSERY SCHOOL EXPERIENCE

Nursery school can be a useful addition to your own education program in the home. Most communities have excellent nursery school facilities. There is a great deal of variability in the ages at which parents send their children to nursery school. Nursery schools also differ in the lower age limit that they accept, but most do not take children under age three. For those of you who are interested in considering sending your child to nursery school during toddlerhood, read ahead to the discussion on pages 639, 814–18.

PREPARED PARENTHOOD CHECK LIST

MOTHER	FATHER	UNDERSTANDING YOUR TODDLER'S DEVELOPMENT
—	—	Have any new sources of friction developed between you and your toddler?
—	—	Is your child showing signs of wanting more independence in some areas?
—	—	Are you working at developing a good relationship with your child?
—	—	Have you made specific attempts to increase your toddler's self-confidence?
—	—	Can you see your toddler discovering new ways to solve problems through active trial and error experimentation?
—	—	Is your child's behavior becoming more purposeful?
—	—	Have you been offering your toddler plenty of opportunities to explore your home and interact with a wide assortment of ordinary household objects and toys?
—	—	Does your child try to imitate some of your behavior?
—	—	Have you observed your child's increased understanding of language?
—	—	In what ways are you trying to foster your child's language development?
—	—	What changes has your toddler's new walking ability brought about in her life? In yours?
—	—	Does your toddler want to be on the go constantly, practicing her new physical abilities?
—	—	Can you see more signs of co-ordinated motor activity?
—	—	Do you notice signs of your child's improving ability to release an object?
—	—	Are you offering your toddler ample opportunities to play by herself, with you, and with all kinds of playthings?
—	—	What are some of the important considerations in selecting toys for your toddler?
—	—	Does your child have a favorite plaything and activity?

BASIC CARE

—	—	What are the childhood illnesses that can be prevented by immunization during toddlerhood?
—	—	Are you familiar with some of the methods that make it easier to give your child medicines?

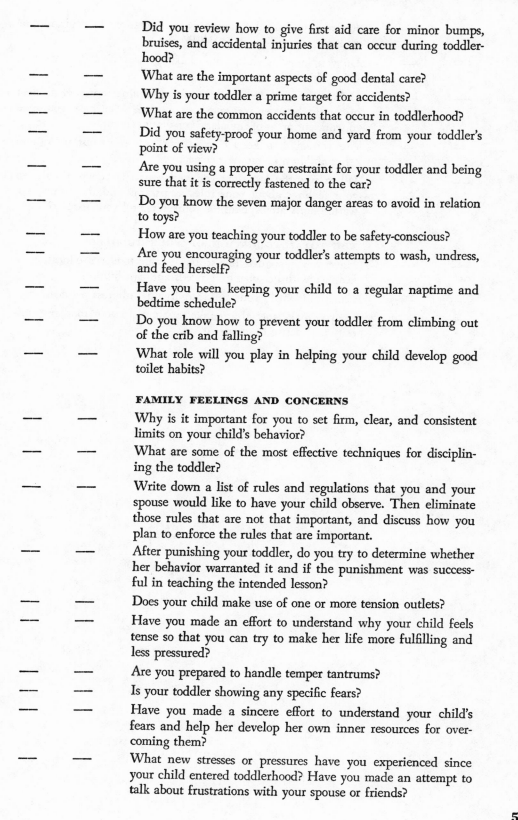

—— —— Did you review how to give first aid care for minor bumps, bruises, and accidental injuries that can occur during toddlerhood?

—— —— What are the important aspects of good dental care?

—— —— Why is your toddler a prime target for accidents?

—— —— What are the common accidents that occur in toddlerhood?

—— —— Did you safety-proof your home and yard from your toddler's point of view?

—— —— Are you using a proper car restraint for your toddler and being sure that it is correctly fastened to the car?

—— —— Do you know the seven major danger areas to avoid in relation to toys?

—— —— How are you teaching your toddler to be safety-conscious?

—— —— Are you encouraging your toddler's attempts to wash, undress, and feed herself?

—— —— Have you been keeping your child to a regular naptime and bedtime schedule?

—— —— Do you know how to prevent your toddler from climbing out of the crib and falling?

—— —— What role will you play in helping your child develop good toilet habits?

FAMILY FEELINGS AND CONCERNS

—— —— Why is it important for you to set firm, clear, and consistent limits on your child's behavior?

—— —— What are some of the most effective techniques for disciplining the toddler?

—— —— Write down a list of rules and regulations that you and your spouse would like to have your child observe. Then eliminate those rules that are not that important, and discuss how you plan to enforce the rules that are important.

—— —— After punishing your toddler, do you try to determine whether her behavior warranted it and if the punishment was successful in teaching the intended lesson?

—— —— Does your child make use of one or more tension outlets?

—— —— Have you made an effort to understand why your child feels tense so that you can try to make her life more fulfilling and less pressured?

—— —— Are you prepared to handle temper tantrums?

—— —— Is your toddler showing any specific fears?

—— —— Have you made a sincere effort to understand your child's fears and help her develop her own inner resources for overcoming them?

—— —— What new stresses or pressures have you experienced since your child entered toddlerhood? Have you made an attempt to talk about frustrations with your spouse or friends?

—— —— Are you aware of the important considerations in beginning or returning to work outside the home?

—— —— Do you know a child who is being abused? What are you doing about it?

—— —— Does sharing the responsibility for discipline represent an area of conflict between you and your spouse? What have you done to work out areas of imbalance or disagreement?

—— —— Are you able to keep comparisons between your child and other children in proper perspective?

—— —— When was the last time you and your spouse openly shared your feelings about your roles as parents and the value of a warm family atmosphere for yourselves and your toddler?

THE TOTAL EDUCATION OF YOUR TODDLER

—— —— Have you expanded the scope of your toddler's education to keep up with her changing needs and capabilities?

—— —— Can you identify your child's individual interest patterns?

—— —— Do you make special attempts to stimulate your toddler's curiosity and desire to learn?

Toddlerhood 2

PERSONAL-SOCIAL DEVELOPMENT

Getting to Know Your Toddler

The Toddlerhood 2 child is more independent than he was in Toddlerhood 1. Through his actions, the need and desire to do things by himself is made clearer to his parents. His increasing ability to assert himself and attempts to express his individuality can make handling him more complicated.

MOVING FURTHER ALONG THE ROAD TOWARD INDEPENDENCE. In a variety of contexts and situations, your toddler will demonstrate his need to assume greater independence. It will be hard for you to ignore or suppress his demands to take over some responsibility for doing things on his own.

Mrs. Schenker, the mother of eighteen-month-old Brandon, noticed her son's growing desire to become more independent at mealtimes. When she attempted to spoon-feed him, he would often take the spoon out of her hands, whine, and try to take over for himself. It was obvious to Mrs. Schenker that Brandon could not manage entirely on his own, but she refrained from immediately taking the spoon away from him since she respected his need to feel more grown-up.

After several minutes of struggling to spoon-feed himself, Brandon usually became frustrated and allowed his mother to feed him again. Occasionally, when she offered assistance he would refuse to accept her help. He did this by saying, "No, me do," and clutching the spoon tightly, making it impossible for her to take it from him.

Like most toddlers during this phase, Brandon was exercising his ability to assert himself. He was more insistent upon attempting to do things himself that his parents had previously done for him, despite his inability to do them as efficiently or quickly. This was his way of strengthening his individuality and sense of being a separate person.

BECOMING MORE OPINIONATED. Your child has been expressing likes and dislikes since early infancy, but now he will begin to express more definite ideas about many specific things. His greater awareness of his surroundings and his feelings of being separate from you set the stage for "little Mr. Opinionated." In no uncertain terms, he will voice his preferences for particular activities, toys, and foods.

His main focus of energy and attention centers around getting whatever he wants, and getting it immediately. He will express his demands more clearly and frequently than the Toddlerhood 1 child. Having his wishes and ideas acknowledged means a great deal to him, since this makes him feel as though he is important. He needs reassurance that he is entitled to have his say in matters that concern him, even though he cannot always have what he wants.

His ability to express his opinions far exceeds his ability to comprehend your reactions to his requests. If you refuse to satisfy his demands, ask him to postpone them, or ignore them, he will not understand the reasons for your behavior. As a result, he may become very frustrated and lose his temper. Coping with minor refusals and frustrations is extremely difficult for him due to his immature intellectual abilities and lack of self-control.

Even a benign suggestion that he do something a different way, or that he wait a moment, may be enough to arouse anger and frustration, and trigger a stubborn, antagonistic reaction. He may first tell you, "No," and then resist following your suggestion. This type of negative behavior is characteristic of your child's push for independence.

THE EXPANSION OF NEGATIVE BEHAVIOR. When the Toddlerhood 1 child learned to walk and began to recognize his own abilities, he took the initial steps toward greater independence. He began to demonstrate this through his occasional demanding, testing, and stubborn behavior. This independence was new to him, however, and he did not seem to feel entirely comfortable with it. His attempts to voice his separateness were probably not strongly or consistently expressed, since he was unsure of his own individuality.

Entering the Toddlerhood 2 phase, your child will be more experienced and confident about his emerging abilities. He will feel more comfortable with his own independence. This will allow him to assert himself more strongly. He may resist your suggestions or defy your commands. This negative behavior often emerges more prominently during this phase. It can be a major source of tension between parent and child.

Your toddler may rely heavily upon the use of the word "No" in voicing his independence. He will often say "No" when you suggest, request, or even order him to do something. This is one of the most common indications of his negative behavior. From the frequency with which he says this word, it will be clear to you that he actually enjoys the feeling of expressing his opposition.

Despite his use of the word "No" when you tell him to do something, he may still do what you ask. There is likely to be a game-like, teasing quality to some of his verbal refusals. Some of his "No's" may be voiced while he conforms to your wishes. When you tell him that it is time for dinner, he may say "No" while he climbs up on the chair at the kitchen table. Simply saying this word over and over again appears to give him the feeling of being more independent and allows him to practice his new ability to talk.

There will be occasions when he will strenuously refuse to do what you ask, or simply ignore you and continue doing what he pleases. You cannot expect too much from him in terms of his always following your advice or instructions. As his sense of independence matures, he may become increasingly obstinate and contrary.

These changing aspects of the toddler's personality and behavior are often puzzling to parents. Friction between parent and child also becomes a primary focus of discussion and concern in most homes. An awareness of the factors contributing to negativism can help alleviate your concern.

In order to understand your child's attitude and behavior better, it helps to put yourself in his shoes. Your ability to walk has improved, and you are now feeling more assured of your emerging independence. You have also learned how to say a few words, and decided that your favorite word is "No," since this is the one that seems to get you the most attention.

Suddenly your parents and other people tell you not to wander away, not to touch the dog, stay out of the kitchen, don't wet your pants, and numerous other rules. Freedom to behave and act spontaneously appear gone. All the restrictions begin to produce feelings of shock and anger. These feelings prompt you to rebel. You develop a very negative attitude.

All toddlers experience these kinds of feelings, but in varying intensities. Even though it is not fully possible to know what may be going on in the child's mind, it can be assumed that part of the turmoil and stress during toddlerhood is the result of so many parental and cultural pressures on the child at a time when he is beginning to realize and assert his independence.

Most psychologists feel that obstinacy and antagonism, especially toward his parents, are a toddler's way of showing that he is an individual, and stating his need for independence. Negativism, which surfaces periodically throughout toddlerhood, is considered to be a normal and essential part of growing up. When a child rebels or does the opposite of what his parents wish, he is learning about being his own person, and strengthening his sense of identity.

In many ways the child is testing his parents' rules and standards to see what they expect from him. This helps him learn about how to create boundaries and controls for himself. Although he began to distinguish between himself and other people during infancy, it is not until toddlerhood that this difference is more clearly established. As he goes about clarifying this distinction, he more strongly asserts himself and becomes obstinate and rebellious. Negativism, when viewed in this light, is a healthy indication that he is becoming more aware of his own individuality.

Your child's negativism will not interfere with your entire relationship with him. Most of the time he will probably abide by your wishes, and will be pleasant to have around. Be aware, however, that while going along with your wishes, he may abruptly change his mind, or insist upon doing something himself. You should prepare yourself for a certain amount of tension between you and your child during this phase.

EXPRESSING FRUSTRATION AND ANGER. Do not be surprised if your toddler has difficulty controlling his frustrations and aggression. Whenever he is feeling very angry or frustrated, he cannot control his temper and needs to "blow off steam." Children react to feelings of anger and frustration in a number of ways. They may pout, frown, scream, cry, or stamp their feet. They may also kick, punch, bite, struggle, throw objects around, throw themselves on the floor, hold their breath, or break toys. These forms of expression in various combinations make up the child's temper tantrums, and demonstrate his inability to exercise self-control.

Even though each child may have his own individual combination of behavior patterns to release stored up anger and frustration, most Toddlerhood 2 children show these feelings through physical forms of release. They are just beginning to express themselves through simple phrases or words, and are not yet able to release their feelings of tension through verbal means. They must rely on body movements and loud screaming to release their emotions. To assist you in dealing with your child's temper outbursts and aggressive actions, suggestions are provided on pages 536–37.

It is easy to be put on edge by your child's changing personality. Do not mistake the signs of his emerging individuality as a challenge to your authority or an intentional desire to irritate you. Look upon this behavior as a healthy, normal aspect of his personal-social development.

Self-awareness

As your toddler becomes more aware of himself and his own abilities, the results of his actions will fascinate him. His familiarity with his body is becoming more evident, and this allows him to continue developing as an independent person. Together, these new developments add a further dimension to his self-concept.

INCREASING AWARENESS OF ACTIONS. The Toddlerhood 2 child is better able to associate his actions with their outcome. Your child is growing more sensitive to the results of his activities. He will begin to recognize that certain things that he does can cause you to become upset. Other activities will make you show him affection or support. Through these observations and experiences, he is gradually beginning to understand the difference between acceptable and unacceptable behavior. You should not expect too much of him, since learning how his actions affect himself and others is a slow process.

LEARNING ABOUT OWNERSHIP. As a part of establishing his own identity, your toddler must become aware of what does and does not belong to him. The Toddlerhood 2 child is starting to learn the difference between what is his and what belongs to others. He may now understand that "this purse is Mommy's," "this scarf is Grandma's," and "this toy is mine." One little toddler took great pleasure in walking around the house, picking up particular objects, and saying to whom they belonged, for example, "Daddy shoe," "Mommy hat," "mine." Many toddlers enjoy saying the word "mine." In fact, "mine" may be their favorite word next to "No."

One mother's twenty-month-old son, Steve, had recently begun to distinguish between his and his parents' possessions. One afternoon he was in the kitchen with his mother watching her bake cookies. While he was eating some of the finished cookies, his mother went over to the sink to get a drink of water. Suddenly his expression changed and he shouted out, "No, mine." At first his mother was caught off guard and was confused at his response. When she looked down at the glass in her hand and recognized the picture of Steve's favorite cartoon character, she realized that she was using his favorite glass.

Steve, like most children his age, was very possessive about one of his favorite objects. He was sensitive about having other people, even his mother, use what he clearly regarded as his glass. When your child develops a sense of ownership, he may like to have some of his objects in a few rooms of the house. He may also enjoy having some of his playthings in his own box in the living room or in a drawer in the kitchen.

Realizing that their children were becoming more sensitive and protective about their possessions, some parents have found that their children had great fun with labels during this phase. Mr. and Mrs. Burn placed the name of their child, Toma, on colored labels which they attached to drawers, cabinets, shelves, toy chests, and so forth, that were designated as being his. This, they reported, helped him keep track of what was his.

Toma took great pride in having certain places in the house that he could call his own. The Burns also said that the labels were useful to them when Toma was older. Whenever it was time to clean up a mess of playthings, they could tell him to "put your toys away in Toma's drawer in the kitchen." Labeling Toma's toys and storage areas was useful to the Burns in helping reinforce Toma's sense of ownership.

Despite your child's increasing awareness of what belongs to him, he will not be ready to respect the rights or property of others. Do not be surprised if he occasionally takes an object that is not his and treats it as though it were.

GREATER FAMILIARITY WITH PARTS OF THE BODY. The Toddlerhood 2 child's familiarity with his body has grown. He appears to be more interested in body parts, as well as in simple games involving pointing to or naming parts of the body. One father took pleasure in playing the following game with his twenty-three-month-old son, Harper.

He propped Harper on his lap so that Harper was facing him and had Harper point to his facial features. After Harper pointed to his eyes, nose, mouth, and so on, he also pointed to his father's and laughed with joy and surprise as if he were proud of the fact that he realized the two of them were similar. Discoveries like this will be going on daily, and more and more your child will show you that he is aware of the similarity between you and himself. By engaging in this type of give and take interaction with him, you will not only be fortifying his feeling of being a person, you will also be encouraging him to identify with you.

Once he is able to talk, you can add a new dimension to this game. Point to various parts of his body and encourage him to say their names. Do not expect perfection from him during this phase. It is not uncommon for children occasionally to mix up names or forget them, even though they can name many parts of their bodies. This confusion will diminish as their language and memory improve.

Social Sensitivity and Interests

Your toddler's abilities to deal effectively with other people are still quite limited. Interpersonal relationships are not his strong point. One major reason for this lies in his lack of ability to communicate on a verbal level. Another major reason is his self-centered point of view.

He makes social contact with people mainly when he wants something. He expects others to cater exclusively to his needs and whims. Despite these limitations, he is definitely more conscious of others than he has been. In fact, he may show you that he wants to be consulted in making decisions and included in family activities.

His interest will be evident as he begins to follow you around the house or imitate your activities. You will notice that his social sensitivity is increasing, even though he is immature in his dealings with people.

GREATER AWARENESS OF YOU AND YOUR WHEREABOUTS. The Toddlerhood 2 child shows a high interest in his parent or the person who consistently cares for him during the day. Your toddler's strong interest in where you are in your home and what you are doing will be difficult to ignore. Even when he is having a good time playing by himself in his room, he may frequently call you just to make sure that you are still around.

His capacity for independent activity seems closely tied to his knowledge that you are present in the home. You provide the security that enables him to branch out on his own. Once he has made verbal contact with you, he will once again continue to play happily by himself.

YOUR RELATIONSHIP WITH YOUR TODDLER. When you and your child are in the same room, he will interact with you more frequently. He may come to you to show you his toys, ask you to help him with something, or make various requests for attention, affection, food, a drink, or a toy. Since his abilities to speak are limited, his requests may be in the form of pointing or gesturing to whatever he wants. Occasionally he may take hold of your hand and pull you toward the kitchen, back door, or wherever he wants to go.

He has learned to use you for getting things that he needs or wants. The requests and demands that he makes upon you may come in a steady stream. Many of his requests will be preceded by "Mommy" or "Daddy." Unless you satisfy his demands right away, he will become increasingly impatient and frustrated.

Living with him may not be easy. He expects you to satisfy his wants immediately, but is generally unwilling to offer you the same treatment. When you ask him to do something, he may ignore you or even do the opposite of what you told him to do. He has not fully developed the ability to appreciate other people's needs and respect their wishes. Your child's primary relationship with you will center around his frequent demands of you.

Not all of his contact with you will be based on his self-centered point of view. Demonstrations of concern for your feelings may be seen through his displays of affection. One twenty-month-old child, Kurt, showed his sensitivity to his mother's feelings by offering her a piece of cookie that he was eating.

His mother was initially surprised at his gesture, because normally he was very possessive of his food or toys, and would not share them with others. Most Toddlerhood 2 children's behaviors will appear selfish, but you will occasionally notice that your child is slowly developing a concern for your feelings.

Your child's attachment to you is very strong. One of his major interests is likely to involve watching you work, and imitating your speech and behavior. As you clean house or work in the yard, he will take great pleasure in mimicking whatever you are doing, using his own toy equipment.

Being the focus of your attention will be very enjoyable for him. You will be a captivating audience for his "show-off" play. He will relish the attention and affection that you shower on him. He still needs a strong emotional security base so that he can develop his own independence. Your relationship with him, although seemingly one-sided, will be very important in fulfilling his emotional needs.

GETTING ALONG WITH OTHER FAMILY MEMBERS. Your child's self-centered nature makes it difficult for him to co-operate in family situations. This is an age when he will probably argue and have a hard time getting along with brothers and sisters. It's best not to set your expectations for peaceful family relations too high, or else you may be quite disappointed.

Fights and jealousies among siblings are common. It is usually advisable not to interfere during their arguments and not to take sides unless it is absolutely necessary to protect one child. Your toddler can learn a lot about getting (and not getting) along with other people through the time that he spends with his brothers and sisters, even if much of it centers around disagreements. Relationships that do not involve co-operation and sharing are generally smoother and more peaceful. Toddlers who have older siblings may spend a lot of time imitating what they do and say without actually interacting with them. Toddlers can learn a great deal from watching and copying older siblings.

DEALING WITH OTHER CHILDREN. The Toddlerhood 2 child usually is not very interested in other children, although some toddlers like to play near other children at the park or playground. Most toddlers are happier playing by themselves. This suits them just fine. When you take your child to a place where there are other children his own age, you may be surprised at how immaturely he deals with them. He may occasionally grab at them or their toys, or even hit or push them.

Nagging him to play with his peers or to share his playthings will not bring positive results. Most Toddlerhood 2 children are simply too immature for this. They usually do not care very much about playing with other children, and show little or no respect for their feelings or property rights. Friendly, social exchanges among children are not characteristic during this phase, although some toddlers will play nicely with other youngsters.

As your child grows older, he will find it easier to play alongside another child, and later will be able to co-operate in play. It is a good idea to allow him to spend time in the company of other children, especially if he has had very little contact with them until now, but at this early stage you should not try to push him to play with other youngsters if he prefers simply to watch them, have fun by himself, or play with you.

Separation Anxiety

The anxiety that many children feel upon being separated from their parents during the latter part of infancy was discussed on pages 363–64, 427. Most children's separation anxiety diminishes between the ages of about one year and a year and a half, as they gradually become more accustomed to dealing with short separations from their parents.

Separation anxiety may once again become very noticeable among Toddlerhood 2 children. In fact, during Toddlerhood 2 and 3, and Preschool 1, it is fairly common for children to experience anxiety when they are apart from their parents, even when the separation is limited to a few hours or overnight.

HOW DO CHILDREN EXPRESS SEPARATION ANXIETY? Most children become tense and upset when their parents leave them, and they start to cry. This reaction may be prompted by even short separations such as when parents leave them alone for a few hours to go out to dinner, shop, or go to work. A common time for separation anxiety to surface is in the evening at the child's regular bedtime. An occasional child may even become fearful if his parents leave the room in which he is playing to go to another room in the home.

Mrs. Pullman, who worked as an accountant during the day, had the following experiences with her daughter, Janie. She said that Janie had never before become upset when the two of them were separated. Suddenly at around eighteen months, her daughter's reactions changed. Janie began to cry and repeatedly call out, "Mommy, Mommy," each morning as Mrs. Pullman prepared to leave. According to the regular baby-sitter, Janie would keep this up for at least half an hour each morning, and sometimes longer.

These reports from the baby-sitter concerned Mrs. Pullman, and, for the first time, she began to feel guilty about working away from home. She felt badly for Janie, but still thought it best to continue leaving for work as she had been doing all along.

After a couple of months, Janie's separation anxiety subsided, and she seemed much more capable of coping with her mother's necessary absences from the home. You may notice that your toddler becomes panicky, emotionally upset, and clingy whenever he thinks that you are going to leave him or whenever you actually leave him, even temporarily. Thinking that your child has outgrown his anxiety over separations from you, the re-emergence of this behavior may come as a surprise. One father was puzzled by his son Jerry's behavior. Jerry would cry for hours when he was separated from his mother at eight months of age, causing a great deal of concern. He gradually outgrew this behavior by twelve months, to the delight of both parents. Separations no longer produced difficulties during the next several months.

As Jerry approached twenty months, he suddenly became frightened and tearful whenever his father left home for work, or walked outside to the garage. Jerry's father could not understand his son's reaction to separations, since he thought Jerry had outgrown this behavior at the end of infancy. This father's experience is similar to that of many parents during Toddlerhood 2 and 3. Separation anxiety may be more of a problem at this time, since the child is better able to express his feelings and create more of a scene. Parents often wonder if something is wrong with their child, or if his behavior is a sign of regression or maladjustment.

You should not interpret your child's fear reaction of clinginess when you leave him as evidence that he is overdependent upon you, or that something is wrong with him. His reaction may simply be evidence of his close attachment to you. Try to understand that his concerns and needs are real even if, in your opinion, they are exaggerated.

There is much speculation as to why toddlers become fearful and upset over separations from their parents. Children during this phase are quite dependent upon their parents for emotional support. A child who has been consistently cared for by his parent has become very attached to him or her. The security that his parent provides is very important to the child. Without his parent, he feels tense and insecure. As he becomes more certain that he will not be abandoned, and that each time his parent leaves him he or she will always return, his anxiety over separations will gradually subside.

Separation anxiety in a child who is otherwise developing well should not be a major cause for concern, but it can still be an annoying and frustrating experience for parents. Understanding how other parents have handled this behavior will help you determine how best to handle your child.

HANDLING SEPARATION ANXIETY. Separation anxiety appears to need to run its course with most children. How long it persists and how intensely it is experienced varies from child to child. Of utmost importance is trying to understand that your toddler's feelings, fears, and anxieties about your departures are very real to him. He will need all of the support and patience that you can offer. You should avoid punishing or ignoring him, even if his clinginess, crying, and fearfulness are trying on your nerves.

Preparing your child prior to your departures should help him cope with them. If you or your spouse, or both, are going away without him for an evening, weekend, or a longer trip, let him know in advance that you will be leaving, and also reassure him that you will be back soon. Make arrangements for him to be cared for by someone he knows and likes. Reassure him before you go that you will be back soon, and do not drag out your good-bys. Acting guilty or overly concerned when you are about to depart may add substance to his own concerns about separations.

A child who is upset over the briefest separations from his parents may have a much more intense emotional response to a major separation. If you are planning a long vacation away from your toddler, you may decide to postpone it for a while until he is mature enough to handle separations. Similarly, if you are thinking of returning to a full-time job away from home, and have a choice about this matter, you may conclude that it will be easier on your child to postpone this for the time being.

There is no reason for you to feel guilty about not being with your child 100 percent of the time. It is not advisable to cancel your normal activities outside the home simply to remain at home with him. These alterations in your routine probably will not help him, and may only contribute to further dependency upon you.

Toddlers are often anxious in new situations or with new people that they face alone. Having a parent nearby generally helps reduce their fears and anxieties, and enables them to adapt to new situations more easily. It is a good idea to get your toddler gradually used to being around different people and new situations, remaining close by to reassure him and reduce his worries.

Allowing him to express his dependency upon you is more advisable than ignoring his feelings or telling him to act more grown-up. The extra emotional support and reassurance that you can give him will not make him more dependent. Rather, it should allay his anxieties so that he will be able to go out into the world once again, the brave little explorer.

DEALING WITH SEPARATION ANXIETY AT BEDTIME. Separation anxiety is often very noticeable at bedtime, and is a common reason for a child's resistance to going to bed. He may be upset about being in his bedroom alone, and also frightened by the prospect of awakening in the morning and discovering that his parents are gone. After being tucked in bed, he may cry out for "Mommy" or "Daddy," and keep this up until he either becomes exhausted and falls asleep, or his parents return to comfort and reassure him.

This behavior can be irritating, and parents are often uncertain about how to deal with it. There are a few different approaches that can be taken; a popular one is to sit by his side or remain in his room until he falls asleep. Leaving the room before he is fully asleep may trigger another crying spell. After several weeks, he should overcome his fear of leaving the family.

However, some parents do not have the time to do this. It is also inconvenient in cases where the child's anxiety lasts more than a few weeks. Children who become accustomed to having a parent present when they go to sleep may occasionally have difficulty outgrowing this dependency. Experienced parents advise against sitting by a child's bedside for weeks on end, lest the child become too dependent upon this pattern.

Another common alternative is to spend a few minutes with the child at bedtime, soothing and reassuring him, and then leave. The child, once reassured, is forced to learn to adapt to unavoidable separations from his parents at bedtime. This method seems reasonable to some parents, although also difficult, because an anxious child may cry for hours at a time, even though he is completely worn out and overtired.

The approach that you select is really a matter of personal preference. You might try a combination of approaches, or try one method and be prepared to move on to the next if the first does not do the trick. What works well for one child may not work as well for another, so try to take your child's individual personality and needs into account, as well as your own, in determining which approach to use.

INTELLECTUAL DEVELOPMENT

The Developing Mind

Now that your toddler can move about more easily, his interest in the environment and his own actions will increase. Despite his rapid movement from one activity to another, he is more aware of the world around him and is better able to concentrate than he was in the past. His curiosity and desire to learn may seem limitless as he goes everywhere, gets into everything, points, talks, and asks simple questions. He will no longer be willing to play for hours at a stretch in a cramped area such as a playpen, because he is anxious to satisfy his need to pioneer and explore.

YOUR CHILD'S THINKING BECOMES MORE EVIDENT. The Toddlerhood 2 child shifts from working through problems solely by direct trial and error activities, to also solving them in his head. He is better able to remember images of objects and familiar action patterns. He can hold these images in his head and begin to relate them to one another. This allows him to "think" about particular activities and consider what the outcome of his actions would be before engaging in them.

Observing your child at play will enable you to appreciate the progress he is making in his intellectual abilities. One Toddlerhood 2 child, David, was playing with his ball on the floor and accidentally rolled it underneath a deep couch that was pushed up against a wall. David surveyed the situation and realized that the ball was beyond his immediate reach. He was surrounded by other objects, including a stick and a truck, but he wanted to retrieve his ball. His facial expression revealed his determination and obvious concentration on this task.

During earlier phases David was not able to think about the best way to get his ball by reflecting upon previous action patterns. In attempting to retrieve the ball, he would have had to experiment directly with various methods of reaching it. At this level of intellectual development, in which thinking emerges more clearly, he can not only remember previous experiences in playing with objects, but can also combine them in his mind and come up with new behaviors that will allow him to solve this problem and get his ball.

Through previous experience David learned that he could hit an object with a stick and cause it to move. He also learned that he could strike a ball with another object and cause it to roll away. He is now able to recall these previous experiences with objects and relate them in his mind in order to come up with a solution to his problem. He realizes that by taking the stick and hitting the ball with it in a sweeping motion, the ball will roll out from under the couch to a point where he can probably reach it. This is indeed what he did after examining the situation, and pausing for a moment to think.

Your toddler, like David, will begin to solve simple problems by thinking through a couple of alternatives without having to act them out physically by trial and error experimentation. Although this new ability to relate simple ideas or memories of experiences in his mind is a major step forward, he is still very limited in his ability to think through problems.

LEARNING FROM EVERYDAY EXPERIENCES. The Toddlerhood 2 child will continue to explore his surroundings and learn through sensory and motor activity. The more he can see, touch, taste, smell, and hear, the more discoveries he can make about the world around him. As he accumulates more experiences, he will be trying to understand them, interrelate them, and generalize from them. Even though he is better able to notice similarities and differences in objects, and form his own conclusions about various things, there is much for him to learn about his environment. He still lacks thinking power and the experience that comes with age.

There are many ways in which you can help him understand ordinary experiences and develop his thinking ability. Simple explanations in the course of your normal conversations and activities with him will encourage him to think, compare, interrelate, question, and draw conclusions. Suggestions for how to promote early thinking and stimulate intellectual development can be found on pages 568–69.

Concept of Objects

Your child began experimenting actively with objects in his environment a long time ago. He banged them together, dropped them, tasted them, and carefully observed them. As a result of his experience through his own experimentation, he is now realizing more and more that objects can and do exist independently of his personal contact with them.

He no longer conceives of objects only as the result of his touching, tasting, hearing, smelling, or seeing them. Even if an object is out of view, it continues to exist for him. Now that his mind has developed more fully, he can follow an object's imaginary movements in space. He can find an object even if he did not see it at the time it was hidden, and can more easily think about objects. This is quite an accomplishment, which provides evidence of his improving memory.

During Toddlerhood 1, page 487, an example about a ball placed in a cookie jar was presented. The jar was hidden behind a couch and the ball was removed. When the jar was returned to the child, the child seemed puzzled that the ball had disappeared, although she probably did not search for it behind the couch.

The Toddlerhood 2 child would not simply continue to stare at the empty cookie jar. He would be more likely to search immediately for the ball in the place where the cookie jar was last seen, behind the couch. The child's new ability to think about an object's possible unseen movements enables him to participate more successfully in games involving hide-and-seek with objects.

Here is a game that you can try with your child. It will enable you to observe his progress in this area. Take his favorite toy and hide it while he is not looking, but not a spot in which he is likely to look first. Then ask him to find the toy or go and get it. He will probably search for it in the place where he last saw it. Then he may search for it in the places in which it is usually kept. If he does not find it in those areas, and is still determined, it is likely that he will continue his search, looking underneath pillows, the table, his crib, and so on, because he now knows that it exists and has to be somewhere. He has reached the stage in which objects are viewed as having a more permanent and separate existence.

What Makes Things Happen

The child is developing a beginning concept of causality as we think of it in an adult sense but does not have a well-organized view of events that take place. Through his past experiences, he has learned that by doing certain things, certain other things will happen.

By pulling a certain chain, he knows that the light will go on. He is aware that if he throws all of his food on the floor at mealtime, his mother will get angry. One little boy, seated in his wagon, was playing with some berries on a bush. He was thoroughly enjoying himself and did not want to leave. Out of the corner of his eye he saw his mother slowly bend down and extend her arm in the direction of the handle on his wagon. Even before the wagon moved, the child screamed, "No, no, no!" He was able to infer that if his mother picked up the handle and pulled it, the wagon would move away. Given a certain action, this child was able to anticipate the outcome correctly.

Children may also be able to look at a given result and have some idea of what caused it. Every time a little boy named Sonny built simple towers of blocks, his dog knocked them over. One afternoon, with his father's help, Sonny built a very elaborate block structure in the den. He was extremely pleased and proud of his accomplishment, and watched it for several minutes. He and his father then went into the kitchen to have a snack. While in the kitchen, Sonny heard a loud crashing noise coming from the den. He rushed in and found that his block structure had been knocked down. No one was around. Although his dog was in another part of the house, he turned to his father and said, "Doggie, doggie!" In a similar fashion, your child will probably indicate to you that he is developing a more practical understanding of cause and effect.

Concept of Space

The child is beginning to experience the world as a more organized place in which all people and objects are interrelated. A new ability emerges around this time. He becomes able to follow or remember a series of his own movements through space, and learns about his own movements in relationship to other objects. He can also keep better track of the movement of objects through space.

Re-examining a situation discussed in Toddlerhood 1 on page 488 may help illustrate the child's new ability. When the Toddlerhood 1 child's ball rolled under the day bed, she only searched for it at the base of the bed, and became frustrated when she did not find it there. During Toddlerhood 2, a child probably would not react in this manner. Chances are that he would assume that the ball passed through one space under the bed to the space on the other side. He would walk around the bed and spot the ball. Your child's improved ability to follow objects and perceive spatial relationships may become evident to you as you watch him play.

Concept of Time

A toddler still lives mainly in the "here" and "now" and is for the most part concerned with the "present." He often uses the word "now," and becomes extremely frustrated when his immediate desires are not satisfied.

In small ways he may indicate that he is developing some sense of future time. He may show signs of understanding comments such as "soon" or "in a minute." As long as he thinks there will be only a momentary delay, he will probably be patient.

Twenty-three-month-old Guy was told by his mother that he could play outside after his nap. Guy went to sleep and as soon as he woke up, he shouted, "Now, out!" This little boy's response indicates that he was able to think ahead and anticipate going outside after naptime.

The Toddlerhood 2 child may show some signs of remembering events that have occurred in the past. Upon hearing someone's name or a name for an object, he may immediately associate a past event with it. A little girl who had been taken to visit her sick grandmother the day before showed signs of remembering this event. When she later heard her grandmother's name mentioned, she said, "Nan sick."

Most toddlers have great difficulty remembering something their parents tell them from one moment to the next. It will be some time before they show signs of being able to remember past events in a clear, well-organized fashion.

Imitation

The toddler has developed some ability to think and handle images or symbols for people, objects, and events in his head. This enables him to imitate models who are not present. When a child is able to copy the behavior of people he has previously seen, but who are no longer in sight, he will be exhibiting a new, significant form of imitation. Although you may have seen some signs of imitation of absent people in the past, you are likely to see more evidence of it during Toddlerhood 2 and 3.

A child's ability to mimic an absent model suggests that he has a mental image or memory of the model. One day a toddler saw another young child systematically piling up her toys and using them as steppingstones in an attempt to climb out of her playpen. A day later his mother observed him doing something he had never done before. She saw him piling up his toys and stuffed animals near the side of the playpen. Then he climbed up on these objects in an effort to escape from the playpen, just as he had seen the little girl do the day before. This child, like others during this phase, has developed a better ability to maintain an image or memory of situations he has seen.

LANGUAGE DEVELOPMENT

Toddlerhood 2 children are beginning to say more real words than at earlier ages. Nonsense talk is still used, but they are learning that actual words are more valuable in bringing them what they want, including attention and praise. Vocabularies are variable and may range from about a half dozen words to way over one hundred words. Some of the words that children say will be parroted rather than used appropriately to convey specific meanings. Their ability to use words meaningfully develops more slowly than their ability to pronounce and mimic words that other people use.

Toddlers frequently use single words and hand motions when they speak. During Toddlerhood 2, parents often notice the sudden emergence of children's ability to put two words together to convey a thought. A few children who are advanced in the area of language development may even put three or more words together into sentences, but you should not expect this in this early phase.

As your child's comprehension of speech expands, it will become obvious to you that he knows the meaning of many simple words that he frequently hears. He will understand short phrases, suggestions, and requests, although it may not always seem so when he ignores what you tell him or does exactly what you told him not to do.

It is important to capitalize on your toddler's growing interest in language. Toddlerhood 2 and 3 children are often enthusiastic about learning new words, trying to understand their meaning, and listening to conversations and sounds. You will find numerous suggestions on how to foster your toddler's language development on pages 570–72 in the Total Education of Your Child During Toddlerhood section.

Active Language Development

VOCABULARIES ARE EXPANDING. How broad your child's vocabulary is at this time partly depends on his own timetable for learning to speak, how much you have talked and interacted with him, and how much you have helped him learn the names of objects. It will be extremely helpful to continue to teach him new words and to encourage him to say the names of household objects, since he will love to imitate you.

You will overhear your toddler spontaneously saying words that he has heard you and other family members using. These words are apt to be repeated until they have lost their novelty. Many of the words that he will pick up will probably apply to his own activities. Words like "play," "go," "out," "now," "want," "more," and "say" are common.

A child who has begun to speak and is learning the names for several familiar household objects will have fun practicing his new verbal abilities, particularly when his parents are around to nod approval and offer words of praise and encouragement. Your child may show an emerging interest in pointing to objects in the home or in pictures in magazines and identifying them by name.

At some point during Toddlerhood 2 he may begin to combine two words to make longer sentences than before. His ability to put two words together to make a complete thought may come as a surprise and will undoubtedly make you beam with pride. He will find that his new ability to use sentences such as, "Gimme candy," "Come, Mommy," "Bye-Bye," "See shoe," "Big car," or "Thank you," comes in very handy in asking for things that he wants, and socializing with you.

SINGING AND MUSIC. Your toddler may enjoy listening to music. Upon hearing often-played children's songs with a clear melody, he may smile, move around, and try to sing. When he tries actually to sing along, he may simply be able to sing only a sentence, or a part of a sentence or a word.

Like many Toddlerhood 2 children, Winston developed a strong preference for a certain record on which there were songs from his favorite children's television program. Whenever he heard this record, he would excitedly bounce up and down and sway back and forth to the beat. The moment his parents would mention that they were going to play this particular record, his face would light up with a big grin, and he would spontaneously begin to "dance," and say a word or two from the song, even before they turned on the record player. See page 500.

OTHER PEOPLE INFLUENCE LANGUAGE DEVELOPMENT. Older children in the family play an important role in influencing a toddler's language development. A toddler often spends a great deal of time playing and interacting with his siblings and shows a strong interest in imitating their speech and behavior patterns. The nature of toddlers' interactions with an older child (children) in the family can vary widely depending upon such factors as their ages, personalities, kind of relationship they have, and other individual circumstances. In many cases toddlers receive a great deal of encouragement from their older brother or sister, perhaps even more than is received from parents, to give up nonsense or baby talk.

Farrah Benson, a year-and-a-half-old toddler, was often with her five-and-a-half-year-old brother, Cory. Cory was aware of his sister's baby talk and "babyish" one word sentences. During the time that the two of them were together, he took it upon himself to help her learn to speak, using techniques that his parents had obviously employed with him in the past. As the two of them played, he pointed to objects in the home and yard and told her their names. Sometimes he handed her toys and objects, one at a time, while he identified them. Occasionally, he even sat down with her on the floor, flipped through picture storybooks, and pointed to pictures as he labeled them.

Cory strongly encouraged Farrah to speak more clearly. Whenever he heard her utter "ba ba," for instance, he would quickly respond by saying "bottle." He found it hard to tolerate her nonsense talk, and in subtle ways pressured her to learn to use intelligible words by providing her with immediate feedback and correct models to imitate.

Once Farrah began using one and two word sentences, Cory encouraged her to expand upon them. One evening at the dinner table, Farrah said, "More," and held up her plate to indicate her desire for an additional serving of meat. Cory immediately turned to her and said, "I would like to have more meat, please."

As a result of her older brother's encouragement, teaching efforts, and correction, Farrah quickly learned to speak more clearly. She also picked up many new vocabulary words, and began to use longer, more complex sentences. Mr. and Mrs. Benson noticed the remarkable strides that she was making in her speech and were aware that their son was influential in stimulating this progress, since they had taken a less active role in fostering their second child's language development than they had taken with their first.

It is not uncommon for an older child to hasten a younger brother's or sister's language development, and spend time teaching, motivating, and correcting mistakes. In some cases in which a child's parent(s) and older sibling(s) are constantly correcting and pressuring her to move toward more mature speech, this can have a less beneficial effect. Too much of this kind of pressure may make a toddler self-conscious and nervous about talking, or hesitant to speak for fear of not living up to everyone's expectations or being constantly criticized.

It is advisable to observe the manner in which your children interact in relation to your toddler's language development. Also examine your own verbal interactions with him. Should you determine that between you and your older child, your youngest is receiving too much pressure to perform, it would be a good idea to discuss ways in which to ease up and create a more relaxed atmosphere. The majority of parents usually find that this is not the case, and discover that their older child is a very positive influence on their toddler's development of speech.

Early Speech Difficulties and Stuttering

The development of language is a gradual process which requires practice and effort on your toddler's part. A very noticeable aspect of a toddler's development is his ability to speak. Parents often get concerned when their child has difficulties in speaking, such as stuttering or poor pronunciation of words. These speech difficulties are more characteristic of Toddlerhood 3 and preschool children, but they can occur earlier in toddlerhood. Just as anyone learning a new task has difficulties, your child will probably develop some initial speech problems.

One mother was concerned that her year-and-a-half-old son, Barry, was beginning to stutter. She had been very proud of her son's ability to speak several words and form simple sentences at fifteen months of age and was now rather surprised and concerned about his stuttering.

Barry would occasionally get excited and have trouble saying words that began with "b" and "m." One morning, he wanted his bottle and blurted out, "Ba, ba, ba, ba, bottle." He also had difficulty asking for more food. He would say, "Mm, mm, mm, mm, more." His stuttering would occur in a variety of situations. Periods of excitement seemed to bring it on.

Barry's mother overcame her initial surprise and did not draw attention to his stuttering. Barry's father, however, was very upset and worried that Barry would have a permanent stuttering problem. He constantly scolded Barry, telling his son to slow down and begin again. After discussing this problem with their friends, Barry's father realized that many children have similar difficulties when they are first learning to speak. Calling attention to his son's problem or scolding him for it was probably only increasing Barry's tension and contributing to further stuttering.

Barry's parents decided to try to ignore their son's problem to see whether it would resolve itself. Gradually, over the next two months, Barry's stuttering became much less common, and occurred only once or twice a week. By the time Barry was two years old, he had apparently overcome his stuttering completely.

Another problem that parents often face is the difficulty some children have with pronouncing certain sounds, such as the letter "y." Jannine always substituted the sound of the letter "b" for the "y" sound. When asking her mother for her yellow ball, she would ask, "Bellow ball?" Such difficulties usually disappear as skill with language improves.

It is important to remember not to panic and become overly concerned about your toddler's minor speech problems. Most of these difficulties are related to learning a new skill which he has not perfected. In the event that your toddler is having speech problems, and you would like some specific suggestions for dealing with them, read ahead to the discussion on errors in speech in the Language Development section in Preschool 1 (pages 729–31).

Passive Language Development

It was previously pointed out that during this phase you will observe noticeable improvements in your toddler's comprehension of language. Try to use short phrases in conjunction with hand gestures rather than complex sentences in giving him suggestions or directions. This will help him get the meaning of what you say.

Another aspect of passive language development includes his awareness of sounds. He is probably beginning to show a greater interest in sounds such as ambulance sirens, car engine noises, ticking clocks, ringing telephones, and sounds produced by his toys. The Magic of Learning Through Sound topic in the Total Education of Your Child During Toddlerhood section (pages 571–72) offers numerous suggestions for providing a child with sound stimulation.

MOTOR DEVELOPMENT

Your toddler's strong need to exercise and improve his physical skills is likely to be more pronounced than in Toddlerhood 1. He will go everywhere, do everything, and constantly move his toys from place to place. Instead of riding in his kiddie car, he will probably prefer to push, drag, or shove it.

One of his favorite activities will be moving around small tables, chairs, and other pieces of furniture. He is apt to be fascinated with stairs and may constantly go up and down until he is exhausted. Even then he may not stop.

Now that he can walk and move with greater speed and skill, he will enjoy zooming around your home, and having you go after him. Over the next few months he will continue to practice and show improvement in his hand skills, but he is likely to concentrate upon gross motor activity.

More evidence of co-ordinated movement patterns will become noticeable. He will constantly be refining his movements and adding new variations to the motor abilities that emerged earlier. A child who attempted to kick a ball forward or walk up steps during Toddlerhood 1 will try to perfect these abilities during this phase. He may also be adding new maneuvers such as jumping in place and riding a tricycle. It should bring you pleasure to watch your child's increasing co-ordination and attempts at more complicated actions.

Gross Motor Activity

WALKING. By carefully observing your toddler's motor behavior, you can see that even though his walking has improved, he still does not move like an adult. He tends to lean forward as he walks, with his feet wide apart. This stance gives him more stability.

The reason that your child still has these slight differences in his walking posture is that his nervous system and muscular system are not fully co-ordinated. The ability to walk and perform complex movements requires millions of nerve signals that have to be co-ordinated and organized. Over the next several months, you will see him becoming more and more comfortable in the upright position.

RUNNING. As your child's ability to walk improves, he can go faster and faster. Speedily moving all around your house, in between chairs and under tables, will give him great pleasure. He will be spending a great deal of time walking very quickly, in a manner that almost looks like running. However, until a child has developed sufficient leg strength and balance to allow him to leave the ground with both feet simultaneously, he is not running. Real running usually develops in Toddlerhood 3.

PUSHING AND PULLING LARGE OBJECTS. The Toddlerhood 2 child will show an endless supply of energy for testing his new physical prowess. He can suddenly stand up and push around large, lightweight objects. Much of his time will be spent playing with and moving objects that lie in his path. These activities will set the stage for many humorous and sometimes anger-producing incidents. You will be delighted seeing your child pulling his wagon or pushing his new red fire engine or doll car-

riage around the house. You may be less pleased when he decides to push your end table with the lamp on top. These can be trying times for most parents, but your anxiety can be greatly lessened by following the suggestions in the accident prevention section, (pages 506–13) and teaching him what he can and cannot play with in your home.

WALKING BACKWARD. While your child is making great progress toward running, he will also be beginning or perfecting his ability to walk backward. He will feel more secure walking in a forward direction, but he may attempt to walk backward to experiment or imitate your behavior. As he gets better and better at walking backward, he will soon realize that under certain circumstances it will be easier to walk out backward than to try to turn completely around and walk forward.

CLIMBING. It will be fun to watch your child as he begins walking up steps. He will initially go through all types of postures and positions in order to get from one step to another. Most children will not yet be proficient at step climbing, and walking down steps is even more difficult for them. Toddlerhood 2 is a time for learning these new skills.

This deserves a word of caution. Your child may gain a great deal of confidence around steps as he develops the ability to climb easily. This confidence can be dangerous, if he attempts to go down a flight of steps too quickly; prevent your child from attempting to go down a flight of steps without supervision.

KICKING A BALL. If your child did not attempt to kick a ball during Toddlerhood 1, it is very likely that he will begin to do so now. As previously discussed, this task requires the co-ordination of many motor actions, and will take considerable practice and time to be mastered. Your child's first attempts may prove disastrous, but with practice he will throw his ball or toys across the room.

THROWING AND CATCHING A BALL. Your child has probably made previous attempts to throw objects, and you have undoubtedly observed them flying in all directions. As his ability to release objects and co-ordinate their release with the movement of his arm improves, he will become more proficient at throwing a ball. Remember that he will not only want to warm up his throwing arm with a ball but at times may hurl any small object he can get into his hand.

Once he develops the ability to throw a ball to you, he will be able to start playing "catch," but you should not expect him to be good at it during Toddlerhood 2. His ability to catch the ball will lag far behind his ability to throw it. During Toddlerhood 2 he may position his arms in a type of cradle and passively wait for the ball to land in the center of the "cradle." Playing with him in this manner can be fun for both of you.

THE DANCING TODDLER. Improved balance on his feet frees your child to use his hands and arms for swinging, circling, and many other motions. He can move up and down and rock back and forth on his feet. These newly acquired abilities set the stage for the toddler's dancing.

A child who has seen people at home or on television dancing to music may try to imitate these dancing movements. Your toddler may suddenly walk into the middle of the room and start moving rhythmically to the sounds of your favorite record.

Toddlerhood 2 children get a great deal of pleasure from listening and dancing to music. They may even develop a preference for a specific song. You may get a kick out of teaching your child to dance and watching his improvised movements as he swings to the beat.

NEW SKILLS MAY EMERGE. Toddlerhood 2 children who are advanced in motor development may develop several new skills. Parents may see their child balancing on one foot or attempting to jump in place. If they have a tricycle at home, he may also attempt to pedal it. A few children may even be able to jump forward a short distance, in addition to jumping in place. Most children will not develop these skills until the next phase of toddlerhood.

Fine Motor Activity

BLOCK BUILDING. By this time your child has developed a good pincer-like grasp with his thumb and forefinger and is getting better at letting go of objects and gently putting them down. This increased co-ordination in hand and arm movements enables him to be more efficient at piling blocks on top of each other. One way to measure his increasing skill is to have him pile block on top of block, creating a mini tower. Most children at this stage can create a three or four block tower, and a few will be able to build even taller structures. Although your child is getting better at his hand movements, he may still be awkward at using his wrists to perform smoother motions.

HAND AND FINGER SKILLS. Your child will continue to show improvement in his hand and finger agility. With a crayon, he will scribble spontaneously and will probably be able to imitate a vertical line within 30 degrees. Although he may paint with a brush, his creations are far from being works of art. If you have introduced him to the world of books, he may turn the pages by himself, but he may turn more than one page at a time.

DRESSING AND UNDRESSING. It is still easier for your child to remove articles of clothing than it is for him to dress himself. You are likely to see him removing his shoes and pants, and perhaps other garments as well, such as his hat and gloves. He may attempt to tie his shoes, but his efforts will be fruitless, because he will not master this task until much later on. He may be able to undo a large zipper, but will still have difficulty with smaller ones.

GROOMING. As a result of his greater proficiency with his hands, you may see your child attempting to care for his body in simple ways. He will probably wash and dry his hands when told, brush his hair, and wash easily accessible parts of his body while in the bathtub. He may also dry the front part of his body with a towel following his bath. Tooth-brushing is a task that many Toddlerhood 2 children undertake. With proper guidance, they may do a fairly good job, particularly when parents or older siblings are brushing at the same time.

LEARNING THROUGH PLAY

Toddlers Have an Endless Supply of Energy

Your toddler's vigorous play activities will be a testimony to his never-ceasing energy. The time devoted to gross motor activity will far exceed that which is devoted to fine motor activity. Keeping tabs on him as he climbs, zooms around, crawls, and moves objects will keep you hopping. Despite his small size, he can cover an incredible amount of ground in the span of only several minutes. Even when a particular object or toy attracts his attention, he may play with it only momentarily before he gets distracted and shifts to another plaything or place. Nearly everything will arouse his interest and sustain his high level of enthusiasm for additional activity.

Your child will find many ways to foster his large-muscle development. Pushing toys and small pieces of furniture around the room may seem to preoccupy him at times. Some parents try to provide toys or objects that foster active play, such as a junior jungle gym, a slide, stairs, and so forth. This kind of equipment can be used either outdoors or indoors. Some junior-sized jungle gyms are specially designed for apartment use, being compact. Should cost or space represent an obstacle, try to take your child to a park or playground occasionally where such equipment is usually available. See pages 925–26 for a discussion of safety tips regarding outdoor equipment. Most toddlers love to play outside because there they generally have fewer obstacles as well as greater freedom to roam.

The Emergence of Pretend Activities

With the emergence of some symbolic thinking, a whole new avenue of make-believe play behavior is open to the child. Images of objects have become fixed in his brain and action patterns are also represented for later recall. He can now think about his actions and play activities, and "make-believe."

Toddlers' play frequently consists of their pretending to be engaged in some familiar action in the absence of "real" objects that would ordinarily be necessary for that activity. A child may say, "Yummy," and pretend to be feeding himself, even though no food is present, or may grab his security blanket, lie down on the floor with it, and pretend to be sleeping. Benjamin pretended to feed his doll many different foods, using only a paper torn in pieces to symbolize the foods. A child's early make-believe play may also consist of treating a familiar pattern of action as a symbol of an event. Chuck, in the absence of shampoo or water, pretended to be washing his hair by massaging and rubbing his scalp with his hands.

You may see several indications of your toddler's ability to enter into pretend play activities. Parents often observe their youngsters "feeding" their dolls, rocking them to sleep, and kissing them good-by. At later stages, when children's intellectual skills are more fully developed, they will become able to engage in more elaborate and complex imaginative play.

Playing with Parents

As your child's awareness of people gradually increases, the amount of time he spends playing alone will gradually decrease, but at this stage most of his playtime will probably be spent alone. He may occasionally turn to you for assistance, especially when he wants a different plaything. Sometimes he will want you around just so that he has enjoyable company.

He will be very interested in imitating you and may stick close by, mimicking your actions. As you cook, he may tinker on the floor with pots and pans. He may dust the furniture with a rag as you dust, or sweep the floors with his toy broom as you do the same. Although these activities are work to you, much of his play may involve imitating your work.

Participating in many of your activities will give him great pleasure. When you go grocery shopping, he may like to have you tell him or point to what you need so that he can bring the items to you. After you come home from the store, he may enjoy making a game of putting away the groceries.

Toddlers usually love to play games with their parents such as hide-and-seek, peek-a-boo, and rolling a ball. Most of all, they will be happy knowing that their parents are nearby and are interested in whatever they are doing at any given moment.

Your toddler's interest in language is expanding. As a result, he will increasingly enjoy naming games. When you point to various toys, objects, people, and parts of his body, he will name them for you. Wherever you are, in the car, the doctor's office, your home, the park, and so forth, he will enjoy having you talk to him and say the names of things. He will also enjoy hearing simple stories, poems, nursery rhymes, and songs, and is apt to want to have them repeated over and over again.

Playing with Other Children

It is a good idea to give your toddler opportunities to play with other children in your home or at some public place such as a playground or beach, since this will promote socialization skills. At this stage, he will primarily be concerned with his own toys and activities, and may make only minimal contact with other children. He may occasionally try to grab an interesting toy away from one of them, or tell another child to stop doing something, but in general, he will probably have a hard time co-operating with his peers in joint activities.

Your Young Artist

Your child may love to paint, but it is too soon for his artistic talents to be either well expressed or recognized by others. Allowing a Toddlerhood 2 child to use paint either indoors or outdoors can be a very messy proposition. His lack of control with a brush can result in paint being splattered on floors, walls, and everywhere but the paper.

An alternative activity to using real paint, yet one that is equally attractive to toddlers is to paint with water. This idea may seem silly at first, but many toddlers and even young preschoolers have loads of fun painting with water.

A large paintbrush and a plastic bucket, tub, or pot to hold water are the only equipment necessary. This activity is best carried on outdoors. Your child can go to work painting the sidewalk, driveway, tree, front steps, or even your apartment building or house. It will be fun for you to watch him painting away to his heart's content. Best of all, the only mess you will have to clean is to hang his wet clothes up to dry.

Another alternative to using real paint is to purchase books similar to coloring books, for which the child uses a brush and water. Brushing on the water makes colors appear on the page. This activity is not as creative as the one mentioned above, but some children enjoy it as an early painting experience.

The Hidden Object Game

Toddlerhood 2 children enjoy playing simple hide-and-seek games. A suggestion for an activity of this nature is presented in the Intellectual Development section (page 598). The following game involving hiding and finding objects capitalizes on your child's newly emerging mental abilities, and also gives him practice in dealing with the properties of objects.

Find three cardboard boxes or pots without lids. You will need a small-, medium-, and large-size box. Place them in a row on a table or on the floor. Then place a ball or some other object underneath the largest box while your toddler is watching. Scramble the position of the boxes, but make sure that the ball remains under the large box. Then ask him to find the ball.

After several games of placing the ball under the large box, place the ball under the medium-size box and try this for several rounds. Once he catches on to selecting the right size, you can alter the game. Find three boxes of the same size, but paint them different colors or wrap them in different-colored papers. Hide the ball under one colored box for several tries and then move on to another. This will give him practice in discriminating colors. There are endless variations to this game that you can devise.

Modified Bowling

The Toddlerhood 2 child is often interested in playing with balls. One activity that capitalizes on this interest and gives him practice in rolling and aiming a ball involves modified bowling. Take a large cardboard box without a lid and place it on the floor so that the open end is facing your toddler.

Have him stand several feet away from the box. Obtain a large ball and show him how to bend down and roll it into the box. Then encourage him to do the same.

It may take him a long time and much practice before he manages to aim the ball so that it rolls into the box. Once he masters this game, you can place a couple of empty, lightweight plastic squirt bottles upright near the opening of the box. These can serve as bowling pins to knock over with the ball, adding a new dimension to this game. He will get plenty of exercise retrieving his own balls, but if you have the time, you can pretend that you are the automatic ball return.

How to Keep an Eye on Your Toddler Without Severely Restricting His Movements

Toddlerhood 2 children still need close parental supervision, but they also need freedom to exercise and try things out on their own. Keeping a toddler cooped up in a small area fosters neither his independence nor his self-confidence.

Parents of active young toddlers often wonder how to keep them within the boundaries of one area of their homes without having to resort to putting them in a small, confining area such as a playpen. This can represent a real problem during those times when parents are too busy or tired to run after their children.

A clever way to accomplish this goal is to section off part of a large room by using several small chairs, a couch, or some large, empty cardboard boxes. Be sure that you arrange the furniture or boxes so that your child has ample room to move, and so that he can see you. Put several of his favorite playthings in his corner or special area of the room. He may be more than willing to play there while you engage in some other activity, as long as he can see you.

For parents who find that rearranging furniture is not feasible, or is inconvenient, here is another suggestion. Try tacking up a very sheer piece of material across a corner or area of a room. This will give your child the feeling of having his own special place to play, and both of you will easily be able to watch one another's activities. He may not feel as if he is being confined, because he will still be able to see you.

Using either of these two suggestions, you will be able to keep an eye on him and talk to him while you busy yourself with other activities. He will have ample space in which to play, but will probably not feel as if his activities are being restricted. Even when the two of you are doing separate things, he will occasionally want to watch you and call out to you. By using your own imagination, you should be able to come up with additional ideas that will allow both of you freedom and closeness at the same time.

HOW TO ENSURE YOUR TODDLER'S SAFETY

The experience you have gained in handling your younger toddler will make it much easier for you to manage him in Toddlerhood 2 and 3. Taking simple precautions to ensure your toddler's safety can allow you to be much more relaxed. As the toddler becomes more mobile and adventurous, it is useful to review the safety precautions discussed in Toddlerhood 1 on pages (506–13) and consider a few additional precautions to ensure your child's safety.

When You Least Expect It . . .

When you do not expect an accident, that is when it is likely to occur. Many parents do not become suspicious and nervous when they think that their children are happily occupied in some play activity, and suddenly realize that there is a period of silence. However, when the normal sounds of play diminish, this should warn you of possible trouble.

There are other circumstances in which accidents are not expected but are likely to occur, such as when you are ill, vacationing, rushed, arguing with your spouse, or preoccupied with your own activities.

KEEPING HOLIDAYS SAFE, HAPPY TIMES. Another very common time to be on guard against unnecessary accidents occurring is during holidays. At these times you should be extra careful. Holiday celebrations can be great fun for both parents and children when everyone is in a relaxed, festive mood. A small amount of prevention can make holidays safe, joyous occasions for all.

It is easy to forget to take appropriate safety precautions when you are busy preparing for holidays, or socializing with friends and relatives. However, there are key precautionary measures that should not be overlooked. During the times when you are unable to keep an eye on your toddler, make sure that he is well supervised, or provide him with a safe place in which to play, so that he does not get his hands into bowls of nuts, popcorn, hard candies, or other potentially harmful foods and objects.

Every time a holiday rolls around—the Fourth of July, Valentine's Day, Easter, Chanukah, Christmas, etc.—it is wise to take a few minutes out to think of special potential hazards to your child. At Christmas time, for example, extra care should be taken to guard against your toddler or preschool child getting his hands on ornaments with small parts that can be swallowed, ornaments with sharp points, or the hooks that hold ornaments on the tree. Some parents have found it helpful to place an expandable, circular "kiddie corral" around the tree to prevent children from getting near enough to touch it. Other parents have decided not to decorate the tree with the usual potentially dangerous ornaments, but instead, tied harmless colored bows on the branches. Still other parents, who were trying to be extra cautious about the dried needles that often drop off trees, decided to use construction paper to make a Christmas tree and holiday decorations to hang on the walls. Decorative candles and other potentially hazardous decorations can certainly give a home a festive atmosphere at holiday time, but with a little ingenuity, it is possible to accomplish the same end without risk to the young child.

Halloween is a holiday meant for children to enjoy, so evaluate possible sources for accidents. Candies that are small enough to be swallowed on which your youngster might choke should be kept out of his reach. Parents who want their children to go "trick or treating" should accompany them, and keep a watchful eye on them during the time they are out. Local police departments often issue a list of checkpoints for keeping children safe during Halloween, including allowing good vision from masks or costumes. It is advisable to inquire about such lists at your local police headquarters as the holiday approaches.

Once back at home with a bag full of "treats," some of which may be harmful, it is a good idea to make a quick survey of its contents, and, if necessary, substitute nutritious, safe goodies for potentially harmful ones. Even if candy is wrapped, be suspicious; cut it and apples, etc., open; unfortunately there are people who put sharp objects into their "treats," to the point where hospitals sometimes offer free X-raying of treats on Halloween.

While their children were young, some parents have found it safer to throw a Halloween costume party in their home, rather than taking them "trick or treating." They claim that the children enjoyed this alternative. A home Halloween celebration had another major advantage in that parents could offer a variety of very nutritious treats as opposed to the non-nutritious treats, loaded with sugar, that youngsters usually collect. In many respects, this is a safe, fun way to enjoy this holiday, particularly for toddlers and preschoolers.

Fourth of July brings with it many potential dangers for children. Fireworks and young children can be an explosive combination (no pun intended). Although individual usage of fireworks is against the law in many areas of this country, each year one hears of unfortunate accidents involving children who were harmed by fireworks. Young children should be kept far away from fireworks. Accidents can occur even if they are only standing within firing range. The safest place for a youngster on the Fourth of July is probably indoors. In some areas fireworks displays or shows are sponsored by groups or by the city, and precautionary measures are generally taken so that onlookers can enjoy the show without personal risk.

Holiday visiting will surely take you to other people's homes. Do not take it for granted that they are safety-proofed. It will be your responsibility to keep an eye on your youngster. It may be necessary to take along a playpen for him, as well as a few of his favorite toys and snacks.

EATING

Your toddler's patterns of eating are likely to remain about the same as they were in Toddlerhood 1. The most obvious change will be seen in relation to his attempts to feed himself. Most toddlers will be determined to participate at mealtime and will be making steady progress in self-feeding.

Self-feeding

Toddlerhood 2 children are making impressive progress in their ability to eat by themselves. Some children will be able to handle a cup and a spoon skillfully, while others will be rather awkward and clumsy with these tools and utensils. You will be lucky, indeed, if your child is able to take over much of the responsibility for feeding himself for all three meals. Do not be surprised if he sometimes wants or allows you to feed him, and sometimes gets angry at your offers to help. Frequently there are days or hours in which a child wants desperately to do everything by himself, and other times when he wants you to do things for him. Be patient with your toddler. He may have difficulty deciding between independence and dependence in the area of eating.

Once a toddler becomes capable of using a cup and spoon with a certain degree of success, it is a good idea to introduce him to a fork. A child will find it most awkward to learn to feed himself with a regular fork, and the possibilities that he might accidentally poke himself in the eye or jab his face are real. A regular-size, sharp fork can be dangerous placed in a toddler's unsteady hands. He does not have sufficient co-ordination or control to be able to handle or use it properly. It is safer and easier for him to learn to use a fork properly if you initially offer him a child-size fork with blunt prongs, and, better still, one with a rounded-type bowl similar to a spoon.

Sometime during Toddlerhood 2 or 3, depending upon how he does with a spoon and fork, you can introduce him to a knife. For safety reasons, it is important to offer him a child-size knife with a very dull edge. When you first give him a knife to use, be sure to be on hand to supervise him. Even a dull-edged knife can be dangerous if it is waved around the eyes.

It is possible to teach him to use the knife to spread food such as margarine, peanut butter, or meat spreads on bread, and cut soft foods. He is lacking the manual skills required to use a knife to cut meats. This ability will not be acquired for several years. How well he does with a knife or any eating utensil partly depends on his level of co-ordination and hand and finger control and on how much opportunity he has had to practice.

Weaning

It is not uncommon for a toddler to continue to want to drink from a bottle, especially after dinner or before bedtime. The same holds true for those toddlers still making demands to breast-feed. Some toddlers, however, will show a strong preference for the cup and indicate that they want nothing further to do with the bottle or breast.

BATHING

Fun in the Tub

Most toddlers really enjoy their baths and some will have such a good time that they object to seeing bath time come to an end. Toys seem to go hand in hand with toddlers and are naturally carried into the tub. Even standard bathtub equipment such as washcloths, sponges, and soap bars become playthings for young children. Toddlers must be carefully supervised in the tub since they may try to drink the tub water or play with the faucets.

The toddler's fascination with kitchen equipment often results in spoons, measuring cups, and small assorted plastic containers and dishes being taken into the tub. Filling and dumping are favorite activities. Rubber ducks and plastic boats are among children's other prized bath time toys. There are a number of educational toys designed to enhance bathroom play. One, for example, involves the child's getting small boat-shaped objects into a U-shaped "harbor." While it is not necessary for you to purchase special educational bath toys, do not overlook opportunities to make learning in the tub fun for your toddler.

In the bathtub, an older toddler can carry out simple pretend activities. He can wash his dolls just like his parent washes him, create mountains out of bubble bath, sink his "battleships," or land "airplanes" in the "sea." Toddlers tend to be very interested in taking bubble baths. Young brothers and sisters may enjoy taking baths together, or taking baths with their parents. You can suggest imaginative activities for your toddler to carry out at bath time. This will make taking baths even more pleasurable for him.

Greater Participation

Young toddlers, desiring more independence at bath time, often make comical attempts to wash and dry themselves. It is a good idea to encourage your child's efforts, although intervention is necessary to get him really clean and dry. A few younger toddlers will be content to sit back and let their parents do all the washing. Children who have been encouraged to assume more responsibility at bath time as soon as they were ready are usually eager to participate and show their parents how much they can do by themselves.

Many Toddlerhood 2 and 3 children are capable of washing their faces and the front of their bodies, and then rinsing off the soap. They may also attempt to wash their hair, ears, and feet. They generally have trouble reaching the center of their necks and backs, because their arms are so short, but with the help of a bath brush, or other device with long tabs they can pull back and forth behind their backs, this obstacle can be overcome. These items foster independence and can help minimize hassles over parental interference from a child who is determined to bathe himself.

It is advisable to take advantage of your child's interest in washing and drying. Let him take over as much responsibility as he can manage, praise him for what he accomplishes, and very tactfully correct the finished job. The more he can do for himself, the easier your job will be.

Fear of the Bath

Not all toddlers are enthusiastic about taking baths. Fears related to baths are common during toddlerhood. Younger toddlers who are not fully confident of their standing or walking abilities may be insecure about falling or slipping in the tub. This insecurity can prompt them to become resistive at bath time. Reassurance and understanding from parents usually help to allay their anxiety, as does placing a grooved, rubber bath mat or rubber decals on the bottom of the tub to make it less slippery.

There is another less obvious reason why some children resist taking a bath, cry, or appear frightened at bath time. Some toddlers develop fears of disappearing down the bathtub drain when the stopper is pulled. This fear is similar to the child's fear of disappearing down the toilet when it is flushed. A toddler has not yet acquired a good understanding of size differences. Given his limitations and lack of experience, it is possible for him to think that he could be sucked down the bathtub drain along with the water.

This fear often becomes evident around the time that he recognizes his own separateness. Before his sense of self-identity is fully realized, the child may have some insecurities related to losing his identity—himself. According to some psychologists, the child's fear of disappearing down the drain may be related to his fear of losing his sense of identity.

The fact that a toddler often cannot verbalize his fear of disappearing down the drain makes it difficult for parents to know if this is causing him to be resistive at bath time. One way to find out is to try to eliminate other possible reasons for the child's resistance. Watch his reaction when you pull out the plug to let the water drain. A look of fear when he sees the water level dropping or hears the sound of swooshing water can be a good clue. Attempt to determine if he is fearful of slipping in the tub by following the suggestions given earlier for helping to allay this fear. Assuming that you have eliminated obstinacy, rebellion, and the fear of slipping, and he continues to resist taking a bath or cry when he is placed in the tub, there is a good chance that he is frightened of disappearing down the drain.

There are several approaches to handling a child who develops this fear. Forcing him into the tub and insisting that he remain there while the water drains might increase his fear. Arguing every night at bath time might result in temper tantrums or increased rebelliousness in other situations. Assuming that he is not so fearful that he will not get into the tub even with reassurance, you can attempt to make taking a bath more enjoyable for him by waiting until he is out of the tub before you let out the water, and by reassuring him that he is safe when he is in the tub.

You can also try to help him overcome his fear by reassuring him that he will not vanish down the drain, and helping him learn about the size of his body in relation to the drain opening in play situations. Encourage him to give his toys or dolls a bath in the sink or the tub. In this situation there will be no threat of danger to him. He can pull out the stopper and see that his toys do not disappear down the drain. Eventually he will realize that if a doll much smaller than himself cannot fit down the drain, neither can he.

This type of learning activity can help a young child overcome his fear. If he won't get in the tub even with reassurance, it is advisable to be patient and give him sponge baths until he feels more confident and secure in the bathtub. Fears related to the tub are usually outgrown early in the preschool years.

CLOTHING

Toddlerhood 2 children are becoming increasingly eager to take on more responsibility in dressing. By the end of this phase most children will be able to undress themselves completely, and may enjoy the activity of undressing for the sheer fun of it.

It is not unusual for a younger, uninhibited toddler who has recently learned how to take off his clothes to want to practice this new task even in public or at other inappropriate times. In handling this situation, avoid overreacting. While you help him back into his clothes, make it clear to your child in a matter-of-fact, firm tone of voice that he must keep his clothes on whenever he is out of the house. This type of behavior is usually short-lived, subsiding as the child grows older. It can be prevented by keeping a close eye on him.

As children move toward greater independence, they make further attempts to put on their own clothes. Mrs. Birney noticed that her daughter, Kristine, was taking a greater interest in dressing. One morning when Mrs. Birney was preparing to get Kristine dressed, Kristine yanked the dress out of her hands and struggled to put it on.

This mother noted that for every occasion on which Kristine put her dress on correctly, there was another occasion on which the outfit was put on backward or inside out. She bought an inexpensive, full-length mirror to fasten to the door in her daughter's bedroom, and tried to teach her the correct way to position and pull on clothes. The mirror helped Kristine see what kind of job she had done, and was of assistance to her in learning to dress herself properly.

When a child is able to see his mistakes, it is easier for him to correct them, but learning how to manage for himself may be a rather slow process, so do not expect perfection in his performance during this phase.

SLEEPING

The Toddlerhood 2 child, particularly during the latter part of this phase, often resists going to bed at his regular hour. He may scream, struggle, and even throw a temper tantrum. Firm handling is required, and it may sometimes become necessary to pick him up and carry him to bed.

When your child is finally tucked in, he may frequently ask for such things as a favorite toy, a special pillow, some food, or to be taken to the "potty." Many parents find that a good way to deal with these requests is to anticipate them ahead of time, and take care of any usual requests before tucking the child in bed.

Mr. and Mrs. Gregg used this approach with their son, Simon. Before they said "good night," they took him to the bathroom, offered him a drink, gave him his favorite pillow, and set his Teddy bear in the crib beside him. Then, as they tucked him in, they told him in a matter-of-fact manner that they had taken care of everything he might need or want, and would see him the next morning for breakfast. The Greggs ignored all further requests and crying without feeling guilty about it. This method of handling dawdling at bedtime is often successful.

Difficulties sleeping through the night may arise during this phase, but this problem more commonly arises in Toddlerhood 3. Waking during the night is discussed on pages 678–79.

DEVELOPING GOOD TOILET HABITS

Parents usually begin to think more seriously about toilet training during Toddlerhood 2. Some, but certainly not all, children will be ready for toilet training during this phase. Parents may notice several signs of readiness. Those parents who recognize indications of their child's capability and desire to co-operate will probably want to capitalize on this and initiate training.

Many parents do not start training until Toddlerhood 3, or even early in Preschool 1, depending upon their child and individual circumstances. There is no need to become impatient with a child who is not ready during this phase. Try to be flexible and relaxed about this issue.

Bowel training and suggestions for how to proceed with it were previously discussed in Toddlerhood 1 on pages 523–26. Before discussing the child's possible progress in toilet training, it is advisable to have a general familiarity with bladder training.

What You Should Know About Urine Training

Bladder control involves two steps: the ability to remain dry during the daytime, and the ability to remain dry overnight. In most cases urine control during the day precedes nighttime control by quite some time, although this is not necessarily the case with every child. Nighttime control is not usually achieved until Toddlerhood 3 or Preschool 1 and is discussed on pages 681–82. Urine control during the daytime can often be accomplished around the same time as bowel control, and some parents may want to initiate bowel and bladder training simultaneously.

CAPABILITY OR READINESS. As the child grows older, his bladder develops the ability to hold urine for longer stretches of time. During this phase he may begin to urinate less frequently for a need to release urine is felt only when the bladder becomes full. To prevent this release of urine, a conscious effort has to be made. The child has to hold back his natural urge to urinate to prevent wetting his pants.

The ability to retain urine until the child is able to get to the toilet requires both the physical control of the flow of urine, and the desire to hold it back. Parents often notice signs of readiness in their toddlers during Toddlerhood 2 and 3. You will probably notice your child's increasing interest in mimicking your behavior, and doing things to gain approval. He may express an interest in the toilet and show a growing awareness of the process of urination.

Other signs of readiness include a child's ability to say the words you have taught him for urine after he has wet or while he is wetting. He may also indicate that he dislikes wet diapers. These are all clues that he is becoming ready to learn to urinate in a toilet.

Between the ages of about two to three and a half, most children are capable and ready for bladder training. There is a great deal of variability in the age at which a given youngster gains bladder control. In general, girls tend to be faster at bladder training than boys.

Try to refrain from becoming impatient or overly concerned with this issue. Your toddler will develop his own "pace" for bladder training, and will benefit from having a relaxed parent who respects whatever pace he sets.

SUGGESTIONS FOR BLADDER TRAINING. As in the case of bowel training, it is most important to develop a personalized training program suited to your child's capabilities and interests. Attempt to select the right timing for him and adopt a relaxed, positive attitude toward helping him achieve the independent ability to control his urine.

There are several principles to keep in mind when you begin to help your child establish bladder control. They are very similar to the principles mentioned in the discussion of bowel training on pages 522–26. The suggestions that follow should be of assistance to you in formulating a program.

The first step is to teach your toddler a word to associate with urination. Many parents use the words "pee pee," "wee wee," or "wet." As in bowel training, you should repeat these words several times daily. Your child will probably start to use them after he has wet his diapers, and then when he is urinating. Gradually he will begin to tell you when he feels the urge to urinate.

Expect some inconsistency when he starts to notify you of his need to urinate. There are bound to be days when he will simply forget to let you know, or will tell you too late. Be patient.

Take advantage of his desire to imitate your behavior in helping him understand how to urinate on the potty chair or toilet. Little boys who have had opportunities to see their fathers or other males standing up to urinate may feel more comfortable doing as they do. Offer your son a small step so that he can easily reach the regular toilet.

Once your child meets with some initial success, it would be appropriate to make the shift from diapers to training pants. Let him know that he is a "big boy" now and can wear more grown-up underwear.

Try your best to keep the teaching process as relaxed and free of emotional tension as possible. Avoid scolding, spanking, or punishing your child in other ways for having "accidents." Training in bladder control takes quite a while, and progress is sometimes slow. Lapses or "accidents" are very common, especially during the "learning" phases. Even after a child has achieved fairly consistent bladder control, "accidents" may occur when he is under stress, very tired, ill, or wrapped up in some activity, particularly those outside the home.

General Progress in Toilet Training

Toddlerhood 2 children are becoming more conscious of the sensations generated in passing a bowel movement and urinating. They are more aware of the purpose of toilets. Their increasing desire to mimic their parents' behavior makes teaching them to use the toilet a realistic possibility.

Greater regularity in a child's elimination habits may emerge during this phase. In the event that your toddler defecates or urinates at specific times of the day, you might try to put him on the potty at those times. Toddlerhood 2 children do not usually object when they are seated on the toilet.

Another factor that improves the chances of parents' training efforts meeting with success is their child's growing ability to say words like "pooh pooh" and "pee pee" and associate these words with what they represent. Occasionally a toddler may tell his parents in advance that he has to "make," or even go to the toilet all by himself. This is the exception, rather than the rule. It is not uncommon for a Toddlerhood 2 child to become upset when he soils his diapers or training pants, and this desire for cleanliness can help in training him.

However, many children do not exhibit these signs of readiness for training in Toddlerhood 2. Trying to train a youngster who is unco-operative or irregular in his patterns of elimination can be very difficult, and is not advisable. On the other hand, this might be a good age to start teaching words for his bowel movements and urine, and to encourage him to tell you when he feels the urge to "go." Remember that at first he is likely to notify you after he has already wet or dirtied his pants. Be patient with your toddler, and do not expect him to catch on immediately.

It is very important not to rush your toddler or place too much pressure upon him to become trained, although encouragement and some motivation are often helpful. A casual, low-keyed, pleasant approach should prevail. Given ample time and a little help from you, he will learn to use a toilet, but it often takes time for children to adjust to this new way of life.

Resistance to Toilet Training

Assuming a toddler has shown signs of readiness, there are still factors and circumstances that can result in his resistance to toilet training. Objections may be voiced by a youngster who has difficulty sitting still on the toilet seat long enough to perform. A child who has associated the potty with something unpleasant such as being forced to sit there too long or has bowel movements that are hard to pass may be unco-operative during toilet training. Resistance can also arise when parents put too much pressure upon their child.

The Toddlerhood 2 child often has a strong desire to exert his autonomy. Being overly pressured or controlled by his parents at a time when he wants to exercise his own control can irritate him and undermine his desire to be co-operative. Quite frequently a child's normal rebellion and negative attitude spill over into the area of toilet training, especially when his parents are making too big an issue over it, or are insisting that he live up to their expectations when he is not able or willing.

A toddler who was co-operative in the past may now become obstinate and resistive to the toilet. It is not uncommon for a child to tease his parents by indicating to them that he has to "make," and then, after the parent has placed him on the potty, deliberately refuse to defecate or urinate. Other children may play games with their parents and hide from them when they have to "go." Still others may purposely refuse to pass a bowel movement or urinate while on the potty, and then soil or wet their pants as soon as they are off it. These children are aware of the fact that their behavior is frustrating and infuriating to their parents, and they are using the toilet training issue to irritate, get back at their parents, or assert their independence.

Arguing with or punishing a toddler who is using toilet training as a means of getting to his parents gets the parents nowhere, except more frustrated and angry. The child's resistance does not usually last very long, so it may be best to ease up on the pressure or even postpone further attempts to train him until he becomes more co-operative. This attitude will probably save unnecessary aggravation, and toilet training will not become an issue of winning or losing. Avoid pressuring and arguing, even if it means a short delay in training.

Occasionally a child who strongly objects to his parents' attempts to train him may withhold passing his stools for a day or two or longer. This behavior is a type of constipation, but the underlying reasons are psychological. It is advisable to treat the matter casually, rather than turn it into an argument. His condition will cure itself in time, and will not harm him.

Toilet Training Before or After the Arrival of a New Baby?

Parents who are expecting a second child during the latter part of their toddler's second year often ask whether they should initiate toilet training prior to or after the arrival of their new baby. There is no right answer to this question. It all depends on factors such as the child's readiness and attitude, the parents' attitude, and how much time is left before the new baby arrives. Knowing that they will be extra busy with their new baby, some parents decide to try to toilet train their toddler or young preschool child ahead of time. A child who can be successfully trained by the time the new baby arrives will make things easier on his parents, who can save on energy, time, and laundry.

Toilet training may take several months, and it is a big step for a child. He needs to be permitted to go at his own pace, without being pushed. Getting prepared for and accustomed to a new baby brother or sister is often a big enough adjustment for a child, without being pressured to master toilet training at the same time. In the event that you want to toilet train your toddler before your new child arrives, allow him to proceed at his own rate, and do not press him to succeed.

Parents should be prepared for a possible regression in their toddler after the new baby is brought home. Even a preschool child who had previously been trained may temporarily return to dirtying and/or wetting his pants during the period of adjustment to a new sibling.

There is no need for parents to be overly concerned about this. A short period of regression is not uncommon. The child who regresses in toilet training needs reassurance from his parents that he is still loved, and that he is not a failure. Deliberate soiling or wetting in a child who has been successful in developing good toilet habits usually indicates that he wants more attention. Rather than belittling, reprimanding, or punishing, which may only aggravate the situation, parents should concentrate upon trying to find ways to fulfill his needs and make him happier.

Some parents who have had little or no luck in helping their child learn to use a toilet before the arrival of a new baby find that he suddenly trains himself in a matter of a few days or weeks after the new baby is brought home. Comparing himself with the new baby may make him feel very big and grown-up. This may stimulate his desire to follow the more grown-up pattern of using a toilet.

DISCIPLINE

Disciplining your child during this phase is apt to become more difficult. He may sometimes be unco-operative in an effort to exert his independence from you. He may also try your patience and test your limits. This is quite normal behavior for a child of this age.

Requests alone will probably not motivate him to stop an annoying activity or stay away from a dangerous place. Perhaps the most effective way to get him to stop is to lift him up and take him away while you tell him why you have to do this. You might also try distracting him by giving him one of his favorite playthings, or finding a replacement activity that he will enjoy equally as much as the objectionable one.

In attempting to direct your toddler verbally, keep your commands and questions short and sharp. Show him what you want him to do by motioning or pointing. The simpler the request, the more likely he will be able to follow it. Environmental discipline as described on pages 324, 506–7, 510 should come in very handy during this phase, and will make life more peaceful for both you and your toddler.

How to Handle Negativism in Your Child

Many of the restrictions you impose on your young child's behavior are likely to be met with objections (verbal and physical) and outbursts of temper. The child may run away when you call him, put up a physical struggle when you ask him to do something, or throw a temper tantrum. There is no way to avoid antagonizing him completely during toddlerhood, even if you try your hardest. The simple fact that you are attempting to change your child's behavior puts you in a position that is opposite of your toddler's.

Throughout toddlerhood your child will have to face what you want him to do versus doing what he pleases. He will test your limits from time to time to find out what you expect of him so that he can decide how to react to your restrictions.

Negativism is a healthy and normal sign in a child of this stage. Refusing to comply with his parents' commands and requests often helps convince the child that he is a separate person. Trying to make your child obey your every request without permitting him to express the normal amount of negativism which is typical and important at this stage of development is a mistake. In a very real sense, you should be pleased when your child exhibits this kind of attitude and begins to assert himself. However, his behavior must not be allowed to get out of hand.

There are ways to maintain firm limits without completely suppressing his individuality or causing him to "lose face." It is important to be able to tell the difference between "real" negative behavior, and the playful kind of "back talk" that toddlers often use with parents. A child who is really displaying negative behavior, for example, will run away, kick, push, or vigorously defy your directions or requests. A child who is playing games with you and simply wants your acknowledgment that he is an individual with his own will acts much differently. He may say, "No," or, "Don't want to," when you ask him to do something, but he will then do it anyway. Some children will say no to everything. If you mistake your child's playful "back talk" for "real" negative behavior, and react to it by becoming overly upset with him, you can create a problem where none previously existed. Some parents find that getting upset over this type of behavior can draw attention to it and even reinforce it. It is advisable not to become overly upset with your child's testing behavior.

Real displays of obstinancy are harder to deal with than playful teasing, especially when it is imperative that your child do something, and he is vigorously refusing to do it. The child's resistance and the parent's insistence usually turn into an argument, which can be extremely frustrating to both parties. As a parent, you must usually maintain the upper hand, and not "give in" or abdicate your authority.

RESPECTING THE CHILD'S NEGATIVE FEELINGS WHILE MAINTAINING CONTROL. By letting your child know that you understand how he feels, you will be permitting him to maintain his self-esteem. How is this done? Assuming that your child refuses to put on his socks and shoes, you could say something like, "I know that you're angry and don't want to get dressed, but I must insist that you put on your shoes and socks," while you put his feet into his socks. This enables you to permit the child to save face, but makes it clear that he is expected to do what is necessary. Many parents who have employed this technique have found that it works very well.

AVOID ASKING QUESTIONS THAT CAN BE ANSWERED WITH "NO." If you ask a young child whether or not he wants to do something that he may not find pleasurable, such as picking up his toys, eating his peas, or "going" on the potty, his most probable reply will be a flat "No." After all, during toddlerhood, "no" is likely to be his most often used word. Once your child responds with "no" (assuming he is not just saying it in a playful manner), persuading him to change his mind and do what you want him to do may be nearly impossible. You may end up feeling frustrated and having to argue with him unnecessarily. It is important to offer your child some choices, such as which toy he prefers to play with or whether or not he wants to go to the park, but it is advisable not to offer him choices when it comes to things that are necessary, such as getting dressed, brushing his teeth, or taking a bath. If you want him to wear a hat outside, for instance, avoid the following question: "Do you want to wear your hat?" Rather, it might be more effective to say something like, "Would you rather wear your red or blue hat on our walk?"

Teaching Good Manners

An important area of discipline includes educating your child about manners. Good manners are learned, and since learning is such a slow process for children, it is advisable to begin teaching them when they are young. Manners include such things as respecting the rights of others, learning to share, co-operate, say "please" and "thank you," hold and use eating utensils in an acceptable manner, and so forth.

You can initiate training efforts during toddlerhood, but toddlers are not ready for rigorous training in manners. Many aspects of acquiring good manners require readiness in addition to training. A child must have adequate control and co-ordination before he can be expected to manipulate eating utensils properly. He must have a sufficient awareness and understanding of property rights before he can learn to respect others' belongings.

Toddlers need to have some opportunities to mess with their food and experiment with taking objects that belong to other people, since these experiences will help them learn. They also need to have a chance to be provocative and negativistic, simply to learn about themselves and others' expectations of them. Most youngsters, even by age two, are not deliberately rude to others. They simply have a lot to learn about dealing with other people.

There are several small ways in which to encourage your child to develop good manners. Through your program of discipline, attempt to teach him about respecting other people's belongings, respect for authority figures, and so forth. Encourage him to be around other people so that he will learn to get along with them. Chances are that if he likes others, he will want them to like him too, and will be motivated to be polite, share, and co-operate.

Most importantly, set a good example for your child. Having an appropriate model is a great aid in learning good manners. Politeness among family members and an atmosphere of love and respect for everyone's rights in the home will probably do more for him in terms of promoting good manners than nagging, or giving him a long list of do's and don'ts. Go easy on manners training during toddlerhood, and keep your expectations to a minimum.

Does a Toddler Steal?

The answer to this question is no, since stealing implies an intentional act of wrongdoing, with a definite understanding of right versus wrong. The toddler does not deliberately steal. He is strongly motivated to grab and handle everything that happens to interest him. It is not uncommon for youngsters occasionally to take things that do not belong to them. The Toddlerhood 2 child is first beginning to learn to distinguish between what is his and what is not his. Developing a sense of property rights takes a long time, and even after a child becomes aware of ownership rights, he still has to learn the harder lesson of respecting those rights.

Handling a toddler who cannot resist taking others' belongings is fairly straightforward. In a matter-of-fact way, take the object out of his hands and firmly remind him that it does not belong to him. Tell him that it must be returned to its rightful owner, and help him bring the object back.

Avoid looking shocked or extremely angry. This may result in your toddler's making a game of taking others' property just to see whether you will become upset again. Harsh shows of disapproval involving punishment are not really appropriate, since your child does not yet understand that what he did was unacceptable.

Discipline and Responsibility in the Home

Another aspect of disciplining a young child includes teaching him to assume some minimal responsibility for the care of his room and his home when he is ready and able. Within the scope of his abilities, he can be encouraged to help you in small ways as you work around the home and yard. A young child who is able to carry his toys from place to place, for example, can certainly help you put them back where they belong when he is through playing with them. When encouraging your toddler to assist you, do not overburden him or expect too much from him. The idea is to capitalize on his interest in mimicking you and participating in your activities, and to give him the feeling that he is needed.

A child, even as young as eighteen months, is likely to be showing a natural interest in household activities and a desire to participate in them because he wants to imitate his parents. He will enjoy watching his parents sweep the floors and wipe the table and then imitating them. This makes him feel grown-up and gives him a chance to please his parents. It also allows him to feel that he is an important member of the family.

A Toddlerhood 2 or 3 child who is able to remember where some of the groceries belong may be eager to help his parent put them away. Helping out in this respect allows him to practice his new skills and makes him feel proud of himself. By working along with another family member to straighten up the house or carry objects from place to place, he is learning a new skill, and also learning to co-operate with another person in an activity. Wiping up his water messes in the bathroom along with Mommy or Daddy, or putting his toys away as his parent does the same, are not "work" for him; they are enjoyable activities.

Your young assistant may get on your nerves at times. Ed Pelligrino, for example, enjoyed making fancy desserts for the family. He used a special technique to roll out strudel dough that his father, a professional baker, had taught him. One afternoon Ed was in the process of rolling the dough when his son, David, wandered into the kitchen to help. David immediately grabbed a hunk of dough and formed it into a ball. At first Ed was not annoyed. He explained what he was doing, and showed his son the proper way to roll out the dough. He even let David hold the rolling pin along with him. David listened with interest, and for a few minutes he was content to watch his father working. After a short while, however, David began to pick up pieces of dough again and make them into "things."

Ed realized that he was not getting anywhere with his little helper. Rather than getting upset, he offered David a small piece of strudel dough, told him to sit at the other end of the table, and gave him an opportunity to do whatever he wanted to with it. David was delighted to have his own special piece, and played happily with it while his father completed his cooking project.

Being tolerant of his son's good intentions and also being practical, Mr. Pelligrino was able to work around his son's interference. Allowing your toddler to participate in your household activities can be trying at times, but with a little patience and ingenuity you can usually manage to get the job done and also provide an excellent learning experience for your child.

SEX EDUCATION

Why Discuss Sex Education During Toddlerhood?

Most parents would agree that toddlers are too young and immature to be offered anything but the broadest, most basic type of "sex education." Parents who have tried to present facts about sexual function to their toddlers frequently find that they are simply not interested, and are not capable of understanding this kind of information. Some precocious children who are advanced in verbal abilities may begin to ask questions about birth, conception, pregnancy, and so forth, during Toddlerhood 3, but most children do not start asking sex-related questions until the preschool stage. Suggestions for answering children's questions are provided in Preschool 2 on pages 865–76.

There are other ways besides verbal explanations in which parents can convey positive or negative messages to their toddlers and teach them about the "facts of life." Parents can influence their toddler's feelings about relationships between people of the same sex as well as the opposite sex. Toddlers are in a good position to watch how their mothers and fathers get along with one another, get along with members of the opposite sex, and interact with persons of the same sex. Mothers and fathers can also influence their children's feelings about their bodies and themselves during toddlerhood by the way they react to their children's touching their genitals, labeling of the sex organs and organs of elimination, and, in part, by how they interact with their toddlers. Sex education, in an adult sense, is usually not an issue during toddlerhood, but the child will be receiving a more subtle form of sex education through his daily interactions with his parents, other family members, and peers.

Sex Education Is a Personal Matter: A Controversial Topic

It is up to you to decide what type of sex education you want your child to receive based upon your own personal, moral, and religious convictions. You must inevitably teach your child what you feel is right, when you feel that your child is "ready."

Sex education is, indeed, a controversial subject. The minute some parents hear the words "sex education" they get nervous or embarrassed. Perhaps this is because when they were young, their own parents ignored this issue, offered them untrue facts about sex, or caused them to feel guilty about expressing a normal curiosity about their genitals or sexual issues. It is understandable, then, why some parents might feel uncomfortable having to educate their own children about sex. Yet regardless of what may have happened in the past, these days there are many parents who appear to be more relaxed in their attitudes about sex. They are looking forward to having the opportunity to teach their children about sex-related issues in a way in which they wish they had been taught when they were young.

Those of you who are concerned and doubtful about your ability to do a good job should try to relax. Offering your child a healthy, positive type of sex education need not be very difficult or complicated. The material in both the toddlerhood and preschool Sex Education sections will help you by offering guidelines and suggestions which you can utilize in developing your own, personalized approach to "sex education."

Toddlers Are Not Sex Maniacs

To a fourteen-month-old little boy who is naturally exploring his environment and his body, touching his penis seems as interesting to him as touching his fingers or his nose. To a sixteen-month-old little girl, poking her finger around her vaginal area represents an expression of her normal curiosity about her body, just as does poking her finger into her ear or into her navel. Even if toddlers knew that there was such a word as "sex," they would not know the meaning of this word, because their minds, their bodies, and their experience are not sufficiently well developed to enable them to comprehend what is meant by "sex."

Adults often attach sexual meanings and shameful interpretations to toddlers' normal, natural explorations of their bodies, specifically their genitals. Some parents frequently treat their children's normal desires to investigate areas of their bodies as a sex problem. Toddlers do not feel the least bit guilty or inhibited about investigating and playing with their genitals, but they may learn to feel this way if their parents convey the message that handling their genitals is "naughty," "dirty," or "harmful," and that these areas of the body are taboo. When they play with their genitals they are not masturbating in the adult sense of the word. Little boys are not capable of having an ejaculation until their bodies undergo changes during puberty, and children's self-stimulation does not culminate in orgasm.

Some books and parents refer to the young child's playing with his genitals as masturbation. The word masturbation, however, often has negative implications. It is a misleading label for the kind of activity which occurs during toddlerhood. Toddlers exploring their genitals may find that touching feels good, but they do not experience the same kind of sexual and sensuous feelings in fondling their genitals as would an adult.

Parents' Reactions to Toddlers' Genital Play

It may be difficult for you to predict with any certainty just how you would react if you found your infant or young child playing with his genitals. Depending upon your personal feelings, you may be surprised, shocked, embarrassed, angered, or not bothered by it at all. Fewer parents these days seem to regard this as a problem. You may also be inclined to react differently depending upon how frequently and where you see your child playing with himself—in the privacy of his room, in the middle of the living room, or out in public. Some examples may help illustrate the variety of reactions parents may have when they discover their children touching their genitals.

Sharon had always prided herself on the fact that, unlike her parents, she was liberal about sex. She vowed to herself and her friends that she would treat her child's normal genital investigation and sex play casually, and would be totally open and honest in answering her son's questions about sex. One evening, while Sharon was in the midst of changing her son Timmy's diapers, she noticed him playing with his penis. In spite of her preplanned reaction, she was surprised, slightly disgusted, and embarrassed by Timmy's behavior. She grabbed his hand, slapped it lightly, and said, "No, dirty boy!" Timmy began to cry, and she picked him up to comfort him. After this incident she felt ashamed of herself and guilty that she had let both herself and Timmy down.

This parent's honest reaction is not atypical. It seems apparent that despite her strong desire to overcome the negative feelings about sex conveyed to her during her own childhood, she could not completely leave the past behind, at least on this first occasion which called for a quick response.

Parents who consciously decide to take a casual and relaxed approach about this issue, and then react with shock or embarrassment when actually faced with the situation, need not worry that their toddler's future sexual development will be stifled as a result of their reaction on one occasion. You will undoubtedly have numerous chances to convey your attitudes about sex and morals to your child during early childhood, and it is your over-all attitude that will be transmitted over a period of time.

Parents who have been told untruths about sex-related issues by their own parents, sometimes pass "old wives' tales" on to their toddlers. Mr. Levine was giving his daughter, Ellen, a sponge bath one evening when he saw her fondling her genital region. He became very concerned about this behavior. When he was younger, he had been told that playing with the genitals can make you become emotionally disturbed. This father did not realize that the information he had been given by his own parents was not correct. His misunderstanding led him to want to protect his daughter. He picked her up, spanked her, and said, "No, don't touch—you'll hurt yourself!" Ellen looked startled and began to cry. Like many other children, she was being punished for expressing a natural, wholesome interest in her body.

Toddlerhood 2 is a phase in which some parents begin to toilet train their children. Parents who are extremely anxious for their youngsters to be trained often misinterpret children's exploratory interest in the genitals as signs or clues that they have to urinate. This was the case with Mrs. Crowley, who had recently begun toilet training her eighteen-month-old son, Don. Whenever she observed him holding and playing with himself, she immediately lead him to the bathroom and sat him on the potty, under the assumption that he had to pass urine.

Some parents react very casually when they notice their children playing with their genitals. One afternoon, Mr. Engle observed his eighteen-month-old son, Kurt, fondling his penis while they were romping around together in the nude in Kurt's bedroom. Mr. Engle was rather amused and actually delighted that his son had discovered his own penis and testicles. He pointed to his son's penis and casually said, "Kurt, this is your penis; here are your testicles." Kurt stared downward toward his genitals. Then Mr. Engle pointed to his own penis and testicles and said, "See, Kurt, Daddy has a penis and testicles, too. Your body is like Daddy's." Kurt smiled with utter delight, and then glanced back and forth between his own and his father's sex organs. This father took advantage of the opportunity to teach his son the names for his sex organs and point out the similarity in their bodies. He did not convey anything but positive messages to his toddler.

Guidelines for Dealing with Toddlers' Genital Play

Openly negative reactions to children's normal, natural genital play may create unhealthy attitudes and associations with sex which would not be favorable to children's sexual adjustment either now, or later in their lives. The taboo on genital handling in our society is strong, and these kinds of parental reactions have tended to be the norm, rather than the exception. Actively interfering with children's normal genital interest and play clearly transmits this taboo to them. In some children genital interest and handling may actually increase when parents display their concern or call an undue amount of attention to genital exploration, although they are likely to engage in this activity secretly, and feel ashamed, anxious, and guilty about what they are doing. Other toddlers may suppress their desire to handle their sex organs, leaving them feeling generally anxious and tense, and fearful of their own normal impulses. Negative parental treatment of children's genital handling might also, in some ways, hinder children's later ability to understand sex-related issues or their own sexual feelings.

Young children are not as likely to develop guilt, shame, and anxiety in relation to their bodies when parents take a relaxed attitude and react casually to genital handling. Parents who discover their youngsters playing with their genitals should try to look at this as a natural, healthy experience. Toddlers are simply curious about their bodies and the sensations accompanying touching the genital region. Parents can let their child know that they know what he is doing, and then try to ignore the situation. Should his activity bother them, perhaps they can casually suggest an alternative activity. Slapping his hands, yanking them away from his genitals, or calling undue attention to the activity may make him more determined to persist.

In cases where a child plays with his genitals frequently or seems very engrossed in this activity, parents should check to see whether their youngster has had enough contact with them and stimulation from external sources, or whether there is something causing him to feel unusually pressured or anxious. By eliminating the possible source of tension, and making sure that he has ample opportunities to engage in other activities, parents might be able to minimize a toddler's need to engage in self-stimulation.

A child who plays with his genitals in public can be told that it is not appropriate to play with one's genitals in front of other people. The vast majority of parents will want to set limits on this kind of behavior. Ignoring this behavior will undoubtedly result in someone else's calling attention to it, perhaps in a way that is distasteful.

Further research on childhood sexuality is sorely needed. Well-documented, scientific evidence that harsh, punitive, or negative treatment of childhood genital play has undesirable consequences for sexual adjustment is lacking, although many professionals feel that there is some justification in this hypothesis. Having no solid facts to help guide you in deciding what kind of atmosphere in the home would best foster normal sexual adjustment, you must come to your own conclusions about whether or not to accept this hypothesis. The important factor to keep in mind is that your reaction to your child's genital handling can influence the way he feels about his body and himself.

Helping Your Child Acquire a Healthy, Positive Attitude Toward His Body

When a child feels good about his body, he generally feels good about himself. At this stage in your child's development, he should be gaining confidence in himself, and you will be instrumental in helping him do so. For example, you will help him master language skills by teaching him the names for parts of his body as well as names for people and objects in his environment. Once he masters them, he will feel good and more confident about his own abilities.

Most parents readily teach their child names and functions of objects and people. When it comes to certain parts of the child's body, however, some "educational programs" are not as comprehensive as they should be. Parents may not hesitate to teach their toddler words such as eyes, ears, nose, mouth, shoulder, fingers, hair, tongue, and teeth, but they may fail to teach him the names for his organs of elimination and sex organs. Nearly every parent has heard another parent, at one time or another, playing a word game with a toddler such as the following: "Mary, point to your nose; now point to your toes." However, it is unlikely that you have overheard a parent telling a little girl to point to her vagina, or a little boy to point to his penis. Parents do not hesitate to tell their children that they smell with their nose, but they might never dream of telling them that their rectum allows them to pass a bowel movement.

Why some parents fail to provide their toddlers with proper labels for their sex organs or their organs of elimination is not exactly clear. Perhaps parents feel that by teaching children labels such as penis, testicles, vagina, and anus, children's attention will be drawn to those parts of their bodies, and they will develop an unusual interest in sex or elimination. A common worry is that by teaching toddlers labels for these body parts, they will repeat words like "penis" or "anus" in public and thus embarrass their parents.

Some parents have noticed that despite casual, open teaching of labels and functions, two toddlers gleefully converse in public about penises, etc. This behavior is normal and nothing to be particularly concerned about. Many young children go through a phase in which they enjoy talking about, pointing to, or even exposing their genitals. Unless parents become overly upset and draw further attention to the behavior, chances are that it will subside rather quickly. Ignoring the behavior or distracting the youngsters by engaging them in a fun activity often helps. Whether or not parents teach the correct labels for the genitals, children who are interested in these areas of the body will talk about them anyway.

Many adults, perhaps out of embarrassment, and perhaps out of politeness, refer to the vaginal area as the area of the body "down there," or refer to a man's penis as a "thing," although it is clear to everyone that they mean vagina and penis.

It appears that the sex taboo in our society frequently includes not teaching children the names of their sex organs and organs of elimination. Children who have not been provided with correct labels for these organs may, according to many psychologists, take longer to accept and understand the functions of these parts of their bodies. This, in turn, may influence their ability to understand sex and elimination activities in the future.

"Forbidden" objects and places and taboo words often become a focus of attention. From their parents' attitudes and reactions, children quickly learn what labels and areas of the body are taboo. These labels and body parts may then become particularly fascinating to them, since their parents get upset every time these words are spoken and these areas of the body are touched. By not teaching children about these areas, parents may actually draw youngsters' attention to their genitals and organs of elimination, and strengthen their curiosity.

Teaching toddlers names for these areas should not stimulate their curiosity. Merely because parents matter-of-factly teach toddlers words like "arm" or "nose" children do not become unusually fascinated with these body parts. They might, however, develop such an unusually strong interest if parents purposely avoided teaching them labels for their arms and nose, and reacted negatively or tried to distract them every time they touched these parts of their bodies.

Casually teaching a toddler words like "penis," "vagina," "breast," and "anus," just as he is taught words like "leg," "arm," "nose," and "hair," is certainly a good idea. The way in which you educate your child about these areas of the body is a personal matter, but most professionals would advise you to refrain from instilling in your child the idea that these areas of the body are taboo.

Nudity in the Home

Some parents today seem to have fairly relaxed attitudes toward nudity, or at least partial nudity, in the home. There has certainly been a significant move away from the modesty of previous generations. Most professionals feel that casual attitudes are more advisable, and that occasionally seeing their parents nude can be a healthy experience for toddlers. Watching his parents get undressed and bathe, or walk around the home with no clothes on, allows a child to be exposed to the unclothed body in a perfectly natural way and learn something about the different forms the body takes in males versus females.

According to many authorities, when a child nears the age of three, and his own sexual feelings begin to develop, he may experience some emotional arousal upon seeing his parents naked, and may be upset by such exposure on a regular basis. Furthermore, parents are advised against behaving seductively or erotically toward their child, because of the possibility of such experiences causing emotional tension and ultimately having an unfavorable psychological effect upon him.

The decision as to whether to allow your child either occasionally or regularly to see you in the nude is a personal one. Whatever your decision, you need not be too concerned with your toddler.

A common question that parents have is whether or not it is all right to allow siblings of the same or opposite sex to take baths together or to see each other getting undressed. Again, this is a question of parental judgment, since there is no clear scientific evidence on this subject. In some homes, small children regularly bathe and dress together. Some youth organizations and local swimming groups that teach young children to swim often do not require bathing suits in the pool, although this is more common with groups of children of the same sex. It is not generally regarded as unhealthy for young children occasionally to see one another in the nude, since this allows them to learn about each other's bodies. As the child's sexual identity begins to emerge, usually during the preschool years, he may become embarrassed or respond differently to being seen in the nude or seeing other adults or children in the nude; this is described in the Sex Education section in Preschool 2 (pages 878–80).

FEARS

Overprotection and Fears

It is not uncommon for children who have been overprotected to be more susceptible to developing fears than those who have been encouraged to give up their dependence according to signs of readiness. An overprotective parent generally exaggerates possible dangers. Accidents, hazards, illnesses, and so forth, are often blown out of proportion. The parent hovers over the child to protect him at every turn, and limits the independent exploring the child can do. When the child falls or incurs even a minor injury such as a scraped knee or a cut finger, the parent may become unduly concerned and worried, and/or may feel as if what happened were his or her fault for not watching the child more closely.

The parent's guilt, overconcern, and fearful attitude become obvious to the child. He, in turn, becomes convinced that there is good reason to be fearful of his surroundings and may cut short his explorations because he is afraid that he will be injured.

Sometimes parents who have to leave their child in order to work during the day feel guilty about doing so. This guilt, be it well founded or unrealistic, may result in overprotective feelings on the part of these parents during the time that they spend with their child. Parents who tend to be overprotective of their children may be well-meaning, but this pattern of behavior can increase or reinforce children's fears.

Try to allow your child independence that is consistent with his abilities and needs. Take advantage of signs of his readiness to give up his dependence upon you. When minor accidents occur, do not show him that you are overly anxious and concerned. Strive to develop a happy balance between protecting him from real dangers and allowing him to function freely in his explorations and learning experiences.

Common Fears

The fears that the child of this age develops are generally similar to those that were discussed during Toddlerhood 1, although each child may develop individual fears other than those previously mentioned depending upon factors such as his personality and experiences. Certain fears seem to change with age and may diminish or reach a peak at particular times. Fear of separations from parents, for instance, tends to be heightened during this phase. A child's increasing awareness of himself and his environment often contributes to his insecurity and fearfulness. A parent's presence when a child is in a new kind of situation or different surroundings allays his fears and enables him to be more adaptive.

The toilet, for many toddlers, represents an interesting piece of equipment to explore. They may play with the water in the toilet bowl, steer toy cars around the rim of the seat, and have fun repeatedly flushing the toilet. Having learned something about this bathroom fixture, they may not be frightened by it once their parens begin toilet training them. These youngsters may even express a desire to flush their own feces down the toilet.

On the other hand, some children react with shock or fear when the toilet is flushed. Their fears may be related to the sound of the water going down the drain. Noises that do not prompt fear reactions in older children may be very frightening to toddlers or even young preschoolers.

Toddlers' fears of the toilet flushing may also be related to the disappearance of their bowel movements. During the time when a child's sense of "self" is emerging, he may consider his bowel movements to be a part of himself. He may not want to part with them knowing that they will vanish down the drain. Seeing his feces disappear may make him fearful that he has lost a part of himself. This can make him avoid the toilet.

Another possible reason for a child to be frightened when the toilet is flushed is the thought that he, too, might vanish down the drain if he happened to fall into the toilet bowl. As we have seen, the young child does not have a concept of the relative size of his body in comparison to other objects such as the toilet bowl or the drain opening.

In cases in which a child is very fearful when the toilet is flushed, it is generally best to flush it after he is off the toilet seat, or even out of the bathroom. Occasionally a toddler reacts with fear when his parent does the flushing but is less uncomfortable about doing this by himself. Try to take advantage of any available opportunities to help your toddler learn about space relationships and how much room his body occupies in comparison to other objects and spaces. This may help him realize that he could not possibly fit down the drain.

It is not unusual for a curious or fearful toddler to experiment with the toilet by throwing his socks, dolls, or other objects into the bowl to see if they go down the drain when it is flushed. You will obviously have to limit this behavior carefully, but, at the same time understand that your toddler's experiments are important to him as a way of dealing with his curiosity or fear of the toilet. Fear of the toilet flushing often emerges around the time toilet training is begun, and normally diminishes between the ages of two and three.

FRICTION BETWEEN PARENT AND CHILD

Toddlerhood, like the developmental stage of adolescence, is known for the friction that develops between parent and child. During this stage, your toddler will be coming to the significant realization that he is an independent individual.

The result of this new view of himself is different with every child and family situation, although most toddlers strongly state and demand some independence. They usually accomplish this by insisting upon doing things by and for themselves, testing your limits, and not yielding to all of your wishes and requests. In short, they become obstinate and rebellious. This is the time when temper tantrums are likely to develop. The onset of this campaign for independence may come suddenly and vigorously, or it may develop more gradually, over a period of months.

It is a rare parent who makes it through toddlerhood without feeling some frustration, anger, and resentment toward his or her child. These feelings are normal, just as toddlers' obstinacy, contrariness, and rebellion are normal. Trying to deny these feelings would not be the best thing for either you or your child.

Feeling guilty about heated arguments with your toddler is also very natural. Through these confrontations, he will be discovering how much you will tolerate. This enables him to begin slowly to learn something about how far he can go, and in what situations he must control his actions.

Living with your toddler is not likely to be easy, since you will frequently find yourself at odds with him. Mrs. Morgan was fast losing patience and understanding with her two-year-old son, Louis, who was becoming more contrary and defiant. As managing him became more difficult, she felt increasingly frustrated and alone. These feelings were not easy for her to deal with or express, because she thought they were unique to her situation with her child. After hearing about troubles her friends were experiencing with their toddlers, she felt much less uneasy, embarrassed, and isolated. It is helpful to keep in mind that you are not alone in your trials with your toddler.

Being able to express your feelings about your abilities as a parent honestly without embarrassment, shame, or doubt is extremely important. Talking about your reaction to your child and his behavior, and trying to understand it, will allow you to view the situation in the proper perspective. Your thoughts, feelings, and needs are no less important than your toddler's. Parents react in different ways to the stress and turmoil during toddlerhood. In Toddlerhood 3 parents' reactions to their toddlers' behavior are more fully explored with the hope that this will heighten your awareness of your own feelings and enable you to be more comfortable with them.

PARENTS' PET PEEVES

Complaints and expressions of annoyance from parents of toddlers are common, if not universal. While many complaints center around children's testing behavior and refusal to do what parents ask, there are other aspects of toddlers' behavior that can be highly irritating.

Living in a small apartment setting with a toddler who wants to explore to his heart's content can set the stage for heightened tension, irritation, and resentment. Being stuck indoors in a crowded apartment or home with him, you may find that your home and furniture show an incredible amount of wear as a result of his activity, and that you and he are regularly getting on each other's nerves.

Both you and your toddler need space to call your own, even if it is only a corner that is partially partitioned or separated from the rest of the room. There you can retreat when the going gets rough and you need some breathing space. With a bit of ingenuity, even a small apartment can be arranged this way.

It would be unreasonable to expect your young child to treat your furniture as you do. Parents who are concerned about the wear and tear that their home is showing as a result of their toddler's activity find it useful to avoid buying new furnishings or reupholstering the couch. This is the time to put blankets or inexpensive throws on your upholstered furniture or protect it in other ways.

Another common source of annoyance to parents is their toddler's repetitive behavior patterns. Toddlers seem to reap great pleasure from performing an activity over and over again, long past the time their parents become bored to tears and ready to scream.

Mr. Logan made this comment, "Tia is slowly driving me crazy. She's got a new thing now where she's interested in opening and closing doors. The other evening while I was trying to read the newspaper in the kitchen, she began opening and closing the back door. At first it didn't bother me that much, and I tried to ignore it. But the slamming of the door seemed to get louder and louder as the minutes passed. After several minutes of this I had had it. I shouted at Tia to stop and remarkably, she listened. I returned to the article I was reading, but all of a sudden I heard another repetitive slamming noise. I glanced over my shoulder to find her concentrating on opening and shutting the closet door. Tia's preoccupation with opening and closing doors has really gotten to me. My nerves are shot!"

This kind of complaint seems almost humorous on a printed page, but few parents of toddlers consider their child's repetitive behaviors a laughing matter. It is easy for you to lose sight of the significance of movement and repetition as a means by which your young child learns, especially when his activity is annoying. Keeping this in mind may prevent you from taking your frustration out on your toddler or becoming overly impatient with him.

The gripes discussed above may mirror your own, but chances are that you have at least a few others on your list. In some cases friends who have no children or even spouses never really seem to understand why you are so bothered by a certain aspect of your child's behavior. Do not let this add to your troubles. Spending lengthy blocks of time with a toddler is quite different from being around him for only an hour or two, or even several hours each evening. Rest assured that most of your child's bothersome behaviors will be outgrown as he matures. Patience and tolerance are necessary to living peaceably with a toddler.

THE STRESS OF DISCIPLINING A TODDLER

One area of rearing a toddler that seems to concern parents the most is discipline. No one would argue with the fact that a toddler needs some discipline, but parents often feel insecure about their ability to do a good job in setting appropriate limits and controls. There are few parents of toddlers who do not have some doubts about whether they are doing right by their child. Walking the thin line between being too strict and too lenient can surely put you in a vulnerable and awkward position.

Arguments over how best to discipline a child are very common. Couples may not always agree about what to do or say, and one parent may unknowingly undermine the other's attempts to establish certain rules and limits. Single parents may receive even more advice than couples from well-meaning relatives and friends as to how best to manage their toddlers. Finding yourself disagreeing with your partner, your relatives, or your friends over the subject of discipline is not unusual, but can create feelings of insecurity and resentment, as well as additional stress.

The issue of discipline becomes more prominent now, and contributes to the pressure and stress of parenting, because of the child's need to exert independence. He is probably testing the limits of your tolerance and patience by ignoring the rules you have set. He is also going to break rules, defy wishes, and whine, cry, or struggle when he does not get his way.

When he says "no" or does not listen to you, this may naturally cause you to think that he is deliberately being stubborn or mean. This is not the motive underlying his actions. It often helps to look at his "no's" and testing of your limits as positive ways in which he can courageously stand up to you and tell everyone that he is separate—his own person. This is highly significant in terms of his future development as a person who can stand on his own two feet.

Your child is confronting you and your expectations of him. This helps him more clearly determine who he is and establish his own limits. Each time he pushes you into scolding him, blowing your stack, or giving him a slap on his hand or buttocks, you may feel a bit guilty afterward. You may also feel angry at yourself for not maintaining your composure. This is very natural, but your open expressions of feeling about his bothersome behavior will gradually enable him to regain control and learn your limits.

A certain amount of tension and conflict over discipline should even be expected. Despite the negative aspects, establishing reasonable guidelines should be very rewarding, since you are helping to shape certain attitudes and behaviors in your child that will eventually enable him to become a self-controlled individual.

YOUR FEELINGS ABOUT SEPARATIONS FROM YOUR CHILD

Children's demands for their parents' physical presence and attention surely play on parents' emotions. Many toddlers are now fearful and anxious about brief separations from their parents, such as separations at bedtime. The possible reasons for this were discussed in the Personal-Social Development and Sleeping sections.

Some parents, especially those who would secretly like to have their toddler stay young and dependent, and those who have mixed feelings about their toddler's demands for independence, actually relish their child's emotional reactions to their departure. Mrs. Reilly said:

> For many reasons, too long and complicated to go into, I've always felt pretty insecure about my abilities to be a good mother. My daughter is going through a stage now where she is becoming harder for me to handle day by day. She

seems to want to do everything for herself, and if I try to help her or interfere, she gets stubborn and angry. This bothers me terribly, and makes me feel really insecure—as if I'm doing something wrong. The more independent she becomes, the more I wish she needed me as much as she did when she was younger. Last week I went out to dinner with some friends, and left her with her regular baby-sitter. She cried before I left, but I went anyway. At the restaurant I received a call from the baby-sitter asking me to come home because my daughter was screaming for me, and was really in bad shape. I decided I'd better go home, and I have to admit that I got a lot of pleasure out of thinking that she needed me that much. Announcing to my friends that my daughter needed me, and that I had to leave, was like showing them that I was a good mother. Last week wasn't the first time I left friends to go home to my child. It's been happening quite a lot.

Parents sometimes consciously or unconsciously foster their child's dependency in order to fulfill their own needs. It sometimes helps to understand that it is not that toddlers do not need their parents any more, it is that they need them in different ways. If you are ambivalent about your toddler's growing need to express his independence, you should take care not to be too sympathetic and oversolicitous, or go overboard in the opposite direction by disregarding his real needs.

Quite often a toddler's reaction to separations causes his parents to feel guilty. For example, Mr. Dansky, a single parent, stated:

It tears me apart inside when I have made plans to go out on a Friday or Saturday night, and my son, Billy, starts crying and throwing temper tantrums. As much as I love him, I have my own needs, too. Having female companionship on the weekends is important to me. I have to leave him in someone else's care during the day, since I have to work to support us both. There is no way to get around it. When he starts up on the weekends with his crying, it makes me feel awfully guilty.

Mr. Dansky's reactions echo that of many parents working outside the home. Doubts about whether or not you are spending enough time with your child, coupled with his anxieties about even brief separations from you, can trigger a variety of feelings, particularly guilt. In the majority of cases, these feelings are not well founded. Seeing that your child is well cared for in your absence, and offering love and attention when you are with him, is what really matters.

Guilt feelings can emerge even with parents who spend full time with their toddlers. Children's anxieties about separations from their parents are often an emotional issue which prompts a variety of responses from both parent and child. Feelings should definitely be sorted out and explored.

Sometimes all that is necessary is some extra patience, and a willingness to give your child the understanding and reassurance that he may need during this difficult period in his life. Additional suggestions for ways of handling a child who is having a hard time dealing with separations were provided on pages 595–96. There is no need to feel guilty about not spending all of your time with your toddler. He needs to learn to accept inevitable separations from you gracefully, and get along well in your absence. This is a natural part of growing up and becoming more independent.

WHO IS TO TAKE CARE OF YOUR TODDLER IN YOUR ABSENCE?

If you are seeking a child care arrangement different from the one which prevailed during the infancy stage, it is important to consider some of the alternatives. For the most part, the options discussed on pages 27–32 during infancy are still appropriate and open to you during toddlerhood. Two alternatives, which may or may not be available to parents of infants, but which usually become more prominent as the child grows older, becomes able to walk, and learns to use a toilet, are the day care center, or day nursery as it is sometimes called, and nursery school.

Deciding who is to care for your child in your absence requires very careful thought and planning. Much worry, guilt, and doubt can be eliminated by ensuring that he will be safe, happy, well cared for, and sufficiently stimulated during the time you are away. Whatever care arrangement you choose, you are still primarily responsible for him, and should continue to make the major decisions regarding his upbringing.

An Individual to Care for Your Child

Parents who either choose or are forced to leave their toddlers in someone else's care during the day often consider arranging for one person to act as a parent figure in their absence. Toddlers benefit from having a great deal of individualized attention and establishing a one-to-one relationship with a care-giver.

Depending upon individual circumstances and finances, there are many possibilities for finding a loving, dependable parent figure. Suggestions for how to select a suitable person to care for your toddler in your absence are essentially the same as described in Preparing for Parenthood on pages 29–31. It is important to select someone who shows a genuine interest in your toddler, his over-all development, education, and well-being. Discipline and training are two issues that become more prominent during toddlerhood, and you should discuss these issues with the person caring for him. You should feel comfortable with this person's methods of handling your child.

In many cases hiring a person full time to care for a child can be prohibitively expensive. Some parents have been fortunate in being able to reduce the cost. Occasionally neighbors, friends, or relatives may enjoy caring for your child on a full-time or part-time basis, either in your home or theirs, and ask for no or much less money.

Finding someone like this with whom your child is familiar can often work out very well. Such an arrangement may be mutually beneficial for the care-giver and the child, and may be much easier on your budget than hiring an unfamiliar person. If you are lucky enough to find someone in your apartment building or within walking distance of your home, it will also be possible to save on transportation costs.

The fact that the person you are considering to care for your child will be caring for other children in addition to yours need not be a major disadvantage. Women licensed by the state to provide day care in their homes often have several youngsters to care for at one time. Your friends or relatives may also have children of their own. Whether or not this would be a good arrangement for your toddler largely depends upon the number, age, and health of the other children, and how much time the person can devote to your toddler.

Decisions must be made on an individual basis. In some cases toddlers, particularly Toddlerhood 2 and 3 children, who have had little or no contact with other young children around their age can benefit from a small group care arrangement. Additional factors to consider are space, equipment, safety of the surroundings, and adult supervision.

A toddler may be easily upset by frequent shifts in the people caring for him. In making your selection, try to find someone, preferably one person, who wants a permanent position. Maintaining continuity in this regard is important to your young child.

Day Care Centers

Day care centers represent a viable alternative arrangement for child care for parents who either cannot or do not want to spend every day with their child. The concept of day care centers has changed, expanded, and gained in popularity as an increasing number of mothers pursue careers outside the home. They are also very important for single parents who need or want to continue working.

Originally, day care centers were established primarily to provide a baby-sitting service for parents whose work took them away from the home during the day, but many day care centers offer more than just a baby-sitting service. Many have evolved into centers that also provide excellent intellectual and developmental activities, similar to those provided in a nursery school. These centers often prefer to be called day nurseries.

Emphasis is placed upon offering the child a good early educational experience in the parent's absence. A high priority is given to satisfying the child's intellectual, social, language, and motor needs along with his needs for a safe environment, food, warmth, rest periods, and toys. This type of child-oriented day care center is in great demand. Unfortunately, the demand still outweighs the supply.

The suggestions for selecting a day care facility provided in Preparing for Parenthood on pages 30–31 should assist you in making a decision. Based upon the experience of parents who have used day care facilities, the following condensed list of things to look for in a center may also be of help.

GUIDELINES FOR EVALUATING A DAY CARE CENTER
A center should:

• be licensed by the state
• have highly trained, experienced staff members who care about children's welfare and over-all development

- have ample playthings and equipment for indoor and outdoor use
- offer nourishing lunches and snacks
- be equipped with child-sized furniture and bathroom facilities
- have ample play space indoors and outdoors
- have space and facilities enabling children to nap or rest
- provide children with adequate supervision
- offer a regular routine including a good balance between unstructured and structured activities
- take a philosophical approach geared to each individual child developing to his fullest potential
- work in conjunction with parents and encourage parental involvement
- be equipped to offer medical attention should an emergency arise or in the event that a child becomes ill

The above list should offer you a starting point from which to set your own standards for selecting a quality day care center for your child. You are the best judge of your toddler's needs, and being confident that they will be fulfilled in your absence is of vital importance to him and to you.

Co-operative Day Care Centers

Co-operative day care centers, in which parents take an active part in management, have become increasingly popular. They can be organized along very different lines, but parental participation and involvement are emphasized, encouraged, and in many cases required. The availability of co-operative day care centers varies from community to community. Parents who are interested may get together and form a co-op on their own, taking care to investigate state licensure requirements.

In many co-operative day care centers, parents rent a building or appropriate structure and hire a trained professional to be present on a full-time basis and co-ordinate a daily program. Each parent is often required to take turns caring for the children, putting in a certain number of hours a week as their schedules permit. In some cases parents who cannot participate themselves may pay the other parents to take over their turns. In some co-ops parents who cannot or are unwilling to take their turns on a regular basis are not permitted to join. Parents are often required to attend business meetings and take turns buying and preparing food and snacks.

Parents usually govern the center themselves. Rules and requirements are established according to their needs and preferences as a group. Together, parents determine the philosophy and curriculum of the center.

A major advantage of a co-operative day care arrangement is that parents make their own decisions regarding its operation, and are directly involved in caring for their children. A second advantage is a financial one. Parental participation considerably reduces the cost of child care.

Should the concept of co-operative day care appeal to you, it is advisable to evaluate those centers in your area carefully. You may use the same general guidelines for selecting a day care center on pages 30–31, preceding page 637 and above. Be sure to find out how much parental participation is required. In cases in which parents cannot adjust their working schedules to fulfill obligations to the center, and/or cannot attend meetings, a co-operative arrangement may not be the best choice. Weigh the advantages and disadvantages for both you and your toddler.

Nursery Schools

Not all nursery schools accept children under age two and a half to three, although many do accept younger toddlers. Nursery schools are primarily designed to accommodate children on a part-time basis. Youngsters usually attend for half a day, two or three times a week, or every day. This can vary considerably depending upon the policies of individual schools. There are some nursery schools equipped to handle children on a full-time basis, although this can be extremely costly.

Parents of older toddlers who want more freedom from child care, or who work outside the home part time, may want to consider enrolling their children in nursery school. The discussion on pages 814–18 will assist you in your selection and in preparing your child to attend.

ARGUMENTS AND FIGHTS IN THE HOME: HOW THEY AFFECT TODDLERS

Arguments occur in almost every family. Most confrontations end with parents making up, and do not involve physical or emotional abuse. These squabbles usually do not have a major effect upon the strength of the family unit, although they are not pleasant either for parents directly involved or children observing or overhearing them.

In some cases arguments go beyond everyday squabbles, and are much more serious in nature. These conflicts can have detrimental effects on a marriage, and eventually lead to separation or divorce, and can negatively affect a toddler. A child who regularly overhears or witnesses his parents being verbally or physically abusive toward one another, or abusive to objects and furniture in the home, may understandably be very disturbed by this.

Children react differently to their parents' arguments. Toddlers are more aware of and sensitive to marital stress in their homes than infants, and older toddlers tend to be more affected by marital disagreements than younger toddlers. The effect of arguments upon the child is largely dependent upon factors such as how often parents argue, how severe their arguments are, what type of personality the child has, and how much he understands about the events occurring around him.

Exposure to severe arguments on a regular basis can create anxiety in the toddler which needs to be expressed. Toddlers can discharge this anxiety in different ways. Parents may notice an increase in the use of tension outlets. Some children may become more aggressive or destructive. Signs of depression, apathy, fearfulness, and insecurity may be observed. It is not uncommon for children to display a loss of appetite, diminished interest in play and exploration, and sleeping difficulties punctuated by frequent fears and nightmares. Sometimes parents involved in marital conflict overlook either subtle or obvious signs that their toddler is emotionally upset and needs help, comfort, extra attention, and reassurance.

Couples who are very involved with their own needs and personal problems may either consciously or unconsciously fail to fulfill their responsibilities as parents, and fail to offer their toddler good care on a daily basis. In some cases parents blame their child for their marital conflict, take their frustrations out on him, or use him to get back at one another in arguments. This can have detrimental effects upon the child and may result in disturbances in his normal behavior pattern and emotional development.

Couples experiencing severe marital difficulties must not overlook the possibly harmful effects that this is having upon their child. When the atmosphere in the home is marked by coldness and hostility, the child can suffer. Being under emotional stress yourself, it may be difficult to consider the feelings of your child. Attempt to put things into proper perspective, and do not lose sight of his needs. Signs of anxiety and emotional stress in your toddler, or a breakdown in normal communications between you and your spouse, are indications that you may need help in resolving marital discord. If attempts to resolve problems on your own are not successful, do not hesitate to seek outside help.

THE SINGLE PARENT FAMILY

A parent rearing a toddler alone, whether by choice, accident, or the result of a separation, divorce, or death, can provide a warm, stable family framework within which both parent and child can flourish and develop. Life as a single parent of an active toddler, particularly one during the period of the "Terrible Two's," has both its rewards and pleasures, and its stresses and problems.

The substantial number of families composed of single parents with toddlers have much in common with two parent families, but there are differences that are important. Some of the emotional and practical considerations for the single parent family discussed in Preparing for Parenthood (pages 11–14) are still pertinent for toddlerhood, but other factors arise during this stage of development. The toddler's greater need for discipline, expanded awareness and mobility, and sensitivity to separations from his parents raise new issues that are of special interest to the single parent.

Social Life for the Single Parent

Rearing a child alone does not necessarily place added strain upon one's social life, but some single parents find this to be the case. Problems related to loss of social contacts, loneliness, and loss of spontaneity which may have previously been experienced may persist or arise in the course of caring for a toddler. For some these problems may diminish during toddlerhood as the child changes and becomes more independent and sociable.

Toddlers look at their parents from a highly self-centered point of view. They are generally regarded as being all important, as well as all powerful. Toddlers' social lives mainly revolve around being with their parents. In single parent families a child's relationship with his parent may be even more precious to him. It is understandable why he might become upset when his parent leaves him to go out with friends or entertains other adults in the home. He may resent not being the sole focus of his parent's attention. This can prompt him to behave poorly, call out to his parent in insistent tones of voice, throw a temper tantrum, show off, or act silly in an attempt to gain attention.

Should his parent show affection toward a guest, this may heighten the jealousy that he feels. Elinor, a single parent, experienced great difficulty bringing a man, whom she had been dating, into her home. Whenever Elinor and her date held hands on the couch or her date put his arm around her, Elinor's son, Joseph, climbed up between them in an attempt to capture his mother's attention. Elinor said that he was the world's best chaperone, but that this became annoying to both her and her boy friend. It also made spending time with a date in her home very awkward and uncomfortable.

Parents who are dating often have some concerns about how to handle their relationships in their toddler's presence. This generally becomes an even more important issue during the preschool years (pages 889–90) as the child's awareness, curiosity, and ability to ask questions increases. It is generally advisable to be discreet in sexual practices, although this is a highly personal matter that each parent must find answers to on an individual basis.

A genuine concern for your child's feelings should be shown if he is to be included or is present when you are with a date or entertaining friends. Parents who have a steady stream of overnight guests in the home will probably want to examine the possible effects that this practice either might have or is having upon the child.

Children who are experiencing difficulties dealing with separations, particularly those who are troubled by the recent departure of one parent, should be given the utmost consideration. A child who has just enough time to get to know and become attached to his remaining parent's boy friends or girl friends, and then suddenly sees them leave, may understandably find this a painful emotional experience.

There is no one right way in which to conduct your social life. You must determine what feels right and comfortable for you. If you decide to socialize in the presence of your child, it is important to respect his needs and feelings. Being sensitive to your own needs and his, it will be easier to develop a pattern of socializing that works well for your family. Parents, through actions as well as words, often have to convince their children that they need adult companionship, but that nothing will threaten their love for them.

Rather than pushing your toddler to accept or respond positively to your dates, give him plenty of time to get to know them on his own terms, and in his own way. Sometimes, without realizing it, parents are so engrossed with their dates that they ignore their toddlers completely, and make them feel totally excluded. This often encourages the child's jealousy, resentment, and bids for attention. If your child is not yet ready for bed, try to include him in your conversation and engage him in activities that you know he enjoys. Your date can participate. Make your toddler feel welcome in his own home.

Even in cases where parents give their toddlers no just cause to feel jealous or threatened by their dates, children may still have these feelings. Remember that they are very immature. From their limited perspective, they tend to think of their parent's affection as being exclusive. You will have to be understanding of your youngster's limitations and be patient with him. Giving him added reassurance that he is loved and special to you may help in allaying his fears of losing you to one of your dates.

LEAVING THE CHILD TO GO OUT. A common concern among single parents centers around the toddler's separation anxiety interfering with their social life. Fear and anxiety about a parent's departure are not just felt by children reared by one parent. Children with two parents also experience these feelings, but with many single parents, particularly those who work outside the home, their child's reaction may have a more powerful effect.

Marta became very concerned about leaving her daughter, Shana, to go out in the evenings or on weekends. Shana always cried and became highly distressed whenever Marta was preparing to leave. Like many parents who work outside the home and have only evenings and weekends to spend with their children, Marta was torn about whether or not to leave.

She worried about the possibility that she was not devoting enough time to her daughter, and felt rather guilty about leaving in the evenings or on weekends after not being home during the week. On the other hand, she felt that it was necessary to have a social life apart from her life as a parent.

The extra sense of responsibility that single parents sometimes assume as their child's only parent can heighten feelings of worry and guilt about leaving. These feelings may become more apparent during toddlerhood, especially during Toddlerhood 2 and 3, as the child acquires verbal and social skills that enable him to communicate through words his strong desire for his parent not to leave.

Ms. Williams was a divorced mother of an older toddler named Herbert, who had occasionally thrown temper tantrums and cried when his mother had to leave him to attend social functions. Ms. Williams was concerned about leaving him at those times, but was able to put this into perspective and not let it interfere with her enjoyment of activities outside the home. One evening, as she was going out for dinner with a male companion, having arranged to have a baby-sitter stay with her child, her son became upset and cried out, "Mommy, no go. Love you."

Herbert's verbal expression of his love and need for his mother and his increased fear of separation from her were hard for her to handle. His newly emerging ability to put his feelings into words made her feel even more guilty about leaving him than she had before he learned to talk. Ms. Williams still went out in the evenings, but had difficulty having a good time, knowing how much Herbert needed and loved her.

Many single parents share Ms. Williams' guilt and concern about going out without their children when this obviously disturbs them. The child's intense anxiety about separations generally diminishes during Preschool 1, and need not cause a parent to feel that all free time should be spent with his or her child.

While a toddler's real need for parental time and attention should not be ignored, it often seems as though no matter how much time parents spend with their children, youngsters never feel that it is enough. A balance between meeting your toddler's needs and your own can and should be achieved.

Building and maintaining relationships in addition to the special relationship that you share with your toddler is important. Depending upon individual feelings and circumstances, this can be worked out in any number of ways. Some parents feel more comfortable separating parenthood and their social life. They rarely entertain friends in their home unless their toddler is asleep, and almost never include him in social activities outside the home. These parents often believe that as long as they do not leave their child to go out every night, or even every other night, and are always certain that he is well cared for in their absence, he will simply have to adjust to separations.

Other parents take a different approach. Given the child's anxiety over separations during a certain developmental stage, some parents try to take the child's needs into account without denying their own by including him in many of their social activities. This becomes more feasible during toddlerhood, because of the child's ability to walk.

Friends and people with whom you socialize will vary considerably in their reactions to your wanting to have your child take part in social activities. Those without children may resent your wanting to bring your child along, although this is certainly not always the case. Single parents often find that other parents are more understanding of their desire to include their youngsters in social situations.

This can work out quite well for everyone. Adults can socialize while the children play in another room. The cost of baby-sitters can be eliminated, and parents who wish to have an active social life can accomplish this without feeling badly about having to leave their child or impose upon their friends.

The desire of unmarried parents to socialize with one another and also include their youngsters in some social activities has prompted the establishment of many social clubs and groups for parents without partners. In many communities there are centers where single parents can meet. Organized groups often offer lectures, trips, dinners, dances, cooking classes, and a wide variety of other activities for both parents alone and parents with their children.

Parents living in communities with no organized groups, or those who prefer socializing in smaller groups, can form one of their own. There are endless possibilities for how social groups for single parents can be arranged. Baby-sitting services may occasionally be shared to minimize cost, or parents may want to form a baby-sitting pool whereby they take turns caring for each other's children (pages 155–56).

Activities can be as specialized or as broad as the members prefer. While parents socialize with one another, children have the opportunity to do the same. Sharing experiences with other parents in similar positions can be of enormous benefit to you. Your child should profit from a broadened social sphere as well.

Single Parents May Have a Hard Time Exercising Authority

The single parent often has special needs concerning the issue of discipline. Making decisions alone about how to handle your child gives you complete freedom to do whatever you feel is best. With this freedom comes the responsibility of making judgments by yourself. Some single parents feel burdened with this responsibility, which can create family and personal problems. Being aware of the experiences of other single parents in disciplining their children should be helpful in developing your own program of discipline.

Carissa, a divorced mother of a year-and-a-half-old boy named Barry, had a great deal of trouble establishing rules for his conduct. She was not very strong in the area of decision-making, particularly when it came to deciding what limits were the most necessary to establish. She often changed her mind about a limit in midstream, because she was never certain that she was doing the right thing.

As a result of her vacillation, Barry became very hard for her to manage. He sensed her indecision, and his behavior became increasingly provocative, week by week. It was almost as if he was regularly testing her limits in an effort to clarify them for himself. Mentioning the problem during Barry's check-up at the doctor's, Carissa heard the doctor point out that what Barry needed were clear guidelines for conduct, and that his constant testing behavior stemmed from her inability to provide this for him. He offered to help her determine what limits to set, and urged her to be consistent in adhering to them.

Difficulty in setting consistent limits is not an uncommon problem among single parents. If you are unable to deal with this alone, it may be necessary to find someone, perhaps a relative, friend, or physician, to assist you in deciding which limits to set, and to offer you the encouragement and support you may need to make these decisions.

Being both "mother" and "father" to a child is not easy. There is a tendency to be overly lenient and to avoid antagonizing the child. The whole issue of assuming responsibility for discipline and enforcing limits is harder on the single parent, who usually has no one else to count on to balance out or complement his or her relationship with the child.

Mrs. Larsen, a young widow, had difficulty being firm when her son, Robert, obviously needed external controls. Throughout his infancy she had not found disciplining Robert too much of a burden. His negativistic, testing behavior during toddlerhood, however, presented constant tests of her ability to handle him. She sometimes resented the fact that she alone had to bear the brunt of his occasional aggressive outbursts. She was very afraid of arousing Robert's resentment, and could not seem to enforce the limits that she had established. Quite often after she had relaxed the limits or let Robert take advantage of her, she rationalized her too-lenient approach on the grounds that what Robert needed was more love and understanding, not stricter limits.

When Robert broke the rules, she would threaten to spank him, but she rarely carried through with her threats. Punishing her son was a painful and anxiety-producing experience for her, and she usually backed away from it. As a result of her failure to enforce her program of discipline, Robert began to take more advantage of her. This continued for a couple of months until she could no longer tolerate his behavior. One afternoon, she finally lost all patience with him. She spanked him. Immediately afterward she felt an overwhelming sense of guilt and remorse. Through her tears, she hugged and kissed him in an effort to apologize.

Mrs. Larsen was very aware of the difficulties she was having in regard to the issue of disciplining Robert. She recognized the need for her to assume the role of an authority figure for Robert's sake, but had trouble doing just that. Her wish was that someone else could share the responsibility. After discussing these issues with a family guidance counselor, who confirmed her own feelings about Robert's need for guidance and controls, she felt more sure of herself and her ability to do what had to be done.

It is understandable that the issue of discipline is a harder one to deal with in one parent households. In families where one parent bears the sole responsibility for disciplining and punishing a child, that parent must serve as a symbol of authority. A parent who gives up this responsibility is short-changing the child, and is likely to have increasing difficulties managing him.

Assuming the role of disciplinarian is necessary and important in terms of your child's future adjustment. At times, you may have to be strict and firm simply to teach your child a lesson, or emphasize your authority, even though doing this makes you feel uncomfortable. You must be confident of your ability to discipline your child. It is possible to be a symbol of authority to him while maintaining a close, positive parent-child relationship. For your child's sake, and your own, do not let unwarranted fears and feelings of insecurity interfere with your judgment and ability to exercise your authority.

PREPARED PARENTHOOD CHECK LIST

MOTHER	FATHER	UNDERSTANDING YOUR TODDLER'S DEVELOPMENT
—	—	In what respects is your child asserting himself and voicing his individuality?
—	—	Is your toddler expressing any rebellion or negativism? Does this change in his behavior and attitude create friction between you?
—	—	Does your child have difficulty controlling physical expressions of anger and aggression?
—	—	Do you see evidence that your toddler is becoming more aware of his possessions?
—	—	Does your child occasionally pause for a moment and appear to be thinking about a situation or problem before plunging in and moving or acting?
—	—	What evidence do you see that your toddler is learning from his previous experiences?
—	—	When you hide your child's favorite toy, does he make repeated attempts to find it?
—	—	Is your child showing signs of understanding simple cause and effect sequences?
—	—	Have you observed indications of improvements in your toddler's memory?
—	—	Has your child begun to make one or two word sentences?
—	—	Have you been talking to and with your child as often as you can and helping him learn the names of people and objects?
—	—	Does your toddler experience any difficulties when he speaks? How do you handle this?
—	—	Is your child showing a driving need to exercise and practice his physical skills?
—	—	Does your toddler enjoy pushing, shoving, and carrying large objects?
—	—	Do you notice signs of increased co-ordination in finger and hand movements when your child plays with blocks and engages in other tasks requiring fine motor skills?
—	—	Does your toddler devote more time and energy to vigorous physical activities or more subdued activities?
—	—	Have you noticed your child carrying on any pretend activities in his play?

Toddlerhood 2

— — Have you made arrangements for your toddler to play with other children his age?

— — What kinds of play activities and playthings does your child enjoy the most?

BASIC CARE

— — Are you offering your toddler sufficient supervision without stifling his freedom?

— — Have you familiarized yourself with some of the danger traps to avoid at holiday time?

— — What signs of progress is your toddler showing in his ability to handle a spoon and cup?

— — Does your child enjoy playing in the tub or does he seem resistant? If he resists, why might this be happening and how do you handle the situation?

— — Is your toddler interested in undressing himself? Dressing himself?

— — Have you given your child access to a full-length mirror as a tool to help him learn how to dress himself properly?

— — Has your toddler become increasingly resistive at bedtime?

— — Are you on the lookout for signs that your child is ready to learn to use the toilet?

FAMILY FEELINGS AND CONCERNS

— — Do you know how to handle negativism?

— — Does your toddler occasionally take things that do not belong to him?

— — Are you encouraging your child to assist you in activities around the house?

— — Have you thought about what type of "sex" education you are offering your toddler?

— — Do you know that a toddler's interest in touching his genitals is a normal indication of his curiosity about his body?

— — Are you helping your child acquire a healthy, positive attitude toward his body?

— — What is your stance on nudity in the home?

— — Are you aware that overprotecting your child may make him more susceptible to developing fears?

— — Is your child's fear of separation from you becoming more prominent and intense?

— — Which aspects of your toddler's behavior annoy you the most?

— — In what ways has disciplining your toddler created added stress for you?

— — Have you explored your feelings in relationship to separations from your toddler?

---   ---   When you and your partner argue, what effect does this have upon your child?

---   ---   What are some of the special concerns of the single parent?

---   ---   Are you familiar with the common alternatives for child care during toddlerhood?

Toddlerhood 2

Toddlerhood 3

PERSONAL-SOCIAL DEVELOPMENT

Toddlerhood 3 is a time for change. Early during this phase toddlers generally appear to be less negative and more pleasant to live with compared with Toddlerhood 2 children. As they approach the transition between Toddlerhood 3 and Preschool 1, their behavior usually changes again. They pass through a stage that has become known as the "Terrible Two's," a time when they are less co-operative and harder to manage.

At the beginning of Toddlerhood 3 you may find that your child is easier to handle, since her intellectual, language, and motor abilities have expanded. She will be happier practicing her new abilities, and may seem like a more capable and interesting person. Just watching her make new discoveries and listening to her as she speaks will bring you a great deal of pleasure and pride.

Her new abilities will also bring with them a greater desire for independence and self-expression. She may suddenly refuse to abide by your wishes and become rebellious. The demanding and negative behavior that was evident to some extent in Toddlerhood 1 and 2 may reach new heights toward the end of this phase, which is often a time for increased tension and stress. There is a great deal of variability in children's personalities, but by being aware of common changes that occur in many toddlers, you will be able to understand and manage your child better when her behavior becomes less co-operative.

"The Terrible Two's": Negativism Reaches a Peak

Negativism often becomes a highly prominent aspect of the Toddlerhood 3 child's behavior, since improvements in her language and intellectual abilities make her much more capable of resisting you both verbally and mentally. Her obstinance, defiance, and use of the word "no" may rise to new heights.

Some tension between parent and child seems to be unavoidable. As we have said before, the negativism and rebellion that a toddler directs toward her parents is the normal and probably essential way in which she establishes and confirms her individuality and independence.

It is by no means easy to live with a child whose desires and activities seem to conflict with yours at frequent intervals. She is apt to object to many things that you say; when you ask her either to do something or to stop what she is doing, she will probably do the opposite. Opposing you fortifies her feelings of being her own, separate person. Your child's contrariness, rebellion, and defiance will be impossible to ignore. When you ask her to play inside your house, she may head for the back door. Then, if you tell her that she can play outdoors, she may immediately run back into the house. She will find it terribly difficult to follow your suggestions, since this undermines her feeling of having a mind of her own.

The back talk and physical struggle that she is likely to display whenever you give her an order can be a constant source of conflict between you. From the time her daughter, Shelly, reached twenty-seven months, Hanna Lopez found their relationship strained. According to this mother:

We simply haven't been getting along with each other lately. No matter what I say, she says the opposite. Even when I suggest that she do things she usually likes to do, she turns around and makes it seem as if she doesn't want to do them any more. When I say "yes," her reply is "no."

Shelly's behavior is like that of most children her age. She is not deliberately being contrary to spite her mother, but is simply trying to find her own way and assert herself. As your child cements her own sense of identity as an individual who is like but different from others, she, too, will go through a stage of heightened contrariness and resistance. Her opposition and rebellion are her way of making it clear to both you and herself that she is different from you, and has a mind and will of her own.

MORE DEMANDS FOR INDEPENDENCE AND DECISION-MAKING. Your child's will to become more independent will emerge much more strongly than in the past. She will demand to make many more of her own decisions. Unfortunately, she is not fully prepared to handle the difficult tasks that she has set forth as goals for herself.

In earlier phases of toddlerhood the child frequently contradicted her parents. Now she not only finds herself at odds with her parents, she also finds that she is in conflict with herself when she tries to make a decision. She is beginning to realize that she is capable of making her own choices about what clothes to wear or what to eat for lunch, but she has not had much experience with the decision-making process.

Difficulty arises when she has to choose between alternatives. Choices often confuse her, as shown by her shifts from one extreme to another. One toddler had a hard time deciding whether or not she wanted a particular toy. After much delay and deliberation, she concluded, "I want it." A moment later, however, she suddenly changed her mind and decided, "I don't want it."

It may take your toddler a long time to make decisions such as what clothes to wear or whether or not she wants to play with blocks or with balls. This trouble making choices tends to leave her feeling tense and confused. Being aware of her difficulties and wanting to help her to speed things up, you may make a decision for her. This may only create more tension between you. Chances are that she will strongly resent your interference and will let you know this by rebelling against you, putting up a real struggle, and perhaps throwing a temper tantrum.

INSISTENCE UPON DOING THINGS HER WAY. Your toddler is acquiring a clearer sense of her uniqueness and independence, and wants to be the one who makes decisions and gives commands. She will relish being the boss, a mini-dictator who decides things not only for herself but for everyone else. When she wants to do something alone, she may not let anyone else help her, even when she finds she is incapable of handling the task. Not only will she not accept your help, but she will tell you what to do and what not to do. Once she makes up her mind that you should do something, she may voice strong objection to having someone else do it. You are apt to react with disdain to her demands and orders.

Mrs. Colson, mother of twenty-eight-month-old Cynthia, suddenly noticed that her daughter had become very bossy. She insisted on telling her parents and brother what to do. She was unable to be neat and orderly, yet she wanted everyone else in the family to be this way. Everyone was told where things should go, and how things had to be done. Things had to be done her way, or else she would lose her temper. One activity had always to follow the next. No change in routine would be tolerated.

Everyone in the Colson family found Cynthia's behavior aggravating. Mrs. Colson tried to help other family members understand why her daughter was acting this way, but tensions still ran high in the household until Cynthia passed through this stage.

During the "Terrible Two's," toddlers have very definite wants, which they make perfectly clear. Their ability to change their ways or accept suggestions from others is extremely limited.

THE EMERGENCE OF RITUALISTIC BEHAVIOR. Ilg and Ames of the Gesell Institute have noted that during this phase children are ritualistic and demand repetition. An example will help to illustrate this behavior. One little toddler named Marshall was quite set in his ways. When his mother offered him a particular plate at lunch time, he insisted that the same plate be used at dinner. For the next several days at lunch time he did not want to eat his lunch unless it was served on the same plate.

Changes are hard for the Toddlerhood 3 child to accept. She tends to go on and on with whatever she is doing whether her activities involve playing with a special toy, listening to a favorite record, or saying a certain phrase. This need for repetition and clinging to old, set ways of doing things makes her an unlikely candidate for anything unfamiliar or different.

You may have to be careful about introducing new haircuts, clothes, routines, foods, or rearranging her bedroom. She will be more comfortable having the security of familiar objects and living patterns, and it is advisable to respect her needs temporarily. This type of ritualistic behavior usually diminishes during Preschool 1, or early in Preschool 2.

THIS IS A TENSE, EMOTIONAL PHASE. Toward the end of Toddlerhood 2, tensions are likely to run high within the child. These tensions stem from her immaturity and the changes taking place within her. She is first beginning to consider alternatives, regulate her emotions and behavior, and make decisions for herself. Mastering these tasks is difficult and time-consuming. Her negative attitude, indecisiveness, and easily aroused frustration and anger frequently result in increased inner tension and confusion. When inner tensions mount, she has to blow off steam through tension-releasing behaviors such as temper tantrums.

The need for tension outlets is very common among Toddlerhood 3 children. The many ways in which youngsters discharge pent-up anxiety and frustration and comfort themselves are examined on pages 534–42. Understanding your toddler's tension-releasing behaviors will help you avoid becoming overly concerned about them.

DIFFERENCES IN PERSONALITIES ARE COMMON. Individual differences in children's personalities often become more pronounced during Toddlerhood 3. As was noted earlier in Toddlerhood 1, nearly all children go through a phase of increased negativism. While most enter this phase near the end of Toddlerhood 3, there are some who entered it earlier, and some who will enter it during Preschool 1.

The intensity and expression of negativism can also vary from child to child. Some children will appear to be more negative and rebellious than others. The fact that your child is either more or less obstinate and defiant than your neighbor's child should not be a cause for concern.

There are differences in the timing and duration of the "Terrible Two's," as well as in children's behavior during this phase. Normal variability is to be expected. Try to bear with your child when she enters this phase. The change is as hard on her as it is on you. Avoid overreacting to or misinterpreting her normal, negativistic behavior as problem behavior. She is not out to annoy you or challenge your authority. Her negativism is a normal, positive sign that she is growing up.

Self-awareness

Continued expansion of your toddler's awareness of her body parts, her actions, and her belongings will be evident during Toddlerhood 3. Increased verbal and intellectual abilities allow her to broaden her knowledge of herself in relationship to others.

AWARENESS OF HER NAME. Your child will show a greater awareness of her name. When she hears her name spoken, she will know people are speaking about her or to her. Her ability to understand and use pronouns such as "I," "you," and "me" is still limited, and if she does use them, she may do so incorrectly. When you speak to her, you may find that it helps to preface whatever you say with her name, rather than referring to her as "you." Hearing her name first may result in a greater willingness on her part to listen as well as follow instructions.

Children of this age do not usually use the pronoun "I" when referring to themselves. They use their first names. As their self-awareness and sense of identity increase, generally around age three, they begin to use the pronoun "I."

KNOWLEDGE OF ABILITIES INCREASES. Understanding what she can and cannot do is one aspect of your toddler's self-awareness that is beginning to develop. Previously she may have persisted in her attempts to tackle a project that was clearly beyond her abilities.

Mr. Reynolds observed this growing awareness in his daughter, Ellen. Ellen often tried to copy the behavior of her older sister, Tania. Whatever Tania did, she had to try to do, too. One morning as Tania put together a very difficult puzzle, Ellen watched her very closely, as if she were trying to understand this complex task. Later, her father looked on as Ellen attempted to put the puzzle together herself. Ellen worked hard trying to put a few pieces of the puzzle together. After several minutes, she left the puzzle and returned to her own toys, as if she realized that this task was too difficult. According to Ellen's father, earlier in the year she would have struggled unsuccessfully for half an hour over a task that she could never successfully complete.

Most children at this stage no longer persist for very long at tasks that are far beyond their capabilities, although they may still try to perform tasks clearly appropriate for older children or adults. Formulating a fairly accurate notion of one's own abilities and limitations takes a long time.

THE BEGINNINGS OF CONSCIENCE DEVELOPMENT. Having a conscience generally implies that a person has a built-in system for controlling her behavior according to standards or ideals for acceptable behavior. When these standards are not lived up to, the person feels guilt or shame. Many psychologists feel that the Toddlerhood 3 child is beginning to develop a conscience. Either during this phase or the next, she may stop as she reaches out for an object that she has been warned not to take, say the word "no," and think to herself that she should not take it. This will indicate that your toddler is starting to build an inner set of controls. Before she reaches the point where she can block impulses to break rules, she will pass through various preliminary stages.

As a first step, you may occasionally hear your child say "no no" or "don't" aloud after she has done something that you warned her not to do. This is progress, although it may not seem so at first. She realizes that she has done something that she was warned by you not to do, but her realization comes too late. Still, she has recognized the fact that she has been naughty, and this, in itself, is a noteworthy accomplishment.

She may soon mutter your warning while she is doing something "naughty," and later, she will be able to say aloud your previous warning and refrain from breaking specific rules. This is similar to the steps most children take during toilet training. First they tell you after, then while, and finally before they "make" in their pants. Each small, successive step in the desired direction is a sign of improvement.

You will play an important role in helping your child develop a conscience by helping her learn "right" from "wrong," and "good" behavior from "bad." Important lessons will not be learned unless you discipline her. By consistently showing that you disapprove of unacceptable behavior, and showing your approval of acceptable activities, she will gradually realize the difference between the two.

Already she has become very sensitive to your displays of approval and disapproval. This is invaluable in terms of her conscience development. An example should help to illustrate this point. One day, twenty-seven-month-old Andy was playing with his toys on the kitchen floor. His mother was talking on the telephone, but she kept her eyes on him at all times, ready to intervene if he got into any mischief. Twice he approached the stove in order to play with the knobs, and each time his mother rushed over to him and loudly said, "Don't touch!" She then tried to distract him with a toy. These diversionary tactics worked only briefly. A few minutes later he went for the knobs once again.

The third time he was hesitant in his approach. He looked at his mother several times as he came closer to the oven, and seemed to go forward and then backward in his approach. When he was within a foot of reaching the oven, while glancing at his mother, he raised his arm partly, turned red in the face, and said loudly, "Don't touch." Then he turned his back to the oven and walked away. Had his mother not been physically present in the room the third time he headed for the stove, one can assume that he would have played with the knobs. He was able to avoid touching the knobs, not because he thought that this would be naughty or dangerous, but presumably because he feared that his mother would show her disapproval if he touched them again.

Avoidance of unacceptable behavior out of fear of parental disapproval is a prelude to conscience development, but is not indicative of a real conscience. Andy has not, yet, developed an inner system to help him exercise self-control and stay on the right track when his mother is not around to watch him. Andy's sensitivity to his mother's disapproval is nonetheless significant. At this time he still relies mainly upon her to control his behavior. By consistently showing approval and disapproval, she has provided him with a reason to change his behavior and exercise self-control. Andy cares about how his mother feels toward him, and tries to live up to her expectations to maintain her approval and avoid her disapproval. Eventually, as a result of her teaching efforts, he will learn to distinguish between proper and improper behavior, and control his own actions as she controls them now.

Despite your toddler's sensitivity to your approval and disapproval, progress in this area is often very slow. When she disobeys your warnings and breaks established rules after you have shown disapproval, you should not conclude that she does this because she does not care for or respect you. The Toddlerhood 3 child is still forgetful and very immature, and has not developed a good control system of her own or acceptable conduct. She has strong urges. It is particularly hard for her to refrain from doing something when her desire to do it is so pressing.

It may take months of your having to repeat rules and warnings before you notice positive results for your efforts. Your child still needs close supervision and discipline, particularly in situations where her safety is at risk. Even after you notice signs of conscience development, you should not expect her to follow her conscience consistently, since this would be expecting too much from such a young child.

Patience on your part is important. As she acquires a broader vocabulary, this will help her incorporate your verbal rules and warnings into her own inner control system. Further identification with you will also result in additional incorporation of your values and rules for conduct into her conscience.

Social Sensitivity and Interests

INTERACTIONS WITH YOU AND OTHER FAMILY MEMBERS. You continue to be of primary concern to your toddler. She senses your importance in her life, and is very closely attached to you, even when she rebels and provokes you.

As she strives for independence, she sometimes is not sure that she is ready to assume the added responsibilities and pressures that accompany growing up. She may occasionally want to stick close by you and want you to baby her. The fact that she wants to be both dependent and independent can make living with her unpredictable and annoying. Nevertheless, by allowing her to express her need for dependence and by being responsive to her, you will be providing the security base that will enable her to move toward independence.

When your toddler enters the "Terrible Two's," you can prepare yourself for inevitable conflicts and family stresses. You can also be fairly certain, if she has brothers or sisters, that they will fight. While she is trying to make some of her own decisions and come to grips with the demands you are placing on her, she will find it difficult to get along with siblings. Despite these difficulties, she may enjoy playing with them and may be quite able to express affection.

You will notice that she is increasing her attempts to imitate your behavior, as well as the behavior of others. She will be most eager to mimic your actions as you work around the house and yard. She may also tag along beside you wherever you go, dragging her toy housekeeping equipment as she follows. If you are not careful, she will pick up your curse words and bad habits, and delight in showing off her new behavior and vocabulary words in front of strangers.

INTERACTIONS WITH STRANGERS AND OTHER CHILDREN. Do not be surprised if she is initially shy around strangers. Once she has had an opportunity to become acquainted with an unfamiliar person, however, she may quickly act friendly toward him or her. She might offer cookies or some other token of acceptance and affection to the stranger. How your child reacts to strangers will largely depend upon whether you are nearby when she encounters them, and how many opportunities she has had to be around unfamiliar people.

The Toddlerhood 3 child may begin to take a real interest in her peers, which will strengthen as she grows older. She has finally reached the stage where she likes playing near her contemporaries, and sometimes with them, although she may not yet be able to interact with them very well. Even though she mainly plays by herself, she may like to play parallel to (alongside of) another child. She will occasionally spend time watching what other children are doing, and may even be affectionate toward another child. You may see her run over to a playmate and give the child an affectionate squeeze or a big kiss.

It is very common for children to want to see and explore each other's bodies when they're playing together, although they do not fully understand the difference between the sexes. Often their exploration includes aggressive behavior. Grabbing each other's toys, pulling each other's arms, or even kicking each other is fairly common at this age.

Toddlerhood 3 children are still quite immature and lack the social skills that enable them to play well and get along harmoniously together. As long as they play next to each other without interacting, they do just fine. When they try to play with each other, problems usually arise.

Since they are just beginning to develop more positive feelings for one another, it is advisable that you or another adult be there to supervise when youngsters of this age play together. This will help keep fights to a minimum while allowing children to get the social benefits of each other's company.

As your child becomes more social and more interested in her peers, you should encourage her social activities. If there are children around your child's age in the neighborhood, she can play with them every day. Otherwise, you might want to start bringing her to a park, playground, or local Y so that she can have an opportunity to play with her contemporaries.

Many parents organize play groups for their children. Several parents, who want their children to be exposed to other youngsters around their ages, may decide to form a play group during one or more mornings or afternoons a week. Parents take turns having the play group meet at their homes, and also take turns in supervising the children.

Play groups are a good way to offer a child opportunities to observe youngsters her age and interact with them. As adult supervisors change, she will also experience different methods of discipline. Exposure to varied types of handling is often beneficial for a child. Social skills will gradually develop through repeated association with other adults and children.

INTELLECTUAL DEVELOPMENT

The Developing Mind

The Toddlerhood 3 child is entering a level of development that marks the beginning of a type of thinking more like an adult's. An important advance is her ability to develop symbols (words) to represent or stand for people, objects, and events that she sees in her surroundings more easily. This allows her to deal with her environment on a symbolic or representational level. She can begin to play with images and symbols for concrete things in her mind, without having to see or handle the actual objects.

RAPID EXPANSION OF SYMBOLIC THOUGHT. Prior to this phase the child has dealt primarily with actual things that she could see, touch, hear, smell, and taste. Problems could be solved practically, through physical experimentation and handling objects, rather than by thinking them through.

Reflecting upon alternatives or playing with ideas in her head was not an activity that she engaged in to any great extent in infancy or early toddlerhood, although this new thinking ability does have its roots in her earlier sensory and motor experiences. It is helpful to view the development of her symbolic thinking as a gradual process that started earlier in her life. These earlier experiences laid the foundation for the rapid expansion of symbolic thought that will begin to emerge during Toddlerhood 3.

RECOGNIZING NEW INTELLECTUAL ABILITIES. Your toddler's ability to remember and interrelate simple ideas in her head in order to come up with new ways of solving problems will be improving and expanding rapidly. You will probably notice that she is becoming less a creature of impulse and more of a thinker.

When faced with a new problem for which she has no familiar response pattern to rely upon as a solution, she may not immediately experiment with various physical methods of solving it such as handling or moving objects. Rather, she may pause for a moment or two to think what her next move should be. After she has reflected on the problem, she will then attempt to carry out the solution that she has decided upon.

You will not only notice that she is reflecting upon events before she takes action, but will also see other signs of her improved intellectual abilities. Make-believe play activities, imitation of people who are no longer present, and a tremendous advance in language generally become more obvious during Toddlerhood 3. These exciting developments reflect the use of images and symbols, and show that your child is no longer limited to direct action involving real (concrete) objects. She can now think

657

about objects and events and, through the use of symbols, manipulate them in her mind.

Your toddler has become a thinker, but her ability to hold and interrelate symbols and ideas in her mind is still at a primitive level. At this early stage she will basically be concentrating upon developing symbols for objects. As she plays, she will focus upon learning the names of her playthings and their properties. When you take her outside your home, she will be anxious to learn the names for people, animals, buildings, and so on, that she sees.

Once these names or symbols become firmly established, she stores this information in her mind. Symbols and memories of experiences can gradually be organized and interrelated. This will enable her to think and speak on a more sophisticated level.

Watching your child at play and interacting with her will enable you to observe these changes in her mental abilities indirectly, because they will be reflected in her speech and behavior. By paying close attention to what she says and does, you cannot help but be struck by the rapid progress she is making.

Concept of Objects

Memory for objects, even when they are no longer in sight, is becoming well established. Now that your child's memory has improved, the number of objects that she can remember seeing or dealing with has grown markedly. Through exploration, she is continuing to learn more about objects and their characteristics.

Take, for example, her understanding of a given object such as her ball. She may know that the name of this object is "ball," and that it is big, red, can be thrown, rolled, or bounced. Despite her awareness of several characteristics of the ball, she still has a limited capacity to cope with many different properties of this object at once in her mind. She can say that the ball is "big," or "red," or "pretty" on different occasions, but at any given time she is not able to tell you that it is "big, red, and pretty."

The child is learning the names of many objects, and learning to record and remember symbols for different properties of objects in her mind. It is difficult for the Toddlerhood 3 child to interrelate and organize these symbols, and it will be several years before she is capable of doing this well.

What Makes Things Happen

Through her everyday experiences, the toddler has now developed a practical understanding of many simple cause and effect situations. Turning the faucet makes the water come out. Turning the dial on the radio makes the music louder or softer. She knows that if she teases you, you will probably react in a certain way.

A main interest of hers is learning about the consequences of her actions. Just as she is building a word vocabulary that enables her to communicate with others on a more sophisticated level, she is also developing numerous action and result experiences that will help her to better understand how things happen around her.

SURPRISES STIMULATE CURIOSITY. The simple cause and effect sequences that your child has learned allow her to anticipate or expect a certain result to follow her action. She has become so familiar with particular consequences of her actions that she takes them for granted. It is usually when something unexpected occurs that she becomes interested in why things happen.

Marsha, early in toddlerhood, learned that by turning the dial on the radio, she would hear music or voices. She did not seem to be concerned about the radio itself, or why it played. Her main concern was that she could listen to the music.

One afternoon, Marsha went over to the radio and turned the dial, but heard no music. This had never happened before, and took her by surprise. Disturbed that her immediate need to listen to music was not satisfied, she first played with the dial and twisted it all the way to the right. When this produced no results, she picked up the small radio and shook it, as if trying to understand why it was not working.

When an expected consequence of your toddler's action does not occur, you may see indications that she is very surprised and puzzled. Toddlerhood 3 children, who take simple cause and effect patterns for granted, frequently show a beginning interest in why things happen, especially when an expected event does not occur. Under these circumstances they may explore and question in order to find out why something they had anticipated did not happen.

BEGINNING TO REALIZE THAT SHE DOES NOT CAUSE EVERYTHING. The Toddlerhood 1 and 2 child's view of cause and effect relationships was highly self-centered. Nearly everything that happened around her was thought to be related to or caused by her. To a large extent, this self-centered point of view is still taken by the Toddlerhood 3 child, although she is slowly beginning to realize that there are events which are beyond her limited range of influence, and that not everything that happens is the consequence of what she does. Her active experimentation and experience in dealing with the environment allows her to develop a more objective concept of causality.

A little boy standing in a park saw an apple fall from a tree. Previously he would have related this event to himself. He would have concluded that he caused the apple to fall by wishing it, or merely by the fact that he was looking at it when it fell. Now that he is moving away from the highly self-centered position taken in infancy and early toddlerhood, he is able to realize that he did not cause this event. The event happened independent of his wishes, thoughts, or presence. From his point of view, the apple fell of its own accord, just as he might fall if he were in a tree. In his eyes, the apple, like himself, is capable of causing something to happen.

Your child may be able to recognize that she does not cause everything to take place around her. This new realization about what makes things happen takes time to develop, and will become a more prominent aspect of her view of cause and effect sequences during the early preschool years.

Concept of Space

By Toddlerhood 3, the child has developed at least some notion of space in which people and objects are related to each other. This notion will gradually become more sophisticated as she learns about perspective, variations in sizes of objects, how objects can be taken apart and put together, where objects belong, how to get from one place to another, and so forth. To a large extent, her knowledge of space depends upon her own movements and dealings with objects.

As your child moves about in her surroundings, she is becoming more and more familiar with spatial relationships. She can speedily get from one area of your home to another, and knows where many things are kept. If asked to do so, she can respond correctly to requests to get objects for you or return them to places where they are normally kept. She may even show a strong preference for having objects placed where they belong, to the point of getting angry if you leave objects lying around.

In her play with toys and objects, you will also realize that she is becoming more aware of spatial relationships. She not only may be able to take apart objects such as a plastic jar with a lid, but she may begin to put them back together. If you give her a series of graduated cups, she might be able to fit them together correctly. In her play with blocks, she can probably balance them neatly one on top of the other in order to build a tower consisting of many blocks.

Her abilities to deal with objects are improving, but she may continue to have difficulty placing or fitting things together. Although she is able to recognize obvious differences in size, she may have trouble noticing smaller differences. You may see her trying to fit a large object into a smaller one, since her perception of the comparative sizes of objects is not well developed.

The Toddlerhood 3 child is also not yet aware of the fact that one object cannot be in two places at the same time. Juanita was being pulled along in her new red wagon, when she happened to spot another red wagon just like her own. Her parent jokingly said to her, "Look, somebody took your new red wagon." Juanita began to cry, seemingly unaware that she was sitting in her own wagon. It will take some time before she will have a realistic understanding of spatial relationships.

Your child will probably begin to use many words that refer to space, both of her own accord, and in response to questions that you ask. She will use words such as "over," "upstairs," "up high," "in," "out," "down," "under," and "around."

As she plays with objects such as blocks, she is likely to talk about where to place them. Many of her questions and demands will also include the use of space words. "Mommy, up" or "Go out" are phrases that are frequently heard.

You may notice that she has become more familiar with how to get from your house to nearby places such as a relative's house, the playground, or the grocery store. The child who "knows" the familiar route to a specific location may become upset if the route her parent ordinarily takes is varied. If on your way to the corner grocery store where you often take your child, you make a left turn where you usually make a right turn, you may be surprised at her response. She may shout "no" and get all worked up in an attempt to inform you of your mistake.

Despite her familiarity with one or two routes connecting familiar locations, she may not be able to lead the way to the grocery store by herself. She also will not be able to find her way to most places outside of the home.

At this early stage in development, she is not ready to comprehend the way in which different locations make up a total picture of space or can be organized to make a map. The toddler's perception of space is closely tied to her own movements and travels. There is much more about space for her to learn as she enters the preschool years.

Concept of Time

During Toddlerhood 3 you will be able to observe your toddler's awareness of simple time sequences. There is a good chance that she will begin to use the words "yesterday," "today," and "tomorrow" to indicate past, present, and future time, even though when she uses them she often gets them mixed up. Most children are not able to state that "yesterday" comes before "today," which is followed by "tomorrow."

Living from moment to moment is your toddler's main concern, but she will show some signs of remembering past events and anticipating future events. New words that refer to future time can be heard. You may hear her say things like "maybe soon," "not now," "in a minute," and "gonna," whenever she wants to refer to the future or the delay of an activity. Her vocabulary is likely to include several words that refer to present time such as "today" or "now."

Some understanding of the concept "simultaneous" is emerging. When you say things like, "While you play with your blocks, I'll cook dinner," or, "Go play with these pots, while I do the laundry," she will show you by her actions that she comprehends your remarks. She is also learning to take turns with you in performing tasks or playing games in which you do something first while she waits, and then she does something while you wait.

Your toddler's procrastination can be annoying, especially when you are trying to get her away from her play activities in order to come indoors or go to bed. Unlike the majority of adults, toddlers are not terribly aware of or concerned about time pressures and schedules, except when there is something that they want to do. Then they will be aware of and annoyed about any attempts to make them wait or postpone their plans.

Toddlers are slowly learning the important lesson that immediate fulfillment of their wishes is not always possible. They are better able to wait when told "In a while," "Not right now," or "We'll do it after lunch." At this time do not expect too much, since your toddler will find it difficult to postpone her desires.

Imitation

Imitation is increasing and becoming more accurate. Through imitation, you will notice that your toddler is gradually learning to use the bathroom, feed herself, comb her hair, and wash and dry her hands. She is also learning to brush her teeth, use language effectively, dress and undress herself, put away her toys, and deal with other people and objects more effectively. She takes great pride in mimicking you, and will listen eagerly while you attempt to show her the proper way to accomplish certain tasks.

Copying the actions of absent people, which began during Toddlerhood 2, should now be seen more often, since your child is better able to remember someone's behavior. You will notice her mimicking the behavior and sounds of different people, animals, or even objects she has previously seen in person or on television. As her intellectual abilities increase, her imitation of others becomes more elaborate and sophisticated. By mimicking other people's behavior she is discovering many things about herself, and how to deal with others more appropriately.

Curiosity

It will seem as if your child's desire to learn is insatiable. She will be a great pioneer who wants to practice her abilities and explore her environment without restrictions. She is becoming more independent, and you may have great difficulty keeping up with her as she goes about her daily business of quickly moving from one activity to the next, and one room to another. Your Toddlerhood 3 child is likely to be interested in nearly every object and event that she sees. The tiniest pebble or speck of grass may arouse her curiosity.

Toddlerhood 3 children begin to ask questions. Their questions may be very simple and are often accompanied by pointing or other gestures. Twenty-six-month-old Linda was becoming very interested in the plants in her mother's garden. She would point to a flower, look up inquisitively, and ask, "What," or, "What this?"

Her mother would tell her the names of the flowers and explain what color they were.

This was so exciting to Linda that she kept asking her mother about the same three flowers over and over again. It is not uncommon for children to ask questions in a game-like, repetitive fashion. Linda was just learning how to ask questions, and her curiosity compelled her to practice this new skill repetitively.

Toddlers who have larger vocabularies will be asking questions more complex than Linda's simple ones. They may string together several words, and be more specific in their requests. They will want to know where things are; "Mommy, where big truck?" "Play with me?" or "Daddy fix it?" or "One more time?" are questions that reflect a child's desire for assistance or company. They may ask where people have gone or for permission to do certain activities.

These questions are a sign of your child's inquisitive nature and increasing intellectual abilities. When she asks a question, she is presenting you with a perfect opportunity to offer an explanation. Your response can be very helpful to her in expanding her knowledge and promoting her ability to speak.

The questions that your child asks are significant, despite their simplicity. They reflect not only her strong, increasing curiosity, but also her attempts to socialize with you, seek assistance, use you as a resource for learning, and practice thinking and talking. Knowing this, you will not want to ignore her questions.

The way in which you handle her questions can influence her feelings about learning, as well as the frequency with which she approaches you with additional questions. Try to respect her requests for information, and look upon them as creating opportunities to promote her intellectual, language, and personal-social development.

When she approaches you wanting to know something, or you recognize an inquisitive or puzzled expression on her face, do the best you can to show enthusiasm and offer answers that will satisfy her curiosity. Take time giving replies, and put some genuine effort into them. She will appreciate your attention and interest.

Striving to Be Good at What She Does

With the development of each new physical ability, your child has a strong need to practice constantly until she is skillful. The same holds true for thinking and language abilities. Repetition of words, questions, and demands will reflect her need to practice using these new skills.

A Toddlerhood 3 child named Jake was very verbal and began to ask the same set of questions over and over. At first his mother was amused and enjoyed answering his requests, but after an hour or two she became tired of responding. To Jake, however, this was a new and exciting way to spend his time. He was having great fun talking with his mother.

Being able to carry on a conversation and interact with her verbally for relatively long periods of time was a new experience for Jake. His mother realized the importance of his repetitive behavior. She knew that by giving him opportunities to practice, he would become more proficient and gain confidence in his new ability, so she made an effort to be patient and tolerant.

Your child's repetitive behavior is evidence of her attempts to master new skills. It reflects her determination to practice until she feels comfortable with her verbal, physical, and intellectual abilities. Her need to be good at what she does and her growing curiosity are the strong motivating factors underlying her desire to learn.

Improvements in Memory

An important advance will take place in your child's memory during Toddlerhood 3. In a variety of day-to-day situations, you can observe that her ability to retain information for longer periods of time has rapidly expanded. This retention of information goes hand in hand with the development of symbolic thinking.

You will notice that she is better able to remember stories and nursery rhymes that you have read to her. Games that you have taught her will not be forgotten as quickly as in the past. When she hides her own toys, or you hide them, she will have less difficulty than before in finding them, since her image of the toy is more permanently fixed in her mind.

Parents often notice improvements in their child's ability to remember and follow directions. When told to, "Go to the living room, get the keys on the table, and give them to Mommy," the Toddlerhood 3 child will probably remember this sequence of directions well enough to be able to carry it out correctly. Other frequently noticed signs of memory improvement include remembering people who have not visited the house for a couple of months, and repeating words heard on television commercials. If you watch for signs of memory improvement with your child, you will be amazed at the progress she has made.

LANGUAGE DEVELOPMENT

As your child enters Toddlerhood 3, you are likely to notice that her ability to speak is rapidly increasing. Her "nonsense talk" will drop out, and her immature, one word sentences will remarkably evolve into longer sentences. She is fast becoming more confident about speaking, since she has had prior experience and chances to practice. The strong interest that she will show in learning to speak will be hard for you to ignore. Her ability to tell you what she wants, needs, or thinks should not only make spending time with her more pleasurable, but should also make your job easier.

Marked improvements in her speech will be the most obvious and dramatic difference that you will observe between this phase and the one that preceded it, although she is also making commendable strides in her comprehension of language. She will be much better able to understand conversations, questions, suggestions, and directions.

Toddlers, Television, and Language Development

Toddlerhood 3 children show a stronger interest in watching television than at earlier ages. They may sit for relatively long periods of time with their eyes glued to the screen. Programs and commercials with a lot of action, loud talking, and lively music tend to capture the child's attention the most.

Television viewing can influence a child's language development. It may be of some assistance to her in learning to say new words and learning the meanings of words. Children often imitate words that they hear on television, particularly words that their favorite characters use, or those frequently heard in commercials.

Parents are sometimes quite surprised by the number of new words and even jingles their children pick up from watching television. One working mother came home late one afternoon and was greeted by her toddler, Jaime, in a most unusual manner. Jaime, who had been watching an educational program for children for the past couple of months, stood at the door and said hello to his mother in Spanish. Other parents note with amusement that their toddlers have learned to pronounce several long and difficult words as a result of watching television.

Despite the poor quality of some television shows and the violence that prevails on the screen, there are several excellent educational programs designed for young viewers. Among these programs, a few make special efforts to stimulate children's vocabulary development, comprehension, and interest in language learning. If you permit your child to watch television, it would be wise to check on which educational children's programs are available in your area.

While your toddler sits spellbound viewing her favorite children's show on a regular basis, you will have some freedom to engage in other activities, and you may even notice some modest improvements in the size of her vocabulary, understanding of words, or grammar. Certainly you can do more to foster your toddler's language development than can television, but in limited doses, it can provide her with an additional source of language stimulation and serve as an educational tool. Some of you may wish to refer back to the earlier discussion of television on pages 261–62.

Active Language Development

THE DEVELOPMENT OF GRAMMAR. Now that your child will probably begin speaking in sentences of two or more words, it is appropriate to expand upon the development of grammar. Grammar provides us with specific rules for combining words into sentences. Between early toddlerhood and the end of the preschool stage, children accomplish the amazing task of learning the rules for combining words into sentences. Your child's ability to produce grammatically correct sentences will emerge, even though you do not give her formal lessons in this area.

There are numerous ideas about how the child learns to speak in grammatically correct sentences. One theory states that the child learns grammar by simple imitation, and that she says only what she has heard other people say. However, when a child comes up with sentences such as, "I maked a pie," or, "I saw some mices," it seems unlikely that she is parroting sentences that she has heard.

This seems to indicate that simple imitation is not enough to account for how children learn grammar, but it is most difficult to prove that the child's correctly produced sentences as well as her grammatical errors are not directly copied from a model.

Another theory stresses reinforcement principles in learning grammar. It claims that the child initially combines words at random, but since she is only praised when her sentences are properly constructed, ungrammatical sentences begin to diminish and eventually drop out entirely. Research by Ursula Bellugi and Roger Brown suggests that this is not the case. Findings from their investigation of the structure of children's early sentences indicate that the toddler's initial two word sentences are not just randomly chosen from the broader group of words in her vocabulary. Her phrases have a structure and also express a thought.

Take, for example, the phrase, "All gone milk." It communicates a complete thought, even though it is brief and grammatically incorrect. Researchers have established that the child's two word verbalizations frequently consist of both a modifier word and a subject word. In the three word sentence just mentioned, the subject word is "milk" and the modifier is "all gone." Some examples of subject words are as follows: truck, plate, mommy, bird, house, box. Some examples of modifier words are: my, see, tall, pretty, big.

The majority of toddlers' sentences are composed of a modifier and a subject, but they may also combine two subject words to make a sentence such as "House, Mommy!" Sentences made up of two modifier words are rare. Researchers have thus suggested a rule that explains the young child's early sentence construction: their sentences consist of a modifier and a subject, or a subject and a subject.

You will probably hear your child experimenting with sentence construction and the position of words as she learns to produce sentences of greater length. You might hear the following sentences, one right after another: "I want bottle." "I want candy." "I want truck." This type of sequence presumably indicates her attempts to try out different nouns as endings on her sentences. The development of this aspect of language, independent of "formal instruction," has been an exciting area for researchers to study.

It is interesting to get a feel for how some researchers have viewed the development of correct sentence structure. It should be stressed, however, that they still do not know the precise, underlying means by which a child develops grammar. You have a wonderful opportunity to make your own observations about the development of grammar by speaking and listening to your child. More information on the topic of grammar can be found in Preschool 2 (pages 841–42).

VOCABULARIES ARE EXPANDING. Children's vocabularies are likely to increase significantly during Toddlerhood 3, although the number of words they are able to say varies from child to child. Part of this variation in vocabulary size may be due to inborn differences in toddlers, but environmental factors such as having appropriate language stimulation, opportunities to interact verbally with parents, and encouragement also play a role. Toddlerhood 3 children are eager to learn new words, be involved in family discussions, and play games with words. Therefore, by all means take advantage of your child's enthusiasm, willingness, and interest, by including her in your discussions and engaging her in activities designed to promote language learning.

Most youngsters quickly learn words that assist them in telling their parents what they need or want. Their vocabularies often include words that refer to playthings, specific objects that they use every day, foods, and places. Toddlers are frequently able to recognize and name shapes such as stars, crosses, circles, or diamonds. They are also learning names for common colors, including red, blue, and orange.

Your child may now be able to tell someone her first and last name when asked. This is an accomplishment that can be of great help to her in the event that she gets lost. It also adds a new dimension to her self-identity.

SPEECH OFTEN ACCOMPANIES PLAY. Youngsters often talk as they play. They tell simple stories or even tell themselves or their playthings what to do. A toddler may say aloud the steps required in putting a lid on a jar, or in playing a record. As she goes to touch the basement door, an off-limits object, she may say "no-no" aloud as a warning or reminder to herself to keep hands off.

CONVERSATIONS. Toddlers communicate with others, even though their ability to enter into conversations is very limited as well as comical. They will make attempts to talk, say something funny to get a laugh, and even sometimes tease their parents or brothers and sisters.

It can sometimes be frustrating for parents to try to keep track of what their child is trying to tell them, since she does not have the necessary words at her command to fit all of her ideas. She talks slowly, and now and then loses her train of thought. Communication skills will improve with practice.

Passive Language Development

UNDERSTANDING THE MEANING OF WORDS. Your child's vocabulary will increase during this phase, but you will notice that she understands far more words than she can say. This is perfectly natural. Her ability to comprehend language will always exceed her ability to use words. You will also observe that she understands a great deal more language than in the past, and will pick up on things you say to other adults, sometimes to your surprise and dismay.

LISTENING. Toddlers of this age love to listen to conversations and stories. They are especially delighted when the stories are about them; it makes them feel special and important to hear their own names mentioned. Your child will probably listen with interest when you read to her from simple children's books, and will take pride in identifying the pictures.

FOLLOWING DIRECTIONS. Your toddler will be able to follow simple suggestions or instructions such as, "We will read books after eating dinner," or, "Please pick up your socks," although she may not always choose to carry out the expected behavior. It may be harder for her to understand general directions such as, "Let's put your toys away," than for her to understand specific directions such as, "Trucks go on the shelf," or, "Put Teddy bear on the bed."

In talking or reading to your child, it may become obvious that she does not understand what you are saying; try to slow down and use simpler, more familiar words. When talking to her or giving instructions, avoid continually using words that are above her level of comprehension.

MOTOR DEVELOPMENT

Between the beginning and end of this phase, your toddler's motor activity will be better organized. She will be more sure of herself than she was in the previous phase, and will be less worried about maintaining her balance when walking and running. The skills that she has been developing earlier in toddlerhood will be further refined over the next few months.

Her activities will more closely resemble those of an adult. You will be able to interact and play with her more readily. She will seem to understand more of what she's doing, and thus her motor activities will seem to be more goal-oriented. She will still have an enormous amount of motor energy, and will be placing increasing demands on your time to participate in her activities.

You will also see signs of improved fine motor co-ordination. As she gains further control over her hands and fingers, she will want to tackle new, more difficult manual tasks, and become more independent in the basic care areas.

Gross Motor Activity

WALKING. Your toddler will be much more at ease on her feet, although she may still watch how she places them so that she does not trip over objects in her path. She will be assuming a more correct posture as she walks. Her ability to stop, turn around, and walk backward will be greatly improved. You may also see her walking sideways and on tiptoe. She will now be able to bend and pick up objects from the floor more rapidly and easily. Although she has not as yet become a soccer star, she is becoming more adept at kicking a ball or other objects.

CLIMBING. Children are now rather efficient at walking up steps. They will further develop their ability to walk down steps during this phase. Your toddler will most likely be able to walk down a flight of steps while holding your hand or the side railing. This is a difficult task to master, and may still not be completely developed during this phase. She will also be more efficient at sitting in a chair, and is now likely to be able to lower herself down onto a small chair smoothly, in an adult-like fashion.

RUNNING. Sometime during Toddlerhood 3 the child gains enough leg power and balance to permit her briefly to leave the ground with both feet at the same time. She becomes capable of running. For a while, her running may appear awkward, with a stiff and flat type of gait. Given ample time, she will become more adept at this activity. Once she has begun to run, she will constantly travel in this fashion.

This will be a difficult time for you, if you are an anxious parent. Your little toddler will still have trouble co-ordinating starting, stopping, and turning movements, and thus is in store for many crash collisions. The way in which she will turn a corner in a hallway is very amusing. She will probably run straight into the wall, bounce off it, change directions, and then continue running. This behavior may also be typical of young preschool children.

BALANCING. Your toddler may now attempt to perform several new motor tasks. You may see her balancing on one foot for about a second or two. Her ability to maintain her balance is in its early stages. She may try to stand on one foot, but she may begin to sway and sometimes fall. With persistence, however, she may be able to balance on one foot for a short period of time.

JUMPING. Jumping is another skill that your child is beginning to acquire. When she first attempted to run, one of her feet always remained in contact with the ground. The same holds true for her first attempts to jump, in which she simply stepped off low objects. During the last phase, you probably observed her stepping off low objects with one foot, remaining suspended in the air for only an instant. At this time she may use a two-feet take-off.

Watch her arms closely as she jumps. Older children swing their arms forward when they jump. The Toddlerhood 3 child is less adept at this new skill, and will tend to retract her arms to the rear instead of swinging them frontward. Your child will also be able to jump in place, and may derive a great deal of pleasure from practicing this activity.

Still another type of jumping involves jumping forward for short distances (better known as broad-jumping). In order to test your child's ability to broad jump, lay a piece of standard-size typing paper in front of her feet and tell her to try and jump over it. According to the Denver Developmental Screening Test, less than 50 percent of the children tested were able to jump over the piece of paper at this age.

RIDING A TRICYCLE. Riding a tricycle is a favorite activity of many toddlers. If you have not already bought one for your child, you may want to do so now, or borrow one for the time being. By the end of this phase, most toddlers will be able to pedal a tricycle, although some children are three years old before they are capable of pedaling. Parents tend to swell with pride as they watch their toddlers take off for the first time on a tricycle. Safety precautions must be taken to prevent unnecessary accidents when she is riding.

THROWING A BALL. Your child's ability to throw a ball should be improving, despite the fact that she is still rather inefficient at this complex motor task. By the end of this phase most children will be able to throw a ball near a target not too far away. They generally use a forward and backward motion of the body and arm when they throw. Their bodies usually face the direction of the throw, and they tend not to shift their weight.

Just for the fun of it, try throwing a ball as your child does. Imitate her arm and body movements. See how much this position hampers the distance you can throw, as well as your aim.

CATCHING A BALL. The ability to catch a ball is still crude, although it, too, shows improvement. Rather than cradling her arms, she may now hold them straight in front of her body, elbows stiff. It is no wonder balls that happen to fall into her arms often bounce right back out.

Fine Motor Activity

BLOCK BUILDING. Your child is much more efficient at releasing objects, and, therefore, you will have fun interacting with her in numerous skill games. She will show increasing dexterity when handling blocks, and will probably be able to build a tower of six or seven blocks.

DRAWING. Drawing skills will rapidly develop during this phase. You will spend many interesting moments trying to determine what your child has created. Her attempts to draw the sky, your house, or copy simple designs will seem very purposeful, but her drawings will still be unsophisticated, and may show little resemblance to the objects that she is drawing. She should be able to copy a simple vertical line, and may be able to copy a circle. In order to test this, draw a circle on a page while your child is watching. Then hand her a pencil and tell her to draw a circle. Consider her attempt successful if she draws any enclosed form resembling a circle. If she makes continuous round motions, then she is unsuccessful at this task. The majority of children will be able to copy a circle by Preschool 1.

DRESSING AND UNDRESSING. As her dexterity improves, your child will become able to undress herself completely. You may also see great progress in her ability to dress herself. She will take great pride in her ability to put on her own clothes. Some of her initial attempts may lead to putting her shirt on backward or attempting to put the right shoe on the left foot, but gradually she will become more skillful at dressing.

TURNING PAGES. Your toddler will derive great pleasure from mimicking the way you sit and read a book. She may sit in a chair and turn the pages of her favorite book, carefully noting the pictures and colors on the page.

EATING. During this phase your child will be more efficient at feeding herself. She will be better able to handle a spoon, dropping only small pieces of food as she brings it to her mouth. She may also be learning how to use a fork and knife, although the ability to use these utensils proficiently comes later.

TAKING OBJECTS APART. Now that her manipulatory skills have improved, she will enjoy taking apart objects such as puzzles, an old, empty stapler or coffee pot, and then attempting to put them back together. At this point she is still probably better at taking things apart.

WRIST-TWISTING. Toddlerhood 3 children develop the ability to rotate their forearm. This allows them to twist their wrist. They may now be better able to turn on water faucets, twist doorknobs, and most importantly, unscrew the caps of medicine bottles.

Your toddler is still unable to co-ordinate this twisting motion with other movements such as pressing down. This is the basis for the "child-proof" medicine bottles that have recently been developed. Most of these bottles require the combined, simultaneous motions of twisting and pushing to open the cap. A toddler cannot perform these two movements together, although she can perform each one separately. She will not be able to open this type of special bottle cap. For her complete safety, however, you must continue to lock up all medicines, even those in "child-proof" containers.

HAND PREFERENCE. Is your child right-handed, left-handed, or ambidextrous? Handedness is an area of study about which there is some knowledge, and quite a lot of speculation and controversy. Certain problems arise when considering hand preference which make it difficult to evaluate. When children and adults are exposed to one-handed tasks, for example, they often fail to show consistent hand preference.

Many authorities believe that hand preference is initially determined by heredity, and is later influenced and molded by subtle cultural and social pressures. They generally agree that once a child shows a definite preference for her right or left hand, parents should not force her to change her natural preference.

Often a child's preference for one hand or the other can be detected during the first year. By Toddlerhood 3, her handedness is more clearly seen. Once a child reaches the age of five or six, she has usually developed a more consistent preference for one hand or the other. Even then, a right-handed child, for example, may eat, write, and bat with her right hand and throw with her left. Some people are completely right- or left-handed in everything that they do, and others are ambidextrous.

LEARNING THROUGH PLAY

Varied Play Activities

Your child's activities will vary throughout the day. Much of her play will involve gross motor activity. She will love to romp, run, climb, push, pull, shove, and carry. You will see her dangling from the low bars on a child-sized jungle gym, climbing three-step ladders, crawling over rocks and piles of logs, attempting to balance on her wooden planks, rolling balls, and pulling her wagon. One of her favorite pieces of play equipment is apt to be her kiddie car.

The very active play which began earlier in toddlerhood will continue throughout this phase. Your Toddlerhood 3 child needs to move around, and will spend much of her time doing just that, although some of her day will be devoted to quiet activities. She will hammer, paint, tinker with pots and pans, look at picture books, and scribble with large crayons.

Creative activities may be among your toddler's newly emerging interests. She may first really begin to concentrate upon constructing a tower or a building with her blocks, shaping her lump of clay into a banana, or drawing a picture. Creative activities will become more prominent and important during the preschool years.

Pretend or make-believe activities are also emerging to a greater extent than in Toddlerhood 2. She will create imaginary situations in her play and assume various roles. This will be discussed further in Preschool 1 on page 672.

Fun with Language

The Toddlerhood 3 child's interest in language is rapidly expanding. Games involving the repetition of words, sounds, and even jokes are not only a good way to foster her language growth, but can be thoroughly enjoyable for both parent and child. Quiet activities such as reading her stories, picture-word cards, rhymes, and poems are very useful in breaking up large periods of active play. Further suggestions for having fun with language are presented on pages 798–801.

Stringing Objects

A good way to give your toddler practice in using her hands and fingers is to introduce her to stringing activities with different objects. Several old, long shoelaces are ideal for safe stringing games when one end is knotted. Empty spools of thread can be strung on the shoelace.

For variety, string a large, flat circular shape with a hole in the center on the shoelace first. Then she can string different objects with larger center holes afterward. Appropriate objects to string might include curlers, empty toilet paper tubes, or stale bagels.

At holiday time you can help your child paint these "ornaments" and display them around your home. This type of activity will require her utmost concentration, so avoid pressuring her if she occasionally misses her aim.

Matching Lids and Containers

The following activity will give your toddler practical experience in dealing with lids and containers. It will also give her practice in using her hands and wrists, and making discriminations. Gather several different-sized containers with lids, such as boxes, plastic jars, and plastic bottles.

Place the containers in a row on the table or floor, and put their appropriate lids in front of them. Show your toddler how to place the top on each container. After she has mastered this task, try something new.

Scramble the containers and tops. Then encourage her to unscramble the "puzzle" by matching the lid to the right container. This activity may prove to be very difficult for her at this early stage. If it appears that she is getting frustrated and is unable to manage the new aspect of this game, help her finish the task and then reintroduce it when she is older.

Helping Out Around the House

Many toddlers love to play wherever their parents are, and they often want to do what they see their parents do. Whether you are working with foods, straightening up, or washing the cabinets or floor, you will be able to find several simple tasks for your child to carry out. She will enjoy being her parent's little helper.

When preparing a salad, for example, you could allow her to assist. Have her wash her hands first, and then hand her several leaves of lettuce to tear into small pieces. There will undoubtedly be occasions on which small pieces of cheese or other foods have to be covered and stored in the refrigerator, and she may be interested in helping you tear off pieces of foil and wrap the foods. You can also encourage her to help take food out of grocery bags, hold small cans for you while you put them away, or help you carry non-breakable items.

It will make her feel both needed and proud to be able to lend a hand. Helping you, even in small ways, will also aid in building her self-confidence, and introducing her to many practical tasks. As you work in other areas of the house or yard, you can also find numerous ways to involve her in your activities. She will have great fun imitating you, and will not consider helping as work or a chore.

Activities with Suitcases

Toddlers' interests in hauling things, working hinged objects, filling and emptying, and pretending are all taken into account in the following activity. You will need to have a small, lightweight travel bag or suitcase and objects such as small toys, or clothes that need to be washed.

First show your toddler how to open and close the suitcase, and give her plenty of opportunity to practice on her own. Have her pick it up and carry it while it is empty. Then suggest that she pack it with the toys or clothes. If she overloads it, encourage her to remove items one by one, until it will close.

She will probably have loads of fun packing and unpacking it and parading around the house with it. Point out to her the difference in weight between a packed and an empty suitcase. You can also encourage her to pretend that she is preparing for a trip. She may have an easier time with a suitcase or duffle bag with a zipper, and this will give her chances to practice working zippers.

Music and Rhythm Activities

Activities that involve music and rhythm will also be thoroughly enjoyed by your child. She may like to dance to music or walk along to the rhythm while holding onto someone's hand or while holding objects such as blocks or bells.

Youngsters often show an interest in playing with objects that give them the feeling of using real musical instruments. You can give your child some boxes along with spoons to pound on them or some saucepan lids to clang together. She may also be interested in using a simple record player, or simply selecting records that she likes to hear.

Most toddlers sit spellbound watching parents sing and dance, so now is your time to discard your inhibitions and show off your hidden talent. Rest assured she will not be put off if you are rusty, slightly out of step, or off key. If you are a music lover, chances are your child will love music, too. Why not introduce her to a wide variety from Elvis Presley to the Beatles to Bach, and let her listen to music as she takes a bath, eats dinner, or helps you around the house.

Play with Other Children

Children often show an interest in being around other children and playing near them during Toddlerhood 3. As soon as this interest emerges in your child, it is advisable to encourage it by giving her opportunities to play with youngsters her age. Having ample contact with her peers is important to her personal-social development. More information on play with other children can be found on pages 803, 830–31.

Imaginative Play

Your child's dramatic play is likely to be more noticeable around this time. She may pretend to be you, a baby, or another person with whom she is familiar. She might pretend that her doll or Teddy bear is a baby and play "house" with it, but at this early stage her ability to play imaginatively is not well developed. You are likely to see her do simple things to her doll that you have done to her such as tucking it in bed, naming objects for it, or even placing it on the toilet.

She may also play with imaginary objects. In her imaginative play, a toy hammer may become a gun, or a cardboard box may become a hat. Her lump of mud might become an animal, and through her play this inanimate object may come "alive." An extensive discussion of imaginative play is provided in the preschool sections on play (pages 839–40, 848–52, 919–20).

Suggested List of Playthings

housekeeping equipment for children
toy lawn mower and gardening tools
non-toxic, water soluble paint
large paintbrushes
dough
clay
finger paint
puzzles—large, simple
wooden and plastic transportation toys
costumes and old clothes for dramatic play
large cardboard boxes
books
simple record player and records
toys that can be put together and taken apart
large, non-toxic crayons
paper of any kind
children's desk, table and chair
tricycle
felt-tip markers (non-toxic)
empty spools of thread
long shoelace
containers with lids
small, lightweight suitcase or duffle bag
bells
chalk
blackboard
easel

HOW TO ENSURE YOUR TODDLER'S SAFETY

Safety and Tricycles

Many parents purchase a tricycle for their toddlers during Toddlerhood 3 or Pre-school 1. Toddlers often regard their tricycles as their favorite outdoor plaything. In order to keep tricycle riding a safe, fun activity for your toddler, you should be aware of a few simple precautions.

MAKING A WISE SELECTION. For parents wondering what kind of features to look for when selecting a tricycle, here are some suggestions. Choose a tricycle that is well constructed, and designed. It should be able to withstand a great deal of wear and tear.

Avoid purchasing a tricycle with sharp or pointed edges. Fenders should be smooth. Pedals and handle bars should have rough or grooved surfaces to help prevent your toddler's hands and feet from slipping and becoming entangled in the moving parts of the tricycle.

Stability in a tricycle is a key factor to take into account. Tricycles should be suited to your child's size. Those that are too large for her size will be hard for her to control properly. Instability may also result when a child is too large for the tricycle. All such riding toys should be marked by the manufacturer as to suitable maximum weight. Two additional features that will offer your child added stability are widely spaced wheels and a low seat.

TAKING PROPER CARE OF THE TRICYCLE. Proper maintenance of your child's tricycle will help ensure her safety. Examine the tricycle from time to time to check on its condition. Look for loose parts such as the seat, handle bars or pedals. Missing or worn hand grips can also be dangerous. Be sure rough edges are covered or sanded. Repair broken or damaged parts promptly before permitting your child to use it again. Try to keep the tricycle indoors overnight to prevent rust from accumulating and metal parts from deteriorating.

TEACHING YOUR CHILD HOW TO PROPERLY USE THE TRICYCLE. Either you or another responsible person should closely supervise your child when she is riding her tricycle. Tell her to avoid hills, sharp turns, steps, and curbs, and *never* to put her hands and feet near turning spokes. Make a concerted effort to teach her safe ways of conducting herself when riding. A child who can comprehend simple verbal explanations should be given reasons why not following these safety rules is dangerous.

Tricycle-related accidents are more common than most parents think. By selecting a good tricycle that is well matched to your individual child, keeping it in proper shape, and carefully supervising her whenever she uses it, many unnecessary accidents can be prevented.

EATING

Over the past several months you have observed your toddler's steadily increasing desire and ability to participate at mealtimes. With additional hand control and chances to practice, she will make further progress in eating on her own, and may even be able to assume much of the responsibility for feeding herself. You have observed many changes in her needs and abilities in the area of eating, although your responsibilities have remained essentially the same. It is still up to you to offer her healthy, well-balanced meals, and to try to keep the atmosphere at mealtime enjoyable and relaxed. Your job as a dietician is likely to be less taxing, since she will basically be eating the same foods that you eat.

The Fussy Eater

To many parents' dismay, this is the approximate age at which toddlers tend to become very selective about what they will and will not eat. They are apt to have great difficulty making up their minds about what they want to eat. When parents serve them what they say they want, they may suddenly decide that they want no part of it, and would rather have some other food instead.

According to Ms. Snead: "My son, Freddie, is driving me nuts at mealtime. First he says he wants Cheerios, so I pour some into a bowl. No sooner do I put it in front of him when he says 'No, want flakes.' So, I throw out the soggy Cheerios and give him corn flakes. Then he doesn't want corn flakes, either." Freddie, like many toddlers, is showing a desire to make his own decisions. Not having had much practice in this, he finds it necessary to change his mind several times before making a final decision.

Along with difficulties in making choices about what they want to eat, Toddlerhood 3 children often become fussier in their eating habits. Mrs. Spencer used to shop at a store where they stocked a particular well-known brand of soup. One day she shopped at a different supermarket that carried its own store brand of instant chicken soup. Despite the similarities in taste between the well-known brand and the store's, her daughter refused to eat the latter because of the difference in the appearance of the package.

This little girl's reaction is not unusual. Toddlers often become brand- or label-conscious during this phase. As they grow more aware of their individuality, it becomes important for them to express their opinions and assert themselves. They do not like change, and often insist upon having things remain as before. Refusal to eat because a particular brand was not purchased, or because a food was not prepared or served in a certain, familiar way is not uncommon.

Mr. Hall, the father of twenty-eight-month-old Leon, made the following remarks:

> My son is a riot when he eats. Lately he's been very finicky about foods. He spends a lot of time separating the foods on his dish. If a little gravy from the meat happens to touch his green beans, he won't eat the beans. I think it's funny to watch him, but my wife says he's impossible to please. She must know what she's talking about, since I only help with meals on weekends, and she takes care of our son every day.

A toddler's fussiness may be amusing to those who are not responsible for food shopping or preparation. To the parent caring for her on a full-time basis, her choosiness and mealtime antics can be annoying.

Understanding some of the reasons underlying her new mealtime behavior may enable you to put it into perspective, so you will not overreact to it. Her finicky, fussy attitude and eating practices will probably diminish by Preschool 1. In the meantime, a little extra patience and tolerance on your part may be helpful in minimizing confrontations at meals. It may become necessary to set some limits should her demands get out of hand, or cause you too great an inconvenience.

Your Child's Diet Is Expanding

As your child gets older, her diet can gradually be expanded. How and when to introduce new foods into a child's diet is extremely variable. Some physicians have rigid timetables for when and how to add new foods, and others take a more flexible stance. In general, whenever you think that it is time to add more variety to your child's diet, it is best to play it safe and ask your doctor's advice.

The most important thing to keep in mind when adding new foods is to do so slowly. By offering them one at a time, in very small amounts, you will be able to see if your child develops an allergy to them, or how well she is able to digest them. When introducing new foods, strive to keep her diet well balanced. Offer her a healthy selection of meats, vegetables, fruits, milk products, breads, and cereals.

A Toddlerhood 3 child is in some ways eating like a mini-adult. At this time you may want to introduce certain fresh berries, unusual fruits, and melons into her diet. When adding new fruits, it is advisable to mash them first or cut them into small pieces to make them more easily digestible for the young child. At the first sign that a child has trouble eating or digesting any new fruits, or if she develops hives or a rash, a parent should stop giving them right away. To prevent the possibility of her choking, always remove pits and seeds from fruits. Core and pit apples that you offer.

Many children dislike strong-tasting vegetables such as onions or broccoli or eggplant. They may enjoy other blander-tasting vegetables, especially if they are presented in attractive ways. Now that your child is better able to chew, she can be given larger pieces of vegetables than before, but certain vegetables, such as kernels of corn, should be split open before they are offered to her to make them more easily digestible. Raw vegetables can be served in place of cooked vegetables. Peel them well, and offer them in small bits and pieces first, until you are sure that she is well able to chew them and swallow them.

Go slowly when introducing new meats and fish into her diet and stick to the simpler varieties. Very fatty meats and heavily fried foods are not easily digestible, and may cause the child some problems. Tuna packed in water, for example, can be added, but try to steer away from introducing food like bacon or even perhaps rich fish like crabmeat or lobster.

Milk products such as yogurt, cottage cheese, and cream cheese are healthy for a young child. Cottage cheese and unsweetened canned fruit can be arranged to look like a funny face or an animal. Young children enjoy foods that are attractively prepared, especially when they seem fun to eat. Syrups, such as chocolate, or powdered chocolate, fortified with vitamins, can be added in small amounts to milk, assuming that the child prefers it served that way, but it is best to serve milk plain.

There are so many natural, nutritious foods that can be offered, even as snacks, that there should be no real reason to offer unwholesome or highly sweetened foods. "Junk foods" can take away a child's appetite for regular meals and contribute to tooth decay. In place of candy, for example, you can give raisins, fresh fruit, or bits of cheese. It is important to help your child develop good eating habits, and the best way to accomplish this is to serve only healthy foods, plan well-balanced meals, and set a good example for her to follow.

Self-feeding

Many Toddlerhood 3 children will be managing to feed themselves fairly well. You should be encouraging your youngster to take over the responsibility for feeding herself as she shows you that she is able to do so. At times she may want and ask for your help, and at other times she may be very insistent upon managing alone or with little aid from you. It is a good idea to have a relaxed attitude, and let her lead the way. Try to be patient and avoid pressuring her to assume more independence, if she cannot handle it. She will eventually learn how to hold and use eating utensils properly, so there is no real need for you to apply unnecessary pressure. The main thing is to arrange for her to have plenty of opportunities to practice in a relaxed, friendly atmosphere.

CLOTHING

Now is really the time to encourage your toddler to dress herself, in the event that you have already done so. A good way to assist her in learning to put clothes on properly is to lay them out on her bed in the right position, so that when she picks them up and pulls them on, they will be facing the right direction.

Mrs. Doyle used this method and found it to be quite successful with her toddler, Kevin. Each morning she laid out his clothes and shoes, and then left the room, since Kevin liked to manage all by himself. Occasionally he would still end up with his T-shirt on backward, or his pants twisted, but his over-all performance had improved after his mother began laying his clothes out for him.

Dorothy Tucker, a single parent, hit upon a marvelously ingenious way to help her daughter, Dina, learn to put her shoes on correctly, using nail polish and colored stickers. Dorothy painted Dina's right toenails pink, and placed a pink colorfast sticker inside her right shoe. Dina's left toenails were painted white, and a white sticker was placed in her left shoe.

Dorothy showed Dina how to match the colors, and within a day or two Dina learned to put her shoes on correctly. Colored labels, even used without nail polish, can come in very handy in teaching a child right from left, or simply how to put her shoes on the right feet. They can also be useful in teaching a toddler to tell the difference between the front and back of a garment, or to learn to match clothes that go together well. With a little imagination, you may be able to devise your own, unique approach to helping your toddler learn to dress herself properly.

CLOTHES FOR DRESS-UP PLAY. Your toddler will be most appreciative to have some old, adult clothes to use for dress-up play. Dress-up play often begins in a small way in toddlerhood. It becomes even more prominent during the preschool years.

Caution should be taken to ensure your child's safety whenever she is parading around in adult clothing. Dangling shirttails and long scarves can be a tripping hazard. High heels can be dangerous, and even flat shoes that are two or three times the size of her feet may be a potential source for falls. Be sure to make stairs off limits when she is wearing shoes that do not fit, and, if necessary, supervise her dress-up play to minimize the possibility of accidents.

SLEEPING

Going to bed is something that most youngsters strongly dislike, particularly active toddlers. Arguments at bedtime are common, and parents may have to be very firm and set clear limits as to how much acting up, "back talk," and stalling they are willing to tolerate.

Bedtime Patterns

Many young children find going to bed easier if a consistent pattern is established. Mr. Wagner followed the same ritual each night. First his daughter's Teddy bear was kissed and tucked in, then her favorite pillow was fluffed. Next her special blanket was placed over her and then the child was kissed and tucked in. Some parents sing a lullabye, say a simple prayer, or have a nice chat before finally turning off the light and leaving the room. Other parents read their children a short story each night at bedtime.

It is not advisable to hurry your child to bed, although it is also not a good idea to prolong these going-to-bed patterns. Elaborate bedtime patterns are frequently seen between Toddlerhood 2 and Preschool 1. When a child is very insistent upon carrying out each step in the ritual, it is advisable to go along with her, rather than get into an argument about it.

Waking During the Middle of the Night

Waking during the night may become a problem. Fear of separations from her parents and loneliness were previously discussed as possible reasons for the child's sleeping difficulties during the night. A child who has been overstimulated on a particular day may find it hard to relax and sleep through the night. Children are often soothed and relaxed by taking a bath or listening to music or stories before bedtime. It is usually best to avoid playing roughly with a child before bedtime, since this can get her "wound up." Preventing her from getting overstimulated on a regular basis should help minimize this kind of problem.

FEAR OF THE DARK. Fear of the dark is a rather common cause of sleeping difficulties among young children. Reassurance from parents may help, although if the fear is strong, it may be wise to leave a night light on in her room during the night, or leave a light on in a hallway. Some children enjoy having a flashlight near their bed, since this gives them a sense of extra security.

BAD DREAMS. Children who have had a bad dream or a nightmare may wake during the middle of the night and refuse to go back to sleep for fear of having a recurrence of the dream. Remaining at the child's bedside until she drifts back to sleep is a good solution. A parent's comfort and reassurance generally help ease the child's anxieties so that she can go back to sleep. Particularly in this situation, it is not a good idea to allow the child to watch frightening television programs or listen to scary stories before she goes to bed. These activities may be causing some of her bad dreams.

FEAR OF WETTING THE BED. It is also not uncommon for a child who is being toilet trained to wake during the night out of fear that she is going to wet her bed. Such a child may need to be reassured that she will still be loved even if she has an accident, and that it is okay if she does have one. Sometimes too much parental pressure on a child who is simply not ready to stay dry at night may cause these kinds of anxieties and fears, and parents may have to readjust their teaching methods so that it is consistent with what can be reasonably expected from their child at a given stage.

Taking a Nap

Some children may now object to taking a nap altogether. Others will sleep so long that they have to be awakened. When a toddler refuses her nap, there is no sense trying to force her. Encourage her to use the regular nap period as a time for quiet play, looking at books, or listening to records.

Climbing Out of the Crib

Between the ages of two and three, many young children will become able to climb out of their cribs. The possibility of their falling as they climb over the rail is a real one, and therefore some adjustments in sleeping arrangements may have to be made. A child's new ability to climb out of her crib can create other problems. Occasionally, a child may simply refuse to go to bed and keep climbing out each time her parents put her back. A firm approach is often necessary to alleviate this problem.

When a child has trouble sleeping through the night, she may now climb out of her crib, go out of the bedroom, and even perhaps wander outdoors. This can present numerous problems. A primary problem is her physical safety. Another problem may arise if she insists upon climbing in bed with her parents. The pros and cons of allowing your child to sleep in your bed when she wakes during the night are discussed in Preschool 1 on pages 858–59.

There are several ways to deal with the problem presented when your child is able to climb out of her crib. To prevent falls, many child care experts recommend lowering the crib mattress and side rails, or shifting the child to a regular or youth bed. A regular mattress can also be placed directly on the floor. Other experts recommend the extreme solutions of tying a net across the top of the child's crib, or using other restraints to prevent her from climbing out. Strapping the child in bed at night or "caging" her with a net is not something we would recommend. Lowering the crib rails or switching the child to a regular bed seems to be a much better solution, allowing the child freedom to move around at night.

The child who is unrestrained and gets up during the middle of the night can now get around the house, and when alone, can get herself into trouble. A few children who get up during the night may be content to play by themselves in their rooms. Even then, parents must be absolutely sure that windows are locked, and the room is completely safety-proofed. More likely than not, children will want to be up and exploring the entire house.

One obvious solution is to lock the door to the child's room at night. She will have plenty of freedom to move around and explore, but, at the same time, she will be contained within the safe boundaries of her room. Some parents and psychologists who object to locking a child in her room have suggested an alternative solution. It entails closing the child's door after she is in bed, and tying a metal object or bell on it. Should she get up and open the door, the sound of the bell will warn her parents that they had better get up too. This solution seems to be a good one, unless you are a very sound sleeper. Another idea is to place a safety gate across the door to her room. You should consider the alternatives and make your own decision as to how to handle this situation.

The child who wakes during the night and gets up may simply be restless, and may want to play, have a snack, or go to the bathroom. Often she will settle down and go back to bed once her needs have been met. Waking during the night because of the need for activity is common in young children, and often diminishes by the time they are about four years old. Punishing a child for what is generally considered to be natural behavior is not recommended, although you may have to take a firm stand as to how much nighttime activity you are willing to accept.

DEVELOPING GOOD TOILET HABITS

Many children now become regular in their bowel movements, and more capable of holding urine for longer periods of time. The majority of children are able to tell their parents that they need to go to the bathroom, using different words for bowel and bladder functions. They may even get upset when they have "accidents." Some youngsters cry when they wet their pants, while others quickly take off wet pants and put them in a hamper. This interest in cleanliness and in imitating people are signs of readiness that can help parents' training efforts.

Despite the fact that each child will set her own pace, bowel control and daytime bladder control can often be established during Toddlerhood 3, provided a child has had appropriate parental guidance and assistance. Occasional daytime "accidents," however, should be expected until she is about three years old, or sometimes even older than three, particularly when she is overtired, or under stress.

Youngsters who still want an adult to take them to the bathroom and undress them may wish to be left alone while they are on the potty chair, and may ask their parents to leave the bathroom. When they have finished, they may call their parents for assistance. Others are more independent and capable. These children may refuse to defecate or urinate unless they go to the toilet by themselves. If your child still needs help in undressing, but refuses to "go" unless she gets on the potty by herself, you can undress her and leave her alone in the bathroom at about the time she usually has a bowel movement. When she is ready, she will probably manage quite well without outside assistance. Try to avoid clothing that is difficult for her to remove by herself.

You should now want to teach her how to wipe herself, if you haven't already. After a child is able to get herself to the bathroom on time, pull down her pants, "go," and wipe herself, she will then be much less dependent upon you, and delighted with the feeling of being so grown-up. Do a good job of training your youngster to wipe after elimination. Girls should be taught to wipe from the front to the back: it is felt that this method minimizes getting feces from the anal area into the vagina.

Overnight Bladder Control

In most cases, nighttime bladder control is spontaneously achieved several months after a child has gained daytime control, although it may take longer than this. Children generally learn to stay dry while they are awake before they develop the ability to hold back urine during sleep, or to wake when their bladders are full in time to urinate on the toilet. Youngsters stop urinating at night when their bladders are sufficiently mature and they have learned that urine goes in an appropriate receptacle. This happens naturally, except in instances in which physical or emotional problems interfere with control of elimination functioning.

Once a child has gained consistent daytime urine control, she may be ready and motivated to take the next step and stay dry at night. Nighttime dryness can often be achieved during Preschool 1, but there is wide variability in the ages at which children are able to remain dry during the night. Some perfectly normal youngsters do not stay dry until age four or five, or even later than this. Little girls tend to achieve sleeping bladder control earlier than boys.

Parents often wonder about the possibility of doing something to promote nighttime bladder control. Actually, you do not have to do anything about this except casually encourage it, praise your child for her successes, and refrain from putting undue pressure upon her to stay dry.

In an attempt to speed up nighttime dryness, some parents wake their children and take them to the toilet between 10 and 11 P.M., or whenever the parents are ready to retire. If your youngster does not mind having her sleep interrupted and has no trouble falling back to sleep, this technique may help her stay dry through the night.

Waking children to take them to the bathroom is not always a good idea. Having their sleep interrupted can upset some children. They may have trouble urinating on demand and may have difficulty getting back to sleep. In the morning, their beds may still be wet, even though they were toileted between 10 and 12 p.m. If this is the case with your child, it is advisable to discontinue waking her, and relax and let nature take its course.

It is too early to expect consistent overnight bladder control, although some children may achieve it during this phase. Some who are picked up and taken to the toilet before their parents go to bed will be dry the following morning. Occasionally, a child will get up several times in the middle of the night and ask to go to the bathroom of her own accord.

Training Problems

DEALING WITH A CHILD WHO HAS TROUBLE SITTING STILL ON THE TOILET AND PREFERS TO STAND. Some Toddlerhood 2 or 3 children strongly dislike having to sit still on the toilet, even though they did not object to this earlier. As a result, they may suddenly begin to wet or soil their pants, despite their former "success" in toilet training. They may also sit down on the toilet at their parents' request, but not "go" as long as they are there. After they get up off the seat, they may then urinate or defecate.

Parents often attribute the child's sudden change in behavior to obstinacy or rebellion. In most cases this does not explain the child's behavior. It is quite normal for a toddler who is lacking in self-control and is very active to prefer to "make" while standing. Sitting on a toilet and being expected to perform may make her feel nervous or uncomfortable. Perhaps she simply feels less pressured and more relaxed off the potty. In such a case you might wish to postpone toilet training for a while until she is in a more relaxed, co-operative frame of mind, and is better able to sit still.

HOW TO HANDLE A CHILD WHO DOES NOT READILY GRASP WHAT IS EXPECTED OF HER. A few children are slower than others in understanding what toilet training is all about. They may still be somewhat irregular in their patterns of elimination, may not express any interest in learning, and may not be the least bit disturbed by soiled diapers. It could be that the child is simply not yet taking notice of her bowel movements or what is happening to her.

Some professionals suggest that you can help your child develop an awareness of her feces by removing her diapers or training pants, and letting her play in the bathroom around the time when she is most likely to move her bowels. Sooner or later she is bound to have a bowel movement, see it, and perhaps for the first time be made more aware of what has happened. This is where you can be of assistance. Tell her what happened, and show her where her bowel movement belongs by dropping it in the toilet or potty.

Assuming that this method does not appeal to you, there is an alternative. As you are changing your child's diapers, you can remove the bowel movement, explain to her what has taken place, and show her where it belongs by depositing it in the toilet. After a few such experiences, she will probably get the idea. In the event that she still seems bewildered by the whole thing, do not despair. There is no reason to push her to learn to use the toilet at this time. Each child has her own pace for becoming trained.

FEAR OF USING THE "BIG" TOILET. Some parents who are now introducing their children to the "big" toilet will find that their children are fearful of it. At the parent's insistence the child may sit on the seat, but may hold back her bowel movements. This deliberate refusal to perform on the toilet is not the same as the resistance discussed earlier.

Considering the child's prior success in toilet training, her new refusal to use the "big" toilet often puzzles parents and disappoints them. This behavior is not uncommon at this stage of development. Many children, as was described on page 631, come to value their bodily waste products as part of themselves. Seeing their bowel movements disappear down the toilet bowl drain may make them fearful that they, too, may fall in and disappear.

When a fearful child is forced to use the toilet, she may continue to hold back her stools and become constipated. Her fear of using the toilet can then become coupled with a fear of discomfort that she associates with passing a hard bowel movement. In such a case, parents have an even more complicated problem. The physician may prescribe a mild laxative, stool softener, or alteration in diet to alleviate the child's physical constipation, but she may continue to withhold her stools should her fear of the toilet persist.

Suggestions for how to handle this fear were provided on page 631. Sometimes reassuring a child and allowing her to return to using her potty or diapers for a short period of time will help until her anxiety subsides. When she is more relaxed and less afraid, parents can gently encourage her to return to the toilet.

Diaper Rash

Diaper rash is more commonly thought of as a problem of infancy. Some parents are surprised to find that their toddler may be developing diaper rash. Diaper rash is not a major problem during toddlerhood, although many parents find that their youngster, who is not completely toilet trained, may begin to develop a diaper rash. Diaper rash is the result of an irritation of the skin around the diaper area. Irritating detergents, prolonged contact with urine and/or feces, and increased skin sensitivity often can result in a diaper rash.

During infancy, parents are usually very conscious of the possible problem of diaper rash, and go to great lengths to keep their child dry and protect her skin with lubricating lotions, powders, and non-irritating diapers. Thus, the problem of diaper rash is usually short-lived, and often disappears before the child enters toddlerhood.

The young toddler, who is not yet completely toilet trained, may wet her pants at night or during the day without her parents' knowledge. It is not uncommon for some toddlers to spend prolonged periods of time with wet or soiled pants. This prolonged contact with urine or feces may irritate the child's skin, producing a rash similar to diaper rash. It is also possible that new clothing or the use of a different detergent may contribute to the sudden appearance of diaper rash in toddlerhood. Also bear in mind that underpants of synthetic materials can be more irritating than those made of cotton.

The approach to alleviating diaper rash during toddlerhood is similar to the approach during infancy. Parents may want to check their child more often during the day to see if her diapers need changing, and attempt to use more absorbent diapers on her at night, while she is asleep. It often helps to protect her skin with powder or lubricating oils. Some physicians recommend that when these initial attempts fail, disposable diapers should be used, since some of a child's urine may not be completely removed during washing.

Teaching Little Boys to Urinate While Standing

Most small boys between two and three have little or no difficulty learning to stand up to urinate in the toilet. Parents can provide their child with a sturdy step placed in front of the "big" toilet, and show him how to hold and aim his penis. Having a male model to imitate, such as his father or an older brother, will provide him with an added incentive for learning how to urinate while standing.

The Child Who Seems Too Interested in Bowel Movements

Toddlerhood 3 children generally do not express an unusually strong interest in bowel movements, but it is not abnormal for some youngsters to seem overly interested in feces when in public places. Maria Sanchez was walking down the street with her parents when she happened to spot animal feces on the edge of the sidewalk. She pointed to it and talked on and on about it, much to the surprise and embarrassment of her parents.

This kind of behavior is not unnatural, and may possibly stem from the fact that her parents have made her extremely aware of her own stools at home. Therefore, she is likely to be more aware of the "products" of others or of animals. Expressing an unusual fascination with feces is a temporary phase that occasional youngsters go through. It is short-lived and should not cause you undue concern.

Stool Smearing

A child who occasionally touches, smears, or plays with her feces is probably expressing a natural, normal curiosity about her bowel movements in much the same manner that she expresses her desire to find out about other things in her surroundings. This is nothing to be overly concerned about, and is probably best handled in a matter-of-fact manner. Tell her that playing with feces is not an acceptable behavior, but there is no need to get very angry and upset with her.

Stool smearing often occurs at the end of a nap. When a parent does not get to the child fast enough, she may have a bowel movement, remove her pants, and play with her feces. Probably the best way to prevent this from occurring is to go to her sooner or see that her diapers or training pants are snugly fastened, making it more difficult for her to remove them.

Constipation or Painful Bowel Movements

A constipated child who experiences discomfort or pain when she defecates may put up a struggle when she is placed on the toilet the next time, probably because she is afraid that the same thing will happen again. This can represent a minor obstacle to a parent who is anxious to continue toilet training. When hard movements persist, it is best to notify your doctor, who may prescribe a medication or a change in diet to alleviate this situation. Offering your youngster extra reassurance may also be helpful in allaying her fears.

It Is Important to Keep Toilet Training Low-keyed

Parents sometimes notice an increase in temper tantrums or obstinate, defiant behavior in areas of the child's life other than toilet training around the time that earnest efforts to teach a child to use the toilet are begun. The child may willingly cooperate with toilet training in order to live up to her parents' expectations and stay in their favor, but her angry and resentful feelings may crop up in relation to a different aspect of her life. Parents may be puzzled by her cranky, stubborn, and resistive attitude at bath time, not realizing that her behavior has anything to do with toilet training.

In some cases sleep is affected. A child may become very obstinate at bedtime, or she might have trouble sleeping through the night. The child who is trying hard to please her parents may be afraid of having an accident while she sleeps, and thus awaken in the middle of the night. A few children who have been making a major effort not to "make" in their pants become excessively fussy about cleanliness. They suddenly refuse to engage in messy play activities or to continue feeding themselves for fear of getting their fingers or clothes dirty.

These types of problems are often confusing to parents. On the surface they appear to be totally unrelated to the area of toilet training. However, they sometimes stem from the fact that parents are placing too much pressure on their child to become trained early. This can make a child nervous, fearful, angry, and resentful. Despite her success with toilet training, her feelings are often expressed in relation to other areas of her life such as sleeping, eating, bathing, or dressing.

You will not be able to link all of your toddler's fears, temper tantrums, bedtime resistance, negative behavior, and other bothersome traits to your toilet training methods, nor should you even attempt to make these associations. On the other hand, it is important to be aware that an occasional problem that is very puzzling to you might be the result of tremendous pressure exerted in toilet training.

The best way to find out is to lower your expectations of her in toilet training, keep the atmosphere in relation to it as low-keyed as possible, or even postpone training her for a period of time. Assuming that her problem stemmed from the pressure she felt to learn to use the toilet quickly, it should diminish or disappear once this pressure is lifted.

The value of being casual, relaxed, and friendly during the time when you are helping your toddler learn to use the toilet cannot be overemphasized. By approaching it with this attitude, you will not give her cause to be tense, frightened, or antagonistic toward you, and will be able to maintain a positive relationship with her during the training period.

DISCIPLINE

Managing the Child During the "Terrible Two's"

Handling a child during the temporary, difficult stage of the "Terrible Two's" is not only a challenge, it is an art. Many of the techniques for handling negativism outlined in previous Discipline sections on pages 621–22 should continue to be very helpful to you at this time. Try to allow your toddler some "elbow room" for expressing negativism, without continually giving in to her demands.

Switching from one activity to another is something that your child may not like to do, especially when she is enjoying an activity and you try to interfere or stop her from continuing with it. Therefore, you can expect a certain amount of dawdling and stalling, and should not expect her to make an immediate shift. Be patient, and give her a little extra time to make necessary changes. A reminder that it is "almost time" for another activity several minutes before you plan to have her shift to something new may be useful in minimizing her resentment when you finally interrupt her activity.

Now that your child is better able to speak and understand your verbal rules, limits, and directions, you can tell her what it is that you want her to do, and offer her some explanations as to why certain objects or areas of your home are unsafe or "forbidden." These verbal techniques are not as effective with toddlers as with preschoolers, since toddlers are still immature. You may find that distracting her, substituting one activity for another, and picking her up and carrying her or leading her to another area of your home are still the most effective methods of dealing with her.

Sharp commands, substitution techniques, and physical intervention are not the only effective methods of motivating a Toddlerhood 3 child. The value of using praise, affection, and compliments should not be overlooked. Toddlers often respond very positively to these approaches.

Chances are that you will not have an easy time getting your child to abide by your rules without her putting up an argument or struggle of some kind. Try not to allow her to have her own way out of fear of antagonizing her further, since this can result in her taking advantage of you. Once this happens, it may be harder to regain your position of authority and get her to listen to and follow your directions. A child who has learned few, if any, lessons of obedience and conformity during this stage of her life, will probably have trouble when she enters school or has to deal with other authority figures.

Fostering Self-control and Conscience Development

The majority of children, as has been discussed, need to have their parents set guidelines for their conduct. Some may even beg indirectly for some rules and regulations by deliberately behaving so badly that they press their parents into "laying down the law." Knowing exactly where they stand in terms of limits relieves their anxiety, protects them, makes them feel more secure, and fosters their own self-control.

It is important at this stage in your toddler's life to set firm and consistent but reasonable limits on her behavior, and encourage her to assume responsibility for her actions. This will promote your child's conscience development. By beginning to take responsibility for her behavior, she will start to feel guilty when she breaks rules or behaves poorly. Occasionally parents go to extremes in their management, and are either overindulgent or overly strict and punitive. This approach to discipline may discourage their child from assuming responsibility for her own wrongdoing. Such a child may never develop the appropriate guilt feelings which will assist her in not yielding to the temptation of breaking rules in the future. More information on the development of conscience is provided in both the Personal-Social Development sections of Preschool 1, 2, and 3, and the Discipline sections of Preschool 1 and 2. Keep in mind that while you want a child to feel some guilt when she violates the rules, you do not want her to feel too much guilt, since this might damage her self-esteem or stifle her urge to learn.

Your toddler is beginning to develop a conscience, but her ability to keep her unacceptable impulses in check is still very limited. Given the fact that her conscience is only starting to emerge, do not expect too much from her in terms of exercising self-control. Assuming that you maintain a consistent program of discipline, and work to keep a good relationship with her, over the next several years she will not only fully develop a conscience, but will learn the value of following it. In the meantime, until she shows evidence of being able to inhibit her own "unacceptable" actions, be patient with her, and willing to repeat rules and warnings as often as this seems necessary.

Overprotecting the Toddler Can Make Discipline Harder

A child who is developing new abilities wants and needs to have an opportunity to practice them. She must have a chance to feed herself, dress herself, explore, and so forth, without interference when she is ready, providing she is in no *real* danger. A parent who constantly stands over a child and interferes with her activities in order to "protect" her may contribute to a child's feelings of resentment, stubbornness, and rebellion. By not permitting the child freedom to do things for herself, a parent may retard the child's development of self-reliance, competence, and self-regulation.

Children seem to be much more tolerant of and willing to comply with parental restrictions if they are offered in a context in which the child, within certain reasonable limits, can have freedom to explore, to learn, to make mistakes, and to breathe! From this phase on, parents should guard against the possible tendency to prevent the child from moving forward and to keep her from having the experiences that are necessary to her development by overprotecting her.

Allowing Your Child to Express Her Feelings

Now that your child's self-concept is emerging strongly, she will want to exercise her new independence; it is important for her to enjoy freedom in the way she feels, even though she will not have full freedom to do as she pleases. So that neither one of you loses "face" in situations involving arguments over her poor behavior, and so that your program of discipline can be maintained, try to make it clear to her that you understand and sympathize with her feelings, even though you have to insist that she keep her behavior within whatever limits you have established.

All children, like adults, have feelings of anger, hostility, jealousy, and so forth. The feelings a child has cannot be controlled by her parents, although the manner in which a child acts or expresses these feelings can be managed and restricted. When a child is angry, her anger is usually expressed as antisocial behavior (hitting, biting, kicking, etc.). Parents can set boundaries on a child's actions, so that antisocial behavior does not occur, and can teach a child to express her feelings in a more acceptable manner, but they should not try to deny the fact that their child's feelings are real.

Let's take an example of a child, John, who is angry at his sister, Jane, for taking his favorite toy. John runs over to Jane, kicks her, and yells, "Bad Jane." A parent who realizes the value of allowing his child to express his feelings, and at the same time realizes the importance of encouraging him to learn socially acceptable behavior, might say something to this effect: "John, I understand that you are very angry at Jane, and I know how you must feel, but I have to insist that you not kick your sister."

Another parent, on the other hand, who is either afraid to allow the child to express his feelings openly and honestly, or who does not realize the value of this, might say something like, "John, how can you say that you hate your sister? You know that you love her. You don't hate your sister, and you had better stop kicking her or else!" In this case, the parent is trying to deny that the child's feelings exist, although both parent and child know that is simply not true. What may happen is that the parent will succeed in teaching the child to be untruthful about his feelings. Or, the parent may force the child to bury his feelings, which may result in his expressing them in a subtle, hostile way over a longer period of time, or expressing them when the parent is not around. Either of these results is not particularly good.

It is possible for you to stand firm and insist that your child obey household rules and regulations, even though she puts up an argument. At the same time you can allow her to express her feelings, and tell her that you understand how she feels. Do not fall into the trap of assuming that if you discipline her, and enforce rules, you are in some way restricting her freedom or personality development.

Allowing a child to express her feelings is often hard on parents. There will be times when you do not even care to listen to what she has to say, or do not want to understand her negative feelings. You will get angry with her and will act accordingly. It may be difficult not to prohibit your child from expressing her feelings, particularly if you were not allowed to express yours as a child. Chances are that you will understandably feel threatened about allowing her to express her mildly negative feelings about you, because you think that she will lose all respect for you. However, she will not lose respect for you just because she is upset with you on occasion, and is allowed to tell you so. Despite the fact that it may be hard for you to give your child freedom to express her feelings in an "acceptable" manner, it is something for which to strive.

It would not be beneficial for your toddler to have you constantly undermine (even if only in subtle ways) her sense of self-worth and individuality by arbitrarily giving her orders. Her feelings should be taken into account. By making an effort, you can continue to assume the role of an authority figure and firmly enforce your limits while allowing her to express her feelings. It is important to limit your child's behavior when necessary, but not her feelings.

FEARS

Children May Adopt Their Parents' Fears

Researchers have shown that there is a relationship between parents' and children's fears. Fears are, for the most part, believed to be acquired through learning, and a great deal of a child's learning takes place at home. Her parents' fears may be adopted through simple observation of the environment and learning, or through identification. The two-year-old is anxious to be like her parents, and because she learns a lot from observing them, this may be a prime time for her adoption of their fears.

Mrs. DeMatteo had always been afraid of bugs. The sight of an insect, even a tiny spider, made her fearful. She was unable to kill an insect in her home, or even remain in the same room in which she had spotted an insect. Soon after her daughter Trish turned two, she also began to fear insects. Mrs. DeMatteo recognized this right away, and felt guilty that she was to blame for her daughter's fear. She wished that somehow she could make insects less fear-provoking for Trish, but this was not easy, since she was unable to control her own fear.

It is difficult for a child who adopts her parent's fear to overcome it. Her parent cannot help in this regard by teaching her to respond differently to the feared object. He or she has not learned to react more maturely when faced with the frightening object, and thus cannot provide a different kind of model, one who is not afraid, for the child. Perhaps the other parent or a friend can help the child learn to react more maturely to the feared object. As the child grows older and spends more time away from her parent in the company of people who do not share her parent's fear, she may gradually overcome the fear.

Common Fears

Some children who had not previously exhibited fears may develop them at this time. The two-year-old's fears are generally similar to those discussed in the previous fear sections in Toddlerhood 1 and 2. Their fears may center around various things they see, noises they hear, animals (especially wild ones), and unfamiliar places and people. Many children fear separations from their parents, even when the separation is short-lived. Others fear sudden loud noises like those that come from trains, large moving vans, and vacuum cleaners. Fear of dogs, cats, dreams, a specific person, or moving to a new home sometimes emerges in Toddlerhood 3. Fearfulness at night often arises during this phase, and is discussed in the Sleeping section.

As the child becomes better able to understand language, parents' explanations about why the child need not be fearful may become more useful in helping to allay her fears. At this early stage, however, explaining the fear to the child may not by itself be an effective method of reducing her fear.

FEAR OF FIRE. It is not uncommon for a young child to develop a fear of fire, especially one who has been burned on a stove, or has had or witnessed others having an unpleasant experience with fire. This fear may one day save her life, so parents should try to help her put this fear into proper perspective. Allowing the child to blow out candles on a birthday cake, help roast hot dogs over a campfire, or visit the local fire department may help to alleviate intense anxiety. Under no circumstances should a young child be able to play with matches unsupervised. Even with close adult supervision it is not advisable to allow the child of this young age to play with matches.

FEAR OF AIRPLANES, TRAINS, AND OTHER FORMS OF TRANSPORTATION. Some children are extremely frightened by the sight and sounds of airplanes, trains, large trucks and busses, and so on. They may cling tightly to their parents or try to hide from these vehicles whenever they hear, see, or have to ride in them. It frequently helps to allow a child to play out her fears. Buying her toy models of trains, busses, or whatever she fears, and encouraging her to make their sounds may assist her in overcoming her fear. There are many excellent children's books about various forms of transportation with stories about how particular children have gotten over being afraid of them. Reading such stories to a frightened child may also help to allay her fears. These kinds of fears are only temporary.

"I HATE MY TWO-YEAR-OLD"

At a recent party a loving mother boldly announced to her friends, "I hate my two-year-old!" This mother was expressing an honest feeling that reflected the difficulties she was having in dealing with her child. Many of you, although you love your child dearly, will have similar types of reactions at some point over the next year, if and when your child passes through the stage of development often referred to as the "Terrible Two's."

The period of several months during which your child is in the "Terrible Two's" will place a great strain on you as well as on family relationships. Your child will be at a most exasperating age when she will be extremely difficult to deal with, let alone live with.

Mrs. Long made the following comments:

I really can't say that I like my daughter very much lately, or myself for that matter. Nearly everything she does irritates me, and I think that the opposite is also the case. I constantly feel tired, and emotionally drained. As a result of the things she does, I'm always on edge, or better yet, at the end of my rope. Living with her under one roof, day in and day out, is really getting to me. I don't think my husband really understands how I feel, and I resent the fact that he only gets a taste of it after he comes home from work. All I seem to do is complain to him about her, from the moment he steps in the door, until the moment we get into bed. I'm aware that my relationship with him hasn't been perfect either lately, since I'm always in a bad mood. I'm seriously thinking of taking a part-time job. Maybe being away from my daughter for a couple of hours a day will be the best thing for all of us. I know I need some sort of relief.

In trying to analyze what to many parents is a puzzling situation, you will probably begin to ask yourself, "Why?" Doubts or insecurities about your ability as a parent, and resentment toward your toddler or spouse may emerge around this period. You may put all of the blame for your child's behavior on yourself, feeling guilty that somewhere along the line you have made a grave mistake in rearing her. On the other hand, you may feel that your child is consciously trying to make life difficult for you by deliberately acting badly. This is the time when couples may blame one another for difficulties, and say to one another, "She's *your* child!"

Understanding some of the changes that your child may be experiencing may be of some help. It is also consoling to realize that many other parents are going through the same thing with their children. Try to find parents who are experiencing similar difficulties and discuss your respective problems. The possibility exists that all of the support in the world may not seem like enough to help you through those situations in which your child is pushing you to the wall. Such is the nature of the "Terrible Two's." But rest assured that you will get through this.

EARLY RELIGIOUS TRAINING

The Toddlerhood 3 child's capacity to understand concepts of God, heaven, prayer, and religion are extremely limited. Nevertheless, parents who are religious may want to introduce their child to early religious training at some point during toddlerhood. A child's ability to remain quiet or sit still through church or synagogue services is doubtful, although some parents may want to take their child with them to their place of worship occasionally, especially on major holidays.

Festive holidays, on which families get together to celebrate, are an important aspect of many people's lives. Parents often wish to involve their toddlers in such occasions. Older toddlers may enjoy listening to religious music and learning to sing simple songs appropriate to particular holidays. They may also enjoy watching holiday preparations in the kitchen, helping to decorate their homes or Christmas trees, and of course receiving gifts.

Some parents begin teaching their youngsters words such as "Christmas," "Easter," "Chanukah," "God," "church," "pray," and "heaven." A toddler's ability to repeat such words does not necessarily indicate her understanding of their meaning. Very often parents will point to places of worship as they pass by them while riding in a car. This helps the child associate the word "church" with particular buildings that she sees on a regular basis. In teaching words like "God" and "heaven," parents often point to the sky.

It is not uncommon for parents to include prayer as part of their toddler's nightly going-to-bed pattern. They may show their child how to kneel down at the side of the bed and cup her hands in prayer. The parent may do the same and, while kneeling, say a few simple prayers. Some toddlers enjoy learning to say "Amen" after their parents have finished reciting prayers.

TODDLERS' REPETITION OF BAD LANGUAGE

It is not unusual for a toddler to latch on to a "dirty" word, often to the surprise of her parents. The child becomes fascinated with a particular swear word because of people's response to it, not because she completely comprehends its meaning. The use of "bad" language does not represent a major problem during this phase, but it can occasionally cause parents some embarrassment when a child says a four-letter word in public.

Toddlers of this age are like parrots. Whatever they hear, they tend to repeat, and this includes "bad" language. They seem especially adroit at mimicking words that they know will arouse a fairly strong reaction from you or other people. They enjoy saying these words over and over again, each time more loudly than the next. At the same time, they concentrate upon the faces of those around them so as not to miss people's responses.

Mrs. Varga often used swear words when she was angry. One afternoon, when her son, Carl, was upset, he repeated the swear word he had heard his mother use on many occasions. At first Mrs. Varga said that she was rather amused, and she laughed at this. Carl took his mother's response as encouragement to continue saying this word, and repeated it constantly throughout the day. He even shouted it out several times at the grocery store.

This mother said that she was very embarrassed by Carl's behavior, and decided thereafter to ignore him whenever he said the swear word. Within two weeks she noticed that this word was no longer used by her son.

It is not fair to blame your toddler for using swear words now and then. If their use is bothersome to you, drawing attention to them will only tend to make them seem more special. The best treatment is just to act as if these words are not any different from any others. Parents who swear on a regular basis should think twice about their own behavior if their child's mimicking of their swear words causes them embarrassment.

SEPARATION AND DIVORCE

Marital friction cannot be viewed in isolation from the whole family structure, since all members of the family are affected. Separation and divorce affect an older toddler differently from an infant or younger toddler. The Toddlerhood 3 child is more aware of people and events taking place in her immediate surroundings. She is more sensitive to others' feelings and changes in the home atmosphere, and capable of more sophisticated emotional responses. Time has also enabled her to build stronger attachments to her parents. A major life change such as a separation or divorce must be examined in this light.

Dealing with a separation or divorce can be a delicate issue for both parent and child. Parents and children who have been through this share certain experiences, even though each situation surrounding a separation or divorce is unique. Your awareness of some other parents' experiences should assist you in making the emotional adjustment to this change easier on both you and your child.

Recognizing and caring for your own needs is the first step toward being able to do an effective job in caring for your child. It will be difficult to give of yourself to her, unless your life is relatively stable and your needs are satisfied.

Caring for a Toddler Alone May Not Be Easy

Rearing a toddler is not an easy profession, even under the most ideal conditions. Bearing the sole or major responsibility for a child's upbringing, particularly when a person has been unprepared for this, can create additional pressures and stresses upon a newly separated or divorced parent. A parent who has been used to making joint decisions must now decide upon everything alone. Doubts and fears that never before existed may suddenly emerge.

Having confidence in one's own abilities, judgments, and convictions is of vital importance to the parent responsible for the child. Insecurities, doubts or lingering feelings of guilt can make child rearing all the more difficult. Trust in one's good judgment may not come readily in some cases. It is often very helpful to talk about insecurities and questions with other parents who have been through a separation or divorce, or discuss the situation with your child's physician.

Handling a child during the period of the "Terrible Two's" is trying on a parent's nerves, particularly when that person is struggling to resolve his or her own personal problems. It is easy to take the toddler's obstinacy and rebellion personally and over-react to it. Expressing your own needs and honest feelings is important, but it is equally important for your child to have freedom of expression. How this can be worked out to your mutual satisfaction will be a very individual matter.

Despite the new trials and stresses that you face with your child, it should be of comfort and reassurance to you that many parents in your position have noticed improvements in their relationship with their children after a separation or divorce. Out of working together with your child to resolve problems and build a more satisfactory life, you can establish a special closeness and honesty with her that can strengthen the relationship that you share.

A major worry among parents about to obtain a divorce is that the breakdown of the two parent-child family (nuclear family) will have detrimental effects upon their child. This need not be the case. While a family composed of a mother, father, and child is considered by many to be ideal for child rearing, there are situations in which this arrangement is not the best for the particular individuals involved. When incompatibility leads to divorce, a different family setting has to be established.

Single parent families can work well in providing a child with a strong family base. It is not uncommon to rear a child in this type of framework. The major concern should be that the relationship be stable and mutually satisfying for parent and child. The love, warmth, security, and close emotional attachment that a child needs can be well nurtured in the single parent family home. The single parent family is discussed on pages 640–44, 889–91 where issues such as social life, financial concerns, who is to care for the child, separation anxiety, discipline, and other topics of special interest to parents rearing children alone are explored.

Telling Your Toddler About Your Separation or Divorce

Parents who have decided to separate or obtain a divorce are often anxious and uncertain about how to break this news to their child. This is understandable in parents who are concerned about their child's feelings. Many parents find that offering simple verbal explanations is not as difficult as they had anticipated.

Telling a young child about a separation or divorce is very much a personal matter. You must use your own best judgment and knowledge of your child in determining when, how, and what to say. There are, however, certain general guidelines that should be of help to you.

Adequate advance preparation can help lessen the trauma of a sudden shift in lifestyle, although there are limitations in how thoroughly you can prepare a young child. Even though a Toddlerhood 3 or a Preschool 1 child is capable of understanding simple verbal explanations, it is unlikely that she will receive a good grasp of the situation. Preparation should be given with the awareness that your child may not fully realize what you are trying to tell her until after your separation or divorce has become a fact, and she has lost day-to-day contact with one parent. Explanations should be geared to your child's level of understanding. Keep them very simple. Your attitude and the feeling with which you speak will be more important than the exact words you use.

Either you alone or you and your spouse, together, should inform her. Hearing such news from people whom she loves and trusts is important. Avoid having her learn about what is happening from relatives, or overhearing it in conversation.

It is not advisable to speak to your child about a separation or divorce unless you are certain of it and have finalized plans with your spouse. Talking about this with her long before a final decision has been made may lead to extra worry on her part, and should a change in plans be made, this could leave her feeling insecure and confused. As soon as you are sure of your plans, you can inform her of them.

Break the news to her at a time when you are composed and thinking clearly of her needs, rather than when you are crying and emotionally upset. She will need your understanding and reassurance to help her deal with news of this nature. A genuine concern for her feelings should be apparent in what you tell her.

Go slowly, and give her as much time as necessary to try to digest each small bit of information before going any further. Use familiar words that she knows. It is advisable to stick to the truth. In the case of a separation where a reconciliation is a real possibility, a child can be informed of this. When there is no realistic possibility, it is not a good idea to give her false hopes.

In explaining about her divorce, Mrs. Jacobs told her daughter, "Daddy and Mommy are unhappy together. We argue a lot. We can't live together happily in the same house. Daddy is going to live in another house, but he will still see you often. Daddy and I both love you and will take care of you always." Mrs. Jacobs was nervous about approaching her child with this news, but she found that a short explanation satisfied her daughter.

Giving truthful information to her child, this parent still spared her from possibly disturbing details and from the feelings of resentment, anger, or bitterness between her and her spouse. She reassured her youngster that she was loved and would be cared for, and made it clear in simple terms the child could understand that the parent who was leaving was not deserting the child.

Depending upon the child's comprehension, other parents often include in their explanations a statement to the effect that the child was in no way to blame for their separation or divorce, since it is not uncommon for older toddlers and younger preschoolers to think that their parents are splitting up because they have been bad or naughty. When visitation rights are clearly known, parents will probably also want to tell the child how often she will be allowed to visit with the parent who is leaving.

Children react differently to hearing about a separation or divorce. Those who do not fully realize the significance of their parents' words may appear slightly puzzled or even rather undisturbed by the information. It is not unusual for a Toddlerhood 1 or 2 child to return to her play activities as if nothing is the matter. Parents should not immediately jump to the conclusion that she simply does not care. More than likely the significance of the message that they are trying to get across simply has not been fully understood.

Among older toddlers who are able to understand more of what has been said, responses may vary from their being mildly disturbed to highly emotionally upset. A youngster might become tearful, fearful, or angry upon learning the news. Additional questions may be asked of parents either then or later. These should be answered truthfully and to their satisfaction.

Youngsters who are upset will need substantial emotional support, understanding, and physical comfort. They should be permitted complete freedom to express their feelings. Patience on the part of parents is very important. Be prepared to have more than one discussion on this subject with your child, since it will take time for her to comprehend what to you are simple explanations, and her ability to retain information is not well developed.

A child whose parents are having marital problems or are obtaining a divorce is apt to show changes in her behavior patterns. Other care-givers that she may have, including baby-sitters, nursery school teachers, etc., should probably be informed that this is a stressful time for her. In this way they will be on the lookout for possible adjustment problems that she might experience, and can bring them to her parents' attention, if need be. It is a personal decision whether or not to discuss divorce plans with these persons prior to telling the child. A lot depends upon their trustworthiness. If care-givers are informed in advance, it is important to tell them not to discuss the divorce, especially with the child, if she has not as yet been told.

How Will Separation or Divorce Affect the Child?

Assuming a separation or divorce is final, parents often wonder how this will affect their child. This is a very complicated question for which there is no easy answer. There are numerous factors that will play a role in the child's reaction, such as her ability to comprehend the events, her personality, the nature of the conflict and atmosphere in the household preceding the separation or divorce, and whether or not the child has been prepared for a parent's departure. The ability to care properly for the child and the emotional stability of the parent who assumes primary responsibility, as well as the kind of living situation and visitation arrangements that have been made following her parents' split, can also be important in determining how a child is affected.

No longer having one parent around on a daily basis is usually the most significant disruption in the young child's life. Through the years, she has built up close emotional ties to that parent. She has also established special, familiar ways of interacting with the parent that have become firmly entrenched as an important part of day-to-day living.

The loss of daily contact with one parent who represents a significant aspect of her life can come as a rather sudden emotional jolt. This trauma should be viewed in perspective. The Toddlerhood 2 and 3 child, as discussed in the Personal-Social Development sections, is often very upset over separations from her parents. Even being apart from a parent for a relatively short length of time may cause her to become anxious and upset. It is understandable that a major separation, with no hope of the parent's return, would cause a substantially more severe reaction.

Youngsters are affected differently by separation or divorce. Even children within one family may have vastly different responses, and there is no way to predict this with any certainty. The separation of parents or dissolution of a marriage does not necessarily affect children in a negative way. Children for whom the period of time prior to the marital split has been particularly traumatic and disruptive may actually feel happier, more relaxed, and even relieved afterward.

In many cases, children *are* upset by the changes in their lives; however, with sufficient parental support and time to adjust to new life circumstances, the majority of these problems can be worked through and satisfactorily resolved, without any long-lasting ill effects on the child.

It is important to be aware of some common reactions. Recognizing signs of distress in your toddler will enable you to be more aware of her needs.

1. *Feelings of depression*

The departure of one parent often represents a significant emotional blow to the child that affects her behavior. According to Ms. Nelson, a newly separated mother, her toddler became tearful and withdrawn after her father left the home. She wandered around the house for days calling out, "Dada, Dada," and searching for her father. Her depression interrupted her normal eating and sleeping behavior. She ate little and had difficulty sleeping through the night. After several weeks, with an abundance of reassurance, love, and comfort from her mother, she seemed to pull out of the depression. Tearfulness, depression, and eating and sleeping difficulties are not uncommon reactions.

2. *Insecurity and fear*

A major separation from a parent can cause the child to feel frightened and insecure. Losing one parent shakes her family security base, and can plant seeds of doubt that the remaining parent will also disappear and abandon her. The fear of being left all alone can be highly disturbing to such a young child, and can greatly influence her behavior.

3. *Greater reliance upon the remaining parent*

A marked change in the behavior patterns of a toddler who has been working to establish greater independence can be expected. She may suddenly become fearful of the briefest separations from the parent who is caring for her. A noticeable increase in dependency and displays of affection are not unusual responses. More frequent demands for her parent's affection and attention may also be seen, along with regression in her behavior. A child who was toilet trained may suddenly begin to soil or wet her pants, or she may act like a baby in other ways.

These changes in a child's behavior should not be ignored. They are signs that she needs help in dealing with her fears and emotions. Feelings of being deserted by the parent who is gone can make her relationship with her other parent more important to her than before. Sometimes this can place an additional burden upon the remaining parent, making a smooth adjustment all the more difficult upon both.

4. *A decline in negativism*

As a result of the loss of a parent, some toddlers do not express the testing behavior and negativism that is normal for a child at this stage of development. Instead of working at establishing themselves as separate individuals, they may work hard to please the remaining parent by conforming to all wishes, requests, and limits. This is probably because they are afraid that obstinate, rebellious behavior may anger and drive away the parent whom they so desperately need.

Extra reassurance from the parent caring for them is especially important at this time. Parents should try to help and encourage their child to realize that their love will be there and that she will not be abandoned should she periodically express negativism or behave badly. Getting this message across may take some time.

5. *Feelings of anger*

Anger is another type of response to the departure of a parent. It is not uncommon for an older toddler or younger preschool child to feel angry and resentful toward the parent who has left home. These feelings of anger can prompt her to lash out at the lost parent, or at some substitute target, such as her remaining parent, brothers and sisters, or playmates.

Unprovoked aggressive outbursts or destructive behavior in the home or at nursery school can sometimes occur. A child should be encouraged to use acceptable rather than unacceptable outlets for her hostility and aggression, as discussed on pages 531–34, 687–88, but her feelings should not be denied. It would be a mistake for the remaining parent to attempt to make the child suppress her emotions.

6. *Loss of self-confidence*

A young child, from her naïve perspective, views her parents as able to find solutions to or "fix" all problems. She may therefore feel that if the parent who left her had really loved her and wanted to stay at home to be with her, this parent would have done just that.

The fact that the parent left her can contribute to a child's lowered self-esteem and loss of self-confidence. A child should be reassured that her poor behavior, naughty thoughts, or wishes in no way caused her parent to leave. As she matures, it will be easier for her to understand that her lost parent was not all powerful. In the meanwhile attempts can be made to help her regain her self-confidence by reassuring her that she is loved, and praising her for genuine efforts and achievements.

How to Help Ease Stresses on Your Toddler Following a Separation or Divorce

Stress accompanies sudden, significant disturbances in a child's living patterns. The following suggestions should be of assistance to you in lessening possible emotional trauma to your child, and helping her make an easier adjustment.

PROVIDE A LOVING EMOTIONAL CLIMATE. Shortly after a separation or divorce your child will need extra warmth, reassurance, and emotional support. A loving, caring atmosphere in the home would certainly make the transition easier for her. While it is not necessary for you to hide your own feelings from her if you are upset, frustrated, or depressed, try to be responsive to her needs and feelings.

Some parents find this to be difficult. They may be preoccupied with their own troubles and in need of a great deal of emotional support. Under these circumstances, they may have a hard time giving of themselves to their toddlers. It is important for parents responsible for their toddlers' care to be aware of this, and to seek support from family, friends, or professionals following a separation or divorce. Talking out your own problems will help relieve your tensions, and make it easier for you to provide a warm and happy family atmosphere for your toddler.

DO NOT TAKE YOUR FRUSTRATIONS OUT ON YOUR TODDLER. It is not uncommon for parents who have recently separated or obtained a divorce to feel bitterness, anger, or resentment toward each other. During the stressful period of adjustment that follows, feelings tend to be intense. When the parent who is primarily or fully responsible for the child's care can no longer direct feelings at a spouse, hostility may be shown toward the child. This can sometimes occur without the parent realizing it.

You should guard against using your child as a substitute outlet for your hostility toward your former spouse. Taking anger or frustration out on her is destructive to her emotional well-being and mental health. She should not be given the impression that she was to blame for your unsuccessful marriage.

Following your separation or divorce, you may have some adjustment problems.

Parents who have experienced feelings of shock, anger, depression, rejection, loneliness, fear, guilt, or an overwhelming sense of responsibility at being left to care for a child alone have often found that their behavior changed as a result. Your child will notice these kinds of changes in what you say and do, and how you look.

An older toddler or younger preschool child is often very attuned to the feelings and behavior patterns of her remaining parent. Seeing her parent look so unhappy, she may offer comfort by being very affectionate and generous. She may also go to her parent for frequent cuddling and offer other kinds of physical comfort.

The capacity for offering consolation and sympathy to a parent in obvious distress is admirable, and is a compliment to the toddler's emotional development. When a child is placed in the position of consoling her parent either occasionally, or only very temporarily, it is doubtful that this kind of interaction will in any way have a detrimental effect upon her. Assuming a new, "grown-up" role may even be beneficial for her.

Should a child have to assume this role in her interaction with her parent very frequently, for extended periods of time, this would be unfair to her. A child who spends a great deal of her time and emotional resources trying to reassure and comfort her parent may have little left over to spend on working through important developmental tasks during toddlerhood or preschool. Forcing her into taking on an adult-like role, either consciously or unconsciously, would be placing too much responsibility upon her.

Parents who are in emotional distress and are finding it difficult to adjust should not rely to this extent upon their young child. Rather, they should discuss problems with other adults, or seek appropriate professional help.

TRY TO MAINTAIN YOUR TODDLER'S DAILY ROUTINE AND LIVING QUARTERS. A toddler finds a great deal of security in her familiar daily schedule and her home. An older toddler knows what to expect in terms of her meals, activities, bath, bedtime, and so forth. This predictability adds a certain sense of stability and structure to her life.

Her home is the place where she spends the major part of her time. She knows where things belong, and how to get from one room to the next easily. In her home she finds comfort, security, and control. Abrupt changes in regular living patterns, in conjunction with the major disruption of a parent's departure, can be very stressful for a child. Unnecessary changes in schedule or living situation can make a smooth adjustment more difficult. The child between Toddlerhood 3 and Preschool 1 may be particularly disturbed by these kinds of changes, even when the family structure is very stable, and the atmosphere in the home is warm and peaceful. Following the separation or divorce, it is important to try to keep your child's routine and surroundings much as they were before.

CONTINUE WITH YOUR REGULAR PROGRAM OF DISCIPLINE. Following a major life change, it is often hard for a parent to maintain the usual mode of discipline. Parents who are feeling very sorry for their children or perhaps guilty over the breakup of the family sometimes become overly lax in an effort to "make it up to them." Unnecessary guilt or sympathy can cloud a parent's judgment when it comes to setting limits and enforcing them.

Toddlers need parental limits and guidance. They find security in knowing the rules of the house, and may be confused by their parents' abrupt change in approach. Attempts should be made to maintain the disciplinary approach that was established prior to the separation or divorce.

The tendency for a person who has lost a spouse to become overprotective of his or her child also exists. Overprotecting a toddler can stifle her emerging independence, initiative, and curiosity. More information on special problems that the single parent may have in disciplining the child can be found on pages 643–44.

Your Relationship with Your Ex-spouse

It seems strange to some parents even to explore the subject of their relationship with their ex-spouse following a divorce, but consideration should be given to this matter. There can be enormous variation in the relationships that former marital partners establish. Some couples end marriages on friendly terms, although others never wish to see or speak to one another again.

The type of relationship that ex-spouses develop can affect their child. Even though a man and woman have decided to dissolve their marriage, their child may still feel love and loyalty to both parents. A toddler who has grown up loving and feeling loyal to both parents still wants to have these feelings after one parent has left the home. Remaining loyal to both parents helps her keep a firm hold on her identity as well as her security base.

Except under unusual circumstances, parents should respect their child's right and need to remain loyal to both of them. Hostile, derogatory statements about a spouse should not be made in front of a toddler. A spouse should also refrain from doing this during visits or phone calls. Neither parent should try to win the child over to his or her side by going overboard with affection, attention, or gift buying. A child's feelings and her wish to love both her parents should be respected.

When parents refrain from trying to cloud their child's judgment negatively about one another or members of the opposite sex, and remain on amiable, or at least civil terms, this can often make it easier for the child to adjust and maintain emotional ties. This is not always possible, but, for the child's sake, some discussion of how parents' treatment of one another following their divorce could possibly affect her should occur before the divorce becomes finalized.

In most situations involving divorce, the parent who is not awarded custody of the child is granted visitation rights. Visitation rights are important to both parent and child, and should be utilized to their best advantage. The conditions under which visits can occur, and how often they occur differ widely, and in large part depend upon the child and the individual circumstances of each case. Although it is most common for one parent or the other to retain custody of the child, some kind of shared or joint custody arrangement is gaining in popularity. With this arrangement, it is even more important for both natural parents to try to respect one another and remain on friendly terms for their child's sake.

Parents who are openly antagonistic to each other and who refuse to talk may find the period of time immediately prior to, during, and after visits extremely uncomfortable, and in some cases, painfully disturbing. Their reactions are bound to affect their child, and she may come to regard visits or shifts in homes as frightening or upsetting experiences.

The parent caring for the child on a regular basis should avoid preventing visits from taking place, making derogatory remarks about his or her ex-spouse in front of the child, or giving the child the "third degree" after visits. Emotions should, if possible, be kept under control in the child's presence out of respect for her need to feel positively toward the parent with whom she is no longer living.

Parents who are not caring for their children on a full-time basis should also show respect for their ex-spouses as well as consideration for their child's feelings, as we've discussed. Should a visit have to be postponed or missed, the parent should try to maintain contact with the child through phone calls or letters. It is important that she not believe that she has been abandoned or deserted.

Some children adapt well to visits as well as after them, while others are disturbed for days or even weeks following visits. Toddlers and younger preschoolers often have considerable difficulty dealing with separations, and each time they visit with and then have to leave their parents, the separation can be upsetting.

Parents should try to view a child's response to visits objectively. They should carefully consider her feelings and behavior in relation to them, and be considerate about making adjustments should this become necessary for her well-being.

Help Your Toddler Maintain a Strong Family Base

The family comprises a significant part of your child's life. It provides her with a strong sense of identity and security. Following the departure of one of her parents, it is especially important to make an effort to preserve her feeling of belonging to a family.

It is desirable for children from a family to live together in one household, rather than be split up. It can be traumatic for brothers and sisters to be thrust apart suddenly and lose daily contact with one another. Make an effort to preserve your child's relationship with your spouse's relatives. Maintaining continuity in her relationships with brothers, sisters, grandparents, and other relatives will help to minimize the child's emotional stress.

Separation or divorce need not prove to be devastating to either you or your toddler. A substantial number of men and women with children have been through similar experiences and have raised happy, healthy children. By recognizing small problems that may arise, and seeking solutions to them without too much delay, they will not have a chance to develop into major problems.

PREPARED PARENTHOOD CHECK LIST

MOTHER	FATHER	UNDERSTANDING YOUR TODDLER'S DEVELOPMENT
—	—	Has your toddler entered the stage commonly referred to as the "Terrible Two's"?
—	—	Does your child seem very set in her ways, and cling to old, familiar methods of doing things?
—	—	Is your toddler demanding when it comes to having her way?
—	—	Do you see any signs of conscience development?
—	—	In what ways are you encouraging your child to be sociable?
—	—	Judging from your toddler's speech and behavior, what evidence do you see that her ability to think and deal with symbols has rapidly expanded?
—	—	Is your child doing more talking about space and time relationships?
—	—	Does your toddler frequently approach you wanting to know things? How do you respond to her questions?
—	—	Why is repetition so important for your child?
—	—	Have you observed a remarkable increase in your child's vocabulary and ability to speak?
—	—	Has your toddler picked up any new words as a result of watching television?
—	—	Do you ever hear your child experimenting with sentence construction or the position of words as she talks?
—	—	Is your child getting better at following directions?
—	—	Is your child more self-confident in regard to her motor ability and becoming more skilled at walking, running, and other coordinated movements?
—	—	Does your toddler show improved ability to stop, turn around, walk backward, kick a ball, walk up steps, and dance?
—	—	What evidence do you see that your toddler is more efficient at turning pages of books, taking objects apart, twisting doorknobs, and eating by herself?
—	—	Is your toddler showing a preference for her right or left hand?
—	—	Does your toddler enjoy activities which involve fun with language, music, rhythm, and imitation?
—	—	Are you providing your child with opportunities to "mess"?
—	—	Have you noticed your child taking a new interest in creative activities?

Toddlerhood 3

—— —— Are you encouraging your child's make-believe play?

—— —— Is your toddler better able to play with other children her age?

BASIC CARE

—— —— Are you aware of the important safety precautions to take in relation to tricycles?

—— —— Has your child become a fussy eater?

—— —— Does your toddler have a lengthy going-to-bed pattern that she insists upon sticking to night after night?

—— —— Is your toddler having difficulty sleeping through the night? If so, have you been able to come up with a reason for this?

—— —— Have you made attempts to help your child develop good toilet habits?

—— —— Is your toddler making noticeable headway in gaining bowel and bladder control?

FAMILY FEELINGS AND CONCERNS

—— —— Have you been allowing your child to express her feelings and, at the same time, not giving up your authority as her parent?

—— —— Do you take care not to undermine your toddler's sense of self-esteem when you are disciplining her?

—— —— Are verbal rules and explanations becoming more effective now that your child is better able to understand what you say to her?

—— —— Have you established reasonable expectations and limits?

—— —— Are you consistent in your methods of discipline?

—— —— Are you honest about possible negative feelings aroused in you by your toddler's behavior?

—— —— Have you prepared yourself for family strain during the phase called the "Terrible Two's"?

—— —— Is your toddler parroting "bad" language that she has picked up? Do you know how your reactions to her bad language can influence her behavior?

—— —— What are some of the special issues of concern to parents involved in separation or divorce?

Preschool 1

PREPARING FOR THE PRESCHOOL YEARS

The preschool stage has been divided into three phases roughly corresponding to the ages of two and a half to three (Preschool 1), three to four (Preschool 2), and four to five (Preschool 3). There is nothing rigid about these phases, and parents are encouraged to read according to their own child's developmental trend rather than any artificial timetable. As many of his personal characteristics begin to emerge more clearly, individual variation from one preschool child to another becomes more noticeable.

In just about all respects, the preschool child is a very different individual from the one he was during toddlerhood. Parents often describe their preschooler as being more adult-like than the toddler in appearance and behavior. Added time and maturity have enabled him to become more attuned to his culture, more sensitive to his surroundings, and more aware of himself and his relationship to his family. Abilities that emerged during toddlerhood are further refined and expanded, giving the preschooler a greater sophistication.

A major difference between the preschooler and toddler is the child's astounding progress in language development. Parents are quick to notice their youngster's sudden ability to converse well with them and tell elaborate stories. The older preschooler, in particular, offers his own continuous commentary about the goings on around him, even when there is no one but himself around to listen. A strong interest in speech, words, sounds, and games involving language is characteristic of the preschool child.

Marked improvements in the preschool child's ability to think, remember things, make associations, and solve problems also set him apart from the toddler. He has a very active, imaginative mind that enables him to make-believe and imagine to a greater degree than in the past, and he may occasionally lose sight of the boundaries between reality and fantasy.

The preschool child's behavior is sometimes quite puzzling to parents. He can be very mature on the one hand, and then suddenly seem to be off in the magical world of make-believe. Fears, especially imaginary fears, are prominent during the preschool years, since it is easy for the child to confuse internal events with external ones and believe that his dreams actually happened. Witches, giants, bogeymen and bears hiding in the closets may seem very real to the preschooler whose mind allows him to believe in the unbelievable.

In toddlerhood the child worked hard to establish his initial declaration of separateness and independence. Having accomplished this developmental task to some degree, usually early in the preschool years, the child is then faced with a new personal task—that of establishing a firmer sense of identity. He tries out a variety of roles in dramatic play-acting, and he absorbs many of his parents' attitudes, values, and mannerisms through identification with them. In trying to strengthen his sense of self or "I," he often asks questions about his origin, and goes through a temporary phase of wanting to relive his babyhood. This is a time when his sexual identity becomes more fully established, and he develops a conscience, albeit inefficient.

As the preschooler acquires his own system of self-control, parents find it much easier to discipline and reason with him. During this stage he becomes more capable of conducting himself in a responsible manner with respect to his parents' safety rules and home regulations. They have to continue to limit certain of his behaviors for his own protection, but this is not as time-consuming a task as it was in toddlerhood, and the child is usually more co-operative and receptive to reasonable explanations.

It is during this stage that the child emerges as a more social being with a more stable, identifiable personality. He shows rapid gains in his ability to relate to other people, especially other children his age. Having playmates around is important to the preschooler. He genuinely enjoys their company and friendship and is well able to play co-operatively with them.

Parents and family are still extremely important to the preschooler, but he is less dependent upon them than the toddler, whose major social interest was probably his parents. Most preschool children find it easier to leave their parents for short periods of time each day or week to play in the park with other youngsters, go to visit a friend at another house, or attend nursery school or a special activities program for preschoolers.

Besides being better able to handle temporary separations and function well outside the immediate family, the child can take over more responsibility for his own care than in toddlerhood. By the age of three, most children are pretty much able to feed themselves, wash themselves, brush their own teeth and hair, dress and undress themselves, and take care of their own toilet needs. This gradual shift of responsibility from parents over to their youngsters seems to suit both very well.

A major factor underlying the preschooler's greater maturity is his pressing wish to understand the world around him, acquire new skills, and refine the skills he previously acquired. Between the ages of two and a half to five the child's ability to absorb information and discover things for himself increases enormously. He asks constant questions, most of which begin with "why."

This is a stage in which the youngster is receptive to learning and to other people's, particularly his parents', efforts to teach him new things. Parents will want to take advantage of his quest for knowledge about himself and the world at large, and of his boundless energy and curiosity, by expanding his educational opportunities and trying to provide an excellent learning experience for him during the time they spend together.

The Total Education of Your Child section in Preschool 1 applies to the entire preschool stage. A central premise on which this section is based is that many parents can provide an excellent educational experience for their child at home, and can find this immensely enjoyable, rewarding, and challenging. Even if they cannot provide for their child's complete education at home, they can make it possible for him to have the benefit of receiving a total education through other resources, and offer him what they can during their times together. Some of the important guidelines for teaching young children are discussed in the hopes that this will stimulate parents to take an active part in coming up with their own individualized educational program for their child that can be carried out in a spontaneous way in the relaxed home atmosphere.

Sex education becomes a more prominent issue during the preschool years. Youngsters often show a heightened curiosity and interest in their own and other people's bodies, and in sex-related issues. It is during the preschool years that many engage in sex play and body exploration games with their peers. Frequently, children begin to ask their parents questions about where they came from, or about pregnancy, birth, fertilization, and the differences between males and females.

The Sex Education section in Preschool 2 applies throughout the preschool years. It offers information on how the child develops basic attitudes toward sexuality, suggestions for how to answer questions on sex, and guidelines for handling genital play, sex play, and nudity in the home. It provides theories, facts, and practical advice that should answer questions and allay parents' anxieties and doubts about their ability to do a good job in their roles as sex educators. A main objective of this section is to assist parents in devising their own personalized plan for providing their child with a positive, wholesome sex education.

Many preschoolers not only begin to ask questions about sex-related issues, but also about other topics including God and religion, and death. It is not unusual for parents to have new concerns during the preschool years as their child's ability to speak and his awareness of people and of events taking place around him markedly expand. Parents often feel uneasy about answering their child's questions and frequently wonder about how to explain certain life changes to him, such as separation or divorce, or wonder how these changes might affect him.

As the child becomes more aware, more capable, and more inquisitive, parents will find new challenges in child rearing. They will have to make numerous adjustments in the manner in which they talk to him, conduct themselves around him, handle him, and react to him as an individual. Even though he is growing more independent, the attitudes that parents convey and the example that they set will continue to play an influential role in shaping his development.

In many respects, the fact that the preschool child is more social, goal-oriented, imaginative, co-operative, and creative than he was during toddlerhood makes spending time with him very pleasurable for parents. Keeping him stimulated and happily occupied will be a challenge, but enjoying his company and taking pride in his daily accomplishments should come naturally.

PERSONAL-SOCIAL DEVELOPMENT

Your child's personality will become more well defined and identifiable during the preschool years. Her ability to think and speak will improve, and she will acquire new habits and different attitudes about herself, other people, and her surroundings. These changes enable her to develop more highly complex patterns of interacting with family members as well as people outside the family.

The preschool child is still quite dependent upon her family. You and other family members will continue to play an influential role in shaping your child's personality. To a much greater degree than before, however, her social contacts will broaden during the preschool stage. She will meet many more people at your place of worship, nearby parks, play groups, and nursery school. These non-family members will also play a role in her personality development.

The "Terrible Two's"

The reasons why children commonly go through a temporary phase called the "Terrible Two's" were explored in Toddlerhood 3. Youngsters who entered this phase earlier may now become less obstinate, negative, and rebellious, while others will first enter such a phase in Preschool 1.

Mrs. Klatskin said that her child, Sara, was a pleasure to have around when she was between two and two and a half years old. When this mother compared Sara's "good" behavior with that of her sister's twenty-five-month-old child, Ginny, who had already entered the "Terrible Two's," she was proud and delighted that Sara had skipped over that "awful" phase. Mrs. Klatskin took most of the credit for this, and convinced herself that her fantastic abilities as a mother had made a real difference.

As Sara approached thirty-two months, however, Mrs. Klatskin noticed a rather radical change in her behavior. Sara became contrary, rebellious, and domineering. At the slightest reprimand, she would fly into a rage and throw temper tantrums. Mrs. Klatskin was shocked, hurt, and rather perplexed.

In comparing notes with her sister, Mrs. Klatskin learned that Ginny, by contrast, was becoming more co-operative and pleasant day by day. This made Mrs. Klatskin feel guilty; she was afraid that she had not handled Sara properly. Thoughts about the possibility of having been too lenient, too strict, too distant, or too affectionate with her daughter troubled this mother each day.

Had Mrs. Klatskin been aware that almost all healthy, normal youngsters between Toddlerhood 3 and Preschool 1 go through the "Terrible Two's," much of her confusion and guilt about how she had somehow mismanaged Sara would have been alleviated. In observing children between two and three years of age, you will probably notice the wide variability in their personalities and behavior, and that some entered this "negative" phase earlier than others. From speaking with other parents, you will learn that some children give their parents an incredibly hard time during this phase, while others are easier to manage.

Do not be discouraged if your child is in the midst of expressing negativism and is behaving like a little rebel or overbearing boss. This stage is only temporary, and during Preschool 2, you can expect some turn-around in behavior making her more co-operative, settled, and easier to handle. Once your child gradually starts to put her "negative" behavior behind her, a new level of maturity will be reached. She will be surer of her individuality, more comfortable with independence in decision-making, and more aware of both external and internal boundaries. This achievement makes the struggle that preceded it seem very worthwhile.

Self-awareness

FORMING AN IDENTITY. Your Preschool 1 child has, to some extent, declared her separateness and independence. This major developmental task, once finally achieved, enables her to move ahead to a new task: becoming more conscious of herself as a person. It is generally in the third year of life that the process of forming an identity prominently emerges.

Many authors and psychologists have actually referred to the preschool child as a mini-adolescent, since the tasks of finding out more about who she is and strengthening her self-identity are similar to those faced by adolescents. During the preschool stage your child will develop a sense of identity that will make it possible for her to function well and socialize outside of the immediate family setting.

Along with an increasing sense of identity comes the initial use of the word "I." Chances are that your toddler usually referred to herself by her first name. When two-year-old Susie, for example, wanted to go outside to play, she would say, "Susie wanna go out." When Susie's parents wanted to get her attention or call her to them, they would address her by name, rather than by the pronoun "you."

The Preschool 1 child, who is becoming more sure of her identity, begins to refer to herself as "I." Still feeling a bit uncertain about her identity, as well as unsure of the correct usage of pronouns, however, she may occasionally confuse "you," "I," and "me."

A NEW INTEREST IN RELIVING THE PAST. In connection with their growing self-awareness, Preschool 1 children often become extremely interested in learning what they were like when they were "little." Your youngster may ask you to tell her what she was like when she was a "baby." She may relish flipping through the family photograph album to see what she looked like as an infant and toddler, and will probably enjoy hearing tales of things she did at earlier ages. By asking you questions about her past, looking at pictures, and listening to stories of what she was like, she will be able to relive the past.

Helping your child learn about her past will heighten her emerging sense of identity. Feelings of self-pride should also be stimulated upon her discovery that she is so grown up as compared to the tiny, helpless infant in the photographs.

WORRIES ABOUT THE BODY. The more conscious your young preschooler becomes of herself as an individual, the more aware of her body she becomes. During the latter part of the third year of life, as the child starts to develop a sense of identity, she will value her body more highly, and show greater concerns about its intactness. Her sense of identity is closely linked to the condition of her body. When even minor scratches or cuts are sustained, she may no longer feel "complete" as a person. Injuries to the body are regarded as injuries to her "self."

Your child's normal concerns about her body should be easily recognized. This is the phase when bandages appear to take on special importance to the child. One mother made the following observations about her Preschool 1 child.

Thank goodness for Band-Aids. I don't know what I'd do without them. Ever since Brian turned two and a half, he gets upset and frightened every time he gets a tiny scratch, bruise, or mosquito bite. All I have to do is take out a Band-Aid, plaster it on the cut, and he calms down. They work like magic!

This little boy's reaction to minor insults to his body is quite normal. Many Preschool 1 children go through a period in which they overreact to minor scratches, cuts, and bruises. Earlier, these benign injuries probably resulted in a few tears, but now the child may react with an unusual degree of fear and concern. This concern usually continues throughout the preschool stage, and is likely to become even more pronounced during Preschool 3.

Bandages or adhesive strips placed over a child's "boo boo," or even simply the promise of this, are often enough to allay fears and concerns. Once her body is "patched up," she feels complete again as a person. Bandages have an almost "magical" effect upon youngsters, since in the mind of the young child, they can instantaneously restore both her body and her sense of "self."

It is a good idea to keep an extra box of adhesive bandages around the house. This will save your preschooler from unnecessary worry, and you from having to listen to her crying. Many youngsters enjoy playing with adhesive bandages, and at some point you are likely to see your child slapping bandages on both herself and her playthings, particularly dolls and stuffed animals. She will want to cover the tiniest nicks, both real and imaginary, so keep that box of bandages within easy reach.

THE PROCESS OF IDENTIFICATION. During the early preschool stage, your child will begin to pick up many of your values, habits, attitudes, and standards and make them a part of her own personality. This is a gradual, subtle process commonly referred to as "identification." She will be assuming some of your personality characteristics, without consciously trying to. Identification is believed to play an important role in the child's personality development and behavior traits, sexual identity, and conscience development.

A parent plays a major role in the process of identification by serving as a model for the child to follow. You will see increasing evidence that your child is closely identifying with you as she progresses further into Preschool 2 and 3, although the foundations of identification have been developing since early infancy with her imitation of your behavior.

Dramatic play represents a major avenue through which your youngster's identification with you can be explored, strengthened, and expressed. A major portion of a child's early dramatic play is devoted to assuming the role of her parent(s). At first your child will simply dress up in your old clothes and walk around the house, presumably feeling a great deal like you.

As her awareness of you increases, her dramatic play will become more complex. She will move, walk, and gesture like you. Her mannerisms, tone of voice, and inflections may be surprisingly similar to yours. While outfitted in your clothes, she will even soothe, scold, and converse with her dolls and stuffed animals in a way that resembles your interactions with her. As she "plays out" your role, she will behave as though she actually has some of your attributes, and is experiencing feelings and emotions similar to those you would have in the same situation. Thirty-four-month-old Margie, for instance, talked to and caressed her doll in the same way her mother often cared for her. As Margie played with her doll, she felt grown-up and controlled, and experienced the same warm, tender, and proud feelings that she believed her mother had in interacting with her.

From watching your youngster at play, it will become clear to you and other family members that she has picked up not only many of your obvious speech and behavior patterns, but also some very subtle traits that even you may not have previously recognized as being characteristic of yourself.

In dramatic play a child can put herself in her parents' as well as other people's shoes, try out their roles, and experiment with behavior, attitudes, and personality traits that are peculiar to them. As a result of this kind of play, she can learn a lot about other people, find out more about herself, and determine which attitudes and characteristics of others she would like to take and make a part of her own personality.

It is easy to see why most children would have a desire to be more like their parents. From a very young age, children develop strong emotional attachments to their parents. The majority of youngsters think that their parents are the strongest, most wonderful, loving, powerful, intelligent, and competent people in the world. By emulating their speech and behavior, the youngster is "able" to take on their power, strength, and intelligence, as well as their feelings of warmth, pride, and love. Parents who express sincere love and affection to their child will quite naturally be fostering her desire to imitate them.

A youngster's feelings of being like her parent may come from other people's comments about similarities. One little boy, who had regularly been told by his grandmother and other relatives that he had his father's handsome looks and athletic ability, had good reason to feel a strong similarity and close bond with his father.

Another factor that can influence the process of identification is a child's belief that she is similar to her parent. This belief can stem from her own observations. For example, Mitzie, whose hair was long and dark like her mother's, and who was often dressed in mother-daughter look-alike dresses, had good reason to believe that she and her mother were similar. A child who has the same haircut, dress, facial features, name, and so forth, as a parent will notice these similarities, and feel like that parent in many different respects.

Usually, the child will feel more similar to the parent of the same sex. Johnny, upon discovering that he and his father both had a penis and were made differently from his mother and sister, realized that he was a boy and would someday grow up to be a man like "Daddy." He closely watched his father's behavior and tried hard to be as much like him as he could.

Some identification with the opposite sexed parent is also likely to occur. As a child's social contacts outside the family increase in Preschool 2 and 3, she may also, to a lesser degree, identify with relatives, teachers at school, other adults with whom she spends a lot of time, and her playmates.

Each time that the child sees some similarity between herself and her parent, and every time other people tell her that she is similar, her identification with the parent is fortified. As her identification grows stronger, she thinks, feels, and acts as though her parent's personality traits, values, attitudes, and mannerisms really do belong to her. Eventually, the many small aspects of her parent's behavior that she has been imitating since birth become incorporated into her own character and personality. She does not make a conscious effort to be more like her parent. It happens spontaneously.

INTERRACIAL CONSIDERATIONS. When a child and parent are not of the same racial backgrounds, as expressed by obvious differences in skin color or other characteristics, this may result in some confusion. Youngsters are usually quick to pick up on differences, especially those as obvious as skin color. The differences that they observe often arouse their curiosity and prompt them to ask questions.

Carrie Parsons, nearly three, was very inquisitive about the differences between her appearance and her mother's. Carrie's skin was dark brown, like her father's. She also had short, bushy dark hair whereas her mother had long, straight hair. One afternoon, this little girl asked why she did not have skin and hair like her mommy. Mrs. Parsons explained that Carrie simply looked more like her daddy and encouraged Carrie to be proud of that fact. She went on to say that even though their skin color and hair were different, they were alike in many other ways, such as in their sex, interests, and last name. She tried to instill in Carrie the notion that despite obvious differences in skin coloring, people are very similar.

Children's questions should be answered to their satisfaction. Mrs. Parsons respected her child's curiosity and observations. She addressed herself to the differences in appearance that Carrie noticed, but emphasized the similarities between herself and Carrie.

There are many other ways in which a child can feel similar to her parent other than by observing likenesses in complexion, hair color, or facial features. The youngster may note similarities in dress, mannerisms, interests, name, styles of gesturing, and sex. A child can, indeed, develop a strong identification with a parent unlike herself in appearance, and the parent can assist in this by emphasizing the things they have in common and the ways in which they are alike.

Children of one race who are adopted by parents of another race may have some confusion about which group they belong to. As close as they may feel to their parents, they will notice differences in appearance. They will also hear other youngsters or adults comment about racial differences.

Parents of these youngsters should try to instill in them a feeling of self-pride and respect for people of their own race as well as people of other races. Care should be taken to ensure that the children learn something about their racial background and cultural heritage. Children can be given ample opportunities to associate with and form friendships with people of their own race from an early age. In cases in which this is not possible in the neighborhood, they can be exposed to children of their own race and others through activity programs for preschoolers offered by day care centers, play groups, or nursery schools that are racially mixed.

There are several ways for parents to assist children to identify with others of their racial background. Mr. and Mrs. Whelan adopted a child named Ernie, who was of a different race. As a way of helping him develop a sense of pride and positive feelings for members of his race, they saw to it that he had frequent chances to play with children of his own race and opportunities to develop friendships among them. The Whelans also selected some dolls for Ernie made with his skin color. In choosing picture storybooks, they purchased a few with children of the same race as main characters, and others that were interracial.

Toys and books that reflect the child's image or color can help her build self-esteem and pride, as well as positive feelings for her racial background. Parents who treat members of the child's race with the same respect they show members of their own and who provide ample social contact with persons of her race, help the child learn the value of mutual respect. This approach also sets the stage for her to learn to live in harmony with persons of all races.

DEVELOPING A SEXUAL IDENTITY. One of the many developmental tasks that your child undertakes during the preschool stage is forming a more well-defined sexual identity as a male or female, and beginning to develop attitudes about sex differences. This is a very complex task, influenced by a combination of genetic, environmental, social, and even intellectual factors that have been shaping her attitudes and behaviors since the time she was conceived, and throughout infancy and toddlerhood.

Parents' initial reactions to and interactions with their child are often considered to be consciously or unconsciously influenced by sex. Fathers, for example, may speak to and handle little girls more tenderly than boys. From a very young age, parents usually begin to treat little girls differently from boys, and reward children positively for behaving in ways that parents and society consider appropriate for that sex. Social expectations about a child's sex role are generally felt by the child during infancy and toddlerhood. By the time a youngster is of preschool age, he or she may have already adopted many interests and behavior patterns that are similar to the parent or parent figure of the same sex, and are considered acceptable for that sex.

Prior to Preschool 1, most youngsters do not have a clear concept of the differences between the sexes. They may say that a person is a boy or girl or "Mommy" or "Daddy" based upon looking at variations in clothing and hair styles, or listening to tones of voices. Older toddlers pick up on differences in the way their parents dress, talk, or even use the toilet, but distinctions between their mother and father, men and women, or boys and girls are probably quite fuzzy and naïve.

During the early preschool period, the child usually pays more attention to his or her genitals. This often stimulates interest in other people's genitals, and ultimately leads to some new discoveries about differences between boys and girls—mainly that boys have a penis and girls do not.

Learning About One's Own Sex. A young girl may think that everyone's unclothed body looks like hers. A little boy, on the other hand, may imagine that everyone he meets has a penis as he does. It is understandable why children who have such notions might, at the very least, be surprised when they find out that their theories were incorrect. Children's reaction to this discovery will naturally vary depending upon their sex and also upon factors such as their ages and personalities.

Sue, almost three, while watching her younger cousin, Johnny, being undressed, realized that he had something that she did not. She asked her aunt, "What is that?" and was told that Johnny was a boy and had a penis like other boys. She then asked, "Where is my penis—did somebody take it?" At this point, her aunt explained that boys have a penis and girls do not because this is the way God made them.

Sue seemed to understand, and did not say anything further. To her mother's surprise, the next day Sue confronted everyone she met with a very fearful expression and the question—"Do you got a penis? . . . Mine's gone!" This behavior persisted for about a week and caused some embarrassment and concern around the house.

This little girl's reaction to finding out that boys have a penis and girls do not is not abnormal or unusual. Upon seeing a boy undressed, a girl is likely to wonder, "What's that thing?" referring to his penis. She may show some confusion over the fact that she does not have one. Feelings of fear that something is "missing" on her body may arise. In an attempt to make some sense of this, her immature thought processes may lead her to the conclusion that she was originally born with a penis, but someone must have taken it away or even, perhaps, cut it off because she was naughty.

A girl's worries that she is the only one without a penis may prompt her to ask others whether or not they have one. Learning that there really are two different types of bodies often alleviates her anxiety.

Boys often react differently upon learning that girls do not have penises. Ronnie, age three, and three-year-old Clarise, while playing together outside, decided to pull down their pants to show one another what was underneath. Ronnie was surprised to discover that his friend Clarise had no penis. He quickly pulled up his pants, ran home, and asked his five-and-a-half-year-old sister, Angie, "Where's your penis?"

"I don't have one," she replied.

"You do too have a penis!" he insisted. Then he demanded to know where she had hidden it. He still did not believe her when she said, "I'm a girl, dumb dumb, and girls don't have penises."

After several hours of constantly questioning his sister about her missing penis, he finally gave up and then began to hold onto his penis as if to protect it. He was obviously afraid that something would happen to his own penis.

From a little boy's point of view, he sees something "missing" on a little girl's body, and usually wonders what happened to it. Given his intellectual limitations and lack of experience, a common belief is that someone took away or cut off her penis, leaving her in this less-than-whole, or as one little boy put it, "broke" condition. It is not uncommon for a boy to begin to worry that his own penis will be removed if he is a bad boy.

Fears of possible injury to his penis may prompt some changes in a young boy's behavior. For example, one youngster became very anxious whenever his playthings broke. Every broken toy that he saw reminded him of the possibility of his body being damaged.

Not every child will have fears of this nature, but they are not uncommon. Young children's minds may lead them to some incorrect and anxiety-producing explanations about genital differences, particularly since concerns about body wholeness tend to run high in Preschool 1, and throughout the entire preschool stage.

Helping Your Child Feel Comfortable with Her Body. Knowing that the child may become anxious and fearful upon realizing that boys are made differently from

713

girls, you will probably want to make the child's first real observation of anatomical differences between the sexes as comfortable and positive an experience as possible. This will be more easily accomplished if she makes her discovery in your presence, but in the event that you are not around, there are still some things that you can do.

Should your young preschooler ask questions, offer simple, honest answers. In the event that no questions are asked, you can offer to explain things anyway, since fear may underlie the child's reluctance to question a parent. Before giving any explanation, pump your child a bit to find out what she knows or thinks. Assuming that her ideas about genital differences are incorrect, then you will have a good opportunity to set her thinking straight. Avoid laughing at her questions or comments, since she takes them seriously.

Little girls can be told that they never had a penis, but have other body parts that boys do not have such as a uterus, vagina, and breasts. This may be a good time to explain that when little girls mature, they can grow babies inside of them, if they wish to do so. Some parents find this a good time to explain about the function of the uterus and breasts.

Girls should know that they are made just like Mommy, Grandma, Aunt Rose, and so on. A little girl undoubtedly loves Mommy very much, so learning that she is made like Mommy should make her feel proud of her body—of herself. In a very natural sort of way, it is important to convey the message that your daughter is loved as a female, and that being a female is a positive attribute.

Little boys, on the other hand, can be told that girls and grown-up women, like Mommy, are not born with a penis. They are made differently from boys and men. Further simple comparisons of bodies can be drawn, depending upon how much information you want to give. Most of the time a boy's fears that something will happen to his genitals will naturally subside, although he may need some extra reassurance from you should he seem especially worried.

A boy should be told that he is made just like Daddy, Grandpa, Uncle Dave, and so on. Learning about the way in which he and his father or father figure are alike should promote self-pride. Conveying to him that he is loved as a boy should also encourage positive feelings about the male gender.

I Am a Boy Just Like Daddy. A little boy's knowledge that "I am a boy" adds another important dimension to his self-awareness, and helps him establish a more solid identity. His self-image is further fortified by the awareness that he and his father are of the same gender. By the time a boy is three years old, he will have a more definite understanding that he is a boy who will grow up to be a man like his father.

With this realization, he will probably begin to pay more attention to the activities of other males, especially his father. He will also become increasingly motivated to mimic his daddy, to dress and act like him, and may even adopt his father's special interests.

A father with woodworking as a hobby may notice his son's growing interest in learning to hammer, nail, and build things from wood. In dramatic play, a little boy may often assume the role of his father, and perhaps drive an imaginary truck or pretend to be a judge in a courtroom trial like his daddy. A child may even try to lower his voice when he talks so that he sounds more like Daddy, and move in his father's characteristic manner.

He will not only want to be like his father in these respects; he will also want to have the same relationship with his mother that his father has. When a little boy sees his father being affectionate toward his mother, sleeping with her, and going out alone with her, he may want to have the same kinds of opportunities. His love for his mommy, until now, has been mainly non-romantic and largely based upon his dependency on her to satisfy his needs. In his attempts to imitate his father's relationship with her, however, his love becomes more romantic. This new development may create tensions and conflicts which are discussed in Preschool 2.

I Am a Girl Just Like Mommy. Similar events occur with little girls. A girl will make further attempts to increase the similarity between herself and her mother, and is likely to want to imitate her mother's relationship with her father. During Preschool 1 and 2, she becomes envious of her mother's position with her father. This can cause her relationship toward her daddy to become more intense and romantic. Along with this development come new tensions and conflicts that are explored on pages 827–28.

Spending Time with Father. Having ample chances to spend time with his father can facilitate a boy's positive identification with his dad as well as males in general. In the event that a young boy's father has died, or in a single parent family, a mother can often arrange for her son to spend some time with another man or "big brother." Most of the time a young boy will be naturally encouraged to feel positively about his own sex by being around his father, or father figure, and doing things with this person.

The young boy also needs to spend time with his mother. Through everyday interactions, she will encourage him to feel good about his gender identity and his masculinity, and will respond with approval when he attempts to emulate his father. This, too, will serve to strengthen good feelings in him about being a boy.

Spending Time with Mother. A little girl should have an opportunity to spend time with an older female whom she can imitate and with whom she can identify. This helps her establish her gender identity. Most of the time a girl will be encouraged to feel proud about being a female as a result of being around her mother or mother figure. Being with her father is also important, since he will encourage her to identify with other females by showing her in subtle ways that her femininity is appreciated.

DEVELOPING A CONSCIENCE. Your Preschool 1 child is still very impulsive, although she is becoming less so as she grows older. Her conscience is still in the formative stages; her inner system of self-discipline is not well developed. Through your program of discipline, you provide limits and necessary controls. When you are not around, she will have great difficulty refraining from yielding to the temptation to disobey your warnings or rules. After doing something that you warned her against, she may not even feel guilty, unless you discover her misdeed.

Feeling guilty after doing something wrong is part of having a conscience. If your child looks guilty when you talk with her after you find out that she has broken your rules, this is a sign of a developing conscience. Once a child's conscience is more fully established, guilt feelings will arise not only after she has done something wrong, they will also arise the moment she thinks of violating a rule. Ultimately, this will help prevent her from acting on impulses that are unacceptable.

Improved Language Skills Aid Self-discipline. As your child's vocabulary base broadens, she will be able to put new words to use in regulating her own behavior. She will do this by saying your warnings and rules out loud, just as you would if you were around, and thinking to herself that she should not disobey them. By repeating your warnings in the circumstances in which they would apply, she may be able to stop herself from approaching an off-limits place or object, and thus refrain from violating a rule.

At the age of two, when Vicky wanted a cookie from the jar kept on the kitchen counter, she simply climbed up and took one, whether or not her parents were in the room, even though they warned her time and again that the cookie jar was off limits. Several months later, she took cookies from the jar only when her parents were not around. She seemed to have remembered their previous punishments and was trying to avoid them. By the time she entered Preschool 1, Vicky had incorporated her parents' warning into her own system of self-discipline. This time, when she went into the kitchen in her parents' absence, she glanced longingly at the cookie jar, said, "Don't take cookie. No, No!" and turned away with a strained, but triumphant, expression on her face.

Words that this little girl had heard her parents repeat were recalled when she was just about to break a rule. Saying them served as a needed reminder to keep her hands out of the cookie jar. As your child's vocabulary begins to expand, it will be possible for her to say and appropriately use many of the verbal warnings that you have been patiently repeating. You will probably begin to hear her say these warnings occasionally and then refrain from doing wrong. When you are not around, she may say the warnings, but still disobey. Remember that her ability to control her impulses is just emerging. Once she develops greater self-control, it will be easier for her not only to say your warnings but heed them as well.

Identification with a Parent Influences Conscience Development. Your child's observation and imitation of your behavior, and her identification with you, will play an important role in the development of her moral standards, values, and ideas about unacceptable actions. During this phase you may see indications that she is beginning to develop some attitudes that are similar to yours.

In her dramatic play with a doll, for example, she may take on your role as a parent and scold the doll (supposed to be her) for doing all of the bad things that she herself does and for which she is reprimanded. One little two-and-a-half-year-old, Lana, was overheard to say, "You naughty little girl! You played with Daddy's pipe. You need to be punished!" This little girl then picked up her doll and spanked the doll's bottom.

The manner in which this little girl talked to her doll is very important. It clearly shows that the child is beginning to identify with her parents' rules of behavior, and the taboos they want her to uphold. Identification with parental standards for conduct, just like the development of a conscience, is a gradual process. It will still be some time before your child absorbs and adopts your behavior standards and value system, but you will see small signs of progress in this direction.

Social Sensitivity and Interests

RELATIONSHIP WITH YOU AND OTHER FAMILY MEMBERS. Your Preschool 1 child's ritualistic tendencies and other personality characteristics may place a strain on your relationship. Nevertheless, she may be a lot of fun to be with, since she will probably be energetic, more talkative and independent, increasingly anxious to imitate you and learn from you, and a greater help around the house and yard.

Parents often notice that their child is not as warm, friendly, or affectionate toward them as she was in Toddlerhood 3. Rather than offering you spontaneous hugs and kisses, she may give them in what appears to be a dutiful manner. Children quite often express affection only at bedtime, as a regular part of their rigidly followed bedtime pattern.

The child continues to become more independent from her parents while at the same time her interest in playmates grows. Some children at two and a half, and many more at age three, will be ready to spend more time apart from parents and the home setting for several hours each day by attending nursery school or entering into play groups with their peers. Being able to separate from her parents is a big step for a child. Nearly all children experience some anxiety or at least ambivalence about being apart from their parents, although some children feel separation anxiety more intensely than others. This topic was more fully discussed on pages 594–96, 634–35.

Do not expect your child to be very adaptable at this stage. She is still self-centered and socially immature and is likely to have some difficulty getting along with brothers or sisters. Parents should be prepared to witness numerous fights and conflicts, some verbal and some physical.

GETTING ALONG WITH OTHER CHILDREN. The Preschool 1 child shows a greater interest in other children than at earlier ages. Your child will usually play parallel to another child, although you will see more co-operative play between her and her playmates. Several children often group together to play a game or participate in some activity. Both real and imaginary play will be seen. Often when one child starts to do something, such as climb on the jungle gym, or make believe she is a bird, the others quickly decide that they want to do the same thing. Should one youngster decide to act silly, the others are apt to follow suit. When one child starts laughing hilariously, her laughter is likely to be "contagious," for soon every child in the bunch is laughing, too. The copying that you will see going on during this phase becomes more prominent in Preschool 2 and 3.

Youngsters are often inconsiderate and aggressive in their dealings with each other. Without being provoked, one child may launch an attack against another, physically or verbally. Children may purposely crash into one another, knock down and wreck each other's products and creations, rip apart each other's drawing materials, and snatch each other's crayons. Fights and arguments are very common. This is the age when parents must listen to screaming and arguing over playthings, and when they find themselves having to resolve their children's fights. This is also the age for broken toys, so be sure to buy the sturdiest you can find.

REACTION TO UNFAMILIAR PEOPLE. The child's reaction to strangers is difficult to characterize. She may no longer be as shy as she appeared to be in toddlerhood. However, she may now fluctuate between being hostile toward a stranger, and being shy and quiet. She may try to hide behind her mother's legs and refuse to speak, or she may approach an unfamiliar person and strike out at them for no apparent reason. Your child's behavior toward strangers reflects her emotional instability and social immaturity, and therefore it often works well not to overreact to it. It should be made clear to her how you expect her to behave when she meets a new person, but punishing her severely for occasional displays of hostility or forcing her to make friendly contact during a shy period is not a good idea.

INTELLECTUAL DEVELOPMENT

The Developing Mind

One of the major differences that you will notice in comparing your child now with the Toddlerhood 3 stage is her increasing ability to understand verbal explanations and instructions and to talk. As her language skills improve, you will undoubtedly begin to think of her as being both more intelligent and more adult-like. This change in her is bound to be very exciting for you.

Improvements in language development provide evidence of the rapid progress the child is making in formulating symbols (words) to stand for people, objects, and experiences, and in combining them in new ways in her mind to solve problems. For her to be able to accomplish this, information about her past experiences has to be translated into symbols and images and stored in the brain. At some later date, it can then be remembered. Her brain must also have developed a method of processing or organizing this information so that when it is recalled in the future, it not only makes good sense, but can be applied to new situations. Bear in mind that the actual mechanisms or physiological basis for intellectual improvement and development are not understood, although it will become clear to you that your child's memory is improving along with her ability to associate things and speak.

An example will help to illustrate this improvement in mental capacity. A mother gives a suggestion to her little boy Tommy: "Let's play with your truck." Tommy says, "Okay, I'll get my truck," walks quickly from the living room into his bedroom, and heads directly for the cabinet in which his truck is kept.

When he opens the cabinet door, he finds that the truck is not in its usual spot on the lowest shelf, but is on a shelf beyond his reach. He pauses for a moment, presumably to think about the problem. He then gets a low chair from the corner of his room, drags it over to the cabinet, climbs up on it, and is able to reach his truck. He brings it back into the living room and starts moving it across the floor, making the noise of a truck engine.

For Tommy to behave in this appropriate manner, one has to assume that there are many complex things going on in his brain. To understand his mother's verbal suggestion, he had to know what the words "play" and "truck" meant. These symbols probably then triggered his memory or recall system, because he had to know how to play, as well as remember where his truck was normally kept. Then he had to combine several symbols in his mind in order to solve the new problem of how to get the truck. Finally, he had to remember how to bring it back to his mother, play with it, and make the appropriate sounds associated with a truck.

The complex changes taking place in the mind of the Preschool 1 child enable her to behave more appropriately, and function on a higher plane intellectually than during toddlerhood. Your child's new ability to carry on simple conversations, remember things for longer periods of time, and find solutions to problems that she encounters from day to day should provide you with evidence that she is more of a "mental being" than she was at earlier ages. Yet, there are many things her mind cannot do.

Despite your youngster's strides forward, her ability to think and reason is still at a relatively primitive stage. By listening carefully to her comments, and by asking her questions, you will discover that her knowledge is extremely limited, and her ideas about events taking place around her are often rather strange or ridiculous.

The Self-centered World: Egocentrism

The toddler's view of the world closely revolved around her own experiences, movements, needs, and wishes. To a large degree she maintained the self-centered, or egocentric, view of her surroundings instilled in infancy. She made things happen, and influenced objects and events.

It is with this self-centered approach to life that the child embarks into the preschool stage. The Preschool 1 child's views of objects, space, time, and what makes things happen are less self-centered than they were in toddlerhood, but still closely tied to and influenced by personal considerations.

As you are probably aware from watching children's programs, or listening to your youngster's statements, "Children often say the funniest things!" The self-centered thought process of the preschool child often creates humorous interpretations of events, because the child looks at events differently from the way an adult would look at them. Her frame of reference is vastly different, because of limited knowledge and experience.

One night, while walking home from her aunt's house with her mother, Sally, nearly three, asked why that big light in the sky was following her home. Sally's mother seemed rather surprised and puzzled, looked up, and realized that Sally thought that the moon was trailing her. This humorous and seemingly unusual interpretation makes sense when considered from Sally's frame of reference. From her own self-centered view, Sally felt that the moon's presence and pathway related personally to her. It is not too farfetched to be able to see how Sally could think that the moon was following her home, not recognizing that the moon is in the sky whether she is outside or not.

The concept of egocentricity in intellectual development during the preschool years is important to understand, because it is a prominent feature of the way the preschool child thinks and relates to the environment and interprets events. Even adults never fully leave behind the self-centered attitudes that were prominent in infancy and early childhood.

Understanding the World of Objects

Much of the Preschool 1 child's vocabulary growth will involve learning the names for things that she sees or with which she plays. As she handles objects, she is continuing to learn symbols for them along with their many characteristics. Learning labels and verbal descriptions helps her focus on particular aspects of an object and plays an important role in making the picture of the objects and their characteristics more permanent in her mind. It also influences her behavior toward those objects and her ability to think about them. Yet she still has many limitations in dealing with objects and various substances in her environment. Many of these limitations, which are quite fascinating to observe, may go unrecognized, unless you know how to look for them.

FOCUSING ON ONE ASPECT OF A PROBLEM. The Preschool 1 child's ability to deal with information from more than one source at once is extremely limited. This characteristic of her thought process clouds her judgment, and sometimes allows her to form very inaccurate conclusions about objects and events. In order to observe this characteristic of the preschool child's thinking in your own child, you may want to try the following experiment during Preschool 1 or 2.

Pour equal quantities of juice or some other liquid into two identical jars. Place them in front of your child, and ask her whether or not the amount of juice is the same or different in the jars. In order to be more certain that she understands the meaning of the word "same" you might say something like, "If I drank the juice in this jar and you drank the juice in that jar, would I have as much juice in my tummy as you have in your tummy?" She will probably tell you that they are the same.

Next obtain another jar that is shorter and broader than the original jars. While she is watching, pick up one of the original jars, and pour the juice from it into the short jar. Place the other filled original jar and the short jar next to each other on the table. Ask her whether the amount of juice has remained the same or is different. She will probably tell you that the amount of juice in the tall container is greater than the amount in the shorter jar.

Most preschoolers base their answer upon either the height of the juice in the jar, or the height of the original jar. The preschool child frequently states that the tall jar has more juice because it is "taller" or "bigger," or that the new, short jar has less juice because it is "shorter" or "littler." They do not even seem to be bothered by the fact that no one added to or took anything away from the original amount of juice.

The next step is to pour the juice from the short jar back into the original container. Once again, ask her to compare the quantity of juice in the two original jars. Chances are that she will say that the amounts are the same, or equal.

No matter how many times you carry out this simple experiment, your child's responses are likely to remain unchanged. She will not realize that her conclusion is incorrect, or that it does not make sense. Based upon her replies, you will see that she is not able to take both height and width into account simultaneously.

The young preschool child is usually able to concentrate upon only one feature of an object or event at any given time. This interferes with her judgment, since other important features quite often cancel out or make up for the distortions that go along with paying attention to only one feature at a time. If she were able to consider both height and width simultaneously in the experiment above, she would have realized that one compensated for the other.

When you see something take place around you, and she sees the same event, given her limitations, she may perceive it very differently from you. Tasks or explanations that are simple for you may often be extremely complex for her. It will be years before she develops the ability to process information from several different sources simultaneously.

THINKING FORWARD AND BACKWARD. Another characteristic of your child's thinking is that she has difficulty thinking forward and backward. She can take a few steps forward in her thoughts, but cannot change directions and think backward to the original problem. The following simple game should allow you to observe this aspect of your child's thought process.

Make up a batch of dough (clay or some other similar substance will also work well). Divide it into two equal balls, and hand them to your child. Tell her that the balls are exactly the same, having equal amounts of dough.

Next tell her to take one ball and pound it flat with her hand. Then ask her to compare the flattened piece with the ball. Ask her whether the amount of flattened dough is the same as, more than, or less than the amount in the ball.

A preschool child almost always denies that the quantities of dough remain the same. She is unable to realize that the amount of matter is "conserved" or remains the same despite changes in form or shape. You know that if she took the flat piece of dough and shaped it into a ball, she could return it to its original form, since no dough was added or taken away. Your child cannot reason this out as you do, since she is unable to reverse the steps in her mind. Upon request, she will probably tell you that you did not add or take away any dough, but even this knowledge will not lead her to change her statement that the amounts of dough are not the same. The contradiction escapes her.

The final step in this experiment involves your taking the flattened dough and forming it back into a ball. Hand it back to your child, along with the original ball, and once again ask her to compare the amounts. Chances are that she will tell you they are the same.

The concept of the quantity of matter being conserved is beyond her level of comprehension, because of her inability to reverse her thinking. Some of the illogical and incorrect opinions that your child will form about things going on in her surroundings will stem from the irreversibility of her thinking. Even simple facts that seem obvious to you will be hard for her to grasp. When she sees you pour water into an ice cube tray, for instance, and later examines the frozen cubes, it will be difficult for her to understand that the quantity of matter has remained the same, despite alterations in its form and shape. Now that you are aware of this limitation in her thinking, you will undoubtedly see evidence of this as you interact with her.

DIFFICULTIES WITH OBJECT GROUPING. Your child has difficulty understanding the concepts of how objects are grouped together into major classes and then subclasses based upon their properties. For example, your child may look upon every dog that she spots as an example of "dog." She is not likely to be able to distinguish between types of dogs. She shows little evidence of understanding that each dog she sees is an individual dog with its own unique characteristics, and, at the same time is a member of a group of dogs such as dachshunds, bulldogs, or cocker spaniels.

The notion of categorizing things is generally beyond the scope of the child's comprehension for several reasons. One reason is that she has trouble holding several ideas in her mind at once.

Her ability to see relationships among objects and events is at a rather immature level, and she has great difficulty dealing with abstractions. She knows that she rides in a car, but she does not know that a car is a form of transportation. She may know the word "pear" and apply it correctly to every pear that she sees, but she may not be able to tell you that a pear belongs to the class of fruits. The preschool child is beginning to form concepts, but her ability in this area is extremely limited.

A young child who is offered a number of balls which could be placed into separate groups according to properties of size, color, and texture, will not usually group them in this manner. Rather, she may group together several small balls and two large balls into a "family," designating the larger balls as the "mommy" and "daddy," and the smaller balls as the "children." She has used size as her criterion for grouping these objects, but she does not use size properties objectively, as an adult would. Based upon her own limited frame of reference, she groups the balls according to size differences that she has observed in members of her own family. This is immature and self-centered thinking at work. You can probably see numerous examples of this type of object grouping in your child's play activities.

"LIVING OBJECTS." Still another characteristic of the young preschool child's thought is that she perceives many inanimate objects as being alive. In the immature mind of the Preschool 1 child, objects, particularly those that move or are moved, are believed to be capable of thinking, feeling, and even wishing. Piaget described this aspect of the child's thinking, and referred to it as "animism."

A little girl who feels sorry for her Teddy bear and believes that it must be hurt when its stuffing begins to pop out at the seams can feel this way only if she believes that the toy is alive and feels pain upon being injured. As you observe your youngster playing with her toys, you will probably see evidence that she thinks of them as having human attributes similar to her own.

Mrs. Rodell saw signs indicating that her son, Ray, looked at a stuffed deer's head hanging on the wall as though it had life-like qualities. One afternoon while she was dusting, and Ray was playing nearby in the same room, she accidentally knocked the deer's head off the wall. She picked it up and placed it near the edge of the coffee table, in a precarious position.

Ray stared at the hollow head on the table, with a slightly fearful expression. Mrs. Rodell encouraged Ray to examine it and play with it. He shook his head no. A moment or two later, he hesitantly walked over to it. Just as he approached, it fell off the table. He not only jumped back, but began to cry. The movement of the deer's head presumably convinced him that it was really alive. His mother, understanding the reason for his fear of this object, immediately rushed over to comfort Ray and reassure him that the deer's head was not alive.

Given the child's limited knowledge and self-centered point of view, it is not surprising that she regards objects as having qualities or characteristics similar to those that she possesses. This type of immature thinking about objects will be outgrown as the child moves further into the preschool stage. An awareness of this aspect of her thinking should enable you to appreciate her reactions to objects more fully.

What Makes Things Happen

Older toddlers moved further away from the self-centered belief that they caused everything to happen. It is usually during Preschool 1 that the child more fully recognizes that objects can move and events can occur beyond her sphere of influence. She sees objects changing position even when she is not acting on them. Once the child becomes aware that things can happen independently of her influence or actions, she develops another way of explaining cause and effect relationships.

The child's new explanation about what makes things happen relates to her belief that objects, particularly those that move, are living. When she sees objects move, independent of her moving them, she presumably assumes that they can move of their own accord because they are alive, and wanted to shift positions. A little boy who sees a lawn chair blown over by the wind may think that the chair simply decided to flip itself over.

Immature thinking, coupled with the youngster's self-centered viewpoint, enables her to give human-like character traits to inanimate objects. She knows that when she feels like moving she acts on those desires. She naïvely assumes that objects, like herself, have their own inner feelings, wishes, and thoughts, which motivate them to move. Your child probably watches events take place around her, and pretty much takes them for granted. Her theories about what makes things happen generally do not stimulate her curiosity about "why." She "knows" why, since, in her opinion, objects move because they feel like moving.

This early view of cause and effect will be gradually outgrown as the child progresses from Preschool 1 to the next phase. Once she outgrows the primitive notion that objects that move are alive, you are likely to hear her ask you more questions about what makes things happen.

Concept of Space

KNOWING WHERE OBJECTS IN THE HOME BELONG. You will notice that your child is becoming more and more familiar with the space within and immediately surrounding your home. This should be of some help to you. She may enjoy working with you to straighten up the house and put away groceries and toys, since she now knows where practically everything belongs.

Many Preschool 1 children are quite rigid when it comes to dealing with change. They insist upon a "status quo" approach to spatial arrangements, and strongly dislike having the familiar places for objects moved or rearranged, particularly things in their bedroom. Should parents move a plant from one table in their child's bedroom to another, she may express a desire for the plant to be returned to its old, familiar spot. Even minor shifts in the location of objects may make her feel uncomfortable and insecure.

This personality trait can be a nuisance to other members of the family, especially those to whom being neat does not come easily, and those who are prone to a monthly urge to rearrange furniture.

An occasional child will carry this desire to have all objects remain in their familiar spots to an extreme. She may become quite upset by the tiniest changes in spatial relationships in the home. When she sees a dining room chair moved slightly away from the table, she may rush over and push it back into its proper place. Seeing a picture on the wall that is not hanging properly may motivate her to climb up on a chair and attempt to straighten it. The child's recognition of these kinds of minor differences in spatial arrangements in her home provides evidence of her growing awareness of space, improving ability to notice minor details, and ability to retain information for longer spans of time.

MORE APPROPRIATE IN DEALING WITH OBJECTS. By observing the manner in which your child uses toys and other objects, you will notice that along with learning more about space inside your home, she is learning more about spatial relationships between objects. She will find it somewhat easier to put objects and playthings back together once she has dismantled them. She may delight in putting together simple puzzles, although she will still have some difficulty orienting the pieces so that they fit in their proper spaces.

In her play with blocks, she will be piling them one on top of the other to build taller "buildings," and will also experiment with shaping them into "bridges" and "trains." Do not expect too much from her in terms of intricate, sturdy, or very tall constructions, since this requires, among other things, a more extensive knowledge of space, as well as improved co-ordination. As her awareness of space increases, her dealings with playthings and household objects will become more sophisticated.

IMPROVING ABILITY TO DESCRIBE SPACE TO OTHERS. The Preschool 1 child will not only be more aware of and sensitive to changes in space, but will be able to talk about spatial relationships in more detail, because of her expanding vocabulary. She is likely to learn words like "kitchen," "attic," and "garage" as symbols for these spaces in your house.

Many of the new words that she begins to use go along with her interest in having objects remain in their proper places. She will frequently use phrases such as "right here," "over there," "up here," "near here," "out there," "down in," and "right over there." By putting two or more words referring to space together, she is able to be more exact in describing specific areas of location. Parents may also hear her use expressions like "way away from" or "far away" in talking about spaces that she cannot see, and knows are not easily reached.

DIFFICULTY THINKING ABOUT FAMILIAR ROUTES. Despite improvements in the child's ability to learn words as symbols for locations, her ability to manipulate these symbols in her mind when she is not moving within or seeing the actual spaces is quite limited. A child standing still in the kitchen, for example, will have great difficulty thinking about how to get from the kitchen to the attic, even though she would know how to get there once she started to move.

The child's knowledge of space is basically tied to her own movements and current sensory perception. It is easy for her to go from one place to another in her home and yard, but thinking accurately about her movements through space or remembering them is beyond the scope of the Preschool 1 child's abilities.

Concept of Time

MORE SIGNS OF REMEMBERING THE PAST. The young preschool child is becoming more aware of the past, even though her memory of things that happened in the past is not well developed. Occasionally you may be surprised by your youngster's ability to remember a detail of an event or specific episode that occurred long ago, and that you had forgotten.

Clara Sutton had been hospitalized for several weeks when she was approximately fifteen months old. When she was almost three, she had to return to the hospital for a series of tests. Clara was brought to the pediatric floor and seemed to be in good spirits until she spotted a particular nurse. Suddenly, she burst into tears and started to scream. It was obvious to Mr. and Mrs. Sutton that their daughter was terrified of this nurse, but they could not think of why. Later, they chatted with the nurse and learned that she had been the person who had drawn blood every day from Clara during her last hospital visit.

Your child's ability to recall aspects of past events will increase during the next few years and gradually she will start to organize them into a clearer memory. During this phase she will show signs of remembering bits and pieces of past events, but will not be able to organize them or place them in chronological order. You will also notice that her memory for the immediate past is improving. She will be better able to remember things that you teach her from one day to the next, and will have less difficulty remembering instructions that you give her.

During this phase, those preschoolers who did not show a previous interest in learning about their past may ask questions about what they were like as babies. This interest in personal history reflects the child's concern about the past, but more importantly, her acknowledgment of the fact that she changes as she grows older. However, despite children's temporary interest in this aspect of the past, they are mainly interested in the present.

GREATER ABILITY TO TALK ABOUT TIME. As the Preschool 1 child's vocabulary and understanding of time expand, she will learn and use more words and phrases to describe past, present, and future time. Most youngsters feel more confident and at ease when talking about things that they are doing, or that they see others doing. This is understandable, since their main concern centers around present activities and events. Words such as "morning," "now," or "today" are often used in talking about the present.

In referring to the past, children may discuss events that took place "way before," and begin to speak of what happened "yesterday." Future time may be indicated by statements such as "soon," "gonna do it," or "next is mine." Many Preschool 1 children learn some of the names of the days in the week and use them when they speak. However, in Preschool 1 it is doubtful that they will use words that refer to telling time, since words such as "bedtime" and "dinnertime" usually emerge in Preschool 2.

The Imaginary World of the Child

You will notice an enormous increase in your child's use of her imagination during the preschool years. A whole new world of fantasy and make-believe will open up to her. The development of imaginative skills is closely related to the development of the child's ability to learn word symbols, manipulate these symbols in her mind, and treat objects and activities as symbols for other objects and activities. These intellectual abilities began to emerge during toddlerhood, but become much more prominent during the preschool stage, particularly in Preschool 2 and 3.

PRETEND ACTIVITIES BECOME MORE PROMINENT. Your Preschool 1 child will be playing with ideas in her mind to a greater extent than at earlier ages. As a result, you will see her engage in more role-playing and pretend activities. She may make believe that she is you or an infant in her play, and pretend that her doll is a real child. The child's early imaginative play often involves playing "house."

Children who are verbal may begin to tell simple imaginative stories based upon their own experiences or things that happen at home. Further into the preschool stage, when imaginative skills rapidly expand, the themes of her make-believe stories and play activities will involve people, situations, and places that are unrelated to her own experiences.

Your child's new powers of imagination will often serve as a substitute source of satisfaction for her. When her wishes cannot be fulfilled in the "real" world, she can always find some degree of fulfillment by temporarily escaping from reality and entering into daydreams, dramatic play, and pretend activities. In the world of fantasy, every wish that she has can be fulfilled.

Mr. Tate, the father of two-and-a-half-year-old Robby, was rather surprised one day by his son's make-believe activity. He walked into Robby's bedroom and found him pretending to be eating an ice cream cone. Robby was holding a small paper cup into which he had placed a tennis ball, which he licked as though it really were a scoop of ice cream.

This father thought for a moment about his son's amusing activity, and then came up with an explanation for it. Earlier in the day, Robby had begged Mr. Tate to take him to the ice cream parlor down the street so that he could have a cone, but his father had refused. Having his request denied, however, did not lessen Robby's desire for an ice cream cone. Being resourceful, he found substitute satisfaction in creating a make-believe cone.

This child's use of his imagination as an outlet was helpful to him in dealing with a frustrating situation. At this stage children are also likely to turn to make-believe activities from time to time as a means of overcoming fears; this is described on pages 772–73. Your child's imaginative skills will serve a useful purpose in helping her cope with life's pressures. By assuming different roles in her dramatic play, she can learn more about herself and the world in which she lives.

LIVING IN A WORLD IN WHICH ANYTHING IS POSSIBLE. A major difficulty that the young preschool child has is knowing where reality stops and fantasy begins. She is not able to look at things objectively or clearly distinguish real events and objects from those that she creates in her mind. This is because of her limited experience, skill in thinking, and knowledge. When you and your child simultaneously watch something happen, there is a good chance that her perception and explanation of the event will be vastly different from yours. Not being able to separate what is real from what is not enables her to think that anything is possible, and that her wishes can come true.

One morning Mrs. Haskell told her daughter, "Angie, tomorrow we're all going to drive to Grandma's house." Angie looked puzzled, but continued to play with her blocks. That evening, when her father came home, she demanded that he show her how to drive the car. He appeared surprised and said to Angie, "Little girls are too young to drive cars."

Angie immediately burst into tears and blurted out, "I want to go to Grandma's." Angie's mother remembered what she had told Angie earlier, and found it rather humorous that Angie had taken her statement so literally. She explained to Angie that she could come to Grandma's, since Daddy would drive the car.

What often allows youngsters like Angie to take what their parents say literally is their lack of a good hold upon reality, and their ability to believe in the unbelievable. In the mind of the child, fact and fantasy can be intertwined, and things that adults say can become very distorted.

Toddlers and preschool children also tend to regard things that happen in their dreams as though they are real events. They do not realize that they have dreamed, nor do they comprehend that dreams originate within their own mind. The child frequently confuses dreams, feelings, wishes, and thoughts with reality. When she wishes that something would happen, or thinks about it, she believes it will actually happen.

Being aware that young children cannot fully separate things that they imagine, wish, or dream from actual events in the "real" world should make it easier for you to understand why they develop certain fears that seem nonsensical to adults, and why they believe they can really cause something to happen by wishing it were so. Your young preschool child does not live in a world that is regulated by objectivity, the laws of science, reason, and logic. Rather, as a consequence of her primitive thought process, she lives in a magical, mysterious kind of world in which fact and fancy are frequently blended in peculiar ways.

LANGUAGE DEVELOPMENT

You will be impressed by how well your child can speak and how her understanding of language has grown. Communicating with her will be more pleasurable than in previous phases, because she will be much more involved in carrying on conversations. Each day she will probably learn new words, and this will be reflected in her vocabulary expansion. An increase in the length of her sentences can be expected, along with more sophisticated sentence construction. Her improved comprehension of language will make it much easier for you to try to reason with her and get her to follow simple instructions.

Fostering Your Child's Language Development

It is important for you to be aware of the many ways in which you can foster your youngster's language skills. Throughout the remaining sections on language development, suggestions for stimulating her interest in both oral and written language are given. The Total Education of Your Child section on pages 798–801 focuses on specific suggestions that will help you share your child's enthusiasm for learning new language skills.

Slow or Late Talkers

The subject of children who are slow to talk was previously discussed on pages 550–51. Throughout this book it has been emphasized that the age at which normal children begin to talk is variable. During Preschool 1, it is important to broach this subject in a new light. There are some perfectly normal children, usually boys, who do not talk very much up to this rather late date. The late development of speech may be a family characteristic, and this sometimes explains why a child is slower in this area. In some cases in which a child is not speaking by the age of three or four, there may be some problem in the mechanism of speech or in the child's emotional state.

In the event that this slow talking or seeming lack of speech worries you, check with your doctor or a speech specialist. A thorough examination should reveal whether the absence of speech or the presence of faulty speech is the result of an organic problem or a psychological problem. Recommendations about treatment methods and appropriate education programs for your child may be suggested.

Active Language Development

VOCABULARIES ARE EXPANDING. Each and every day your child will be learning new words. She may pick them up from listening to you, other family members and adults, her peers, or television and radio. As she learns new words, she will take great pride in saying them for you.

Her vocabulary of words referring to time and spatial relationships is rapidly expanding. She may learn many new words which imply past, present, and future situations. You will also hear her using new words in talking about distances, locations, and the interrelationships between objects.

Children may now know the names of several colors, as well as the shapes of many objects, such as stars, circles, and squares. Most will be able to say their first and last names. As they are read to from storybooks, they often enjoy filling in words or phrases of sentences they know. By Preschool 2, they will be frequently using pronouns, adjectives, and adverbs. Gradually they are beginning to use all parts of speech, even though they sometimes use them incorrectly.

WORDS THAT HAVE SHOCK VALUE. Most children do not use obscenities until later in the preschool stage, around the age of four. There are some Preschool 1 children who happen upon curse words or obscenities by accident, and use them without really understanding what they mean. It is usually advisable to react casually or ignore the child upon hearing such language, rather than becoming aggravated, laughing, or looking very embarrassed. The use of "bad" language, as discussed earlier on pages 691–92, should not be of major concern during this phase.

SENTENCES. Toddlerhood 3 children were speaking in two word sentences or very brief phrases. Now that they have a better command of words and their meanings, sentences will be three or more words in length. You may hear your child saying phrases such as: "I'm a big girl now!" "See, I made a pie!" "She's got my truck." "Wow, watch me!" "I did it all by myself." "Help me! I want to get down." "I'm gonna ride my bike."

Your preschooler's broader vocabulary paves the way for easier self-expression. She will love to tell you about what she is doing or is about to do. She will also be able to ask for your help, complain, and "tattle" on her siblings.

As your child develops her ability to speak, she will devote a great deal of time to asking questions. You are likely to hear questions such as, "What is that?" "Who made it snow?" or "How do you do it?" As was previously discussed, it is important to answer her questions. These questions provide you with a great opportunity to offer information and foster language development.

When she approaches you with a particular question or interest, try to answer it right away through words and actions. Rest assured, you will have an attentive audience. Many children enjoy having parents ask them questions, particularly when parents ask silly questions on purpose, knowing that children know the correct answers. Having occasional opportunities to prove a parent wrong, or look more intelligent than a parent, can be a terrific ego booster for a young child.

CONVERSATIONS. At this early phase in your child's language and social development, you cannot expect her to converse well with other children. Arguments between them are common.

Preschool 1 children's conversations often seem to be mainly one-sided. Experiencing the enjoyment of expressing herself through language is the child's primary objective, while interacting in a meaningful way with another child takes second place. What one child says is often not related to what the other child says. One youngster may focus on something minor that the other said and use it to develop a new train of thought that has nothing to do with the other child's original comments. Observing children who are engaged in such one-sided "conversations" can be amusing. They may position themselves near one another and politely wait for their turn to talk. This type of verbal exchange, often called a "collective monologue," is commonly seen in young preschool children.

Not all preschool children have the type of conversations just described. Often the child will really try to communicate with her playmate. She will listen carefully to what her friend is saying, and then address her next comments to the points that were just made. Meaningful conversations will take place, but conversational skills are not well developed.

Self-centered thinking represents one of the child's major problems in carrying on conversations with others. The effect of egocentric thought upon speech is discussed in the Intellectual Development section (page 908). Another problem stems from the child's inability to maintain her original train of thought and build upon it logically. The young preschooler often goes off on tangents, even in the middle of a sentence. It can be very difficult for other people to follow what she says unless they are extremely patient and spend a great deal of time with her.

Do not be discouraged if you have trouble following your child's stories or discover a communication gap between you. Her conversational skills will gradually improve during Preschool 2 and 3. In the meantime, try to be a tolerant, respectful listener to encourage her to want to speak both to and with you.

SONGS AND RHYMES. Your child may attempt to sing simple songs, especially those that are repetitive and very familiar to her. Chances are that she will only be able to remember some words or parts of a song rather than the entire song. Some children who are rather embarrassed about singing in front of other people sing loudly and boldly when they are alone.

Preschool children sometimes like to memorize short nursery rhymes. When interrupted in the middle of reciting a rhyme, many will not be able to resume where they left off. They usually end up going back and starting at the beginning. Their ability to repeat what they have heard is rapidly expanding.

SPEECH ACCOMPANIES PLAY ACTIVITIES. Children tend to do quite a bit of talking aloud while they play. Sometimes they tell themselves what to do or comment on their own activities. Parents standing in the next room or listening at the door to their child's room may also hear her speaking to her playthings, particularly toy animals and dolls. Now is a good time to tape record some of your child's repetitive, delightful speech. Years from now the tape will be fun to play back.

Errors in Speech Are Common

In learning to speak, children have to perfect their articulation, master new vocabulary words, and combine words into grammatically correct sentences. As they are striving hard to absorb and use the intricacies of spoken language, mistakes will be made along the way. Common errors of speech include mispronunciation of words, repetitions of syllables, improper timing of sounds, stuttering, and grammatical errors. These mistakes are characteristic of normal speech development, and most, if not all, young children make them at some point prior to perfecting their speaking abilities.

The vast majority of these speech errors are outgrown or naturally corrected by children themselves as they grow older. Certain of these errors may be due to defects in the speech apparatus, causing articulation difficulties. If your child has ongoing speech problems, a specialist should be consulted.

Most youngsters have little or no idea that they are making mistakes or having trouble speaking until others bring this to their attention. A child whose attention has been constantly called to her errors, or who has received strong pressure to correct her errors, may become self-conscious when speaking. In some cases this can result in increased speech difficulties.

The child's initial errors in speech should be treated very casually or overlooked. There is no need for you to become overly worried or concerned about the possibility that something is wrong with her. At this early stage it would be an unfortunate mistake to label your child as a "stutterer," or as being "tongue-tied" or "neurotic." It is important not to nag her to stop making errors when she talks, or call attention to her difficulties in other ways.

STUTTERING. Many preschool children pass through a temporary stage during which they may stutter. This is particularly common during Preschool 2. Parents often hear various pauses, repetitions of syllables and sounds, or prolongations of sounds in their child's speech.

Their child's initial stuttering often causes parents to become concerned and upset over the possibility of it being a permanent problem. The first thing parents usually want to know is what is causing their youngster to stutter.

There is no one answer to what causes stuttering, although numerous possible theories have been proposed. Some theories suggest that stuttering results from tension and/or emotional upsets in a child's life. Others suggest that there are physiological or biochemical differences between the stutterer and the non-stutterer. Still others postulate that stuttering is due to various experiences that the child has had, emphasizing the role of environmental differences between children who do not stutter and those who do.

Another theory relates stuttering to the development of the speech center in the brain. Right- or left-handedness develops because one side of the brain becomes dominant over the other. The speech center has been shown to reside mainly in the dominant side of the brain. Thus, the development of the speech center appears to be related to the development of brain dominance and handedness. Some researchers feel that before the establishment of the fixed speech center in the dominant side of the brain, the child will be more susceptible to making errors in speech such as stuttering.

This theory also suggests that some forms of stuttering usually disappear as the child's handedness becomes established, simultaneously establishing the speech center in the brain. It has been observed that stuttering difficulties often persist in children who do not have a consistent preference for their right or left hand. It has also been observed that some children begin to stutter when they are forced to switch from using their left hand to using their right hand.

These theories indicate that there is probably more than one cause for stuttering during early childhood. It is important to stress that the vast majority of preschool stuttering is not a problem that should arouse undue concern in parents. Most cases are the result of some minor difficulty in learning the new task of speaking. Stuttering can be handled in the same way as other errors in speech described below. Parental attitudes and methods of handling this problem can often influence the course of stuttering.

By using the simple guidelines described below, most stuttering problems should be resolved in a short period of time. The rare forms of more persistent stuttering should be handled by consultation with your pediatrician and appropriate speech specialists.

WHAT TO DO IF YOUR CHILD MAKES ERRORS IN SPEECH. There are several things you can do to help your child become more fluent in speech, without calling attention to her difficulties.

1. Relax—and remember that normal children learning to speak make errors. Avoid becoming preoccupied with your child's speech or overanxious about her errors. She may sense your anxiety and become anxious herself.
2. Be attentive, and listen with patience and understanding when she speaks.
3. Let her finish talking without interrupting her.
4. Avoid making an issue of her difficulties by asking her to "think before you speak" or "slow down."
5. Do not label her errors or speak of them in her presence. Doing this may make her self-conscious about her speech, which may increase her difficulties. Even though you may not be aware of your facial expressions, they can be a dead "giveaway" that you notice her difficulty in speaking.
6. Avoid making the child feel uncomfortable in verbal situations. You should not force her to recite in front of company, or apologize to others for the problems she is experiencing.
7. Don't punish her for making errors in speaking; this is not a constructive way to help her learn to speak correctly.
8. Try to see to it that the atmosphere in your home is relaxed and conducive to speech. If your child must always vie for a chance to say something, it may be difficult for her to speak comfortably. Eliminate possible sources of frustration or tension in her life which may heighten her troubles.
9. When you speak to her, it will be helpful to speak clearly and distinctly so that she has a correct model to imitate.

Passive Language Development

The child's rapidly increasing comprehension of language has brought her to the point where she will have little difficulty understanding most simple day-to-day conversations. There will be many words that are beyond her current comprehension, just as there are at any age, but your child will show you by her actions that she understands most everything said to her.

LISTENING. Children of this age love to listen to stories and nursery rhymes. They often show particular interest in rhythm and the repetition of familiar words and phrases and stories. They enjoy hearing detailed stories of their own life, or stories built around what they or their playmates are doing. Short, simple stories about familiar subjects, or those which tell about the world, are also among their favorites.

FOLLOWING DIRECTIONS. Your youngster's ability to comprehend language has markedly improved, and she will be more capable of understanding your questions, comments, suggestions, and simple instructions. You will notice this improvement each day. Here are a few activities that should give you direct evidence of her growing understanding of the meanings of words. First, ask her to show you what "we drink out of." She will most likely point to a glass or cup. Then, as a second task, ask her what she does when she is "hungry?" . . . "tired?" . . . "cold?" She will probably respond appropriately. Finally, ask her to "Put the Teddy bear *on* the table; *under* the table; *in front* of the chair; and *behind* the chair"; she is apt to complete these tasks with little or no difficulty.

In attempting to get your child to do something that you want, you are likely to notice that some techniques are more effective than others. Certain phrases such as "let's get going," "right away," "hurry up," or "it's getting late," can often be helpful in motivating a child to stop procrastinating. As in the past, it is advisable to avoid giving directions that can be easily answered with "No," thus making it difficult to direct your child. Rather than give instructions in the form of a question, such as, "Can you put your toys away?" you might say, "What do you do with your toys when you've finished playing?" or, "Where do your toys go?" She will know the answer to these questions, and phrasing them in this manner can motivate her to follow your directions more readily.

LEARNING THE MEANINGS OF WORDS. As your child picks up more new words, she will be anxious to learn what each one means, and how it can be used. You are likely to hear her experimenting with new words in sentences, and sometimes using them incorrectly.

In developing her language and thought processes, the child starts attaching word labels to objects. This represents meaning on a concrete level. The word "doll," to her, will mean her own favorite plaything. Any time the word "doll" is mentioned she will take this as meaning her particular doll. As the child sees many other dolls, she will gradually apply the word doll to any object that looks like a doll. This form of thinking represents the generalization of the meaning of the word doll. Instead of being limited to describing her own doll, the word comes to describe any doll-like object.

The process of learning the meanings of words and learning to generalize their meanings is gradual, and you should be able to observe this process in your own child.

Fabienne's grandfather owned a blue truck, and she loved to ride around in it with him. Whenever her parents said the word "truck" at home, Fabienne always thought that they were referring to Grandpa's truck. As her awareness of other trucks grew, she realized that the word "truck" was appropriate to use with trucks other than her grandfather's. She also learned to differentiate between trucks on a more sophisticated level, and describe them in more detail when talking about a specific truck.

Your own child will gradually become more sophisticated in differentiating between objects and properties of objects. This can only come with experience and verbal interaction. Try to teach her more about the properties of objects and the difference between objects, since this will allow her to expand her vocabulary and label objects in her surroundings correctly.

During the preschool years, your child will still have to work at discovering the meaning of new words. You can help her by taking the time to explain what words or phrases mean. Point out to her the similarity and differences between objects as well as words, and continue to teach the names of various objects. When she says a new word, try to show her how it can be used in a variety of sentences and contexts. Do your best to make it enjoyable for her to learn new words and their meanings. This will foster both her language and intellectual development.

Regulating Actions Through Language

The child between the ages of two and five slowly learns to use language to help modulate her behavior. The toddler may say "don't" aloud as she approaches an object that she knows she should not touch. You are likely to hear your preschooler talking to herself with more complicated instructions as she performs certain activities. She may use language to ask herself questions, to give herself instructions, or to plan out what she will do in constructing a building with blocks. Sandy, attempting to put together a puzzle alone in her room, was overheard to say, "This one goes here. No, it doesn't fit. Where does it go? Maybe over here. We have to start all over again. It needs to go in a different hole." Young children are believed to be capable of regulating their own behavior and inhibiting their actions by means of self-commands that they have often heard their parents use in disciplining them.

Talking to oneself is considered to be a key factor in being able to carry out more complex tasks. As the child becomes increasingly able to use and understand language, she becomes more capable of controlling her actions, and also makes progress in her ability to perform more difficult tasks that require the self-discipline that language provides. By observing your child, you will discover on your own that the ability to use language effectively and the ability to regulate actions, think, reason, and solve problems are very closely related.

You will be able to observe the development of your child's ability to reason and solve problems out loud during the preschool years. Usually after the age of six or seven, most children do not do as much talking aloud to themselves when performing complex tasks. Reasoning through words becomes internalized in their thought process.

Learning a Second Language

Parents are sometimes interested in having their child learn more than one language. In some families, either one or both parents may be bilingual, and they may want to pass this skill on to their children. In other families, parents often want to maintain the traditional language and customs of their ethnic culture. There are also instances in which monolingual parents wish to have their children become bilingual to broaden their educational backgrounds.

The subject of second languages was previously discussed in detail on pages 108–10. Those parents who are seriously considering exposing their child to a second language often want to know whether or not the preschool stage is a good time to introduce it. Most researchers agree that the time between ages three and six represents a favorable period to introduce a second language. The child's ability to absorb a second language is felt to be maximal during these years. By allowing the child first to master the primary language, the second language is less likely to compete with the development of the first language.

Another common concern among parents is who should teach their child. Introducing the second language between the ages of three and six allows a great deal of flexibility in how the language can be taught. At this age the child can be taught by her parents or another adult at home, or a teacher in nursery or grade school. A major consideration in deciding who should teach the child is that the "teacher" should be fluent in the language, and should speak it correctly.

Once an appropriate teacher has been selected, a teaching program should be designed. Interacting with the child in a natural way in the second language is of primary importance. Some parents approach this in a very structured way, and set aside one to two hours each day when only the second language is spoken with the child. Another approach is to speak with the child in the second language only in certain areas of the house. Some parents choose to have the child learn a second language while at school, assuming this opportunity is available.

Recently, a few television programs for children have introduced educational sessions in a second language. Records and tape recordings designed to teach different languages are also available, although these methods alone are generally less effective than a personalized teaching approach.

It is felt that having an introduction to a second language when a child is young and most receptive will facilitate her ability to become fluent in that language later in her life. There may be minor problems associated with introducing a second language between three and six, after the native language has been well established. To avoid difficulties, it is best not to put too much pressure on the child to learn the second language. Teaching a foreign language in a comfortable, relaxed way during the preschool years has not been observed to have any major detrimental effects on the development of the child's native language, or her performance in school.

MOTOR DEVELOPMENT

This phase marks the transition from toddlerhood to the preschool years, and there are many physical changes that occur between two and a half and five which greatly affect a child's motor development. Before learning about the progress your child will be making in refining motor skills previously acquired and developing new skills, it is helpful to know some facts about how her body will change during the preschool years.

New Strides in Motor Development as the Child Grows

Your child's progress in physical development during the preschool years will be very evident to you. Children's over-all growth rate decreases from the first to the fifth year. An "average" child, during her first two years, adds about fifteen inches to her height. Thereafter, she adds a couple of inches per year. During the first year, the child essentially triples her birth weight. After her first year, the rate at which she gains weight declines.

The child's proportions also change dramatically during the preschool years. Head growth, for example, markedly slows down. A two-year-old has a proportionately large head which accounts for about one fourth of her total height. By the time the child is five and a half, her head accounts for only about one sixth of her total height. Limb growth during the preschool years is rapid.

Important changes in the child's muscles also occur during the preschool years. From birth to about four years, muscle growth is approximately proportional to the rate of over-all body growth. After the first three years, the muscles develop at a faster pace so that muscular development during the fifth year accounts for a larger proportion of a child's weight increase.

All of these changes in size, proportion, and muscular strength and co-ordination significantly influence your child's ability to move and the kinds of activities she can participate in. As her legs lengthen and become more capable of supporting her weight, she outgrows the immature posture and "drunken sailor" walk typical of a toddler, and gradually walks more erectly. Her ability to maintain her balance also gradually improves. During the preschool years the child's head no longer looks overly large compared to the rest of her body. As shoulders broaden, arms lengthen, and co-ordination improves, she becomes able to throw objects more efficiently and accurately.

In the area of fine motor co-ordination, you will also see signs of improvement. As her nervous system develops, she becomes capable of making finer and more accurate movements. The child who used to handle objects awkwardly will become capable of using a fork and knife, brushing her teeth, and drawing with a crayon or pencil.

Many motor skills such as rolling over, sitting, and walking tend to be acquired at rather predictable phases as a child grows and matures. Lack of training seems to affect such abilities only in minor ways. There are other motor skills that are influenced to a greater extent by training.

PRACTICE, ENCOURAGEMENT AND TRAINING: THEIR EFFECT ON MOTOR SKILL DEVELOPMENT. As your child's nervous and muscular systems mature, her potential for developing new motor skills increases, but her ability to perform more complex skills would be influenced by practice and special training. Children do not naturally learn to ski, tap dance, swim, roller skate, and ice skate. They must have special training in these activities, as well as necessary equipment.

There are other fairly common, but also complex, activities that can be influenced by practice, encouragement, and training, although the exact manner in which training may modify certain abilities is not well documented. A child's ability to throw a ball, for example, will partly depend upon whether or not a child is encouraged to play with balls, and how much opportunity she has to practice throwing. A father who dreams of his child's becoming a Little League star pitcher is apt to place a ball into his child's hands at a very early age, and urge her to practice throwing it whenever she has the opportunity. It is only natural that his child might be much better at throwing a ball after a year or so than a child who is not encouraged or afforded opportunities to practice.

A child's ability to draw or engage in fine hand and finger manipulations also partly depends upon what kinds of opportunities she has for practice. In cases in which a child is not offered crayons, pencils, pens, and other writing tools with which to practice, and/or is not given any encouragement in these activities, she may never learn to use these tools as well as another child who has had plenty of chances to handle writing instruments and receives parental encouragement to draw and print.

As your child grows older, do not lose sight of the importance of offering her ample opportunities to utilize both previously and newly acquired motor abilities. Encouraging her to refine motor skills and develop new abilities will also be very valuable in helping her develop to her fullest potential. You might give some thought as to whether or not you think she would enjoy and benefit from learning specific motor skills such as swimming. In your area there may be fairly inexpensive swimming, gymnastics, and dancing or other classes specially designed for preschoolers.

Gross Motor Activity

WALKING. Your child will be much more skilled at walking and running. These basic skills will enable her to participate in numerous activities. She will take great pleasure in exploring your home. The ability to cover greater distances will allow her to explore your yard and beyond. Now when your child walks, she will no longer have to watch her moving feet as closely as before. As her balance improves over the next several phases, she will become more able to walk erectly, in an adultlike fashion. An improving ability to vary body movements in an upright position will probably enable her to walk backward, sideways, and on tiptoe. These are not activities to which a great deal of time will be devoted, but she may use them on occasion.

RUNNING. Running may be your child's favorite method of getting around. Many youngsters rarely walk once they learn to run. Running is apt to be a rather recently acquired skill, and your child may still appear awkward when she runs. She will continue to lack the ability to start and stop quickly, and may still have difficulty pivoting in order to change her direction. When, in the midst of running, she decides to play with a toy on the floor, she may suddenly drop to her knees and slide to a halt in front of the toy. You may see her using her hand to guide her around a piece of furniture or push against a wall in order to make a turn.

CLIMBING. Your child will probably be able to walk up and down a staircase, although she may still want to hold onto a railing or your arm. Instead of her one-step-at-a-time method, she may begin to alternate her feet as she climbs upward. Similarly, she may now be able to climb a ladder, jungle gym, or a tree with low branches, alternating her feet rather than placing both feet on one step before going to the next higher step. Keep in mind that a child who is slower in her motor abilities, or is still a bit uneasy about stairs, particularly steep and narrow ones, may use the less sophisticated method a little longer. Going downstairs by alternating feet is a harder task, and one which takes considerably longer to master.

BALANCING. The Preschool 1 child's balancing ability is not fully developed. Most children will be able to maintain their balance on one foot for only a second or two. A few may be able to maintain this position a bit longer. Your child can probably walk between two parallel lines about one foot apart, although she is probably not yet ready to walk a balance beam several inches wide and raised off the ground.

JUMPING. Most children love to jump up and down in place. They use a two-foot jump when jumping from low objects such as the bottom step of a stairway, and may broad jump short distances. Once your child starts to jump down from low heights, she will begin to jump over low objects. The ability to hop on one foot is usually not acquired until later in preschool.

THROWING A BALL. Assuming that you have been encouraging your child to practice throwing a ball, she may be throwing with greater skill than in previous phases. She will probably be able to throw a distance of several feet. Greater skill with balls is generally more obvious in Preschool 2 and 3. Children of this age continue to have difficulty catching balls. Their arms are generally held straight with elbows stiffly positioned in front of their bodies.

Fine Motor Activity

BLOCK-BUILDING. In the area of fine motor control you will notice that your child is making small but nevertheless important gains. Using small blocks, your child may now be building more impressive-looking towers consisting of eight or nine cubes, or building a simple bridge-type structure.

DRAWING. Drawings will still be crude, and will mainly consist of marks scribbled on a page. Your child may attempt to enclose a space, producing a rather shakily drawn circular or spiral-type pattern. Many Preschool 1 children are able to copy a circle. Your child will probably be able to imitate a vertical line, although chances are that she will be off by about 40 degrees. Drawing two intersecting lines in imitation of a cross will be a harder task. Do not expect her to accomplish this until later in preschool.

DRESSING AND UNDRESSING. Now that your child is becoming skillful with her hands, she will be more capable of dressing herself. Many children will now be capable of working simple zippers and buttoning large buttons. Giving your youngster plenty of chances to practice putting on clothes will result in an improvement of her performance.

EATING. In the area of self-feeding, your child will be more efficient with her spoon and fork. She may now be able to spread jam on bread with a knife, although cutting her own food is probably too difficult a task for her. Do not expect her to be able to cut with a knife until she is five or six years old.

GROOMING. Children are definitely improving in their ability to groom themselves. Many are able to wash and dry their hands, brush their hair without messing it up, and brush their teeth with some degree of success. In the bathtub, most children will be washing the front part of their bodies.

WRIST-TWISTING AND OTHER SKILLS. Your child's ability to twist her wrist is now more fully developed. Tasks such as turning doorknobs, unscrewing bottle caps, and turning on water faucets should be easier for her.

As her ability to manipulate objects improves, she will become better at putting objects she has taken apart back together. She may enjoy putting together simple puzzles and kitchen equipment that she has spread out all over the floor. If you hand your child a piece of candy that is wrapped, she should be able to unwrap it more smoothly and quickly than in previous phases. It is likely that she will want to begin using a scissors, but she has not developed sufficient hand and finger control to allow her to use this tool skillfully and without close supervision.

LEARNING THROUGH PLAY

Play will be very important to your two-and-a-half-year-old. Playtime activities and equipment are very similar to those in Toddlerhood 3. Vigorous physical activities will still probably be her favorites. Climbing equipment, both outdoors and indoors, is valuable and should be enjoyable for her. Your little acrobat will love to climb on low wooden ladders and steps and swing from a jungle gym. Large hollow boxes or blocks will be hauled around, stacked, and arranged so that she can scramble over them. As she exercises and climbs, she will be developing the large muscles of her legs, arms, and trunk. She will also enjoy a swing set, and may even try balancing by attempting to walk across a wooden plank raised several inches off the floor.

The Preschool 1 child will often carry large, lightweight objects from place to place, and any well-sanded pieces of lumber that you provide her with should be greatly appreciated. She will also like to crawl underneath tables and through tunnels made from combining large cardboard boxes. You are likely to see her trying to do exercises such as jumping jacks or knee bends.

This is usually a good age to provide your child with a tricycle. Having already learned how to pedal kiddie cars, most children, with some adult assistance, quickly learn to pedal away on their tricycles. The pleasure your child will experience from riding a tricycle will be worth every penny that you will have to pay for one. This might be a good time to review the safety tips for tricycles presented on page 674.

When your youngster is in the mood for more subdued types of play, there are a wide variety of activities that she will engage in. She will love to look at books, listen to records, paint, scribble, finger paint, and work with dough. She will thoroughly enjoy her play with water, dirt, and sand. Putting together simple puzzles should interest her more than before, and now she may begin to enjoy stringing large beads. At this stage, her dramatic play becomes more prominent, and she frequently creates imaginary situations in her play activities.

Toys will be prized possessions that no one else can touch. When it is time for you to clean your child's room, she may stand near her toys so that you cannot disturb them in any way. She will enjoy having a variety of toys, but she may become slightly confused and overstimulated when surrounded by too many toys at once. Your child may also like to have her playroom arranged so that one corner or area is for doll play, one corner is for climbing equipment, one corner is for books and puzzles, and one area is for her art work.

The Improving Young Artist

PAINTING. Assuming you are the daring sort who is not bothered by a mess, you may want to offer your child a chance to use some real, non-toxic paint. Your child will need a large paintbrush. Probably your best bet is to give her a large brush with a handle that is wide enough for her to grasp. When buying paint, it is a good idea to purchase powder or poster paint. To prevent excess dripping, you can thicken the paint with wallpaper paste. Obviously, you will have to protect your child's clothing with some kind of vinyl smock, and also protect your floors with a large dropcloth. At this stage there is no need for you to buy paper, since newspaper will do just fine. Your child can paint on the floor or on a low table. A low easel is another piece of equipment that you can make if you are so inclined. An older preschool child finds it easier to paint against an easel, but the younger child usually likes to paint on the floor.

Your child will probably be satisfied using only one or two colors in the beginning, whereas at later stages she will want a variety. You will probably see her transfer the large brush from hand to hand and experiment with some different strokes, such as lines, arcs, circles, and dots. She will not concern herself with painting a picture of something at this early stage in her painting career. Most of her pleasure will come from the activity itself, rather than making an actual picture.

Do not expect your young child to be neat when she paints. In the event that you intend to encourage her in this activity, be prepared to cope with the messes that she produces. While she is painting, you might try turning on some music, and asking her to paint according to how the music makes her feel. Youngsters often enjoy painting to music.

Painting and scribbling with crayons are wonderful rainy day activities. They also serve as marvelous expressive outlets, especially for youngsters who cannot express themselves well through language. You might let your youngster paint with her fingers, or a sponge, if she has difficulty holding a paintbrush.

FINGER PAINTING. For variety, you can also introduce your child to the joys of finger painting. Some children take readily to this experience, while others are initially reluctant to dirty their hands.

It is simple to make your own finger paints. Start with some flour and a little salt, and gradually add water while stirring, until the mixture is of the desired consistency. A few drops of food coloring finishes the job. This finger paint is safe when eaten, whereas some others might not be. Investigate the ingredients of finger paints before giving them to your child since there is a good chance that she will do a little tasting as she paints.

Finger painting need not be done only on paper. A formica table top or counter top is also suitable. Finger painting is definitely a messy activity, so you will have to dress your child appropriately and protect your floors. You, too, had better put on your oldest clothes. When you see how much fun your child is having finger painting, you may want to join in.

DRAWING AND SCRIBBLING. Preschool 1 children will delight in scribbling, even if that is all they can do—scribble. Most children will not be drawing very much of anything, although a few may draw a crude picture of some figure or object. Your child may try to imitate some marks or lines that you make with a large crayon, and, although you may buy her a coloring book or two, you should not expect her to be able to color within the lines. Keep a close eye on her, so that she does not stray from the paper and mark up your floors and walls.

You should not make your child feel as if she has to draw a picture that looks like "something" to you. Again, it will be the activity that she enjoys, not necessarily the end result. If she talks about what she drew, and you see no resemblance whatsoever between what she says she drew and the actual drawing, withhold your negative remarks, and do not try to correct her drawing or insult her by making a better drawing yourself. Try to compliment her on her initial attempts or at least encourage her to continue. Give her opportunities to practice manipulating crayons, magic markers, and pencils, since the skills she will develop will help her enormously when she is learning to print.

INTRODUCING A BLACKBOARD. This is a good age to introduce your child to a large blackboard. It is a valuable piece of equipment, and a wonderful learning tool, and it will be used throughout her preschool years. Provide her with colored non-toxic chalk and an eraser, so that she can scribble to her heart's content, erase her marks, and then start again. It will be most helpful to give your child plenty of opportunities to scribble, since scribbling will later evolve into drawing and writing.

DOUGH AND CLAY. Your child may enjoy playing with clay or dough. Dough is not only less messy than clay, it is also easy to make at home by mixing two parts flour to one part salt and adding water to make the consistency of bread dough. A few drops of food coloring can make the dough even more appealing. By adding a couple of drops of oil, the play dough will be preserved for quite a long time. Wrap it in plastic and store it in your refrigerator. It may last for a month.

Large lumps of clay can usually be purchased at art stores. Your child will delight in pounding clay or play dough, pulling it apart, squeezing, twisting, and molding it into various shapes. You might even show her how to use a rolling pin, cookie cutters (preferably the plastic ones, to avoid sharp edges), and popsicle sticks or tongue depressors to make indentations and designs when working with clay or dough. A large piece of wood can make an excellent surface for working with clay or play dough.

Imaginative Play

Imaginative play, which emerged in a rudimentary way during late toddlerhood, continues and blossoms during the preschool years. It becomes more and more elaborate during Preschool 2 and 3. The world of make-believe is very important to a child. Taking on different roles helps her to understand more about other people and herself. It also gives her an outlet for expressing her feelings. Therefore, it is a good idea to encourage this type of play, and not worry that her activities are not "true" or "real."

You can provide a place in your home where your child can engage in imaginative play. By throwing a blanket or a cloth over a table or her climbing apparatus, she can have an excellent place in which to play "house." Or, she can pretend that this area is a doctor's office or a teepee. You can even take part in her play by telling her to imagine, for example, that her plastic or paper plate is a steering wheel, and have her take it from there. You might also push two wooden crates together so that both of you can sit down, and have her make believe she is driving you around town. You can even combine two types of educational play and sing a song like "The Wheels of the Bus Go Round and Round."

To promote her dramatic play further, you can provide her with appropriate dress-up clothes and props. She will love to have a box full of your old clothes that she can put on when she assumes your role in her play. She will also like to have a doll carriage, a play vacuum, a cardboard box big enough for her to climb into, a toy iron and ironing board, plastic dishes, a toy telephone, and any other objects and toys that may help to stimulate her ideas for imaginative play.

Puzzles

Preschool 1 is an excellent time to introduce your youngster to the world of puzzles. Puzzles that are simple, large, and colored are probably the best for the beginner. Toy stores are filled with puzzles that are appropriate for children between two and three, but you can make them yourself out of ordinary materials that you have in your house. Draw a large square on a cardboard box, cut it into four or more smaller squares, paint each square a bright color, and you have an excellent puzzle. Or you can find a large colorful picture of a person or an object in a magazine, and paste it onto a piece of cardboard. Then cut the cardboard into a few, large, differently shaped pieces. You could also use some of your child's artwork for this purpose.

If you are handy, another interesting type of puzzle can be made from wood. Obtain a large board and draw several different shapes on the board such as a circle, stars, squares, or triangle. You might even attempt to draw an outline of a house, a person, a tree, a car, or a cat. These shapes can then be cut out of the wood, sanded, painted with non-toxic paint, and then used as puzzle pieces to be fitted back into the holes from which they were cut.

Fun with Words

Your child is making rapid progress in her ability to speak and understand language. She delights in talking to herself and her toys as she plays, learning new words, mimicking what you say, playing with the sounds of words, rhyming words, and listening to stories, songs, poems, and nursery rhymes. Given her increasing desire to hear and experiment with sounds, words, and repetition, she will probably enjoy language activities.

Now is a good time to play some new word games with her. Wherever you are, you can point to objects, and ask *her* to say their names. You can say, "I'm thinking of an object in this room that is yellow—what is it?" You can also vary the game by telling her you are thinking of objects with certain shapes or sizes. Another game is to say to her, "I'm thinking of a word that starts with the same sound as Tommy." (Use many different sounds both at the beginning and ending of words.) This will sharpen her listening skills and her awareness of different words and sounds. It should also provide her with a good foundation for learning to read later on.

Here is another game that will help make your child more aware of sounds. Encourage her to close her eyes and remain as quiet as possible so that she will be able to hear the sound you make and try to identify it. Once she has closed her eyes, you can produce a variety of sounds and ask her to tell you what they are. For example, you could dial the telephone, turn on the water faucet, eat a potato chip, bang a spoon against a glass, or ring the doorbell.

In order to help her see relationships and similarities as well as learn the names of objects you might also ask her to point to all of the objects of a certain color, shape, or size. There are actually an infinite number of games to play that will stimulate her language development, and it should be easy for you to come up with many games on your own. Be sure not to make games too difficult for her. She will enjoy playing these games with you, and will feel a genuine sense of accomplishment when she responds correctly and learns new words.

Fun with Felt

The Preschool 1 child may now enjoy playing with a felt board, which you can make easily and inexpensively. Buy several colorful pieces of felt. Take one piece and paste it on a large square of heavy cardboard or wood. The other pieces of felt can be cut into various shapes. Should you be artistically inclined, you can cut out the shapes of people, animals, or your child's favorite cartoon characters. Once you have shown your child how these forms can be placed on the felt board, she will probably have loads of fun playing with it. Later on, when she is able to use a pair of scissors, she can cut out pieces of felt on her own. This makes an excellent rainy day activity, and there is not much to clean up after your child has finished playing.

Your youngster can play with her felt board without your assistance, but you can also join in this activity. Cut out a variety of shapes around which you can build a story. With the shapes of a little girl, a man, a woman, a dog, a tree, and a house, you can make up a story about a family that will delight your child. Begin by placing one object, for instance, the house, on the felt board. Then, after you have run out of things to say about the house, introduce a new shape such as the little girl. With each new shape that you introduce, you can elaborate upon your story. Once your child is able to speak well, she can make up her own story, or you can each take turns building on a story and putting new shapes on the felt board.

Play with Other Children

Previously we discussed the type of play referred to as "parallel" play (page 656). Now that your child will be more interested in her friends, she may engage in what is referred to as "associative" play. Associative play describes the type of play in which children engage in the same activity in close proximity to one another, but they still have little to do with or say to one another.

Your child and two other children may all play in the same sandbox, with each child making "mountains," but there is likely to be little social interaction among them. When you invite several youngsters to your home for an afternoon, they may all sit together on the floor playing with clay, each one having her own lump, but there will probably be little interchange among them. Gradually, toward the age of three, your child may engage in more co-operative play with her friends. Her ability to play with and get along with other children will partly depend upon how many opportunities she has to be with her contemporaries, and it is hoped that you are making it possible for her to play often with other children.

Shoving, hitting, pushing, and grabbing are all to be expected when children of this age play together. They may show very little, if any, respect either for one another, or for each other's toys. This is the phase when half of your child's toys are likely to end up being broken. Due to the rough nature of children's play, you or another adult should always be on hand to supervise.

Water, Sand, and Dirt Play

Your child will continue to be very interested in playing with water, especially when soap flakes and bubble bath are added. She will enjoy washing and wringing out her doll outfits, scrubbing her toy dishes with a sponge, and blowing soap bubbles. Even if you have introduced her to real paint, she may still enjoy painting outdoors with water.

With her mixtures of sand and water, and dirt and water, she will be more creative. Her lump of mud may now be fashioned into a ball or squished down into a pancake. She will shape and smooth her handfuls of sand into cupcakes, birthday cakes, pies, and hamburger sandwiches, and name her creations as she goes along. As you watch her play with sand and water, you will notice that she is becoming more creative and imaginative.

Music and Rhythm Activities

Your youngster will like listening to all kinds of music, and moving rhythmically to the beat. She may especially enjoy learning the words to simple songs, and then attempting to sing them. By now she is likely to have developed certain preferences for records and songs, and will be able to recognize many familiar ones. She may also derive a great deal of pleasure from experimenting with musical instruments that you can make for her at home. Suggestions for homemade instruments are provided in Preschool 3.

KEEPING YOUR PRESCHOOL CHILD HEALTHY

The child's growth rate slows down during the preschool years. Body proportions of the preschool child begin to resemble those of an adult more closely. Head size decreases in relationship to the body size. The proper maintenance of good personal hygiene and diet discussed in toddlerhood is of continued importance during the preschool years (see page 502).

Teaching the Value of Personal Hygiene

The older preschool child is much more capable of understanding how to care for her body properly. Teaching her how to brush her teeth and keep her body clean is an important part of well child care. Most children will take an interest in health care instruction if it is presented in an enthusiastic and enjoyable way.

When encouraging their children to learn to bathe themselves, for example, some parents make up songs about washing the parts of the body. Others play games with what gets washed next. Using your imagination, you should be able to provide instruction for personal hygiene in an enjoyable way. Changing dirty clothes on a regular basis is another simple task that can be taught to the child. She can learn that socks, underwear, and clothing should be changed at least daily.

Children often resist personal hygiene routines because baths and other habits of cleanliness are usually forced upon them in a way that is not fun or when they are more interested in doing something else. Every child, at times, would rather be doing something else than taking a bath. However, if her parents are enthusiastic and personal hygiene is made enjoyable, she will be more likely to perform the required tasks without putting up a fuss. Many youngsters take considerable personal pride in developing new skills related to taking good care of their bodies. Acquiring this kind of attitude at an early age will be of assistance in ensuring their continued good health throughout life.

Teaching the Importance of Preventive Health Care

It is important for children to develop a positive attitude toward preventive health care at an early age. They are more likely to place importance upon their personal health if parents set a good example and convey a positive attitude toward health care during the preschool years. Many children enjoy playing doctor or hospital during dramatic play. This is often a useful way for them to work out their fears of doctors. It also represents a time when parents can teach the importance of good health care.

Three-year-old Peter Osteroff was very afraid of visiting the doctor. One afternoon Mrs. Osteroff became concerned about this. Peter developed an ear infection and refused to get into the car to go to his doctor's office. So as not to miss the appointment, his mother ended up having to carry him into the car and later into the doctor's office while he struggled and cried. After Peter and his mother returned home, he refused to take the medicine that was prescribed. Mrs. Osteroff had to use all sorts of tricks to keep him on his antibiotics. Mrs. Osteroff was very frustrated, but rather than punish him, she thought of ways to try to help him overcome his fear of the doctor.

Mrs. Osteroff bought Peter a doctor's kit, with numerous colorful objects, needles, stethoscope, light, mirror, and other equipment. Then she encouraged him to play doctor and offered to be his patient. He really seemed to enjoy giving his mother needles and other numerous tests. During these play sessions, Mrs. Osteroff would discuss with Peter the importance of seeing the doctor. She would pretend that she needed help and only the doctor could give it to her. Peter indirectly began to learn how important it was to go to the doctor to get well, and his fear of visiting the doctor subsided gradually.

Preventing Illness by Immunization

During the preschool years, your child's immunization program must be extended to ensure her continued immunity against specific diseases. The table on page 947 of the Health Care Guide presents the program for routine immunizations of normal preschool children. You should record where and when your child receives these immunizations in the spaces provided in this immunization table.

It is recommended that preschool children routinely receive DTP and TOPV immunizations between four and six years of age. These repeat immunizations will strengthen the child's immunity to diphtheria, tetanus, pertussis, and polio. Your doctor may also recommend a repeat tuberculin test during the preschool years, depending upon the incidence of this disease in your community.

It should be mentioned that children who received their measles immunization before fifteen months of age should be immunized again against measles before they enter school. When children are immunized before fifteen months, it has been found that some of those children still develop measles. Research has demonstrated that before fifteen months of age some children have pre-existing maternal antibodies to measles virus in their bodies. These antibodies, obtained from the mother, have been shown to prevent the measles vaccine from producing adequate immunization. After fifteen months, these antibodies are usually gone and the measles vaccine will produce effective immunization. Discuss obtaining a repeat measles immunization with your doctor if your child was immunized before fifteen months.

Dental Care During the Preschool Years

The young preschool child should be encouraged to begin brushing her teeth if this was not already begun in toddlerhood (see pages 503–4). Most youngsters are anxious to do what they see grownups doing, and look upon brushing their teeth as a fun task rather than simply a chore. If possible it is advisable to have your child brush after meals.

Now is a good time to teach your child why proper brushing and tooth care are important. She may ask questions about teeth that you should try to answer. Your dentist will be able to recommend or provide pamphlets or short storybooks designed for young children.

Many young preschool children who have not had their first visit to the dentist will now be ready for it. The importance of regular dental exams cannot be over-emphasized. By helping to take proper care of your child's teeth at home and arranging for her to see the dentist at regular intervals, you will be promoting the healthy development of her teeth.

Common Illnesses and Problems During Preschool

The illnesses and problems encountered during the preschool years are usually minor and self-limiting and are similar to those seen in toddlerhood. The preschool child is better able to tell you when she feels ill or in pain, and this may make it easier to recognize problems much earlier. Colds, ear infections, fevers, and sore throats (see pages 954–59) are still commonly seen. The preschooler is a target for minor accidents or poisonings (pages 985–1005), but toward the end of preschool the child should be somewhat more capable of recognizing and avoiding danger.

As the child spends more time with tasks such as drawing, working puzzles, and looking at picture books, problems with vision may be more easily detected. It is important for parents to recognize signs of visual problems, since in most cases the child will not complain that she is having any difficulty. Squinting, headache, and stumbling over objects may be early warning signs that a visual exam is necessary. Some of the more common eye and visual problems of childhood and how to recognize them are discussed on pages 980–82.

Some preschool children develop allergies, even though they did not have them in infancy and toddlerhood. The more common allergic conditions seen during childhood are discussed on pages 970–74. When there is a family history of allergy, learning how to help minimize allergies may be useful.

Constipation sometimes becomes a problem during preschool. There are several causes for constipation and it is advisable to discuss this problem early in its development with your doctor. Soiling of the child's pants with feces occasionally occurs during preschool and should be evaluated by your doctor since this problem may be due to more than just poor toilet habits. These and other common elimination problems are discussed in more detail on pages 963–66.

HOW TO ENSURE YOUR CHILD'S SAFETY

The preschool child is still lacking in the ability to exercise good self-control and look out for her own safety, although she is probably making some progress in these areas. You should continue to set limits on objects, areas, and your child's behaviors that might be dangerous or harmful. Also continue to take safety precautions within your home and yard. A quick review of previous accident prevention sections should serve as a reminder of specific things you can do to help ensure your child's safety. Again, you will want to encourage her to be careful, without causing her to become too afraid of her surroundings. Between two and four years of age, most accidental fatalities result from automobile accidents, fire, drowning, poisonings, and falls, so pay particular attention to these areas in your program of accident prevention during the preschool years.

Your Child's Needs Are Changing

As your child's capabilities change, you will have to grant her greater independence in certain areas. When she first became interested in feeding herself with a spoon, you were probably worried that in waving it around, she might accidentally poke her eyes, and for a long time, while she was learning to use a spoon, you supervised her until you were certain she could be trusted to use it properly. Similarly, when you first began encouraging your child to develop good toilet habits, you probably led her into the bathroom, and remained with her to ensure her safety.

During this phase in her life, or in Preschool 2, she may show you that she is quite capable of performing many tasks, such as going to the bathroom, alone. Many older preschoolers will demand privacy while they are in the bathroom. Obviously, there eventually comes a time in each child's life when she would find it embarrassing or even humiliating if her parent remained with her in the bathroom, continued to operate the water faucets for her, or prevented her from using pens, blunt scissors, and other tools. You know your child better than anyone else. You know what her abilities are, and how well she follows instructions and obeys rules, and these factors, along with good common sense, help you in determining how much she can be trusted to do certain things by and for herself.

Allowing your young preschool child more independence requires some advance preparation by you. First, you will want to continue to safety-proof your home. No matter how mature and obedient your child is, she is still lacking in experience as well as self-control, and is still limited in her ability to tell the difference between what is safe and what is not safe. There is no reason why you should not allow your two- to three-year-old to go to the bathroom by herself, providing you have safety-proofed the bathroom (be sure that she cannot lock herself inside), and you keep your ears open as well as keep a mental note of the time. In the event that she has been in the bathroom beyond what you determine to be a reasonable length of time, or you hear unusual noises coming from the bathroom, you should check on what she is doing.

In addition to safety-proofing your home, you should also train your child to handle utensils and tools properly, and to operate basic pieces of equipment. When, for instance, you decide that she is ready to use the water faucets in the bathtub and sink, you should show her several times how this is safely done. First, the cold water is turned on, and then gradually the hot water, until the desired degree of warmth is reached. Next, allow her to do it on her own on several occasions with your supervision. Until you are as certain as you can be that she knows how to work the faucets properly, do not allow her to do this on her own. The same general rule applies to other tools, pieces of equipment, and so on.

Imitation and Accident Prevention

Preschool children are interested in and more capable of imitating their parents. Therefore, it becomes especially important for parents to set a good example for their child in regard to accident prevention.

Mrs. Case had the habit of throwing various objects around the home whenever she was angry or extremely upset. Her two-and-a-half-year-old son, Mason, picked up on this. One afternoon, while playing outside on the patio with several other children, Mason became angry at one of his playmates, picked up the wooden car that he had been playing with, and hurled it in the air. It struck one of the youngsters, causing her to cry, but fortunately did not injure the child.

Mason's angry gesture with his toy may have nothing to do with his mother's method of dealing with anger, but there is good reason to believe that he was picking up her habits. Prior to this incident, Mrs. Case had no reason to think that her habit of throwing objects in anger was influencing her son, but after seeing him behave in a similar manner, she vowed to refrain from expressing anger this way, in the hope that her son would alter his behavior as well.

Young children are great imitators, and when parents act in potentially dangerous ways, it becomes more difficult to teach youngsters to be safety-conscious. Mrs. Case had some trouble explaining to Mason that his behavior was not very responsible, since he had observed her doing the same thing.

Children should not be left alone with potentially dangerous tools and substances that they are not ready to use properly, since they have seen parents using them and will probably want to imitate their parents' actions.

Mr. Rodnight took his son, Webster, outside with him so that they could talk while he trimmed the bushes. At one point Mr. Rodnight had to go back into the house to receive a phone call, leaving three-year-old Webster alone with a pair of hedge clippers. Suddenly from within the house Mr. Rodnight heard his son screaming. He rushed outside to find Webster bleeding from a wound on the leg, obviously inflicted by the hedge clippers. This father should have foreseen that his son would try to imitate him.

Your child's strong desire to imitate you can be very useful in teaching her to avoid accidents. It will come in handy in motivating her to behave in responsible ways, hold and use tools properly, and return objects to their proper storage places after she is finished using them. However, if potentially dangerous objects that you use regularly, such as sharp garden tools and lighter fluid, are left in easily accessible places around your home, chances are that your child's imitation of your actions could prove to be harmful.

Safety in the Car

Car accidents are still a leading cause of injury and death for the preschool child. It is important for all parents to restrain their children properly when traveling in the car. The child car seats or shields described in Toddlerhood 1 (pages 512–13) will be used through most of preschool depending upon the type of device obtained. Be sure that these safety devices are properly installed.

When the child weighs approximately forty pounds or more it is usually time to use the car seat belt. This most frequently occurs after four years of age, during Preschool 3. The older child may need a little added height to use the lap belt properly. It is recommended that the older preschool child be placed on a firm cushion not more than two inches high and strapped in with a lap seat belt, while sitting upright. By raising the child up on the cushion, the lap belt will be more correctly positioned, low across the hips. The lap belt should *not* slip up and rest around the abdomen.

Shoulder straps that are available with most lap seat belts are designed for adults. The preschool child may not be tall enough for a shoulder strap. If the shoulder strap crosses the child's neck or face, that part should obviously not be used, but allowed to rest beside or behind the child who has the lap seat belt buckled. When your child is big enough, the shoulder strap will cross the chest and should be used for added protection. If your car is equipped with some other type of seat belt system, consult your child's physician or contact Physicians for Automotive Safety (page 42) to determine if this seat belt system provides adequate protection for your child.

Teaching Your Child to Become Safety-conscious

Carrying out the second phase of your responsibility in regard to accident prevention is important at this time. Environmental prevention is not sufficient. You must help your child learn to be safety-conscious and to recognize and avoid danger. Try your best not to overprotect your preschooler. Wanting her to feel positively about herself and eventually become a person who can assume responsibility for her own safety, you must gradually give her more freedom and independence when she demonstrates to you that she can handle it wisely and safely.

In Preschool 2 and 3, your child will undoubtedly be leaving you for periods of time each day or week to spend time with other children in the neighborhood, or attend an activity class for preschoolers, or nursery school. During the time that she is away from home, it will be impossible for you to eliminate every danger that she may encounter. Knowing this, you will want to prepare her to spot potential dangers and help her learn how to avoid unnecessary accidents by taking safety precautions.

Now that your child is more capable of understanding what you say to her, it is time to offer her more specific verbal explanations and demonstrations as to why certain activities, objects, and places are dangerous. Tell her why certain places are off limits, and why specific objects should be used only when an adult is present to supervise. It will help her immensely if you explain the value of safety devices such as seat belts, lights informing pedestrians when it is safe to cross the street, and so forth. If you and your youngster enjoy taking a walk after dark, it is a good idea for both of you to wear reflector clothing or patches and stripes so motorists can see you. Again, you can offer your child an explanation of this so that she understands the importance of the reflectors. It would not be advisable constantly to call attention to potential dangers, or go overboard in explanations, since this might make her too afraid or insecure. Rather, casually point out signs and equipment having to do with safety precautions. By doing this, you will be educating her in accident prevention in ordinary, everyday situations, and will be encouraging her to be safety-conscious.

General Guidelines for Training a Child to Avoid Accidents

Remember the general rule not to permit your child to handle objects or operate equipment alone until you are confident that she knows what she is doing. Below is a brief list of some areas that you will want to touch upon in devising a personalized educational approach, but you will surely come up with additional ways to teach her to prevent accidents.

—show her how to use water faucets properly

—train her how to use tools such as blunt knives and scissors properly

—encourage her to watch for cars when crossing the street or riding a tricycle

—teach her not to play near an excavation site or deserted building

—tell her not to throw stones or sharp objects during play activities with other children

—tell her not to play in the street or in other unsafe places such as near railroad tracks

—teach her to recognize and avoid poisons

—instruct her to ask you, her other parent, or care-giver before eating any substance with which she is unfamiliar

—tell her that medicine is not a food, drink, or candy, and should never be taken without adult supervision

—explain why certain substances, such as bug repellent, cleaning fluids, etc., are to be used by adults only

—show her how to use her toys and play equipment properly

—teach her where to go and what to do in case of a fire in your home. If you are installing or have installed an alarm system (e.g., smoke alarm), tell her about this.

EATING

Food requirements change during the preschool years. The Preschool 1 child is more aware of what is going on around her when she eats, and is also more capable of voicing her opinions about what she wants and does not want to eat. These factors may result in the child eating less, becoming more distractible, and becoming choosier at mealtimes.

This is an age when children commonly exhibit what, to parents, may seem like poor eating habits. Parents should not expect completely regular eating patterns from their child, and they should take care not to treat normal behavior as if it were problem behavior. A calm attitude and a great deal of patience will help see you through this phase, and should prevent you from creating problems that do not exist. On the other hand, you may have to set some firm limits on your child's behavior at the table, so that it does not get out of hand.

Your Preschool 1 child is probably eating the same foods other family members eat, with only a few exceptions (see pages 465–68). Highly spiced foods may not appeal to some young children, and you may have to season your own food to taste after a portion has been set aside for your youngster. She will undoubtedly have an easier time eating if you keep her food easy to manage, and offer her assistance when needed. Many parents may now really begin to teach their children table manners, but it is important not to expect too much from the young child in this regard.

Appetite Fluctuations

Your child's appetite may heighten or diminish from meal to meal. This is normal. How she feels will, to a large extent, influence how much she wants to eat. When she is tired, cranky, or sick, she simply may not have much of a desire to eat. As long as your doctor tells you that she is gaining weight properly, there should be no reason for concern over her swings in appetite.

Trying Her Hand at Selecting Foods

The child's preferences for certain foods and avoidance of others are apt to be very similar to those during Toddlerhood 3. One of the most annoying aspects of her behavior is that she may have quite a bit of difficulty making up her mind about what she wants to eat. Just as soon as she has made a choice, she is apt to change her mind again. As soon as you pop a piece of chicken in the oven she is likely to decide that she would rather have a hamburger. A way to get around this is not to offer a choice, or tell her that whatever her initial selection is, she will have to stick to it.

Preschool 1 children tend to develop rather rigid patterns of behavior. Your child may insist upon having a tuna sandwich every day for lunch for a week, or a particular brand of cereal at a particular time, in a certain colored bowl. Again, you should not be too concerned about what she eats, as long as her meals over the course of several weeks are generally wholesome and well balanced. Should you feel strongly about not giving in to her food preferences, as some parents do, be consistent in presenting a healthy variety of foods each day. She will be forced to choose between eating or going hungry. Do not worry about the possibility of her starving in the presence of food.

Between-meal Snacks

A desire for between-meal snacks may increase as your child grows older. Whether or not you allow your child to snack between meals is really a matter of personal preference. However, as at earlier ages, there are certain guidelines that nutritionists often urge parents to observe. Assuming that your child is eating three good meals a day at her regular mealtime, and she still gets hungry between meals, there is no harm in offering her snacks. Many children will not need to eat between meals, and this is the best of all circumstances, but when you do give your child snacks, use good common sense.

Try to set regular times for her snacks that are not right before her next regular meal. Certain kinds of foods, including sweets, often spoil a child's appetite for her regular meals and should be avoided. Instead, offer snacks that are better for the child such as vegetables and bits of cheese. Crackers and dried or fresh fruits also make good snacks. Naturally, you will have to limit the amount of these foods. Do not allow her to have as much of them as she pleases.

Parents whose child eats small portions or only "picks" at her regular meals, but seems ravenous between meals, often wonder if this is because they have gone overboard in offering her between-meal snacks. Often this is not the reason. Sometimes a parent makes a child so uncomfortable during regular mealtimes that she tenses up and cannot eat.

Mr. Fried was a well-meaning parent, but he tried to force his son to eat foods he disliked. This made his son so nervous and upset at dinnertime that it was impossible for him to relax and eat. Each night when dinner was over, his son would play for a while. Half an hour later he would be starving.

Mealtime atmospheres, as we have previously emphasized, should be relaxed. The child's regular dinners should be more appetizing to the child than snacks that you might offer in between regularly scheduled meals.

Feeding Problems

Assuming that you have been meeting your responsibilities in the area of eating outlined on pages 128–29, and have not been infringing upon your child's responsibilities, feeding problems during the preschool years should be kept at a minimum. In case you feel that there is some problem in this area, you should review the materials on Feeding Problems and How to Avoid Them in Infancy 12, pages 464–66. Should a pressing eating problem arise that really concerns you, the best thing to do is to consult your pediatrician or family doctor.

Good Table Manners

During the preschool years, parents generally make more earnest efforts to teach their children table manners. Sloppy eating habits are something that parents are quick to attempt to correct. They try to teach their youngsters not to throw or fling their food, and to wipe their dirty mouths and hands on their napkins, rather than on their sleeves. Many parents are adamant about having their children wash up before a meal.

Another aspect of table manners is knowing how to use utensils properly. The child must learn that certain foods, such as fried chicken, can be eaten with her hands, and others must be eaten with appropriate utensils. She also has to learn the acceptable pattern of holding eating utensils. When you first teach your child to use a knife, you have to show her how and in which hand to hold it, and how to use it in conjunction with a fork. Some parents teach their child to transfer the fork back to the right hand, and some will allow the child to hold the fork with her left hand.

Keep in mind that nearly every young child who is learning how to eat with utensils will initially run into some problems. Until she gets the hang of how to pick up food with her fork, bits of food will probably drop onto her lap and the floor. When she begins to cut with a knife, pieces of food are apt to fall off her dish accidentally onto the table. Table manners also include learning not to talk with a mouthful of food, and learning to ask politely to have food passed to her rather than reaching for food that is at the other end of the table.

You cannot expect perfection from your young child. Table manners will not come naturally to her; she must be taught acceptable eating patterns. This, as you know, will not be accomplished overnight, or even in a year. Children must have the skill and co-ordination to use utensils properly. They must also have developed some self-control that will allow them to inhibit particular unacceptable impulses. Having an awareness of and some respect for other people's feelings will also be of assistance.

Preschool children are gradually acquiring these abilities, but they take considerable time to master. The vast majority of children will show poor table manners from time to time, and there is no need for a parent to fly into a rage when a child exhibits bad manners. Simply show her the acceptable way of doing something in a matter-of-fact tone of voice, and allow her to continue eating.

The child who wants very much to be like her parents will watch them carefully as they eat, and imitate what they do. When parents have good table manners, chances are that their child will adopt them, too. Sensing that your child is capable, and knows what is proper, but is intentionally doing something the wrong way to defy you or get attention, you may have to set firm limits as to how much you are willing to tolerate.

Experienced parents claim that scolding or embarrassing the child at the table does not accomplish anything. You may have to isolate her at mealtimes, or simply not permit her to finish her meal, unless she is willing to behave in a more acceptable manner. If you give your child guidance, and keep your expectations at a reasonable level that is consistent with her capabilities, she should make progress in establishing good table manners during the preschool years.

BATHING

Taking a bath is usually among the Preschool 1 child's favorite activities. Your child may love to scoot forward and backward in the water, and talk as she plays with her toys. Her play in the tub is likely to become more imaginative. She may sink her toy battleships and perhaps have her imaginary airplane land on water, all the while making appropriate noises to accompany her play. She may enjoy her baths so much that you have to invent excuses for getting her out of the tub.

Most children will probably insist upon washing themselves without any assistance from their parents, even though they are not capable of doing a very good job. Do not be surprised if your child establishes a set pattern of washing and drying her body. Many Preschool 1 children develop elaborate rituals at bath time, and insist upon sticking to them day after day.

Your child could easily burn herself by turning on the hot water, so you will have to remain close by to supervise her activities and ensure her safety. Training her to use the water faucets properly is discussed in the section on How to Ensure Your Child's Safety. You might want to turn down the temperature of your hot water to prevent any severe burns.

CLOTHING

Preschool 1 is a phase during which you may have difficulties getting your child dressed. One day she may refuse to lift a finger to help, and the next day she might insist upon doing everything by herself. Her fluctuations between wanting to be independent and then wanting to be dependent are likely to be very annoying.

Another source of irritation to parents is the fact that as soon as they start to get their child dressed, she may run away and refuse to return. She often makes a game out of running away. To her this is very funny, but to a parent with better things to do than chase a child around the house holding a shirt in one hand and a pair of pants in the other, this game is not the least bit amusing. Arguments and temper outbursts over getting dressed are likely to occur fairly frequently.

The Preschool 1 child can most likely take all of her clothes off, but will not be adept at putting them on. She may attempt to squeeze her head out of an armhole, or end up with her pants inside out and backward. Despite these minor problems, she will now be learning to put her shoes on the correct foot, something that she was probably incapable of doing at earlier ages since she had not learned her left from her right foot. She will make further attempts to fasten buttons and snaps, and zip up zippers, but do not expect her to tie her shoelaces. You will have to help her make adjustments in her clothing after she has finished, provided that she will stand still.

Selecting Clothes for Your Child

In selecting clothes for your child, it is important to take her needs and opinions into account. Assuming that she is extremely active and loves to play outdoors, it would not be advisable to force her to wear frilly dresses or clothes which soil easily and are difficult to clean. This may seem obvious, but there are parents of active children who dress them in good clothes and threaten to punish them if they get their outfits dirty. Many conflicts can be avoided by taking your youngster's needs and not your own into account when purchasing clothes for her.

As your child becomes more independent and skillful at dressing, she is apt to take more pride in her clothes. She may want to have a say in what clothes to buy when she is out shopping with you, and will want to choose which outfit to wear on a particular day. Some children are very fussy about the color, newness, texture, and style of their clothes, whereas others could care less about these things. The child who attends nursery school or a play group may want to dress like her playmates, since being dressed very differently from her peers is likely to result in her being ridiculed by them.

A young child is not capable of selecting her own clothes entirely, but she should be allowed to make simple choices and decisions. While shopping, you can select several outfits that would be acceptable for your child, and then allow her to make the final choice. Or, knowing her favorite color, you can try to select clothes of that color. In the event that you sew her clothes, she can help select the pattern, the color of the fabric, and the buttons. Give her a certain amount of autonomy in selecting her own clothing. Taking her needs and likes into account when purchasing or making clothes for her should increase her feelings of being an individual and boost her self-confidence.

There are also certain other guidelines which may be useful to keep in mind when selecting clothes for your child. They should preferably:

- fit well
- be suited to the weather or temperature so that the child is not uncomfortable
- permit full freedom of movement
- be easy for her to put on by herself
- be sturdy and made of easy-to-care-for materials that are washable and need little, if any, ironing
- have extra seams, tucks, and cuffs that can be let out or down as she grows

SLEEPING

Bedtime still represents a problem for many Preschool 1 children. The child tends to be somewhat rigid in her behavior patterns, and rituals emerge quite clearly in the evening, before she goes to bed. Other problems which were previously discussed (pages 678–80), such as waking during the middle of the night and climbing out of the crib, may still be evident at this time. Most children during this phase will be ready to change to sleeping on a "youth" or regular bed.

Going-to-bed Patterns

The child's strict and lengthy going-to-bed patterns often postpone bedtime. Marisa, like many Preschool 1 children, developed very definite and complicated going-to-bed behavior, which usually took about forty-five minutes to carry out. She began by kissing and saying good night to her brothers and sisters, her two dogs, her fish, her parakeet, and last but not least, her father.

Next she was ready to march upstairs to brush her teeth, and this took at least ten minutes. After this, she had a set pattern of taking off her clothes and putting on her pajamas. Then she would say good night to all of her dolls and stuffed animals, kiss each one, and make certain each was put in its proper place in her room.

Following this, her favorite Teddy bear was picked up, for she refused to get in bed without it. Holding "Teddy" in her arms she was finally ready to hop into bed. This did not represent the end of her complex bedtime pattern, however, for she then insisted that her mother tucked her in a certain way, and read her the same three stories, night after night.

Do not be surprised if your child also insists upon a set going-to-bed pattern. Nightly rituals can be as elaborate as Marisa's, and are common during Preschool 1. Children often have some difficulty shifting from being awake and active to sleeping, and the lengthy going-to-bed patterns that they sometimes establish seem to help them make this shift.

Knowing this in advance may not change the situation, but it may make you more patient with your child and more tolerant of her behavior, if she insists upon such bedtime rituals. It may also help you to avoid setting up a long, complicated going-to-bed pattern which she may want to follow every night. See whether you can somehow shorten bedtime patterns and activities, before she reaches the stage when she is likely to develop a strict pattern around each activity related to going to bed. Usually by the time the child is three, these bedtime rituals diminish, and other than being an inconvenience, they should not be a cause for concern.

Taking a Nap

Naptime may also represent a problem. Some children periodically or regularly refuse to take a nap. When a parent insists that the child climb into bed, she may not readily fall asleep. She may play for a while until she tires herself out and then, perhaps, she will go to sleep. On the other hand, she may never fall asleep.

It is not uncommon for a child of this age to refuse to take a nap in her crib. She is apt to be able to climb out of the crib, and may do so as soon as her parent leaves the room. Sometimes the child will more readily take a nap in another person's bed, in a sleeping bag on the floor, or in other places—anywhere but in her crib.

Upon waking from her nap, your child may cry and appear grouchy, and irritable. When you try to comfort and quiet her, she may continue to cry, more loudly and vigorously than before. It sometimes helps to ignore her and simply wait until she quiets down on her own. Not all children will be grouchy after their naps.

Some appear quite contented and pleasant. Again, individual differences among children are evident.

When is it time to eliminate the child's nap? Some youngsters have already given up their naps, and others want and/or need to have an afternoon nap until they are five or older. How will you know? You cannot rely solely upon what your child says. She is likely to insist that she does not want or need a nap, even when she needs the rest, and may simply be showing a normal amount of resistance to established routine.

It is far better to use your child's behavior as the criterion for whether or not to continue the nap. Sometimes asking yourself the following questions helps. How is she when she skips her nap? Is she very irritable at dinner and in the evening? Does she seem overtired? Does her behavior improve or deteriorate when you insist that she take a nap? Does she really fall asleep, or rest, or does she simply play in bed and keep getting up? Does insisting that she take a nap cause a great deal of conflict between you and her?

These kinds of questions can help you determine whether or not it would be a good idea to eliminate her nap, but you should also take your own needs into account. Assuming that she does not put up a huge argument at naptime, and at least plays quietly, you may want to continue her nap simply because it gives you a break every afternoon. Having this time to yourself may be so important to you that you will decide to keep her naptime going as long as she is willing to go along with it. Your child is not the only person in the family whose needs should be satisfied.

DEVELOPING GOOD TOILET HABITS

Most Preschool 1 children will achieve daytime bowel and bladder control. Accidents in which a child soils her pants are rare; more common are accidents in which the child wets her pants, although even these occasions will be fewer in number. Children are likely to be very aware of their accidents, and may feel very bad when they occur. Some children still require their parents' assistance getting undressed or dressed, and wiping themselves, although many younger preschoolers are capable of performing these tasks on their own. Children may also tell parents when they have to "make" or ask permission to go to the bathroom. Two-and-a-half-year-olds often request privacy while they are in the bathroom, and you should oblige if your child asks you to leave the room and close the door.

Now or in Preschool 2 should be a good time to introduce your youngster to "grown-up" toilet facilities, if you have not already. Despite the fact that children may prefer to "go" on the familiar potty, they can generally be encouraged to use the regular toilet. Some children will still be fearful of the toilet, although this fear will probably subside by the time they are three.

Nighttime Bladder Control

Generally, as the child nears Preschool 2, she will experience some success in nighttime control. Boys tend to lag behind girls in this area, but there is no specific age for remaining dry at night. Some children will persist in wetting their beds beyond the age of three. If your child is not staying dry during her afternoon naps, and is not aware of or concerned when she wets her pants, chances are that she is not ready for nighttime control. Waking her up during the night may be useless if she is still wet when she gets up each morning.

Nagging a child who is not ready for nighttime control may make her feel terribly guilty each time she has an accident. It is generally advisable to ignore her accidents. Put her in padded rubber pants, and place a protective covering on her bed. The child who is disturbed by her accidents may need reassurance that in time she will achieve control, and that she is still loved even though she cannot stay dry at night.

Your child may show signs of being almost ready to remain dry at night (is dry after her naps, is mildly upset when she has an accident, is occasionally able to remain dry at night). Under these circumstances, there are a few measures you can take to help matters along. Assuming that she is agreeable to this, waking her up at night before you go to sleep may help ensure that she stays dry. Some parents leave a night light or a potty chair in their child's room to make it easier when she wakes on her own and wants to urinate. A few parents have found that setting an alarm clock as a reminder to children to get up and urinate helps them to remain dry. Parents are not advised to use these or other similar measures with a child who is not at all ready to achieve nighttime bladder control, since this may place too much pressure on her.

DISCIPLINE

Your preschooler's mental and language capacities will be constantly expanding, along with her ability to imitate you, identify with you, and learn from you. These changes will play an important role in allowing her to begin to regulate her behavior to a greater extent than was possible during toddlerhood, although she will still be very limited in self-control. As she matures, you will have to modify some of your techniques of discipline as well as your expectations so that they are in line with her changing ability.

Changing Your Expectations

During the preschool years, you will gradually make more extensive and determined attempts to motivate your youngster to behave in an acceptable manner. This will involve teaching her the difference between proper and improper forms of behavior and helping her inhibit unacceptable actions. You will also be more insistent that she postpone immediate satisfaction of certain whims and impulses, and develop substitute or indirect ways of deriving pleasure and alleviating pressing needs.

In order to accomplish these educational objectives, it will be important to continue to establish reasonable and consistent limits for your child's behavior. She will slowly become more capable of changing, delaying, and blocking some of her impulses as her conscience develops. Yet, as is emphasized in the Personal-Social Development section, the preschool child's conscience will not be well developed, nor consistently followed by her.

The utmost patience on your part will be required in your program of discipline. Positive results will not be seen right away. You will find yourself regularly having to repeat warnings and rules, and to intervene when she goes astray and violates them.

Between Preschool 1 and 3, your child will make impressive gains in her ability to control her actions in specific situations. As a result, her reliance upon you constantly to oversee and manage her behavior will gradually diminish. The child's improving ability to regulate her own actions with respect to your rules and commands will necessitate granting her more independence and freedom, according to how much she demonstrates she can handle.

Despite improvements, there will still be a strong need for you to provide your youngster with guidance, reasonable controls, and explanations for those controls. This will assist the further development of your preschooler's own inner system of regulation, as well as prevent her from straying too far from the path of acceptable behavior whenever her conscience fails to work effectively.

Improvements in Language Ability Make Disciplining Your Child Easier

As your child acquires a better understanding of what you say to her, and a better ability to speak, disciplining her should become easier. Verbal methods in managing her behavior are already beginning to work as well as or better than physical methods such as picking the child up and carrying her away from a "forbidden" to an "unforbidden" area in the home. Being able to motivate your child through words will be of great help to you in getting lessons in discipline across to her, and will be far less taxing on you physically.

Language will assist your child in acquiring control over her impulses, because it enables her to repeat your limits and warnings more easily and employ them for her own self-control. She may now show some signs of being able to regulate her actions by saying your limits aloud, and thinking to herself that she should not go beyond them, as discussed on pages 715–16. As her comprehension and use of language continue to improve rapidly during the preschool years, you will see evidence that her conscience is operating more effectively, and on a more sophisticated level.

Your child's growing ability to understand language also enables you to make further use of the techniques of explaining limits to her, and enables you to try to reason with her. A child who is able to understand why certain actions must be controlled, or why particular objects or places might be dangerous, is likely to accept her parent's reasonable limits and comply with them more willingly than a child who cannot comprehend the reasons behind particular limits.

Extremes in Disciplining Your Child Should Be Avoided

In helping your preschooler learn to behave in an acceptable manner, it is important to avoid being either too lax or too strict in disciplining her. Extremes in discipline may interfere with her learning to take responsibility for her own behavior and difficulties can arise.

Mr. and Mrs. Baxter were afraid to set firm, consistent limits on their son Claude's behavior for fear of losing his affection. They constantly gave in to his whims. Whenever Claude broke rules or went beyond their limits, Mr. and Mrs. Baxter tried to overlook his violations, and eased up on rules and expectations.

Claude, as a result, learned to evade responsibility for improper behavior, since his parents saw to it that he had no reason to be concerned about ignoring their standards for conduct. It is understandable that this little boy felt no remorse or guilt about behaving in an unacceptable manner. Mr. and Mrs. Baxter did not hold him accountable for his wrongdoings, and he, therefore, saw no need to hold himself accountable.

The Baxters did their son an injustice. As Claude grew older and entered school, he had a great deal of trouble getting along with other children and his teacher, since he had always gotten his own way with his parents. This little boy also had difficulty following directions in class and obeying certain rules, presumably because he never learned to exercise self-control or to obey and respect authority figures during the preschool stage.

At the opposite end of the spectrum are those parents who are overly strict and generous with punishment. Mr. and Mrs. Curran expected far too much from their daughter, Dierdra, in terms of exercising self-control and obeying their rules than she could manage. They imposed unusually harsh restrictions on her behavior. Whenever Dierdra disobeyed them or broke even a minor rule, they punished her severely by withholding their love and affection for unreasonably long periods of time.

No matter how hard Dierdra tried, she could never live up to her parents' expectations. After breaking some rule and being punished, her self-esteem was lowered considerably, and she felt rejected. To avoid these feelings, which were terribly hard for her to deal with, she began to deny her own wrongdoings, and became sneaky about breaking rules so that her actions were not easily discovered, and she could avoid extreme forms of punishment.

This little girl could not accept the responsibility for defying her parents' rules for conduct, since admitting this would mean a great loss of parental love and self-esteem. Dierdra did not develop appropriate means of controlling her own behavior as a result of her parents' too-strict approach to disciplining her. The only way that she could maintain her self-esteem was to deny that she did anything wrong, and continue to misbehave behind her parents' backs.

It is important to be aware that extremely lenient and extremely harsh methods of discipline are not the best way to promote conscience development or the development of self-regulation in the young child. An approach to discipline that is reasonably in line with a youngster's ability, and is flexible, firm, and consistent, is more appropriate for preschoolers. Such an approach is believed to foster the child's conscience development, ability to take responsibility for her own misbehavior, and ability to govern her actions. It should also promote her self-esteem and enable her to function more independently.

Punishment During the Preschool Years

It is worth reconsidering the topic of punishment as it relates to the preschool child. Between two and a half and five, the child will be developing self-control and forming her own conscience. Like disciplinary measures, the types of punishment employed during this phase of the child's development should be designed to foster conscience development and promote self-control.

As was discussed previously, there is no one correct way to punish a child. Each family usually establishes its own guidelines as to how punishment should be administered. Whatever the form of punishment used, parents should attempt to respect the importance of maintaining the child's self-esteem in order for her to develop internal standards for regulating her own behavior.

The goal of punishment during the preschool years should be to teach the child right from wrong, and to encourage her to establish an internal means for regulating her own actions. It is obvious that harsh, severe forms of punishment may often keep the child in line out of fear. However, when the threat of punishment is not present at a given moment, she may revert to her previous behavior, assuming that she has not already learned to regulate her own actions. External punishment alone, without fostering some internal standard within the child, is not the best means of punishment. It is important to be aware of some of the pros and cons of different forms of punishment so that you will be in a better position to develop an effective, personalized approach for punishing your preschool child.

THE CHILD'S OWN GUILT AND REMORSE MAY BE ENOUGH PUNISHMENT. Occasionally there are circumstances in which no punishment from parents is necessary. Four-year-old Brad had been repeatedly warned by his parents not to play with matches. One afternoon, while playing outdoors, he lit a match and set fire to a bush. The fire spread quickly to some nearby trees. Brad was filled with guilt and terror over his actions. He ran to tell his mother, tears streaming down his face.

Luckily, in several minutes the fire trucks arrived. No one was injured, and the firemen were able to put the fire out before real damage to the family's property had been done. Brad, however, had seen the damage caused by the fire, and seemed very upset and emotionally drained by the incident. It was clear by the expression on his face that he was horrified by the fire that he had caused. He kept crying to his mother that he was sorry and would never play with matches again.

Brad's mother felt that her son's feelings of remorse and suffering, which he had experienced as a result of the fire, seemed to be quite sufficient punishment. She did not spank him or scold him harshly. Rather, she reinforced his own awareness of how wrong it was to play with the matches by discussing with him how dangerous matches can be.

Following this episode, Brad stayed away from matches completely. The punishment that resulted from his own suffering had taught him a good lesson, and helped develop his internal standard of discipline. Most wrongdoing is not accompanied by a potentially serious outcome. However, when it appears evident that your child has clearly been "punished" by the results of her own actions, it is usually not necessary for you to punish her further with harsh measures. Some psychologists even suggest that if parents punish their child after a painful experience, they might simply alleviate the child's own concern about the outcome of her own actions, and interfere with the development of the child's conscience. By keeping this concept in mind in disciplining your child, you will be able to judge when and what type of punishment, if any, is best suited to a given situation.

PHYSICAL PUNISHMENT. Spanking and slapping are still the most commonly used forms of punishment during the preschool years. As long as they do not become excessive, they can be effective deterrents to the young child. After all, these forms of punishment have been employed by parents for many generations.

At this time, you should carefully evaluate whether your physical forms of punishment are excessive. There is a fine line between effective physical punishment and counter-productive physical punishment. It is obviously difficult to give a single set of guidelines to determine how much physical punishment is excessive. In evaluating the effectiveness of your own punishment, it can be helpful to consider some of the problems that can result from excessive physical punishment, or physical punishment that is applied improperly.

In cases in which a child is regularly beaten or physically abused, her feelings of self-worth and self-confidence will diminish. Not only will her self-image be affected, but she may also begin to feel helpless, just at a time when she should be gaining confidence in her own effectiveness and skills. Excessive physical punishment does not just mean severe physical abuse, since this mainly falls under the category of child abuse. It can also refer to steady, almost daily spankings and slappings.

In a child who has a strong sense of self-esteem and feels that her family really cares for her despite the physical punishment, punishment should not interfere with the normal development of her self-concept. A child who does not have strong self-esteem and tends to be insecure may be more sensitive to physical punishment. This type of regular punishment may further weaken the child's self-concept, and diminish positive feelings she has for her parent. It is not just the amount of punishment that determines whether or not it is excessive; the child's sensitivity to it must also be taken into account. What is an overly severe punishment for one child may not be for the next.

Spanking and beating during the preschool years are generally not believed to be as effective in fostering conscience development as some other forms of punishment. The child who has been severely spanked for deliberately misbehaving may temporarily shape up and behave more reasonably, but shortly thereafter she may seem to forget whatever the punishment was supposed to teach her.

There are several factors that may account for this behavior. Spanking frequently has no relationship to the child's violation of her parents' standards for conduct. Let us say a child deliberately acts up at the dinner table, and is spanked. The spanking itself is not logically related to her misbehavior, and the main lesson she may learn, at least temporarily, is to avoid the behavior out of a fear of being spanked again. Her reason for not misbehaving again is external, coming from her parents, rather than internal, coming from her own conscience. A fear of punishment by her parents, rather than her own inner feelings about what is right or wrong, determines how she will react in a given situation in which she is tempted to violate her parents' rules.

You will want to achieve a healthy balance between your desire to control your child, and wanting her to develop her own self-control. If you rely too much upon managing her behavior through physical punishment, she may decide to sneak behind your back the next time, so that her bad behavior is not discovered. Or she may consider the risks and decide to misbehave again, even though she must suffer the consequences, since being punished will ease her guilt feelings. A child who establishes a pattern of misbehaving and feeling as though being punished automatically "cancels" her wrongdoing is not likely to develop guilt feelings that will assist her in refraining from doing wrong again, particularly when her parents are not looking. At times, in order to rid herself of guilt feelings, it may seem as though she is deliberately misbehaving and provoking her parents so that they will spank her. When a child feels as though she has paid for misbehaving, she may have no qualms about repeating the act again, because she has no remaining guilt feelings or remorse about it.

Feelings of shame or guilt are believed to be essential for the development of a conscience. Physical punishment, as illustrated in this example, may not be the best way to foster conscience development. The child who has no conscience will need to have her parents around in order to ensure that she behaves properly. This child may not do anything wrong as long as her parents are around, simply because she fears being caught and punished. But when she is alone, and not in any fear of physical punishment, she may act differently. The child who has a conscience will have her own inner system for regulating unacceptable impulses, and will not need to rely upon her parents to ensure that she behaves in an acceptable manner.

TEACHING A LESSON THROUGH PUNISHMENT. There are other categories of punishment that, when properly applied, appear to be valuable in fostering conscience development and self-control. These forms of punishment are often more successful in teaching a lesson than physical punishment, because they have a greater relationship to the child's misbehavior.

Sally Frank was frequently told by her mother not to ride her tricycle past the end of their driveway onto the street. Despite the fact that Mrs. Frank always supervised Sally whenever she was on her tricycle, this little girl frequently defied her mother's warnings and rules. On several occasions, in response to Sally's disobedience, Mrs. Frank slapped her as a punishment. This type of punishment, however, did not seem to teach Sally the intended lesson.

Realizing that slapping had not been successful in deterring her daughter from disobeying, Mrs. Frank decided to try a different approach. The next time she saw Sally riding past the end of the driveway, she warned her that she would not be allowed to continue riding her tricycle until she was ready to obey the rules of safety and not to ride onto the street. Mrs. Frank locked her daughter's tricycle in the garage for a couple of hours. Then she asked Sally whether or not she was now ready to ride in an appropriate manner. Sally told her mother that she was ready, and so Mrs. Frank allowed her to ride it again.

This episode did not immediately stop Sally from disobeying the rules of safety on her tricycle, but it did have a more dramatic effect than did slapping her. After a few more episodes similar to the first, in which the privilege of riding her tricycle was denied when she misbehaved, she gradually learned to use it properly consistently. Riding her tricycle was very important to her, and being denied this privilege was a much stronger motivating factor for her to change her behavior.

Punishments that are closely tied to the child's misconduct are often more effective in teaching the child a lesson than physical forms of punishment. It is important to realize that, with a few exceptions, when there is no connection between the child's misbehavior and the punishment meted out, it is likely that no "lesson" will be learned. When the punishment lasts too long, or is too severe in comparison to the rule or limit that the child defied, she may feel angry and resentful toward her parents for treating her unfairly. Again, the "lesson" is almost sure to be lost.

In order to help ensure that your punishments are effective, it should be helpful to review the basic principles about punishment on pages 330–31, 532–33. With a little imagination and good common sense, you should have little or no difficulty in developing your individual methods of punishing your child.

Nearly Every Parent Experiences Some Difficulties with Discipline

It takes a long time and consistent reminders of rules and limits from parents for even simple lessons in proper behavior to be learned. This gradual process is often taxing on parents' patience and difficult for them to tolerate. Many parents experience frustration in disciplining their preschool child, and feel that they are not succeeding in teaching their child to behave properly.

Even the most conscientious parents usually become flustered at some point during the preschool years, feeling that they have not done right by their child in handling her, or believing that the child has a behavior problem. These feelings can be extremely bothersome and anxiety-producing when they arise, but when these parents talk to other parents, they realize that these feelings are experienced in some form by nearly all parents of preschool children.

It is easy to feel insecure about your ability, especially when you do not see your child responding to your efforts immediately. Do not let these natural feelings of insecurity interfere with your judgment and management of your child. Also be realistic in your expectations, recognizing that positive results for your daily efforts may not be clearly seen for some time.

Knowing yourself, your family situation, and your child as well as you do, you are in the best position as her parent to offer needed behavioral guidance and controls. Trust yourself and be confident of your ability to do right by your preschooler.

WAYS THAT PRESCHOOLERS RELEASE AND REDUCE TENSION

The preschool child, like the infant and toddler, has to find ways of releasing tension and comforting herself. Preschoolers face certain new tasks that can contribute to feelings of tension and frustration. Being older and more capable, they are expected to assume additional responsibilities. Pressures to become more independent and leave their parents to play with neighborhood children or perhaps attend nursery school are felt by most children.

All children experience a certain amount of pressure from their parents, siblings, playmates, and possibly teachers. Some of the pressure and anxiety that they feel may also be self-initiated as they strive to grow up and acquire new skills. Both internal and external pressures can make them feel nervous and frustrated.

Variability in Tension Outlets and Parental Concern

Reactions to tension outlets largely depend upon how frequently they are used and how long they persist. Some children rely very heavily upon an activity such as thumb-sucking, engage in it for hours during the day and night, and do not outgrow it after several months. Other children may use this particular tension-releasing activity intermittently, and only for very brief periods.

Parents of children who rely heavily on tension-reducing behavior are likely to be much more disturbed by these activities than parents whose children use tension outlets only occasionally. They may also be anxious to intervene and correct the situation. These parents often experience feelings of disappointment, impatience, embarrassment, and even guilt about their child's "bad" habits. These feelings often increase the longer the activity persists.

Over the next two and a half years, the amount of tension your child feels may fluctuate. Ilg and Ames of the Gesell Institute have done work demonstrating that there are certain peaks and valleys of tension corresponding to specific ages. They indicate that a high point for tension occurs during the transition between Toddlerhood 3 and Preschool 1, at approximately two and a half years of age. Tension may subside for a period of time, and then increase again toward the middle of Preschool 2 (three and a half years of age). You can expect to see heightened use of tension-reducing behaviors around these times.

There are some differences also in the ways preschoolers and toddlers discharge tension. The preschool child, being more verbal, does not have to rely solely on physical forms of release. She can also discharge pent-up feelings and anxiety through language, particularly through name-calling, swearing, and bragging. Nail-biting, nose-picking, twitching, and hair-pulling are more common outlets during the preschool years, although they can also be seen earlier.

Many children have outgrown some tension-releasing activities that they employed during toddlerhood. However, with some, these habits continue or, occasionally, first begin. Parents who may have expected their youngster's habits to decline after Toddlerhood 3 often become very impatient and concerned over them when they realize how persistent these activities still are.

It is difficult to keep from becoming concerned when you notice that other preschoolers do not appear to have such habits. The temptation to think that something must be wrong with your child is often very strong. While these feelings are understandable, it is important to refrain from jumping to incorrect conclusions.

Some children simply need to make longer and more frequent use of outlets for tension than others. Both types of children may be perfectly normal, and well adjusted. There is a great deal of variability in the intensity, frequency, and duration of tension-releasing activities. Individual differences in this area, as in others, are evident.

Most of the outlets for tension utilized by the preschool child are healthy and useful in helping her discharge excess energy and anxiety, and comfort herself. You need not become concerned about these behaviors if your child appears to be content and well adjusted over-all. In the majority of cases these habits will be outgrown as the child matures and her need for them diminishes.

General Guidelines for Handling Tension Outlets

It is usually more effective and easier on you and your child to try to make her life more relaxed and rewarding, rather than concentrating your efforts on putting an end to the undesirable behavior. Punishing, nagging, or ridiculing her can make her feel more tense, frustrated, and emotionally upset than before, and can result in increased reliance upon her form of release. By finding possible major sources of stress, and eliminating them, you can frequently hasten the disappearance of her bothersome activity. If you cannot locate a source, it is advisable to be supportive, and offer your child reassurance and understanding.

Simply asking or encouraging your older preschooler to give up her habit sometimes works well. Enabling her to spend more time with other children in a playground or nursery school setting may also help improve the behavior in question. She may receive enough direct pressure from her playmates to motivate her to discontinue its use.

In some cases parents simply have to be patient and allow tension-releasing behaviors to work themselves out. Most of the time these habits will be outgrown naturally, whether or not action is taken to speed up this process.

VERBAL OUTBURSTS. As the child's command of language improves between Preschool 1 and 3, you can expect to see an increase in her use of speech as an avenue for releasing tension and frustration. A peak time for verbal expression of tension is during Preschool 3, although this can be observed at earlier ages, particularly in children who are early talkers.

The most common forms of verbal release include bragging, boasting, use of bathroom terms (toilet talk), name-calling, and swearing. Children often mimic curse words that they hear their parents and older siblings or playmates use. Parents who are generous in their use of swear words or name-calling when they are frustrated or angry can expect to hear some imitation from their preschoolers.

Preschoolers' verbal outbursts frequently arouse their parents' concern, and may even shock them. It is particularly disturbing to parents when children direct their name-calling and swearing toward them. Youngsters have to learn the difference between acceptable and unacceptable verbalizations, just as they have to learn to distinguish between acceptable and unacceptable actions. A certain amount of bragging, boasting, and name-calling should be expected and perhaps even tolerated, particularly since it is so common and typical of Preschool 3 children. Should a child's expressive language get out of hand, however, parents will probably want to set firm limits upon her speech.

THUMB-SUCKING. Thumb-sucking often continues well into the preschool stage. During Preschool 1, if your child is a thumb-sucker, you may notice that this activity is less commonly seen during the daytime. Nighttime sucking, especially with a favorite object such as a blanket, will probably be very persistent.

Patterns of thumb-sucking are variable, but certain common characteristics can be observed. All three of the following thumb-sucking patterns are commonly observed and are part of the usual variability seen with this tension outlet.

Some children are not fascinated with their thumbs, and have only a short interest in this finger. Thumb-sucking usually becomes very infrequent in these children during the Preschool 1 phase and may be seen only at night.

Dedicated thumb-suckers continue to show interest in their thumbs throughout the preschool years. They may continue to suck rather regularly during the daytime into Preschool 2 and will still show a strong desire to suck their thumb at night throughout Preschool 3.

Most children fall into the middle of the road group, and are still interested in their thumbs during Preschool 1. These children will usually suck during the daytime when they are tired or lack something interesting to do. Watching television, listening to music, or resting on the couch may prompt them to begin to suck. At night these preschoolers still use their thumb to help them get to sleep. Comforting objects are often used with the thumb to relieve their tension before bed, and may be carried around the house during the day. During Preschool 2 and 3 these children lose interest in their thumbs during the day and gradually stop sucking before falling asleep. The decrease in thumb-sucking often goes in spurts. They may seem to have stopped for several weeks and then start again. Gradually they make less and less use of this tension-reducing behavior until it is only rarely employed.

Children who continue to suck their thumbs well into Preschool 2 and 3 often arouse parental concern. Some parents are embarrassed by their child's "disgusting habit." Thumb-sucking is generally regarded as very undesirable, especially in the later preschool years.

A major worry among parents is that thumb-sucking is harmful to the structure of the child's mouth. In most cases thumb-sucking does not cause the child any harm. Most dentists agree that thumb-sucking does not have any detrimental effect in children who have a normally shaped mouth or bite. With those who have some distortion of the mouth or teeth to begin with, persistent thumb-sucking may, in rare instances, make this condition worse. Your preschooler's dentist will bring to your attention any potential problems.

It is easy to become impatient with a child who persistently sucks her thumb. As was indicated in the general guidelines for handling tension outlets (pages 765–66), you should first attempt to find out whether your child is experiencing too much pressure in a specific area of her life, and then alleviate it if possible.

Having ruled out unusual stresses in her life, it is usually advisable to be patient.

Let thumb-sucking run its natural course. The experience of many parents is that if they ignore thumb-sucking and do not draw the child's attention to it, sucking will eventually be outgrown.

Discussing this habit with the older preschool child, and letting her know that you would like her to give it up can be effective in some cases. Playing with other children may also influence her to stop this habit, since teasing can be a powerful motivator to act more maturely.

Punishing, nagging, or ridiculing your child is usually not effective. Parents often find that harsh disciplinary measures rarely help to eliminate this problem. When they are successful in decreasing thumb-sucking, a new method for releasing tension, just as bothersome as thumb-sucking, usually develops. Measures involving putting substances on the thumb or restraining it (page 538) meet with little success.

It is advisable to put your child's late thumb-sucking into proper perspective. Unless it is getting extremely out of hand, you should not worry that this activity is having a detrimental effect upon her. Taking a relaxed attitude toward it may make life with a dedicated thumb-sucker a lot easier. There is no need to become embarrassed by her thumb-sucking or to apologize for it in front of other adults.

NAIL-BITING. Nail-biting is a common tension outlet during the preschool years. It usually begins toward the middle of Preschool 2 (around age three and a half), and frequently continues long beyond the preschool stage. The natural course of nail-biting is variable, but this form of releasing nervous tension and frustration is often begun in the preschool years and may continue into the school age stage.

Some youngsters employ this method of release only when they are under a great deal of pressure. It may emerge in response to a specific upsetting event such as a shift in living quarters or a new addition to the family. Nail-biting may also occur when a child is very excited, such as when watching a particularly captivating or scary movie or television program.

A useful course of action is to try to determine if there are specific stresses that are prompting a child's nail-biting. Lessening or eliminating pressure areas may result in the gradual discontinuance of the activity in question. This may not always be possible, and even when areas of stress are eliminated, nail-biting may continue out of habit rather than a need to discharge tension.

Occasionally it helps simply to discuss nail-biting with the child, and encourage her to give it up. Repeated reminders to take her fingers out of her mouth may work in a few cases, but when nail-biting becomes a habit, reminders or constant nagging are rarely successful. Belittling a child or using harsh punishment as a way of getting her to stop nail-biting rarely works. These tactics often add to the tension and frustration that she feels, and ultimately result in increased reliance upon this behavior.

An older preschool girl may be motivated to discontinue biting her nails for beauty reasons. Parents can point out to her how much prettier she would look if her nails were longer. A promise from mother to file her daughter's nails and allow her to wear nail polish just like a grown-up lady can sometimes be an effective motivator.

There is a chance that nothing parents do to help their child give up this activity will bring positive results. While this can be discouraging, it is a fairly common occurrence. Nail-biting may simply have to run its natural course with some youngsters, particularly if it has become a habit or represents your child's need to release tension on a regular basis. Unless the child appears to be unusually tense or unhappy, parents need not be too concerned about her nail-biting. Many perfectly normal preschoolers bite their nails. If nothing in particular appears to be bothering the child, and attempts to make her life less pressured or more rewarding do not result in a decrease in nail-biting, parents should relax and stop worrying.

MIDDLE-OF-THE-NIGHT ACTIVITY. It is not unusual for children during Preschool 2 to have difficulty sleeping through the night, although this can occur earlier or later. Night waking may result from the tension that they are experiencing, or from fears, bad dreams, or nightmares.

Upon waking, a youngster may wander around her house. Middle-of-the-night activity is particularly common in three-year-olds. Some children simply go to the bathroom, the kitchen for a snack, or play quietly by themselves until they are ready to return to sleep. This may not represent a real problem as long as appropriate measures have been taken to safety-proof the home.

Nighttime wandering can present a problem in some cases. Youngsters are capable of getting into mischief when they are unsupervised. They have even been known to open doors and latches and go outdoors. Parents' major concerns about this behavior are for their child's safety.

Suggestions for how to deal with middle-of-the-night activity are presented on pages 678–80.

TEMPER TANTRUMS. Children are apt to throw more temper tantrums around age two and a half than at any other stage in their lives. Coping with inner as well as outside pressures is difficult for people at any age, but especially for children who do not really have the ability to control their own impulses or put their feelings into words.

The Preschool 1 child is beginning to develop a better command of language and some self-control, and may occasionally inhibit her urge to throw a temper tantrum. It is advisable to tell her to express her feelings verbally, rather than through physical means. You cannot expect all of her temper tantrums to disappear by the end of this phase.

Temper tantrums are occasionally seen in the Preschool 2 child, especially when she is fatigued or very tense and frustrated, or during temporary phases in which she regresses or acts babyish. In most children temper tantrums gradually diminish as a form of tension release after age four as the preschool child learns more sophisticated ways of discharging tension. General guidelines for handling temper tantrums were presented on pages 536–37.

STUTTERING. Stuttering is especially common between two and three, and in many cases can be viewed as a form of releasing tension. Tension is generally high in children of this age group and may underlie stuttering, although there are certainly other reasons for this behavior. Stuttering causes parents to become concerned about their child, and worried about the possibility of a permanent problem.

The vast majority of young children outgrow their stuttering after a period of several weeks to several months. Nearly all youngsters learning to speak stutter from time to time, particularly when they are tense, bothered by something, extremely excited, or frustrated.

Stuttering occasionally emerges after or in reaction to an upsetting event, such as a parent's departure, separation from a parent, the death of someone with whom the child has had a close relationship, a move to a new home, or the birth of a sibling. Offering the child extra affection, reassurance, and support may help make her feel less tense and lessen her stuttering.

There are many other possible pressures that may result in stuttering. It is useful to examine the child's life both in and outside the home for unusual or new areas of stress, and try to eliminate unnecessary pressures if any are evident. When possible causes of tension are eliminated, her stuttering may diminish.

A more complete discussion of stuttering and suggestions for how to handle it were presented on pages 729–31. If your child's stuttering is an ongoing problem, discuss it with your doctor or a speech therapist.

NERVOUS HABITS (TICS). Nervous habits (tics) such as nose, facial, or shoulder twitches, throat-clearing, blinking, dry coughing, or sniffling may emerge during the preschool years, although they are generally more characteristic of the school-aged child. These tension-releasing behaviors involve quick, repetitive movements that occur on a regular basis. Other nervous habits that are commonly seen include nose-picking and ear-pulling.

The duration of nervous habits is variable. In some children they disappear after a matter of days or weeks, or are seen only intermittently. Nervous habits can last longer in other children. They may be seen for several months or as long as they are useful.

Constantly calling a child's attention to her nervous habit by nagging her, scolding her, or talking negatively about it to others in her presence is rarely helpful. These measures can contribute to her nervous tension, and perhaps result in an increase in her habit. Concentrating your efforts upon making her life less pressured and more fulfilling is a more constructive approach to attempting to eliminate the behavior in question.

BITING. The child who bites others during the preschool years is likely to do so out of intense anger and frustration. Biting is not a common form of tension release, although an occasional child may employ it. This behavior should not be ignored or allowed to continue, and attention should be given to possible ways in which it can be eliminated. Parental intervention is appropriate and recommended.

A preschool child who bites other people is unlike the infant or even young toddler, in that she is more aware of what she is doing. Parents should do their best to explain to their child why her behavior is unacceptable and can no longer be tolerated. This is often effective in motivating a child to give up her behavior.

When reasoning with a child and setting firm limits on her behavior are unsuccessful, parents should try to discover the reasons why their youngster feels the need to lash out at others in this unacceptable manner. Perhaps she is having difficulty getting along with a particular child with whom she plays. Maybe she bites other children whenever she is in too large a play group. She may feel frustrated or very uncomfortable if she regularly plays with children older than herself.

If parents are able to determine a specific situation that is contributing to this form of tension release, they should attempt to correct or eliminate it. Offering more adult supervision when a child is playing with other children sometimes helps to prevent this unacceptable behavior. Employing reasonable punishment may also be effective. One way to punish a child who bites is to isolate her from her playmates after every occasion on which she bites.

In the rare event that parents cannot get to the root of the problem, and no attempts on their part are successful in getting their child to discontinue biting, it would be advisable to discuss this problem with the child's physician or a child psychologist. It may be that something is troubling her that her parents simply cannot recognize or deal with effectively.

GENITAL HANDLING. Children who frequently manipulate and handle their genitals may do so because they are tense or bothered by something. The genital area can be rhythmically touched just as hair can be pulled, or thumbs can be sucked. Genital handling can be a natural tension-releasing activity.

There is no need for undue concern over this tension outlet. If your child handles her genitals in private, it is probably best to ignore this behavior and treat it as you would most other tension outlets (page 764). Genital play in public is not regarded as acceptable. Most parents find that explaining this to their child works well.

Genital manipulation during Preschool 2 and 3 may be related to children's concerns about their genitals. Young children who first realize that boys are made differently from girls may begin to fear that something has or will happen to their genitals (pages 712–14). This appears to be a reason why children suddenly start to fondle their genitals. Young boys may fear that something will happen to their penis to make them look like little girls. Little girls may worry that they are missing something. These and similar concerns may focus the preschool child's attention on the genitals. Talking to your child about sex education as discussed on pages 713–15 may help alleviate this tension. Clearing up misconceptions and offering reassurance usually help children relax; this often results in a decrease of genital manipulation.

In a few cases of very frequent or persistent genital handling, parents' attempts to help their child may fail to bring desired results. If the child appears to be obsessed with this activity, or appears to be rubbing the genitals because of pain or itching, you should bring this activity to the attention of her doctor.

ROCKING. Rocking movements at bedtime or while a child is sleeping are less commonly seen during the preschool years, but persistent body-rocking may continue during Preschool 1 and 2, and even into the Preschool 3 phase in an occasional child. Suggestions for handling this outlet for tension were provided in the toddlerhood stage on pages 540–42.

In some children it is helpful to shift their bedtime to a later hour, and precede it with exercise or another activity that enables them to release excess energy and tension. This may diminish their need to rock once they are put to bed.

A Preschool 2 or 3 child may be motivated to give up her rocking activity if she is given a grown-up bed. This approach works with some who are nearly ready to give up this behavior on their own, but if their need to release tension through rocking is still strong, a shift to a new bed may not bring the desired results.

Patience is often necessary on the part of parents. Rocking is a natural form of release that should not cause undue worry. In the majority of cases it is outgrown prior to or during Preschool 3.

HAIR-PULLING. Playing with the hair as a form of releasing tension can be seen during the preschool stage. This activity is often annoying to parents and can take different forms.

Rhythmic, gentle pulling or fingering of the hair while watching television or looking through a book is not uncommon. Parents sometimes become concerned that their child is picking up a bad habit, but children usually outgrow this outlet on their own. A mild form of hair-pulling should be viewed and handled like thumb-sucking (pages 765–66).

More vigorous forms of hair-pulling can become more worrisome to parents. The child may pull one or more strands of hair in a repetitive pattern. In some cases children concentrate on one area of their head. Regular hair-pulling often results in a small balding area or general thinning of the hair. Persistent hair-pulling to the point of hair loss is a behavior that parents will want to try to eliminate. It is important to recognize that this activity is a form of tension release. Even though the consequences of vigorous hair-pulling represent a cosmetic problem, the behavior itself in an otherwise happy child is not a sign that something is wrong with the child. The hair that is removed will eventually grow back.

In dealing with this activity, try to locate sources of tension or pressure in the child's life either at home or away from home. If a child pulls her hair only in specific situations, this can be of help in pinpointing and possibly eliminating the source of her tension. Hair-pulling that occurs on a regular basis and not under specific circumstances may indicate that a child's life is not as satisfying as it could be, or that she is experiencing a more generalized kind of tension. A constructive approach would be to attempt to make her life less pressured and more satisfying over-all. Engaging her in activities designed to foster relaxation and pleasure may help.

The child who is aware of her habit and wants to give it up but is unable to do so may be willing to pull on a substitute object such as a fuzzy cap. Wearing a fuzzy hat around the house can offer her the release of pulling on something, while at the same time preventing her from pulling her own hair. A child who is unwilling to accept a hat may be willing to pull on another object such as the hair of a doll.

Hair-pulling may simply continue in some youngsters until they are ready to give it up of their own accord. In these cases parents will have to be patient and not let their child's hair-pulling interfere with friendly parent-child relations.

HEAD-ROLLING. Head-rolling is a tension-releasing activity that may appear during the preschool stage. It involves the rhythmic rolling of the head from side to side, and is often seen at bedtime. This outlet for tension was previously discussed on page 335.

FEARS

Fears May Increase

Parents are likely to notice an increase in the number of fears their child displays during the preschool years. There are numerous factors which may account for this. The child is now more independent, and the anxiety that often accompanies her growing awareness of her new responsibilities may result in increased fears. She is more aware of her surroundings, and along with this comes a greater knowledge of potential dangers and harmful situations. As her intellectual skills increase, she will not only be more able to recognize dangers, but is likely to spend more time worrying about them. Her very active imagination will carry her into a world where make-believe figures and situations may sometimes seem real and threatening. As the child's self-awareness grows, she will be more susceptible to developing additional fears such as those related to bodily injury.

There are many possible sources of anxiety for a child during the preschool years. She will be exposed to more new people, as well as to more new situations, at home and possibly at nursery school. As a result, there will be additional opportunities for her to become anxious. More will be expected from her during the preschool years. She must, for instance, learn to control aggressive actions. Too much pressure from parents in this area or in other areas of training, such as toilet training, may contribute to a child's real and imaginary worries.

Untruths from parents may also give rise to fears. A preschool boy, for instance, who is told that he will go blind if he handles his genitals may actually believe this, and may become fearful about any matters connected with touching the genital region. Exposure to scary television programs and movies may also result in fears. These dramas can provide fertile source material for bad dreams and anxieties, and the young child may have difficulty sorting out what can really happen from what happens on the television programs that she watches. Children whose parents have been overprotective or who have not had sufficient opportunities to be around many different people may become fearful whenever they are exposed to new situations such as when they enter nursery school.

"Love conflicts" are also believed to contribute a great deal to the emergence of new fears in children. During the preschool stage, the child may become romantically attached to the parent of the opposite sex, and develop aggressive, hostile feelings toward the parent of the same sex, who stands in the way of the child's wish fulfillment. Imagining that the parent of the same sex feels the same way about her (or him), and feeling rather guilty, the child may fear retaliation or punishment from that parent. These frightening thoughts and guilt feelings may be suppressed during the day, but at night, while the child is sleeping, they may be a source for bad dreams and nightmares. This is more fully explained in Preschool 2 on pages 827–28.

Parents may do their best to protect and shield their child from overly frightening and unpleasant experiences during the next few years, but it is very likely that the child will develop some fears anyway. No parent can shield a child from imaginary or irrational fears.

Common Fears

Between the end of toddlerhood and the end of the preschool stage, changes develop in the child's fears. The number of fears that children have generally increases, the signs of fear (symptoms such as panic, crying, and trembling) tend to decline, and the kinds of fears children exhibit often change. Fears of objects, settings, or people, for instance, frequently diminish, while imaginary fears usually increase. Despite these changes, many of the fears previously mentioned in the toddlerhood Fears sections may persist or emerge during the preschool years. The remaining sections on fear will concentrate upon new fears that may develop.

Imaginary and irrational fears are quite common during the preschool years. Shadows in a child's room at night may take the form of animals, ghosts, or robbers. She may interpret the movement of the drapes in her room by the wind as being evidence of an invisible monster. This is the time when the child may fear the dark, and believe that a monster is hiding in her closet. She may also be convinced that a wild, fierce animal is camping out underneath her bed, and think that little creatures are congregating underneath her sheets.

The child who is learning to control her own unacceptable wishes, such as those to bite, destroy things, or hit people, may project these wishes onto animals, people, or monsters who haunt and come after her in her dreams. A little boy's wish to hit his father, for example, which he strains to control during the daytime, may be projected onto a tiger whose aim is to harm him in his dreams. This child may develop a fear of tigers, or may generalize this fear to include all wild animals. The dreams seem real to him. He does not recognize that they are created in his mind.

A child's attempts to control her impulses are believed to give rise to many imaginary fears. Fear of the rain or of water may be interpreted by some psychologists as representing a child's fear of wetting her pants at night, especially if her parents have been pressuring her to stay dry. The love conflicts during the later preschool years are believed to be a source of fears, especially the fear of dangerous animals. Professionals often warn that too much parental pressure on a child to control her impulses can sometimes cause the child to become very fearful. Assuming that this is correct, lessening this pressure may result in the disappearance of these fears.

Many fears seem to be related to the child's developmental stage. It is important for you to try to understand why your child is fearful, since this may be useful in helping her resolve the fear; however, it is sometimes very difficult to track down the cause of a child's fear. In such cases it may help simply to offer support, comfort, and understanding. Most imaginary fears are naturally outgrown as children grow older.

Fears related to movement of objects or even people may also emerge at this time. The child of this age tends to resist change, and may become fearful if objects are moved from their familiar spots. This may not be a good time to take your child on a long trip, or to rearrange the furniture in your home, especially the furniture in her room. The child may also be afraid of big moving objects such as trains, airplanes, busses, or moving vans.

How Children Handle Fears

Children differ not only in their level of susceptibility to fear, but also in their reactions to whatever it is that they fear. One child may tremble and shake, while another may cry and have a sinking feeling in her stomach. Every child will also have her own methods of dealing with fears on an intellectual level. The preschool child is better prepared than the toddler to utilize her intelligence and creative abilities in resolving her own fears.

It can be helpful to look briefly at some of the different ways in which a child may attempt to overcome her fears on her own. Imaginative play is one of the most useful and effective methods for some children. Terry, who was afraid of dogs, created an imaginary companion, a dog, who was very friendly and tame. With a box of raisins in hand, he "fed" his imaginary animal named Sparky. After several weeks of playing with Sparky, his fear of dogs seemed to subside. During his next encounter with a dog, he seemed more relaxed.

Having opportunities to act out frightening situations through play can help a child feel less afraid. In her play, she can control what happens, and the threat of harm to her is removed. Like Terry, who feared dogs, some children will create a likable, obedient dog who does everything that they want it to do. Others might assume the role of the dog and, in doing so, their fear of this animal may diminish.

Some children use other approaches in dealing with their fears. Brandon Etkind, for example, was very curious about how things operated. At the age of three he became fearful of having his teeth worked on at the dentist's office. The sound of the drill seemed to fill him with horror. Attempts by his parents to reassure him, prepare him in advance for what would happen at the dentist's office, and encourage him to play at being a dentist, did not seem to help.

Mr. and Mrs. Etkind finally ended up taking him on a special trip to the dentist's office between his regular check-ups, not to be examined or to have his teeth cleaned, but simply to give him an opportunity to get to know his dentist and learn about the dentist's equipment and instruments. Their understanding dentist spent a few minutes talking about the drill and showing Brandon how the drill worked. Brandon was then allowed to press the pedal which turned on the drill, and was shown how to operate the chair all by himself. Brandon was delighted and even told the dentist that on his next visit he would try to act more bravely, and he did. For some children, trying to understand events or trying to discover why things happen seems to make them feel more in control of a situation in which they previously felt helpless and afraid.

Play, imagination, experimentation, and investigation are some of the most common methods or means by which children during the preschool years may try to overcome their fears. Each child uses her own approach, the one which is most well suited to her. Knowing how your child generally handles her fears may help you understand certain aspects of her behavior that might otherwise seem puzzling or disturbing, and should offer you clues as to how you might assist her in overcoming some fears.

Helping Your Child Resolve Her Fears

Recognizing the means by which your child attempts to overcome her own fears should enable you to assist her in her efforts to resolve them. Knowing that your child enjoys day trips and is afraid of trains, you might try taking her to a museum where she will be able to see some actual trains, perhaps go inside a train, and learn something about them. Or you might take her to the library and find some books about trains to read to her. If she is more play-oriented in dealing with frightening experiences, you might encourage her to play at being a train conductor, and to play with toy trains. Another technique might involve creating a "train" with a string of cardboard boxes being the "cars," and your child being the "engine" who makes appropriate train and whistle sounds.

Supporting and encouraging your child's natural methods of dealing with frightening experiences is one of the most effective ways in which you can help her overcome fears. Developing her own inner resources to handle anxiety and fears is extremely healthy and positive from a psychological point of view.

At times, simply having you nearby may help to allay your child's fears. Your reassurance and expressions of understanding can put her at ease. Explanations as to why a fear-provoking object, person, or situation is really harmless should become increasingly useful as your child gets older. There may be times when you think that you are putting a little too much pressure on your child to control her impulses, and suspect that this is resulting in her developing fears. On such occasions, the solution is fairly obvious—lessen the pressure.

Whatever you do, try not to blame yourself if your child develops fears, because nearly all children are susceptible during the preschool years. If your child, after a reasonable period of time, does not show signs of being able to overcome a fear on her own, you will surely want to try to help her. With or without your help, most of the child's fears will automatically be outgrown as she grows older and gains in knowledge and experience. If your child's fear persists despite your efforts to help her overcome it, and becomes a strong interference in her daily life or emotional health, then you should consult her doctor.

RESPECT FOR THE ENVIRONMENT

Nature is one of the greatest gifts that we all enjoy. Yet, there is abundant evidence that many of the problems that nations are facing appear to be the result of the unnecessary pollution of the environment, the needless killing of particular species of wildlife, and the excessive waste of energy and natural resources. Young children should learn to respect their environment. If children were taught a positive appreciation and respect for nature at an early age, perhaps things would be different when they grow up.

There are many ways in which to help instill in your child an appreciation of nature and a respect for her environment. An important place to begin is by setting a good example for her to follow. Rather than letting the water run for several minutes while you brush your teeth, show her that you are opposed to wasting this essential resource. Turn it on only to wet your brush, and then shut it off. When you are through brushing, turn it on again, only for a brief period of time to rinse out your mouth. Show her how to do the same when she brushes her teeth.

Saving water while brushing your teeth may seem like a trite example in teaching conservation, but it is the type of lesson that is easy for your child to understand. The preschool child learns well from simple explanations that are related to her daily activities and experiences. Learning about conservation in her simple daily activities will make it easier for her to understand your message.

To help make her daughter aware of the importance of not wasting natural resources, Mrs. Sarason came up with another idea. Her four-year-old daughter, Nancy, happened to be finicky about the foods she would and would not eat. Whenever Mrs. Sarason cooked mashed potatoes or french fries for dinner, Nancy would insist upon having a baked potato instead.

For a long time Mrs. Sarason catered to Nancy's wishes, and put a single baked potato in the oven for her, but this mother became concerned and irritated about the fact that lighting the oven for only one baked potato was a terrible waste of energy, in this case natural gas. She finally explained this to Nancy, and told her that in many parts of the world natural gas is scarce. Mrs. Sarason went on to say that if everyone did not stop wasting gas, some people might not have enough gas to heat their homes and stay warm in the wintertime. She asked Nancy to remember how cold it had been the previous winter and pointed out how terrible it would be not to have heat in cold weather. Nancy listened carefully to what her mother said, and seemed interested in learning more ways in which she could help conserve energy. The next time her mother prepared potatoes that were not baked, Nancy did not insist that a single potato be put in the oven for her, and explained to her family that she was saving gas.

This parent's approach to helping her preschooler learn the value of conserving natural resources was very good. Rather than speaking in generalities, she related her discussion to her daughter's own experiences, and pointed out how much their family depended upon natural gas.

Encouraging your child to respect the environment might also include teaching her not to litter. One afternoon while fishing off the shore, Mr. Quincy saw his little boy, Travers, who loved the sand, throw a candy bar wrapper onto the beach. Mr. Quincy adamantly pointed out to Travers that he had littered, that this was not acceptable behavior, and that litter should only be placed in the proper receptacles for that purpose. This father then told Travers that if everyone constantly dropped candy wrappers and other litter onto the beach, he would no longer be able to play there. This seemed to hit close to home, and, according to Mr. Quincy, Travers began eagerly to pick up other food wrappers and empty cans and deposit them into the appropriate nearby garbage cans. If everyone, parent and child, made a conscious effort not to litter, and to pick up others' litter, our environment would surely be cleaner and safer.

A child who develops an appreciation for nature will undoubtedly have a greater respect for it. There are numerous ways in which to introduce your child to the joys of nature. Camping trips, fishing trips, hiking trips, and even back yard nature walks can help your child learn what nature is all about. You can encourage your child to smell the flowers, handle the rocks that she finds, feel the damp ground, and breathe the clean air. Some children like to collect rocks, sea shells, or leaves on these outings. Many youngsters like listening to stories about nature and looking at picture books of flowers, insects, or trees.

You should help your child learn about nature's gifts. During the course of day-to-day living, you will come across many opportunities to encourage her to enjoy the marvels of nature and appreciate what nature has done for her. If you take an interest in teaching your child to respect the environment, we will benefit from the lessons that she learns.

FAMILY HERITAGE

Growing up with a strong family base and some knowledge of one's family background provides a child with a wonderful and very basic early sense of security, self-esteem, and uniqueness that she will carry with her throughout life. Family contacts may not always be strong and closely knit. When family members are spread out across the country, and even when relatives live in the same town, children very often never really have an opportunity to get to know their grandparents, aunts, uncles, and cousins. A surprising number of adults have no idea of the names of their cousins, where their grandparents or great-grandparents came from, or where their families originated. Growing up with a real feeling of belonging to a continuing family structure can enrich a person's life.

One way to provide your child with a knowledge of the family is, if possible, to allow her to spend time with her grandparents or other older relatives. The love and emotional attachments of a grandparent for a grandchild and vice versa are a wonderful asset. During their times together she can ask her grandparents many questions about what their lives were like, where they grew up, and who their parents were, or they may spontaneously offer this information. Grandparents frequently enjoy teaching their grandchildren many skills and useful practical tips that parents themselves may not be able to provide for their children.

Arrange for family celebrations, picnics, and informal get-togethers in which children are included. These gatherings will present marvelous opportunities for your child to get to know who her relatives are, and what they are like. It is unfortunate that many family members never really get to know one another, and only gather on sad occasions in hospital rooms or funeral parlors.

Another thing you can do is to pass on to your child family traditions or heirlooms. Perhaps there is a certain simple song, prayer, or saying that your grandmother taught to you when you were young that you would like to pass on to your child. Or you may have some old clothes, a locket, or a tie clasp that belonged to a family member who has passed away. Chances are that your child will treasure such heirlooms, and enjoy hearing about the persons to whom they previously belonged. When you use old family recipes to cook particular traditional foods on religious holidays, be sure to let your child know their origins.

Preschool children love to hear stories about people in past generations and faraway places. Many parents tell their youngsters stories in which they trace their family backgrounds as far back as they themselves are aware. A common mistake that parents often make is feeling that their own backgrounds are not interesting enough or important enough to talk about with their child. Simply because a family is not wealthy or has not attained national prominence does not mean it has not had an important role in society. The real building blocks of most nations are the people who work hard on a daily basis to provide a better life and future for their children.

Rebecca came from a very poor immigrant family. Her parents took great pride in telling her how her great-grandparents risked the dangerous ocean crossing to start a new life in this land. They then described how the grandparents worked long and hard hours just to provide their family with food and shelter. Rebecca was fascinated with the stories of what life was like at earlier times. She especially liked to hear these stories from her grandparents, and would often ask questions and become excited when they shared even seemingly trivial details with her.

It is not important what your family has done, or where they originated. Preschool children often derive great pleasure from hearing about their family and heritage. This can often fortify the child's sense of self-pride and self-identity.

VIOLENCE ON THE SCREEN

It is becoming more and more difficult to ignore the fact that the world of violence is abundantly depicted on the television and movie screens. One need attend only a few movies or tune in on one night's television programs to see bloody, violent scenes depicting armed robbery, muggings, rape, and murder. Even cartoons for children often have more than their fair share of violence.

Whether or not a young child should be exposed to this is a controversial issue.

One point of view, held by both parents and professionals, is that the more violence a child sees on television, the more accepting of it she will become, and that a child who accepts violence will be more prone toward violent actions. Young children often imitate many adults to whom they are exposed. Watching superheroes on the screen consistently commit violent actions may result in children's behaving more violently as well. Children for whom television is used as a major source of entertainment frequently emulate these role models, and have little incentive to block hostile, aggressive actions toward other people.

Another point of view is that children's exposure to mild violence on the screen does not really determine whether or not they will be more or less accepting of and prone toward violent actions. According to some professionals and parents, children are not as easily influenced by the fantasy situations depicting violent actions on the screen, and merely enjoy watching these particular cartoon, Western, and detective shows because they love action. These people claim that whether or not a child has difficulty controlling violent impulses has a great deal more to do with how her parents behave and what kind of training they offer her than what she sees on the screen. Rather than blaming violence on the screen for children's violent actions, they blame parents for not providing proper non-violent role models for their youngsters to emulate, and not giving adequate training in self-control.

No matter which point of view you suscribe to, it is important to consider carefully what programs or movies you allow your young children to see. Even people who control the media are realizing that many programs in which violence is depicted may not be suitable for young children. At the beginning of such programs there are warnings to parents indicating that the material about to be shown may not be suitable for young children to hear and observe.

The ultimate decision about whether or not to allow your child to see certain movies or shows is yours, but you should heed network warnings and ratings of movies. Moderation and good common sense appear to be the most advisable approach. The most important thing to understand is how a child's mind functions in relation to what she sees and hears on the screen, so that you can more easily and intelligently interpret her reactions, form your own opinions, and establish healthy guidelines.

Your preschool child views violence on the screen differently from an older child or teen-ager. This is partly because of her limited experience. She does not analyze and look at what she sees and hears with an adult frame of reference. When watching a television program about a bank robbery, she does not realize that the bank robber's behavior is socially unacceptable, or that it is the exception, rather than the rule. Her knowledge of people and right versus wrong is not sufficiently well developed for her to sit back and say to herself that robbing a bank is very bad, and not an acceptable way of behaving. Her ability to sort out what she sees on the screen from what she knows is real from her own range of experience is limited. This is why she may sometimes get confused and frightened about what she sees on television or at the movies. Your youngster is much more vulnerable than you are to the violence she sees on the screen.

Realizing this, you will undoubtedly want to pay attention to her reactions to movies and the programs she watches on television. Children, like adults, react differently to what they see and hear. After seeing a particularly violent scene portrayed on television, one child may develop related fears and nightmares, while the next child may not be affected in the least. One child may emulate the role of the good guy while the next may imitate that of the bad guy. Carefully observe your child's responses to violence on the screen, and try to determine what effect, if any, it is having upon her.

Do not hesitate to exercise your authority as a parent in controlling the kind and amount of programs and movies that you permit your child to watch. Some parents are so afraid of the possibility of antagonizing their child that they go against their own instincts and better judgment and let her watch whatever she pleases. This is a mistake, and one which may ultimately have a detrimental effect upon the child's personality. A constant diet of violence on the screen may undermine the very morals, values, and behaviors that you are undoubtedly trying hard to shape in your child. Therefore, be discriminating in what programs and movies you allow your child to watch.

HAPPINESS IS GETTING SOME TIME OUT FROM CHILD CARE

Some parents find it hard to admit to others that their child is growing more difficult to handle. Perhaps part of the reason for this is that they do not want to let other people know that they do not exactly fit the image of the parent as always calm and patient, and overflowing with understanding. It is doubtful that there is a single parent who could fit this picture, so there is really no reason to keep feelings and troubles bottled up inside.

Caring for your child at this phase may be more demanding a job than it has been in the past. Her greater ability to assert her likes and dislikes, her desire to voice her independence, and her demands for your time, energy, and attention can make living with her rather trying. This is the phase when parents often long to be alone for a getaway weekend, or even to have just half an hour a day all to themselves. Parents should not hesitate to admit that they need some freedom from the responsibility of child care.

Dealing full time with the child's "no's," temper tantrums, and demands can challenge even the most tolerant person's patience, and can be both physically and emotionally draining. If the child could talk well and understand more of what you say, as well as more about how you feel, this might ease some of the pressure and tension that can really escalate after several hours with her. Unfortunately, she probably cannot.

Talk to your spouse or friends, and voice your complaints and feelings. Every parent has the right to complain, and to seek support from others, particularly when his or her child's behavior becomes very bothersome. Also take advantage of baby-sitters, parents' baby-sitting exchanges, or neighborhood play groups to take some of the burden of caring for your child off your shoulders in the event that you are having a difficult time going it alone.

Seeing to it that your own needs as an individual are satisfied along with your child's will make your role of parent more enjoyable. Self-sacrificing parents who completely deny their own needs to cater to their child's are not doing either themselves or her a favor. It is important to achieve a healthy balance in the family structure so that parent and child are both happy as individuals, and as family members.

BEGINNING OR RETURNING TO WORK OUTSIDE THE HOME

Whether for economic reasons, personal fulfillment, or the need for more freedom from the responsibility of child care, some parents will either begin or return to work outside the home during the preschool years. Many of the special considerations involved in supplementing child care with a job outside the home were previously explored on pages 559–62, but there are some new considerations that often arise during this stage that should be examined.

Separations Are Often Easier on Both Parent and Child

Preschoolers, particularly during phases 2 and 3, are much better prepared to cope with temporary separations from their parents than toddlers. They have acquired greater independence and social skills that enable them to develop interests and relationships outside the immediate family setting. In many ways it is much easier on both parent and child to be apart for periods of time each day than it was in previous stages.

Parents making the decision to work during the preschool years receive less overt or subtle pressure from family members to remain at home with their child. This, coupled with the knowledge that their child is better able to adjust to separations, works to eliminate some of the guilt that they might have previously felt about leaving her. In cases in which parents have a choice as to whether or not to work, it would still be important to weigh both their own individual needs as well as their child's special needs to determine if working is the right or best approach for them and the entire family.

Many preschool children adapt very well to temporary absences from their parents, and parents often notice their youngsters becoming more self-sufficient as a result. When both parent and child are able to make a positive adjustment to separations, their over-all relationship may be enhanced, and the time that they do spend together may seem more precious as well as enjoyable. Of primary importance is to take into account both your own and your preschooler's needs, and then determine how each can be simultaneously satisfied.

Some Children Still Find Separations Difficult

There are some preschool children who will still have difficulty with separations from their parent. Not all children are able to react adaptively to their parent's absences at age three or even at four or five. There is no exact age at which a child develops the ability to deal effectively with separations. Some youngsters handle them quite well at an early age, while others simply require more time.

Preschoolers are better equipped than toddlers to express verbally the negative feelings they may have about their parent's decision to begin or return to work. They may verbalize their anger or resentment. A child who resents her parent's leaving her may employ guilt-inducing tactics, sometimes sufficient to cause her parent to give up the notion of leaving and remain at home.

In some cases children have justifiable reasons for wanting their parent to stay with them. Following major upsets within the family structure, such as separation, divorce, death, a move to a new residence, or the entry of a new baby into the family, it may be advisable to delay a decision to seek employment outside the home until your child has had ample time to make a satisfactory adjustment. The child needs extra emotional support from you during these difficult times.

It is important to observe your child's responses to your absences from the home. Watch for possible signs of loss of appetite, depression, acting out, or increased insecurity and fear. These symptoms can indicate genuine difficulties and a real need on the child's part for closer contact with her parent.

Part-time or Full-time Employment

Those parents who have a choice as to whether to work part time or full time often wonder which alternative to select. No one is in a better position to weigh the alternatives than you are. Lengthier separations are likely to be easier upon preschoolers than toddlers, but a great deal depends upon how strong your needs are to work full time, and how well you feel that your child will adapt.

Parents who are considering full-time employment, but have reservations about what effect this would have upon their youngster might, if possible, want to return to work gradually. Begin on a part-time basis and see how it goes. Should both you and your child adapt well to being apart, then you could try increasing your work hours to build up to a full-time job eventually.

Another alternative is to try to arrange your work schedule around your child's activities away from home. In situations in which a child attends nursery school three mornings or afternoons a week, it might be possible for her parent to adjust his or her schedule to work when she is gone from the home.

Parents who have little choice but to work full time may be able to arrange their work schedules to have occasional lunches with their child, if lengthy separations are difficult for her. Even a phone call or two during the day can help to reassure a child and bridge the loneliness sometimes imposed by a parent's full-time employment outside the home. See also pages 560–61 where part-week versus part-day employment was considered.

Alternatives for Child Care in Your Absence

The alternatives available for child care arrangements while you work are basically very similar to those explored during infancy (pages 636–39). One option that is now probably more viable because your child is older is to enroll her in a nursery school or preschool. The topic of nursery school is more fully discussed on pages 814–18.

There may also be some special classes for preschoolers offered in your community built around play activities, learning to swim, early gymnastics training, and so forth. Some require a parent's presence, but others do not. You may want to investigate this avenue for part-time child care, if a part-time work schedule can be arranged to coincide with the hours during which your child would attend such classes.

Feel free to find and work out your own child care arrangements if those available in your community do not appear to be well suited to your needs and those of your child. Whatever arrangements you make, try to be sure that she is happy, well cared for, stimulated, and safe in your absence. You will feel more comfortable and relaxed in the knowledge that you have made proper arrangements for her care.

Preparing Your Preschooler for the Separation from You

Just as it was during toddlerhood, it is very important to prepare your preschooler in advance for any necessary separations from you. This can make adjusting to the time spent apart from one another somewhat easier on her. Preschoolers are much more capable of understanding verbal explanations than toddlers. The explanation that you offer should definitely take this into account. Also realize that a Preschool 3 child will want more information than a Preschool 1 child.

Most often, children are interested in concrete facts about what changes will occur as a result of their parent's decision to work. It is advisable to talk to your child about what you will be doing, where you will be working, how long you will be gone, your work schedule, who will care for her in your absence, and so forth. Give her ample time to express her feelings and ask questions. Do not be surprised if your older preschooler wants to know such things as where you will eat lunch, and other details that you consider trivial. Give simple honest answers that satisfy her curiosity.

Top on your list of priorities should be to convey the message that you love her, are not abandoning her, and that you will be thinking of her whenever the two of you are apart. This reassurance and reconfirmation of your love along with concrete facts should help to put her mind at ease. In informing her of the impending changes in both of your lifestyles, try to be confident and cheerful. A sad or guilty expression on your face may arouse her worry and concern when the purpose of your discussion is to put her at ease. If she does seem upset over your decision, let her express her anger or concerns without passing judgment. There is nothing wrong with telling her that she might feel uneasy about the changes at first, but that chances are that these feelings will subside once she has adjusted to the new situation.

After giving your child an explanation, you might find it helpful to suggest an excursion to the office or place where you will be working. Following her verbal explanation, Sheila Krenshaw asked her son, Craig, if he would like to see the place where she would be working. He nodded "yes." Sheila had previously decided that it might be reassuring for Craig to see where she would be when they were apart. In consideration of his feelings, she had hung two pictures that he had painted on the bulletin board and placed a framed photograph of him on her desk.

When Craig and she entered her office, his attention was immediately drawn to his paintings and picture. It was apparent from the expression on his face that he was delighted and also reassured. Sheila made a point of showing her son the phone on her desk, and told him that she could call home to talk to him from time to time.

This mother's approach to preparing her preschooler was quite successful in alleviating some of his anxieties about their separation. In her own way, Sheila had made it clear to her son that he was loved and would be in his mother's thoughts when they were apart. The importance of getting this message across to your child cannot be overemphasized.

Feeling secure in your love will make coping with your absences much easier for your child. It will be up to you to determine exactly what to say to your youngster and how to prepare her, but remember that your attitude will play a far more important role than your words.

STEPPARENTHOOD DURING THE PRESCHOOL YEARS

When someone marries a widowed or divorced person with a preschooler, he or she becomes a stepparent to the youngster. The general discussions about assuming the role of a stepparent previously presented in the Preparing for Parenthood section on pages 14–22 should be of assistance to prospective or new stepparents of preschool children. The young preschool child's reactions to a stepparent are similar to the toddler's, and stepparents should benefit from reading the material on Stepparenthood During Toddlerhood found on pages 556–59. On the other hand, the older preschool child has had more time to cement relationships within her family. She has also had more experience, and has a much better ability to comprehend the new events and changes in her life. These factors, along with her ability to speak and ask questions, will all play a role in her response and require the stepparent to be responsive to the child's special needs.

The preschool child, much more so than the toddler, is likely to be disturbed by having a new parent and show greater resistance to this person. The feelings of resentment, jealousy, and fear that she may have about her stepparent, which were discussed in toddlerhood, are often more intensely experienced by the preschooler, and can now be verbalized. For example, a child who fears that she will lose her natural parent once the stepparent arrives or who feels a strong sense of rejection may ask her parent over and over again, "Do you really love me?" or beg her parent not to leave her alone.

Having had more time to form stronger attachments to her natural parent(s), the preschool child is apt to be more resentful of her stepparent, whom she may not be willing to accept as a substitute for the real parent. If the parent's departure was a painful experience, and the child cannot fully accept the fact that the parent is not returning, a stepparent can represent a threat. Loyalty issues are often difficult for the preschooler to handle. Being nice to her stepparent may be hard for the child since she may feel that this represents an act of disloyalty to the natural parent or to the parent's memory. Thus, she may also feel that accepting the new parent may require her to break the bonds with her original parent.

Bear in mind that the preschool child may harbor the childish dream of her absent parent's returning and being reunited with her other parent, even in the case in which a parent has died. The hopes of this dream coming true must be put aside once the new stepparent is accepted. This can be a difficult and very upsetting realization for the child.

A young child who is very upset about having a new parent may express this verbally, or through other avenues. She may, for example, stage temper outbursts, cry, become overanxious and withdrawn, deliberately misbehave or engage in destructive behavior, or act up at nursery school. She may also return to soiling or wetting her pants, have frequent nightmares, and rely heavily upon outlets for releasing tension that have been previously outgrown. Both parents should be on the lookout for signs that indicate the child is having adjustment problems or deep inner conflicts, and do their best to help alleviate them. Should this not prove fruitful, it may be necessary to seek guidance from a professional.

It is usually not a case of immediate love and acceptance for either the child or the stepparent. The stepparent should realize that there will be an adjustment period before a new family can achieve a certain stability. In the meantime, both parent and child will have to get to know and understand each other. There will be a good deal of testing and family ups and downs in the process. In time, many of the initial obstacles encountered in the relationship may gradually be reduced or overcome.

The period of adjustment can be stressful for all members of the family, but it represents a time for exploring each other's feelings and emotions, both positive and negative, and each other's likes and dislikes, as well as different ways of doing things. There are some ways in which a stepparent can handle things during the early stages that may make the adjustments and transition easier on the child.

A prospective or new stepparent, for instance, might be able to learn a great deal about the child's special ways by talking with her doctor, regular baby-sitter, or teachers at nursery school. These care-givers can often provide important information about the child that will add to that which the new spouse offers. It is also helpful to learn as much as possible about the child's phase or stage of development before meeting her or assuming responsibility for her care. This is particularly important for stepparents who have never been parents before.

It is advisable to prepare the child very gradually during the dating period for the introduction of a new parent into the family. The child's natural parent can explain his or her need for companionship and love from another adult, just as the child needs to make friends with other children.

A child should be told about her parent's plans for remarriage as soon as the final decision has been made. It would be terribly hard if she found out about these plans from someone other than her parent, or if her parent made a quick announcement without adequate advanced preparation and explanation. It is important to allow the child to ask questions, and to provide her with answers that satisfy her curiosity.

The child who maintains a good relationship with the natural parent who does not live with her may be particularly confused by the prospect of having two mommies (or daddies). Simple explanations should be given to help her realize that it is possible to grow to love and care for different people in different ways, and that although her natural mother (or father) and her "at home" mother or father are different, it is okay to love both of them, and her natural or *real* mother will always remain so. The child may need help in understanding that by liking or loving her stepparent, she is not being unfair or disloyal to the absent natural parent. From time to time parents may have to offer more detailed explanations or repeat the initial explanations, since the child may forget them and is bound to want more information as she grows older.

The child will surely have some questions about how to address her stepparent. Both the child's and stepparent's feelings should be considered in this regard. The discussion on page 20 about how a stepparent should be addressed should be of assistance.

A natural parent who tries to pressure the child to like his or her new companion often finds that this approach backfires. The same holds true for the future or new stepparent who, in an attempt to win the child over right away or make friends quickly, goes overboard in physical shows of affection and/or gift-giving. Children are often overwhelmed and confused by such well-intentioned efforts from a relative stranger. They may feel threatened by this, and may even turn down these advances or presents, leaving the stepparent feeling hurt.

It is of the utmost importance to proceed slowly. Genuine offers of friendship and caring from a future or new stepparent can and should be given, but it's best to follow the child's lead. Give her ample time to size up and get to know her stepparent well.

A stepparent must be patient with his or her stepchild. Should the child show jealousy, resentment, or open hostility toward the stepparent he or she should try not to overreact. When the child's negative attitude or actions make a stepparent withdraw from further attempts to love her, or respond with rejection, this can only make matters worse. It is far better to try to determine reasons for the child's reactions or the motives underlying her behavior, and be sensitive to her needs and feelings. Bear in mind that some stepparents represent a scapegoat for a child. Rather than expressing anger at a natural parent or herself, she may project this onto her stepparent. Although this can be very hard upon a stepparent, there is no easy solution to this problem. The stepparent's continued extensions of interest and friendship over a period of time will reduce the child's anger and enable her to outgrow the need to use the stepparent as a scapegoat. Eventually, the child will learn to accept the stepparent, and will realize that her natural parent has room in his or her heart for her as well as her stepparent.

Discipline tends to be a sensitive area for both stepparent and stepchild. The stepparent who suddenly enters the family and quickly begins to set limits and discipline the child is likely to be in for some very rough times. The child may resent a relative stranger telling her how to behave and may react with open defiance. She is also likely to do a lot of testing of her stepparent's limits. Even though a stepparent should assume some parental responsibilities, it is advisable to go slowly and cautiously on matters of discipline. In the early stages of the relationship, it is often wise to allow the child's natural parent to assume the greater responsibility for discipline, at least until the child has had ample time to adjust to the new living arrangement and the idea of having another parent. During the adjustment period, the stepparent can try to understand the child's special feelings, moods, and behavior patterns. With a more sophisticated awareness of the child, discipline is apt to be somewhat easier.

Occasionally a child will make a statement such as, "You can't tell me what to do. You're not my *real* parent," or, "Mommy didn't make me do that." However, it is important for a stepparent not to be intimidated by such remarks. An appropriate reply might be something like, "You're right that I'm not your original parent, but I'm your parent *now*. Everybody likes to do things differently, and this is the way I want to do this." Even though children are entitled to their angry feelings about their stepparent or his or her rules and requests, a stepparent should still expect youngsters to stay within the boundaries that he or she and the spouse have established.

Stepparents should also be cautioned against making too many changes at once in other areas besides discipline. A child is likely to be quite upset over sudden shifts in routine, diet, wardrobe, and living quarters. It is advisable to allow the child to continue with her familiar patterns of living at least for a while, since they can offer her comfort and a sense of security at a time when major life changes are occurring.

It is wise to be considerate of the child's feelings when parent and stepparent display physical affection toward one another in front of her. Preschool children often feel very uneasy seeing their parents kissing and embracing, particularly when there are sexual overtones to this behavior. The preschool child, trying to work through the fantasy of having the opposite sex parent all to herself (himself), may be very possessive about that parent, and feel rejected and threatened by the parent's physical involvement with another adult. Conflicting emotions and even guilt feelings may be aroused in the child at the sight of such displays of affection, particularly when a stepparent is involved.

Children need to know that they cannot have the opposite sex parent to themselves, and that the kind of love parents share is different from the love between parent and child. However, in deference to their feelings, it may be advisable for parents to go easy on physical embraces, etc., in the child's presence, at least until she has had time to adjust to sharing the natural parent's affection with a third party.

It is also important to understand that the child may regard her natural parent's sleeping with her new stepparent as an assault to the memory of the parent she has lost, or as an act of disloyalty to the natural parent who is no longer living in the home. In general, parents should try to be somewhat discreet, especially during the adjustment period. Some simple explanations and reassurance may be necessary, if the child seems very upset.

Even though a stepparent may receive resistance from the preschool child, very often youngsters are glad to have an intact or complete family once again, and need the security, love, and guidance that their stepparent can provide. Given ample time, most children will be able to make a healthy adjustment. The stepparent's continuous offers of friendship, trust, and understanding will be instrumental in enabling the child to regard him or her as not just a parent, but also a close friend.

HOW TO PROVIDE A SOUND EDUCATION FOR YOUR CHILD

Between the ages of two and a half to five, when the child's curiosity and desire to understand the world around her are strong, and her ability to absorb information increases, the possibilities for educating her expand far beyond those in toddlerhood. You should be able to provide your child with a sound, total education that will help her make the most of her potential during the time when she will be particularly receptive and sensitive to learning.

One of the problems with educational guidelines is that some parents take them too literally and feel that unless they follow every activity exactly as suggested, they are doing wrong by their children. Their approach to their children becomes artificial and they do not relax. They become preoccupied with teaching their children, but really do not enjoy them. It is hoped that the material that follows will stimulate your imagination and interest in helping your child learn without making you overly self-conscious. Bear in mind that you don't have to do something with your child every minute to be a good parent.

Having the opportunity to take part in your child's education, and to watch her develop, should bring you satisfaction and should greatly enrich the unique relationship that you share. Those of you who are fortunate enough to be able to take advantage of this challenging opportunity to be involved in your preschooler's education will want to make the most of it.

This section, which applies to the entire preschool stage, offers you a basic framework which can be modified in formulating your own educational program to best suit your child's individual needs, interests, and ability. Some of the activities are more appropriate for the younger preschool child, and others should be introduced during Preschool 2 or 3. Use your own good judgment about when to introduce activities and experiences, taking your lead from your child.

How to Be an Effective Teacher

In order to help your child achieve important educational goals, and develop to her fullest potential, she will need a teacher. You need not have a college degree or certification as an educator in early childhood to be a good teacher. Many, if not most, parents make the best teachers for their preschool children because they love them and have their best interests at heart. They have experience, know their child better than anyone else, and can offer their child individualized attention as well as immediate feedback as to how she is doing. Teaching your child at home makes it possible for her to learn in a relaxed, informal, and familiar atmosphere. Furthermore, since you have established a positive relationship with her, she will be very anxious to imitate you and will learn a great deal by following your example.

Some parents decide that they are not well qualified to be solely responsible for their child's education. Perhaps this is because they are tied down with caring for other children in the home, have to work, or have other pressing responsibilities, leaving them with little time to devote to their child's education except during some evenings and on weekends. They may consider themselves too impatient, and not dedicated or enthusiastic enough to assume the responsibility for their child's education. During this phase, nevertheless, your child will be learning very basic principles, and you can be an excellent teacher for her.

Whether you consciously plan to be your child's main teacher or not, you will still play a large role in educating her. During the time that you spend with her, even if it is only a few hours during the evenings, or several hours each weekend, you will be helping her learn many things, partly by the example you set, and partly through your natural, enjoyable interactions with her. Even if her social sphere is broadening, and she has another teacher, she is still closely tied to you and to her home. What your child will be learning from another teacher will simply serve as a supplement to what she will be learning from you during the time you spend together.

Given the role that you will be assuming in helping your preschooler learn, you should be aware of some of the basic guidelines for teaching. Familiarity with them should be quite useful to you in helping her get the most enjoyment and learning out of her early years.

LET YOUR CHILD LEARN WITH REAL OBJECTS. Children seem to learn best when they are given opportunities to work with actual objects in their environment. This includes objects that can be seen, heard, touched, and so forth. You can spend an hour telling a child how to make a bed, but if she cannot see the bed and the bedspread in front of her, and does not have a chance to practice working with the sheets and bedspread, chances are that your attempts to teach will not be as effective as they could be. By allowing your child to work with actual things, she will gradually and naturally progress to making associations about those things, and formulating her own abstract concepts about them. Let her abstract thinking, limited as it may be as compared to an adult's, come from her own everyday experiences in interacting with her surroundings.

PERMIT YOUR PRESCHOOLER TO DISCOVER THINGS ON HER OWN AND PARTICIPATE IN HER OWN EDUCATION. Whenever possible, allow your child to discover things on her own. You can constantly offer information and train her to memorize facts, but she will derive more pleasure and will probably remember what she has learned for longer periods of time when allowed to find things out for herself. This is not to imply that you should leave her on her own all day and not interfere. Rather, you can gently guide and encourage her in the direction of certain activities that will allow her to discover things by and for herself. The aim is to let her do, accomplish, and learn as much as she can on her own so that she will be actively involved in her own educational process. After all, a person will not become an independent, original, and imaginative thinker if she does not learn how to learn, and is not given opportunities to be independent.

In deciding what learning tools, activities, and demonstrations to introduce, it is advisable to let your preschooler's needs, interests, and abilities guide you. Always try to be patient with her, and custom-make learning experiences so that they are well suited to her. Let her educate herself at her own pace, and in her own style. There should be no rush, and very little pressure.

Make her as happy, comfortable, and relaxed as you can. Let her know that you are enthusiastic about learning, and about helping her learn. Help her to understand that mistakes are inevitable, and it is possible to learn from one's errors. Above all, remember that no two children develop or learn in exactly the same way. Respecting her individual strengths and weaknesses is very important.

STRUCTURE AND ORDER WITHIN A CONTEXT OF FREEDOM. Be aware that she should develop an awareness of order, timing, and routine. Try to assist her in establishing good work as well as living habits, and help her to realize the value of finishing a project that she starts, to the best of her ability. She should be learning that there is a proper way to go about each task that she undertakes.

Within certain routine and stable activities, allow her some freedom of choice as to what she would like to do and to learn. Respect her interests and do your best to encourage and support them. Children usually reap more enjoyment from learning when certain structured educational experiences are offered in a relaxed atmosphere of freedom and personal choice.

KEEPING YOUR CHILD STIMULATED. Two of the main things to guard against are boring your child and allowing her regularly to undertake and fail at tasks that are too difficult and complex. You can avoid boring her by watching her closely. Should she show any signs of boredom, restlessness, or fatigue during your educational efforts or demonstrations, discontinue them. Also make sure that you have a wide enough variety of stimulating learning materials, playthings, equipment, and activities so that you can easily make shifts when necessary. Remember that certain activities and playthings that you think are interesting may bore her and vice versa.

PROCEED WITH HER EDUCATION ONE STEP AT A TIME. A child who regularly fails at tasks soon feels inferior and incompetent and can grow disinterested in learning. The idea is to "turn your child on" to learning, not to "turn her off" to it. In teaching her, it is a good idea to go from simple to complex. Break each task down into small, manageable, successive steps. Introduce her to the first step, and allow her to have as much time as she needs to practice it. Only after she has mastered the first step should you introduce the next one.

Dividing a complex task into its component parts, and letting your child proceed one step at a time, will enable her to experience success at each step along the way. This approach to teaching fosters a good self-image. Receiving positive feedback after each step will motivate her to continue, and instill in her the ideas that she is competent and that learning is fun.

Bear in mind that occasional failure is inevitable. Do not try to protect your child from ever failing to accomplish a task. When she fails, let her know that you still love her, and everyone, even you, cannot do everything right all of the time. Try to turn a negative experience into a positive one by helping her learn from mistakes. Continual failure can undermine a child's self-esteem, but occasional failure can strengthen her self-awareness by giving her a better notion of the boundaries of her abilities.

A GOOD LEARNING ENVIRONMENT

Your preschooler's learning environment should nourish her development and suit her needs. She should have access to all different kinds of safe learning materials that will promote her development in all areas. Examples of such materials are described in the Learning Through Play sections in Preschool 1–3. The learning environment should also provide access to various community resources, including the public library, the zoo, and other places of interest to young children such as those outlined on pages 792–93.

Adequate space is another criterion for a proper learning environment. Your child needs plenty of space in which to run, move, and explore, not just indoors but also outdoors. Some of this should be open or unstructured space. Other areas should be designated for different types of play and learning experiences. There might be one corner of a room for dramatic play, one for block construction, and another for arts and crafts. A fourth corner could be designed for music activities or books and puzzles. To ensure that she has complete access to all learning materials, equipment and furnishings should be suited to her proportions and her size.

Finally, your child's learning environment should provide her with ample opportunities to play with and learn from other children her age, and sometimes even older or younger children. This will be instrumental in enabling her to develop the social skills necessary to deal with her peers, to form friendships with some of them, and to learn to respect other people and their differences. You can provide an excellent learning environment in your own home or apartment with little or no expense.

TEACHING RESPECT FOR OTHER PEOPLE AND THEIR DIFFERENCES

The child's attitudes toward other people are shaped at a very early age. Now is the time when your child will be growing more aware of other people and their differences. You will play a very important role in shaping your child's attitudes toward other people, and it is hoped that you are teaching her a healthy respect for all people and their differences (see pages 935–37).

TEACHING RESPECT FOR THE ENVIRONMENT

Your preschool child can learn to respect her environment, and you will be instrumental in teaching her. Helping her acquire an appreciation for nature is one way to do this. Try to help your older preschooler learn something about natural resources, wildlife reserves, energy conservation, air pollution, and water pollution. Also try to impress upon her the fact that every person has a responsibility to herself and to others to respect the environment (see pages 774–75). Nature study for the young is one activity that comes to mind that would provide learning opportunities and an appreciation for nature at the same time.

HOW TO STIMULATE YOUR CHILD'S MIND

Encouraging Curiosity

During the preschool years there will be a steady, remarkable increase in your child's ability to speak and manipulate ideas in her mind. Early in the preschool phase, her curiosity about the world around her will be aimed mainly at exploring objects and the environment in general. Later, at three and a half to four, it will be directed at trying to understand "why" things happen. Her active mind and curiosity will prompt her to seek answers, and try to discover solutions to problems. She may often come to you for help, asking "why" questions.

When your child approaches you with questions, it is important for you to try your best to answer her immediately, and not put her off. Questions reflect her curiosity, and they provide you with perfect opportunities to give her your own, more sophisticated ideas about various subjects. Offering her explanations is extremely important for mental growth, so make a good effort to pass your knowledge and ideas on to her.

Helping Your Child Learn How to Solve Problems

Your explanations will be of enormous help to your child in understanding and interpreting her experiences, but whenever possible, encourage her to discover things on her own. Helping her learn how to learn and how to seek answers to problems and questions will be of greater value to her in the long run than simply feeding her answers and factual information. In the event that she comes to you wanting to know why the rock she found in the playground will not float in her wading pool, you could just offer her a simple answer. This simple answer to the question will probably satisfy her curiosity, although it will do nothing to help her learn how to learn.

Why not occasionally encourage your Preschool 2 or 3 child to pretend that she is an explorer trying to seek an answer to a problem? The Preschool 1 child will not be doing much in the way of investigation, but the older preschool child is likely to enjoy making believe that she is about to make a new discovery, with a little help from you.

You can first determine with your youngster what question she is going to try to answer. Then think of an experiment or several activities to provide information about the subject. In the case of the rock that will not float, you could have her gather all kinds of objects, such as a leaf, an apple, a sponge, a small block of wood, a plastic measuring cup, and a metal spoon. Next fill her bathtub up with water, and allow her to experiment and discover for herself which objects float, and which objects sink.

As your youngster tests each object, you can jot down the information in a notebook. This will help her learn that keeping records of her findings is an important aspect of investigation. When she has completed her experiment, you can ask her to put all of the objects that float into one pile, and all of those that sink into another. Then encourage her to observe carefully the differences in the objects in the respective piles. Finally, together, you can help her draw conclusions, and find the answer to the initial question.

Do not expect your preschooler to comprehend fully the reasons why certain objects float and others cannot, but she can learn that some objects do not float because they are not supported by the water. Of even greater significance than her learning the actual answer to a problem is that by helping her plan, set up, and carry out several activities, she will be learning how to approach questions and attempt to find solutions to problems.

A person does not have to have all of the facts and answers crammed in her brain in order to show intelligence. Rather, a person should be aware of how to deal with a problem, and know how and where to seek information that will help her find answers to her questions. Learning how to learn is one of the most valuable things that you can teach your older preschool child.

The simplest projects or activities often bring the most pleasure. Do not feel that you do not know enough to help your child solve problems. Be imaginative; you will be amazed how much you can teach your child about everyday experiences.

Teaching Your Child How to Use Resources to Her Advantage

You not only can, but should help your child learn how to use resources effectively. To a young child, her parents are a marvelous resource. Your child will often come to you for assistance and for answers. Mainly offer her assistance after you are certain that she has made a sincere effort to try to help herself and is not just relying upon you to do something for her because she is lazy.

In the case of a young child, she can also learn to direct some questions to her grandparents and other relatives, assuming that they are close by and she sees them regularly. She should discover how to use adults as resources, since they can supply her with both experience and specific information. Seeing you asking other adults for information or directions from time to time will also show her that it is occasionally useful to turn to other people for assistance.

An older preschool child can learn about the value of libraries. You can take her to a local branch and show her around. There will probably be times when she comes to you with questions that you do not know how to answer. On such occasions you might propose a trip to the library to try to find out the answers.

Many parents who have purchased a children's encyclopedia for their home believe that this has been of tremendous benefit to their child. Having such a readily available reference text, they claim, was valuable to them in seeking immediate answers to their young child's questions, and they could read to her from the text. Later, when their child was able to read, she could use the encyclopedia whenever she wanted to learn more about a subject, or needed to find an answer to a question.

Other reference texts can be gradually introduced to your child as well. A good children's dictionary should be an asset for your home. She may enjoy looking at the pictures in an atlas. By the example that you set, she will learn that books, newspapers, and magazines are valuable sources of information.

By helping your child develop learning skills, and showing her how to use resources effectively both at home and in the community at large, you will be providing her with great tools which she will utilize and which will be of benefit to her throughout the remainder of her life.

HOW TO FOSTER THINKING ABILITIES

Dramatic increases in your child's mental abilities will be observed during the preschool years. The abilities to think, solve problems, and form opinions and explanations are rapidly and steadily improving. Most parents want to know if there are any measures that they can take to nourish their child's mind. The answer is yes.

Stimulation of the Five Senses

One of the steps you can take to stimulate your child's intellectual development is to encourage her to be more aware of her surroundings by using her five senses. In order to provide her with opportunities to build up numerous sensory experiences, offer her toys and ordinary household materials to work with and learn from. In the preschool Learning Through Play sections, there are suggestions for playthings, games, and activities that will increase her sensory awareness.

The child's ability to think arises out of her early sensori-motor experiences. You can encourage her to touch, smell, see, hear, taste, and move inside your home, on nature walks, and short trips. Encourage her to use all of her senses to appreciate things around her. Help her notice tiny details such as the subtle changes in the colors of a small rock. Tell her to close her eyes and try to identify the different sounds that she hears such as the rustle of the leaves, the water rushing over rocks, the chirping of birds and crickets, and so on.

Broadening Your Child's Experience

Another excellent way to expand your child's mind is to broaden her experience. Experiences can be both firsthand and secondhand. A marvelous way to expand her firsthand experience is to take her on numerous field trips. There are an infinite variety of places to visit both in your own community and in other communities: a historic home, ethnic restaurant, place of worship, greenhouse, museum, hobby store, bread factory, bookstore, train station, airport, zoo, harbor, planetarium, gym, old age home, farm (if you live in a city), city (if you live in the country), hospital, and so on.

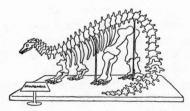

Community resources are unlimited and you should take advantage of them. While you visit these places, encourage your youngster to ask questions, and talk with her about the experiences. Offer her explanations and specific information. Field trips will not only provide firsthand experience, they will also provide good source materials for conversations, and will stimulate her mind and interests. Travel can also greatly expand the young child's firsthand experiences.

Secondhand experiences are also very important. Your child can get them by listening to other people talk, listening to stories, records, and tapes, by watching television, attending movies and plays, and so forth. All of these are excellent means of nourishing your child's mind, expanding her horizons, and encouraging her ability to think.

Helping Your Child Formulate Concepts

The young child needs to understand and make sense out of her everyday experiences, and she strives hard to do so. As she keeps accumulating more and more information about her surroundings, she will be making attempts to form associations, integrate this information, and come to her own conclusions about things going on around her. You can assist your child in this regard by helping her interrelate information, clearing up incorrect notions, filling in gaps in her information, and introducing her to certain concepts that should help her understand events.

Your younger preschooler's ability to think on an abstract level will be quite limited. The older preschooler, between three and a half and five, will be better able to think and will, even if only in a small way, begin to search for explanations and form some of her own immature conclusions about things that she sees. There are numerous ways to help your Preschool 3 child formulate concepts out of her concrete experiences in dealing with her surroundings but, given her limitations in abstract thinking, you should not expect her to grasp explanations fully.

One significant concept that you can introduce to the older preschool child is the concept of gravity. Have your child pick up an apple and toss it upward in the air. Then ask her why she thinks it landed on the ground. Listen carefully to her answer, as this will guide you in first clearing up her misconceptions, and then offering new information.

You can explain that there is an invisible force called gravity that pulls objects down toward the ground. Point out that leaves on the trees fall down, rather than up, and that when water faucets are turned on the water flows downward rather than upward, just as raindrops fall down toward the ground.

When introducing your child to abstract concepts, it is advisable to relate your explanations to her daily experiences. In explaining the concept of money, you could give her some play money and encourage her to play "store." You can be the customer, and she can manage the "cash register." Through this play activity, show her how to make change, and help her understand how money is offered in exchange for goods. Then go on from there to show her real money, and teach the names of coins and bills.

A short field trip to a bank might add to her enjoyment and stimulate further interest. Afterward, you might offer explanations about earning money, borrowing money, saving money, saving coupons, hunting for sales and bargains, keeping a budget, and so forth, linking all of your explanations to her ordinary experiences in dealing with money. It is a good idea to encourage her to save her own money in a piggy bank. With a little help from you, your older preschool child may enjoy setting up her own money-making enterprise such as a lemonade stand. You can also pay her for doing extra work, other than her regular chores around your home and yard. You might even develop a payment system whereby the child earns points for a job well done, and each point equals a penny earned. When a job is not completed or done poorly, points are subtracted or put in a minus category. The Preschool 3 child can also be given a modest allowance. These kinds of real experiences with money will expand her concept of money, as well as stimulate her interests in other areas as well.

By helping your youngster understand certain concepts, you will be enabling her to understand more about the world around her. There are many concepts that can be introduced during the preschool years including the following: birth, death, friction, shadows, wheels, hot and cold, hard and soft, large and small, numbers, letters, money, marriage, transportation, and so on. In your local library and bookstores you will find numerous excellent books that are useful in explaining many important concepts to preschool children in terms that they can understand. Reading to your child from books may serve as a good supplement to her own activities and your explanations. In reading them to her, you may learn or relearn a thing or two as well.

Expanding Your Child's Concept of Time

There are numerous ways in which to increase your child's awareness of time, and expand her concept of time. One way involves talking with her about the past. Tell her what she was like when she was just a baby, and what life was like when you were just a young child. Encourage her to ask her grandparents or older people what life was like when they were growing up. Youngsters often sit spellbound listening to stories their parents and especially their grandparents tell them, and from these stories they will learn many things about "history."

A marvelous way to help your Preschool 2 or 3 child develop an awareness of history is to take her to a museum of natural history. There she will see fascinating things like skeletons and lifelike models of prehistoric animals. She will learn something about how prehistoric men and women lived, what kinds of primitive tools they used, how they dressed in animal skins, and how they made fire by rubbing sticks of wood together. She will probably be so fascinated and awed by the things she sees that she may ask to visit the museum again. You can also teach her about the past by reading her stories from history books for children.

Youngsters tend to be primarily concerned with the present. In order to keep your child up to date on what is happening now, you can teach her about current events. Making a monthly collage of pictures from front page news articles is one suggestion. Tell her that newspapers, and news programs on the television and radio are specially designed to inform people about important and sometimes not-so-important events that take place every day. Encourage her to talk to you about her current activities, and keep her informed about your activities as well.

You can gradually make attempts to teach your child to tell time, although even an older preschool child will have difficulty learning this task. There are many toys available that can help a child learn to tell time, and a quick visit to your local department store will convince you of this. It will be easier for your child to learn to tell time if you obtain a clock that has a second hand, a minute hand, marks for each minute, and large numbers on the face.

Tell your youngster that there are sixty seconds in each minute and that each time the second hand goes around in a full circle, the minute hand moves a notch. Then explain how there are sixty minutes in an hour. Mention that when the minute hand makes a half-circle, a half an hour has gone by, and when it makes a full circle, an hour has gone by. Many children are able to learn that when the "big" hand points to a certain number, it is time for a particular activity. They may learn to use a clock or a wristwatch to keep track of turning points in the daily schedule or activities.

Children often talk about what will happen in the future. A good way to expand your child's awareness of future time is to teach her about calendars. Tell her that there are seven days in the week, four weeks to a month, and twelve months to a year. Show her on the calendar how many days, weeks, and months it will be until her next birthday, the trip you are planning, the next major holiday, and so forth. Teach her the names of the days of the week, the twelve months, the seasons, and major holidays. You can also help her plan out a daily and a weekly schedule of activities. Talk to her about your plans for the future, and ask what she would like to do in the future. All of these kinds of activities should be helpful in expanding her concept of time.

Expanding Your Child's Point of View

The preschool child tends to view things solely from her own, limited point of view. She generally cannot imagine herself in someone else's place, or imagine that something would look different if she were viewing it from another perspective. Despite her limitations in this regard, you can try to teach that there are several different ways to examine a problem or situation, and that the world often looks different from someone else's point of view.

Should she complain about not liking a toy that her relative gave as a gift, you might point out to her that to a child who rarely receives a new toy, and often wishes for one, her brand-new toy would look awfully good. In the event you are getting dressed and discover that the belt you had intended to wear is too tight, you might point out that on her it would be too loose.

Still another way to expand her perspective is to explain how you feel about something she has done that bothers you. Assuming that she has taken one of your favorite possessions, you can tell her how hurt you are and how inconsiderate this action was. Then point out how bad she would feel if someone took her favorite book or toy or whatever she treasures. You should come across numerous opportunities throughout the preschool stage to broaden your child's limited point of view and expand her thinking horizons.

HOW TO FOSTER CREATIVITY

It is important for you to encourage your child to be logical in her thought processes, but it is also important for you to encourage her to use her imagination to come up with creative, original ideas of her own. There are numerous ways in which to foster original, creative thinking.

To the Preschool 1 child, thinking about things is still a rather new ability, and her thought processes are still rather closely tied to her actual experiences in dealing with people and objects. Later, in Preschool 2 and especially Preschool 3, when the child's ability to play with ideas in the mind rapidly increases, it is more likely that you will observe your youngster being more creative, and hear her coming up with some original ideas.

Most parents are quick to notice when their child comes up with a terrific new idea, but they often fail to reinforce her positively for this inventiveness. A major way in which to promote creative thinking is to offer your child positive feedback, and show her that you are enthusiastic about her ideas when she comes up with new ones. Saying something to her like, "That was a wonderful, new idea—I'll bet you're the first person who ever thought of that," will stimulate her to do more thinking for herself.

Another approach is to encourage her to look at things, think about them in a new light, and explore further possibilities. When she comes to you with some object that she has been playing with in an old, familiar way, you might ask her "What else could this be used for?" or "Can you think of any other ways to play with this?"

You can also help stimulate her imagination by playing "What if" kinds of games, in which you make comments such as, "What if flowers could talk?" or "What if when you turned on the water faucet milk came out instead of water?" Thinking about nonsensical possibilities is appealing to the imaginative nature of the young child. This type of activity encourages her to look at ordinary things that she takes for granted in a new light.

You, too, can show her how to use ordinary items in multiple, resourceful ways. Let's say that you are baking cookies, and cannot find the right size cookie cutter, you can use old tin cans or lids from jars to cut out shapes in the dough. Your use of materials in various ways will give her a good idea of how resources can be used effectively and imaginatively.

Creativity with Unstructured Materials

Your Preschool 2 and 3 child will combine materials in all sorts of interesting ways to make constructions and new products. This requires creativity, resourcefulness, and originality. It is advisable to praise her "creations," and provide her with all kinds of unstructured toys and materials such as paints, dough, wooden blocks, sand, dirt and water, and a variety of objects for collage. There are an infinite number of things your child can do with unstructured materials. She can experiment with them, combine them in limitless ways, and utilize her own ideas and imagination in dealing with them. She will be doing all of the thinking, talking, and working, not the toys.

Art as a Medium for Creative Expression

It is very important to encourage creative expression. Unstructured art materials provide an excellent medium for creative expression of one's feelings and ideas. Coloring books and connect-the-dot paintings are generally too structured and confine the child's creative talents. Providing your child with a bowl of fruit and asking her to draw it is also rather confining, because the ideas and structure are already there, and the possibilities for originality are limited. These activities are fine on occasion, but it is far more stimulating for a child to have complete freedom to put her own feelings and ideas into a drawing or painting, to use materials in unconventional ways, and to make her own artistic creations.

In working with art materials, encourage your child to experiment and express her feelings through color, shapes, brush strokes, and textures. You can try playing music while she is engaged in art activities, and encouraging her to paint or draw according to how the music makes her feel. Another enjoyable activity is to hold up various pictures of paintings, or take her to an art museum or gallery, and ask how particular paintings, colors, lines, and brush strokes make her feel.

Music as a Medium for Creative Expression

Music is another wonderful medium of expression, and there are all kinds of interesting activities that promote creative expression using music. You can play different kinds of music for your older preschooler, and ask her to tell you how the music makes her feel. You can also encourage her to create new songs, or think of lyrics to go along with melodies without words.

Movement as an Avenue of Creative Expression

There are unlimited possibilities for creative expression through movement. When you play different kinds of music for her, explain that she can do anything that the music makes her "feel" like doing, or "tells" her to do. She can bounce, jump, run, clap her hands, rock, sway back and forth, stretch, twirl, and make use of all parts of her body. You can also play games in which you say a word or a name of an animal and ask her to act out the word or "be" the word through facial expression, gestures, and body language. For instance, if you say the word "elephant," she will have to assume the posture of an elephant and move like an elephant moves. If you say the word "pole," she will have to stiffen up and stand straight like a pole.

Language as an Avenue of Creative Expression

Language is another excellent medium through which she can express feelings and be original and creative. Three- and especially four-year-olds tend to be great talkers and storytellers. You can encourage your child to create her own stories and help her write her own books. Variations on these activities are numerous. Verbal activities not only give your child opportunities to practice speaking and communicating with others, they will also encourage her to think, to be imaginative, and to be original.

Encouraging Dramatic Play

Through dramatic play, your child will extend her experiences as well as re-create and organize them so that they make more sense. Thus, it would seem advisable to encourage dramatic play by providing opportunities for it as well as giving her props such as dress-up clothes in order to enrich it. You can also offer her suggestions and occasionally join in her pretend activities. In addition to dramatic play, you can also provide puppets and equipment for doll house play. These will encourage creative thinking and expression.

Telling Your Child Imaginative Stories

Still another way in which to foster creativity is to tell your child stories. You have it within you to come up with all kinds of fascinating tales of imaginary characters in imaginary places. Sometimes you can make them spooky and eerie and sometimes you can make them absolutely wonderful and delightful using good fairies and elves. Your child will probably be fascinated with the stories you create, and may want you to repeat them. You can also find books of fairy tales to read to her. Fictional materials will help to expand her imagination further and stimulate her to be creative in her thinking.

HOW TO STIMULATE LANGUAGE ABILITIES

You will be spending a great deal of time with your preschooler. It is important for you to be aware of some ways in which you can promote her language abilities, and her interest in oral and written language.

The Importance of Conversing with Your Child

Whenever you are together, talk with her about whatever either of you are doing, thinking, or feeling. Short excursions outside of your home such as a trip to the museum or the zoo will give you interesting things to talk about. Mealtime may also be a good time for discussion when each family member can have an opportunity to tell what he or she did that day. By conversing often with your child, you will be helping her learn about language, giving her a chance to practice speaking, and stimulating her intellectual development.

After your child has watched a program on television, or has seen a movie, encourage her to discuss what she has seen with you. Assuming that a television program has motivated her to want information about sports events or animals, talk to her about these general topics and obtain magazines or books for her about them. By discussing programs with her, you will not only be fostering her language development, you will also be clearing up any misunderstandings she might have, helping her to sort out fact from fiction, and encouraging her to be critical about what she sees and hears. By pinpointing what is interesting or important to her, and then discussing it, you will be making effective use of conversation.

Stimulating Your Child's Vocabulary Development

One of the ways in which you can help expand your child's vocabulary is to generate within her a curiosity about words. Wherever you are—riding in a train, doing a load of wash, shopping in a store—you can name objects for her. In a grocery store, you could say the names of the products on the shelves. When you place a product such as a cereal box in your cart, you can read the labels. Another way to aid her vocabulary development is to introduce her to new words. Teaching new words and even something about the origins of some words can be fun, and once she is able to pronounce a new word correctly, she will be very proud of herself.

Reading to Your Child

Reading to your child can be a pleasurable and educational experience for both of you. It is as much a social as an intellectual experience, so it is advisable to hold your child on your lap or snuggle up beside her as you read. Hold the book so that she can easily follow along and see the pictures. Talk to her about the pictures and encourage her to do the same with you. Always allow her to interrupt you with questions and comments about the material.

It will help your child learn to use books properly if you read her the title of the book and tell her the author's name. Other details such as who published the book, or who created the illustrations, or photographs, may also interest her. Knowing how to examine books and attend to important details will come in handy once she enters school.

As you read to her, try to be expressive. There is nothing more boring than listening to someone who constantly speaks in a monotone. Your child will appreciate changes in your tone of voice and in your facial expression.

During Preschool 3, you may want to start taking your child to the children's room of your local library. The librarian can be a help to you and your child, and may offer to give your child a grand tour of the library. If not, you can show your child around on your own. Be sure to inquire if there are any story hours or movie hours for preschool children. Many libraries provide such special services. At first you or the librarian will probably play the major role in selecting appropriate books for your child. Later, she may select some of her own books.

When it is time to check out the books, show your older preschool child how this is done. Let her see your library card, and explain to her about borrowing books. Also explain to her that she must take good care of the books so that others can enjoy them after they are returned.

Besides reading to your youngster from library books, you can buy her some books of her own. Short excursions to a good bookstore will be fun for her. Her books will probably be among her most prized possessions, and they should be kept in a special place. Building or buying a bookcase for your child should stimulate her interest in books.

It is important to be selective in choosing books to read to your child. Many books will state whether or not they are recommended for youngsters her age. There are even prepared book lists that present books appropriate at different ages. These can be used as general guides, but it is always advisable to scan a book before you buy it, and determine its appropriateness yourself, considering your child's interests and responses. They will probably be the best guide as to what books would be appropriate for her. When a book is too difficult or too easy for her, she will probably get fidgety and tune you out or move away. If the vocabulary level of a book is too high but the story is appealing, you can paraphrase it. Watch closely for signs of disinterest or boredom, and upon seeing such signs, discontinue the activity.

The time of day when you read to your child does not really matter. Many children enjoy hearing bedtime stories. They also enjoy being read to in place of an afternoon nap. It may be helpful to try to set aside a certain period of time each day in which to read to her. She should also enjoy a quiet period of "reading" books on her own.

Where you read to your child is completely a matter of personal preference. The main factor to keep in mind is that both of you should be very comfortable. When the weather is nice, you might read to her outdoors. It would be a good idea to bring along a couple of books when you anticipate a long wait at the airport, shoe repair, or doctor's office.

It is important to show your child that you enjoy reading on your own, aside from reading to her. Discuss with her what you read, since this may encourage her to do the same. By letting her see that you read books for pleasure as well as to obtain information, she will learn that books can serve more than one purpose. On special occasions such as your birthday, you might suggest that her gift to you be a book. Likewise, on her birthday you might occasionally want to buy her several books instead of a toy or a new outfit.

You can stimulate your Preschool 3 child's interest in both oral and written language by reading her signs, symbols, and labels such as traffic signs, menus, your shopping list, reminders that you leave by the phone, and so forth. This will help expand her vocabulary by arousing her interest in words and their meanings, and will help her realize that letters make up words that have meanings.

Not all children at this age enjoy reading. Some more active children may not be able to sit still long enough, and may be much more interested in riding their tricycle or kicking a ball. Do not force the issue, if your child does not seem interested in listening, since this will defeat the purpose of reading to her. There are so many different ways in which you can stimulate her language development (e.g., word games, naming games, etc.), that you should not be concerned about her disinterest in any one activity.

Your Child's Own Magazine Subscription

Many Preschool 2 and 3 children enjoy being read to from children's magazines. There are several magazines available to choose from, and they may provide stimulating material for your child. They cater to the young child, including jokes, riddles, pictures, stories, and puzzles.

One of the most exciting aspects of a magazine subscription to your child is having the order placed in her name. Chances are that each time the magazine arrives, she will be thrilled that she received something especially for her in the mail. Any other household magazines, colorful books, or pictures may also be useful in fostering your child's interest in language.

Your Child the Author

Many nursery schools conduct projects where the children create their own books. Children between the ages of three and five often enjoy and take great pride in creating their own books. Common household items such as cardboard for book covers, typing paper, glue, string, and scissors are usually all that are necessary to begin.

To foster your child's creativity (pages 797–98) several suggestions were given to encourage her to make up her own stories. You can record these stories by writing them down or typing them, often leaving spaces for adding pictures and drawings after the story is finished. The pictures in her book can be from magazine or newspaper cutouts, or her own artwork drawn in between your writing or typing. Your enthusiasm in helping her with this project will further stimulate her interest and enjoyment.

After the text is completed, you can make a cover and back for the book out of cardboard. Then, talk to her about what she wants to call the book. Try to stimulate her imaginative thinking by discussing her ideas for the title. After putting the title on the cover, and adding some pictures or illustrations as well, your child may take great pride when you place her name, as the author, on the front cover.

As your child becomes older and more sophisticated in her ability to tell stories, you can help her make books about some of the field trips you take to the zoo, museum, or library. When she learns to write her name, or print some letters or words, she may also enjoy adding her own printing to the book, or signing the cover in her own handwriting.

Encouraging Your Child's Listening Abilities

Preschool children show a beginning interest in the sounds of words. You can increase your child's interest by engaging her in word games that will expand her awareness of sounds and sound patterns. You might ask her to say as many words as she can think of that begin with the "K" sound as in "candy." Or you might have her listen as you say several words that end the same way as "crop." There are many games which help to refine a child's listening skills. Games in which you give directions and she has to follow them are appropriate. Other activities that will encourage your child's listening abilities and foster language development are presented in the play sections of Preschool 1 and 3.

Teaching Your Child a Second Language

Preschool children tend to be very receptive to learning a second language. If you are interested in teaching your child another language, we suggest that you read pages 733–34 in the Language Development section.

HOW TO PROMOTE PHYSICAL PROWESS

Learning New Skills

Some complex physical activities such as skiing, ice skating, and swimming are not naturally acquired as a child grows and matures. The development of such abilities depends upon special training. A child's ability to engage in other common activities such as throwing a ball and drawing or writing with crayons, pens, and pencils also depends, in part, upon whether or not she has been encouraged in these skills, and how much opportunity she has had to practice them. It is hoped that you are encouraging your child to develop both gross motor and fine motor abilities, and are providing her with opportunities for practice, since this will enable her to develop to her fullest potential. You may also want to offer her training in specific activities such as gymnastics, swimming, ice skating, and skiing.

HOW TO FOSTER PRIDE IN PERSONAL ACHIEVEMENT

By the time your child is three, she will probably begin to show even more pride in personal achievements and accomplishments than in the past. After she has created, built, or drawn something, she may talk about how well it turned out or how pleased she is with it, and may come to you with a proud look on her face seeking your approval and praise. It is important that she learn to differentiate between a job well done and a job poorly done, and that she learn the value of trying to complete tasks that she starts.

Should your Preschool 3 child bring you a piece of paper with some scribbling on it seeking your praise, and you know that she is capable of producing a more sophisticated drawing based upon her abilities and past performance, it would be advisable to explain that you know she is capable of doing better, and not offer your praise. By praising her for a job poorly or hastily done, she may develop unrealistic or inappropriate standards for personal achievement and accomplishment. On the other hand, when she brings you a sample of work which is indicative of a real effort on her part you will want to express your approval and probably show her how proud you are of it by displaying it in your home.

While you should not expect things from her which are far beyond or above her real capabilities, it is also unadvisable to set standards and expectations that are below her capabilities. By keeping your expectations for her "creations" and accomplishments at or slightly above the level of her abilities, and by doling out praise when it is well deserved, you will be helping her set appropriate standards for achievement and aspiration.

HOW TO PROMOTE SELF-AWARENESS AND SOCIAL SENSITIVITY

Suggestions for fostering gender identity and identification have been given previously on pages 709–15.

Promoting Conscience Development

Scientific research on conscience development is relatively scarce. Some of the many factors that are believed to promote effective conscience development are outlined in both the Personal-Social Development sections of Preschool 1, 2, and 3 and the Discipline sections of Preschool 1 and 2. In general, you should strive to maintain a warm, loving relationship with your child so that she will work to maintain your approval as well as build up her own self-esteem. Having a good relationship with her will encourage her to identify with you and incorporate your attitudes toward her unacceptable impulses and actions into her own personality. You should also encourage your child to accept responsibility for her own unacceptable behavior, and try to maintain a program of discipline that is neither extremely lenient nor extremely harsh, since these methods may not promote normal conscience development and the development of an inner system of self-control.

Encouraging Independence

It should become clearer to you day by day that your child is growing more independent. As she becomes more capable of taking over some of the responsibility for her own basic care, and as she becomes better able to handle herself in responsible ways, you must offer her more freedom and opportunities to do things by and for herself. It is hoped that you are encouraging her to become more independent, and are not holding her back by positively reinforcing overdependency upon you in order to fulfill your own needs.

Broadening Your Child's Social Sphere

Generally around the age of three the child begins to express a desire to separate from the parent who has been taking primary care of her and become more independent. She is usually ready to be apart from her family for a few hours or more a day, to spend time with her peers and perhaps other adults such as teachers at nursery school or Sunday school. Her social sphere can, and probably should, be expanded at this age, at least to enable her to play regularly with children of her own age. In interacting with them, she will develop numerous social skills that would not be developed otherwise. It is important for you to encourage your child to expand her social contacts, even if you are ambivalent or reluctant about accepting the fact that she is growing up and is not as dependent upon you as she was during infancy and toddlerhood. She also needs opportunities to learn to deal effectively with adults and children her own age, other than those in her immediate family.

HOW TO FOSTER YOUR CHILD'S SENSE OF SELF-ESTEEM

It is important for your child to emerge from the preschool stage with a good sense of her value as a person. You will play a major role in shaping her attitudes about herself. There is no magic formula for helping a child build self-esteem, although there are several time-tested guidelines to assist you. Knowing your child better than anyone else will put you in the best position to help her build self-esteem, and enable you to think of additional ways to accomplish this.

Of primary importance is to make your youngster feel likable, loved, wanted, and worthy of your and other people's respect. This is achieved through a combination of words and actions. Compliment her for a job well done, and praise her for tasks at which she tried her best. Guard against expecting too much from her, since not being able to live up to your expectations can lead to feelings of self-doubt and failure.

Your youngster will surely fail at some tasks. When she does, help her accept the failure, learn from it, and not take one failure in a particular area or task as an indication of failure as a person. Occasional failure, put into proper perspective, can be enlightening, so do not try to protect her from it altogether. Also, keep your doubts about her abilities to yourself. Statements such as, "I don't think you'll ever learn," or, "I doubt that you'll do it right this time," lead to insecurity and self-doubt.

Give your preschooler freedom to be herself. Do not try to mold her into some preconceived pattern of what you want her to be. Constant comparisons between her and her siblings or relative's or friend's children the same age in which she always turns out to be the "loser" slowly diminish her self-esteem. Comments like, "Why can't you be more like so-and-so?" can be devastating to a young child, particularly when they come from her parents, whom she desperately wants to please.

Calling attention to a child's every mistake undermines her sense of self-worth and her positive feelings about her own abilities. So, too, can giving her negative labels such as "stupid," "clumsy," "fatso," "squirt," "beanpole," "bad girl," or "brat." Such names often stick with a youngster, interfere with her ability to develop a positive self-image, and sometimes become a self-fulfilling prophecy.

Avoid constantly belittling your child, embarrassing her, and putting her down in front of other people, especially her playmates. Comments such as, "Can't you do anything right?" or, "You'll never be good at anything," will not only shame her in front of others, but breed insecurity, low self-esteem, and resentment toward you. Just as you should avoid putting her down in other people's presence, you should also refrain from apologizing to others for her difficulties, appearance, or bothersome habits.

Another way in which to promote your child's sense of value as a unique person is to listen to what she has to say. Do not just put on the pretense of hearing her. Pay attention, and give her respect. Your child needs to feel that her ideas and opinions count. If you are a good listener and respect her comments, she will learn that what she thinks, feels, and says is truly important.

Do not always take your child's words or actions at face value. Quite often there are motives and hidden meanings underlying what she says and does that are far more important than what appears on the surface. A child who engages in some bothersome activity or misbehaves may do so for a variety of reasons, not just to spite her parents. For a child to feel worthy of respect, she must first be understood, so do your best to get to know your child well. Then it will be easier for you to guide her, discipline her, and talk to her without hurting her feelings or damaging her self-esteem.

Parents are often unaware that their words or actions are working against their child's establishment of a positive self-image. They do not maliciously or intentionally try to undermine her sense of self-esteem, but they still do so. Your preschooler should feel your positive acceptance and respect, since this will assist her in respecting herself, developing a positive self-concept, and a sense of self-worth as an individual.

HOW TO ENCOURAGE SELF-REGULATION

Your preschool child is much more capable than she was during toddlerhood of being trained to delay, change, and block certain unacceptable impulses. Two of the major aspects of becoming a self-regulating person that you will be teaching your child include talking about her aggressive feelings rather than acting upon them, and taking the responsibility for her own misconduct. Suggestions for how to encourage your child to develop an effective internal system for self-control are provided in the Discipline sections of Preschool 1 and 2.

Helping Your Child Acquire Good Moral Standards

Most parents desperately want their children to grow up with a good set of morals and standards for conduct. Your preschool child should learn "right" from "wrong," but moral standards are acquired very slowly, and are very specific rather than general. You, as her parent, will be instrumental in helping her learn the difference between right and wrong. Suggestions for how to accomplish this can be found on page 932.

Continuing Manners Training

A child who has not been encouraged to acquire good manners will be at a great disadvantage in her dealings with other people. You should be continuing to teach your child good manners (see pages 622–23), and not tolerating purposely rude behavior or disrespect toward yourself or others. It is also important to establish yourself as a good model for her to follow in regard to having good manners.

Responsibilities in the Home

Your Preschool 2 and 3 child is old enough to be expected to assume some responsibility for the care of her own room and possessions, and to be given certain simple chores to perform for which she will not be materially rewarded. The goal of giving her household chores to perform is to help her develop a sense of responsibility. See also pages 623–24.

HOW TO CONTINUE EDUCATING YOUR CHILD ABOUT HEALTH CARE AND SAFETY

Teaching Your Child to Be Safety-conscious

The preschool child is more interested in imitation, so it is extremely important to set a good example for her in regard to accident prevention. Especially now, when she is becoming more capable and independent, and will be occasionally journeying out into the community without you, it is necessary for you to prepare her to cope with an unsafety-proofed environment. Specific suggestions for how to accomplish this are provided on pages 748–49.

Teaching a Respect for the Body and the Importance of Preventive Health Care

A knowledge of and respect for one's own body, and a general awareness of the importance of health care, when learned at a very early age, can become a well-ingrained aspect of one's character. It is very important to help your preschool child learn about her body, feel good about her body and herself, and become aware of the value of preventive health care.

You can teach your Preschool 3 child something about the human body by using simple pictures and diagrams. She may show an interest in learning the names for all of her outer body parts as well as some of the names for inner organs, and what they do. You can help her learn about bones, muscles, how food is digested, what enables her to breathe and talk, and so forth, in simple terms that she can understand. Many kits are available in toy stores for building three-dimensional models of the body, or parts of the body, and these can be useful in teaching your child. Do not expect her to be able to put such models together.

You should help your child appreciate the advantages and pleasures of keeping herself in excellent physical condition. Teach her about physical fitness, and show her how to do exercises that will help her stay in shape. Tell her that it is important to get a certain amount of exercise each day, and encourage her to perform a set of exercises on a regular basis.

Keeping oneself clean is another aspect of staying healthy, and you should explain this to your child. She should learn how important it is to take regular baths, to wipe thoroughly after elimination, to wash her hands thoroughly after using the toilet, to brush her teeth, to change underwear daily, to refrain from cooking or eating unless her hands are clean, and to avoid putting dirty fingers into her mouth or near her eyes. Besides teaching these things, you should encourage her to assume as much independence for her own basic care as she is capable of handling.

Good nutrition is another essential aspect of preventive health care. You can introduce your child to the concept of good nutrition by teaching about which foods are healthy to eat and which to avoid. Help her learn to identify various foods.

It is also important to teach your child the value of getting proper amounts of rest and relaxation. Tell her that her body should not be too overtaxed if she is to remain healthy, and therefore she should go to bed at a regular time each night so that her requirements for sleep will be adequately fulfilled.

You can explain the value of going for regular check-ups to the pediatrician or family doctor and the dentist—an important part of preventive health care. When teaching your child about her body and health care, try to make learning as pleasurable as possible for her. Encouraging her to feel happy and positive about her body should also strengthen her self-concept and her pride in her appearance. By teaching her to respect her body, and involving her in preventive health care, you will help her to establish habits and attitudes that will serve as the foundation for good health throughout her life.

HOW TO CONTINUE TO PROVIDE HEALTHY SEX EDUCATION

Your child's attitudes about her body, her sex, herself, members of her own sex, and the roles of men and women will become more well established during the pre-school years. Your own behavior, comments about the roles of men and women, and reactions to her behavior will influence the kinds of attitudes that she develops. You should be fully aware of the role that you will play in shaping her feelings, and aware that you are helping her to feel good about her body, her sex, and members of her sex as well as the opposite sex. In regard to attitudes about men and women, you are likely to want to teach her to respect their differences and similarities.

Most children show an increased interest in and curiosity about sex-related issues during the preschool years. Should your child approach you with questions, give her simple, honest answers that she can understand, for this is one of the best ways to impart information about sex to a young child. Avoid instilling in your child the no-tion that her curiosity and interest in sex are perverted, dirty, or disgusting, or that sex is a taboo subject. See pages 865–80.

TEACHING YOUR CHILD ABOUT YOUR FAMILY

Teaching your Preschool 3 child about your family heritage should be fun for both of you, and educational for her. It is important for a child to be taught as much as is known about her roots, because this will help foster her sense of identity and her sense of self-pride. Ways in which you can help your child learn about your family background and origin are discussed on pages 775–76.

TEACHING PRACTICAL SKILLS

Now that your child is more capable, the list of practical skills that she can be taught expands enormously. You can teach your older Preschool 2 or 3 child how to handle and use many more utensils and tools properly, how to wash and dry dishes, how to pour liquids and other substances from one container into another and measure them, how to operate a water faucet, how to lace and tie her shoes, how to help set a table, how to help prepare simple dishes and make sandwiches, how to ice a cake, how to unscrew lids of jars and replace them, how to help care for pets, how to wrap a present, and so forth. The list of practical skills that you can teach her is virtually endless. We hope that you are teaching your child numerous practical skills as her mastery of them will be of immense value to her not only now, but also in the future.

THE THREE R'S (READING, WRITING, ARITHMETIC)

Some parents want to teach their Preschool 2 and 3 children the fundamentals of how to read, write, and do simple mathematical computations. There is still controversy about whether these skills should be taught before the child enters grade school. Some educators recommend that children receive training in the Three R's prior to entering school, while others are opposed to this on the grounds that even Preschool 3 children are not "ready." Not all parents will be interested in teaching these skills, and if either you or your child is not enthusiastic about engaging in activities which promote the Three R's, forego them for the time being.

There is even disagreement among educators who favor teaching the Three R's, with some claiming that parents can do an effective job of teaching their children, and others insisting that these skills should be taught only by qualified teachers in nursery school. There are some nursery schools that offer children instruction in or "preparation" for reading, writing, and arithmetic, but many of them do not.

The most important thing seems to be that many older preschool children enjoy learning the fundamentals of the Three R's before they enter kindergarten or grade school, especially when these skills are presented in enjoyable ways. Some Preschool 2 and 3 children, even without parental encouragement, show a spontaneous interest in words, sounds, letters, the alphabet, learning to recognize simple words, numbers, counting, or printing. Should your youngster display one or more of these interests, you may wish to encourage her by teaching her fundamental or preliminary aspects of reading, writing, or arithmetic. The following material should help you understand how you can initiate instruction in these areas, and will offer some brief suggestions for how to take advantage of your child's interest.

The Proper Attitude Is What Counts

Learning the preliminaries of reading, writing, and arithmetic can be enjoyable for some Preschool 2 and 3 children, particularly when the atmosphere their parents create is happy and relaxed, and they are provided with stimulating learning materials. By introducing your child to the basic skills underlying reading, writing, and arithmetic through interesting activities and games, you will not only be setting the stage for the continued development of these three important skills once she enters grade school, when she will be expected to learn them, you will also be helping her acquire positive attitudes about learning.

Whether the child learns to read, write, and count to one thousand is not as important as how she feels about learning these skills. She can always learn the fundamentals once she enters grade school, but the attitudes about learning which she is acquiring now may not be as changeable later on, and may be carried with her for many years.

This is why you are cautioned not to force or pressure her into learning the Three R's, or, for that matter, any other subject. Your attitude is very important. If you present materials and activities with the attitude that learning arithmetic is sheer drudgery, or is difficult, but that she must learn to count before she enters school so that she will be ahead of her classmates, you will be doing her a great injustice. Similarly, in the event that she seems to dislike reading, and you force her to sit still for even five minutes sounding out words, you will be doing more harm than good. She will probably begin to resent not only you but the activity and subject matter as well.

Some parents think that by pushing the Three R's on their child at a young age, she will be smarter than her classmates once she enters school. Their intentions may be good, but they often force tasks on their child in a very uninteresting and anxiety-provoking manner. Their plan to have her be a "star" pupil, and have her excel in the Three R's at school may quickly backfire on them. A child who has been forced to learn the Three R's, and for whom early learning has not been enjoyable, is likely to be "turned off" to reading, writing, and arithmetic in school.

Let's say that your Preschool 3 child seems more interested in learning about nature than she is in letters. This does not mean that she is less likely to do well in school than a child who shows an early interest in letters or words. The most important thing is that your child is interested and enthusiastic about learning, and that you support and encourage her interests. Tailor your teaching to go along with her interests. Assuming that she is interested in nature and enjoys collecting leaves, and you want to introduce her to reading and writing, you could do this in ways that she might enjoy, using her interest in leaves. You could help her learn the names of the leaves that she finds by obtaining some simple books on trees and leaf-collecting. This may indirectly stimulate her interest in words, names, and reading. You might also help her mount and label her collection, and show her how to copy the letters you made. Eventually, she will be able to label her leaf collection all by herself.

Activities designed to introduce your child to the Three R's should be enjoyable for both of you. Should either of you lose interest, or dislike a given activity, stop and move on to another activity that you find more pleasurable. Try your best to keep the atmosphere surrounding each activity happy and relaxed, and make learning the fundamentals of reading, writing, and arithmetic fun for your child. A preschool child who is excited and enthusiastic about learning the Three R's is likely to want to develop these skills further once she starts school, not because her teacher tells her that she must learn them, but because of her own interest.

Learning to Recognize Letters Can Be Fun

Many older preschool children enjoy learning and playing with letters, when this is made interesting for them. There are unlimited ways in which you can introduce your child to letters. There are individual letters that can be purchased in art stores, wooden blocks with letters imprinted on them, blackboards on which letters are printed, and puzzles with letters. You can cut out letters from newspapers, magazines, and rough paper or other textured materials. Many parents have enjoyed introducing their children to letters by serving them alphabet cereal or soup, and teaching them the names of the letters. Letters are everywhere—in books, on signs, typewriters, on the television screen, on the labels of food products, and on the back of cereal boxes.

In introducing your child to letters, you can help her learn to recognize the forms and individual letters of the alphabet. It is a good idea to use colorful, large-size, textured letters. Encourage her to look at them and feel them. By using her eyes to see the letters, and her fingers to feel the form of the letters, she will, through her senses, learn to recognize the letters which comprise the alphabet.

Teaching the Sounds of Letters

Becoming familiar with the forms and the sounds of letters of the alphabet will prepare your child for printing and, later, reading words. Many Preschool 2 and 3 children seem to be fascinated with sounds and language in general. Sounds of the letters can usually be introduced without difficulty. There are phonics training cards which have the letters printed on one side, and the sounds that are to be taught on the back side. Or you can simply teach your child the sounds of the individual letters.

When teaching the sounds, try to make learning them as much fun as possible for your child. Teaching the letter "d," you can tell her several words that start with the "d" sound, such as "dive," "dog," "drum," and "daddy," and have her repeat the sound of the letter "d." Ask her if she can think of any other words that start with the "d" sound and write the letter "d" for her. Try to think up games involving letters and sounds that she will enjoy playing. You could tell her to browse through the pages of a magazine, and point to pictures of things that start with the "d" sound.

Teaching Your Child to Print

Many Preschool 3 children are anxious to learn how to print letters. You can use felt or paper shapes (curved and straight lines, etc.) and have her construct letters to familiarize herself with their forms. After you have given her opportunities to handle letters and to feel them with her fingers, then you can show her how to print them. Begin with the upper case first, and then teach the lower case. Do not expect perfection. It takes time and much practice before children become proficient at printing. As she becomes able to trace and print the letters fairly well, you can say a letter such as "A," and then encourage her to print the letter. You can also say simple words such as "bat," sound them out slowly, and ask her to print the letters for the sounds that she hears.

Teaching the Alphabet

Once your child is familiar with letters and can recognize them, you can teach her the alphabet. Many parents like to teach the alphabet in song form, using the tune of "Twinkle, Twinkle Little Star." There are alphabet records that you can play for your child, and all kinds of toys and games that can be useful and enjoyable in helping her learn the alphabet. You can also think up games on your own.

Enjoyment of Books and Printed Material

Frequently, youngsters who have learned to recognize letters and their sounds begin to focus spontaneously on words and try sounding them out. They spell out the letters in words, and ask their parents what the words say, or copy words down on paper, show them to their parents, and ask what the words mean. There are numerous ways in which to stimulate your child's curiosity about words and what they mean. One way to do this is by reading to your child, and allowing her to look at the printed material as you read.

Another approach is to point out signs as you are driving, and tell her what the words say. As you prepare dinner, show her the instructions printed on the sides and backs of food products. At breakfast time, point out words on the backs of cereal boxes, and encourage her to sound them out. At restaurants you could teach her what the menus say, and what is printed on placemats and special cards placed on the table.

You can start by showing her simple words such as "hat," "dog," "run," "stop," and "go" written down on cards, and ask her to sound the words out as quickly as she can. Making up picture-word cards is a fun activity. Cut out colorful pictures of animals, people, and various objects, and glue each picture onto a square of cardboard. Underneath each picture write the word for it. Another enjoyable activity is to show her a picture, such as one of a cat, tell her what letters to look for, and have her hunt through her pile of individual letters to find the correct letters that when put together spell "cat." Still another activity is to print simple words on cardboard, such as "run," "stretch," "open the door," "close the door," "shake hands," "wipe your feet," "touch your toes," "raise your right hand," "turn around," "smile," "blink your eyes," and so forth. As you hold up each card, encourage her to sound out the words with you and then do whatever the words tell her to do.

After your preschooler has had practice in putting sounds together, and can recognize several words by sight, you can buy her some beginner reading materials that use large-size print and have good, simple illustrations. The feeling of mastery, self-pride, and pleasure that comes with acquiring the ability to read, along with the praise and encouragement that you offer, will probably motivate her to try to read any printed material that she can get her hands on.

Your Preschool 3 child may enjoy reading simple books, searching through magazines and reading familiar words, and reading labels on food products. At this early stage in her reading career, it is a good idea to let her read anything that she seems enthusiastic about reading, from the comic strips in the newspaper, to the educational books that you bring home from the library. The most important thing is to share in her enthusiasm for reading, not to worry about what she is, or is not, reading.

You Don't Have to Be a Genius at Math to Teach Your Child

Some parents automatically shy away from teaching their children the fundamentals of arithmetic, perhaps because they feel insecure about their own mathematical skill, and doubt their ability to teach anything about math to their children. This is a shame. You can do a good job of teaching your child; it is really quite easy to introduce your older preschooler to the fundamentals of math and to arouse her curiosity and interest in learning math. There are all sorts of games and activities that will make helping her learn about numbers and mathematical concepts pleasurable for you. And by utilizing these resources she will find learning a lot of fun.

In selecting materials that will introduce her to mathematical ideas, try to choose those with which she will enjoy playing. The object is not to teach her to recite the numbers from zero to one hundred by rote, or to teach her to memorize that one plus one equals two. Children often learn to memorize things without really understanding the meanings behind what they say. The real goal is to give her concrete objects to see and manipulate, and let her discover for herself general concepts that arise from her actual experiences.

TEACHING HER NUMBERS CAN BE FUN. Teaching your child to say the names of numbers and to recognize them can be accomplished in many different ways. There are blackboards on which numbers are written, wooden blocks with numbers, numbers on the telephone, and large individual numbers that can be purchased in art stores. You can, of course, simply write numbers on paper, or cut numbers out of textured paper. Encourage your child to handle cutout numbers, and trace them with her fingers. Do not forget that zero is a number, too. While she looks at and feels each number, tell her its name.

You could write down the numbers from zero to ten, and ask her to point to number "four," or give her a pile of individual numbers and ask her to find and hand you number "six." Wherever you are, you can point to numbers such as those on houses or buildings and encourage her to tell you their names. When the two of you are in an elevator you can ask her to push the button that is marked number "five." As she learns to identify numbers, she may enjoy circling all of the "2's" that she can find on a page, or cutting out and naming numbers that she finds in old catalogues or magazines.

TEACHING YOUR CHILD TO COUNT. A child who can quickly say the numbers from one to twenty-five does not necessarily know how to count. In teaching your child how to count, you should help her learn to associate the name of a number with the quantity to which it refers. There are numerous games and activities that can be helpful in introducing counting.

Offer your youngster "real" objects to count, objects that she can see and feel. You might use raisins, seedless grapes, large buttons, apples, oranges, spoons, small pieces of paper, and crayons. One kind of activity that can be used to teach her to count might involve raisins and cut out number symbols.

Put the raisins into ten piles. The first pile would be comprised of one raisin, the second pile would have two raisins, and so forth. Teach her that there is one raisin in the first pile, and place a cutout number "1" above that pile on the table. Then count the raisins in the second pile, and place the number "2" above that pile. Continue with this until the number symbol for the quantity of raisins in each pile is placed above them on the table.

Then encourage her to count the raisins in each pile by herself. Next, leaving the number symbols intact on the table, gather up the raisins and put them in a bowl. Tell her to look at the number symbol and place the correct quantity of raisins below each symbol. It will take some time for her to be able to accomplish this, so be prepared to offer your assistance or discontinue the activity if she is becoming too frustrated.

Wherever you are, you will be able to think up counting games. While walking down the street, you can encourage her to count mailboxes, bicycles, and fire hydrants. When the two of you are in the store, you can ask her to count all of the grocery carts that she sees in one aisle. While she is helping to put away the groceries, she can count the objects as she removes them from the bag. When you take clothes to the cleaners, you can ask her to count the number of shirts, and put them into one pile, and count the number of sweaters, and put them into another pile. These activities will be enjoyable for her, and will give her practice in counting.

TEACHING YOUR CHILD HOW TO WRITE NUMBERS. As your Preschool 3 child learns to count, you may want to show her how to print the numbers that she is counting. Some youngsters do not show an interest in printing, even at age five, so do not pressure her to learn to print if she is not ready or seems disinterested. Should she be enthusiastic about this activity, you can teach her how to form the numbers, one at a time, and then have her try to write each one. You could also have her learn by tracing the numbers. Some children have a harder time learning to write numbers than they do learning letters, but given enough opportunities to practice, and enough encouragement, they will eventually become proficient.

Try to think of games that will help your child practice writing numbers. A simple game is for you to call out a number, and for her to write it down. Once she is able to count and write numbers, you can think of activities involving both skills. You might interest her in helping you take inventory of the various pots in your kitchen cabinets. A more purposeful activity might involve taking stock of canned goods before you go grocery shopping. You can write the words for the food products in a column. Let's say that the first entry is soup. Then you would ask her to count the number of cans of soup. Next, point to the empty space beside the word "soup" on your inventory sheet, and have her write in the number of cans that she counted. By giving her opportunities to practice her new skills, and by showing her how these new skills of counting and writing numbers can come in handy, you will be helping to promote their further development, as well as her interest in mathematics.

INTRODUCING OTHER SIMPLE MATHEMATICAL CONCEPTS. Preschool children can learn many fundamental mathematical concepts by working with actual materials and objects, and playing simple games. There are specially designed kits for teaching simple concepts of mathematics to preschool children, such as "Montessori" rods, and "Cuisenaire" rods. These kits can be very useful, and you may want to invest in one of them.

Preschool children can be introduced to the concepts of odd and even, addition, subtraction, short division, fractions, and so forth in very natural ways. When it is time for dessert, and you are serving cake, you might slice it up in eight pieces while your child watches. Have her count the number of pieces, and tell her that there are eight pieces that make up the whole cake. Then remove one piece and tell her that you have taken one eighth, or one piece out of eight, of the cake away.

Another activity might involve giving her a one-cup measuring cup. Then give her a half-cup measuring cup. Tell her to fill the half-cup measure with tap water and pour it into the one-cup measure. Then have her fill the half-cup measure again, and pour the water into the one-cup measure. Help her to realize that two half-cups equal one cup. Even older children of five or six often have difficulty realizing that two one-half cups equal one cup, so go slowly and do not expect her to comprehend even simple fractions readily.

You can even make up your own games that involve numbers, counting, and other mathematical concepts if you are so inclined. Some parents have introduced their youngsters to the metric system in a small way. By giving your child opportunities to learn about math through interesting activities, she will probably learn to enjoy math. You will be helping to set the stage for further learning once she enters grade school. The object is not to try to turn her into a mathematical whiz. Rather, it is to capitalize on her spontaneous interest in numbers and simple mathematical concepts, and instill in her an enthusiasm for learning about this subject.

NURSERY SCHOOL: AS A SUPPLEMENT TO THE HOME EDUCATIONAL EXPERIENCE

Teaching your child in your home should be rewarding as well as challenging. It should greatly enrich your relationship with her by bringing the two of you closer together, and should promote very open, positive communication between you. Many parents can provide an excellent educational experience for their child in their own home, but some parents work outside the home, do not have the time, the resources, or the desire to be responsible for their child's total education, and they need more freedom from child rearing. These parents sometimes decide that it would be in their child's best interest to supplement her educational experience at home with additional educational experience outside the home.

A child's first experience with school outside of her home often occurs at a nursery school, sometimes referred to as a "preschool." The quality of nursery schools varies greatly, but many communities have first-rate nursery schools that provide a good supplemental educational experience for the child. Nursery schools usually operate on a half-day schedule, but there are some that enroll children on a full-time daily basis. It can be expensive, and some parents may not be able to afford it. Parents who investigate alternatives may find a day care facility or day nursery that operates similarly to a good nursery school.

One alternative to a traditional nursery school is known as a co-operative nursery school. A salaried professional person is frequently employed as a manager or director, and parents themselves rotate in teaching the children. Parents are not placed on a salary. They must take a regular turn teaching the group, of which their child is a member. (See also page 638.)

What Are Some of the Benefits of Nursery School in General?

A good nursery school should offer a child many opportunities, one or all of which may be lacking in the home situation. Many schools offer a child chances to be with and learn to deal effectively with her peers and chances to utilize a wide variety of playthings and equipment. They also provide more space for movement and exploration, the opportunity to deal with adults other than her parents, and the opportunity to separate from her parents and establish social contacts and activities of her own away from home.

As far as parents are concerned, nursery school often provides them with much needed time out to work, relax, attend school, or take care of their own needs. Any relief from their twenty-four-hour "on-call" schedule, and their role as the child's sole teacher, may be greatly appreciated. Sending a child to a nursery school with well-trained, experienced, and conscientious teachers can also offer parents opportunities to discuss their concerns about their child or problems that they may be having with her.

A good nursery school should broaden a child's horizons. When the nursery school is devoted to providing the child with an enjoyable educational experience, and works closely with parents to furnish specific kinds of experiences that the child is not receiving at home, then it should be of great benefit in relation to her over-all development.

Selecting a Nursery School

Parents considering enrolling their child in nursery school often have many questions. One is certainly: At what age is a child ready to attend nursery school? There is no one answer to this question since each child and family situation are unique. "Readiness" can vary a great deal from child to child. Many children start nursery school at around two and a half or three years of age, and are quite capable of making a positive adjustment. A few may start as early as eighteen months, or two years, although most children are not ready to begin until they are around two and a half to three years old. There are nursery schools that will not take youngsters under the age of three.

By the age of three, the majority of children have been weaned and toilet trained, and they are more easily able to cope with separations from the parent who has been taking primary care of them. Around the age of three, most children are very interested in their peers and are able to co-operate and interact with one another in positive, meaningful ways. A few nursery schools make it a point to evaluate a child's readiness to enter, although parents themselves should make their own evaluation based upon good common sense and their knowledge of their own child.

Choosing a nursery school is often not an easy task. There are good ones and not-so-good ones, very costly ones and less expensive ones, convenient ones and inconvenient ones. When you first begin to consider sending your child to nursery school, it is a good idea to determine what resources may be lacking in your home, and in what ways you hope the nursery school will be able to supplement the kind of educational experience your child is receiving at home. Assuming that you are able to provide her with everything except the opportunity to spend time with her peers, then you may want to find the type of nursery school that focuses on promoting the child's social skills.

Perhaps the best way to begin narrowing down the possibilities is to ask your friends and neighbors who have preschoolers who are attending, or have recently attended, nursery school for their honest evaluation. In the event that your friends cannot be of assistance, you might phone a local family social agency to see if they have any recommendations. As a last resort, turn to the Yellow Pages.

It is a good idea to make a list of questions so that when you talk on the phone with the directors of various nursery schools, you will be sure to find out what you want to know. Below is a brief list of some of the kinds of questions that you may want answered.

- Is the nursery school licensed by the state?
- What does the school feel it can offer your child?
- Does it have well-qualified teachers?
- Does it have a regular curriculum, and, if so, what kind?
- What is the ratio of children to teachers?
- Does it operate on a half-day or full-day basis?
- How much does it cost?
- What is its philosophy of handling and educating children?
- Does it have adequate play space, toys, and equipment both indoors and outdoors?
- Does it have a nurse or physician on call in case a child gets sick?
- Does it ever take children on field trips?
- What age requirements, if any, are there?
- Are children of the same age range separated into groups?
- Does it encourage parental involvement or maintain communication between home and school?
- Does it have rest periods for the children?

After you have narrowed down the possibilities, visit each nursery school to see what goes on during the day; judge for yourself if you like what you see. A visit will enable you to determine whether or not the atmosphere is friendly and relaxed, and will give you a chance to talk with staff members.

Your Child's Reaction to Nursery School

Attending nursery school represents a big step forward for your child. She should be adequately prepared for it. It is important to tell her in advance that she is going to go to school. You should tell her when she will start, and offer her information about what goes on at nursery school. Also let her know how much time she will be spending there each day, and how she will be dropped off and picked up. Knowing a little about what she can expect should help to make the transition from home with you to school without you less anxiety-provoking for her.

In giving her a description of nursery school, you should paint an optimistic, but realistic, picture of it. Some children love school from the very beginning, others are unhappy, feel insecure, and are frightened and uncomfortable there. A child who has been told that she will "love" school and that it will be "a lot of fun" may be disappointed and resentful if she finds the opposite to be true during even the first few days. While you should avoid painting a totally negative picture of school, because this might make her apprehensive, you could tell her that she may feel uncomfortable there during the first few days, but that her uneasiness will diminish and things will get better as time goes on. You can also tell her that she, like most children, will probably learn to enjoy going to nursery school.

CHILDREN'S REACTIONS TO SCHOOL VARY, AND OCCASIONAL PROBLEMS MAY ARISE. Most children adapt easily to nursery school, and really enjoy it, while others take longer to adjust, and some never like nursery school. Occasionally, children feel as though they are being pushed out of the house because they have been bad, or are no longer wanted, and these feelings are apt to be strong when they are enrolled in nursery school shortly after the arrival of a new baby into the family. Some children, particularly those whose appearance differs from the norm or who are fragile, are "bullied" or "picked on" by the others at school, and this may be the reason for their reluctance or negative attitude toward going to school.

Many children, especially very young ones, are anxious about being separated from their mothers or fathers. When this is the case, it is often helpful for a parent to accompany the child to school for several days in order to ease the transition. Once the child feels more secure there, she can be left alone. Many teachers do not object to a child's bringing a favorite toy or object for comfort. Whatever you do, it is not advisable to belittle your child or make her feel ashamed of herself for being afraid to attend school. Rather, try to encourage her to tell you her feelings, and then do your best to understand them and help her deal with them.

Sometimes the manner in which parents prepare their child for school can prompt the child's negative reaction. When parents are particularly anxious about what will happen to their child at school, or are the overprotective type, they may unknowingly convey to her the message that the school experience is not really positive, or is something for her to worry about. They may send such messages by dropping their child off at school with a look that says, "I wish you weren't going," or by prolonging their good-bys. It is advisable to say a pleasant good-by and then leave promptly.

Parents occasionally have a difficult time adjusting to their child's absence. Accustomed to having their children at home during the day, they may find it hard to get used to being alone, and may secretly long to have their preschooler home again, and dependent upon them. These parents may not feel as though they are conveying their "secret" wish to their children, but the children may sense that their parents would prefer to have them at home, and, as a result, may become reluctant to return to school.

WHAT TO DO IF YOUR CHILD DISLIKES SCHOOL. If your preschooler does not adapt well to nursery school, check with her teacher. The teacher may be able to offer some explanation, as well as suggestions to assist your youngster in making a more positive adjustment.

Should a conference with your child's teacher reveal little about possible reasons for her dislike, then try to determine whether or not your own ambivalence about being separated from her is contributing to her reluctance to attend school. If this is not the case, try to get her to talk about her feelings, and help her get over her worries as best you can. A little extra understanding, support, and reassurance may be all that is needed. In the event that she is young, and is simply not ready to separate from you, or is not benefiting from or enjoying the nursery school experience, there is no sense forcing her to continue.

The majority of children adapt well to nursery school, although nursery school is not for every child. Before you hurriedly come to the conclusion that nursery school is not for her, give both her and it a chance. Some children simply need more time

Preschool 1

than others to adapt, and some need more gentle persuasion and encouragement from their parents than others. Most parents need not worry about their child's reaction to the nursery school experience, because most children are eager to attend, and will find school enjoyable as well as educational.

PREPARED PARENTHOOD CHECK LIST

MOTHER	FATHER	UNDERSTANDING YOUR CHILD'S DEVELOPMENT
—	—	Has your child passed through the phase of the "Terrible Two's," or is she entering it now?
—	—	Some children show an interest in reliving the past. Has yours?
—	—	Have you seen any indications that your preschooler is worried about her body's condition? Does she become upset over the tiniest hurt or scratch?
—	—	Is your child beginning to identify with you?
—	—	In what ways does your youngster show that she is developing a sexual identity?
—	—	Have you observed any improvements in your child's ability to control her behavior in regard to specific rules that you have established?
—	—	Can you see evidence of the further development of symbolic thinking in your child's behavior and speech?
—	—	Are you aware of the self-centered nature of your preschooler's thinking?
—	—	What limitations in your child's understanding of the world of objects have you observed?
—	—	Does your child react to some moving objects as though they are alive?
—	—	In what ways have your child's concepts of space, time, and cause and effect expanded?
—	—	How has your child become more imaginative?
—	—	Are you able to communicate verbally with your child?
—	—	Is your preschooler making rapid strides in her ability to speak and understand what you say to her?
—	—	Have you been making sincere attempts to foster your child's language development by conversing with her, reading to her, and teaching her new words?
—	—	Does your child make any errors in speech? How do you react when you hear them?
—	—	Are you aware that the preschool stage is a favorable period in which to introduce a second language?
—	—	Have you been allowing your child to move about freely and practice her physical skills?
—	—	Do you see evidence that your child is becoming more co-ordinated in gross motor tasks such as walking, running, climbing, kicking a ball, and throwing a ball?

Preschool 1

— — What signs of progress in your child's hand and finger control have you noticed?

— — Does your preschooler enjoy art activities?

— — Are you doing anything to promote your child's imaginative play?

— — Has your youngster's interest in playing with other children increased?

— — Have you been offering your child a wide assortment of playthings and activities suited to her interests and abilities?

— — Does your child enjoy playing with you?

BASIC CARE

— — What booster immunizations need to be given during the preschool years to continue to prevent certain illnesses?

— — Are you teaching your child a positive attitude toward health care and cleanliness?

— — Have you been offering your child proper dental care and instruction in caring for her teeth?

— — Are you able to grant your child more independence and responsibility in certain activities?

— — Have you been setting a good example for your preschooler to follow in regard to accident prevention?

— — In what ways are you teaching your child to become safety-conscious?

— — What efforts are you taking to ensure your child's safety in the car, around water, and in the home?

— — Is your youngster eating less, becoming more distractible, and becoming choosier at mealtimes?

— — Have you been taking your child's preferences into account in selecting clothes for her?

— — Are you encouraging your preschooler to assume more independence in regard to eating, bathing, and dressing?

— — Does your child have a nightly going-to-bed ritual?

— — What progress is your child making in developing bowel and bladder control?

— — Is your child ready to make a shift from a crib to a "youth" or regular-size bed?

FAMILY FEELINGS AND CONCERNS

— — Are you altering your expectations of your child to go along with her changing abilities?

— — Is your child's ability to regulate her own actions in specific situations improving?

— — Do you avoid going to extremes in your approach to discipline?

—— —— What is your philosophy of punishment?

—— —— Have you been experiencing any difficulties in disciplining your child?

—— —— How does your preschooler discharge tension?

—— —— Are you aware of the more common tension outlets often used by preschool children as well as the general guidelines for handling them?

—— —— Have you noticed an increase in the number of fears your child displays?

—— —— Does your preschooler have any imaginary fears?

—— —— Are you encouraging and supporting your child's natural ways of dealing with frightening experiences?

—— —— Have you thought about how to help your child develop a healthy respect for the environment?

—— —— Why is it beneficial for your child to grow up with a strong family base and some knowledge of her family background?

—— —— How does watching violence on the screen affect your preschooler? Are you discriminating in what programs and movies you allow her to watch?

—— —— Is your child becoming more difficult to handle? Do you share your frustrations with your spouse and others?

—— —— What are some of the new considerations that arise in relation to beginning or returning to work outside the home during the preschool stage?

THE TOTAL EDUCATION OF YOUR CHILD

—— —— How do you plan to offer your preschool child a personalized, total educational experience?

—— —— Are you aware that you can be an excellent teacher for your child even though you do not have formal training as a teacher?

—— —— What are some of the major areas of education, and are you familiar with the basic teaching techniques that are successful in helping the child learn?

—— —— Have you been making a sincere effort to teach your child to respect other people and their differences?

—— —— In what ways do you try to foster your child's curiosity, creativity, and enthusiasm for learning?

—— —— How do you try to make learning fun for your preschool child?

—— —— If you plan to supplement the home educational experience with nursery school or preschool, do you know how to select a good one?

Preschool 2

PERSONAL-SOCIAL DEVELOPMENT

Preschool 2 children have finally passed through the rough and stormy stage of the "Terrible Two's," or are at least headed in this direction, much to their parents' relief. Temporarily around age three, most youngsters are not as uneasy and tense as they might have been in Preschool 1, and may seem more relaxed and emotionally well balanced. The child feels more independent and secure, and no longer needs the security of "set" patterns of behavior, inflexible routines, and old methods of accomplishing tasks. He is not only able to use language more effectively in communicating his needs and wishes to others, he is beginning to utilize words to regulate his own behavior to a greater extent than in the past.

Your three-year-old has achieved the more sophisticated level of maturity and autonomy that he fought so hard for during toddlerhood. He no longer has to be as defiant, bossy, and obstinate, because he has proven to himself and you that he is separate and can act independently from you. Now he is better able to make some independent choices and decisions, and express personal thoughts and ideas. You will still hear your child use the word "no," but you will gradually hear the word "yes" more often. More attempts will be made to gain your approval. In general, he will be more even-tempered, and more pleasant to have around. You are likely to discover that your child is better able to comply with your wishes and live up to your expectations.

Socializing with you and other family members, and establishing friendships with other youngsters, is more important to your child during this phase. His peers mean a lot to him, and he spends a large portion of time each day playing co-operatively with them. Greater awareness of other people, added maturity, and increased verbal abilities contribute to his stronger interest in social activities.

BEHAVIOR CHANGES AROUND THREE AND A HALF. The greater security and more relaxed attitude that is usually seen following the stormy phase of the "Terrible Two's" is often short-lived. Once the Toddlerhood 3 or Preschool 1 child resolves his early push for independence and emotional security, he must face new challenges in Preschool 2. He will begin to develop a sexual identity and have to learn to cope with new situations outside the security of his home.

It is not uncommon to see a change in your child's behavior during Preschool 2, around the age of three and a half. Once again, he may not feel comfortable within himself and his feeling of confidence and security might suddenly diminish. Feelings of inferiority may emerge. This is a time when he will regularly ask you whether or not you really love him and want him around. He is apt to crave more of your attention and affection, and make increasing demands on your time. Insecurity may result in his becoming bossier in dealing with you and others, and he will frequently insist upon telling you and his friends what to do. This will be a time for more complaining, arguing, whining, and crying.

Your three-and-a-half-year-old's emotions are likely to be more unstable. One moment he will be laughing, and the next moment crying. He may be friendly to a stranger for a moment, and then quickly shift to being extremely shy and quiet. As a result of his rapidly changing and unpredictable emotional state, you will have to be a bit more patient with him.

Feelings of uncertainty are not only expressed in the area of personal-social development. You may also notice that he is unsteadier on his feet, more ill at ease in new situations, and more subject to fears and nightmares. Heavy use of outlets for tension and minor speech difficulties often arise during Preschool 2. Like the "Terrible Two's," this phase of insecurity often seen during Preschool 2 will gradually subside. It represents a natural sign of your child's constant emotional and intellectual growth. The insecurity and emotional change reflect the tension that the child feels as he progresses from one level of development to the next, similar to that which the infant experiences before major developmental milestones are achieved. Extra reassurance and support from you can make it easier for him to meet new developmental challenges during this phase.

TEMPER TANTRUMS MAY DIMINISH. At long last your child's temper tantrums are probably subsiding. Some lapses in emotional control can still be expected, although immature methods of discharging tension through temper outbursts and tantrums are likely to be seen much less frequently than before. Your youngster is better able to listen to you when you try to reason with him, and can accept suggestions without feeling threatened or flying into a rage.

Improved ability to use and understand language enables him to exercise self-discipline more easily. He is developing an increasing capacity to be patient and not let temporary frustrations get him down. Improving mental abilities are opening up new doors for him. When you tell him that he cannot go to the zoo, for instance, he can make use of his imagination and play that he is at the zoo, or just sit and daydream about being there. The fact that your child's temper tantrums have diminished will make your life more settled. It is easy to take his more mature behavior for granted, but if you remember back to earlier phases when flying off the handle was a frequent occurrence, his behavioral improvements will be more appreciated.

Self-awareness

A MORE SECURE IDENTITY. The Preschool 1 child began to use the word "I," although he probably did not feel totally comfortable using this pronoun. Chances are that this was partly due to the fact that he did not have a good understanding of this new vocabulary word, and partly due to the fact that the distinction between himself and others was not entirely clear in his own mind. The distinction is likely to be more obvious to him during Preschool 2. His sense of identity is stronger. This enables him to refer to himself as "I" with greater self-assurance. He now knows for sure that he is a boy like his father and other boys with whom he plays. When asked whether he is a boy or a girl, he may even find this question silly, and will say with the utmost confidence, "I'm a boy."

THE TEMPORARY DESIRE TO ACT LIKE A BABY AND RELIVE HIS PAST. The child of this age is apt to show an interest in returning to his past, assuming that he has not already done so in Preschool 1. After learning about his past, your preschooler will probably go through a temporary period in which he acts like an infant. He may want to drink out of a bottle, play with his "baby" toys, talk "baby talk," or be held just like when he was a baby. This behavior often takes an exaggerated form in families in which a preschool child feels threatened by or jealous of a new baby. With all of the subtle and not-so-subtle pressures that the child feels to act more "grown-up," it may be easier for him to slip back into the past for a brief period of time than to continue to live up to parental and social expectations.

In the event that your child goes through a temporary phase such as this, there is no need for you to worry that he is in any way abnormal. It is quite common for children to want to relive their babyhood and regress for a brief period of time. Once he has had his fill of being a baby again, he will quickly move forward to more mature ways of behaving. Having had an opportunity to slip back in time can be a beneficial experience for a young child. When he starts acting his own age again, he should feel a stronger sense of identity and self-pride in all of the progress he has made since early infancy.

WHERE DID I COME FROM? Now that your child has some sense of identity, he will probably become interested in knowing where he came from, and where he was before he was born. Such an interest usually prompts youngsters to ask many questions like, "Where did I come from?" Questions pertaining to where babies come from are also very common. These questions reflect a child's increasing curiosity and attempts to clarify his own identity. Receiving satisfactory answers should strengthen his sense of "I" and add a new dimension to his expanding awareness of himself. Suggestions for how to handle these types of questions are provided on pages 868–74.

Before answering questions of this nature, it is always a good idea to find out where your child thinks babies come from, or how he thinks they are made. Be prepared for some strange theories. Knowing his thoughts on the subject, you will be in a much better position to clarify his naïve, incorrect notions. Hearing what he already knows or does not know can help you shape your replies so that they are more in tune with his level of understanding.

Upon learning that a baby grows inside a mother, children are often very anxious to grow a baby themselves. When a little girl says that she wants to grow a baby, her parents think this is adorable. When a little boy announces that "I want to grow a baby, too!" his parents are less thrilled. This should not represent any cause for alarm. A young boy simply does not have enough knowledge about the differences between men and women to prevent him from making this kind of statement. Eventually, you will convince your son that this wish can never be fulfilled, but for a while, at least, he may continue to believe that he is going to grow a baby inside him when he gets older.

HEIGHTENED CONCERNS ABOUT THE CONDITION OF HIS BODY. Concerns about body safety and "wholeness" that emerged during Preschool 1 are apt to increase. Your youngster may show a sudden interest in people he sees who are ill, crippled, or injured, and ask all kinds of questions about their condition as well as the factors that might have contributed to it. These questions probably reflect his worry that he will get sick or that a similar mishap or injury will happen to him. He may even become upset over minor changes in someone's appearance. Should a familiar woman have her waist-length hair cut short, or a nursery school assistant teacher show up in class wearing contact lenses in lieu of her regular glasses, the Preschool 2 child may misconstrue these changes and regard the person as being deformed, injured, or not whole.

These concerns are normal, and most children have them. Knowing that preschool children have worries about body intactness, it is easy to understand why a visit to the doctor, dentist, or hospital (even when someone else is the patient) may heighten their concern. Having a tooth or tonsils removed at this time may be terrifying to a young child. A great deal of reassurance from you as well as correct information should help in allaying fears.

FURTHER IDENTIFICATION WITH PARENTS. You will see more evidence of your child's identification with you, especially the parent of the same sex, as he talks to other children or engages in dress-up play. He is gradually beginning to incorporate small aspects of your behavior and attitudes into his own personality. As he spends more time apart from you and the home setting, you will probably see evidence that he is identifying with non-family members as well, although to a lesser extent. His ability to identify with others is still in its embryonic stages during Preschool 2, and more evidence of this will be seen in the next phase.

SEXUAL IDENTITY IS MORE WELL-ESTABLISHED. Part of establishing a firm sexual identity involves learning about the differences between the sexes and simple aspects of reproduction. Your child now knows his sex, and will state it when you ask, but a clear sense of sexual identity is still forthcoming. He is apt to ask questions about the anatomical differences between boys and girls, and also may be curious about the different urination positions males and females use in the bathroom.

It is not uncommon for little girls at this age to try urinating "like Daddy" or an older brother. After a short period of experimentation, they usually give up. Many children become fascinated with looking at and touching their parents' bodies when they are undressed, probably focusing on their father's penis and mother's breasts, since differences in size and shape will catch youngsters' attention.

LOVE AND THE MARRIED WOMAN. A little Preschool 2 boy, striving to be like his father, may want to have a love relationship with his mother that is just like Daddy's. He begins to develop new feelings toward his mother—romantic feelings. These feelings are normal, and most little boys are believed to have them. A boy may think and fantasize about being alone with his mother, and marrying her when he grows up. He may act on his fantasies in the sense of being very affectionate toward his mother and insisting that "When I grow up I'm going to marry Mommy." Some boys keep their feelings and wishes to themselves, whereas others are much more demonstrative about them.

When a boy loves someone as much as he loves his mother, it is only natural for him to want to have her all to himself. Realizing that his father is an obstacle to having Mommy all to himself, he becomes jealous and resentful of Daddy and probably wishes that his father would go away. Competitive and aggressive feelings toward his father are troubling to a young boy because he needs, loves, and admires his father, and is afraid to think of what would happen in the event that his wish really came true. Contradictory feelings about Daddy make a boy feel very tense and guilty.

A little boy often imagines that his father has similar aggressive and jealous feelings toward him. Knowing that his father is so much bigger and stronger, he begins to fear that his father will punish him or seek other revenge. Frightening thoughts such as these may not bother him during the daytime, but can provide fertile material for a child's bad dreams and nightmares during the preschool years.

According to psychologists, a child may project his fear of his strong and powerful father onto terrifying figures such as giants and wild animals that come after him in his dreams. Many psychologists attribute the child's occasional antagonistic behavior toward his father, nightmares, and strong guilt feelings to this competition or conflict with his father over his mother. The universality of this "love" conflict has been questioned, but it is common enough to warrant your attention.

LOVE AND THE MARRIED MAN. A similar "love" conflict usually occurs with the little girl, although her father is the basis for her romantic feelings. Some little girls, like boys, cover up their feelings and wishes, whereas others voice them openly. Recognizing that Mommy is her arch rival, she becomes jealous and resentful of her. These feelings create the same conflicts for the little girl as they did for the boy. She may also feel tense and guilty, and imagine that her mother feels hostility toward her. In dreaming, girls may project their fear of their mothers onto figures such as witches or wild animals that come after them. This conflict may result in periodical excessive guilt feelings as well as antagonistic or competitive behavior toward mother.

The young child must eventually learn that the romantic love attachment to the parent of the opposite sex, and wish to replace the parent of the same sex, cannot be fulfilled. The resolution of the child's conflicts is discussed in Preschool 3 (pages 900–1).

STEREOTYPING SEX ROLES. How many times have you heard statements like the following: "Boys don't cry." "Jerry's a little boy, so he doesn't have to help with the dishes." "Dolls are for girls." "Elinor's a tomboy; she likes to play football with the boys." "Trucks and erector sets are for little boys to play with—not girls."

Society often dictates very rigid stereotypes of "masculine" and "feminine" roles. Men have traditionally been expected to be better at sports and heavy work than women and were also supposed to be less expressive about fears and emotions. In the past, competitive and aggressive sports such as football, hockey, and baseball were off limits to women, and even certain careers such as medicine, law, mechanics, plumbing, truck driving, and so on, were considered strictly for men. Men, on the other hand, were forced to avoid typically "feminine" activities such as cooking, sewing, housework, child care, and so forth.

This situation has changed. More women have entered what were formerly considered only male occupations and professions. Women have become the providers in many families, and some men are staying home and taking a more active role in child rearing. Roles have changed and are continuing to change. It is now more difficult, if not impossible, to describe clearly completely "feminine" or "masculine" occupations or styles of living.

It is important not to become threatened by these changes. Each individual family should not feel pressured to function in a given way. The role of the husband and wife in a family setting should be a personal decision.

As children develop a sexual identity, it is not uncommon for them occasionally to want to take on both male and female roles in their dramatic play. It is also fairly common for a little girl to want to try to urinate standing up like her father, or for a little boy to want to try on his mother's hat or purse. Young children, under the age of about three, are often not too aware of the distinction between "masculine" and "feminine" activities (whatever they are). Labeling a young boy as a "sissie" or punishing him for occasionally exploring a female role is a mistake. It is also a mistake to label a young girl or punish her for occasionally exploring "male" activities.

After the age of three, youngsters generally become more aware of the "conventional" male and female activities. As they begin to identify more with the parent of the same sex, they are more likely to imitate the behavior of that parent. The adoption of sex roles occurs naturally and should not cause any major concern at this early stage.

Some parents grant their children greater freedom to explore aspects of both male and female roles. However, when a child is granted too much freedom at this age, some confusion and conflict about his or her sex role can result. While parents may want to guard against forcing their child into a rigid stereotyped sex role, they will also want to avoid going to the opposite extreme of not providing a clear role model to follow.

DEVELOPING A CONSCIENCE. The child's conscience is still in the early stages of development, but his ability to control his actions in some situations will become more evident. Your child's conscience is still new and immature. He may follow his conscience on one day, and then be swayed by temptation on the next. His system of self-control is not always working as it should. Try to be patient with him in this regard, and do not expect his conscience to work effectively twenty-four hours a day.

Children's ability to regulate their own behavior will continue to fluctuate during Preschool 2. They are still, for the most part, trying hard to control their urges to do as they please on a conscious level. Once their consciences are further developed, they should not even have to stop to think about whether or not to do something parents have warned them against doing, since doing it would be unacceptable to them as well.

As the young child begins to recognize that some of his behavior patterns are unacceptable to his family and even to himself, internal tensions and pressures often arise. A youngster may know that a behavior is "wrong" but want to do it anyway. Johnny, for example, who is jealous of his younger sister, wants to hit her and thus release his aggression. His parents have told him that he should love his sister and take care of her. He is caught between his feelings of anger toward his sister, and his knowledge of the way he *should* treat her.

Unable to control his feelings one day when he was especially jealous of his mother's affection toward his sister, Johnny pushed her, causing her to fall out of her infant seat and cry. At first, Johnny felt relieved by his action, but he soon realized that he had done something wrong. He then felt ashamed at having gone against both his parents' and his own standard of how he should behave.

It is common for young children who are first assuming some of their parents' attitudes toward their own behavior to have difficulty dealing with their own unacceptable desires and/or actions. No one likes to admit to others or to himself that there are things he did that were wrong, or aspects of himself that he does not like. Owning up to this would probably cause a loss of "face." Accepting responsibility for one's own behavior requires a certain maturity that children of this age generally do not have.

Young children, in dealing with their unacceptable actions, often regard a violation of the rules as if it did not belong to them. A child has trouble thinking that he was a "bad" boy, and believes that naughty behaviors come from someone else. He usually does not accept the fact that unacceptable desires to do wrong "belong" to him, and for this reason may not feel ashamed of himself after he has been "bad."

Another way of dealing with his unacceptable desires is to project (transfer) them onto another person or object. The Preschool 2 child may behave as though his Teddy bear or his younger sister were to blame for his behavior. Using a person or object, either real or imaginary, as a scapegoat for his wrongdoings, he is able to maintain positive feelings about himself. The subject of children blaming imaginary companions for their own wrongdoing is more fully explored on pages 833–34.

Before your preschooler is better able to follow his conscience, he will have to acknowledge his own undesirable impulses, and learn that he is accountable for his wrongdoings. Once this occurs, you will probably notice great progress in conscience development and self-regulation. As he approaches Preschool 3, watch for further signs of self-control, a greater willingness to accept responsibility for his own acts, and more evidence of feeling guilty about his misdeeds. These signs will serve as evidence of the strides he is making in self-discipline.

Social Sensitivity and Interests

RELATIONSHIPS WITHIN THE FAMILY. Your Preschool 2 child will demonstrate greater ability to share, give affection, get along with others, and co-operate with you. His social relationships will reach a more sophisticated level in which he will show greater respect for other people's requests, needs, and wishes. During the first part of this phase, around age three, he is apt to get along quite well with you and even, perhaps, with brothers and sisters. He should feel more comfortable and relaxed in general. This enables easier dealings with other people, particularly family members.

Moving further into this phase, around the age of three and a half, family relationships may deteriorate once again. His bossy, irritable, and rebellious nature is likely to antagonize you and other family members. Unless things are done the way he wants them to be done, he will be furious and probably lose control of his emotions. These and other personality characteristics, such as constant complaining and whining, can make it hard for you to live with him and enjoy his company. The things that he will do during this stage are likely to grate on everyone's nerves.

IMPROVING ABILITY TO GET ALONG WITH OTHER CHILDREN. Most Preschool 2 children enjoy playing with their contemporaries. They are noticeably more interested in other children. Together they will engage in both real and imaginary play, and hold delightful, amusing conversations. Children often converse with one another in a much more friendly manner than in Preschool 1. You may want to record a few of the lively conversations that your child has with his playmates when they engage in pretend activities.

When playing together, Preschool 2 children tend to be less aggressive toward one another. Previously, children appeared to argue most over playthings, but now their arguments will be about social issues. Disagreements over who will play with whom, who will be included in an activity and who will not, who will take on what roles in their dramatic play, and who is friends with whom are very common. Sometimes several children gang up against a particular child. They may call the child names, treat him cruelly, and not allow him to enter into their games or activities. These arguments may result in children physically and verbally abusing one another.

Children are becoming very interested in friendships, and although girls tend to be friends with other girls, and boys mainly become friends with boys, there are also friendships between girls and boys. A child may proudly state, "I have a girl friend," or, "I have a boy friend." Youngsters may go so far as to ask one another for their hand in marriage, and hold a make-believe wedding ceremony with a pretend ring, minister or rabbi, flower girl, and wedding cake.

More play in groups is seen. Parents will notice that in a group of youngsters playing together on a regular basis, roles can be more easily recognized. One child may act as a "leader," while the others become "followers." A "bully" may also emerge in the group. Within the group there may also be a "popular" child as well as one who is not very well liked.

Imitation among youngsters playing together is likely to be strong. When one child does something, the others will feel compelled to do the same. Parents often begin to notice the effect that other children are having upon their preschooler, sometimes with dismay, and sometimes with pleasure. Pressure from peers grows stronger as children grow older and spend more time with their contemporaries.

Imaginary Companions

Preschool 2 children have highly active imaginations. During this phase, the appearance of imaginary companions is common. Imaginary companions might have existed at earlier ages, but parents do not often discover them until their child can talk about them. Even then, some children keep their imaginary companions private. However, there are children who talk to their companions and about them in front of other people. An imaginary companion may take different forms: an imaginary friend to play with (either human or animal), imaginary identities, in which a child pretends to be someone else, imaginary playthings, imaginary scapegoats, or real objects or toys which are believed to be "alive."

Imaginary companions can serve many different functions. They may act as the child's "ideal self," or a well-operating "conscience." One little boy had an imaginary companion that was his extra conscience, threatening to punish him severely if he was naughty. For a period of about a month, this child's companion kept him in line, until he was better able to manage his behavior on his own.

In some cases imaginary companions function as good friends. Murray created an imaginary friend out of loneliness after his family moved to a new city. His make-believe buddy helped keep him company until he was able to make real friends in the new neighborhood.

When a child wants to try out or assume a new identity, he may create an imaginary one for himself. Children who assume a new identity often go to great lengths to act out their roles. One little boy named Keith, according to his parents, assumed a role as a kangaroo. He referred to his stomach as a pouch, began to make animal noises, and jumped around like a kangaroo instead of walking. Keeping up this role was difficult for him, and after two weeks he gave it up, having caused his parents much embarrassment.

Some children may have only one imaginary companion, whereas others have more than one. The child's imaginary companions, in some cases, interfere with family life. Timothy, for example, insisted that a place be set at the dinner table for his imaginary friend, Mark. Whenever he sat down—on the couch, in the car, and so on, he saw to it that a place was reserved for Mark. It is not uncommon for a youngster to want to include his imaginary friend in family activities, and this can sometimes represent both a nuisance and an inconvenience.

DEALING WITH IMAGINARY COMPANIONS. Mrs. Jenner played along with her son Glenn's demands to include his imaginary friend, Jimmy, in family activities, but spoke only to Glenn and never to Jimmy. She let Glenn know from the start that Jimmy was only a pretend friend, but told him that there was nothing wrong with pretending.

One afternoon, when Mrs. Jenner was meeting with a travel agent to finalize plane reservations for the family, Glenn insisted that his mother reserve a place on the plane for Jimmy. When she said that this was not possible, Glenn became very angry and upset. After he had calmed down a bit, Mrs. Jenner explained to him that Jimmy would have to be left behind, since only real people travel on airplanes. He seemed satisfied with her answer.

The day of his airplane trip, Mrs. Jenner encouraged Glenn to say good-by to Jimmy. After a rather sad parting, he and his mother left for the airport, and Jimmy disappeared for good.

This mother's method of handling her son's imaginary friend was quite appropriate. She encouraged him to recognize the difference between "pretend" versus "real," but respected his need for an imaginary outlet, rather than scolding, shaming, or punishing him for it.

Many professionals agree that you should not react to your preschooler's make-believe companions as though they really existed. You can tactfully let your child know that his companion is not real, but still convey the message that you understand it is sometimes fun to pretend. Separating make-believe from reality is not an easy task for a preschool child. Most youngsters probably know that their companions are not real, but some children get rather lost in their make-believe activities.

It is important to try to help your child sort out reality and fantasy, rather than confuse him further. Clearly outline for him where his pretending ends and reality begins, but refrain from denying him permission to engage in any make-believe play. It is healthy for youngsters to have opportunities to pretend, and to make use of imaginary outlets.

Not every child creates imaginary companions, but many perfectly normal children have them. Make-believe companions should not cause you an unnecessary amount of concern. If a child is spending almost all of his time in an imaginary world, and has great difficulty or is unable to establish good relationships with real people, a parent may need to seek professional help in dealing with this problem.

Make-believe companions do not seem to appear merely because a child lacks love, attention, companionship, or is an "only child." Children with siblings and plenty of friends also create these companions. According to the Gesell Institute's *Child Behavior from Birth to Ten,* "Most often it is the well-endowed child of good intelligence and adequate social adjustment, as well as imagination, who has imaginary companions." Imaginary companions are a normal expression of the child's imaginary world, and represent his attempts at learning about the differences between fantasy and reality.

Having opportunities to escape from reality occasionally and briefly enter a world created by one's imagination is a coping mechanism that is important to adults as well as children. Make-believe companions appear to help a child deal with the frustrating demands and pressures that he experiences. They may also assist a child in learning more about himself as well as other people. Dr. T. Berry Brazelton, in his book *Toddlers and Parents,* says that with imaginary friends the child "can explore parts of his personality, parts of himself which he could never learn about otherwise. And he learns about experience with the world this way. He finds out what his parents will or won't allow by letting his 'friend' try things out for him."

Other professionals point out that imaginary companions and imaginary play can help a child overcome his fears. A child, for example, who has a fear of dogs, may try to overcome this fear by becoming a dog in his dramatic play. This is a healthy approach to dealing with his fears. You may want to refer back to the earlier discussion of this which appeared in the Preschool 1 Fears section on page 772.

Imaginary companions seem to fill some temporary need within a child. In the majority of cases, they fade out of the picture when a child's need for them diminishes. Most imaginary companions disappear after a short period of a couple of weeks to a few months, although they may occasionally stick with a child during the early elementary school years. The most common time for make-believe companions is during the preschool stage, especially during Preschool 2 and 3. See also pages 725–26 in the Preschool 1 Intellectual Development section that dealt with the imaginary world of the child.

USING AN IMAGINARY COMPANION AS A SCAPEGOAT. One type of imaginary companion that arouses a great deal of parental concern is the type that functions as a scapegoat for the child. During Preschool 2, when parents expect more from their youngster in terms of self-control and conscience development, they are often quite disturbed by his creation of a make-believe person or animal upon whom the burden of responsibility for his own wrongdoing is placed.

In some cases in which the young child has difficulty accepting his "naughty" urges and actions, and holding himself responsible for breaking rules, he creates an imaginary companion who serves as a scapegoat. A child places the blame on the make-believe figure, and can thus maintain his own self-love. The example that follows should increase your awareness of the function of this special type of imaginary companion, and help you realize that it can represent a child's progress toward developing a conscience.

Ronald Larson was having a hard time dealing with his undesirable wishes and actions. One day, when he was very angry at his father for not taking him to the ice show as he had promised, he deliberately broke his father's favorite model ship in the study. No one else was around at the time.

Mr. Larson later asked Ronald whether or not he had broken the ship, knowing that his son was the only one who could have done it. In response to this question, Ronald turned to his right and said, "Mr. Bear, did you break my daddy's ship?" He paused, and then continued in an angry tone of voice, "You naughty bear—you should know better."

Ronald's father was completely dumfounded. "Who are you talking to?" he asked.

Ronald replied, "I'm talking to Mr. Bear. He followed me home from the playground. He's very big, strong, and mean. He broke your ship 'cause he doesn't like you. I didn't do it."

This father was thus introduced to his son's new imaginary scapegoat, Mr. Bear. That night, when Mr. Larson went to say good night to Ronald, he found all of Ronald's toys scattered across the floor of his room (something he had been warned against on many occasions).

"Why didn't you put away your toys like you were supposed to?" his father demanded.

"I've been a good boy," Ronald reported. "I didn't make a mess." Then he turned and said in an angry tone of voice, "Mr. Bear, did you leave my toys on the floor? You bad bear." Then he turned back to his father and said, "Mr. Bear did it—not me. He doesn't like to put toys away."

Mr. Bear "lived" with Ronald and his family for several weeks, and appeared every now and then as a scapegoat for Ronald's own unacceptable wishes and deeds, and a mean person who "demanded" that Ronald do naughty things. Three and a half weeks after Mr. Bear appeared, he suddenly disappeared.

Ronald's father knew that Mr. Bear did not represent an evil force that "made" Ronald behave poorly against his wishes. Mr. Larson made it clear to his son that it was Ronald, and not Mr. Bear, who had broken the rules of the house. This imaginary friend was useful during this phase of Ronald's life when he had a hard time accepting his own strong tendencies to go against his father's commands and was unable to exercise self-control. Ronald realized eventually that he alone was responsible for his violations, and that his naughty wishes came from inside himself, not his imaginary companion.

It is difficult at first to look upon Ronald's transference of his naughty wishes, thoughts, and actions onto another party as strides toward the goal of developing a conscience. By denying this negative part of himself, however, he is showing signs of recognizing "right" from "wrong." This is an important achievement in and of itself. Evidence of conscience development can be seen in the way Ronald talked to and behaved toward Mr. Bear.

Ronald addressed Mr. Bear in an angry and impatient tone of voice; one which was similar to Mr. Larson's tone when reprimanding his son. In Ronald's interactions with Mr. Bear, he looked at his own undesirable behavior through his father's eyes. This indicates that he has started to identify with his parents' attitudes about proper modes of behavior, although he has not yet incorporated them into his own personality, or conscience.

The disappearance of this little boy's imaginary scapegoat marked a significant step in his self-awareness and his strides toward self-control. In leaving Mr. Bear behind, he was learning to hold himself accountable for going beyond the limits and expectations that his father established. What was an outward conflict between himself and Mr. Bear became an internalized conflict between his urges to do wrong and his conscience. Now that he is realizing that his negative, or "bad" wishes come from within himself, he will be better able to come to grips with his undesirable impulses and will start to feel guilty and responsible for his own wrongdoings. This immature conscience should then begin to prevent him from acting when he feels the impulse to do what he knows is wrong.

INTELLECTUAL DEVELOPMENT

The Developing Mind

The child's mental capacities are changing and expanding. As a result, you will undoubtedly see corresponding changes in your child's behavior.

IMPROVEMENTS IN LANGUAGE ABILITIES. Your Preschool 2 child will probably be capable of carrying on a fairly good conversation with you. This, in and of itself, will make him seem much more intelligent and mature. His capacity for using and comprehending language has grown, and he will be very interested in learning new words, and combining them into longer, more complex sentences.

Rapid progress is taking place in your child's ability to store, interconnect, and play with word symbols in his mind. He will listen more attentively when you reason with him, and will learn vicariously, by listening to stories and explanations. Increases in his comprehension of language and ability to talk will serve as evidence of the progress that he is making in intellectual development.

MORE THINKING: LESS ACTING ON IMPULSES. Few would disagree that the Preschool 2 child is still impulsive, but he is growing less so as higher level mental activity enables thinking and talking to serve as substitutes for quick action. When faced with a problem, he will spend more time considering alternatives before he makes a move. You will observe many more short delays in his responses, during which time his facial expression will indicate that he is probably thinking the situation through.

Improvements in the child's ability to exercise self-control will accompany improvements in his ability to think and speak. Parents are often able to see this in relation to temper tantrums. As the child becomes able to talk about frustration and anger, he can express his feelings through this avenue as opposed to acting them out. Now that it is becoming easier for your youngster to understand what you say, listen to reason, and think about the results of an action before acting, disciplining him may be a less taxing job than in earlier phases.

MAKING DECISIONS IS EASIER. Making simple decisions such as whether to wear his red or green sweater was extremely difficult for the toddler and younger preschool child. Confusion over which of the two alternatives to select quite often led him to choose both, or to change his mind constantly from one minute to the next.

The Preschool 2 child is less prone to having trouble making up his mind. He is better able to remember experiences and hold more than one idea in his mind at a time. Evidence for this lies in his rather new ability to consider two alternatives and choose between them without quickly changing his mind or procrastinating for long periods of time. Simple decision-making comes easier to him now that he has become more of a thinker, has had more practice, and is surer of his opinions.

NEW ABILITY TO DO TWO THINGS AT ONCE. Expanding powers of concentration are making it possible for the Preschool 2 child to focus upon more than one task at once. This can be shown by the fact that some children will be able to play with a toy or engage in an activity and at the same time talk about something unrelated to what they are doing. While a little boy is playing with his fire engine, he may be talking about a trip to the post office that he and his parent took earlier in the day. This is something that he was usually unable to do before. Your youngster's emerging ability to divorce activity from conversation provides still more evidence of his intellectual development.

Understanding the World of Objects

Your child is able to say more about objects, do more with them, and think more about them than in earlier phases. His interaction with objects is becoming more and more appropriate. He knows how to hold and manipulate many more of them properly. Parents frequently notice that their preschooler is more resourceful and creative in his use of unstructured toys and art materials. With his blocks he may build a bridge or create a building. A cardboard box may become a puppet stage or a castle in his imaginative play. Objects are increasingly used as symbols for other

835

objects and make-believe activities. He may pretend that his bed is a car or that his shoes are boats, or that his lumps of clay are birthday cakes.

The Preschool 2 child is also making some progress in his ability to classify objects. He understands many of the names of classes of objects, and may be using these labels appropriately. It is clear to him that a chair is not a table, and that a car is not a bus, although he may not be able to tell you why.

You will notice how much better he is at clearly differentiating among objects in his surroundings, and at talking about objects in his conversations. He may even be able to point to objects of specific shapes, colors, and sizes correctly and pick out the odd member given a set of similar objects. Try giving him three blocks (or other objects) of one color and a fourth block of a different color. Chances are that he will easily be able to separate these blocks by color. In many respects, your child will show greater skill at carrying out simple abstractions related to objects and their properties, even though his classification of objects and people is still more related to his own frame of reference than to the objective properties of the objects themselves.

Despite the continued improvement in the child's ability to talk about objects, and use them more appropriately and creatively, the limitations in his dealings and thoughts about objects and various substances in the environment discussed in Preschool 1 are still evident.

What Makes Things Happen

The Preschool 2 child has an active mind and will show a growing interest in what is happening around him. During infancy and early toddlerhood, he mainly believed that he caused things to happen. Later in toddlerhood and during Preschool 1, his views about causality changed, and were presumably based in the notion that objects moved because they were alive and wanted to move. Now, during this phase, he develops new ideas about why things happen.

When the child sees something going on that has nothing to do with his own activity, he thinks that some "being" or "force" is behind it. He may ask questions about who it was who wanted the event to happen, or inquire about the motives or reasons underlying the changes that took place. Aaron, who heard the noise of thunder, seemed frightened by it. He ran to his mother for comfort and asked her why the man in the sky was angry. Aaron, like many Preschool 2 children, believed that there was some person or human-like force in the sky who was capable of feeling anger just as he did, and who let off steam by producing the roar of thunder. His question was not about what caused the thunder. Rather, he was attempting to discover the purpose behind this event.

It is common for children to see purposes and meanings behind everything that happens around them, because of their assumption that some being or force wills things to happen for a reason. You are likely to see some evidence of this belief in your child's questions, as well as his reaction to events that are accidental.

DIFFICULTY UNDERSTANDING "COINCIDENCES" AND "ACCIDENTS." Parents usually have tremendous difficulty trying to explain to youngsters of this age the idea of things happening by "coincidence" or by "accident." Children who see purposes for every event do not seem to be able to comprehend these notions.

Mr. McAfee took his two daughters, Sue Ellen, age eight, and Lynn, age three, to the movies on a Saturday afternoon. He picked three seats right next to the aisle, and told his children that he wanted the seat closest to the aisle. Lynn immediately plopped down in the seat next to where her father was going to sit. Sue Ellen had to get by Lynn in order to take her seat. As she attempted to move past her younger sister, she accidentally stepped on Lynn's toe. Lynn became furious, since she thought Sue Ellen had deliberately stepped on her. Despite Mr. McAfee's attempts to explain to Lynn that the incident was an "accident," he could not convince her of this, and she remained angry at her sister for the rest of the afternoon.

There is no reason to be discouraged if your child has trouble understanding that it is not always possible to find a purpose behind every event, or that when two events occur simultaneously or one right after another, this does not always imply a causal relationship. He will eventually be able to grasp the notion of "coincidences" and "accidents" when he outgrows his current, immature theories about what makes things happen.

Concept of Space

Your Preschool 2 child will develop a broader vocabulary of words to describe spaces and spatial relationships. Knowing additional words will help him to focus on more detailed spatial directions and relationships between objects and parts of objects. An interest in having objects put in their proper place may still be shown, although the child is usually not as insistent about this or as bothered by new arrangements of furniture as in Preschool 1.

Your child's perception of space is gradually becoming more accurate. He is likely to be able to describe a toy as being "on top of" the shelf, or state that a glass goes "on top." When you ask him to put an object such as a toy car "in back of," "under," and then "on" another object such as a sofa, he will most likely respond appropriately. Among the new words he may learn to describe position are "from," "over," "among," "behind," and "next to."

Other new additions to his vocabulary may include words to describe size and shape, such as "littlest," "biggest," "larger," "highest," and "lowest." From his use of these words it will be apparent that he is developing a better awareness of the comparative sizes of objects and playthings. In regard to distant places, he may more accurately describe something as being "way down there" or "far away."

Assuming that you have been teaching your child to distinguish "left" from "right," he may now begin to use these words in telling you how to get to a specific location and show an interest in directions. While in the car on the way to the supermarket several blocks away from home, he might give you directions such as, "First turn right and then turn left," or, "Make a left turn over there." When you ask him where a nearby relative lives, he may no longer give a simple reply like, "At her house." Instead, he may begin telling you, probably in a disorganized fashion, how you could get to this person's house. Your child may even display the new ability to tell you or other people the name of the street on which he lives, and possibly even the name of the city in which he lives. This ability comes more slowly with some youngsters, so you should not expect it at this particular phase.

In addition to his new ability to give directions, the child will also show his growing grasp of spatial concepts in his other activities. He may be able to fit forms into their proper places on a puzzle or form board and build more well-balanced buildings with his blocks. His use of art materials and objects will be more creative. Despite these advances, it is difficult for him to understand how all of the specific places that he knows can be organized into an over-all map. His abstract knowledge of space is still not well developed.

Concept of Time

Between Preschool 2 and 3, you are likely to notice marked increases in your child's awareness of time and the words that refer to time. He will learn many new time words and use them spontaneously in talking about the past, present, and future.

Two behaviors that parents will readily see is their child's ability to tell someone else how old he is, and his eagerness to have his next birthday. These rather new developments suggest his growing awareness that he changes as time goes on. His ability to assume the role of an older child or an adult in his dramatic play suggests his awareness that he, too, will someday be grown-up.

The child's reference to time in speech will become more precise or exact. He probably has little or no idea about how to tell time using a watch or a clock despite possible attempts by you to teach him, although he may now begin to use many different time words and phrases such as "bath time," "bedtime," or "time for me to play." Sometimes he will use silly or incorrect time phrases. When a child is asked at what time he usually plays outside, he may say "at sixty-four o'clock." Even though he is making an attempt to tell someone when he plays outside in terms of time, his desire to answer in a grown-up fashion far exceeds his knowledge of clock time.

Phrases such as "in a minute," referring to very brief periods of time, are frequently heard during this phase. Longer spans of time may be expressed by such words and phrases as "always," "for years and years," and "a whole year." Over the next two years he will start to parrot some common adult expressions of time words as when he says, "When I was little," "In the old days," "A long, long time ago," or, "Forever and ever." By listening carefully to your child's descriptions of time, you will be able to hear evidence of the further development of this concept.

The Self-centered World: Egocentrism

Your Preschool 2 child's frame of reference will still be self-centered, although usually not to the same degree as during infancy and toddlerhood. He watches what goes on around him with curiosity and enthusiasm. Then he forms his own opinions about things that happen and tries to explain them. Many of his opinions and explanations are still inaccurate and seem strange to adults, since adults can, for the most part, separate their personal and emotional considerations from the objective properties of objects and events that they observe. They can reason things out logically and rationally. The child has still not acquired these abilities. This is not only because of his limited practical experience and limited intellectual capacities, but also because his ability to perceive events objectively is clouded by his self-centered attitude and position.

DIFFICULTY IMAGINING HIMSELF IN ANOTHER PERSON'S SHOES. One of the major differences between a younger preschool child and an adult is that the child has a limited capacity to put himself in the place of another person. The young child, looking at his front lawn from inside his house, tends to have great difficulty thinking about what the view in front of him would look like to someone standing across the street, or someone in an airplane flying overhead. An adult, on the other hand, knows that the view of a landscape changes depending upon one's perspective or point of view and can imagine how different the lawn would look from another position.

By observing the child's behavior toward other people, it is often possible to see evidence of the difficulty he has in considering other viewpoints besides his own. Mrs. Perkins noticed signs of this in her three-year-old son, Warren.

While playing nicely with another child, Marleen, in his back yard, Warren suddenly grabbed Marleen's toy and smashed it. His playmate began to cry. Mrs. Perkins, obviously disturbed by her son's lack of consideration, rushed over to him and said, "Warren, you should be ashamed of yourself. That was not a very nice thing that you did. How would you like it if someone grabbed your toy and broke it?" Warren did not seem to reflect upon her remarks and did not appear to be concerned in the least about how his behavior had affected Marleen. His mother could see that her son simply did not care about his friend's feelings, and could not understand why this was so, since she had tried so hard to teach him the importance of respecting other people's feelings and property.

A major reason why this little boy, like other young preschool children, could be so inconsiderate of others, and could remain unfazed by his mother's comments, was his inability to put himself into Marleen's shoes and think about how he would feel in her place. Since his position was self-centered, the only thing that mattered to him was himself; he was unable to identify with his playmate's feelings.

Most Preschool 2 children have not developed the ability to identify with other people's feelings or points of view, although they are gradually acquiring the intellectual, emotional and social skills that will enable them to do so in the near future. Right now, they tend to view the world exclusively from their own point of view. Their own feelings, desires, and needs are generally put above other people's. This self-centered perspective occasionally explains their rude and aggressive behavior toward others. Knowing that your child has trouble imagining how his outlook and feelings might change if he were seeing a situation from another's viewpoint, it should be easier for you to understand specific aspects of his behavior that are bothersome.

The Imaginary World of the Child

Your child's increasing ability to deal with symbols in his head enables his imagination to develop more fully. The Preschool 2 child spends considerably more time playing with ideas in his mind than in the past. He has a very active imagination.

Dramatic role playing and make-believe activities become more prominent during this phase. By himself or in a group situation, your child may pretend that he is a policeman catching a thief, a father scolding his son, a fireman rescuing a woman in a burning building, or a doctor taking care of a sick patient. Blocks, cardboard boxes, toy brooms and mops, and so forth, may imaginatively be used as part of his dramatic play.

As your child plays, you are likely to hear him talk about his pretend activities as though they were real. The stories that he makes up will be colorful, and will reflect his expanding imaginative abilities. He may begin to invent characters and talk about situations and faraway places unlike any that he has ever seen, although many children continue to base the themes of their stories upon their own experiences.

You may occasionally see evidence that your child actually believes things that he imagines. A little boy named Cory, according to his parents, began to eat the birthday cake that he had shaped out of sand and water, presumably believing that it really was a cake. As is discussed in the Personal-Social Development section on pages 831–34, many preschool children may create imaginary companions, and behave in ways indicating that their companions are real to them.

Preschool 2 children still do not realize that thoughts and wishes cannot cause real events. A child may worry and feel guilty about his own "bad" wishes about another person, because he believes that wishing can really cause things to happen. Your child's inability to distinguish adequately between actual events and those created in his mind enables him to think that his dreams are real. It is not uncommon for a child to awaken from a dream in the middle of the night convinced that there is really a monster hiding in his closet, a rattlesnake under his bed, a witch who is trying to harm him, or a mean-looking burglar peering at him through his bedroom window. He may be so totally convinced that his dream actually happened that he will refuse to go back to sleep in his own room unless his parents "kill" the snake under his bed or "chase" the monster out of the closet. Do not feel bad or become too impatient if you have a hard time making him believe that the things he dreamed about are not real and are only a product of his imagination.

Young preschoolers attending magic shows do not usually react to the magician's tricks in the same way adults react to them. Adults never cease to be amazed when the magician pulls a dove out of a hat, or makes a woman in a box first disappear, and then reappear. Young children, however, may not be particularly fazed or entertained by such incredible feats of magic, presumably because they see "magical" things occurring each and every day in the world around them, and because they themselves, like a magician, can use their own form of "magic" and cause things to happen.

The child's increasing ability to assume different roles in play situations, fantasize, engage in make-believe activities, and interact with imaginary characters is a testimony to his creativity and expanding capacity to think. It is true that he is learning more about the "real" world, but he still lives in a world where even the impossible is possible.

LANGUAGE DEVELOPMENT

The Preschool 2 child tends to be much more fluent in his speech than the Preschool 1 child. His command of words often impresses his parents. He loves to repeat new words and try them out in varying combinations in sentences. In contrast to the two-year-old's sounds, which, at times, may have been slurred and difficult to decipher, the three-year-old's articulation of words has markedly improved.

Listening to children of this age talk should convince you that they have already mastered certain basic grammatical rules. The child will be more talkative, and his conversations will be lively and lengthy. The stories that he will tell are bound to be imaginative, reflecting new mental abilities. His occasional use of silly language will reflect his growing sense of humor.

Active Language Development

VOCABULARIES ARE EXPANDING. By Preschool 2, the child generally has a fairly extensive vocabulary, although he understands many more words than he can say. During Toddlerhood 3 he was interested in repetition of the same words and phrases. Now he shows a growing interest in learning new words and new ways in which to use them.

Occasionally, when the child cannot find the proper word to express himself, he may alter words that he knows to fit a new situation. Three-year-old Amy, for example, one day announced, "I'm not uptight, I'm downtight!" She had invented an antonym. Preschool children are able to form such contrasts for words long before they can use proper antonyms. The regular use of correct antonyms usually emerges around age six or seven.

THE PRONUNCIATION OF NEW WORDS. Most of your child's speech will now be intelligible. His ability to articulate shows rapid improvement. You may still hear "baby talk" from time to time. As he pronounces words, some of the sounds and syllables may be misplaced. Preschool children often have difficulty pronouncing the word "spaghetti." They often say "psghetti" instead. "Animal" is another word that tends to be mispronounced as "aminal."

A good way to guide your child toward more accurate pronunciation is to offer proper models to imitate. In the event that he announces a desire to have "psghetti" for dinner, you could say, "Yes. I think spaghetti would be a good choice." Stopping a child in the middle of a sentence to point out his mistake, scolding him for the error, or making him repeat the word several times can cause worse problems than the parent is trying to correct. These methods tend to make a child learning to speak more self-conscious and reluctant to pronounce the word again.

TEACHING YOUR CHILD NEW WORDS. Assuming that your child really enjoys learning new words, you can help introduce him to some "big" ones, just for the fun of it. Words such as "symphony," or "investigate," although difficult to remember and pronounce, can be great fun to say once they are learned. Being able to say "big" words is a boost to a child's self-confidence, and can be pleasurable for him, particularly if his parent teaches him big words and explains their meanings in simple terms.

SENTENCES. The sentences your child will be using should offer evidence of the improvement in his language abilities. They are probably growing longer. Nouns, articles, verbs, prepositions, and conjunctions will appear in his sentences, and a greater number of sentences are likely to be compound or complex. You may now hear him saying sentences such as the following: "I couldn't tie my shoes last year and I can't tie them now." "Mommy, I'm awfully hungry today." "Please show me where my dolly is." "I'm not a baby 'cause I don't drink out of a bottle!" "No one as old as Daddy could fit in my pants!" "No. There aren't any kids as old as I am, and I'm going home." "I help you clean this big mess up."

Questions are also becoming more sophisticated. The child may ask, "Do you have any brothers?" or, "Why is that big boy drinking out of a bottle?" "Do you like me?" tends to be a frequently asked question by children of this age.

GRAMMAR. The grammatical system of any language is highly complex, but even three- to four-year-olds have mastered certain basic rules of grammar. How do we know this? Researchers have studied many of the grammatical mistakes that the

841

young child tends to make. These studies indicate that he is making use of the rules of grammar which enable him to produce new sentences.

Take, for example, the sentences "I maked a hole," and "I saw some mices." "Maked" and "mices," of course, are not being used correctly, and it would be difficult to assume that the child was imitating words he had heard. After examining the words "maked" and "mices," one can guess how the child came up with such creations. The child has treated the irregular verb "make" in a way similar to regular verbs such as "rake" or "bake," which form the past tense by attaching a "d" on the end. He has also treated "mice" as if it were a noun like bike, which uses a regular plural ending "s." The child has handled the irregulars in the English language as if they were regulars, and investigators have concluded from this that he has used the rules of grammar that he has learned through experience to generate new sentences.

Jean Berko, as part of her doctoral research (1958), devised an interesting "game" in which young children would hopefully indicate their understanding of the rules of grammar. The children were shown a picture of a small animal(s) and were told things like: "This is a wug. Now there are two of them. There are two ———." A child, having to complete the sentence, normally filled in the word "wugs," pronouncing the "s" with a "z" sound (wug/-z). For a different animal the child was given the fictitious name "bic." The child went on to supply the correct plural "bics," pronouncing the "s" with an "s" sound (bic/-s). The plural "s" endings were pronounced differently depending upon the example given to the child. The children in Berko's study put the correct endings on words they heard for the very first time. Thus, they revealed their knowledge of forming plurals. Using similar materials, Berko's investigations showed that children as young as four could employ regular rules of English to construct plural and possessive endings on nouns, comparative and superlative forms of adjectives, and the past tense of verbs. Other studies have shown that even younger children know certain grammatical rules.

Your child will be acquiring and using grammatical rules, even though he will not be able to tell you what they are. Grammar gradually appears in early childhood, and is a truly remarkable accomplishment. Exactly how children learn grammar remains a mystery, and presents a great challenge for researchers devoted to the study of language acquisition.

Many preschool children have trouble with pronouns. The child may forget that the pronoun "he" is used for males, and the pronoun "she" is used for females. Earlier, he may have confused the pronouns "you" and "I," but now he may confuse the pronoun "we." When he asks, "Are we going out to eat?" he may mean, "Are Daddy and Mommy going out to eat?"

Negatives are also apt to be confusing to the child, who often ends up using double negatives. He may produce sentences such as, "I didn't see no boat," or, "He never does nothing." Even though these sentences are grammatically incorrect, he has made much progress since the time when he said, "No. I want," or, "No wash hands."

Children are bound to make mistakes as they attempt to speak correctly, and it is impossible to predict exactly at what age a child will stop making errors. Generally, by the time the child enters school, he has mastered most of the common grammatical forms and constructions, at least those to which he has been exposed in his particular language environment. Further refinement, of course, will then be made according to elementary school standards.

CONVERSATIONS. With better language ability and a greater interest in their peers, children are beginning to converse meaningfully with one another. Collective monologues as described in the previous period still persist, but more and more you will hear social, two-sided conversations. Youngsters frequently talk to one another about play activities. "Mary, make believe this is a doghouse and you're the dog; say, 'Bow-wow, bow-wow.'"

Sometimes children talk about trading things with one another, or make joint decisions as to who will be allowed to enter in a group activity or game: "John, you can take my truck. I'll use your boat." "You can't play with us." "Get out of here." "You're a bad girl." There also tends to be conversation about secrets: "Do you know what we have?" "It's a secret." "Want us to tell you?" At times they may resort to calling each other names and fighting about toys: "You're stupid!" "You dummy!" "Get your own dolly." "That's mine!" "Take your hands off!"

Your child will probably make numerous daily attempts to engage you in conversation. You may hear him brag about things he has made. "Look at the pretty picture I made." He is likely to point out how grown-up he is: "I can do it myself." Other discussions will involve telling about his activities: "I built a house, and now I'm going to make a cake"; and asking for assistance: "Please help me fix the car. It's broke." He will also turn to you to gripe about his playmates: "Daryll took my elephant," or, "Sean stole my piece of cake."

Children of this age frequently bombard parents with questions. At times their questions are embarrassing. Mr. Bunn carried his three-year-old child Susan piggyback style into a bookstore. When they approached the person at the checkout counter, Susan asked, "Daddy, is that a boy or a girl?"

Mr. Bunn would have been only too happy to respond had he known the answer. Unfortunately, even he could not determine whether the person was male or female. Much to his dismay, Susan repeated her question over and over again, each time more loudly and demanding than before. Instead of saying something like, "I'm busy now, but I'll answer you in a moment when we're outside," this father's only thought was to ignore her questions.

Taking the time to address your child's questions and carry on simple conversations will not only be helpful to him, but also to your relationship. Try to observe his activities and areas of interest, and use them as a basis for conversation. Keep in mind that his language abilities are rapidly increasing. As a result, you should adjust your own language so that it is neither too far above nor below his level of understanding.

SONGS, JINGLES AND RHYMES. Children usually enjoy singing songs. Some may now sing many songs, even though not always on pitch. Their ability to carry a tune should show some improvement. If your child attends nursery school, he will probably learn a few songs. You may hear him singing them during play activities at home. Children often begin to compose their own songs. While a child pretends he is on a boat, for example, he may "sing" a song about his activity.

Most youngsters really like to repeat nursery rhymes and advertising jingles. They may also enjoy riddles and guessing games. As they become able to retain information for longer periods of time, their ability to memorize phrases, rhymes, slogans, and jingles also improves.

STORYTELLING. Children of this age tend to be imaginative storytellers, and their spontaneously created stories often give us some idea as to how they think and feel about a whole host of things, and what they know and do not know. Their stories are often disorganized and loose. They may go on and on giving endless details, but forgetting to provide information that is relevant.

Violence, injury, and catastrophes of various sorts are frequently among their stories' predominant themes. Parents may be portrayed in a negative role as reprimanding, spanking, or leaving the child alone forever. Sometimes one parent may be portrayed in a negative role, while the other is spoken of as the epitome of goodness.

Not all stories told by children are of the type just described. You will also hear stories with predominantly friendly or social themes. According to the Gesell Institute's *Infant and Child in the Culture of Today,* girls usually have "Mommy," "girls," or animals as the main characters in their stories. The main characters in stories told by boys usually include "Daddy," "boys," or animals.

Toward the middle or end of this phase many stories that children tell will no longer be about real life; fantasy will prevail. They may talk about their imaginary companions, or about imaginary roles and activities, and their impersonations of other people can be award-winning dramatic performances.

You may notice a new touch of humor coming out of your child's stories. Humor in its early forms is often expressed in the use of silly talk or rhyming words. Martin told his grandfather that "the turkey gobbled up the fly. Oh, my. Gobble, gobble, dobble, dobble, robble, robble."

Passive Language Development

It will become more obvious to you that your child understands nearly everything said in the course of ordinary conversations. Even when he does not comprehend a particular word, he will probably get some sense of its meaning from the context in which it is used, and from people's facial expressions and gestures.

LISTENING. You will notice that your child's listening skills have improved. He will be more interested in hearing stories, and will be more attentive during this activity. Books that tell about familiar people, animals, and activities in elaborate detail will probably capture his interest. As he approaches Preschool 3, he may also love listening to stories about the world of fantasy, especially those in which animals "talk" and behave like people. As he listens, he is likely to look at the pictures and explain them to you.

Children's interests in and reactions to music are extremely variable, but music time continues to be enjoyed by most children. They may particularly like having the volume and tempo altered as they listen and move to the music, and will often walk, clap, skip, and jump in time to the music.

Preschool 2 children enjoy the sounds of words. You can expand your child's interest in word sounds by engaging him in word games that focus upon sounds and sound patterns. For example, you could ask him to say as many words as he can think of that begin with the "L" sound as in "land." Or you might have him listen as you say several words that end the same way as "mop." There are many games which help to refine a child's listening skills. Simon Says is an appropriate game for children of this age that helps promote their ability to listen. Other activities to foster language development are presented in the play and educating your child sections on pages 740–41, 798–801.

FOLLOWING DIRECTIONS. Your child will be capable of following directions, even though he will be equally capable of saying "no" and putting up an argument. He may rebel against demands such as, "Pick up your toys," and respond much more readily when he is given reasons for requests and orders: "Please pick up your toys so we'll have more room to exercise," or, "How about picking up your toys so Daddy won't trip over them when he comes home?"

Rather than asking your child to follow vague or general directions, try to give him specific step-by-step instructions: "First wash your hands, and then we can eat lunch," or, "Would you first pick up your sweater and then bring it to me so that I can wash it?" Some parents have occasionally been successful at getting their child's co-operation and attention by whispering when they want him to do something.

MOTOR DEVELOPMENT

Your child's motor system is becoming much more controlled. He will be more confident in an upright posture, and will no longer have to think about maintaining his balance. His proportions are changing, and he is gradually beginning to resemble a mini-adult in appearance. In many ways, which you will observe, his actions and activities are also becoming more adult-like.

In the area of fine motor co-ordination, he has come a long way. His hands and fingers will be under greater control, allowing him to engage in finer, more sophisticated manual activities. For example, he may now control his crayon strokes sufficiently to imitate the drawing of a circle and a cross. In many day-to-day activities, you will see evidence of his improved fine motor co-ordination, and no doubt will take pride in his latest accomplishments.

Gross Motor Activity

WALKING. The Preschool 2 child will walk erectly and turn sharp corners without having to rely upon walls or pieces of furniture to help him change directions. He will go forward smoothly, with arms and legs swinging freely, unlike earlier days when he toddled along in an awkward manner. Gradually, his arm and leg actions are becoming well co-ordinated. When he steps forward with his right foot, his left arm swings forward and vice versa.

Variations in walking behavior may be seen from time to time. Occasionally, your child will decide to walk sideways, backward, or on tiptoe. At times he will move around with much twirling. He may really enjoy spinning round and round with his arms outstretched until he becomes "crazy" from dizziness and excitement.

EXERCISING. From observing you and other people around him, or from watching television, your child is apt to pick up the idea of exercising. You will see him trying to perform sit-ups, jumping jacks, and somersaults. He may picture himself as quite an acrobat, but his attempts to perform these tasks will indicate just the opposite, and should be quite humorous to watch.

DANCING. Your child will probably begin to discover his abilities in the area of dancing. Little "Fred Astaire" may imitate African dances, teen-age dances, ballroom dancing, or ballet steps. His performances may range from hilarious jerking movements to graceful motions. Given the proper music, atmosphere, and audience, he should put on quite a show!

RUNNING. Having had more practice in running, your child will now run with greater smoothness and speed. He will experience less difficulty in getting going, turning around, and stopping suddenly. You can count on fewer crash collisions than in previous phases, now that his ability to shift quickly from running fast to standing still has improved.

CLIMBING. You will see your child going up a flight of steps by alternating his feet as you do. Most children will also be able to walk down stairs without assistance, although they are apt to use the old one-step-at-a-time method. Many children like to make a game of racing up and down stairs.

Your child may be an accomplished stair climber, but do not be shocked if toward the middle of this phase he asks you to "hold my hand" going upstairs or downstairs. This uneasiness about stumbling and falling, which is not uncommon among three-and-a-half-year-olds, represents only his temporary feelings of insecurity, as discussed in the Personal-Social Development section. The child's anxiety about climbing or engaging in other activities that he formerly enjoyed will soon pass.

BALANCING. The Preschool 2 child's balancing ability will definitely improve. Your child should be able to walk a straight path. According to the Denver Developmental Screening Test, more than half of the children tested could walk heel to toe two out of three attempts by the age of four. In order to test your child's ability, here are the brief instructions: Tell your child to walk forward with his heel within one inch of his toe. You may demonstrate to him how this is done. He must walk four consecutive steps. Give him credit if he is able to perform this task correctly on two out of three trials. Some children may be able to walk a line, heel to toe, for as much as ten feet.

Walking backward heel to toe is a harder task, and one which is generally not accomplished until a child is closer to five or six. Some children will be able to walk very short distances on a low balance beam, about five inches wide. Your child may now be able to stand on one foot for several seconds or more without losing his balance.

JUMPING. Many children will be able to jump fairly well. They cannot jump very far or very high, but they will be more co-ordinated at jumping tasks. Your child may enjoy jumping on and down from low objects, couches, or chairs. You are likely to see him jumping over small toys on the floor.

HOPPING. Your child may develop the ability to hop on one foot, although hopping becomes more prominent in Preschool 3. Many children will be able to hop a foot or so on the foot for which they show a preference. Hopping will take time to master, so you cannot expect your youngster to play hopscotch or other similar games during this phase.

RIDING A TRICYCLE. The child's ability to ride his tricycle will improve. Riding a tricycle is a task that many Preschool 2 children are ready to tackle, since they are gaining in leg strength and co-ordination. Adult supervision will be required whenever your child is on his tricycle.

THROWING A BALL. By now you will probably see evidence of your child's greater skill in throwing balls. Many children are able to throw a ball a distance of about seven feet. You might begin to see some body rotation as he throws. He may rotate his body to the left when he throws with his right hand, and may twist his body to the right when he throws with his left hand. Older children shift their weight in the throwing process, but your child is not likely to do this when he throws objects.

CATCHING A BALL. Catching a ball is still difficult for most children. Try standing about four feet away from your child and bouncing a ball to him. He may be able to catch it with his hands. Many children will now be holding their hands in such a way that they are open to receive the ball. Others will continue to hold their arms out stiffly in front of their bodies, trying to catch the ball with their arms, rather than their hands. The more opportunities your child has to practice, the better he will get at catching.

Fine Motor Activity

BLOCK-BUILDING. Your child is making noticeable progress in the area of hand manipulation. In his play with blocks he will show some concern with how high a structure he can build. You will probably see him making fairly tall "buildings" of about ten blocks, as opposed to the two-year-old's shorter structures.

USING TOOLS. As a result of your youngster's improved hand skill he may now be ready to begin using simple tools such as a child-size pair of blunt scissors or a small, lightweight hammer. Adult supervision will be necessary until he develops sufficient control to use these tools properly, efficiently, and safely. Parents who allow their child free access to scissors are asking for trouble. This is an age where a child may attempt to cut his own hair, eyelashes, or eyebrows given the opportunity. It is worth reminding you of how potentially dangerous a tool a scissors can be when used by a child with insufficient hand and finger control.

DRAWING. It should be obvious to you that your child's ability to draw is improving. His strokes will be less repetitive, and may begin to evolve into more well-defined shapes. He can now draw a circle, albeit crude and perhaps somewhat misshapen, and may also attempt to draw a simple cross. Many youngsters enjoy making repetitive crosses with both vertical and horizontal lines. Watch your preschooler's drawings closely, and you will probably see squares emerging. He may attempt to "square off" circles, or start to leave spaces within his repetitive vertical and horizontal lines. Some of his geometric shapes are likely to resemble vaguely familiar things such as a house.

Using stick figures at first, the child will begin to draw a person. By the end of this phase, your child may be able to draw a person with three parts. If you were testing your child's ability to draw a person, you would have to score each pair (two arms, two legs, and so forth) as counting for one part. Assuming that you have been showing him how to print, he may be able to print a few large letters, but you should not expect much from him in this regard at this time.

After your youngster has made a "picture," he may tell you what he has drawn. It is unlikely that his drawings will resemble whatever it is that he tells you. Chances are that they will look like mere scribbles. Do not be surprised if he changes his mind as to what he is drawing before finishing his creation. What started out to be a dog might turn out to be a house or a bird.

It is doubtful that his pictures will be works of art, but they will be meaningful and important to him. Many wise parents, realizing the value of their children's early artwork, display them on the walls in their home for all visitors to see. Your child will beam with pride if you do this for him. Other parents have kept a special scrapbook comprised of their child's drawings. Saving his pictures is a good idea, and years from now it may be great fun for both you and your child to look back at them.

DRESSING AND GROOMING. As your child becomes more skillful with his hands, dressing, grooming, and eating abilities will show improvement. He will probably be able to put on his clothing, including some more difficult garments, but do not expect perfection. He may be able to button up his shirts and sweaters and work a large zipper or hook-type fastener. The ability to lace and tie shoes does not usually emerge during this phase, but some initial attempts to perform these tasks are often made. You can expect your child to brush his teeth successfully, and take a more independent role in other matters related to grooming and bathing.

LEARNING THROUGH PLAY

The Preschool 2 child will continue to enjoy many of the playthings, outdoor and indoor climbing equipment, and activities that were suggested in previous play sections, but now there are additional playthings and activities that you can introduce. Some suggestions for toys, objects, and activities are presented below, but you will undoubtedly come up with your own ideas. As always, you will want to take your child's needs, interests, and responses into account in selecting playthings and activities, and try to offer him a well-balanced diet of play.

Your child will now be more enthusiastic about play and better able to concentrate on activities. He is less likely to change constantly from one toy or activity to the next. When he has been playing at one activity for a long time, you may want to suggest that he move on to another for variety. He will probably be more playful, and may even make a game out of helping you cook or clean the house.

Imaginative, Dramatic Play

Your child's play is becoming more imaginative. He will not only play with toys and art materials for the sake of exploration or enjoyment, he will also combine them and make new "things" and "creations" with them. Dramatic play and pretend activities should be very prominent, and have become much more involved and complex than at earlier ages. Much of his play will revolve around pretend activities.

In dramatic play, he will take on many roles. He may like to dress up and pretend that he is a baby, a police person, a doctor, a musician, a dancer, a cab driver, a chef, or you. It should be extremely amusing for you to watch him acting out these roles, and to listen to him talk as he plays. From observing his dramatic play, you will get a good glimpse of what he feels and thinks about adults and grown-up activities and occupations.

During his make-believe play, he will create imaginary situations in which his dolls and stuffed animals will be treated as though they are alive. He may also create imaginary playmates. His imaginative play will mainly involve his acting out daily activities such as eating, cleaning house, and doing the laundry. Playing "house" and "store" are apt to be among his favorite make-believe activities. Very often he will pretend that objects are present, when, in fact, they are not. He may pretend to be calling various people with an imaginary telephone, or setting an imaginary table with imaginary silverware.

Small-sized versions of adult equipment will be thoroughly enjoyed by your child. He will treat them as though they are the "real thing." With a toy shopping basket filled with empty food boxes and cans, he will pretend that he is an adult going grocery shopping. His toy golf cart will be a "real" golf cart in his imaginative play. His play vacuum cleaner will become a real vacuum cleaner, and dolls will become real babies as he plays. Toys that are replicas of real objects are perfect for pretending.

There are innumerable ordinary household objects that he can also use in imaginative play. Very large cardboard packing boxes, for example, can become a playhouse, a box office, or a store. Below you will find several suggestions for ways in which to stimulate your child's make-believe play by making use of items that you probably have lying around your attic, kitchen, basement, and garage.

You can help your child by gathering appropriate dress-up clothes, props, playthings, and assorted equipment that can be used in his make-believe activities. You can also help him plan activities, and carry them out. Occasionally, you can be an active participant in his pretend activities. Be sure to invite some other children over from time to time to join in the fun. Together they may play "school," "house," or "doctor."

Most importantly, respect your child's need for imaginative outlets, and do not worry that he is losing his grasp on reality if you condone or encourage his role-playing and pretend activities. Dramatic and make-believe play are extremely important avenues for learning, since they help your child learn about himself, other people, and his surroundings. It is a good idea to offer him encouragement to use his imagination in play.

DRESS-UP MATERIALS. A little boy will love to parade around the house wearing his daddy's old jackets, army uniform, shirts, ties, hats, and shoes. With a toy razor and some shaving cream, he can even pretend to shave just the way he sees his father do each morning. A little girl will love to dress up like her mommy. She will delight in wearing Mommy's old dresses, hats, shoes, purses, and junk jewelry. She may also

849

want to try on some of Mommy's make-up, nail polish, and perfume. Keep in mind that little girls may sometimes want to wear their daddy's old clothes in dramatic play, and little boys may like to dress up in their mommy's hats when they take on the "mother" role in their play. This is completely natural at this age and should not represent a cause for concern.

Old uniforms, hats, and other old clothes that you or other relatives had planned to give away will be treasured by your child. You can also purchase them cheaply at tag or garage sales. Costumes and dress-up articles can be put in a large box in your youngster's room. Be imaginative in using materials. An old lace tablecloth with a center slit can make a perfect wedding gown or "fairy" outfit. A stick or baton can be a charming magic wand. Masks and spacesuits can be easily made from grocery bags. Paper plates can also be easily turned into masks. Paint them and cut holes out for your child's eyes, nose, and mouth. A piece of yarn can be tied around the backs of the paper plates to keep them in place. Colored yarn can be glued on for hair.

PLAYING "HOUSE" OR "STORE." A place for your child to play "house" or "store" can be easily arranged using household items. The make-it-yourself kind of playhouse or store will serve the purpose, and will be much less expensive than buying them ready-made at a toy store. One kind of "house" can be made by throwing a sheet or large piece of material over a table or your child's jungle gym. He can pretend that it is a house, a store, a school, a castle, or something else, depending upon what kinds of objects he plays with in it. Do not be discouraged if this idea does not appeal to him. Pile up cardboard boxes for "walls" and section off a corner of his room as a playhouse, or use a tall folding screen. An even better idea is to take a huge cardboard box (you might ask for one at a department or large appliance store) and transform it into a house or a store by painting it and cutting out some windows and a door.

When your child plays "house," he will want small-scale or make-shift versions of the "real" things. Some things that come to mind for use with house play are: dolls, doll clothing, doll bed, doll carriage, doll houses, child-size table and chairs, brooms, dustpans, pots and pans, dishes and cups, silverware, stove, telephone, iron and ironing board, clothespins, napkins, and bits of material for a tablecloth and curtains. A medium-sized cardboard box can easily be painted to look like a stove. Red strips of material or cotton painted red can be glued on the top to look like electric coils or gas flames on your stove.

In playing "store," your child may enjoy having a box or old drawer filled with "play" money. A cash register can be any cardboard box, and large buttons, green pieces of paper, or raisins can serve as money. He will need old empty food boxes with labels attached, canned goods from your kitchen cabinets, something on which to store these items, grocery bags, and even, perhaps, a wagon to serve as a grocery cart.

The same space that your child uses for playing "house" and "store" can also serve many other uses. By changing the insides and props a bit, it can become a doctor's office. Toy doctor and nurse kits can be bought at most toy stores. He may also enjoy having an "examining" table and chair, a box of bandages, some dolls for "patients," a white face mask, an old white shirt or a white poncho as a uniform (use an old white sheet), gauze pads, cotton, a disposable plastic syringe with the needle removed for giving "shots," and bits of dry cereal or Kool-Aid in cups for giving "pills" and "medicine." Many preschool children are somewhat apprehensive of doctors, doctors' offices, and hospitals. Having an opportunity to play "doctor" and "hospital" may help to familiarize them with doctor's equipment, and lessen their fears.

PUPPETS. Hand puppets can make excellent accompaniments to your child's imaginative play. He can make them "talk" and say things that he is not allowed to say. He can also make them "sing." Puppets can serve as an outlet for his positive and negative feelings. They can also become imaginary "friends." You can buy all kinds of hand puppets, but they are easy to make at home. One advantage of the home-made puppets are that they cost very little, and another is that they can be made in a flash.

Making your own puppets can be fun. A small paper bag, when slipped over your child's hand and gathered at his wrists with a string or rubber band, can make a marvelous puppet. You can ask him what kind of face he would like the puppet to have, and then draw or paint the face on the bag. Some glued-on buttons can become eyes, and dyed cotton can become the puppet's hair. "Mateless" mittens, gloves, and socks that you have saved can also make great hand puppets when they are decorated. When using an old glove, cut out a circle from cardboard or material to serve as a "face," decorate it to look like a character, and sew it so that it fits over the middle three fingers of the glove. The "thumb" and "pinky" glove fingers can serve as the puppet's arms.

Another kind of hand puppet can be made from a large green pepper. Cut off the top so that your child's hand will fit inside. Olives stuck into the pepper with toothpicks can serve as the eyes, and a slice of pimento can serve as a mouth. After your child loses interest in this puppet he can eat it for a snack.

You can also cover an empty food can with colored paper and draw a face on it. Top it with some yarn for hair or glue on a small cardboard box to serve as a hat. As a final suggestion, you can draw a face directly on your child's hand with washable, felt-tipped, non-toxic markers. When he moves his hand, he can make this puppet "talk." Or draw a small face on each of his fingers; by wiggling them individually, he can have a whole "family" conference or make "friends" talk to one another.

When playing with hand puppets, your child may enjoy having a stage or little puppet theater. A plain cardboard box can easily be transformed into a great-looking puppet theater. An elaborate theater might even include a drape (piece of material can serve as a curtain). Ordinary cardboard boxes can also be transformed into wonderful doll houses.

Construction Play

Your child will now concentrate on making things with toys, objects, and art materials. Construction play generally emerges around the age of three. His initial attempts to make things are likely to be crude, but it is important to reinforce his attempts positively and not make fun of the finished products. He will no longer be content to bang on his blocks and throw them around the playroom. Rather, he will use them to build taller towers, buildings, and other architectural "triumphs." The bigger the structure that he can erect, the happier he will be. Try to provide your child with a wide assortment of wooden blocks in varying sizes. He will use them by himself, or get together with his contemporaries for co-operative block-building ventures.

There are many other good construction toys, including huge transportation toys, plastic people, and small metal cars and trucks for your child's block villages, that are available for children of this age. It is also possible to provide him with less expensive construction materials based on ordinary household items. Household materials such as a blunt scissors, all types of paper, tissues, rubber bands, crayons, play dough, clay, cooking ingredients, and so on, can be used in many different unexpected ways by you and your child. All that you and he need is a bit of ingenuity and imagination.

It should be fun for you to watch your child using these materials, and shaping them into various things. For your child's safety, when he is using many of these materials, you will have to be there to show him how to use them properly, and to supervise his activities. For example, before you allow your child to use a scissors, even a blunt one, you will have to teach him how it is used, and be on hand to make sure that he is using it correctly. Your preschooler is not ready to use this equipment unless you are there to supervise closely.

There are many safe playthings and raw materials that can be used in making things. Dough, clay, and sand with water may now be used to construct all sorts of things. Your child will not just pound, throw, and squeeze them for the sheer pleasure that he gets from "messing." Increasingly, he will shape, pat, smooth, and mold these materials into houses, animals, cakes, pies, people, and objects. With pencils, pens, crayons, and paper he will no longer scribble. Instead, he will attempt to draw people, animals, trees, flowers, and objects.

The Preschool 2 child will take great pleasure in making things, but may not be as concerned with his finished product. His main enjoyment and reward come from the process of "shaping," "making" and "building." As he grows older, the "things" that he makes will become more important to him.

Helping with Household Chores Can Be Fun

Children of this age make a game of everything. They enjoy helping out with household chores, since assisting Mommy and Daddy with various tasks is not work to them, it is play. Assuming that your child seems interested, let him help you perform various simple tasks. He may or may not be the most efficient helper, but he will have fun and will learn by having an opportunity to help you dry pots and pans, sort laundry, put away groceries, wash vegetables, and wipe the kitchen cabinets. Being a busy parent, you will probably enjoy his company, and his presence should make doing household chores more enjoyable for you.

Artistic Talents Are Emerging

Young children love to engage in projects and activities that deal with art. You will probably want to offer your child opportunities to work with a wide variety of art materials and mediums. Working with various art materials will provide him with opportunities to be imaginative and creative, and to express his feelings and ideas.

Art materials should ideally be stored on low shelves so that when it's time for an art project, your child can go and get the necessary materials on his own. He certainly can and should be expected to help in cleaning up his own messes and putting art materials back where they belong when he is through with an activity. Let him help prepare the materials by doing such tasks as mixing play dough or paint, or gathering together various objects to be used in making collages. The more involved he is, the more he will enjoy artwork.

Give your child ample time to experiment with each art activity. Rather than asking him if he is finished with a certain activity, you can tell him to let you know when he is done. In most cases, he should decide when to stop, not you. When it is almost time for him to finish up an activity for whatever reason, let him know in advance that you will tell him several minutes before it is time to stop. This approach will afford him a chance to finish what he is doing without feeling pressured or rushed to complete a project.

It is best to allow him to use his own imagination and make his own creations. This means not always providing him with models of objects to paint, color, mold, and shape. You may occasionally want to give him a coloring book, but he will probably get far more enjoyment from drawing his own designs and pictures. Whatever he creates will be "something" to him, and will mean "something" to him, even though it does not look like "anything" to you.

Most parents are very proud of their children's creations. Nothing delights a child more than having Mommy or Daddy tack his pictures on the wall or place his other creations in an area of the home for visitors to see. When displaying your child's artwork in your home, it is a good idea to display it at his eye level, rather than at your eye level. This will enable him to see his own work easily without having to climb up on a chair.

PAINTING. Painting is likely to be one of your child's favorite activities. With a different large paintbrush and container for each color of paint, he will go to work. Remember to use only non-toxic paint. Do not expect a masterpiece. He will concentrate hard on his painting as he experiments with using different strokes and colors. He may attempt to make some designs. Chances are that he will tell you that he painted a picture of a person or an object, but most of the time his paintings will bear little or no resemblance to whatever he says that he painted. Nevertheless, he will be pleased with his own work, and will probably pull you by the arm to come look at his finished products. For the sake of economy, the paper that he uses can be newspaper, cardboard, cut-up paper bags, shelf paper, or plain brown wrapping paper. For variety, you might suggest that he paint an old, useless board or a paper cup.

PRINTING WITH OBJECTS. Your child may now enjoy exploring the art of printing. Provide him with an empty TV dinner tray or pie tins, each containing a different color of water soluble paint. He can dip a variety of objects into the paint and then make impressions of these objects on paper or pieces of old sheets or plain colored material. The objects that you provide him with might include sponges, halved pieces of fruits and vegetables, kitchen utensils, and plastic cookie cutters. He can also use his hand to make impressions.

SQUIRT BOTTLE PAINTING. Squirt bottle painting is another fun activity. Show your child how to use a squirt bottle. Then provide him with several different-sized plastic bottles, and he can make interesting designs on pieces of paper. For added variety you can give him an eye dropper or two and show him how to squeeze-a-painting. This is an activity that requires adult supervision.

DRAWING. Your child is likely to want to use a variety of colored crayons. He may begin to draw shapes such as circles, crosses, simple designs, and even, perhaps, crude representations of objects and people. He may also like to draw with pens, pencils, colored chalk, and washable, non-toxic magic markers.

COLLAGE. Collage, a French name, refers to the art technique of gluing or pasting all sorts of objects and materials onto a piece of paper or cardboard. A good recipe for homemade boiled paste is as follows: Take a cup of flour and add cold water to it until it reaches a soupy consistency. Pour it into a pot. Turn your stove on to a low setting, and let it cook for about ten minutes or less. Be sure to stir it as it cooks. This mixture makes a fine paste, and will not harm your child if he happens to put some in his mouth. Place the paste in an airtight container and store it in your refrigerator.

Next you can collect all sorts of objects, including items such as pieces of silver foil, crackers, dry cereals, scraps of materials, cotton balls, cut-up pieces of birthday or greeting cards, and so forth. Give your child a piece of a cardboard box, some paste, and the objects. Let him use his imagination in combining the objects to make a "creation."

He will probably love making three-dimensional pictures. After he is finished pasting objects on the cardboard, he may then enjoy painting them. In the event that he is still putting inedible things into his mouth, offer him only edible collage materials or materials too large to fit into his mouth. By the age of four or five most children will be ready to use paper, glue, and smaller collage materials, but at this age it is best to be safe and stick with boiled paste.

HOW TO ENSURE YOUR CHILD'S SAFETY

You will notice improvements in your child's ability to speak, handle objects more appropriately, and exert self-control in specific situations. Now that he is more mature, you can start to put back some of the breakable objects that you hid from him during infancy and toddlerhood. The Preschool 2 and 3 child should be much more capable of handling the objects in a responsible manner or following your instructions not to touch them than he was at earlier ages. He should also be more capable of following requests to behave in an acceptable manner and being cautious in some situations in which dangers might be involved.

On the other hand, you cannot expect a Preschool 2 or 3 child to assume a great deal of responsibility for protecting himself. Certain objects such as medicines, poisons, and sharp instruments, etc., should still be stored away, locked up, or made off limits. A child should not be permitted to use the stove, washing machine, dryer, garbage disposal, or trash compacter. Do not allow him to go into the garage, workshop, or basement unless these areas have been completely safety-proofed or he is closely supervised.

The utmost precautions should be taken in regard to preventing accidents with poisons, fire, automobiles, from drownings and major falls. Your preschool child should never be left alone in your home under any circumstances. A few of the items on previous "safety check lists" in Infancy may be eliminated, depending upon your child's maturity and obedience, although it is better to be too strict in regard to safety than too lax.

Don't Underestimate Your Child's Ability to Get into Trouble

Some parents underestimate their children's ability to climb, track down forbidden objects that have been hidden, unlock drawers, doors, and cabinets, and, in general, get into trouble. Twenty-eight-month-old Alice Polk disliked taking medicine whenever she was sick. One morning, when Mrs. Polk was in a hurry to get dressed and out of the house for a club meeting, she tricked Alice into taking children's aspirin tablets by telling her that the pills were pieces of "candy." Mrs. Polk left the bottle of pills on the highest shelf in her daughter's room, and hurried to get dressed.

When she returned from her room, she was horrified to discover that Alice had the bottle of pills in her hand and had ingested at least fifteen to twenty of them. Mrs. Polk immediately phoned the Poison Control Center and her pediatrician for instructions. How had Alice reached the pill bottle? She had pulled a nearby chair over to the nightstand so that she could climb up on it and from there she was able to reach the bookshelf. Mrs. Polk compounded her error of telling her child that medicine was candy by underestimating her child's abilities.

Stories about youngsters who find weapons and ammunition around their homes, and actually figure out how to load them and fire them, are not all fictional. Neither are those accounts of how preschoolers managed to start their parents' cars, push the lever into drive or reverse, and step on the gas pedal. Children can, and frequently do, pick up rather sophisticated techniques and ideas from observing their parents or watching television. Stay in touch with your child's abilities from one day to the next, and always try to remain several steps ahead of him in taking precautionary measures to avoid accidents.

Avoid Assuming That Your Preschooler Has an Eight- to Ten-year-old's Judgment

Do not make the mistake of expecting too much from your Preschool 2 child in terms of accident prevention. He will not be able to exercise the same level of caution in regard to safety that you would expect from an eight- to ten-year-old child.

Mr. Moller was thrilled by his son Harper's ability to converse with him, and his strong interest in following and helping him around their home. One Sunday afternoon, Harper sat down near his father on their driveway and watched with interest as Mr. Moller began to strip paint off an old chest of drawers.

Harper was an attentive audience as his father explained all about how to refinish old, painted furniture, and why it was important to wear gloves and have plenty of ventilation when using paint stripper. This little boy asked several intelligent questions as he carefully observed his father at work.

When Mr. Moller had finished the task of removing nearly all of the paint, he put the cap on the stripper and set it aside. Then he told Harper to sit still because he had to go into the garage to find a scraper with which to remove the remaining bits of paint. Harper said "okay," but soon after his father disappeared into the garage, he removed the cap on the can of stripper and brought it up to his lips. Just at that moment, Mr. Moller walked out of the garage, spotted Harper about to drink the stripper, and yelled at him to stop. He had caught his son just in time to prevent a serious accident.

This father expected his son, who spoke and responded so intelligently several minutes before, to respond equally as intelligently when it came to avoiding an accident with the paint stripper.

No matter how mature or intelligent your Preschool 2 or 3 child seems, he is still lacking in knowledge, self-discipline, and experience, all of which represent essential aspects of accident prevention. Do not give him too much to handle in the way of responsibilities, substances, tools, or equipment before he is able to exercise a sufficient degree of caution to behave safely in situations in which dangers exist.

EATING

The Preschool 2 child is more mature, and more co-operative than he was at previous ages. He is usually more well mannered and responsive to his parents' requests and rules in regard to acceptable mealtime behavior. This makes life a lot easier and peaceful for parents, and makes mealtime more enjoyable for all. The child's desire or at least his willingness to taste new foods is increasing, and parents may be able to introduce new foods into his diet, foods which he may have refused to try during Preschool 1. Three- to four-year-olds can be asked to help their parents perform simple tasks in relation to serving foods and cleaning up after meals, but expectations should be kept to a minimum.

The Discriminating Eater

The child's insistence upon having particular foods and upon eating these foods on certain plates may be gradually diminishing, but it is common for children occasionally to refuse to eat what is prepared, and demand to have substitutes. From time to time, out of spitefulness, your child may ask to have foods which he knows you do not have in the house.

Mrs. Connors complained that her son, Webb, would deliberately try to irritate her at mealtimes. When she served Webb's favorite soup in a bowl, he would say that he would only eat it if it were served in a cup. When she sliced a piece of chocolate cake in two, he would complain that he would not eat it because it was not "whole."

Dealing with this kind of behavior, typically seen in three-and-a-half-year-olds, is difficult for most parents. In general, it is advisable to try to remain calm and avoid getting emotional at mealtimes. Offer foods that your child likes whenever possible, and when his demands are unreasonable, it may help to use a firm, "Eat it or go away hungry," approach at mealtime.

SELF-FEEDING. Most Preschool 2 youngsters are quite accomplished at feeding themselves with a spoon, and are getting better at using a fork. Cutting with a knife is usually too difficult for them, and therefore parents still have to cut meat into bite-size pieces for them. Children are more capable of eating on their own, and will be making increasing demands for greater responsibility in this area.

Some youngsters act up at the dinner table when eating with their family. They play with their food, or deliberately act up in other ways. In order to avoid arguments and hassles over meals, it is best to be firm, and tell them that if they are not willing to behave properly at dinnertime, they will have to eat by themselves. Children usually enjoy eating with other people, and isolating them while they eat generally motivates them to discontinue their mealtime antics and behave more maturely. Some youngsters do much better when they eat alone, rather than with other family members.

BATHING

Some of the child's set patterns of behavior in the tub may subside, but his bath times will probably be similar to those during the previous phase. Children who were previously rather passive about washing themselves may now become more insistent upon doing things for themselves.

CLOTHING

The Preschool 2 child will be more skilled at unbuttoning side and front buttons, unzipping zippers, and unfastening snaps than in the previous phase. This will enable him to remove his clothing more quickly. He will also improve at dressing, since he can probably fasten different kinds of buttons, zippers, and so forth, provided they are not too small or located in places which are hard for him to reach.

Characteristically at three and a half, children become resistive when it's time to get dressed or undressed. One of the aspects of dressing that bothers them the most is having clothes put on or taken off over their heads. For this reason, parents usually find it easier to purchase outfits that button or zip in the front or back.

Even at three and a half, a youngster's ability to put on his clothing is still poorly developed. His lack of skill, coupled with his contrariness, can make dressing him aggravating for all concerned. Many children will attempt to tie their shoelaces, although few children are able to complete the task correctly even with guidance. Some three-year-olds will learn to tie their shoes and there are educational toys and dressing frames available to assist you in teaching your child.

SLEEPING

The child's set going-to-bed behavior patterns which were quite apparent in Preschool 1 usually diminish, although some of them may continue to linger on during this phase. Getting the child to bed generally poses less of a problem, although sleeping difficulties during the middle of the night often escalate.

Waking During the Night

Many Preschool 2 children wake during the middle of the night. This is the age when the child is likely to climb out of bed and parade all over the house. His fears and bad dreams occasionally cause him to have difficulty sleeping through the night, although, as was previously discussed on pages 678–79, there may be other reasons for disturbed sleep. Sometimes a child will engage in some activity for a while, and then will go back to sleep.

The Pros and Cons of Allowing Your Child to Sleep in Your Bed

Other children will present more of a problem. Many children who wake up during the night want to be with their parents, and will go into their parents' bedroom and insist upon sleeping there with them. Much controversy exists over whether or not parents should take a child who wakes during the night into bed with them. How you handle this issue will ultimately be your decision, and will partly depend upon your own feelings, your spouse's feelings, and your child's personality. An awareness of some of the pros and cons should provide the insight to help you make your decision.

There are psychologists and parents who advise parents against allowing their child to sleep in their bed, maintaining that their bed is a special place where the child does not belong. The feeling is that parents reinforce their child's dependency as well as his romantic fantasies about the parent of the opposite sex by taking their child into bed with them. While parents can offer him comfort in his own room, the aim is for them to be firm about not letting him sleep in their bed, even if he cries every night for a while. Eventually he will learn that his crying gets him nowhere, and will stop. Once a child establishes the pattern of sleeping in his parents' bed, parents sometimes have a very difficult time getting him to break the habit. Still another reason not to allow a child to sleep with his parents is that this practice may disrupt their sex lives, and/or otherwise invade their intimacy and privacy in bed.

Other psychologists and parents maintain that there is no reason why parents cannot take their child into bed with them when he wakes during the night and is uncomfortable or fearful about sleeping in his own bed. The feeling is that this practice will not necessarily encourage the child's dependency or incestuous feelings in regard to the parent of the opposite sex, and should not, in most normal family situations, cause any major difficulties for him in terms of outgrowing romantic fantasies. In some cases it may do the child who is in distress a lot of good to be able to sleep in his parents' bed. Many times the child's demand to spend the remainder of a disturbing night in his parents' bedroom does not last very long, or may occur only periodically. Once the child is comforted, and falls asleep, he can then be moved back to his own bed.

The vast majority of you will make the "right" decision according to what seems best for you and your child. As always, it is best to consider the alternatives and then exercise your own good judgment. In the event that your child is expressing very strong affection toward the parent of the opposite sex or is making obvious attempts to have this parent to himself, it would probably be better to comfort him in his room and not yours. If your child persists in wanting to sleep in your bed after several nights or a couple of weeks, and this practice is interfering with your privacy or comfort, help him break this habit before it becomes even more well-established by being firm in your refusals to give in to his requests. Assuming that he is only periodically fearful during the night, or experiencing a temporary emotional crisis, it is doubtful that allowing him to sleep in your bed will have any negative effects upon his psychological development. Again, there is no one right method of handling this situation, and how you choose to deal with it is a personal decision.

DEVELOPING GOOD TOILET HABITS

Many children, at three, have already established good toilet habits, and are able to assume some or full responsibility for their needs. Some youngsters still ask for their parents' assistance after they have had a bowel movement. Most children will be staying dry at night on their own, although this may depend upon their being taken to the toilet late in the evening before their parents go to bed. It is not uncommon for preschool children to have occasional accidents or temporary lapses in bladder control. With a few youngsters, nighttime accidents, as well as daytime accidents while they are playing outside, are especially persistent.

Toilet Training Problems

Some parents whose children are progressing more slowly than their peers in caring for their own toilet needs, are probably becoming discouraged or losing patience. In the event that your child is among those who are lagging behind in developing good toilet habits, try not to be too disappointed or impatient. There is a great deal of variability in the ages at which children become fully toilet trained, and there is no "right" age at which a child must remain dry. Some perfectly healthy, normal, and happy children are simply slow to be trained and continue to wet their beds during the night until they are well into grade school. An awareness of some of the problems that can arise during the preschool years may help you understand and handle them should this become necessary. Bed-wetting (enuresis) is discussed in more detail in Preschool 3 on pages 929–31.

Any problems that arise in this area should be discussed with your child's doctor. A doctor's examination can determine whether or not there is anything physically wrong with your child which could be interfering with his ability to be successfully trained. Assuming there is no physical finding, the doctor may tell you that your child is simply a "late bloomer" in this particular area, and that you should try to relax and forget your concerns. The doctor may also offer you suggestions for solving the problem based upon a knowledge of your child and hundreds of others with similar problems.

It is also advisable to evaluate your child's environment to see if there is some aspect of it or some sudden change or disturbance that is causing him to be emotionally upset. It may turn out that he is having temporary difficulty adjusting to a new teacher at school or a new baby at home. It is a good idea to examine all possibilities. Guard against being too quick to attribute all of your child's difficulties to emotional factors; he may simply be exhibiting a normal delay in this particular area of development.

DAYTIME ACCIDENTS WHILE PLAYING OUTSIDE. Some children, otherwise successfully toilet trained, regularly wet their pants while they are playing outside. Experienced parents claim that the solution to this problem is not to be found in warning, punishing, or keeping the child indoors, because the child is not deliberately having accidents. There is a better chance that this problem can be solved through positive measures.

Parents can tell their child that they are going to remind him at intervals that it is time to come inside to use the bathroom. It may also help to urge him to use the bathroom before he goes outside. Frequently a child who is simply excited or wrapped up in a play activity forgets that he has to urinate, or waits until it is too late. This problem is usually short-lived. Eventually the child will be able to remind himself to come indoors whenever he feels the urge to urinate.

LAPSES IN BLADDER CONTROL. It is understandably disturbing to parents when a child of three or four, who has been staying dry for quite some time, suddenly exhibits a prolonged lapse in bladder control. The most common causes for these regressions are excessive external pressures and emotional tensions, which the child may experience in the home or while playing with his peers. Initial steps in resolving this problem should attempt to determine whether the child is under such stress.

Parents may often be unaware that their demands during the day are putting undue pressure on their child, or that peer group pressure to perform in various games or activities is the reason for their child's anxieties. It is not uncommon for the child's lapses in bladder control to disappear when these pressures are alleviated or removed.

Should your initial attempts to deal with possible causes of emotional stress in your child be unsuccessful in restoring his normal bladder function, it would be appropriate to have him examined by your doctor. Urinary tract infections, more common in young girls, may be the cause for the lapse in bladder control. A simple analysis of your child's urine can reveal such a problem.

Occasionally, you may not find any emotional cause, and your doctor may not find any physical reason for the lapse in control. This should not be a cause for alarm, since some children, as they go through major developmental stages, temporarily regress in a few of their previously mastered skills. Assuming that you do not overreact to your child's problem, and have ruled out physical and emotional causes, he should have little difficulty in overcoming his lapse in bladder control.

CONSTIPATION. Constipation may become an exaggerated problem for a few children during the preschool years. This condition can often be alleviated by offering a child prune juice. Changes in diet may also be helpful (see the Health Care Guide). If, in spite of your efforts, the condition doesn't improve or the child becomes even more constipated, it is advisable to have him checked by a physician.

In a few cases, a child's constipation may not be relieved by the usual remedies prescribed by the doctor and may become more severe and prolonged. Assuming that your doctor has ruled out a physical cause, the constipation is likely to be indicative of emotional difficulties, and is sometimes referred to as "psychological constipation." It is not unusual for parents to have trouble trying to determine what factors caused this problem initially, and how to correct whatever is going wrong in their child's life. It is often advisable to seek professional help from a child psychologist or psychiatrist with this kind of problem, in the event that you cannot find a solution, and the constipation persists for long periods of time.

REFUSAL TO USE THE TOILET TO GET ATTENTION. The child who tries to manipulate his parent by deliberately refusing to use the toilet and soiling his pants may be doing this in order to gain parental attention. Whenever he feels he is not getting enough attention, and feels a bowel movement coming, he may produce it in his pants, rather than on the toilet. This may occur when his parent is busy fussing over the new baby, or is otherwise occupied with another person in the home. This is quite effective in drawing his parent's attention, since the parent has to interrupt his or her activities in order to wash him and change his pants.

This pattern of behavior should be changed as soon as possible. When parents themselves cannot find ways of improving the quality of their child's life so that they can overcome this situation, they will probably want to discuss this problem with a professional.

LITTLE OR NO DAYTIME CONTROL. An occasional child of three or four may still not be able to control his bladder or bowel functions during the daytime. This problem should be taken up with your physician. Assuming that you and your doctor have ruled out physical and emotional causes, perhaps the problem stems from the fact that the child, for a variety of reasons, simply is not very conscious of his elimination processes or is unclear about what is expected of him. You may have to start from the beginning and repeat each step involved in encouraging him to develop an awareness of the process of moving his bowels and urinating as though he were still a toddler. It may be helpful to reread the suggestions on pages 522–26, 616–18 for encouraging either bowel or bladder control before you begin again.

Keeping a child who is unsuccessful in bladder or bowel control in training pants may pressure him and contribute to his feelings of not living up to his parents' expectations. It is usually recommended that parents put him back in diapers and rubber pants, and help him feel as comfortable as possible wearing them. Then, whenever he shows more signs of readiness to control his elimination function, reintroduce the training pants to positively reinforce his successes.

Offering your child plenty of reassurance and support may help boost his confidence. Try your best not to rush him or become impatient with him. Let him set the pace of the training. Given this extra time and encouragement in a relaxed and emotionally unpressured climate, your child may make considerable progress in a relatively short period of time.

STRANGE ELIMINATION BEHAVIORS. A few preschool children may display very strange or even bizarre elimination behaviors. One little boy, for example, began to hide his bowel movements in a corner of his bedroom closet. In another case a mother reported that her daughter was storing her bowel movements in the drawer of her nightstand. Other children may regularly defecate in odd areas in the home rather than in the bathroom. If your child is behaving in an unusual way in regard to his toileting habits, you will obviously want to help him outgrow this pattern.

This behavior may not mean too much, assuming that it is the only unusual response in a child who otherwise appears to be happy, well adjusted, and is developing normally. However, these activities may appear among children with slightly abnormal personalities, so it is important to determine the reason for this, and examine your child's over-all behavior patterns. In case this strange behavior is not isolated, but is one of several unusual activities which the child exhibits, you should discuss the situation with your doctor.

DISCIPLINE

Parent-child Relationships and Discipline

Parents who have a warm, loving, comfortable relationship with their child are likely to have an easier time disciplining him than if their relationship has not been very positive. As discussed in the Personal-Social Development section, when parents are loving and warm toward their child, he is more likely to want to identify with and model himself after them, and will thus adopt many of their values and standards of conduct as his own. A good parent-child relationship is believed to promote conscience development. When the child behaves contrary to these standards that he has incorporated into his personality, he is likely to feel a loss of self-esteem, and also feel guilty.

Assuming that the parent-child relationship has been positive, the child will also try to live up to his parents' expectations in order to please them and maintain their love and approval. He will also want to avoid misbehaving because he fears disapproval and loss of their love. The child who loves his parents will probably not object as much to the controls they put on his behavior as he would if he did not trust them or felt that they did not care about him.

Helping Your Child Learn to Control Aggressive Actions

In our society, the expression of aggression through physical means such as hitting, kicking, and biting is frowned upon and generally punished. Therefore, all of us must learn to find more acceptable, substitute outlets for our aggression. Language helps us express anger and aggression through talking rather than acting. A major objective of your program of discipline during the preschool years will be to help your child control his aggressive actions, but you should not expect him to deny his angry, jealous, and hostile feelings, because repressing or burying these feelings might lead to problems in the future.

As your preschooler's ability to use language grows, he will be increasingly able to discharge feelings and emotions through speech, substituting talking for acting on unacceptable wishes and urges. In order for this change in the expression of aggression to take place, he must want to change. This is where you will play an important role.

You will have to motivate your preschooler to talk about his aggressive feelings, rather than scratch, kick, bite, or strike out. Unless he is sufficiently encouraged to give up immature and unacceptable behaviors and replace them with speech, chances are that he will continue to express angry, aggressive, and destructive urges through physical channels, as was the case in infancy and toddlerhood.

Should you catch your child readying to strike out at someone or something, or in the midst of doing so, stop him and make it clear that you want him to talk about his feelings, since you disapprove of his actions and will not tolerate them. Do not reinforce his temper tantrums or other unacceptable physical shows of anger or frustration, such as slapping, but rather, encourage him to put feelings into words. You can also encourage him to express his needs for physical outlets through appropriate channels, such as exercise, other physical activities, and rough play.

It is necessary to make it clear to your youngster that you will not stand for destructive behavior by establishing firm controls, showing your disapproval of improper behavior, and telling him why certain actions are not desirable. There is also another step that you can take to help teach him to control anger and aggression. This is to provide him with a good example to follow.

Parents who employ physical means for discharging their own aggression at the very same time they are trying to teach their child to control his aggression are setting a poor example for him. Why should their child strive to control his behavior when his parents regularly behave in an unacceptable manner? Most preschool children are interested in imitating their parents' behavior. A child who sees his parents using acceptable channels such as language to express aggression and anger will want to release his aggression in this manner, since, in doing so, he will become more like them. By controlling your own violent actions, and setting a good example, you will be doing a great deal to help your child learn to control aggressive behavior.

Do not expect to see immediate results for your efforts, since your child's vocabulary and ability to put his ideas into words will still be limited. Try to be patient and tolerant, while continuing with your educational program. Anticipate that it will take time for important lessons in controlling his own aggression to be learned and consistently put to use. You are likely to achieve greater success in the latter part of Preschool 2 and in Preschool 3, at which time he will have a better ability to express his feelings through speech.

Taking Property That Does Not Belong to Him

The preschool child's sense of property rights and his respect for other people's possessions are still limited. He may occasionally take something that does not belong to him because his ability to refrain from yielding to temptation is not well developed. The child of this age who takes things that are not his is not really doing so deliberately. He has yet to learn the difference between wishing he could have an object that belongs to someone else, and acting upon his wishes. With a little help from you, this difference will become clearer to him in the next few years.

In the meantime, you should show your disapproval clearly, for example, by explaining that what he did was wrong. If you punish your child too harshly, or make too much of an issue over his misconduct, you may make matters worse in the long run. What may concern you even more than your youngster's taking someone else's property, is the fact that he may continue to deny that he took something even after he has been caught red-handed. He may claim that his sister, his cat, his imaginary companion, or some other innocent party (real or make-believe) was the culprit.

This behavior is not unusual for a preschool child who lives in a world where fact and fantasy quite frequently become intertwined. Punishing the child severely may result in more attempts on his part to deny the truth when questioned. You should clearly let him know that you are not able or willing to accept his story, and stress the importance of being truthful and admitting one's mistakes.

Sometimes a parent's overly harsh attitude in quizzing a child about taking things that do not belong to him can frighten him into lying. By asking a child if he took something or *did* something that you are certain he took or did, you may be making it more difficult for him to admit his wrongdoing. Assuming that you are sure that your child took your bottle of nail polish, saying something like, "Harvey, where did you put my bottle of nail polish?" rather than, "Harvey, did you take my nail polish?" may prompt him to return it to you. After he has returned the item in question, you can explain why he should not have taken it in the first place without asking your permission.

There is a better chance that a young child will find discussions about respecting property rights and being honest about his actions more meaningful if you make them relevant to his own life. Perhaps you could talk about how bad he might feel if someone took his favorite toy without asking him beforehand. This would be easier for him to relate to than a long explanation about abstract terms such as truth and morality; as was previously discussed, you should not expect too much at this stage, since your child will probably still have difficulty about respecting other people's property or putting himself in another's place.

SEX EDUCATION

Whether or not to offer your child specific information about issues related to sex is a personal matter. Even if you choose to refrain from having any discussions on the subject of sex with your child or answering his specific questions, you will still be indirectly educating and giving him sex education through your own actions and attitudes. Sex education is a broad subject that is an introduction to life. It is not simply a heart-to-heart discussion between parent and child on where babies come from. Teaching the facts of life is only one aspect of sex education.

Sex Education Begins at an Early Age

The child's sex education begins at an early phase, probably when he first becomes aware of how his parents feel and behave toward him, one another, and his brothers and sisters. It continues throughout childhood, whether or not his parents make a conscious effort to "teach" him about sex per se. It includes, among other things, parents' roles in helping to shape their child's attitude toward his body, his sex identity, relationships between men and women, and the "roles" of men and women in society. It also includes parents' roles and attitudes in handling sex-related situations, such as those involving genital and sex play, and the part parents play in influencing their child's identification with members of his own sex. These additional avenues of conveying sexual information and attitudes to a child are perhaps more important than giving specific factual information about reproduction. They play a major role in molding attitudes and feelings about sex-related matters and in developing the ability to find fulfillment in a given sexual role.

On several occasions Derek Weber's mother had found him playing with his genitals. Her reaction was always one of shock and disgust at his behavior. Each time Mrs. Weber discovered Derek handling his genitals she told him that he was a "bad" or "dirty" boy. When he became curious about sex and began to ask his mother questions, such as, "Where did I come from?" she refused to answer him and told him that he had a "filthy" mind for thinking about sex.

This little boy grew up believing that sex was something "dirty," and this idea was hard for him to outgrow, even though years later he read in books that masturbation was not "harmful" or "dirty" and that sex was a natural function. As we have seen, the early attitudes toward masturbation and sex that parents convey can be carried with a child even into adulthood.

Monique, throughout early childhood, had constantly observed her father abusing her mother, verbally and physically. Her father took advantage of her mother and other women whenever he had an opportunity to do so and frequently reminded his wife and daughter that women were placed on this earth to "serve men." Monique, as a result of this "sex education," grew up resenting her father and had negative feelings about men in general.

This preschool child's early experience with her father and her parents' poor marriage made it difficult for her to enter into any meaningful and lasting relationships with men. Later, once she entered school, she was taught in a health class that marriage was a beautiful relationship between a man and a woman based on trust, love, and respect. It is understandable that she found this concept of marriage difficult to accept.

As was previously mentioned, parents play an influential role in shaping their child's feelings about his gender identity, and his attitudes about himself as well as members of his own sex. Sandy's parents were extremely disappointed when she was born, because they had been desperately hoping to have a boy. Throughout her early childhood they made this fact obvious. She came to feel unloved and unwanted as a girl, and modeled herself after boys in order to receive her parents' love and affection. Sandy's mother's negative attitude toward her own sex and her role as a woman reflected her own unhappiness, and this attitude was passed on to Sandy.

Learning some of the facts of life and that one day she could get married and have a baby did not help her to feel positively toward her sexual identity or women in general. The attitude her parents conveyed to her about members of her own sex and about femininity during early childhood made it difficult for Sandy to identify with her mother and other females and find pleasure in being a girl.

Children's attitudes toward their own sex, their future sexual role, and sexual matters in general are influenced by their parents' attitudes and behavior toward them, and how their parents get along with one another. Teaching children the "facts of life" is important, but even more important in these early years, when the child's ability to comprehend information about sexual matters is limited, is the need to help children develop a healthy positive attitude toward their bodies, their gender identity as boys or girls, and their future roles as males or females.

WHO SHOULD GIVE YOUR CHILD SEX EDUCATION? You know and understand your child better than anyone else, and should be the one to answer his questions as well as offer explanations about sex and reproduction. You are not only more capable of getting information across to him properly, but you are in the best position to translate any information he receives from other sources, so that it is geared to his level of interest and understanding. You can also help clear up any misguided notions that he might have. Parents have a very strong influence on their children, and, in the vast majority of cases, are the best teachers. Parents not only act as teachers by answering their child's questions, but they also provide information about sexual identity, male and female roles, and interpersonal relationships by their example.

Your youngster will want answers from you, if and when he begins to ask questions about birth, babies, and so forth. Many parents worry about explaining sex-related information to their children. This need not be an area of concern provided that you take the time to get the facts straight, prepare yourself in advance for inevitable questions, and realize that your child's curiosity will be satisfied by simple, direct answers. Parents these days tend to do a good job of offering their children sex-related information, since adults appear to be more relaxed about sex and recognize that an early interest in sex-related issues is not unwholesome or unusual.

YOUR ATTITUDE CONVEYS AN IMPORTANT MESSAGE. Toby asked her parent why there were clouds in the sky, and her mother answered her casually, calmly, and matter-of-factly. Toby got the message that it was all right to ask this question and, afterward, could ask her parent more questions, without even thinking twice about it. On the other hand, when Toby asked where babies came from, her parent became embarrassed, looked shocked, and abruptly replied, "They grow in a special place inside a mother's body." Toby got the message that this subject was different from other subjects, and seemed surprised and rather puzzled by her mother's emotional reaction. Did she dare ask any further questions about the origin of babies? She was not sure. From her parent's reaction she sensed that there was something special and fascinating about this subject.

Try to remain relaxed and emotionally neutral when your preschooler asks questions about sex. Do your best to answer him casually and matter-of-factly, and in a friendly tone of voice, just as you would if he questioned you about the clouds in the sky. It is important to convey to him the message that it is natural and healthy for him to be curious, and that expressing an interest in babies or reproduction is really no different from expressing an interest in any other subject.

Keep in mind that your child will have no idea that his question is in any way related to sex, because he does not fully comprehend the meaning of this word. This subject may be emotionally charged and embarrassing for you, but a young child has none of these feelings or associations when he asks sex-related questions. With him it is simply a matter of interest or curiosity. Avoid drawing special attention to this subject by your own attitudes and reactions.

The Child's Comprehension of the Facts of Life Is Limited

Preschool children cannot be fully educated in matters concerning reproduction and other aspects of sex. Their ability to comprehend facts and principles is limited. Their experience is also very minimal, and their bodies are not mature enough to allow for a sophisticated understanding of this subject. In trying to help children learn the appropriate facts, parents often resort to using dolls as models, and showing youngsters anatomical diagrams and pictures. Parents usually repeat the same facts and answer the same questions time and again. Even the utilization of these techniques may not ensure that their children will understand the information that is given, although it is a good idea to try.

Some Preschool 2 or 3 children can recite the simple story about how babies are made, as explained by their parents:

> The Daddy plants the seed inside the Mommy. The seed meets the egg. The baby then grows in a special place inside Mommy, and comes out through a special passage.

This was the case with little three-and-one-half-year-old Betsy.

Betsy had clearly memorized the story of how babies are made and could recite it from beginning to end, but still had no understanding of the process. When stopped in the middle of her recitation, she could not pick up at the point at which she had been interrupted. Upon being questioned as to how Daddy plants the seed inside Mommy, she stated with uncertainty that she figured that Daddy gives Mommy special seeds to eat, and when Mommy eats them, they go into her stomach where they stick to the eggs which are already in the stomach.

Even the brightest preschool child, who appears from her ability to memorize and recite the facts to know all about the process of making babies, may actually comprehend very little. Many preschool children have their own ideas about how babies are made. Many of these ideas, much to their parents' surprise, are related to the processes of eating and going to the bathroom. When their parents offer them simple facts about the birth process, children may combine these facts with their own distorted thoughts on the subject and come up with some highly unusual explanations.

Does all of this imply that giving preschool children factual information about sexual reproduction is a waste of time and effort? No. Just because young children have some trouble understanding facts in other areas of "education," parents do not discontinue all efforts to teach them. Similarly, parents should not refrain from giving sex information just because preschoolers are not capable of fully understanding the facts about procreation. It is important to be aware of children's limitations in comprehending the facts of life—since this will influence what you say, and guide you in how to tailor teaching efforts to suit your youngster's changing needs.

When Children Begin to Ask Questions

During the preschool stage, generally in Preschool 2 or 3, children become very curious about how things are made, and they ask their parents numerous "why" questions. They often express an interest in knowing where they came from and how they were created. Most youngsters start asking simple and direct questions such as, "Where did I come from?" or, "Where do babies come from?" before they enter school. Some children begin to ask questions early, when they are about two to three years old, but most ask these kinds of questions when they are three to four years of age. A few children never ask, but this does not necessarily reflect their lack of curiosity or interest in reproduction. Questions are often asked after a child observes his mother or another woman with an enlarged belly. The arrival of a new baby in the home may also prompt a child to ask questions, as may the sight of animals giving birth.

Children ask a variety of questions about sex, such as those focusing on pregnancy, birth, fertilization, the differences between males and females (discussed in the Personal-Social Development section), and even menstruation. Two of the most common questions preschool children pose are "Where did I come from?" and "How are babies made?" Other examples of the numerous kinds of questions asked are as follows:

Pregnancy and Birth:
"Where did Mrs. Grant get her new baby?"
"Why is Aunt Annie's stomach so fat?"
"Can I make a baby?"
"Where was I before I was born?"
"Do you have a baby growing inside you now, Mommy?"
"How does the baby get out?"
"Can Daddy have a baby?"
"Where does the seed come from?"

Fertilization:
"How did the baby get inside her tummy in the first place?"

Menstruation:
"Mommy, what's in the box?"
"What are those things, Band-Aids? Do you have a cut?"
"Are you hurt, Mommy?"

It is impossible to predict exactly how or in what order children's questions about these subjects will be asked. Each child may add his own individual twist to a familiar question.

ANSWERING YOUR CHILD. When your child asks you a sex-related question, it is always wise to attempt to determine what your child knows or thinks is the answer before offering any information. Be prepared to hear him say some rather unusual and amusing things. No matter how naïve or ridiculous his comments seem to you, show your respect by listening carefully and refraining from laughing or making fun of him.

Listening to your child's ideas first will give you a good opportunity to clear up any incorrect ideas that he might have. This is initially important, because if you do not find out what he thinks, and simply offer explanations, he may misinterpret the new information based upon what he already thinks. He may also take the real facts and insert them into his own distorted explanation, and become more confused.

When Margie Glaser asked where babies come from, her mother replied that they grow in a special place inside a mother's body. Mrs. Glaser essentially offered her daughter a valid explanation. Margie, however, thought that babies grow in mothers' stomachs, and she interpreted this new information about a "special place" as referring to a stomach. Had Mrs. Glaser asked Margie where she thought babies came from before answering the question, Mrs. Glaser might have emphasized the fact that the "special place" was not the stomach, or she might have told Margie that "the special place is called a 'uterus.'"

Besides attempting to discover what your child knows at the time of his first question, it is advisable to ask him what he thinks is the answer to each successive question that he asks, before going further. Children often forget the facts shortly after they learn them, and since the explanations parents give sometimes seem more unbelievable than their own explanations, they may go back to their previous notions.

Despite parents' genuine efforts to offer simple, factual information, children's own incorrect notions may still persist. The stories about reproduction that they believe quite often consist of a mixture of real and imagined events. Just when parents have answered their child's last question, and are fairly certain that he has the whole story about where babies come from straightened out in his mind, they may be surprised when they realize that he has it all confused.

The most appropriate occasion to give information to your child is immediately after he asks for it. To parents' embarrassment and surprise, children's questions seem to pop up unexpectedly in public. Drew, upon seeing a pregnant woman in a restaurant, yanked on his mother's arm and shouted, "Mommy, that lady is fat. Why is her stomach so big?" Drew's mother was rather taken aback by her son's question, but proceeded to answer it right then and there, while the question was still fresh in his mind.

Should your youngster ask a related question at home or when the two of you are alone, it would be best to answer him right away, just as you would immediately reply to a question about why the car moves or the train makes noise. When this kind of question is asked in a public place or when there are many people around, you might want to answer him right then or you might say that you will tell him later, when so many people are not around. Do not use this delay as an excuse to forget the whole issue. Your child's curiosity deserves to be satisfied, and he is likely to keep after you until you offer answers that accomplish this.

LET YOUR CHILD'S QUESTIONS GUIDE YOU IN OFFERING INFORMATION. You will have to determine how best to communicate information about sex to your child. Some parents feel uncomfortable discussing sex with their children, and when their child finally asks a question, they often try to get the whole story of procreation over with all at once. This is not the most advisable approach to take with preschool children, knowing that they generally have a difficult time grasping such facts. It is also a mistake for parents to assume that once they have had one discussion about sex with their youngster that is the last time that they will be involved in such a discussion. Most children ask many questions. More likely than not, they will ask the same question time and again, not always because they forgot their parents' answers, but because as they mature, the same question and the same answers have different meanings to them. You should be prepared to elaborate upon answers as your child matures, since your Preschool 3 child, who asks, "Where did I come from?" will be capable of digesting an explanation that he could not have understood during Preschool 1 or 2.

A youngster who wants to know where he came from is not asking for elaborate information about sexual feelings or intercourse, and most psychologists agree that it is not appropriate for parents to offer exact descriptions of the physical and emotional aspects of procreation to children at this stage of development. The young child does not want a long, drawn-out, and comprehensive lecture on sex when he asks a question. Rather, he wants a simple answer about reproduction that satisfies his curiosity at that particular point in time.

After a child's parent has found out what the child thinks, an appropriate reply might be, "You grew in a special place called a uterus inside Mommy's body." Assuming that he is satisfied with this answer, he is not likely to ask any further questions for the time being. He may consider this new information, and try to comprehend it. It may then be several minutes, a week, a month, or several months before he asks another sex-related question such as, "How did I get into Mommy's body?" When a child asks how he got into his mother's body, his parent, after determining what the child thinks is the answer, might reply that he grew from a very tiny egg that was inside Mommy all the time. Again, assuming that the child's curiosity is satisfied with this answer, it may be some time before he asks another question, or a moment later he might ask, "How does a baby get out?" Then, at that point, his parent can offer still another piece of the total story of reproduction and birth.

This method of using the child's questions as a guide to help you determine how much and what kind of information to tell him is excellent. Offering information step by step, according to what your child tells you he wants to know, will help you avoid giving too much sex information before he is ready for it. This approach will also give him time to try to make sense out of each new aspect of the story, instead of being overloaded with too many facts all at once. Giving too much information at any given time will most likely confuse him, and it may also bore him.

OFFER YOUR CHILD THE TRUTH. Be honest with your child in giving information about sex and reproduction. Your child may overhear bits of older children's and adult's conversations regarding sex and pregnancy, and he may be thoroughly confused when he tries to compare and combine what you have told him with whatever he has heard or imagined. When the stories do not sound the same, he is likely to worry and imagine all sorts of things.

Sooner or later your child will learn the truth. Remembering that you were not honest with him on previous occasions may make him leary about asking you anything else about reproduction. Don't jeopardize your child's trust or confidence in you by telling untruths. By giving him simple, but honest, answers to his questions, you will be in a better position to answer the more sophisticated questions that may arise in the future.

Sometimes parents partially distort the facts by telling their children that babies grow inside a mother's stomach. Giving a child sex information that is anatomically wrong is also not a wise practice. It is not uncommon for a child, on his own, to believe that a baby is created by the mother eating something special. In the event that such a child then asks his pregnant mother where a baby comes from, and the parent replies, "It grows inside Mommy's stomach," this will only add further to the child's own incorrect ideas.

The new fact that a baby grows in his mother's stomach, coupled with the child's awareness that the food he eats goes into his stomach, may convince him that something his mother ate, perhaps something quite large like an orange or hard-boiled egg, settled in Mommy's tummy and then grew to be a baby. Would it be so far-fetched for this child to conclude further that if he eats everything his mother eats, he, too, will make a baby? In figuring out how the baby gets out of his mother's stomach, the child might understandably think that since food eaten goes into the stomach and later comes out through the hole for "wee wee" or "pooh pooh," the baby in Mommy's stomach must ultimately come out of one of these two holes.

The child's mother will later undoubtedly have a difficult time telling her youngster to give up this nonsensical story because the incorrect facts she offered earlier were not only false, but gave substance to the child's fantasies about conception. Telling a child untruths can add to his confusion, make it harder for him to learn the correct facts later on, and cause him to lose trust in you once he learns the truth. It is much easier to be honest with your preschooler.

Guidelines for Giving Answers

Some parents want to know how much and what kind of information on sex is appropriate to offer their preschool child. Since the amount of information as well as the level of sophistication of your answers and explanations will be determined by factors such as your child's age, his ability to grasp facts, and his level of curiosity, the ultimate decision about what kind and how many facts to offer rests with you. However, the following examples of different ways to offer explanations may serve as guidelines or take-off points from which to formulate your own answers and methods of giving information.

THE GARDENING APPROACH. In recent years, the story of a baby's conception from a seed has been likened to a seed that grows in a garden. This "gardening" approach to explaining the facts of life has been and still seems to be one of the most commonly used.

Mrs. Vance used this approach with her four-and-one-half-year-old son, Hector. In response to Hector's question about where babies come from she replied, "A baby grows from a tiny seed in a special place inside the mother's body." When Hector asked how the baby got into his Mommy's body she said, "You know how plants in the garden need to be fertilized before they can grow—it's the same way with the seed in a mommy's body. The seed is there for a long, long time, but it will not grow into a baby until it has some special fluid from a daddy. It takes a mommy and a daddy to make a seed grow into a baby."

A long time passed before Hector asked how the fluid from the daddy got into the mommy. Mrs. Vance's answer was, "The fluid in the daddy comes from a special place in Daddy's body, and he gives the fluid to Mommy." Hector seemed fascinated by all of this and right away asked how the baby comes out. Mrs. Vance went on to explain that when the baby is fully grown, the special hole in the mommy, not the hole where "wee wee" or "pooh pooh" comes out, stretches to let the baby pass through.

A DIFFERENT APPROACH TO OFFERING EXPLANATIONS. Naturally, there are other ways to answer children's questions about reproduction. Mrs. Marcus, for instance, had a wonderful opportunity to explain the facts of life to her four-year-old daughter Alyssa in a very thorough fashion. Mrs. Marcus became pregnant and began to show in her fourth month.

One afternoon Alyssa said, "Mommy, why are you getting so fat?"

"Why do you think I'm getting fatter?" Mrs. Marcus asked her daughter.

"Because you eat so much!" Alyssa retorted.

"No, that isn't right," said Mrs. Marcus. "I'm pregnant and I'm going to have another baby."

Alyssa seemed surprised and delighted, since she had recently shown a great interest in babies.

Mrs. Marcus went on to say, "The reason I look fatter to you is because the baby is growing inside my body."

"Where?" Alyssa asked.

"The baby is growing in a special place inside my body called a uterus. It's not growing in my stomach."

Alyssa then asked, "Did I come from the same place, too, Mommy?"

"Yes, before you were born you grew from a tiny egg inside my body, too."

For several days Alyssa went around telling everyone that the reason her mommy was fat was because she was growing a baby inside her, but she asked her mother no further questions. After a week's time she asked her mother where the baby came from. Mrs. Marcus was surprised at this question, since she had previously told her daughter. Nevertheless, she refrained from telling Alyssa that she had already explained the answer, and replied, "Where do you think the baby came from?"

"From the grocery store," Alyssa answered.

"No, Alyssa," Mrs. Marcus said, "I did not buy the baby at the grocery store like I buy groceries. The baby grew from a tiny egg in a special place inside my body, and little by little it's getting bigger. The bigger the baby gets, the fatter I'll get around my belly, but the baby isn't growing in my stomach. It's growing in another place called a uterus."

Another two weeks passed, and then one morning Alyssa demanded to know whether the baby would be a boy or a girl.

"I wish I could answer your question right now," Mrs. Marcus said, "but we'll have to wait until the baby is born to find out if it's a boy or girl. It's more fun this way since it'll be a surprise."

Right away Alyssa asked another question. "When will the baby come out?"

Mrs. Marcus wasn't exactly clear as to what to say but she replied, "The baby will come out when it's fully grown, and we're hoping that it will be somewhere around New Year's [a valid statement] but we're not sure exactly when the baby will be born. It will take quite a while before the baby is ready enough to be born, but even now I can sometimes feel it moving inside me. If you want to, you can put your hands on my belly sometime and feel the baby kicking. Would you like that?"

Alyssa nodded her head "yes."

Later that week Mrs. Marcus had Alyssa place her hands on her abdomen so that she could feel the baby move. Since Mrs. Marcus knew that her daughter was always fascinated by pictures, she bought a book and showed Alyssa pictures of how a fetus grows and develops, answered any further questions Alyssa had about how a baby gets food and air, and explained when and how it comes out, with the use of gestures and a doll as a model.

For an entire week and a half Alyssa ran around the house sticking her belly out in obvious imitation of her mother. When Mrs. Marcus questioned her posture, Alyssa stated with assurance that she, too, was growing a baby because she had eaten a lot of eggs. Mrs. Marcus found this amusing. She was surprised at her daughter's statement, because it indicated that her educational program was not making things clear.

Mrs. Marcus felt that it was time to offer additional information, but first she knew that she would have to clear up Alyssa's incorrect notions. She explained that the egg from which a baby grows is not the same kind of egg that people buy at the store and eat. To avoid further confusion she decided to refer to it as the mother cell. Alyssa then asked how the mother cell got in, and Mrs. Marcus explained that from the time she was a little girl the mother cell was inside her but it couldn't develop into a baby until she became a grown-up lady and married Daddy, since to make a baby it is necessary to have a mother cell and a father cell. "I want to make a baby, too!" said Alyssa. "Can I?" she asked.

"One day when you grow up to be as big as Mommy and get married, then you will be able to have a baby if you want to."

Alyssa seemed very disappointed, and returned to her normal posture.

Nearly a half year passed after the birth of her brother, John, before Alyssa inquired about what part her father had played in creating the new baby. She had remembered that to make a baby there must be a father cell and a mother cell, but she wanted to know how they got together inside her mother. Mrs. Marcus asked Alyssa how she thought the father cell got into the mother. Alyssa said that she wasn't sure but in the picture which her mother had shown her of father cells, they had looked small like pills, and that she thought the father got the pills from the doctor and gave them to the mother to swallow. Mrs. Marcus found her daughter's answer very amusing, but she did not let her feelings show as she explained the correct information to Alyssa once again. Despite her thorough explanations about reproduction, Alyssa seemed to put together her own version of the process. She appeared satisfied with her understanding and did not persist in asking more questions.

Being pregnant, Mrs. Marcus had a special opportunity to explain the facts of life to her child. However, it was Mrs. Marcus' method of instruction that was excellent, and she most likely would have done equally as well offering Alyssa information about sex whether or not she had been pregnant. Explaining the facts of life can be done by mother or father, and each of you will undoubtedly say and do things differently, depending upon what, to you, seems comfortable and right.

A MORE EXPLICIT TYPE OF EXPLANATION. Mrs. DeCarlo had a very explicit approach to sex education with her child, Sara. At age three, Sara asked her mother where she came from and how she was born. Mrs. DeCarlo explained to her young daughter that she was created inside her mother's uterus. She further explained that Sara grew inside of her mother's uterus until she was ready to be born, and then passed out of a special place in her mother's body called the vagina. Sara seemed to accept this answer without any further questioning, and went back to her play activities.

Several weeks later Sara, again, became interested in the birth process and asked her mother how the baby got in the mommy. Mrs. DeCarlo, again, explained that the baby grew in the mommy's uterus, and that a seed from the mommy was helped to grow by fluid from the daddy. Sara looked puzzled and seemed to be confused. She wanted to know more and asked her mother about how Daddy's fluid got into Mommy. Mrs. DeCarlo explained that Daddy put his penis into Mommy's vagina and the fluid came out from the penis and went into the uterus. Sara seemed satisfied with this answer and asked no further questions.

Mrs. DeCarlo's approach to sex education may seem natural and truthful to some parents, but may seem too explicit to others. Not all parents feel that they want to communicate these details of reproduction to their preschool-aged child, and thus, give less exact explanations. There is no best approach to providing information about reproduction. How much information and what kind to impart is a personal matter and varies greatly from parent to parent.

BOOKS CAN BE HELPFUL. Another route that parents find useful is to read their child a book about reproduction. There are several good books available which explain the facts of life adequately with pictures. These books are especially designed for young children. Before you read such a book to your child, always scan the material to be sure it is appropriate and geared to your child's level of understanding.

Read a book about sex-related issues as casually and naturally as you would books on any other subject. Allow your child to ask questions and make comments. When you have finished, you can put the book in his bookshelf along with his other books. Just as you read other books to him more than once, it may be a good idea to read this book several times. As he matures, the same story will mean different things to him.

ANSWERING QUESTIONS ABOUT MENSTRUATION. In offering information on sex and reproduction, it is worth while mentioning that some preschool children ask questions related to menstruation. A preschool child, who sees his mother's sanitary napkins, may think that these items are like bandages and thus suspect that his mother is cut or injured, especially if he happens upon a used pad that has been discarded. Parents should be prepared to give their child a simple, reassuring explanation about menstruation.

Depending upon the child's level of understanding and curiosity, parents might explain that the box or package contains pads that absorb wetness. Parents may want to emphasize that Mommy is not hurt and that all grown-up women have a discharge of reddish fluid that appears about once every month. The child can be told that this discharge, which is a necessary part of being able to be a mother, contains blood and other substances. When these body substances are not needed, they pass out of a woman's body through the same special passageway from which a baby is born. The sanitary pads are worn to protect Mommy's clothing from becoming stained.

YOU MUST FORMULATE YOUR OWN PERSONALIZED APPROACH. These few examples have given you some idea of how other parents have offered sex instruction and answered sex-related questions in several different ways. You may want to use these examples as guidelines in forming your own approach to giving information. There are certainly numerous other ways in which factual information on sex can be passed on to children.

Start with the basics, for there will be plenty of time later to give further information to fill in the gaps as your child matures. Listen carefully to his questions, since they will help you determine how much and what kind of information to offer. Give sufficient information to satisfy his interest and curiosity at each step. Have confidence that you will do a splendid job.

Do All Preschoolers Ask Questions About Reproduction?

Many, but not all, preschoolers ask about reproduction. The fact that a Preschool 3 child has not asked direct questions about sex does not necessarily mean that he is not curious, or does not have any ideas of his own about where babies come from or how they are made. It could be that he has somehow gotten the impression from his parents that this subject is taboo, and therefore is afraid to ask. He may indicate his interest and curiosity in indirect ways, such as by calling attention to every pregnant woman's enlarged belly that he sees, or by "accidentally" (on purpose) walking into his parents' bedroom several times at night when they are undressing or making love.

Parents should not overlook these or similar indirect indications that their child is ready for some information about sex. Should they arise, it is important to take advantage of such occasions to give explanations. An example comes to mind of a little boy who was visiting the zoo with his parents. He seemed unusually fascinated by a display of newborn guinea pigs and a guinea pig giving birth. He asked many questions about animal babies, and wanted to know where they came from, and how they were born. He did not ask his parents any direct questions related to humans, but his parents suspected that he was also curious about human reproduction.

Parents whose children do not ask questions about reproduction or sex-related subjects should not be concerned. Many children do not show an interest in these issues at this age. Their curiosity will be expressed in other ways. By taking your child's lead you can offer information as he develops an interest and becomes curious about these subjects.

Genital Play

Is playing with the genitals during the preschool years different from genital play in toddlerhood? Many professionals feel that there are some differences. Young children's interest in their genitals usually increases during the preschool stage. Prior to this time children probably had some interest in their genitals and in playing with their sex organs, mainly in order to satisfy their curiosity. Between Preschool 1 and 3, however, many children realize more fully that playing with their sex organs feels good and different from the feelings that they get when they handle their nose, ears, or knees. This area of the body stands out as being different—as being special—and, for a period of time, may become a focus of attention.

Preschool children's bodies and experiences are not sufficiently mature to allow them to have an ejaculation or experience the same degree of sexual arousal as would adults. As during toddlerhood, it would be inappropriate to label this activity "masturbation" in the adult sense of the word. On the other hand, observations of numerous youngsters have revealed that they find it pleasurable to fondle their genitals, and are capable of having pleasant feelings, if only of a childish kind. Some adults fail to recognize their children's feelings, try to deny that they exist, regard them with disgust or shame, or try to suppress them. Other parents appear to recognize their child's feelings and behavior more readily, but still have difficulty accepting them. Seeing their child touching his genitals and obviously enjoying it frequently causes parents to become concerned.

Young children's genital play is a normal aspect of development during the preschool years, and all indications are that this activity is not harmful. Most professionals suggest that parents respond to it much the same as was suggested during toddlerhood by trying to ignore it. In cases where parents feel as if they must interfere because their child's occasional genital play bothers them, they are advised to do so casually, perhaps by calmly suggesting an alternative activity.

Sex Play

Sex play among preschool children should not be regarded as a "sexual" activity, at least not in the adult sense of the word. Rather, these kinds of investigation and examination games should be looked upon as normal ways is which young children sometimes attempt to satisfy their natural curiosity about each other's bodies, specifically each other's genital organs. Preschool children who become involved in sex play are simply exploring each other's bodies so that they can find out what they want to know.

SEX PLAY IS MORE COMMON THAN YOU THINK. Preschool children's curiosity about other people's bodies and the differences between males and females frequently prompts their desire to touch and explore each other's bodies in a group situation. It is not uncommon for parents to find their youngsters engaged in sex play, or to hear about how their child was involved in such a "sinful" activity from an upset parent.

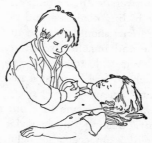

Children's investigatory activities quite often take the form of "playing doctor." Usually one child in the group assumes the role of a doctor who "examines" the other children. They feign illness. After a short while roles are likely to be changed, and the "doctor" becomes a "patient," until each preschooler has had an opportunity to examine and be examined. Sex play between youngsters may also take other forms. Children may pull down their pants and look at, comment on, and touch each other's bodies, probably concentrating on the navel, genital region, and the organs of elimination.

The number of different ways in which children express interest about sexual differences is only limited by their imagination and curiosity.

HANDLING SEX PLAY. Parents' reactions to discovering their child engaged in sex play with another child or other children vary greatly. Some parents are shocked and horrified when they find that their child is engaged in what they refer to as a "disgusting" activity. With a disturbed facial expression, they quickly attempt to put a stop to this activity, and punish their child afterward. Other parents do not attach any special significance to discovering their child engaged in sex play with other children, and they ignore it or treat it very casually. How you react is a personal matter, although there is certain general information with which you should become familiar before you take a stance on this issue.

Sex play among youngsters is common and not unnatural, and many experts suggest that parents, upon discovering their children in such activity, try not to act overly shocked, horrified, or disturbed about it. Taking a harsh, punitive attitude is not recommended. On the other hand, parents need not act as though they approve of such activities, when the opposite is the case. Most parents prefer that their child not engage in sex play, and want to let him know this without making him feel terribly guilty, or stifling his normal curiosity about sex and other children's bodies.

Giving children closer supervision is one approach, since it is less likely that children will engage in such exploratory activities when a parent is looking. What can parents do should they happen to walk in while children are playing "doctor" or "show"? This depends upon how parents feel about sex play between children. Some parents may want to matter-of-factly tell their child and the other children present that since they have satisfied their curiosity, they should not have to engage in this activity again, and then casually suggest that the children do something else of interest to them.

Another approach parents can take is to tell the children right then and there that their curiosity is normal, and is nothing to be ashamed of, but that their questions can be more easily satisfied by asking parents questions, since parents know the answers. Giving children some on-the-spot reassuring explanations about sex differences and similarities can answer their questions and sometimes put them at ease.

Children may find answers to their questions by looking and touching, but many youngsters will be left feeling confused and even uneasy after these group experiences with sex play. Parents should be able to help these children by giving them information about male and female sex differences, and encouraging them to ask questions. Children who are able to ask their parents questions and receive reasonable answers are not likely to feel as great a need to engage in sex play in order to find out what they want to know.

Most parents will want to set some firm but reasonable limits on sex play. This can be done by parents' treating this behavior as casually and naturally as they would other of their child's unacceptable behaviors, such as playing with "forbidden" objects, or disregarding rules for conduct that they have established. Even if you do your best to prevent sex play, you cannot keep your preschooler from being curious or interested in his own body and the bodies of other children. Try to offer your youngster an acceptable outlet for his curiosity through verbal discussions and questions.

Nudity in the Home

During the preschool years, parents often ask again about how much nudity should be allowed in the home. There are often varying opinions among psychologists and psychiatrists as to whether or not preschool children should regularly be permitted to see their parents taking a shower or dressing. One group of professionals sees no harm in parents taking a more relaxed attitude toward nudity in the home during the preschool years. They claim that when parents allow their child to observe them taking a shower or dressing, the child should benefit from having the opportunity to observe the anatomical differences between men and women in a casual atmosphere. They suggest that this approach helps a child satisfy his curiosity about males versus females.

Another group of professionals suggests that since the preschool child, particularly during Preschool 2 and 3, is developing sexual feelings, regularly seeing his parents nude may be too stimulating, may arouse feelings in him that may cause him to feel anxious or may be confusing and difficult for him to handle. Even though the child is very curious about how grownups are made, these professionals claim that there are ways in which his curiosity can be satisfied other than by looking. His parents should be able to help him find out whatever he wants to know by encouraging him to ask questions about the anatomical differences between males and females.

Conflict among professionals as to what is the best approach in large part results from a lack of controlled research on the effects of nudity in the home during the preschool years. Under these circumstances, it is difficult to advise parents as to what approach they should take in dealing with nudity. One thing to consider is the possibility that the small child will have difficulties with behaving one way (permissively) in his own home, and another way (modestly) outside the home. In some cases this can result in confusion. It is reassuring to know that many parents have raised healthy children using both permissive and conservative approaches to this issue.

DEVELOPING A SEXUAL IDENTITY. Whatever your approach to nudity in the home, it is important that you consider the guidelines discussed in toddlerhood on pages 629–30, and be aware of the fact that during the preschool years your child is developing a sexual identity. This can occur without any noticeable signs, or it may be very obvious in some children. Here is where parental discretion and careful observation may be very helpful in determining how to handle nudity with your child. A few examples may help illustrate this point.

Mr. and Mrs. Jones had been in the habit of allowing their toddler, Jackie, to take showers with them regularly. As Jackie began to develop her sexual identity during the preschool years, she became more seductive and affectionate toward her father, and more competitive and antagonistic toward her mother. She refused to take showers with her mother, and insisted upon taking showers with her father. The Joneses discussed at length how to handle their daughter. They felt that it would not be harmful or traumatic for Jackie to continue taking showers with her father, but they also believed that this was not appropriate in view of her current feelings toward her father. They decided to tell Jackie that she was grown-up enough to bathe alone, and would no longer be able to bathe with her parents.

These parents made a very sensible decision regarding the practice of allowing their little girl to bathe with her father. Given her strong affection and attraction for him, and her obvious jealousy toward her mother, continuing to permit her to take a bath with her father might reinforce her fantasies of replacing her mother and having him to herself.

Some youngsters, particularly older preschoolers, are quite open about their interest and attraction to the parent of the opposite sex. This certainly should help guide parents in deciding how to handle the issue of nudity.

Up until Mrs. Cheng's son, Lung-Chu, became a preschooler, she had always felt very comfortable about allowing him to observe her in the nude. Shortly after entering the preschool stage, however, Lung-Chu began to flirt with her and became markedly interested in watching her whenever she undressed or took a bath. Mrs. Cheng was very aware of this change in Lung-Chu's attitude and behavior toward her, and began to feel increasingly uncomfortable allowing him to see her unclothed. She felt that perhaps in some childish way Lung-Chu was becoming sexually aroused by seeing her in the nude. As a result, Mrs. Cheng decided that it was best not to undress in front of her son.

A child's flirtations or strong interest in seeing the parent of the opposite sex nude can often be embarrassing for that parent. It is definitely important that parents observe their child's responses to their nude bodies, and consider whether or not he is possibly being sexually stimulated, even if only in an immature way. In such a case, it would be wise to avoid letting him see you naked, since the feelings aroused in the child may be difficult for him to handle.

It is not uncommon for a youngster, particularly during Preschool 3, suddenly to want to have privacy when he is undressing, and to be embarrassed by seeing his parents or brothers and sisters undressing. Peggy, age four, suddenly seemed to be concerned with modesty in the home, and this puzzled her parents, who had been quite permissive about nudity in the home from the very beginning. Peggy began to insist upon having privacy when using the toilet or dressing. Her parents noticed that she seemed embarrassed whenever they walked around in the nude, or left the door open while bathing. Peggy's parents talked over the issues of modesty and privacy in the home and decided to respect not only Peggy's wish for privacy but also to refrain from appearing without clothes whenever Peggy was around.

Whether your child shows no change or significant changes in his attitude toward nudity during the preschool period, it is important to consider his feelings as well as your own in re-evaluating your policy toward nudity in the home. Should he feel uncomfortable or embarrassed undressing in front of either you, other family members, or other children, forcing this issue might be traumatic for him. In the event that you feel embarrassed by permitting him to see you in the nude, it would also be advisable to undress in private. There is no reason to believe that this practice will have a negative effect on his future sexual development.

FEARS

Some fears which were previously discussed during toddlerhood or Preschool 1 may still persist at this time. Certain fears, such as the fear of the toilet flushing, are likely to decline. Others may increase or emerge at this time, including fear of the dark, animals, bogeymen, dreams, being alone, and people who are extremely old or wearing strange masks.

Fear of Water

Most often the child's first fear of water was related to a fear of the bath. When he was fearful, he simply refused to get into the tub, or cried if you put him in against his will. During the preschool years, when some parents try to teach their children to swim, or enroll them in swimming classes, children may cry and refuse to go into the water because they are afraid. Throwing a crying child into a pool, or shaming him into getting into the water in order to cure him of his fear is not a good approach. It will probably serve only to heighten his fear of the water, and make him distrust the person who forced him to go in.

Some children are unafraid of getting into a small wading pool, but will not get into a full-sized swimming pool. Others respond to gradual entry into a pool, starting with their feet, and gradually easing the rest of their body into the water, inch by inch. Frequently, a child will go into the water providing he is securely held in his parent's arms, and allowed to hold onto his favorite plastic toys. Reassurance and encouragement from a parent may help to allay a child's fears, but it is wise to avoid putting pressure on a fearful child. His fear is often only temporary, and sometimes watching a parent, brothers and sisters, or other children taking swimming lessons and having fun in the water is sufficient to stimulate a child's interest in learning to swim, and to overcome his fear on his own accord.

Fear of Going to Nursery School

Some children initially fear going to nursery school and being separated from their parents. Usually they quickly overcome this fear after they have had a week or two to get adjusted. With a few children this fear may persist and even perhaps grow stronger. Sometimes a parent's unconscious desire to keep the child at home contributes to the child's fear of school. This fear is more fully discussed on pages 816–18.

Fear of the Dark

Fear of the dark is especially common among children between three and four, although it may arise at any time during the preschool years. This fear was more thoroughly discussed on pages 543–44.

TELLING YOUR CHILD THAT HE WAS ADOPTED

Many concerned, loving parents wonder whether or not they should ever tell their children that they were adopted. Most professionals agree that children should be made aware of this fact early in their lives by their adoptive parents. Parents who avoid telling their children that they were adopted run the risk of having their children overhear the facts from some third party. Hearing such news from someone other than one's own parents may not only come as a shock to a child, it may also result in his feeling insecure, fearful, and upset. Furthermore, he may feel as if he can no longer trust his parents to tell him the truth about other important subjects.

How, When, and What to Say

Parents often worry excessively over how, when, and what to tell their child, but this need not be an unusually difficult task. Your knowledge of your child and the love that you feel for him should give you confidence and guidance. You will ultimately decide how to approach this task depending upon what seems best and most comfortable for you and him. A few general guidelines should be helpful in making your own decisions.

Parents are advised to let the truth that their child was adopted come out very casually and naturally. There can be a great deal of variation in the age at which one tells a child. Many children start to ask questions about where they came from during the preschool years, so in answering questions, some initial information can be given. Keep in mind that when a child first asks such a question, he is not usually ready for the whole story, nor is he probably capable of grasping all of the facts.

The kind and amount of information you impart depends upon his comprehension, personality, and desire to learn about his origin.

Should your two- to three-year-old ask you where he came from, you might tell him that he grew from a tiny seed inside a mommy's body or uterus. Either at that point or at some later time he might ask if he grew in your body, at which point you can explain that he grew in a mommy's uterus, but not yours. If he is curious enough to want to know how you became his mommy, you might explain that his mother was not able to care for him. Then you can go on to tell him that you wanted a baby very much, one just like him, and that you chose him especially to be your child. In case your older preschool child wants more information, try to be as honest as you can in satisfying his curiosity without imparting facts that may hurt him.

Your attitude throughout your discussions is very important, probably more important than the specific information you offer. Take care not to act as though you are telling him some bad news or an embarrassing secret. Rather, try to get across to him the idea that he is a special individual who was wanted, and will be your child forever. Most of all, convey to him that you love him, and that whether or not he grew inside you or in your spouse's body, you are his parent and will always be there whenever he needs you.

Be sure to allow your child opportunities to express his feelings on this matter. If he seems insecure about the possibility of your giving him up in the near future, you will have to be very patient and reassuring in trying to convince him that you will never change your mind and abandon him.

There are several good books available that may serve as a guide to telling your child that he was adopted, but as his parent, you are capable of doing a first-rate job of handling his questions and giving explanations.

What If You Give Birth to Your Own Children Later?

There is a possibility that your adopted Preschool 2 or 3 child will feel slighted and rejected. He may think that because you had your own natural child, you no longer love him or want him. This situation need not be all that difficult to resolve, although extra patience on your part may be required.

You must reassure your child that you still love him, and that he is still special to you. Guard against becoming overly affectionate or oversolicitous in your methods of discipline, in order to counter the possibility that he may feel unwanted. He will surely sense the difference in your treatment of him, and this may only heighten his worries and insecurities. In other words, avoid trying to "make it up to him." Do your best to be consistent in your affection, attention, and care, and try to make each of your children feel as if they are special, wanted, and loved as individuals.

TELLING YOUR CHILD ABOUT GOD AND RELIGION

It is very much a personal matter for you to determine whether or not you wish to offer your child any religious education. Assuming that you plan to offer him religious experiences, it is also up to you to decide upon how much and what kind.

When both parents are of the same religious backgrounds, and plan to bring their child up in their religion, this usually presents no problem.

Difficulties may arise when parents have had different religious training and must decide what to do about their child. Parents should try to come to some kind of joint decision about the kind of religious education they want their child to receive, so that there is no conflict or confusion after the child is born. In cases in which there are extreme variances of opinion so that no compromise can be made, a professionally trained counselor may be of some help.

Once parents have made a joint choice, they often wonder at what age a child will be capable of receiving and understanding information about religion. Children during this phase are still extremely limited in their ability to understand an abstract concept such as God or religion. During the preschool years, particularly during Preschool 2 and 3, they often begin to ask many questions, such as "Who made the grass?" or, "Who made Auntie Annie?" which may be interpreted by parents as having relevance to religion. Parents will answer these "why" questions in a manner in which they feel is appropriate, perhaps offering explanations that have to do with God and religion. A preschool child is mostly interested in concrete answers, so explanations must be simple, direct, and kept at his level of understanding.

Answering your child's questions about God may be a rather delicate issue. Do not be surprised if he wants to know what God looks like, or whether God is a man or a woman. It is advisable to offer your child a simple, truthful answer. You might let him know that no one is sure what God looks like. Be sure to give him freedom to express his curiosity, and do not be afraid to tell him that you do not know the answers to all of his questions when this is really the case.

Some children between the ages of two and three will be capable of attending Sunday or religious school. The opportunities to be with peers that a child will receive attending Sunday school may also be very beneficial to him socially. Many youngsters attending Sunday school can be taught simple Bible stories, and can learn to say simple prayers. Young children may enjoy kneeling at the side of their beds and repeating prayers, with or without a parent's encouragement or coaxing. They may also enjoy celebrating religious holidays and learning to sing melodic, religious songs. Growing up with a knowledge of the name of his religion, and some early religious education, may add a new, positive dimension to a child's self-concept and identity, and provide a sense of pride and "belonging."

SEPARATION AND DIVORCE

In toddlerhood, some of the ways in which a separation or divorce might affect the child were explored and suggestions for dealing with these life changes in order to minimize problems were offered. Many of the general issues discussed on pages 692–700 are still applicable during the preschool years.

The preschool child is more mature than the toddler, has had more time to form solid emotional attachments to parents, and is better able to understand explanations. During this stage the child will not only be more aware of his surroundings, but will be going through many personal and family adjustments such as the love conflicts that arise, the development of a sexual identity, and the move beyond his family to enter into relationships with other children. It is important to examine some of the special circumstances and problems that can arise as a result of separation and divorce, as well as the ways in which to help your child make a good adjustment.

Greater Awareness of Marital Conflict Preceding a Separation or Divorce

Preschool children are more aware than toddlers of parental arguments, tensions, and marital troubles during the period of time prior to a separation or divorce. Parents often try to argue in private and disguise their hostility toward one another, thinking that their preschooler will not discover that their marriage is deteriorating. Attempts to conceal serious marital problems from children are rarely effective.

Bedrooms are not soundproof. Children are often able to hear arguments taking place, and are not apt to be fooled by parents' attempts to hide the fact that they have been fighting.

Barbara Schultz had this to say about the period of time before she and her husband, Todd, decided to become legally separated.

> My husband and I were going through some really tough times. Although we tried hard to argue in private, so as not to involve or upset Ricky, our son, he obviously heard us arguing in our bedroom night after night. Often, when we'd come out of the bedroom after an argument, we'd find him curled upon his bed, sobbing his little heart out. Sometimes while Todd and I were arguing in the middle of the night, Ricky would come tearing into our bedroom and would beg us to stop fighting and make up. Occasionally he would even ask us why we were mad at each other, and it was obvious that he thought he was to blame for our marital difficulties.
>
> It was no use trying to hide things from Ricky. He knew what was going on, so I offered him a simple, but truthful explanation for our arguments and marital problems, and did my best to reassure him that he had not caused them.
>
> Once our separation was finalized, and I told Ricky about it, the fact that we had decided to live apart did not come as a total shock to him. He knew that our arguments stemmed from our unhappiness about living together in the same house, and seemed to understand why we wanted to try living in separate homes for a while. This is not to say that he was happy about our separation. He wasn't. But at least he was more prepared for it than if I had never told him about our problems before.

Depending upon the circumstances, it may be possible and advisable to shield your child from learning the details of your arguments, but it is doubtful that you could or should keep the fact that you are having serious marital disagreements a secret, particularly when one spouse moves out of a shared bedroom to sleep elsewhere in the home, or leaves the home. Most youngsters feel the strain and tension created when their parents argue or are cold and antagonistic toward each other. They are sensitive to the interactions between their parents as well as to the emotional climate in the home.

Even when parents try to argue in private and put on a happy front in their child's presence, there is a good chance that he will sense that something is different or wrong and wonder what is happening. When a child is not informed of serious marital difficulties and sees that his parents are no longer talking to one another or sleeping in the same bedroom, or living in the same house, this can breed confusion and anxiety greater than would be aroused by learning the truth.

Am I to Blame?

From a child's self-centered perspective, he may think that his own poor behavior or bad wishes or thoughts are causing his parents to turn against one another. He may feel guilty every time they argue, or think that his parent's departure was his fault. A child should be told that he is not to blame for arguments and conflicts, and he may need frequent reassurance about this fact.

Be Aware of Your Child's Feelings

As a result of living in a home in which the atmosphere created by parents is hostile or cold, a child may become fearful, insecure, confused, withdrawn, depressed, or overly aggressive. Children often try to get their parents to stop arguing and make up, or become angry, tearful, or upset whenever they hear their parents fighting. It is important to observe what effects your marital conflicts are having upon your child. He may need extra attention, physical comfort, emotional support, and reassurance during the period of time when you are giving serious consideration to a separation or divorce.

Do your best not to overlook or neglect your youngster's physical, intellectual, or emotional needs. This sometimes occurs unconsciously because parents become totally immersed in their own pressing problems and have little time, energy, or interest in seeing that their youngster's needs are adequately satisfied. While this is understandable, a special effort to consider your child's feelings and needs should be made. Guard against shirking your responsibilities as his parent. Your child is bound to be affected by the strains of your deteriorating marriage, but by placing a high priority upon his welfare and emotional well-being, it may be possible to minimize emotional trauma for him prior to your separation or divorce.

Telling Your Preschooler About Your Separation or Divorce

As in toddlerhood, it is important to tell your preschool child about your separation or divorce as soon as it becomes a certainty. A preschooler is better able to understand language and feelings and is entitled to receive more sophisticated verbal explanations than a toddler. Your child should be given a simple, truthful account of events without hearing details that might hurt him or create additional anxiety or insecurity.

The young child will probably be interested mainly in learning about how his life will change as a result of the separation or divorce, but before saying anything, it would probably be a good idea to find out what he thinks a divorce or separation is. Youngsters sometimes have misconceptions about the meaning of such words that should be cleared up from the start. In defining a divorce or separation, use easy, familiar terms that he can comprehend, and to which he can relate.

Once you have informed him of what it means to separate or get divorced, you can go on to tell him something about the reasons why you and your spouse have been unhappy living together and have decided that it would be better to live apart either temporarily, while you try to resolve problems, or permanently, as in the case of divorce. Avoid giving him the impression that the decision was made on the spur of the moment. He should be made aware of the careful thought behind your decision as well as the efforts that went into trying to work out marital problems before concluding that a separation or divorce was the only solution.

Of utmost importance is to help your child understand that he is still loved by both you and your spouse. Convincing him of this may not be easy, since he may feel that the parent who is leaving is doing so because he or she no longer loves him, or is deserting him because of something that he did, thought, or said. It is not uncommon for a preschooler to feel guilty about his parents splitting up, and blame himself for their problems. Vigorous attempts to convince him of his innocence in this regard should be made.

It will be useful for you to discuss this issue with your spouse and try to come to a mutual decision about how to explain things to your child. This can help prevent your child from becoming confused by two different stories, and may also minimize further conflict between you and your spouse. Try to be patient and considerate of your child's feelings.

Your youngster will naturally want to know where and with whom he will be living, and will also want information regarding how often he will be able to see the parent who is leaving. Give him as clear a picture as is possible about living and visiting arrangements. Be sure to emphasize that he will be spending time with both you and your spouse individually.

Give your preschooler ample time to understand each new bit of information before going further. Questions will arise either at the time of your initial explanation or later. Answer them as best you can so that his curiosity is satisfied.

Do not expect your child to adjust easily to your separation or divorce. There is a good chance that he will find such news very disappointing as well as upsetting. Allow him to express his anger or unhappiness freely without passing judgment. He has a right to express feelings and emotions and should be given opportunities to do so.

There is a strong possibility that one explanation will not be enough. Your child may return to you from time to time wanting to know more about your separation or divorce, particularly as the months and years pass. On each occasion you will be able to add to your initial explanation, adjusting what you say to his level of understanding.

Helping the Child Resolve Love Conflicts During a Separation or Divorce

During the preschool years, the child's sexual identity becomes more well defined, and he commonly develops some romantic fantasies about the parent of the opposite sex that create love conflicts as discussed on pages 827–28 in the Personal-Social Development section. There are certain situations that can arise when family relationships are disrupted by separation or divorce that make forming a positive identification with members of the same sex and resolving love conflicts more difficult for a child. Special attention should be given to these situations so that the child's personal-social and psychological development are not impeded.

Let's first examine a little boy's position. A young boy's strong romantic fantasies about having his mother all to himself often prompt him to wish that Daddy would go away. In a two parent family situation, Daddy never leaves and the boy must realize that his desire to take his father's place can never be fulfilled. Instead of replacing his father, he learns to be more like him and develops a positive identification with him.

In the majority of divorce cases, mothers gain custody of children, and fathers leave the home. It is understandable why a young boy who believes that wishes can come true might misconstrue this event as the fulfillment of his wish for Daddy to leave and feel very guilty about causing his parents' divorce. His feelings of guilt may be very strong, and parents may notice how hard he is trying to apologize or make up to them for breaking up their marriage. Both parents should make a special effort to help their son realize that he was not responsible for their divorce.

A mother must take care to avoid encouraging her son's romantic fantasies after the divorce. Feeling lonely and rejected, and craving affection, an occasional mother will unconsciously give substance to her son's romantic inclinations by treating him as a substitute spouse. This reaction on her part would not be healthy or beneficial for him, since it could interfere with his ability to outgrow the fantasy of replacing Daddy in her heart and actions.

It is also important for a mother to refrain from constantly making derogatory statements about her ex-spouse, since this can hinder her son's ability to identify positively with his father. Divorce may leave a woman feeling quite bitter toward her former partner, but an effort should be made not to put Daddy down regularly in the child's presence, and to make the child's visits with his father go as smoothly as possible. It is important for a boy to respect his father and continue his relationship with him. In the event that this is impossible, a mother should try to arrange for her son to spend time with an older male with whom he can identify and establish a stable relationship.

The situation for girls tends to be quite different, since it is less common for a father to gain custody of his children in a divorce case, and spend a great deal of time alone with his daughter. If a little girl ends up living with her father, he should refrain from encouraging her romantic fantasies toward him, and also do what he can to help her identify positively with her mother and other women. A little girl's relationship with her mother should, if possible, be maintained, or else she should be given opportunities to form a good relationship with a mother figure with whom she can identify.

How Will Separation or Divorce Affect the Preschool Child?

The process of accepting and adjusting to a separation or divorce takes on different courses and varies in duration from child to child, and from parent to parent. Some children are emotionally upset from the moment they learn about the changes that are going to take place within the family structure. With others, the full impact of what has happened is not experienced until a parent actually leaves the home. Occasionally a child seems indifferent to altered life circumstances for several months, and then, suddenly, appears to lose emotional and behavioral control. There are also, of course, a few children who are happier and rather relieved after their parents have split and all the fighting is over. It is doubtful that you will be able to determine accurately how your youngster will react, since each child has his own, personal reaction in such circumstances.

Many of the points brought out in the previous discussion about how a separation or divorce will affect a child (pages 695–97) are still applicable to the preschool child. It is important to listen carefully to what your child has to say during the first several months following your separation or divorce, and pay close attention to the feelings and possible hidden meanings behind his words and comments. Also watch for changes in his normal pattern of behavior both inside and outside the home.

Do not just take every piece of behavior at its face value. A child who never before caused trouble at nursery school may not be just an "impossible child" who needs to be punished. Behaving poorly or aggressively may be his way of discharging intense emotions resulting from the stresses and changes in his life brought on by his parents' separation or divorce.

It is not uncommon for some children to lose their appetites, have trouble sleeping, or wet their beds after they have gained bladder control. They may go through a temporary period of depression, withdrawal, clinginess, regression, or overaggressiveness following the breakup of their parents' marriage.

According to Mrs. Sanchez, a newly divorced mother of three-and-a-half-year-old Maria:

> Maria suffered a lot before our divorce and even now she still seems very disturbed by it. She keeps asking me when her father and I will make up, and when he'll come back here to live. She seems to think that she caused us to separate, in spite of our attempts to tell her otherwise. Lately she's almost too good to me. She bends backward trying to please me, as if she's trying to make something up to me. She is also very afraid and insecure every time I leave the house, even to go to the store. She cries and gets really upset, as if she thinks that I'm never coming back. I've tried my best to make her understand things, but a month has gone by and she just can't seem to realize or accept what's happened.

It may take quite a while for some youngsters to accept the fact that one parent is no longer living in the home, and until this happens the remaining parent may be questioned about the absent parent's return. Feelings of insecurity, denial, rejection, anger, grief, fear, and anxiety are common and can cause a variety of disturbances or changes in a child's behavior. Rather than punish or shame a child for his unacceptable actions or "babyish" ways, it is important to try to get to the root of his problems by encouraging him to verbalize his feelings.

Assuming that your attempts to encourage your child to talk about his feelings and emotions are successful, try to refrain from passing judgment or behaving as though his feelings are not real or are silly. It will mean a great deal to him to have a supportive parent who makes a sincere effort to understand how he is feeling and help him resolve problems.

How the parent who is primarily responsible for the child's upbringing reacts to the separation or divorce will play an important role in influencing the child's reaction, and subsequent adjustment. The suggestions for how to help ease stresses on a toddler following a separation or divorce presented on pages 697–700 also apply to a great extent to preschoolers. Understanding your child's feelings about each parent and his own special needs will help make the transition easier and assist you in providing a happy single parent family environment.

Special Concerns of the New Single Parent

A newly separated or divorced parent often shares many concerns of the single parent and the working parent. These topics are explored on pages 640–44, 778–81, and it may be helpful to you to read them.

THE SINGLE PARENT FAMILY

Many common concerns among single parents have been previously discussed in toddlerhood (pages 640–44). Issues of importance to working parents and alternatives available to them are explored on pages 778–81. Those of you who have only recently become single parents may find it useful to review this material.

A major concern among single parents of preschoolers is the possibility that the absence of a second parent will be difficult for their child. Growing up with one parent need not be a major obstacle.

You can do a splendid job of providing for your preschooler's needs rearing him alone, and should not be insecure about your ability to do right by him. Now that your youngster is more aware, curious, and opinionated, and will be establishing a sexual identity, there are several issues that you will want to pay closer attention to in the preschool stage than in toddlerhood.

Your Child May Question You About Your Lifestyle

As your preschooler becomes more independent and ventures outside the home into the neighborhood, he will be exposed to many different family structures and settings. His awareness of obvious differences in families, lifestyles, and relationships is likely to arouse his curiosity and prompt him to make comparisons as well as ask you questions about your status as a single parent. It is not uncommon for a child to want to know what happened to his mother or father, or why his friend has two parents instead of one.

These questions are important and should be treated with respect, since they reflect his intellectual curiosity. Try to answer them as best you can, shaping your explanations to his level of comprehension. Simple, honest answers should suffice. Some single parents who feel guilty about their status, or are embarrassed or ashamed of the fact that they are rearing their child alone, may transmit these feelings to him in giving explanations, or overreact to questions by becoming very defensive or emotional. This can make a child feel insecure or embarrassed about the fact that he has only one parent.

A cheerful, confident, matter-of-fact approach to answering your child's questions should satisfy his curiosity and make him proud of his family structure and of you. Refrain from making value judgments about the single parent versus the two parent family, and underplaying the obvious differences that he has observed. Simply help him understand the truth and learn about some of the differences in family structures that exist without feeling the need to justify or defend your status as a single parent to him.

Your child, at some point, will recognize that there are families that consist of both a mother and father caring together for their children, and may express some jealousy over the fact that he has only one parent. Assuming that he is happy and you have provided him with a loving, stable home life, there should be no reason for you to feel threatened by his comments or questions; they merely reflect his normal curiosity.

Handling Your Social Life

Many of the aspects of establishing or maintaining a social life of your own that were discussed in toddlerhood (pages 640–41) are still applicable during the preschool years. The preschool child, however, is more aware of people and events. He is more curious about what he sees, and is also better able to ask questions and verbalize opinions. For these reasons, parents often pay closer attention to how they handle intimate relationships in their child's presence.

Each parent must make his or her own decisions, since a person's social life is a personal matter that is best approached on an individual basis. It is important to consider your youngster's vulnerability. His trust in you and close attachment to you makes you a very influential person in his life. Through your actions and words, you will not only be setting an example, but also helping to shape in him certain attitudes, values, and standards for conduct as regards himself, other people, and handling interpersonal relationships. The friends, lovers, or companions that you expose your youngster to on a regular basis will also have some influence upon him.

It is important to consider what effects your sexual and general social practices may be having upon your child. Also think about how he is possibly being influenced by the people with whom you associate. This is not to imply that you should deny your own needs or feelings, but you should not lose sight of his. You should take this into account when entertaining guests in your home or including him on dates or in your social activities.

You should anticipate numerous questions about your social life and friends. Being more verbal as well as more curious, older preschoolers often bombard their parents with questions on this topic. Often their questions prove to be quite embarrassing. Try to give your child simple, truthful answers. His questions should give you some insight into what he thinks and feels about your actions and reactions and those of your companions. In the event that the manner in which you are conducting intimate relationships in your child's presence appears to be confusing him or having a detrimental effect upon him, it would be advisable to alter your practices or be more discreet.

The Child's Reaction to a New Parent Figure

If your partner has died or left you, or if you are separated or divorced, you may wish to develop another close relationship, but may be worried about how this will affect your child. The topic of stepparenthood is explored on pages 782–85.

Helping Your Child Put Male and Female Relationships into Proper Perspective

As the child becomes more aware of the differences between males and females, and more capable of developing opinions about them, it becomes important for the single parent to help his or her child establish healthy attitudes toward members of the same and opposite sex. Single parents who themselves have had emotionally upsetting or painful experiences with a spouse or person(s) of the opposite sex sometimes generalize their bitterness or resentment to include all persons of the opposite sex. Parental opinions and feelings play an influential role in the child's development, particularly during the formative years between two and a half to five.

In situations in which a little child, girl or boy, never hears a kind word about persons of the opposite sex from the parent, and never sees the parent develop friendly relationships with members of the opposite sex, it is doubtful that the child will be able to put male and female relationships into proper perspective. Assuming that the child is also never given opportunities to form significant relationships with persons of the opposite sex from the parent, this would cloud the youngster's attitudes toward members of that sex, and make a healthy adjustment more difficult.

Let's take the case of a young boy being reared by his mother. He will benefit greatly by seeing his mother relate positively to men, and by having chances to play with boys around his own age. He may also enjoy forming a close, stable relationship with an older man or father figure, such as a grandfather, uncle, neighbor, etc. He needs to develop positive feelings for members of his own sex, and also needs to relate to one or more father figures with whom he can identify. If he hears his mother constantly express bitterness toward all men, and is not allowed to socialize with them, this would be an unhealthy atmosphere.

A similar situation would exist in the case of a single father rearing a little girl. It is important for him to refrain from showing bitterness toward all women, and to give his daughter plenty of opportunities to spend time with other young females as well as develop a close, continuous relationship with someone who can serve as a mother figure. This person might be a female relative, friend, neighbor, paid caregiver, or teacher at school.

The situation is somewhat different when the single parent and child are of the same sex. A little girl should see her mother interact with men on a friendly, social basis, from time to time, and should be encouraged to spend time with one or more men who can serve as a father figure(s).

Likewise, a father rearing a little boy alone should refrain from giving him a negative view of all women. He should try to offer his child opportunities to spend time with an older woman who can serve as a mother figure, and allow his little boy to occasionally see him socializing with women.

Single parents should strive to expose their children to some balance between male and female social contacts. During the preschool years, children are in a vulnerable position. They will be absorbing many of their parents' attitudes and incorporating them into their own personalities without having had firsthand experiences upon which to base their own judgments. Try to give your youngster a positive view of male and female relationships, since he is not mature enough nor intellectually capable of understanding and analyzing the complex ideas, emotions, and feelings that underlie your attitudes.

THE OVERWEIGHT CHILD

Children who are markedly overweight and of normal height are occasionally this way as a result of glandular problems, but there are many other factors that can contribute to a child's weight problem.

Possible Causes

It is not uncommon for overweight infants to develop into fat children. Research on obesity indicates that overfeeding or forced feeding during early infancy may play an important role in the child's developing an unusually large number of fat cells. These individuals seem to be prone to gaining weight more easily later in life. The chronic tendency toward being overweight can usually be countered with proper amounts of exercise and more careful supervision of the kinds and amounts of foods the child eats. Obesity later in life can lead to a higher incidence of certain diseases and thus should be avoided. A good place to start to prevent obesity is during childhood.

Heredity can also play a role in a child's tendency to be overweight. It often seems that weight problems are a family affair. In a family where parents have always been overweight, there appears to be a greater chance that the child will also be overweight. This can also arise because of family eating habits.

In some cases a child's weight problem seems to be related to his anxiety, unhappiness, loneliness, or dissatisfaction in one area of his life. There are children as well as adults who overeat when they are very tense and troubled as a way of reducing tension and deriving satisfaction. Parents should avoid calling the child names such as "porky," "fatso," or "piggy," and nagging him or shaming him in front of other people. These approaches can damage a child's sense of self-esteem, result in his developing a poor self-image, and heighten the tension and unhappiness that he feels, leading to further overeating.

A much more constructive approach is to try to determine the underlying reason for the child's need to use food as a form of tension outlet. In most situations, with some investigation, parents will be able to pinpoint whatever is triggering the child's unhappiness. Then they can put their energies into finding ways to make his life more fulfilling by attacking the cause as opposed to the symptom.

Another possible factor to consider in an overweight child is whether or not he is getting proper amounts of exercise. A child who eats very large quantities of food and does not burn off enough calories through regular daily exercise will have more calories left over at each day's end for his body to store as fat. Parents should encourage such a child to get more exercise each day through vigorous play and sports activities. Enrolling the child in a community exercise program for preschoolers may be a good idea.

Feelings of Isolation from Other Children

Unfortunately, in many cases the more overweight the child is, the harder it will be for him to enter into vigorous play or sports activities, derive pleasure from them, and do well at them. This can lead to an unfortunate situation in which the child feels uncomfortable participating in active games with other children, begins to sit on the sidelines, gets less exercise, and gains more weight, leading to his having an even harder time exercising in the future. An added problem is that the child may be picked on or ridiculed by neighborhood children.

Young children can be very cruel in their treatment of a fat child. They may call him names, laugh when he has trouble doing as well as they in certain games and tasks, and, in general, make him feel like an outcast. Ridicule from playmates in the neighborhood or at nursery school can be devastating to the preschool child. Feelings of being rejected by the other children can result in his further desire to remain at home and not enter into his friends' activities. A youngster who is regularly picked on at school often expresses a strong aversion to school.

Parents of a child who feels isolated from other children and rejected should be understanding about his feelings. He needs to feel a continuing sense of love and acceptance from his family. He also needs his parents to help him with his weight problem.

How Parents Can Help Their Child Lose Weight

A first step is for parents to examine their own eating patterns. In some cases parents themselves have poor eating habits and constantly eat fattening foods as well as eat frequently between meals. They may be consciously or unconsciously contributing to their child's problem. These parents are setting a very poor example for their youngster, and should realize that in order to help him they will have to change their eating habits.

A preschool child should not be expected to exercise will power on his own, or put himself on a diet. It would be unfair for parents to continue to eat fattening foods and snacks that their youngster enjoys in front of him but not give him any. This may arouse his resentment and anger, and heighten his desire for the foods that he is not being permitted to eat.

A better approach is for the parent cooking meals to prepare less fattening foods, eliminate high calorie desserts, and offer only one helping at meals. Frequent between-meal snacking can be gradually curtailed and fresh vegetables and fruits can be offered, only if the child is really hungry. Candies, cookies, cupcakes, ice cream, and other foods should not be kept around the house to tempt either parents or their preschooler. The entire family should make an effort to help the child lose weight gradually, by setting a good example for him to follow. There is a much greater chance that he will be more willing to accept the alterations in diet and develop better eating patterns if he has the support of his family.

In the event that parents' normal attempts to help their child reduce are unsuccessful, they should discuss this problem with his doctor. He or she may be able to offer more insights into the child's weight problem and be of assistance in developing a more effective weight reduction plan. Placing a child on a crash diet or giving him any medications to help him lose weight without first consulting a physician may be injurious to the youngster's health.

PREPARED PARENTHOOD CHECK LIST

MOTHER	FATHER	UNDERSTANDING YOUR CHILD'S DEVELOPMENT
——	——	Most children at age three are no longer as rebellious, demanding, and negative in their attitudes. Is your child more mature?
——	—	In what ways is your child's sense of identity strongly emerging?
——	—	Is your child becoming increasingly concerned about his body? Why?
——	—	Do you see evidence that your child is identifying with you and/or your spouse to a greater extent than in the past? Is he also identifying more with members of his own sex?
——	——	Have you familiarized yourself with the love conflicts that generally occur between the ages of approximately three and six?
——	——	Does your child have an imaginary companion?
——	——	Is your child more aware of and sensitive to other people, and able to play co-operatively with other children?
——	——	In what ways are your child's mental capacities expanding? Is he less impulsive, better able to solve problems, and able to make simple decisions?
——	——	Have you noticed an increase in your child's use of imagination, and improvements in his ability to remember things?
——	——	Has your preschooler's interest in what makes things happen increased?
——	——	Does your child have trouble understanding "coincidences" and "accidents"?
——	——	Can you think of any examples of your child's self-centered view of the world?
——	——	Does your preschooler occasionally believe things that he imagines?
——	——	What improvements have you observed in your child's speech? Is his speech more fluent? Are his sentences longer and more complex? Has he mastered certain grammatical rules?
——	——	How well does your child understand what you and other people say to him?
——	——	Does your youngster like conversing with you and telling you stories?
——	——	In what ways are your child's actions and activities becoming more adult-like?

— — Is your preschooler ready to begin using simple tools such as a child-size pair of blunt scissors or a small, lightweight hammer under your close supervision?

— — Can you see improvements in your child's ability to draw?

— — Is your youngster able to button his shirts and sweaters and work a large zipper?

— — Is your child more enthusiastic than before about play?

— — Has your child's play become more imaginative? In his dramatic play, which roles does he most often assume?

— — Are you providing your child with appropriate dress-up clothes and props to enhance his dramatic play?

— — Does your child enjoy making constructions or "creations" from toys, objects, and art materials?

BASIC CARE

— — Why is it important not to overestimate your child's ability to avoid accidents?

— — Have you noticed improvements in your child's ability in the areas of eating, bathing, dressing, and grooming?

— — Does your child have trouble sleeping through the night? Do you know why?

— — What are some of the pros and cons of allowing your child to sleep in your bed?

— — Are you familiar with some of the more common problems that may arise in relation to toilet training?

FAMILY FEELINGS AND CONCERNS

— — How is the quality of your relationship with your child likely to influence how he responds to your program of discipline?

— — In what ways are you helping your child learn to control aggressive actions?

— — What evidence do you see that your preschool child is still limited in his sense of property rights and his respect for other people's possessions?

— — Now that your child's comprehension of language has increased, is it easier for you to reason with him and manage him by using verbal techniques?

— — Do you recognize your child's limitations in comprehending the facts of life?

— — Are you familiar with the kinds of sex-related questions preschool children ask, and the general guidelines for answering these questions?

— — Why is it important to be truthful with your youngster in answering his questions?

— — How do you intend to approach the issues of genital play, sex play, and nudity in the home?

Preschool 2

— — What are some of the considerations in telling a child that he was adopted?

— — Have you thought about whether or not to offer your child a religious education or to send him to religious school?

— — Are you aware of some of the special circumstances and problems that can arise as a result of separation and divorce, as well as the ways parents can help the child make a good adjustment?

— — What are some of the concerns shared by single parents of preschool children?

Preschool 3

PERSONAL-SOCIAL DEVELOPMENT

The Preschool 3 child moves out in many directions at once. Her high energy level keeps her in constant motion, and she searches for new challenges and activities. Always on the move, she is ready to go at any time, often without any idea about where to go. During this phase your child will probably not be easy to handle.

Gesell has called this an "expansive" age, and has described the child's behavior as being "out-of-bounds." In her motor behavior, for instance, she often tugs and runs away from her parents and home. She wants to cover as much ground as she can. Her verbalizations frequently cause raised eyebrows, and may be too crude for her parents' liking. She may use bad language, and seems to take pleasure in everyone's reactions to her speech.

Boasting and bragging are typical of the Preschool 3 child. Through this kind of communication she is able to assert and compliment herself although her toughness, brashness, and brave manner probably mask some of her feelings of insecurity.

Self-confidence Grows

In many respects, the child seems almost too secure and self-confident. You are likely to notice that your child has outwardly moved from being unsure and ill at ease in Preschool 2 (around age three and a half) to the opposite extreme. She will not only call people names, issue ultimatums, refuse to follow orders, brag, and curse, but will also tell you what to do, and laugh at warnings. In exercising her strong need to test her new abilities, she is apt to go overboard.

Chances are that your youngster will move beyond the limits that you set on her behavior and language, and also travel beyond the limits of reality into the exciting world of fantasy. The exaggerated, fantastic stories that she will tell are likely to seem like outright lies, but it is best not to overreact to them. Children during this phase still have trouble differentiating between what is and is not real, and sometimes really believe what they dream or imagine. Their assertiveness makes their stories seem almost believable.

In your child's opinion, no task will be beyond her capabilities. Nearly every task will be undertaken, even those at which failure is inevitable. In the face of defeat, most Preschool 3 children do not give up. They simply try again.

This is a time when the child's behavior and emotions are often labile. They unpredictably change from one minute to the next. She is independent and seems to do what she wants. An "I love you" can swiftly change to an "I hate you." A hysterical bout of laughter can quickly turn into a display of tears.

Living with Your Preschool 3 Child

Your four-year-old's confident, imaginative, inquisitive, and adventurous nature will make her a lively member of the family. With a Preschool 3 child in the household, there is rarely a dull moment. She will go forward with enthusiasm to learn, experiment, and make new discoveries.

You will have to offer your child some elbow room, both literally and figuratively.

It is important to recognize and be tolerant of her desires to try things out for herself, exert her growing independence, and assert herself. While it will be necessary to give her space and freedom to satisfy these desires, do not be afraid to set firm limits and controls when they are required.

As your child approaches her fifth birthday, she will begin to become more settled, and will probably have a more realistic plan about how to achieve destinations and goals. As she becomes more persistent and goal-oriented, she will be better equipped to follow through with plans without getting sidetracked.

You will still notice her trying hard to sort out what is and is not real. Her tendency to believe her own fantastic statements is apt to diminish as she develops a firmer grip on reality, so be patient. As she becomes more self-confident and secure from within, her bragging, rebelliousness, and need to boss other people will also subside. By the age of five, she will be more mature and well adjusted.

Living with your Preschool 3 child can be an exciting and educational experience. The degree to which a child asserts herself or expresses her personality varies considerably from one child to the next, but you should be able to observe many of the new changes in her personality in one form or another. Being aware of these remarkable advances can often make it easier and more enjoyable to live with your child during this demanding time in her life.

Self-awareness

The Preschool 3 child has developed a firmer sense of identity. She recognizes herself as being similar to others around her, but also different. Being more in touch with her own feelings, she becomes more sensitive to her parents' changes of heart, moods, and ideas. This awareness does not mean that consideration for other people's feelings will always be shown.

LEARNING MORE ABOUT THE BODY. Your child's knowledge of her body has increased. When questioned about the purpose of her ears, nose, and mouth, she will probably reply that she hears with her ears, smells with her nose, and tastes with her mouth. Names for outer body parts can usually be stated with assurance by the child, along with a few names for inner organs such as heart, stomach, uterus, and so forth. Should you ask your child how her inner organs function, or how they are arranged within the body, be prepared to hear some mighty strange answers.

Having had an opportunity to learn something about men versus women, the child now recognizes the two different ways in which bodies are made, and knows whether her body is male or female. Feelings of similarity with persons of the same sex are apt to be stronger during this phase than in the past.

DIFFERENCES ARE CLEARER. An improved ability to perceive similarities and differences between herself and others and a growing awareness of parental as well as cultural demands result in her showing a greater capacity for self-examination and criticism. To a greater extent than before, she will realize that unacceptable behavior stems from unacceptable impulses within herself. This knowledge leads to an improved ability to wait, postpone satisfaction of her immediate desires, and exercise self-restraint.

Reliving her past in Preschool 1 and 2 gives the child a new perspective about her identity and heightens her awareness of the changes taking place within and around her. During Preschool 3 she will be more sensitive to expectations and responsibilities that accompany growing older. When pressures and demands to act more maturely build, temporary periods of crying, babyish behavior, and clinginess sometimes occur. You will notice how conscious of birthdays your child has become. She may frequently tell you about her wish to be more grown-up, or talk about being five years old.

AM I ALL RIGHT? Concerns and worries about the body often become more prominent in Preschool 3. The child who is more aware of her body and her identity usually becomes more conscious of illness, injury, and death. This is the phase in which initial questions about death may arise, often to parents' surprise. Simple, truthful explanations accompanied by plenty of reassurance are helpful in allaying the child's fears that she or persons whom she loves will soon die.

EXPANDING GENDER IDENTITY. The child continues to show a strong interest in the differences between males and females, which will probably subside when she is around five years old. Some children now like to play games where they expose their genitals to one another, or watch one another urinating. These games of "show" or "doctor" take place both indoors and outdoors.

On the other hand, many children become more modest about showing off their bodies. Even children whose parents have taken a relaxed approach toward nudity in the home may want privacy when they are undressing. One four-year-old girl, Tara, who was touring an art museum, saw a statue of a nude woman and whispered to her mother, "Mommy, she's naked! She must feel funny 'cause everybody's staring at her!"

Children, being more conscious of gender identity, often show a preference for playing with members of the same sex. In any large group of little girls and boys, smaller groups are likely to form, with segregation of girls and boys. Activities that girls and boys engage in may differ.

Children seem to be extremely interested in watching other people go to the bathroom, although they themselves may insist upon having privacy. There is much conversation about bathrooms and "products" among children. Statements involving crude elimination words such as "You big fat dudy!" are quite common.

RESOLVING LOVE CONFLICTS WITHIN THE FAMILY. In most normal family situations, the child gradually gives up the dream or unrealistic idea of having the parent of the opposite sex to herself, stops feeling rivalrous toward the parent of the same sex, and identifies more closely with the same-sexed parent. Usually, by the age of about six, this major task is accomplished. The exact age varies, depending upon individual and family circumstances.

How is this conflict resolved? A little girl must learn that she cannot take her mother's place with her father or have a romantic love relationship with him because this is not acceptable to the family. Both of her parents will play an important role conveying to her that this is not possible.

Through their actions and attitudes, parents make it clear to their children that their wishes are not based on reality, and can never be fulfilled. As discussed in the Intellectual Development section on page 909, children of this age are learning to distinguish between reality and fantasy in many aspects of their life. Their desired or imagined relationships with their parents have to be gradually put into perspective, so that their interactions with family and other individuals will be appropriate and acceptable.

When a little girl proposes marriage to her father, he may act flattered so as not to hurt her feelings, but he will let her know, in a gentle and understanding way, that he is already married to her mother. He may also explain that someday, when she is grown-up, she can find a man of her own to love and even, perhaps, marry. When a little boy becomes jealous and resentful of the fact that his daddy and mommy are going out together for an evening, his parents, instead of feeling uncomfortable about excluding him, matter-of-factly explain that when two people love each other the way they do, they occasionally need to be alone with one another.

Mother and father help their child realize that they have a type of relationship with one another that is different from the relationship they have with her. This happens quite naturally in subtle and sometimes not-so-subtle ways. Parents teach their child that she cannot be a part of the private, intimate, love relationship that they share with one another. They do not, for example, encourage her to sleep in their bed at night, nor do they generally allow her to intrude upon their privacy when they are making love. Should the child, out of jealousy or rivalry, begin to question the authority of her parent of the same sex, this parent should not react as though the child's flirtatious behavior is a threat to the marital relationship. Rather, the parent should handle such challenges by being tactful, matter-of-fact, and firm. The child will eventually get the message and develop an appropriate relationship with both parents.

By parents not giving substance to their child's immature wishes to have the opposite-sex parent to herself, she eventually realizes that these wishes are, indeed, fantasies. The little girl realizes that she cannot have Daddy all to herself, but she can use him as the model for the man she will love and even, perhaps, marry when she grows older. She cannot take her mother's place, but she can probably find someone like her daddy by becoming as much like her mother as possible. A similar situation exists for the little boy. He replaces his unrealistic ideas of sending his father away and having his mother to himself with realistic ones of being more like his father, and falling in love with, and possibly marrying, a woman like his mother when he grows older.

The consequences of the child's early love conflict are very positive in the majority of cases. The child identifies more closely with the parent of the same sex, and the emotional and psychological groundwork is laid that will allow the child to form love relationships with persons of the opposite sex in adolescence and adulthood. Having outgrown her childhood love for the parent of the opposite sex, she is now able to move on to other interests during the school years, and eventually develop more mature love relationships in the future. Many psychologists believe that after resolving this love conflict in the family, the child's sexual identity is firmly established.

It should be of reassurance to you that in the majority of family situations, parents will, without even having to think about it, discourage their child's fantasies in many subtle ways. In certain families, such as those in which the relationship between parents is unstable, marked by deep-rooted feelings of antagonism, or otherwise disturbed, it may become more difficult for the child to outgrow her fantasies about love relationships within the family. A parent may either consciously or unconsciously encourage a child's flirtation or romantic affection, behave seductively toward the child, try to alienate the child from the parent of the same sex, or in other ways give the child reason to believe that the desire to have an exclusive relationship with the parent of the opposite sex will be fulfilled.

These types of unusual reactions by a parent should be guarded against for the child's sake. Again, this represents the exception rather than the rule, and chances are that in your spontaneous reactions to both your spouse and child, you will help **your child to resolve early** love fantasies effectively and successfully.

FURTHER IDENTIFICATION WITH PARENTS. Your child will be conscious of your speech and behavior, and will be striving harder than before to make herself more like you. She has already absorbed many of your mannerisms, attitudes, and values, and will be closely identifying with you in Preschool 3. As she begins to realize that her immature dreams of having the parent of the opposite sex all to herself are unrealistic, this will fortify her identification with the parent of the same sex.

FURTHER PROGRESS IN CONSCIENCE DEVELOPMENT. During your child's fifth year of life, you will undoubtedly see more evidence that she has a conscience. Her ability to regulate her own behavior in specific situations will increase. When she violates the standards for behavior that you have established, you will notice further indications that she feels sorry or guilty afterward.

The Preschool 3 child's mental abilities make it easier for her to deal with frustrations. When her desires cannot be fulfilled, or her impulses cannot be expressed through direct action, she utilizes other ways of deriving satisfaction. She can think or daydream about her wishes coming true. Her ability to make use of substitute outlets such as these is a sign of significant progress toward the goal of becoming a self-disciplining person.

The older preschooler is leaving behind the behavior patterns of infancy and toddlerhood, when her primary objective was to have immediate needs and whims fulfilled, and do whatever she wanted at any given moment. Still, she has a long way to go in her conscience development. Her conscience operates on a limited basis and is not always successful in preventing her from doing wrong.

A little girl knows that she is not supposed to go into the attic, hit her younger brother, touch the stove, operate electrical appliances, wander away from home without asking permission (the list goes on and on), but aside from heeding familiar parental warnings, her knowledge about the ways in which she should behave is incomplete. This is, in large part, due to intellectual limitations and lack of more experience.

An older child is capable of understanding abstract concepts such as honor, truthfulness, and morality. This enables her to incorporate these concepts and ideals into her conscience. The preschool child, who cannot fully comprehend such concepts, is unable to make them a part of her own personality and put them to work in guiding her behavior. Her mental abilities are limited, and successful conscience development partly depends upon the child's intellectual development.

Your Preschool 3 child is still self-centered in her thinking. She has trouble being considerate of other people's feelings, since her perspective is narrow, and she is unable to imagine what it might feel like to be "in their shoes." Once she develops a better capacity to identify with others and consider something from different perspectives, it will be easier for her to respect their feelings.

From this phase on into the middle childhood years, your child's conscience will continue to develop and operate more effectively as her mental capabilities expand. She will not just avoid doing wrong because you told her not to do something, or because she fears loss of your approval, or being punished, but will avoid acting because she herself considers the behavior wrong and intolerable. Through further identification with you, she will be acquiring many more of your moral values and standards. These will become a part of her conscience, serving as an "ideal" self. They will help her regulate her behavior from within, and motivate her to behave in an acceptable manner.

Social Sensitivity and Interests

The Preschool 3 child is not only more social in the sense of showing a stronger interest in being with people, but also in the sense of being more effective in her dealings with others. Her speech and behavior are more appropriate than in the past, and provide evidence that a higher level of social interaction has been reached.

RELATIONSHIP WITH FAMILY MEMBERS. In many respects the child is still closely tied to her family and dependent upon them. Yet, she is capable of functioning for short periods of time outside the family sphere such as at nursery school or at a neighbor's home. Even when apart from her parents, it is apparent how much they mean to her. In conversations with her friends, she quotes Mommy and Daddy as all-powerful, all-knowing sources of authority.

When she is visiting another family, or is in an unfamiliar place, she often compares it to the familiar home situation. Most Preschool 3 children think that they have the best family and home in the whole wide world, and brag and boast about them to other people. Despite the child's underlying positive feelings for her parents and brothers and sisters, her loud-mouthed, domineering, bossy manner often places a strain upon family relationships and creates tension in the home.

GREATER INTEREST IN PEERS. The Preschool 3 child is so interested in being with children around her own age that when her parents go visiting and ask her to come along, the first question that she may ask is whether there will be children her age there. Should her parents say no, she may object to going with them.

She is much more mature in her ability to deal with other children, having acquired additional social and verbal skills. Much to your surprise and delight, you are apt to see your child sharing a toy with her playmate, taking turns at a game, and showing her friend some courtesy such as asking permission to play with a toy that is not hers. Playing together with her friends will make your child happy, as long as you keep introducing new games and exciting activities, and provided that she is not the target for their biting criticism.

Friendships have become more important to the child than in the previous phase. Out of a group of youngsters who have known each other for a while, two children may form a rather tight friendship. It is common for youngsters to use the word "friend" themselves, and become jealous if their "best friend" begins to pay more attention to another child than to them.

Children may also form cliques or exclusive groups. Much discussion often centers around who they want to be in the group, and other similar social difficulties. The issue of popularity becomes more prominent in Preschool 3.

Large groups of children often divide up into smaller groups. In many instances girls still migrate to one area, and boys head to another. Play in a group is generally easier for the child now than it has been in the past.

It is common for children to try to get each other in trouble, call each other names, or criticize each other's abilities, characters, or families. This behavior often triggers fights. More often than before, children are able to resolve their own disputes, but parents should be on hand just in case some last-minute intervention becomes imperative.

In any group of Preschool 3 children, parents supervising them are bound to hear a great deal of boasting, bragging, cursing, name-calling, and "toilet talk." Children often try to "outdo" one another, for example, in their "bad" or silly language, gymnastic or athletic prowess, tall tales, artistic talents, or constructions. Competition among children is likely to be highly prominent during this phase. Learning to deal with other children under difficult, as well as ideal circumstances, is all part of the child's learning process.

INTELLECTUAL DEVELOPMENT

The Developing Mind

There are striking differences in mental ability between a Preschool 1 and a Preschool 3 child, and these differences are reflected in their behavior. The Preschool 3 child's greater effectiveness with words, rapid acquisition of grammar, and enormous growth in vocabulary all testify to advances in her intellectual abilities. She is not only better able to speak and comprehend language, but, as a result of the expansion of language skills, is also better able to learn, regulate her own behavior, think, reason, form concepts, and solve problems.

You will notice that your child is mastering many new tasks that she was previously not able to perform. She will ask never-ending questions which represent her increasing curiosity and awareness of the world around her. Her interest in learning and ability to learn from firsthand experiences as well as from listening to people talk or read to her will be difficult to ignore.

In nearly every respect, the child during this phase will seem more mature than she has in earlier phases. Underlying her more appropriate and sophisticated behavior patterns are improvements in intellectual capabilities that pave the way for greater self-control, ingenuity, and use of imagination.

The Preschool 3 child will move further away from being highly dependent upon immediate sensory input and will be less self-centered in her thinking. These changes enable her to develop a more organized, thoughtful, sensible, and realistic view of people and objects in her surroundings. Your child is entering a higher level of intellectual development that will carry her through the early elementary school years. She will begin to formulate more concepts than before, and will be developing more complex symbolic representations, images, and ideas. Despite the rapid strides that she will make in her ability to think during this phase, it will be obvious to you that her mind has not developed to a point which allows her to think in a logical, consistent, abstract, adult-like fashion.

What Makes Things Happen?

"WHY" QUESTIONS. The Preschool 3 child's curiosity about what causes things to happen will be stronger than at earlier ages. She will ask frequent "why" questions related to clouds, wind, rain, colors, ice, birds, insects, the origin of babies, and so forth. These questions reflect her increasing awareness of the environment, and quest for further knowledge of how things run.

At least on the surface, your youngster may seem satisfied with your answers, but her ability to comprehend explanations, particularly those related to science, will be extremely limited. Her thought process is still self-centered and concrete. It will be difficult for her to look at things objectively and grasp abstract concepts such as those dealing with gravity, electricity, simple principles of physics, and so forth. When she hears your explanations, there is a good chance that she will take what you tell her and combine this information with her own primitive ideas and explanations. This can lead her to form new, but also distorted, views about why events occur, based on half fact and half fantasy.

MAGICAL BELIEFS. Keep in mind that your child does not have a good grasp of the "real" world. She still believes that thinking or wishing can cause things to happen, and she may still explain some natural events in terms of her own appearance, feelings, and the functioning of her body. Four-year-old Harmony asked her father why there was a little ghost following her around. Her father realized that she was frightened by her own shadow, and asked her why she thought that a ghost was following her.

According to what Harmony told her father, she believed that the ghost was out to get her because she had misbehaved and thought bad things about her mother. Her father proceeded to correct these primitive beliefs by explaining to Harmony how shadows are cast. She listened carefully, but was not convinced that the shadow was not a ghost who would eventually punish her for having bad thoughts.

Harmony's thinking was still based on her childish, "magical" beliefs that ghosts really do exist, that bad thoughts can cause real events to take place, and that there was a purpose underlying the shadow that she saw. Despite her parents' attempts to clear up these distortions of reality, she continued to believe in these fantastic notions. Like many Preschool 3 children, she viewed things that happened subjectively and continued to confuse events in the mind with actual events. She also searched for purposes to explain natural events in her surroundings, and frequently saw human or monster-like forms in shadows.

LESS SELF-CENTERED. As your child approaches age five, her ideas about why events happen will gradually become less self-centered. She will slowly start to separate thoughts and wishes from actual happenings and will develop at least some initial understanding of the cause of several natural events that she sees. However, her knowledge, ability to grasp abstract concepts, and grasp of reality will still be limited.

Whenever the child has trouble understanding her parents' explanations or interpreting things that happen based upon her knowledge and experiences, she will occasionally slip back to her unsophisticated notions about cause and effect. At certain times she will still find purposes behind "coincidences," "accidents," and natural events, and believe that wishing something will make it so. This is not unusual, since buried within the mind of even the most rational adults is a primitive approach to causality that has its roots in the "magical" thinking characteristic of young children.

Concept of Space

Your child's understanding of space, particularly on a practical level, has grown rapidly during the past four years. Her vocabulary during this phase will include numerous words that describe specific locations, directions, comparative sizes of objects, and spatial relations among objects. She will move easily from place to place and, to a greater extent than before, think about as well as talk about where she is planning to go or where she has been. Direct evidence of her increasing awareness of space will be seen in her improved ability to tell someone else her home address, including both the street on which she lives and the city.

In many respects the child's concept of space is becoming more sophisticated and refined. Old fears about the possibility of being lost down the bathtub or toilet bowl drains have been outgrown, since the child has a better notion of the comparative sizes of objects and spaces in relation to the size of her body. Former notions that an object could be in two places at the same time have also been outgrown. She no longer believes that objects actually shrink in size as they move farther away from her, since she realizes that faraway objects and people appear to be much smaller than those right in front of her.

Improvements will be seen in the manner in which the child handles and uses toys, simple tools, and unstructured play materials. Her block constructions will be taller, more well balanced, and more complex than in previous phases. The ability to draw or paint objects, people, and events accurately usually emerges much later in life, but some small signs of progress in this regard may be seen. New abilities to cut and paste, saw, hammer, and make things from arts and crafts materials and pieces of wood will all testify to the progress that she has made in understanding basic spatial relationships related to objects and parts of objects.

Preschool 3 children are still lacking in their knowledge of space, and it will be years before their concept of space becomes well developed enough to enable them to read a map or draw a fairly accurate map of familiar spaces such as those in their homes. Children's understanding of spatial relationships during this phase will still be closely tied to their own movements through space.

Concept of Time

IN YOUR CHILD'S MIND, TIME IS NOT THE SAME FOR EVERYONE. Youngsters do not realize that time is exactly the same for everyone and that as they grow older, so do their parents. Chances are that your child will find it hard to imagine you as ever being her age, or think of you as being forty years older than you are now. From her viewpoint, time stands still for you, but continues to pass for her. It is for this reason that a Preschool 3 child may actually believe in the possibility of catching up with her parent's age and appearance, or marrying the parent of the opposite sex. The realization that time is the same for every person will probably emerge sometime during the early school years, although this varies from child to child.

UNDERSTANDING OF TIME AS IT RELATES TO HERSELF. Your child will be more conscious of time in relation to her own development, despite the immature notion that time stands still for you. Throughout the year she may talk on and on about her next birthday, not forgetting to mention the presents she would like to receive when she turns five, and whom she will invite to her birthday party. In her dramatic play, she will often play-act at being an adult since her interest in pretending that she is older will be strong. You are likely to hear her talk about what she will do when she becomes a grown-up person like you. Questions about death often crop up during Preschool 3, as another indication of the child's increasing consciousness of time in relation to her development.

The Preschool 3 child is still most concerned with her own current activities, although her ability to exercise self-control and do something now in anticipation of being positively rewarded in the near future are rapidly developing. Nearing age five, she will become more goal-oriented. Your child is likely to develop the ability to plan a project that takes several days to complete, and see it through to its completion. With your assistance, she may even take pleasure in planning a schedule of regular activities, or planning a weekly menu. As her concept of time increases, her actions will probably seem more deliberate, purposeful, and well thought out.

At this phase in development, the child's concept of time is still self-centered in that from her point of view, time revolves around her own whims and activities. Sabrina had recently learned that when the "little hand" on the clock pointed to four, it was time for her snack, and when the "little hand" pointed to six, it was time for her dinner. One evening, around five-thirty, without looking at the clock, Sabrina told her mother that she was very hungry and that it was time to eat. Her mother knew that it was not yet six o'clock, and told Sabrina to look at the clock and see if the "little hand" was pointing to six. Sabrina looked up at the clock on the kitchen wall and, upon seeing that the "little hand" was not yet pointing to six, became very angry at the clock. "You mean old clock," she said, "your little hand is supposed to point to six!"

It is apparent from Sabrina's comments that she believed the "little hand" followed her needs and daily activities. One can also see from her anger toward the clock, and the fact that she called it "mean" and "old," that she was giving it human-like emotions and characteristics.

KNOWLEDGE OF PAST EVENTS IS LIMITED AND DISORGANIZED. The Preschool 3 child knows little or nothing of history. The notion of time extending backward long before she was born is an extremely difficult concept for her to understand. You may try to introduce her to history in a small way by reading her stories about things that happened years ago, or by taking her to a museum, but there is a good chance that she will have a hard time believing that people existed and events occurred before her birth.

The child's memory for past events in her own life is still limited and disorganized, although some signs of improvements will be seen. More things that happened to her in the past will be recalled, but experiences that she can remember will be incomplete. They will also not be put into chronological order. Your child may remember certain details of things that she did "last week," "last month," or "last winter," but she will probably not be able to manipulate memories in her mind and arrange them into correct time sequences.

TELLING TIME. You may try to teach your Preschool 3 child how to tell time using a clock, but you should not expect her to accomplish the task at this early phase of life. As a result of your teaching efforts, she is likely to learn a few "times" on the clock that represent important shifts in her routine.

Four-and-a-half-year-old Paul knew that when the little hand pointed to "8," and the big hand pointed to "12," it was time for him to get out of bed. He also learned to recognize his bedtime hour on the clock. One Sunday evening Paul's parents wanted to put him to bed early, since they were expecting company. He did not want to go along with their wishes, since the "big" and "little" hands were not pointing to the correct number. This little boy's initial knowledge about telling time came in very handy when he stated a good case for staying up later.

GROWING ABILITY TO TALK ABOUT TIME. Many children will be able to say the names of days of the week, seasons of the year, and important holidays. In their conversations, they will probably talk about what will take place "tomorrow," "next month," "next year," and "next summer," even though their concepts of a month, year, or season are not well developed. Similarly, children will frequently use the words "yesterday," "today," and "tomorrow," without having a clear understanding of this sequence of time. On a Monday afternoon, Laura was overheard to say, "It did not break yesterday cause my daddy said it broke on Sunday!" It will be clear to you that your child's ability to use words referring to time is developing at a faster rate than her comprehension of the meanings of those words.

The Self-centered World: Egocentrism

YOUR CHILD'S SPEECH REFLECTS SELF-CENTERED THINKING. Now that your child's ability to express ideas through words has rapidly expanded, you will probably notice evidence of her self-centered point of view in her speech. The Preschool 3 child rarely tries to take the point of view of the listener into account when she talks. Betty Moore, according to her father, talked on and on to him about a person whom he had never met, and knew nothing about. His daughter made no attempt to tell him who she was talking about, and apparently took it for granted that because she knew who she was talking about, so would her father. Later, Mr. Moore found out from his wife that Betty was talking about a character on her favorite television series. In telling a story to another person, your child is likely to leave out information that is necessary for that person to know in order to follow the story.

PERSISTENT DIFFICULTY CONSIDERING OTHER POINTS OF VIEW. Most children of this age still have a hard time realizing that their viewpoint is merely one of many conceivable points of view. A classic example of the preschool child's difficulty in considering other viewpoints beside her own is as follows: Corinne, who had two sisters, was asked how many sisters she had, and she answered that she had "two." But next, when this little girl was asked how many sisters there were altogether in her family, she still answered that there were "two." Corinne's failure to count herself as a sister clearly suggests that she could not look at her family from any perspective but her own.

Your child's personal considerations, feelings, and emotions still distort her reasoning and thinking ability, but she is making further headway in outgrowing her egocentric position. By identifying with you, your attitudes about respecting other people's rights and showing consideration for their feelings will become ingrained into her personality. Before being able to show consistent, genuine appreciation for the rights and feelings of others, however, she must be able to put herself in the place of another and imagine how feelings might change from another's point of view. This ability may not be developed for some time.

The Imaginary World of the Child

Your Preschool 3 child will be extremely imaginative in her play, in her use of arts and crafts materials, and in the stories she tells. Her ability to play with ideas in her mind and create make-believe situations and places beyond the scope of her own experience has markedly grown.

The world of fantasy is alive and thriving in the mind of the child. Creation of imaginary friends and companions often reaches a peak during this phase. A good portion of your child's day may involve role-playing and other make-believe activities. Her powers of imagination will reach a high point early in this phase. You can expect her to exaggerate real events, boast, tell fantastic tales, and pretend that she is someone else, sometimes believing that she is a different person. Included in her typical afternoon conversation with you may be the following kind of remark: "Guess where I went this morning? A man with pointy ears and a green face came and took me on a ride in his space ship!"

SEPARATING FANTASY FROM REALITY. At some point between the ages of four and five, your child will probably begin to sort out fact from fancy, and things she sees on television from what are real. She may continually ask you whether or not various things are real. Imaginary companions often persist, but they are not as likely to be brought into family activities as in Preschool 2, and may also not be spoken to as much.

Beyond the age of about four and a half, your child is not as likely to believe her own tall tales. In her play, she is less likely to think that she really is a doctor, and when pretending to be a doctor, she is apt to insist upon having realistic props—a stethoscope, a white jacket, perhaps a mask, and a bag for her equipment. It is as though your child will need these props in order to be able to assume a new character role.

Most youngsters will not have an easy time sorting the real world from the world of make-believe. At times they will become quite confused. Even after your child recognizes that her thoughts and wishes cannot cause actual things to happen, she may sometimes forget this. It is safe to say that even the most logical, objective adult never fully outgrows the belief that wishing for something may influence the course of events and cause the wish to come true. This belief may occasionally come out of its secret hiding place in the adult's mind.

LANGUAGE DEVELOPMENT

Your Preschool 3 child will be quite a talker. She will give drawn-out explanations about anything and everything, even when she is the only one listening. Her mouth will keep going until she runs out of things to say, gets tired, or is ordered to be quiet. Stating her ideas and point of view will be important to her. Frequently, she will talk about things she knows little about, but once in a while, she may appear to know much more about life than would be expected from such a young child.

The child of this age has a strong drive to talk, and speech tends to be a necessary part of just about everything she does. She will talk while assuming imaginary roles in her play, taking a bath, and getting undressed. One of her recent accomplishments may entail talking and eating at the same time. She will carry on just the same whether she is playing alone in a room or speaking to her friends. The frequency with which she will tell stories, enter into conversations, try her hand at jokes, and ask questions has increased by leaps and bounds. You will undoubtedly be delighted and very impressed by the progress that she has made in both speaking and understanding language.

Active Language Development

VOCABULARIES ARE EXPANDING. With each passing week, your child will be saying new words. Her more extensive vocabulary will afford her greater flexibility in what she can say, and in the manner in which she expresses feelings, ideas, opinions, and emotions. As her vocabulary expands, you will notice an increase in rhyming, joking, creative storytelling, and detailed description.

Children often latch on to particular words as their favorites, and use them very frequently. Words such as "secret," "new," "really," "present," "strange," "surprise," and "party" are often heard, although your child may have her own favorites. Adverbs, expletives, and other parts of speech will be used in the course of her conversations.

Your preschooler is likely to be excited about the prospect of learning unusual, new, and "big" or sophisticated words. She will go about adding these kinds of words to her vocabulary with enthusiasm and determination. You will hear her doing a great deal of experimenting and playing with the sounds of words. Mr. Haire was raking leaves in the back yard near where his daughter, Mandy, was sitting and playing with mud and water. He heard her say, "This sure is ooshy, squooshy, gushy, mushy."

Mandy was having fun rhyming words and inventing them. You are apt to hear your child doing similar things with language. Her interest in words often results in an eagerness to engage in all kinds of word games with you, especially those that involve silly language, absurd rhymes, and learning "grown-up" words.

HELPING YOUR CHILD LEARN NEW WORDS. Assuming that your child takes an interest in building her vocabulary, you can capitalize on it by thinking up activities designed to foster vocabulary growth. Mrs. Renda devised her own game, which she claimed was particularly enjoyable and educational for both her and her child. She called it the "Point to a Page" game.

Every afternoon Mrs. Renda would hold her child, Kenneth, on her lap and have him open up a dictionary to any page. She then had him close his eyes and point.

Wherever his finger landed, that became the word of the day. She would say the word aloud, and he would repeat it.

Sometimes the words were easy for Kenneth to pronounce, but many had to be repeated several times before he could say them correctly. Assuming that the word was not too far beyond his level of comprehension, Mrs. Renda would discuss its meaning, and show him how it could be used in a variety of sentences. She would occasionally ask him to make up a sentence using the word.

Mrs. Renda engaged in this activity mainly because she and Kenneth had fun together, but she was delighted to see that as a result of this game his curiosity about words and their meanings was stimulated, and his vocabulary began to increase. Occasionally, when Kenneth asked the meaning of a new word, she took out the dictionary, looked it up, and gave him a simplified explanation. By the time he was ready for school, he had obviously learned that a dictionary is a valuable tool.

Further suggestions for activities to stimulate vocabulary development are given in the Total Education of Your Child section on pages 798–801. Naturally, it is important to select activities that are well suited to your child's interests in language, and refrain from pressuring her to engage in language-oriented activities if she seems disinterested or bored.

THE PRONUNCIATION OF WORDS. Many children mispronounce a few speech sounds until they attend kindergarten or first grade, and you should not be concerned about these kinds of minor mistakes. When a child rushes to say something, she is likely to stumble over sounds, mumble, or skip certain syllables. By being a respectful, patient listener, you will help prevent her from feeling pressured to talk very quickly.

In a few cases, children have persistent difficulty pronouncing words, to the point where their parents or other people who know them very well cannot understand their speech. In the event that this is the case with your child, you should discuss it with your pediatrician or a speech therapist.

SENTENCES. The Preschool 3 child no longer speaks in the short, simple sentences common in toddlerhood and the early preschool period. She uses a wide variety of parts of speech to generate longer, more sophisticated sentences. The following sentences will give you an idea of the types of comments made by children during this phase: "That enormous bug flew down here and bited me on my toe." "Maybe if I'm a good boy you'll take me to the zoo." "Really, Daddy, you can be so careless with your clothes!" "I know a secret, but you'll never guess what it is in a million-billion years." "You see, you can't button your sweater if you put it on backward."

RUDE, FRANK LANGUAGE. The language of the older preschool child can be frank and sometimes rude. To her parents' surprise and dismay, she may also pass on family "secrets" to others. Without realizing that she is being rude, the child may comment upon another person's weight problem, bad skin condition, handicap, or unusual appearance loudly enough for that person to hear. In the majority of cases, youngsters are not deliberately rude; they simply do not know any better. Attempts should be made to teach the child why her comments are rude, and help her be more respectful of other people's feelings. Do not expect immediate results.

Mr. Edwin overheard his four-year-old daughter make the following remarks to her friend Donna. "My daddy came home drunk last night. Mommy got very mad. She started to cry. Mommy made me go to bed, but I heard her fighting with Daddy."

This father was shocked to learn that his daughter was not keeping certain household events private. Children rarely keep things that they see or hear in their homes confidential. Whatever they hear inside their homes tends to be repeated in front of non-family members.

Preschool 3 children are also adept at boasting and bragging, as well as exaggerating things to make a point. Statements such as, "I live in the biggest, prettiest house in the whole world!" or, "No one could throw as far as I can!" are quite common. The competitive nature of their statements rings through loud and clear.

THE USE OF "BAD" LANGUAGE AND "TOILET TALK." It is not uncommon for older preschool children to go through a stage in which they seem preoccupied with "four-letter" words and "toilet talk." They are aware of the shock value of curse words and the crude use of words dealing with elimination and anatomy, and frequently use them just to upset adults or aggravate parents. The use of the four-letter words referring to sex organs or sex acts does not usually occur until the child attends school, but preschool children may occasionally pick up these words by accident, or from older children, not really understanding what they mean.

Parents' reactions of shock or distress tend to encourage the use of "bad" language. It is initially advisable to ignore a child who uses language of this nature, or casually discuss the reasons why you do not want her saying such words. Should this approach be unsuccessful, you will probably want to set definite limits on her speech. Violations of the rules can then be backed up with some form of mild punishment, such as temporarily denying her some privilege or isolating her from her friends.

QUESTIONS. This is a peak phase for question-asking. Preschool 3 children ask their parents "how" and "why" questions about nearly every imaginable subject, including those that are often considered "taboo." Eileen, age four and a half, while attending her first funeral, asked her mother, "How can Uncle Mac get to heaven if the bugs and worms eat him up first?"

Your child's strong curiosity and constant desire to know things will probably leave you drained at the end of an afternoon with her. Try to look upon her questions as presenting you with a good opportunity to discover what she thinks and feels, and knows and does not know about various subjects. Her questions also provide evidence of her growing interest in learning, so do your best to answer them right away.

IMPROVEMENTS IN GRAMMAR. The Preschool 3 child uses many of the basic grammatical rules of her native language when she speaks. Your child's speech is still not exactly like yours, however. Adults frequently produce complex sentences by placing simple sentences inside other sentences. Complex sentences do not generally occur among children of this age. Children occasionally leave out parts of sentences as in, "I want to go McDonalds." On the other hand, they may include more words than are necessary, as in the sentence, "She swept it away the mess."

When you hear your child making grammatical mistakes, you will probably feel like telling her where she went wrong. As at earlier ages, it is advisable to offer her some corrective feedback, rather than criticisms or formal lessons about syntax. After she makes an error, try not to point out her mistake. Simply provide the correct sentence model without saying anything else. Should your child say something like, "He taked it with him," you might say, "Yes, you're right. He took it with him when he went outside." Criticism often makes a child hesitant to speak, whereas this approach helps a child learn without making her feel inadequate or self-conscious.

912

STORYTELLING. This is a time for "tall tales" and long, disorganized, fantastic stories. Children build stories about almost everything. Give them a topic, and they will create a story about it. Their stories are imaginative creations, often set in make-believe lands.

Parents are often disturbed about the stories their children tell, in particular those that revolve around death, violence, sickness, and other not very pleasant themes. This preoccupation with unpleasant experiences is not uncommon during this phase. As children tell stories, they often act them out. Their dramatic talents are encouraged by appreciative audiences.

Your youngster's stories or accounts of movies or television programs are likely to be rather hard to follow. She will probably shift from one idea to the next without any warning or appropriate transition except to say "'n' then" this or that happened. She will also shift from offering elaborate, detailed descriptions to offering little information to clue you in about the plot, characters, or action.

From listening to your child's stories and descriptions of her experiences, you will gain insight into her feelings and her impressions of the world. By being an especially good listener, you will discover many things about her that might otherwise go unnoticed.

Passive Language Development

Your child's comprehension vocabulary will be enormous in comparison to her ability to use words. Parents sometimes fail to realize this discrepancy, and mold their language to the type of language that their child uses. You should not be afraid to use words that are more sophisticated than those that you hear your child using, or those that she does not immediately understand. After all, when she was just a young infant who had no understanding of language, everything that you said was beyond her level of comprehension. This did not stop you from talking to her, and gradually, she learned the meaning of the simple words that you used.

For your child's comprehension of language to expand, it is important for her to hear a variety of speech, some of which, at any given point in time, is above her level of understanding. Given ample time, she will grasp the meaning of what she hears spoken, and her comprehension vocabulary will continue to show improvement.

DEFINITIONS OF WORDS AND SIMILARITIES. The Preschool 3 child will try to establish a relationship between a word and the concept to which it refers. Her ability to understand the meanings of words far exceeds her ability to define them, but she will probably offer definitions for certain familiar words.

When asked, she is likely to be able to define several words such as house, lake, banana, and ball in terms of their shape, use, composition, or general classification. Many of her definitions will be practical. "An apple is to eat," or, "A house is to live in." You will notice that most of your child's definitions are concrete, since abstract concepts are difficult for her to understand. In time, she will start to offer more sophisticated definitions. Rather than defining a banana as yellow, long, or something to eat, she will say that it is a fruit.

The child's similarities are also likely to be concrete. When asked how a knife and a scissors are alike she will probably say something like, "A knife is used to eat with. A scissors is to cut." An adult would easily draw the analogy that a knife and scissors are both cutting utensils, but this requires abstract thinking that is not characteristic of the Preschool 3 child.

On the other hand, youngsters who would perform poorly on a similarities test might occasionally draw their own fairly sophisticated analogies. Sally, age four and a half, was visiting a relative who lived on a farm. Each morning at 6 A.M. the roosters crowed and awakened her. On her third day there, when the roosters awakened her, she remarked, "It's like an alarm clock." As your child's ability to perceive similarities between objects and events and to form concepts improves, it will be easier for her to draw analogies beyond the concrete or practical level.

At this stage it should be less difficult for your child to understand problems involving opposites than in the past. You may want to ask her to complete the following sentences. "If fire is hot, ice is———." "Mother is a woman, Dad is a———." Chances are that she will be able to provide appropriate answers.

LISTENING. Preschoolers like asking questions and listening to answers. Chances are that your youngster will listen attentively as you answer her questions, and sometimes follow your explanations with other questions. She will also be a more courteous, patient audience when you talk to her. Her improving self-control and growing interest in stories may enable her to sit still while you read as many as four or five short books in succession.

Children's tastes in books are extremely variable, so you must use your child's interests and responses as a guide to the type of books to select. Many Preschool 3 children enjoy books of fairy tales, books that explain things, humorous books, and those containing nonsense words and rhyming.

MOTOR DEVELOPMENT

From the time your infant was born until the present, you have seen obvious as well as subtle changes in her ability to move. You have also seen steady improvements and refinements in her performance of many day-to-day tasks. Once a relatively immobile infant lacking in voluntary body control, she has developed into a child who can sit, walk, run, climb, throw, balance on one foot, walk up and down stairs, hop, and engage in a variety of more complex activities.

By the time your child reaches five years of age she will run with good speed in a well-co-ordinated manner, and maintain good balance both in a stationary position, and while moving. She should begin to throw more efficiently, and be able to catch a large playground ball. Jumping, riding a tricycle, and hopping will show rapid improvement. Her motor behavior, in general, will resemble that of an older child, due to the further maturation of her nervous and muscle system. Over-all, only more experience and training will continue to foster her capacities for movement.

In the area of fine motor activity you have watched your child make equally amazing progress. At birth her hand-eye co-ordination was almost absent. She gradually gained some voluntary control over her hands, and then co-ordinated hands and eyes, enabling smooth, quick, accurate reaching and grasping. She went on to develop the abilities to drop and throw objects, pick them up between thumb and forefinger, and handle objects in a more sophisticated manner. Still later you watched her scribble spontaneously, build towers of ever-increasing heights with small blocks, and imitate simple marks and shapes with a crayon or pencil.

By the time the child is five years old, she will be capable of even finer hand and finger control. She will build taller towers and more complex structures with her blocks. With proper adult supervision, she will be able to use such tools as children's hammers, scissors, and some staplers. You can expect to see her draw recognizable circles, crosses, and squares, and perhaps a picture that actually looks somewhat like a person. She may even be able to print her first name and many numbers and letters. The Preschool 3 child still has more difficulty performing tasks that involve finer co-ordinations than those requiring large movement, but her progress in manual skills since early infancy is nonetheless amazing.

Gross Motor Activity

EXERCISING. Many Preschool 3 children like to do exercises. Those exercises that require good arm and leg co-ordination such as "jumping jacks" are generally difficult for a child of this age. You may still be surprised at the variety of exercises your child will attempt. Children who attend special exercise and gymnastic classes may develop abilities and routines that amaze their families and testify to greater body control and co-ordination.

RUNNING. Over the next year, you can expect your child's running ability to increase. She will run more smoothly and her arm and leg actions will become more co-ordinated. By the age of five, most children will be running with greater confidence and reasonable speed. They will easily start running, at a fast pace from a standing still position, and will also be able to come to a sudden halt when their destination has been reached.

CLIMBING. Your child will be faster and more proficient at climbing upward as well as downward. She will develop the ability to go up and down stairs smoothly, in an adult-like fashion. Most Preschool 3 children enjoy climbing jungle gyms, ladders, and trees with low branches. You should keep an eye on your child when she climbs, especially if she is the daring sort and likes to climb.

BALANCING. Your child's balancing act will probably show signs of promise. She is likely to be able to walk forward and backward, heel to toe, for at least four consecutive steps, and walk a line around the outside of a circle. She will balance on one foot for about ten seconds, and may be able to walk across low wooden beams that are only a few inches wide. By the age of five, most children have a fairly mature sense of balance.

JUMPING. The Preschool 3 child will be moderately skillful at jumping. She should be able to make reasonably good running and standing broad jumps. By the time a child is five years old, she should be able to broad-jump a distance of two to three feet, jumping and landing on two feet. When asked to jump over low objects, a child, using a two-foot jump, will probably jump almost one foot in the air.

HOPPING. Your child is also improving in her ability to hop. Between the beginning and end of Preschool 3, most children will progress from four to six consecutive hops to about eight to ten. Hopping from one foot to the other foot in fairly rapid succession is difficult for a child during this phase. By the time many children are five years old, they possess greater strength and balance, enabling them to hop for greater distances at a fairly rapid pace.

SKIPPING. You may see your child attempting to skip. Her first attempts to skip should be comical to observe, because she will probably skip on one foot and walk with the other. Skipping is a complex locomotor activity, and you should not expect your youngster to be adept at this form of movement until she is about six to seven years old.

RIDING A TRICYCLE. The majority of children become skillful at riding a tricycle during Preschool 3. You may now see your child performing various stunts on her tricycle. This is a major reason to watch her when she is riding it, and teach her safe ways of handling the tricycle as described on page 674.

THROWING A BALL. The child's ability to throw a ball continues to improve. During this phase she will probably develop the ability to throw a small ball about twice the distance she was able to throw it during Preschool 2. You will notice that your youngster still does not take a step and shift her weight as she releases the ball. Throwing a ball relatively long distances in an adult-like fashion is a very complex task which most children do not master until they are considerably older.

CATCHING A BALL. Most children continue to have trouble catching a ball. Their elbows are usually still stiffly positioned in front of their bodies, and only their hands are open to receive the ball when it arrives. By the age of five, many children can catch a large playground ball that is bounced to them.

Fine Motor Activity

Your child's fine motor abilities will be more well controlled. She will probably enjoy performing various manual tasks, and sticking with them until they are completed. Being intent upon perfecting her skill with her hands and fingers, she will strive to master each task she sets for herself, and will constantly search for new challenges.

BLOCK BUILDING. Your child's play with blocks is now becoming more sophisticated. Rather than concentrating on how high a tower she can build, she will now be concerned with matters of construction—combining blocks to make a particular structure. Early in her "building" career, her structures will be spread out, loosely held together, and rather easily knocked over. By the time she is five, her structures should be more stable and well balanced. You may be amazed by the great height of her buildings, as well as their sophisticated over-all construction and design.

DRAWING AND PRINTING. You will definitely see signs of improvement in your child's ability to draw. At this age she will draw and color with increased concentration. Your child will now probably be capable of drawing fairly straight strokes in a variety of directions. She will be copying circles and drawing fairly good crosses. Squares are also reproduced by many children of this age. Triangles, when attempted, are generally poorly drawn, but by age five, the child will draw a reasonably accurate triangle.

Children whose parents have been showing them how to print are likely to be able to print various numbers and letters by the end of Preschool 3. Each child will have her own unique manner of writing her letters and numbers when she begins to print. Some numbers are often drawn without the child's lifting the pencil off the paper to complete them. Others that adults print using a continuous stroke are often written using two separate strokes. Numbers, instead of being printed neatly in a row, are usually placed all over a piece of paper. They are also quite large in size. Letters may be placed sideways, and are apt to be slanted. Do not be surprised to see your child's numbers and letters reversed in a wide variety of ways. By the age of five, or even earlier, many children are able to print their first names. Those who have been printing letters for some time may even be able to print the alphabet, but you should not expect this.

By examining your child's pictures, her improvement in the area of fine motor control should be obvious. Many of the simple forms that she draws or paints will, according to her, represent familiar objects. Circles drawn with extra lines may become "suns" or "faces," and crude squares or rectangles may become "houses" or "buildings." A circle attached to a square with several lines sticking out of the circle may be a "cat." By the time she is five, her drawings and/or paintings will be much more elaborate. Many children spend a great deal of time on a particular "creation," painting scenes of complex activities. These drawings often contain items such as the sky, sun, moon, stars, clouds, trees, grass, flowers, and animals.

She will also make more attempts to draw people. Her figures will be crudely drawn, but she may be able to draw the human form; torsos are usually left out. The "head" will often be just a circle with scattered marks inside to represent the eyes, nose, and mouth. Sometimes she will draw hair by scribbling at the top of the head, or by making a series of loops around the circle's edge. The child may also draw a mark for a mouth in the circle that is either upturned or downturned to indicate whether the person is happy or sad.

Youngsters often draw "stick-like" arms and legs. Legs may end in a circle that is supposed to represent a foot. Next, a child might add fingers and a torso. Following this, she might refine her figure drawing by adding parts of the face, and may particularly emphasize the eyes, fingers, feet, and facial expression of the person. Last but not least, she may draw the limbs and body with some width.

USING TOOLS AND UTENSILS. The Preschool 3 child will be more adept in her use of tools. She should be able to cut on a line with a small blunt scissors. With close adult supervision, she may also be able to use some simple carpentry tools. Her wood constructions are likely to be poorly made. By age five, the child will take more time to plan a project, build it very carefully, sand it, and paint it. She will probably enjoy making replicas of familiar objects.

DRESSING AND GROOMING. In the area of dressing, your child is likely to be able to dress herself completely without your assistance. Many children will learn to lace their shoes. Your youngster should be assuming greater independence in caring for her own body. By now she will probably be able to brush and comb her hair successfully, wash her body, including her hair, dry herself after taking a bath, and do a good job of brushing her teeth.

LEARNING THROUGH PLAY

The Preschool 3 child's play will be quite socially oriented, imaginative, and lively. She will constantly want to be involved in new projects and activities. Keeping her and her playmates stimulated and occupied by helping them plan different activities should be a real challenge.

Your child is more capable of independent play, although she will prefer to play with her peers rather than play alone. She will need less of your assistance than previously in getting out materials, starting activities, executing them, and cleaning up her messes after she is finished. She will still be very spontaneous in her speech and actions, but less impulsive in her play than at earlier ages. Her activities are gradually becoming more purposeful, and goal-directed.

Most of the playthings and activities suggested in the previous preschool play sections are still appropriate for your child. She will continue to enjoy outdoor play with toys and equipment that promote large-muscle development such as a tricycle, a football, a wagon, a ladder, a slide, large hollow blocks, a swing, a sled, rings, a jungle gym, a seesaw, jump ropes, roller skates, and ice skates. With her friends, she can play tag, catch, touch football, King of the Mountain, hide-and-seek, and numerous other co-operative games.

Indoors, either alone or with other youngsters, your child will enjoy all kinds of arts and crafts, role-play and fantasy situations, activities that involve music and rhythm. She will also derive pleasure from working puzzles, listening to stories, making up her own stories, looking at books, playing matching games, using construction toys, and playing dominoes and simple board games that involve counting. Most Preschool 3 children like to play word games, quiz games, and lotto games, use Montessori-type dressing frames, cook, have an ant farm, use a magnifying glass and magnets, and play with toys and equipment that enable them to imitate adult work and activities.

By now you surely have discovered that it is possible to come up with all sorts of interesting playthings and toys out of ordinary household materials and ready to be discarded items. The best part about such playthings is that they cost next to nothing, and are readily available. Journeying back a few generations, when store-bought toys were unheard of, children still played, but, out of necessity, parents and children were forced to be more creative. They had no choice but to make their own toys out of ordinary materials, and use their imaginations in coming up with games and activities.

There are many excellent toys available in toy stores, and you will no doubt purchase some of them, but with a little bit of effort and imagination, you and your child can create many of your own playthings, and devise your own activities. They will stimulate her interest and provide her with virtually endless opportunities to learn and develop her own inner resources through play.

Pride in Finished Products and Creations

Your child is now likely to be much more interested than before in making her own "constructions," and also more capable of handling equipment with your supervision. She will be resourceful and creative in combining and using various objects, materials, and substances, and transforming them into new products. She will not only admire her own artwork and finished products, she will also want you and other people to admire them as well. After she has finished using blocks to build a fort or a castle, she may not want to disassemble the blocks, and may insist that her structures not be touched for several days until she decides to make something new and more exciting out of them. The pride that she will take in making things will motivate her to do the best she can.

Play with Others

Your child may want to spend very little time in play by herself, since she probably prefers to play with friends. With her playmates she may build sand castles, hold tea parties, construct elaborate block buildings to house tiny plastic dolls and metal cars, play with musical instruments, and shape and mold clay into various objects. She and her friends may also paint murals together, hold delightful conversations on nearly every subject, look at books, seesaw, "race" with tricycles, and play "hospital."

It is important for you to try to make your child's friends feel welcome and comfortable in your home. Many of their group activities may be dreamed up and carried out without their asking for help, but you should remain close by, ready to suggest a new activity, and to get them started on it. You should have little or no difficulty finding interesting activities for your child and her playmates when she laments, "We don't have anything to do!"

Imaginative, Dramatic Play

Your youngster has an active imagination. She loves to re-enact situations she has experienced in dramatic play and pretend activities. As you know, make-believe play can help her learn many things, including something about the "real" world. You can be of great help to your child by providing her with numerous opportunities for dramatic play, encouraging her to assume many different roles, and seeing to it that she has an adequate supply of props. Your child will probably want to have many more accessories and props for dramatic play than she needed or wanted in Preschool 2.

With her friends, she may enjoy conducting an orchestra, putting on a puppet show, playing "house," "supermarket," "beauty parlor," "post office," "hospital," "gas station," or "cops and robbers." When she assumes various roles, she will probably insist upon having appropriate costumes to wear and accessories to make her play more successful. In the event that she decides to assume the role of a "fire person," she may want to wear a badge, a raincoat, boots, a hat, and carry a fire extinguisher (a squirt gun filled with water) as well as a ladder (step stool).

CREATIVE SELF-EXPRESSION THROUGH LANGUAGE. There are virtually unlimited possibilities for projects and activities that will allow your child to use her imagination and be creative. A worth-while activity that she may enjoy involves language and creative expression. Cut out pictures from magazines depicting various scenes. You might, for instance, find pictures of a man reading to a little boy, two adults embracing, children happily playing games, and so forth. Hold the pictures up one at a time, and encourage your child to create a story around what she sees and thinks is going on in the pictures. You might cut out pictures of people's faces —some laughing, some crying, some looking angry, some looking surprised, and so on. Then hold each one up and encourage your youngster to imagine how the person in the picture feels, and tell why the person might feel that way.

Preschool 3 children love to talk and make up their own imaginative stories.

Preschool 3

These kinds of activities will help them learn to imagine, project feelings, recognize feelings, and express them verbally. Other activities to stimulate creative expression might include helping your child create her own books, encouraging her to express feelings through movement to music, and showing her how to play pantomime games.

Expanded Play Area

Your child is likely to need more room than before in which to play. Do not underestimate her ability, for she can easily slip through the gate if you accidentally leave it unlocked. At this age your child should be allowed greater freedom, independence, and responsibility, but you should also set firm boundaries with her safety in mind, and be prepared to enforce them. You can now try to establish rules and boundaries verbally, for example, by telling her not to play in the street or wander any further than the fence or the big pile of wood in the back yard without first asking your permission. Most of the time she will obey your rules, but you will still have to keep a watchful eye on her to make sure that she is safe, and has not wandered into the street or another area that is off limits. Keep in mind that she may occasionally forget your limits and rules, and can be tempted to go beyond your boundaries by her friends.

Cooking Can Be Fun and Educational

Little girls and boys love to do the things they see their parents do, and they especially enjoy working with "real" food products and "real" cooking utensils. Assuming that you have the time and inclination, there are many ways in which to make cooking a terrific learning experience for your child as well. One or more of the following suggestions may be of interest to you and your child.

• Talk to your child about good nutrition and proper eating habits. Have her cut out pictures of foods from the different food groups, and paste them on cardboard.
• Teach her to handle (with your supervision) and name various cooking utensils. Tell her what purpose each one serves.

• Teach her the meanings of simple, basic cooking words such as "knead," "peel," "cream," "fold," "sauté," and "dice," by allowing her to help knead bread or peel a carrot with a vegetable peeler, etc.
• Show her your cookbooks and talk about the different kinds of cookbooks available in bookstores. Take her to a bookstore and try to find one especially for preschool children.

- Talk about foods eaten in different countries. Occasionally try to prepare foods from a different country and culture, and point out that country on a map.
- Let her decide upon a dish that she would like to make from her very own cookbook. You may select three or four that you feel are best-suited to her abilities in advance, and allow her to choose from among these.
- Show her how you make a shopping list of needed ingredients, and have her shop for the ingredients with you. Teach her how to select fresh fruits and vegetables. Show her how they are weighed. Talk about how much they cost.
- Teach her about the importance of washing hands before cooking and cleanliness when cooking.
- Show her how to follow the step-by-step instructions in the recipe. Help her learn about units of weights and measures.
- Allow her to do as many things as she can on her own, including cleaning up her own mess.
- Let her eat the dish that she has prepared. Try to eat some yourself, or invite her friends over to taste the food.
- Have discussions about the importance of storing particular foods in the refrigerator so that they do not spoil. Also talk about how to wrap foods properly so they will stay fresh longer, and how to freeze foods. Let her help you defrost the freezer and clean out the refrigerator.
- Encourage her to feel the different textures of foods, smell the different odors and the aromas of foods being cooked, see the various shapes, sizes, and colors of foods, hear the noises that foods make when they are being cooked, and enjoy the different tastes of foods.
- Show her how to use a food timer and talk about the importance of keeping track of the time when cooking and baking.
- Talk about where food comes from, and how certain food products are made.
- Plant a small vegetable or herb garden, and encourage her to observe its growth.
- Find appropriate material to read to her about good nutrition, food products, and so on.
- Encourage her to observe how foods can be transformed from one state to another (e.g., a stick of butter can be melted, frozen juice can be thawed).
- Allow her to participate in planning weekly menus.
- Show her how leftovers can be utilized so that foods do not go to waste.

With your guidance, encouragement, and supervision, cooking will be more than just fun for your child. The enjoyment she derives from learning and doing, and the satisfaction and sense of accomplishment that she gets from examining and tasting the finished products will be well worth your time and effort.

Your Improving Young Artist

Your four-year-old is likely to enjoy a wide variety of arts and crafts activities, since they provide opportunities for practicing skills, exploration, and creative expression. She will continue to enjoy many of the activities suggested in the previous play sections, but now that she is more mature, more capable, and less likely to be putting things into her mouth, there are many new activities that you can introduce.

Many children of four and older are ready to use paste, glue, tape, blunt scissors, and a paper punch. The ability to work with these adhesives and tools varies greatly from child to child, and you must decide whether or not your child is capable of handling them. In making your decision, you should also consider how much time you have to supervise her activities.

PAINTING AND DRAWING. Your child will concentrate for longer periods of time than before on a particular painting. Now that she is able to hold a paintbrush like an adult, it will be much easier for her to apply paint more precisely. She is likely to change her mind frequently about what she is painting when she is halfway through with a painting, and this, in addition to her unusual use of colors and proportions, can result in some funny-looking finished products. Nevertheless, your little artist is making progress in her ability to represent people and objects on paper, and she may surprise you by painting or drawing a picture that you recognize as being "something." You might hear her begin to criticize her own artwork. She will adore having others positively reinforce her own feelings about her artistic talent.

COLLAGE AND OTHER "CREATIONS." Equipped with a blunt scissors, paper, glue, some tape, paint, and bits and pieces of anything and everything that you and your child can find, she will use her imagination and come up with all kinds of interesting collages. Assuming that she is no longer putting inedible objects into her mouth, she can now use assorted pebbles, shoestrings, scraps of styrofoam and material, dry macaroni, nut shells, corks, pipe cleaners, string, and straws. Sequins and glitter will add sparkle to her creations.

Naturally, all of these materials can be used for purposes other than making collages. For example, little toys can be made from nut shells, interesting figures can be made from pieces of styrofoam, and dolls can be made using scraps of material, yarn, paint, and wooden spoons. With shoestrings she can string pieces of straws and tubular pieces of dry macaroni in order to make jewelry. Colored construction paper cut into shapes can be used to make paper dolls. Colored pipe cleaners can be twisted into a variety of interesting human and flower shapes.

With scissors and a variety of paper, your child can make all kinds of animals. Paper can be folded to make paper airplanes and hats. With crayons or paint and paper she can make her own holiday greeting cards, birthday party invitations, and valentines. Offer her a hanger and some wire or string, and show her how to use a combination of items mentioned above to make mobiles. At Christmas time, Chanukah, or other holidays she can make an endless variety of her own home decorations.

Music and Rhythm Activities

While listening to music, you can encourage your youngster to let her imagination run wild. She may like to make up her own different interpretations of the music through various movements and facial expressions. In addition to moving and dancing to music, she may enjoy music participation and singing games that she can play with her friends. Some of the old favorites include "London Bridge," and "Humpty Dumpty."

Many children like to play with musical instruments, and experiment with the sounds that they produce. If you have a musical instrument at home that you can play for your child, she will be an attentive listener, and you may even want to encourage her to try the instrument out for herself. Most youngsters are delighted with homemade instruments, too.

HOMEMADE MUSICAL INSTRUMENTS. Cymbals can easily be made by offering your child two pot lids to bang together. Fill an empty container such as a small box or a plastic bottle with dried peas, rice, marbles, gravel, or dried macaroni, and your child can have a fine shaker or "rattle." Another idea is to fill partially a large paper cup with rice or any of the substances just mentioned. Then place another paper cup over it and tape the edges of the cups together so that no spaces are left. This makes a fine shaker.

Several small bells on a piece of elastic tape also makes a fine instrument. With some different-sized metal pots and spoons your child will be able to bang away to her heart's content. Even two metal spoons can make a fine ringing sound when they are banged together.

A good plucking instrument can be made by removing the lid of an old deep box and stretching rubber bands of various widths around it. In your child's make-believe play, she can pretend that it is a violin or a banjo. Another instrument can be made from two wooden blocks and sandpaper. Attack a piece of sandpaper, rough side facing up, to each block. When your child rubs the sandpaper together, she will hear a shuffling sound. Empty, round, sturdy cereal cartons with lids attached make excellent bongo drums.

You will probably come up with many other kinds of homemade instruments. The suggestions given above will give you a start. Your child can play with the instruments alone, or get together with her friends and form a band.

Sorting Games

Many children, given a mixed group of objects, will naturally begin to sort them. If you happen to have a box filled with assorted threads, you can put your child to work in organizing them for you. Give her an empty candy box, or another carton with divisions, and she can sort the spools according to their size, shape, color, and according to the thickness of the thread. You can also give her other objects to sort such as colored marbles, leftover pieces of different-colored materials, or mixed nuts. She may like to sort piles of laundry. Sorting games can help her develop manipulative skill and co-ordination, and can also give her practice in counting.

Sewing

Little girls and boys may enjoy having opportunities to sew. A good way to introduce your child to sewing is to give her sewing cards. Cut a large piece of cardboard into several smaller pieces, perhaps each one having different "clothes" shapes. Punch holes around the edges of each piece. Give her a sewing card, and show her how to sew with a shoelace, a piece of string, or yarn. When using string or yarn, wrap the ends with tape, since this will make it much easier for her to lace with them.

Making Doll Clothes

Boys and girls do not have to know how to sew to be able to make clothes for their dolls. They can make simple wrap-style dresses by wrapping material around a doll and gathering it at the waist with a rubber band, ribbon, or piece of yarn. A stapler and glue, providing that a child knows how to use them, can also come in handy in making doll clothes.

Your Little Carpenter

Little girls and boys frequently love to make "constructions" with wood, and many are now ready to learn to use "real" carpenter's tools just like those that they see Mommy and Daddy use. Assuming that you feel your child is ready, you can show her how to cut soft pieces of wood with a small saw, nail them together, smooth pieces of wood with sandpaper, and paint them. With your help, guidance, and encouragement, she can make all sorts of things with wood, including simple boats, boxes, book holders, and blocks. Do not forget that glue comes in handy when working with wood, and in cases where a child is not ready for carpentry tools, glue can be used in making things from wood.

Like any carpenter, your child will need a good, sturdy, and low workbench or table, as well as plenty of space in which to work. Start out slowly. First teach her how to handle tools properly. Next give her opportunities to practice hammering nails into wood. Take one step at a time, and make sure that she has mastered each step before you introduce a new task. Your four-year-old's first "constructions" may be rather quickly built and primitive, but by the time she is five, you may be surprised at how well many of her constructions turn out.

Indoor Fun with Magnets

Your child may have a lot of fun and, at the same time, learn many things by having an opportunity to play with a magnet. One activity using a magnet involves letting her "fish" for small metal objects such as bobby pins, paper clips, and nails in a tub. You have probably seen this fishing game on numerous children's programs, since it is a very popular activity. Magnetic alphabet letters are also fine playthings.

A Detective in Disguise

A magnifying glass is one of the most fascinating pieces of equipment that you can give your child. Encourage her to walk around the house and yard and observe what various objects and substances look like under her magnifying glass. Giving her this piece of equipment is like giving her a bit of magic. Even the tiniest ant, or particles of dust, will take on new meaning when they are magnified. Give her an old cape, a cap, and a pipe, and she may play detective for a whole afternoon.

HOW TO ENSURE YOUR CHILD'S SAFETY

Safety Precautions and Playground Equipment

Older preschoolers, who will be spending more time with playmates at their homes or in neighborhood playgrounds, are frequently exposed to playground equipment. This equipment can be a potential source of danger to a young child, but there are several ways in which you can protect your child and her friends from accidents.

SELECTING PLAYGROUND EQUIPMENT. If you are going to buy playground equipment, it is important to examine it thoroughly, paying close attention to the following features. Most playground sets do not come preassembled. Before you purchase a set, make sure that clear, specific instructions for its assembly are included in the box.

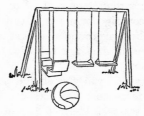

A playground set that is unstable will be very dangerous. The set that you purchase should be equipped with special devices that will enable it to be securely anchored to the ground.

Any protrusions from the playground set, including bolts and screws, can be dangerous, and should be covered. Some sets provide specially designed caps to fit over the protrusions. If not, it will be up to you to place tape or some other protective covering over the objects sticking out.

There are several other features to be wary of in shopping for playground equipment. Do not purchase sets with pointy edges or rough bars or seats. Rings greater than five inches but less than ten inches in diameter represent danger to a young child whose head may get caught in them. Sets that utilize S-shaped or open-ended hooks of other shapes are unsafe and should be avoided, as should those with moving parts in which a child's finger might get trapped or pinched. By being aware of these features, and purchasing a set that is sturdy, well-designed, and safe, your child will have loads of fun in your back yard, and you will feel more at ease when she is using her playground set.

INSTALLATION AND MAINTENANCE. Properly installing and maintaining your youngster's playground equipment is extremely important for her safety. Do not position her playground set near a fence or wall. Allow ample room, at least six feet, preferably more, from any obstruction. For a set to be securely anchored to the ground, it must not be installed over concrete or other hard surfaces.

Check on the condition of the playground set from time to time, preferably every couple of weeks. Clamps, nuts, screws, and bolts should be securely fastened. Any rusted parts or hardware, including swings and chains, should be replaced. Areas on the metal tubes or poles that have rusted or are rough should be sanded and repainted with non-lead-base paint for outdoor use.

PROPER ADULT SUPERVISION. All youngsters of preschool age and younger must be closely supervised whenever they are using or playing near playground equipment. Many unnecessary accidents can be avoided by having an adult oversee their play activities.

TRAINING YOUR CHILD TO PROTECT HERSELF. An important aspect of your educational program in accident prevention will be to help your preschooler learn how to conduct herself in responsible ways when she is using or playing near a playground set. Let her know that there are specific rules that should be observed. Tell your child that pushing, fighting, and shoving are not permitted around a playground set. Warn her not to sit off to one side of a swing, but rather, always to sit in the middle of the seat. Let her know why it is dangerous to walk in front or back of moving swings, set empty swings in motion, or twist the swing when she is using it.

Inform your child about possible dangers of other playground equipment as well. For example, warn her that standing in front of a sliding board is a safety hazard, since another child coming down might collide with her. Be sure to tell her that when she is at a public playground she must take turns with the other children, and not copy their actions if they are behaving improperly on the equipment or are doing dangerous things.

Rules and warnings that you give should be accompanied by appropriate explanations as to why those specific practices can be dangerous. Be prepared to repeat warnings, rules, and reasons. They will eventually sink in, and when they do, your child will be in a better position to conduct herself in safe ways.

EATING

The Preschool 3 child tends to be more enthusiastic than in the past about dining both in and outside the home. Her interests in eating and experimenting with new things make her a better candidate for her mother's or father's original recipes. At last her parents may be able to introduce new taste experiences without hearing her complain. She may even beg them to buy a new kind of cereal or frozen vegetable that she has seen advertised on television, or other food products that she has heard about from people or seen in magazine advertisements.

Her ability to behave reasonably at the dinner table and to interact with other family members is also improving, despite the fact that she may occasionally dominate the dinner conversation and have difficulty sitting still in her chair. When encouraged to do so, she may love to help plan menus for the week, participate in cooking simple dishes, and place non-breakable dishes and glasses on the table.

Your child is better able to regulate her own behavior than she was in previous phases, and is undoubtedly anxious to imitate you. As a result, you may see a noticeable improvement in her manners. However, it would be unreasonable to expect perfection from a four- to five-year-old child.

Everyone is subject to cravings for particular foods from time to time, especially four-year-olds. Do not be surprised if your child gets "hooked" on a particular food for breakfast or lunch, and insists upon having it every day for a while. Provided that the food is healthy for the child, some parents decide that it would probably avoid unnecessary arguments simply to go along with her preferences. Other parents are less tolerant of this mealtime behavior. They offer their child a well-balanced meal, and if she does not eat it, they promptly remove it. When she eventually gets hungry enough, she will eat whatever they have prepared, and at the same time will learn about the value of a well-balanced diet.

BATHING

Children are now much more capable of washing and drying themselves, and many will be doing a good job. They are anxious to assume greater responsibility, and may actually enjoy pulling the plug to let the water drain, and helping to clean the tub and floor after their baths.

Give your child as much leeway to be independent at bath time as possible within the scope of her abilities. She should be able to do just about everything on her own from shampooing her hair to washing between her toes. Taking care of her own needs will give her a feeling of responsibility and pride in her appearance.

Many Preschool 3 children find it humiliating to have their parents hover over them at bath time. Quite often they demand some privacy in the bathroom, and are embarrassed about undressing in front of others. Provided that your bathroom is safety-proofed, and that your child can be trusted to operate the water faucets safely and climb in without help, there is no need for you to interfere. Or, you could put the water in the tub first, help her into the tub, and then leave. Still, you should check on her from time to time to make sure that she is all right, and listen for periods of silence or strange noises that might indicate trouble.

CLOTHING

Most children can now dress and undress themselves with little, if any, need for help from their parents. Many children are skillful at fastening different kinds of fasteners, and are able to tie their shoes. Children of this age, boys as well as girls, especially enjoy having dress-up clothing for their dramatic play.

The Preschool 3 child is ready to assume some responsibility for taking care of her clothes. She can be taught to collect her dirty clothes and put them into a basket or a pile to be washed, and to put her shoes away on a shelf or rack in the closet. You can also encourage her to hang her clothes on low pegs after she wears them, and to wipe off her shoes or boots when she enters the house so as not to track dirt on the floors. Do not expect her to assume all of these responsibilities immediately, since this would be demanding too much from her at once, but you can expect her gradually to become more responsible in caring for her clothes.

SLEEPING

The four- to five-year-old is much easier to manage at bedtime in comparison with her behavior during the earlier preschool periods. Much to her parents' astonishment, she may occasionally say that she is sleepy and ready to go to bed. She knows her bedtime, and is generally more willing to accept it.

Many children like to take their time getting into bed. Once in bed, they enjoy having a period in which to play quietly, talk, look at books, or engage in some other activity before the light is turned out. It generally does not take a Preschool 3 child too long before she falls asleep.

The Crib Is a Thing of the Past

Assuming that you have not shifted your child from a crib to a "big" bed, you will want to do so now. Most children of this age love new things and new challenges, and a regular bed represents both. Sometimes a child who has persisted in her middle-of-the-night demands to sleep in her parents' room or wander around may be motivated to sleep alone and stop wandering by the promise of having a "big" bed providing that she acts more grown-up. Having a regular bed may act as an incentive to an immature child to alter her behavior. If this shift does not accomplish the desired result, try not to make her feel like a failure.

Waking in the Middle of the Night

Especially during the latter half of this phase, the child may wake during the night as a result of bad dreams and nightmares. These dreams may often be about wild creatures such as lions or tigers chasing her. Depending upon how vividly she recalls the events in her dream, she may simply get up and then either go back to sleep, or else scream for her parents. If a parent comforts and reassures her, she may go back to sleep right away, but she may occasionally awaken again yelling in a terrified manner. Even when her parents offer a great deal of comfort, she may refuse to go back to sleep unless they sit by her side until she is asleep again, or she may insist upon sleeping with them.

Some children will be fearful of the dark. Suggestions for handling this problem were provided on pages 678–79. Other children will be fearful of the shadows on the walls or ceiling of their rooms, which may sometimes appear to them as monsters, ghosts, or other frightening figures. Parents may be able to change the lighting, window shades, or drapes in the child's room so that the shadows disappear. Hooking up a night light or changing the position of her bed should help. If all else fails, parents may find it helpful to show the child how to cast her own shadows on the ceiling or walls of her room. This may help to convince her that she doesn't have to be afraid of shadows.

Many parents are very understanding in regard to their children's fears, but others are less solicitous. Whatever your approach to handling your child's fears, be aware that they are real to her. Often with parents' help and understanding, children's fears will subside after a short while; even if parents do nothing, chances are that, in time, the fears will gradually begin to diminish.

A child will occasionally get up during the night because she has to go to the bathroom. Some children call for their parents' help, whereas others go all by themselves. Sometimes children need their parents to sit beside them for a while in order to get back to bed. By the end of Preschool 3, this help may no longer be necessary.

DEVELOPING GOOD TOILET HABITS

The majority of children are now able to assume total responsibility for their own elimination needs. An occasional daytime accident may occur, especially when a child tries to "hold it in" too long, and then discovers that it's too late. Nighttime accidents are more common, although most Preschool 3 children do not wet their beds at night. In cases in which a child is having some success staying dry at night, awakening her once during the night and taking her to the bathroom, or setting an alarm clock to awaken her a couple of hours after she has fallen asleep so that she can get up and go to the toilet on her own, may be effective in helping her remain consistently dry.

It is fairly common for some children of this age to express a strong desire for privacy in the bathroom, although these same youngsters often want to observe other people urinating or moving their bowels. When away from home children may show a strong interest in unfamiliar bathrooms. This desire to investigate other people's bathrooms has caused many parents some embarrassment when they take their Preschool 3 children to their friends' homes for visits.

"Toilet talk" is also quite common among children during this phase, as described in the Language Development section on page 912.

Toilet Training Problems

A few children will continue to have difficulties in the area of toilet training. If you feel that your child has a problem, we suggest that you reread the section on toilet training problems in Preschool 2 on pages 859–62, and discuss the problem with your child's doctor.

BED-WETTING: ENURESIS. Occasional bed-wetting is common throughout the preschool years. A child who is sick, or overly excited, frightened, or under stress, may begin to wet her bed at night, even though she achieved nighttime control a long time ago. Once the reason for the temporary lapse in control has been eliminated, the child usually has no trouble regaining control. Reassurance, support, and understanding from a parent can often help to alleviate the child's feelings of shame and doubt, and lessen her anxiety.

Chronic or late bed-wetting poses a greater problem, and often causes parents to become very concerned. Sometimes this delay in achieving nighttime control is simply a matter of slow development in this particular area. The child's family history may even show that one or more immediate family members also wet their beds beyond the age at which the average child is able to remain dry. The majority of children achieve nighttime control by Preschool 1 or 2, although some children, who are perfectly normal, do not achieve control until several years later.

Once in a while, a thorough medical examination will reveal some physical cause for the child's difficulty, and this possibility should be explored before parents start jumping to their own conclusions about reasons for their child's problem. Quite often when no physical reasons for enuresis can be pinpointed, doctors will suggest that parents try to be patient and give children more time, since some children are just slower to mature than others in their ability to remain dry at night. If this is the case with your child, relax and let nature take its course. Given sufficient time, your child will gradually begin to stay dry at night. When she begins to acquire some nighttime control, you may want to follow the suggestions on page 756 for possible ways to speed up this process.

Punishing, shaming, scolding, and threatening a child for wetting at night are methods that may cause anxiety and resentment, and can contribute to a child's feelings of shame and failure. Emotional pressure resulting from these methods may even interfere with her ability to remain dry during the daytime as well as prolong her inability to remain dry at night. Most of the time children are already very ashamed about their bed-wetting, and would do anything to overcome this problem.

Many children express a desire to keep their problem a secret between themselves and their parents. Parents should respect their child's feelings, and go along with her wish for them to keep her "secret." Older brothers or sisters and other relatives should not be permitted to make fun of her.

The child will need to be reassured that many children have had this kind of problem and have overcome it in time. This may help her to be more confident and optimistic about the future. Patience, understanding, and support from parents can be very helpful.

It is common for a Preschool 3 child to feel bad about wearing training pants or underpants plus rubber pants, so try to make her feel as comfortable as possible in them. Make sure that her rubber pants are not airtight, since this may cause a skin irritation such as a diaper rash. You may also want to purchase a waterproof sheet and pad in order to protect her mattress.

There are professionals in the field of child mental health who believe that emotional factors underlie bed-wetting problems. Undue emotional pressure and stress can certainly play a part in some children's problems, and this avenue should also be explored.

Children who are late bed-wetters are quite often reported to be very sound sleepers. In deep sleep, messages to the brain that the bladder needs to be emptied are either not sent or are not transmitted in time for the child to wake up and urinate in the proper place. The child is therefore unaware of her bodily sensations while she's asleep, and only realizes what has happened after she wakes up and discovers that she has wet her bed.

There are numerous mechanical apparatus available that can warn a child when she is urinating. Several of these devices are put on the child's bed, and work in the following manner. The salt in a child's urine produces a short-circuit, which then prompts an electrical current to ring a buzzer, turn on a light, or activate some other stimulus that awakens the child. Gradually, provided that this method is successful, she will wake on her own before the stimulus awakens her. The signal that the youngster's bladder is full and needs to be emptied will be sent before her bladder sphincter relaxes, and in sufficient time for her to get to the toilet.

Such "conditioning" devices can often be effective in helping children who have previously been unsuccessful in learning to control their bladders during the night. However, a mechanical conditioning device may not always work, especially if the child is unwilling to accept its use, or is simply not ready to achieve nighttime control.

There appears to be controversy about whether such mechanical devices should be used with children under the age of seven or eight. Young children take great pleasure in accomplishing the goal of remaining dry at night by themselves, and if there is any chance for them to do so of their own accord in the next few years, it is often suggested that parents should not interfere. In cases in which a child is not physically capable, is unwilling to go along with it, or is wetting her bed due to an emotional problem, it is doubtful that a mechanical device will be successful, and, therefore, it may not be advisable. In the event that you have questions regarding the use and possible effectiveness of a mechanical device with your child, or are thinking of purchasing one, consult your doctor first.

DISCIPLINE

Transmitting Your Values to Your Child

In the course of each day or each year, you will have innumerable opportunities to convey your values and moral attitudes to your preschooler in a most natural, relaxed way. At this stage of development, when abstract concepts about being honest and moral will be difficult for her to grasp through words, your actions will most definitely speak louder than verbal explanations. Giving her a lecture about the value of being kind to others will probably not mean as much to her as would watching you behave kindly toward other people, or offer to help a handicapped person cross the street. Similarly, telling her about the value of being honest and respecting other people's belongings is not likely to have the same impact upon her as seeing you return a ring that you found on the sidewalk, or give back an extra dollar that a cashier gave you by mistake.

It will be very helpful for you to show as well as tell your youngster how you feel about being honest, morally upstanding, and respectful and considerate of other people and their property. You need not resort to employing severe punishment, threats, and fear-arousing warnings in order to transmit your values to her when there are so many positive ways in which to accomplish the same educational objective. Setting a good example is half the battle.

Distorting the Truth—Lying

Lying is common during the preschool years. Even before Preschool 1, a child may playfully pretend she is sick or hurt so that her parents will hold her and shower her with their attention. During toddlerhood the child may occasionally play simple tricks on her parents or siblings such as telling her father that "doggie gone" when the dog is really tied to a post in the back yard.

The toddler may also be able to tell simple lies by shaking her head and emphatically stating "no" in an attempt to deny doing something her parents have correctly accused her of having done. After the age of about eighteen months, when the child's ability to think and imagine increases, she often confuses dreams and real events, wishes and actions, or make-believe and reality.

During the preschool years, especially in Preschool 3, when the child's imagination is expanding very rapidly, she may develop an imaginary companion and tell untrue tales. Many of her statements and stories may sound like small lies to her parents, but the child who has difficulty separating fact from fantasy may not really be telling lies. She may merely be exaggerating or distorting reality to make it more exciting or transforming actual events into an elaborate, imaginative story. There is a good chance that she will even think that a few of her own made-up statements and stories are true.

Should parents take their children's "lies" too seriously, and treat "normal" behavior as problem behavior by punishing her, the child may have difficulty learning to separate fantasy from reality, and may begin to lie more often. Most children do not completely believe their own stories, and therefore do not really think that their parents will believe them either. They are testing out what is real and what is fantasy. Parents provide the guidance for teaching what is real. In situations where parents act as though they believe that their youngster is deliberately trying to deceive them, they give substance to the child's fantasies. This can confuse her and even cause her to wonder whether or not the imaginative statements she made were real.

Mrs. Jackson was planning to go out for dinner with her husband and had arranged for her mother to care for her son, Carl. When Carl heard that Grandma was going to baby-sit he said, "Grandma always hits me and is mean to me." Mrs. Jackson knew that this was not true, but was puzzled by her son's reaction. Carl then said, "Let Aunt Joan baby-sit, because she always brings over David and Lisa," two younger cousins.

It became clear to Mrs. Jackson that Carl was making up a bad story about his grandmother so that he could have his favorite aunt as a baby-sitter. She was annoyed at her son's behavior, but realized that he was confusing his wishes with reality by distorting the truth. She told Carl that Grandma was coming over and that she knew that Grandma would not hurt him because she loved him. Carl was disappointed, but eventually accepted the situation.

There may be a few occasions on which your youngster will try to deceive you by lying her way out of a situation. Many children occasionally deny their own misconduct even when their parents have direct evidence substantiating their accusation. Lying in order not to have to suffer the consequences or not to lose self-esteem is common in young children, and should not cause parents to worry that their children will become permanent liars in the future. Parents, under these circumstances, should make it clear to their child that they know she is saying things that are not true, and that they disapprove of lying.

You need not be concerned about your youngster's tall tales, fantastic statements, and small fibs, unless lying becomes so constant and extreme that it appears that she really believes all of her own lies or has lost touch with reality. This happens only in very rare situations. In such cases parents should try to discover why their child feels the need to retreat constantly to an imaginary world. Perhaps she is dissatisfied with her life, or feels very pressured, or frightened. A professional may be able to assist parents in exploring the possibilities and finding a solution to the child's problem.

Mention should be made of the "white lie" or "social lie" often used by parents in front of young children. This can cause a youngster some confusion.

Mr. Grenell and his wife were driving with their preschool daughter, Marie, over to a business associate's house for dinner. They were discussing how much they hated having to attend this social engagement. The Wallaces always tried to show off at their parties by impressing everyone with how much money they had. The Grenells wished they didn't have to go, but they had to attend for business reasons. Mr. Grenell kept saying to his wife how much he disliked the Wallaces. Marie was listening to this conversation in the back seat and she obviously was developing a bad opinion of the Wallaces.

When they arrived, Mr. Grenell introduced Marie to Mrs. Wallace and said how pleased he was to be invited over for dinner. He complimented the Wallaces' house and said how much he enjoyed working with Mr. Wallace. Mr. Grenell was obviously being polite and not really saying what he truly felt. Marie, however, was very confused. She assumed that her father was lying, but kept quiet.

Children at this stage often have great difficulty understanding the difference between lies of some consequence, and little white lies. To them, there are no "degrees" of lying. The issue is black or white, never gray. It is often easier to avoid such conversations if your preschool child is present. In some cases it can be very embarrassing, since the child may blurt out what you really said at an earlier time. If Marie had told Mrs. Wallace how her father really felt, he would have been rather upset. Preschool children are not able to understand the meaning of the word tact. Be prepared to be embarrassed if you let your child overhear your social or white lies.

A child's eagerness to imitate her parents should also be considered in relation to telling white lies. When confronted about her own lying by her parents, she may try to justify her behavior, claiming that Mommy or Daddy lies. Hearing them lie can give her the impression that lying is acceptable behavior. Using common sense and setting a good example are the best ways to avoid any difficulties with white lies.

Handling Bragging and Boasting

It is very common for four-year-olds to brag and boast about themselves and their accomplishments. Many parents are uncomfortable when their children boast, and feel that they must put a stop to this behavior lest their children grow up to be "obnoxious, conceited brats." Parents may also feel slightly guilty that they have failed to do a good job in this aspect of rearing their children.

These feelings are understandable, but you should not overreact to your Preschool 3 child's natural tendency to boast. Try to take it in stride. Most Preschool 3 children do not really believe the exaggerated statements that they make about themselves and their abilities, and soon outgrow this tendency to brag and boast excessively.

FEARS

Fears which were previously discussed may also apply to the child between four and five. Fear of certain noises, such as the sound of sirens, which may have subsided for a period of time, are likely to be prominent again during this phase. Among the other most common fears are a fear of wild animals, fear of the dark, fear of a parent's departure in the evening, and fear of injury to the body.

Fear of Bodily Injury

Fears about injury to the body are quite prominent during the preschool years, particularly during Preschool 3. As the child's self-awareness grows, and she realizes more and more that she is vulnerable, minor cuts, small scrapes, or bruises may be blown out of proportion, and bandages may take on special importance. Being examined at the doctor's office may cause her to become very frightened. She may also begin to point to or ask questions about people who are crippled, or deformed, and she may fear that she will incur a similar injury or disease. The child's concerns about bodily safety may increase as she becomes more aware of the physiological differences between males and females. A more thorough coverage of these types of fears and concerns can be found in the preschool Personal-Social Development sections.

Fear of Death

Fears about death sometimes emerge during the preschool years. The child, upon being exposed to the death of a pet, friend, or relative, or simply realizing that people and animals die, may begin to fear that she, too, will soon die. Often the child begins to ask questions about death, either her own or her parents'.

Parents sometimes feel that it is best to keep young children from learning about death. In an effort to shield them from this taboo subject, they may refuse to discuss death when the child is present, or deny the fact that a close relative has died. Parents sometimes lie to the child about death by saying that Grandma is asleep forever, or Grandma has taken a very long vacation. Parents often try to cover up their own grief over the loss of a dear friend or relative. Children are not as oblivious to what goes on around them as some parents naïvely think they are. Frequently, children's own conclusions and theories about death are more frightening and anxiety-producing than if they were told the simple truth in terms that they could understand. Suggestions for how to tell a child about death are provided on pages 938–39.

PREJUDICE

There are many studies on what causes prejudice. One generation often passes on their prejudices to the next. It is well accepted that children acquire many of their families' opinions, beliefs, and values. As a parent, you will play a large role in shaping certain of your child's attitudes about persons of different nations, religious backgrounds, cultures, sexes, and races.

A great deal of what your child learns from you about how to treat people will be the result of listening to what you say about people of different races or religions, and observing whether or not you respect them. Your speech and actions will influence her opinions. When a parent continually makes sarcastic or derogatory jokes about members of a certain ethnic background, his or her child will pick up on this. When parents do not treat members of a different race as equals, they send their child the message that people belonging to this race are inferior. Parents may not even make any disparaging or negative remarks about people of a different race, but the fact that they never associate with persons of a certain race may convey an indirect message to their older preschool child.

Preschoolers are very quick to notice differences in people. This recognition can occur quite independently from anything their family may have said or done. Young children interacting with one another in nursery schools or in other settings usually approach each other in a curious, but unbiased way. They often have questions as to why certain children are of a different color, or are dressed differently, but they do not tend to have preconceived ideas regarding children of other nationalities, races, or religions. Often the negative or derogatory remarks that some youngsters make seem to be very similar to those that they have heard their parents make at home.

Many parents are interested in learning how they can foster respect for people of other religions, races, and cultures. One obvious way to do this is by setting a good example for your child. Merely telling your child that she should respect people who are different is not enough, especially if you turn around and treat handicapped persons, or persons of other races or religions, as though they are inferior. Your appropriate actions must accompany your words in transmitting a meaningful message to her.

Three-and-a-half-year-old Tim Hammond, who had just started nursery school, asked his father the following question one evening while they were playing ball together: "Why is Johnny black?" Mr. Hammond asked Tim who Johnny was, and Tim told his father that Johnny was a boy in his class at nursery school. In a very calm and matter-of-fact way, Mr. Hammond said that Johnny's family had originally come from a different part of the world from their family and that this was the explanation for the fact that they had different color skin. He went on to say that all people are different and unique in certain ways. "Daddy is tall, and Mommy is short, Grandpa is fatter than Grandma, and some people have blue eyes, while others have brown eyes."

Tim's father concluded by saying that a person's skin color is just one of many differences that make each person unique, and that although each person in the world is different, they are all very similar. Mr. Hammond's answer was easy for his son to understand, and seemed to satisfy Tim's curiosity.

Parents can take advantage of natural opportunities to explain something about not only racial but religious differences, and convey to their child a respect for these differences. Three-year-old Maegan came from a home in which religious training in Catholicism had been stressed by her parents. From the time she was a year old, Maegan's parents had taught her words like "God," "heaven," and "hell," and had taken her to church with them every Sunday. One Sunday morning when Maegan and her family were walking to the corner church, Maegan spotted a little boy whom she recognized.

The little boy, dressed in shorts and an old T-shirt, was riding his tricycle, and was obviously not headed for church services. Maegan wondered why, and asked her mother the following question: "Mommy, why doesn't Jerry Stein go to church on Sunday? Is he bad?"

Maegan's mother explained that not all people have the same religion and that there are Catholics, Jews, Moslems, Protestants, and so forth. "We all worship differently," she said, "and although our family goes to worship services on Sunday, Jewish people go to services on a different day of the week." She went on to explain that even though people have different beliefs and different styles of worship and conducting their lives, this is personal choice, and everyone is entitled to his or her own beliefs.

This parent did not underplay the difference that her preschool child picked up on, but used the observations her daughter made to help her learn more about religion. Young children usually regard religion from a very self-centered viewpoint, thinking that everyone else has the same religion that they do. When questions about religious practices arise, it can be healthy to make the child aware that there is more than one religion, and that people of a different religion are not "bad" or inferior—just different.

Youngsters are not only quick to notice racial and religious differences, they are also quick to recognize differences in people's dress and customs. Mr. and Mrs. Fowler and their daughter, Sandie, were invited to a new neighbor's home for dinner. Their neighbors, now American citizens, were originally from India, and they had promised to cook a traditional Indian meal. When the Fowlers arrived, they were delighted to find their new neighbor clad in a traditional sari, and a vast assortment of Indian rice and vegetable dishes set on the table.

Sandie was obviously puzzled by all of this, and she was unusually quiet during dinner. At one point during the meal, she leaned across the table to her mother and asked, "Mommy, why is that lady dressed so funny, and why aren't we having any meat?" Mrs. Fowler, somewhat embarrassed by her daughter's comments, nevertheless went on to explain that their new neighbors came from a country where people dress differently, and where many people do not eat meat. She told her daughter that in every country people have their own customs, just as Americans do, and that this is what makes each country special. Sandie seemed pleased with this explanation, and was quite talkative about her new friend's unusual customs.

It is not uncommon for children who have grown up in homes where there is prejudice toward different races, religions, or even economic classes to convey this prejudice toward their peers at nursery school, play groups, or social gatherings. It is important to consider how you would handle a situation in which your child came home crying from the park because she was picked on by one or two of her peers for being "different."

Parents of children who have been verbally tormented by other youngsters often have similar reactions. A common initial reaction among parents is one of anger, and they may fight prejudice with prejudice by making a derogatory remark about their child's playmate that is aimed at the youngster's racial background or religious affiliation. This reaction accomplishes nothing except to perpetuate prejudice. Parents who resort to fighting bigoted remarks from others with bigoted remarks in return are setting a poor example for their youngster.

To make a sincere effort to overcome prejudice, people have to avoid fighting prejudice with prejudice. This is not always easy, since it may be difficult for parents to know how to react to these situations except through the gut reaction of anger. Stopping and thinking for a moment often makes it clear how to handle this type of situation. Reassure your child and explain that there are some people in this world who do not respect the differences between people. One parent told her daughter, "Don't worry about what Randy said. If he calls you another name tomorrow, try to ignore him, since he is being very inconsiderate of you. Daddy and I don't act like Randy, and hope that you will not call him names. It is important to be nice to people, no matter how they look, or what their religion or background is. Everybody deserves respect."

Explaining to your child that there are some people who do not respect her rights, feelings, and so forth, but that you do not do the same, not only teaches her respect for others and their differences, but also prepares her for future interactions of a similar nature. Unfortunately for all of us, prejudice exists in many societies on different levels. In your discussions with your child, it is important not to behave as though the obvious differences that she recognizes for herself do not exist. When appropriate, emphasize how people are alike, since this will help her to learn that although every human being on this earth is completely unique, we are all similar in many ways. Try to instill in your child a positive feeling toward all mankind, and a healthy respect for differences in people. If all children were taught this at a very early age, it would be bound to have a positive effect upon human relations.

TALKING TO YOUR CHILD ABOUT DEATH

Death is often one of the hardest topics to deal with, for adults as well as children. Parents often wonder about the age at which a child is capable of understanding the concept of death. There is no hard and fast rule, since the level of understanding varies from child to child. Youngsters under the age of about three usually have a very difficult time understanding the concept of death, although they may frequently use words such as "kill," "murder," "dead," and "died" in their play or conversations. Even an older preschool child will have trouble understanding the meaning of death, and may think of death in the sense of a person leaving town, disappearing, or simply going away.

Questions About Death

Preschoolers do not usually begin to ask questions about death until the Preschool 3 phase, although questions may arise at any time. A young child who is curious about death often wants simple answers and facts geared to her concrete level of thinking. She may want to know where people go after they die, where they are now, how they go there, and whether they will come back again. These kinds of questions often surprise parents and seem strange or silly to them. To a young child who knows little about the meaning of death, these questions represent her genuine curiosity and concerns, given her limited knowledge and experience.

Answering Questions About Death

Some parents avoid giving simple, truthful answers, and describe death to a child as being in "a deep sleep" or "asleep forever." Unfortunately, this may result in a child's becoming afraid to go to bed for fear of not waking up, or may result in bad dreams. It is better to describe death in terms of the following: A person or a pet simply got very old, weak, or sick, could not keep going, and couldn't get better again. Tell the child that every effort was made to keep this person or pet alive, but even the doctors and nurses could not help.

If you are religious, your beliefs about life after death may be helpful in explaining death to your child. However, if you have never before discussed religion with your child, she may be even more confused by a religiously oriented explanation.

Mrs. Brewster, who had not previously brought up the topic of religion, responded to her child's questions about where Aunt Hilda went after she died by telling him that she went to heaven. "Will I go to heaven, too, when I die?" her son demanded to know. To this Mrs. Brewster replied that if he were a good boy, he, too, would go to heaven like Aunt Hilda.

For two weeks this little boy became increasingly difficult to manage. He broke his parents' rules, was mean to his younger brother, and did the opposite of what his mother and father wanted him to do. Finally, his parents sat down together to discuss their son's behavior and try to figure out why he had turned into such a "terror."

After ruling out other unusual occurrences, it finally dawned on Mrs. Brewster that her discussion of death might have disturbed her son in some way. After exploring this possibility with him, she realized that he had been behaving as poorly as he possibly could so he would not die. He believed that being a good boy meant that he would die and go immediately to heaven like his aunt Hilda. Once Mrs. Brewster understood the motivation for his bad behavior, she explained to her son that he would not die for a "very, very, very long time." Gradually his behavior returned to normal.

Introducing additional abstract concepts into a discussion of death can, in some cases, confuse a child and produce further anxiety. A preschool child is not equipped to comprehend anything but limited explanations of death geared to her level. Offering too many facts or details at once is not a good idea. What you tell her and how much you tell her will largely depend upon her level of comprehension, how much she appears to want to know by her questions, and the particular circumstances that prompt her questions or your explanations.

How the Death of Someone Close Affects the Child

Children have different reactions to the death of someone with whom they have been close. Some accept it readily and matter-of-factly. Others may be very disturbed at the death of a pet, relative, parent, or sibling. Each child will react to the loss in her own unique way, depending upon factors such as her age, understanding, and relationship with the deceased. Quite often children show symptoms of depression, withdrawal, clinginess toward the remaining parent, loss of appetite, overaggressiveness, fearfulness, or loss of interest in daily activities. During the period of adjustment following the death of someone close, it is also not uncommon for a child to behave as though nothing unusual has happened for days, weeks, or even months, and then suddenly fall apart.

You must exercise great patience and understanding when informing your youngster of the death of someone she has formed a close emotional attachment to. Upon learning that someone close to her has died, there is a good chance that your child will express concern over the possibility of your death or her own death. It is best to be truthful but cautious in giving explanations, knowing that your child will fear being left alone.

In the event that your child asks you if, or when, you will die, you might say something like this: "Yes, I will die, but not for many, many, many years. Most people do not die until they are very, very old." A similar response should suffice if she asks questions about her own death. The emphasis should be upon "many," and "very old," so that your child's anxieties will be lessened.

Youngsters quite often feel that death is reversible. They believe that their parents are capable of righting any situation. When they are told that this is not so, they may get angry and even refuse to believe this fact. Learning that their parents cannot fix every situation, and bring a dead pet or person back to life, can make even the most secure child feel somewhat insecure.

If a child's parent has died, the youngster may also feel anger and resentment toward the dead parent. Perhaps believing that the deceased parent is all-powerful and could have done anything, including coming back to life, she may feel that her parent wanted to die and abandon her. Despite repeated explanations that this is not the case by the parent who remains, a child may continue to believe this for some time.

Preschool children sometimes have feelings of guilt after the death of a close family member, such as a parent or a sibling. In the past they may have experienced feelings of resentment or been openly antagonistic toward that person, and even hoped that the person would die or go away. The person's actual death may be misconstrued by the child as the realization of her hopes, thoughts, or wishes, or punishment for her poor behavior. This can be a terrible burden for any child to bear. Therefore, since it is not unusual for preschool children to believe that their wishes and thoughts can make actual events come true, it is important to make it clear that the child in no way is responsible for or prompted the person's death.

Helping Your Child Adjust

After a death of a person to whom a child has been particularly attached, she will need love and reassurance to help her cope with her feelings and adjust to such a great loss. She will also need opportunities to express her feelings freely. Parents may themselves be grieving and depressed following a death in the family, but their child's feelings should be acknowledged. Patience, love, and understanding from you are most important following the death of someone your child loved.

In the event that someone close to your child dies, it is beneficial for her to see "normal" amounts of grief being expressed. This will make her aware of the fact that the person (or pet) was loved and that now that the person is gone, those people that loved the deceased are unhappy and affected by the loss. Expressing grief is a healthy reaction following death, and a child will benefit from seeing this natural part of life. It would not be wise to try to hide grief reactions from your child, but allowing a very young child to witness intense expressions of grief is of no benefit, and may be extremely upsetting and frightening.

As to whether or not to take a young child to a funeral, there are no clear-cut answers. A young child under the age of three may be very frightened by such an experience, so it is probably best to spare toddlers, younger preschool children, and perhaps even older preschool children from this experience, depending, of course, upon how well you think that your child can handle it. However, if you feel that your older preschool child is emotionally capable of attending a funeral, and that this experience will help her adjust to the person's death, then do not hesitate to take her with you.

Besides offering your youngster reassurance and plenty of opportunities to express her feelings, it is important to let her know that the dead person or pet could never be completely replaced. Also tell her that it will probably take a long time before she adjusts to the absence or the feeling of missing the person or pet. Memories of a person or pet should be cherished and can be kept alive through discussions and by keeping pictures or mementos. Removing every reminder of a loved one or immediately rushing out to replace a child's dead pet with another is not advisable. In essence, this would be denying the person's or pet's existence as well as their importance to her. The best way to help her adjust to a loss is to enable her to express her feelings and give her ample time to work through her grief while providing emotional support, comfort, and reassurance.

PREPARED PARENTHOOD CHECK LIST

MOTHER	FATHER	UNDERSTANDING YOUR CHILD'S DEVELOPMENT
——	——	Does your child seem almost too secure and overly confident in her abilities? Despite this, does she seem insecure underneath?
——	——	Can you give examples illustrating how your child's awareness of her body and herself has increased?
——	——	Do you see evidence that your child is identifying with you to a greater extent than in previous phases?
——	——	Are you aware of what part you will play in helping your child outgrow the notion of having the parent of the opposite sex to herself, and develop a more realistic idea of family relationships?
——	——	Is your child, like most children her age, showing more evidence of having a conscience?
——	——	What evidence do you see that your youngster is becoming more social, especially as regards other children her age?
——	——	In what ways is your child's ability to perceive, think, and reason becoming more sophisticated?
——	——	Your child's "why" questions are a testimony to her growing curiosity and interest in understanding what makes things happen. How often does she approach you wanting to know, "Why"?
——	——	Make a list of all of the words your child uses that refer to time and space in the course of half an hour. Are you aware of how her awareness of time and space has rapidly expanded?
——	——	Does your child have any "magical" beliefs?
——	——	Do you see evidence that your child is trying to separate reality from fantasy? Is she having any trouble with this?
——	——	Now that your youngster has a more extensive vocabulary and command of language, have you noticed her doing more rhyming, joking, creative storytelling, and questioning?
——	——	Are you helping your child learn new words?
——	——	Does your child seem to enjoy using "bad" or crude language and "toilet talk"?
——	——	Have you heard your preschooler boasting and bragging?
——	——	Are you able to see signs of improvement in nearly every area of gross motor activity?
——	——	What evidence do you see that your child is trying hard to perfect her skill with her hands and fingers?

941

Preschool 3

— — Does your child enjoy drawing? Have you been giving her plenty of opportunities to engage in this activity?

— — Are you providing your child with ample opportunities to play with other children now that playing with her friends has become more important as well as easier for her?

— — Have you noticed that your youngster's activities are becoming more goal-directed, and that she needs less help from you than before in carrying out play activities?

— — Does your preschooler take personal pride in her constructions and "creations"? Do you praise her finished products and display them in your home?

— — Has your child's dramatic play and use of materials become increasingly imaginative?

— — Is your child better able to stick with a certain toy or activity for longer periods of time than before?

BASIC CARE

— — Do you realize how much more adept your child has become in the areas of eating, bathing, dressing, and grooming?

— — Have you switched your child to a "youth" or regular bed?

— — Does your preschooler occasionally wet the bed at night?

— — Are you aware of the problem of enuresis and how to deal with it?

FAMILY FEELINGS AND CONCERNS

— — What are some of the ways in which you are transmitting your values and moral standards to your child?

— — Does your child occasionally lie to you? How do you handle situations in which you know she is telling untruths?

— — Has your youngster developed a fear of bodily injury or a fear of death?

— — Is your preschooler quick to notice differences in people? Are you trying to teach her to respect differences in people?

— — Has your child asked any questions about death? If so, have you been truthful in answering them?

Health Care Guide

Contents for Health Care Guide

YOUR CHILD'S MEDICINE CHEST

Many parents find it is useful to have some common health care supplies at home. It is very important to emphasize that medicines or treatments should not be given to your child without first seeking the advice of your physician. See page 946 for a discussion of why this is so important. The following list of health care aids can be obtained from most pharmacies or retail stores. Discuss this list with your doctor. He or she will be able to recommend additions or modifications.

General First Aid Supplies:

Supply of bandages of different sizes (commercially available Band-Aids are most convenient)
Absorbent cotton
Gauze pads
Nasal aspirator and medicine dropper (for clearing the nose during colds or giving nose drops if recommended by your doctor)
Tweezers
Antiseptic (if recommended by your doctor)
Ice bag (for bumps and sprains—not for high fevers)
Petroleum jelly (Vaseline)

Reducing a High Fever:

Thermometer
Children's aspirin (St. Joseph's, Bayer, etc.) or aspirin substitute (Tylenol, Datril, Liquiprin, or Tempra) as recommended by your doctor.

Treating a Poisoning:

Discuss with your doctor if he or she recommends keeping syrup of ipecac (to induce vomiting) or powdered activated charcoal (to bind up poison) in the home. Your doctor or health care professional will give you instructions for their use if they are indicated. These medications should be used with the advice of your physician.

Medicines Spoil

It is important to emphasize that some medications spoil when stored. Certain antibiotics in liquid form are especially unstable and should not be stored for prolonged periods. Throw out medications that are left over. If your child develops a mild illness, it is best to consult with your doctor and obtain the appropriate medications. Do not use old prescriptions to treat new symptoms.

Check with Your Doctor First

The basic and well child care you give your child will be a major factor in ensuring his health. Most medications that parents give their children are designed to reduce symptoms or make the child feel better if he becomes ill. Medications given improperly or for the wrong reasons, however, can do more harm than good.

It is important to take advantage of modern medicine. Your doctor is trained to take care of your child. During your well baby check-ups, or by phone, you should ask his or her advice about medications you have at home before you give them to your child. Many doctors recommend having on hand certain medications for treating common symptoms.

You should place extra emphasis on the importance of working together with your physician. This allows your doctor to assist you in providing the best possible care for your child.

RECOMMENDED SCHEDULE OF IMMUNIZATIONS AND TESTS FOR NORMAL INFANTS AND CHILDREN[1]

INFANCY	IMMUNIZATION OR TEST	DOCTOR OR CLINIC GIVING IMMUNIZATION	REACTIONS	DATE RECEIVED
2 months	DTP	_____	_____	_____
	TOPV	_____	_____	_____
4 months	DTP	_____	_____	_____
	TOPV	_____	_____	_____
6 months	DTP	_____	_____	_____
	TOPV (optional)[2]	_____	_____	_____
12 months	Tuberculin Test[3]	_____	_____	_____
TODDLERHOOD				
15 months	Measles, Rubella, Mumps[4]	_____	_____	_____
18 months	DTP	_____	_____	_____
	TOPV	_____	_____	_____
PRESCHOOL				
4–6 years	DTP	_____	_____	_____
	TOPV	_____	_____	_____
OTHER				
_____	_____	_____	_____	_____
_____	_____	_____	_____	_____
_____	_____	_____	_____	_____

Abbreviation: DTP: diphtheria and tetanus toxoids plus pertussis vaccine
TOPV: trivalent oral polio vaccine

[1] This schedule is based upon the recommendations of the American Academy of Pediatrics. Immunization schedules are subject to modification or supplementation with new information and research, since new vaccines may be added through the years. Your doctor will be able to advise you on the best schedule to meet your child's individual needs.

It is important to keep good records of your child's immunizations. Record the place where the immunization was received, the date, and any reactions to the immunization. If your doctor recommends additional immunizations to meet special needs in your community, record this information in the space provided under *Other*. DTP (Diphtheria, Tetanus, Pertussis)—sometimes also abbreviated DPT. TOPV (Trivalent Oral Polio Vaccine).

[2] The third dose of TOPV may be optional in some areas, depending upon the incidence of polio in that area.

[3] The tuberculin test is often repeated at one or two year intervals, but the frequency of repeated tests depends on the risk of exposure to tuberculosis in your area. Your doctor will advise you when repeat tests are appropriate. Record additional tests in the extra space provided.

[4] Immunizations for measles, rubella, and mumps may be given as measles-rubella or measles-rubella-mumps combined vaccines.

EMERGENCY REFERENCE LIST

Child's name: _____

Address _____

Phone _____

Parent's Name(s): Mother _____

Father _____

Parent's Work Phone: Mother _____

Father _____

Doctor: Name _____

Address _____

Phone _____

Poison Control Center Phone: Day _____

Night _____

Hospital: Name _____

Address _____

Phone _____

Nearest Emergency Room: _____

Phone _____

Local Emergency Phone Number (if available, e.g., 911): _____

Police: Phone _____

Fire Department: Phone _____

Pharmacy: Name _____

Phone _____

Person to be contacted if parents not available: Name _____

Phone _____

Current Medications: _____

Allergies: Medicine _____

Foods _____

Other _____

Illnesses: _____

_____

Other: _____

_____

SICK CHILD CHECK LIST

When your child is ill and you call your doctor, it is very helpful to know certain important facts concerning the child's condition. This information can be very useful to the doctor or nurse. Quickly go over the following check list so that you will have all the pertinent information on hand when you call your physician (see pages 118–21).

The major complaint is _____.
Temperature is _____.
Temperature has been elevated for _____ hours.
Child is _____ lethargic _____ restless _____ irritable.
Breathing is _____ normal _____ noisy _____ difficult _____ rapid _____ slow.
Child is _____ hoarse _____ coughing _____ sneezing.
Child's appetite is _____ good _____ bad. (He has skipped _____ feedings.)
Bowel movements are _____ normal _____ abnormal. (Color _____ consistency _____ odor _____ frequency _____)
Urination is _____ normal _____ abnormal. (Color _____ frequency _____ painful _____)
Child has vomited: force _____ amount _____ color _____ frequency _____.
Body movements are _____ normal _____ abnormal. (Twitching _____ stiffness _____ immobility _____ convulsions _____)
Appearance is _____ normal _____ flushed _____ pale _____ perspiring _____ rash. (Color _____ itchy _____ patchy _____ even _____)
There are signs of pain _____ crying _____ screaming _____ ear pain _____.
Eyes are _____ normal _____ watery _____ red _____ dull.

Medications or treatment already given: _____.

YOUR CHILD'S MEDICAL RECORD

Name _____ Date of Birth _____

Birth Weight _____ Apgar Score 1st_____ 2nd_____

Obstetrician _____ Pediatrician _____

Difficulties at Birth _____ none _____

_____ Type _____

Caesarean Delivery _____ yes _____ no

Premature Delivery _____ yes _____ no

Illnesses, Accidents, or Surgery During the First Year of Life:

	DATE		DATE
_____	_____	_____	_____
_____	_____	_____	_____
_____	_____	_____	_____
_____	_____	_____	_____

Illnesses, Accidents, or Surgery from 1–5 Years of Age:

	DATE		DATE
_____	_____	_____	_____
_____	_____	_____	_____
_____	_____	_____	_____
_____	_____	_____	_____

Allergies:

CAUSE	REACTION	MEDICATION OR PRECAUTION
_____	_____	_____
_____	_____	_____
_____	_____	_____

FEVER AND TAKING A TEMPERATURE

Most parents are familiar with taking their own temperature, but some become apprehensive when it comes to taking their baby's. Taking the temperature of a baby or young child is very easy. You should know how to take your child's temperature when you suspect illness. If you have never taken an infant's temperature, it is best to obtain practical instruction from a nurse or other health professional.

How to Take a Temperature

The only correct way to take a temperature is with a thermometer. Feeling the child's forehead will give you some idea of his temperature, but this technique is not an accurate way to measure the body temperature. The thermometer is an essential item to have in your child's medicine chest.

THE THERMOMETER. There are basically two types of thermometers: oral and rectal. The shape of the bulb is the only difference between these thermometers. The oral thermometer has a long thin bulb. The rectal thermometer has a round smooth bulb that is not as pointed as the oral type.This makes it easier to insert the thermometer in the rectum, because the round bulb slides in more easily without catching in the wall of the rectum.

The scale on rectal and oral types of thermometers is the same. The scale can be marked in degrees Fahrenheit (°F) or degrees Centigrade (°C). A long mark indicates each degree and the five spaces between each degree marked off by the short lines each represents a fifth of a degree (0.2°). Usually only the even numbered degrees are marked on Fahrenheit scales. Most thermometers commonly used by parents in the United States have °F scales and to avoid confusion we will use °F throughout the book; °F can be converted to °C by using the conversion table shown below.

Temperature Conversion Table

CENTIGRADE	FAHRENHEIT	CENTRIGRADE	FAHRENHEIT
35.0	95.0	38.6	101.4
35.1	95.4	38.8	101.8
35.4	95.7	39.0	102.2
35.6	96.1	39.2	102.5
35.8	96.4	39.4	102.9
36.0	96.8	39.6	103.2
36.2	97.1	39.8	103.6
36.4	97.5	40.0	104.0
36.6	97.8	40.2	104.3
36.8	98.2	40.4	104.7
37.0	98.6	40.6	105.1
37.2	98.9	40.8	105.4
37.4	99.3	41.0	105.8
37.6	99.6	41.2	106.1
37.8	100.0	41.4	106.5
38.0	100.4	41.6	106.8
38.2	100.7	41.8	107.2
38.4	101.1	42.0	107.6

The thermometer can be easily read by slowly rotating it until you can see the silver mercury (silver line) on the scale. The band of mercury will start from the bulb and go up to a certain point and stop. This is the thermometer's reading.

THREE WAYS TO TAKE THE TEMPERATURE. The three ways to take the temperature depend on where you place the thermometer: oral (in the mouth), rectal (in the anus or rectum), or axillary (under the arm). A rectal or oral thermometer can be used for all three methods. A rectal thermometer is preferred for taking rectal temperatures, since it usually slides in easier, although an oral thermometer can be used if inserted carefully into the rectum. An oral thermometer is usually preferred for oral and axillary temperatures.

Rectal or axillary temperatures are the preferred method for the infant. As the child gets older and it is easier to take the oral temperature, this method is usually preferred.

After cleaning the thermometer, the first step before taking the temperature is to *shake down* the thermometer. Hold the end of the thermometer (end away from bulb) and shake it. Using a quick snap of the wrist is usually the most effective way to accomplish this. Shake the thermometer until the mercury level is below 95° F. Then use one of the following methods that is best suited for your child.

Rectal method. Put some petroleum jelly (Vaseline) on the end of the thermometer to lubricate it for easy insertion into the rectum. Putting the baby or young child on his stomach on the dressing table or over your knee is the most common position. Sometimes laying the child on his side with the knees tucked to the chest works well. After trying to relax the child, gently insert the thermometer into the baby's rectum with light pressure so that it will slide in on its own. It should be approximately one inch into the rectum. If you find resistance, do not try to use force—STOP. The thermometer is probably stuck on the side of the rectum. Remove it and gently try again. Most parents find that it is very easy to insert the thermometer with a little practice. The nurse in the hospital after your delivery or during a well baby checkup can give you additional assistance if necessary.

Once the thermometer is in the rectum, try to keep the child calm and hold the thermometer gently in place for approximately two or three minutes. This is more than enough time to take a reading. If the baby is squirming and you cannot keep it in for a minute, you can probably get a fairly accurate reading in twenty to thirty seconds. Remove the thermometer, wipe it off with a tissue, and read the temperature from the scale.

Axillary (under the arm) method. The axillary (armpit) method is often useful in the young infant or older child who will not sit still or who fights the oral or rectal methods. After shaking down the thermometer, hold it under the baby's or child's arm. This is done by holding the arm against the chest wall so that the bulb of the thermometer is sandwiched between the arm and the chest wall. It usually is best to read the thermometer after three to four minutes. This method is occasionally preferred over the rectal temperature for the toddler since it is often more easily tolerated by the child.

Oral method. The oral method is preferred when the child is old enough to cooperate, usually in the preschool years. After shaking down the thermometer, insert it under the tongue and wait for two to four minutes. Be sure that the child keeps his mouth closed.

Normal Temperature Versus Fever

The normal temperature for an adult is 98.6° F. This is the temperature that is usually maintained by the body. The normal temperature of an infant and young child is also 98.6° F, but the temperature is more easily influenced by daily activities. A normal, healthy baby's temperature is not fixed at 98.6° F. It goes up and down, depending on the time of day and what the child is doing at a given instant. Thus, the "normal" temperature is really a range of values.

In the morning the temperature is usually lower than in the afternoon. Activity such as violent crying or rapid movements can cause the temperature to rise. Younger toddlers can also show normal variations in body temperature. After strenuous play the body temperature may reach 99° or even 100° F. The preschool child's temperature is becoming more carefully regulated and is less influenced by activity. The older child is less likely to show significant rises in body temperature after activity.

It is unusual for the temperature to climb above 101° F because of increased activity by the infant or excessive play by the young child. Temperatures above 100° to 101° F indicate that the child is running a fever. Smaller increases in temperature above 98.6° F may reflect increased activity in a young child, but could also indicate that the child is running a low grade fever. Babies often do not run high temperatures when they are ill (see page 955). A temperature of more than 100° F, especially in the first few months of life or when the child looks ill, should be brought to your doctor's attention.

Treatment of High Fever Until You Can Get Medical Assistance

Children between the ages of one to seven years often have a tendency to run very high fevers when they are ill (see page 505). It is best to discuss the treatment of high fever with your doctor. He or she will recommend an appropriate treatment for your child. Remember never to give medicines to a child, especially to a baby less than six months of age, without first checking with your doctor.

In the rare event that you cannot get in touch with your doctor and you have not previously discussed how to treat a high fever, the following guidelines should be of assistance in reducing the fever until you can contact a doctor.

The fever can be brought down by giving the child children's aspirin or children's aspirin substitutes (Tylenol, Tempra, Liquiprin, etc.). The proper doses for a given age are clearly marked on the container. Do not give the infant or young child adult medications since these preparations are much stronger.

It is also helpful to take a few simple steps to allow the excess body heat to escape from the body and thus lower the temperature. It is best not to overdress or cover the child with a heavy blanket. This traps the body heat. Undressing the child and covering him with a light sheet in bed will help allow the heat to escape without overchilling.

Gently rubbing an arm or leg for a few minutes with water at room temperature will help bring the blood to the surface and further cool the body as the water evaporates. It is often convenient to put some water into a bowl and use a washcloth (wrung out) to wipe off the child's body. Then rub the back, chest, and other arm and leg, one after the other. The reason for not rubbing or wetting a larger body area all at once is that this may cause too rapid a heat loss and lead to excessive chilling. It is also important not to use cold water, since this will shrink the blood vessels in the skin and decrease the body's ability to release the heat.

Occasionally the temperature will rise very rapidly even before you are aware of it. High fevers can sometimes cause a convulsion (see pages 984–85). In most cases you will be able to keep the fever under control until you contact your doctor.

COLDS, EAR INFECTIONS, AND COMMON RESPIRATORY ILLNESSES

Colds, ear infections, and respiratory illnesses are commonly seen in the first five years of life. Many of these illnesses are fought off by the child's natural defenses against disease. These illnesses are self-limiting in nature except in rare situations.

Colds

The cold is the most common illness during the first few years of life. Babies usually catch colds from exposure to other infected individuals. It is important to protect your baby from exposure to other adults or children who are ill. Colds are also very common in toddlerhood and preschool children. They are more prevalent in the winter and spring. Undue exposure to sick individuals at this time should be avoided.

CAUSES OF THE COMMON COLD. The common cold is caused by a virus. Viruses are very small germs. There are over one hundred types of cold viruses, mainly called rhinoviruses. This makes it almost impossible to develop one vaccine to protect against colds.

A cold virus usually infects the upper respiratory tract (nose and throat) and produces a mild inflammation, causing a clear nasal discharge and sometimes a mild sore throat. The body can fight off the cold in a few days and often no other symptoms occur. The duration and the symptoms of the cold depend partly on the type of virus and on the defenses of the body.

The mild illness produced by a cold virus is believed to lower the body's resistance to infection, especially in the nose and throat. Other germs and bacteria that can cause respiratory infections often inhabit these regions of the body, especially during the winter and spring months. These organisms are usually held in check by the body's defenses and do no harm. When the defenses are lowered by a mild cold, these bacteria can begin to multiply and possibly lead to other infections and respiratory illnesses: pneumonia, bronchitis, sinus infections, sore throats, croup, laryngitis, and ear infections.

A cold can set the stage for these other infections. This is why it is important to keep the infant or child with a cold away from individuals who might be ill and spreading other possible sources of infection.

COLDS DURING INFANCY. Colds are so common that it is very likely that your baby will have at least one cold during the first year of life. Colds in infants produce different symptoms from those in older children. The infant usually gets a mild cold with some sneezing or a stuffy nose. Infants do not usually run a high fever with colds and may not even develop a fever.

The most obvious symptoms of the infant's cold are his runny or stuffy nose. Sometimes the mucus around the nose forms bubbles as the baby breathes. In many cases the baby seems fine and does not mind his bubbly or runny nose. Sometimes the nose gets congested or plugged with mucus so that the baby can only breathe through his mouth. This may cause him to cry or become fussy, especially when he has to use his mouth to suck, since he will not be able to take in air and eat at the same time.

Mucus in the nose that is irritating the baby and making it difficult to breathe can be gently removed with a nasal rubber syringe. The syringe is used by squeezing the bulb, inserting the tip in a nostril, and then slowly releasing the bulb to suck up the mucus. This technique can alleviate most minor cases of stuffiness. Occasionally the baby develops more severe congestion. Your doctor may want to prescribe some nose drops to use before feeding so that the baby can breathe while eating. Sometimes oral medications are recommended.

Most colds in infancy are mild, but some can become more severe. It is important to recognize that a baby can be sick without a fever. If the infant looks sick with a cold, or develops a bad or wheezy cough, you should contact your doctor, even in the absence of a fever. This is especially true in the first three to four months of life.

COLDS DURING TODDLERHOOD AND PRESCHOOL. Some children have the same types of mild colds during toddlerhood and preschool that they had in infancy, but others will have a tendency to develop high fevers with their colds. The temperature may suddenly shoot up to 102° to 104° F. In some cases the child seems restless or sick while in others he is just a little flushed.

The symptoms of a cold during this time can vary greatly. Some colds last only one day, while others linger for a week or more. Runny or stuffy noses are common, but occasionally the child just appears flushed and does not want to eat. You should not become overly alarmed if your child suddenly develops a high fever with the cold, since this is common at this time. It is important, however, to contact your doctor when the child runs a high fever and/or looks sick, because occasionally the child has a more vigorous infection (see page 957).

It is not clear why toddlerhood and preschool children get more colds and complications from colds than at other times, but they do. Do not be alarmed if your child has five to eight colds per year, since this is about average in the northern United States. Taking simple measures to help avoid colds and providing some comfort and relief of symptoms after the cold develops is about all parents can do to take care of this mild illness.

It is not common, but some children develop a convulsion with the sudden onset of a high fever (see pages 984–85). If other members of your family had seizures with fever as a child, or if your child has a tendency to run high fevers, you should discuss this with your doctor. It is helpful to make a more vigorous attempt to keep the temperature down during this sensitive period to try to prevent a convulsion.

HELPING PREVENT COLDS. There is no generally accepted treatment that can cure or shorten the length of a cold. Colds usually come and go no matter what you do. Although there is nothing for parents to do to cure the cold once it is started, there are some preventive measures that they can take to help maintain their children's natural resistance to colds.

A good diet. Good nutrition with adequate food and vitamin intake ensures the child of having the necessary building blocks to maintain his resistance against disease. Deficiencies in certain vitamins or other food products may increase the susceptibility to colds or raise the chances for developing such complications as pneumonia or bronchitis. A proper diet will ensure good nutrition and thus maintain a strong body. It is not clear whether excess amounts of some vitamins can help prevent colds. There is some preliminary evidence that vitamin C may help prevent colds in adults, but this has not been satisfactorily shown in children. Providing good nutrition is the first line of defense against the cold.

Helping natural defenses in the nose and throat. The moist mucous linings of the nose and throat provide a protective barrier against germs and contain antibodies against certain organisms. Living in a very dry environment can dry up the mucus in the nose and respiratory system. This reduces the effectiveness of the mucous membrane in resisting infection. Rooms that are kept hot and dry in the winter may dry out the nose and throat. Keeping the humidity in the home around 35 to 45 percent can help maintain the body's natural defenses against colds. Avoid keeping the temperature above 70° F; air above this temperature usually becomes much drier.

Avoiding exposure. Many colds are caught when an individual is exposed to others who are sick. If a family member comes down with a cold, take precautions. Try not to expose the child to the sick person directly. Evidence suggests that colds are often transmitted by direct contact with the sick person. Special care should be given to washing eating utensils. A good tip is to have the sick person use disposable utensils and tissues and avoid handling the children.

Emotional Stress. Tension and stress are believed by many psychiatrists to wear down the body's defenses against colds. Although this is difficult to prove, it is possible that increased anxiety or stress may affect some body functions that resist colds. It is well known that these factors can cause diarrhea, cold clammy hands, increased heart rate, and other changes in body function. It is not unreasonable to suspect that they might also alter the body's defenses against colds.

HELPING RELIEVE COLD SYMPTOMS. Colds will run their course of a few days to a week no matter what you do. Once the cold is caught, all parents can do is to help relieve the symptoms and make the child comfortable.

Many doctors recommend plenty of fluids and as much rest as possible as the best way to treat the common cold. The child's appetite often decreases during illness. Thus, fluids should be encouraged. As long as the child is taking them well, it is not harmful if he does not eat his regular diet for a time while he is sick. See pages 961–62 for guidelines concerning diet during illness.

It is often difficult to keep a young child in bed. Do not force the child to lie down if he resists, since the excitement will only tire him out. Parents often find that when a child is not feeling well, he will usually take it easy on his own. If the child refuses to relax and remain in bed, rather than force him to rest, try to occupy him with quiet or less-strenuous activities.

It is advisable to avoid putting the child through extremes of temperature. Keeping the room at a comfortable 68° to 70° F is adequate. It is not necessary to over-dress the child or put many blankets on him. This will only overheat him and cause excessive perspiration and possibly chilling.

If the air in your home is too dry, your doctor may recommend adding moisture with a humidifier or a vaporizer to help relieve congestion in the nose and throat.

This is especially useful in the winter with the dry air produced by most central heating systems. Extra moisture in the air can be helpful in treating a cough, especially croup (see pages 959–60). If the child develops a high fever with his cold, you should try to reduce the fever. Your doctor will give you advice for treating a high fever (see pages 953–54).

Stuffy nose. The treatment of a stuffy nose with a nasal aspirator (syringe) is discussed on page 955; medications that are taken by mouth can also relieve congestion and may be recommended by your doctor. Occasionally your doctor may recommend nose drops to relieve congestion. Children often rebel against nose drops. In situations where the nose and sinuses are so congested that they cannot drain on their own, the nose drops are very helpful in allowing drainage. When the eustachian tube (an opening from the back of the throat to the inside of the ear) is blocked by congestion, nose drops can help to open the tube. This is especially important if the child has an ear infection. A doctor will often recommend using nose drops for an infant or child who is very upset and cannot breathe, or for a baby who has difficulty nursing because he cannot breathe through his nose while sucking.

Nose drops come in two major types. One type contains medications that actually shrink the tissues in the nose, allowing the child to breathe more easily. The effect of the medication gradually wears off and the linings of the nose swell again. If used in excess, these medications can irritate the mucous membrane in the nose. It is best to use these drops only for the types of conditions described above and only with the advice of your doctor. It is not advisable to treat minor congestion that is not bothering the child. The other type of nose drops help kill some of the germs in the nose that can cause secondary infections and thus eventually allow easier breathing. These drops do not shrink the linings of the nose and thus will not rapidly improve breathing.

Administering nose drops is easy, if the child is co-operative. Try to clean out some of the surface mucus from the nose to allow the drops to get further back into the nose. Have the child lie on his back or hold him and tilt his head back as you carefully insert the drops. Keep the head in this position for a short time, if possible, to give the drops a chance to start working.

Never use the drops more often than recommended (usually no sooner than every four hours) and do not continue using nose drops for more than a week without checking with a physician.

The cough of a cold. A cough is the body's natural way of bringing up mucus or other material that is blocking or irritating the airway. Medications to treat the cough do not cure it. Some medicines simply suppress the mechanism in the body that causes the cough. You should not rush to treat a minor cough occurring at infrequent intervals with cough suppressants since this type of cough is productive and helps to clean out the mucus and pus in the throat. When a cough becomes so frequent and persistent that it is wearing the child out or interfering with sleep, a cough suppressant may be needed. However, you should discuss this with your doctor, who will recommend an appropriate treatment (see page 946).

Ear Infections

Ear infections are common in young infants and children and often accompany a cold or respiratory tract infection. During the first five years of life, the ears are much more sensitive to infection. It is important to learn to recognize the signs of an ear infection as early as possible, so that proper therapy can be initiated to help prevent chronic infections from developing.

RECOGNIZING AN EAR INFECTION. It may be difficult to diagnose an ear infection in a young baby who cannot directly complain to you. The following signs should make you suspicious that an ear infection may be present: increased prolonged crying, rubbing the ear, pain when the ear is touched, and discharge from the ear. Older children usually complain of pain in the ear or they can be seen rubbing or scratching it. Fever may also accompany the infection. In external ear infections redness around the outer part of the ear can also be seen.

In some cases, the ear infection causes pain behind the ear (the mastoid bone area). This is not always an indication of a mastoid infection (infection in the mastoid bone behind the ear) or a more severe ear infection. The pain is just localizing to this area in some children. Chronic mastoid infections or abscesses are complications that can occur with ear infections, but these conditions take time to develop and are rarely seen with an initial ear infection.

Ear infections are recognized by their symptoms. Pain in the ear is often the main symptom. A child may also experience a temporary decrease or loss of hearing during an infection. Occasionally ear infections cause very little in the way of symptoms in the beginning. Your first clue of the infection may be pus on the pillow in the morning. This is not common, but you should be aware that it does happen.

CONTACT YOUR DOCTOR. If you think your child has an ear infection, contact your doctor's office as soon as possible. Most ear infections occur in the middle ear behind the eardrum. In many ear infections pus builds up behind the drum and can easily be seen by the doctor during an examination. An ear inflammation resulting from viral or allergic causes can produce a clear fluid discharge behind the drum, which can also be seen by examination.

Prompt medical treatment of ear infections can prevent chronic infections and complications from developing. Abscess formation and mastoid infections are rare if medical treatment is properly obtained. The doctor will determine if a medication is indicated. Modern drugs can effectively stop bacterial infections and prevent complications, especially if treatment is started early in the course of the infection.

The importance of seeking medical help early in treating ear infections cannot be overemphasized. Do not try to treat these infections at home without the advice of your doctor. Allowing an ear infection to go untreated can lead to a chronic infection and even permanent hearing loss (page 1019).

Sore Throats

Sore throats are common in childhood and can be caused by several agents. The most common cause of sore throats is a virus. Viral sore throats are usually caused by the cold viruses, but other viruses can also produce sore throats. There is no treatment for this viral illness and it runs its course no matter what you do. Occasionally a viral sore throat develops into croup or laryngitis. These conditions are described below.

Bacteria are the second most common cause of sore throats. A "strep throat" is a bacterial infection caused by a type of streptococcal bacteria. It is important to diagnose strep throats. Strep throat infections, especially if left untreated, can occasionally lead to the development of other illnesses such as rheumatic fever (page 1034) or a kidney problem (glomerulonephritis, page 1029). Your doctor will treat a strep throat with antibiotics to prevent these complications from developing.

A child who develops a sore throat should be examined by his doctor. Since it is not always possible to diagnose a strep infection by simply examining the throat, the doctor or nurse will often take a throat culture. A throat culture is the best way to determine if the child has a strep infection and can usually be done in the doctor's office. It then takes approximately twenty-four hours to get the result.

In most cases the culture is negative since the child usually has a viral sore throat, which requires no further treatment. If the culture is positive, your doctor will treat the strep throat with antibiotics.

Sore throats can also be caused by allergic or irritative factors. A good medical examination is the best way to diagnose these conditions (see Allergies on pages 970–74).

Flu

Flu is viral illness characterized by different symptoms. Fever, headache, nausea, respiratory illness, and muscle aches are some of the more common signs of flu. The disease is often epidemic in character and tends to occur in cycles.

There are several types of flu, each of which causes slightly different symptoms. Mild cases of the flu are indistinguishable from the common cold, but many cases of flu produce a more severe illness than the usual cold. Your doctor can advise you if your child should be immunized against a particular type of flu.

Laryngitis

Laryngitis is an infection or inflammation of the larynx (voice box). It causes hoarseness and occasionally complete loss of the voice. If the infection is bacterial, your doctor will prescribe an appropriate antibiotic. Rest and supportive care are important in fighting off the infection.

Coughs

Coughing is a symptom of many problems and illnesses. Infections or allergic reactions in the respiratory passages can cause a cough. Objects or food caught in the throat can also be a cause. Most common coughs can be easily recognized as mild and usually clear rapidly. If the cough is severe or persistent, you should seek medical advice. Croup causes a special bark-like cough. Since croup is fairly common and can be rather alarming to new parents, it is discussed in more detail below.

Croup

Croup refers to several illnesses that produce a readily recognizable barking cough associated with difficulty in breathing as the result of obstruction of the airway (breathing passage). The blockage in the airway is usually at the level of the voice box (larynx). There may be a bluish color around the lips and a widening of the nostrils during each breath. The child will often look scared. It is not hard to recognize croup.

SPASMODIC (MIDNIGHT) CROUP. Spasmodic or midnight croup is the most common type of croup. It occurs most commonly in the winter months and between two to four years of age. As the name implies, this form of croup often occurs at night. The usual history is that a child develops a mild cold with a runny nose and slight sore throat. He may go to bed without any problem but then suddenly awaken in the middle of the night with the barking cough and other signs of croup. The child will be very frightened and worried about his difficulty in breathing and hoarse voice. He usually has a low grade fever of 100° to 101° F.

The important thing for parents to do is to remain calm and try to comfort the frightened child. Bring him into the bathroom, close the door, turn on the hot water in the sink and tub, and let steam build up in the room. The steam that builds up will help relieve the symptoms and allow the child to breathe more easily. In most cases he will calm down and his cough will subside along with the breathing difficulties. The symptoms should clear in about thirty minutes. If they do not, your child should be evaluated by a doctor immediately, since you may be dealing with a more severe form of croup that requires emergency medical attention.

When the symptoms clear, the child can be put back to bed and a vaporizer with either hot or cold vapor should be used in his room. The next day he should be fine, with the exception of a mild cough and a hoarse voice. If your child develops croup, it is important to recognize that this condition may recur with his next cold. It will help to begin using a vaporizer as soon as the child shows signs of a new cold to help prevent the recurrence of croup.

MORE SEVERE FORMS OF CROUP. Most cases of croup clear with the steam treatment described above. Occasionally the croup is caused by acute epiglottitis or laryngotracheobronchitis. These causes of croup produce a more persistent problem. The child will develop the bark-like cough and difficulty breathing, but he often runs a higher fever (104° F). The child's breathing and cough will not improve after thirty minutes of steam treatment and he will continue to look sick and may have to lean forward to breathe. Your doctor must be notified immediately, since these persistent forms of croup need emergency medical treatment to keep the airway open. If you cannot reach your doctor, take the child immediately to the nearest hospital emergency room or medical facility.

These more serious forms of croup are usually caused by a bacterial infection and may require antibiotic treatment. Diphtheria was a major cause of serious croup many years ago, but this illness no longer is a common cause of croup since it is prevented by proper immunizations during childhood.

Most cases of croup are not serious and respond well to simple treatment, but some cases can be dangerous. If you are concerned about the seriousness of your child's croup, most doctors recommend that you call them. The doctor can assess the situation and advise you of the best course of action.

Tonsils and Adenoids

The tonsils and adenoids are located on the sides of the throat. They gradually enlarge in the young child until about ten years of age. After ten they gradually decrease in size. Tonsils and adenoids are part of the body's defense system against infection. These body tissues are part of the lymph system which helps ward off disease. The glands under the neck and in the armpits and groin that may swell with local infections are also part of this lymphatic system. When an infection such as a sore throat or cold occurs in the throat, the tonsils may swell or look inflamed. They are helping to stop the illness. This is their natural response.

In the past, tonsils and adenoids were blamed incorrectly for many illnesses and problems. Today it is only under very rare circumstances that these organs are removed. There is no reason to remove the tonsils in children with routine colds and sore throats. As discussed above, children during the toddlerhood and preschool years often have frequent colds each year. The presence of enlarged tonsils in a healthy child who gets several colds a year is no reason to remove them. Ear infections, frequent colds, and even recurrent tonsillitis (infection of the tonsils) are also not indications for removal of the tonsils, since medical management can successfully treat almost all cases of tonsillitis.

The tonsils can become very red and swollen when infected and occasionally have white patches on them. Many cases of tonsillitis are caused by streptococcal infections and should be seen by a doctor, since antibiotics are necessary to stop the infection and prevent complications from developing.

The adenoids are harder to see than the tonsils, since they are located far back on the top of the throat near where the nasal passage enters the throat. Adenoids also can become infected and enlarged like the tonsils. These conditions are treated medically today and it is only under very rare circumstances that the adenoids need to be removed surgically.

Pneumonia

Pneumonia is an infection in the lungs and can follow a cold. Pneumonia can be caused by bacteria, viruses, or other germs. Usually your baby's temperature will be very high (over 103° F). Chills, weakness, and cough are also common symptoms. Pneumonia can cause respiratory difficulty or rapid breathing. Some pneumonias persist as a mild cold for several weeks and go undetected. A high fever with signs of respiratory distress or a cold that appears to be lasting "too long" may indicate that pneumonia is developing. This condition should be evaluated and treated by your doctor.

Bronchitis

Bronchitis is an infection or irritation of the bronchial tubes that go into the lungs. It is most commonly caused by a cold that has spread down the bronchial tubes. The illness produces a dry cough and can occur with or after a cold. It can also cause chest pain, poor appetite, and fever. Most cases of bronchitis are mild and are treated like a regular cold. They usually go away by themselves. When the bronchitis is more severe, the child will look sick, have increased coughing, and/or run a temperature. Consult your doctor for advice. Sometimes it is necessary to treat more serious cases of bronchitis with medications. A young infant can have bronchitis even though he has no fever. A frequent cough will most likely be the most common symptom and should be brought to your doctor's attention.

DIET DURING ILLNESS

There is no best diet during illness. You must be flexible about your child's eating habits and tailor the diet to be appropriate to his needs. There are a few common dietary suggestions that may be used as guidelines. Your doctor is your best guide to diets during illness and will be able to add to or modify the following guidelines to suit your child.

Diet with a Cold or Fever

Some children eat normally during a mild cold and require no change in their diet. Others lose some of their appetite. This is common and should not cause undue concern. Supplementing the child's diet with fluids will be adequate until his appetite returns. Mucus is often aggravated by milk or formula and the child or infant may resist these liquids. Clear liquids as tolerated can be given. Mild decreases in appetite do not last for more than a few days.

A child who is running a fever from a cold or one of the contagious childhood diseases will probably lose much if not all of his appetite for solid foods during the time when his temperature is high. Do not try to force your child to eat. Giving plenty of fluids, such as fruit juices and water, is helpful. These drinks are usually tolerated by children and will help replace some of the body water lost by perspiration. Your doctor will be able to assist you in caring for your sick child and suggesting appropriate fluids to drink.

PROBLEMS WITH DIGESTION

Occasionally babies and young children have difficulties with digestion. Most of these difficulties are not persistent and occur infrequently. It is important to discuss your baby's difficulties with your doctor. Recurrent spitting up, vomiting, hiccoughs, gas, and stomach cramps can have many different causes. Digestive problems can be complex. Your doctor can help you try to determine the cause and eliminate it if possible.

The following brief discussion of a few of the common problems of digestion is presented to familiarize you with the kinds of situations that can arise. Do not attempt to diagnose or treat digestive problems on your own. Having some familiarity with the symptoms of these conditions should alert you to seek medical advice if they occur.

Vomiting or Spitting Up

Vomiting is familiar to most adults. If your child spits up his food, you must determine whether he is "really vomiting" or just spitting up some of his dinner. Many young infants spit up some of their feedings and this is not vomiting. The young infant's digestive system is not functioning as smoothly as an older child's. It is common for the stomach, when it is full, to let food flow back up to the mouth, since the ability to hold food down takes time to develop. If after the baby has eaten you squeeze or move him suddenly, you will notice that food is often spit up. During early infancy, bringing up breast milk or formula is common. Spitting up of most of the feeding or very regular bringing up of food should be brought to your doctor's attention.

Vomiting refers to the more forceful ejection of food from the mouth. Occasionally young infants will vomit feedings, especially if they are overfull or very active. The milk may shoot out of the mouth a few inches. In a healthy baby, infrequent vomiting of feedings probably reflects the infant's immature digestive system, but it is advisable to discuss this with your doctor to be sure that nothing else is causing it. Vomiting can also occur during illness or for other medical reasons. Always advise your doctor of any persistent or severe episodes of vomiting.

VERY FORCEFUL VOMITING. In rare cases a baby will begin to vomit very forcefully, projecting the vomitus some distance out of the mouth. This may be caused by a condition called pyloric stenosis, which means that the valve at the end of the stomach is not opened far enough to allow the normal passage of food into the intestines. The food builds up in the stomach and is forcefully vomited out by reflex action. This condition usually is seen in the first two months of life. It can be successfully treated with an operation. Other obstructions in the intestines or illnesses can also cause forceful vomiting. This should always be brought to a doctor's attention without delay.

Hiccough

Hiccoughs are common in young infants. They are often seen after meals in the first few months and should not cause alarm. They have even been observed to occur while the infant is in the womb. Hiccoughs are also seen in the young child. Only if hiccoughs persist for a long time should you become concerned. Persistent hiccoughing should be brought to your doctor's attention.

Stomach Aches

Stomach aches can occur for many reasons. The child may have eaten too much or he may have an intestinal virus. Constipation may also cause a bloated-achy feeling in the stomach. Most of the usual stomach aches are minor and go away on their own. Occasionally stomach aches or cramps can occur as the result of an illness or a more serious medical problem. Consult your doctor if your child has severe or frequent abdominal pains. Appendicitis can cause pains in the abdomen and is a condition that needs to be evaluated by your doctor without delay.

Appendicitis

The appendix is a small pouch that is attached to the intestines. It can occasionally fill with feces or other material and become infected or inflamed. An inflamed or infected appendix may cause sharp or cramp-like pains in the abdomen, vomiting, and special tenderness usually in the right lower part of the abdomen. The abdomen is often very tender to the touch. Acute, severe, abdominal pain should always raise the suspicion of appendicitis. Your doctor should be consulted to make the diagnosis. The symptoms may also be unusual or vague. Abdominal pain is the most common symptom. If the appendix becomes very swollen, it may rupture, causing an infection in the abdominal cavity. Do not hesitate to seek medical assistance for severe abdominal pain followed by fever and/or change in behavior. Appendicitis is uncommon under five years of age, but does occur, and the child should be promptly examined medically.

COMMON ELIMINATION PROBLEMS

Problems with elimination are among the more common difficulties that arise during the first five years. Almost all of these elimination difficulties are minor and self-limiting and respond well to medical treatment. It is important not to try to treat these conditions without medical assistance, since in many cases this leads to more chronic and difficult to handle problems.

Being familiar with the signs of diarrhea, constipation, and related problems will allow you to recognize these difficulties and seek the assistance of your doctor early in the course of the problems. Proper dietary and sanitary techniques can also help minimize the occurrence of these conditions. Problems with urination are less common, but occasionally occur. Having some familiarity with the signs of urinary tract infections and other conditions will help you recognize a problem and seek appropriate assistance from your doctor.

Diarrhea

Diarrhea refers to an abnormal increase in water content of the stools and often is associated with more frequent bowel movements. Mild forms of diarrhea cause looseness of the stool from excess water, but the stools still appear somewhat intact and only a small amount of fluid is lost through the rectum. More severe forms of diarrhea can cause large amounts of watery stools to be passed at frequent intervals.

This situation can cause a rapid loss of body fluid and certain electrolytes (important minerals in the body), especially in a young infant. Severe forms of diarrhea are easily recognized and should be brought to your doctor's attention without delay. Milder forms are not as pressing, but you should contact your doctor for advice in managing the diarrhea and replacing the lost fluids and electrolytes.

The young infant is more susceptible to some forms of diarrhea. Diarrhea is usually caused by an infection of the gastrointestinal tract by either bacteria, viruses, fungi, protozoa, or possibly some other micro-organisms. It is important to keep these germs from infecting the infant and young child by taking standard sanitary precautions when storing or preparing foods. Diarrhea can also be caused by the common cold. Certain types can be contagious. In most areas with good sanitary conditions, diarrhea is not usually a major problem and is often a self-limiting condition.

Contact your doctor for proper treatment of diarrhea. Do not try to treat diarrhea on your own. Giving fluids should be done under a doctor's guidance. In case you cannot reach a physician and the child is having very severe diarrhea, take the child to the nearest hospital or medical facility for treatment. The following simple guidelines should be helpful if you cannot seek medical assistance in a reasonable length of time. The main concern is to replace the body fluid and salts lost through the diarrhea so that the child does not become dehydrated. It is best to give clear liquids to the older child such as tea, non-carbonated (flat) soda, and Kool-Aid as tolerated. Do not force the child to take fluids. The infant can be given a diluted formula consisting of sugar water (usually one tablespoon of sugar [granulated] in four cups of water). These suggestions should allow you, in a rare situation, to manage a severe case of diarrhea until you can get medical assistance.

Constipation

Constipation is a symptom, not a disease. It has attracted the attention of mothers and grandmothers for centuries. The concept of daily bowel movements has been ingrained in the heads of most parents.

It is important to recognize that there is a great deal of normal variability in patterns of elimination. Some infants and young children have a bowel movement at almost the same time every day, while others have them at unpredictable times or every one to two days or more. This variation in a healthy baby is not constipation and should cause no concern for parents.

Constipation is a condition in which bowel movements are hard, infrequent, and difficult to pass. All three of these signs may be seen, since slow passage of the food through the intestines can cause infrequent stools and more water absorption from the stools making them hard and more difficult to pass. Occasionally constipation results in a relatively frequent and difficult passage of firm, little pieces of stool.

In some cases infrequent movements or difficulty passing a stool occur independently. A marked decrease in food intake may cause infrequent but easy passage of stools. A constriction (anal stenosis) or sore (anal fissure) in the anus may cause a soft stool to be passed only with difficulty. These situations are usually not considered true constipation.

CONSTIPATION DURING INFANCY. Breast-fed babies usually have frequent bowel movements, since breast milk has a natural mild laxative effect. Sometimes breast-fed babies pass stools every other day, but the bowel movement is usually soft and is passed without difficulty. This is not constipation and represents normal variation in elimination patterns.

Bottle-fed babies tend to have bowel movements that are harder and less frequent than breast-fed infants. Many bottle-fed infants have no difficulty passing their stools, but constipation is a relatively common problem in bottle-fed babies. Discuss your baby's constipation with your doctor, who will be able to help you deal with the problem.

CONSTIPATION DURING TODDLERHOOD AND PRESCHOOL. Providing your child with a well-balanced diet containing adequate bulk and fiber content (vegetables, bran, fruits, grain products) will help prevent constipation. Occasionally a child on a proper diet will still develop constipation. It is advisable to discuss this early with your doctor before it gets out of hand.

Bringing the problem to a young child's attention can often make matters worse. Do not scold, nag, use enemas and laxatives, or force the child to sit on the toilet for long periods of time to try to get him to have a bowel movement. These efforts often create tension and resentment and turn a temporary episode of constipation into a real problem. Try not to draw attention to it and consult your doctor for advice.

A toddler or preschool child who is going through a phase of rebellion and negativism may strongly resist efforts at toilet training. Occasionally these children will even hold back their movements. This can lead to distention of the rectum, resulting in an increased ability to withhold larger amounts of stool before the urge to "go" is experienced.

Very hard movements can sometimes cause pain or an anal fissure (see below). The child may then come to dread going to the bathroom and hold in his movements. Your doctor will be able to recommend an appropriate treatment for the child's constipation. It is best not to let the situation get out of hand. Seek your doctor's advice early in the course of constipation before the condition becomes chronic.

Overflow Soiling (Encopresis)

Prolonged, chronic constipation can cause stools to become lodged (impacted) in the rectum. When this occurs, watery fluid often leaks out around the mass of stool in between bowel movements and soils the pants. This condition is most commonly seen with older preschool children.

It is not uncommon for parents to mistake this condition for a behavioral or hygienic problem. Scolding or punishing the child for soiling his pants can only make matters worse. The leakage of fluid is not intentional and is the result of the blocked rectum. The main consideration is to be sure to seek medical advice if your older preschool child begins soiling his pants. This condition can be corrected and should not be ignored or overlooked.

Anal Fissures

An anal fissure refers to a split or cut in the wall (lining) of the anus. It can be painful and may bleed, producing blood on the diaper or on the toilet paper. Fissures are most common in the first year of life. They may be caused by hard large stools, infection, strong laxatives, or picking at the rectum.

Fissures can cause pain at the time of bowel movements and can be very troublesome to the young child learning to control his bowel function. They may also lead to constipation, since the child will avoid passing a stool. Anal fissures are usually treated by the administration of stool softeners.

Urinary Tract Infection

These infections are abnormal and are often more common in young girls than in young boys. They should always be evaluated by your doctor. Pain and burning on urination can be an early sign, but often the symptoms are less specific.

In younger children and infants, the only sign of infection may be a fever. Frequency and urgency of urination and low abdominal pain may also be signs. The cause of the infection must be determined and treated. Chronic urinary tract infections, left untreated, can lead to more serious infections of the kidneys.

Vaginal Discharge

Most newborn girls have a small amount of mucus-like vaginal discharge for approximately ten days or so after birth. Occasionally the discharge may contain tinges of blood. A small amount of discharge that clears after the first several days should not cause alarm. More persistent or unusual discharges can be discussed with your doctor.

Occasionally in girls a slight vaginal discharge occurs for a day and then goes away. This is not uncommon and is usually the result of a mild inflammation or infection that clears on its own. A milky discharge that lasts for several days or a very thick, foul, or large discharge should be brought to the doctor's attention.

These signs may reflect an infection that requires treatment. Sometimes a young girl will put something in her vagina and forget about it. This may cause a foul or bloody discharge in time. Try not to scold or ridicule the child if this occurs. The object can be removed by your doctor.

Difficulty with Urination

This is not a common problem. From time to time a baby (usually a boy) may have difficulty passing urine. The child will have to push excessively hard to pass his urine. The urine may even come out very slowly or in dribbles.

Consult your doctor for this condition. The hole in the tip of the penis may be too small and need enlarging by a simple procedure. It is important to be aware of any persistent difficulties with urination.

Sores on the Penis

Sometimes a baby develops a sore on the tip of the penis from irritation due to the products in his urine. This is a type of diaper rash. In some cases the irritated tip of the penis will swell, closing over the hole for urination. This makes urinating difficult. By keeping the baby's diapers free of toxins from the urine, such as ammonia, this condition can be avoided. Your doctor will be able to advise you about how to treat the sore.

CONTAGIOUS AND INFECTIOUS DISEASES

One of the great triumphs of modern medicine has been the suppression of some of the major common childhood illnesses. Polio, measles, mumps, German measles (rubella), diphtheria, whooping cough (pertussis), and tetanus have all succumbed to immunizations. Many of these diseases caused fear and anguish to parents for centuries, but now they can be prevented by proper well baby and child care.

The importance of properly immunizing your child (see pages 215–16) cannot be overemphasized. Some parents become lax about having their child properly immunized because they feel that these diseases no longer exist or could not strike their child. This is a tragedy, since these illnesses still pose a threat to children, and unnecessary illness and harm can be prevented by simple immunization. Providing a young child with appropriate immunizations is a responsibility that all parents should meet.

Two fairly common contagious diseases of childhood, chicken pox and scarlet fever, are still without immunizations. These illnesses do not usually produce serious harm, although both diseases can give rise to complications. Tuberculosis is a contagious disease that also affects children, but it can be effectively treated by your doctor. This disease can be detected by a simple test and it is important that your child receive appropriate tuberculosis testing by your doctor to detect this illness early (see pages 947, 968–69). The following discussion summarizes some of the common features of these diseases and of the other preventable childhood illnesses.

Chicken Pox (Varicella)

Chicken pox is a contagious illness caused by a virus. It usually occurs in children after two years of age, but can be seen earlier and is even seen in the newborn or young infant. Children, fortunately, are not usually very ill with chicken pox.

A low grade fever of 100° to 101° F usually develops. A rash appears as individual, pimple-like red spots. This is the hallmark of the disease. The red dots enlarge to about an eighth of an inch and then form a small blister. These little blisters can itch very intensely. When the blisters are broken they form small scabs or crusts. New crops of these lesions appear over the first three to five days.

Most of the pox marks are found on the body, but they can surface on the scalp and face. Infants may seem to get more marks on the diaper area. The lesions can also occur in the mouth or on the genitals, but are less common on the arms and legs and rare on the soles of the feet and palms of the hands.

The period of maximal contagiousness is from one to two days before the onset of the rash to five to six days afterward, when all the little blisters have broken and formed crusts. The illness can last longer in children with lowered ability to fight off disease.

Your doctor can help you manage your child. After the diagnosis is made the doctor will recommend medicines, if necessary, to help relieve the itching. It is advisable to keep the child's fingernails short to prevent excessive scratching. Bathing regularly is also useful to minimize secondary bacterial infections of the lesions and reduce itching. Proper treatment for the fever and an appropriate diet will be suggested by the doctor.

Other children should be isolated from the sick child. This will help prevent the spread of illness. In most cases chicken pox runs its course and clears up without any complications. Occasionally, however, complications do arise. A very high fever (103° to 104° F) lasting for several hours, severe headache, persistent coughing or vomiting, extreme tiredness, or bruising of the skin without injury (appearance of blue-purple blotches on the skin) should alert you to contact your doctor.

Scarlet Fever

Scarlet fever is nothing more than a streptococcal (see pages 958–59) throat infection with a rash. A toxin (poison) is produced by the bacteria that causes a red-colored rash to develop. The rash is made up of numerous tiny red dots that are close together. The dots are so close that they give the skin a red color. This is usually seen as a red flush over the chest, cheeks, abdomen, and groin. The tongue often gets red and may appear very rough with some white coating.

With the antibiotics that are available today, scarlet fever is no longer a major problem. Your doctor will prescribe penicillin or another appropriate antibiotic to be taken for over a week in order to eliminate the streptococcus from the throat. It is very important to follow the doctor's instructions exactly. Even though the child may look fine after a few days of treatment, the antibiotic must still be given as directed by the doctor. This is necessary to wipe out the streptococcus and prevent further or chronic infections.

The illness is usually diagnosed by the red rash and sore throat, but a throat culture is needed to make the final determination. The child is contagious for approximately one day following antibiotic treatment. Your doctor may want to culture the throat of other family members, since they may also have been infected with the streptococcus bacteria.

It is important to obtain medical treatment, for medication will not only help your child to get well, but will also help prevent some of the complications that can occur as a result of chronic streptococcal infections. These complications can include rheumatic fever (page 1034) and kidney difficulties (glomerulonephritis, page 1029).

Tuberculosis

Tuberculosis is an infection that is caused by a specific organism (tubercle bacillus of Koch). It may involve almost any part of the body. The most frequent source of infection for infants and children is contact or close association with an adult who has the disease. Infection through milk still occurs in areas of the world where unpasteurized, raw milk is used.

The onset of infection is rarely noticed. The baby or young child may become infected and not be sick. It may take some time before it is recognized that the child has tuberculosis. The infection may start in the lungs, but can occur in other areas of the body. Unrecognized or untreated tuberculosis is a dangerous disease.

Tuberculosis can be effectively treated today with a combination of medications taken over a prolonged period of time. Your doctor will be able to detect tuberculosis before any symptoms of infection occur by administering a simple skin test (see page 947). It is important that your child receives regular tuberculosis testing. This will detect the disease even though the child shows no signs of illness. A positive test does not always mean that the child will need treatment. Sometimes a person is exposed to tuberculosis, but does not develop an infection. If treatment is necessary, your doctor will discuss this with you and prescribe appropriate medications.

Preventable Contagious or Infectious Diseases

The following paragraphs give a brief description of preventable illnesses. Proper immunization can protect your child from these diseases.

DIPHTHERIA. Diphtheria is an infection caused by a toxin (poison)-producing organism. It causes a membrane-like inflammation to form in the upper airway (the throat) and can cause degenerative changes in the body's organs and the nervous system. The disease is transmitted by direct contact with an infected person. It usually starts with a sore throat and fever and produces the characteristic grayish-white deposit on the back of the throat. Serious complications may occur. This illness should be prevented by proper immunizations.

GERMAN MEASLES (RUBELLA). Rubella is the mildest of the more common viral contagious diseases in childhood. It is characterized by a generalized mild rash and some swelling of the lymph glands behind the ears and neck. Fever is also commonly seen. The disease takes on major significance because it can cause a high incidence of congenital defects in children whose mothers get rubella during early pregnancy. Deafness, heart difficulties, cataracts, and retardation are some of the congenital defects that can be produced.

The danger of a pregnant mother catching rubella has been reduced by the use of immunization programs against the disease. Immunizing children against rubella (page 947), as well as women who have not developed immunity before deciding to have children, has greatly reduced the risk of congenital defects due to this illness. Women can tell if they are immune to rubella by having a simple blood test.

MEASLES (RUBEOLA). Measles used to be one of the most common contagious diseases. With the development of the measles vaccines, the occurrence of this disease has been reduced. Fever and feelings of illness signal the onset of the disease. This is usually followed by a cough, itchy irritated eyes (conjunctivitis), and runny nose (coryza).

The fever gets worse over the next few days and then a rash develops. The rash gradually resolves and the symptoms clear in several days. Measles can run a mild course, but numerous complications of the disease can occur. Measles and its complications can be prevented by proper immunization (see page 947).

MUMPS. Mumps is a contagious viral infection that causes swelling and tenderness of the glands under the jaw (parotid glands) and sometimes other salivary glands. The disease can involve the testicles in men who have reached puberty and it can also involve the nervous system. The disease is recognized by the swelling and soreness of the glands, but it also can cause fever, vomiting, headache, and body aches. Involvement of other body organs may also occur. Mumps can now be prevented by immunization.

POLIO (POLIOMYELITIS, INFANTILE PARALYSIS). Polio is a viral infection that produces fever, stiffness of the neck and back, vomiting, headache, and sometimes paralysis in some of the patients it infects. More often the disease produces a mild fever. The severe results of this disease, causing paralysis of muscle groups and even death, made it one of the most dreaded diseases of this century for parents. The development of a vaccine against polio was a major scientific discovery. Polio can now be prevented by proper immunization programs (see page 947).

TETANUS (LOCKJAW). Tetanus is an infection, usually from contamination of a wound, caused by a specific bacteria that produces a powerful poison. This poison causes stiffness of the muscles of the body and convulsions. Tetanus is a very serious illness that is difficult to treat and can be fatal. Proper immunization during childhood can prevent this illness.

WHOOPING COUGH (PERTUSSIS). Pertussis is an acute infection of the breathing system that is caused by a bacteria. The disease begins with a mild runny nose and is initially indistinguishable from a cold. A slight fever is seen and these symptoms can last for about a week.

Following this initial period the child develops a series of severe explosive coughs. The coughs come one after another (usually ten to fifteen) and the child may have difficulty getting his breath. Following the coughs, the child takes a long breath, producing a sound described as a "whoop" (whooping cough). Then another series of coughs may begin.

A child may have several attacks of coughing (as many as twelve to fifty in a day). Vomiting also may occur. The child looks very ill and is usually exhausted by the attack. In infants the coughing attacks may stop their breathing, although in some cases coughing attacks are milder.

This phase of the disease may last for a month. Gradually the coughing subsides but the child usually has symptoms like a chronic cold for some time. Whooping cough can result in many complications and can be very serious in infancy. This illness can be prevented by immunizations during early infancy (see page 947).

ALLERGIES

An allergy is an unusual reaction of the body to an ordinary or foreign substance that would not usually cause a problem in the average person. The irritating substance can contact the body in several ways: for example, through the skin, nose, mouth, or by injection. The type of allergies that affect the child can differ depending upon the child's age. There is enormous variability in the type and severity of allergic reactions in children. Despite these differences, certain general patterns of allergies emerge. The young infant is more likely to develop an allergy to what he eats. Allergies during the toddlerhood and preschool years often seem to have a relationship to colds or other infections and are more often caused by substances the child breathes.

Food Allergies During Infancy

Most of the allergies that occur during infancy are to foods. Infants are almost never allergic to their mother's milk, but they can develop an allergy to cow's milk. The signs of allergy in a baby are often difficult to detect. They are usually mild at first. Mild sporadic diarrhea may be the first sign of an allergy to cow's milk in one baby. Another may become irritable and spit up more frequently. Sometimes the baby develops mild congestion or a slight runny nose. The symptoms can vary in severity and type.

These initial symptoms of a food allergy may seem unrelated or very mild. More obvious reactions will include persistent colic, crying, vomiting, and even respiratory congestion. Wheezing may also occur in more pronounced reactions. These marked allergic reactions to food are easy to recognize. The milder reactions are harder to associate with the food allergy. Diarrhea, vomiting, and colic pain may be signs that the baby is allergic to his formula, and this should be discussed with your doctor.

After six months of age, when new foods are introduced to the baby's diet (see page 305), is a common time for food allergies to appear. By offering one food at a time, you will be better able to tell if the baby is allergic to that food.

Other Allergies in Infancy

Asthma and other allergic reactions to substances in the air or that contact the skin can occur in infancy, but they are less common than food allergies. Eczema (see page 974) can also develop in infancy.

Helping to Prevent Allergies

There are a few simple ways to help prevent allergies from developing. This is especially important in families in which many members have allergies. Babies will be more prone to develop allergies if their parents suffer from allergic reactions or conditions.

It is often recommended that parents with strong allergic tendencies seriously consider breast-feeding their child. Rarely, if ever, does a baby develop an allergic reaction to breast milk. Mothers who cannot breast-feed can try formulas that are less likely to cause allergies, such as commercial soy and animal formulas as recommended by their doctor. Sometimes starting with these formulas will prevent a sensitive baby from developing an allergy.

Whole cow's milk can often produce an allergic reaction in sensitive babies. The protein in cow's milk is only partially digested by the young infant's immature digestive system. Some of this partially digested protein can cause allergies in an allergy-prone infant. As the baby's digestive system matures, cow's milk can be more completely digested and is less likely to cause a problem. A baby who would have developed an allergy to cow's milk during the first few months of life may be able to tolerate it after four to five months of age. Milk protein is partially digested during the processing of most prepared and evaporated milk formulas. These sources of protein are less likely to cause allergic reactions than regular whole cow's milk.

Once a baby develops an allergy, it may make him more prone to have allergic problems later in life. By feeding the infant the food least likely to provoke allergies, it may be possible to prevent the development of early allergic reactions to food in an allergy-prone baby.

When other foods are added to the baby's diet, special attention should be given to avoiding the early introduction of foods that are known often to cause allergies at a young age. Some of these allergy-provoking foods include: eggs, chocolate, fish, wheat, and corn. It is best to avoid these foods or products containing them before an allergy-prone child is a year old.

Simple measures to reduce the presence of allergy-provoking substances in the home environment can also help prevent respiratory or skin-contact allergies from developing. A child who is prone to allergies can benefit from minor changes in the home environment. A few useful suggestions include avoiding dust-catching items in the child's room, such as heavy shag carpets, ornate furniture, or animal furs. Stuffed toys, foam rubber, furniture, or mattresses can also harbor dust and mold. It is usually advisable to obtain rubber pillows, cushions, and mattresses that are well-sealed in plastic covers. Even foam mattresses can absorb body moisture and harbor molds as they age, unless they are properly covered. Plants and aquariums can also give rise to molds and are not advisable. Maintaining adequate humidity in the home and not keeping the temperature too high can help reduce dust. Your doctor will be able to suggest several other useful measures to reduce possible allergy-causing substances in the home that are appropriate for your local area.

Allergies in Toddlerhood and Preschool

During toddlerhood and the preschool years, allergies affecting the respiratory system, such as hay fever and asthma, become more common. Allergies to poison ivy, oak, and sumac are also seen. A skin inflammation called eczema may begin, although this condition also can start in infancy. The older child can still develop allergies to foods and allergic reactions to certain medication.

Hay Fever

Hay fever is the most common allergic disorder. The seasonal variability of hay fever symptoms is familiar to most parents and reflects the differences in the type and duration of exposure to sensitizing substances. Sneezing, an itchy runny nose, sniffling, tearing and itching of the eyes, and nasal congestion are some of the more common signs of hay fever.

The symptoms of hay fever can occur at any time of day, but are usually more intense in the early morning or late evening. Hay fever can develop in infancy, but this is uncommon. It does not usually develop until after the first or second year. The severity of the symptoms often correlates with the pollen count. Many different causes for hay fever exist.

A child with chronic allergies can develop bloody noses more easily (see pages 989–90). Headaches from pressure in the nasal sinuses are often a common symptom. Your doctor will be able to help evaluate your child's allergy and may recommend medications, special allergy injections, skin tests, or just taking certain precautions in the home. It is usually difficult to completely cure an allergy, but the doctor will be able to help reduce the symptoms.

Other Allergies Similar to Hay Fever

Hay fever is a special type of allergy, usually to pollens. It occurs with a seasonal variation. Other substances can also enter the nose and throat that cause allergies in a sensitive person and produce similar symptoms to hay fever. Household dust is a common cause of allergies. Dust is often highest in the home during the fall when the heat is first turned on. The air in the home becomes dry and carries more dust. Allergy-prone children often develop an itchy nose, a cough, or a mild form of bronchitis. There are numerous other common household substances that can irritate the respiratory system. Smoke, paint fumes, and soot from burning leaves are just a few more common ones.

It is impossible to keep your house free of dust. Making an effort to minimize dust and other big offenders, however, can help prevent allergic reactions from developing. Changing air filters and cleaning the air ducts in forced air heating systems may be helpful. Trying to avoid exposure to very dry air by using a humidifier may be useful in protecting an allergy-prone infant.

Asthma

Asthma is an allergic condition that affects the airways (bronchial tubes). When an irritating substance is breathed by a sensitive individual, the linings of the small air passages in the lungs become inflamed and swell. This partially blocks the airways and makes it more difficult to breathe. The child may feel a tightness in the chest and complain of difficulty breathing. The sound of wheezing, a whistling sound, can often be heard as the child breathes.

Your doctor will assist you in managing this condition. The symptoms of asthma can be relieved with medication. It is important to try to identify the cause of the asthma so that exposure to it can be eliminated or minimized. This may produce excellent results if the cause can be easily identified and avoided.

Asthma attacks can vary considerably, but they are more common at night and are often affected by climate, emotional tension, and temperature. An attack can be brought on by a cold. Stresses in the home can also cause or accentuate an attack. An asthmatic child does not need to be babied or completely sheltered, but it is helpful to try to prevent attacks by reducing or eliminating obvious irritating factors.

Each asthmatic attack can vary considerably. After the first attack, your doctor will advise you how to handle future episodes. Treatment varies with the severity of the attack, and many minor episodes resolve on their own. More severe attacks, making it difficult to breathe, usually require an injection or oral medication for temporary relief. Asthma that begins in early childhood often clears up on its own as the child gets older. It is not uncommon for a child with asthma to develop other allergies as well, especially hay fever.

ASTHMATIC BRONCHITIS. During colds, some infants and young children develop difficulty breathing accompanied by wheezing. The mild infection seems to trigger an asthma attack. These attacks of asthma never develop without a cold. This special type of asthma is asthmatic bronchitis. It is most commonly seen in children during the first three years of life and usually disappears on its own a few years after it starts. The medications used to treat asthma often have no effect on this condition. It is usually not serious, but should be brought to you doctor's attention.

Hives

Hives are a common skin problem characterized by a raised area of skin surrounded by redness. These raised areas may appear in crops or singly. They usually itch and disappear in a short time (minutes to hours) leaving no trace on the skin. Some cases are more chronic but these are rare. Hives can be caused by an allergic reaction.

Some people almost never get hives, while others get them rather frequently. Sensitivity to certain foods, injections, and infections are common causes. Most of the time the cause is not found. Your doctor can help relieve the itching or symptoms with medications, if necessary.

Eczema

Eczema is an inflammatory skin problem that causes redness, roughness, oozing and crusting of the skin. It is often associated with asthma and hay fever. Eczema often begins in infancy during the first few months of life, but it can start later during the second or third year. The skin problems often begin on the cheeks, spread to the rest of the face, neck, hands, and the areas around the knee and elbow. Sometimes it can involve the body. In infants it is usually seen on the face and in the older child it is more common in the creases of the skin.

This "red rash" is very itchy. Preventing scratching of the lesions helps avoid crusting and scaling. Children usually try to scratch intensely. Secondary infections of oozing or open lesions are the main complication to avoid.

Eczema usually lasts a few years if it begins early in infancy. Mild cases go into remission before age three, others sometime within the next few years. This remission may be complete or may be incomplete with reappearance of the eczema throughout childhood. The condition can flair up again during puberty and occasionally persist into adulthood.

There is no complete cure for eczema. There are a number of treatments available that can be very helpful; your doctor will discuss this with you. The goal of treatment is to reduce the symptoms, especially the itching, and improve the appearance of the lesions. Removal of a number of substances from the home environment that seem to aggravate eczema, such as house dust, feathers, animal hair, and wool, may help reduce the severity of this condition. It is not clear whether food allergies play a role in aggravating eczema. Your doctor will be able to assist you in taking preventive measures in your home and treating this condition. In most children eczema is self-limited and subsides in a few years.

RASHES AND COMMON SKIN PROBLEMS

Skin problems can be very confusing and new parents often have questions about them. This material is not intended to make you diagnostic experts. Skin changes result from many different causes, and it is always best to consult your doctor about these conditions. Many parents, however, find it useful and reassuring to have some basic information about some of the more common skin conditions.

Rashes and skin problems are common in infancy. Babies can develop diaper rash, prickly heat, hives, eczema, allergic skin reactions, and other skin conditions. During toddlerhood and the preschool years the previously common rashes of measles and rubella should no longer be seen because of immunizations, but the rash of chicken pox may still appear. Allergic rashes to contact irritants (poison ivy, poison oak, poison sumac, etc.) are also very common. The following description of different rashes should help you recognize these illnesses and seek appropriate medical care.

Diaper Rash

The infant's skin is very sensitive and is susceptible to many types of irritation. The skin under the diaper is especially susceptible to developing the common skin problem called diaper rash. Diaper rash refers to a number of conditions that cause irritation of the skin around the diaper area. There are three main causes for diaper rash that should be familiar to parents.

The skin under the diaper gets soiled with urine and stools. These body wastes remain in contact with the skin for varing periods of time. Sometimes they remain on the skin for several hours, especially during the night.

This situation often irritates the baby's tender skin and produces a reddish, irritated-looking rash in the area under the diaper. This is the most common cause of diaper rash in early infancy. Occasionally the skin will form small red pimples, which can become infected, producing small whiteheads.

This type of diaper rash is very common and does not necessarily mean that you are not keeping your baby clean. Some infants are just more susceptible than others. When a diaper rash of this type develops, it is best to be especially careful about avoiding prolonged contact with wet, soiled diapers. Do not use rubber pants, since these can trap moisture and aggravate the problem. Using absorbent cloth or paper diapers is best.

At night or other times when you cannot quickly change the baby, use two or three diapers at once. This will absorb more moisture and leave less in contact with the skin. Try to check the baby more frequently so that he will spend less time in wet diapers.

It is important to keep the skin clean. Gentle washing after each diaper change will help prevent infection and remove excess waste material from the skin. Your doctor will probably recommend using baby powder to help dry the skin after each change and the occasional use of a mild skin cream or lotion, usually before bed or nap times, to help protect the irritated skin.

Another common cause of diaper rash is the presence of ammonia in the urine. Some babies produce more urea in their urine, which is then converted to ammonia. The smell of the ammonia on the diapers will be obvious. These infants often develop skin irritation that is caused by this substance. The ammonia can cause the skin to become bright red in color, especially if it remains on the skin overnight. This problem is often the cause of diaper rash in the older infant. The same basic guidelines given above are useful in handling this condition. Sometimes washing the diapers at home does not remove all the ammonia-producing bacteria. Your doctor will be able to recommend a special antiseptic that can be added to the washing machine rinse cycle that will prevent the growth of bacteria.

Disposable diapers will also eliminate the build-up of ammonia-producing bacteria. Diaper services sterilize the diapers so that these bacteria are killed.

Another cause of diaper rash is a fungal infection. The fungus that produces thrush (see pages 1035–36) in the child's mouth can also cause an infection of the skin around the anus. This infection usually starts from the anus and spreads out to infect the skin around the diaper area, producing numerous small red pimples that eventually come together to form a red rash with sharply outlined borders. Your doctor will be able to give you special medication to control this infection.

Occasionally a diaper rash can become even more irritated and infected. Do not hesitate to contact your doctor about these conditions, especially if small blisters are developing (see Impetigo, below). Your doctor will give you special instructions for handling these situations. In some cases it may be best to expose the skin to the air without diapers to allow the rash to heal. With proper medical advice, diaper rash can usually be easily controlled.

Cradle Cap

Cradle cap is a common mild skin disorder of early infancy. The skin on the scalp becomes crusty and scaly and looks dirty. Do not be alarmed by these changes. This condition usually subsides later in infancy. Cradle cap is a seborrhea that is similar to dandruff in the adult. The best treatment is to wash the scalp regularly with soap and water. Ask the advice of your doctor in treating this condition. A special seborrheic shampoo may be recommended to help treat this skin problem.

Impetigo

Impetigo is a bacterial infection of the skin. In the newborn or young infant the bacteria infect the skin and produce a small blister on the skin surface. The blister contains a yellow-white fluid that is mainly made up of pus. The skin around the blister is usually red.

When the blister breaks, it leaves a raw area. The fluid from the blister can spread the infection. These skin changes are most commonly seen on the moist areas of the body, such as the diaper area, under the arm, or around the groin. This condition requires medical treatment. Your doctor will advise you of how to treat the skin lesions and clean the baby's clothes and bed linens to avoid reinfection.

In older children impetigo often looks different. It produces a crusty change in the skin that forms a scab, usually light yellow or brownish in color. The infection may start from a pimple and can be spread from one skin lesion to other areas of the skin. It is contagious and can spread rather quickly. Your doctor will be able to treat this condition and prevent further spreading.

Do not hesitate to seek medical advice for any scab-like lesions on the child's skin. Scabs on the face or other areas of the body with no history of injury should make parents think of impetigo. Early detection is helpful in preventing the spread of this condition. If ignored or untreated, impetigo can lead to kidney disease or generalized infection. These complications can be avoided by seeking early medical attention.

Birthmarks

There are several types of birthmarks. The most common include the mole or nevus. These marks often appear as small round black or brown spots. They are not usually present at birth, but develop after several months.

The port-wine stains that appear as purple discolorations mainly result from dilation of the small blood vessels in the skin. A tiny red spot that emerges a few days after birth should be brought to your doctor's attention, if it was not seen on the initial examination. This could be a strawberry hemangioma. These marks often grow rapidly for a time in infants and then usually go away on their own, leaving little trace. Other birthmarks of the newborn are discussed on pages 79–80. Most birthmarks are harmless. Your doctor will explain them to you when he or she examines your child at birth or during well baby check-ups.

Facial Rashes in Infancy

The skin on the young infant's face is delicate and mild face rashes in early infancy are common. Some infants develop a few red spots or small pimples on the cheeks that can last for a while. These minor irritations usually fade with time.

Small white pimples are also seen on the cheeks. These spots also clear up with time. Your doctor will advise you if any special treatment is needed.

Eczema

Eczema produces a rough, red, scaly rash that is very itchy (see page 974).

Poison Ivy and Other Similar Conditions

One of the most common causes of allergic contact sensitivity in children is the result of exposure to certain plants, poison ivy, poison oak, and poison sumac being the most common. The skin develops an acute inflammatory reaction, often with large blisters. These skin changes are extremely itchy. Exposure to the plants most often occurs by direct contact, but indirect contact through exposed animals, clothing, firewood, or other objects contaminated with the plant oil has also been shown to cause this condition occasionally. Smoke from the burning plant can also spread the oil.

The plant oil is often initially spread around the body by the hands, especially to the face and genitals. Once the plant oil is removed from the skin by washing, it is important to recognize that the fluid from the blisters that form does *not* spread the irritation.

The skin changes produced by contact with these plants last approximately two to four weeks, depending on the amount of exposure and the degree of sensitivity. The skin reaction appears several hours after contact with the skin. The best treatment is to remove the plant oil from the skin by vigorously washing with soap and water immediately after exposure. After an hour or more of exposure to the skin, washing is probably ineffective in preventing the development of irritation, but it removes the oil from the skin and prevents further spreading.

Once the skin condition develops, seek the advice of your doctor. Medications can be given or applied to help decrease the itching and promote cleaning of the lesions. Some children have a more extensive reaction to this condition and develop a puffy face and swollen eyes. These reactions indicate that the person is extremely sensitive to poison ivy, and it is important for them to avoid future contact with these plants. The doctor will be able to advise you on the best methods for preventing exposure in your community.

Ringworm

Ringworm is caused by a fungus infection of the skin. It produces round areas of rough skin about a half inch in size, giving the infection its name. The rim of the ring is usually rough and bumpy and the center is smoother and scaly. Ringworm can also infect the scalp and produce the same round areas. The hair over these areas will often fall out temporarily.

Your doctor will be able to give you appropriate medications to treat this condition. Ringworm can be spread from one person to another, so do not hesitate to seek medical advice and start treatment before everyone in the house catches the infection.

Scabies

Scabies is a skin condition resulting from infestation of the skin by mites. Scabies is fairly common during the late summer and early autumn. It is often picked up in the woods during camp outings and the mites can readily migrate from one person to another.

The mites burrow into the skin and the female lays her eggs. After a few weeks, the person becomes sensitized to irritating substances from the mite, and itching begins. A chronic inflammatory process gradually develops producing skin changes.

The first complaint is usually itching at night. Genital areas and body creases are the most often affected. The condition is not usually recognized early and leads to skin changes that look like pimples covered with scabs.

Scabies needs special treatment. Your doctor will be able to prescribe medications to get rid of the mites and offer suggestions to eliminate them from clothing and the home surroundings. Other family members may also need to be treated.

Prickly Heat

This form of rash is common on hot days. It most often begins on the neck and shoulders and spreads to the chest and up to the face. The skin usually has small, pink pimples. This rash is best treated by keeping the baby from becoming overheated.

Rashes from Contagious Childhood Diseases

The previously common rashes from measles and rubella (German measles) can now be prevented with immunizations (see page 969). The rashes produced by chicken pox and scarlet fever are still seen and are described on pages 967–68.

Hives

Hives are itchy skin changes that can occur over the entire body (see page 974).

Warts

Most warts are believed to be caused by viruses. There are many different types of warts. Some are very small and flat, while others can become very large and rounded. They are commonly seen on the hands, feet, and face.

One type of wart is contagious, producing small, round, flat warts that often have an indentation in the center. Early treatment can help get rid of those warts before they spread. Most warts seem to spread very minimally, if at all. Warts on the soles of the feet (plantar warts) can be painful and may require removal. There are many different ways to treat these skin problems. It is best to discuss treatment with your doctor before trying to treat the warts yourself.

ANEMIA

Anemia is a condition that occurs when the hematocrit (percentage of red blood cells in a given volume of blood) and hemoglobin (oxygen-carrying protein in the blood cells) are below the normal range for the age of the child. There are many causes for anemia. Iron deficiency anemia is the most frequent cause of anemia in infancy and is often seen in the age period from six months to two years. The iron stores in the normal full-term infant are usually enough to prevent anemia for the first four to six months of life, even if the baby receives no iron in his diet. After this time the infant needs a regular supply of iron.

Iron deficiency anemia can be prevented by being sure your baby receives an adequate supply of iron. Your doctor will recommend iron supplements or an adequate source of iron in the regular diet to prevent this common cause of anemia. Other less common anemias can result from vitamin deficiencies such as the lack of vitamin B_{12}. This vitamin is usually adequately supplied to the baby by cow's or human milk, since these food sources contain vitamin B_{12}. Vitamin supplements are routinely given to babies and young children to increase the daily intake of vitamins to prevent deficiencies from developing.

Other forms of anemia can occur. Your doctor will be examining your child for any signs of anemia during his well baby and childhood check-ups. The hemoglobin test and examination of the blood cells can help the doctor detect other anemias.

Sickle Cell Anemia

Sickle cell anemia results from the formation of an abnormal form of hemoglobin. The red blood cells containing this hemoglobin become crescent or "sickle" in shape, giving the name "sickle cell." This condition can be diagnosed by a simple blood test to see if the altered form of sickle hemoglobin is present or if sickle cells are in the blood. It is seen almost exclusively in Negroes living in particular areas of Africa or in people whose ancestors originally came from this part of the world. The high frequency of sickle cell anemia in this group has been attributed to a selective advantage of the sickle cell trait against malarial infections, common in Africa.

Sickle cell anemia is a hereditary anemia. The sickle cell trait describes the condition where the individual has one normal and one sickle cell gene and does not have major effects from this gene, since many red blood cells have normal hemoglobin. This is called the carrier condition.

In sickle cell disease the individual inherits two sickle cell genes and does not have the regular hemoglobin gene. Signs of this disease rarely appear before the fourth or sixth month of life. Early symptoms may include unexplained fever, swelling of hands and feet, and anemia.

It is important for young Negro children to have the benefit of an early test for sickle cell anemia, especially if they are anemic. If there is sickle cell disease in the family or there is a possibility that one parent is a carrier, a young married couple can have the sickle test to determine if they are carriers of the sickle trait. Their physician can then counsel them as to the odds that their children will have the more serious form of the disease. A great deal of research and public effort is being put into understanding and possibly curing sickle cell disease.

EYE AND VISUAL PROBLEMS

In most cases, excluding trauma and acute infections, eye problems do not represent emergencies, but they almost always require the advice of your doctor. In infancy it is important to recognize crossed eyes (strabismus). Later in childhood visual problems can be recognized by the child's behavior.

A toddler who keeps running into objects or rubbing his eyes needs an examination. Headaches, pain in the eye, and inflammation or redness of the eyes are symptoms that suggest a possible visual problem. Tilting of the head, squinting, or holding books very close to the eyes are other signs that the child's vision should be evaluated.

The preschool child will probably be able to tell you about visual problems such as blurriness or double vision. Children, however, are noted for not always complaining about eye problems, and it may be up to the parent to recognize that something is wrong.

Crossed Eyes

Babies' eyes occasionally cross (squint) in the early months of infancy. One eye may seem to turn in or out too much. This transient difficulty may just represent the infant's initial difficulty in co-ordinating eye movements.

A very steady or persistent (fixed squint) problem should be brought to the attention of your doctor. If the eyes are not fixing properly on an object, the child will see double. The infant's brain mistakenly compensates for this by suppressing the image from one eye. Letting this condition persist for a long time can lead to a type of blindness in the suppressed eye that may not be correctable later on.

Recognizing fixed or permanent squints is important during infancy to avoid permanent visual problems. A child with this condition can be successfully treated by the doctor. It may be possible to correct this problem by wearing a patch over one eye for periods of time or special corrective glasses. A minor operation may be recommended to adjust the imbalance if the other techniques are not successful.

Sometimes a baby will appear to have crossed eyes, but will actually not. Infants have a large skin fold coming out from the nose that covers the inner corners of both eyes. A baby who looks to one side may appear cross-eyed, since one eye will partially disappear under the fold of skin.

The eye under the fold will have white showing on only one side of the pupil, while the other eye will have white on both sides. It might appear at first glance that the eyes are not moving equally. If you feel your child has a fixed squint, it is best to let your doctor examine him and not try to make the diagnosis by yourself.

Conjunctivitis (Pink Eye)

Pink eye is an infection or inflammation of the white part of the eye (conjunctiva). It can be caused by a generalized viral infection, allergies, irritating substances in the eye (i.e., silver nitrate in the eyes of newborns), or by numerous types of infections in the eye without infection elsewhere in the body.

Pink eye usually refers to a localized infection in the eye and can spread from one person to another, in some cases by direct contact (through towels, etc.). It often causes redness of the eye and production of mucus. This mucus can build up and become sticky. Sometimes a child will wake up in the morning and find that his eyelids are stuck together. Gently dabbing the lids with cotton or gauze soaked in warm water will dissolve the mucus and make it easier to open the eyes.

Contact your doctor for this condition. Special eye drops may be recommended, depending on the cause of the infection. In some cases no treatment is necessary since many infections can be overcome by the body's natural mechanisms. The doctor will evaluate the condition and recommend appropriate treatment based on the nature of the irritation.

Nearsightedness (Myopia)

Nearsightedness refers to the condition in which it is not possible to see clearly at a distance, while near vision is intact. The condition is usually hereditary. Nearsighted children tend to squint when looking at distant objects. They may also develop headaches from the eye strain. If a child manifests these symptoms, he should have his eyes checked. This condition is easily corrected with glasses.

The most common visual acuity problem in childhood is nearsightedness. It most commonly develops late in childhood, but it can occur as early as toddlerhood. A toddler who stumbles over objects or walks into things should be suspected of being nearsighted. The doctor will be able to evaluate even the younger child with visual tests that do not require reading skills. It is important to correct this visual problem with glasses before the child goes to school to avoid problems with learning or reading.

Farsightedness (Hyperopia)

Farsightedness is a visual problem in which near objects are blurry, but distance vision is intact. Farsightedness is common in older adults, but is uncommon in childhood. It does occur later in childhood and should be recognized, since it can be easily corrected with glasses. Squinting, headaches, or sore eyes may develop after the child does close work. These signs should be taken as a reason to have his eyes checked.

Astigmatism

Astigmatism is a visual defect caused by an alteration in the normal curvature of the eye lens. Some parts of the field of vision are distorted while other parts are intact. Astigmatism can cause squinting and headaches. This condition is easily corrected by glasses. It is not commonly seen in early childhood.

Color Blindness

Color blindness is a hereditary defect of vision in which the eye cannot see certain colors. There are several types of color blindness, depending on what colors are not seen. Most color blind individuals cannot tell the difference between red and green. This condition is much more common in boys than girls. Color blindness is not a serious problem, but it should be recognized so that teachers can be aware of the child's inability to perceive certain color differences. Most families with color blind children have a family history of color blindness. Parents who are color blind should be on the lookout for this condition in their children.

Eye Glasses for Children

A child who has trouble reading the blackboard, complains of not being able to see the baseball until it is on top of him, or is always squinting and complaining of eye strain certainly is ready for glasses if this visual problem is due to problems with visual acuity. The problem that arises in later childhood is that youngsters are often embarrassed to wear glasses. They may fear ridicule by their friends.

In most situations where a child has significant visual difficulty, his appreciation of what the glasses can do for him usually outweighs his reservations about how they will affect his appearance. Children do not become dependent on glasses. The glasses only correct a visual problem that is already present.

It is important to obtain glasses that are made with shatter-resistant glass. The young child is prone to accidents, and his glasses will be subjected to some rough treatment. The slight increase in cost to obtain safety-proof glasses is well worth it to protect the child from unnecessary injury.

Stye

A stye is an infection in the glands of the eyelid. It appears as a small pimple at the base of an eyelash. If the stye is small, it is best left alone and it will usually clear on its own. A stye that is large or painful should be evaluated by your doctor. Warm soaks will often relieve the pain and help the stye come to a head. Try to discourage the child from rubbing his eye, since this could further irritate the stye and sometimes lead to conjunctivitis.

YOUR CHILD'S HEARING

The ability to hear is important for the development of speech. A child learns to speak by first listening and then imitating sounds. Hearing is also an important aspect of a child's ability to learn. Problems with hearing can interfere with a child's relationships with other children. Hearing difficulties in infancy and childhood are not uncommon and represent a significant disability that may go unrecognized for a long time. Thus, many parents express an interest in understanding some of the major causes of hearing loss and how they might be able to detect this disability in their children.

There are many causes for hearing loss in children. Malformation, disease, or damage to any part of the hearing system during pregnancy, infancy, and childhood can result in hearing difficulties. The following table outlines some of the major causes for hearing disability.

Common Causes for Hearing Loss

DURING PREGNANCY

1. German Measles (Rubella). A mother who develops German measles early in pregnancy has a higher risk of her child's having a hearing disability. This illness can be prevented by vaccination.
2. Rh Incompatibility. This cause is also preventable by proper diagnosis and serum treatments.
3. Prematurity. Premature birth increases the chances of hearing loss.

INFANCY—TODDLERHOOD—PRESCHOOL

1. Middle Ear Infections (otitis media). These infections can be treated by your doctor.
2. Fluid Build-up in the Middle Ear (serous otitis media). This condition often follows a cold and can lead to a ruptured eardrum.
3. Childhood Diseases. Certain childhood diseases that cause a very high fever (scarlet fever, whooping cough, mumps, meningitis) can result in hearing loss. Most of these illnesses can be prevented by immunization.
4. Injuries. Injuries to the hearing system due to a very loud noise near the ear, a sharp blow to the ear, a child putting an object into the ear, or a head injury with a skull fracture can all result in hearing loss. Proper consideration of accident prevention will greatly reduce the possibility of these injuries.

OTHER

1. Some hearing difficulties or tendencies to develop them can be inherited.

Many parents want to know how to evaluate their child's hearing disability. Your doctor will be looking for hearing difficulties during well baby and childhood check-ups. However, there are several simple ways to evaluate your child's hearing at home. It is important to recognize that the signs of hearing loss can vary with age. The following guide may be of help to you in assessing your child's hearing ability.

Warning Signs Suggesting that Your Child Has a Hearing Loss

INFANCY

1. Baby does not startle or react to hand claps up to three to six feet from his ears.
2. Baby does not respond to sounds by looking to the noise later in infancy.
3. Infant doesn't turn head to a familiar sound in late infancy.

TODDLERHOOD—PRESCHOOL

1. Child can follow simple commands with visual clues but cannot follow only voice commands.
2. Child can't imitate any sounds.
3. Child does not use a few simple words (mom, dog, car, etc.).
4. Child can't locate the source of a sound.
5. Delayed development of language skills (usually beyond two and a half years).
6. Can't follow simple verbal directions in preschool.

If your child has some of the simple signs listed above you should discuss your observations with your doctor. The doctor can further evaluate your child's hearing ability or refer you to a hearing specialist.

SEIZURES AND CONVULSIONS IN CHILDHOOD

A seizure is an episode of disruption of regular brain function produced by excessive firing of certain groups of nerve cells. Seizures can be caused by a great variety of conditions. Some seizures produce unconsciousness, marked shaking and stiffening of the body, and clenching of the teeth. These types of seizures are often called grand mal seizures or convulsions. Witnessing a convulsion can be a very frightening experience for a parent. It is important to recognize that most convulsions are not harmful and stop on their own after a brief time.

Other types of seizures may not be obvious to parents. Brief staring spells or short lapses in consciousness without body movement can also occur. Sometimes a seizure can look just like a fainting spell. The child often is not aware that something unusual has occurred.

Epilepsy is the name given to the numerous conditions that cause repeated seizures. In the past, epilepsy was not well understood and many epileptics and their families were the targets of social prejudice. This situation has greatly improved. Today the majority of people with epilepsy can be treated with medications and lead very normal lives. Public awareness of this condition has also lessened the social pressures that once existed.

The majority of children will not have seizures, but there are a few who will. It is useful to be aware of some of the more common types of seizures during childhood in the event that either your child or someone else's has a seizure. A common type of seizure in childhood is brought on by a sudden high fever (febrile convulsions). Staring spells (petit mal seizures) can also occur in childhood. Other types of seizures can develop, but are much less common.

Febrile Seizures (Convulsions)

Febrile seizures usually occur between the ages of one to three years of age. Approximately one to two percent of all children have a tendency to have a seizure when their body temperature is elevated above 101° F. This tendency to have febrile convulsions is usually outgrown by six to seven years of age. Febrile seizures are fairly common, so it is important to be able to recognize them.

Recognizing a febrile seizure is usually not difficult. Suddenly the child will become rigid or stiff and have jerky movements of the arms and legs. The eyes may appear to roll back in the head at the beginning of the convulsion. The seizure may last from thirty seconds to three to four minutes. Urine or stools may be passed. Some children become cyanotic (the skin develops a bluish color) for a brief time during the seizure. These seizures often occur before the parent even realizes that the child has a fever.

Try to prevent the child from hurting himself by keeping him from banging his arms, legs, and head against hard or sharp objects. Do not attempt to force a sharp or very firm object into his mouth, since this will probably do more harm than good. It is best to let the child lie flat on the floor with his head to the side, checking to maintain the airway. The main thing is to try and remain calm, since these seizures usually are very short and will stop by themselves.

After the seizure has stopped, the child may appear sleepy or confused for a period of time. It is important to try to lower the fever. Contact your doctor for advice in controlling the fever and preventing additional convulsions. In case you cannot reach the doctor, begin to lower the fever as discussed on pages 953–54 until you can contact the doctor.

The physician will most likely want to examine your child to be sure that there is no other cause for the convulsion. Special tests may be suggested to rule out other problems. Medications to control or prevent further seizures may be recommended by the doctor along with special suggestions on how to avoid these episodes in the future. When there is some warning of illness, an effort should be made to control the child's temperature as a way of preventing a future seizure.

In most cases febrile convulsions are harmless problems. When properly controlled and not allowed to occur frequently they are not often followed by any permanent ill effects or damage. Be sure to consult your doctor about this condition. With proper, prompt treatment these episodes can usually be prevented and the child will usually outgrow them.

Petit Mal Seizures

Petit mal seizures develop in childhood and cause brief loss of contact with the environment. These seizures are more common after four years of age, but they can occur earlier. The importance of discussing this type of seizure is that it is often not recognized by parents.

The actual seizure may only last a few seconds and the child will appear to be staring off into space, daydreaming, or not listening. Slow, jerking movements of the body or blinking of the eyes may occur. The child will have no recollection of the seizure.

Short lapses produced by this condition can make it difficult for the child when he enters school because he will miss things in class. If you observe your child having prominent, short staring spells or unusual daydreaming-like episodes, discuss this situation with your doctor. Petit mal seizures can be well controlled with medical treatment, and in some cases they are outgrown.

FIRST AID AND ACUTE MEDICAL PROBLEMS

In the event that an accident occurs or an acute medical problem arises involving a child, it is important to know where to call or go for help (see pages 123, 948). Being prepared to seek assistance is the first step. The second step is to be able to provide simple supportive care until medical help is available. These are skills that all parents should want to acquire.

If it is possible, always consult a doctor before administering any treatment or care in acute situations. Emergency medical care can be quickly obtained in the vast majority of situations. Most cities have special phone numbers to get rapid emergency care. In the unusual circumstance that you cannot immediately obtain medical help, the following guidelines for providing supportive care for some common acute problems should be helpful. Recommendations are also included for giving first aid for common minor injuries and when the injuries require medical attention.

Many parents find it very useful to take a first aid or a CPR (Cardiopulmonary Resuscitation) course. Most communities offer such courses through organizations such as the American Red Cross, YMCA, YWCA, JCCA, hospitals, or other similar certified organizations. Obtaining firsthand experience in administering simple first aid and life-support techniques is a worth while investment of time, and is recommended.

How to Handle Burns

Burns are a common accidental injury. Many advances have been made in the treatment of burns in the past years. Immediate use of cold water to treat the burn is the best form of supportive first aid care. It will lessen the pain and help reduce the severity of the burn until you can obtain further medical treatment if that is necessary.

Try to comfort the child. Run cold water from the tap over the burn or pour it from a pitcher. Some doctors find it best to immerse the burned part in cold water or cover it with a wet cloth filled with ice until the pain subsides. If you immerse the burned area in cold water, it is recommended that the part be removed from the water after approximately ten minutes. It is not advisable to keep it in very cold water for much longer than ten minutes since the tissue may be damaged from overexposure to cold. After ten minutes, you can use cool water to relieve the pain. Pain from minor burns or from sunburn often responds well to aspirin or an aspirin substitute, if recommended by your physician.

Do not apply any medications to the burn without your doctor's advice. It is no longer recommended that ointment or petroleum jelly be applied to burns before contacting a physician. The sensitive burned skin is very fragile and it is best not to irritate it with medications or rubbing. Applying cold water is the best way to relieve the pain and keep the burn clean.

A minor burn causing only some redness to the skin may require no further treatment (first degree burn). More severe burns will cause blisters (second degree burn) or raw and darkened areas on the skin (third degree burn). More severe burns usually require further treatment by a doctor. Do not try to break the blisters. The raw skin under the blister or around the burn is susceptible to infection. This area is also very sensitive to any form of treatment. Never apply antiseptics such as iodine or ointments to this broken skin without medical advice since these agents can cause further harm. If a burn is more serious, do not panic. Immediately apply cold water for basic first aid and seek medical assistance.

Sunburn

The best way to handle sunburn is to prevent it. Severe sunburn is very painful. It is unnecessary for an infant or young child ever to suffer from sunburn. This condition can be easily and completely avoided by not allowing your infant or child to be overexposed to the sun.

Do not expose young infants to direct sunlight for more than six to twelve minutes at a time. Avoid the maximum twelve-noon sunrays. A very fair-skinned baby should be carefully shielded from long exposure to direct sunlight for at least eight to nine months. Fair hair and skin can serve as a clue to the child's increased sensitivity to the sun. After approximately a year of age children can tolerate longer exposures to direct sunlight, but be cautious. Severe burns can still occur.

The toddler is very sensitive to strong sun exposure. Keep his skin covered with a light shirt or towel, or let him play in the shade of an umbrella. Clouds do not block out the sun's burning rays, and cloudy days are the most dangerous, since parents often leave their children unprotected.

Sunscreen preparations are occasionally used by parents to decrease harmful effects of exposure. Several products contain screening agents to protect the skin from sunlight (i.e., Pre Sun or Uval). Be careful. Suntan lotions and baby oil do not contain sunscreens unless they clearly state that on the label. If you use a tested sunscreen preparation, also be aware that it can wash off and that it is only a partial protection. Keeping a careful eye on the child to avoid serious overexposure is the best way to prevent sunburn, but do not use the redness of your child's skin as a guide to sun exposure. It usually takes several hours for the full effect of the sun to show and you can underestimate the amount of sun your child is getting.

Sunburn has an effect on the skin similar to a burn from heat. Mild burns will redden the skin and produce pain. More severe burns can cause blisters or discoloration. If blisters form, do not break them. The same treatment that was suggested for burns should be applied to sunburns. Ask your physician for advice in treating mild sunburn at home. He or she may recommend aspirin or an aspirin substitute to relieve the pain.

Do not allow sunburned areas to be further exposed to the sun until the skin has healed. Occasionally, with a more severe case of sunburn a child may look ill or have the chills or a fever. You should immediately seek medical advice for this situation, since it is similar to heatstroke (see page 1030).

ELECTRICAL BURNS. Electrical burns deserve special attention. A child who receives a burn from an electrical source such as a wall outlet, plug, or an electrical appliance, should always be seen by a doctor. Electrical burns can be very misleading. They may seem to have little effect at first, but occasionally can be more serious. It is advisable to check with your doctor for all electrical burns.

Taking Care of Cuts and Bruises

Nearly all youngsters sustain minor cuts and bruises as they grow up. Injuries such as these are common, especially among active children. Small cuts should be well cleaned with soap and water. This helps remove germs and prevents infections. Tap water or water suitable for drinking is usually appropriate for cleaning small cuts.

Gently wash the wound with soap and then rinse it well with water. Many doctors do not recommend strong antiseptics such as iodine for minor cuts. These agents can be very irritating to the wound and are not usually any better than soap and water. Ask your doctor if he or she recommends any other treatment besides soap and water.

Once the cut has been cleaned, it needs time to heal and should be kept free of dirt. Applying a simple bandage is the best way to keep a cut clean. Keeping the cut dry, clean, and undisturbed helps to promote healing.

Most parents prefer commercially available bandages such as Band-Aids. These come in an assortment of sizes and shapes to accommodate most minor cuts and scratches. Some Band-Aids also have the advantage of stick-free absorbent areas so that the scab that forms over the cut does not stick to the pad. Band-Aids are usually inexpensive and are readily available from many suppliers.

Elaborate bandaging using gauze wrapping and adhesive is often best left to professionals and is not necessary for minor cuts. If you must improvise and use gauze and tape, be sure not to wrap the wound too tightly. Never tightly wrap the fingers or toes with a bandage, since this could stop the blood flow. This also applies to bandages around the leg and arm. Ready-to-use Band-Aids save a lot of difficulty.

It is important for your child to be protected against tetanus, which could arise from infection in a small wound. If bacteria start to grow in a wound, they can produce a dangerous poison (toxin) that causes tetanus. This harmful illness can be completely prevented or minimized by seeing to it that your child is properly immunized against tetanus (see page 947).

FACIAL CUTS. It is advisable to call facial cuts to the attention of your doctor. Even small cuts on the face can produce scars. Scars on the face are very noticeable and should obviously be avoided if possible. Your doctor can carefully clean and protect the cut and minimize scarring. Cuts on the scalp that are not particularly serious often bleed heavily and require sustained pressure to stop the bleeding. This area of the body is very rich in blood vessels and normally bleeds more heavily.

LARGE CUTS. Large cuts or puncture wounds (from darts, arrows, and knives, etc.) should be brought to your doctor's attention. These wounds require more careful cleaning, since they are deeper and can trap bacteria. Occasionally a larger wound will need stitches to promote healing.

DIRTY CUTS. Cuts that are contaminated with dirt, pieces of rock, or animal or human feces should be brought to your doctor's attention. These wounds must be more carefully cleaned to remove possible sources of infection. Germs that cause tetanus (lockjaw) may be present in this dirt, especially in feces. Your doctor may want to give your child extra protection against tetanus in addition to the routine tetanus immunization program by giving a tetanus booster shot.

Recognizing and Dealing with Infections

By giving proper first aid to small cuts and consulting your doctor when appropriate, infections will be kept to a minimum. Occasionally a small wound will become infected. The skin around the wound will look reddened and inflamed and pus may form. Your child has natural defenses against infections, but special treatment can be given to speed healing time and prevent the infection from getting out of control. Ask your doctor's advice in treating infections. He or she may have specific recommendations.

Localized infections such as abscesses, boils, infected finger- and toenails, or infected small cuts need to drain so that the pus and debris can be cleaned from the wound. If the infection is very minimal, it is usually best treated by soaking the infected area in warm water. Soaking helps soften the skin and aids the body in opening the wound, and allowing the pus to escape.

Keeping a young child still for long periods of time to soak an infected area of his body is not an easy task. Soaking for shorter time periods (fifteen to twenty minutes) several times each day (three to four times/day) is a way to get around this problem. Some parents find it helpful to amuse the child by reading a story or playing a game while soaking an infection.

After soaking, cover the infected area with a dry clean bandage. Do not attempt to puncture the skin with a needle or knife. Do not apply medications without your doctor's advice.

A SPREADING INFECTION. A localized infection can spread into surrounding tissues, the blood, or the lymph system. Fortunately this condition is rare, if you take proper care of minor infections and seek the advice of your doctor. Fever, chills, swollen glands, or red streaks running up an arm or leg are signs that an infection is spreading. This situation requires immediate medical attention and special drugs may be needed to fight the spreading infection.

What to Do for Bleeding

Small cuts naturally bleed for a few minutes and then stop. Bleeding of this type is beneficial, since it helps clean out some of the bacteria and dirt in the wound. Most injuries will stop bleeding by themselves after the wound is cleaned. Occasionally a wound bleeds more persistently and needs extra attention.

Direct pressure applied over the wound is the best way to stop the bleeding. Using a gauze pad or clean piece of cloth, press down on the wound. The pressure will help stop the flow of blood and allow the blood-clotting mechanism to seal it off. It may take several minutes for the bleeding to stop.

Do not keep removing the pad from the cut to look at the bleeding. The blood takes time to clot. Frequently removing the pad interferes with clot formation. Apply firm pressure for several minutes (five to seven) by the clock before peeking. This technique gives enough time for the clotting mechanism to work. If the bleeding continues after the first attempt, apply pressure for a longer period of time.

Try to elevate the wound if it is on the arm or leg, while you apply direct pressure. This decreases the flow of blood to that area and helps allow the blood-clotting mechanism to overcome the bleeding. A wound on the extremities (arms, legs, feet, and hands) can be easily elevated by having the child lie down and then lift up the injured area. Calming the child helps lower the blood pressure that will naturally be increased from excitement. This will also decrease the bleeding rate.

Under rare circumstances a wound may cause severe bleeding at an alarming rate. Apply pressure to the wound immediately to prevent blood loss and seek medical assistance. Ask someone else to obtain bandages in the meantime. Use the cleanest cloth you have handy to make a pad to stop the bleeding (handkerchief, shirt, pieces of clothing, etc.). Hold this pad in place over the wound with pressure. If the first cloth is soaked with blood, take a second one and place it over the original pad and continue applying pressure. Do not remove the first pad since it is starting to help form a clot. Try to elevate the wound if possible and continue to apply pressure until help arrives.

It is very unusual for bleeding to continue if adequate pressure is applied. Always seek medical assistance for any wound that continues to bleed or causes significant blood loss.

Stopping Nosebleeds

Nosebleeds are often seen in childhood. Most bleeds occur in the front part of the nose and usually stop by themselves or with minimal treatment. Applying direct pressure to the bleeding site is the most effective way to stop the bleeding. Gently pinching together the nostrils with your fingers or with a gauze or cloth for one to two minutes is recommended as the first approach for all nosebleeds. If the bleeding starts again or is not completely stopped, the most effective way to stop a more persistent nosebleed is to reapply firm pressure to both nostrils by pinching them together for a full ten minutes by the clock—without peeking to see if the bleeding has stopped. This treatment should allow the blood to clot and stop the bleeding. Call your doctor if you cannot stop the bleeding. You should discuss the technique for treating nosebleeds with your physician, who may make additional recommendations.

The blood from the nose can often be swallowed by the child. This blood in the stomach can cause nausea. Do not be alarmed if your child vomits blood after a nosebleed, because of the blood that he swallowed. The most effective way to stop the swallowing of blood is to: 1) have the child sit up and lean forward (do not tilt the head back) and 2) stop the bleeding by applying firm direct pressure as described above.

Nosebleeds often occur as the result of trauma or picking at the nose, especially in children with chronic allergies or colds. They may also be caused by constant nose-blowing. Very dry air can dry out the lining in the nostrils and increase the frequency of nosebleeds. Most of these factors can be easily identified and corrected. On rare occasions nosebleeds can result from medical illnesses or blood-clotting abnormalities.

It is usually advisable to keep a record of the frequency of your child's nosebleeds and discuss this with your physician. If they are occurring very frequently or in the absence of an obvious cause, such as trauma, your doctor will want to examine your youngster more closely.

Sprains and Small Fractures

Minor ankle, knee, and wrist sprains are fairly common in childhood. They often occur during strenuous sport activities or after falls. The sprained joint usually becomes swollen in ten to thirty minutes after the injury and turns "black and blue" in the next twenty-four to forty-eight hours. Occasionally a bad sprain or bruise will turn purple almost immediately. This is usually the result of small blood vessel and capillary rupture with minor bleeding into the tissue.

Treatment of a sprain or bruise normally consists of resting and elevating the injured area, and applying cold compresses or soaking the part in cold water immediately after the injury. These measures decrease blood flow and prevent inflammation in the acute phase (first half hour). This helps minimize swelling and further tissue damage.

If the injury cannot be treated with cold compresses in the first half hour, it usually swells more extensively. Following this phase, the sprain often becomes more painful. At this point, warm compresses are useful. They increase blood flow to the injured area and thus help remove the damaged tissue and promote healing.

Most sprains heal quickly and require little more than loving care, but occasionally they are so severe that the child is in a great deal of pain and/or cannot use the injured arm or leg. These sprains should be seen by your doctor. A splint may be necessary to immobilize the injury to allow the stretched ligaments and tendons to heal.

It is also possible that a small fracture (broken bone) may have occurred. This can be seen on an X-ray. Small fractures are painless initially and then become very painful at a later time when the injured part is in use. Always be alert to the possibility of small fractures with any painful injury and seek medical advice. The care and handling of more severe fractures are discussed below.

Fractures (Broken Bones)

An injury that causes severe or persistent pain raises the possibility of a fracture (broken bone). These injuries should be evaluated by a doctor. There are many different types of fractures, depending on the bone that is injured and the type of injury.

A severe fracture is easy to recognize because it usually causes a deformity in shape. In a severe fracture of a long bone of the arm or leg, the limb will be bent out of position and the child will be in severe pain. If a bone is only slightly cracked, there may be no obvious change in shape of the part involved.

Fractures in the bones of the wrists, ankles, and chest area often do not cause an obvious deformity in shape. You can recognize these fractures by other symptoms such as severe or chronic pain, swelling, and possibly "black-and-blue" discoloration. The fingers and toes are especially susceptible to small fractures because these body parts are often injured during play. Falls from high places or head or neck trauma may cause back or neck fractures. Persistent back or neck pain following an injury should alert you to this possibility and the need to seek medical advice.

The first step in supportive care is to avoid further injury by keeping the broken bones from moving until you get medical assistance. Also try to calm the child until you can obtain appropriate help. If the child will not remain still, employ a firm object (splint, wooden spoon, heavy cardboard, etc.) that will fit along the leg or arm to achieve immobilization. Wrap a bandage (gauze, cloth, towel, etc.) gently around the broken limb and splint so that the fractured region is immobilized. Be sure not to wrap too tightly, since this can stop the flow of blood.

For severe injuries suffered in falls from high places or automobile accidents where neck or back fractures may have occurred, do not attempt to move the child, since this may cause further injury. Try to keep him still and await the arrival of proper emergency care personnel. If he must be moved, first try to immobilize the head and neck. Then slide him carefully onto a flat, hard surface such as a board, door, or tray, with as little movement as possible. Once the back and neck are supported on the flat surface, the child can be carefully moved by lifting the board.

Giving Artificial Respiration

Artificial respiration should be initiated immediately if a person stops breathing. Fortunately this is a rare event with children. Drowning, poisoning, electric shock, suffocation, and other emergencies, however, can occasionally cause normal breathing to stop. Knowing how to perform artificial respiration can be lifesaving in one of these emergency situations.

If you live near water or do a lot of swimming with your family, this technique is especially important, because drownings are a major cause for a child to stop breathing. There is no substitute for personalized instruction in this technique and it is strongly recommended that parents take a first aid course in their community (see pages 985–86). The discussion of artificial respiration given below is only intended to give a brief presentation and acquaint you with this technique, and is not meant to be used in place of personalized instruction.

The two basic steps of artificial respiration are:

Opening the air passage
Restoring breathing

These two steps can be performed quickly without special equipment and under almost any circumstances when a person stops breathing. Call for emergency aid at once or have someone else do this while artificial respiration is being initiated. Do not use this technique on a person who is breathing.

OPENING THE AIR PASSAGE. The first step to restore breathing is to open the airway. Special care must be taken with accident victims (see pages 994–96). The unconscious victim should be placed on his back. If mucus, food, or other obstructions are present in the mouth, quickly tilt the head to the side and clean them out of the mouth with your finger before beginning. Then open the airway and see if the person starts breathing.

Opening the Air Passage

To open the airway tilt the head back and lift up the neck: this is accomplished by (1) putting one hand under the neck and the other hand on the forehead and (2) lifting the neck with one hand while tilting the head back with the other. This simple maneuver opens the air passage and lifts the tongue off the back of the throat.

Extra care must be taken in opening the airway of an infant or young child. Their necks are so flexible that too much tilting can obstruct the airway. Do not exaggerate the head tilt in this situation. It might be easier to put the supporting hand under the neck and shoulders and then lift up gently.

When the airway is opened, listen, look, and feel for the movement of air. Sometimes just opening the air passage will start the breathing. You may see the abdomen and chest moving or feel or hear air being taken in and out of the victim's mouth.

Begin artificial respiration if you do not see or hear any spontaneous breathing after opening the airway.

RESTORING BREATHING: MOUTH-TO-MOUTH RESUSCITATION. To restore breathing, begin mouth-to-mouth resuscitation. Keep one hand under the back of the neck and the other hand on the forehead to keep open the airway. Use the thumb and index finger of the hand on the forehead to pinch the victim's nostrils together. Place your mouth over the victim's, forming a tight seal with his lips. Then blow into the victim's mouth. Because you are holding the nostrils closed, the air should enter his lungs and expand the chest. This method is effective for most older toddlers and preschool children. In an infant or very small child, you might not be able to cover only the child's mouth with your mouth. In that case, you would cover both his mouth and nose with your mouth. Remember that an infant's and young child's lungs are much smaller than yours. You will not have to breathe out completely to fill their lungs. Use shallow breaths to inflate their lungs.

Next remove your mouth and allow the air to come out (exhalation). Watch the chest come down and listen for the return of air from the mouth or nose. This cycle is repeated at your regular breathing rate (twelve to fourteen times/minute or every five seconds) for an adult and at a slightly faster rate (sixteen to twenty times per minute or every three to four seconds) for an infant or young child, as long as the person continues to have trouble breathing. Once the procedure is started, it should proceed rhythmically.

Mouth to Mouth Respiration

You will know that you are producing adequate ventilation if (1) the chest rises and falls (2) you can feel the resistance and air flow as you expand the victim's lungs, and (3) you can hear the return of air during exhalation. If air does not seem to be getting into the victim's lungs, check to be sure that the air passage is open and that nothing is obstructing the airway in the mouth (tongue, food, etc.).

RESTORING BREATHING: MOUTH-TO-NOSE RESUSCITATION. The mouth-to-mouth method is preferred when it can be performed. Occasionally it may not be possible to open the mouth or breathe into the mouth because of injury to the jaw or mouth. In these situations the mouth-to-nose technique can be used. Open the airway as described above and put your mouth over the victim's nose, forming a seal with your lips. Then blow air into the victim's lungs through his nose. The same procedure is followed as described above for determining whether the victim is breathing.

It is usually best to use the following technique to open the airway, and, at the same time, keep the victim's mouth closed. Place one hand under the chin, holding the jaw closed, and lift up and back. Put the other hand on the forehead to assist in tilting back the head. Keeping the mouth closed prevents the air that you breathe into the nose from coming out of the mouth. It is occasionally necessary to slightly open the victim's mouth as he exhales, if the air does not easily exit through the nose.

ACCIDENT VICTIMS. Extra care must be exercised before considering resuscitation when there is the possibility of a neck fracture. Neck fractures should be suspected in automobile accidents or when there is obvious trauma to the head and neck. In these situations do not move the neck.

Learning About Cardiopulmonary Resuscitation (CPR)

Cardiopulmonary resuscitation (CPR) is a supportive first aid technique that combines artificial respiration and artificial circulation (movement of the blood). CPR should be started immediately by a trained individual when an emergency occurs in which a person stops breathing and/or circulation of the blood by the heart ceases.

993

This technique has been used successfully for some time by health care professionals. It is currently recommended that as many members of the general public as possible learn CPR.

Cardiac arrest (stopping of the heart) is recognized by the lack of pulses in the large arteries in an unconscious victim who has stopped breathing. In first approaching an unconscious victim who is not breathing, open the airway and quickly start artificial respiration. If you suspect that the heart has stopped as well, feel for the pulse. The absence of a pulse suggests that the heart has stopped and that CPR should be started to produce artificial circulation along with artificial respiration. Although the technique of performing CPR is not difficult, it requires in-person instruction and practice to perfect.

Several communities are organizing courses in CPR. The American Red Cross and other medical organizations are now offering courses in this technique. Many victims of respiratory or cardiac collapse are being saved because CPR was begun at the scene to stabilize them until medical assistance could be obtained.

Fortunately, the need to use CPR in children or infants is very rare. Drowning, suffocation, electric shock, and severe trauma are among the causes for pulmonary and/or cardiac arrest. Heart attacks are the most common situation requiring CPR in adults. Learning how to support respiration and circulation in an injured child or adult is a useful skill. We strongly recommend that you take a course in CPR to learn this simple, lifesaving technique.

What to Do for Choking

When something gets caught in the windpipe, the child or infant has difficulty getting air into the lungs because the airway is blocked. Choking is the body's natural defense against these obstructions. Air is forcefully expelled from the windpipe during choking in an attempt to dislodge the object and force it out of the airway. If something is accidentally swallowed or breathed into the airway, the child will usually cough for a short time and expel the obstruction by himself. In rare situations the natural choking response may not free the airway and assistance is needed to help dislodge the obstruction.

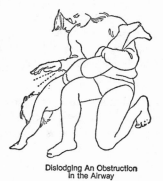

Dislodging An Obstruction
in the Airway

An infant or young child who is choking and is not able to clear the airway rapidly on his own needs assistance in getting out the blockage. Quickly pick up the child and invert him over your arm while you strike his back firmly. Be sure to tilt his head down so that gravity will also help dislodge the obstruction. Avoid using too much force. If an older child cannot cough up an object, it may also be helpful to deliver firm slaps with the heel of the hand between the shoulder blades. Slapping the back is a simple procedure that often helps dislodge objects from the airway. However, slapping the back may lodge the object deeper in the throat. The most effective way to clear the airway is to be perform the Heimlich Maneuver.

The Heimlich Maneuver is named after Dr. Henry Heimlich, who developed it, and is a simple procedure that can be performed on an adult or child to clear the airway more effectively. The best way to learn this procedure is by practicing it under supervision in a first aid course. For an adult or child the following steps are performed:

1. The rescuer quickly stands behind the choking individual and wraps his arms around the victim's waist.
2. Make a fist with one hand and place the thumb side of the fist against the victim's abdomen—below the rib cage and slightly above the belly button.
3. Grasp this fist with the other hand and press into the victim's abdomen with a quick upward thrust and then relax the hug.
4. Repeat the upward thrust several times if necessary.

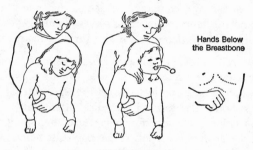

Hands Below
the Breastbone

Heimlich Manuever

This procedure is very effective, since the sudden hug increases the air pressure under the diaphragm, causing the lungs to exhale. The air that is forced out of the windpipe by this technique will help dislodge the blockage. Do not use extreme force or squeeze the rib cage since it will not compress and you can injure the ribs. Thus, be sure you hug below the rib cage. Less force is required for a child than an adult.

The Heimlich Maneuver can also be performed on the infant or young child, but this requires more care, since you do not want to injure the infant's more delicate ribs. For the infant or small child:

1. The infant is held facing away on the rescuer's lap or laid face up on a firm surface with the rescuer at his feet.
2. Place the index and middle fingers of both hands on the child's abdomen, well below the rib cage and slightly above the navel.
3. Gently press into the abdomen with a quick upward thrust and then relax.
4. Repeat the procedure if necessary.

Obtain in-person instruction on how to perform the Heimlich Maneuver. Be especially careful in performing this procedure on infants so that you do not use too much force and injure the ribs. Discuss this procedure with your doctor or nurse during a well baby check-up. A useful pamphlet can be obtained, which discusses this procedure in some detail (see Henry Heimlich and Milton Uhley, Additional Reading & Bibliography).

Occasionally, a sharp object such as a fishbone or a jack may lodge in the wind-pipe and may cause persistent choking. As long as the child is getting enough air and is not turning blue he will be fine. Your doctor will be able to remove the object. Do not attempt to reach in the throat to remove an object that is lodged deep in the back of the throat. This may just push the object further into the windpipe. Keep in mind that persistent choking or coughing can be caused by an illness. See page 959.

Handling Eye Injuries

CAUSTIC LIQUID IN THE EYE. Children may accidentally splash toxic or caustic liquids in their eyes (drain cleaner, detergents, medicines, etc.). In these situations, immediately flush the eye with water. This dilutes the substance and helps prevent damage to the surface of the eye. The important thing is to act immediately. Tap water can be quickly splashed, poured, or run over the eye to dilute the toxin. Irrigate thoroughly. It takes almost fifteen minutes to wash out lye or acid. When you have flushed out the eye, contact your doctor. After any accidental splashing with a potentially toxic substance, your child's eyes should be examined by your physician. He or she will be able to determine if any further treatment is necessary.

TRAUMA TO THE EYE. A blow to the eye can sometimes cause an abrasion (scrape) or cut on the surface of the eye. In rare situations an object (stone, dart, etc.) may be accidentally projected into the eye, cutting or lodging in the surface. These injuries should always receive medical attention.

In many situations, eye injuries look worse than they really are, since the tissue around the eye can quickly swell or become discolored with blood. It is important not to panic. Try to calm yourself and your child and seek medical attention. Thanks to the advances of modern medicine, most eye injuries can be successfully treated.

SMALL OBJECTS IN THE EYE. Handling routine situations when small specks or objects get in the eye will be the most common eye problem you will deal with as parents. Dust, mucous, crusted eye matter, and dirt often get trapped in the eye and produce minor, temporary discomfort. A foreign body (small piece of glass, stone, etc.) can also get in the eye, and these objects should be removed by a doctor if they do not wash out of the eye on their own.

The eye has its own natural way of removing these objects. Tears immediately begin to flow in the involved eye to wash out the particle. Blinking starts in an attempt to try and wash away the material. These natural mechanisms are usually sufficient to clear out the foreign material.

Occasionally, a small speck will not be washed out by these natural responses and your child will come to you complaining of discomfort. Keep him from rubbing the eye. Rubbing can cause further irritation by forcefully pushing the object over the surface of the eye. Do not try to probe the object loose with a swab. Most young children or infants will not be very co-operative and will not sit still. It is not uncommon for well-meaning parents to injure the eye accidentally while they are probing for an object because of a sudden jerk or movement by the child.

A simple maneuver can be performed that will help the eye's natural mechanisms remove the irritant. Hold the upper lid by the eyelashes and gently pull it away from the eye and down. Wait a few seconds and then release the lid.

This technique helps produce tears and flush the particle out of the eye. Try this simple maneuver three or four times. If this does not work, water may be used to wash the eye gently to help the body's natural mechanisms flush out the particle. Some parents prefer using an eye cup to wash out the small particles, but this is not absolutely necessary. Simple irrigation can work just as well. Occasionally, the small speck will be persistent and refuse to come out. In these circumstances, let your doctor remove the particle.

Recognizing and Handling Objects in the Ears or Nose

Toddlers and even preschool-age children occasionally put small objects in their ears or nose. These objects may become lodged in place and not come out. The best rule of thumb in handling this situation is to remain calm and not rush ahead. Do not try to pull on the object. Small firm objects are usually difficult to remove by hand and will probably be pushed in further as a result of your hurried attempts.

If your child is not in any pain or discomfort, take your time and evaluate the situation. Try to use gravity to your advantage. Tilt the head so that the object can fall out of the ear or nose. Sometimes this simple maneuver along with a mild tap will dislodge the object. If the object is soft or can be grasped with a tweezers, your doctor may be able to remove it without difficulty. Care must be taken in using a tweezers, especially in the ear, since the point can be pushed in too far, causing damage to the eardrum. The child may suddenly jump or move, making removal more difficult. Let a trained individual remove objects with a tweezer.

Another trick, if the object is in the nose, is to try to have the child gently blow it out when he blows his nose. This method can be used if the child is old enough to be able to blow his nose without first breathing in through his nose. Having the child inhale pepper held under the nose will cause him to sneeze. This may help blow out the object.

If these initial attempts fail, do not persist. You are likely to do more harm than good. Call your doctor or take the child to the nearest hospital emergency room.

Sometimes you may not know your child put something in his ear or nose. Be on the lookout for bloody discharges, foul-smelling odors, or pain from these sites. These signs often appear several days after an object has been in the ear or nose. Be especially suspicious of foreign objects in the ears and nose during toddlerhood.

Head Injuries

Mild head injuries as a result of routine minor bumps during play are common in early childhood. The toddler who is in constant motion is especially susceptible to minor injuries. Following most of these injuries, the child cries for several minutes and then returns to his normal activities. A small bruise may appear, but he is otherwise fine.

An infant who rolls or falls off a high dressing table and hits his head or receives a hard blow to his head for another reason may appear fine, but is at risk for a more serious injury involving delayed bleeding. The infant should be observed after such a fall or injury and the doctor should be informed if the child begins to behave abnormally.

Head injuries that result in unconsciousness, fever, or unusual behavior (excessive sleeping, agitation, personality change, severe headaches, blurred vision, dizziness, loss of vision, nausea, or vomiting, etc.) should be brought to the attention of a doctor. It is important to recognize the possible relationship between these signs and the head injury. In some situations the symptoms arise immediately following the injury, but in others they do not surface until several days afterward.

Loss of Consciousness

Loss of consciousness is not very common, but it causes concern when it occurs. Occasionally, a child will pass out for a few seconds during a breath-holding spell. On rare occasions a child may faint momentarily from exhaustion or being overheated. If the child appears to "faint" for only a brief moment and is otherwise fine, you should pay careful attention to the details of the episode and inform your doctor about it. Infrequent spells of this nature may be benign, but it is important to know that the child's faints were not due to convulsions or another medical problem.

A child who loses consciousness for a prolonged period of time as the result of head injury, illness, or unknown causes should receive prompt medical attention. This is a rare occurrence. Be sure that he is breathing (see pages 991–92) and attempt to transport him carefully to the nearest medical facility. If head, neck, or back injuries are suspected, do not move the child (see page 993), but arrange for medical assistance.

What to Do for Swallowed Objects

Children and babies occasionally swallow small objects that they have put in their mouths. Round, smooth, small objects such as pits, marbles, buttons, or small coins usually pass through the digestive tract without difficulty once they get past the throat. In fact, almost anything the child actually swallows will pass through the stomach and intestines and come out in the bowel movement. Watch the bowel movements carefully to see if the object comes out. Be alert to any changes in the child's behavior or signs of pain or vomiting.

Straight pins or other sharp objects may be more difficult to pass and are more dangerous. Consult the doctor if the child swallows a sharp object or has any signs of pain or nausea and vomiting after swallowing such an object.

Do not give laxatives to try and speed up the passage of an object. Laxatives do not help very much and can occasionally be harmful. The body will pass most objects naturally without difficulty.

Taking Care of Bites

Occasionally, young children receive animal bites, especially when there are numerous pets in the area. Most minor bites from dogs, cats, birds, and house pets are not serious. However, it is advisable to consult your doctor about an animal bite. For a minor bite, he or she may just recommend simple first aid. In case of a more severe bite, treatment in the doctor's office may be advised. Bites on the face should be seen by your doctor, since they can lead to noticeable scars unless treated properly.

In situations in which the animal was very vicious, bit without provocation, or was a stray or wild, it is very important to capture the animal and observe it for ten days to be sure it does not have rabies. Most communities have city facilities for such purposes. Your doctor may decide that rabies innoculations are indicated in the event that the animal was wild and can not be found.

Human bites are often more of a problem than animal bites. Believe it or not, human saliva will produce an infection much more commonly than an animal bite. Human bites that puncture the skin should be brought to the attention of your doctor. Careful cleaning and antibiotic treatment may be indicated. Animal or human bites can produce deep puncture wounds that are seeded with germs. Being sure your child is immunized against tetanus will prevent this illness from occurring as a result of germs in the wound. A very dirty bite may prompt your doctor to give a tetanus booster.

Drowning

Drowning is a major cause of injury and death during childhood. Toddler and preschool children are especially susceptible to drowning accidents. Drownings occur mainly because of a lack of proper adult supervision, overconfidence on the child's part, absence of sufficient protection, or bad judgment. Young children usually drown while left unattended in bathtubs or swimming areas or after a fall through the ice on a pond. Older children more commonly get into difficulty while playing in the water without proper supervision or experience.

The first and best way to handle drownings is to prevent them. Do not allow toddlers and preschool children to play unsupervised in the water, and this includes the bathtub. Even at a public pool or beach, the supervision on a crowded day is not likely to be adequate. Always carefully watch or play with the young child if he is in the water. Teaching him respect for the water and water safety is important. Learning how to swim and handle himself in the water is also very important, especially if the family lives near a lake or other body of water.

HANDLING A NEAR DROWNING. Artificial respiration (pages 991–93) should be started immediately if a person is found in the water and is not breathing spontaneously. It is important not to delay. While giving artificial respiration, try to send for medical assistance. Even if the victim is revived before help arrives, he should be examined by a doctor. In some cases, the function of the heart as well as the lungs must be supported. These situations require the immediate initiation of cardiopulmonary resuscitation (pages 993–94).

Insect Stings

Bee, wasp, hornet, or other insect stings occur fairly often in childhood. The child usually comes into the house crying with a red mark on his arm, leg, face, or neck; look to see if the stinger is still in the skin. If the stinger is still present, remove it with a fine tweezer or fingernail. The site of the bite may also begin to swell, hurt, and itch because of an inflammatory reaction. Other insect bites or stings may not be as bothersome. Mosquito or fly bites often itch or burn but do not cause as much pain.

There is no one remedy for all insect stings. There are several commercially available sprays and lotions that claim to reduce the pain, itching, and swelling. Your doctor will be able to recommend additional treatments for very painful or itchy stings.

The main danger from insect stings is that some children may suffer a generalized allergic reaction: hives, difficulty breathing, and/or shock or collapse. These generalized reactions are rare, but when they occur they require immediate medical attention. Hives are an indication that the child is allergic to the sting and this suggests that future stings may produce a more serious generalized reaction. Your doctor will be able to advise you how best to handle this situation.

Shock

Following exposure to extreme cold, infections, blood loss, trauma, near drownings, or other serious injuries, shock may develop. Shock can be recognized by the symptoms that it produces. The child will appear very sick and weak and look pale and sweaty. The pulse is usually rapid and weak. In some situations breathing will become shallow and labored. Shock is a medical emergency. Lay the child flat on a comfortable surface and keep him warm (with a blanket or cover). Obtain medical assistance as rapidly as possible.

HOW TO HANDLE POISONINGS

Most accidental poisonings can be greatly diminished or prevented by safety-proofing the home and taking the necessary safety precautions with toxic substances and medicines. The suggestions provided in the How To Ensure Your Child's Safety sections should help you prevent poisonings before they occur. Child-proof medicine bottles, locked cabinets, and Mr. Yuk stickers are a few of the ways in which you can help prevent accidental poisonings during the ages when children are most likely to put everything into their mouths.

Occasionally, a child will still manage to eat a poisonous substance. It is very difficult, if not impossible, for parents always to determine what to do when their child eats something he should not have eaten. Fortunately, it is no longer necessary to guess, since you can almost always obtain immediate medical advice on how to handle the problem.

Know Where to Call for Help

Today the majority of ingestions of potentially poisonous substances by children can be easily handled and the danger to the child greatly reduced. Medical advice on how to manage poisonings is immediately available to all parents except under very exceptional circumstances. If you suspect that your child has ingested a poisonous substance, call your doctor at once. He or she will be able to assist you in managing the situation. If your doctor is not in or you cannot get through to the office, call the Poison Control Center in your area for advice.

Poison Control or Poison Information Centers are major resources for parents to obtain quick information on what to do in case of a poisoning. These centers can be contacted by phone twenty-four hours a day. A doctor or other specially trained professional is available to answer your questions and assist you. There is a network of

Poison Control Centers across the United States, and even if you live far away from a center, you can quickly reach one by phone.

Between calling a doctor or Poison Control Center, every parent has immediate access to medical advice for handling poisonings, except in the rare situations where the phones are out of order or a phone cannot be reached. The development and accessibility of Poison Control Centers represents a major advance in emergency medical care. Every parent should be prepared to obtain medical assistance for handling poisonings by having the phone numbers of their doctor and Poison Control Center readily available (see page 948).

Ask your doctor for the location and phone number of the nearest Poison Control Center. Numbers are often listed in local phone directories under Poison Control or Poison Information Centers. You might also want to call your Poison Control Center to ask for any available literature and to familiarize yourself with the center's services.

Be Prepared in Advance

In addition to avoiding accidental poisonings by safety-proofing the home and knowing where to call for assistance, it is very important to have syrup of ipecac and activated charcoal in your medicine chest. Syrup of ipecac, when taken by mouth, causes vomiting and is used in some situations to remove a poison from the stomach before it can be absorbed into the system. Activated charcoal is a substance that when ingested can bind many poisons in the stomach, preventing their absorption into the body.

When you call the Poison Control Center or your doctor in an emergency, the recommendation may be to induce vomiting immediately with syrup of ipecac and/or give powdered activated charcoal. If you have these items in the home, you will be prepared to give treatment at once. However, these medications should be given only after you obtain medical advice. Inducing vomiting and giving activated charcoal are not the best ways to treat all poisonings and can be dangerous if used with some substances (see page 1003).

It is recommended that you discuss obtaining *syrup of ipecac* and *activated charcoal* with your doctor. He or she can tell you where to obtain these substances and how to use them. They are readily available in most drugstores.

Managing a Poisoning

RECOGNIZING A POISONING. How will you know your child has ingested a potentially harmful substance? In some cases this will be obvious. You may actually see your child swallow or eat something. You may find an empty container on the floor. Even though your child seems fine, you should suspect that he has ingested the contents of the container. Occasionally, an older child will tell you he has eaten something and feels sick.

Sometimes it will be more difficult to recognize a poisoning. The child may ingest something without your knowing it. You will suspect something is wrong only if he becomes sick or behaves in an unusual way.

The signs and symptoms of poisoning can vary greatly, depending on the substance and amounts ingested. If the substance was not very toxic, no obvious signs of illness may be apparent. Other substances can be very irritating to the stomach and mouth, possibly causing vomiting, cramps, burns on the lips, or pain. Confusion, difficulty breathing, or marked change in behavior may occur with some substances such as overdoses of medication or some plant or insect sprays.

In case you suspect a poisoning, immediately look around the area in which your child was playing to see if there is any evidence that he consumed a toxic substance. An older child can be asked what he ate. Empty containers should be examined so you can try to determine what and how much your child has ingested.

CALL FOR HELP. Call the doctor or Poison Control Center immediately if you think your child has ingested a toxic substance. Keep your child close at hand while you call, so that you can observe his behavior.

Be prepared, if possible, to tell the doctor or trained professional what, when, and how much your child has swallowed. If you are not sure of what was ingested, describe the child's condition or why you suspect a poisoning. Recommendations can then be given by phone as to how to handle the situation.

It is reassuring that many of the substances ingested by children are not dangerous. Your doctor or Poison Control Center will be able to tell you if the substance ingested was a poison. Non-poisonous substances will pass through the digestive system without causing any difficulties. Ingestion of these substances requires no special treatment.

Occasionally, a child will ingest a poisonous material. Your doctor or Poison Control Center will be able to advise you on how best to handle this situation. In some cases no treatment will be recommended and you will be asked to bring your child immediately to your doctor's office or hospital. In other cases the recommendation may be to start treatment in the home and then bring the child in for evaluation.

DO NOT BE FOOLED BY A LACK OF SYMPTOMS. In some cases parents see their children eat a poisonous substance or have evidence that they have ingested one, but do not see any immediate symptoms or side effects. Do not be fooled by the apparent lack of symptoms. Be sure to call your doctor or Poison Control Center immediately to find out if the substance ingested is poisonous.

Some substances such as aspirin take longer than parents would think to produce obvious effects in the child. It is well worth a phone call to be sure that the substance the child has eaten is not harmful. Many ingestions of substances by children do not cause any serious problems, but it is very important to be certain of this fact. Do not hesitate to inquire any time, day or night.

IF YOU CANNOT OBTAIN IMMEDIATE MEDICAL ADVICE. In the very rare event that you cannot immediately reach your doctor or Poison Control Center, and it will take you only twenty to thirty minutes to get to the hospital or other medical facility, it is best to start off without delay. Bring along the empty container of medicine or other pills or substances that might help the doctor identify what was eaten.

If you are more than half an hour away from a hospital or medical facility and unable to obtain medical advice, you can begin to manage the poisoning and provide supportive care. Some substances when swallowed are very irritating to the mouth and throat or can be dangerous if they get breathed into the lungs. The more common irritating substances that can be found around the home are listed in the following table. Strong acids and bases (lye, ammonia, etc.) and caustic cleaning solutions can irritate or injure the mouth and throat, especially if they are vomited. Petroleum products (hydrocarbons) that are consumed are potentially dangerous if they are vomited and breathed into the lungs.

Some Common Substances for Which You DO NOT Induce Vomiting

CAUSTIC SUBSTANCES

Ammonia
Bleach
Caustic Lime
Drain Cleaners (containing lye—i.e.,
 Drano)
Lye
Oven Cleaners
Strong Acids (carbolic, formic, nitric,
 sulfuric)

PETROLEUM PRODUCTS (HYDROCARBONS)

Benzene
Carbon Tetrachloride
Cleaning Fluids
Gasoline
Grease Cleaners
Kerosene
Lighter Fluid
Liquid Auto Polish
Liquid Furniture Polish
Oil Base Paints, Paint Solvents and
 Thinners
Wood Stains and Strippers

Ask your doctor for any additions to this list that might be common in your community.

DO NOT induce vomiting if your child has ingested one of the types of substances listed in the table. Be supportive by trying to calm him and head off to the nearest hospital or medical facility without delay. If the child has swallowed a strong acid base, or other caustic substance, it is best to give water or milk to drink, since this will dilute the caustic substances in the stomach and help diminish further irritation. It is best not to initiate any treatment of ingestions of hydrocarbon substances without medical advice.

Never induce vomiting in a person who is unconscious or having a seizure, because the material that is brought up may be breathed into the lungs.

If your child has ingested a poisonous substance that is not in the table, you should try to get him to throw up the poisonous substance, if you have syrup of ipecac in the house. Give three teaspoonfuls (one tablespoonful) of syrup of ipecac to a child over one year of age, followed by four to six ounces of water (about half an average-size glassful). Then start off to the nearest medical facility and bring a container to catch the vomitus, if possible.

For infants from six to twelve months of age, reduce the dose to two teaspoonfuls of syrup of ipecac followed by three to four ounces of water to induce vomiting. Do not repeat this treatment in this age group and do not give syrup of ipecac to infants less than six months of age. Bring along a container to catch the vomitus so it can be analyzed by the doctor.

It should be comforting to know that it is extremely rare for parents who are prepared to call their doctor or Poison Control Center ever to have to manage a poisoning alone. Being able to obtain rapid medical assistance for poisonings twenty-four hours a day is a great help to parents and markedly reduces the risk to the child.

LEAD POISONING

It is important to be aware of the problem of lead poisoning, especially as your child nears the age at which he gains access to several rooms in your house. Lead poisoning can be a serious matter about which every parent should be informed. If you live in an older building or have old painted toys or furniture, it is very likely that some of the paint in your home contains lead pigments. This source of lead can be a danger to your child. Relatives or friends may also have sources of lead paint in their homes. Care must be taken to prevent your child from having access to these sources on a regular basis.

Some children enjoy eating chips of leaded paint and you, as a parent, can be unaware that your child is indulging in these harmful snacks, unless you happen to catch him in the act. Lead poisoning is a cumulative process. A child who eats small chips of leaded paint on a daily basis from the baseboards or furniture will gradually build up a high amount of lead in his body. This lead accumulates in the blood and body tissues and unless the intake is stopped, it can reach toxic levels and produce signs of illness and even serious harm to the child.

When Is Lead Poisoning Most Often Seen?

Lead poisoning is most prevalent in children between one and three years of age. It can occur earlier or later. The toddler and the young preschool child are the most likely to eat paint flakes that contain lead. During this time children often eat unnatural foods including dirt, clay, paper, ashes, string, and paint chips.

This is a time when the child is exploring and often uses his mouth to learn about his surroundings. In this age group, it is a natural tendency for him to put things in his mouth, and he should not be blamed for his behavior. It is up to the parents to be sure that his home does not contain accessible sources of lead-base paint.

Symptoms of Lead Poisoning

There are several different ways lead poisoning can produce symptoms, but the following sequence of events is most common in children under three, especially in the summer months. The child loses his appetite, becomes more irritable, and seems more tired than usual. This can gradually lead to episodic vomiting, loss of newly learned skills, anemia, and problems with balance. These symptoms slowly increase over four to eight weeks.

A child who develops these symptoms should be seen by a doctor. If these earlier symptoms of lead poisoning are not recognized, they can lead to an acute involvement of the brain called encephalopathy. Persistent vomiting, unresponsiveness, and finally coma and convulsions mark the onset of encephalopathy. This condition almost always follows the other symptoms described above. It rarely occurs without numerous previous symptoms.

In most cases the symptoms of lead poisoning diminish or go away when the abnormal eating of lead stops. This can add to parents' confusion. The early signs of irritability, tiredness, and loss of appetite may subside after the child stops eating lead for a while. Then they may reappear several months later when he again has access to lead paint chips. Thus, the child can suffer recurrent episodes of these earlier symptoms without developing encephalopathy. Parents may attach little importance to these milder symptoms and the chronic ingestion of lead can continue.

A child who eats lead without getting encephalopathy can develop other difficulties. The chronic accumulation of lead in the nervous system can cause degeneration of brain cells, mental retardation, convulsions, or behavioral disturbances. Other signs of chronic lead poisoning can also develop, such as muscle weakness and nerve damage.

Symptoms of lead poisoning, especially mild ones, must not be overlooked or be regarded as unimportant. They should be brought to the attention of your doctor.

Prevention of Lead Poisoning

The identification and elimination of environmental sources of lead are the keys to treating lead poisoning. Even though there are medications to remove some of the lead from the body (chelating agents), these drugs usually cannot prevent the occurrence of permanent brain damage if the child continues to be chronically exposed to lead. Eliminating the source of lead ingestion and preventing further exposure is essential in treating this condition.

Parents living in newer homes and using new furniture and toys have a better chance of providing a lead-free environment for their child. It is much less common today for lead-base paints to be used.

Older homes, furniture, and toys require more special attention. The child's room, play area, and equipment should be free of sources of lead. Paint on the walls, window sills, and baseboards in these areas should be lead-free as well.

Should you observe your child eating chips of paint and/or developing some of the milder symptoms of lead poisoning described above, discuss this with your doctor. It is important to find out whether or not your child is being chronically exposed to lead. The doctor can examine your child and perform some simple tests to determine this. The amount of lead in the blood can be directly measured.

Substances in the urine that are increased as a result of lead poisoning can be detected by a laboratory test. The presence or absence of anemia, a sign of lead poisoning, can also be determined by analyzing the blood (see page 979). Your doctor will select the appropriate tests, if necessary, to evaluate your child's condition.

In the event that the doctor determines that your child has been ingesting excessive amounts of lead, it is especially important for further exposure to be prevented. Examine your house thoroughly, looking for possible sources of lead. Sometimes it is easy to pinpoint the source, while in other situations it may be less obvious. You should obtain assistance in evaluating your home, if you cannot determine the source of lead by yourself. Your doctor or local health department will be able to suggest the best methods for evaluating and removing the sources of lead from your home.

Depending upon the amount of lead in the body and the type of symptoms the child is having, the doctor will decide whether or not further treatment is necessary. Sometimes chelating agents that bind the lead and hasten its removal from the body will be recommended. By recognizing the symptoms early and dealing with the situation properly, it will be possible to avoid the more severe and harmful effects of this condition.

HYPERACTIVITY IN CHILDREN

Many parents have become concerned about the syndrome called the "hyperactive child," since it has recently been given a great deal of public attention. The hyperactive child syndrome has also been referred to by several other names such as MBD (minimal brain dysfunction), hyperkinetic syndrome, and several other descriptive terms. There has also been much controversy about how to treat the hyperactive child and even how to be sure the child really is hyperactive. The hyperactive child syndrome refers to a condition that includes more than increased activity and should be distinguished from the behavior of the child that is just very active.

Distinguishing Between Increased Activity and the Hyperactive Child Syndrome

Parents usually become concerned about their child when he appears to be much more active than a friend's child of comparable age. The question, "Is my child hyperactive?" becomes a major worry. Suddenly all the natural dynamic activity of the child becomes viewed as abnormal behavior and some parents even attempt to discourage the child's active exploration. Given that there is a great variation between children, it is the rule rather than the exception that most children vary in their levels of activity. Comparing your child at play with another child, you should expect to see differences in the level of activity, just as you would expect to see differences in personality.

As discussed in the toddler and preschool development sections, one of the major characteristics of a normal, healthy developing child is often the high level of activity that is displayed in exploring and probing the environment. If the criterion of constant activity alone was used to diagnose the hyperactive child syndrome, most parents would certainly say that their toddlers and even preschool children fit into this category. Obviously all those active children do not have the hyperactive child syndrome and in fact are demonstrating a natural desire and curiosity to learn and develop.

Being very active does not mean that a child has the hyperactive child syndrome. What differentiates the normal active child from a child who fits in the hyperactive child syndrome is the presence of other common problems. The active child is motivated by curiosity and an "excited" mind and usually can "turn his motor off" when necessary. He can act clearly and follow tasks to completion. He is also efficient in his activity and is not excessively clumsy. The child who fits the hyperactive child syndrome, on the other hand, does not usually function well. His activity is often misdirected or less efficient. He has excessive difficulty paying attention and following and completing tasks that he starts. Clumsiness and poor motor skills are often seen in his activities.

The hyperactive child syndrome is a loose term that describes a collection of abnormalities in the child's performance, only one of which is increased activity. Your doctor or a pediatric neurologist can determine these signs with a simple neurological examination. The syndrome is characterized by excessive activity that cannot be easily controlled, inability to complete projects, lack of certain motor skills, inefficent activity, lack of attention, and several clear neurologic signs that can be evaluated on examination.

Confusion in the Name

Unfortunately the name of this condition does not clearly describe what it really means, and many parents with active children have worried without cause that their child has this problem. More recently this condition is being called minimal brain dysfunction (MBD) to avoid confusion. Although this name is more descriptive, it has also caused excessive anxiety in parents because it sounds like a much more serious problem. Until better descriptive terms are developed, it is best to understand what this condition means and put it into proper perspective, rather than being concerned about its label.

What Causes This Condition

At the time this book is being written, there is no clear cause of the hyperactive child syndrome. There is no blood test or diagnostic procedure that clearly confirms the diagnosis. A great deal of research is being conducted on this disorder and some interesting results are emerging.

Most experts agree that this syndrome is probably a general category of symptoms that can be produced by a whole host of causes. Some suggest that trauma at birth, lack of oxygen to the brain during delivery, problems during pregnancy, and so forth, may injure the brain in a very minor way producing minimal brain dysfunction later in life. Some researchers feel that heavy alcohol abuse or drug abuse by the pregnant woman can also contribute to this condition. There may be a psychiatric basis for some cases of MBD.

A growing concern has emerged that certain food additives and colorings, if they are eaten in large quantities, can cause hyperactivity in children. Several studies suggest a role of specific substances in causing hyperactivity in children. At the time this book is being written there is no clear direct evidence that these food additives cause hyperactivity in children, but there is a good deal of experimental evidence suggesting that food additives, especially certain food colorings, can produce behavioral changes in animals. Thus, there is growing information suggesting that certain food additives may contribute to the cause of hyperactivity in some children. This is an important topic for medical research, and several prominent scientists are investigating the role of food additives in influencing the behavior and development of the child.

In summary, it is fair to say that although the exact cause of the hyperactive child syndrome is not known, there is some evidence suggesting that this condition represents a minor dysfunction of the nervous system that produces a variety of symptoms. The severity, cause, and location of the initial insult to the nervous system probably determines the extent of the symptoms seen in the child.

What to Expect

Most children with minor forms of the hyperactive child syndrome go on to develop normally. They were probably difficult for their parents or teachers to control, but they often grow up to lead normal, productive lives. Children with this syndrome usually have normal intellectual functions. It is mainly their motor skills and attention span that are affected. Many children with this condition can overcome these minimal dysfunctions of motor control and be productive individuals in our society.

The major problem that must be avoided relates to learning difficulties. Children with this syndrome often have great difficulty in concentrating and following the normal lesson plans in school. They may daydream or be easily distracted by other activities in the classroom. The cars outside, the birds, or the movement of other children can all distract the child while he is attempting to learn.

It is important to be sure that the child does not fall behind because of his inability to learn. When this occurs, it can be very frustrating for him, his parents, and his teachers. Some children are more severely affected than others and have more difficulty performing in school. This problem must be immediately handled by competent professionals as discussed below.

How to Handle the Mild Hyperactive Child Syndrome

How to handle the hyperactive child is the most important yet usually the most controversial question that arises. Parents often ask about drug therapy, special education, diets, or psychotherapy.

The best approach is to work together with your doctor. The hyperactive child syndrome does not usually require treatment during toddlerhood or much of the preschool years. It requires special attention mainly when the child enters school, if he is not able to concentrate and learn in class. Sometimes parents are not able to tolerate their child's increased activity even though he is doing fine. This creates added tensions.

Mrs. Fletcher complained that her four-year-old daughter, Kim, was driving her crazy. Kim was seen by her family doctor, who observed several signs and symptoms of the hyperactive child syndrome and made the diagnosis at that time. Kim was very active, but she also had difficulty with motor control, attention span, and with several specific neurological tests. Her over-all development and intellectual skills, however, were above normal. Thus, her doctor did not recommend any medication or other treatment. Since Kim's mother was anxious about this condition and wanted her daughter treated to calm her down at home, she asked to be referred to a specialist.

Kim's examination on referral confirmed her doctor's findings. Although Kim was hyperactive and manifesting other signs of this condition, she was functioning well with her peers and not falling behind in her developmental or intellectual functions. No treatment was recommended. Kim's mother was upset, however, and insisted that her daughter be given medication to "cure" her hyperactivity.

This example brings up an important problem in handling this condition. Why do you treat the child? To prevent serious learning disabilities or developmental problems, or to produce a quiet, docile young child that is a pleasure for parents to handle? The answer should be obvious. Kim was doing fine in her developmental progress and showed no evidence that her minor motor difficulties were interfering with her development. Under these circumstances she did not need any medical treatment.

Mrs. Fletcher was reassured that Kim was getting along well and given some support and encouragement to try and be tolerant and patient with Kim's active behavior. Although later on Kim's mother and sometimes one of her teachers occasionally needed reassurance about Kim's activity, Kim continued to develop normally and did well in school.

Many children like Kim can do well with this condition, if given a little extra understanding and patience. By working together with the doctor, school officials, and teachers, the child will get a good education. Most of these children with mild symptoms outgrow this condition with time.

Dealing with More Difficult Problems

Some cases of the hyperactive child syndrome are more difficult to control. Difficulties with attention span or easy distractibility make it almost impossible for these children to function well in school. These problems do not usually become significant until the child enters school, but occasionally, they can be recognized during late preschool when the child is attending nursery school.

Herb, a four-year-old, had marked trouble concentrating on simple tasks and had several of the obvious signs that fit the diagnosis of this condition. He was referred by his mother and the head of the nursery school to his doctor for evaluation, because he was having a great deal of difficulty performing in nursery school. Herb's mother was not only complaining about handling his hyperactivity at home, but was also very worried about his difficulties in school. Herb was unable to keep up with the other children in learning simple games and tasks. He was highly distractible in class and rarely paid attention to what the teacher was explaining.

This child's experience in nursery school indicated that he might have difficulty learning when he entered regular school. Herb's doctor did not feel that medications were necessary at this early stage. The doctor did say that once Herb entered regular school he could fall behind his peers if his poor attention span interfered with his ability to learn.

What Herb needed, according to the doctor, was some special attention. Therefore, arrangements were made for Herb to have closer supervision at nursery school. Children with short attention spans and difficulties with concentration often perform much better with one-to-one, pupil-teacher contact than in classroom situations. Herb seemed to do better under these conditions and was more able to perform at a level equal to his potential.

When Herb later entered grade school, he attended regular classes, but also had special classes with closer supervision. He seemed to hold his own up until third grade when his performance began to slip. At this time it was necessary for his parents, doctor, and teachers to work together to try and alleviate this problem. When special education techniques did not seem to work, Herb was started on medication. This improved his attention span and he was able to continue with his class.

Many children, like Herb, respond well to special educational attention in school and the careful use of medications when absolutely necessary. In the rarer situation where the child has an even more difficult problem, these measures may not be completely effective. Occasionally, it is necessary to put the child in a special school or education program. In some cases it may be helpful to keep the child back for one year to allow him to catch up with the learning. A co-ordinated effort among parents, doctors, and school personnel is the most advisable approach to ensure that the child gets the best help for his individual needs.

What to Do During the Preschool Years

Special education and the use of medications are usually reserved for children who are having difficulties learning in school. It is very unusual to have to treat children during the preschool years in any special way. In case your child has been diagnosed by your doctor as having the hyperactive child syndrome, you will have opportunities to see how his learning abilities are affected when you interact with him at home. Providing an interesting, one-on-one educational experience in the home may be all that is needed for your child to do well.

If your child is having difficulties with learning during the preschool years, this should alert you to be on the lookout for problems when he goes to school. Discuss your concerns with your doctor, who can reassure you and give you guidance. Be patient. Your child may do well in school without a great deal of extra support, but if he has difficulties in kindergarten, or first grade, you should immediately seek proper co-ordinated assistance from the school and your doctor.

Parents who have had the diagnosis of the hyperactive child syndrome confirmed by their doctor should try to be patient and calm during the preschool years. See how the child develops and do not make him self-conscious by showing him your concern or labeling his difficulties.

BABIES WITH SPECIAL PROBLEMS

Sometimes babies are born with certain problems which require that they have special handling and care. Parents should become familiar with these problems so that they will be better prepared to cope with them in the event that they arise. Most of these problems are medical in nature and will be discussed with you by your physician. The topics of premature, low birth weight, and postmature babies are a few of the more common problems.

Premature Babies

About 6 to 7 percent of the babies born today are premature. A baby who is born ahead of the mother's full-term expected date of delivery (nine months) is called a premature baby. Premature babies are usually less mature, smaller, and weigh less than full-term babies.

The cause for early delivery of a baby is not always clear. Sometimes it is due to early rupture of the membranes, infections in the mother, the condition of the womb, or poor health of the mother. In most cases, however, the mother seems to be having a normal pregnancy and for no apparent reason goes into labor and gives birth to a premature infant.

PREMATURE BABIES USUALLY NEED SPECIAL CARE. There is a great deal of variability in how premature the baby is. Some infants are only a week or two premature and others are born a month or more prematurely. By examining the infant and knowing the expected date of delivery, the doctor can fairly accurately determine how premature the baby is and estimate how much, if any, special care is needed.

A baby who is only slightly premature may not require extra care and may even be able to go home with the mother as anticipated. More commonly, premature infants need some degree of extra care and observation during the first few weeks of life. Your doctor will discuss your baby's individual situation and determine the type of care required. In general, the more premature the infant, the longer he will have to stay in the hospital.

A premature baby has a much better chance today of developing normally because of the advances in medical care and the availability of newborn special care nurseries. These facilities are managed by highly trained teams of doctors, nurses, and other health care professionals. The special nursery has equipment that will provide the child with an environment that is best suited to his unique needs, and is in some ways similar to the environment he had in the womb.

Depending on the baby's needs, this equipment can help control his body temperature, help him breathe and obtain adequate nourishment. The infant is usually put in an incubator that keeps him warm and is designed to provide additional support if needed. The infant graduates from the incubator to a nursery in the newborn special care unit.

As the baby matures and develops, he will gradually need less special care and be more able to survive on his own. By carefully evaluating the baby's progress at regular intervals, the doctor will be able to determine when the infant can be transferred to the regular nursery and is ready to go home.

PREMATURE BABIES OFTEN LOOK DIFFERENT. The head of the premature infant usually looks disproportionately large in comparison to the rest of the body. This is normal. The head grows faster than the rest of the body in the womb, and at the time of birth the body is just beginning to catch up. The more premature the baby is, the greater will be the disproportion between head and body size.

Another noticeable feature of the premature baby is that he will appear very slim. Body fat takes time to develop. He will have less body fat than a full-term baby. This will make him look less plump and round than you might have expected. The skin is also more delicate and, with less added fat, it is more transparent. Small veins may be more visable through the skin. These are all normal findings that reflect the child's stage of development.

Full-term babies often have a temporary lack of a liver enzyme. This causes a mild case of jaundice, giving a yellow coloring to the body around the second or third day after birth. Mild jaundice is more common in premature babies. The jaundice may appear a few days after birth and last a little longer, reaching a maximum at about five to seven days. The doctor will be able to monitor the child and help treat the jaundice. Treatment with light (phototherapy) assists the body in lessening the severity of the jaundice.

In the womb a baby is usually covered with fine hairs called lanugo. The amount of hair varies from baby to baby. By the time the infant reaches full term, most, if not all, of this early body hair is gone. Premature infants may have more of this lanugo hair at birth. It disappears with time.

PARENTS' EMOTIONS AND CONCERNS. Parents are often unprepared for the premature baby. They anticipate a certain time for an expected delivery. When the delivery is early, and the baby has to be kept in the hospital for a while, they are put under a great deal of stress. It is disappointing and sometimes depressing for parents to have to leave the hospital without their baby.

Parents' instincts are to protect and remain with the child. Having to leave their infant in the hospital under the major care of others can leave parents feeling helpless and left out. They have prepared themselves for a close involvement with their child after birth. When they have to wait several weeks or more before they can bring him home, this can create an emotional as well as a physical distance. It is useful for parents to recognize that they are not alone in their concerns. Talking with other parents of premature infants can often reassure them and allow them to talk out some of their concerns.

It is also important for parents to discuss their feelings and worries with their doctor. Under certain circumstances doctors allow parents to take a more active role in caring for the baby. A mother who wants to breast-feed may be able to express the milk from her breasts and have it fed to the child in the special nursery. This can be very beneficial for the baby who can be fed in this manner, because he will receive added protection from the antibodies he will absorb from his mother's milk.

Almost all special care nurseries permit visiting privileges for parents. This is very important in establishing an early parent-child bond. The advantages of fostering early parent-child contact are recognized by most special care nurseries. Many of these facilities are encouraging more active roles for parents, whenever possible, in helping to care for the infant. This not only promotes the infant's early emotional development, but it also reduces parents' anxieties and enables them to feel more like parents.

CARING FOR YOUR BABY ONCE HE COMES HOME. Once you bring your baby home from the hospital, you will want to take basically the same initial precautions taken by parents of a full-term baby. Like any newborn infant, your baby is more susceptible to catching illnesses. It is advisable to keep people who are sick away from him and to avoid bringing him into rooms crowded with people.

In caring for your baby, you may find that he gets tired more easily than full-term babies. He may demand to be fed at more frequent intervals, and require longer mealtimes for a while. Your baby may also have to urinate more frequently during the early weeks, so be prepared for rather constant diaper changes. Even though premature babies tend to lose more weight initially after they are born, they gain weight very rapidly once their body has adjusted to life outside the womb.

Other baby care routines should be essentially the same. You may find that regular cloth diapers are a little too large, in which case you can fold them in half, or cut them to fit. During the early weeks your daily routine will be anything but regular and predictable. This is normal, and things will eventually settle down as your infant matures. All parents find the first few months tiring and hectic, but also quite exciting.

TREATING THE PREMATURE BABY NORMALLY. After the doctor allows the baby to go home, you will be given any additional instructions for his care, if they are needed. In most cases the baby will be handled as a term baby and no extra precautionary measures need to be taken.

It is common for parents who have spent time worrying about their child to be overprotective. Feeling anxious and protective are natural emotions. Once parents realize that their infant is doing well, these feelings gradually diminish, enabling them to treat him normally.

In some situations parents have difficulty in overcoming these emotions. They continue to be overanxious about the infant's health and activities. This can cause unnecessary tensions in the family. It is important to discuss these feelings, especially with the doctor, who can help put them into proper perspective.

CONCERNS ABOUT THE BABY'S DEVELOPMENT. It is natural for parents to worry about their baby's development, whether or not their baby is premature. These concerns tend to be stronger in parents whose babies arrived ahead of schedule.

The premature baby has a normal capacity to grow and develop, but he will initially have some catching up to do. It generally takes a premature baby a year or two to catch up with babies who were older and stronger at birth. After that any differences that parents might have previously noticed are no longer likely to be seen.

In the meantime, parents will have to make certain allowances in terms of the rate of his development, and not try to compare him with other infants who were full term. If he was one month early, for instance, he may be acting like a four-month-old baby at five months. Just like all babies, he will develop at his own individual pace and style. Your doctor will evaluate your baby's growth and development with you at the time of your regular well baby visits. He or she will be able to answer any questions that you might have concerning the baby's developmental progress.

Low Birth Weight and Postmature Babies

Premature babies almost always have a low birth weight and they are born before term. Some babies are born at the expected time of birth, but have a low birth weight. These babies are smaller in size and weigh less, primarily because their growth rate in the womb was slowed down. They have certain similarities and differences when compared with premature infants that your doctor will discuss with you. Like the premature baby, the low birth weight baby sometimes requires special care and observation after birth. The feelings and concerns of parents are often the same as for a premature baby.

Postmature babies are born after the expected date of delivery. They spend more time in the womb before birth than a term infant. In many cases this creates no special problems. Sometimes these babies also need special care, depending upon the cause of the delayed birth and how delayed the birth was. Your doctor will evaluate the baby at birth and advise you if any special problems exist.

THE HANDICAPPED CHILD

The child with a handicap sometimes requires special management and can place additional stresses on parents and other family members. Rearing a handicapped child can bring with it rewards and challenges as well as understandable worries and frustrations. The subject of handicapped children deserves a great deal of attention from parents, physicians, health professionals, and educators. Co-operative efforts can help improve the quality of life for the child and his family and raise public consciousness about the needs of the handicapped.

With early medical attention, special educational training, and parental care, many handicapped children are able to lead fulfilling and productive lives. In some instances, early treatment, medications, nutrition, physical therapy, and so forth, can help alleviate problems or lessen their severity. Your doctor will discuss possible treatment plans with you, if they are indicated in your child's case. In many areas of the world there are organized clinics which are specially established and equipped to help children with handicaps. Some of the more common handicaps are discussed on pages 1017–19 along with organizations that can be helpful.

Parents with a handicapped baby must realize that they are not alone. In fact, in many communities groups are organized so that parents whose children have similar problems can discuss them, share feelings, and receive emotional support as well as practical advice. State or local health departments can be helpful in finding out what is available in your community.

The emotional strains on both the child and the parents require consideration. It is helpful not to bottle up feelings. The following discussions present some of the more common concerns of parents with handicapped children.

Emotional Considerations: Learning of Your Child's Handicap

Parents may learn of their child's handicap at birth or later in infancy, toddlerhood, or the preschool stage. Finding out a child has a handicap normally comes as a shock and a tremendous disappointment. Some parents have an easier time dealing with this kind of news than others. Reactions vary, depending upon parents' personalities and upon the severity and nature of the child's problem.

Nearly all parents during the pregnancy period worry about the possibility of giving birth to a handicapped child at one point or another. These concerns often appear and disappear, and few parents actually believe that their child will be anything but perfectly healthy and "normal."

Hearing that this is not the case arouses all kinds of thoughts, feelings, and emotions in parents besides shock. It is not uncommon for them to feel angry. The anger may be directed at the child, other family members, or even the doctor. Other emotions can be even more troubling to deal with.

FEELINGS OF GUILT. Some parents worry excessively that they may have caused their child's problem in one way or another. In the vast majority of instances, the doctor has reassured them that they are in no way to blame for the handicap. Yet, in the back of their minds, they continue to feel responsible for whatever is wrong with their youngster. It is not uncommon for parents to feel as though their child's handicap is some kind of punishment they must endure for past wrongdoings.

In most cases it is difficult for parents to deal with or discuss their guilt feelings, so they bury them or keep them bottled up inside. This is not healthy. Excessive, unjustified feelings of guilt can often cloud a parent's judgment in seeking proper treatment or medical assistance for the youngster and in rearing him at home.

Difficulties can arise when parents, out of guilt, keep searching for miraculous cures offered by unqualified persons at outrageous costs. This can place a financial drain on family resources, as well as disrupt normal family functioning. It is doubtful that the child will benefit in any way from the "treatment," and there is a strong chance that improper medications, therapies, and other inappropriate procedures could make matters worse or bring harm to him.

Parents who feel personally responsible for their child's handicap may also be overly lenient. They may shower him with excessive amounts of attention, affection, and materialistic possessions in a misguided effort to make up for his problem. This type of treatment is not helpful to the developing child. It can also prove to be a disruption in the family, creating marital tension or heightening feelings of jealousy, rivalry, and resentment in other children.

Being alert to possible needless feelings of guilt should help parents in making appropriate and sound decisions in child rearing as well as selecting the best type of outside help for their child. Parents who continue to feel excessive guilt even though their doctor has told them over and over that they are not to blame should seek professional help in dealing with these feelings.

DENIAL MAY BE STRONG. Upon learning of their child's problem, some parents have a very difficult time accepting the fact that something is wrong. Parents may refuse to believe what their doctor(s) says and deny that the child has a problem.

It is only natural and sensible for parents to want to get a second opinion, or even several "expert" opinions. On the other hand, there are parents who refuse to believe anything confirming their child's handicap; they travel from one doctor or clinic to the next in the hope of finding someone who will either claim that nothing is wrong with their child or offer a "magical cure."

This can be time-consuming, and expensive, both financially and in terms of emotional resources. There is nothing wrong with parents wanting to do anything they can to help their child, but it is important not to lose sight of other family members' needs and carry the search for a cure to unreasonable extremes.

Avoid Neglecting Other Children

Other children in the family may suffer a great deal when parents give the handicapped child nearly all of their time, attention, and affection. It may be hard for parents to maintain a proper sense of perspective and not become overly wrapped up in the handicapped child at the expense of other family members. This is especially difficult when he needs special care at home and requires frequent medical treatment or therapy.

Parents should make an effort to consider all of their children's needs, and not concentrate solely on meeting the handicapped child's special requirements. This is crucially important to the other children's emotional development and well-being, and also to their feelings about their handicapped brother or sister.

Resentment and rivalry can usually be minimized if parents try to meet their children's individual needs and give ample time and attention to each child. There is no need to try to or promise to treat each child equally, since this will probably be impossible to achieve, particularly when one needs special management. On the other hand, each child needs to feel loved and wanted, and parents should try to be as fair as possible in their treatment of all their children.

Marital Stress

Other children in the family are not the only ones who may suffer when the handicapped child becomes the focus of attention. A spouse may feel similar neglect when one parent concentrates all of his or her energy upon the child. Sometimes one parent takes the entire responsibility for the handicapped child's care out of guilt feelings of having caused the problem. In an attempt to make it up to the child, all of the parent's time and energy is devoted to meeting the child's needs to the neglect of the partner's needs.

This situation often places an enormous strain upon the marriage, creating resentment between partners. The spouse who feels rejected may find it hard to ask for more emotional support and attention out of fear of being called selfish and immature. When communication lines break down, an even further distance between partners is created, sometimes sufficient to cause serious marital problems.

Parents of a handicapped child should often talk about their honest feelings. They should not hesitate to ask for more support and affection from one another when this is necessary. Worries and guilt feelings related to the child's condition need to be shared and dealt with. Keeping these feelings to oneself can create barriers that slowly drive a couple apart.

There are cases in which parents have difficulty meeting each other's needs, as well as preserving their relationship while caring for their handicapped child. In the event that problems arise and escalate to the point where they cannot be resolved by a couple alone, parents should not feel embarrassed about seeking outside help from their clergyman or a marriage counselor or some other professional adviser.

Accept the Child for Himself

The life of a child with a noticeable handicap is accompanied by several stresses not usually experienced by others. Handicapped youngsters are often subjected to people's pity, stares, derogatory remarks, unnecessary offers of assistance, and whispered questions and comments. These reactions can naturally make them feel somewhat self-conscious. How self-conscious, uneasy, or unhappy they feel depends more upon their family's attitude and treatment of them from the start than upon the severity and nature of their handicap.

Some parents are very embarrassed by their child's handicap and are basically ashamed of him. They criticize him, wish he were different, and keep him away from other people as much as possible. Other parents are overprotective of their youngster, and try to shield him as much as possible from other people so that he will not have to be subjected to stares and whispers. Parents who are ashamed of their child, overprotective of him, or who try to isolate him from others may find that he grows up feeling alone, unloved, and ashamed of himself. When parents are overly self-conscious about him, chances are that he will grow up feeling very unhappy and self-conscious.

Like any other child, the youngster with a handicap needs to feel positive acceptance from his parents. He deserves to be loved and to feel worth while for what he is. Parents should give him ample opportunities to be around other people and children his age, and try to treat him naturally, without making apologies for his handicap or attempts to hide it.

A handicapped child, most importantly, needs a stable emotional foundation and a positive self-image, both of which parents can help offer him early in his life. While not underplaying his handicap, parents can help him concentrate upon his strengths to compensate for his weaknesses. As much as possible, he should be treated as any child without a handicap, since this will make him feel less self-conscious and unusual. It will be much easier for him to take other people's stares and whispers in stride if he has had early opportunities to socialize with non-family members, feels positively about himself, and is secure in his family's love.

Parents' attitudes and treatment of him set the stage for how he feels about himself and his surroundings. His brothers and sisters are also likely to react to him in a manner that is similar to their parents'. It is very important for parents to assist their handicapped child in developing self-esteem and confidence and a positive outlook on life.

Understanding, Not Pity

A handicapped child needs understanding, not pity. Pity does not encourage him to accept new challenges and make the most of his potential. Rather, a steady diet of pity becomes an addiction.

It is understandable that parents whose child has an obvious or disfiguring handicap would naturally feel sorry for him. This attitude, when carried too far, will not do the child any good, and can be a hindrance. Parents may set their expectations for him far below what he can reasonably achieve. Since they do not provide the incentive or encouragement for further progress, he comes to be satisfied with doing less than he is able. Thus, while it is not advisable to set unrealistically high expectations for the child who cannot possibly measure up to them, it is also not beneficial to underestimate his abilities.

Parents should not automatically assume that he cannot perform a given task with proper guidance and sufficient encouragement. They can greatly assist their child by motivating him to want to learn and acquire new skills.

When parents are confident and hopeful, this sustains their youngster's drive to maximize his potential and do the best he can at any given task. He does not sit around feeling sorry for himself, nor does he thrive on pity that others are willing to offer. His self-pride and respect do not allow for this.

Home Care Versus Institutional Care

Some children are born with severe medical problems. The question can arise in these cases of whether or not to institutionalize the child. This is a difficult decision and one which cannot be easily made. Each case is individual and depends upon the illness, the family structure, financial resources, religious background, and so forth. If you are involved in such a situation, you should seek the advice of physicians, friends, family, and staff members at available institutions. Then make your own decision based upon what feels right in your case.

Do Not Hesitate to Seek Help When This Seems Necessary

Parents sometimes have a rough time coping with a handicapped baby and may need some help and guidance when difficulties arise. Whatever the problem is, parents should feel comfortable about getting help, especially if the situation is more stressful than they can easily handle on their own.

Asking for assistance when it is needed is not a sign of inadequacy. It shows good judgment. Parents often find it helpful to discuss their problems with their doctor or social workers and staff members in family and children's social agencies or special clinics. The names of such agencies and clinics are usually available from various state Welfare Departments or local Community Chest organizations. A few of the more common handicaps are briefly discussed below.

Genetic Diseases

There are over two thousand genetic diseases that have been identified. In the past, inherited birth defects were surrounded with fear and superstition. Some of these feelings are still present today, but the many advances in diagnosing and managing genetic diseases have greatly reduced the fears about these diseases in parents with a family history of a genetic illness or a child with a genetic disease.

If your child is born with a genetic disease, or if you have a family history of genetic illness, you may find it helpful to receive genetic counseling. Counseling for genetic diseases has become increasingly available over the past ten years. Most major medical centers now have physicians who can provide this service.

When a disease is genetic in nature, it is important to know what the chances are of having other children affected by the same problems. An illness or handicap that is not genetically produced may indicate that there is no unusual risk of having another child born with the same condition. Genetic counselors can be of great assistance to parents with these problems. The National Foundation—March of Dimes, 1275 Mamaroneck Avenue, White Plains, New York 10605, may be of further assistance in locating local services that provide information and counseling for genetic diseases.

Mental Slowness

Mental slowness or mental retardation (MR) is a general term used to describe an abnormal progression of mental development. Usually these children develop much more slowly and never reach the full normal range of mental development. There are numerous causes for MR, including birth injuries, lack of oxygen at birth, specific enzyme defects, infections of the brain, and metabolic disease. Over 70 percent, however, of the cases of MR have no clear cause that can be determined at this time.

Mental slowness is most noticeable in early toddlerhood. This is when parents become worried about how poorly their child is learning to talk or walk. Concerns about late development are common at this time and many parents whose child is a little behind a neighbor's child in development may become very upset and begin to wonder if he is mentally retarded.

As has been emphasized, there is an enormous variation in the sequence of development among normal children. The mentally retarded child, however, is usually outside the limits of normal variation. Your doctor will be aware of this condition if it exists. If your pediatrician notices signs of significant developmental delay, a careful medical evaluation will be conducted to rule out any treatable causes. Sometimes a specialist (pediatric neurologist) is asked to evaluate the child further.

There are many new advances and facilities for helping the mentally retarded child. The initial emotional and psychological shock of learning that your child is mentally retarded is often difficult to handle, especially alone. We have found that bringing together groups of parents with mentally slow children to discuss their problems and feelings has been very helpful. Your doctor will be able to give you guidance and assistance. The National Association for Retarded Citizens, 2709 Avenue E East, P. O. Box 6109, Arlington, Texas 76010, is an organization that may provide further assistance.

DOWN'S SYNDROME (MONGOLISM). Down's Syndrome occurs as a result of a chromosome abnormality that produces numerous physical and biochemical changes. The child usually has slanted eyes, flat nose, protuberant tongue, malformed ears, and problems with several internal organ systems. He is often retarded.

The chromosome abnormality is not usually inherited, but the result of changes in the chromosomes in the egg. The older a woman is, the greater the chance that this defect can occur. The occurrence of mongoloid births in women under thirty-five is very low; for women over thirty-five it is much higher.

Amniocentesis is a procedure to sample cells that come from the amniotic fluid surrounding the fetus while it still is in the womb. By examining these cells it can be determined if the child has Down's Syndrome before the child is born. This technique is being employed in many major medical centers as a diagnostic screening test for pregnant women over thirty-five years of age.

Partial or Complete Blindness

Visual difficulties are common handicaps. Special training programs are now available for blind children that help them to lead much more normal lives. Your State

Commission for the Blind or your doctor should be able to assist you in obtaining education for your child. The American Foundation for the Blind, 15 West Sixteenth Street, New York, New York 10011, can also be very helpful. Some of the costs for special programs and equipment may be paid by the United States Government. Write to American Printing House for the Blind, 1839 Frankfort Avenue, Louisville, Kentucky 40206, for more information on educational materials.

Hearing Difficulties (Deafness)

Hearing difficulties can occur as a result of congenital (in the womb) or acquired problems (infections, trauma, etc.). Your doctor will be able to determine the cause of the hearing difficulty. Sometimes the cause is in the ear itself. A damaged eardrum or ear bones may be responsible. These difficulties can often be corrected surgically. In other situations the ear is fine, but the nerves that carry information from the ear to the nervous system are not working properly. The ear sends information about sound to the brain along special nerve cells. If these cells are damaged or destroyed, hearing difficulties are experienced. These conditions cannot usually be corrected unless the damage to the nerves is not permanent.

There are many programs that can help the deaf child and his family. A child who is totally or partially deaf from birth may even learn to speak with a great deal of training from a qualified person. The doctor will be able to assist in arranging learning programs for the deaf child. The Alexander Graham Bell Association, 3417 Volta Place, Washington, D.C. 20007, can be of assistance if you cannot find appropriate support or advice in your community.

Muscular Dystrophy

Muscular dystrophy is a degenerative disease of the muscles of unknown cause. There are actually many different types of muscle disease that can occur in childhood. Although there is presently no specific cure for these diseases, certain symptomatic treatments and physical therapy may help. The Muscular Dystrophy Association of America, Inc., 810 Seventh Avenue, New York, New York 10019, and the National Easter Seal Society for Crippled Children and Adults, 2023 West Ogden Avenue, Chicago, Illinois 60612, may be helpful.

Cerebral Palsy

Cerebral palsy is the name given to many different conditions that affect the brain and cause impairment of motor function. The causes of cerebral palsy are varied. Lack of oxygen at birth is one of the more common causes. The condition is usually caused before, during, or soon after birth. The signs of the disease vary depending on the parts of the nervous system that are damaged.

Your doctor will be able to help alleviate some of the symptoms of this condition and offer suggestions for school placement and physical therapy. The United Cerebral Palsy Associations, 66 East Thirty-fourth St., New York, New York 10016, will be able to give suggestions for therapy and special treatment available in your community.

THE CHILD WHO MUST GO INTO THE HOSPITAL

Parents whose children are ill and must be admitted to a hospital for diagnostic tests or surgical procedures may naturally have many questions and concerns about how to handle this situation in order to minimize emotional trauma to their children. Obviously, all caring parents are concerned about their children's well-being and are anxious to help their children cope as effectively as possible with the hospitalization.

Hospitalization During Early Infancy

A younger infant is not likely to be as disturbed as an older infant or young child by a hospitalization. Older infants, toddlers, and preschoolers are usually more fearful of separations from their parents, and more upset by unfamiliar people and unusual settings. If an infant becomes ill during the first few months of his life, he is usually not sufficiently aware of his surroundings to have a markedly negative response to being hospitalized, but he may react negatively to being separated from his parents and familiar home environment.

Parents should try to stay with their baby at least for some time during the day. Interacting with him and perhaps being involved in aspects of his care help develop the parent-child bond and can make the hospitalization less uncomfortable and anxiety-provoking for both infant and parent. Remaining near the child is not always possible and depends upon the baby's condition. In this situation the nurses and doctors caring for the child will let you know as soon as you can begin interacting with your baby.

Older Infants and Hospitalization

An older infant may be quite fearful of being separated from his parents and placed in a stange place. His understanding of language is so limited, however, that parents will find it extremely difficult if not impossible to prepare him in advance for his stay at the hospital. In order to help make the experience less traumatic for the infant, there are a few things that parents can do.

Many hospitals allow parents to stay with the child both during the day and night. The love, physical closeness, and reassurance that his parents can offer should help to ease the child's fears and anxieties, and make him feel more secure. Parents can also bring several of the infant's favorite possessions, such as toys, special blankets, and so forth, to the hospital in order to make the unfamiliar surroundings seem more familiar. Furthermore, parents can try to act cheerful and confident in front of their infant, even though they may be worried and anxious about the whole situation. If their baby senses that they are worried and fearful, this may heighten his own fears.

Preparing the Toddler and Preschool Child for Hospitalization

An older toddler or preschool child who is capable of understanding simple verbal explanations should be told in advance about the fact that he will have to go to the hospital. Adequate preparation will help him get ready for the experience. In the simplest of terms he should be told about when he will have to be hospitalized, and why this is necessary.

A child's parents should be honest with him, although he should be spared the "gory" details. It is important to be truthful with the child. Lying to him about what will happen may undermine his trust in his parents or hospital staff members, and may leave him quite unprepared to cope with the experience. It is possible to be confident and reassuring while still being truthful.

In situations in which a child will be having an operation, it is important for him to learn about this in advance. He should be informed that the surgery will take place only after he has been put to sleep and that no pain will be experienced during the actual operation. Feelings, discomforts, and pains that he might experience after the operation should be discussed with him, without frightening him.

A youngster who is not told in advance about an operation and later discovers that he was operated on while he was asleep may understandably associate going to sleep with having another operation. As a result, he may put up a great deal of resistance at bedtime, show a strong fear of sleep, or other sleep disturbances. By giving the child truthful information in advance, this type of problem may be avoided.

Answering the Child's Questions

A preschool child may have all kinds of questions related to hospitals, doctors, being separated from his parents, what he will eat in the hospital, how long he will have to be there, etc. His questions should be answered in terms that he can understand. When, what, and how much information to impart depends upon the child's curiosity and capacity for understanding. If a child will be having particular tests or will be undergoing surgery, he should be given an honest and easy-to-understand description of what he will be experiencing by either his parents or an understanding doctor or nurse.

Taking Advantage of Preparation Programs Offered by the Hospital

Some major hospitals have special programs designed to prepare young children for hospitalization. Quite often these programs include a tour of the hospital or the pediatric floor, a movie about a child going to the hospital, and a question-answer session in which children are encouraged to participate.

There are hospitals that have more thorough programs of preparation for young children who will be undergoing specific tests and procedures, or having surgery. As a technique of explaining more about a procedure or operation, members of the hospital staff often use dolls and small-sized replicas of hospital equipment. They demonstrate to the child exactly what events will transpire a day or so in advance, and often encourage him to participate by taking on the role of the nurse or doctor in the doll play. These programs can be helpful in lessening a child's fears.

Such sessions can be extremely useful in heightening a child's awareness of what to expect prior to, during, and after surgery, and in allowing him to express apprehensions and even angry or aggressive feelings. By having a clearer idea of what will happen to them, most children are better prepared to cope with what might have otherwise been a terribly frightening experience.

In the event that your hospital offers no preparatory programs, it would be advisable to learn about what will take place while your child is hospitalized, and pass this information on to him in terms that he can understand. You may also want to engage him in "doctor" play as an added form of preparation.

Preparation Through Reading Stories About Hospitalization to Your Child

Reading stories to an older toddler or preschool child about going to the hospital can be another aspect of his preparation. There are many good books available that tell about children's experiences in the hospital and their honest feelings and reactions to it. Some books are specially written to explain about operations in terms that are easy for children to understand. It is advisable to check local libraries and bookstores for specific listings of such books.

Dealing with Your Child's Fears

A child may have many fears and worries about what will happen to him in the hospital, and may be unhappy about the prospect of being there. Some of his concerns may be realistic but parents should be aware that imaginary fears and worries are quite common, especially in older preschool children. The child should be encouraged to talk about his fears and concerns, and to voice negative feelings about being hospitalized. Parents should try their best to be understanding and reassuring, and to try to allay his anxieties or clear up any misconceptions he might have about doctors, hospitals, and operations.

It Is Important to Stay with Your Child as Much as Possible

A child may, indeed, be frightened by being in the hospital, and therefore he will need parental patience, emotional support, and extra reassurance. Parents, or at least one parent, should try to remain with him. Some hospitals permit parents to stay overnight. Young children are generally disturbed by separations from their parents and being placed in unfamiliar territory. Having parents close by usually helps them adapt and alleviates many of their tensions and fears. Parents can provide understanding, words of encouragement, and security at a time when their child needs all of these in great abundance. If it is not possible for parents to remain overnight, they should tell their child why they cannot stay, and should visit him regularly each day.

In some cases children who are hospitalized may become angry and hostile toward their parents when they visit, but their feelings should be accepted and understood as being normal and natural. In order to make the transition from home to hospital easier on the child, it is wise for parents to bring along his favorite toys, blanket, or other objects that will make his room seem more familiar.

Youngsters React Differently to Being Hospitalized

Children's reactions to hospitalization vary. Some children fare very well and do not appear to be upset by the experience, especially when hospital personnel have been truthful, compassionate, understanding, and reassuring, and when their parents have remained close by their side to give them support, comfort, care, and attention. Other children, due to a variety of factors, may be very upset by such an experience, and may show some disturbed behavior patterns once they are released. They may cling to their parents, have difficulty sleeping, and be very insecure for a while. Do your best to minimize your child's anxiety both before he is admitted to a hospital, and while he is there. Chances are that the hospitalization experience will cause him a minimum amount of difficulty.

OTHER PROBLEMS IN CHILDHOOD

Parents often have many questions about problems that can arise during childhood. They may have heard or read certain terms or names and want to know something about them. There are numerous topics of interest. Some of the more common topics that parents ask about are included in the following material. These subjects are only briefly discussed to give parents some basic familiarity with them.

Abscess

An abscess is a localized infection that usually becomes walled off by the body. Abscesses can occur almost anywhere in the body, but are more commonly seen on the skin. See pages 988–89.

Airsickness

Airsickness is a form of motion sickness. It can occur while riding in airplanes, but is most commonly seen in children who are riding on circus or carnival rides.

Arthritis

Arthritis is an inflammatory disease that mainly affects the joints and connective tissues of the body. There are many types of arthritis. This disease is often considered an illness of old age, but it can occur in children. Juvenile arthritis is a rare disease in childhood. Arthritis can also occur as a complication of other diseases. A form of arthritis is sometimes seen with rheumatic fever (page 1034).

Athlete's Foot

Athlete's foot is a fungus infection between the toes or on the bottom of the feet. It is most commonly seen in the summer months, and can be caught in showers or other infected sources. The skin becomes red and itchy. Cracks may develop between the toes. The fungus of athlete's foot is similar to the fungus that causes ringworm. There are numerous antifungal powders, sprays, and creams available. Your doctor will be able to recommend an appropriate treatment. Some of the more common antifungal preparations are Tinactin, Desenex, or Caldesene.

Aura of Seizures

Sometimes before a seizure a person experiences an unusual sensation. This warning feeling is called an aura. It may be a smell, a sound, a pain, a visual disturbance, or one of many possible feelings.

Blood Poisoning

Blood poisoning generally refers to the spread of infection into the blood from a localized area. This condition is discussed under infections on page 989. It can also more loosely refer to the presence of any toxic substance in the blood.

Breath-holding Spells

Occasionally infants or young children get very angry or excited and stop breathing for a short time. The exact cause for this behavior is not known, but it is believed to be a reflex phenomenon similar to the "startle" response. Seeing a baby stop breathing when excited and turn slightly blue or grayish around the mouth and face for a few seconds can be a very traumatic experience for any parent, especially the first time.

In rare prolonged episodes a child may twitch and even have a convulsion. The attacks usually start at the end of the first year, but can occur as early as six months. Usually they disappear by the fifth year. They commonly accompany temper tantrums. This behavior is not serious, but the first attack or any very severe or prolonged episodes should be brought to the attention of your doctor to be sure that these episodes are not mild seizures.

Older children often recognize that these episodes generate a great deal of excitement in the home. The child may begin to throw temper tantrums more frequently to get attention and this may lead to an increased frequency of breath-holding spells as the child works up his excitement. Suggestions for handling these situations are given on pages 434–35.

Cancer

Cancer refers to a group of illnesses that are characterized by an overgrowth of particular cells in the body. The specific type of cancer depends on the cell type that is involved. Cancer of the blood (leukemia), eye, and abdomen are the types most frequently seen in children. Many new treatments are being developed for these diseases and the possibility of remissions and occasional cures is gradually increasing.

Car Sickness

Car sickness is a type of motion sickness that occurs while riding in the automobile. It can cause nausea and vomiting. Some individuals are more sensitive to motion than others and are more likely to develop this problem. Your doctor can recommend medications to help decrease or prevent the symptoms from occurring.

Cerumen

Cerumen is the scientific name for earwax. Some children accumulate more wax than others. This may interfere with hearing. The doctor can prescribe special drops to help dissolve the excessive wax. Do not try to clean a young child's ears with a sharp or pointed object. A sudden movement can cause the eardrum to be punctured.

Charley Horse (Cramp)

Cramps occur when a muscle goes into tight contraction. They are very painful and are relieved by heat and massage. Cramps often occur when the muscle becomes tired. They are also commonly seen when the child swims or participates in strenuous activity.

Chorea

Chorea is the name given to a movement disorder that produces jerky, involuntary movements of the body or face. It has many causes, but in childhood it is usually seen as one of the rarer symptoms of rheumatic fever. The chorea seen with rheumatic fever is referred to as St. Vitus' dance.

Circumcision

Circumcision is the most common urologic operation performed in infancy. It consists of cutting off the skin that normally covers the tip of the penis, the foreskin. Whether or not a child is to be circumcised is a personal decision. It is advisable for parents to discuss circumcision with each other and with their doctor. The circumcision is usually performed on the newborn baby before he leaves the hospital.

Cleft Palate and/or Lip

Cleft palate and/or lip are congenital malformations that result when a portion of the roof of the mouth (palate) fails to develop completely. This condition can vary in the extent of the involvement of the mouth structures. Some only involve the roof of the mouth. Others can involve the lip or beginning of the nose. Your doctor will diagnose this condition at birth and discuss the possible methods of treatment. These defects can be partially or completely corrected by plastic surgery.

Club Foot

Club foot is usually an obvious malformation that will be identified at birth by your doctor. In mild cases this condition is treated by putting the foot in a cast. Surgical procedures are occasionally necessary to correct severe malformations.

Coma

Coma is a condition in which the child is unresponsive. He may or may not be breathing normally. Coma is obviously serious and requires immediate medical evaluation. Coma can result from metabolic diseases, diseases of the brain, following a seizure, or from head trauma.

Concussion

Concussions usually result from head injuries which cause no obvious damage to the brain or skull, but which leave the child slightly lightheaded or dazed. Headache is often seen with most concussions. More severe head injuries resulting in transient loss of consciousness should be brought to the attention of your doctor. Most concussions are very mild and are treated with rest for a day or so. Occasionally a more severe concussion can occur, requiring a more extensive recovery period. Your doctor will be able to evaluate the child and determine if any further treatment or tests are necessary.

Congenital Heart Disease

Congenital heart disease refers to several abnormalities of the heart that are present at birth. These abnormalities in the heart are usually caused by developmental problems that produce alterations in the normal anatomy of the heart. Depending on the type of defect or alteration present, the child will develop certain symptoms that will alert the doctor to the presence of an abnormality. Many of these defects are detected at birth, but they may not become apparent until later in childhood. Modern medical and surgical research have made major breakthroughs in treating and correcting many of these heart defects.

Crib Death

See Sudden Infant Death Syndrome (page 1035).

Curvatures of the Spine

Curvatures of the spine sometimes develop in childhood, but they are relatively rare. These conditions should be evaluated by a doctor. Scoliosis is the most common cause of curvature of the spine, but it is rare in children less than five years of age. In this type of curvature, the spine curves to one side or the other in an abnormal way. Other types of curvatures of the spine (kyphosis, lordosis) can also develop, but they are less common.

If you notice that your child's spine is developing an unusual curvature, see your doctor soon so that he or she can evaluate the condition. Some cases of spinal curvature can cause marked deformity if not taken care of at an early stage. With early evaluation and proper medical treatment, many of these problems can be improved or corrected.

Cyanosis

Cyanosis refers to the bluish color of the skin that can occur when the child does not get enough oxygen. The blood turns a darker color when it does not have high levels of oxygen. This gives the skin a dusky, bluish color. Cyanosis may be seen in congenital heart disease, breath-holding, convulsions, or in other problems or illnesses.

Cystic Fibrosis

Cystic fibrosis is an illness characterized by the production of abnormally thick secretions from various glands in the body (pancreas, respiratory lining cells), and an excessive excretion of salt in the sweat. The condition is usually recognized in early infancy, although some cases are not seen until later in childhood. Cystic fibrosis is a hereditary disease.

This disease often causes problems with the digestive and respiratory systems. Chronic respiratory tract infections requiring medical treatment occur rather frequently and these children require close medical follow-up.

Some progress has been made in recent years by dedicated physicians and parents in managing this disease. Antibiotic therapy and oral digestive enzymes have helped control the illness. Some children are reaching adulthood at this time due to these remarkable efforts.

Parents should seek advice concerning their chances of having other children with cystic fibrosis. Genetic counseling is usually very helpful in understanding this disease and knowing what to expect.

Cystitis

Cystitis is the medical term for an infection or inflammation of the urinary bladder.

Dehydration

Dehydration refers to the loss of body fluid. It is usually seen with severe diarrhea, vomiting, sweating, or poor fluid intake. This condition should be evaluated by your doctor.

Dizziness

Dizziness refers to a vague feeling of "lightheadedness" or true vertigo (room spinning around). The most common form of dizziness occurs when the child runs or is swung in circles. His attempts to walk following such behavior are often humorous. Sometimes a child will feel dizzy after getting up quickly. This is often the result of a short fall in blood pressure as the child rapidly changes position (postural hypotension). Some children become nauseated and dizzy when riding in a car, boat, or plane. These symptoms are characteristic of motion sickness, and are also common to many adults. Your doctor may recommend medication to treat motion sickness if it is a persistent problem.

If the child complains of persistent dizziness or spinning of the room, and has difficulty keeping his balance for prolonged periods of time, take him to your doctor for an evaluation. Infections in the inner ear, nervous system diseases, or other problems could be the cause of these symptoms.

Encephalitis

Encephalitis is the medical term for an infection or inflammation of the brain that can be caused by bacteria, viruses, fungi, protozoa, or other infectious or toxic agents. Many viral forms of the disease are epidemic and often are carried by insects. The symptoms include fever, muscle aches, tiredness, headache, and nausea. In rarer severe cases coma, seizures, or paralysis may develop.

Enuresis

Enuresis is the medical term for nighttime bed-wetting. This is often common in toddlerhood and the early preschool years. See pages 929–31 for a full discussion of this condition.

Epistaxis

Epistaxis is the medical term for a bloody nose (see pages 989–90).

Fainting

Fainting refers to a brief loss of consciousness. It usually results from lack of blood flow to the head as the result of pooling or collecting of the blood in the legs following rapid position changes or other causes. Exhaustion, heatstroke, prolonged standing, and rapid position changes can all increase the chances of fainting. If fainting occurs infrequently and the child is only unconscious for three to ten seconds and feels fine shortly afterward, there is no need for alarm. Discuss the episodes with your doctor on your next visit. If the spells are frequent, produce long periods of unconsciousness, or leave the child confused or dazed for prolonged periods, you should seek the advice of your physician. Other medical causes of loss of consciousness must be ruled out by the doctor.

Flat Feet

Flat feet refer to fallen arches. They are common and usually hereditary. Flat feet are not really of significant medical concern. Good arch supports may be recommended to help support the foot, but most children with this problem have little or no difficulty in walking. Most infants under a year old appear flat-footed. Infants have extra fat in their feet and this tends to cover the natural arch of the foot, making it appear less apparent. The full formation of the arch usually takes some time to appear completely and often is not fully apparent until the second year.

Food Poisoning

Food left unrefrigerated or that is improperly canned or preserved can support the growth of bacteria. Some types of bacteria give off toxins or poisons that can be harmful if eaten. Botulism is a type of food poisoning that can result from improperly preserved food. The poison in botulism is very dangerous and attacks the nervous system. The symptoms start with an upset stomach beginning twelve to forty-eight hours after the ingestion of the contaminated food. The child may then develop confusion, double vision, inability to swallow or talk, and tiredness. There are other food poisons that produce diarrhea, vomiting, or intestinal infections. These are common in people who travel to countries that have contaminated food. Mushroom poisoning is also a danger. Seek the advice of your doctor if you suspect food poisoning. Proper care and refrigeration of foods in the home will help prevent this problem.

Frostbite

Frostbite refers to damage to body tissue that can occur when parts of the body are exposed to cold temperatures. Frostbite occurs during prolonged exposure to severe cold, resulting in decreased circulation of blood, most often in the ends of the arms and legs and exposed areas. The lowering of temperature in the body parts involved gradually causes damage. The most common areas of involvement are the toes, fingers, nose, and ears. These body parts are often exposed to more severe cold and are also among the first to lose good circulation in cold weather.

The best way to handle frostbite is to prevent it. Do not allow a child to play outdoors in cold weather without proper protection. Warm gloves, socks, and ear muffs help protect sensitive areas. Prolonged exposure to cold weather should also be avoided, even if the child seems properly dressed.

Overexposure to cold can produce varying symptoms. Most cases are mild and cause some redness and tingling of the involved areas. In more severe situations the skin may become very pale or even gray-looking. Seek the advice of your doctor for treating frostbite.

Glomerulonephritis

Glomerulonephritis is a term used to describe a number of diseases of the kidney which primarily affect the glomeruli (a part of the kidney that is involved in "filtering" the blood). This disease shows marked variations in the intensity of symptoms that it produces. The more common clinical signs include urinary abnormalities (such as bloody urine or protein in the urine), edema (retention of body fluid), and hypertension (high blood pressure).

Many types of glomerulonephritis may be caused by an immune reaction where antibody products against foreign materials in the body deposit in the kidney and cause an inflammatory reaction. Although there are many causes of this disease, parents should be aware that it can occur as a complication of strep throat infections (page 1932). Thus, it is very important to have sore throats evaluated by a doctor.

Gum Cysts

Gum cysts are small cysts. They usually contain clear fluid and develop on the gums of some infants before the teeth come in. They are not cause for undue concern, and will subside in time. It is best to mention them to your doctor.

Headache

Headaches are the result of a large number of illnesses or problems resulting in head pain. Visual difficulties, head trauma, migraine, tension, infections, and allergies are among just a few of the possible causes of headaches. An occasional headache is not unusual, but persistent headaches in childhood are not common and should be evaluated by your doctor to determine the cause.

Heart Murmurs

Heart murmurs are sounds produced by the blood moving through the valves and chambers of the heart and its major blood vessels. There are several types of murmurs which your doctor can recognize. Some of these murmurs are called functional or innocent heart murmurs. These sounds are not produced by problems in the heart and are not cause for alarm. This type of murmur is fairly common during early childhood. Most of these sounds disappear as the child grows up.

Murmurs can also be caused by congenital malformations in the heart or blood vessels and by diseases that affect the heart. Rheumatic fever causes an inflammation in the heart, usually located in one of the heart valves. This can cause a heart murmur. Your doctor will be able to detect these murmurs during routine well child check-ups.

Not all murmurs are easy to hear, especially in a young infant who will usually be less than co-operative during the physical exam. It is not unusual for your doctor to have to examine your child more than once to be sure of presence or absence of murmur. Many doctors send their patients to a pediatric cardiologist (a heart specialist), if they feel that it is difficult to be sure of the cause of the murmur. Going to this specialist does not necessarily mean that your child has a serious problem; it just means that your doctor wants to evaluate the murmur in more detail.

Many advances have been made in detecting and treating congenital malformations and other problems of the heart. Early detection and proper treatment of these conditions can often improve or correct the difficulty.

Heat Exhaustion

Heat exhaustion causes the child to become tired and weak, especially after vigorous exercise in warm weather. The symptoms usually result from excessive loss of body salt and water by perspiration, which is not adequately replaced by fluid intake.

Heatstroke

Heatstroke is a rare severe form of heat exhaustion. It is an emergency condition. The child may develop a very high fever (103° to 106° F) and become hot, dry, and flushed. Call the doctor immediately.

Hernia

Hernia refers to a weakness in the abdominal wall which can allow an internal organ to protrude into the hole. Hernias occur in several special locations. Umbilical hernias result from the protrusion of the lining in the abdominal cavity through a weakness in the abominal wall left by the umbilicus (navel). These hernias can enlarge with prolonged crying spells. The condition is rarely serious, and the hernia usually subsides without treatment.

Inguinal hernias occur in the groin or inguinal area. A loop of intestine often protrudes down into the scrotum in a boy, or into the thigh area in a girl. This condition is more common in boys and requires surgical treatment. If the intestine is severely pinched and loses blood supply as it protrudes out of the abdominal wall, it can become strangulated, producing a serious condition. A painful lump in the groin region should be evaluated by your doctor.

Ingrown Toenail

Ingrown toenails are a relatively common problem. They usually occur when the toenail grows into the flesh of the toe. It is more commonly seen with the big toe. Picking or pulling at the toenails is a common cause. Occasionally ingrown toenails become infected and are very painful. Soaking the toe in warm water may be helpful. If a persistent problem develops, your doctor should evaluate the condition.

Insomnia

Insomnia refers to an inability to sleep at night. During toddlerhood this is not uncommon, and often occurs when the child is overtired. Excitement may also keep a child awake at night. In some cases emotional strain can cause insomnia. Most cases of insomnia are short-lived and well handled by the parents. Never give your child sleeping pills used by adults. If the condition persists and no clear solution appears to surface, discuss the situation with your doctor.

Leukemia

Leukemia is a cancer involving the white blood cells that is seen in childhood. The bone marrow produces too many of a specific type of white cell and this overproduction interferes with other functions of the bone marrow and other organs. Anemia, tiredness, or clotting defects are often among the first signs. Modern pediatric hematology has made major advances in the control of this disease through chemotherapy. Remissions of the disease are often possible for long periods of time, and "cures" may be obtained in some cases.

Lice

Lice are small insects that can get into the hair or on the body. Body lice cause small hive-like lesions as the result of their bites. The bites are very itchy. Head lice can cause intense itching of the scalp. Eggs can often be seen around hair roots.

Lice are common in some areas and are easily spread from one child to another. If you suspect your child is infected with lice, take him to your doctor for evaluation. The doctor can prescribe a simple treatment. Kwell is a common delousing agent that usually achieves good results. Try to have the child avoid extensive scratching since this can lead to infection.

Lisping

Lisping is a speech disability which results in difficulties in pronouncing certain sounds. Lisps are not harmful, but they can be emotionally traumatic for the preschool child if his playmates ridicule his speech defect. Consultation with a speech therapist may be helpful.

Mastoiditis

Mastoiditis refers to an infection of the mastoid bone, which lies behind the ear. This illness is sometimes seen in children with repeated ear infections. Mastoiditis can be a serious problem that can cause chronic infections and eventual hearing loss. It needs medical evaluation and treatment.

Meningitis

Meningitis is an infection or irritation of the membranes (meninges) surrounding the spinal cord and brain. It can cause a high fever and a stiff neck, but in many cases the first sign may be fatigue or lethargy. This condition needs to be evaluated by your doctor. Some forms of meningitis are contagious. It is important to have the doctor evaluate the child as soon as possible, since meningitis (mainly bacterial meningitis) may require antibiotic therapy. The risks of this disease have been greatly reduced by the development of modern treatment techniques, especially if the child receives proper medical care early in the course of the illness.

Migraine

Migraine headaches are uncommon in early childhood, but they can occur. The symptoms include sudden severe headaches which may be localized on one side of the head. They may be accompanied by nausea, transient loss of vision, seeing spots or flashing lights, and occasionally weakness over one side of the body. There is usually a family history of migraine. Your doctor should evaluate these symptoms and may prescribe medications to help prevent or control the headaches.

Nephritis (Glomerulonephritis)

Nephritis is the medical term for an infection or inflammation of the kidneys. In childhood the most common type of nephritis is acute glomerulonephritis, which sometimes occurs following a streptococcal throat infection.

Nightmares

Nightmares are dreams that are very frightening. They are common in toddlerhood and in the preschool years. Eating late or increased excitement before bedtime can often increase the frequency of nightmares. See pages 679, 827–28 for a full discussion.

Night Terrors and Sleep Walking

Night terrors are more severe than a nightmare. The child usually wakes up terrified and screaming. Usually the child does not remember having a bad dream. Occasionally, the child will appear to be in a trance when you run to comfort him. Some children get out of bed, walk to the bathroom to urinate, and then fall asleep on the floor or on the living room couch. When they wake up the next morning they do not know how they got there.

Most parents become extremely concerned at the first episode. Try not to panic, since this condition is usually not serious. In some children it may be due to emotional stress, but it is more frequently just related to a sleep disorder that is not completely understood at the present time.

Be patient with the child and remove dangerous obstacles in the house at night that could cause him harm. Supportive care and reassurance are usually all that is necessary. The child often outgrows this condition. Discuss it with your doctor to be sure he is not having an unusual seizure disorder.

Peritonitis

Peritonitis refers to an infection of the abdominal cavity, usually producing abdominal pain and abdominal stiffness (see Appendicitis). This condition is a medical emergency and requires immediate medical attention.

Rabies

Rabies is a viral disease of the central nervous system. It is usually transmitted to humans by the bites of infected dogs, cats, bats, and wild animals. In areas where house pets are vaccinated to prevent rabies, the disease is mainly caused by wild animals. It is important to try to capture the animal, but avoid being bitten yourself.

An animal that bites without provocation or any wild animal that bites should raise the suspicion of rabies. Your doctor will advise you how to handle this situation.

Not all animals that bite have rabies. An animal that has rabies will die in a few days to a week. If the animal dies, its brain should be examined for signs of rabies infection. If the animal was infected, the bitten individual will need to be immunized with a rabies vaccine to prevent the disease from developing. In situations where the animal could not be captured, the doctor will advise you how to deal with the problem. Immunization may be recommended. Rabies is a fatal disease. It is important to seek the advice of your doctor for all animal bites so that steps can be taken to prevent this serious illness from developing.

Rh Factor

The Rh factor is a substance found in most red blood cells given the designation of Rh positive. Some individuals do not have the Rh factor in their red blood cells, and they are called Rh negative. The majority of people are Rh positive. The difficulty with the Rh factor arises with blood transfusions or during pregnancy.

When Rh positive blood is given to an Rh negative person, the immune system of the Rh negative individual recognizes the Rh factor on the transfused blood as "foreign" to the body. Antibodies are made that attack this "foreign" Rh factor. These antibodies attach to the "foreign" blood cells and destroy them in a massive way, usually producing a transfusion reaction. Blood typing must include the Rh factor so that the proper blood is given during a transfusion.

The Rh factor also becomes important during pregnancy. The Rh factor is a genetic trait. If both parents are Rh negative, their children will all be Rh negative. Parents who both have only Rh positive genes will have Rh positive children. The danger arises when the mother is Rh negative and the father is Rh positive, since the baby will have a chance of being Rh positive. When this occurs, the Rh negative mother's immune system may react to the Rh positive blood of the baby as "foreign."

A father who is Rh positive either has two Rh positive genes or one Rh positive and one Rh negative gene. When both of the father's genes are Rh positive (homozygous condition) the baby in the womb of the Rh negative mother will always be Rh positive. A father who has one of each gene will have a 50 percent chance of having an Rh positive and a 50 percent chance of an Rh negative child.

An Rh negative mother carrying an Rh positive child can be immunologically sensitized to the Rh positive factor in her baby during the delivery of her first Rh positive child. If some of the child's blood enters the mother's blood stream at the time of birth, the mother will develop antibodies against Rh positive red blood cells. If this sensitized mother has a second Rh positive child, these antibodies could affect (actually attack) the red blood cells in the second Rh positive fetus. This produces the condition called erythroblastosis fetalis, which can cause a hemolytic anemia in the fetus. Depending on how severe the effect on the fetus, this condition can result in miscarriage, stillbirth, or a living infant that is ill at birth.

Recent advances have almost completely reduced the risks of pregnancies involving Rh negative mothers and Rh positive fathers. It is now possible to prevent the mother's immune system from becoming sensitized to the Rh positive fetus by the use of the substance called RhoGAM. RhoGAM is given to the Rh negative mother after the birth of her first Rh positive baby to prevent the development of antibodies.

By knowing the blood type of the mother and father, most problems due to Rh incompatibility can now be prevented by proper treatment. Your doctor will discuss this with you if you are at risk.

Rheumatic Fever

Rheumatic fever is a chronic inflammatory disease which affects connective tissue in the body, especially in the heart and joints. It occurs following an infection of a special type of bacteria (Group A beta hemolytic streptococci), which cause a "strep" throat. In some children infections with this bacteria, especially if prolonged, cause rheumatic fever. This is why it is very important to have your doctor examine your child and take a throat culture whenever the child develops a sore throat. Detection of "strep" throats and their proper treatment will greatly reduce the risk of developing rheumatic fever.

Rheumatic fever is less common during infancy or toddlerhood, but becomes more common in the preschool and older child. There are many ways for the illness to develop; some of the symptoms include respiratory tract infections; heart difficulties (carditis), arthritis, unusual movements (chorea), small lumps under the skin, a red blotch rash (erythema marginatum), and persistent fever. Your doctor will make the diagnosis. If the heart symptoms are severe, the child may have to be hospitalized. Proper treatment, usually with penicillin, can help prevent further attacks and often avoid some other complications.

Round Worms

Round worms are fairly common in young children who play in contaminated soil or eat contaminated food in areas where these worms are found. Round worms can be treated with specific medications. The appearance of worms in the child's stools may be the first clue of infection. Seek medical advice if you suspect that your child is infected with round worms.

Scoliosis

See Curvatures of the Spine (page 1026).

Sinusitis

Sinusitis is an infection or inflammation of the sinuses. The sinuses are located above and below the eyes. Sinusitis can cause headaches and is usually seen with other mild illnesses such as the common cold. Sometimes chronic sinusitis develops. Your doctor will be able to recommend appropriate treatment. Most of the time the use of decongestants will allow the sinuses to drain and alleviate the problem.

Smallpox

Smallpox is a serious viral illness that is highly contagious. This illness has been almost completely abolished in the world since the development and use of smallpox vaccinations. It is not currently recommended that infants be vaccinated against smallpox since the risk of complications from the vaccine, although very low, is greater than the risk of getting the disease.

Splinters

Small splinters in the skin can often be removed with a tweezers or with the fingers. Occasionally, soaking the skin in warm water makes it easier to remove the splinter. It is not recommended that parents attempt to remove splinters by digging at the skin with a sharp instrument. It is much safer for your doctor to handle any splinters that cannot be removed by simpler methods. Prolonged probing and digging at a deep splinter by an inexperienced person can often lead to infection.

Sudden Infant Death Syndrome

The Sudden Infant Death syndrome is a condition that causes a seemingly healthy infant to die suddenly, usually during sleep, for no apparent reason. This problem has also been called "crib death." It occurs most commonly between two and four months of age, but can occur earlier or later. The cause of this condition has not been clearly established, although a great deal of research is being directed at the problem. Some medical centers are attempting to determine if risk factors can be identified that will indicate which infant will develop this problem. This is done by monitoring the infant's breathing patterns, especially during sleep. In these research programs, babies that have a higher risk for breathing difficulties are often selected for monitoring. It is hoped that medical research may offer more answers about this condition through continued study.

Swimmer's Ear (External Otitis)

Swimmer's ear is a fairly common complaint of young children who spend a great deal of time engaging in water activities. This condition is an infection of the external ear canal, usually involving the skin and sometimes including the eardrum. This condition does not usually result in infections of the middle ear. It also does not occur in everyone who swims a great deal.

Infections of the ear canal are usually first recognized by the pain they produce. In most cases of swimmer's ear, it hurts to wiggle the external ear. Contrary to most beliefs, swimmer's ear is not usually the result of swimming in dirty pools. It is more likely a fungus infection that begins in the ear canal because the ear stays warm and wet for prolonged periods of time during the swimming season. When external ear infections become bothersome, they are often also secondarily infected with bacteria. These infections can cause swelling of the canal and extreme tenderness.

Swimmer's ear is easily treated and you should consult your doctor for proper medications. Most of these infections are cleared up with appropriate ear drops. Occasionally, a case of swimmer's ear does not respond to treatment for prolonged periods of time and may extend beyond the swimming season. This should raise the possibility of ear canal eczema—an allergic reaction of the skin in the ear canal. Your doctor can prescribe a different type of medication to be used as ear drops to clear up this condition if it has developed.

Thrush

Thrush is a fungus infection that commonly occurs in the mouth, on the tongue, and on the skin of the diaper area (see page 976). The medical term for this fungal infection is moniliasis. It often occurs in the first few months of life. Early symptoms of thrush are that the infant develops white spots or areas on the tongue. As the condition worsens, the entire tongue can become white in color. The infection can also involve the lips and lining of the mouth. Thrush is not serious if brought to the attention of your doctor. There are several antifungal agents that clear up this condition.

Toeing Out—Toeing In

Some children have a tendency to toe out or toe in when they walk. Minor deviations from center are not significant. If the child has a pronounced defect, you should discuss the situation with your doctor.

Twitch (Tic)

A twitch is a rapid, jerky movement of the arms, legs, shoulders, or face. Most twitches result from anxiety and emotional stress. Do not direct your attention to the tic. Try to ignore it and see whether or not it persists. If the tic does not subside, it should be evaluated by your doctor. Twitching of the eyelids may indicate fatigue of the eyes and suggest the need for an eye exam. Rheumatic fever can also cause a persistent twitching disorder (see page 1034).

ADDITIONAL READING AND BIBLIOGRAPHY

American National Red Cross. *Advanced First Aid and Emergency Care*. Garden City, N.Y.: Doubleday & Company, Inc., 1973.

Ames, Louise Bates, and Chase, Joan Ames. *Don't Push Your Preschooler*. New York: Harper and Row, 1974.

Ames, L. B., and Ilg, F. L. *Child Behavior*. New York: Harper and Row, 1955.

————. *Your Two Year Old*. New York: Dell Publishing Co., Inc., 1980.

————. *Your Three Year Old*. New York: Dell Publishing Co., Inc., 1980.

————. *Your Four Year Old*. New York: Dell Publishing Co., Inc., 1980.

Apgar, Virginia. *Is My Baby All Right?* New York: Pocket Books, a division of Simon & Schuster, 1974.

Arnstein, Helene S. *What to Tell Your Child*. New York: Condor, 1978.

Baker, Augusta. *The Black Experience in Children's Books*. New York Public Library; revised edition, 1971.

Banks, A. J., and Grambs, J. D. *Black Self-concept*. New York: McGraw-Hill, Inc., 1972.

Baughman, E. Earl. *Black Americans*. New York: Academic Press, 1971.

Beadle, Muriel. *A Child's Mind*. Garden City, N.Y.: Anchor Books, Doubleday & Company, Inc., 1971.

Beck, Joan. *How to Raise a Brighter Child*. New York: Pocket Books, a division of Simon & Schuster, 1975.

Boston Children's Medical Center. *Pregnancy, Birth and the Newborn Baby*. New York: Delacorte Press, Seymour Lawrence, 1972.

Boston Children's Medical Center, and Feinbloom, Richard I., M.D., et al. *Child Health Encyclopedia: The Complete Guide for Parents*. New York: Delacorte Press, 1975.

Boston Children's Medical Center, and Gregg, Elizabeth M. *What to Do When There's Nothing to Do*. New York: Dell Publishing Co., Inc., 1968.

Boston Women's Health Book Collective. *Our Bodies, Ourselves*. New York: Simon & Schuster, 1973.

Brazelton, T. Berry, M.D. *Infants and Mothers*. New York: Delacorte Press, 1972.

————. *Toddlers and Parents*. New York: Delacorte Press, 1974.

Caine, Lynn. *Widow*. New York: William Morrow, 1974.

Carlyle, Nancy. *Child Care Tips for Busy Mothers*. New York: Simon & Schuster, Essandess Special Editions, 1970.

Carson, Mary. *The Womanly Art of Breast Feeding*. Franklin Park, Ill.: La Leche League International, Inc., 1963.

Castle, Sue. *The Complete Guide to Preparing Baby Foods at Home*. Garden City, N.Y.: Doubleday & Company, Inc., 1973.

Chess, Stella; Thomas, Alexander; and Birch, Herbert G. *Your Child Is a Person*. New York: Penguin Books, 1978.

Cratty, Bryant. *Perceptual and Motor Development in Infants and Children*. New York: The Macmillan Co., 1970.

Croft, Doreen J., and Hess, Robert D. *An Activities Handbook for Teachers of Young Children*. Boston: Houghton Mifflin Co., 1975.

Dember, William, and Jenkins, James. *General Psychology: Modeling Behavior and Experience*. New Jersey: Prentice-Hall, Inc., 1970.

Despert, J. Louise. *Children of Divorce*. Garden City, N.Y.: Dolphin Books, Doubleday & Company, Inc., 1962.

Dodson, Fitzhugh. *How to Father.* Los Angeles: Nash Publishing Corporation, 1974.
——. *How to Parent.* New York: Signet Books, 1971.
——. *How to Discipline With Love.* New York: New American Library, 1978.
Ervin, Jane. *Your Child Can Read and You Can Help.* Garden City, N.Y.: Doubleday & Company, Inc., 1979.
Ewy, Donna, and Ewy, Roger. *Preparation for Breast Feeding.* Garden City, N.Y.: Dolphin Books, Doubleday & Company, Inc., 1975.
Faber, Adele, and Mazlish, Elaine. *Liberated Parents Liberated Children.* New York: Avon Books, a division of The Hearst Corporation, 1974.
Fitzgerald, Hiram, and McKinney, John. *Developmental Psychology: Studies in Human Development.* Illinois: The Dorsey Press, 1970.
Fraiberg, Selma H. *The Magic Years.* New York: Lyceum Edition, Charles Scribner's Sons, 1968.
Frank, Lawrence K. *On the Importance of Infancy.* New York: Random House, 1966.
Fromme, Allan. *The ABC of Child Care.* New York: Pocket Books, a division of Simon & Schuster, 1969.
Furth, Hans G. *Piaget and Knowledge: Theoretical Foundations.* New Jersey: Prentice-Hall, Inc., 1969.
——, and Wachs, Harry. *Thinking Goes to School: Piaget's Theory in Practice.* New York: Oxford University Press, 1974.
Galper, Miriam. *Co-Parenting.* Philadelphia: Running Press, 1978.
Gerber, Mrs. Dan. *Bringing Up Baby.* New York: Pocket Books, a division of Simon & Schuster, 1972.
Gersh, Marvin. *How to Raise Children at Home in Your Spare Time.* New York: Stein & Day, 1973.
Gesell, Arnold, M.D. *The First Five Years of Life.* New York: Harper and Row, 1940.
——, and Ilg, Frances, M.D. *Infant and Child in the Culture of Today.* New York: Harper and Row, 1974.
Ginott, Haim G. *Between Parent and Child.* New York: The Macmillan Co., 1965.
Gordon, Ira J. *Baby Learning Through Baby Play.* New York: St. Martin's, 1970.
——; Guinach, Garry; and Jester, R. Emile. *Child Learning Through Child Play.* New York: St. Martin's, 1972.
Hardwood, Michael. *Games to Play in the Car.* Des Moines, IA: Meredith Press, 1967.
Heimlich, Henry J., and Uhley, Milton H. *The Heimlich Maneuver,* CIBA Clinical Symposia, Vol. 31, No. 3, 1979.
Hend, David. *Save Your Child's Life!* Garden City, N.Y.: Dolphin Books, Doubleday & Company, Inc., 1974.
Homan, William E. *Child Sense.* New York; London: Basic Books, Inc., 1969.
Howells, J. G. *Modern Perspectives in Child Psychiatry.* New York: Bruner-Mazel, 1971.
Hurlock, Elizabeth B. *Child Growth and Development.* St. Louis: McGraw-Hill, Inc., Webster Division, 1970.
Ilg, Frances L., M.D., and Ames, Louise Bates, of the Gesell Institute. *Child Behavior from Birth to Ten.* New York: Harper and Row, 1955.
Kalt, Bryson, and Bass, Ralph. *The Mother's Guide to Child Safety.* New York: Grosset & Dunlap, 1971.
Kaluger, George, and Unkovic, Charles. *Psychology and Society.* St. Louis: C. V. Mosby, Co., 1969.
Kelly, Marguerite, and Parsons, Elia. *The Mother's Almanac.* Garden City, N.Y.: Doubleday & Company, Inc., 1975.
Klaus, Marshall H., M.D., et al. "Human Maternal Behavior at the First Contact with Her Young," *Pediatrics* 46 (1970).
Klein, Carole. *The Single Parent Experience.* New York: Avon, 1973.
Krantzler, Mel. *Creative Divorce.* New York: Signet Books, 1972.
La Leche League International, Inc. *Breast Feeding and the Premature Baby.* Franklin Park, Ill., 1971.

Lamaze, Fernand, M.D. *Painless Childbirth: The Lamaze Method.* New York: Pocket Books, a division of Simon & Schuster, 1972.

LeShan, Eda J. *Natural Parenthood.* New York: Signet Books, 1970.

Liepmann, Lise. *Your Child's Sensory World.* Baltimore, Md.: Penguin Books, 1973.

Lipsitt, Lewis, et al. *Learning Capacities of the Human Infant.* New York: Academic Press, 1969.

McKeachie, Wilbert, and Doyle, Charlotte. *Psychology.* Reading, Mass.: Addison-Wesley Publishing Company, Inc., 1970.

McLaughlin, Clara J. *The Black Parents' Handbook.* New York; London: Harcourt Brace Jovanovich, 1976.

Marzollo, Jean, and Lloyd, Janice. *Learning Through Play.* New York: Harper and Row, 1972.

Matterson, E. M. *Play and Playthings for the Preschool Child.* New York; Baltimore, Md.: Penguin Books, 1974.

Melton, David. *How to Help Your Preschooler Learn . . . More . . . Faster & Better.* New York: David McKay Co., 1976.

Munsinger, Harry. *Fundamentals of Child Development.* New York; Chicago: Holt, Rinehart and Winston, Inc., 1971.

Mussen, Paul; Longer, John; and Kagan, Jerome. *Child Development and Personality.* New York: Harper and Row, 1969.

Neumann-Neurodede, D. Revised by Wendula Kaiser. *Baby Gymnastics.* Oxford, London: Pergamon Press, 1967.

Piaget, Jean. *The Construction of Reality in the Child.* New York: Basic Books, 1954.

———. *The Origins of Intelligence in Children.* New York: International Universities Press, 1952.

———. *Play, Dreams and Imitation in Childhood.* New York: Norton, 1962.

Pomeranz, Virginia E., M.D., and Schultz, Dodi. *The Mothers' and Fathers' Medical Encyclopedia.* Boston: Little, Brown, 1975.

———. *The First Five Years.* Garden City, N.Y.: Doubleday & Company, Inc., 1973.

Pomeroy, Wardell. *Your Child and Sex.* New York: Delacorte Press, 1974.

Prenatal Care. U. S. Department of Health, Education, and Welfare, Children's Bureau Publication No. 4, 1962.

Princeton Center for Infancy. *The First Twelve Months of Life.* New York: Grosset & Dunlap, 1973.

———. *Parents Yellow Pages.* Garden City, N.Y.: Anchor Books, Doubleday & Company, Inc., 1978.

Pryor, Karen. *Nursing Your Baby.* New York: Pocket Books, a division of Simon & Schuster, 1973.

Pulaski, Mary Ann Spencer. *Understanding Piaget.* New York: Harper and Row, 1971.

Ramos, Suzanne. *Teaching Your Child to Cope with Crisis.* New York: McKay, 1975.

Rozdilsky, Mary Lou, and Banet, Barbara. *What Now? A Handbook for New Parents.* New York: Charles Scribner's Sons, 1975.

Rutherford, Frederick W. *You And Your Baby.* New York: New American Library, Signet, 1971.

Salk, Lee. *Preparing for Parenthood.* New York: McKay, 1974.

———. *What Every Child Would Like His Parents to Know.* New York: McKay, 1972.

———, and Kramer, Rita. *How to Raise a Human Being.* New York: McKay, 1972.

Schwartz, Felice N.; Schiffer, Margaret H.; and Gillotti, Susan S. *How to Go to Work When Your Husband Is Against It, Your Children Aren't Old Enough, and There's Nothing You Can Do Anyhow.* New York: Simon & Schuster, 1972.

Shiller, Jack, M.D. *Childhood Illness.* New York: Stein & Day, 1973.

Shuttlesworth, Dorothy. *Exploring Nature with Your Child.* New York: Hawthorn, 1952.

Society for Research in Child Development. *Cognitive Development in Children.* Chicago; London: The University of Chicago Press, 1970.

Spencer, Thomas D., and Kass, Norman. *Perspectives in Child Psychology*. New York: McGraw-Hill, Inc., 1970.

Spock, Benjamin, M.D. *Baby and Child Care*. Rev. ed. New York: Pocket Books, a division of Simon & Schuster, 1972.

Steinfels, Margaret O'Brien. *Who's Minding the Children?* New York: Simon & Schuster, 1973.

Stone, L. Joseph, and Church, Joseph. *Childhood & Adolescence*. New York: Random House, 1968.

Sutton-Smith, Brian, and Sutton-Smith, Shirley. *How to Play with Your Children*. New York: Hawthorn, 1974.

Talbot, Toby. *The World of the Child*. Garden City, N.Y.: Anchor Books, Doubleday & Company, Inc., 1967.

The American Red Cross. *Cardiopulmonary Resuscitation*. Pamphlet available from the American Red Cross, Library of Congress Catalog Card Number: 74-82395, 1974.

The Better Homes and Gardens Baby Book. New York: Bantam Books, Inc., 1969.

The Concise Home Medical Guide. New York: Grosset & Dunlap, 1972.

Toy Safety. Bureau of Product Safety, U. S. Department of Health, Education, and Welfare Publication No. 73-7009.

Turtle, William John. *Dr. Turtle's Babies*. New York: Popular Library Edition, W. B. Saunders Company, 1973.

U. S. Department of Health, Education, and Welfare, Office of Child Development, Children's Bureau. *Infant Care*. Washington, D.C.: Superintendent of Documents, U. S. Government Printing Office, DHEW Publication No. (OCD) 73-15, 1973.

U. S. Government Book of Infant Care. New York: Award Books, 1968.

Weaver, Kitty. *Lenin's Grandchildren*. New York: Simon & Schuster, 1971.

White, Burton L. *The First Three Years of Life*. New Jersey: Prentice-Hall, Inc., 1975.

INDEX

Emergency and First Aid

Artificial respiration, 991–93
Bites, 998–99
Bleeding, 989–90
Broken bones (fractures), 990–91
Burns, 986–97
Choking, 994–96
Concussion, 1025–26
Convulsions (seizures), 984–85
Croup (severe coughing), 959–60
Cuts, 987–88
Diarrhea, 964
Drowning, 999
Ear infections, 957–58
Eye infections, 981
Eye injuries, 996–97
Fever, 951–54
Food poisoning, 1028
Frostbite, 1028–29
Head injuries, 997–98

Heatstroke and heat exhaustion, 1030
Infections, 988–89
Loss of consciousness (fainting), 998, 1027
Nosebleeds, 989–90
Objects in the eye, 996–97
   in the nose, 997
   in the ear, 997
Poisoning
   Lead poisoning, 1004–5
   Managing poisoning, 1001–3
   Where to go for help, 1000–1
Rashes, 974–79
Shock, 1000
Stings, 999–1000
Swallowed objects, 998
Visual problems, 980–82
Vomiting, 962–63

A

Abscess, 1023
Acrocyanosis, 79
Adenoids, 960–61
Adoption, 23–25
  agencies, 23–24
  availability of babies, 23
  giving birth after, 882
  government agencies, 23, 24
  interracial, 25
  older babies, 24
  older children, 24
  single parents and, 24–25

  by stepparent, 20–21
  telling the child about, 881–82
Airsickness, 1023
Allergies, 970–74
  asthma, 973
  eczema, 974
  hay fever, 972–73
  hives, 974
  in infancy, 122, 467, 971
  in preschoolers, 745, 972
  preventing, 971–72
  solid foods, introduction of, 305

  strawberries, 312
  in toddlers, 972
Alphabet, teaching in song, 811
American Academy of Pediatrics, 139, 215, 304, 502
Ames, L. B., 652, 763
Anal fissures, 966
Anemia, 979–80
Animals
  fear of, 543
  See also Pets
Apgar, Virginia, 83
APGAR Test for newborns, 83
Appendicitis, 963